APB Statements

FINANCIAL ACCOUNTING STANDARDS BOARD, FASB (1973 to present)

Statements of Financial Accounting Standards

INTERMEDIATE ACCOUNTING

INTERMEDIATE

PRENTICE-HALL, INC., Englewood Cliffs, New Jersey 07632

ACCOUNTING

PAUL DANOS

University of Michigan

EUGENE A. IMHOFF, Jr.

University of Michigan

Library of Congress Cataloging in Publication Data

DANOS, PAUL (date)
 Intermediate accounting

 (Prentice-Hall series in accounting)
 Includes bibliographical references and index.
 1. Accounting I. Imhoff, Eugene A. II. Title.
III. Series.
HF5635.D19 1983   657'.044   82-15004
ISBN 0-13-469338-8

INTERMEDIATE ACCOUNTING
Paul Danos and Eugene A. Imhoff, Jr.

Material from Uniform CPA examination questions and unofficial answers,
copyright © 1969, 1970, 1971, 1972, 1973, 1974, 1975, 1976, 1977, 1978,
1979, 1980, 1981 by the American Institute of Certified Public Accountants,
Inc., is reprinted (or adapted) with permission.

Material from the Certificate in Management Accounting examinations, copyright © 1969, 1970, 1971, 1972, 1973, 1974, 1975, 1976, 1977, 1978, 1979,
1980, 1981 by the National Association of Accountants, is reprinted (or
adapted) with permission.

Development Editor: Raymond Mullaney
Editorial/Production Supervision by Pamela Wilder
Interior and Cover Design by Janet Schmid
Manufacturing Buyer: Raymond Keating

Printed in the United States of America
10 9 8 7 6 5 4 3 2 1

ISBN 0-13-469338-8

Prentice-Hall International, Inc., *London*
Prentice-Hall of Australia Pty. Limited, *Sydney*
Editora Prentice-Hall do Brazil, Ltda., *Rio de Janeiro*
Prentice-Hall Canada Inc., *Toronto*
Prentice-Hall of India Private Limited, *New Delhi*
Prentice-Hall of Japan, Inc., *Tokyo*
Prentice-Hall of Southeast Asia Pte. Ltd., *Singapore*
Whitehall Books Limited, *Wellington, New Zealand*

TO OUR FAMILIES
Mary Ellen, Amanda, and Melissa
Barbara, Catherine, and Darren

PRENTICE-HALL SERIES IN ACCOUNTING
Charles T. Horngren, Editor

OUTLINE

CONTENTS

4 The Balance Sheet and the Statement of Changes in Financial Position: Fundamental Concepts 119

5 Compound Interest and an Introduction to Accounting Measurement of Future Cash Flows 147

6 Alternative Valuation Models 176

PART 2 ASSETS 222

7 Cash and Temporary Investments 228

8 Current Receivables

9 Inventories—Basic Concepts and Measurement Procedures

10 Inventory Measurement: Estimation Procedures 346

11 Plant, Property, and Equipment 385

14 Long-Term Investments

15 Leased Assets

18 Noncurrent Liabilities—Long-Term Notes and Bonds 672

19 Pensions 720

20 Stockholders' Contributed Capital 761

21 Stockholders' Earned Capital 794

PREFACE

This text covers the underlying principles, procedures, and reporting requirements necessary to gain an understanding of *both* the preparation and the use of modern financial reports of profit-seeking entities. The number of such factors affecting accounting has grown at an unprecedented pace during the past decade. Mirroring this growth, many accounting texts have expanded the number of subjects covered.

The basic premise of this text is that *conceptual commonalities* tie much of financial accounting together. Emphasizing these commonalities should aid the learning process. Although generally accepted accounting principles (GAAP) contain many important, specific, and sometimes arbitrary, prescriptions, the main goal of this text is to highlight the conceptual foundations of these prescriptions, with ample discussion of why departures from them take place.

OVERALL ORGANIZATION OF THE TEXT

The organization of this text reflects our view of financial accounting. We see the subject matter as a mixture of concepts, procedures, and reporting requirements. Our belief is that covering accounting procedures and reporting requirements without regard for the underlying concepts is not conducive to a thorough understanding of financial accounting. At the same time, some abstract concepts take on much more meaning as specific procedures are illustrated. For these reasons, we have attempted to interrelate concepts and procedures throughout the text.

In Part 1, "An Introduction to Financial Accounting Organizations, Concepts, and Techniques," we cover the fundamentals. Chapter 1 describes the political and institutional setting. Chapter 2 covers the Conceptual Framework Study of the Financial Accounting Standards Board and other key aspects of basic accounting theory. In Chapters 3 and 4 we introduce the more specific concepts underlying conventional financial statements, including such things as how changes in accounting estimates and methods are reported and the concept of funds flow measurement as an economic indicator of the entity's activities. We introduce the present-value measurement concept in Chapter 5 and other accounting valuation models (such as replacement cost) in Chapter 6.

The six chapters of Part 1 introduce fundamental accounting concepts that are important to a full understanding of the specific accounting procedures and disclosure requirements discussed in Part 2, "Assets," and Part 3, "Equities." For example, several chapters in Parts 2 and 3 consider the procedures and reporting requirements to account for an "accounting change" (such as a change in estimate or a change in principles), which were introduced in Chapter 3. Also, each chapter in Parts 2 and 3 ends with a discussion of funds flow effects, thereby relating back to the introduction to funds flow in Chapter 4. Expanded coverage of the conceptual framework of accounting, first introduced in Chapter 2, is found in virtually every chapter of the text, and discussion of many of the specific generally accepted accounting procedures and reporting requirements draws upon an understanding of the valuation concepts introduced in Chapters 5 and 6. Thus, the fundamental concepts of accounting introduced in Part 1 pave the way to a full understanding of the material presented in Parts 2, 3, and 4.

Part 4 of the text summarizes and expands on the key accounting concepts, procedures, and reporting requirements necessary to evaluate and use modern financial reports for decision making. The chapters of Part 4 focus on some of the more complex elements of financial reporting and expand upon topics first covered in Parts 1, 2, and 3. For example, Chapter 23 reviews the revenue-recognition concept introduced in Chapter 3 and applied throughout the book. Chapter 24 provides a wide-ranging review of the financial reporting of accounting changes and expands on the coverage of error analysis and correction. Chapter 25 consists of a comprehensive evaluation of the statement of changes in financial position, which was first discussed in Chapter 4. Chapter 26 provides detailed coverage of accounting for changing prices according to current generally accepted accounting principles and reviews the concepts that underlie the required supplementary disclosures. In this way, Chapter 26 broadens the discussion in Chapter 6. Chapter 27 provides a capstone review of the nature and use of financial statements, including a discussion of interim and segment reporting requirements, an outline of key Securities and Exchange Commission reports, and an introduction to analysis of financial statements.

STRUCTURE OF PARTS AND CHAPTERS

Each part of the text begins with a major *conceptual overview* that highlights the common theme of the several chapters of that part. For example, the overview of Part 2 reviews the general nature of assets. Each chapter has a common structure. Each begins with a *chapter overview* that previews the chapter material and notes its relationship to the underlying accounting concepts. Each chapter of Parts 2, 3, and 4 includes *illustrative material from published annual reports* to provide practical examples of the material being covered. As already mentioned, each chapter in Parts 2 and 3 of the text has a section on *funds flow effects* in order to stress the underlying economic effects of the transactions covered in the chapter. *Chapter summaries* identify the underlying concepts, procedures, and reporting requirements covered.

CHAPTER SEQUENCE AND ORDER OF COVERAGE

Chapters 1 through 5 introduce fundamental accounting concepts and techniques. For this reason, these chapters should be covered before Parts 2, 3, and 4, unless students have had comparable exposure in other courses. Parts 2 and 3 are arranged in a basic balance sheet format. With the exceptions of the natural sequence of Chapters 9 and 10 on inventory and Chapters 11 and 12 on plant, property, and equipment and depreciation, the order of coverage of the chapters in Parts 2 and 3 can be varied to suit a particular course. Although Part 4 builds on previously developed materials, Chapters 23, 24, and 25 may be covered whenever the instructor feels the students have been adequately prepared for them. Chapters 6 and 26 are designed to stand on their own for the most part and may be inserted almost anywhere in the sequence of material depending on the instructor's preference. Chapter 27 seems to work best as a concluding chapter.

QUESTIONS, CASES, EXERCISES, AND PROBLEMS

In addition to the hundreds of questions, cases, exercises, and problems developed specifically for this text, CPA and CMA exam materials are used as important learning tools. We have attempted to provide a wide variety of self-testing materials that are useful both for stimulating class discussions (questions and cases) and for testing comprehension in problem-solving contexts. Some of the exercises and problems are straightforward, relating directly to the chapter material; others are more complex, involving richer contexts from which students must sort out relevant data. Some require logical extensions of the chapter material or are designed to test the student's ability to integrate material from other chapters. Some of the questions and cases are also straightforward, with answers flowing directly from the text, whereas others involve the ambiguities encountered in the real world where no single response is obviously correct. The various levels of difficulty in the questions, cases, exercises, and problems permit the instructor to fashion a mix of assignments according to personal preferences.

SUPPLEMENTS TO THE TEXT

This text is supplemented by the following materials:

1. A solutions manual
2. A set of transparencies
3. An instructor's resource manual
4. A test bank of over 1,000 questions and problems
5. A student guide
6. A practice set
7. A complete set of working papers

The instructor's manual, test bank, and student guide were prepared by Professor Thomas J. Frecka of the University of Illinois who also worked closely with us as a reviewer throughout the development of the text. All supplementary materials have been thoroughly integrated with the text. The instructor's resource manual provides the instructor with materials that supplement and enhance the topical coverage in each chapter. The student guide summarizes key concepts and provides assistance and insights. This guide also contains a series of tests for self-study. The practice set is a simulated case problem that covers all the steps in the accounting cycle reviewed in the early chapters.

These supplements have been carefully designed to provide a challenging and useful package of materials to enhance the usefulness of the text.

The writing of any textbook is a challenging and demanding task. Throughout the long period of writing, reviewing, rethinking, and rewriting, our persistent goal has been to provide students of intermediate financial accounting with the most comprehensive, up-to-date, and clearly written text available. We feel that we have reached that goal. If you find that here and there we have fallen short, we would appreciate your writing us with your comments and suggestions for improvement.

PAUL DANOS
EUGENE A. IMHOFF, JR.

ACKNOWLEDGMENTS

We owe a great debt of gratitude to the many colleagues who provided us with comments, suggestions, and insights at various stages in this project. The following reviewers provided invaluable assistance in the development of various parts of the text:

Richard E. Baker
Northern Illinois University

Floyd A. Beams
Virginia Polytechnic Institute and State University

David M. Beuhlmann
University of Nebraska, Omaha

Gyan Chandra
Miami University

Daniel W. Collins
University of Iowa

Gary M. Cunningham
Virginia Polytechnic Institute and State University

John W. Eichenseher
University of Illinois, Urbana-Champaign

Joe D. Icerman
Florida State University

Paul A. Janell
Northeastern University

James C. McKeown
University of Illinois, Urbana-Champaign

Gale E. Newell
Western Michigan University

Gary John Previts
Case Western Reserve University

John R. Robinson
University of Kansas

Michael B. Sheffey
University of Wisconsin, Parkside

E. Dan Smith
University of Florida

Robert J. Swieringa
Cornell University

Albert Wright
California State University, Northridge

Martin E. Taylor
University of South Carolina

In addition, several reviewers were involved with the project from start to finish and deserve special thanks for their effort and interest in the development of this book:

Thomas J. Burns
The Ohio State University

Thomas J. Frecka
University of Illinois, Urbana-Champaign

Alfred R. Roberts
Georgia State University

We want to also acknowledge the valuable contributions of Professor Harold E. Arnett of the University of Michigan and Doris Holt who was a Ph.D. student at Michigan during the development of this book.

At Prentice-Hall, several very competent professionals made our labors easier. The contributions of Ray Mullaney, development editor, were outstanding. His dedication and skills cannot be overstated. Pam Wilder, production editor, displayed competence and patience throughout a very hectic production schedule. Janet Schmid, designer, deserves credit for the book's attractive and functional format. We would like also to thank Paul Misselwitz, Jack Ochs, Elinor Paige, and especially Ron Ledwith, all of whom have convinced us that our choice of publishers was well-founded.

INTERMEDIATE ACCOUNTING

AN INTRODUCTION

ACCOUNTING

CONCEPTS.

OVERVIEW

Financial accounting is a complex information-generation process that is a building block in free-market economic systems. It is concerned primarily with the information needs of persons outside the entity, whereas managerial accounting is designed to fill the needs of management. It is integral to communication activities within and across all types of economic entities. The first six chapters of this text analyze the basic ideas that must be understood if the more technical material that follows is to be put in proper perspective.

Because financial accounting is so pervasive and complex, no one vantage point can provide a satisfactory place to begin. We have arranged the chapters of Part 1 in terms of several core ideas. In Chapter 1 we discuss the environ-

PART 1

TO FINANCIAL

ORGANIZATIONS,

AND TECHNIQUES

ment of accounting—the individuals and organizations most deeply involved with users and providers of financial accounting information. Here, the varying needs, skills, and levels of authority are emphasized. An understanding of the historical evolution of financial accounting is particularly critical here. We depict the past and present relationships among authorities and users and providers of accounting information as dynamic, ever-changing networks of interested parties. It is likely that future relationships among these parties will be based on their past relationships.

Chapters 2, 3, and 4 are reviews of basic accounting concepts, definitions, and procedures. We stress the notion that generally accepted principles are to a certain degree rooted in a conceptual framework. A solid grounding in

the theoretical concepts allows the reader to appreciate the many specific applications that are introduced in later chapters. These chapters provide a conceptual perspective and an introduction to the specific measurement, recording, summarization, and communication techniques that are at the heart of conventional, historically based, financial accounting.

The last two chapters in Part 1 introduce techniques of measurement and modification of financial data that are indispensable tools in modern financial accounting. Compound-interest techniques are used as basic measurement devices of future asset flows. Price-level adjustments and current-valuation techniques have become important as inflation has accelerated in recent years.

The Development and Environment of Financial Accounting

OVERVIEW

Financial accounting is an information-generating system designed to measure and report upon economic aspects of entities that are relevant for decision making. Because each entity is unique, each information system must likewise be unique. Decision makers and their information needs are equally varied. Therefore, if financial accounting is to be useful to as many decision makers as possible, it must be a flexible system. This text, while acknowledging these diversities, focuses on the **generally accepted accounting principles (GAAP)** that are applicable to broad groups of entities and result in information that is relevant to the various groups who will use this information. If you are to understand fully the strengths and weaknesses of financial accounting, you must first understand the environment that shaped its development. That environment is characterized by a tension created by the different kinds of information needed or desired by several major groups: business managers, external users of accounting information, auditors, and accounting policy makers.

Financial accounting must be applied to complex and dynamic economies throughout the world. Such an accounting system must be adaptable to varying interests, and, therefore, it needs a broad conceptual base. As you shall see throughout this text, GAAP are based on fundamental conceptual notions, but they are not bound by them. All GAAP must be adaptable to varying needs of decision makers and the diverse interests of concerned parties pursuing their own interests. Accounting policy making, therefore, is conducted in a dynamic sociological, economic, and political setting and within a framework of basic accounting theory. In this way, different information needs may be satisfied.

In this chapter we survey the environment of financial accounting. We analyze the nature of financial accounting information in terms of the needs and desires of the primary parties who are directly involved. In addition, we take a close look at several major groups that have influenced the development of contemporary accounting. This background will help you gain a better understanding of current financial accounting.

ACCOUNTING INFORMATION AND USER GROUPS

Decision makers form groups of consumers of accounting information. Table 1−1 suggests that all types of entities have groups of individuals who are interested in using the entity's accounting information. These user groups can be divided into two broad classes: "**internal**" users (those within the entity) and "**external**" users (those outside the entity). Generally, internal users have access to all data on transactions affecting an entity. External users, on the other hand, generally rely on accounting statements incorporated in publicly available annual and interim reports or on special statements designed to provide specific information. Internal users often can influence the structure of their entity's information system and can usually retrieve as much information as their system is designed to produce. In contrast, external users typically have access only to financial data released to the public.

In this book we shall be concerned primarily with the information needs of external users and with the information systems of business entities. We shall not explicitly deal with special accounting techniques for not-for-profit and governmen-

TABLE 1−1

COMMON PATTERNS OF ACCOUNTING INFORMATION USER GROUPS		
ENTITY TYPE	**INTERNAL USERS**	**EXTERNAL USERS**
1. Publicly held business[a]	Management Board of directors	Owners Creditors Nonmanagement employees Government bodies Other interested parties
2. Privately held business[b]	Management Owners	Creditors Nonmanagement employees Government bodies Other interested parties
3. Not-for-profit and governmental units	Management	Creditors Nonmanagement employees Government bodies Voters Other interested parties

[a] Publicly held businesses are those corporations with stock sold on exchanges or the over-the-counter market.

[b] Privately held businesses are closely held corporations with no public trading of stock, partnerships, and sole proprietorships.

tal units. We also shall not study at length the special kinds of information used specifically by internal management in its decision making. This is not to say that concepts and techniques that make up GAAP are not important to all groups of users. To the contrary, understanding financial accounting is basic to an understanding of all other forms of accounting, for example, cost accounting and income tax accounting.

External Users　It may seem odd that in Table 1–1 the owners of publicly held entities are designated as external users. This separation of owners and management, which became common in the nineteenth century, is due largely to the need for managerial specialists and for the division of responsibilities among management. The increased size and complexity of businesses, the wide distribution of ownership shares, and many other factors all helped to separate managers from owners.

　　Today, large amounts of resources are invested in publicly held companies, and in most of these, managers are usually separate from owners. As a result, owners are an outsider group along with bankers, customers, and others. Management is required to report information to the owners. This information flow from management to outsider user groups includes the reporting of financial accounting information, which is the subject of this text.[1]

　　Although considerable attention is given to the information needs of the owners, that group is not the only important external user group. Any party or group that has current or potential contractual relationships with the reporting entity—such as investors, creditors, bondholders, and even employees—is an important consumer of accounting information. Decisions concerning investments, employment, and credit granting can be influenced by financial accounting information.

　　The information needs of all external user groups is the primary concern of **financial accounting,** while the needs of internal users (managers) is the primary concern of **managerial accounting.** The management of an entity can obtain the accounting information it needs for internal decision making. However, external users must to some extent rely on financial accounting policy-making bodies, such as the Securities and Exchange Commission (SEC) and the Financial Accounting Standards Board (FASB), to ensure that they are provided with the information they need. These bodies prescribe accounting policy in many cases and, in essence, ensure a certain minimum level of financial disclosure by entities under their jurisdiction.

　　Actually, the information needs of external users and internal users are not necessarily different. For example, both user groups are interested in the financial statements; however, managers of firms (internal users) typically have access to detailed information that supports and supplements the financial statements. Such detail is ordinarily not made available to external users. Managerial accounting data thus differ from financial accounting data in the level of detail available. Accounting policy-making bodies set a minimum level of disclosure required for external users, whereas internal users generally can obtain any information they feel is required for internal decision making. External reports, therefore, are more general, less detailed, and more constrained than are those available to internal users.

---

[1] The view that external users are the principal party to consider in establishing financial accounting rules and policies has been expressed in several reports, including *A Statement of Basic Accounting Theory* (Evanston, IL: American Accounting Association, 1966) and the *Report of the Study Group on Objectives of Financial Statements* (New York: American Institute of Certified Public Accountants, 1973).

Information

"Information" is a key term in the discussion of the objective of financial accounting, which is to provide the information needed by external user groups. Indeed, accounting is often defined as an *information system.* **Information** is derived from the Latin verb *informare,* meaning "to give form to." Information is defined here as data that have been so structured that they have the potential to influence a decision maker's actions. Data that are not considered in a decision-making context do not have the potential to influence decisions and are not considered information. A key word here is "potential." Data that are collected and evaluated for possible use in decision making are considered information, even though they may not result in an action in every case.

What information do external users need? This question is difficult to answer. Different decision makers may be interested in making different types of decisions, and therefore they may need different kinds of information. For example, the information necessary to make a short-term credit decision may not be the same as that needed to make a long-term investment decision. Owners of a corporation's securities may desire information that differs from information desired by the corporation's employees. Security analysts who evaluate the performance of a firm for investment potential may need one kind of information, whereas those holding the firm's securities and considering selling them may need another kind of information.

Still, some common aspects of information needs provide financial accounting with some direction for satisfying the diverse groups it serves. For example, most interested parties wish to assess and compare the future cash-generating abilities of business entities. This is so even though there may not be complete agreement among external users as to what information best predicts future cash flows. Thus, one external user may feel that past cash-flow trends best predict future cash flows. Another user may feel that past net-income trends are a better indicator.

Information must in some way pertain to future states. Because accounting is basically a measurement and communication process based on past events, how can accounting provide information? The answer is that knowledge of past events is relevant if it influences decisions about future actions. Why do people decide to buy stock in a company or to accept a receivable from a company or to work for a company? Without the expectation of future dividends or price appreciation, why hold stock? Without the expectation of future payment, why grant credit? Without the expectation of a job in the future, why not seek employment elsewhere? The value of accounting information is based on the assumption that past performance can predict future performance. As a result, the accounting-information system that reports to a large extent on the past economic activity of an entity is considered to be one of the more important sources of information for external users.

Interrelationships Among User Groups

The information-generation process just described operates in a context where several groups of individuals have influence: (1) external users, (2) managers, and (3) independent auditors. In this section we shall discuss these three groups and their interrelationships. In subsequent sections we shall review the history and current makeup of several organizations that influence financial accounting.

Because financial accounting information is strongly shaped by the needs of external users and because managers and auditors are primarily agents of external users, we can conclude that the most important group is the external users. They can be termed the "principals" in a principal-agent setting. The second group includes managers; they are "agents" in that they are responsible to the external users. Strictly speaking, stockholders are the true principals who (through their represen tatives on the board of directors) hire management to run the corporation. However, we include other external users, such as lending institutions, among the principals.

External users want management reports that are accurate and comprehensive. At the same time, management may want to limit both the accuracy and the completeness of their reports, in order not to damage the entity's competitive status or in the event that they have mismanaged resources entrusted to them. As a result of this potential conflict of interest, there is a third party to the process of reporting accounting information, the independent auditors. **Independent auditors** review management's financial statements and other disclosures and attest to their fairness of presentation in conformity with GAAP. In this sense, auditors provide a monitoring function. These three groups are represented by the three circles in Figure 1–1.

Each party is represented by a circle or "information set" in Figure 1–1. Missing is a fourth major group, the financial accounting policy makers, which we shall discuss in the following sections. The corporate-management circle represents the information that management is willing to provide. The user circle represents the information that users would like to obtain. The auditor circle indicates the information about which auditors are able and willing to make attestations.

Intersection I in Figure 1–1 represents information that at a given time (1) management is willing to provide, (2) users desire, and (3) auditors will attest to. This information is currently included in the audited financial statements made available to the public.

Intersection II represents information that at a given time (1) management is willing to provide and (2) users desire, but that (3) auditors will not attest to. Management forecasts are an example of this type of information. Even though users may be quite interested in this formation, auditors may not be willing to attest to it at this time.

Intersection III represents information that at a given time (1) management is

FIGURE 1–1
The interrelationships of three primary parties involved in providing financial accounting information
Source: R. M. Cyert and Y. Ijiri, "Problems of Implementing the Trueblood Objectives Report," *Supplement to the Journal of Accounting Research,* 1974, p. 30.

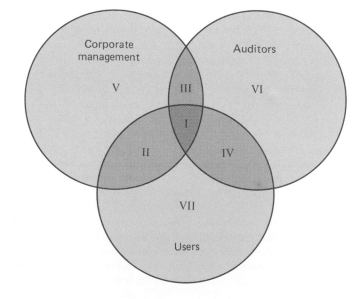

willing to provide and (2) auditors will attest to, but that (3) users do not desire. This might include information regarding the number of employees and their average age, the budgeted cost of specific materials used in production, and other information too detailed to be of concern to external users or irrelevant to their needs.

Intersection IV represents information that at a given time (1) users desire and (2) auditors will attest to, but that (3) management is not willing to provide. This could include data that management feels would harm the firm's competitive position in the market—for instance, detailed cost data for major products.

Because external users are considered to be the principal party, information in areas V and VI is of little significance. Area VII indicates information that (1) users desire, but that (2) management is not willing to provide and (3) auditors will not attest to. This area should be the focus of accounting policy makers as they seek to satisfy the needs of users of financial accounting information.

ACCOUNTING POLICY-MAKING GROUPS

How are the positions taken by managers, external users, and auditors converted into a process that generates GAAP? This is the realm of accounting policy making, which can be considered from social, economic, political, and conceptual points of view. The conceptual underpinnings that influence accounting policy making are explored in Chapter 2. The social, economic, and political aspects of accounting policy making are covered here. These will be best understood if we review the history of accounting policy making and study the organizations that have been concerned with, and influential in, the development of current accounting practices.

The discussion of policy making will start with the principal public- and private-sector bodies that have the explicit authority to decide on what constitutes GAAP. Then we shall review other influential organizations that have been active in the accounting policy-making process.

Private-Sector Policy Makers

The history of ways various private groups have influenced accounting policies and procedures in the United States is marked by gradual evolution and change. As businesses grew in size and the separation of managers and owners became more pronounced, a demand arose for standard policies regarding the disclosure of financial information.

The **New York Stock Exchange (NYSE),** established in 1792, was the primary mechanism for trading ownership interests in corporations. As such, it established specific requirements for disclosure of financial information that served as accounting policy for corporations whose shares it listed. It served as the principal authority in establishing accounting policies for externally distributed financial information until the stock market crash of 1929.

During the Depression of the 1930s the federal government became convinced that the collapse of the stock market was due in part to the lack of meaningful requirements for reporting financial and economic information to investors and creditors.[2] Furthermore, many felt that economic conditions would not improve until the investing public regained confidence in the financial markets.

In an effort to bolster public confidence and restore order to the securities markets, Congress enacted the **Securities Act of 1933** and the **Securities Ex-**

[2] For an interesting discussion, see Edward R. Willet, *Fundamentals of Securities Markets* (New York: Appleton-Century-Crofts, 1968), pp. 208–214.

change Act of 1934, which established the **Securities and Exchange Commission (SEC).** These acts and the decisions of the SEC required that publicly traded firms be audited by independent certified public accountants (CPAs), which naturally led to the increased influence of the independent accountants' professional organizations.

Certified public accountants have long played an important role in the U.S. economy. In 1877, the **American Association of Public Accountants (AAPA)** was established. This group represented the core of the accounting profession in the United States. The name of the organization was changed to the **American Institute of Accounting (AIA)** in 1917 and finally became the **American Institute of Certified Public Accountants (AICPA)** in 1957. Accounting organizations were active in influencing accounting policy prior to the 1930s, but the securities acts accentuated the need for more formal accounting standards and for systematic promulgation of those standards.

The Committee on Accounting Procedures   In 1939, the AIA formed the **Committee on Accounting Procedures (CAP),** which was to establish, review, and evaluate accepted accounting procedures. The policy-making authority of the CAP was indirect. Once the public accountant's attestation became a requirement for publicly traded entities, accountants began to look for more guidance in the area of financial accounting standards. Public accountants belonged to the AIA, and through the CAP the GAAP were identified. Through this indirect process, public accountants began to identify GAAP that formed the basis for auditor attestations.

The Accounting Principles Board   After issuing a total of 51 pronouncements, called Accounting Research Bulletins (ARBs), between 1939 and 1959, the CAP was replaced in 1959 by the AICPA's **Accounting Principles Board (APB).** It was hoped that the APB, made up of 18 AICPA members who served on the board part-time, would be a more effective policy-making body than the CAP had been. A total of 31 APB opinions defining GAAP were issued between 1962 and 1973, along with 4 APB "statements," which expressed the views of the APB on specific topics but did not require compliance by the profession.

The APB, like the CAP before it, was discontinued because of criticisms of its pronouncements and the belief that a new, more effective organization was possible and needed. As with most regulatory bodies in a free society, it is necessary that the majority of the affected parties accept its rules and regulations.[3] If the majority is displeased and a viable alternative is proposed, change must occur. The groups most affected by the APB—primarily the management of publicly held corporations, industry groups, and investors—were not completely satisfied with many of the APB's pronouncements. They at least believed that a different structure for private-sector policy making would be an improvement. Furthermore, there was substantial disagreement among AICPA members regarding many of the APB opinions. Other important beliefs that played a role in the replacement of the APB were the following: (1) the authoritative body should be more independent of the CPA profession; (2) full-time members would be better than part-time members; (3) more staff support was needed; and (4) a new push for a comprehensive statement of basic concepts was called for.

[3] For a discussion of this situation, see David Solomons, "The Politicization of Accounting," *Journal of Accountancy,* November 1978, pp. 65–72.

The Financial Accounting Standards Board (FASB) In 1971 the AICPA appointed the Wheat Committee (headed by Francis M. Wheat) to study the procedures for formulating accounting standards. The committee eventually proposed the establishment of a new private-sector policy-making body.[4] In 1973, the AICPA membership adopted the committee's recommendations, and the **Financial Accounting Foundation (FAF)** and the **Financial Accounting Standards Board (FASB)** were established. As can be seen in Figure 1–2, major functions of the FAF include financing the FASB and appointing its members.

The nine trustees of the FAF are charged with generating sufficient funds from business, industry, professional organizations, and individuals to support the FASB and thereby keep it financially independent of all special-interest groups. The FAF does not have any authority over policy making, and therefore it plays no role in the actual work of the FASB. The FAF collects approximately $6,000,000 a year to support the work of the FASB.

The FASB is made up of seven full-time members, only four of whom are drawn from among practicing CPAs. The other three members represent other private-sector interests. In addition to the seven board members, who are appointed for 5-year terms, renewable once, the FASB has the support of over 35 full-time technical staff members to assist in research and analysis of current accounting issues. The FASB also commissions outsiders in the academic and business community to conduct research projects so that it can receive as much evidence and substantive input as possible before ruling on controversial topics.

One of the primary tasks of the FASB is the issuing of official pronouncements that set financial accounting standards. Each of these pronouncements is known as a **standards statement.**[5] A three-stage policy-making schedule has been established to encourage interested parties to provide their views and comments during the standard-setting process. Thus, most of the standards statements issued by the FASB go through the following steps:

1. *Discussion-memorandum stage:* After the board and its staff have considered a topic on its agenda, and perhaps consulted with experts on this topic or with other interested parties, a **discussion memorandum** is issued. This memorandum outlines the key issues involved and includes the preliminary views of the board. The public is invited to comment on the memorandum, with public hearings sometimes held to permit those interested to express their views in person.

2. *Exposure-draft stage:* After further deliberation and modification of the proposed statement by the board and its staff, an **exposure draft** of the standards statement is issued. During this exposure period, which lasts not fewer than 30 days, further public comment is requested and evaluated.

3. *Voting stage:* Finally, the board votes on whether to issue the standards statement as contained in the exposure draft or to revise it and reissue a new exposure draft. For a proposed standard to become an official standards statement and a part of generally accepted accounting principles, four of the seven board members must approve it.

[4] The official name of this committee was "Study Group on Establishment of Accounting Principles."

[5] These primary pronouncements of the FASB are technically called *Statements of Financial Accounting Standards* (SFAS) but are commonly referred to as *"FASB No. ____"* or *"FASB Statement No. ____"* in the professional literature. This text will refer to these standards as "FASB Statement No. ____." In addition to Statements of Financial Accounting Standards, the FASB issues two other kinds of pronouncements: Statements of Financial Accounting Concepts and FASB Interpretations.

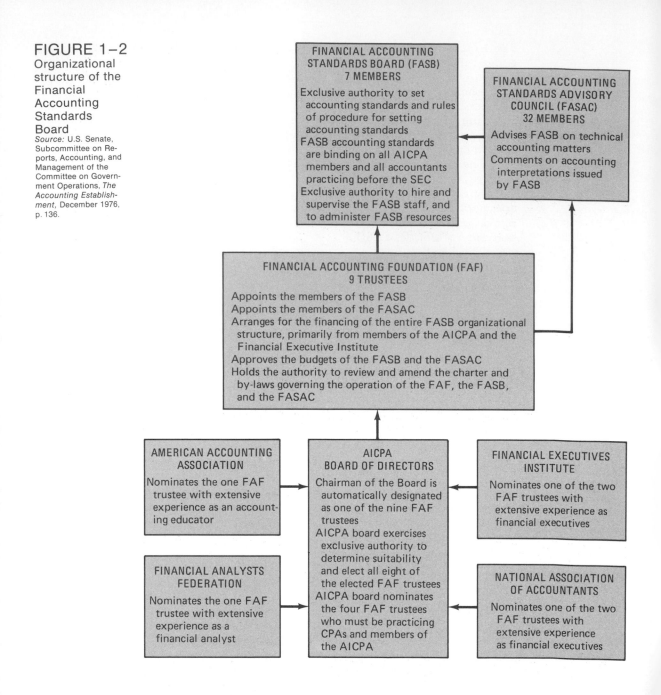

FIGURE 1–2
Organizational structure of the Financial Accounting Standards Board
Source: U.S. Senate, Subcommittee on Reports, Accounting, and Management of the Committee on Government Operations, *The Accounting Establishment,* December 1976, p. 136.

FINANCIAL ACCOUNTING STANDARDS BOARD (FASB)
7 MEMBERS
Exclusive authority to set accounting standards and rules of procedure for setting accounting standards
FASB accounting standards are binding on all AICPA members and all accountants practicing before the SEC
Exclusive authority to hire and supervise the FASB staff, and to administer FASB resources

FINANCIAL ACCOUNTING STANDARDS ADVISORY COUNCIL (FASAC)
32 MEMBERS
Advises FASB on technical accounting matters
Comments on accounting interpretations issued by FASB

FINANCIAL ACCOUNTING FOUNDATION (FAF)
9 TRUSTEES
Appoints the members of the FASB
Appoints the members of the FASAC
Arranges for the financing of the entire FASB organizational structure, primarily from members of the AICPA and the Financial Executive Institute
Approves the budgets of the FASB and the FASAC
Holds the authority to review and amend the charter and by-laws governing the operation of the FAF, the FASB, and the FASAC

AMERICAN ACCOUNTING ASSOCIATION
Nominates the one FAF trustee with extensive experience as an accounting educator

AICPA BOARD OF DIRECTORS
Chairman of the Board is automatically designated as one of the nine FAF trustees
AICPA board exercises exclusive authority to determine suitability and elect all eight of the elected FAF trustees
AICPA board nominates the four FAF trustees who must be practicing CPAs and members of the AICPA

FINANCIAL EXECUTIVES INSTITUTE
Nominates one of the two FAF trustees with extensive experience as financial executives

FINANCIAL ANALYSTS FEDERATION
Nominates the one FAF trustee with extensive experience as a financial analyst

NATIONAL ASSOCIATION OF ACCOUNTANTS
Nominates one of the two FAF trustees with extensive experience as financial executives

Since it was established in July 1973, the FASB has issued over 55 FASB standards statements as well as many interpretations that elaborate on fine points or uncertainties in the standards. In addition, the FASB has retained many of the APB and CAP pronouncements, and they have the same status as the FASB standards. A list of all standards currently in effect can be found on the endpapers of this book.

Many feel that the FASB must continue to be successful if the private sector is to remain the major contributor to the development of accounting practices and procedures in the United States. At the same time, without the support of the public accounting profession, business, and industry which are affected by its standards, the FASB cannot remain viable. History has demonstrated that developing accounting policy in the private sector, for the guidance of the private sector, and with the necessary support of the private sector is an ambitious and difficult task.

Public-Sector Policy Makers

The FASB and its predecessors have created an impressive body of promulgated GAAP that, along with other generally accepted procedures and concepts, guide accounting practices. These private-sector efforts are both sanctioned and mirrored in the public sector. The most prominent public-sector accounting policy maker is the SEC.

The Securities and Exchange Commission The SEC was created to serve as an independent regulatory agency of the U.S. government. The commission consists of five commissioners, appointed by the president of the United States and approved by the Senate for five-year terms. The terms overlap, with the term of one commissioner expiring each year. To guarantee balanced political representation on the commission, no more than three of the five commissioners may be from the same political party. The SEC has the absolute legal power to prescribe the nature of accounting and other financial information distributed by a corporation under its jurisdiction. If a corporation does not comply with SEC rules, the SEC can suspend trading of the corporation's securities or can take other actions to force compliance.

Formation of the SEC was not the first attempt to establish public policy concerning the regulation of financial information. During the period 1900–1922, congressional commissions dealing with business and industry introduced several bills that were designed to regulate disclosures included in annual financial reports. However, prior to the stock market crash of 1929, public sentiment was in favor of leaving business pretty much to itself, with a minimum of formal government regulation. It was not until after the crash of 1929 that government regulation of business became a feature of public policy. Congress, responding to the public mood, began an investigation of the securities industry in 1932, and a report to the House of Representatives in early 1933 clearly supported the need for federal legislation.

As mentioned earlier, the SEC was established as a result of the 1934 Securities Exchange Act and was charged with the responsibility of ensuring that publicly traded entities provide disclosure of all significant financial information in their public reports. Congress believed that improved disclosure rules would improve the operations of the capital markets and would thereby decrease the likelihood of another massive market failure.

The SEC currently is a rather large organization as can be seen by the organization chart in Figure 1–3. Regulating the securities market is obviously a complex and demanding task that requires the skills of various professionals, including accountants.[6] In addition to its primary pronouncement, **Regulation S-X,** which contains the principal formal financial-disclosure requirements for registrants, the SEC has issued over 300 *Accounting Series Releases* (ASRs), which include filing require-

---

[6] For a good discussion of the function of various divisions of the SEC and a detailed history and analysis of its activities, see K. Fred Skousen, *An Introduction to the SEC* (Cincinnati, OH: Southwestern, 1980).

SECURITIES AND EXCHANGE COMMISSION

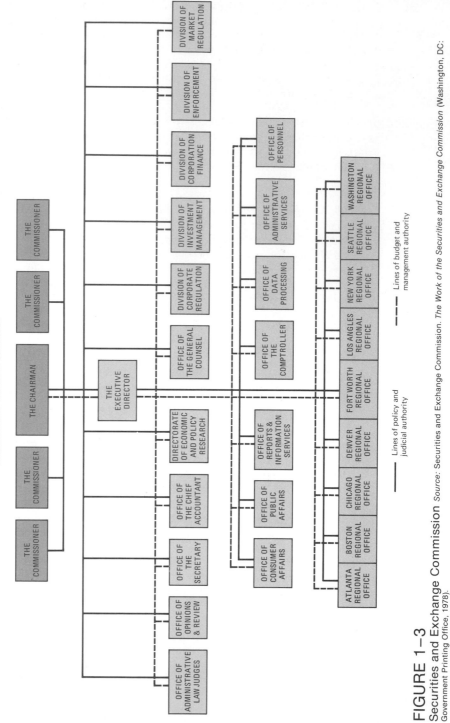

FIGURE 1–3

Securities and Exchange Commission Source: Securities and Exchange Commission. *The Work of the Securities and Exchange Commission* (Washington, DC: Government Printing Office, 1978).

14

ments passed by the commission. Regulation S-X and the ASRs are the major public-sector authoritative pronouncements on financial accounting.

Although it has set its own rules through numerous ASRs starting in 1937, the SEC has generally allowed the private sector to take the lead in formulating major accounting principles. The CAP, which first issued statements regarding accounting principles in 1939, the APB, and the FASB have worked closely with the SEC. However, during the transition period between the APB and the FASB, the SEC seemed to take on a more active and aggressive role in policy making. The APB, during its last 9 months of operation (October 1972–June 1973), tried to complete its agenda of in-process considerations of accounting principles and policies. It issued 7 opinions during these last months. The SEC, for its part, issued 14 ASRs during this same period.

This flurry of activity continued during the FASB's first year. During that period the SEC issued another 20 ASRs. More important, however, was the fact that these ASRs concerned major policy issues such as lease accounting and current-value accounting. This caused concern in the private sector that government policy makers were taking on a leadership role in developing generally accepted accounting principles. The chairman of the FASB charged that the SEC was preempting the FASB in the establishment of GAAP in the area of current-value accounting policy, for instance.[7] Other leaders in the accounting profession publicly expressed concern over the apparent expansion in the role of government.

At the same time, different signals were received from the SEC. In **ASR No. 150** (December 1973), the SEC made explicit its support for the pronouncements developed by the private sector in establishing GAAP. **ASR No. 150** further stated that the SEC had always looked to the profession to provide leadership in establishing GAAP and would continue to do so in the future. However, the SEC had in the past suggested in public releases that the private sector had failed to establish workable accounting policies and that perhaps the commission should take the lead.[8]

The SEC's degree of involvement and the volume of its policy-making activity have varied through time as its membership has changed. A most important challenge came in 1978 over the controversy concerning oil and gas accounting methods. The FASB had studied the issue of oil and gas accounting for some time and, after a lengthy development stage, issued **FASB Statement No. 19** in December 1977, which identified a single method of accounting that was to be followed by all affected parties.[9] In August 1978, the SEC ruled that a new method of accounting for oil and gas reserves needed to be developed and that in the meantime companies could use any method that had been generally accepted prior to **FASB Statement No. 19**. This directly contradicted the FASB and required the issuance of **FASB Statement No. 25** to bring the SEC and FASB into conformity with one another.[10]

It is doubtful that the SEC could ever be the sole source of GAAP without the participation of the private sector. The ability of the SEC to issue timely pronounce-

[7] Marshall Armstrong, "News Notes," *Journal of Accountancy,* March 1974, pp. 9–10.

[8] Securities and Exchange Commission, "The SEC and the FASB: Their Roles" (Washington, DC: Government Printing Office, 1974). This is an SEC news release dated January 21, 1974.

[9] *Statement of Financial Accounting Standards No. 19,"* Financial Accounting and Reporting by Oil and Gas Producing Companies" (Stamford, CT: FASB, December 1977).

[10] *Statement of Financial Accounting Standards No. 25,* "Suspension of Certain Accounting Requirements for Oil and Gas Producing Companies" (Stamford, CT: FASB, February 1979).

ments can be questioned by a review of the SEC–FASB disagreement in the oil and gas situation. The FASB deliberated on the oil and gas issue for well over a year. During this time the SEC had ample opportunity to provide its input at both the discussion-memorandum and exposure-draft stages of **FASB Statement No. 19.** Yet it was not until 8 months after a legal deadline that the SEC was able to issue a statement disagreeing with the FASB.[11]

We doubt whether the SEC has the ability or desire to deal with the numerous complex accounting issues being handled by the FASB. It is likely that the SEC's organizational and institutional burdens along with public support for less government regulation will result in the private sector's retaining its dominant policy-making role. In addition, as we shall discuss further in Chapter 27, the SEC's current attempt to streamline reporting requirements seems to be headed toward more direct authority for the FASB in establishing GAAP for SEC reporting purposes.[12]

OTHER INFLUENTIAL ORGANIZATIONS

The American Institute of Certified Public Accountants
When the APB was setting accounting policy, the AICPA played a substantial role in accounting policy making. After all, the APB was part of the AICPA. When the FASB replaced the APB, the AICPA's role changed because the FASB is an independent organization. Still, because it is the national professional association for CPAs, the AICPA remains an important force in the establishment of GAAP. As suggested earlier, independent auditors (members of the AICPA) must make an attestation to certain financial information that external users seek and management is willing to provide. Instances will be found throughout the text where the auditor's need to attest helps to explain, at least in part, the underlying justification of certain reporting practices.

The AICPA is a very large organization representing over 150,000 CPAs in public practice, business, education, and government. As Figure 1–4 shows, the AICPA is governed by a broadly based council representing several groups of members. The organization is made up of permanent staff and several committees and boards whose members are selected from the AICPA membership.

In order to make the views of its members known, the AICPA has established the Accounting Standards Division to draft and communicate positions on accounting policy issues. Within the division, a senior technical committee, the **Accounting Standards Executive Committee (AcSEC),** actually carries out the task of setting the AICPA's official position and commenting on the proposals of the SEC and FASB through its *Statements of Position.* The AICPA also has had an impact on accounting practice through its **Auditing Standards Board,** formerly the **Auditing Standards Executive Committee (AudSEC).** Its accounting and audit guides have strongly influenced the practice of accounting and auditing.

Among the AICPA's several publications is *The Journal of Accountancy,* the major accounting journal for practitioners in public accounting. The *Journal,* with a

[11] A public law effectively required an investigation and action on the state of oil and gas accounting rules by December 25, 1977. Public concern stemmed from the oil-supply crisis of 1973–1974, which was created by the cartel of oil producing and exporting countries (OPEC). This public concern resulted in this unusual legal deadline in connection with the process of setting account standards.

[12] See Jeremy Wilsen, "Reporting Concepts for the 1980's," *Journal of Accounting, Auditing and Finance,* Summer 1980, pp. 309–324, for a review of the SEC's current and future directions in this regard.

CHAIRMAN OF THE BOARD

Appoints committees
Speaks for AICPA
Presides at meetings
Recommends candidates for nominations committees
Trustee of Financial Accounting Foundation

SENIOR TECHNICAL COMMITTEES

Independently speak for the AICPA in their respective subject areas

COMMITTEES AND BOARDS

Perform work for the AICPA in various subject areas

VICE CHAIRMAN OF THE BOARD

Designated as the next Chairman
Recommends candidates for nominations committee

BOARD OF DIRECTORS

Makes policy and administers resources of the AICPA
Approves appointments to senior technical committees
Reports to the Council
Elects Financial Accounting Foundation which controls Financial Accounting Standards Board

PRESIDENT

Executive authority over all policies and programs of the AICPA
Speaks for AICPA

AICPA STAFF

COUNCIL

Holds ultimate authority over AICPA

OFFICERS OF THE AICPA	ELECTED MEMBERS	MEMBERS AT LARGE	MEMBERS OF THE BOARD OF DIRECTORS	PAST PRESIDENTS/ CHAIRMEN OF THE BOARD	DESIGNATED COUNCIL REPRESENTATIVES OF STATE SOCIETIES
Nominated by the Nominations Committee Elected by the Council for a 1-year term	Nominated by the Nominations Committee Elected automatically unless independent nominations are filed Elected to 3-year staggered terms	Nominated by the Nominations Committee Elected by the Council for 3-year staggered terms	Nominated by the Nominations Committee Elected by the Council for 3-year staggered terms	Members of the Council for life, provided membership in the AICPA is continued	Chosen by the state societies according to their own rules

NOMINATIONS COMMITTEE

Selects official nominees
Apportions the number of elected council members from each state

FIGURE 1-4

Organization of the American Institute of Certified Public Accountants *Source:* U.S. Senate, Subcommittee on Reports, Accounting, and Management of the Committee on Government Operations, *The Accounting Establishment,* December 1976, p. 136.

readership of 165,000, provides factual information on current professional developments, news affecting the profession, and articles expressing opinions and providing evidence on controversial or current topics of interest. Another major service provided by the AICPA is continuing professional education. Literally hundreds of thousands of course days are taken each year under the auspices of the AICPA.

Perhaps the most dramatic changes in the AICPA in recent years have come in response to the congressional investigations that took place in the mid 1970s. Committees of both the U.S. Senate and the U.S. House of Representatives criticized the accounting profession for what they perceived to be a lack of independence from their clients, too much auditor concentration in large CPA firms, and a failure to review auditing practice regularly and objectively.

In response to these criticisms, the AICPA established two new divisions: (1) the **SEC Practice Section** and (2) the **Private Companies Section.** As the names suggest, this put into two separate categories (1) those AICPA members serving clients who are publicly traded entities listed on an exchange and who are responsible for compliance with SEC regulations and (2) those members serving private clients who need not adhere to SEC regulations.

The AICPA believed that these two groups called for different kinds of review procedures, with members of the SEC Practice Section needing more specific requirements and guidance in the areas of peer review, continuing education, and quality-control standards in auditing practices. In order to enforce guidelines, the **Public Oversight Board** was established to ensure that the standards of the SEC Practices Section are adhered to and that penalties are imposed on individuals and firms who violate these standards.

The AICPA also administers a program of peer review aimed at self-regulation of the quality of the audit function. In the peer-review process, CPA firms audit one another and issue peer-review reports at the end of the audit to both the AICPA and the firm being reviewed.

Although the SEC publicly approved of these efforts toward self-regulation, in July 1978, Congress considered establishing a government body to regulate the accounting profession. This attempt to involve the government directly in regulating the accounting profession was rejected largely due to the SEC's testimony before Congress in support of the AICPA's efforts at self-regulation.

In addition to the AICPA, several other organizations have an impact on financial accounting standards. Some of these are listed in Table 1–2. The three listed under "policy makers" have rule-making authority that is peripheral to mainstream financial reporting. Sometimes these organizations develop policies that indirectly affect or influence financial accounting practices.

The Cost Accounting Standards Board

The Cost Accounting Standards Board (CASB) was established in 1972 to achieve uniformity and fairness in defining product cost for major governmental defense contracts. After approximately 8 years of operation, it was terminated, and the U.S. General Accounting Office took over the duties of enforcing CASB standards. In a strict sense, the CASB's rules related only to certain government contracts. However, in practice, many businesses are involved indirectly in CASB-related government contracts. Therefore, CASB rules have influenced many cost accounting systems used as the basis for both internal and external inventory measurement and reporting.

TABLE 1-2

OTHER GROUPS THAT AFFECT FINANCIAL ACCOUNTING

GROUP	REPRESENTING	METHOD OF INFLUENCING FINANCIAL ACCOUNTING	MAJOR VEHICLES FOR INFLUENCING FINANCIAL ACCOUNTING
Policy Makers			
1. Cost Accounting Standards Board (CASB)	Public interest	Sets rules and regulations on cost accounting systems used for companies with major government contracts.	Cost Accounting Standards
2. Internal Revenue Service (IRS)	Public interest	Indirectly influences financial accounting to the extent that financial accounting principles and procedures follow those required for tax accounting.	Internal Revenue Code
3. Other government bodies	Public interest	Set rules and regulations for form and content of special-purpose financial reports to regulatory agencies.	Agency regulations
Interested Organizations			
1. CPA firms	Members of their firm	Respond to FASB standards. Forging practice. Provide input to all accounting-related policy-making bodies.	Numerous in-house publications. Sponsoring research projects.
2. National Association of Accountants (NAA)	Controllers, management accountants, and related parties	Sponsors research projects. Publish monographs on current topics and issues. Committee on management accounting practices provides position papers to policy-making bodies. Testifies at public hearings of the SEC and FASB.	*Management Accounting*
3. Financial Executives Institute (FEI)	Chief financial officers, financial managers, and other related parties	Supports Financial Executive Research Foundation, which conducts research into various current topics. Provides input to policy makers. Testifies at public hearings of the SEC and FASB.	*The Financial Executive*
4. American Accounting Association (AAA)	College professors and practicing accountants in industry and public accounting	Supports research into current issues of academic interest and publishes research monographs on specific topics. Provides input to policy makers. Testifies at public hearings of the SEC and FASB.	*The Accounting Review*

The Internal Revenue Service

The Internal Revenue Service (IRS) has had a significant impact on the tax-related aspects of financial accounting. In this way it has had an influence over accounting procedures used for financial reporting. When tax accounting requires specific accounting procedures that are acceptable but not *required* for financial reporting purposes, companies often select the alternatives required for tax purposes. This will be pointed out in several places throughout the text.

Other Government Bodies

Other government bodies have the authority to require firms to provide certain information in a specific format for their own purposes. For example, the Civil Aeronautics Board required airlines to report lease information before either the SEC or the FASB sets procedures for such reporting. State securities laws often require specific reports and registrations. The Federal Reserve Board administers the banking system and prescribes financial accounting procedures for member banks. Insurance and utility commissions have many specialized rules affecting financial reporting. However, these various government agencies have not been a major factor in the development of GAAP.

CPA Firms and Other Interested Organizations

CPA firms are probably the most influential of the interested organizations listed in Table 1–2. In their responses to FASB exposure drafts and their participation at public hearings and other forums that allow interested parties to provide input to accounting policy making, CPA firms play a more active role than any other non-authoritative body. The major CPA firms carefully monitor policy-making activities and provide the firm's views as input to accounting policy. It is critical for CPA firms to keep abreast of policy-making activity because they must be aware of GAAP before they can test for compliance with GAAP. Although CPA firms may have been more directly influential in policy issues before the FASB was set up, they still have a strong indirect impact on accounting policies and the establishment of GAAP. Given their current level of interest and involvement in policy-making activities, CPA firms are likely to continue to be an important force in the development of GAAP.

The other interested organizations listed in Table 1–1 all have similar means of influencing the policy-making process. Because these organizations represent rather broad groups with diverse interests and preferences, it is likely that they will continue to contribute to accounting policy in an indirect way. The American Accounting Association (AAA), for instance, has been active in developing the conceptual foundation of financial accounting for many years through its research programs and publications. In addition, many AAA members serve on various professional and policy-making boards. The other listed organizations have also used these means to contribute to financial accounting.

SUMMARY

Financial accounting serves the needs of diverse users—investors, creditors, taxing authorities, employees, and others—who make decisions based on financial information provided by businesses and other economic entities. How these information needs are translated into specific accounting policies and how those policies are used to generate accounting information involves both conceptual and institutional elements. In its analysis of the historical foundations of accounting and accounting institutions, this chapter has attempted to demonstrate that the complex environment of accounting has a great impact on the accounting policy-making process.

The accounting principles, practices, and procedures to be discussed in coming chapters are, at least in part, functions of the accounting environment. An awareness of this environment will help to give you the perspective necessary to appreciate some of the practical limits of accounting information. It is as important to know the limitations of accounting as to know its strengths. A knowledge of the current rules alone will not make you a competent professional accountant or even a competent user of accounting information. The rules are apt to continue to change in ways that will force the users and providers of financial information to reach a more basic understanding of the context and the framework of accounting as the basis for decisions.

The conceptual framework of accounting can be understood only in the context of the accounting environment and policy-making process. Similarly, the conceptual framework and environment of accounting are crucial to an understanding of accounting procedures. For this reason, we shall refer back to the accounting environment discussed here and to the conceptual structure to be discussed in the next chapter, as we progress through the remainder of the text.

QUESTIONS

Q1-1   What is the objective of financial accounting?

Q1-2   Who are the three main parties involved in the financial accounting information system? Discuss their positions concerning information they would like to see disclosed in the financial statements.

Q1-3   Who are the authoritative accounting policy-making bodies today? What is the exact nature of their authority?

Q1-4   What is the role of the AICPA in accounting practice and policy making? What is the source of the AICPA's strength or authority?

Q1-5   What is the major publication of the AICPA? How often is it issued and how many people subscribe to this publication?

Q1-6   Which groups have played a role in private-sector policy making over the last 50 years? How long were they each involved and what was their apparent source of authority?

Q1-7   Explain why the private-sector policy-making bodies have changed so often while the public-sector group has not changed. Try to support your explanation with historical facts whenever possible.

Q1-8   You are an accounting major having dinner with you father and his boss. Your father's boss, Mr. Muchbucks, has learned from your father that you are an accounting major and has asked you to explain what accounting is all about. Prepare your answer. Don't feel intimidated, Mr. Muchbucks was a marketing major at Yell Well back in the 1940s.

Q1-9   What is the role of the IRS in setting accounting standards?

Q1-10   What is the role of CPA firms in setting accounting standards?

Q1-11   What is the FASB procedure for developing and issuing accounting standards?

Q1-12   What organizations, without having specific authority to do so, have been influential in accounting policy making? How? Can you cite instances of how this influence was exercised?

Q1-13   What are the differences between financial accounting, managerial accounting, and auditing?

Q1-14   What are the similarities between financial accounting, managerial accounting, and auditing?

CASES

C1-1   Different economies throughout the world are often characterized by different financial accounting systems. For example U.S. and Canadian companies provide external users with information that differs substantially from that provided by their counterparts in the Soviet Union. Even among Western countries, procedures for financial disclosure vary widely. What do you think are the major factors in an economy that influence financial accounting disclosures of economic entities operating in that economy?

C1-2   Presume you are a member of a U.S. senator's staff. A Senate subcommittee is scheduled to debate the proposition that financial accounting procedures should be set by a government agency. The senator you work for is a middle-of-the-roader who doesn't have a strongly held position on this issue. He asks you to draw up two short position papers. One is to support purely private-sector control and the other is to support purely public-sector control. After completing the two papers, discuss where you think the current system as described in this chapter fits in relationship to the two.

C1–3 Financial accounting reports have many standardized elements, that is, certain financial statements and other forms of disclosure are common to most information packages periodically distributed to external users. In addition, the specific techniques used for measuring financial statement items are often prescribed by accounting policy makers. There has been a longstanding debate concerning the cost and benefit of standardization versus flexibility. In the past half century, there has been a trend toward more standardization under the auspices of the FASB and its predecessors and the SEC. Make lists of the pros and the cons of standardization in financial accounting and give your overall assessment of benefits and cost of standardization.

C1–4 Financial accounting statements are used by a wide variety of people, from sophisticated bankers and financial analysts to lay people such as employees and owners or managers of small businesses. Discuss the propositions that there should be different accounting policy-making groups for each major class of user. What problems and benefits would you foresee in instituting such a multitiered system?

C1–5 On a visit to your home, a friend who owns a travel agency picked up your text and read Chapter 1. Being fascinated by the discussion, she quizzed you as follows: "I think I see how accounting information, as defined in this book, would be of importance to those interested in large publicly held businesses, but I don't think that such a concept applies to my local travel agency." How would you respond to such a statement? Be specific about potential external users who might want accounting information about her business.

Framework of Accounting Theory and Practice

2

OVERVIEW   Chapter 1 provided the necessary background for an understanding of the environment of accounting. Understanding the primary forces responsible for, and involved in, the development of accounting will be useful for understanding various aspects of accounting theory and practice throughout this chapter and the remainder of the text. This chapter describes the conceptual foundation of financial accounting.

The primary source of the theoretical framework described in this chapter is the Financial Accounting Standards Board (FASB). The FASB, one of the most influential organizations in financial accounting discussed in Chapter 1, is involved in articulating accounting theory through its **Conceptual Framework Project** and its **Statements of Financial Accounting Concepts (SFAC).** The resulting framework is not unlike the frameworks developed in previous authoritative pronouncements and scholarly works, but it is directly relevant to current accounting policy because of its adoption by the FASB.

The framework for accounting theory is designed to provide some common underpinnings to current and future practices and procedures followed in accounting. Without some common basis for relating accounting procedures and practices to one another, accounting would be nothing more than a disjointed set of rules. While some have argued that accounting can survive as a useful element of business and society without a conceptual framework, most agree that a set of rules, practices, and procedures that may be explained in the context of a theoretical structure is preferable.[1]

This chapter considers the framework of accounting theory and practice as it exists today. It is a framework that has evolved over many decades and is expected to continue to undergo change. The importance of the underlying concepts discussed here cannot be fully appreciated until the text has been completed, and it is very likely that the reader will refer back to the framework material throughout the book.

To the extent that the underlying framework of accounting is understood and can be viewed as the basis for accounting practices and procedures, accounting will be a subject that makes sense; it will be a subject that enables one to think through to an acceptable solution to accounting problems. Alternatively, if the underlying framework is not understood or does not provide a logical way of explaining practice and procedures, accounting will be treated as a mechanical process calling for memorization. In the final analysis, we shall probably conclude it is made up of both conceptual and mechanical elements. By design, this text attempts to focus on the former and minimize the latter.

BASIS FOR ACCOUNTING PRONOUNCEMENTS

The body of rules, procedures, and practices that constitute accounting today are referred to throughout the text as **generally accepted accounting principles (GAAP).** The published financial reports of many business entities must be prepared in conformance with GAAP. But where do GAAP come from? How are they developed? In a narrow sense, the body of practice called GAAP came from the pronouncements of policy-making organizations such as the FASB and its predecessors, the SEC, and other influential organizations discussed in Chapter 1. Yet in a broader sense, these rules have been developed using certain guiding concepts and notions that have been informally accepted by policy-making organizations as standards by which accounting pronouncements might be judged.

PURPOSE OF ACCOUNTING

The FASB's
Conceptual
Framework
Project

Since its inception the FASB has been involved with the development of a framework for accounting theory. The framework is intended for the use of the FASB in establishing **Statements of Financial Accounting Standards** and **FASB Interpretations** and is expected to provide guidance to the board in the development of conceptually consistent accounting standards. The framework was designed to draw commonalities from existing accounting practice, taking what is known as a basis. It was not the purpose of the framework study to change existing accounting practices. Rather, the goal was to observe common dimensions of accounting practices and procedures and to identify those that were expected to provide the most suitable framework for guiding the future development of accounting.

The outline of accounting theory in Exhibit 2–1 identifies the major compo-

---

[1] N. Dopuch and S. Sunder, "FASB's Statements on Objectives and Elements of Financial Accounting: A Review," *The Accounting Review,* January 1980, pp. 1–21.

EXHIBIT 2-1

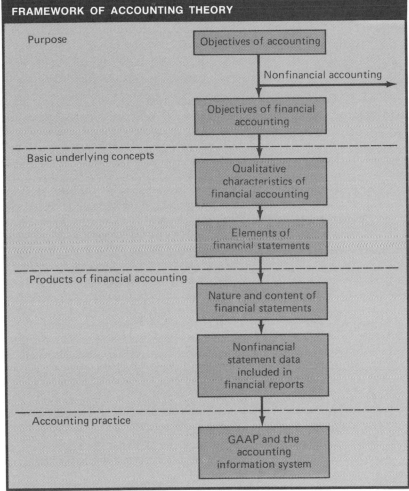

FRAMEWORK OF ACCOUNTING THEORY

Purpose — Objectives of accounting
— Nonfinancial accounting
— Objectives of financial accounting

Basic underlying concepts — Qualitative characteristics of financial accounting — Elements of financial statements

Products of financial accounting — Nature and content of financial statements — Nonfinancial statement data included in financial reports

Accounting practice — GAAP and the accounting information system

nents of the framework. These components will be discussed according to their hierarchical ordering, with detail added at each stage of the outline.

Objectives of Accounting

The overall objective of accounting must be stated in such a way that it does not exclude any type of accounting information, if possible. An objective statement at this level of generality is necessary. While the FASB has confined itself to one subset of accounting—financial accounting—other accounting bodies that have examined accounting theory have defined the overall objective of accounting as follows: **To collect, measure, and communicate relevant economic information for decision making.**

In its broadest form, **accounting** is defined as an information system concerned with aiding the decision-making process of any interested decision maker whose decision is based, in part at least, on economic data. This objective would include a wide variety of internal and external users with many different decision making needs, and this gives the objective statement its general applicability. However, the notion that accounting is a systematic means of collecting information, recording it through measurement, and communicating it by way of somewhat standardized transmission formats is not peculiar to the broad objective statement. Even for narrower statements of objectives, accounting is still a system of processing and reporting information.

Objective of Financial Accounting

As discussed in Chapter 1, external users, managers (internal users), and auditors are the three primary groups concerned with accounting information. Financial accounting is designed primarily to satisfy the information needs of external users. In **SFAC No. 1,** two major categories of external users were identified as being most prominent: (1) **investors and potential investors;** and (2) **creditors and potential creditors.**[2] It was not the intention of the FASB in **SFAC No. 1** to provide a single-sentence definition of the objective of financial accounting. However, as outlined in Exhibit 2–2 and discussed below, the objective of financial accounting might be summarized as follows: **Financial accounting should provide investors and creditors with financial reports that contain information useful for making business decisions and other decisions based on economic data.**

Components of Objective of Financial Accounting

Reporting unit **SFAC No.** 1 begins by stating that financial accounting data are not ends in themselves but are designed to provide data about the business entity to assist external users. This is sometimes referred to as the **entity assumption.** The **business entity,** as opposed to the individual owners of a business, is the reporting unit of concern.[3] The external user group identified would contain those investors and creditors who normally lack the authority to determine the accounting data provided them by managers of the business entity.

Measurement unit The "financial reports" are the vehicles by which accountants provide the desired information. These financial reports focus on the formal financial statements that are expressed in terms of **monetary units** of measure.[4] However, given the nature of the data, the fact that in some cases the measures are approximations, and the general limitations required by letting the numbers in the statements speak for themselves, other financial data not reported in the formal statements are considered to be an integral part of the financial reports.[5]

[2] *Statement of Financial Accounting Concepts No. 1,* "Objectives of Financial Reporting by Business Enterprises" (Stamford, CT: FASB, November 1978).

[3] The focus on the **entity** as the accounting unit rather than the owners of the entity or the industry of the entity was known as the **entity assumption** in most theoretical outlines that preceded *SFAC No. 1.* The fact that the entity assumption is taken for granted by most users probably explains its reduced prominence in *SFAC No. 1.*

[4] The monetary unit identified in *SFAC No. 1* is not the same as that previously embodied in the "monetary assumption" (or the "stable unit of measure assumption") in that it does not require that the dollars used in financial statements be defined as any one type of dollar units (for example, historical-exchange dollars, constant-purchasing-power dollars, and so on). This increase in the generalizability of the measurement unit provides the framework with a degree of flexibility not possible in prior frameworks. It permits the framework to apply to the alternative valuation methods to be considered further in Chapter 6 and Chapter 26.

[5] *SFAC No. 1,* "Objectives of Financial Reporting by Business Enterprises," pars. 6–7.

EXHIBIT 2-2

Users The **investment decisions** and **credit-granting decisions** are considered to be of primary interest to users of financial accounting data. Where accounting data are considered to have utility in such decision situations, the "usefulness" test is considered to be met.

Economic flows SFAC No. 1 places emphasis on information that would be useful in assessing the future cash flows of the business entity. This emphasis on cash flow is supported by the fact that expected cash flows are considered to be the most important factor in decisions regarding investments and the issuing of credit. A generally accepted valuation model for economic entities is **the net present value of future cash flows.**[6] **SFAC No. 1** also focuses on the way in which the financial reports may be used to evaluate the performance of the entity and its managers.

Capital maintenance The capital-maintenance concept, which views financial reports as a record of the resources of an entity at a point in time and the flow of resources over time, is a fundamental concept underlying financial reporting. Figure 2–1 illustrates how the basic financial reports fit into this capital-maintenance concept for a 1-year period. This "stock-and-flow" view of financial reporting provides statements with details regarding both the "stocks" (balance sheets) and the "flows" (various statements of changes), permitting users to focus on either the position or the nature of changes in position or both.

BASIC UNDERLYING CONCEPTS

Qualitative
Characteristics
of Financial
Accounting Data

SFAC No. 2 addresses the question of the qualities that financial accounting data should possess.[7] These qualities are relevance, reliability, and comparability. The concepts identified in **SFAC No. 2,** which are outlined in Exhibit 2–3, provide the details of the qualitative characteristics of financial accounting.

Relevance **Relevance** is considered to be the primary attribute of accounting information. For accounting information to be helpful to users' decision-making

___

[6] This net present-value concept is developed more thoroughly in Chapters 5 and 6. Put very simply, net present value of future cash flows is the amount an investor would pay now for future cash amounts given a certain interest rate. In essence, the emphasis on cash flows in *SFAC No. 1* suggests that users make decisions based largely on the net present value of the *expected* future economic benefits. These *expected* economic benefits are closely related to *the economic flows of the entity* they are evaluating for investment or credit-granting purposes.

[7] *Statement of Financial Accounting Concepts No. 2,* "Qualitative Characteristics of Accounting Information" (Stamford, CT: FASB, May 1980).

FIGURE 2–1
Capital maintenance and financial reporting

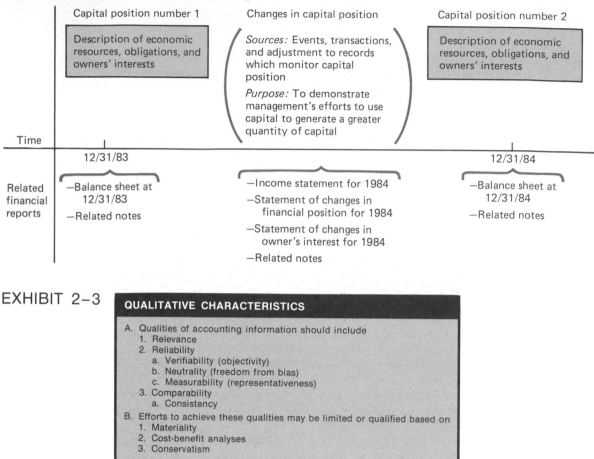

EXHIBIT 2–3

QUALITATIVE CHARACTERISTICS

A. Qualities of accounting information should include
   1. Relevance
   2. Reliability
      a. Verifiability (objectivity)
      b. Neutrality (freedom from bias)
      c. Measurability (representativeness)
   3. Comparability
      a. Consistency
B. Efforts to achieve these qualities may be limited or qualified based on
   1. Materiality
   2. Cost-benefit analyses
   3. Conservatism

needs, it must first be relevant. Relevant information is considered to represent a trade-off between **timely information** and **useful information.** Data that are capable of reducing uncertainty are "useful information." Data regarding a future outcome that are received far enough in advance of the outcome for users to respond to it in a decision-making sense are "timely information." In many cases, the more timely the information, the less useful it is (that is, the less capable it is of reducing uncertainty about a future outcome of interest to decision makers). This common trade-off is illustrated in Figure 2–2. As the future outcome becomes closer to being realized, information will frequently become more certain but will become less timely. Information about events that have already occurred is usually certain but has little value in terms of timeliness. The trade-off between timeliness and usefulness does not always hold true but seems to apply in many situations. Although relevant information is not always predictive, it often enhances predictions.

Reliability The concept of **reliability** is perhaps the most complex of the three qualitative characteristics. Reliable information has the following attributes: **objec-**

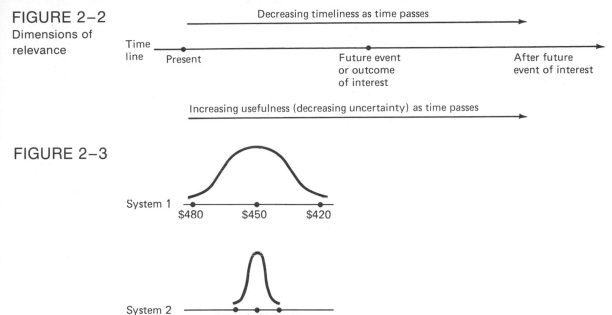

FIGURE 2–2
Dimensions of relevance

Decreasing timeliness as time passes →

Time
line

Present   Future event   After future
                   or outcome   event of interest
                   of interest

Increasing usefulness (decreasing uncertainty) as time passes →

FIGURE 2–3

System 1
$480 $450 $420

System 2
$420 $400 $410

tivity (or verifiability); **neutrality** (or freedom from bias); and **measurability** (or representativeness). What do these attributes mean and how do they determine reliability? In a conceptual sense, these attributes are related to one another. Objectivity (or verifiability) may be represented conceptually by a distribution of measurements from a particular measurement system, such as the two distributions shown in Figure 2–3. Assume these two distributions represent the results of 110 independent measurements of a particular asset. System 2 is more objective (or verifiable) than system 1 (all else assumed to be equal) because there is more of a consensus as to the value of the asset being measured. System 1 is less objective because there is more uncertainty about the value of the asset using whatever measurement process is called for by system 1.[8]

The concepts of neutrality and measurability can be thought of as two different sources of measurement error, one being attributable to the measure being used, the other to the measurer, as illustrated in Figure 2–4.

In total, these errors account for the difference between the average or expected value (for example, $450 in system 1) and the "true value" of the object being measured ($A). These errors may be represented by the distances D-1 in system 1 and D-2 in system 2. Because system 2 is both more verifiable, less biased, and more measurable it can be said to be more *reliable* than system 1.[9] If one measurement system was more objective but resulted in greater bias and measurement error, it would be necessary to determine whether measurement errors or objectivity were more important in order to judge reliability.

[8] These two systems might be viewed as two different ways to measure inventory, such as LIFO or FIFO, or two different depreciation methods.

[9] These representations of the attributes of reliability are based on Yuji Ijiri and Robert K. Jaedicke, "Reliability and Objectivity of Accounting Measurements," *The Accounting Review*, July 1966, pp. 480–483.

FIGURE 2-4

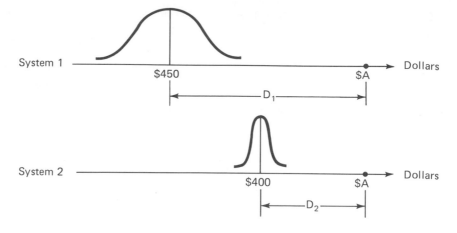

These abstract representations of the concepts of objectivity, bias, and representativeness are useful in providing an understanding of the complex concept of reliability. Certainly, if we knew the true value of the items we were attempting to measure, there would be no need to consider any of the qualitative characteristics. Although the conceptual relationship between measurement errors and objectivity may have little practical significance, it is important to have a grasp of the nature of reliability in order to use it as a means of evaluating accounting alternatives.[10]

Comparability A third quality that accounting data should possess is **comparability,** the ability to portray accurately important common dimensions of the items being reported. Information that meets the test of comparability will report like objects to be alike and will permit the economic (or real) differences between unlike objects to be accounted for in such a way that users will understand the differences. The comparability of accounting information is heavily dependent on a clear communication of similarities and differences in reported items. If, for example, original cost is an important dimension of two different assets, the accounting information system that reliably measures the original cost of these assets will permit a meaningful comparison to be made. Comparability also encompasses the notion of the **consistency of measurement methods** or procedures. Consistency of information within an entity as well as between entities is essential to the comparability of accounting information.

Qualitative Limitations Certain limitations may reduce the need for, or importance of, the qualities of relevance, reliability, and comparability. Three such limitations are **materiality, cost-benefit considerations,** and **conservatism.**

Materiality Accounting data that can be expected to have an impact on the economic decisions or judgments of a reasonably knowledgeable user of those data are said to be **material** in nature. Accounting data that, had they been presented to a reasonably knowledgeable user, would not have affected that user's judgments or decisions are said to be **immaterial.** To the extent that there is no precise definition

---

[10] For a more complete conceptual model that integrates relevance, reliability, and comparability, see E. Imhoff, "Evaluating Accounting Alternatives," *Management Accounting,* October 1981, pp. 56–71.

of what constitutes a "reasonably knowledgeable person," there is no exact definition of materiality. Except in those instances where the FASB or others have identified specific materiality limits, the notion of materiality depends on the judgment of the individual applying this standard. Information that is relevant, reliable, and comparable may be omitted from accounting disclosures or may be treated in what would be considered an otherwise inappropriate way if the nondisclosure or incorrect treatment would not have an impact on decisions.

Cost-benefit considerations   Like materiality, this is a somewhat difficult limitation to explain and to apply in that it calls for individual judgment. In essence, if the cost of producing information that is otherwise qualitatively desirable exceeds the expected benefits, there is no need to provide the information. Like materiality, application of the cost-benefit considerations to some event will result in either the disclosure or nondisclosure of that event as a result of the cost-benefit considerations. Since the *judgment* affects the disclosure (outcome), it is difficult to evaluate these judgments either before or after the fact.

Conservatism   The concept of conservatism relates primarily to the quality of reliability and, to a lesser extent, comparability. If information is relevant but not reliable due to various potential uncertainties, more conservative alternative measures might be used in their place. The concept of conservatism cannot be employed to achieve a deliberate understatement of the net asset position or the net income of an entity. However, when there is a high degree of uncertainty in accounting measurements, the use of conservative alternatives, that is, those resulting in lower assets and/or income amounts, may be the most prudent course. In terms of the concept of reliability, conservatism attaches greater importance to verifiability than to neutrality or measurability.

Elements of Financial Statements   **SFAC No. 3** describes the components of the financial statements of the business entity.[11] These components, which are listed in Exhibit 2–4, are directly related to the capital-maintenance concept illustrated in Figure 2–1. They define the elements that are the basis for measuring the position of the entity (the balance sheet) and the elements that report on the changes in an entity's position that permit users to assess the performance of the entity and its management. Although the list of elements

EXHIBIT 2–4

ELEMENTS OF FINANCIAL STATEMENTS

A. Elements for describing position measurement
   1. Assets
   2. Liabilities
   3. Equity
B. Elements for describing position changes
   1. Investments by owners
   2. Distributions to owners
   3. Comprehensive income
   4. Revenues
   5. Expenses
   6. Gains
   7. Losses

[11] *Statement of Financial Accounting Concepts No. 3*, "Elements of Financial Statements of Business Enterprises" (Stamford, CT: FASB, December 1980).

appears to consist of terms with which we are already familiar, the meaning of these elements should be studied with care. Many of the specific problems and controversial issues in accounting practice are based on the inherent difficulties encountered in the application of these elements. We shall refer back to the definitions of these basic elements to help resolve real-world accounting issues discussed elsewhere in the text.

The first three elements measure the position of the entity, whereas the last seven indicate how changes in position have occurred. These two types of elements are related to one another in that a change in one of the three elements of position (assets, liabilities, and owners' equity) often results in a corresponding change in one or more of the seven elements that describe change. This enables users to determine the underlying causes of the change in position. The ten elements are all defined in the context of their description of a particular entity and its business affairs.

Position measurement

ASSETS "Assets are probable future economic benefits obtained or controlled by a particular entity as a result of past transactions or events."[12] In order for future benefits to be recorded as assets, they must be likely to occur and must be reasonably measurable. They must also be controlled by the entity in such a way that other entities may not have access to the benefits without consent. The transaction or event that provided the entity with the future benefits must have already occurred.

Perhaps the most important criterion that assets must meet is the measurability of the future economic benefits. Unless these future benefits are measurable with a reasonable degree of precision (objectivity), they may not be recorded. This can be a problem even for relatively common assets, such as accounts receivable. Accounts receivable represent claims to future cash payments. The collectibility of these future payments normally involves some uncertainty, even in the case of preferred customers with excellent credit ratings. To allow such uncertainties to be reflected in statements, **valuation accounts,** such as Allowance for Uncollectibles, are established. The use of valuation techniques permits assets, the net expected future benefits, to be measured objectively and with a reasonable degree of precision. Complete certainty regarding the amount of future benefits is not required for the expected benefits to be recorded as assets.

Assets do not necessarily represent legally enforceable claims to economic resources. The legal title to an economic resource is not a requirement for asset recognition. For example, leased equipment is an economic resource that *might* qualify as an asset of an entity other than the entity that holds legal title to the equipment.

LIABILITIES "Liabilities are probable future sacrifices of economic benefits arising from present obligations of a particular entity to transfer assets or provide services to other entities in the future as a result of past transactions or events."[13] Entities often incur liabilities when obtaining cash, goods, or services required to operate their business. These liabilities are normally the results of formal and informal contractual agreements with other entities and are generally incurred in the activities of all but the most simple businesses.

Like assets, liabilities are not confined to legally enforceable claims against the entity. If the probable future sacrifice of economic benefits can be estimated with

[12] Ibid., par. 19.

[13] Ibid., par. 28.

reasonable precision, and if an event that establishes the obligation is expected to result in a future outflow of goods or services, it may be recorded as a liability. Here again, valuation techniques are sometimes used in order to satisfy the measurability requirement.

It should be noted that the term "probable" is a key element in defining both assets and liabilities. There is no precise statistical meaning for the term as it is employed here. The probable nature of the future inflow or outflow of economic resources is to be based on the available evidence and the judgment of the individuals determining assets and liabilities. Thus, the net asset position of the business entity may be based, in part at least, on human judgment.

EQUITY "**Equity is the residual interest in the assets of the entity that remains after deducting its liabilities. In a business enterprise, the equity is the ownership interest.**"[14] The equity holders of a business entity take the highest risk but stand to receive the highest rewards if the entity is successful. The high risk is attributable to the fact that the claims of owners are subordinate to the claims of creditors upon liquidation of the entity. Also, most ownership contracts represent an investment for an indefinite period of time, whereas most liability contracts represent investments for a limited time period. At the end of this period, the entity must eliminate the obligation by transferring some of its resources. There are three basic types of ownership structure in business: **proprietorships, partnerships** and **corporations.** Partnerships and proprietorships are considered to be the most risky because they do not allow the ownership interests to limit their liability. The corporate form of business is presumed throughout this book since it is the dominant form of business used by entities that must comply with GAAP. The overall balance sheet category of ownership interests is normally referred to as **stockholders' equity.** Within the stockholders' equity category, different types of stock certificates represent different degrees of risk. Generally the voting common stock is the equity security with the greatest amount of risk. Common stockholders might lose their entire investment in certain cases.

The rewards of equity interests should have an expected value greater than that of liabilities to compensate for the greater risk. Because the equity holders must wait until the profits are sufficient to cover the interest payments to the creditors before receiving any cash dividends, they are taking a greater risk. However, unlike the creditors, the returns (dividends) to the equity holders are not limited. Creditors will receive a maximum of their stated interest payments no matter how successful the entity is, while common stockholders are normally able to receive unlimited returns.

The equity accounts represent three types of owner capital: original invested capital; capital contributed from time to time from various types of nonroutine activities (for example, a new stock issue or gifts to the corporation); and net income generated by the entity from all sources and retained in the business. From a simple perspective, equity at a point in time is equal to total assets minus total liabilities.

Position changes The seven terms describing how positions may change are all capable of being defined in terms of assets, liabilities, and equity. Keep in mind that net assets is the term for assets minus liabilities.

INVESTMENT BY OWNERS **Owners' investments** result in an increase in net assets and a corresponding increase in the owners' capital accounts. They may result

[14] Ibid., par. 43.

from various types of transactions between the owners and the entity, but the result of these transactions is to generate additional net assets and additional ownership interest.

DISTRIBUTIONS TO OWNERS **Distributions to owners** are the result of transactions between the entity and its owners that cause a decrease in net assets. The most common distribution would be through cash dividends to shareholders.

COMPREHENSIVE INCOME **Comprehensive income** is the result of changes in net assets resulting from events and transactions other than investments by, or distributions to, owners. Comprehensive income includes the inflows from revenues and gains, the outflows from losses and expenses, and the various intermediate measures of these inflows and outflows (for example, gross margin, net income before tax, and so on).

REVENUES **Revenues** are inflows of net assets that result from the operating transactions and events of the entity over a specified period of time. Revenues represent the benefits, or expected future benefits, to be derived from the business entity's activities, such as selling goods and services to customers. These benefits are expected eventually to be converted to an inflow of liquid assets, which in turn are returned to operations or used to fulfill obligations or to provide returns to the ownership interests.

EXPENSES **Expenses** represent the measures of future benefits that have expired during the operating process, resulting in an outflow of net assets. They are the "costs" side of the cost-benefit analysis of the entity's operations. Expenses are frequently identified by considering the revenues that are being recognized during a specified time period and then determining the costs that were necessarily incurred in order to generate the revenue. This approach, known as **matching,** is the basis for resolving many practical questions regarding expense determination and measurement. Expenses represent past outflows or expected future outflows of liquid assets consumed or to be consumed in the process of generating revenues.

GAINS AND LOSSES **Gains** and **losses** are generally the result of unplanned events that are either unrelated or only indirectly related to the normal operating activities of the entity. Like revenues and expenses, gains and losses result in inflows or outflows of net assets, respectively. Gains and losses may occur as a result of events and transactions that are controlled by the entity (for example, the sale of securities held as a temporary investment of idle cash) or events and transactions that are beyond the control of the entity (for example, storm damage or thefts). Because of the tremendous variety of gains and losses, it is important to describe them as accurately as possible so that users can evaluate the nature of the inflow or outflow of resources. Several types of special disclosure for gains and losses are discussed in Chapter 3.

PRODUCTS OF FINANCIAL ACCOUNTING

The products of financial accounting are either formal financial statements or other data included in an entity's financial reports (see Exhibit 2–5). Among the formal statements are the balance sheet, the income statement, the retained earnings statement (or statement of changes in owners' equity), and the statement of changes in financial position. Other data in financial reports might appear in management's letter reviewing the entity's performance, in the notes to financial statements, in the auditor's report, or in a historical summary or review. In the following two chapters we'll discuss formal financial statements in detail, and in the remaining chapters of

EXHIBIT 2–5

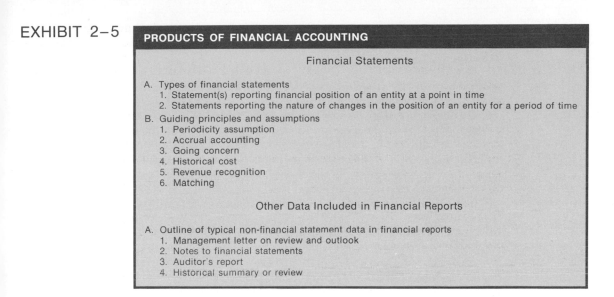

PRODUCTS OF FINANCIAL ACCOUNTING

Financial Statements

A. Types of financial statements
   1. Statement(s) reporting financial position of an entity at a point in time
   2. Statements reporting the nature of changes in the position of an entity for a period of time
B. Guiding principles and assumptions
   1. Periodicity assumption
   2. Accrual accounting
   3. Going concern
   4. Historical cost
   5. Revenue recognition
   6. Matching

Other Data Included in Financial Reports

A. Outline of typical non-financial statement data in financial reports
   1. Management letter on review and outlook
   2. Notes to financial statements
   3. Auditor's report
   4. Historical summary or review

the book, specific aspects of the statements and other nonstatement data will be considered. Here we will focus our attention on some common principles and assumptions that guide and support the preparation of financial statements. Included are the periodicity assumption, the accrual basis of accounting, the going-concern assumption, the historical-cost principle, the revenue-recognition principle, and the matching principle.

Principles and Assumptions Guiding the Preparation of Financial Statements

The periodicity assumption and the accrual basis of accounting The financial reports issued by the business entity, which is the unit being accounted for, are prepared annually and quarterly based on the assumption that information about the entity is required periodically for decision-making purposes. This **periodicity assumption** is an important one which actually provides the basis for **accrual accounting.** A business entity may be viewed as a series of business cycles during which a pool of resources (net assets) is converted into a larger pool of resources (for example, by making a unit of inventory and selling it for more than what it costs to make). This cycle can be viewed as the process of converting cash to goods and services and then back to cash, with ending cash expected to be more than beginning cash.

At any point in time we may view the entity as a series of business cycles, some just starting, some just ending, and some in process. As a result, the periodic reports needed for business decisions must be based on business cycles that are incomplete. Accrual accounting is the method used to prepare reports about incomplete business cycles on either an annual or a quarterly basis. If it were not for the periodicity assumption, which calls for periodic reports, we would not need to employ the accrual accounting model.

Because of the accrual basis of accounting, productive equipment that is not completely consumed, inventory that is not sold, salaries that are not paid, and other assets or liabilities that represent various aspects of incomplete cycles need to be measured and accounted for in the periodic financial reports measuring performance of the entity and its managers. The accrual model, which is an alternative to the less-sophisticated cash-based model,[15] is necessary in order to permit the definitions of the elements of financial statements discussed above to form the basis of financial reporting.

The going-concern assumption The **going-concern assumption** simply suggests that the entity being accounted for will have an indefinite life. In one respect, the going-concern assumption justifies the periodicity assumption, as well as the accrual basis of accounting. Accounting for business entities would be very simple if one could wait until the end of the entity's life to have an accounting report prepared. Accrual accounting would not be required, and the measures of position and performance would be relatively simple because "cash in" and "cash out" would be the basis for such measures. However, the entity typically has no planned ending point.[16] Therefore, reports on performance cannot wait until the end of the entity's life, and the periodic reporting and accrual concepts are required to supply needed information to decision makers.

The historical-cost principle The **historical-cost principle** requires that all transactions and events be recorded at their cost and that the *financial statement data be based on historical-cost measures of the original transacted values*. Virtually all information in conventional financial statements is determined using the historical-cost principle.

The going-concern assumption tends to justify the use of historical costs as the basis for measuring the position (and change in position) of an entity. To the extent that the recorded historical amount may not always represent the most relevant measurement of the economic value of an asset, the historical-cost principle may not provide the most relevant information about the asset. However, these measures of assets other than cash represent incomplete cycles that will eventually be completed (converted back to cash) under the going-concern assumption. Thus the use of historical cost will not result in different or inappropriate performance measures (measures of the increases in net resources) in the long run when the cycles reported in any given balance sheet are completed.[17]

Historical cost is a *highly reliable* basis for accounting record keeping because measurements based on historical cost may be *objectively determined* and *readily verified*. Although numerous exceptions to historical cost are either permitted or required by GAAP, original transacted costs form the basis for conventional accounting.

[15] The cash-based model simply accounts for cash inflows and outflows. A purchase of an asset with a 10-year life would be recorded as an expense under the cash basis of accounting and sales on account would not be recorded as revenues until cash was received from credit customers. Note that the definitions of the elements of financial statements are not consistent with the cash basis of accounting since they are not confined to measuring cash.

[16] The major exception to this statement is a limited joint venture between two or more corporations. For example, a mining company and a real estate holding company might form a joint venture that would be dissolved upon the completion of the extraction of natural resources from a specified area.

[17] The following example may help you to understand this concept. Assume you bought a house for $80,000 in 1978. By 1983, the fair market value of your house is $140,000. Because of the historical-cost principle, you have the house (which represents an incomplete cycle) on your personal balance sheet for $80,000 *less* depreciation, well below the fair value. However, once the cycle is completed by selling the house for cash, the correct value (in cash) and profit (selling price less $80,000 plus depreciation) will be measured within the historical-cost framework. This concept is covered in greater detail in Chapter 6.

Note that when the going-concern assumption is not appropriate, as in the case of a company that is expected to become bankrupt, the historical-cost principle becomes inappropriate. For companies expected to fail, historical cost is normally replaced by liquidation value as a basis for measuring the net assets of incomplete cycles. The going-concern assumption is implicit when historical costs are employed, and it is a fundamental part of every auditor's report. If the assumption is not expected to apply to any given entity, the auditor must note this in the auditor's report. Exhibit 2–6 illustrates an auditor's report that is qualified because of the going-concern assumption, thereby questioning the use of historical cost.

The revenue-recognition and matching principles The **revenue-recognition principle** and the **matching principle** both relate to the process of measuring net income, a key element of performance evaluation. Revenue recognition is the basis for determining the benefits derived from the profit-making activities of the business entity, whereas the matching principle is used to determine the costs of such activities. Revenues are said to be *recognized* when they are *actually recorded* on the books of the entity. In order to recognize revenues, the entity must be able to measure *objectively* all of the benefits and the associated costs involved in the profit-making activities of the entity. This recognition point is normally at the time goods or services are provided, usually considered to be at the point of sale, but it may occur at other times as we will find in Chapter 3 and Chapter 23.

Once revenues are recognized (recorded), the matching principle is invoked to determine the expenses to be "matched" against the recorded revenues. The appli-

EXHIBIT 2–6

AUDITOR'S REPORT—BARCLAY INDUSTRIES

Board of Directors and Stockholders, Barclay Industries, Inc.
Lodi, New Jersey

We have examined the consolidated balance sheets of Barclay Industries, Inc. and subsidiaries as of July 31, 1980, and August 31, 1979, and the related statements of operations, stockholders' equity (deficiency in assets) and changes in financial position for the eleven months ended July 31, 1980, and the year ended August 31, 1979. Our examinations were made in accordance with generally accepted auditing standards and, accordingly, included such tests of the accounting records and such other auditing procedures as we considered necessary in the circumstances.

The aforementioned financial statements have been prepared using generally accepted accounting principles applicable to a going concern which contemplates the realization of assets and the liquidation of liabilities in the normal course of business. However, continuation of the Company as a going concern is dependent upon its ability to maintain adequate financing and achieving profitable operations. At July 31, 1980, adverse operating results and the disposal of certain operations resulted in a working capital deficiency of $1,143,900 and deficiencies in net assets of $808,100. The financial statements do not reflect any downward adjustments (presently not determinable) to the carrying value of assets which could be required in the event of disposal other than in the ordinary course of business. Should losses continue or the Company not be able to maintain adequate financial arrangements with its lenders, the realization of assets and order of maturities of liabilities may be adversely affected.

In our opinion, subject to the affects of such adjustments, if any, as might have been required relating to the Company's continuation as a going concern referred to in the preceding paragraph, the consolidated financial statements referred to above present fairly the consolidated financial position of Barclay Industries, Inc. and subsidiaries at July 31, 1980, and August 31, 1979, and the results of their operations and the changes in their financial position for the eleven months ended July 31, 1980, and the year ended August 31, 1979, in conformity with generally accepted accounting principles applied on a consistent basis.

TOUCHE ROSS & CO.
Certified Public Accountants
Newark, N.J.
October 15, 1980

EXHIBIT 2-7

OUTLINE OF FINANCIAL ACCOUNTING

I. Objective
  A. Useful information for economic decisions of external users
    1. Investor and creditor decision needs
    2. Expected economic flows
    3. Facilitate performance evaluation
II. Qualitative Characteristics
  A. Desirable qualities
    1. Relevance
    2. Reliability
      a. Verifiability
      b. Neutrality
      c. Measurability
    3. Comparability
      a. Consistency
  B. Limiting qualities
    1. Materiality
    2. Cost-benefit analyses
    3. Conservatism
III. Elements of Financial Statements
  A. Position measurement
    1. Assets
    2. Liabilities
    3. Equity
  B. Describing position changes
    1. Investments by owners
    2. Distributions to owners
    3. Comprehensive income
    4. Revenues
    5. Expenses
    6. Gains
    7. Losses
IV. Financial Statements
  A. Statements
    1. Reports on position
    2. Reports on changes in position
  B. Common aspects
    1. Periodicity
    2. Accrual accounting
    3. Going concern
    4. Historical cost
    5. Revenue recognition
    6. Matching
V. Non-Financial Report Data
  A. Typical financial report data
    1. Management letter
    2. Notes to statements
    3. Audit report
    4. Historical summary or review

cation of the matching principle is often accomplished by answering the following question: What costs were incurred in order to permit the revenues to be recognized? As we will see in many cases throughout the text, the matching principle often provides the primary theoretical justification for expense-recognition procedures.

The complete outline of financial accounting discussed in the preceding sections is summarized in Exhibit 2–7. Review this before we go on to a discussion of the details of the processing of accounting information.

THE ACCOUNTING CYCLE

In the previous section the conceptual framework of financial accounting was introduced and discussed. This framework is used in conjunction with conventional techniques to develop the information that is communicated to decision makers. If the objectives of financial accounting are to be achieved, a rigorous system of information collection and processing must be maintained. This system generates financial statements that are period-end summaries. For example, the **balance sheet** summarizes the financial position of an entity at the end of a period. The **income statement** and **statement of changes in financial position** summarize activities during a period. The **accounting cycle** is the pattern of accounting actions (journalizing, posting, summarizing, and so on) that are performed during a reporting period. In this section, we shall describe (1) the role of the conventional accounting system in achieving the objective of financial accounting and (2) the steps in the accounting cycle.

Stages of the Accounting Cycle

Exhibit 2–8 provides an overview of the steps in the complete accounting cycle, identifying some of the major outputs and systems concepts that are part of the process of producing accounting information.

The cycle begins with the **journal entries.** At this stage, events and transactions affecting the entity are recorded in the journal in chronological order. Periodically, journal entries are posted to **ledger accounts.** These provide a means of summarizing the impact of all events and transactions on a particular item of interest, such as a specific asset or expense account. Until financial statements are desired, the entering of events and transactions in the journal and the periodic posting of journal entries to ledger accounts are the only required accounting-system activities.

When statements are prepared, the current ledger account balances are listed in a document called a **trial balance.** The preliminary trial balance enables the accounting system to view the preliminary position of the entity and to summarize its activities prior to applying the adjustment procedures called for by the **accrual-accounting** convention used in financial reporting. The **adjusting journal entries** are then recorded and posted to the ledger accounts, and a new trial balance, called the **adjusted trial balance** is prepared. The adjusted trial balance is the listing of all accounts after they have been adjusted on the basis of accrual-accounting procedures. This listing of accounts forms the basis of the financial statements.

Many accounting decisions are necessary concerning data manipulation if the ultimate goal of satisfying informational needs of interested parties is to be reached. An accountant must identify those events that are relevant to that goal among all the events that affect the entity. If an event affects the financial position of the entity and is relevant to the information needs of users of accounting data, such an event is an **accounting transaction.** Accounting transactions are the basic inputs to the accounting system. The data regarding an accounting transaction are then organized on the basis of the double-entry accounting system.

Double-Entry Accounting

Double-entry accounting requires that those events identified as accounting transactions be measured and recorded in such a way that the following equality is maintained:

Total dollar amount assigned to assets — Total dollar amount assigned to liabilities and equities

EXHIBIT 2–8

OUTLINE OF THE ACCOUNTING CYCLE

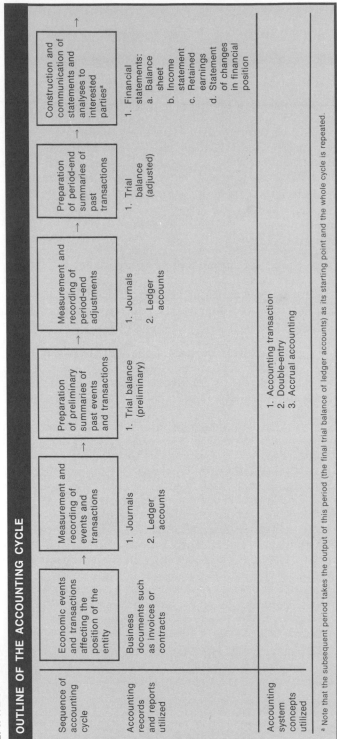

Sequence of accounting cycle	Economic events and transactions affecting the position of the entity	Measurement and recording of events and transactions	Preparation of preliminary summaries of past events and transactions	Measurement and recording of period-end adjustments	Preparation of period-end summaries of past transactions	Construction and communication of statements and analyses to interested parties[a]
Accounting records and reports utilized	Business documents such as invoices or contracts	1. Journals 2. Ledger accounts	1. Trial balance (preliminary)	1. Journals 2. Ledger accounts	1. Trial balance (adjusted)	1. Financial statements: a. Balance sheet b. Income statement c. Retained earnings d. Statement of changes in financial position
Accounting system concepts utilized		1. Accounting transaction 2. Double-entry 3. Accrual accounting				

[a] Note that the subsequent period takes the output of this period (the final trial balance of ledger accounts) as its starting point and the whole cycle is repeated.

TABLE 2–1

TYPES OF ACCOUNTING TRANSACTIONS		
	EFFECTS OF ACCOUNTING TRANSACTIONS	
TYPES OF ACCOUNTING TRANSACTIONS	**($) ASSETS = ($) LIABILITIES AND EQUITIES**	
Type 1	$(+) = (+)$	
Type 2	$(-) = (-)$	
Type 3	$(+) (-) =$	
Type 4	$= (+) (-)$	

This is equivalent to the balance sheet equality: assets equal liabilities plus equities.

The double-entry system provides a basis for assigning dollar amounts to financial statement elements in order to maintain the equality just mentioned. For each accounting transaction resulting in a net change on one side of the equation there must be an equal net change on the other side of the equation. The various types of accounting transactions and their effect on the balance sheet equation are listed in Table 2–1. For transactions of types 1 and 2, the total dollar amounts of both sides of the balance sheet change by equal amounts. For transactions of types 3 and 4, there is both an increase and a matching decrease on one side of the balance sheet; the balance sheet totals remain the same. Of course, in all cases the equality is maintained.

An example of a type 1 transaction would be the investment of $10,000 by Jones and Smith in the J & S Corporation. The position of the entity after the transaction would be as follows:

ASSETS	=	LIABILITIES AND EQUITIES
Cash $10,000		Common stock $10,000

This position can be interpreted as follows: The J & S Corporation controls assets (cash) of $10,000 and is responsible to the owners (evidenced by their ownership of common stock) for $10,000.

The purchase by the corporation of office equipment for $2,000 cash is an example of a type 3 transaction. Only the form of assets would be affected, not the balance sheet total.

ASSETS		=	LIABILITIES AND EQUITIES	
Cash	$ 8,000		Common stock	$10,000
Office equipment	2,000			
	$10,000			$10,000

Cash is reduced by $2,000 and Office Equipment is increased by the same amount, resulting in no changes in total assets and total liabilities and equities.

If the corporation were to borrow $5,000, a type 1 transaction, the following changes would occur:

ASSETS	=	LIABILITIES AND EQUITIES	
Cash	$13,000	Loan outstanding	$ 5,000
Office equipment	2,000	Common stock	10,000
	$15,000		$15,000

If the corporation then paid off part of the obligation with $2,000 in cash, a type 2 transaction, the balance sheet would show the following:

ASSETS	=	LIABILITIES AND EQUITIES	
Cash	$11,000	Loan outstanding	$ 3,000
Office equipment	2,000	Common stock	10,000
	$13,000		$13,000

A type 4 transaction, which increases and decreases the liabilities and equities, would take place if the company paid off its outstanding debt of $3,000 by issuing common stock to the creditor. This would result in the following equality:

ASSETS	=	LIABILITIES AND EQUITIES	
Cash	$11,000	Common stock	$13,000
Office equipment	2,000		
	$13,000		$13,000

Although there are only four *types* of changes in the position statement or balance sheet, the examples of each type shown are certainly not the only ones that can occur. There are virtually unlimited possibilities, depending on the complexity of the entity and degree of detail one desires in the description of the classifications of assets, liabilities, and equities.

Journals and Ledgers
To keep information in an orderly form, accounting systems (1) maintain a record of each transaction chronologically and (2) maintain a record of every transaction that has affected any given account. The first step is carried out through the maintenance of a **general journal,** which is used to record the accounting transactions and the subsequent adjusting entries. The second step is carried out through the use of a **general ledger,** which summarizes all the transactions or adjustments that have affected each separate account. Illustrated below is an example of a typical general journal:

DATE	ACCOUNT	DEBIT	CREDIT
1/1/84	Cash	10,000	
	Common stock		10,000
1/2/84	Office equipment	2,000	
	Cash		2,000
1/10/84	Cash	5,000	
	Loan outstanding		5,000
1/20/84	Loan outstanding	2,000	
	Cash		2,000
1/25/84	Loan outstanding	3,000	
	Common stock		3,000

Recall from introductory accounting that a **debit** in a journal records an increase in an asset or expense account and a decrease in a liability or equity or revenue account. A **credit** decreases an expense or asset account and increases a liability, equity, or revenue account. The nature of the specific accounts affected by an event must be known before the meaning of the debit or credit entry in the journal can be understood. This relationship may be illustrated by the following diagram:

ASSETS AND EXPENSES			LIABILITIES, EQUITIES, AND REVENUES	
DEBIT	CREDIT	=	DEBIT	CREDIT
Increase	Decrease		Decrease	Increase

While the general journal provides a chronological record of all the transactions of the entity, information is also needed regarding the impact of all transactions on specific accounts, such as cash. Converting these date-oriented records to account-oriented records involves a procedure called **posting to the ledger.** For example, the first journal entry illustrated above is:

DATE	ACCOUNT TITLE	DEBIT	CREDIT
1/1/84	Cash	10,000	
	Common stock		10,000

Cash is an asset classification and Common Stock is an equity classification. All activity in each account is maintained in a **ledger account,** as illustrated below:

CASH		COMMON STOCK	
DEBIT	CREDIT	DEBIT	CREDIT
1/1/84 10,000			1/1/84 10,000

Viewed individually, ledger accounts give the history and current status of each account in the system. After the journal entries have been posted to the ledger, the combined ledger accounts form the components of the financial statements.

The journal entries listed on page 42 are reported in the following ledger accounts:

Assets

CASH				OFFICE EQUIPMENT		
DEBIT		CREDIT		DEBIT		CREDIT
1/1/84	10,000	1/2/84	2,000	1/2/84	2,000	
1/10/84	5,000	1/20/84	2,000			
	11,000					

Total assets − $13,000

	Liabilities			Equities	

LOAN OUTSTANDING		COMMON STOCK	
DEBIT	**CREDIT**	**DEBIT**	**CREDIT**
1/20/84 2,000	1/10/84 5,000		1/1/84 10,000
1/25/84 3,000			1/25/84 3,000
	0		13,000

Total liabilities plus equities = $13,000

When a transaction occurs, the accountant must enter the transaction in the account that most closely relates to the event being recorded. If none of the existing ledger accounts is appropriate, a new account must be started.

It is important to understand the following facts about ledger accounts and journals:

1. All amounts that appear in ledger accounts are first recorded in a journal.
2. The journal entry requires equal debits and credits, and, therefore, at least two ledger accounts are affected by each journal entry.
3. As long as equal debits and credits are transferred from the journals to the ledgers, the basic equality will be maintained.

Preliminary Trial Balance

The ledger account balances, when listed together, form a **trial balance.** The total debits of all ledger accounts should equal the total credits of all ledger accounts if posting has been properly accomplished. Asset and expense accounts will normally have a debit balance. Liabilities, equities, and revenues will normally have a credit balance.

Relationship of Accounts

The trial balance will typically contain a list of the primary accounts that make up the balance sheet, the income statement, and the retained earnings statement. The income and retained earnings statements are normally prepared first so that the balance sheet will reflect the updated figures for retained earnings. Income statement and retained earnings statement accounts are sometimes considered to be a part of the Retained Earnings account, providing details about the changes in retained earnings. These statements are interrelated as follows:

ASSETS		=	LIABILITIES	+	EQUITIES	
DEBIT	**CREDIT**	**DEBIT**	**CREDIT**	**DEBIT**	**CREDIT**
+	−	−	+	−	+

	RETAINED EARNINGS	
	DEBIT	**CREDIT**
	−	+

EXPENSES		REVENUES	
DEBIT	**CREDIT**	**DEBIT**	**CREDIT**
+	−	−	+

FIGURE 2-5
Relationships among financial statements

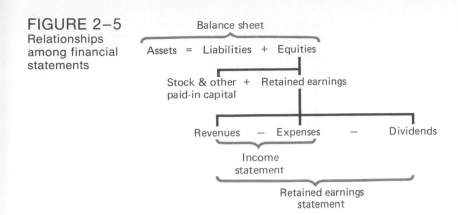

An alternative formulation of this relationship without considering the interrelationships of increases and decreases is illustrated in Figure 2-5. This illustration shows revenues and expenses as two types of accounts that not only provide the details of changes to retained earnings but also make up the details of the income statement. The **income statement** describes the reasons for the changes in retained earnings that resulted from the inflows and outflows of net assets. The **retained earnings statement** consists of the net inflows (income) or net outflows (loss) from the income statement along with dividends to account for all three items affecting retained earnings.

The **balance sheet** directly or indirectly encompasses all of the various types of accounts listed in the trial balance. However, only balance sheet accounts (assets, liabilities, and equities) are reported in the balance sheet. The revenue, expense, and dividend accounts are **nominal accounts,** which record the details of the causes of net asset inflows (revenues) or outflows (expenses and dividends). Sometimes these nominal accounts are designated "temporary", because they are all periodically eliminated (closed out) and netted against the beginning retained earnings balance in order to arrive at the ending retained earnings balance.

It should be noted that the **statement of changes in financial position** (SCFP) is also developed based on the amounts in the trial balance. The SCFP analyzes the changes in the balance sheet, using both the income statement and balance sheet accounts listed in the trial balance, as well as the balance sheet account balances from the previous trial balance. Although there is no need to develop a separate set of nominal accounts to facilitate the construction of the SCFP, it is certainly possible to do so, just as the nominal accounts are developed for income statements. The SCFP evaluates changes in all financial resources of the reporting entity, whereas the income statement focuses on changes in resources that resulted from inflows and outflows of net assets.

Recording Events, Transactions, and Adjusting Entries in the Accrual Model

Accrual accounting is the system of procedures that has evolved to cope with the problem of incomplete business cycles created by the periodicity assumption. The resulting accounting statements, therefore, reflect not only cash-flow effects (from completed cycles) but also the effects of transactions that are somehow incomplete.

This accrual system calls for the recording of events and transactions, as well as certain modifications or adjustments to balances in ledger accounts at the end of each accounting period. The required adjusting entries are identified by reviewing the preliminary trial balance, focusing on the balance sheet accounts and asking the following questions:

1. What asset, liability, or equity amounts are recorded but do not reflect the asset, liability, or equity positions at this time?
2. What asset, liability, and equity amounts are not recorded at this time but should be?

The answers to these questions will suggest the adjusting entries that need to be made in order to state accurately the financial position of the entity at a given point in time. Techniques of accrual accounting answer these questions by accomplishing the following two objectives:

1. Identify the assets of the entity.
2. Identify the liabilities of the entity.

These objectives are less elaborate than one might expect, and their simplicity stresses the central nature of the balance sheet. The objectives consider only assets and liabilities (two of the elements of financial statement defined earlier) because all other elements are related to these two key components. Recall that equity is represented by net assets and that components of the income statement and the statement of changes in financial position are defined in terms of changes in the balance sheet accounts. Due to their interrelationships and the double-entry system, the adjustment process may be completed by accomplishing these two objectives. Let us consider some examples of how accrual accounting works.

Objective 1: Identify the assets of the entity   Clarke Company performs a service for its customers and sends an invoice for $1,000 on July 1, 1984. The journal entry would be:

7/1/84	Accounts receivable	1,000	
	Sales		1,000

The debit to Accounts Receivable indicates that an asset has been established as a result of the claim to future cash receipts. The credit to Sales, which may be considered a subcomponent of the retained earnings account, does not require the receipt of cash but is recorded when the revenues are considered to be recognizable. This example illustrates the impact of the accrual system on the recording of *events or transactions* involving business cycles that have not been completed. Accrual procedures account for events and transactions by recording assets and liabilities of incomplete business cycles.

Another situation involving receivables demonstrates a common accrual activity that does not involve the recording of an event or a transaction. On December 31, 1984, the end of the accounting period, Clarke Company owns a 6 percent, $10,000 maturity value government bond that pays semiannual interest on May 1 and November 1 each year.[18] Accrual objective 1 would require the following journal entry on December 31, 1984.

[18] Note that the 6 percent interest is an annual rate, which is how interest is normally stated.

12/31/84	Interest receivable	100	
	Interest revenue		100
	($10,000 × .06 × 2/12 = $100)		

This entry is suggested by a review of the pre-adjustment trial balance and asking question 2: What asset, liability, and equity amounts are not recorded at December 31, 1984, but should be? In this case, we should have an asset, Interest Receivable, that has not been accrued until the above entry is recorded. As in the previous example, the revenue account is credited when the claim to future cash flows is considered to be recognizable. Note that this entry was not triggered by an event or transaction between the entity and some other party of interest as in the first example. Also, there is no document, such as an invoice, entering or leaving the entity that lets the accounting system know that an entry should be recorded. Such a **period-end journal entry** is prompted by the accrual model and is called an **adjusting journal entry**.

Accrual objective 1 may also require an adjusting entry to eliminate all or part of an asset. For example, assume Clarke Company has prepaid a total of $12,150 in various selling costs during 1984. At the end of 1984, Clarke reviews the asset Prepaid Expenses and asks question 1: What asset, liability, or equity amounts are recorded but do not reflect the assets, liabilities, or equity position at December 31, 1984? In this case, assume that Clarke determined that $3,038 of the Prepaid Expense account no longer represents a future benefit but had been consumed during 1984. The following adjustment would be required:

| 12/31/84 | Selling expense | 3,038 | |
| | Prepaid expense | | 3,038 |

This entry accomplishes objective 1 above by *reducing* an existing asset account for the amount of the future benefits that has expired. In one sense, adjusting entries are practical applications of the definitions of assets and liabilities. Whenever an asset is consumed in operations, that asset account is credited and an expense account is debited.

Sometimes, for record-keeping convenience, the recording of the expense is made periodically instead of at the time the asset is consumed. Recall from your introductory accounting course the *periodic inventory method*, where inventory was not revised after each sale but was measured only at the end of an accounting period after a physical count of inventory. The following formula is typically used:

PURCHASES ACCOUNT ONLY		PURCHASES ACCOUNT DETAIL	
Beginning inventory (1/1/84)	$ 40,000	Beginning inventory	$ 40,000
+ Purchases (net)	175,000	+ Purchases	198,500
Cost of goods available		+ Freight in	3,750
for sale	$215,000	− Purchase returns and allowances	24,000
− Ending inventory (per		− Purchase discounts	3,250
count)	52,000	Cost of goods available	
Cost of goods sold	$163,000	for sale	$215,000
		− Ending inventory (per	
		count)	52,000
		Cost of goods sold	$163,000

The Purchases account may be used to record all purchasing activity (for example, freight on purchases, purchase returns, allowances, discounts), or separate accounts may be developed to account for purchase details. The results are, of course, the same. These accounts do not record costs until the end of the period when the ending inventory count is taken and "costed out" using a cost-flow assumption such as LIFO or FIFO. This periodic inventory method arrives at the Cost of Goods Sold expense through the following adjusting entry:

Inventory (ending)		52,000	
Cost of goods sold		163,000	
Purchases			175,000
Inventory (beginning)			40,000

Until this adjusting entry is made at the end of the period, only the beginning inventory account and the purchases account(s) will appear in the ledger or the before-adjustment trial balance. Recall the difference in the perpetual inventory method, which continuously updates both the Inventory account and the Cost of Goods Sold account throughout the accounting period. Whether an entity uses perpetual or periodic inventory may be determined by reviewing the before-adjustment trial balance. When a Cost of Goods Sold account is listed, perpetual procedures are being used. When a Purchases account is listed, Cost of Goods Sold will be established through an adjusting entry required by the periodic method.

Assets are recorded initially at cost and are kept at cost unless it becomes apparent that the assets' economic potential has declined. For example, on January 1, 1984, Clarke Company purchases a delivery truck for $10,000. On December 31, 1984, 80 percent of the truck's original economic potential remains. The asset account should be made to reflect a balance of $8,000 at year-end:

1/1/84	Delivery equipment	10,000	
	Cash		10,000
12/31/84	Depreciation expense	2,000	
	Accumulated depreciation		2,000

This is another example of addressing question 1: What asset value is included at December 31, 1984, but is no longer an asset? The December 31, 1984, adjusting entry accomplishes objective 1 by reducing the remaining net asset value from $10,000 to $8,000, and matching the $2,000 depreciation on the asset against the 1984 revenues. The December 31, 1984, adjusting entry reduces owners' equity through a debit to an expense account. What governs the amount of the allocation from an asset account to an expense account? The general rule may be stated this way: When assets are used up in the process of revenue generation, the asset should be credited and an expense account should be debited for an amount that is proportional to the amount of the future benefits consumed.

Objective 2: Identify the liabilities of the entity This objective is the basis for recording obligations to pay cash in the future. For instance, on January 1, 1984, Clarke Company receives $1,000 of supplies from a supplier. The journal entry to record this event is:

1/1/84	Supplies	1,000	
	Accounts payable		1,000

This is an example of accounting for events and transactions that results in the recording of a liability and an asset of an incomplete business cycle. Although this type of entry helps accomplish both objectives 1 and 2 above, it is not an adjusting entry.

Adjusting entries are also used to accomplish this second objective of accrual accounting. Clarke Company has not paid wages since December 28, 1984, the last payday. Workers earned $1,000 during the period from December 28 to December 31, and the company has an obligation to pay that amount plus any subsequent wages at the next payday. On December 31, 1984, the adjusting journal entry would be recorded:

12/31/84	Wages expense	1,000	
	Wages payable		1,000

This entry addresses question 2: What liabilities are not recorded at December 31, 1984, but should be? Since the wages payable represent an objectively measurable obligation of the entity that has accrued since December 28, 1984, the adjusting entry recorded above is necessary to accurately report the financial position (balance sheet) of Clarke at December 31, 1984. This journal entry not only records the liability but also reduces owners' equity by the amount of the expense, thus recording the expense in the year in which the labor services are used.

Another common adjusting entry involving liability balances is the adjustment of a previously recorded unearned revenue liability. For example, on November 1, 1984, Clarke Company received $6,000 for 6 months' rent in advance from a tenant. The following journal entries are necessary for the recording of the initial liability and the necessary adjusting entry at year-end:

11/1/84	Cash	6,000	
	Unearned rent		6,000
12/31/84	Unearned rent	2,000	
	Earned rent		2,000

The initial transactions establish a liability (Unearned rent) on the entity's part to either perform the service or pay back the cash. At December 31, 1984, 2 months of rental service have been supplied, thereby reducing the obligation by one-third. Revenue has been earned, and therefore an adjusting entry is required in order to properly state liabilities as of December 31, 1984. This adjusting entry addresses question 1 regarding liabilities that are on the books as of December 31, 1984, but no longer represent obligations of Clarke Company at that date.

Evaluating the Accounting Cycle	Referring back to Exhibit 2–8, we see that the following steps are necessary in the accounting cycle:

1. Journalizing events and transactions
2. Posting journal entries to ledger accounts
3. Summarizing ledger accounts in a trial balance
4. Recording and posting adjusting journal entries
5. Summarizing adjusted ledger accounts in an adjusted trial balance
6. Placing the accounts in the adjusted trial balance into the financial statements

The entire cycle can be viewed as consisting of two major steps. The two steps in the cycle are (1) recording journal entries in a way that most meaningfully captures the economic impact of the relevant events and transactions affecting the entity and (2) posting, totaling, adjusting, retotaling, and organizing accounts. The first step, recording the journal entries, is the most difficult; it requires skill, judgment, and a thorough understanding of the framework of accounting. Once the necessary journal entries are properly recorded, the second step may be viewed as a straight-forward process that is largely mechanical. It requires much less skill and accounting expertise. The most difficult aspect of the second step is in recording those adjusting journal entries needed to *complete* the two objectives of accrual accounting.

In short, journal entries that record the events and transactions of the entity, along with adjusting journal entries, are the most challenging aspects of the accounting cycle. Many accounting problems and issues are centered on the proper recording of unusual events, transactions, and adjustments. Alternatively, those steps involving posting journal entries to ledger accounts, totaling ledger accounts, listing trial balances, and preparing statements from the adjusted trial balance are relatively mechanical procedures. Many modern accounting systems perform these latter steps with computers that are programmed to generate financial reports, using journal entries as the single input.

The Worksheet   Most of the second step in the accounting cycle can be illustrated in a **worksheet,** which is a relatively standard form of documentation used in the preparation of financial statement information. Exhibit 2–9 illustrates a worksheet, which summarizes steps 3 through 6 in the accounting cycle.

     3. Summarizing ledger accounts in a trial balance (columns 1–2)
     4. Recording adjusting entries (columns 3–4)
     5. Preparing adjusted trial balance (columns 5–6)
     6. Preparing financial statements
       a. Income statement (columns 7–8)
       b. Retained earnings statement (columns 9–10)
       c. Balance sheet (columns 11–12)

Note that the key to the worksheet is in the adjusting entries recorded in columns 3–4. The twelve adjusting entries (which for convenience have been paired by the numbers in parentheses) are typical entries required by the accrual process in order to state the position of the entity properly. There are many slight variations on this basic worksheet formula. The version illustrated here prepares the income calculation by way of a closing-type entry found in columns 7–8. The exact form is not of particular importance. The basic procedure is first to pull off from the adjusted trial balance (columns 5–6) the income statement accounts in order to compute net income (columns 7–8). Net income (from columns 7–8) is then closed to retained earnings along with dividends (columns 9–10), and the updated retained earnings balance is finally added to the remaining balance sheet accounts (columns 11–12). Column 13 is a type of a mathematical proof sometimes used.

Use of a worksheet enables business entities to prepare financial statements without formally going through the **closing process,** which eliminates the balances in all nominal accounts. The trial balance in columns 1–2 can be taken from the current ledger balances, and the worksheet enables one to proceed from there to the financial statements without affecting the journals or ledgers of the entity.

Closing Entries   The worksheet is convenient for interim financial reports, such as monthly or quarterly statements, because closing is not required except at the end of a year. At year-end, as a seventh step in the cycle, closing journal entries would need to be recorded in the journal and posted to the ledger accounts. The following closing entries

EXHIBIT 2-9

CLARKE COMPANY WORKSHEET, DECEMBER 31, 1984

Worksheet
Clarke Company
December 31, 1984

General ledger accounts	Trial balance Debit	Trial balance Credit	Adjustments Debit	Adjustments Credit	Adjusted trial balance Debit	Adjusted trial balance Credit	Income statement Debit	Income statement Credit	Retained earnings statement Debit	Retained earnings statement Credit	Balance sheet Debit	Balance sheet Credit	Add across Debit (Credit)
Cash	$ 25876				$ 25876						$ 25876		$ 25876
Accounts receivable	78220		(3) 8360		86580						86580		86580
Allowance for uncollectibles		$ 1180		$ 4077 (1)		$ 5257						$ 5257	(5257)
Inventory	115910		(8) 1135	5610 (2)	111435						111435		111435
Prepaid expenses	12150			3038 (12)	9112						9112		9112
Land	45000				45000						45000		45000
Building	178375				178375						178375		178375
Accumulated depreciation		39225		7650 (4)		46875						46875	(46875)
Furniture and fixtures	31000				31000						31000		31000
Accumulated depreciation		14000		2000 (5)		16000						16000	(16000)
Equipment	97280			11000 (6)	97280						97280		97280
Accumulated depreciation		33000		11000 (6)		44000						44000	(44000)
Intangible assets	10785				10785						10785		10785
Accumulated amortization		3280		820 (7)		4100						4100	(4100)
Accounts payable		49870		1135 (8)		51005						51005	(51005)
Interest payable		8125		4063 (9)		12188						12188	(12188)
Taxes payable		16000		1150 (10)		17150						17150	(17150)
Short-term notes payable		30000				30000						30000	(30000)
Long-term notes payable		165000				165000						165000	(165000)
Common stock (to par)		100000				100000						100000	(100000)
Retained earnings		43103	(b) 20000			43103			(b) 20000	$ 66390 (a)		89493	(89493)
Sales		1352176		8360 (3)		1360536		$ 1360536					0
Cost of goods sold	853668		(2) 5610		859278		$ 859278						0
Selling expense	187320		(12) 3038		190358		190358						0
Administrative expense	127000		(11) 14875		141875		141875						0
Tax expense	48000		(10) 1150		49150		49150						0
Interest expense	24375		(9) 4063		28438		28438						0
Dividends	20000				20000					20000 (b)			0
Bad debt expense			(1) 4077		4077		4077						0
Depreciation expense			(4) 7650 (5) 2000 (6) 11000		20650		20650						0
Amortization expense			(7) 820		820		820						0
Wages and salaries payable				14875 (11)		14875						14875	(14875)
	$1854459	$1854459	$ 63778	$ 63778	$1909589	$1909589	$1294146	$1360536			$595443	$595443	0
Net income							66390 (a)		(a) 66390				
							$1360536	$1360536	$86390	$86390	$595443	$595443	

would be recognized in order to close out the nominal accounts illustrated in the worksheet in Exhibit 2–9.

12/31/84	Sales		1,360,536	
	Cost of goods sold			859,278
	Selling expense			190,358
	Administrative expense			141,375
	Tax expense			49,150
	Interest expense			28,438
	Bad debt expense			4,077
	Depreciation expense			20,650
	Amortization expense			820
	Retained earnings			66,390
	(To close income statement accounts)			
12/31/84	Retained earnings		20,000	
	Dividends			20,000
	(To close dividend account)			

After closing entries are made, only the balance sheet accounts will have a balance, and the balance sheet equality should hold.

Reversing Entries Some systems also have an eighth step in the cycle, which occurs at the start of the following year when certain year-end adjusting entries are reversed. Reversing entries are optional and are not required in order to account for events and transactions properly. They tend to be used most frequently for adjustments relating to accrued receivables (for example, interest receivable) and accrued payables (for example, wages payable) where some follow-up flow of cash or other liquid assets is expected. Consider the $100 accrued interest receivable of the Clarke Company for the year ending December 31, 1984 (see page 47). The $100 adjusting entry made at December 31, 1984, would be reversed on January 1, 1985, if reversing entries were used. If reversing entries were not used, no entry would be required. The following entries illustrate the recording of interest income for Clarke with and without reversing entries:

WITHOUT REVERSING ENTRIES

12/31/84	Interest receivable	100	
	Interest revenue		100
1/1/85	No entry		
5/1/85	Cash	300	
	Interest receivable		100
	Interest revenue		200
	(To record receipt of 6 months' interest and 4 months' interest revenue		

WITH REVERSING ENTRIES

12/31/84	Interest receivable	100	
	Interest revenue		100
1/1/85	Interest revenue	100	
	Interest receivable		100
5/1/85	Cash	300	
	Interest revenue		300

ACCOUNT BALANCES AT MAY 1

WITHOUT REVERSING ENTRIES		WITH REVERSING ENTRIES	
Interest receivable	0	Interest receivable	0
Interest revenue	$200	Interest revenue	$200

In this text, reversing entries are never used or required. However, students should feel free to use them if so desired. The single, most important point to be made about reversing entries is that, whether they are used or not, the final account balances should be the same in terms of their impact on the financial reports of the entity.

Completed Cycle

The completed cycle contains the following seven steps:

1. Journalizing events and transactions
2. Posting journal entries to ledger accounts
3. Taking a trial balance
4. Recording and posting adjusting journal entries
5. Taking an adjusted trial balance
6. Preparing financial statements
7. Recording and posting closing entries to leave all non-balance sheet accounts with a zero balance

SUMMARY

Accrual accounting objectives flow directly from the informational assumptions of the theoretical framework. In accomplishing the stated objectives, accountants, guided by the qualitative characteristics and elements of the theoretical framework, have formulated many specific procedures for recording the economic activities of the entity and for maintaining its accounting records. It is often tempting for students to look at these specific procedures as prototypes that are to be copied and memorized for use in analogous situations. This approach is counterproductive if the accrual objectives are lost sight of or if the role of specific procedures in the overall information-production process is disregarded. The recording of depreciation at year-end or of revenues at the time of credit sale is done to facilitate the reporting of the entity's economic status and operations in conformance with the conceptual framework of accounting. The student, therefore, should continuously reflect on the underlying reasons for specific procedures, reasons that should be sought in the theoretical structure considered in this chapter.

Accounting is motivated by the demand for relevant information. In order to provide the desired information in a manner that is cost effective for both the providers and users of that information, accountants typically work within the boundaries of the theoretical structure and a system of specific rules and industry practices that together provide the basis for accounting decisions. As a result, accounting information is generated in the form of general-purpose accounting statements that are more or less standardized. This is not to say that they are simple or easy to interpret, but they do have many commonalities.

This book is designed to show how the theoretical framework, the conventional procedures, and the appropriate rules and industry practices are brought to bear on classes of transactions. Each transaction affecting an entity demands an accounting decision. The sum of all such decisions, in turn, results in the accounting information made available to decision makers.

APPENDIX A
Special Journals

OVERVIEW

In Chapter 2, a simple manual journal-entry and posting system was used to describe how accountants translate certain economic events into accounting records. In businesses of any significant size, various timesaving devices are used to reduce clerical effort, ranging from the machine-assisted systems that use bookkeeping machines and electronic computers to the purely manual systems using special journals.

No matter what timesaving devices are used, the major elements of the accounting process remain the same:

$$\text{Source documents} \rightarrow \text{Data processing} \rightarrow \text{Accounting outputs}$$

The source documents—invoices, checks, inventory records, and so on—are evidence of relevant economic events. Accounting outputs are the reports and statements that convey accounting information to users. These end points in the accounting system can include the same documents no matter how complex the clerical functions. Data processing, however, which includes all the intermediary steps, shows tremendous variations across various-sized businesses, usually depending on the volume of transactions. Great economies in the clerical activities of journalizing and posting of transactions are available as the volume of those activities increases. Of course, the same is true of all kinds of accounting-related clerical work, such as the preparation of payrolls, inventory records, and invoices.

One very common type of timesaving device, which is identical in concept to the single-journal manual system introduced in Chapter 2, is the manual system of multiple special journals. Keep in mind that although we cover manual systems in this text because they are useful in demonstrating concepts, all of these procedures can be and are commonly combined with computers.

We shall analyze a manual system of multiple special journals including the sales journal, the purchases journal, the cash receipts journal, the cash payments journal, and the general journal. As the names imply, the first four journals are designed to save recording and posting time for specific types of transactions, whereas the general journal is used to record all other journal entries.

Sales Journal The sales journal has the following format:

DATE	INVOICE	SUBSIDIARY ACCOUNT	POSTING	AMOUNT (DEBIT ACCOUNTS RECEIVABLE; CREDIT SALES)
7/1/84	1010	Swingling, Inc.	√	$ 1,100
7/1/84	1012	Broadoor Co.	√	501
7/2/84	1013	Chelsea Corp.	√	8,050
.	.	.	.	.
.	.	.	.	.
.	.	.	.	.
7/31/84	2120	Sisters, Inc.	√	10,400
				$440,200
				(√) (√)

Such a system allows for one posting per time period (in this case, a month) to the Accounts Receivable and Sales accounts. Note that subsidiary accounts, one for each customer, are also posted for sales transactions. Subsidiary records, those that do not directly impact on the accounting equation, are usually used to keep track of receivable amounts from individual credit customers and, in the purchases journal, payable amounts to individual suppliers. Subsidiary records are desirable no matter what type of journal system is used, and this is true of both manual and machine-assisted data-processing systems.

Purchases Journal The purchases journal has the following format:

DATE	SUBSIDIARY ACCOUNT	POSTING	AMOUNT (DEBIT PURCHASES; CREDIT ACCOUNTS PAYABLE)
7/2/84	Acme Supply, Inc.	√	$ 830
7/2/84	Johnson Metals	√	7,419
7/3/84	Interstate Distributors	√	601
.	.	.	.
.	.	.	.
.	.	.	.
7/31/84	Sinclair Company	√	6,600
			$338,621
			(√) (√)

The purchases journal bears a striking similarity to the sales journal, and the advantages are the same. Only two postings per period to the Purchases and Accounts Payable accounts are required, along with the necessary subsidiary ledger postings.

Cash Payments Journal

The cash payments journal has the following format:

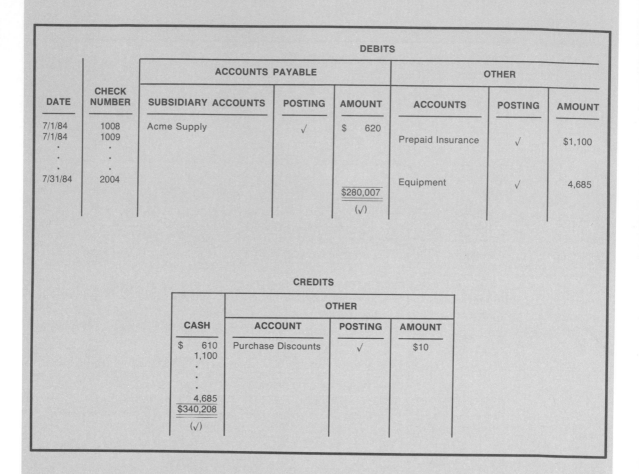

| | | DEBITS | | | | | |
| | | ACCOUNTS PAYABLE | | | OTHER | | |
DATE	CHECK NUMBER	SUBSIDIARY ACCOUNTS	POSTING	AMOUNT	ACCOUNTS	POSTING	AMOUNT
7/1/84	1008	Acme Supply	√	$ 620			
7/1/84	1009				Prepaid Insurance	√	$1,100
.	.						
.	.						
.	.						
7/31/84	2004				Equipment	√	4,685
				$280,007			
				(√)			

| | CREDITS | | |
| CASH | OTHER | | |
	ACCOUNT	POSTING	AMOUNT
$ 610	Purchase Discounts	√	$10
1,100			
.			
.			
.			
4,685			
$340,208			
(√)			

The cash payments journal is used to accumulate the effects of all payments for which checks (vouchers) are written. Only one posting each to the Cash and Accounts Payable ledger accounts is necessary per period. Many more single-account columns could be and are used in practice depending on the normal volume in ledger accounts. In this case the $340,208 credit posting to the Cash account represents the total of all July 1984 checks, and the $280,007 debit posting to Accounts Payable represents the total amount paid to suppliers from whom purchases on credit were made. The difference between the Cash and Accounts Payable accounts postings is the net effect of all debits and credits to all other accounts shown in the journal.

The cash receipts journal has the following format:

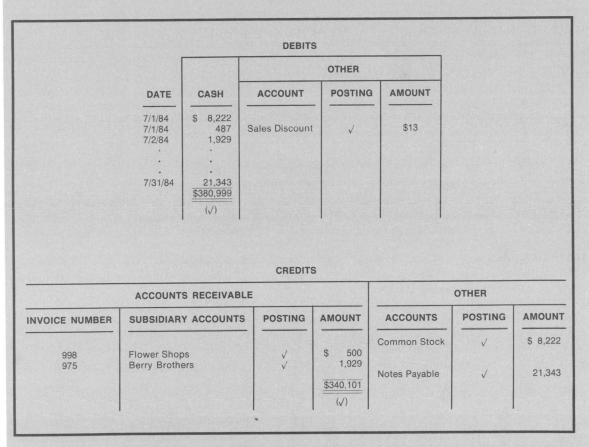

DEBITS

| DATE | CASH | OTHER | | |
		ACCOUNT	POSTING	AMOUNT
7/1/84	$ 8,222			
7/1/84	487	Sales Discount	√	$13
7/2/84	1,929			
.	.			
.	.			
.	.			
7/31/84	21,343			
	$380,999			
	(√)			

CREDITS

| ACCOUNTS RECEIVABLE | | | | OTHER | | |
INVOICE NUMBER	SUBSIDIARY ACCOUNTS	POSTING	AMOUNT	ACCOUNTS	POSTING	AMOUNT
				Common Stock	√	$ 8,222
998	Flower Shops	√	$ 500			
975	Berry Brothers	√	1,929	Notes Payable	√	21,343
			$340,101			
			(√)			

The cash receipts journal serves exactly the same purpose for cash receipts as does the cash payments journal for cash payments.

The General Journal and Other Journals

The general journal is of the type shown in Chapter 2. It is necessary because many transactions do not fall into recurring patterns in sufficient volume to make maintaining a special journal worthwhile. For instance, most of the adjusting entries, such as the ones for depreciation, require only one entry per period and, therefore, would not necessitate a special journal. It is important that sufficient explanation and reference to documentation be given for each general journal entry, because the format of the journal itself, unlike the special journals, does not indicate the nature of the transactions.

Journals other than the five mentioned above are often found in practice. For a company with a great deal of activity in notes receivable and/or payable, for example, special journals relating to those transactions would be possible.

Q2–1   Identify the components of the framework of accounting theory and explain the role of theory in accounting practice.

Q2–2   Many different types of decision makers are potential users of financial accounting information. How does accounting deal with the challenge of providing relevant information to these many groups of decision makers?

Q2–3   Define *generally accepted accounting principles* (GAAP).

Q2–4   What assumptions about the uses of information by decision makers are implied by the conventional accounting model?

Q2–5   Define *assets, liabilities,* and *equity,* and explain their role in the conventional accounting model.

Q2–6   How are revenues and expenses related to assets, liabilities, and equity?

Q2–7   How are gains and losses related to assets, liabilities, and equity?

Q2–8   Explain the qualitative characteristics of accounting and their components.

Q2–9   Why is the periodicity assumption important to decision makers?

Q2–10   In what ways does the going-concern principle direct accountants in their recording of transactions?

Q2–11   Explain the role of the concepts of materiality and conservatism in accounting.

Q2–12   What are the major steps in the annual accounting cycle? Explain the relationship of the cycle to the periodicity assumption.

Q2–13   Give an example of a situation requiring an adjusting entry and explain why such entries are necessary.

Q2–14   Is the double-entry system a necessary part of conventional accounting? Can you think of a different system for recording and summarizing transactions?

Q2–15   What is the objective of accrual accounting?

Q2–16   Why are equity holders considered to be taking a greater risk than are investors who purchase a corporation's bonds?

Q2–17*[19]   What is a special journal and how is it different from a general journal?

Q2–18*   What is the relationship between subsidiary ledgers and the ledger accounts that are reflected on balance sheets?

C2–1   The Newell Construction Company is a developer of real estate. Newell buys land and old buildings in major metropolitan areas, destroys the buildings, and builds high-rise apartments for lease or sale. One project in the heart of New York City had been underway for some time. Newell was slowly acquiring the last few parcels of a square-block area in an old residential neighborhood and was planning to construct a major complex of modern apartments with shopping facilities. The zoning for the project had been approved 4 years earlier.

The total costs incurred and assigned to the asset account to date amount to $12,500,000. The total cost of the completed project is estimated at $80,000,000, which will probably represent about 25 percent of Newell's assets at that future date. The property is expected to generate over $10,000,000 profit per year.

About two weeks prior to the scheduled construction start, the city council voted to order that work on the project be stopped so that the council could reconsider the zoning. A local citizens group was urging that the area be converted into a city park. It is estimated that no more than $6,000,000 of the costs could be recovered from the city if the park plan is approved.

REQUIRED   How should the property be disclosed in Newell's annual report and what, if anything, should be reported in the income statement?

[19] An asterisk following a question, case, exercise, or problem number indicates that the topic was covered in the appendix to this chapter.

C2-2 Sterling National Bank was organized as a publicly owned bank in 1985 with an initial stock offering. A few months after the bank opened, arrangements were made to make loans to six of the original stockholders who also were officers or directors of the bank. The published policy of the bank is to permit employees to receive loans at a slightly favorable rate of interest. The unsecured loans to the top six officers and directors totaled 125 percent of their total original investments.

REQUIRED As the auditor of Sterling, how do you think these loans should be disclosed in the financial statements? Should the loans reduce owners' equity? Should the loans simply be added in with the other Loans Receivable? Should any special footnote disclosure be provided? Should the relationship of the owners as borrowers be reported? Explain the basis for your answer.

C2-3 Based on your understanding of the elements of financial statements, identify which of the following would qualify as an element to be included in one of the financial statements, (for example, assets, expense, and so on). State which element(s) are involved.

1. The $6,000,000 contract between the Detroit Lions and Billy Sims for services over a 5-year period
2. The prepayment of $20,000 cash for 1 year's rental of an office in the Sears Tower
3. A signed contract from a renter agreeing to pay rent of $10,000 at the end of each month for the next 5 years for space in the World Trade Center

C2-4 You have just learned of an invention by an auto company of a battery that will run a 2,000-pound automobile for a year without recharging. The total cost of the research was $12,500,000. The total cost of the battery itself (the prototype) is $2,000. The total expected future revenues from the invention are $100 billion, and the cash value today (based on bids from other competitors and oil companies) is about $2.5 billion.

REQUIRED How would you record this invention, if at all, on the books of the auto company? Explain.

C2-5 In evaluating the alternatives below, you are to use only those concepts identified in the outline of qualitative characteristics of financial accounting data and discussed in the chapter. Do your best to apply these concepts to the alternatives in order to choose between them.

1. Several movers wish to measure the dimensions of an exit door of a building whose contents they have been hired to remove. They have a string, a 1-foot wooden ruler, and a 10-foot-long piece of floor molding made of wood. Evaluate the alternatives.
2. A farmer passed away leaving his entire farm and worldly possessions to his three grandchildren. The three grandchildren want to know what the cash value of the farm is before they decide whether to sell it or keep it for farming (using hired help). One grandchild suggests that they hire their grandfather's accountant, another suggests that they hire their grandfather's lawyer, and the last suggests that they hire the grandfather's realtor. Evaluate the alternatives.

C2-6 Identify the elements of the accounting model that are evident in each of the following situations.

1. In setting the value of its temporary investments in marketable securities at year-end, a company uses market value, which is lower than cost.
2. During the year, inflation of 15 percent took place. No adjustment for this change is recorded on the books.
3. Joe Namath owns a motel, a restaurant, a night club, and a clothing store. He has separate financial statements prepared for each of the businesses.
4. A charge is recorded to *Bad Debts Expense* for *expected* write-offs of accounts receivable.
5. Jay Corp. purchased ten waste barrels with an expected life of 5 years each for $20 per unit on January 1, 1984. The waste barrels were charged to Supplies Expense.

C2-7 On January 31, 1984, X Corporation has an unresolved issue about which its accountant is very uncertain. It relates to a parcel of land that originally cost $50,000 ten years ago and currently has a fair market value of $100,000. Management questions whether or not it would be appropriate to value the land at $100,000 in order to fully disclose its status on the balance sheet. The accountant decided that two alternatives were possible: (1) Increase the book value to $100,000 by making the following entry:

Land		50,000	
Owners' equity			50,000

or (2) increase a receivable account in anticipation of the sale of the land, which the accountant feels will come about some time in the future as follows:

Receivable		50,000	
Revenue			50,000

REQUIRED   Explain to the accountant what is wrong with his two alternatives by pointing to the aspects of current financial accounting that govern this situation.

C2–8   In your audit of the Goddard Sporting Goods Company, you noted that several inventory items had not changed much since the previous year. Specifically, you found the following items:

ITEM	1984 PURCHASES	INVENTORY COUNT 1984	INVENTORY COUNT 1983
Wallenda Hi-Wire Sets #287	0	750 sets	750 sets
Glass Shafted Golf Clubs #4736	0	560 sets	578 sets
B. J. King Tennis Racquets #8753	0	1,340 units	1,389 units
Fuzzy Folner Golf Carts #2387	0	425 units	429 units
H. Aaron Autograph Ball Bats #723	0	1,190 units	1,193 units

Goddard is a major chain in the Midwest, with stores in 50 locations. Their sales were $25,000,000 this year, with profits of $3,000,000 and total assets of about $30,000,000. Inventory represents about 15 percent of assets. The items identified above have a book value of $150,000. You believe these items should be written off as obsolete inventory, but the controller of Goddard does not agree.

REQUIRED   Identify what additional information you would like to have to make a decision whether to go along with the Controller or force the write-down issue. Next, assume you have no additional information and arrive at a decision. What aspects of the framework did you use in arriving at your two decisions?

C2–9   The following sets of alternatives provide data that might be considered as substitutes for one another. Consider each set of alternatives and select the alternative you believe provides the *most relevant* information. In order to make your selection, you should assume that you are a bank loan officer and that you are evaluating accounting data in an effort to determine the credit worthiness of the client company. A major loan is involved. Support your choice by identifying what makes the information you selected more relevant for lending-decision purposes.

1. a. Inventory valued at LIFO.
   b. Inventory valued at FIFO.
2. a. Book value of the asset "land held for future plant site."
   b. Real estate agent's estimated value of "land held for future plant site."
3. a. Historical cost, less accumulated depreciation, of the equipment used to manufacture the principal product line of the company.
   b. Current replacement cost of the equipment used to manufacture the principal product.
4. a. Historical cost of stocks and bonds purchased for investment purposes.
   b. Market value of stocks and bonds purchased for investment purposes.
5. a. Sales staff salaries and advertising expense reported separately.
   b. A combined expense for both salaries and advertising.

6. a. Research and development expense and other administrative expenses as separate items of the income statement.
   b. Research and development expense as a part of the single amount for administrative expense.
7. a. A management forecast of income and cash flows for the next 5 years.
   b. Management's analysis of the operating results for the past 3 years and their explanation of why the results were below or above expectations.

C2–10* Oklahoma City Printers specializes in printing stationery for commercial customers. In the past, the company has used a manual, general journal system for all transactions. Overall volume has increased to such an extent that their one experienced clerical worker is in need of assistance and has suggested that an inexperienced person be trained on a new multiple, special journal system. The following schedule gives a breakdown of the kinds and monthly volume of accounting transactions currently being experienced:

	TOTAL
Sales invoices processed	1,200
Purchases invoices processed	50
Checks written	75
Number of individual credit customers	200
Number of suppliers	5

One problem that keeps recurring is the reconciliation of the amounts owed by individual customers to the total amount of accounts receivable.

REQUIRED Suggest a special journal system that would be appropriate for Oklahoma City Printers, and provide examples of the suggested formats. Give reasons for your suggestions.

EXERCISES

E2–1 The following items are presented for your consideration in preparing financial statements. Identify which of the elements of financial statements (if any) each item represents:

1. Investment in a hotel by a lumber company.
2. An order to buy $5,000 worth of inventory from a supplier.
3. Receipt of cash for services to be performed by you next month.
4. Payment of cash for rent of facilities for the month now ending.
5. Payment of an insurance bill for insurance on your inventory for the next 18 months.
6. A check from an insurance company for $1,000 to settle a claim resulting from an automobile accident. The car, which was totaled, had a book value of $800 at the date of the accident.
7. A bill from a customer for the damage done by one of your employees to the customer's car. The court has recently ruled in favor of the customer.
8. An invention of a new electronic paring knife.

E2–2 Listed below is a series of events and transactions that took place during the month of December for the Foster Salvage Company

1. The company acquired land worth $5,000 in exchange for 1,000 shares of $2 par value stock.
2. The president of the company borrowed $5,000 from the company's cash funds. He was not required to sign a note.
3. The company purchased 15 new wastebaskets for $2 cash each for new offices that are a part of a $5,000,000 expansion of facilities.
4. The company constructed a tool shed at the rear exit of its plant using company labor ($3,000) and supplies

($2,600) for a total cost of $5,600. Contractors outside the company had bid on the project, with a low bid of $7,200, but the company decided to build the shed itself.

5. The company borrowed $10,000 from one of its wholly owned subsidiaries on a short-term basis.

6. The company sold $8,000 in goods that had cost $5,000. The terms of the sale called for the company to pay the transportation cost. The goods left the plant on the last day of the month and were due to arrive at the customer's in 2 days.

7. The company sold a fully depreciated generator for $700. The generator originally cost $6,000.

REQUIRED

1. Record these events.
2. Identify which parts of the theoretical framework (if any) helped you decide how to record each item.

E2-3 Accounting principles and procedures may frequently be related to the framework of accounting theory. One element of the framework is the notion of "conservatism."

REQUIRED Define what is meant by conservatism and indicate how it is related to accounting practice. Give several examples of accounting procedures that might be based, in part at least, on the notion of conservatism.

E2-4 The following are the ledger account balances of the Waco Corporation after adjustments as of December 31, 1984:

	DEBIT	CREDIT
Cash	$ 53,725	
Revenue received in advance		$ 4,292
Wages payable		16,400
Services provided to customers		87,630
Product sales		150,290
Patents	3,000	
Dividends	17,000	
Dividends payable		4,000
Supplies	38,500	
Equipment and furnishings	135,200	
Rent paid in advance	15,000	
Stock		120,000
Retained earnings		23,163
Accumulated depreciation		40,000
Land	45,000	
Selling and administrative expense	137,000	
Income tax expense	10,000	
Bonds (mature in 1994)		80,000
Supplies used	71,350	
	$525,775	$525,775

REQUIRED Prepare the income statement and balance sheet for Waco.

E2-5 The Jasper Corporation uses a periodic inventory procedure for valuing inventory. The inventory at the start of the year was $15,876. The total invoices received from vendors for goods shipped to Jasper amounted to $276,854. Bills received and paid for transportation charges on inventory purchased totaled $13,271. At year-end, Jasper has its employees make a count of the inventory on hand, with the following results:

INVENTORY ITEM NUMBER	COUNT
18705	300 units
22763	653 pounds
00154	250 units
33428	360 sets
97653	738 boxes
05072	734 cartons

Jasper's accountant looks up the most recent invoice price of the ending inventory and computes the value of the ending inventory to be $18,356.

REQUIRED

1. Compute Cost of Goods Sold for Jasper.
2. What inventory method (assumed cost flow) is being used by Jasper? Explain.

E2–6 Compute cost of goods sold based on the following data:

	DEBIT	CREDIT
Inventory 1/1/84	$ 76,294	
Salesmen's commissions	118,005	
Purchases	397,247	
Purchase returns		$16,329
Freight on sales	9,280	
Freight on purchase	12,604	
Allowance for bad debts		15,300
Sales returns	8,150	
Purchase discounts		2,975
Inventory 12/31/84	64,928	

E2–7 (CPA ADAPTED)[20]

E 1. Which of the following is not considered to be a qualitative characteristic of accounting information?
  a. Objectivity
  b. Freedom from bias
  c. Relevance
  d. Comparability
  e. Materiality

C 2. Assets may be defined as
  a. Economic resources
  b. Items that have future value
  c. Economic resources whose future benefits are objectively measurable
  d. The production and service potential of the firm
  e. Items with debit balances in their accounts

C 3. The entity assumption
  a. Refers to the name of the company required in the heading to the balance sheet
  b. Refers to the owners of the entity who must account for their interest in the entity in their personal holdings
  c. Indicates that the accounting unit being reported on is the business itself, separate from its owners
  d. Takes the view that the business is made up of many separate components which are accounted for separately but reported collectively in the financial statements

B 4. The primary characteristic of accounting information should be
  a. Predictive ability
  b. Relevance
  c. Objectivity
  d. Economic significance
  e. None of the above

C 5. The periodicity assumption
  a. Refers to the limited life of a joint venture
  b. Suggests that corporations need to report on a periodic basis, when all operating cycles are complete
  c. Suggests that corporations report on a systematic time interval, even though the operating cycle(s) of the entity may be incomplete
  d. Refers to the fact that adjusting entries must be made before financial statements are prepared periodically

[20] The words "CPA adapted" indicate that this exercise has been adapted from the CPA examination.

_B_

6. Which of the following accounting concepts suggest that an accounting transaction should be supported by sufficient evidence to allow two or more qualified individuals to arrive at essentially similar measures and conclusions?
   a. Matching
   b. Verifiability
   c. Periodicity
   d. Monetary unit

_C_

7. The valuation of a promise to receive cash in the future at present value on the financial statements of a business entity is valid because of the accounting concept of
   a. Entity
   b. Materiality
   c. Going concern
   d. Neutrality

PROBLEMS

P2–1 Record the following selected events of the Dallas Company in the general journal:

1. Received $1,000 on March 31 upon the sale of equipment. The $1,000 is for a service contract that states Dallas will service the equipment for 5 years, charging the customer only for parts in the event of a breakdown.

2. Entered into a 5-year lease with a real estate company, paying $5,000 down on June 30 and agreeing to pay $800 rent per month for the next 5 years.

3. Acquired land for a future building site, paying $10,000 cash on July 1 and signing a 1-year, 10 percent note for $50,000. Payment is to be made in full on July 1 next year.

4. Paid an advertising agency $34,500 on September 1 for an ad campaign that is being developed to be run on TV between December 1 and February 28.

5. Paid employees $15,000 in travel advances on November 15 for their expected costs of attending professional meetings. These advances cover the period December 1 to December 31. The actual travel costs incurred during December were $14,850.

6. On November 18, a credit agency called Dallas to inform them that a customer, Mr. J. Farnswell, had filed for bankruptcy. Farnswell owes Dallas $6,000 on an open account.

7. A delivery van was purchased on March 1 of this year for $10,000 with an expected life of 5 years and no scrap value. On December 1 the van was totaled in a head-on collision. The insurance company is expected to pay Dallas $8,000 for the accident.

REQUIRED Record any adjusting entries at December 31 that seem appropriate for items 1–7 above.

P2–2 The R. Malcom Company has prepared the following partial trial balance as of December 31, 1984:

	DEBIT	CREDIT		DEBIT	CREDIT
Accounts receivable	$ 87,620		Sales returns	$15,720	
Allowance for bad debts		$ 486	Notes payable (10%)		$120,000
Purchases	398,260		Freight in	17,630	
Sales discounts	19,276		Undeposited checks	14,000	
Inventory (1/1/84)	79,650		Prepaid postage	3,780	
Purchase returns		14,329	Supplies inventory	1,500	
Unearned rent revenue		16,250	Supplies expense	11,250	
Wages payable		2,900	Sales		839,254

ADDITIONAL DATA

1. The ending supplies inventory is $3,120 per the physical count.
2. The ending inventory is $64,950 per the physical count.
3. All revenues received had been earned as of year-end.
4. No interest had been paid on the note since June 30.
5. Bad debts typically are set at ½ percent of net sales.
6. $1,210 in postage is on hand at year-end.

REQUIRED   Record any entries necessary in order to prepare year-end financial statements for the R. Malcom Company.

P2-3   Assume that the balances in the ledger accounts for the AC–DC Linen Company for the year ending December 31, 1930, are as follows:

	DEBIT	CREDIT
Cash	$ 3,225	
Accounts receivable	650	
Trucks	2,000	
Building	4,000	
Land	1,000	
Accounts payable		$ 1,600
Bonds (1%)		2,000
Common stock		6,000
Dividends	100	
Interest expense	10	
Service revenue		3,100
Gasoline expense	250	
Advertising expense	140	
Salaries expense	1,200	
Soap expense	125	
	$12,700	$12,700

ADDITIONAL DATA

1. Depreciation is computed on the straight-line basis, and no salvage values are assumed.
2. A building purchased on January 1, 1930, was believed to have a useful life of 40 years.
3. Trucks purchased on April 1, 1930, were believed to have a 10-year life.
4. The bonds were issued on April 1, 1930, and interest will be paid on April 1 and October 1 each year until 1940 when the bonds become due.
5. The Advertising costs were for billboards that were put up on July 1, 1930, and that will be torn down on June 30, 1931.
6. AC–DC owed one of its customers $125 worth of services, which the customers had paid for but not yet received.
7. Unpaid and unrecorded bills for gasoline totaled $35.

REQUIRED   From the above information prepare the *adjusting* journal entries, the income statement for the year 1930, and the balance sheet as of December 31, 1930.

P2-4   Acme Travel, Inc., has operated from June 3, 1984, through the end of its first year, December 31, 1984. The following ledger accounts and balances exist at December 31, 1984:

	DEBIT	CREDIT
Cash	$ 40,500	
Accounts receivable	33,040	
Supplies	1,750	
Buildings and equipment	120,200	
Land	5,000	
Accounts payable		$ 14,700
Notes payable		10,000
Common stock		100,000
Sales		105,700
Expenses	29,910	
	$230,400	$230,400

The following events have *not* yet been recorded:

1. Supplies of $500 were delivered to Acme on December 30, 1984, but the invoice will not be paid until January 5, 1985.
2. Salaries were paid on December 24, 1984, and properly recorded, but $2,500 of salaries related to the period December 24–31 were not recorded.
3. On December 15, 1984, a major customer sent Acme a check for $6,000 as a prepayment for a tour which will take place in March 1985. As of December 31, 1984, Acme has not performed any services for this tour.
4. The economic life of the building, which cost Acme $40,000 on June 30, 1984 and has no salvage value, is felt to be one-thirtieth used up by December 31, 1984.
5. The equipment, mostly office equipment, has an expected useful life of 5 years and cost $10,500 on December 30, 1984. It has no salvage value.

REQUIRED For each of the five items above, (1) discuss which elements and common aspects of the financial statements, as included in the theoretical framework, guide the accountant's action; (2) record the necessary adjustment entries, if any; (3) prepare an adjusted trial balance; (4) construct a balance sheet and income statement.

P2–5 The following trial balance as of December 31, 1984, for the Kinnear Corporation is presented to you by your boss, the controller:

	DEBIT	CREDIT
Cash	$ 25,879	
Accounts receivable	30,104	
Notes receivable	6,700	
Allowance for uncollectibles		$ 847
Inventory	59,276	
Prepaid insurance	4,500	
Plant and equipment	248,302	
Accumulated depreciation		87,480
Property	68,000	
Notes payable (current)		17,150
Accounts payable		21,200
Interest payable		4,000
Taxes payable		785
Long-term note payable		150,000
Common stock (no par)		100,000
Retained earnings		31,864
Sales revenue		1,287,350
Cost of goods sold	729,600	
Selling expenses	172,190	
Administrative expenses	288,600	
Interest expense	11,000	
Tax expense	18,375	
Depreciation expense	13,150	
Dividends	25,000	
	$1,700,676	$1,700,676

After examining the account details and supporting documentation, you discover the following facts:

1. The year-end inventory value, based on the actual physical count, was $57,328.
2. The allowance for uncollectibles should have a balance equal to 10 percent of total receivables (both accounts and notes).
3. The prepaid insurance is for a 3-year policy, and the $4,500 was paid in cash at the start of this year.
4. The notes payable (current) were taken out at the start of the year, with total interest for the year amounting to $2,550 payable on January 1 next year when the loan matures.
5. The long-term note calls for interest payments of $7,000 twice each year on July 1 and January 1.
6. Sales revenue includes $9,875 for an order of goods (costing $4,387) which are still in inventory, scheduled to be shipped on the next available train. The sale was made on account.
7. Taxes are calculated at 40 percent of net income before tax.
8. Depreciation expense for the year is $15,000.

REQUIRED

1. Prepare the necessary adjusting entries.
2. Prepare the 1984 income statement.
3. Prepare the year-end balance sheet.

P2–6 The following events took place during the first 3 months of operations of the JFI Nursery:

Mar. 1   Sold 1,000 shares of no-par stock for $60,000 cash and $100,000 in land.

Mar. 15   Purchased for cash and installed a shed to house equipment and furnishings at a cost of $2,500. Expected life is 10 years.

Mar. 18   Paid $600 cash for utilities hookup (phone and electricity).

Mar. 18   Acquired hand tools, a desk, three chairs, and a work bench for $1,875 cash. Expected life is 5 years.

Mar. 19   Purchased supplies for $750 cash.

Mar. 20   Purchased a tractor with a backhoe and a delivery truck for $25,000 and $7,800, respectively. The tractor has an expected life of 15 years, and the truck 5 years. Paid cash for both.

Mar. 23   Received a shipment of $4,800 in trees and $6,500 in shrubs from a wholesaler, paying $6,000 cash and the balance on an open account. A perpetual inventory accounting system is used.

Mar. 31   Paid wages of $4,925 cash.

Apr. 1   Purchased a 3-year insurance policy on all assets (except land) for $6,000.

Apr. 15   Sold to date trees costing $3,000 and shrubs costing $2,000 for $10,000 in cash and $6,000 on open account.

Apr. 18   Paid wages of $2,850; paid gasoline bills of $650.

Apr. 19   Purchased fertilizer for $925 on open account.

Apr. 30   Borrowed $16,000 from the bank on a 1-year note, with 1 percent interest due each month on the unpaid balance.

May 3   Sales since April 15 were: $1,500 in trees (at cost) and $1,800 in shrubs (at cost) for $7,100, of which $3,500 was cash sales.

May 8   Received shipment of $7,000 in trees and $3,000 in shrubs from wholesaler. Paid $7,000 cash on account with wholesaler.

May 15   Collected $6,000 from customers and deposited in bank.

May 20   Purchased additional supplies for $385 on account.

May 21   Sales since May 3 were: $4,800 in trees (at cost) and $1,900 in shrubs (at cost) for $14,820, of which $9,650 was cash sales.

May 22   Paid wages of $5,780, and salary of $9,000. Paid gasoline bills of $725.

May 30   Received $3,950 from customers and deposited in bank. Paid bills for gas of $275.

ADDITIONAL DATA

1. Wages due on May 30, but unpaid, totaled $2,700.
2. Unrecorded sales were: $2,700 for trees and $2,780 for shrubs. One-half of these sales were for cash.
3. Undeposited and unrecorded checks from customers on account totaled $2,950.
4. Salaries payable amounted to $3,800.
5. Inventory of fertilizer was $375 at cost.
6. Inventory of supplies was $220 at cost.
7. Inventory of trees was $1,320 at cost.
8. Inventory of shrubs was $2,300 at cost.

REQUIRED   Assume that all depreciable assets have no scrap value and that JFI uses straight-line depreciation.

1. Record all the events and transactions.
2. Post journal entries to ledger (T) accounts.
3. Prepare a trial balance.
4. Record necessary adjusting entries at May 31 and post to ledger (T) accounts.
5. Prepare an adjusted trial balance.
6. Prepare an income statement and a balance sheet for the period ending May 31.

P2–7   Speedo Company was organized on January 1, 1920, for the purpose of providing transportation for companies without horses or cars. Data in summary form from the first year's operations are given below:

1. Transportation revenue earned from services performed on account		$2,500

2. Cash receipts for the year:

Jan. 10	From stockholders for shares of stock	5,000
June 30	From bonds issued (1 percent bonds, maturity date, June 30, 1930)	2,000
Jan. 1–Dec. 31	From customers representing collections on account	1,850
		$8,850

3. Cash disbursements for the year:

Jan. 1	For purchase of land	1,000
July 1	For advertising (1 year paid in advance)	3,400
Dec. 30	For dividends	100
	For bond interest	5
Jan. 1–Dec. 31	For gasoline	250
July 1	For advertising (1 year paid in advance)	140
Jan. 30–Dec. 15	For wages	1,200
Jan. 30–Dec. 31	For repairs	125
Nov. 1 and Dec. 1	For auto payments	400
		$6,620

4. Purchased five autos costing $2,000 total on October 1 for no down payment. These autos were expected to have a 10-year life and no scrap value. The autos were to be paid for in ten monthly payments interest free.
5. Unpaid wages as of December 31 were $100.
6. Unpaid invoices as of December 31 were $60.

REQUIRED

1. Prepare the journal entries necessary to reflect the summary of events described above and post to the T-accounts.
2. Prepare the trial balance as of December 31, 1920.
3. Prepare the adjusting entries and post to the T-accounts.
4. Prepare the adjusted trial balance.
5. Prepare the income statement for 1920.
6. Prepare the balance sheet and retained earnings statements for 1920 year-end.

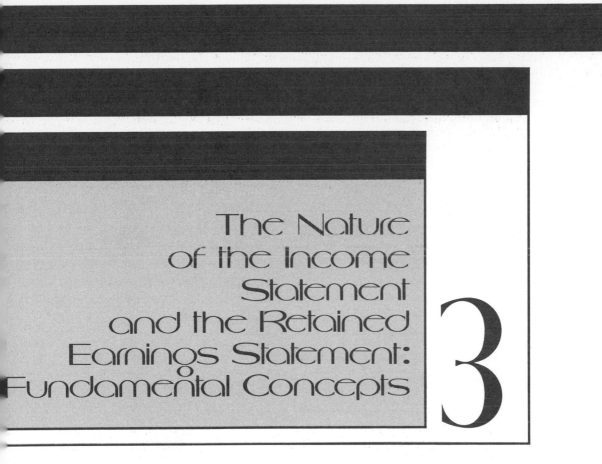

The Nature of the Income Statement and the Retained Earnings Statement: Fundamental Concepts

3

OVERVIEW   The objective of accounting is to provide useful information to investors and creditors for decision making. This objective is accomplished largely by issuing periodic financial statements. The balance sheet, or position statement, was identified in Chapter 2 as the primary statement, with the income statement, retained earnings statement, and statement of changes in financial position all representing ways in which accountants describe the nature of changes in the balance sheet from one period to the next. Although the balance sheets of an entity report its position at various points in time, the other statements tell what caused the changes and what impact the various activities of the entity had on income, changes in net assets, flows of funds, and other financing and investing activities. These "change" statements can aid users in evaluating the performance of the entity and its management.

This chapter focuses on two of these change statements; the income statement and the statement of retained earnings. The development of these statements has been guided by the qualitative characteristics and elements defined in Chapter 2 as well as by the principles of historical cost, revenue recognition, and matching. The format of these statements has also been an important consideration, as we shall show in this chapter.

INCOME STATEMENT

The **income statement** reflects the results of operating activity for a designated period of time. The income statement summarizes a firm's operations, reflecting certain results from its production and sales activities. Four *major* elements make up an income statement: revenue, expense, gain, and loss.

Revenue   **Revenue** was defined in Chapter 2 as the inflow of net assets that results from the productive activities of the entity over a specified period of time. As a result of these productive activities, the entity recognizes an increase in net assets. This increase in net assets is offset by an increase in owners' equity in order to maintain the balance sheet equality: Assets = Liabilities + Owners' equity. Consider the case of an entity that purchases a single asset, land, valued at $20,000, for $20,000 in stock. The balance sheet equation would show:

ASSETS	=	LIABILITIES	+	OWNERS' EQUITY
Land $20,000	=	$0	+	$20,000 Equity

Assume that the entity rents the land to a farmer who pays $1,000 cash at the end of the season for use of the land. The only *real* impact on the entity is that it received $1,000 cash. The balance sheet equation would now be as follows:

ASSETS	=	LIABILITIES	+	OWNERS' EQUITY
Cash $ 1,000	=	$0	+	$20,000 Equity
Land 20,000				
$21,000				

This temporary imbalance in the equation is remedied in the double-entry system by using a plug account, Retained Earnings, which allows the balance sheet to balance:

ASSETS	=	LIABILITIES	+	OWNERS' EQUITY
Cash $ 1,000	=	$0	+	$20,000 Equity
Land 20,000				1,000 Retained earnings
$21,000	=	$0	+	$21,000

In complex entities there are numerous inflows of net assets from revenue-generating productive activities. These inflows need to be accounted for, and often many different types of activities are involved. Also, other activities of the entity may result in outflows of net assets (expenses) in the process of generating more revenues. Using the Retained Earnings account alone to balance out all the inflows and outflows would enable the accountant to maintain the basic balance sheet equality. At the end of an accounting period, however, explaining to someone why the net assets for the period increased or decreased would be complex and would require a detailed analysis of all the entries affecting the Retained Earnings account. To facilitate this explanation process, the details of the inflows and outflows of net assets are first accumulated in the revenue, expense, gain, and loss accounts of the entity. These accounts provide the details of the entries to the Retained Earnings account and thereby facilitate the periodic explanation of why net assets increased or decreased during a specified period of time.

Revenue accounts provide the details of the increases in net assets that will require the eventual increases in retained earnings to maintain the balance sheet equality. They are **temporary,** or **nominal, accounts** in that they will eventually be closed out to the Retained Earnings account. For example, consider the case where land is rented for $1,000 per year, and the cash is received at the end of the rental period. The following entry would record the revenue:

| 12/31/84 | Cash | 1,000 | |
| | Rent revenue | | 1,000 |

Net assets have increased from the inflow of cash. The Rent Revenue account is to be closed out to Retained Earnings through the following closing entry:

| 12/31/84 | Rent revenue | 1,000 | |
| | Retained earnings | | 1,000 |

Now consider the case where the $1,000 land rental is prepaid 1 year in advance. The following entry would be recorded at the beginning of the rental period:

| 1/1/84 | Cash | 1,000 | |
| | Unearned rent revenue | | 1,000 |

The Unearned Rent Revenue account is a liability that represents the claim of the renter to receive the right to use the land for 1 year. No revenue has resulted from the inflow of cash. At year-end, revenue is recognized by decreasing the liability account:

| 12/31/84 | Unearned rent revenue | 1,000 | |
| | Rent revenue | | 1,000 |

In this entry, revenue is accompanied by a decrease in a liability account. In both situations above, revenue resulted from an increase in *net* assets. And in both situations, the end result is to increase Cash and Retained Earnings by $1,000.

Revenue recognition In most major industries, accountants recognize revenue only when that revenue has been **realized.** (To "recognize" revenue means simply to "record" it in the accounts and reflect it in financial statements.) Revenue is normally realized **when the earnings process is substantially complete** and the product or service of the entity is transferred to the customer. Thus, realization generally occurs at the point of sale. Recognition of revenue at the point of sale is applicable to most situations because that is the first point in the entire process of production, sale, and collection **where both the costs and the benefits of the process can be measured with a reasonable degree of objectivity.** Although this **revenue recognition principle** has been stated in various ways, recognition is essentially a function of the measurability of the net asset inflows and outflows from revenue-generating activities.

What if revenue and related costs can be measured objectively at a point earlier than the sales point? Or what if revenue or associated costs cannot be measured objectively until beyond the sales point? Many alternatives to the point of sale exist, and therefore the point of sale itself cannot be used as the sole basis for revenue recognition. The basic principle is that revenue can be measured at any point in time when both the costs (expenses) and the benefits (revenues) can be measured with a reasonable degree of certainty. As with many of the difficult questions in accounting, the accountant's professional judgment is a key ingredient in determining when to recognize revenue.

Some of the common revenue-recognition alternatives are summarized in Exhibit 3–1. Note that not all of these examples are uniformly accurate for all cases. For example, not all installment sales agreements are recognized beyond the point of sale. Only for installment sales where the conversion of accounts receivable to cash is uncertain would revenue recognition be delayed beyond the point of sale. The guiding concept is that the outflows of net assets from expenses and the inflows of net assets from revenues must be **measurable with a reasonable degree of certainty.**

Revenue recognition *before* the point of sale and *after* the point of sale are discussed in Chapter 23. To develop illustrations of every alternative to point-of-sale revenue recognition at this point would go beyond the scope of this chapter. Understanding that the delivery of goods or services or the actual occurrence of net asset inflows or net asset outflows (or both) or the signing of legal contracts is *not* pivotal

EXHIBIT 3–1

REVENUE-RECOGNITION ALTERNATIVES

Status of inflow and outflow of resources involved in revenue-generating activities:	Both inflows and outflows of resources are incomplete	Either inflows or outflows of resources are incomplete	POINT OF SALE	Either inflows or outflows of resources are complete	Both inflows and outflows of resources are complete
Time line					
Revenue-recognition examples:	1. Long-term construction contracts 2. Timberland development 3. Livestock development 4. Aging of wine and liquor	1. Mining of precious metals 2. Sale of services (for example, ticket agents) 3. Agricultural products 4. Leases	Most goods and services	1. Retail land sales 2. Installment sales (certain types) 3. Exchanges of similar productive assets that result in gains	1. Installment sales (certain types) 2. Exchanges of fixed assets with unknown values

	BEFORE POINT OF SALE	AFTER POINT OF SALE
Typical reasons or conditions for recognizing revenue before or after point of sale identified:	1. Stable market price of commodity. 2. Contracts make yet to be incurred costs and benefits known and measurable with a reasonable degree of precision. 3. Products have no unique features to differentiate one from another, making them highly uniform (for example, gold, wheat, corn). 4. Use of valuation accounts to measure expected inflows and/or outflows.	1. Uncertainty as to inflows or outflows remains significant even though goods have been transferred. 2. Valuation accounts not feasible for reducing uncertainty. 3. Conservatism in certain accounting rules prohibits recognition (for example, *APB Opinion No. 29*). 4. Status of ownership has been legally demonstrated to not relieve seller from obligations regarding sold goods or services (for example, land sales).

in determining revenue recognition will prove much more beneficial at this point than a review of the alternatives to point-of-sale revenue recognition.

Expenses

Expenses were defined in Chapter 2 as outflows of net assets that are incurred in an effort to generate inflows of net assets from the productive activities of the entity. Expense accounts are also nominal or temporary in that they describe the details of the decreases to the Retained Earnings account from operating activities. The expense accounts may shed light on how efficient and effective management was in generating revenue.

Another way to look at an expense is as a measure of the future benefits consumed during the year in pursuit of revenue. To understand this statement, two things must be kept in mind. First, the **matching principle** requires that expenses be matched with (deducted from) the revenues they are related to. Revenue is the controlling classification. Once the decision is made to record revenue in a given accounting period, the accountant must attempt to match the expenses that caused it against that revenue. Second, an asset is defined as something with anticipated future benefits—something that can be utilized in the future to generate income. An expense is a benefit that has been utilized, and as such it may be viewed as an asset that was consumed to generate revenue in the current year.

Consider the following situation involving a manufacturing concern. As a manufacturing machine is being utilized to produce a product, the service utility in the machine is being consumed, but the utility is not gone from the entity until the product produced has been sold (assuming recognition of revenue at the point of sale). Therefore, as we record depreciation on the machine, a current asset is debited:

3/31/84	Work-in-process inventory	500	
	Accumulated depreciation		500

In essence, this is a reclassification from a noncurrent to a current asset. Then, after other costs for material, labor, and so on have been added to the product and the product is finished, the following entry is made:

4/10/84	Finished-goods inventory	4,000[a]	
	Work-in-process inventory		4,000

[a] Includes $500 depreciation on machinery.

This is a reclassification within the current-asset section. Note that no expense has been recognized in the accounts and will not be recognized until revenue is recognized, perhaps not until the next accounting period. Certain costs must be carried forward until the period in which the related revenue is recognized. They must then be recognized as expenses and matched with the revenues they cause at that time:

1/19/85	Cost of goods sold expense	4,000	
	Finished-goods inventory		4,000

As illustrated, expenses represent efforts that have been made to bring about revenue. From this purely conceptual view, an entity wants expenses because it must make efforts in order to generate revenue, although it strives to minimize expenses for any given level of revenue.

Gains and **losses** are generally associated with nonoperating activities of the entity. They occur in most entities but are not a result of the entities' normal efforts to accomplish specific operating objectives. For example, a manufacturing concern may have an overall objective of maximizing profit from the production and sale of products that it can competitively produce. In attempting to achieve this overall objective, the entity may temporarily invest idle cash with a *secondary* objective of achieving some growth in the value of the idle cash. Changes in the value of the temporary investment are considered to result in gains or losses rather than revenues or expenses because the entity is not in business to buy and sell temporary investments. However, changes in value of the identical type of investments might be considered revenues and expenses (cost of sales) for a bank trust fund manager whose principal business consists of buying and selling such investments to earn a profit.

Revenues and expenses result from the entity's seeking to accomplish its principal business objective, whereas gains and losses are involved with changes in values of an entity's assets or liabilities that occur as a secondary result of business activity. These gains and losses are often simply the result of holding certain assets or liabilities that have experienced favorable or unfavorable price changes between the time of acquisition and the time of disposal. Such gains and losses are often due to events that are beyond the control of management.

Although expenses might be viewed as something that the entity seeks to incur because they imply that effort has been expended to generate revenue, losses are not desired. Like expenses, losses measure service utility consumed during the period. Unlike expenses, however, losses do not produce or cause revenue. Distinguishing between a loss and an expense in a given circumstance can be difficult. Distinguishing between a loss and an expense as a concept, however, is not difficult and can help us understand the information in an income statement. As an example of a loss, assume that a machine originally costing $10,000 is sold for $4,000. Accumulated depreciation at the date of sale is $5,000. The following entry would be appropriate:

7/1/84	Cash	4,000	
	Accumulated depreciation	5,000	
	Loss on sale of machinery	1,000	
	Machinery		10,000

A gain would be recorded in the above example if the asset were sold for, say, $6,000, resulting in the following journal entry:

7/1/84	Cash	6,000	
	Accumulated depreciation	5,000	
	Gain on sale of machinery		1,000
	Machinery		10,000

Once again, revenues and expenses are ordinary operating items, whereas gains and losses are not ordinary operating items. However, revenues and gains both increase net income (and retained earnings), whereas expenses and losses both decrease net income (and retained earnings).

Even though a basic understanding of revenues and expenses and gains and losses is necessary for interpreting the information conveyed by the income statement, both the sources and the causes of those items can vary considerably. These causes must also be understood. Some items are ordinary, recurring, operating items. Others are unusual, nonoperating, nonrecurring items, which we shall refer to as "unusual" for ease of discussion. As a consequence, not all types of revenues, expenses, gains, and losses convey the same messages about the firm, and distinctions must be made between them if the statements are to convey their specific messages. Accountants have long debated the nature of income statement disclosure. Some accountants believe that the **current operating** approach to disclosure is the most appropriate; others prefer the **all-inclusive** approach.

Current operating concept of income   Advocates of the **current operating concept of income** argue that all unusual items should be recorded directly in the Retained Earnings account and reflected in the retained earnings balance at year end. They feel that since unusual items are not part of the normal, ongoing operations of a firm, such items are not representative of the firm's future earnings potential. Placing them in the income statement, therefore, might cause some users to include these items in future projections, which might lead to incorrect economic decisions. In other words, many users would have difficulty distinguishing the "usual" from the "unusual." Recording them directly in the Retained Earnings account, however, makes the distinction clear.

All-inclusive concept of income   Advocates of the **all-inclusive concept of income** argue that all items of an income-determining nature should be reported in the income statement. Not to do so would exclude some items from the total historical income-generating activities of the firm, items considered to be necessary to project long-run, income-generating ability. All such items, whether usual or not, do contribute to the total income of the firm. They feel that unusual items can be separated from normal operations in the income statement in a way that would avoid possible misinterpretation. Furthermore, since judgment is flexible in distinguishing usual from unusual items, the current operating concept of income lends itself to manipulation and leads to other disclosure problems.[1] However, the all-inclusive concept requires that most events, whether usual or unusual, be summarized and disclosed in the income statement.

Supporters of the all-inclusive concept of income have evidently presented the most convincing arguments. Present professional requirements dictate that, with relatively few exceptions, all items of an income-determining nature, regardless of source, must be reflected in the income statement. In other words, most events that occur in the current year and that will have an effect on the Retained Earnings account should be shown on the income statement in the current year. There are two primary exceptions: (1) **dividends** (and other equity transactions) that are considered to be distributions of funds generated by operating activity rather than elements of the earnings process and (2) **prior period adjustments,** which consist primarily of error corrections and the effects of certain types of changes in accounting principles.[2] Two other exceptions to the all-inclusive concept will be discussed in Chapter 24.

[1] For example, see Amir Barnea, Joshua Ronen, and Simcha Sadan, "Classificatory Smoothing of Income with Extraordinary Items," *The Accounting Review,* January 1976, pp. 110–122.

[2] For an early study on prior period adjustments and other types of changes in accounting principles, see Barry Cushing, "Accounting Changes: The Impact of APB Opinion No. 20," *Journal of Accountancy,* November 1974, p. 54. Also see Martin Gosman, "Characteristics of Firms Making Accounting Changes," *The Accounting Review,* January 1973, pp. 1–11.

Introduction to Continuing Operations and Special Items

To avoid confusing the results of operating activities with unusual types of events and transactions, the income statement and retained earnings statement require separate disclosure of certain items. These items must all be given special consideration and can be divided into **income statement items** and **retained earnings statement items** and grouped into five basic categories:

ITEMS REQUIRING SPECIAL DISCLOSURE	
INCOME STATEMENT ITEMS	**RETAINED EARNINGS STATEMENT ITEMS**
1. Discontinued operations 2. Extraordinary items 3. Most changes in accounting principles	4. Errors 5. Certain changes in accounting principles

We'll shortly discuss how the first three of these items are disclosed on the income statement, and then, after introducing the retained earnings statement, we'll discuss errors and changes in accounting principles that need to be disclosed on the retained earnings statement. However, before we treat these special items, which are illustrated by means of actual annual report disclosures in Appendix B to this chapter, we need to discuss two more fundamental issues: (1) intraperiod tax allocation and (2) the format of the income statement.

Special Items and Intraperiod Tax Allocation

Intraperiod means *"within* a period." Thus, intraperiod income tax allocation means that the total tax burden *for* a given period must be allocated *within* that period to the various components of the income statement and the retained earnings statement identified in Exhibit 3–2.[3] This is done as follows: First, the income tax consequences of all *ordinary* revenues, expenses, gains, and losses are deducted as a *single* figure in order to arrive at "income from continuing operations." Then the tax consequences of any *unusual* items (items 4, 5, 6, 7, 9, and 10 in Exhibit 3–2) reflected in separate sections of the income statement or the retained earnings statement are measured and netted individually against those items. The appropriate portion of the total tax burden for the period should be allocated to each of the specific unusual items on the income statement and the retained earnings statement to provide more useful information to financial statement users. Were it not for intraperiod tax allocation, all the tax burden for a period would be reported as a single expense in the "regular" section of the statement, thereby distorting income from operations.

Income Statement Formats

The unusual items that might be found in the income statement must be disclosed after the "regular" part of the income statement, which includes the usual, recurring, and normal operating revenues, the operating expenses, and the ordinary gains and losses.[4] The subtotal at the end of this section is frequently called **income from continuing operations** or **income before extraordinary items**. The exact title of the subtotal will normally depend on whether the entity has any or all of the unusual

---

[3] The accounting for tax allocations is based largely on *Accounting Principles Board Opinion No. 11,* "Accounting for Income Taxes" (New York: AICPA, December 1967). This topic is covered in greater detail in Chapter 17.

[4] Ordinary gains or losses are all of those gains and losses that do not meet the requirements of "extraordinary." Unfortunately, there is no better way to concisely define ordinary gains or losses.

EXHIBIT 3-2

COMPONENTS OF THE INCOME STATEMENT AND THE RETAINED EARNINGS STATEMENT

STATEMENT	COMPONENT	CONTENT
Income statement for the year ended 12/31/84	The "regular" section of the income statement	1. Revenues and expenses 2. Certain gains and losses 3. Taxes on items 1 and 2 only
	Regular subtotal	Income from continuing operations
	Discontinued operations (if any)	4. Net income or loss from the 1984 operations of the discontinued operations, net of applicable taxes if any 5. Gains and losses from the sale of the net assets of the discontinued operations, net of applicable taxes if any
	Extraordinary items (if any)	6. Any gains or losses that are required by GAAP to be disclosed separately, net of applicable taxes if any
	Change in accounting method (if any)	7. Prior years' impact of most types of changes in accounting methods, net of applicable taxes if any
	TOTAL	NET INCOME
Retained earnings statement for the year ended 12/31/84	Prior years' adjustments	8. Beginning balance (1/1/84) 9. Corrections of errors, net of applicable taxes if any 10. Prior years' impact of a selected number of changes in accounting principles, net of applicable taxes if any
	The "regular" section of the retained earnings statement	11. Beginning balance (as corrected and adjusted) 12. Net income for the period 13. Dividends for the period
	TOTAL	ENDING BALANCE

events (identified earlier) to report in its income statement. Each unusual item listed below this subtotal is reported at its net of tax amount, as noted in Exhibit 3–2. Exhibit 3–3 shows an income statement divided into two sections—one for ordinary items and one for special or unusual items.

There are two basic formats for income statements: the **single-step** and the **multiple-step.** The example shown in Exhibit 3–3 is a single-step statement because **only two groups of ordinary items** are reported: revenues and expenses. The expenses are deducted from the revenues to arrive at "income from continuing operations." The multiple-step statement discloses additional relationships before arriving at "income from continuing operations." Exhibit 3–4 shows a multiple-step statement that uses the same basic data as those in the single-step statement.

Note that the statements in both formats show "income from continuing operations" of $12,000 and "net income" of $362,000. The unusual items must be listed in the order indicated. The two basic differences in the formats are the degree of detail usually presented and, more importantly, the fact that the multiple-step statement has intervening "profit" figures before arriving at "income from continuing operations." Some accountants prefer the single-step statement because it is simpler and more easily understood. Other accountants prefer the multiple-step statement because it allows users to evaluate the various sources of operating in-

EXHIBIT 3-3

SINGLE-STEP INCOME STATEMENT EXAMPLE

THE KELLER CORPORATION
Income Statement
For the Year Ended December 31, 1984

Net sales	$ 576,000
Other income	10,000
	$ 586,000
Expenses	
Cost of goods sold	$(342,000)
Sales and marketing	(15,000)
Travel and entertainment	(25,000)
Shipping	(58,000)
Depreciation	(68,000)
Administrative	(35,000)
Income taxes	(11,000)
Ordinary gains and losses (net)	(20,000)
Total expenses, gains, and losses	$(574,000)
Income from continuing operations	$ 12,000
Discontinued operations	
Loss from discontinued division X (net of applicable income	
taxes of $200,000)	(300,000)
Extraordinary gain (net of applicable income taxes of $400,000)	600,000
Cumulative effect of changing from declining balance to straight-line depreciation (net of applicable income taxes of $33,333)	50,000
Net income	$ 362,000

come. It separates the results from regular operations (production and sale of the primary product or service) and those brought about by secondary operations (interest income, gains and losses on the sale of equipment). Disclosing expenses according to their functional classification (selling, administrative, and so on) may provide useful information for comparison with prior years. Both formats are acceptable presentations and are used extensively.

Disclosure of Special Items in the Income Statement

Discontinued operations At times a firm may discontinue a major segment of its business operations. In **APB Opinion No. 30,** the term **major segment** is defined as a "major line of business or class of customers."[5] The impact of such a discontinuation on decision making is different from the results of normal operating items reported in arriving at "income from continuing operations." Users of the income statement must take into account discontinued operations in making judgments about the future earnings of a business. Certainly if results of discontinued operations were reported as a component of regular income, users might be misled regarding the future earnings prospects of the firm. Consequently, the results of discontinuing a segment of a business are reported separately, net of any income tax effects, as an addition or deduction below the subtotal "income from continuing operations."

Judgment must be exercised in applying the broad criterion "major line of

[5] *Accounting Principles Board Opinion No. 30,* "Reporting the Results of Operations" (New York: AICPA, June 1973).

EXHIBIT 3-4

MULTIPLE-STEP INCOME STATEMENT EXAMPLE

THE KELLER CORPORATION
Income Statement
For the Year Ended December 31, 1984

Sales revenue			$ 600,000
Less: Sales discounts		$ (14,000)	
Sales returns and allowances		(10,000)	(24,000)
Net sales			$ 576,000
Cost of goods sold			
Beginning inventory		$ (42,000)	
Purchases	$(400,000)		
Less: Purchase discounts	9,000		
Net purchases		(391,000)	
Total goods available for sale		$(433,000)	
Less: Ending inventory		91,000	
Cost of goods sold			(342,000)
Gross profit on sales			$ 234,000
Operating expenses			
Selling expenses			
Travel and entertainment		$ (15,000)	
Sales and marketing		(15,000)	
Shipping		(58,000)	
Depreciation on sales equipment		(28,000)	
Total selling expenses		$(116,000)	
Administrative expenses			
Travel and entertainment	$ (10,000)		
Depreciation on office equipment	(40,000)		
Office salaries	(14,000)		
Legal services	(11,000)		
Utilities expense	(10,000)		
Total administrative expenses		(85,000)	
Total operating expenses			(201,000)
Income from operations			$ 33,000
Other income and gains			
Dividend income		$ 8,000	
Interest income		2,000	
Gain on sale of investments		10,000	20,000
Other expenses and losses			
Loss on sale of office furniture			(30,000)
Income before taxes			$ 23,000
Income taxes			(11,000)
Income from continuing operations			$ 12,000
Discontinued operations:			
Loss from discontinued division X			
(net of applicable income taxes			
of $200,000)			(300,000)
Loss before extraordinary items and cumulative effect of changes in accounting principles			$(288,000)
Extraordinary gain (net of applicable income taxes of $400,000)		$ 600,000	
Cumulative effect of changing from declining balance to straight-line depreciation (net of applicable income taxes of $33,333)		50,000	650,000
Net income			$ 362,000

business or class of customers." **APB Opinion No. 30** lists events that *never* qualify as discontinued operations:

1. Disposal of *part* of a line of business
2. Shifting of production or marketing activities for a particular line of business from one location to another
3. Phasing out of a product line or class of service
4. Changes caused by technological improvements[6]

Thus, to qualify for separate disclosure, an entire separate line of business or class of customers must be discontinued. The line of business must be abandoned, not merely shifted to a new location. The event causing the discontinuation must be relatively sudden as opposed to a gradual phasing out or a change brought about by technological improvements. And the operations discontinued must have been a significant part of the total activities of the firm. If a firm disposes of one of its ten copper mines for example, it can't consider the closed mine a "discontinued operation."

Even when the disposition of a segment qualifies for separate disclosure, practical considerations sometimes make it difficult or impossible to account for the discontinued operations properly. It is necessary to distinguish the assets, business activities, and results of operations of the discontinued segment physically, operationally, and for financial reporting purposes in order to measure and separately disclose the effects of the discontinued operations. The following example will illustrate the measurement and disclosure to be accorded a discontinued segment.

Shrinking Corporation, a conglomerate corporation with many different types of manufacturing operations, sold the segment of its business that manufactured and marketed office furniture on December 31, 1984. Exhibit 3–5 shows the summarized comparative income statements for 1983 and 1984 for *all* of Shrinking's operations *before* considering the sale of the segment. The net assets that were sold had a total book value of $50,000,000 on the date of sale. The selling price was $70,000,000. The operations of the sold segment for 1983 and 1984 that are included in Exhibit 3–5 are summarized in Exhibit 3–6.

If the discontinued operations of the sold segment are subtracted from all the other operations, the results for Shrinking Corporation *exclusive* of the segment are shown in Exhibit 3–7.

The journal entries to record the sale of the segment and the related income tax effects (assuming a 50 percent tax rate) are recorded below. The first and second entries record the sale of the segment's assets. The third entry records the tax expense on income from continuing operations. The fourth and fifth entries record the final operating activities of the discontinued segment.

12/31/84	Cash	70,000,000	
	Net assets (various accounts)		50,000,000
	Gain on sale of segment		20,000,000
	(To record the disposition of the discontinued furniture operations)		
12/31/84	Tax on gain from sale of segment (50%)	10,000,000	
	Income taxes payable		10,000,000
	(To record tax effects of the $20,000,000 gain)		

[6] Ibid., par. 13.

12/31/84	Tax expense	1,500,000	
	Income taxes payable		1,500,000
	(Ordinary tax expenses for $3,000,000 operating income from continuing operations)		

12/31/84	Revenues (furniture segment)	15,000,000	
	Operating loss (furniture segment)	2,000,000	
	Expenses (furniture segment)		17,000,000
	(To identify separately the operating loss of the discontinued segment)		

12/31/84	Income taxes payable	1,000,000	
	Operating loss (furniture segment)		1,000,000
	(To reflect reduction in total income taxes payable and the after-tax operating loss of the segment because of the tax savings brought about by the operating loss of the segment)		

EXHIBIT 3–5

SHRINKING CORPORATION
Total Operating Results

	1984	1983
Revenues	$ 70,000,000	$ 75,000,000
Expenses		
Expenses (other than income taxes)	(69,000,000)	(70,000,000)
Income before taxes	$ 1,000,000	$ 5,000,000
Income taxes (50%)	(500,000)	(2,500,000)
Net income	$ 500,000	$ 2,500,000

EXHIBIT 3–6

SHRINKING CORPORATION
Office Furniture Segment Results

	1984	1983
Revenues	$ 15,000,000	$ 20,000,000
Expenses		
Expenses (other than income taxes)	(17,000,000)	(18,000,000)
Income (loss) before taxes	$ (2,000,000)	$ 2,000,000
Income taxes (50%)	1,000,000	(1,000,000)
Net income (loss)	$ (1,000,000)	$ 1,000,000

EXHIBIT 3–7

SHRINKING CORPORATION
Total Operations Less Office Furniture Segment

	1984	1983
Revenues	$ 55,000,000	$ 55,000,000
Operating Expenses		
Expenses (other than income taxes)	(52,000,000)	(52,000,000)
Income before taxes	$ 3,000,000	$ 3,000,000
Income taxes (50%)	(1,500,000)	(1,500,000)
Net income	$ 1,500,000	$ 1,500,000

EXHIBIT 3-8

SHRINKING CORPORATION
Comparative Income Statements
For the Years Ended December 31

	1984	1983
Revenues	$ 55,000,000	$ 55,000,000
Operating expenses		
Expenses (other than income taxes)	52,000,000	(52,000,000)
Income before taxes	$ 3,000,000	$ 3,000,000
Income taxes (50%)	(1,500,000)	(1,500,000)
Income from continuing operations	$ 1,500,000	$ 1,500,000
Discontinued operations (see note Z):		
Income (loss) from operations of discontinued office furniture division (less applicable income taxes of $1,000,000 and $(1,000,000))	(1,000,000)	1,000,000
Gain on disposal of office furniture division (less applicable income taxes, of $10,000,000)	10,000,000	
Net income	$ 10,500,000	$ 2,500,000

The comparative income statements illustrated in Exhibit 3–8 would be published at year-end, 1984. Note that as a result of the required tax allocation within a period, the tax effect of discontinuing the segment is shown with the disclosures concerning the discontinued segment. This is an example of intraperiod tax allocation as previously discussed. Note that the segregation of discontinued operations allows statement readers to determine the current operating results of the continuing operations, which is more relevant for making projections regarding future operating results. A footnote to the income statement must be used to identify and explain all the important facts concerning the discontinued segment.

Extraordinary items An **extraordinary item** is defined in **APB Opinion No. 30** as one that is **highly unusual in nature and not expected to occur again in the foreseeable future.**[7] Both requirements should be fulfilled for a gain or loss to be considered extraordinary. They are material items "of a character significantly different from the typical or customary business activities of the entity" and "which would not be expected to recur frequently and which would not be considered as recurring factors in any evaluation of the ordinary operating processes of the business."[8] The definition of extraordinary items is such that few items encountered in practice qualify as extraordinary.

APB Opinion No. 30 provides additional guidance on what is extraordinary by identifying the following as items that *do not* qualify as extraordinary:

1. Write-down or write-off of receivables, inventories, equipment leased to others, deferred research and development costs, or other intangible assets
2. Gains or losses from exchange or translation of foreign currencies, including those relating to major devaluations and revaluations
3. Gains or losses on disposal of a segment of a business

[7] Ibid.

[8] Ibid. It should be noted that specific pronouncements can be and have been issued to identify items that are required to receive treatment as extraordinary but that do not otherwise qualify. In fact, these exceptions tend to be the rule in practice. These exceptions are identified at the end of this section.

4. Other gains or losses from sale or abandonment of property, plant, or equipment used in the business
5. Effects of a strike, including those against competitors and major suppliers
6. Adjustment of accruals on long-term contracts[9]

The listed items are considered ongoing, usual, and recurring as a consequence of customary and continuing activities, according to **APB Opinion No. 30,** and thus cannot be considered extraordinary. However, items 1 and 4 can be classified as extraordinary if they result from an unusual, nonrecurring casualty, such as an earthquake, an expropriation, or a prohibition under a newly enacted law or regulation, all of which clearly meet the tests of unusual and infrequent.

The environment within which the entity operates is important in determining whether an event is unusual and infrequent. This means *total* environment and encompasses such things as geographical location, the characteristics of the industry within which the firm operates, and the nature and extent of governmental regulations. As examples of extraordinary items, **APB Opinion No. 30** lists the destruction of a tobacco manufacturer's crop by a hailstorm where hailstorms are rare; the earthquake destruction of an oil refinery owned by a multinational oil company; and the sale of a large block of common stock that was the only security investment the selling company ever owned.[10]

However, assume that a business has an orange grove in central Florida. In a given year, a frost may damage the orange crop. Is such an event extraordinary? The answer depends on whether, given the geographical location of the grove, the damaging frost is or is not considered highly unusual and can or cannot be expected to occur again in the future. Since such damage to citrus groves in Florida is not unusual and will probably occur again in the future, it is not a likely candidate for treatment as an extraordinary item. Gains and losses resulting from such "nonextraordinary" events must be added or deducted in arriving at "income from continuing operations."

The following two items are exceptions to the general rule in that they are always considered extraordinary, even though they do not meet either the "unusual" or the "infrequent" criterion: (1) the net amount of gains and losses from early extinguishment (retirement) of debt (bonds or notes payable) and (2) the realization of tax-loss carry-forward benefits.[11] The exceptions were developed because it was expected that such items, if used in determining "income from continuing operations," would make the statements less useful to decision makers in evaluating the ongoing, normal results of operating activity and, consequently, less useful in making future projections of cash flows.

The following example illustrates the appropriate treatment of an extraordinary item. One of American Agri Company's many plantations is located in Revolt-prone, a small, unstable country. The government there expropriates the company's

---

[9] *Accounting Principles Board Opinion No. 30,* "Reporting the Results of Operations," par. 23.

[10] Ibid.

[11] These exceptions stem from other pronouncements. Specifically, the retirement of debt is addressed in *Statement of Financial Accounting Standards No. 4,* "Reporting Gains and Losses from Extinguishment of Debt" (Stamford, CT: FASB, March 1975); and the tax-loss carry-forward is addressed in *Accounting Principles Board Opinion No. 11,* "Accounting for Income Taxes," and is exempted from change in paragraph 7 of *Accounting Principles Board Opinion No. 30,* "Reporting the Results of Operations."

EXHIBIT 3-9

> **AMERICAN AGRI COMPANY**
> Income Statement
> For the Year Ended December 31, 1984
> (not including Revoltprone operations)
>
> | | |
> |---|---|
> | *Revenues* | |
> | Sales | $ 200,000,000 |
> | *Expenses* | |
> | Cost of goods sold, etc. | (75,000,000) |
> | Income before taxes | $ 125,000,000 |
> | Income taxes (40%) | (50,000,000) |
> | Net income | $ 75,000,000 |

assets, which consist of land valued at $10,000,000. Given a tax rate of 40 percent, the income statement for American Agri *before considering* the income of the Revoltprone operations is shown in Exhibit 3-9. The entry to reflect taxes on these operations would be recorded as follows:

12/31/84	Tax expense	50,000,000	
	Income taxes payable		50,000,000

American Agri Company would also record the following entries regarding the expropriation of its land in Revoltprone:

12/31/84	Extraordinary loss—expropriations	10,000,000	
	Land		10,000,000
	(To write off lost net assets)		
12/31/84	Income taxes payable	4,000,000	
	Extraordinary loss—expropriations		4,000,000
	(To recognize reduction in current taxes payable (40% × $10,000,000) and reduction in loss from expropriations due to tax saving)		

The complete income statement in Exhibit 3-10 takes these entries into account. A footnote giving additional details regarding the expropriation should also accompany the income statement.

Changes in accounting principles Consistency and comparability, two of the qualitative characteristics of accounting, require that once a method of accounting (such as **declining balance depreciation** or the **FIFO** inventory valuation method) has been adopted, that method should be followed year after year unless there are compelling reasons for using another method.[12] Changes in business circumstances may, for example, cause changes in the way the service utility of an asset used to produce a product is consumed. This, in turn, generates a need to change depreciation methods. Also, in some instances a firm may change from one inventory method to another because that is what most of its competitors are doing.

[12] Changes in accounting principles discussed here consist of (1) changes in accounting methods (often called principles), (2) changes in accounting estimates, and (3) changes caused by errors. These changes are governed primarily by *Accounting Principles Board Opinion No. 20,* "Accounting Changes," (New York: AICPA, July 1971).

EXHIBIT
3–10

AMERICAN AGRI COMPANY
Income Statement
For the Year Ended December 31, 1984

Revenues	
Sales	$ 200,000,000
Expenses	
Cost of goods sold, etc.	(75,000,000)
Income before taxes	$ 125,000,000
Income taxes (40%)	(50,000,000)
Income from continuing operations	$ 75,000,000
Extraordinary Item	
Expropriation of Revoltprone operations (less applicable income taxes of $4,000,000—see note X)	(6,000,000)
Net income	$ 69,000,000

Though accounting method changes may be justified by varying economic and financial circumstances, such changes lead to inconsistency. As a consequence, following the new principle or method for the current and future years causes some loss in comparability between the current year's and the prior years' statements. To counterbalance this effect, present rules require that the income statement disclose the "cumulative catch-up adjustment" (net of taxes) as a separate item to be reported in arriving at net income. Present rules also require that the income statement and balance sheet data that would have been reported in prior years had the change (the new method) been applied in those prior years be disclosed in the financial statements. These disclosures are called **pro forma** disclosures. (*Pro forma* is a term used in accounting to mean "as if.") In other words, the pro forma disclosures should provide prior years' financial statement data concerning the new method *as if* the method had been used in the past. This enables users to observe the impact on the financial reports both with and without the change in method.

The basic objective of using the cumulative catch-up adjustment in the income statement is that the *current year's* "income from continuing operations" should be shown as if the new method had always been in effect. The following events describe such a situation. Tentative Incorporated has previously reported the income statements illustrated in Exhibit 3–11. During 1984 the company decided to switch from the straight-line depreciation method to the double-declining-balance depreciation

EXHIBIT
3–11

TENTATIVE INCORPORATED
Comparative Income Statements
For the Years Ended December 31

	1983	1982
Revenues	$1,200	$1,000
Expenses		
Cost of goods sold, etc., except depreciation	$ 600	$ 500
Depreciation (straight-line)	100	100
	$ 700	$ 600
Income before taxes	$ 500	$ 400
Income taxes (50%)	250	200
Net income	$ 250	$ 200

method for book and tax purposes. The following depreciation amounts would have been applicable in 1982 and 1983 using declining-balance and straight-line depreciation:

YEAR	DOUBLE-DECLINING BALANCE	STRAIGHT-LINE	DIFFERENCE
1982	$200	$100	$100
1983	160	100	60
Total	$360	$200	$160

Assume that 1984 revenues are $1,400; cost of goods sold, and so forth, are $700; and double-declining-balance depreciation is $128. The 1984 depreciation expense amount will be deducted in the "regular" part of the income statement for 1984 in arriving at "income from continuing operations."

The following journal entries would be recorded in the year of the change:

12/31/84	Depreciation expense	128	
	Accumulated depreciation		128
	(To record depreciation for 1984 using the double-declining-balance depreciation method)		
12/31/84	Cumulative effect of accounting change	160	
	Accumulated depreciation		160
	(Cumulative catch-up adjustment [before tax effects] up to the beginning of 1984 resulting from a switch to double-declining-balance depreciation from straight-line)		
12/31/84	Income tax expense	286(a)	
	Cumulative effect of accounting change		80(b)
	Income taxes payable		206(c)

These journal entries are arrived at as follows:

1. Income tax expense (item a):

Revenues	$1,400
Expenses	
Cost of goods sold, etc.	700
Depreciation	128
	$ 828
Tax base	$ 572
	× 50%
Income tax expense—1984	$ 286(a)

2. Tax effects of change in accounting method for book purposes and tax purposes—years ended December 31, 1982 and 1983 (item b):

Original depreciation	$ 200
Revised depreciation	360
Difference	$ 160
Income tax rate	× 50%
Reduction in federal income taxes of prior years	$ 80(b)

3. Federal income taxes currently payable—1984 (item *c*):

Revenues	$1,400
Expenses	
Cost of goods sold, etc.	700
Depreciation	288
	$ 988
Taxable income	$ 412
	× 50%
Federal income taxes payable	$ 206(c)

The comparative income statements for the years ended December 31, 1983 and 1984, are shown in Exhibit 3–12.

A footnote should be used to describe the reasons for the change and other pertinent information related to it. The disclosure should include the "as if," or "pro forma," information regarding 1983 (and perhaps 1982). In this case, the following pro forma data would also be reported:

PRO FORMA	1983	1982
Depreciation expense	$160	$200
Net income	$220	$150

These pro forma amounts would be computed as follows.

The new method of depreciation would have increased 1982 depreciation expense by $100 to $200, thereby reducing 1982 tax expense by $50. Net income would have been reduced by a net of $50 (from $200 to $150).

The new method of depreciation would have increased 1983 depreciation expense by $60 to $160 and reduced 1983 tax expense by $30. Net income would have been reduced by a net of $30 (from $250 to $220).

Many feel that the pro forma numbers are useful in making projections regarding net income and cash-flow figures. Earnings-per-share figures must also be computed and disclosed based on the pro forma numbers. This will be discussed in greater detail in Chapter 22.

EXHIBIT
3–12

TENTATIVE INCORPORATED Comparative Income Statements For the Years Ended December 31				
		1984		**1983**
Revenues		$ 1,400		$ 1,200
Expenses				
Expenses other than depreciation and taxes	$700		$600	
Depreciation	128		100	
Taxes	286	(1,114)	250	(950)
Income from continuing operations		$ 286		$ 250
Cumulative prior years' effect of change from straight-line to double-declining method (less applicable income taxes of $80)		(80)		
Net income		$ 206		$ 250

Changes in accounting estimate An important and common type of accounting change involves *changes in estimates.* These changes *do not* receive special disclosure in either the income statement or the retained earnings statement. One might ask what accountants have to do with estimates. Accountants actually make many estimates throughout the accounting cycle. Examples include such things as the lengths of service lives and salvage values for depreciable and depletable assets; estimated uncollectibles; and write-downs of inventory because of estimates of obsolescence. Economic and financial circumstances regarding business firms change frequently, making it necessary to alter such estimates. For example, bad debts frequently increase during periods of economic slowdown, requiring an increase in the estimate for uncollectible receivables. This does not mean that the old estimate was wrong. Given the economic and financial circumstances at the time it was made, the old estimate may have represented the best available forecast. However, new circumstances may require revisions in accounting estimates. Such revisions are called **changes in accounting estimate.** *No* special disclosure is made in the body of the income statement when changes in estimates occur. These changes are accounted for on a prospective basis, affecting operations for the current year (the year of the change) and future years. Consider the following example.

In 1979 a depreciable asset was purchased for $10,000. The estimates made were (1) salvage value, $1,000; (2) useful life, 10 years. The following depreciation was charged through 1983:

1979	1980	1981	1982	1983	TOTAL
$900[a]	$900	$900	$900	$900	$4,500

[a] $\dfrac{\$10,000 - \$1,000}{10}$

During 1984, due to a perceived decline in demand for the product produced by the depreciable asset, it is estimated that the asset has a remaining life of 3 years from the beginning of 1984 and no salvage value. The following facts, therefore, exist at the beginning of 1984:

	BALANCE 1/1/84
Asset—cost	$10,000
Accumulated depreciation	4,500
Book value	$ 5,500

The remaining book value (net of salvage, if any) must be expensed over the remaining life of the asset. Thus, annual depreciation expense for 1984–1986 would be $1,833 ($5,500/3 years). The 1984 depreciation expense would be recorded as follows:

12/31/84	Depreciation expense	1,833	
	Accumulated depreciation		1,833

Again, changes in estimate affect the current year (year of change in estimate) and future years. No cumulative catch-up adjustment applicable to prior years is permitted or required. Thus, the $1,833 for 1984–1986 would be deducted in arriving at "income from continuing operations." In the year of change, however, a footnote is required explaining the nature of the change and the impact on earnings per share, if material in amount.

THE STATEMENT OF RETAINED EARNINGS

The **statement of retained earnings** is a reconciliation statement that summarizes what brought about the increase or decrease in retained earnings during the year. The two major items bringing about this change are **net income** and **dividends**. Net income is added to the beginning balance, and dividends (both cash and stock dividends) are deducted in arriving at the ending balance. Certain items other than net income and dividends may also affect retained earnings. Here we will consider only **prior period adjustments** and certain accounting principle changes, which are generally the only items besides dividends and income that affect retained earnings.

Prior period adjustments consist primarily of the cumulative prior years' effects of errors. These errors are disclosed as adjustments to the beginning balance in retained earnings of the year in which an error is discovered.

In addition to prior period adjustments, the beginning retained earnings balance may also be adjusted for the prior years' effect of certain select accounting principle changes. The normal treatment for a change in accounting principle was illustrated in Exhibit 3–12. However, certain special accounting principle changes are treated like prior period adjustments in that the cumulative prior years' effect is reported as an adjustment to retained earnings.[13] These special cases include:

1. A change *from* the LIFO inventory method to any other method.
2. A change in the method of accounting for oil and gas reserves.
3. A change in the method of accounting for long-term construction contracts.

While it is not feasible to elaborate on these special cases at this point, it is worth noting that certain special accounting principle changes are treated like prior period adjustments.[14]

Prior Period
Adjustments

Errors are misstatements of facts, either deliberate or accidental. They may arise from mathematical mistakes, the change from an unacceptable to an acceptable accounting procedure, an oversight (such as not accruing a liability at the end of an accounting period), or an incorrect classification (such as the recording of an expense as an asset or vice versa). Exhibit 3–13 illustrates the way that prior period adjustments must be reflected in the statement of retained earnings.

The *calculations* of cumulative catch-up adjustments for errors and the changes in accounting principles, which must be recorded directly to the Retained Earnings account, are identical to those illustrated previously for Tentative Incorporated. However, there is an important difference regarding disclosure requirements. Retroactive application, illustrated below, is required for prior period adjustments and

[13] For a more complete discussion, see Chapter 24 and *Statement of Financial Accounting Standards No. 16*, "Prior Period Adjustments" (Stamford, CT: FASB, June 1977).

[14] These exceptions to the general rule for changes in accounting methods are specified in *Accounting Principles Board Opinion No. 20*, "Accounting Changes," and are considered in greater detail in Chapter 24.

EXHIBIT
3–13

Statement of Retained Earnings

Retained earnings, January 1, 1984, as reported		$500,000
Correction resulting from recording an expense as a purchase of an asset	$50,000	
Less: applicable income tax effect	15,000	35,000
Retained earnings, January 1, 1984, as adjusted		$465,000
Net income for 1984		275,000
		$740,000
Less: Dividends		125,000
Retained earnings, December 31, 1984		$615,000

special cases of accounting principle changes. Once the catch-up adjusting entries are recorded in the Retained Earnings account, the retained earnings balance is correct. Income for the current year is not affected by the catch-up adjustment, and the items for income determination purposes for the current year are stated on a correct basis. However, prior years' reports provided for purposes of comparison in the current period must be corrected by way of retroactive adjustment.

Presentation of prior period adjustments in comparative retained earnings statements and income statements When statements of income or retained earnings from a previous period are reported again in a following period for comparison purposes, the numbers reported in previous years are *changed* to reflect the retroactive impact of the prior period adjustments. To do this, journal entries *are not necessary.* As stated above, once the catch-up adjustment is closed to the Retained Earnings account, the ledger accounts are correct. Comparative statements are corrected *in an illustrative sense only* by changing those items in the statements that were previously reported incorrectly in prior annual reports.

To illustrate retroactive adjustments, consider the following case. Assume that Goofproof, Inc., presented comparative income and retained earnings statements in its annual report for the year ended December 31, 1983, as shown in Exhibit 3–14. During 1984 it is discovered that depreciation on a machine purchased January 1, 1981, was incorrectly recorded as $100 per year through 1983. The amount should have been $200. Assume that this is the only depreciable asset Goofproof, Inc., owns and that the error was made on the tax returns as well as on the books.

Calculation of the catch-up adjustment is as follows:

	1983	1982	1981	TOTAL
Depreciation recorded	$100	$100	$100	$300
Depreciation that should have been recorded	200	200	200	600
Understatement of depreciation	$100	$100	$100	$300

Some time during 1984, whenever the error is discovered, the following entry would be made to record the prior period adjustment:

Retained earnings	300	
Accumulated depreciation		300

In addition, because depreciation has been understated on the tax return for $300 in total, taxes have been overpaid by $150 (50% × $300) during the 3-year period. If

EXHIBIT
3–14

GOOFPROOF, INC.

Summarized Comparative Income Statements
For the Years Ended December 31

	1983	1982	1981
Revenues	$ 3,000	$ 2,000	$ 1,000
Expenses			
Expenses (other than depreciation and income taxes)	(1,500)	(1,000)	(500)
Depreciation	(100)	(100)	(100)
Income before taxes	$ 1,400	$ 900	$ 400
Income taxes (50%)	(700)	(450)	(200)
Net income	$ 700	$ 450	$ 200

GOOFPROOF, INC.

Summarized Comparative Retained Earnings Statements
For the Years Ended December 31

	1983	1982	1981
Beginning balance	$ 550	$ 200	0
Add: Net income	700	450	$ 200
Subtract: Dividends	(300)	(100)	0
Ending balance	$ 950	$ 550	$ 200

we assume that the $150 can be used to reduce 1984 income taxes payable, the following entry would also be made:

Income taxes payable	150	
Retained earnings		150

To illustrate the consequences, first assume that Goofproof, Inc., *does not* prepare comparative statements for 1984. Only an income statement and a retained earnings statement for the year 1984 are reported (see Exhibit 3–15). Note that the 1984 depreciation expense is correctly stated as $200. The $300 cumulative prior years' impact of the error, net of the $150 tax effect, is reported as a correction to the January 1, 1984, retained earnings balance.

To illustrate retroactive disclosure, assume that Goofproof, Inc., presents 3-year comparative statements for the years 1984, 1983, and 1982. This means that retained earnings on January 1, 1982, must be corrected for the effects of the error in 1981, net of taxes ($100 − $50), that depreciation expense must be reflected at $200 in 1982 and 1983, and that income tax expense must be reduced by $50 in the 1982 and 1983 comparative income statements. The comparative statements are shown in Exhibit 3–16, which should be compared with Exhibits 3–14 and 3–15.

Note that no catch-up adjustment is necessary at January 1, 1984. Since a $50 adjustment was made to retained earnings at January 1, 1982, and the net income figures of $400 and $650 for 1982 and 1983 are *correct* figures, then the $800 beginning retained earnings at January 1, 1984, must be correct. Note that such corrections were made by merely writing down the correct figures for printing purposes. To do this, no journal entries are necessary on the books. The books were corrected

EXHIBIT
3–15

GOOFPROOF, INC.

Summarized Income Statement
For the Year Ended December 31, 1984

Revenues	$ 4,000
Expenses	
Expenses (other than depreciation and income taxes)	(1,800)
Depreciation	(200)
Income before taxes	$ 2,000
Income taxes (50%)	(1,000)
Net income	$ 1,000

Summarized Retained Earnings Statement
For the Year Ended December 31, 1984

Beginning balance, January 1, 1984, unadjusted	$ 950
Correction for understatement of depreciation expense (net of income taxes of $150)	(150)
Beginning balance, January 1, 1984, as adjusted	$ 800
Income for 1984	1,000
	$ 1,800
Less: Dividends	(540)
Ending balance, December 31, 1984	$ 1,260

EXHIBIT
3–16

GOOFPROOF, INC.

Summarized Comparative Income Statements
For the Years Ended December 31

	1984	1983	1982
Revenues	$ 4,000	$ 3,000	$ 2,000
Expenses			
Expenses (other than depreciation and income taxes)	(1,800)	(1,500)	(1,000)
Depreciation	(200)	(200)	(200)
Income before taxes	$ 2,000	$ 1,300	$ 800
Income taxes (50%)	(1,000)	(650)	(400)
Net income	$ 1,000	$ 650[a]	$ 400[a]

[a] Note that net income declined by $50 in both 1982 and 1983. This results from the *increase* in depreciation expense of $100 and a *decrease* of $50 in income taxes (50% × $100) in each of those years, a net decrease of $50. (Compare these statements with those in Exhibits 3–14 and 3–15.)

GOOFPROOF, INC.

Summarized Comparative Retained Earnings Statements
For the Years Ended December 31

	1984	1983[a]	1982[a]
Beginning balance, as reported	$ 800	$ 450	$ 200
Reduction for understatement of depreciation (net of income taxes of $50)			(50)
Beginning balance, as adjusted			$ 150
Add: Net income	1,000	650	400
Deduct: Dividends	(540)	(300)	(100)
Ending balance	$1,260	$ 800	$ 450

[a] Compare these statements with those in Exhibits 3–14 and 3–15.

EXHIBIT
3–17

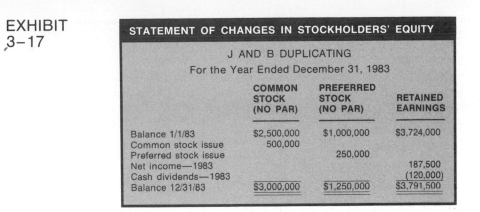

STATEMENT OF CHANGES IN STOCKHOLDERS' EQUITY

J AND B DUPLICATING
For the Year Ended December 31, 1983

	COMMON STOCK (NO PAR)	PREFERRED STOCK (NO PAR)	RETAINED EARNINGS
Balance 1/1/83	$2,500,000	$1,000,000	$3,724,000
Common stock issue	500,000		
Preferred stock issue		250,000	
Net income—1983			187,500
Cash dividends—1983			(120,000)
Balance 12/31/83	$3,000,000	$1,250,000	$3,791,500

once and for all when the journal entries were made in 1984, as shown on pp. 90–91. Earnings-per-share calculations would also be based on these corrected figures. In addition, if comparative position statements are presented, the accumulated depreciation, total plant, property, and equipment, and total asset figures would have to be restated to the correct amounts, as would ending retained earnings.

THE STATEMENT OF CHANGES IN STOCKHOLDERS' EQUITY

Many corporations report a **statement of changes in stockholders' equity** (SCSE) in place of a statement of retained earnings. The SCSE statement includes all of the information contained in a statement of retained earnings plus information concerning changes in all *other* accounts within the stockholders' equity section of the balance sheet. If changes occurred in the number of shares of common or preferred stock, for example, these changes would be reported as adjustments to the beginning balances in the stock accounts. Exhibit 3–17 illustrates a hypothetical statement of changes in stockholders' equity that includes changes from net income, cash dividends, and the sale of additional shares of common and preferred stock. More complex examples of the SCSE require an understanding of the material presented in Chapters 20–22.

INTERRELATIONSHIPS OF BALANCE SHEET, INCOME STATEMENT, AND STATEMENT OF RETAINED EARNINGS

Operating activity certainly has financial consequences, and these net financial consequences are reflected in the balance sheet through the closing of the income statement accounts to retained earnings and the change in net assets resulting from operations. Thus, there is a direct tie-in between the balance sheet and the income statement through the Retained Earnings account.

The connections between the balance sheet and the income statement extend far beyond the change in retained earnings, however, and are ongoing. The time periods utilized in the preparation and presentation of financial statements often hide this fact. When products are sold, there is an impact on retained earnings *in-directly* through the Revenue account, as well as an impact on cash or accounts receivable and inventories. Note the following:

Cash	XXX	
Accounts receivable	XXX	
Sales revenue		XXX

Cash and/or accounts receivable increase to reflect the inflow of assets from sale of the product or service of the entity as measured by the sales revenue reflected in the income statement. As expenses are accrued, there is an indirect impact on retained earnings through the expense accounts. Note the following example:

| Wages and salaries expense | XXX | |
| Wages and salaries payable | | XXX |

The current liability increases, reflecting an ultimate outflow of assets of the entity that takes place when the liability is paid, as measured by the wages and salaries expense that is reflected in the income statement in arriving at net income for the period. Whenever income is affected, retained earnings will ultimately be affected.

Many other examples might be used. The important point is that the balance sheet and the income statement are interrelated and interdependent, and these relationships are continuous. The income statement is not a subsidiary to the balance sheet but, rather, an important statement in its own right. It presents information that could not be obtained easily, if at all, from comparative balance sheets. This fact is not altered by recognizing that all the events and transactions with which the accountant is concerned in the income determination process have an ultimate effect on the balance sheet.

SUMMARY

In this chapter we have presented a conceptual overview of the income statement and the retained earnings statement. The major purposes were to aid in understanding the principles and standards that underlie their preparation and disclosure, and the meaning of the elements making up the statements. An effort was made to present this material without making excessive use of complex procedures, techniques, and examples in order to avoid becoming so mired in detail that the essential meanings would be overlooked. In the various chapters throughout the book we shall focus on details that are related to the basic concepts of this and previous chapters.

Various concepts from Chapter 2 were drawn upon in considering the income statement and the retained earnings statement. These include the entity assumption, the periodicity assumption, the monetary unit, accrual accounting, and the elements of revenue, expense, gains, and losses. These statements also draw upon the other elements and concepts discussed in Chapter 2 in a less direct way. Perhaps the most important and obvious aspect from Chapter 2 that provides the basis for the income statement is the matching principle in conjunction with revenue recognition discussed earlier in this chapter. Given the application of the revenue-recognition principle to the specific situation faced by a given entity, the income determination process matches all expenses necessary to generate the revenues in order to arrive at net income.

Although some accountants believe that the income statement is the most important financial statement, this chapter emphasized that income statements describe changes in balance sheets from one point in time to the next and that the two are closely related. The retained earnings statement formally merges the balance sheet with the income statement.

APPENDIX B
Illustrations of Special Items
in Financial Statements

This appendix provides real-world illustrations of the special items that were discussed in Chapter 3 as they are actually reported in corporate annual reports. Specifically, we illustrate:

1. Discontinued operations
2. Extraordinary items
3. Changes in accounting principle
4. Statement of stockholders' equity
5. Changes in accounting principle that need to be treated like a prior period adjustment
6. Pro forma disclosure

It is important to note that we concentrate on the form of these disclosures and *not* on the substantive accounting topics that they are illustrating. The *topics* are discussed in greater detail and illustrated in other sections of the text.

DISCONTINUED OPERATIONS

Exhibits B–1 and B–2 both illustrate how discontinued operations are disclosed. In Exhibit B–1, note that GTE discloses the discontinued operations as a single-line item in the income statement without separating the amount of *operating loss* ($1,404,000) from the amount of loss on sale of net assets ($140,000,000 net of taxes). The breakdown between operating loss and loss on sale of assets is provided in the footnote, however, in some detail. Alternatively, Exhibit B–2 illustrates a slightly different presentation made by Fleming Companies, Inc., which separates the operating results and the loss on sale of assets in the income statement.

EXTRAORDINARY ITEMS

Exhibits B–3 and B–4 illustrate extraordinary items. In B–3, McIntyre Mines, Ltd., discloses the tax benefits of prior years' operating losses as an extraordinary item. As noted in Chapter 3, this is one of two exceptions to the general definition of extraordinary items since it is *neither* highly unusual nor unlikely to reoccur in the foreseeable future. It is one of the most frequent examples of an extraordinary item encountered in practice.

In Exhibit B–4, Banner Industries, Inc., reports both an extraordinary item and a change in accounting principle. Even though the accounting change took place in 1980, it is still reported and explained again in 1981 when the 1980 statement is reported for comparison purposes. The extraordinary item in Banner's case is the result of tornado damage. Note that the insurance proceeds *exceeded* the

REPORTING DISCONTINUED OPERATIONS

GENERAL TELEPHONE & ELECTRONICS CORPORATION AND SUBSIDIARIES
Years Ended December 31

	1980	1979	1978
	(THOUSANDS OF DOLLARS)		
Revenues and Sales			
Telephone Operations	$5,927,958	$5,219,764	$4,599,235
Other Operations	4,050,917	3,678,721	3,136,829
	9,978,875	8,898,485	7,736,064
Costs and Expenses			
Telephone Operations	4,247,414	3,719,894	3,204,062
Owner Operations (including cost of sales of $3,231,959,000, $2,868,989,000 and $2,411,334,000 respectively)	3,784,990	3,346,401	2,806,960
	8,032,404	7,066,295	6,011,022
Operating Income	1,946,471	1,832,190	1,725,042
Other (Income) Deductions			
Interest Expense	870,429	658,980	547,164
Interest Income	(60,596)	(40,873)	(30,559)
Minority Interests	21,035	17,949	13,236
Preferred Stock Dividends of Subsidiaries	59,266	51,314	46,385
Other—net	(80,947)	(49,791)	(50,957)
	809,187	637,579	525,269
Income Before Income Taxes	1,137,284	1,194,611	1,199,773
Income Taxes (Note 6)	518,004	538,001	589,535
Income From Continuing Operations	619,280	656,610	610,238
Discontinued Operations (Note 10)	(141,404)	(11,540)	11,949
Net Income	477,876	645,070	622,187
Preferred Stock Dividends of Parent	32,284	32,877	33,348
Net Income Applicable to Common Stock	$ 445,592	$ 612,193	$ 588,839
Average Common Shares (in thousands)	151,805	145,661	141,303
Earnings Per Common Share			
Primary			
Continuing Operations	$ 3.87	$ 4.28	$ 4.08
Discontinued Operations	(.93)	(.08)	.09
Consolidated	$ 2.94	$ 4.20	$ 4.17
Fully Diluted			
Continuing Operations	$ 3.69	$ 4.03	$ 3.84
Discontinued Operations	(.87)	(.07)	.08
Consolidated	$ 2.82	$ 3.96	$ 3.92

See notes to Financial Statements.

10 Discontinued Operations

During the year, GTE established provisions of $140 million, net of tax benefits of $80 million, for estimated losses on disposition of its worldwide Consumer Electronics business. The caption "Discontinued Operations" in the accompanying statements of income includes these provisions and the results of operations discontinued during the year (prior to discontinuance) as shown below (in thousands of dollars):

	1980	1979	1978
Sales	$558,000	$1,052,000	$985,000
Net Income (loss)	(1,404)	(11,540)	11,949

REPORTING DISCONTINUED OPERATIONS

FLEMING COMPANIES, INC., AND CONSOLIDATED SUBSIDIARIES

	1980	1979	1978
Net sales	$2,816,958,000	$2,507,684,000	$2,210,731,000
Costs and expenses:			
Cost of sales	2,681,297,000	2,394,659,000	2,110,664,000
Selling and administrative	94,173,000	79,122,000	70,603,000
Interest (Note G)	6,356,000	6,342,000	5,784,000
	2,781,826,000	2,480,123,000	2,187,051,000
Earnings before income taxes	35,132,000	27,561,000	23,680,000
Federal and state income taxes (Note J)	15,265,000	12,015,000	10,452,000
Earnings of Fleming Companies, Inc. and consolidated subsidiaries	19,867,000	15,546,000	13,228,000
Earnings of unconsolidated finance subsidiary (Note I)	837,000	845,000	648,000
Earnings from continuing operations	20,704,000	16,391,000	13,876,000
Discontinued operation (Note C):			
Earnings, net of income taxes of $600,000 and $693,000	—	644,000	707,000
Loss on sale, net of tax benefits of $684,000	—	(596,000)	—
Net earnings	$ 20,704,000	$ 16,439,000	$ 14,583,000
Earnings per share:			
Continuing operations	$3.25	$2.60	$2.22
Discontinued operation:			
Earnings	—	.10	.11
Loss on sale	—	(.09)	—
Net earnings per share	$3.25	$2.61	$2.33
Weighted average shares outstanding	6,364,000	6,303,000	6,264,000

C. Disposal of Business Segment:

On July 30, 1979, the company sold the business and substantially all of the assets, subject to certain liabilities, of its trailer manufacturing subsidiary, American Trailers, Inc., for cash of $6,300,000 and a note receivable for $2,500,000 due in equal annual installments over 10 years. Operating results of American Trailers prior to the sale have been reclassified in the Statements of Earnings as earnings from discontinued operations, net of income taxes. Revenue of American Trailers were $14.6 million in 1979 and $22.5 million in 1978.

net book value of the assets destroyed, resulting in a gain from the tornado damages.

CHANGES IN ACCOUNTING PRINCIPLE

As noted in Chapter 3, most disclosures of changes in accounting principles report the net cumulative prior years' impact of the change as a separate item in the lower portion of the income statement net of any tax consequences. In Exhibit B–5, Southwest Airlines Co. reports the change in the accounting method for recording maintenance on aircraft, resulting in a $735,000 gain. In Exhibit B–4, Banner changed its method of accounting for tires on equipment from direct expensing to

REPORTING AN EXTRAORDINARY ITEM

MCINTYRE MINES, LIMITED

Consolidated Statement of Earnings (Loss)
(in thousands of Canadian dollars, except per share data)

	YEAR ENDED DECEMBER 31, 1980
Revenue:	
Coal sales	$62,667
Less: Coal Royalty	(442)
	62,225
Expenses:	
Operating costs	46,303
Administration	1,504
Exploration	333
Interest	8,620
Depreciation	9,005
Amortization of deferred development	1,909
Foreign exchange gain	(402)
	67,272
Loss from operations before deferred income taxes	5,047
Deferred income taxes (recovery)	(2,306)
Loss from operations	2,741
Equity in earnings of affiliates	39,226
Earnings before extraordinary item	36,485
Extraordinary item: Tax benefits of operating losses of Falconbridge	7,424
Consolidated earnings	$43,909
Earnings (loss) before extraordinary items	$ 15.33
Extraordinary items	3.12
Net income	$ 18.45

capitalization as assets, with amortization taken over 3 years. This resulted in a $264,000 after-tax gain in 1980.

STATEMENT OF STOCKHOLDERS' EQUITY

The material in Chapter 3 noted that sometimes the retained earnings statement is included as a part of a more comprehensive statement called the statement of changes in stockholders' equity, or just statement of stockholders' equity. Exhibit B–6 illustrates such a statement for Southwest Airlines for a 3-year period. The column labeled "retained earnings" is equivalent to a statement of retained earnings, with net income added and cash dividends deducted in each of the 3 years illustrated.

PRIOR PERIOD ADJUSTMENT TYPE OF DISCLOSURES

As noted in Chapter 3, errors and certain special changes in accounting principles are reported as adjustments to the retained earnings balance in the statement of retained earnings. Errors are prior period adjustments that are reported as adjustments to retained earnings. Those special accounting principle changes that are treated *like* prior period adjustments are more common in practice. Two illustrations

**REPORTING BOTH AN EXTRAORDINARY ITEM AND A CHANGE
IN ACCOUNTING METHOD**

BANNER INDUSTRIES, INC. AND SUBSIDIARIES

Consolidated Statements of Income

For the Years Ended June 30, 1981 and 1980

(in thousands, except per share data)

	1981	1980
NET SALES AND REVENUES	$208,687	$187,124
COST AND EXPENSES:		
Cost of sales and operating expenses	$174,422	$154,255
Selling and administrative expenses	24,462	22,656
Interest expense	4,646	3,189
	$203,531	$180,100
INCOME BEFORE TAXES ON INCOME, EXTRAORDINARY GAIN AND CUMULATIVE EFFECT OF CHANGE IN ACCOUNTING PRINCIPLE	$ 5,155	$ 7,023
PROVISION FOR TAXES ON INCOME:		
Current	$ 710	$ 1,650
Deferred	650	650
	$ 1,360	$ 2,300
INCOME BEFORE EXTRAORDINARY GAIN AND CUMULATIVE EFFECT OF CHANGE IN ACCOUNTING PRINCIPLE	$ 3,795	$ 4,723
EXTRAORDINARY GAIN ON INSURANCE SETTLEMENT, NET OF INCOME TAXES OF $368,000 (Note 2)	432	
CUMULATIVE EFFECT ON PRIOR YEARS (to June 30, 1979) OF CHANGE IN ACCOUNTING FOR TIRES ON REVENUE EQUIPMENT (Note 3)		264
NET INCOME	$ 4,227	$ 4,987
NET INCOME PER SHARE:		
INCOME BEFORE EXTRAORDINARY GAIN AND CUMULATIVE EFFECT OF CHANGE IN ACCOUNTING PRINCIPLE	$ .94	$ 1.17
EXTRAORDINARY GAIN ON INSURANCE SETTLEMENT	.11	
CUMULATIVE EFFECT ON PRIOR YEARS (to June 30, 1979) OF CHANGE IN ACCOUNTING FOR TIRES ON REVENUE EQUIPMENT		.07
NET INCOME PER SHARE	$ 1.05	$ 1.24

2. Extraordinary Gain on Insurance Settlement

In October, 1980, inventory and plant and equipment at one of the company's subsidiaries were severely damaged by a tornado. Substantially all losses were covered by insurance, and insurance proceeds received in excess of the net book value of assets destroyed ($800,000) have been recorded as an extraordinary gain in 1981, net of applicable income taxes.

3. Change in Accounting Principle

In the fourth quarter of fiscal 1980, the company changed its method of accounting for non-radial tires on revenue equipment used in its transportation operations from the expensing as installed method to a method of capitalization as installed with amortization of the capitalized cost over three years. This new method of accounting was adopted to recognize that the useful life of these assets exceeds a one-year period, and has been applied retroactively to tires installed in prior years. An adjustment of $264,000 (after reduction for income taxes of $234,000) to apply the new method retroactively is included in 1980 net income.

EXHIBIT B-5

CHANGE IN ACCOUNTING PRINCIPLE EXAMPLE

SOUTHWEST AIRLINES CO.
Consolidated Statement of Income
(in thousands except for share and per share information)

	YEARS ENDED DECEMBER 31,		
	1980	1979	1978
Operating revenues:			
Passenger	$ 205,764	$ 131,573	$ 78,537
Package express	6,080	4,057	2,364
Other	1,204	484	164
Total operating revenues	213,048	136,114	81,065
Operating expenses:			
Fuel and oil	61,887	37,598	16,509
Flight operations	16,101	12,689	7,049
Maintenance	14,319	7,675	5,711
Passenger services	7,992	5,868	3,723
Terminal operations	22,170	15,321	9,221
Promotion and sales	10,061	6,749	3,718
Insurance, taxes, and administrative	12,224	8,444	5,223
Depreciation	12,172	8,482	6,436
Employee profit sharing (Note 5)	7,293	4,302	2,353
Total operating expenses	164,219	107,128	59,943
Operating income	48,829	28,986	21,122
Nonoperating expense (income):			
Interest and other income	(1,697)	(441)	(194)
Interest expense (Note 4)	9,236	8,713	5,882
Net non-operating expense	7,539	8,272	5,688
Income before gain on disposition of aircraft and federal income tax	41,290	20,714	15,434
Gain on disposition of aircraft	—	—	8,522
Income before federal income tax	41,290	20,714	23,956
Provision for federal income tax (Note 6)	12,843	4,062	7,687
Income before accounting change	28,447	16,652	16,269
Net cumulative effect of accounting change (Note 8)	—	—	735
Net income	$ 28,447	$ 16,652	$ 17,004
Income per common share:			
Weighted average common shares outstanding (adjusted for 1979 and 1980 stock splits)	7,006,000	6,750,000	6,750,000
Income before accounting change	$4.06	$2.47	$2.41
Net income	$4.06	$2.47	$2.52

8. Accounting change

In years prior to 1978, the Company provided an airworthiness reserve for major aircraft maintenance and overhaul costs. These costs were accumulated in the reserve on a per-flight-hour basis. Actual expenditures for major aircraft maintenance and overhaul costs were relieved from the reserve as incurred.

Effective January 1, 1978, the Company changed its method of accounting for major maintenance and overhaul costs from the reserve method to that of expensing such costs as incurred. The change was made to conform the Company's accounting for such costs to the predominant method in the airline industry and, in anticipation of possible interstate route awards, to utilize the established accounting policies of the Civil Aeronautics Board (CAB). The Company believes that the direct expense method is preferable because of changes in the physical manner in which airframes and engines are now being maintained and an increase in the Company's fleet size.

Net income for the year ended December 31, 1978, has been increased by approximately $735,000 (net of applicable federal income taxes and profit sharing of approximately $388,000) which represents the cumulative effect on years prior to 1978 of the aforementioned change.

EXAMPLE OF A STATEMENT OF STOCKHOLDERS' EQUITY

SOUTHWEST AIRLINES CO.
Consolidated Statement of Stockholders' Equity
(in thousands except for per share information)

THREE YEARS ENDED DECEMBER 31, 1980

	COMMON STOCK	CAPITAL IN EXCESS OF PAR VALUE	RETAINED EARNINGS	TOTAL
Balance at December 31, 1977	$2,000	$12,367	$12,240	$ 26,607
Three-for-two-stock split	1,000	(1,000)	—	—
Cash dividends, $.11 per share	—	—	(770)	(770)
Compensation element of executive stock options	—	48	—	48
Net income—1978	—	—	17,004	17,004
Balance at December 31, 1978	3,000	11,415	28,474	42,889
Three-for-two stock split	1,500	(1,500)	—	—
Cash dividends, $.19 per share	—	—	(1,260)	(1,260)
Compensation element of executive stock options	—	131	—	131
Net income—1979	—	—	16,652	16,652
Balance at December 31, 1979	4,500	10,046	43,866	58,412
Three-for-two stock split	2,287	(2,287)	—	—
Proceeds from issuance of common stock	615	15,836	—	16,451
Contribution of common stock to profit-sharing trust	174	5,275	—	5,449
Cash dividends, $.27 per share	—	—	(1,924)	(1,924)
Compensation element of executive stock options	—	129	—	129
Net income—1980	—	—	28,447	28,447
Balance at December 31, 1980	$7,576	$28,999	$70,389	$106,964

See accompanying notes.

of how such disclosures of special accounting changes might appear in the retained earnings portion of a statement of shareholders' equity are illustrated in Exhibits B–7 and B–8. Note that in Exhibit B–7, the opening retained earnings balances are actually adjusted in the statement, whereas in Exhibit B–8 the adjustment is *not* illustrated in the statement but is explained in the footnote. The treatment given to this prior period adjustment *type of disclosure* in Exhibit B–7 is the preferred treatment.

PRO FORMA DISCLOSURE

Exhibit B–9 illustrates the most preferable treatment for pro forma disclosures, where they are actually reported at the bottom of the regular income statement or statement of income and retained earnings. These pro forma disclosures enable users of financial statements to determine the impact on statement data of both the current year and prior year(s). Such information is designed to facilitate the comparability of accounting reports over time.

REPORTING A CHANGE IN ACCOUNTING PRINCIPLE THAT CALLS FOR PRIOR PERIOD ADJUSTMENT TYPE OF TREATMENT

EATON CORPORATION AND SUBSIDIARIES
Statements of Consolidated Shareholders' Equity

YEAR ENDED DECEMBER 31	1980		1979		1978	
	SHARES	THOUSANDS OF DOLLARS	SHARES	THOUSANDS OF DOLLARS	SHARES	THOUSANDS OF DOLLARS
4¾% Cumulative Convertible Preferred Shares—600,000 authorized; par value $25.00 a share; convertible into one and one-half Common Shares; redeemable at $25.00 a share; liquidation value $25.00 a share:						
Balance at January 1	58,017	$ 1,450	80,119	$ 2,003	87,190	$ 2,180
Converted into Common Shares	(8,258)	(206)	(22,102)	(553)	(7,071)	(177)
Balance at December 31	49,759	$ 1,244	58,017	$ 1,450	80,119	$ 2,003
Serial Preferred Shares—5,000,000 authorized; $2.30—Series A—convertible into one and one-half Common Shares; redeemable at $43.00 a share; stated value $.50 a share; liquidation value $40.00 a share:						
Balance at January 1	445,170	$ 223	604,932	$ 302	692,894	$ 346
Converted into Common Shares	(66,751)	(34)	(159,762)	(79)	(87,962)	(44)
Balance at December 31	378,419	$ 189	445,170	$ 223	604,932	$ 302
Common Shares—50,000,000 authorized; par value $.50 a share:						
Balance at January 1	26,115,508	$ 13,058	17,277,145	$ 8,639	17,211,418	$ 8,606
Issued in connection with three for two stock split	0	0	8,676,199	4,338	0	0
Issued for conversion of convertible debentures and preferred shares and exercise of stock options	470,522	235	386,240	193	265,861	133
Issued in acquisitions of businesses	138,708	69	75,874	38	265,861	49
Purchase of shares for treasury	0	0	(299,950)	(150)	(298,300)	(149)
Balance at December 31—excluding shares in treasury of 2,017,635 in 1980, 2,020,014 in 1979 and 1,720,064 in 1978	26,724,738	$ 13,362	26,115,508	$ 13,058	17,277,145	$ 8,639

Capital in Excess of Par Value			
Balance at January 1	$103,381	$ 98,100	$ 91,553
Common Shares issued for conversion of convertible debentures and preferred shares and exercise of stock options	6,574	4,372	4,881
Excess of fair value of Common Shares issued in acquisitions of businesses	0	2,612	3,301
Adjustment related to company acquired	(57)	0	0
Purchase of shares for treasury	0	(1,703)	(1,635)
Balance at December 31	$109,898	$103,381	$ 98,100
Retained Earnings			
Balance at January 1 as previously reported	$818,280	$720,533	$638,367
Adjustment for cumulative effect of an accounting change	(5,762)	(4,960)	(4,562)
Balance at January 1 as adjusted	812,518	715,573	633,805
Net income	115,784	153,264	130,876
Cash dividends paid	(46,435)	(43,083)	(40,365)
Purchase of shares for treasury	0	(8,898)	(8,743)
Transferred to Common Shares in connection with three for two stock split	0	0	0
Adjustment related to company acquired	(1,453)	0	0
Balance at December 31	$880,414	$812,518	$715,573

REPORTING A CHANGE IN ACCOUNTING PRINCIPLE THAT CALLS FOR PRIOR PERIOD ADJUSTMENT TYPE OF TREATMENT

NORTH AMERICAN ROYALTIES, INC.
Statements of Common Stockholders' Equity
For the Years Ended April 30, 1980 and 1979

	COMMON STOCK	PAID-IN SURPLUS	RETAINED EARNINGS (RESTATED—NOTE 1)	TREASURY STOCK
Balance, April 30, 1978	$3,696,000	$140,000	$35,144,000	$(3,575,000)
Net Income	—	—	10,627,000	—
Dividends on Stock—				
Common, $.20 per share	—	—	(657,000)	—
Preferred—				
$5 series	—	—	(47,000)	—
8⅞% series	—	—	(239,000)	—
Exercise of stock options, 6,800 shares	—	1,000	—	58,000
Balance, April 30, 1979	3,696,000	141,000	44,828,000	(3,517,000)
Net Income	—	—	8,515,000	—
Dividends on Stock—				
Common, $.24 per share	—	—	(788,000)	—
Preferred—				
$5 series	—	—	(47,000)	—
8⅞% series	—	—	(217,000)	—
Exercise of stock options, 2,500 shares	—	14,000	—	21,000
Balance, April 30, 1980	$3,696,000	$155,000	$52,291,000	$(3,496,000)

(1) Summary of Significant Accounting Policies:

Oil and Gas Properties and Accounting Change—

The Company follows the full cost accounting method of capitalizing for financial reporting purposes all direct costs incurred in the acquisition, exploration and development of oil and gas properties, including nonproductive drilling and exploration costs. The capitalized costs of all properties are being amortized on a company-wide, composite, unit-of-production method using proved oil and gas reserves determined annually by independent petroleum engineers. Under the full cost method of accounting, no gains or losses are recognized upon sale or disposition of oil and gas properties, except in extraordinary transactions. In addition, net capitalized costs of oil and gas properties will be reduced by a charge to operations should the costs incurred on oil and gas properties, or revisions in reserve estimates, cause the total net capitalized cost of the properties to be in excess of the estimated future discounted net revenue of the total proved reserves.

In December 1978, the Securities and Exchange Commission adopted rules which allow oil and gas exploration and producing companies to continue to follow the full cost method of accounting for costs incurred in exploration and development of oil and gas reserves and, in connection therewith, established uniform financial accounting and reporting requirements for companies following such method of accounting. The Company plans to continue to follow the full cost method of accounting and effective May 1, 1979, retroactively adopted the new accounting rules. The change in accounting did not require a restatement of previously reported net income for years subsequent to 1974. The Company did, however, record $1,900,000 of deferred federal income taxes on the unamortized oil and gas exploration and development costs incurred prior to May 1, 1974 by a charge to retained earnings.

EXHIBIT 5-3

PRO FORMA DISCLOSURE EXAMPLE FOR CHANGE IN ACCOUNTING PRINCIPLE

NL INDUSTRIES, INC.
Consolidated Statement of Income and Retained Earnings
(in thousands, except per share amounts)

YEARS ENDED DECEMBER 31	1980	PER SHARE OF COMMON STOCK	1979	PER SHARE OF COMMON STOCK	1978	PER SHARE OF COMMON STOCK
Revenues:						
Net sales	$2,117,552		$1,810,235		$1,538,412	
Equity in partially-owned companies (Note 4)	33,443		16,855		7,722	
Other income (loss), net (Note 9 and Page 25)	(7,324)		(574)		(3,974)	
	2,143,671		1,826,516		1,542,160	
Costs and expenses:						
Cost of goods sold	1,392,925		1,221,773		1,034,295	
Selling, general and administrative	439,710		364,424		312,145	
Interest (Note 11)	41,975		48,876		34,468	
Minority interest	4,565		2,869		1,745	
	1,879,175		1,637,942		1,382,653	
Income before items shown below	264,496		188,574		159,507	
Provision for income taxes (Page 27)	96,823		73,998		72,334	
Income from continuing operations	167,673	$4.94	114,576	$3.36	87,173	$2.55
Discontinued operations (Note 1):						
Income (loss) from discontinued operations, net of income taxes—$3,517,000 in 1979 and (3,362,000) in 1978	—		6,469		(897)	
(Loss) from disposal of discontinued operations, net of $28,227,000 income tax benefit	—		(35,359)			
Income before cumulative effect of accounting change	167,673		85,686		86,276	
Cumulative effect of accounting change (Note 3)	—		26,257			
Net income	167,673	4.94	111,943	3.28	86,276	2.52
Retained earnings at beginning of year	641,447		573,224		530,274	
Less dividends paid:						
Common: 1980, $1.30 per common share; 1979 and 1978, $1.20 per common share	42,993		39,407		39,013	
Preferred	4,313		4,313		4,313	
Retained earnings at end of year	$ 761,814		$ 641,447		$ 573,224	
Pro-Forma Information (Note 3):						
Income from continuing operations (Pro-Forma)	$ 167,673	$4.94	$ 114,576	$3.36	$ 92,922	$2.72
Net income (Pro-Forma)	167,673	4.94	85,686	2.48	93,026	2.73

3. Investment Tax Credit:

In 1979, the Company changed its method of accounting for the investment tax credit from the deferral method to the flow-through method. The effect of this change was to increase income from continuing operations $7,919,000 ($.24 per common share) and net income $7,321,000 ($.23 per common share) for the twelve months ended December 31, 1979. The cumulative effect of this accounting change applicable to prior years aggregated $26,257,000, or $.80 per share of common stock. The 1978 pro-forma information, which assumes the change was made retroactively, increases income from continuing operations by $5,749,000 ($.17 per common share) and net income by $6,750,000 ($.21 per common share).

SUMMARY

These examples, which show how the special items discussed in Chapter 3 become incorporated in the financial statements and their accompanying footnotes, are meant to help you better understand the subject of special items. They also serve to point out minor variations in terminology and presentation that invariably occur in practice.

Throughout this book, we frequently use such actual examples from corporate reports to illustrate real-world applications of accounting concepts, practices, and procedures. While these practical examples can serve to enhance our understanding of the accounting subject matter covered in the text, it is important to keep in mind that the examples are just that, *examples*. They are not provided to illustrate *what must be reported* or *how something must be reported*, but rather they are simply illustrations of how a given entity has *elected to report*, given the framework provided by GAAP.

As we shall observe in many of the examples throughout the text, the uniformity of presentation, terminology, and format is not as great in practice as most text illustrations suggest. For example, in the text we might use the account Cumulative Effect of Accounting Change to report the cumulative catch-up effect from prior years of a change in accounting principle. In practice, we might observe that in any given sample of three or four annual reports where entities have changed accounting methods, several *different* captions (besides the account title used in the text) might be used to describe the change. Among these titles are Accounting Change, Gain from Change in Depreciation Procedure, Impact of Switch to Preferred Accounting Method, and several others. These variations in terminology and presentation emphasize the need to focus on issues of substance rather than form. Seeing such variations will help you to move smoothly from text problems to real-world problems.

QUESTIONS

Q3–1 What does the income statement depict, and what major elements of the conventional accounting model are applicable to that statement?

Q3–2 The income statement must be constructed with periodicity in mind. Why is it important that a uniform period be used in constructing income statements?

Q3–3 Is a single-step income statement more informative than a multiple-step income statement? Would it be advisable to switch from one to the other from one period to another? Explain.

Q3–4 When is revenue recognized?

Q3–5 Give an example of a situation in which both an accrual objective (see Chapter 2) and the revenue-recognition principle provide support for a journal entry recorded by an entity.

Q3–6 Why are adjusting entries necessary if an income statement is to be properly presented?

Q3–7 Discuss the relationship between retained earnings and the revenue and expense ledger accounts.

Q3–8 Compare and contrast *revenue* and *gains*.

Q3–9 Compare and contrast *expenses* and *losses*.

Q3–10 What is the connection between the retained earnings statement and the income statement?

Q3–11 Certain "unusual" items are shown separately on the income statement below the "regular" section. List these items and tell why they are not included in "income from continuing operations."

Q3–12 Why is the technique of intraperiod tax allocation often necessary in constructing income statements?

Q3–13 Can a gain or a loss be "very unusual" and still be reported as a part of "income from continuing operations"?

Q3–14 What impact does a material clerical error in computing depreciation expense from a prior year (discovered this year) have on the current financial statements?

Q3–15 When are "pro forma" disclosures necessary? Of what benefits are pro forma disclosures to financial statement users?

CASES

C3–1 On March 23, 1984, the Wonch Battery Company, a client of yours located on the banks of the Red Cedar River, experienced a flood on its premises as the result of a 5-day period of heavy rainfall. The company had been in business for only 5 years and had just begun to show good profits from operations, with 1983 income reported at $75,000 after taxes for an 11 percent return on assets. The flood damage was uninsured and resulted in a net loss before taxes of $215,000, mostly due to lost inventory and damage to the furniture and equipment.

The water had risen to 8 feet in the first story of the two-story office facility and to about 6 feet in the manu facturing facility. The local press has called the flood, which caused millions of dollars in damage to homes and businesses in the community, an "11,000-year storm," meaning that such a storm would not be expected but once every 11,000 years.

As the auditor of Wonch Battery, you must determine how to treat the loss from the flood damage. Wonch management has suggested that the flood should qualify as an extraordinary loss, arguing that a second storm like the recent one would surely put the company out of business. The junior auditor on the engagement tells you he agrees with the client but is unsure how GAAP apply to this situation.

REQUIRED How should the loss be reported in this case? What is the support for your decision?

C3–2 The Fly-by-Night Travel Service, located in California and New York, has branch offices on each campus of the University of California and the State University of New York. Fly-by-Night was formed by some business students in January 1984 but did not begin operations in earnest until the fall term of 1984. The operations were simple, requiring little in the way of facilities. The service hired agents on each campus to book reservations on advertised tours to attractive locations, such as Fort Lauderdale, Daytona Beach, Hawaii, Bermuda, and St. Croix, during the various school holidays and breaks (for example, Thanksgiving). Sometimes the agents operated out of rented facilities, and sometimes the agents would simply use their own apartments. The tours were negotiated by the top executives of Fly-by-Night with the major airlines, and their advertised night-flight rates were at a deep discount price compared with the prices quoted to individuals. However, these discount prices were available through the airlines only if the flights were booked to 100 percent of capacity by Fly-by-Night.

The fall term of 1984 was very successful. A total of 127 tour flights were conducted by the 23 Fly-by-Night offices. By the end of its first year of operations (December 31, 1984), Fly-by-Night had begun to schedule 206 deep discount tour flights for spring break. Tickets for these spring-break flights were, on average, 50 percent sold, and like all tickets they had been purchased in advance.

Fly-by-Night management has prepared an income statement for 1984 which reports its commissions from the airlines for sales of tickets for the spring flights as part of "commissions revenues." You are the senior auditor on the engagement, and your audit supervisor asks you to state your opinion regarding the treatment of the commissions revenues for the flights that have not yet occurred.

REQUIRED State your opinion and support it with whatever justification you can come up with from your accounting coursework.

C3–3 The Good Neighbor Insurance Company, located in Omaha, employs 25 insurance salespersons who deal exclusively in life insurance policies. As an incentive for salespersons to sell policies, they are paid a commission equal to the first year's insurance premiums paid by the customer. For example, a 38-year-old customer buying a $10,000 life insurance policy must pay $350 per year in advance until age 65, at which time the insurance policy will return $10,000 plus some additional amount based on the success of the insurance company's investments. The first

$350 payment of premium is the amount of commission paid to the salesperson who sells the policy. As a result, in the first year of a policy the insurance company would report premium revenues of $350 and would incur various processing expenses (telephone, secretarial, and so on) plus a $350 cash payment to the salesperson.

REQUIRED The key accounting question you've been asked to answer is, How should the $350 payment be treated? Is it an asset or an expense or both? Note that if the $350 is expensed in the year of "sale," there is a loss from the sale of additional insurance policies! A growing insurance company could report very poor income despite its being very successful.

C3–4 On June 30, 1982, Ashton, Inc., acquired equipment that had an estimated useful life of 15 years and no salvage value. Ashton selected the straight-line method of depreciation to account for the write-off of the equipment. Because of technological improvements, Ashton revised the useful life on January 23, 1984, estimating the *total* useful life to be no more than 7 ½ years (6 more years from January 1, 1984). The asset is now expected to have a $10,000 salvage value. Ashton reports on a calendar-year basis.

REQUIRED What type of change is involved in this case, and how should it be accounted for?

C3–5 BWM is a conglomerate holding company that controls many diverse operations. As assistant to the controller, you are asked to prepare a first draft of the financial statements for the year ending December 31, 1984. Included in the results for the year are several unusual transactions: an expropriation of the company's Chilean mining operations by the government of Chile; sale of the I. C. railroad operations (a wholly owned subsidiary); a change to straight-line depreciation; and a very large gain on the sale of land held for speculation (which will approximately double the bottom-line income figure for 1984). In the process of preparing your rough-draft reports, you are unsure of how to handle these items. Also, although the tax accountant for BWM has provided you with the total tax obligation for 1984 for all of BWM's activity, you're not sure how to report it in the financial statements.

REQUIRED Indicate the appropriate financial statement disclosure for the items identified, and explain how the taxes should appear in the statements. Why are taxes reported in the way you have suggested?

EXERCISES

E3–1 (CPA ADAPTED)

_____ 1. Revenue recognition
  a. Takes place at the point of sale
  b. Takes place when goods are received
  c. May take place only after a purchase order is signed
  d. Is an objectively determinable point in time requiring little or no judgment
  e. None of the above

_____ 2. The determination of expenses of an accounting period is based largely on
  a. Application of the cost principle
  b. Application of the consistency principle
  c. Application of the matching principle
  d. Application of the objectivity principle
  e. None of the above

_____ 3. A transaction that is material in amount, unusual in nature, but *not* infrequent in occurrence should be presented separately as
  a. A component of income from continuing operations, but *not* net of applicable income taxes
  b. A component of income from continuing operations, net of applicable income taxes
  c. An extraordinary item, net of applicable income taxes
  d. A prior period adjustment, but *not* net of applicable income taxes

_____ 4. An extraordinary item should be reported separately as a component of income
  a. Before cumulative effect of accounting changes and after discontinued operations of a segment of a business

b. Before cumulative effect of accounting changes and before discontinued operations of a segment of a business
c. After cumulative effect of accounting changes and after discontinued operations of a segment of a business
d. After cumulative effect of accounting changes and before discontinued operations of a segment of a business

E3-2 (CPA ADAPTED) At the beginning of the year, Smack Cereal Company launched a sales promotion program. For every 10 box tops of Smack cereal sent in to the company, customers would receive a plastic squirt gun. Smack believed that 30 percent of all box tops from sales would be sent in by customers for redemption. The following data are now available:

	UNITS	AMOUNTS
Cereal sales	2,000,000 boxes	$1,400,000
Purchases of squirt guns	36,000 guns	18,000
Prizes sent to customers	28,000 guns	

At year-end, Smack recognized a liability equal to the estimated cost of unredeemed box tops outstanding from sales that had occurred during the year.

REQUIRED Record the entries related to the purchase and distribution of prizes, and the entry (if any) to record the prize obligation at year-end. Explain why the "squirt gun promotion expense" must be based in part on a forecast of future redemptions of box tops. Why can't the accountant wait until redemption to account for this expense?

E3-3 (CPA ADAPTED) Hottentote Stove and Refrigerator Sales estimates its warranty expense at 2 percent of annual net sales. The following data are reported for 1984:

Net sales	$4,000,000
Warranty liability account (1/1/84 balance)	$ 60,000 credit
Payments made during 1984 for warranty parts and service by Hottentote	$ 75,000

REQUIRED Record the 1984 warranty expense. What is the estimated warranty liability as of the end of 1984. Explain why warranty expense must be estimated.

E3-4 The following data are taken from a current income statement and retained earnings statement:

	DEBIT	CREDIT		DEBIT	CREDIT
Prior period adjustment due to error		$ 60,000	Gain from early retirement of debt		$79,000
Gain on sale of net assets in discontinued operations		100,000	Operating loss on discontinued operations	$148,000	
Income from continuing operations		950,000	Loss from earthquake	410,000	
Gain from change in accounting method		180,000	Beginning retained earnings	666,000	
Gain from sale of temporary stock investment		38,000	Dividends declared (but unpaid)	30,000	

None of these data have reported the impact of taxes, which are at a 40 percent rate.

REQUIRED Using proper intraperiod tax allocation, prepare a partial income statement beginning with "Income before taxes" and a retained earnings statement.

E3-5 The following data are taken from the adjusted trial balances of Brenda Guzal Office Supplies, Inc., at the end of 1983 and 1984:

ACCOUNT	($000) BALANCE 1984	($000) BALANCE 1983	ACCOUNT	($000) BALANCE 1984	($000) BALANCE 1983
Revenues from sales and services	$5,876	$5,127	Donations to charity	$ 40	$ 38
Sales returns and allowances	41	36	Rental of office equipment	101	93
Sales discounts	18	17	Depreciation on salespeople's autos	346	321
Beginning inventory	281	232	Advertising expense	177	162
Purchases	2,461	2,380	Loss on sale of autos	58	0
Freight-in	161	157	Gain on sale of office equipment	0	71
Purchase returns and allowances	13	18	Depreciation—furniture and fixtures	403	396
Gain on bond retirement	357	0	Administrative salaries	687	658
Dividend income	63	63	Entertainment expense	71	59
Salespeople's salaries	887	818	Ending inventory	300	250
Salespeople's travel	97	89	Taxes	40%	40%

REQUIRED Compute the tax expense for 1983 and 1984 and prepare comparative income statements for 1983 and 1984 using the single-step format.

E3-6

REQUIRED Refer to the Brenda Guzal Office Supplies, Inc. data in Exercise 3-5, and after computing the tax expense for 1983 and 1984, prepare comparative income statements for 1983 and 1984 using the multiple-step format.

E3-7 During an audit of Theta Corporation in 1984, it was discovered that the depreciation on a machine that cost $20,000 (10-year life, straight-line depreciation, no residual value) had inadvertently been omitted for the past 3 years (*including* 1984). Ignore income tax effects.

REQUIRED

1. What type of an accounting change is involved in 1984?
2. Give the entry, if any, to record the change in 1984 (show all computations).
3. Give the entry, if any, to record depreciation for 1984.
4. Explain *where* the entries made in items 2 and 3 would affect the financial statements (that is, regular income, extraordinary income, retained earnings adjustment).

E3-8 Prior to 1984 Darren Corporation had never had an audit. At the end of 1984, before the arrival of the auditor, the company accountant prepared comparative financial statements for 1983 and 1984. According to these statements, Darren had income of $44,000 in 1983 and $46,000 in 1984, and retained earnings of $180,000 at the end of 1983 and $205,000 at the end of 1984. No dividends were paid in 1983.

During the audit, it was discovered that an invoice dated January 3, 1980, for $10,000 (paid in cash at that time) had been charged to "operating expense," although it was for the purchase of Machine X. Machine X has an estimated life of 10 years and no residual value. Darren uses straight-line depreciation.

REQUIRED

1. What type of accounting change is involved?
2. Prepare the necessary entry or entries for 1984. Ignore any tax effects.
3. Illustrate how the change would be reflected in the comparative financial statements. Use the income and retained earnings figures to help you illustrate. Ignore any tax effect.

E3-9 Stober Corporation switched its inventory method from LIFO to FIFO during 1985. The following data are available.

	1985	
	ON A LIFO BASIS	ON A FIFO BASIS
Revenues	$47,865,000	$47,865,000
Cost of sales	26,347,000	28,318,000
Net income	4,718,250	3,240,000
Earnings per share	2.36	1.62

The retained earnings balance at the beginning of 1985 was $128,000,000. No dividends were paid out in 1985, but $2,000,000 in cash dividends were declared on December 31, 1985.

REQUIRED

1. Illustrate the summarized 1985 income statement and retained earnings statement assuming the change to FIFO resulted in a $1,000,000 increase in beginning inventory for the after-tax effect of the change.
2. Illustrate the pro forma disclosures.
3. Assuming no other information, what happened to Stober's inventory costs during 1985?
4. What is the apparent tax rate for 1985?
5. What is the apparent number of shares of stock suggested by the earnings-per-share data?

E3-10 (CPA ADAPTED)

_____ 1. Boa Constructors, Inc., had an operating loss carryforward of $100,000 at December 31, 1984, for which the tax benefit was fully realized at the end of 1984, when the income tax rate was 40 percent. For the year ended December 31, 1984, the tax benefit should be reported in the income statement as
a. A $40,000 reduction in income tax expense
c. An operating gain of $40,000
b. An extraordinary item of $40,000
d. An extraordinary item of $100,000

_____ 2. Marvel Construction Co., Inc., had a net income of $600,000 for the year ended December 31, 1984, after inclusion of the following special events that occurred during the year:

1. The decision was made on January 2 to discontinue the cinder block manufacturing segment.
2. The cinder block manufacturing segment was actually sold on July 1.
3. Operating income from January 1 to June 30 for the cinder block manufacturing segment amounted to $90,000 before taxes.
4. Cinder block manufacturing equipment with a book value of $250,000 was sold for $100,000.

Marvel was subject to income tax at the rate of 40 percent. Marvel's after-tax income from continuing operations for the year ended December 31, 1984, was
a. $360,000
c. $600,000
b. $564,000
d. $636,000

_____ 3. Based on the information presented in the preceding question, Marvel's aggregate income tax expense for the year ended December 31, 1984, should be
a. $216,000
c. $264,000
b. $352,000
d. $400,000

_____ 4. On January 1, 1984, Belmont Company changed its inventory cost-flow method to the FIFO cost method from the LIFO cost method. Belmont's inventories aggregated $4,000,000 on the LIFO basis at December 31, 1983. Supplementary records maintained by Belmont showed that the inventories would have totaled $4,800,000 at December 31, 1983, on the FIFO basis. Ignoring income taxes, the adjustment for the effect on changing to the FIFO method from the LIFO method should be reported by Belmont in the 1984

a. Income statement as an $800,000 debit
b. Retained earnings statement as an $800,000 debit adjustment to the beginning balance
c. Income statement as an $800,000 credit
d. Retained earnings statement as an $800,000 credit adjustment to the beginning balance

_____ 5. Shannon Company was formed on January 1, 1982, and used an accelerated method of depreciation on its machinery until January 1, 1984. At that time, Shannon adopted the straight-line method of depreciation for the machinery previously acquired as well as for any new machinery acquired in 1984. Information concerning depreciation amounts under each method is as follows:

YEAR	DEPRECIATION IF ACCELERATED METHOD USED	DEPRECIATION IF STRAIGHT-LINE METHOD USED
1982	$400,000	$300,000
1983	530,000	375,000
1984	600,000	400,000

Assume that the direct effects of this change are limited to the effect on depreciation and the related tax provisions, and that the income tax rate was 40 percent in each of these years. What should be reported in Shannon's income statement for the year ended December 31, 1984, as the cumulative effect on prior years of changing to a different depreciation method?

a. $0
b. $153,000
c. $255,000
d. $273,000

PROBLEMS

P3-1 Forwardlooking, Inc., has accumulated the following pretax data for the year ended December 31, 1985:

Operating income	$ 2,876,000
Gain on sale of assets of a discontinued segment	347,000
Prior years' impact of a change from the double-declining-balance method to straight-line depreciation	520,000
Gain on the early retirement of debt	250,000
Prior years' impact of an error in recording assets (debit)	382,000
Operating loss of the segment whose operations were ended in 1985	186,000
Retained earnings (as reported on 12/31/84)	17,943,000
Dividends declared and paid in 1985	1,000,000

REQUIRED Assuming a 45 percent tax rate, prepare the partial income statement and retained earnings statement of Forwardlooking, Inc., for the year ended December 31, 1985, using proper intraperiod tax allocation procedures.

P3-2 Fleetwood, Inc., has a hotel that is being depreciated on a straight-line basis. The original estimated useful life of the hotel was 50 years, with a $1,000,000 salvage value. The hotel, which originally cost $146,000,000, had a net book value of $82,200,000 as of December 31, 1984. During 1985, Fleetwood made certain improvements to the hotel. These improvements cost $12,000,000 and were added to the Building account during 1985. They also revised the expected *total* useful life from 50 to 60 years, and the salvage value from $1,000,000 to $3,000,000.

REQUIRED Record the depreciation expense on the hotel for 1985.

P3-3 Each of the following items has occurred during the current year. Indicate the specific financial statement, if any, in which each would appear, and briefly discuss where and how each item would appear in that statement. Assuming that comparative statements are presented, indicate how, if at all, the item would impact on comparative statements. State any assumptions made in arriving at your decisions.

1. Adjustment of extraordinary items reported in prior years
2. Loss from insurance proceeds for tornado damage
3. Losses from sale of assets of a discontinued segment
4. Loss on discontinuance of certain operations that are not a segment of the entity
5. Gain on sale of marketable securities properly classified as a current asset
6. Condemnation settlement
7. Resignation of the company's president
8. Relocation of plant
9. Losses on planned disposal of certain product lines that are not a segment of the entity
10. Write-off of a material amount of intangible assets
11. Loss from unsuccessful registration of new securities
12. Gain on sale of fixed assets
13. Error in recording depreciation for the past 3 years
14. Catch up adjustment in changing from sum-of-the-years'-digits depreciation method to straight-line
15. Loss on early extinguishment of long-term debt
16. Write-down of accounts receivable
17. Catch-up adjustment in switching from the FIFO inventory measurement method to LIFO
18. Gain on sale of intangible assets
19. Loss due to the effects of a strike
20. Loss on disposal of a major segment of an entity—the only segment producing furniture

P3–4   The following data are for the Manda Corporation at December 31, 1984:

Common stock (par $100)	$ 400,000	Selling expenses (exclusive of depreciation expense)	$280,500
Purchases	143,000		
Merchandise inventory, December 31, 1984	147,000	Administrative expenses (exclusive of depreciation expense)	91,400
Sales returns and allowances	3,000		
Sales revenue	615,000	Merchandise inventory, January 1, 1984	137,000
Plant, property, and equipment	3,200,000	Freight-in, on merchandise purchased	2,500
Accrued wages payable	20,000	Gain on sale of office equipment (pretax)	11,000
Purchase returns and allowances	6,400	Loss on sale of long-term investments (only sale	
Accumulated depreciation	1,350,000	of long-term investments the firm has ever	
Depreciation expense (60% administrative; 40%		had; the firm does not anticipate acquiring any	
selling)	98,000	more of such investments) (pretax)	8,500
Dividend revenue	7,500	Income tax expense	?
Interest expense	11,000	Error in calculating prior year's depreciation	
Long-term bonds payable	765,000	(pretax)—debit	40,000
Unamortized discount on bonds payable	15,000		

Assume an average income tax rate of 40 percent on all items.

REQUIRED

1. Prepare a multiple-step income statement.
2. Prepare a single step income statement.
3. List and briefly discuss the advantages and disadvantages of each format.

P3–5   The following data were taken from the books of Suspect, Inc., on December 31, 1984:

| | DECEMBER 31 | |
	1984	1983
Sales revenue	$1,250,000	$1,000,000
Cost of goods sold	875,000	700,000
Selling expenses	95,000	80,000
General and administrative expenses	52,000	40,000
Depreciation expense	60,000	60,000
Retained earnings	?	3,000,000
Dividends declared	400,000	300,000

It was discovered late in 1984, after most adjusting entries for the year had been made, that equipment purchased on January 1, 1983, at a cost of $100,000 and no salvage value was being depreciated over 20 years when 10 years should have been used. The straight-line method is used both for book and income tax purposes. The income tax rate is 40 percent on all items. Income tax expense has not been recorded for 1984. It was recorded for 1983 but is not shown in the data above.

REQUIRED

1. Assuming the books have not been closed for 1984, prepare any entries necessary for Suspect, Inc.
2. Prepare an income statement and retained earnings statement for 1984 only.
3. Prepare comparative income statements and retained earnings statements for 1983 and 1984.

P3-6 On December 30, 1985, the Hasselback Corporation decided to switch from straight-line depreciation to the sum-of-the-years'-digits depreciation method for both book and tax purposes. All depreciable assets (furniture and fixtures) were acquired on January 1, 1983, and were expected to have a 10-year life with no residual value. The original cost of the assets was $1,500,000, and the current replacement cost is $2,000,000. Hasselback reports on a calendar-year basis. *Net income* for the year 1985 after considering *all* items except taxes and depreciation was $5,000,000.

During 1985, Hasselback also experienced a $250,000 gain (before tax) from the early retirement of $1,000,000 face value of 5 percent long-term debt. This gain was included in the net income of $5,000,000 above and is subject to a 30 percent tax rate. The total tax payable for 1984 from all taxable income was $2,075,000. The tax on the depreciation method change should be accounted for at a 40 percent rate.

REQUIRED

1. Record any necessary entries to account for 1985 depreciation and the change to sum-of-the-years'-digits depreciation, including the tax effects.
2. Prepare a partial income statement that includes the following items *if* appropriate:
   a. Pretax income from continuing operations; income tax expense on income from continuing operations; net income from continuing operations
   b. discontinued operations (if any)
   c. extraordinary items (if any)
   d. accounting changes (if any)
   Be sure to label the figures clearly, and use proper intraperiod tax allocation procedures.
3. Prepare a partial comparative balance sheet for 1984 and 1985 as it would appear in the 1985 financial statements. Include the following information:

	1985	1984
Furniture and fixtures		
Less accumulated depreciation		
Net book value, furniture and fixtures		

CURRENT SITUATION	MAY DIRECTLY AFFECT			
	REGULAR INCOME (CURRENT YEAR)	IN INCOME STATEMENT BELOW EXTRAORDINARY ITEMS	IN THE RETAINED EARNINGS STATEMENT	IN THE COMPARATIVE INCOME STATEMENT OF THE PRIOR YEAR
1. It was discovered this year that an asset has been on the books for 5 years with no depreciation recorded. Asset is expected to be useful for 10 more years.				
2. Straight-line depreciation has been used for 5 years. It is currently decided that an accelerated depreciation method is to be used because it more accurately reflects the benefit derived from fixed assets.				
3. An asset costing $5,000 was purchased 11 years ago. This asset had an estimated life and scrap value of 10 years and $200, respectively. It became obvious this year that our estimates were not correct because we sold the fully depreciated asset for $600.				
4. It was determined that the ending inventory value from last year was overstated. Goods acquired on a consignment basis (not owned by our company) were *not* included in "purchases" but *were* included in "ending inventory."				
5. Three years ago, our company established a liability account equal to 1 percent of sales for *expected* costs of service on product warranty. It was determined this year that actual costs have amounted to 3 percent of sales.				

P3–7 The following situations relate to *Accounting Principles Board Opinion No. 20,* "Accounting Changes." Fill in the grid above using *Y* for "yes" and *N* for "no."

P3–8 On January 1, 1984, Cathy Company purchased a machine for $40,000. The machine was estimated to have a 5-year useful life and no salvage value. Depreciation was by the straight-line method.

Assume that on January 1, 1986, the following "accounting changes" were made. (*Note:* These are *independent* alternatives.)

1. The useful life of the machine was changed to a revised total useful life of 8 years on January 1, 1986.
2. The double-declining balance method (200 percent of the straight-line rate) was adopted on January 1, 1986.
3. Depreciation recorded in years 1 and 2 was computed at an annual straight-line rate of 25 percent of original cost per year.

REQUIRED (Consider each change separately; ignore taxes.)

1. Record the entry, if any, for change 1, and the entry for 1986 depreciation in 1986.
2. Record the entry, if any, for change 2, and the entry for 1986 depreciation in 1986.
3. Record the entry, if any, for change 3, and the entry for 1986 depreciation in 1986.

P3-9 The following income statement data relate to the Robert Magee Management Company for the year ended December 31, 1984:

	DEBIT	CREDIT		DEBIT	CREDIT
System development revenue		$1,250,000	Advertising expense	$ 124,000	
Consultation revenue		2,115,000	Administrative expenses	1,322,000	
System service revenue		765,000	Depreciation expense	175,000	
Bond interest revenue		138,000	Cumulative prior years' effect of		
Cost of system developments sold	$895,000		change in depreciation method	396,000	
Cost of information service sub-scriptions	196,000		Bad debt expense	10,000	
			Legal fee expense	103,000	
Wages and salaries—temporary employees	827,000		Loss on sale of used equipment	200,000	
Supplies expense	83,000		Gain from retirement on bonds payable before maturity		$63,000

Magee is taxed at the rate of 40 percent, and taxes have not yet been considered in the data listed above.

REQUIRED

1. In conformance with disclosure requirements, prepare a single-step income statement for 1984 using appropriate intraperiod tax allocation.
2. In conformance with disclosure requirements, prepare a multiple-step income statement for 1984 using appropriate intraperiod tax allocation.

P3-10 The following items relate to the adjusted trial balance of the Seymour Corporation at December 31, 1984:

	DEBIT	CREDIT		DEBIT	CREDIT
Revenues from service contracts		$2,565,000	Travel and entertainment—home office	$ 127,000	
Revenues from products		15,876,000	Utilities expense	61,000	
Dividends	$ 125,000		Patents	77,000	
Accounts receivable	875,000		Sales returns	131,000	
Uncollectible accounts expense	13,000		Loss on early retirement of bonds	415,000	
Prepaid advertising	38,000		Purchase discounts		$51,000
Advertising expense	75,000		Sales discounts	72,000	
Wages payable		63,000	Purchase allowances		22,000
Selling and marketing expenses	2,137,000		Change in accounting method	486,000	
Rent expense—office	98,000		Depreciation expense—selling	1,854,000	
Interest income		105,000	Beginning inventory	578,000	
Purchases	8,753,000		Depreciation expense—home office	237,000	
Freight-in	206,000		Dividends received		48,000
Legal expense	57,000		Loss on sale of equipment	71,000	
Office salaries	2,981,000		Outside consultants' fees	13,000	
Travel and entertainment—salespeople	408,000				

Inventory per the physical count at year-end was valued at $632,000. The taxes have not yet been computed but are 40 percent of total income before taxes except for the change in accounting method, which has *no* tax consequences.

REQUIRED

1. Compute the 1984 tax expense.
2. Prepare an income statement for the year ended December 31, 1984, using the single-step format.
3. Prepare an income statement for the year ended December 31, 1984, using the multiple-step format.

P3-11 (CPA ADAPTED) Barrow Company, a publicly held regional manufacturer of western-style clothes, uses a calendar year for financial reporting. During 1983 Barrow purchased a small chain of retail specialty clothing stores. The retail stores were privately owned and had been a good customer of Barrow's for a number of years.

The controller of Barrow prepared a detailed comparison of the 1984 performance (current year) with the 1983 actual figures as reported. Through this analysis he discovered the following items, which affected the reported figures for 1983:

1. Accounts receivable at December 31, 1983, were understated by $63,000. Accounts receivable were reduced by this amount in the adjusting entries for 1983. The sale giving rise to the receivable was recorded in 1984. Ending inventories were correctly stated both years.

2. In May 1984, $60,000 was received in settlement of a $130,000 claim against a supplier for defective merchandise. The claim was filed in March 1983, but no receivable was recorded by Barrow because the supplier's financial condition was very weak.

3. Barrow paid $48,000 of additional income tax in 1983. This was the amount of additional tax due for 1980 as determined by an IRS audit of the 1980 federal income tax return. This additional tax was treated as an extraordinary expense.

4. Barrow paid $75,000 in August 1984 to settle an employee discrimination suit filed by the labor union in September 1983. No liability had been recorded in 1983, but the suit had been disclosed in the footnotes to the 1983 annual financial statements (assume this treatment was correct).

5. The retail chain Barrow acquired in 1983 should have recorded an estimate for bad debts of $50,000 in 1983 but didn't. The adjustment is made in 1984.

REQUIRED Discuss how each of the five items listed above should be handled in conformity with GAAP. Include the pretax impact, if any, on 1983 and 1984 "income" to support your answer.

P3–12 (CPA ADAPTED) The Missy Corporation's condensed combined statement of income and retained earnings for the year ended December 31, 1984, is shown below.

Following the statement are three *unrelated* sets of events involving certain "unusual" items. Each is based on Missy Corporation's condensed statement of income and retained earnings and requires revisions of that statement.

THE MISSY CORPORATION

Condensed Statement of Income
and Retained Earnings
For the Year Ended December 31, 1984

Sales revenue	$ 4,000,000
Cost of goods sold	2,240,000
Gross profit	$ 1,760,000
Selling, general, and administrative expenses	1,200,000
Income before extraordinary item	$ 560,000
Extraordinary item	(400,000)
Net income	$ 160,000
Retained earnings, January 1	640,000
Retained earnings, December 31	$ 800,000

SET OF EVENTS—I

At the end of 1984, Missy's management decided that the estimated loss rate on uncollectible accounts receivable was too high. Because of a depressed economy, the loss rate used for the years 1982 and 1983 was 4 percent of total sales. The economy has strengthened considerably in 1984, justifying a reduction in the rate to 2 percent of total sales. The amount recorded in bad debt expense under the heading of selling, general, and administrative expenses was $72,000 for 1982 and $120,000 for 1983.

The extraordinary item in the statement for 1984 relates to a loss incurred because of the abandonment of outmoded equipment formerly used in the business.

SET OF EVENTS—II

On January 1, 1982, Missy acquired equipment at a cost of $160,000. The company adopted the straight-line method of depreciation for this equipment and has been recording depreciation over an estimated life of 10 years, with no residual (salvage) value. At the beginning of 1984, a decision was made to switch to the sum-of-the-years'-digits method of depreciation for this equipment. Owing to an oversight, however, the straight-line method was used for 1984. For financial reporting purposes, depreciation is included in selling, general, and administrative expenses.

The extraordinary item in the statement relates to shutdown expenses incurred by the company during a major strike by its employees during 1984.

SET OF EVENTS—III

During the latter part of 1984, the company discontinued its retail and apparel fabric divisions. The results of such operations and the loss on sale of these two divisions amounted to a total loss of $400,000. This amount was considered part of selling, general, and administrative expenses. The event meets the criteria for discontinued operations treatment.

The extraordinary item in the statement relates to a loss sustained as a result of damage to the company's merchandise caused by an earthquake, which severely damaged its main warehouse.

REQUIRED For each of the three unrelated sets of events, prepare a revised condensed combined statement of income and retained earnings for the Missy Corporation. Ignore income tax considerations and earnings-per-share computations.

P3–13 (CPA ADAPTED) The Century Company, a diversified manufacturing company, had four separate operating divisions engaged in the manufacture of products in each of the following areas: food products, health aids, textiles, and office equipment. Financial data for the years ended December 31, 1984, and December 31, 1985, are presented below:

	NET SALES		COST OF SALES		OPERATING EXPENSE	
	1985	1984	1985	1984	1985	1984
Food products	$3,500,000	$3,000,000	$2,400,000	$1,800,000	$ 550,000	$ 275,000
Health aids	2,000,000	1,270,000	1,100,000	700,000	300,000	125,000
Textiles	1,580,000	1,400,000	500,000	900,000	200,000	150,000
Office equipment	920,000	1,330,000	800,000	1,000,000	650,000	750,000
	$8,000,000	$7,000,000	$4,800,000	$4,400,000	$1,700,000	$1,300,000

On January 1, 1985, Century adopted a plan to sell the assets and product line of the office equipment division and expected to realize a gain on this disposal. On September 1, 1985, the division's assets and product line were sold for $2,100,000 cash, resulting in a gain of $640,000 (exclusive of operations during the phase-out period).

The company's textiles division had six manufacturing plants that produced a variety of textile products. In April 1985, the company sold one of these plants and realized a gain of $130,000. After the sale, the operations at the plant that was sold were transferred to the remaining five textile plants, which the company continued to operate.

In August 1985, the main warehouse of the food products division, located on the banks of the Bayer River, was flooded when the river overflowed. The resulting damage of $420,000 is not included in the financial data given above. Historical records indicate that the Bayer River normally overflows every 4 to 5 years, causing flood damage to adjacent property.

The company had interest revenue earned on investments of $70,000 in the year ended December 31, 1985, and $40,000 in the year ended December 31, 1984. The company's net income was $960,000 for the year ended December 31, 1985, and $670,000 for the year ended December 31, 1984. The provision for income tax expense for each of the two years should be computed at a rate of 50 percent.

REQUIRED Prepare in proper form a comparative statement of income of the Century Company for the two years ended December 31, 1985, and December 31, 1984. Footnotes are not required.

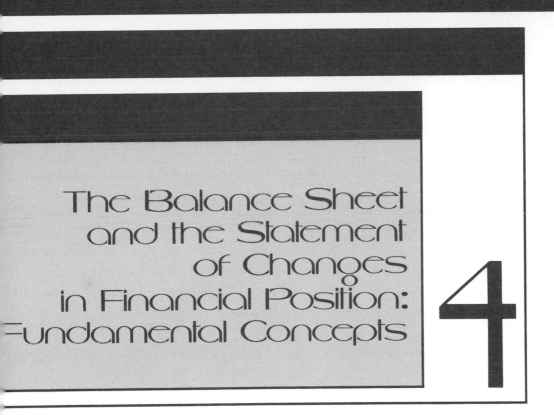

The Balance Sheet and the Statement of Changes in Financial Position: Fundamental Concepts

4

OVERVIEW   Accounting output communicates information to users to aid them in making rational economic decisions. Different financial statements communicate different types of information about the entity's accomplishment and current status.

The balance sheet is an *attempt* to reflect the financial position of the firm at an instant in time. It is intended to be a snapshot of where the firm stands at that point. The use of the word "attempt" is deliberate. Given the complexities and uncertainties that affect even relatively small entities, it is apparent that the financial statements are approximations rather than a reflection of the one true state. Thus, the balance sheet attempts to reflect the financial position of a firm, given (accepting) all the underlying concepts, principles, assumptions, and estimates necessary to accomplish that objective.

Many users of financial statements consider the balance sheet the most important statement because it identifies the status of the entity at a point in time. The three other primary statements are used to explain changes in the balance sheet from one point in time to the next. The statement of changes in financial position, the income statement, and the retained earnings statement are all "change" statements, and they all provide information that, among other things, describes changes in balance sheet items from the beginning to the end of an accounting period. In the preceding chapter we focused on the income statement and the retained earnings statement and discussed their relationship to the balance sheet. In this chapter we focus on the balance sheet and what it represents, as well as on the statement of changes in financial position and its relationship to the balance sheet and income statement.

The balance sheet reports on the financial state of the entity. The basic classifications reflecting this state are assets, liabilities, and equities. In the first part of this chapter, we examine the similarities between assets, liabilities, and equities that appear on balance sheets. The statement of changes in financial position analyzes how certain balance sheet classifications changed during an accounting period. Usually cash or working capital (current assets minus current liabilities) is the balance sheet element under scrutiny. In the final section of this chapter we introduce the fundamental ideas of funds flows as communicated in the statement of changes in financial position.

ASSETS

The Similarities Among Assets

What thread of similarity runs through all types of assets? What makes cash similar to buildings, machinery, and patents? Such similarity must exist because all assets are added together and called *total assets* in the balance sheet. Without such a unifying thread, the total would be meaningless. We can start observing the similarities by noting that assets represent anticipated future benefits. A firm's assets enable it to accomplish its economic and financial objectives. The types and amounts of specific assets needed vary depending upon the product or service to be provided. For instance, compare the complex machinery in an automotive assembly plant with the office furniture in an attorney's office. The assets are held to accomplish specific economic objectives—in one case, to assemble automobiles, in the other, to provide legal advice.

Another way to express this idea is to say that assets are the income-generating base of the firm. Assets have earning potential. They reflect the service potential available for use in the future in the attempt to generate income. In this sense, the balance sheet is a futuristic statement, with estimates of future states having a strong influence on the current presentations.

But does this mean that all elements of a firm having these characteristics are measured and reflected as assets of a firm? Does the accountant claim to reflect *all* future service potential of a firm in the balance sheet? The answer is no, and the reason is simply stated. Many of the firm's assets cannot be measured objectively. For example, human resources often provide important future benefits to a firm; however, reliable measurements of such benefits have not as yet been developed.

Major Classes of Assets

Current assets A **current asset** is one that is expected to be used up, its entire service utility consumed, within 1 year or within the normal operating cycle of the business, whichever is longer. A **noncurrent asset** is one whose service utility extends beyond 1 year or beyond the normal operating cycle of the business. Although many accountants have debated exactly what is meant by **normal operating cycle,** it is sufficient to define it as the time it takes to go from cash to other assets and back to a cash position. For example, in a manufacturing concern the firm's operating cycle is the time it takes to acquire raw materials for cash, convert them into finished goods, sell the finished goods on account, and collect the cash. Some firms, such as a supermarket, may have hundreds of such cycles in a year, whereas others, such as firms that do heavy construction, may have an operating cycle that extends beyond a year. When a firm has more than one cycle in a year, any asset that lasts longer than a cycle but less than a year is a current asset. When the cycle runs longer than a year, the longer period is used to define current assets.

At the balance sheet date, the accountant must review all assets and determine which are to be classified as current. Let us see how that decision process might proceed for certain assets that are often found in a balance sheet.

CASH AND BANK DEPOSITS **Cash and bank deposits** are shown as current assets except when management has designated them for use for some noncurrent purpose. For example, cash that is set aside for payment of a specific current obligation is still classified as current, but disclosure must be made of the restriction because the cash is not available for general operating purposes.

Current assets		
Cash and bank deposits		
Restricted to pay current installment contract	$15,000	
Unrestricted	45,000	$60,000

If set aside for a noncurrent purpose, cash must be classified as a noncurrent asset, usually in the long-term investment section of the balance sheet, as follows:

Noncurrent assets	
Long-term investments	
Cash fund for payment of long-term bonds payable	$100,000

SHORT-TERM INVESTMENTS When a firm has cash that will not be needed in the near future, management may invest the cash in order to earn income on it during the period until the cash is needed for operating purposes. **Short-term investments** are current assets because management *intends* to convert them to cash during the coming period. If such is not the intention, then the securities should be classified as noncurrent in the long-term investment section of the balance sheet.

Short-term investments must be measured at **lower of cost or market** (the detailed rules governing this measurement will be discussed in Chapter 7), and the basis of measurement must be disclosed in some appropriate manner, such as the following:

Current assets	
Short-term investments—at market (cost—$100,000)	$90,000

RECEIVABLES **Receivables** arise from a number of sources. **Trade accounts receivable** reflect in financial terms the promises of customers to pay for goods or services they have bought from the entity on credit. Such payments are usually made within a short period of time, such as 30 to 60 days. **Trade notes receivable** arise in the same way as accounts receivable but are of longer duration and usually bear explicit interest. **Nontrade accounts receivable** and **notes receivable** may arise from such events as dispositions of plant, property, and equipment or loans to officers and employees.

Receivables should be disclosed according to their source. Any restrictions, such as receivables pledged as security for a loan payable, must be indicated.

Current assets		
Trade accounts receivable ($25,000 pledged as security for a loan payable)	$125,000	
Trade notes receivable	50,000	
Notes receivable from officers and employees	10,000	
Nontrade accounts receivable	15,000	
	$200,000	
Less: Allowance for uncollectibles	20,000	$180,000

Note that the items classified as current assets are expected to be converted to cash or used up entirely within 1 year or within the operating cycle, whichever is longer. In certain situations, this rule may require reclassification of items between noncurrent and current. For instance, at December 31, 1984, a note receivable with principal due in two installments of $1,200 on December 31, 1985, and $1,000 on December 31, 1986, would be classified as $1,200 current and $1,000 noncurrent in the balance sheet at December 31, 1984. On December 31, 1985, the remaining $1,000 would have to be reclassified from noncurrent to current.

INVENTORIES In our earlier discussion of the operating cycle, we saw that the life cycle of inventories is included as one component of the overall operating cycle of a business. By definition, then, inventories are classified as current:

Current assets		
Inventories—at lower of average cost or market		
Finished goods	$60,000	
Work in process	40,000	
Raw materials	75,000	$175,000

Inventories represent a very important and complex area of accounting. This subject is covered in detail in Chapters 9 and 10.

PREPAID ITEMS Firms will often pay for such services as rent, insurance, and wages in advance. If these services will be used up during the next year or operating cycle, if longer, they are current assets. Otherwise, they should be classified as noncurrent assets. As in the case of receivables, a **prepaid item** may have current and noncurrent portions.

All of these concepts and classification techniques for current assets will be discussed in depth in other parts of the text.

Noncurrent assets A **noncurrent asset** is one that will be used up or consumed or converted to cash over a period of time extending beyond 1 year or beyond the normal operating cycle of the business, whichever is longer. In some cases, noncurrent assets are reclassified to current on a piecemeal basis. For instance, the portion of a long-term note receivable due within a year of the balance sheet date would be classified as current, while the remainder of the receivable would be classified as noncurrent. Most other noncurrent assets are not reclassified on a piecemeal basis, even though a portion may be used up during the next accounting period. For example, the depreciation for the coming year is still part of the total service utility in the machinery and equipment; it has not yet been released through usage. When it is consumed, the amount will become expense or work-in-process inventory, depending upon the purpose for which the asset is used. Noncurrent assets are generally subdivided into (1) investments, (2) plant, property, and equipment, and (3) intangible assets.

INVESTMENTS **Long-term investments** represent commitments of the firm's resources for substantial periods of time. There is no intent on the part of management to dispose of them within 1 year or within the normal operating cycle of the business, if longer.

The main items making up long-term investments usually are (1) common stocks, bonds, and long-term notes where the intent is to retain the investment for the long term; (2) tangible fixed assets, such as land, that are not presently needed for operating activity and are, therefore, held for investment purposes; and (3) various types of funds, such as a bond sinking fund accumulated to retire bonds as they come due or a plant expansion fund accumulated to expand plant capacity at some time in the future.

Management's intent is very important to the accountant in determining the nature of an item and how it should be classified. For example, an investment in the common stock of another entity, although it may be highly marketable, is classified as a long-term investment if management intends to maintain the investment for more than 1 year of the normal operating cycle, if longer.

Investments		
Investment in ABC Company's common stock (at cost, which is lower than market)	$130,000	
Investment in XYZ Company's bonds	45,000	
Sinking fund for bond retirement	60,000	$235,000

PLANT, PROPERTY, AND EQUIPMENT **Plant, property, and equipment** are relatively long-lived assets that are directly associated with business operations. Most have physical substance and most depreciate with use or with the passage of time.

Also included in this category are **depletable assets** such as mineral deposits and timberlands. As the minerals are being mined or the timber is being cut, these long-term assets are reduced, and current assets, such as ore or timber inventory, are increased. Accountants use the term **depletion** for this process rather than *depreciation*. Conceptually, however, there is little distinction between depreciation and depletion because both reflect the consumption of long-term assets.

Plant, property, and equipment			
Land		$ 70,000	
Buildings	$200,000		
Less: Accumulated depreciation	45,000	155,000	
Machinery	$175,000		
Less: Accumulated depreciation	80,000	95,000	$320,000
Mineral Deposits			
(Net of accumulated depletion)			200,000

INTANGIBLE ASSETS The word *intangible* means "without physical existence or substance." The assets listed in this category, such as patents, copyrights, and goodwill, fulfill this criterion. **Intangible assets** represent certain rights and privi leges; they are frequently a measurement of the competitive advantages the firm has over its rivals. For example, a firm may have an exclusive franchise to operate a fast-food store or to sell a given product in a certain area.

But not too much should be made of these assets' lack of physical substance. That is not the critical reason why they are set out in a separate category. They are acquired rights and privileges of a firm and may be among its most important assets.

Intangible assets		
Patents (less $4,000 amortization)	$28,000	
Franchises (less $7,500 amortization)	46,000	
Goodwill (less $11,000 amortization)	34,000	$108,000

Note that "amortization" is the term used in conjunction with intangibles to represent the same process as depreciation and depletion. Here, the amounts listed as amortization represent the total amount of the original cost of each asset that has been charged to expense since its acquisition.

LIABILITIES AND EQUITIES

The
Similarities
Between
Liabilities
and Equities

As is true of assets, there is a thread of similarity running through all the liabilities and equities of a firm. There are also distinctions that must be understood if we are to interpret the balance sheet properly for decision-making purposes. Liabilities and equities are similar in that they **represent claims against the assets** of the entity and, for the most part, represent the sources of the firm's assets. They indicate where and how the firm obtained the assets. This does not imply that each asset at a balance sheet date could be traced to any given source. It simply means that as individuals and as a group, certain persons and organizations have made their capital available to the entity and, consequently, expect to receive a return.

There are some exceptions to this general concept. For example, what if the firm has been found liable in court for $1,000,000 as a result of personal injury to one of its customers? The customer has a claim and this would be recorded as a liability, although this customer certainly did not make any assets available to the firm. All liabilities and equities represent claims against, or interests in, the assets (resources) of the entity.

Determining
When a
Liability Exists

Conceptually, **liabilities** represent claims against the entity resulting from past transactions or events involving the entity. These claims will have to be satisfied by the disbursement of assets, the performance of a service, or some combination of the two at some time in the future. Although this may be a good conceptual description of liabilities, there are practical problems involved in implementing it. If we think of a continuum running all the way from absolute certainty that a claim exists to absolute certainty that a claim does not exist, the question is, At what point on that continuum is there sufficient evidence indicating that there is a claim that must be recorded in the accounting records? Figure 4–1 illustrates the problem.

Professional judgment is very important in determining where a particular situation falls on the continuum shown in Figure 4–1. Accountants must determine whether some event or circumstance has taken place or exists at or before the balance sheet date and might require a future disbursement of assets to satisfy the claim. For example, if an entity goes to the bank and borrows $10,000 on a 90-day, 12 percent note before the balance sheet date, such an event falls at point w on the

FIGURE 4-1

Point w	Point x	Point y	Point z

Absolute certainty that a claim exists. Claims are recorded and reflected in the body of the basic statements.

Some uncertainty exists, but claims must be recorded and reflected in the body of the basic statements.

Considerable uncertainty exists, and claims must be reflected in footnotes or by other means but are not recorded in the accounts or reflected in the body of the basic statements.

Absolute certainty that a claim does not exist.

continuum. The event is the borrowing of money. The accountant knows for certain to whom the money is owed, knows for certain the amount that must be paid at maturity ($10,000 plus interest of $300), and knows the exact date on which payment is to be made. A number of other liabilities fall into this same general category. In this group are bonds payable, wages payable, accounts payable, accrued interest payable, and customers' advances.

Moving to the right of point *w*, the question of reasonable measurement is more difficult. For example, consider estimated federal, state, and local income taxes payable. If the entity has income during the period subject to income taxes, the event (earning of the taxable income) giving rise to the claim has taken place on or before the balance sheet date, so conceptually income taxes payable is as much of a liability as notes payable to a bank. The difference is the accuracy of measurement. Because many alternatives and estimates are necessary in filing income tax returns, such calculated amounts are often subject to revision. Therefore, on the balance sheet date, income taxes payable may be estimated only and are often labeled as *estimated* income taxes payable in the balance sheet. Other elements have similar characteristics, such as accrued employee vacation pay and pensions payable.

At this stage, we can determine that certain events have taken place before the balance sheet date, thus giving rise to the claim. Although the measurement problem is somewhat more difficult as we move from point *w* to the area of point *x*, no further evidence is needed to validate the claim itself, although future events may affect the amount.

As we move even farther to the right of point *x* toward point *y*, we enter the realm where some future event must occur before the claim arising from an event or circumstance taking place on or before the balance sheet date is considered a liability. To record a liability, the future event must be both (1) likely to occur (probable) and (2) reasonably measurable.[1] Claims that are dependent upon future events are called **contingencies,** and both conditions above must exist if a contingent liability is to be recorded. If both conditions are not present, the contingency is disclosed in the financial statement footnotes, which discuss the situation creating the potential loss.

Items to the right of point *y* are less likely to receive footnote disclosure because of either the greater difficulty involved in estimating the potential claim or the greater uncertainty that a valid claim will exist in the future.

[1] The discussion on contingencies is based on *Statement of Financial Accounting Standards No. 5,* "Accounting for Contingencies" (Stamford, CT: FASB, 1975).

In summary, many liabilities are legal obligations of the firm in a strict sense. Most of these fall at or near point *w* on our scale. As we move from point *w,* we encounter liabilities that are not as fixed but that may have to be recognized in order to ensure that the financial statements convey the best estimate of the possible claims against the firm's resources. For example, **warranties** are likely to give rise to claims that should be recognized in the balance sheet. It is probable that customers will make claims under the warranty provisions, and it is possible to prepare a reasonable estimate of the dollar amount of such claims. The warranty liability is estimated in the year of sale of the product and is recorded as a liability. Accountants do this not because a legal liability exists at the balance sheet date but because of the matching concept and to accomplish the objective of disclosing all significant obligations of the entity.

Major Classes
of Liabilities

Just as assets are divided into current and noncurrent, depending on when they are expected to be used up, so are liabilities divided into current and noncurrent, depending on when the liability is expected to be paid off or eliminated. This distinction is clarified in the following sections.

Current liabilities   If a claim is expected to be liquidated, paid off, or otherwise eliminated through the use of a current asset within 1 year or within the normal operating cycle of the business, if longer, it is a **current liability**. This usually implies the use of something properly classified as a current asset in payment of the obligation or the providing of a service.

Let us test the concept by assuming that 1 year is the normal operating cycle of the business. If, for example, some portion of an obligation classified as long-term debt will fall due within 1 year, it must usually be reclassified as current. The word "usually" is important because there are major exceptions. If a bond sinking fund has been built up for use in payment of the long-term debt when it comes due, then the portion of the long-term debt coming due within 1 year would be reclassified as short-term debt only if the portion of the bond sinking fund (a noncurrent asset) needed to retire the debt is reclassified as a current asset. Under these conditions, neither is generally reclassified as current.

Recall that a current liability is one "expected" to be paid off within 1 year. If management expects to refund the portion coming due with another liability properly classified as noncurrent, and assuming the entity has the ability to refinance, then reclassification to current status is not required.[2]

Current liabilities	
Accounts payable	$165,000
Customer advances	30,000
Notes payable	45,000
Current maturity of bonds payable	80,000
Dividends payable	35,000
Taxes payable	15,000
	$370,000

Noncurrent liabilities   **Noncurrent (or long-term) liabilities** are those that are expected to be liquidated at some time in the future beyond 1 year or beyond the operating cycle, if longer. Lease obligations, notes payable, bonds payable, and pen-

[2] Chapter 16 discusses such reclassifications in detail.

sion obligations (which are due beyond 1 year of the current balance sheet date or operating cycle, if longer) are common noncurrent liabilities.

Noncurrent liabilities		
Bonds payable—12%, due in 1990	$3,000,000	
Lease obligations	1,500,000	
Pension liability	2,000,000	$6,500,000

Stockholders' Equity

Although stockholders' equity is somewhat similar to liabilities, there are many distinctions. Ownership implies risk taking. Owners do not have a specific claim against the assets of the firm except at the time of liquidation, and even then their claims are usually satisfied only after all the debt of the firm has been paid off. Unlike liabilities, there is normally no specific point in time or period of time when owners can demand their capital investment back from the entity. If they wish to dispose of some of their stock, they must find a willing buyer in the marketplace.

In contrast to many types of debtors, stockholders receive no promise of a fixed rate of return on their investment. Since the stock market is relatively volatile, stockholders can often suffer large "paper" losses, or have substantial "paper" gains, by changes in the market price of their stock. And whether the entity has high or low profits, the board of directors is not legally bound to declare dividends. Thus, the stockholders do not have a legal claim against the funds of the entity provided by operations until declared by the board of directors in the form of dividends.

Of course, the owners of common stock do enjoy voting privileges proportionate to their stockholding—the right to vote for members of the board of directors and on certain other issues. Through such votes they can exert influence on the firm's policies.

Stockholders' equity is divided into three major categories:

1. Capital stock—the par or stated value of the shares issued
2. Additional paid-in capital—primarily the excess of the amounts received on issuance of the stock over the par or stated value
3. Retained earnings—primarily a measurement of the excess of accumulated past earnings of the entity over dividend declarations

In any listing of stockholders' equity, details on such matters as the following must be provided: the par value of shares; shares authorized, issued, and outstanding; treasury stock acquisitions; and any restrictions on retained earnings. The following example lists some of the required detail, which will be discussed in detail in Chapters 20 and 21:

Stockholders' equity		
Common stock, par value $10, authorized and issued		
200,000 shares, outstanding 198,500		$2,000,000
Additional paid-in capital		1,500,000
		$3,500,000
Retained earnings		
Appropriated for plant expansion	$250,000	
Restricted by purchase of treasury stock	30,000	
Unappropriated	450,000	730,000
		$4,230,000
Less: Treasury stock, at cost (1,500 shares)		30,000
Total stockholders' equity		$4,200,000

THE BALANCE SHEET FORMAT

We have already covered many of the major elements of the balance sheet. As shown in Exhibit 4–1, all of these elements constitute one of the primary means of communicating financial information about entities. The sequencing of categories shown for the Atkinson Corporation is common but by no means universal. Sometimes the claim is made that assets are listed in order of liquidity. While this may be true in a very rough sense, it is obviously not a strictly followed norm. For instance, some inventory items may generate cash before some receivables do.

THE STATEMENT OF CHANGES IN FINANCIAL POSITION AND ITS RELATIONSHIP TO THE BALANCE SHEET

Financial statements provide three basic types of information: (1) the firm's financial position, (2) the firm's increase or decrease in net assets as a result of profit-seeking operations, and (3) the flow of funds during a given period.

The balance sheet provides a picture of the financial position of the firm at a *point* in time. The income statement describes the nature of the changes in the balance sheet accounts that resulted from the operating activities of the entity over a period of time. In addition to financial position and operating results, users of financial statements seek information concerning funds flows. This information, which is provided in the statement of changes in financial position (SCFP), describes where the entity obtained new funds and how it utilized funds during a specified *period* of time.

The Accounting Principles Board described the relationship of the statement of changes in financial position to the balance sheet and income statement in **APB Opinion No. 19:**

> [The SCFP] is related to both the income statement and the balance sheet and provides information that can be obtained only partially, or at most in piecemeal form, by interpreting them. . . . The funds statement cannot supplant either the income statement or the balance sheet but is intended to provide information that the other statements either do not provide or provide only indirectly about the flow of funds and changes in financial position during the period.[3]

The purpose of the SCFP is to reflect, by major category and for a given time period, the sources of funds to the entity and its uses of funds. In so doing, it provides information to help the user assess changes in the structure of the entity's assets, liabilities, and stockholders' equity, with particular emphasis on changes in its liquidity.

Basic concepts, definitions, and statement formats used in conjunction with the SCFP are introduced here. The more detailed techniques of preparation and interpretation of the SCFP are covered in Chapter 25.

There are a variety of possible definitions of funds. Here we shall think of funds as either cash or working capital. When funds are defined as **cash,** the major objective of the SCFP is to describe the changes in the cash position of the firm between the beginning and the end of the period. For example, if the firm's cash

---

[3] The discussions in this section reflect some of the basic requirements of *Accounting Principles Board Opinion No. 19,* "Reporting Changes in Financial Position" (New York: AICPA, March 1971), par. 5.

EXHIBIT 4-1

THE ATKINSON CORPORATION
Balance Sheet
At December 31, 1984

ASSETS

Current assets			
Cash			$ 44,000
Short-term investments—at lower of cost or market (cost, $71,000)			64,000
Accounts and notes receivable			
Trade accounts		$253,000	
Trade notes		27,500	
Installment accounts		111,000	
		$391,500	
Less: Allowance for uncollectibles		38,500	353,000
Inventories			
Finished goods (LIFO cost)		$ 88,000	
Work in process (LIFO cost)		176,000	
Raw material (LIFO cost)		37,000	301,000
Prepaid expenses			46,000
Total current assets			$ 808,000
Noncurrent assets			
Investments			
Bonds and notes of United Corporation		$ 131,000	
Sinking fund for bond retirement		70,000	
Total investments		$ 201,000	
Plant, property, and equipment			
Land		$ 91,000	
Buildings	$985,000		
Less: Accumulated depreciation	275,000	710,000	
Machinery	$490,000		
Less: Accumulated depreciation	150,000	340,000	1,141,000
Intangibles			
Patents (net of $6,000 amortization)		$ 68,000	
Goodwill (net of $23,000 amortization)		61,000	129,000
Total noncurrent assets			1,471,000
Total assets			$2,279,000

LIABILITIES AND STOCKHOLDERS' EQUITY

Liabilities			
Current liabilities			
Accounts payable		$220,000	
Accrued wages payable		40,000	
Income taxes payable		100,000	
Notes payable		35,000	
Advances from customers		23,000	
Current maturity of bonds payable		60,000	
Total current liabilities			$ 478,000
Noncurrent liabilities			
Bonds payable—12%, due 1991 (net of $60,000 above)		$200,000	
Less: Unamortized discount		30,000	
		$170,000	
Long-term mortgage		375,000	
Total noncurrent liabilities			545,000
Total liabilities			$1,023,000
Stockholders' equity			
Common stock—$100 par value, issued and outstanding, 8,000 shares		$800,000	
Additional paid-in capital		50,000	
		$850,000	
Retained earnings:			
Appropriated for plant expansion	$200,000		
Unappropriated	206,000	406,000	
Total stockholder's equity			$1,256,000
Total Liabilities and Stockholders' Equity			$2,279,000

balance is $5,000 at the beginning of the year and $11,000 at the end, the purpose of the SCFP would be to reflect the major sources of cash inflows during the period and the major causes of cash outflows during the period, which resulted in a $6,000 increase in cash. All transactions that affect cash are reported in summarized form in the SCFP.

When funds are defined as working capital, then the major objective of the SCFP is to reflect what brought about the change in the working capital position of the firm between the beginning and the end of the period. Because working capital is the difference between current assets and current liabilities, the change in working capital during the period can be determined from comparative balance sheets as follows:

	BALANCE SHEET DATA	
	12/31/84	12/31/83
Current assets		
Cash	$ 6,000	$ 5,000
Accounts receivable (net)	13,000	15,000
Inventories	32,000	25,000
Prepayments	1,000	2,000
Total current assets	$52,000	$47,000
Current liabilities		
Accounts payable	$ 6,000	$ 4,000
Income taxes payable	8,000	10,000
Notes payable	5,000	3,000
Wages payable	3,000	5,000
Total current liabilities	$22,000	$22,000
Working capital	$30,000	$25,000

The increase in working capital during 1984 is $30,000 − $25,000 = $5,000. All the events and transactions during the period changing working capital would be reported in the SCFP in summarized form.

Business owners and managers need information on the flow of funds into and out of their firms. External users of the financial statements also need funds-flow data. Such data may aid in answering the following kinds of questions:

1. How was the firm able to increase its funds position in spite of decreases in profits, or the opposite?
2. How did the firm finance large expenditures for plant, property, and equipment?
3. What liquidity constraints were there on dividends?
4. What events caused changes in the long-term debt structure of the firm?
5. How were the funds obtained from capital stock utilized?

Such questions can generally be answered by analyzing the SCFP.

Sources and Uses of Funds

Operations The types of entries made for various routine transactions and events affecting firms will enable us to identify the typical sources and uses of funds for most entities. A major source of funds results from the operating (income-generating) activities of a firm. The data presented in the income statement are based on the accrual concept of accounting. As discussed in Chapter 3, the recognition of revenue does not depend on the receipt of cash or any other working capital item. The recognition of expense follows from the matching concept. Therefore, recognizing expenses does not necessarily follow the outflow of cash or any other working capital item.

For example, an entity might accept land in exchange for its product, resulting in the following entry:

Land (noncurrent asset)	10,000	
Sales revenue		10,000

Neither cash nor any other working capital item is affected by such a transaction. On the expense side, the following entry is common in reflecting depreciation for a period:

Depreciation expense	2,000	
Accumulated depreciation		2,000

Neither cash nor any other working capital item is affected by such an event.

However, the operating activities of a firm often do involve cash and some other working capital items. Most sales, for example, result in an increase in cash, accounts receivable, or notes receivable. Examples of expenses that could directly affect funds would be the recognition of cost of goods sold expense resulting in a credit to inventory and the accruing of salary expense resulting in a credit to salaries payable. Cash or working capital is involved in the majority of recorded transactions that affect the income-generating activities of a firm.

Operations are an important net source (or net use) of funds for a period whether funds are defined as cash or working capital. Many analysts believe that the "funds provided (or used) by operating activities" is the most important single item in the SCFP. Generally, over an extended period of time, operations must provide positive net flows if a firm is to be viable. Net inflows of funds can be used to pay dividends, repay debt, and acquire productive assets. Over the long run, firms must generate funds through operating activity if they hope to attract and retain capital suppliers.

Nonoperating sources and uses Many firms obtain significant amounts of funds through the issuance of long-term obligations, such as bonds, preferred stock, and common stock. The repayment or retirement of such securities often requires the use of funds. Additionally, funds are consumed by the acquisition of noncurrent assets such as plant, property, and equipment; copyrights; patents; and long-term investments. These items represent the major uses of the funds for nonoperating purposes. Although the disposition of noncurrent assets can provide funds, such asset sales are typically not a significant source.

Dividends usually represent an ongoing repetitive use of funds because the market value of a firm's stock may depend in part upon the amount and consistency of dividend payouts by the firm. As a result, management is reluctant to either reduce the amount of dividends or interrupt the consistency in paying dividends.

The Funds Pool Funds (whether cash or working capital) can be significantly increased or decreased by a major single event, such as the sale or retirement of bonds. Funds are also affected by continuous processes, such as when funds are provided by, or used in, operating activities. As a result, the pool of funds is constantly flowing, even though the dollar balance of fund accounts may stay relatively constant over long periods of time. This is often overlooked when considering the balance of funds at a point in time or even comparing the change in the balance between two points in time. Yet, these funds flows provide important information that accountants attempt to report in the SCFP. Remember that **the basic objective of the SCFP is to reflect the nature of the changes in funds** for a period of time. The SCFP captures these dynamics in the pool of funds. These inflows and outflows from the pool overlap. As they become a part of the pool, they usually lose the identity of their specific sources. From the pool of funds, specific uses are identified. Yet it is difficult, if not impossible, to trace a given source of funds to a given use. Figure 4–2 depicts the dynamic nature of the pool of funds and identifies the major inflows and outflows.

In Figure 4–2 the solid-lined circle for the pool of funds indicates the relatively constant dollar amount of funds maintained by firms over a number of years. This basic pool will normally expand and contract as the firm goes through its operating cycles. The concentric dashed circles inside and outside the solid-lined circle depict these short-run increases and decreases in funds. The arrows into the pool reflect the major sources of funds, and the arrows leaving the pool represent the major uses of funds. These flows reflect the constant, ongoing, overlapping sources and uses of funds. The lack of connection between the lines depicting sources and the lines depicting uses indicates the difficulty normally encountered in tracing specific sources to specific uses.

Preparing a Statement of Changes in Financial Position: An Introduction

The Richard Corporation began business on January 1, 1984. Its accounting period ends on December 31, 1984. You have calculated that cash increased $87,000 and working capital increased $54,000 during the period. Following, in summary form, are the transactions that took place during 1984:

Sales on account	$300,000
Sales for cash	150,000
Collections from customers on account	280,000
Purchases of inventory on account	275,000
Payments to suppliers of inventory	255,000
Cost of goods sold expense	245,000
Wages paid	35,000
Wages accrued but unpaid, 12/31/84	8,000
Income taxes accrued, 12/31/84	50,000
Depreciation expense	15,000
Other expense accrued, 12/31/84	5,000
Issuance of common stock for cash	300,000
Issuance of long-term debt for cash	100,000
Dividends declared and paid	20,000
Acquisition of land for cash	110,000
Acquisition of buildings for cash	220,000
Acquisition of machinery and equipment for cash	103,000

These data are used in Exhibit 4–2 to compute income for 1984 (column 1), the summarized SCFP for 1984 using *working capital* as the basis of funds (column 2), and the summarized SCFP for 1984 using *cash* as the basis of funds (column 3).

Because Richard Corporation began operations on January 1, 1984, there were no beginning balances of cash or working capital, so the $54,000 and $87,000 figures representing the *changes* in working capital and cash, respectively, are also the *ending balances* of working capital and cash. Let us analyze the items in order to understand why working capital and cash were or were not affected.

SALES REVENUE Under accrual accounting, revenue is normally recognized at

FIGURE 4-2
The funds pool

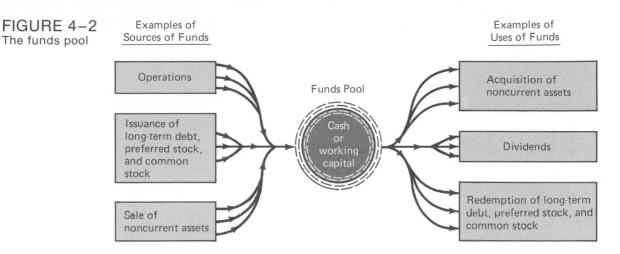

Examples of Sources of Funds

Operations

Issuance of long-term debt, preferred stock, and common stock

Sale of noncurrent assets

Funds Pool

Cash or working capital

Examples of Uses of Funds

Acquisition of noncurrent assets

Dividends

Redemption of long-term debt, preferred stock, and common stock

the point of sale. What is received by the entity in the sales transaction is irrelevant to the timing of revenue recognition. It could be cash, receivables (accounts or notes), or any number of other assets. In this case, cash of $150,000 and accounts receivable of $300,000, a total of $450,000, was received; and this figure is the sales revenue for the period. Note that both cash and accounts receivable are current

EXHIBIT 4-2

RICHARD CORPORATION

ALTERNATIVE SCFP ILLUSTRATIONS

	INCOME STATEMENT FOR YEAR ENDED 12/31/84	STATEMENT OF CHANGES IN WORKING CAPITAL FOR YEAR ENDED 12/31/84	STATEMENT OF CHANGES IN CASH FOR YEAR ENDED 12/31/84
Sales revenue	$450,000	$450,000	$430,000
Less expenses			
Cost of goods sold	$245,000	$245,000	$255,000
Wages	43,000	43,000	35,000
Depreciation	15,000	—	
Other	5,000	5,000	—
Income taxes	50,000	50,000	—
Total expenses	$358,000	$343,000	$290,000
Net income	$ 92,000		
Working capital provided by operations		$107,000	
Cash provided by operations			$140,000
Issuance of common stock		300,000	300,000
Issuance of long-term debt		100,000	100,000
Total working capital available for use		$507,000	
Total cash available for use			$540,000
Dividends		$ 20,000	$ 20,000
Acquisition of land		110,000	110,000
Acquisition of buildings		220,000	220,000
Acquisition of machinery and equipment		103,000	103,000
Total uses of cash and working capital		$453,000	$453,000
Total increase in working capital		$ 54,000	
Total increase in cash			$ 87,000

assets (working capital items), and, therefore, working capital is increased $450,000 as a result of sales activity. Cash received from sales activity is not the same as working capital. In the example, $150,000 of sales was made for cash. In addition, of the $300,000 sales on account, $280,000 was collected in cash during the period. Consequently, cash related to sales activity increased by $430,000 during the period. Note that $20,000 of 1984 sales remains uncollected in the Accounts Receivable account.

COST OF GOODS SOLD The general form of the entry to reflect cost of goods sold is

Cost of goods sold	XX	
Inventory		XX

An expense is increased and a current asset (working capital) is decreased. Thus, the same figure deducted in determining net income, $250,000, also reflects the reduction in working capital during the period. The correct figure to reflect the reduction of cash during the period, however, is the amount paid to the suppliers of inventory during the period, $255,000 in our example.

WAGES In determining income, expenses must be matched against revenues in the period in which the revenue is recognized. And this is true whether or not cash is affected and whether or not working capital is affected. Since Richard Corporation began operations on January 1, 1984, there were no assets, liabilities, or stockholders' equity at the beginning of the year. Hence, the $35,000 wages *paid* during 1984 must be wages that were incurred during 1984. All $35,000 should be matched against revenue in 1984. In addition, the $8,000 of wages accrued at the end of 1984 should also be matched against revenue in determining income for the year. Note also that working capital is decreased by the $8,000 representing accrued wages because current liabilities are increased; however, cash is not used to pay the $8,000 accrued wages until 1985. Consequently, *income* for 1984 is decreased by $43,000; *working capital* is also decreased by $43,000; but *cash* is decreased by only $35,000 as a result of wage-related transactions.

DEPRECIATION Depreciation expense measures the service utility of noncurrent assets consumed during a period. Depreciation must be matched against revenue in order to measure net income on the accrual basis; however, neither cash nor working capital is affected by recognition of depreciation expense. Consider the following entry:

Depreciation expense	XX	
Accumulated depreciation		XX

Cash and working capital are affected when the depreciable asset is acquired, and perhaps when it is disposed of, if anything is received for it. However, the use of the asset as reflected by recording depreciation does not affect cash or working capital and, therefore, is not a use of funds. The same is true of amortization and depletion.

INCOME TAXES AND OTHER EXPENSES The analysis of other expenses and income taxes is similar to that of wages. As these expenses are accrued, expenses and current liabilities are increased. Therefore, they are matched (deducted) against revenues to determine net income and, at the same time, working capital is decreased. However, cash is affected (reduced) only when these obligations are paid. Since nothing was paid in 1984 regarding these two items, there was no effect on the cash-based SCFP in column 3 of Exhibit 4–2.

FUNDS PROVIDED BY OPERATIONS   Cash provided by operations (or working capital provided by operations) is a most significant figure. This flow is considered to be a relevant indicator of the funds-generating ability of the firm, which is related to its ability to generate cash in the long run.

Cash increased by a gross amount of $430,000 due to operating activity; and it decreased by a gross amount of $290,000, thus increasing the net cash position by $140,000 because of operating activity during the period.

NONOPERATING CHANGES IN FUNDS   In our example, plant, property, and equipment items were acquired by using cash, and dividends were paid in cash. Cash was received through the issuance of common stock and long-term debt. None of these transactions is revenue or expense and none affected net income directly; however, cash and working capital were affected. Therefore, these activities must be reflected in the SCFP.

The Format of the Statement of Changes in Financial Position

Exhibit 4–3 illustrates the two SFCPs in columns 2 and 3 of Exhibit 4–2 in a more conventional disclosure format. The first statement defines funds as cash, whereas the second is prepared using a working-capital definition.

One other point should be made. Note that certain types of activities, such as the acquisition of inventory from suppliers on credit, are *not* reported in the SCFP when funds are defined as working capital. Such transactions are completely within the working capital framework and, therefore, can neither increase nor decrease working capital, as the following entry indicates:

Inventory (current asset)	XX	
Accounts payable (current liability)		XX

This is true of all other events and transactions whose effects are completely within working capital (current assets and current liabilities), such as collections of customers' accounts receivable, payment of any current liability, acquiring inventories for cash, or making prepayments properly classified as current assets. When *only* current accounts are affected, there is no effect on *net* working capital, and, therefore, such transactions are not reflected in the SCFP when funds are defined as working capital.

Special Transactions Not Affecting Funds but Affecting All Financial Resources

Let us now consider one additional aspect of the SCFP so that we can complete our introduction to this statement. Current rules require that a firm's SCFP "disclose all important aspects of its financing and investment activities regardless of whether cash or other elements of working capital are directly affected. For example, acquisitions of property by issuance of securities or in exchange for other property, and conversions of long-term debt or preferred stock to common stock, should be appropriately reflected in the statement."[4]

Given the facts in our example, either of the SCFPs presented would be acceptable under current requirements. The question is, What must be done when certain events take place, such as those described in the preceding paragraph? Up to this point, the SCFP has been described as reflecting what brought about the *net* increase or decrease in cash or working capital. Therefore, an event such as the is-

---

[4] Ibid, par. 8.

EXHIBIT 4–3

RICHARD CORPORATION
Statement of Changes in Financial Position
For the Year Ended December 31, 1984

CASH BASIS

Sources of cash		
From operations		
Net income		$ 92,000
Items not affecting cash		
Add: Depreciation	$ 15,000	
Accrued taxes	50,000	
Accrued wages	8,000	
Other accruals	5,000	78,000
Subtract: Sales not collected in cash	$ 20,000	
Cash payments for inventory in excess of cost of sales	10,000	(30,000)
Total cash from operations		$140,000
Issuance of common stock		300,000
Issuance of long-term debt		100,000
Total increases in cash		$540,000
Uses of cash		
Dividends	$ 20,000	
Acquisition of land	110,000	
Acquisition of buildings	220,000	
Acquisition of machinery and equipment	103,000	
Total decreases in cash		453,000
Net increase in cash during the period		$ 87,000

WORKING CAPITAL BASIS

Sources of working capital		
From operations		
Net income		$ 92,000
Items not affecting working capital		
Add: Depreciation		15,000
Total working capital from operations		$107,000
Issuance of common stock		300,000
Issuance of long-term debt		100,000
Total sources of working capital		$507,000
Uses of working capital		
Dividends	$ 20,000	
Acquisition of land	110,000	
Acquisition of buildings	220,000	
Acquisition of machinery and equipment	103,000	
Total decreases in working capital		453,000
Net increase in working capital during the period		$ 54,000

suance of common stock for $300,000 is reported only once in the SCFP, as a source of cash or working capital.

Consider two additional events besides those already covered in the Richard Corporation example. First, assume that long-term bonds are converted into common stock. The following entry records the transaction:

Long-term debt	100,000	
Common stock		100,000

Neither cash nor working capital is affected by this transaction, but it is a major financial event. Long-term debt decreased by $100,000, and stockholders' equity increased by $100,000. The debt-to-equity relationship has changed; less of the firm's assets will now be provided by creditors, more by owners. Income will increase because of a decrease in interest charges, all else being equal. Because it is a significant financial event, it must be reflected in the SCFP. But how?

This question is best answered by assuming that intermediate cash transactions take place as shown below, but it must be emphasized that these entries are for discussion purposes only and are not actually recorded:

Cash	100,000	
Common stock		100,000
Long-term debt	100,000	
Cash		100,000

These entries do not represent precisely the same economic event as the one reflected before, but they do indicate more clearly what must be done in the SCFP. Funds (in the sense of "all financial resources") were provided because resources increased as a result of the issuance of common stock. Funds (all financial resources) were also used for the retirement of long-term debt. Neither net cash nor net working capital changed, so the working capital and cash figures will remain the same. Consequently, this conversion of long-term debt into common stock can be reflected as both a source and a use of funds in the SCFP, regardless of whether the cash or working capital basis is used. However, the captions could be changed to "financial resources provided" and "financial resources used" or similar titles, such as the following:

Sources of financial resources:	
Issuance of common stock for long-term debt conversions	100,000
Uses of financial resources:	
Reduction of long-term debt through conversion to common stock	100,000

As can be observed, this event would have no impact on the final net figure of $54,000 working capital increase or $87,000 cash increase in the two forms of the SCFP illustrated above.

Consider a second example. Assume that land is exchanged for buildings and the following entry is made:

Buildings	25,000	
Land		25,000

Again *assuming* that intermediate cash transactions had taken place, the following would have been the result:

Cash	25,000	
Land		25,000
Buildings	25,000	
Cash		25,000

In other words, the final effects are as though we had sold the land for $25,000 cash and then used that cash to acquire buildings. Under this assumption, the event must be reflected both under sources and under uses of funds:

Sources of financial resources:	
Exchange of land for buildings	25,000
Uses of financial resources:	
Acquisition of buildings in exchange for land	25,000

The final *net* figure of $54,000 increase in working capital or $87,000 net increase in cash would not be affected by the above event—the source of $25,000 is exactly offset by the use of $25,000.

SUMMARY

In this chapter we have attempted to develop a better understanding of the preparation, presentation, and interpretation of the balance sheet and statement of changes in financial position (SCFP) and the relationships between the three statements. We have discussed the principles and standards that underlie the preparation and presentation of these statements, the meaning of the elements making up the statements, and the way they aid users, at least generally, in making rational economic decisions. We have tried to do these things without making extensive use of procedures, techniques, and examples. In later chapters, we shall examine the specific elements of the balance sheet, income statement, and SCFP and their interrelationships. In Chapter 25 we shall focus on the preparation, presentation, and interpretation of a detailed statement of changes in financial positon.

The balance sheet reflects the financial position of an entity at a point in time. It is a futuristic statement in that it depicts the resources that can be used to the firm's economic advantage and the liabilities that must be liquidated at some time in the future. The net of the assets and liabilities measures the stockholders' interest (the residual claims) in the entity. This information helps users to judge the financial strength of an entity and its future prospects.

But there is also a need for information that reflects the ebb and flow of funds for a period of time. This information is provided in the SCFP. In the statement, funds can be reflected on a cash, working capital, or other acceptable basis. The statement in total, however, must reflect the changes in all financial resources during the period and the major ways of financing those changes, regardless of whether cash or working capital is affected.

Again, an understanding of the major goal, assumptions, and elements of the conceptual model presented in Chapter 2 is helpful in developing an understanding of accounting practice. The balance sheet covered here is designed to be relevant to decision makers who want timely monetary information about an entity in terms of assets, liabilities, and stockholders' (owners') equity. The standard classifications and subsections are meant to add relevance in that a clear picture of those items results. The SCFP also is a response to perceived information needs. Whether it is viewed as giving more detail about the changes in balance sheet items or as a separate freestanding statement, it obviously addresses reasonable questions about the flows of assets, liabilities, and owners' equity.

Some of the guidelines for accounting action from the conceptual model, including historical cost and going concern, are particularly applicable to the balance sheet. In addition, the general and specific standards play a role in the final determination of items to be disclosed. In fact, as we shall see throughout this text, all the elements in the conceptual structure continuously interact to fashion accounting information.

Q4-1 Balance sheets are also sometimes called statements of financial position. Which term do you think best describes this type of financial statement? Give reasons for your answer.

Q4-2 What is the importance of the various possible classifications of ledger accounts in a balance sheet? Pay particular attention to the role of liquidity and the *current* and *noncurrent* distinction.

Q4-3 What is the difference between the "fair values" of assets and the "balance sheet values" of assets?

Q4-4 Why are income statements and statements of changes in financial position called change statements?

Q4-5 Current GAAP allow for flexibility in choosing a definition for funds to be used in SCFPs. Do you think such flexibility is warranted and why?

Q4-6 Although the balance sheet is considered a representation of the "state" of assets, liabilities, and owners' equity of an entity at a point in time, there are numerous instances where accountants must consider forward-looking data to make balance sheet determinations. List some of these instances, and discuss their importance in constructing balance sheets.

Q4-7 What do you think are strengths and weaknesses of cash and working capital as definitions of funds in SCFPs?

Q4-8 Define the concept of the operating cycle, and discuss its importance in balance sheet construction.

Q4-9 Does the balance sheet reflect all the resources of an entity? What elements of the conceptual model discussed in Chapter 2 can aid accountants in making decisions about what is included on balance sheets?

Q4-10 Not all entity obligations are disclosed on balance sheets. In general, what considerations are used to determine which obligations are included as liabilities on balance sheets?

Q4-11 *Owners' equity* is sometimes referred to as a *source of capital* and sometimes as an *obligations to stockholders.* Discuss the pros and cons of each point of view.

Q4-12 If liabilities and equities on balance sheets describe how entity assets were acquired, why can't each individual asset be identified by its particular source?

Q4-13 Distinguish between the entity's obligations to creditors and its obligations to stockholders.

Q4-14 What is the "all financial resources" concept, and how does it affect the construction of the SCFP?

Q4-15 Both the income statement and the SCFP are used to evaluate performance. List the types of users who would probably be most interested in each, and state your reasons.

C4-1 Axco, Inc., a large distributor of paper products, has grown rapidly in recent years. Axco's president is considering raising capital by selling common stock or preferred stock or bonds. She is very concerned about maintaining good relations with the owners of common stock and the bankers who currently have several large loans outstanding.

REQUIRED You, as Axco's business consultant, have been asked to explain briefly the effects that the issuing of common stocks, preferred stocks, and bonds would have on financial statements, with particular emphasis on balance sheet classifications.

C4-2 For over a century Allegro Corporation has manufactured pianos and organs at one location in downtown Baltimore. The original cost of the land on which the factory is located was $250. This item was never entered in

Allegro's accounting records. The factory building was constructed in 1918 at a total cost of $10,000 and that amount is completely depreciated, although the Factory Building account, with a $10,000 balance, still appears on the company's balance sheet along with the Accumulated Depreciation account and its $10,000 balance. A debate has ensued between the president and the controller about the appropriate designation of the factory building on Allegro's balance sheet. The president argues that the current value of the land and building of at least $2,000,000 is evidence that the company should show the real value of the asset on the balance sheet.

REQUIRED Assume that you are the controller and must respond to this argument. Prepare a brief response giving the concepts that support your arguments.

C4–3 Statements of changes in financial position often rely on the working capital definition of *funds*. Working capital, in turn, depends on the definition of *current* and *noncurrent* assets and liabilities. Assume that you, as the controller of a corporation, are asked by the board of directors to explain why funds should not be defined as "the difference between all liquid assets and liabilities due within the next year." Upon reflection, you conclude that the board's definition is not an appropriate concept of funds for use in a SCFP.

REQUIRED Sketch an argument in favor of this conclusion.

C4–4 Micro-computers, Inc., is planning to locate an assembly plant in Texas. Several municipalities have been contacted, and each has shown considerable interest. In general, they have offered to donate plant sites and give the company property tax concessions if the factory is located in their jurisdiction. The question is, If the company accepts such an offer, what balance sheet effects will such donations create? Some members of the accounting staff feel that because the definition of *assets* encompasses all items controlled by the entity and possessing future economic potential, both the site and the tax concessions would be recorded as assets. Others feel that such transactions cannot be booked because no arm's-length transactions (that is, transactions between independent parties in a normal market setting) would have taken place.

REQUIRED As controller, resolve this debate and propose an-acceptable accounting treatment.

C4–5 Two loan officers of a bank are engaged in a debate as to which financial statement information should be used in a loan decision. One officer states that the forecast of cash flows would be better because future cash is to be used to pay off loans. The other states that historic trends of income statements would be better because operations are the major source of new funds that can be used to pay off loans. To shed some light on the debate, the two loan officers ask you, as someone with a background in accounting, to give an opinion as to which financial statement information, either historic or forecasted, would be more relevant in evaluating a loan application.

REQUIRED Give your opinion on this issue.

EXERCISES

E4–1 Consider the balance sheet of the Atkinson Corporation in Exhibit 4–1.

REQUIRED Identify any account titles that are illustrated in one section of the balance sheet but might, under certain conditions, be included elsewhere or might not be included at all. Indicate why the flexibility in balance sheet disclosure or classification that you have noted exists in each case.

E4–2 Refer to the information provided in the Richard Corporation case starting on page 132.

REQUIRED Reconstruct the beginning and ending balance sheets and discuss why the information in the balance sheet alone does not permit the type of analysis provided in the SCFPs in Exhibit 4–2. As an investor, which basis (cash or working capital) of the SCFP statement would you prefer? Why?

E4–3 XYZ Company reported income of $28,000. Included in this income figure were the following items:

1. A loss of $500 on the sale of "temporary investments" that had cost $2,700

2. An expense of $1,300 for estimated bad debts
3. A gain of $3,000 for the cumulative prior years' effect of a change in accounting from straight-line depreciation to sum-of-the-years'-digits depreciation
4. A loss of $1,500 on the write-down of inventory

REQUIRED Indicate very clearly what the impact of these four items would be in the statement of changes in financial position assuming (1) first the working capital basis and (2) then the cash basis.

E4–4 An examination of the records of the Unbalanced Corporation discloses the following information for 1984:

1. Cash balance at December 31, 1984, is $1,000,000. Of this amount, $250,000 is restricted to pay a short-term note and $300,000 is restricted to acquire a new building.
2. In December a customer fell on a patch of ice while leaving the firm's office building. He began legal action in January 1985, suing the firm for $1,000,000. Competent legal counsel indicates he will probably collect $450,000 in damages some time in 1986.
3. The firm has $2,000,000 of bonds outstanding, and bonds worth $500,000 are due November 1, 1985. The remainder are due November 1, 1993. Assume that the firm intends to refinance $300,000 of the $500,000 due November 1, 1985, with other noncurrent obligations and has proved its ability to refinance.
4. Machinery, with an estimated scrap value of $2,000, is included in inventory.
5. Land is included in plant, property, and equipment. It was acquired at a cost of $500,000 and is being held in the hope that its value will increase.

REQUIRED Indicate how these items should be reflected in the balance sheet, and give reasons for your answers.

E4–5 The following is a simple preliminary SCFP:

Sources of working capital		
From operations		
Net income	$150,000	
Add: Depreciation	30,000	
Total working capital from operations	$180,000	
Other sources		
Sale of common stock	200,000	
Total sources of working capital	$380,000	
Uses of working capital		
Dividend payments	45,000	
Acquisition of equipment	180,000	
Total uses of working capital	$225,000	
Net increase in working capital	$155,000	

Other transactions during the period included the acquisition of a factory building by the signing of a 5-year note with a principal amount of $305,000, and the acquisition of land by issuance of 10,000 shares of common stock with a fair value of $35,000.

REQUIRED How would these two transactions be reflected on the SCFP?

PROBLEMS

P4–1 Following is a list of transactions and events:

1. During the year a patent with a book value of $60,000 became worthless and was written off.
2. Fully depreciated machinery with no scrap value was sold for $1,000 cash.
3. Marketable securities (current asset) costing $1,500 were sold for $1,500 cash.

4. Uncollectible accounts receivable of $750 were written off against the allowance for uncollectible accounts.
5. Retained earnings of $500,000 was appropriated for plant expansion.
6. Long-term investments that cost $10,000 were sold for $15,000 (considered an ordinary event).
7. Long-term bonds payable with a book value of $600,000 were converted to common stock with a fair market value of $600,000.

REQUIRED Assume that these events and transactions are independent of one another. For each item, indicate how it would be shown in a statement of changes in financial position prepared in accordance with *APB Opinion No. 19,* including dollar amounts:

1. Assuming the change in cash during the year is to be emphasized
2. Assuming the change in working capital during the year is to be emphasized

P4–2 Accounts of Dimlight Corporation have the following balances as of December 31, 1984:

	DEBIT	CREDIT		DEBIT	CREDIT
Patents	$ 54,200		Buildings—cost	$3,556,000	
Accounts receivable	913,000		Accounts payable		$723,500
Cash surrender value of life			Allowance for uncollectible		
insurance[a]	95,000		accounts		32,500
Accumulated depreciation—			Cash	202,200	
buildings		$196,000	Common stock—$100 par		2,250,000
Income taxes payable		81,300	Additional paid-in capital		261,500
Inventories (lower of cost or			Bonds payable—due 12/31/94		900,000
market)	1,031,400		Unamortized discount—bonds		
Land	720,000		payable	28,700	
Short-term investments (market			Retained earnings—12/31/84		?
value 180,000)	168,000				
Notes Payable—due 11/1/85		850,000			

[a] Although the company has the right to "cash in" the policy for this amount currently, it does not intend to do so in the foreseeable future.

REQUIRED Prepare a balance sheet in good form as of December 31, 1984.

P4–3 The following data were taken from the records of the Neat Corporation for the year ended December 31, 1984:

Sales revenue	$478,000	Merchandise inventory increase	$5,600
Expenses, other than depreciation	412,000	Cash dividends paid	17,000
Depreciation expense	9,500	Cash received on the sale of equipment[a]	14,000
Accounts receivable decrease	2,500	Common stock sold for cash	21,000
Accounts payable increase	3,200	Issued common stock for land (fair market value of	
		stock)	16,000
Purchase of property and equipment (cash)	22,400	Paid off bonds payable	18,000

[a] Equipment was sold for its book value.

REQUIRED

1. Prepare a statement of changes in financial position as required by *APB Opinion No. 19,* emphasizing the change in cash during the period.
2. Prepare a statement of changes in financial position as required by *APB Opinion No. 19,* emphasizing the change in working capital during the period.

P4–4 The following comparative balance sheets of the Fox Company were presented at December 31, 1984.

```
                FOX COMPANY
                Balance Sheets
          For the Years Ended December 31
                                        ($000)

                                     1984      1983

Cash                                 $ 98      $ 60
Accounts receivable                    41        60
Noncurrent investments                 40        50
Patents                                 9        10
Fixed assets                           55        60
Accumulated depreciation             (23)      (40)
                                     $220      $200

Accounts payable                     $  6      $  2
Bonds payable                          45        90
Premium on bonds payable                2         8
Unfunded pension costs (a noncurrent liability)  30   20
Capital stock                          99        50
Retained earnings                      38        30
                                     $220      $200
```

ADDITIONAL INFORMATION

1. Had a gain of $5 on the sale of noncurrent investment
2. Sold fixed assets that had cost $40 (50 percent depreciated) at a $2 loss
3. Retired half of bonds payable on January 2, 1984, in exchange for capital stock
4. Paid cash dividend of $10

REQUIRED   Prepare a *complete* statement of changes in financial position for Fox Company for the year 1984, using the *working capital* basis.

P4-5   Jensen, Inc., has the following history of current account balances over the last year.

```
                          12/31/84    12/31/83

Current assets
  Cash                   $   2,000   $  14,000
  Accounts receivable      200,000     210,000
  Inventory               300,000     400,000
  Prepaid expenses          12,000      10,000
                         $514,000    $634,000

Current liabilities
  Accounts payable         115,000     110,000
  Taxes payable             65,000      50,500
  Warranties payable        22,000      12,800
                         $202,000    $173,300
```

Jensen's 1984 annual report describes a very profitable year with increased sales revenues

REQUIRED

1. Determine how the funds (defined as both cash and working capital) have changed during the year.
2. Explain how such a funds flow result could possibly be associated with a " very profitable year with increased sales revenues."

P4-6   Avon Shipbuilders is expanding its fabricating facilities in Gulfport, Mississippi, by purchasing an old waterfront warehouse that is adjacent to its current facility. The company is planning to tear down the old structure and construct an addition to the existing building. Avon has two choices for completion of the project. It can (1) have its own employees do the work or (2) hire an outside contractor, with the following estimated costs:

	SELF-CONSTRUCTED	OUTSIDE CONTRACTORS
	DIRECT COST OF LABOR AND MATERIALS	TOTAL CONTRACTOR PRICE
1. Demolition of old building	$ 80,000	$110,000
2. Scrap value of old building	(20,000)	(20,000)
3. Preparation of sites for construction including roads and drainage	40,000	60,000
4. Building	420,000	610,000
Total net cost	$520,000	$760,000

Before choosing which course of action to approve, the board of directors wants an explanation of (1) why the costs of the two alternatives are so different and (2) which balance sheet accounts will be affected by the project, including the implications for future depreciation.

REQUIRED

1. Explain the possible reasons for cost differences.
2. Explain how each item listed above would be accounted for initially and after operation commences.

P4–7 On December 31, 1984, the end of its first year of operations, Bartoli Pasta Importers, Inc., has several accounting issues that the assistant controller is uncertain of:

1. Bartoli is obliged to purchase a minimum of $450,000 of product in each month of 1985. The contract is fixed irrespective of Bartoli's sales. As of December 31, 1984, the best estimate is that sales will use up 90 percent of the deliveries in 1985 with 10 percent being added to inventory, and probable sale of the increase in 1986.
2. A fire in the warehouse on August 13, 1984, caused minor damage, but two noncompany contract workers who were severely injured have indicated that they will sue the company for damages. Bartoli's attorneys strongly feel that an out-of-court settlement of $50,000 each will solve the problem. If the trial goes to a jury, the probable damages are estimated to run from a minimum of $20,000 to a maximum of $75,000 for each worker.
3. Bartoli's employees are unionized and their new contract, effective January 1, 1985, calls for an increase in wages amounting to a total of $2,200,000 per year. Because that contract was signed on June 30, 1984, the assistant controller feels that a liability exists on December 31, 1984, for some portion of the increase.

REQUIRED As controller of the company, tell your assistant about the accounting status of each of the above items.

P4–8 McMillion Bookstores has experienced unprecedented growth in the past fiscal year ending on July 31, 1984. To finance the ten new locations opened during the year, the company took the following actions:

1. Issued common stock for $5,000,000
2. Traded common stock of a major corporation with a book value of $400,000, which had been held as a non-current investment, for two new bookstore locations, which were valued at $300,000 each
3. Borrowed $8,000,000 by a long-term mortgage arrangement on six new bookstores
4. Converted $800,000 in loans due to three major stockholders to preferred stocks with a book value of $800,000

REQUIRED Indicate how each of these transactions would be reported on the statement of changes in financial position for the fiscal year ending July 31, 1984.

P4–9 Pipeweed Tobacco Company owns several tobacco farms in Virginia and North Carolina, along with extensive warehousing facilities. At December 31, 1984, its inventory of tobacco products is as follows:

	COST	ESTIMATED AVERAGE TIME UNTIL SALE TO DISTRIBUTORS
1. Finished product, packaged and ready for shipment	$17,010,000	6 weeks
2. Tobacco in the packaging plant	1,100,000	10 weeks
3. Aged tobacco at various locations, ready for shipment to packaging plant	12,770,000	6 months
4. Tobacco in the aging process at various locations	17,000,000	14 months
5. Unharvested tobacco at various farms	20,500,000	16 months

REQUIRED How would each of the above items be reported on Pipeweed's balance sheet? Pay special attention to the current and noncurrent classifications. Give reasons for your answer.

P4–10 Rocky Mountain Ski Suppliers Corporation has several items on its December 31, 1984, balance sheet whose classification has been questioned by its independent auditors:

ITEM	BALANCE SHEET AMOUNT	BALANCE SHEET CLASSIFICATION	OTHER INFORMATION
1. Notes payable	$ 75,000	Noncurrent liability	Half is due on 12/31/85, and half on 12/31/86.
2. Preferred stocks	$500,000	Long-term liability	Dividends of $50,000 per year have been paid regularly for the last 10 years, and the stockholders can convert the preferred stocks to bonds payable at their discretion.
3. Investment in Boeing common stocks	$ 80,000	Long-term investment	Acquired on 7/1/84 and is expected to be sold on 6/30/85 to pay off a note at that time.
4. Building	$450,000	Long-term investment	Acquired during 1981 for use as a factory. Remodeling is scheduled to commence during 1985.
5. Inventory of coal	$102,000	Long-term plant and equipment	Coal is used to generate power. This amount is the minimum balance maintained as a safety margin. All other coal inventory above this amount is classified as current.

REQUIRED Give the proper balance sheet classification for each of the above items, and state the justifications for each.

P4–11 During 1984 Dill Contractors had net income of $550,000. The company reports its SCFP using the cash definition of funds. The following facts are known:

1. Sales included $1,500,000 of credit sales, of which 20 percent was uncollected at December 31, 1984. Accounts receivable had a zero balance at January 1, 1984.
2. Interest receivable was $20,000 on January 1, 1984, and $40,000 on December 31, 1984.
3. Plant and equipment increased by a total of $51,000 during 1984 as the result of a cash purchase.
4. Depreciation expense amounted to $75,500 during 1984.
5. Accounts payable related to inventory of supplies was $85,000 on January 1, 1984, and $75,000 on December 31, 1984. Inventory of supplies was $402,000 on January 1, 1984, and $315,000 on December 31, 1984. All inventory usage was charged to an expense account.
6. On January 15, 1984, Dill sold idle land for $200,000. This land had a book value of $20,000.

REQUIRED Compute Dill's cash from operations on its SCFP, and show how it would appear on the SCFP.

P4–12 Refer to Problem 4–11.

REQUIRED Construct the "working capital from operations" section of the SCFP for Dill Contractors under the assumption that the company defines funds as working capital. Give an explanation for each event.

P4–13 Angel Imports, Inc., is expanding its facilities in downtown Cleveland. It has acquired an old warehouse structure that requires extensive remodeling. The following information is available:

1. Total cost to Angel Imports, Inc., for the old warehouse including the land	$1,500,000
2. Estimated cost to remodel the old warehouse structure	650,000
3. Resale value of land alone if building were removed	1,100,000
4. Estimated cost to demolish the old warehouse	100,000
5. Estimated cost to construct a new warehouse assuming the old one was demolished	600,000

The president decides to remodel the old warehouse and makes the following statement: "The warehouse should be recorded at $1,500,000, and the $650,000 remodeling cost should be expensed during the construction year." You, as controller, are concerned that the president's suggestion violates the definition of assets and that resulting depreciation charges would be overstated.

REQUIRED Draft a counterproposal and justify your suggestions. Show the balance sheet amounts that would result from your suggestions.

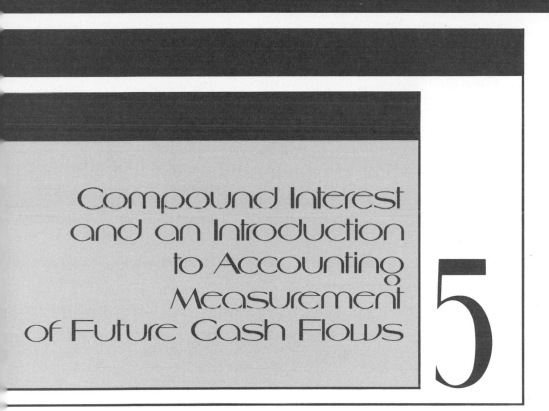

Compound Interest and an Introduction to Accounting Measurement of Future Cash Flows

5

OVERVIEW

In the preceding chapters we emphasized that accounting practices are designed to meet information needs. We also referred to several measurement techniques used to accomplish that goal, including original historic cost, amortized historic cost, and lower-of-cost-or-market value. Other measurement techniques used in accounting as well as in all areas of financial activity are **interest computation** and **compounding.** In this chapter we review the concept of interest and show how many important accounting measurements, including those related to notes, bonds, leases, and pensions, depend on interest computation.

Interest, or **the time value of money,** is a fundamental factor in almost all financial decisions. When money is borrowed, the amount to be paid back at a future point in time will be greater than the initial amount, or **principal.** The difference between the amount borrowed and the total of the payments is the interest charged for the use of money for the period in question. Put another way, the value of money is a function of the time period that elapses between an initial borrowing or lending transaction and the payback of principal. This time value of money concept can be expanded to include all assets to which money amounts are assigned. For example, if a person borrows $1,000 and pays back $1,100 at the end of a time period, $100 is called the interest, or the time value of $1,000 for one period. If a person borrows 2,000 bushels of wheat at the beginning of a period and pays the obligation off at the end of the period with 2,200 bushels of wheat, the 200 bushels can be considered the interest charge for the possession of wheat for one period. In other words, the possession of another person's asset for a time period is seldom free; interest will normally be charged based on the time of possession.

Accountants have adopted a guideline that controls their measurement of future asset flows, which can be stated as follows: In most cases, if the pattern and value of future asset flows is determinable, the time value of money must be considered in any related accounting measurement. As is true of most guidelines, there are exceptions and modifications. In this chapter we introduce various types of compound-interest techniques and show how the "time value of money" affects accounting. In later chapters we discuss the exceptions and modifications.

THE CONCEPT OF INTEREST

Simple Interest   Consider an example of cash flows between Creditor Corporation and Debtor Corporation. The following time line summarizes the transactions:

Transaction	Debtor Corporation borrows $1,000		Debtor Corporation pays $1,160
Time line			
	1/1/84	12/31/84	12/31/85

How was the payment determined? If $1,000 is borrowed and $1,160 is paid back, the $160 is called interest and is the charge for the use of the principal of $1,000. In this case, interest was computed as follows:

Interest charge = (Principal) (Interest rate per period) (Number of time periods)

$160 = ($1,000) (.08) (2)

where $1,000 is the initial amount borrowed, or principal; .08 is the **interest rate** per period demanded by the creditor; and 2 is the number of time periods involved. In this case, the time period is 1 year with the creditor demanding 8 percent per year.

This is an example of **simple interest,** as it involves the payment of interest on the principal only. Debtor Corporation received cash of $1,000 on January 1, 1984, and the payment on December 31, 1985, was for both the principal of $1,000 and the interest charge of $160.

Compound   A more typical contractual pattern occurs when the debtor is charged interest on
Interest   both the original principal and the unpaid interest as of the beginning of a subsequent period. The following time line summarizes transactions involving **compound interest:**

Transaction	Debtor Corporation borrows $1,000	No payment	Debtor Corporation pays $1,166.40
Time line			
	1/1/84	12/31/84	12/31/85

The total interest charge in this compound-interest case is $166.40, which is computed as follows:

```
1984 interest = ($1,000) (.08) (1) =        $80.00
1985 interest = ($1,000) (.08) (1) = 80.00
                 ($80) (.08) (1) =   6.40      86.40
      Total interest charge                 $166.40
```

Again, the total simple-interest charge is $160, whereas the total compound-interest charge is $166.40. The difference of $6.40 is the interest charge on the unpaid interest charge of $80 at the beginning of 1985, which remained unpaid throughout 1985. The dollar amount effect of compounding in this case is $6.40.

The student should carefully compare the two preceding cases, for each is based on unique **contractual terms.** Contractual terms fix the principal, the payback amount, and the time periods. In the simple-interest example, the contractual terms call for one payment that involves interest on the principal only. In the compound-interest example, the terms also require only one payment at the end of the second year including four elements: (1) interest for the use of the principal for the first year, (2) interest for the use of the principal for the second year, (3) interest for the use of the first year's interest for the second year, and (4) the principal amount. Note that the quoted interest rate percentage is the same in both cases, 8 percent, but that the differing contractual terms result in different cash payments.

Throughout this chapter and indeed whenever the time value of money is considered, a clear understanding of the contractual terms is crucial. Notes, bonds, leases, and many other forms of financing transactions have their own typical terms, but even within a category of contracts, such as notes, there can be many different patterns of contractual terms. We will see that in most cases considered in this text, the contracts call for *compound interest.*

FUTURE VALUES AND PRESENT VALUES

Single
Payments

The two preceding examples involved situations in which the payments were known at the outset. Businesses are often faced with the need to compute the necessary payments in accordance with certain contractual terms. For instance, how would the future repayment be computed under the terms of our compound-interest example if it were unknown at the outset?

Transaction   Borrow = $1,000   Repay = Future value
Time line   ├───────────────┼───────────────┤
                      1/1/84   12/31/84   12/31/85

How would the principal be computed if the repayment amount and other contractual terms were known?

Transaction   Borrow = Present value   Repay = $1,166.40
Time line   ├───────────────┼───────────────┤
                      1/1/84   1/31/84   12/31/85

This section introduces the concepts and procedures that answer these and many other similar questions.

The $1,166.40 in the compound-interest example is called the **future value** of the principal of $1,000 with interest at 8 percent compounded annually. For example, if you were to make a single deposit of $1,000 in a savings account that earns 8 percent per year and if you left it there for 2 full years, your savings account balance would grow from $1,000 to $1,166.40 by the end of the second year, assuming no withdrawals were made.

Alternatively, the $1,000 can be viewed as the **present value** of the $1,166.40 future amount, again assuming an 8 percent annually compounded interest rate. An investor who wants an 8 percent return on an investment is said to be indifferent between having the use of $1,000 today and receiving $1,166.40 two years in the future. These relationships can be stated algebraically as follows:

The **future value** (F) of a present amount is expressed as

$$F/P = (P)(1 + i)^n \text{ where } F = \text{ the future value}$$

$$P = \text{ the present value}$$
$$F/P = \text{ the notation for the future value of a present amount}$$
$$i = \text{ the interest rate per time period}$$
$$n = \text{ the number of time periods}$$

Substituting in our example:

$$F/P = (\$1,000)(1 + .08)^2$$
$$= (\$1,000)(1.1664)$$
$$= \$1,166.40$$

The **present value** (P) of a future (F), noted P/F, can likewise be represented algebraically:

$$P/F = (F) \left(\frac{1}{(1 + i)^n} \right)$$

Substituting in our example:

$$P/F = (\$1,166.40) \left(\frac{1}{(1 + .08)^2} \right)$$

$$= (\$1,166.40) \left(\frac{1}{1.1664} \right)$$

$$= (\$1,166.40)(.8573)$$
$$= \$1,000 \text{ (rounded)}$$

Note the inverse relationship of the present and future values, that is, $P/F = 1/(F/P)$. In our example, the factor for P/F is the inverse of the factor for F/P, that is, $.8573 = 1/1.1664$.

Compound-Interest Tables

Rather than make computations for each transaction, it is often convenient to turn to precomputed factors in tables such as those in Appendix H at the end of the book or to enter the variable into a calculator that is capable of making the necessary algebraic computation.

Compound-interest Table H-1 in Appendix H is titled "The Future Value of a Present Amount of 1 (F/P)." The columns are headed so that the appropriate factor can be found if we know the interest rate (i) and the number of periods (n). Recall that our algebraic computation gave us the following:

$$F/P = (\$1,000)(\underline{1.1664}) = \$1,166.40$$

The 1.1664 is the same as the factor in Table H−1 under the column (i) labeled "8%" and across on the row (n) labeled "2."

Compound-interest Table H−2 in Appendix H is titled "The Present Value of a Future Amount of 1 (P/F)." In our example, the algebraic computation gave us the following:

$$P/F = (\$1,166.40)(\underline{.8573}) = \$1,000 \quad \text{(rounded)}$$

The .8573 is the same as the factor in Table H−2 under the column labeled "8%" and the row labeled "2."

Certain calculators are programmed to make the same computations used in computing the factors in compound-interest tables. Typically we are required to input the interest rate, i; the numbers of periods, n; the present or future amount; and the function desired, such as F/P or P/F.

To familiarize yourself with the use of compound-interest tables, consider the case of Mr. Smith, who has $50,000 in cash on January 1, 1984, and is looking forward to his retirement on December 31, 1988. He wonders how much he could expect to accumulate in a savings account if the interest rate were 12 percent compounded annually.

For purposes of communicating, it is helpful to standardize the notation. Let the notation (F/P, n, i) mean "the future value (F) of a present amount (P) at a compound interest rate (i) for (n) periods." This notation makes utilization of the table more convenient:

$$(F/P, 5, .12) = \text{Table H−1 factor when } n = 5 \text{ and } i = .12$$
$$= (1.7623)$$

If Mr. Smith had only $1.00 to invest, the future value of that dollar would be $1.76. The present value of Smith's actual investment is given at $50,000, and the future value would be noted and computed as follows:

$$P(F/P, n, i) =$$
$$\$50,000 \, (F/P, 5, .12) =$$
$$\$50,000 \, (1.7623) = \$88,115$$

Again, the notation $P(F/P, n, i)$ contains the necessary information for location of the factor in a table and the computation for the future value of a present amount. F/P can be interpreted as the process of computing a future amount, F, if we know the present amount, P. F/P can also be interpreted as the identification of the table to be used.

Let us review this notation scheme for the future value of a present amount, as the same general form will be used in all of our other examples.

General notation: $P(F/P, n, i)$				
Interpretation:	P is a known present value	F/P identifies the appropriate table	n identifies the appropriate row in the table	i identifies the appropriate column in the table
Data from our example:	$50,000	Table H–1	$n = 5$	$i = 12\%$

Note the symmetry of the present and future value amounts on a time line:

Transaction	Smith deposits $F(P/F, 5, .12) = \$50,000$	Smith withdraws $P(F/P, 5, .12) = \$88,115$
Time line	1/1/84	12/31/88

On January 1, 1984, the present value of $50,000 is known. In order to compute the value in 5 years given a 12 percent interest rate, the $50,000 is multiplied by the appropriate factor, which is $(F/P, 5, .12)$, or 1.7623. The product of $50,000 and 1.7623 is the future value, $88,115. Alternatively, if on January 1, 1984, it is known that the future value at the end of 5 years is $88,115, the present value could be computed by multiplying the $88,115 by the appropriate factor, which is $(P/F, 5, .12)$, or .5674 (see Table H–2). The factor .5674 means that $1.00 to be received in 5 years is worth only $.57 today. The product of ($88,115)(.5674) is the present value, or $50,000 (rounded).

The impact of varying interest rates The interest rate used in the computations is critical to the determination of present and future values. Interest rate selection depends on a combination of the personal choice of the investor and the range of interest rates available in the market. An investor who feels that an investment is very safe will be satisfied with a relatively lower interest rate. However, an investor who feels that an investment is risky will insist on a relatively higher interest rate. The actual interest rate is determined by the market, which reflects the desires of potential creditors and debtors.

We shall see later that the rational determination of implicit interest rates in some transactions becomes crucial to the proper recognition of certain assets, liabilities, revenues, and expenses.

Every borrowing and lending transaction has an effective interest rate that can be used to equate the present value to the future value. In other words, both borrowers and lenders are assumed to be rational economic people who have computed the value of cash flows at the interest rate they feel they can obtain before they enter into a financial arrangement. In some cases, the effective interest rate is explicit, as in a $1,000 note payable in 1 year with interest at 10 percent. In other cases, the interest rate is not stated explicitly, but it is implied by the contractual terms. For instance, if you purchase an item and promise to pay $1,100 in 1 year, what is the cost of the item today? If 10 percent is the interest rate, then $(P/F, 1, .10)\$1,100 = \$1,000$; but if 10 percent is not stated, how do you know that 10 percent is the true rate? This is usually handled by answering the question, What interest rate equates the future payment with the current fair value of the item? If the current fair value of the item is $1,000, then the true interest rate is 10 percent. If the current fair value, however, is $982, the interest rate necessary to equate $982 to $1,100 a year hence is 12 percent.

This can be computed by use of the algebraic formula for present value and by solving for i. The formula is

$$P/F = F\left(\frac{1}{(1 + i)^n}\right)$$

Solving for i with facts of the current case:

$$\$982 = \$1,100\left(\frac{1}{(1 + i)^1}\right)$$

$$\$982\left(\frac{(1 + i)^1}{1}\right) = \$1,100$$

$$\$982 + \$982(i) = \$1,100$$

$$\$982(i) = \$1,100 - \$982$$

$$i = \$118/\$982$$

$$i = 12\%$$

Unknown interest rates, such as those in the preceding example, can also be computed with the aid of the compound-interest tables as follows:

$$(P/F, 1, i)\ \$1,100 = \$982$$

$$(P/F, 1, i) = \frac{\$982}{\$1,100}$$

$$(P/F, 1, i) = .8927$$

The factor .8927 in Table H−2 for 1 year is closest to the 12 percent factor; therefore, $(P/F, 1, .12)\$1,100 = \$982$. By the same logic:

$$(F/P, 1, i)\ \$982 = \$1,100$$

$$(F/P, 1, i) = \frac{\$1,100}{\$982}$$

$$(F/P, 1, i) = 1.1201$$

Again, the factor 1.1201 in Table H−1 for 1 year is also closest to the 12 percent factor. These equalities demonstrate that the algebraic computation is the basis for the table factors and that it is assumed that there is an indifference between future and present values if the desired interest rate can be earned.

We shall see throughout this book that the determination of the interest rate implicit in a contract is critical to the proper determination of book value and revenue and expense amounts.

A critical point is that varying interest rates will have a direct effect on the present and future values. If Mr. Smith were to invest his $50,000 at a 10 percent interest rate for 5 years instead of 12 percent, the future value of his savings would decrease by $7,590.

	10%		12%
$P(F/P, n, i)$	$= \$50,000\ (F/P,\ 5,\ .10)$	$P(F/P, n, i)$	$= \$50,000\ (F/P,\ 5,\ .12)$
	$= \$50,000(1.6105)$		$= \$50,000(1.7623)$
	$= \$80,525$		$= \$88,115$

In the same vein, if Mr. Smith were to invest in a plan that would result in a $66,911 receipt at the end of 5 years, how much would he pay currently for such a plan if he desired 10 percent? If he desired 12 percent? He would have to compute the present values of the future sum of $66,911 as follows:

	10%		12%
$F(P/F, n, i)$	$= \$66,911(P/F,\ 5,\ .10)$	$F(P/F, n, i)$	$= \$66,911(P/F,\ 5,\ .12)$
	$= \$66,911(.6209)$		$= \$66,911(.5674)$
	$= \$41,545$		$= \$37,965$

Ordinary Annuities

The techniques covered to this point are used to determine the present and future values of single payments; however, accountants must often deal with payment schedules that include series of payments. When these are in the form of equal periodic installments, they are called **annuities,** or **rents.** The present and future values of annuities can be computed using much the same techniques as those previously described. This equal-payment pattern is very common for financing such arrangements as mortgages and leases. Payments that come at the end of each period are called **ordinary annuities;** payments that come at the beginning of each period are called **annuities due.**

Present value of an ordinary annuity   To introduce the techniques of measuring present and future values of annuities, consider the following simple example of an ordinary annuity in which Debtor Corporation borrows $4,000 on January 1, 1984, and pays $1,207.68 at the end of each of four consecutive years:

Transaction	Debtor Corporation borrows $4,000	Debtor Corporation pays $1,207.68	Debtor Corporation pays $1,207.68	Debtor Corporation pays $1,207.68	Debtor Corporation pays $1,207.68
Time line	1/1/84	12/31/84	12/31/85	12/31/86	12/31/87

The $4,000 is the present value of an annuity of $1,207.68 for 4 years at an interest rate of 8 percent with *annual compounding.* An analysis of the components of the four annuity payments gives the interest and principal components. First, what is the total interest charge for all 4 years?

Total payments = ($1,207.68)(4)	= $4,830.72	
Principal	4,000.00	
Total interest charge	$ 830.72	

What is the interest charge and reduction in principal for each year?

		COMPUTATION		DEBTOR'S LIABILITY BALANCE
1984	Unpaid balance at 1/1/84	$4,000.00	1/1/84	$4,000.00
	Interest rate	.08		
	Interest charge for 1984	$ 320.00		
	Payment 12/31/84	$1,207.68		
	Interest charge	320.00		
	Reduction in principal	$ 887.68		887.68
			12/31/84	3,112.32
1985	Unpaid balance at 1/1/85 ($4,000 − 887.68)	$3,112.32		
	Interest rate	.08		
	Interest charge for 1985	$ 248.99		
	Payment at 12/31/85	$1,207.68		
	Interest charge	248.99		
	Reduction in principal	$ 958.69		958.69
			12/31/85	2,153.63
1986	Unpaid balance at 1/1/86 ($3,112.32 − 958.69)	$2,153.63		
	Interest rate	.08		
	Interest charge for 1906	$ 172.29		
	Payment at 12/31/86	$1,207.68		
	Interest charge	172.29		
	Reduction in principal	$1,035.39		1,035.39
			12/31/86	1,118.24
1987	Unpaid balance at 1/1/87 ($2,153.63 − 1,035.39)	$1,118.24		
	Interest rate	.08		
	Interest charge for 1987	$ 89.46		
	Payment at 12/31/87	$1,207.68		
	Interest charge for	89.44[a]		
	Reduction in principal	$1,118.24		1,118.24
			12/31/87	$ 0

[a] Rounded.

Algebraically, the present value of an annuity is computed as follows:

$$A \left(\frac{1 - \frac{1}{(1 + i)^n}}{i} \right)$$

Substituting in the example, the present value of four annual payments of $1,207.68 at 8 percent interest would be computed as follows:

$$\$1,207.68 \left(\frac{1 - \frac{1}{(1 + .08)^4}}{.08} \right) =$$

$$\$1,207.68 \left(\frac{1 - \frac{1}{1.36049}}{.08} \right) =$$

$$\$1,207.68 \ (3.3121) = \$4,000 \text{ (rounded)}$$

As in the case for present and future values of a single payment, tables are available for the present and future values of ordinary annuities. Table H–3 in Appendix H is titled "The Present Value of an Ordinary Annuity of 1(P/A)." Using the same notation as before for the current example, the computation of the present value of the annuity using Table H–3 is as follows:

$$A(P/A, n, i)$$

where A is the annuity amount, and $(P/A, n, i)$ is the factor from Table H–3 that is used to compute the present value of an annuity for n periods at an interest rate i. Substituting in the example:

$$\$1,207.68(P/A, 4, .08) =$$
$$\$1,207.68(3.3121) = \$4,000 \quad \text{(rounded)}$$

Note that the factor 3.3121 is from the column labeled "8%" and the row labeled "4," and that it is the same as the factor from the algebraic computation. The factor 3.3121 (or \$3.31 for monetary computations) represents the present value of 1 (or \$1.00) to be received at the end of the 4 consecutive years. When applied to the four \$1,207.68 annuity payments, these four payments have a present value of \$4,000.

It must be emphasized that the interest rate is an important consideration. If, for instance, in the annuity example a 10 percent interest rate is used, the present value takes on a lower amount:

$$\$1,207.68(P/A, 4, .10) =$$
$$\$1,207.68(3.1699) = \$3,828.22$$

How much would an investor be willing to pay for an annuity of \$1,207.68 at the end of 4 consecutive years under alternative 1, which provides 8 percent interest, and under alternative 2, which provides 10 percent interest?

Alternative 1

Transaction	Pays $A(P/A, 4, .08)$ $\$4,000$	Receives $\$1,207.68$	Receives $\$1,207.68$	Receives $\$1,207.68$	Receives $\$1,207.68$
Time line	⊢	+	+	+	⊣
	1/1/84	12/31/84	12/31/85	12/31/86	12/31/87

Alternative 2

Transaction	Pays $A(P/A, 4, .10)$ $\$3,828.22$	Receives $\$1,207.68$	Receives $\$1,207.68$	Receives $\$1,207.68$	Receives $\$1,207.68$
Time line	⊢	+	+	+	⊣
	1/1/84	12/31/84	12/31/85	12/31/86	12/31/87

We see that the investor would be willing to pay \$4,000 if an 8 percent return is desired and \$3,828.22 if a 10 percent return is desired.

The series of payments presented here is kept simple to facilitate discussion. However, the patterns of payments, the methods of computation, and the considerations regarding time value of money are basically the same for real-world situations such as pension or annuity insurance programs where a series of equal future payments is promised and a current payment is computed.

For instance, how much would an insurance company charge on January 1, 1984, for a fixed annuity of $20,000 per year payable at the end of each year from December 31, 1984, through the death of the beneficiary if the insurer used a 10 percent rate? The first question that must be answered is, How many periods are involved? Assume that the actuaries estimate a 20-year remaining life at January 1, 1984. Computation of the amount of the principal payment at January 1, 1984, is as follows:

Transaction	Insurance company receives $A(P/A,\ 20,\ .10)$ $20,000\ (8.5136)$ $170,272$	Insurance company pays $20,000	Insurance company pays $20,000
Time line	├────────────────	──────┼────────── ↘	↙──────────┤
	1/1/84	12/31/84	12/31/03 (year 2003)

The insurance company would receive $170,272 on January 1, 1984, and would pay out $20,000 at the end of each of the next 20 years starting on December 31, 1984. To the extent that the insurance company can earn more than 10 percent on the investment of the principal, the transaction will make a contribution to its costs and profit.

SEMIANNUAL ANNUITY PAYMENTS   Another crucial factor is the **timing** of payments. Assume that Debtor Corporation borrows $4,000 on January 1, 1984, that eight equal semiannual payments of $594.12 are required, and that the interest rate is 8 percent *compounded each 6 months*. The time line would be as follows:

Transaction	Borrow $4,000	Pay $594.12	Pay $594.12	Pay $594.12	Pay $594.12	Pay $594.12	Pay $594.12	Pay $594.12	Pay $594.12
Time line	├──	──┼──	──┼──	──┼──	──┼──	──┼──	──┼──	──┼──	──┤
	1/1/84	6/30/84	12/31/84	6/30/85	12/31/85	6/30/86	12/31/86	6/30/87	12/31/87

The present value of $594.12 in eight consecutive payments at 6-month intervals at an interest rate of 8 percent compounded each 6 months is computed as follows:

$$\$594.12(P/A,\ 8,\ .04) =$$
$$\$594.12(6.7328) = \$4,000 \quad \text{(rounded)}$$

The following comparison highlights the effects of going from an annual annuity to a semiannual annuity in the example:

	ANNUAL PAYMENTS	SEMIANNUAL PAYMENTS
Number of payments	4	8
Length of period	1 year	6 months
Interest rate	8% compounded annually	8% compounded semiannually
Notation for the present-value factor	$(P/A,\ 4,\ .08)$	$(P/A,\ 8,\ .04)$

As can be seen, both interest rate percentages are 8 percent. The "compounded **annually**" versus "compounded **semiannually**" terms, however, make the crucial difference.

If the interest rate were said to be "8 percent compounded **quarterly**," the present-value notation would be $(P/A, 16, .02)$. Note that the number of periods has doubled over the semiannual case and the interest rate has once more been halved.

Future value of an ordinary annuity   A closely related problem is the determination of the future value of an annuity. For instance, assume that $1,000 was deposited at the end of 5 consecutive years, that is, an ordinary annuity of $1,000 for 5 years at an annual interest rate of 8 percent as characterized by a time line:

Transaction		Deposit $1,000	Deposit $1,000	Deposit $1,000	Deposit $1,000	Deposit $1,000
Time line	1/1/84	12/31/84	12/31/85	12/31/86	12/31/87	12/31/88

If no withdrawals were made, how much would be in the fund at the end of the fifth year? Using the factors provided in Appendix H's Table H–4, which is titled "The Future Value of an Ordinary Annuity of 1 (F/A)," and the standard notation, the future value of the annuity would be computed as follows:

$$A(F/A, i, n) =$$
$$\$1,000(F/A, 5, .08) =$$
$$\$1,000(5.8666) = \$5,867 \quad \text{(rounded)}$$

The $5,867 is the future value of an annuity of $1,000 at 8 percent for 5 years, the factor for which is found in Table H–4. This can be computed algebraically as follows:

$$\$1,000 \left(\frac{(1 + i)^n - 1}{i} \right) =$$
$$\$1,000 \left(\frac{(1 + .08)^5 - 1}{.08} \right) =$$
$$\$1,000 \left(\frac{1.46933 - 1}{.08} \right) =$$

$$\$1,000 \, (5.8666) = \$5,867 \text{ (rounded)}$$

The computation of the present and future values of annuities, therefore, closely parallels the computation of the present and future values of single amounts:

	NOTATION	FACTOR TABLE
The future value of a present amount	F/P	H–1
The present value of a future amount	P/F	H–2
The present value of an annuity	P/A	H–3
The future value of an annuity	F/A	H–4

AN INTRODUCTION TO ACCOUNTING FOR FUTURE CASH FLOWS

In this section we describe how accountants measure, record, and disclose transactions involving future cash flows. First we discuss the general rules that govern the disclosure of receivables and payables, and then we give examples of the schedules, journal entries, and disclosures that are typical for various transactions.

In general, if an entity has the right to receive, or the obligation to pay, cash in the future, the following rules apply:

1. The net book value of the receivable or payable appearing on a balance sheet must be equal to the present value of future cash flows.
2. The interest income or expense appearing on the income statement must be based on the effective interest rate applied to the net book value of the receivable or payable outstanding during the period in question.

These general rules apply to most financing transactions, such as mortgages, notes, bonds, and leases. Although our discussion is in terms of cash flows, it should be understood that receivables and payables may be paid off with other assets. In those cases, the same general rules apply if the future value of the asset is known. For instance, if an entity agrees to accept, as payment of a receivable due in 2 years, title to land that can reasonably be expected to have a fair value of $200,000 at the end of 2 years, the receivable would be carried at an amount equal to the present value of the $200,000. Such situations are not as common as those requiring cash transfers, but they do occur and will be discussed in later sections of this book.

Accounting for Compound-Interest, Single-Payment Transactions

Refer back to the compound-interest example beginning on page 148 pertaining to the Debtor and Creditor corporations. On January 1, 1984, Debtor borrows $1,000 from Creditor and pays back $1,166.40 on December 31, 1985. Note again that nothing is paid on December 31, 1984. The following journal entries and disclosure patterns demonstrate how the general rules are applied:

DEBTOR CORPORATION				CREDITOR CORPORATION			
		DEBIT	CREDIT			DEBIT	CREDIT
1/1/84	Cash	1,000		Notes receivable		1,000	
	Notes payable		1,000	Cash			1,000
12/31/84	Interest expense	80		Interest receivable		80	
	Interest payable		80	Interest revenue			80

Partial Balance Sheet 12/31/84			Partial Balance Sheet 12/31/84		
CURRENT LIABILITIES			**CURRENT ASSETS**		
Notes payable	$1,000		Notes receivable	$1,000	
Interest payable	80	$1,080	Interest receivable	80	$1,080
Partial Income Statement for 1984			Partial Income Statement for 1984		
EXPENSES			**REVENUES**		
Interest expense		80	Interest revenue		80

In this case, the "net" payable on the books of Debtor and the "net" receivable on the books of Creditor are both $1,080. This is consistent with the general rule for valuing future cash flows. On December 31, 1984, the future cash flow is $1,166.40, and applying the factor from Table H−2 it can be seen that the present value (on December 31, 1984) is $1,080:

$$F(P/F, n, i) =$$
$$\$1,166.40(P/F, 1, .08) =$$
$$\$1,166.40(.9259) = \$1,080 \quad \text{(rounded)}$$

In 1985, the following journal entries and income statement disclosures take place:

DEBTOR CORPORATION	DEBIT	CREDIT	CREDITOR CORPORATION	DEBIT	CREDIT
12/31/85 Interest expense	86.40		Cash	1,166.40	
Notes payable	1,000.00		Interest income		86.40
Interest payable	80.00		Notes receivable		1,000.00
Cash		1,166.40	Interest receivable		80.00
Partial Income Statement for 1985			**Partial Income Statement for 1985**		
Expenses			*Revenues*		
Interest expense		$86.40	Interest revenue		$86.40

Recall that the interest charge for any accounting period is based on the interest rate applied to the net book value of the payable or receivable at the beginning of the accounting period. In the current example, on January 1, 1985, the net book value was $1,080, that is, the present value on January 1, 1985, of $1,166.40 in 1 year. The interest computation for year 2 can be viewed as follows:

$$i[F(P/F, n, i)] =$$
$$.08 \ [\$1,166.40(.9259)] =$$
$$.08(\$1,080) = \$86.40$$

Accounting for Annuities   Referring back to the annuity example on page 154, assume that the Debtor Corporation borrows $4,000 on January 1, 1984, and promises to pay back $1,207.68 at the end of each year for 4 years. The journal entries for each party are as follows:

DEBTOR CORPORATION			CREDITOR CORPORATION		
1/1/84 Cash	4,000.00		1/1/84 Notes receivable	4,000.00	
Notes payable		4,000.00	Cash		4,000.00
12/31/84 Interest expense	320.00		12/31/84 Cash	1,207.68	
Notes payable	887.68		Interest income		320.00
Cash		1,207.68	Notes receivable		887.68
12/31/85 Interest expense	248.99		12/31/85 Cash	1,207.68	
Notes payable	958.69		Interest income		248.99
Cash		1,207.68	Notes receivable		958.69
12/31/86 Interest expense	172.29		12/31/86 Cash	1,207.68	
Notes payable	1,035.39		Interest income		172.29
Cash		1,207.68	Notes receivable		1,035.39
12/31/87 Interest expense	89.44		12/31/87 Cash	1,207.68	
Notes payable	1,118.24		Interest income		89.44
Cash		1,207.68	Notes receivable		1,118.24

The book value of the receivable and payable at any disclosure date will be equal to the present value of future cash flows. Take the December 31, 1984, point in time. The future cash flows at that point are $1,207.68 for 3 years. The Table H−3 factor of 2.5771 applied to the annuity of $1,207.68 gives a book value of $3,112.32 (rounded).

An analysis of the notes payable and receivable ledger accounts of Debtor and Creditor corporations would confirm this:

DEBTOR CORPORATION			CREDITOR CORPORATION		
1/1/84	Initial notes payable	$4,000.00	1/1/84	Initial notes receivable	$4,000.00
12/31/84	Entry to reduce notes payable	887.68	12/31/84	Entry to reduce notes receivable	887.68
12/31/84	Net liability	$3,112.32	12/31/84	Net receivable	$3,112.32

These general relationships will apply for all cases where the schedule of payments and interest rates is known. Such relationships can be clarified through the use of **amortization** schedules. The following is such an amortization schedule from the debtor's point of view:

	(1) CASH RECEIPT (PAYMENT)	(2) INTEREST EXPENSE	(3) REDUCTION IN PAYABLE	(4) BOOK VALUE OF PAYABLE
1/1/84	$ 4,000.00			$4,000.00
12/31/84	(1,207.68)	$320.00	$ 887.68	3,112.32
12/31/85	(1,207.68)	248.99	958.69	2,153.63
12/31/86	(1,207.68)	172.29	1,035.39	1,118.24
12/31/87	(1,207.68)	89.44	1,118.24	0
	(830.72)	830.72	4,000.00	

This kind of schedule will be used extensively throughout this book, and, therefore, the basic relationships must be understood.

Column 1 lists the contractual cash flows to and from the specific entity.

Column 2 lists the interest charge for each period. Interest is computed by multiplying the *effective* interest rate by the previous column 4 balance. For example, the interest due on December 31, 1984, is (.08)($4,000).

Column 3 lists the reduction in principal as the result of the payment in question. For December 31, 1984, the payment is $1,207.68 and the interest charge is $320.00. The difference ($1,207.68 − $320.00 = $887.68) is subtracted from the previous amount in column 4 to arrive at the new payable balance.

Column 4 contains the present values of future cash flows at the point of time indicated (with rounding error):

| 1/1/84 | $4,000.00 $= A(P/A, 4, .08)$ |
| | $4,000.00^a = \$1,207.68(3.3121)$ |

| 12/31/84 | $3,112.32 = \$1,207.68(P/A, 3, .08)$ |
| | $3,112.32^a = \$1,207.68(2.5771)$ |

| 12/31/85 | $2,153.63 = \$1,207.68(P/A, 2, .08)$ |
| | $2,153.63^a = \$1,207.68(1.7833)$ |

| 12/31/86 | $1,118.24 = \$1,207.68(P/A, 1, .08)$ |
| | $1,118.24^a = \$1,207.68(.9259)$ |

[a] Rounded.

The particular formats and column headings are often modified because of differing accounting conventions and factual situations, but the basic relationships are quite similar for all applications in this text.

SPECIAL PROBLEMS WITH COMPOUND-INTEREST FACTORS

Annuities Due   When payments for annuities are made at the end of the period, the payments are called **ordinary annuities.** When payments are made at the beginning of the period, the payments are called **annuities due.** Tables H–3 and H–4 in Appendix H, which provide factors for the computation of present and future values of ordinary annuities, cannot be used to compute present and future annuities due without modification. The following example demonstrates how these modifications are made. Assume that Borrower, Inc., purchased office equipment on January 1, 1984. The equipment has a selling price of $4,000 and is paid for in four equal installments of $1,118. The first installment is in the form of a down payment, and the remaining three are paid on consecutive year-ends. The following amortization schedule based on an 8 percent interest rate summarizes the relevant facts (all money amounts have been rounded to the nearest dollar):

	(1) RECEIPT (PAYMENT)	(2) INTEREST EXPENSE	(3) REDUCTION (INCREASE) IN PAYABLE	(4) BOOK VALUE OF PAYABLE
1/1/84	$ 4,000			$4,000
1/1/84	(1,118)		$1,118	2,882
12/31/84		$231	(231)	3,113
1/1/85	(1,118)		1,118	1,995
12/31/85		160	(160)	2,155
1/1/86	(1,118)		1,118	1,037
12/31/86		81[a]	(81)	1,118
1/1/87	(1,118)		1,118	0
	$(472)	$472	$4,000	

[a] Rounding error.

The basic relationships observed for an amortization schedule for an ordinary annuity exist here for an annuity due. The interest charge for each period (column 2) is the 8 percent interest rate multiplied by the book value of the payable at the beginning of the period (column 4); and column 4 amounts are the present value of future cash flows at each point in time. For instance, the interest charge on December 31, 1985, is $(0.8)(\$1,995) = \$160$. The $1,995 amount is the present value of future cash flows on January 1, 1985:

$$A(P/A, 2, .08) =$$
$$\$1,118(1.7833) = \$1,995 \quad \text{(rounding error)}$$

The $3,113 column 4 amount on December 31, 1984, is $1,995 plus the January 1, 1985, payment of $1,118.

The present value of an annuity due can be computed using Table H–3 factors with the following modification: An ordinary annuity assumes year-end payments and is noted $A(P/A, n, i)$, whereas an annuity due assumes beginning-of-the-period payments and is noted $A[(P/A, n - 1, i) + 1)]$.

The factor from Table H–3 would then be $(P/A, n - 1, i)$, or in the example, $(P/A, 3, .08)$, which is 2.5771. The present value would thus be computed as follows:

$$\$1,118(2.5771 + 1) =$$
$$\$1,118(3.5771) = \$4,000 \quad \text{(rounded)}$$

To reiterate, an annuity due has an immediate down payment that is of the same amount as the equal period-end payments. In our example, the time line clearly shows this:

Transaction	Borrow $4,000 Pay $1,118	Pay $1,118	Pay $1,118	Pay $1,118
Time line	⊢—————————	——+———————	——+———————	——————+
	1/1/84	12/31/84	12/31/85	12/31/86

Observe that payments 2, 3, and 4 constitute an ordinary annuity whose present value can be computed using the ordinary annuity table as follows:

$$\$1,118(P/A, 3, .08) =$$
$$\$1,118(2.5771) = \$2,882 \quad \text{(rounded)}$$

What is the total present value of all four payments?

Present value of the three ordinary annuity payments	= $2,882
Plus the present value of the down payment	= 1,118
Total present value of all payments	= $4,000

A slight computational efficiency is gained by the factor modification technique:

$$A[(P/A, n - 1, .08) + 1] =$$
$$\$1,118(2.5771 + 1) =$$
$$\$1,118(3.5771) = \$4,000$$

Put another way,

$$A + A(P/A, n - 1, .08) = A[(P/A, n - 1, .08) + 1]$$
$$\$1,118 + \$1,118(P/A, 3, .08) = \$1,118[(P/A, 3, .08) + 1]$$
$$\$1,118 + \$1,118(2.5771) = \$1,118(2.5771 + 1)$$
$$\$4,000 = \$4,000$$

Sinking Fund Factors

Accountants sometimes must compute the annuity payments necessary to liquidate a future amount or to accumulate an amount of assets to be used for a specific purpose, often called a **sinking fund.** For instance, Investor Corporation must replace an asset at the end of 4 years, and it is estimated that $100,000 will be required at that time. How much should be set aside at the end of each of the 4 years if the interest rate on the money set aside is 8 percent?

This general problem type is noted A/F, or an annuity equal to a future value. In this case, the specific notation is $F(A/F, 4, .08)$. The factor necessary is the inverse of the factor in Table H–4 for the future value of an annuity, or $1/(F/A, 4, .08)$. We solve the problem as follows:

$$F \left(\frac{1}{(F/A, \, 4, \, .08)} \right) =$$

$$\$100,000 \left(\frac{1}{4.5061} \right) =$$

$$\$100,000 \, (.22192) = \$22,192$$

This can be verified by multiplying the $22,192 by the factor for the future value of an annuity:

$$A(F/A, \, 4, \, .08) = \$22,192(4.5061) = \$100,000 \quad \text{(rounded)}$$

Capital Recovery Factors Business owners and managers would often like to know what equal amounts could be withdrawn from a fund over a fixed number of periods. For instance, Company A owns a savings certificate of $50,000, which earns 8 percent interest. How much could be withdrawn in equal installments over a 5-year period? The factors in Table H–3 for the present value of an annuity can be used to solve this problem as follows. The factor for an annuity equal to a present value (A/P) is the inverse of the factor for the present value of an annuity, or $1/(P/A, \, 5, \, .08)$. We solve the problem as follows:

$$\$50,000 \left(\frac{1}{(P/A, \, 5, \, .08)} \right) =$$

$$\$50,000 \left(\frac{1}{3.9927} \right) =$$

$$50,000 \, (.25046) = \$12,523$$

The present value of this annuity is computed as follows as a check on the computation:

$$(\$12,523)(3.9927) = \$50,000 \quad \text{(rounded)}$$

Note that if $12,523 is withdrawn from the fund at the end of 5 consecutive years, the fund will have a zero balance at the end of the fifth year. Capital recovery factors, therefore, allow computation of the *maximum* annuity that could be withdrawn from a fund over a known period and for a given effective interest rate.

To reiterate, both the capital recovery problem and the sinking fund problem can be solved with the inverses of factors in compound-interest Tables H–3 and H–4, respectively:

	NOTATION	TABLE
Capital recovery	1/P/A	H–3
Sinking fund	1/F/A	H–4

COMPREHENSIVE EXAMPLE
OF COMPOUND-INTEREST TECHNIQUES

The following situation demonstrates how many of the compound-interest computation techniques introduced above can be used as investment decision aids. Assume that Ms. Pruitt, the sole owner of a typing service, has an opportunity to expand her business into the areas of quick copying and computer-assisted word processing. She has savings of $80,000 in cash on January 1, 1984, and is contemplating purchasing the necessary equipment from a vendor who requires the following payments based on a 10 percent interest rate:

DATE OF PAYMENT	AMOUNT
1/1/84	$30,000
12/31/84	$30,000
12/31/85	$30,000
12/31/86	$30,000
12/31/87	$30,000

If she decides to purchase the equipment, Ms. Pruitt plans to use $30,000 of her savings for the initial payment. The balance of her savings, $50,000, will be used in the business venture in the form of an initial $10,000 cash-operating fund and a $40,000 investment from which cash-operating requirements can be drawn at the end of 1984, 1985, 1986, and 1987. These additional amounts will be necessary because of the cash drain for the payment of the equipment. After paying off the equipment debt, Ms. Pruitt wishes to set aside an amount sufficient to replace the equipment at the end of its useful life, which is December 31, 1993. She plans, therefore, starting on December 31, 1988, to reinvest equal amounts through December 31, 1993, in order to have a fund for the purchase of new equipment. The salvage value of the old equipment is estimated to be $30,000 at December 31, 1993, and the replacement price is estimated to be $130,000, requiring a fund balance at that time of $100,000.

To summarize, Ms. Pruitt is willing to invest $80,000 in this business venture on January 1, 1984. She has a plan that she feels will supply sufficient cash flow for the early years and will also provide for an asset replacement fund on December 31, 1993. In terms of cash inflow from operations, her best estimate is that $30,000 per year will be generated after paying operating expenses but before any of the debt and fund transactions described above.

Ms. Pruitt has several questions concerning the cash flows for this venture:

1. What is the cash purchase price of the equipment, and how much would be necessary during the term of the loan to pay off the obligation?
2. How much can be withdrawn from the $40,000 fund at the end of each of the first 4 years for current working capital usage purposes?
3. How much must be deposited at the end of each year starting on December 31, 1988, to establish the necessary equipment replacement fund?
4. Is the venture feasible and is it a good business opportunity?

Each question, except perhaps question 4, can be answered in full or in part with the aid of compound-interest techniques. The cash purchase price of the equip ment is the present value of the five $30,000 payments:

Transaction	Payment $30,000	Payment $30,000	Payment $30,000	Payment $30,000	Payment $30,000
Time line	1/1/84	12/31/84	12/31/85	12/31/86	12/31/87

This is an annuity-due computation:

$$A[(P/A, n - 1, i) + 1] =$$
$$\$30,000[(P/A, 4, .10) + 1] =$$
$$\$30,000(4.1699) = \$125,097$$

The current purchase price on January 1, 1984, is therefore $125,097. An amortization schedule shows the present value of payments at several points in time:

	PAYMENT	INTEREST	REDUCTION IN LIABILITY	LIABILITY BALANCE
1/1/84	—	—	—	$125,097
1/1/84	$ 30,000	—	$30,000	95,097
12/31/84	30,000	$ 9,510	20,490	74,607
12/31/85	30,000	7,461	22,539	52,068
12/31/86	30,000	5,207	24,793	27,275
12/31/87	30,000	2,725[a]	27,275	0
	$150,000	$24,903		

[a] Rounding error.

The liability balance is the amount required to pay off the obligation at the several points in time. For instance, on December 31, 1984, the present value of future payments is as follows (assuming that the December 31, 1984, payment has been made):

$$\$30,000(P/A, 3, .10) =$$
$$\$30,000(2.4869) = \$74,607$$

Question 2 can be answered by the application of the capital recovery computation technique. Four year-end withdrawals are made from an initial investment of $40,000 during the period 1984 (year-end) to 1987 (year-end).

$$\$40,000 \left(\frac{1}{(P/A, \ 4, \ .10)} \right) =$$
$$\$40,000 \left(\frac{1}{3.1699} \right) = \$12,619$$

Transaction	Invest $40,000	Withdraw $12,619	Withdraw $12,619	Withdraw $12,619	Withdraw $12,619
Time line	1/1/84	12/31/84	12/31/85	12/31/86	12/31/87

An analysis of this fund follows:

YEAR	BEGINNING BALANCE	+	INTEREST EARNED	−	YEAR-END WITHDRAWAL	=	ENDING BALANCE
1984	$40,000		$4,000		$12,619		$31,381
1985	31,381		3,138		12,619		21,900
1986	21,900		2,190		12,619		11,471
1987	11,471		1,148[a]		12,619		0
1988	0						

[a] Rounded.

Question 3 asks what amounts need to be deposited each year-end from 1988 to (and including) 1993 to ensure a replacement fund. This is an example of a 6-year sinking fund computation:

$$\$100,000 \left(\frac{1}{(F/A, \ 6, \ .10)} \right) =$$

$$\$100,000 \left(\frac{1}{7.7156} \right) = \underline{\$12,961}$$

Transaction			Deposit $12,961	Deposit $12,961	Deposit $12,961	Deposit $12,961	Deposit $12,961	Deposit $12,961
Time line	1/1/84	12/31/84	12/31/88	12/31/89	12/31/90	12/31/91	12/31/92	12/31/93

The fund would grow as follows:

YEAR	DEPOSIT	+	INTEREST EARNED	=	FUND BALANCE
1988	$12,961		—		$ 12,961
1989	12,961		$1,296		27,218
1990	12,961		2,722		42,901
1991	12,961		4,290		60,152
1992	12,961		6,015		79,128
1993	12,961		7,911[a]		100,000

[a] Rounded.

The last question—Is the venture feasible and is it a good business opportunity?—can be partially answered only by analyzing all positive and negative cash flows. The desirability of such a choice will ultimately have to be subjective. In this case, as is shown at the top of page 168, there are positive cash flows.

Whether or not the net cash available in each of the 10 years is sufficient depends on Ms. Pruitt's needs. In other words, the analysis indicates positive cash balances, which is a form of viability. But this is certainly not the entire answer, for it must be remembered that an asset-replacement fund is being created, and the salvage value of the equipment is not insignificant.

One way to approach the overall appraisal of this business opportunity would

| DATE | CASH INFLOW | CASH OUTFLOW | | | NET CASH AVAILABLE |
		INVESTMENT	EQUIPMENT	SINKING FUND	
1/1/84	80,000ª	40,000	30,000		10,000
12/31/84	42,619ᵇ		30,000		12,619
12/31/85	42,619		30,000		12,619
12/31/86	42,619		30,000		12,619
12/31/87	42,619		30,000		12,619
12/31/88	30,000ᶜ			12,961	17,039
12/31/89	30,000			12,961	17,039
12/31/90	30,000			12,961	17,039
12/31/91	30,000			12,961	17,039
12/31/92	30,000			12,961	17,039
12/31/93	30,000			12,961	17,039

ª Initial cash balance.
ᵇ $30,000 net cash from operations plus $12,619 from $40,000 investment.
ᶜ $30,000 net cash from operations.

be to compare the present value of all the amounts made available with the $80,000 initial investment. This would require several computations:

DESCRIPTION OF ASSETS GENERATED	COMPUTATIONAL FORMULA	PRESENT VALUE
1. Initial cash balance	$10,000	$ 10,000
2. Annuity withdrawn from investment for 4 years	$12,619(*P/A*, 4, .10)	40,000
3. Net operating proceeds for last 6 years	$17,039(*P/A*, 6, .10)(*P/F*, 4, .10)	50,685
4. Sinking fund	$100,000(*P/F*, 10, .10)	38,550
5. Salvage value of the equipment	$30,000(*P/F*, 10, .10)	11,565
		$150,800

Note the use of two table factors in item 3 above. This use of multiple factors is necessary when an annuity that commences at a future date must be discounted to the present date. Many such combinations are possible.

Although $150,800 is certainly greater than $80,000, other considerations must be weighed before this project can be deemed a "good" investment. For instance, if the riskiness of the venture is felt to warrant a 20 percent return and the future cash flows were discounted using that rate, $90,990 would be the present value. Again, even though $90,990 is greater than $80,000, the individual decision maker's own subjective judgment as to the desirability of such a return is the ultimate criterion.

SUMMARY

Accounting requires the measurement of assets, liabilities, owners' equity, revenues, and expenses. One class of measurement techniques that accountants and most others involved in financial'transactions use extensively concerns the time value of money. Interest is normally charged on outstanding money amounts, and the terms of contracts involving future asset flows normally consider interest.

Simple-interest computations involve applying interest rates to principal amounts only, whereas compound-interest computations include a computation of interest on principal and previously accumulated unpaid interest charges. Contracts that call for future payments often necessitate the computation of the present value of known future values and/or the future value of known present values.

In this chapter we have analyzed techniques for computing present and future single-payment amounts and annuity amounts. Both algebraic solutions and those involving compound-interest tables were demonstrated. In addition, we surveyed the accounting for future cash flows and the general rules that apply to those kinds of transactions. Finally, business feasibility decisions were shown to be dependent, in part, on several compound-interest techniques. These concepts are frequently used in accounting, and they apply to all assets and liabilities based on contractual arrangements that specify the economic flows and interest rates. Understanding this fundamental concept of the time value of economic flows will be necessary in order to understand the accounting for many of the assets and liabilities encountered in practice.

QUESTIONS

Q5-1 Define and contrast *simple interest* and *compound interest*.

Q5-2 When analyzing a contractual relationship between two parties that involves interest, what part do principal, payback amounts, and time periods play and how do we determine these?

Q5-3 Define the phrase "time value of money."

Q5-4 What part does interest play in the difference between future values and present values of an amount of money?

Q5-5 What is the relationship between the algebraic formulations of present and future values and the compound-interest factors found in tables?

Q5-6 In a situation where a future money amount is fixed, how will the varying of the interest rate affect its present value?

Q5-7 Define *annuities*.

Q5-8 Contrast the difference in contractual terms between "ordinary" annuities and annuities "due."

Q5-9 If you borrow a sum and promise to pay back that sum and all interest at the end of 5 years, will the total cash outflow be more if semiannual compounding is used as opposed to annual compounding? Explain.

Q5-10 Accountants often deal with receivables and payables that have an interest effect. In your own words, what *general* rules are followed for valuing these receivables and payables?

Q5-11 When will the contractual terms for a payable or receivable cause an adjusting entry to be made on the books of a debtor and a creditor?

Q5-12 Describe a business situation that would call for the use of a sinking fund factor. A capital recovery factor.

Q5-13 What is an amortization table, and how does it relate to account balances for receivables and payables?

Q5-14 Can there be an interest factor for a contract that calls for a future payment in an asset other than cash? How would the interest factor be computed?

Q5-15 When a creditor and a debtor agree to contractual terms such as those found in a note, we usually think of a symmetrical relationship. In other words, the receivable on the books of the creditor equals in amount the payable on the books of the debtor, and the interest income on one set of books equals the interest expense on the other set of books. Can you think of a case where the amounts on the books would be different? Explain how this could occur and what effect it would have on the accounting treatment of such an agreement.

C5-1   Contracts that govern payment on loans can take on a great variety of contractual terms. Assume that Mr. Boyle borrows $50,000 to be paid back in 2 years.

REQUIRED   Compose the terms of a contract that calls for repayment of the principal and simple 10 percent annual interest 2 years hence, and the terms that would apply in the case where the principal and 10 percent compounded annual interest would be paid 2 years hence.

C5-2   Salt Lake City Rent-All has two significant liabilities on its balance sheet: wages payable of $68,500 and notes payable of $200,000.

REQUIRED   Explain why the wages payable, which is due within 5 days of the balance sheet date, is shown at the future value of the amount to be paid, whereas the note, which is due within 2 years of the balance sheet date, is shown at the present value of the amount to be paid.

C5-3   On December 31, 1984, the end of the fiscal period, Old Sol Passive Solar Heating, Inc., has a 6-month note payable of $20,000 due on June 30, 1985, with an annual interest rate of 14 percent. Your colleague in the accounting department states that the balance sheet should include a current liability for the note for $21,400, which includes the obligation and 6 months' interest to June 30, 1985.

REQUIRED   How would you respond to this assertion?

C5-4   Claret Winery purchased new equipment on October 1, 1984, and signed a 5-year loan agreement. The payment, 5 years hence, is to be $700,000, including both principal and interest.

REQUIRED   If the note does not explicitly state an interest rate, what evidence could be used to establish the book value of the equipment and the notes payable? How would varying the interest rate affect those balances? Would any income statement items be affected by the choice of interest rates?

C5-5   Describe two business situations where sinking fund factors, capital recovery factors, and annuities-due computations would be useful.

EXERCISES

E5-1   Ansel Photos Company borrows $8,000 on June 1, 1984, and signs a 15 percent, 180-day note with First Bank.

REQUIRED   Show all journal entries and computations necessary to record the loan and payment of principal and interest on both the company's and the bank's books.

E5-2   Use the appropriate compound-interest tables to compute the present values on January 1, 1984, of the two following streams of cash flows, using 8 percent and 12 percent interest rates for each:

		$12,500	$12,500	$12,500
1.	├──────────┼──────────┼──────────┤
		12/31/84	12/31/85	12/31/86
	$5,000	$ 5,000	$15,000	$15,000
2.	├──────────┼──────────┼──────────┤
	1/1/84	12/31/84	12/31/85	12/31/86

REQUIRED Show computations, including the notations for compound-interest factors.

E5–3 A shipping company is undecided as to which of two vessels it should add to its fleet. The initial cost, repair cost, and revenues associated with the 20 years of service estimated for each vessel are as follows:

	INITIAL COST	YEARLY REPAIR	YEARLY REVENUES
Ship 1	$50,000,000	$1,500,000	$10,000,000
Ship 2	$70,000,000	500,000	$11,000,000

REQUIRED If repairs and revenues come at year-end for all 20 years, and all other factors are held constant, which is the better alternative based on the facts given? Show all computations. Assume a 10 percent interest rate.

E5–4 On June 1, 1984, Ms. Morgan was graduated from high school and was given $10,000. She intends to deposit it in an 8 percent annual interest savings account compounded semiannually on July 1, 1984, and withdraw *equal amounts* on December 31, 1984, July 1, 1985, December 31, 1985, July 1, 1986, and December 31, 1986, to finance her first few semesters in college.

REQUIRED What is the maximum she can withdraw, assuming no penalties, at each date if she intends to have a zero balance on December 31, 1986?

E5–5 John Schelfer likes to plan ahead. Upon his graduation from college, he was hired as a staff accountant in a large corporation at an annual salary of $24,500.

REQUIRED What will Schelfer's salary be on his fortieth birthday if he averages a 10 percent raise each year, assuming he starts work on his twenty-third birthday? Show computations.

E5–6 Mrs. Roberts intends to retire at age 60 and would like to be able to withdraw $15,000 per year from her savings account from age 60 to age 80.

REQUIRED How much does she have to deposit each year for the 30 full years between now and her sixtieth birthday if a 10 percent annual return can be earned on her savings? Assume that all payments and withdrawals are at year-end.

E5–7 An insurance contract guarantees a $20,000 retirement annuity at the end of each year from December 31, 1984, to December 31, 1994. The contract costs the policyholder $100,000, and it is known that the insurance company earns 20 percent per year on all of its investments.

REQUIRED What is the present value on December 31, 1983, of the gross profit to the insurance company from this contract?

E5–8 Audio Mart is thinking of selling a deluxe stereo set for $3,000 under a 2-year payment plan that calls for a down payment and four payments at the end of each 6-month period for 2 years. Audio Mart charges 14 percent interest on outstanding balances. The sales manager claims that the following payment schedule is appropriate for such a contract:

Payment	$600	$768	$726	$684	$642
	7/1/84	12/31/84	7/1/85	12/31/85	7/1/86

Audio Mart's accountant, however, claims that the following schedule is appropriate:

Payment	683.81	683.81	683.81	683.81	683.81
	7/1/84	12/31/84	7/1/85	12/31/85	7/1/86

The accountant supports this schedule by stating that the present value of both payment schedules is $3,000 and that his scheme would be easier for customers to understand.

REQUIRED Determine whether these terms are equivalent and discuss your findings.

E5-9 A small California vegetable distributor has an opportunity to sign a contract to become the sole supplier of tomatoes for a large food chain. The contract proposed by the food chain calls for a 3-month delay between invoice date and payment. In the past the distributor has always given its customers a maximum of 1 month to pay invoices with no interest charge. The volume of sales on the proposed contract is approximately $700,000 per year based on the normal terms spread evenly throughout the year. A realistic interest rate is 12 percent.

REQUIRED What kind of adjustment in selling price on the proposed contract must the company make to be in relatively the same position as compared with normal sales?

PROBLEMS

P5-1 On January 1, 1984, Ms. Blair has take-home pay of $23,000 per year. Her total expenditures per year average $18,000, and she therefore feels that she can save a maximum of $5,000 per year in a savings account that will earn 10 percent compounded annually. Her planning horizon is 4 years, and she is contemplating two major expenditures on January 1, 1988: (1) a new car that will cost $6,500 and (2) a European trip that will cost $4,000.

REQUIRED

1. Compare the minimum amount of Ms. Blair's discretionary income that must be saved in order to pay for these expenditures on January 1, 1988. Assume year-end payments into the savings account.
2. Construct a schedule that shows the payments, the interest earned, and the balances in the savings account.

P5-2 On January 1, 1984, Jones Company borrows $1,000,000 from a bank. The agreement for repayment (the note) requires equal payments on June 30, 1984, December 31, 1984, June 30, 1985, and December 31, 1985.

REQUIRED

1. If the payments that include interest are $275,490, what is the effective interest rate assuming semiannual compounding? *Hint:* The present value is $1,000,000, the ordinary annuity is $275,490, and the factor from the appropriate table has the following relationship to these numbers

$$(\text{Table factor})(\$1,000,000) = \$275,490$$

2. Construct an amortization schedule for this obligation.

P5-3 Chef Paré owns a successful restaurant in a small midwestern city. He plans to operate his restaurant for 10 more years and then retire to Key West, Florida. He is concerned about his postretirement financial status and asks you to calculate the amounts he would have to deposit in a savings account at the end of each of the next 10 years in order to be able to withdraw $20,000 per year for 20 years after retirement.

REQUIRED

1. Compute the amount of the 10 year-end payments assuming that the $20,000 retirement withdrawals come at the beginning of each retirement year and 10 percent is the effective interest rate. (*Hint:* Set up a time line for the entire 30-year period and note that there are two annuities. One is an ordinary annuity which builds up the fund, and the other is an annuity due which depletes the fund.)
2. The same as requirement 1 except that the retirement withdrawals are made at the end of each retirement year.

P5-4 Fly Aviation, Inc., is leasing an airplane for 4 years. The lease requires $100,000 to be paid on January 1, 1984, December 31, 1984, December 31, 1985, December 31, 1986, and December 31, 1987. Fly's accountant has constructed the following amortization schedule:

	PAYMENTS	INTEREST	REDUCTION IN OBLIGATION	PRESENT VALUE OF OBLIGATION
1/1/84	$ —	$ —	$ —	$431,213.00(1)
1/1/84	100,000	—	—	331,213.00
12/31/84	100,000	26,497.04	73,502.96	257,710.04
12/31/85	100,000	20,616.80	79,383.20	178,326.84(2)
12/31/86	100,000	14,266.15	85,733.85(3)	92,592.99
12/31/87	100,000	7,407.01(4)	92,592.99	—
	$500,000			

REQUIRED Show how each numbered item, that is (1), (2), (3), and (4), can be computed by the use of compound-interest factors if 8 percent is the interest rate.

P5–5 On January 1, 1984, the production superintendent of a surface coal mine must decide on the replacement of a power shovel. Salespeople from two equipment manufacturers have given him full specifications, estimated useful lives, and other data on their products as follows:

	POWER SHOVEL 1	POWER SHOVEL 2
Cash outlay	$600,000ᵃ	$850,000ᵇ
Estimated useful life	7 years	7 years
Estimated salvage value	$150,000	$300,000
Fuel cost per year	$ 50,000	$ 35,000
Maintenance per year: Year 1	$ 0	$ 0
Year 2	5,000	0
Year 3	5,000	2,000
Year 4	5,000	2,000
Year 5	10,000	2,000
Year 6	10,000	2,000
Year 7	10,000	2,000
Capacity	12¾ cu. yds.	12¾ cu. yds.

ᵃ All paid on 1/1/84.
ᵇ Down payment of $250,000 on 1/1/84, payment of $300,000 on 12/31/85, and payment of $300,000 on 12/31/86.

REQUIRED

1. The superintendent asks you to construct a schedule that compares the present value of cash outflows, assuming a 10 percent interest rate and assuming the above estimates are accurate and all payments for fuel and maintenance are made at year-end. Show supporting computations.
2. Which power shovel is the better buy? Explain.

P5–6 Joy is going to buy a 1925 Ford from Bill. Bill, knowing that the antique car is worth a great deal of money, is looking for a steady stream of cash flow over the next 20 periods to make his retirement more enjoyable. Joy, however, has plenty of cash on hand and would sooner pay all at once instead of over the next 20 periods. Bill agrees to accept either of the following purchase plans: (1) $114,670 cash today or (2) $10,000 cash at the *end* of each period for the next 20 periods.

REQUIRED

1. What implied interest rate is Bill charging Joy *per period?*
2. If Bill suddenly learns that the local savings bank is about to increase its interest rate to 10 percent, which of the alternative purchase plans should he cancel and why?
3. What valuation concept is being used in the problem above?

4. What assets or liabilities permit the use of the valuation concept?

5. Why don't generally accepted accounting principles use this valuation concept for all assets and liabilities?

6. Assume that Joy will pay for the car over 20 periods (option 2). Record the first payment at the *end* of period 1.

P5–7   Dolt Laboratories, Inc., a medium-sized pharmaceutical company, signs a 5-year note for a $1,000,000 loan on January 1, 1984, with the following terms:

Initiation date	1/1/84
Interest payments	6/30 and 12/31 of each year
Annual interest rate	15%
Principal payment	12/31/88

REQUIRED

1. Construct an amortization table for the life of this note.

2. Regardless of your answer in requirement 1, construct an amortization table if the payment was in the form of a 5-year ordinary annuity with payment on December 31 of each year.

P5–8   On January 1, 1984, Timbin Molding Corporation has a 5-year plan to replace its factory equipment. This plan involves major expenditures, but Timbin's management is confident that enough cash can be put aside from operations to cover the projected cash flows.

	EQUIPMENT REPLACEMENT SCHEDULE				
	1985	1986	1987	1988	1989
Estimated cost of new equipment minus salvage value of old equipment	$800,000	$1,100,000	$1,400,000	$700,000	$900,000

The plan consists of putting aside equal amounts of cash (an ordinary annuity) at the end of each month. This would accumulate to just enough at each year-end to purchase the new equipment on January 1 of the following year. Timbin estimates that an average return on fund investments would be 2 percent per month.

REQUIRED

1. Compute the necessary monthly payments into the fund for 1984, 1985, 1986, 1987, and 1988.

2. Show the journal entries necessary for 1984 and 1985 for fund contributions and withdrawals.

P5–9   The city of San Pablo is planning to spend $25,000,000 to construct an all-purpose sports arena. Repairs and maintenance are expected to cost an additional $500,000 per year for the first 5 years after completion, and $600,000 per year for years 6 through 10 after completion.

On January 1, 1984, the city is attempting to decide on the amount of a bond issue to finance both the construction and the projected repairs and maintenance budget given the following time schedule assumptions:

Bond issue	Completion of construction	End of first year's operations	End of tenth year's operations
1/1/84 12/31/85	12/31/86	12/31/87	12/31/96

The proceeds from the bond issue would be invested at an estimated 14 percent annual return rate, and all payments would be made at year-end.

REQUIRED   Compute the minimum bond issue amount necessary to finance the construction and the projected maintenance and repair budget. Disregard interest payments on the bond issue.

P5–10 Investors often have various investment opportunities, each of which may have different contractual terms. Compare the following alternatives for a $100,000 investment on January 1, 1984:

	MONEY MARKET CERTIFICATES	10,000 SHARES OF COMMON STOCK	1,000 SHARES OF PREFERRED STOCK	100 BONDS
Payment schedule	$6,000 semiannually	Quarterly dividends[a]	$8,000 semiannually	$7,000 semiannually
Maturity date	12/31/88	None	None	12/31/88
Security	Guaranteed by an agency of U.S. government	Corporate residual assets	Corporate net assets	Corporate assets after payment of creditors with preference over bonds

[a] Quarterly dividends on common stock have averaged $1 per share in the past 5 years.

Assume that the best current estimates of the market prices for common and preferred stock on December 31, 1988, are $12 and $100, respectively.

REQUIRED

1. Compute the appropriate effective annual interest rate (yield) for each investment.
2. What considerations other than yield must be weighed before choosing an alternative?

P5–11 Grand Isle Company must replace its underground pipeline from its offshore sulfur mine to a storage facility onshore. The alternative is to build a loading facility offshore. The following cost schedules pertain to each alternative:

	PIPELINE	OFFSHORE LOADING
Initial cost	$34,500,000	$47,000,000
Yearly maintenance cost	$ 1,500,000	4,500,000
Estimated useful life	10 years	10 years
Residual value	$ 0	$12,000,000[a]

[a] Offshore loading facility can be sold to other operators after the sulfur deposit is depleted in 10 years.

Assume that Grand Isle Company uses a 12 percent interest rate in making capital expenditure analyses of this kind and that all payments are at year-end.

REQUIRED Which alternative is preferable from a financial point of view? Show all computations.

P5–12 Huron Valley Manufacturers, Inc., sells its heavy equipment for cash, for short-term (30-day) accounts receivable and on a long-term basis with a 2-year payment schedule involving one payment at the end of the 2 year period. The basic selling price for the new Model 11-A crane is to be $250,000, assuming cash payment at the date of sale.

The company charges 12 percent annual interest compounded monthly on all outstanding accounts.

REQUIRED If 1984 sales are estimated to be 360 units for cash, 60 units on the 30-day payment schedule, and 120 units on the 2-year payment schedule, show all journal entries to record sales, interest revenue, and cash collections for 1984 sales. Assume that sales occur at the end of each month, with each month having one-twelfth of the annual sales.

6

Alternative Valuation Models

OVERVIEW   In the first five chapters we reviewed the underlying framework and techniques for the accounting and financial reporting process in practice today. The current process is sometimes referred to as the **conventional accounting model,** which is tied closely to the historical-cost principle. Historical cost is not applied to the exclusion of all other valuation models, however. As we shall see in later chapters, GAAP call for many exceptions to the historical-cost model, both in the formal financial statements and in the form of supplementary disclosures that do not affect the primary financial statements. We shall therefore review the alternatives to historical cost before we consider specific reporting requirements.

Even though these specific reporting requirements will be covered in Parts II, III, and IV, an understanding of this chapter will help you interpret those reporting procedures that draw upon alternatives to historical cost. Moreover, if the current non-historical-cost-based footnote disclosures required by **FASB Statement No. 33**[1] and discussed in Chapter 26 are to be considered in a conceptual context, this chapter will provide useful background information.

[1] *Statement of Financial Accounting Standards No. 33,* "Financial Reporting and Changing Prices" (Stamford, CT: FASB, September 1979).

This chapter considers the general concepts and procedures that pertain to four models of accounting information systems:

1. The historical-cost model
2. The general-price-level-adjusted model
3. The current-entry-value model
4. The current-exit-value model

The first part of this chapter discusses the basic differences between these four alternative models, generally identifying how they are formulated and how they might be used in the context of decision making. The second part illustrates the four models for a simple business situation and evaluates their basic strengths and weaknesses. The objective of the chapter is to provide a basic understanding of the alternative accounting models and their underlying concepts. The intent is not to develop proficiency at generating accounting data using alternative models.

INTRODUCTION TO ALTERNATIVE ACCOUNTING MODELS

Movement
Away from
Historical Cost

Historically, accounting has focused on the accurate reporting of the past events and transactions of the business entity. There is little argument about the ability of the historical-cost-based model to produce an objective measurement of the transactions related to past activities of the entity. However, external users have become concerned about the limitations of this historical perspective because it does not consider general and specific price changes.[2]

Over the past three decades accounting critics have questioned the relevance of historical-cost information. The accounting literature of the 1970s suggested that accounting reports would be more useful if they reduced future uncertainties.[3] Alternative valuation models, such as replacement-cost accounting, were rediscovered, and debates as to the merits of each model became popular among accounting scholars.[4]

[2] See, for example, the following management accounting, financial executive, and auditor publications, which have addressed the question of inflation accounting: *Management Accounting,* December 1977, September 1979, and June 1980; *Financial Executive,* December 1980, February 1981, and May 1981; *Journal of Accountancy,* October 1974, August 1975, September 1975, May 1977, May 1979, and May 1980.

[3] See the report by the Study Group on Objectives of Financial Statements (known as the Trueblood Committee), "Objectives of Financial Statements" (New York: AICPA, 1973), and the 1974 Supplement to the *Journal of Accounting Research* for a series of papers on financial accounting objectives. An early suggestion of the predictive ability criterion can be found in "A Statement of Basic Accounting Theory" (ASOBAT) (Sarasota, FL: American Accounting Association, 1966), for example p. 23. See also William Beaver, John Kennelly, and William Voss, "Predictive Ability as a Criterion for the Evaluation of Accounting," *The Accounting Review,* October 1968, pp. 675–683.

[4] A series of papers by Robert Sterling and John Burton (both February 1975), Lawrence Revsine and James Thies (May 1977), Paul Rosenfield (August 1975 and September 1975), and Raymond J. Chambers (September 1975) in the *Journal of Accountancy* shed light on the kind of debate that took place in the accounting literature during the 1970s.

A sequence of events during the 1970s made these alternative models more appealing. First, the AICPA's Study Group report "Objectives of Financial Statements," which was published in 1973, took a strong stand on the need for current-value information.[5] Then in 1976, the SEC issued **ASR No. 190,** which called for footnote disclosure of the replacement value for inventories and plant assets.[6] Finally, after a great deal of debate, the FASB issued **Statement No. 33,** which requires supplementary disclosures of certain information on the basis of both "constant dollars" (general price level adjusted) and "current costs" (essentially a current-entry or replacement-cost value).[7] All of this was triggered by relatively high rates of inflation during the 1970s.

Criteria for Evaluating Alternatives

The criteria for evaluating the historical-cost-based accounting model and alternative accounting models are based on the information provided to users for their respective decision-making needs. How can we determine which model provides the most appropriate information? Because decision-making needs differ we are not likely to agree on what information is most appropriate, and thus there is no single accounting information system or model that could satisfy all users. The answer, then, is that the most appropriate information is a function of the type of decisions that users make and how they (or others) evaluate the outcome of their decisions. For example, if a manager needed to know the taxable income from the sale of a building, the tax basis (book value for tax purposes) and the market price at the time of sale would be the two required pieces of information. However, if a manager wanted to know the fair value of the building to determine how much fire and casualty insurance to purchase, the market price would be useful, but book values would not. Therefore, no single accounting model is always superior or inferior to another for all users or all decision situations.

In comparing and contrasting the alternative accounting models, the emphasis should be on the inherent differences in the alternatives, not the absolute preferability of one method versus another. Although the strengths and weaknesses of the alternative models will be pointed out, the ultimate means of judging these models cannot be observed in a real sense. Some have argued that the most relevant information is based on the predictive nature of the accounting data, and that the accounting data capable of predicting the future cash flows of the entity are the most desirable.[8] If every decision maker were to evaluate alternative accounting data using this criterion, cash-flow forecast accuracy using accounting data might serve as the sole basis of evaluation.[9] However, not all users of accounting information agree with this cash-prediction criterion, and, therefore, no single condition or set of con-

---

[5] Study Group, "Objectives of Financial Statements."

[6] *Accounting Series Release No. 190,* "Notice of Adoption of Amendments to Regulation S-X Requiring Disclosure of Certain Replacement Cost Data" (Washington, DC: SEC, March 23, 1976).

[7] *Statement of Financial Accounting Standards No. 33,* "Financial Reporting and Changing Prices."

[8] For example, see the papers by David Green and Joel Segall, James Horrigan, and William Beaver in *Empirical Research in Accounting: Selected Studies, 1966,* Supplement to the *Journal of Accounting Research.* See also William Beaver, John Kennelly, and William Voss, "Predictive Ability"; and Robert Eskew, "The Forecasting Ability of Accounting Risk Measures: Some Additional Evidence," *The Accounting Review,* January 1979.

[9] This statement assumes that cash flows represent benefits in an exhaustive sense. Certainly, it is possible to consider noncash benefits, which are sometimes referred to as "psychic income." We ask the reader to assume that cash flows represent all meaningful economic benefits that are measurable.

TABLE 6-1

ALTERNATIVE MODELS AND DEFINITIONS OF WEALTH	
MODEL	**WEALTH DEFINITION**
1. Historical-cost model	1. Original transaction values
2. General-price-level-adjusted model	2. General purchasing power values
3. Current-entry value model	3. Current replacement-cost values
4. Current-exit-value model	4. Current selling price values

ditions can be used to evaluate alternative accounting models. In comparing the alternative models, we shall demonstrate that one model may be preferred to another for certain types of decision needs. These preferences, however, are based on logical arguments rather than scientific proof.

Basis for Alternative Models

The differences between the four models considered here result simply from the basic definitions of wealth. The accounting model is designed to measure the wealth position and changes in the wealth position of the accounting entity through its balance sheet and income statement, respectively. Although the term **wealth** is defined in terms of "well-offness," it may take on a number of alternative specific meanings. Table 6-1 compares the four models considered here and their related specific definitions of wealth. It should be noted that the name of each model is essentially an answer to the question, What do you mean by wealth?

Historical-cost model The **historical-cost** model (or the **conventional model**) measures the wealth position of the entity by using original transaction values as the basis for preparing the financial statements. An entity may own two identical assets, but if each is purchased at a different cost, these assets will generate two different asset values and, when consumed, two different expense amounts. The underlying wealth definition suggests that the users of historical-cost-based financial statements make decisions based on the position of the entity (balance sheet data) and the change in the entity's position (income and funds statements) defined in terms of the original transaction amounts. As a result, different recorded values for similar assets would not be of concern to users of historical-cost data.

The fundamental perspective of decision makers who use historical-cost data is backward looking, or retrospective. Common performance measures when applied to the historical-cost model would measure return based on the original investment amounts. For example, the income would represent the change in wealth based on original investment amounts.

Another commonly used performance measure frequently applied to this retrospective view of the entity is **return on investment (ROI),** which is defined as[10]

$$\text{ROI} = \frac{\text{Net income}}{\text{Net sales}} \times \frac{\text{Net sales}}{\text{Assets}} - \frac{\text{Net income}}{\text{Assets}}$$

An ROI performance measure based on original transaction amounts would differentiate between the performance of two entities that had identical operating activi-

[10] Most finance texts, such as James Van Horne, *Financial Management and Policy* (Englewood Cliffs, NJ: Prentice-Hall, 1977), stress ROI as a key financial measure of performance. Other concepts are also suggested, such as "residual income," but they mostly rely in part at least on financial accounting data.

TABLE 6–2

GENERAL PRICE INDEX CONSTRUCTION		
ITEM	1984 PRICE	1983 PRICE
Butter (1 lb.)	$ 2.07	$ 1.89
Gun (.22-caliber)	48.00	38.57
Tire (size FR78 × 14″)	65.87	67.48
Blouse (size 12)	35.95	32.50
Bread (1-lb. loaf)	1.85	1.70
Fertilizer (20-lb bag)	18.95	15.81
Beer (six-pack of Lite)	2.80	3.05
Total	$175.49	$161.00
Index (1983 = Base Year)	109%[a]	100%

[a] $175.49/$161.00.

ties for some period and used identical plant assets that had different purchase prices (possibly due to the year in which these assets were purchased). The entities whose plant assets had the lowest cost would have the higher ROI measure due to (1) lower depreciation expense resulting in higher net income and (2) lower asset values. The fact that the historical-cost-based model tends to differentiate between entities with identical operating efficiencies but different asset costs is an important feature of this model.

General-price-level-adjusted model   The **general-price-level-adjusted (GPLA) model** defines wealth in units of general purchasing power, which is measured in terms of a price index such as the Consumer Price Index (CPI). General price indexes are constructed by following the changes in the price of a particular group of commodities. Table 6–2 computes a "general" price index based on a group of items and their specific prices.

The index states the relationship between the prices of the current year (1984) relative to some prior year (1983 in this case) and is designed to provide a measure of what has happened to prices *in general* over the last year or some other period of interest. The CPI includes a wide variety of consumer products normally purchased by most consumers. Furthermore, these commodities are "weighted" in proportion to their relative importance to a consumer.[11]

An example of a broader general price index than the CPI would be the gross national product (GNP) index, which also includes nonconsumer durables that enter into the measurement of our national productivity. Alternatively, a narrower general price index would be the CPI–Urban, a version of the CPI that includes commodities relevant to the urban segment of our population and excludes commodities relevant to the rural segment.

The GPLA model provides users with information that enables them to assess their general purchasing power and changes in purchasing power. It measures the performance of an entity exclusive of the impact of general price changes, thereby enabling users to evaluate performance separate from the effects of general inflation

[11] These weights are subjective and are a potentially important factor in evaluating the relevance of any given index. For example, housing costs might be weighted as 20 percent of the total Consumer Price Index, but not every consumer spends 20 percent of income on housing each year. Some consumers may spend 50 percent, others nothing, and therefore the weighting of factors that go into a general price index should be evaluated before an index is applied to any given situation.

or deflation. Net income under the GPLA model measures the amount of assets that can be distributed and still leave the owners or equity holders with the same purchasing power at the end of the period as they had at the beginning of the period, assuming that the mix of assets is similar to the mix upon which the index is computed. If users are interested in accounting data that allow them to assess their wealth in terms of purchasing power, the GPLA model will provide useful data, given the above assumption. Note that the exact nature of the "purchasing power" being accounted for depends on the general price index being employed. Each general price index represents a different definition of general purchasing power.

Current-entry-value and current-exit-value models Both the **current-entry-value model** and the **current-exit-value model** are based on prices and price changes of specific types of assets. They are designed to provide current-value information from the standpoint of how much assets can be sold for (exit-value model) or from the perspective of how much assets cost to own (entry-value model). These models account for the price changes of specific assets, normally by way of specific price indexes. Table 6–3 illustrates specific price indexes for both entry- and exit-value models for a single asset—a steel-belted radial tire, from the standpoint of the tire manufacturer.

The entry- and exit-value models provide two additional types of accounting data that view the entity from two different perspectives. The entry-value model is concerned with the entity's ability to maintain its productive capacity. By measuring the assets of the entity in terms of their current-entry value, or replacement cost, we

TABLE 6–3

CURRENT-ENTRY AND CURRENT-EXIT VALUE PRICE INDEX CONSTRUCTION		
CURRENT-ENTRY MODEL Example: Replacement cost for manufacturer—a steel-belted radial tire		
	COST 1984	**COST 1983**
Material		
Rubber	$12.50	$12.75
Steel	3.80	3.45
Nylon	2.82	2.76
Canvas	4.13	4.09
Material subtotal	$23.25	$23.05
Labor	19.90	18.20
Overhead	8.10	7.60
	$51.25	$48.85
Index—entry value	104.9%[a]	100%
CURRENT-EXIT MODEL Example: Net selling price for manufacturer—a steel-belted radial tire		
	PRICE 1984	**PRICE 1983**
List selling price per unit	$115.00	$104.00
Less commissions and discounts to dealers	29.00	24.00
Net selling price per unit	$ 86.00	$ 80.00
Index—exit value	107.5%[b]	100%

[a] $51.25/$48.85 = 1.0491299.
[b] $86.00/$80.00 = 1.075.

EXHIBIT 6-1

COMPARISON OF DECISION-MAKING PERSPECTIVE OF THE FOUR BASIC
ACCOUNTING MODELS

1. **Historical-cost model:** The retrospective perspective of this model measures assets based on original transaction values. Common performance measures applied to accounting data of this type are in the context of the past invested amount.

2. **General-price-level-adjusted model:** The current perspective of this model measures assets based on units of current purchasing power. Common performance measures applied to accounting data of this type will enable users to focus on the "real" (after general inflation/deflation) change in their purchasing power from their investments.

3. **Current-entry-value model:** The current perspective of this model measures assets based on their current replacement cost. Common performance measures applied to accounting data of this type will enable users to evaluate the individual and comparative operating efficiency of an entity assuming there is a commitment to a certain kind of operating activity.

4. **Current-exit-value model:** The current perspective of this model measures assets based on their current sales value. Common performance measures applied to accounting data of this type will enable users to evaluate their investments, with liquidation of an investment one of the possible decision alternatives.

assume a commitment on the part of the user to a certain type of business activity. The user is able to obtain a performance measure that indicates the profitability of the entity's **operating activities** based on the current cost of the entity's resources. For example, an ROI measure based on the current-entry-value model, applied to two entities with identical operations and identical plant assets but with different purchase prices, would result in identical performance measures. The different historical purchase prices would not influence the **operating results** measured in a current-entry-value, or replacement-cost, model.

The current-exit-value model takes a current investment or divestment decision-making perspective. The exit-value model provides financial data on the liquid or cash-equivalent value of the entity. Unlike the entry-value model, there is no assumption that the user of the accounting data is committed to a given set of assets or resources. The user is provided with data that facilitate the comparison of unlike sets of resources. For example, an ROI measure based on the exit-value model would permit a comparison of the relative performance of a steel mill and a supermarket because the model measures the assets and income in terms of the liquid value of these two investments. The decision to invest more in, or to divest of, either entity would be completely consistent with the accounting data provided by the exit-value model and applied to common performance indicators such as ROI.[12] Note that the exit model, like the entry model, tends to result in identical performance measures for entities that are alike in every respect except for the historical purchase price of their assets. However, the performance measurement using the exit model contemplates liquidation rather than replacement.

Some of the key attributes of the four basic models and their various decision perspectives are summarized in Exhibit 6-1.

Variations of the four basic models   The examples in Table 6-3 have assumed some specific form for the entry- and exit-value models—replacement cost and net selling price, respectively. The general-price-level-adjusted, entry-value, and exit-value models all have a number of minor variations that are identified by various names. Several alternative forms of these current-value models are listed in Exhibit 6-2.

[12] For example, the exit-value model would measure assets in such a way that a decision to sell assets would yield cash equal to their measured value. This is not the case with the other models.

EXHIBIT 6–2

**COMMON VARIATIONS OF THE THREE BASIC ALTERNATIVES
TO THE HISTORICAL-COST MODEL**

GENERAL-PRICE-LEVEL-ADJUSTED (GPLA) MODELS

1. **CPI–U:** A GPLA model based on the Consumer Price Index—Urban, which focuses on the market basket of goods and services typically consumed by urban dwellers, with each item weighted in proportion to its share of urban expenditures. This version of the GPLA model is currently required in practice.
2. **GNP price deflator:** This GPLA model is a version previously supported in *APB Statement No. 3.*[a] The GNP index is broad in that it considers total national productivity at all levels of economic endeavor—from raw materials to manufacturing and wholesale and retail activities. It is less consumer-oriented as a result of its greater breadth.
3. **Retail Price Index:** A GPLA model based strictly on the retail of final consumption stage of the investment production process. It is somewhat broader than the CPI–U in that it is not confined to retail purchases of urban dwellers. However, specific retail indexes that are a part of the overall retail price index also are available for certain categories of retail commodities, such as retail hardware or retail food product indexes.

CURRENT-ENTRY-VALUE MODELS

1. **Current cost I:** Replacement price of identical assets. This concept measures the current reproduction cost of the actual assets held by the entity without considering whether the entity intends to replace such assets with identical assets.
2. **Current cost II:** Replacement price of the equivalent productive capacity. This concept measures the current replacement value of the assets that will be manufactured or purchased to replace existing productive capacity without adjusting for the technological improvements in the assets to be purchased.
3. **Current cost III:** Replacement price of the equivalent productive capacity adjusted for technological improvements. This concept attempts to break down the current replacement cost of similar new productive assets in such a way that an estimate of the current replacement cost net of new efficiencies attributable to new technology can be determined.
4. **Net present value of future costs:** This theoretical concept applies the basic net-present-value notion to the expected future costs. The discount rate for conceptual examples could be represented by the opportunity rate. Actual application of this concept in practice will be observed only when future costs and discount rates are fixed from contractual agreements, such as long-term purchase contracts.

CURRENT-EXIT-VALUE MODELS

1. **Net realizable market value:** This is the current selling price adjusted for any costs necessary to complete the sale (commissions, freight, and so on). The net realizable value is based on the current market-equilibrium price under normal selling conditions.
2. **Current cash equivalent:** This is the estimated cash proceeds from an asset under conditions of orderly liquidation, or the best cash value given the intention to liquidate. The current-cash-equivalent value is also referred to as a proxy for opportunity cost, or the cash forgone by holding the asset.
3. **Liquidation value:** This is the estimated cash proceeds that could be realized under conditions of forced liquidation, or the worst cash-out value given a liquidation posture.
4. **Net present value of future cash flows:** This theoretical concept applies the basic net-present-value notion to the expected future cash flows. Actual application of this concept will be observed only when the future cash flows and discount rates are fixed from contractual agreements.

[a] *Accounting Principles Board Statement No. 3*, "Financial Statements Restated for General Price-Level Changes" (New York: AICPA, June 1969).

RELATIONSHIP BETWEEN ALTERNATIVE MODELS
AND FINANCIAL STATEMENTS

The four alternative models described above form a complete set of basic alternatives for defining wealth. In a financial statement sense, the wealth position of the firm is found in the balance sheet, with changes in the balance sheet explained in the income and retained earnings statements and the statement of changes in financial position (funds statement). We recall from the earlier chapters the following basic relationships as examples:

Statements:	Balance sheet at end of period	− Balance sheet at beginning of period	= Income statement	and Retained earnings statement
Contents:	Net assets at end of period	− Net assets at beginning of period	= Change in wealth position (consumption plus increase)	

Statements:	Balance sheet at end of period	− Balance sheet at beginning of period	= Statement of changes in financial position
Contents:	Total assets, liabilities, and equities at end of period	− Total assets, liabilities, and equities at beginning of period	= Changes in position attributable to funds (cash or working capital) and changes attributable to nonfund activities

As we move from one definition of wealth (for example, historical cost) to another (for example, exit value), the measurements of the assets, liabilities, and equities of the entity change. These changes in wealth measurement in the balance sheet affect the income, funds, and retained earnings statements also because all three statements describe changes in the balance sheet. As a result, each "model" will generate different financial statements that are based on their respective definitions of wealth. In the radial tire example in Table 6–3, assume that the 1984 ending tire inventory consisted of 1,000 units produced in 1983. The four alternative inventory values for the year ended December 31, 1984, would be as follows:

	HISTORICAL COST (LIFO) MODEL	GENERAL-PRICE-LEVEL-ADJUSTED MODEL[a]	CURRENT-ENTRY-VALUE MODEL[b]	CURRENT-EXIT-VALUE MODEL[b]
Alternative asset values for tire inventory (1,000 units)	$48,850	$53,247	$51,250	$86,000

[a] See Table 6–2 for index (109%).
[b] See Table 6–3 for indexes.

Note that although all four measurements of the inventory value are different, they are all "correct" given their respective definitions of wealth.

RELATIONSHIP BETWEEN ALTERNATIVE MODELS AND THE PRESENT-VALUE CONCEPT

In Chapter 5 we reviewed the present-value concept. If we understand this concept, we can properly account for certain assets and liabilities using GAAP in the conventional accounting model framework.[13] However, the present-value concept provides a *theoretically* appropriate measure of the value of any asset at any point in time.

[13] See *Accounting Principles Board Opinion No. 21* "Interest on Receivables and Payables" (New York: AICPA, August 1971).

You'll recall from Chapter 5 that the present value of a future amount (P/F) can be calculated by means of the following formula:

$$P/F = (F)\,\frac{1}{(1 + i)^n} = \frac{F}{(1 + i)^n}$$

where F is the future amount, i is the interest rate, and n is the number of periods. The *total* present value of any asset is simply the sum of the present values of all future benefits:

$$\text{Value of asset} = \frac{F_1}{(1 + i)^n} + \frac{F_2}{(1 + i)^n} + \frac{F_3}{(1 + i)^n} \cdots$$

where F_1, F_2, F_3, and so forth, are the future benefits. For example, assume that property is expected to earn \$12,000 rent at the end of periods 1 and 2 and that the property can be sold for \$100,000 at the end of period 2. In this case, there are three future benefits—two rent payments and a selling price of \$100,000. The value of this property can be measured using the present-value concept once we know what rate of interest or return is appropriate to the individual or the entity seeking to value the property. If a 10-percent interest or return rate is appropriate, the value of this property would be calculated as follows:

$$
\begin{aligned}
\text{Value of asset} &= \frac{F_1}{(1 + i)^n} + \frac{F_2}{(1 + i)^n} + \frac{F_3}{(1 + i)^n} \\[6pt]
&= \frac{\$12,000}{(1.10)^1} + \frac{\$12,000}{(1.10)^2} + \frac{\$100,000}{(1.10)^2} \\[6pt]
&= \$10,909 + \$9,917 + \$82,645 \\[6pt]
&= \$103,471
\end{aligned}
$$

In the context of the notation in Chapter 5, this is the same as:

$$
\begin{aligned}
(P/A,2,.10)\ \$12,000 &= (1.7355)\ \$12,000 = \$\ 20,826 \\
+\,(P/F,2,.10)\ \$100,000 &= (.8264)\ \$100,000 = \underline{82,640} \\
& \underline{\$103,466}
\end{aligned}
$$

The \$5 difference between the two answers is due to the rounding of the P/F factor. At a price of \$103,471, the property described in the example above will return 10 percent. If one desires a higher return for this property, one would have to acquire it for less than \$103,471. Alternatively, if one would settle for a return of less than 10 percent, one would be willing to pay more than \$103,471. The \$103,471 value is capable of representing the replacement cost, the selling price, or the historical cost in various situations.

Although some prefer to consider the present-value concept a fifth alternative to the four basic alternative models identified in Table 6–1, we prefer to consider the present-value concept the theoretical basis of all valuation models.

The present-value model becomes more than just a theoretical model when applied to certain assets or liabilities that, due to their contractual nature, have **known future amounts** (F values) for a **known benefit period** (where n is limited to a specified number of periods) at a **known interest rate** (i). Such was the case in the example given above. Other examples of such assets and liabilities include bonds and notes receivable. Since most assets do not have known future benefits or stated interest rates, the present-value model is more difficult to apply in practice.[14] However, the notion of the present value of future benefits provides the basis for most valuation models and is not peculiar to any single model.

STRENGTHS AND WEAKNESSES OF ALTERNATIVE ACCOUNTING MODELS

The remainder of this chapter will illustrate the four alternative models by considering their strengths and weaknesses. The examples are not designed to give the reader depth or technical proficiency in implementing alternative accounting models. They are meant only to highlight differences and similarities so that the general discussion of strengths and weaknesses may be supported with illustrations. The details of current reporting requirements that involve certain aspects of these alternative models are covered in Chapter 26 of the text.

The Historical-Cost Model

First consider the historical-cost-based (conventional) accounting model applied to a simple example in order to illustrate the measure of wealth and its limitations for decision making:

> During the early 1960s a young lawyer named Tom Dooley purchased (as an investment) automatic car-wash equipment from a friend who had invented and manufactured the first equipment of this type. Dooley purchased land for $25,000 cash in a prime location and installed the washing facility, which cost $100,000 cash. The equipment was expected to have a 3-year life and a zero salvage value by the end of 1963. In 1961, at about the time the facility was placed into operation, the general price index was at 80 percent of the base year. During the 3-year life of the car wash, Dooley did very well, much better than he had expected. He was given a report of operating results by his accountant once a year, and each year Dooley took the net income from operations, paid off some bills that had accumulated from his personal activities, and bought Christmas presents for his family and his best clients. Any cash left in the business after he received an amount of cash equal to net income was left in a savings account earning interest. The car-wash business started slowly but grew rapidly during 1962 and 1963 due to consumer interest in such facilities, and similar businesses began to spring up all over. The orders for car-wash equipment received by Dooley's inventor friend could not be filled on a timely basis, and the price of the equipment skyrocketed, because demand far exceeded supply. Dooley was pleased with the results of his investment, which are summarized in Exhibits 6–3 and 6–4.

> At the end of the 3-year period, Dooley's accountant reported that the utility of the car-wash facility was completely consumed and needed to be replaced. By December 1963 the general price index had reached 96 percent. The cost of replacing the car-wash assets had increased to $125,000. Dooley suddenly realized that he did not have enough capital to replace the car-wash facility. Fortunately, he had received an offer from a local CPA to buy the business for $250,000 at the end of 1963.

The Dooley case provides an example of a major drawback in the historical-cost accounting model, which defines wealth and changes in wealth in terms of origi-

---

[14] Note that the present value of assets such as bonds or leases will be the same for all models that define the benefits to be the contracted future cash flows. In other words, the "benefits" measured in the present-value model are defined in the context of some wealth concept, and the present value *may* vary as the wealth concept varies, or it *may* stay the same.

EXHIBIT 6-3

TOM DOOLEY'S CAR WASH
Income Statement
For the Years Ended December 31

	1963	1962	1961	TOTAL 1961–1963
Revenues				
Operations	$75,500	$59,500	$25,500	$160,500
Interest	8,000	4,000	500	12,500
Total revenues	$83,500	$63,500	$26,000	$173,000
Expenses				
Depreciation[a]	$40,000	$40,000	$20,000	$100,000
Miscellaneous expenses	11,000	7,000	2,000	20,000
Income tax	16,250	8,250	2,000	26,500
Total expenses	$67,250	$55,250	$24,000	$146,500
Net income	$16,250	$ 8,250	$ 2,000	$ 26,500

TOM DOOLEY'S CAR WASH
Retained Earnings Statement
For the Periods Ended December 31

	1963	1962	1961	TOTAL 1961–1963
Beginning retained earnings	$ 0	$ 0	$ 0	$ 0
Plus net income	16,250	8,250	2,000	26,500
Less dividends	(16,250)	(8,250)	(2,000)	(26,500)
Ending retained earnings	$ 0	$ 0	$ 0	$ 0

[a] Depreciation is based on the use of the equipment.

nal transaction values. The financial statements in Exhibits 6–3 and 6–4 measure wealth and change in wealth in terms of Dooley's original investment. Performance measures such as return on assets would seem to suggest that Dooley's investment was profitable. However, Dooley is unable to continue with his business unless he contributes additional capital to the business or borrows capital from another source. Although the historical-cost model accurately measured wealth and change in wealth in terms of original transaction amounts, it did not take into consideration either the general inflation that had occurred or the specific price changes, both of which seem relevant to Dooley's decision concerning what to do with his investment and how to consume the positive net cash flows.

This example might lead us to question the consistency between the historical-cost principle and the going-concern assumption. From the application of the historical-cost principle in the Dooley case and the resulting net income number as a measure of disposable wealth, it was demonstrated that Dooley was unable to replenish the assets at the end of their 3-year life in order to continue the business. Even though the case describes a situation that seemed to be quite profitable, the inability to measure wealth and change in wealth in "real" terms resulted in the probable liquidation of the firm.

The historical-cost model and decision making To better evaluate the historical-cost model, let us consider some very common, yet pivotal, questions regarding invested capital with which investors and corporate management would be concerned.

EXHIBIT 6–4

TOM DOOLEY'S CAR WASH
Balance Sheet as of December 31

	1963	1962	1961
Cash	$ 100,000	$ 60,000	$ 20,000
Equipment	100,000	100,000	100,000
Accumulated depreciation	(100,000)	(60,000)	(20,000)
Land	25,000	25,000	25,000
Total assets	$ 125,000	$ 125,000	$ 125,000
Owners' equity	$ 125,000	$ 125,000	$ 125,000
Retained earnings	0	0	0
Total equities	$ 125,000	$ 125,000	$ 125,000

TOM DOOLEY'S CAR WASH
Statement of Changes in Financial Position[a]
For the Periods Ended December 31

	1963	1962	1961	TOTAL 1961–1963
Sources of cash				
From operating revenue	$75,500	$59,500	$25,500	$160,500
From interest	8,000	4,000	500	12,500
	$83,500	$63,500	$26,000	$173,000
Uses of Cash				
For income tax	$16,250	$ 8,250	$ 2,000	$ 26,500
For miscellaneous expenses	11,000	7,000	2,000	20,000
For dividends	16,250	8,250	2,000	26,500
	$43,500	$23,500	$ 6,000	$ 73,000
Net cash flow	$40,000	$40,000	$20,000	$100,000

[a] Note that this format is not conventional and is used in this chapter for sake of clarity only.

1. How much can the entity pay in dividends, assuming that there is no desire to expand the business?
2. How much of an additional investment should the entity make if it does have a growth objective?
3. What is the fair value of the entity for purposes of mergers or takeover bids by other entities?
4. What was the return on investment last period?

The answers to these and other questions involving the accounting information system depend on our ability to measure the wealth position and the disposable income of the entity given the decision at hand. Based on our example above, it seems that the historical-cost model may not provide the most useful information. By withdrawing the historical-cost-based income from the business, Dooley experienced a need for additional capital in order to stay in business. American industries have experienced similar investment capital needs to maintain their operations. Misunderstanding the information provided by the historical-cost model may easily lead to wrong answers to the questions posed above and may explain some of the economic difficulties that companies have experienced in recent years.

What is the basic problem with the historical-cost model? One significant limitation is that it fails to capture the impact of price changes. Conventional accounting is based primarily on the historical-cost model and generates wealth and disposable income measures that are based on original transaction values. Due to the increased rate of price changes, wealth and disposable income measured in terms of original transaction values have become much less relevant information for many decision-making needs.

General-Price-Level-Adjusted Model

Impact of changing prices One of the major weaknesses of the historical-cost model is its failure to recognize that because of changes in prices, the measurement unit—the dollar—is not a consistent measure. In the 1950s bricks cost about two cents each; today the same bricks cost about eight cents each. There is no real difference in the bricks, but the cost of the bricks as measured in dollars has changed substantially.

If we have an inventory of bricks, or if we must use bricks in constructing buildings during this period, we might be concerned about the impact of this change on our financial measurement of assets. If our brick inventory is measured at $2,000, how many bricks are there? If we have 40,000 bricks, what is their dollar measurement? Without dating the bricks or dating the monetary measurement unit or both, we can become very confused by such a simple situation. Given the price range previously noted, the historical-cost model could yield a measurement of from $800 to $3,200 for several different firms all holding an equal inventory of 40,000 bricks, depending on a number of variables such as the acquisition date and the cost-flow assumption (for example, LIFO or FIFO). However, if bricks remained at two cents during the entire period (1950 to the present), every inventory of 40,000 bricks would have the same value ($800). Price changes make similar assets among similar entities difficult to compare and evaluate.

Measuring in uniform dollars One way to resolve the problem of variable measurement units is to restate all dollar values to a uniform dollar value, thereby eliminating the combining of unlike dollars. This process is normally referred to as **general-price-level-adjusted (GPLA)** accounting, or **constant-dollar accounting.** In the case of a building constructed in 1963 for 200,000 1963 dollars, we could multiply $200,000 by the **ratio** of current dollars to 1963 dollars and thereby restate the building in terms of current dollars. This process is not too difficult once we arrive at the ratio, which is simply a **general price index.**

To measure the GPLA value of our building purchased in 1963 in terms of constant dollars, we must first decide which uniform or standard dollar should be used. To illustrate, assume the following GPL data:

DATE	CPI-U
1963	90.6%
1967	100.0
1975	161.2
1990	287.9

If 1990 dollars were desired, we would compute the CPI–U general-price-level adjusted value of the building as follows:

$$1963 \text{ cost} \times \frac{1990 \text{ index}}{1963 \text{ index}} = \text{GPLA value}$$

$$\$200,000 \times \frac{287.9}{90.6} = \$635,541$$

If 1975 dollars were desired as the standard dollar, the CPI–U adjusted value of the building would be computed as follows:

$$1963 \text{ cost} \times \frac{1975 \text{ index}}{1963 \text{ index}} = \text{GPLA value}$$

$$\$200,000 \times \frac{161.2}{90.6} = \$355,850$$

In GPLA accounting, all historical dollars are usually converted to end-of-current-year dollars. Current dollars tend to have greater relevance for decisions made on the basis of the financial statement data.

Monetary and nonmonetary items To prepare general-price-level-adjusted financial statements, all items must be classified as either monetary or nonmonetary. Only the recorded value of the nonmonetary items will be general price level adjusted because **monetary items represent fixed claims to dollars,** and their numbers remain constant regardless of specific or general price-level changes. **Nonmonetary items** are capable of changing in terms of their current-dollar-value measurement. If the purchase of an asset is followed by a period of inflation, its general-price-level-adjusted measurement will be greater than its historical measurement. Alternatively, if a period of deflation follows the recording of an asset, its general-price-level-adjusted amount will be less than its historical amount.

Classification of monetary and nonmonetary items Table 6–4 lists several common balance sheet items in terms of monetary and nonmonetary classifications. The basic concept of a monetary item alone is not sufficient to resolve all classification problems. Consider a bond held as an investment. Assume that the current market price is $890 and the maturity value 4 years from now will be $1,000. Assume that you purchased the bond 6 months ago for $910. Is the bond a monetary asset or not? The answer is, It depends! If you assume that the asset will be held to maturity, it is a monetary asset because it represents a fixed claim to dollars ($1,000) at maturity. However, if the asset is being held as a short-term investment, it seems more reasonable to treat the bond as a nonmonetary asset because its market price will fluctuate between purchase and sale, and it will not be held to maturity but sold at some interim date instead.

Several other items may differ from their Table 6–4 classifications—for example, inventories produced under fixed-price contracts are a monetary asset, and preferred stocks, convertible securities, prepaid expenses, and deferred revenue may be monetary or nonmonetary depending on circumstances. In each case, we should attempt to determine whether the claim involved is for a fixed number of dollars.

Converting historical-cost statements to GPLA statements The process of converting historical-cost accounting statements into general-price-level-adjusted

TABLE 6-4

CLASSIFICATION OF MONETARY AND NONMONETARY ITEMS[a]

MONETARY ITEMS

ASSETS	LIABILITIES AND EQUITIES
1. Cash on hand and in banks	1. Accounts and notes payable
2. Certificates of deposit	2. Any accrued payables (for example, wages)
3. All accounts receivable—trade	3. Dividends payable (cash)
4. All receivables from employees, subsidiaries, and so on	4. Income taxes payable
5. Allowances estimating losses on receivables	5. Bonds and notes payable
6. Investments in bonds and notes expected to be held to maturity	6. Deferred income taxes
7. Cash value of life insurance policies	7. Deferred revenue from customer advances on fixed price contracts

NONMONETARY ITEMS

ASSETS	LIABILITIES AND EQUITIES
1. Inventory	1. Estimated liabilities (warranties, coupon obligations, and so on)
2. Investments in securities or other assets that do not have fixed prices (land, common stocks, and so on)	2. Advances from customers for contracted sales
3. Plant assets	3. Preferred stock
4. Property and natural resources	4. Convertible bonds and stocks not expected to be redeemed
5. Intangible assets (goodwill, patents, and so on)	5. Common stock and other shareholders' equity accounts
6. Accumulated depreciation, depletion, or amortization	
7. Prepaid expenses	

[a] For an official listing of monetary and nonmonetary items, see **FASB Statement No. 33**, par. 208.

(GPLA) financial statements requires that we answer a series of questions about each financial statement item. This sequence of steps is summarized in Figure 6–1.

To illustrate the application of the GPLA accounting model, return to the example of Tom Dooley's Car Wash. This GPLA application assumes that the events described in the Dooley case have already taken place. The historical-cost financial statements are then restated in terms of general-price-level adjustments. As a result of this assumption, the amount of taxes and dividends paid, along with the other events, will not be affected by the revised GPLA statements. The GPLA statements will simply illustrate the *process* of general-price-level adjustment.

Assume the following year-end and average general price index data are available for the 1960–1963 period:

GENERAL PRICE INDEX DATA		
DATE	INDEX	AVERAGE INDEX FOR THE YEAR
12/31/60	80%	
12/31/61	84	1961 = 82%
12/31/62	90	1962 = 87
12/31/63	98	1963 = 93

FIGURE 6-1
Converting historical-cost statements into GPLA statements

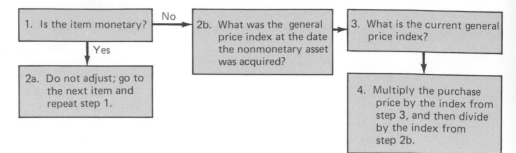

The balance sheet The historical-cost and general-price-level-adjusted balance sheets for 1961 and 1962 are illustrated in Exhibit 6–5. In 1961 the nonmonetary items in the balance sheet are all adjusted by the factor 84/80, which is the year-end index over the index **at the time the nonmonetary item was recorded.** Since land and equipment were purchased at the beginning of 1961 when the index was 80 percent, they must be multiplied by 84/80 in order to convert their amounts to 1961 year-end index (84 percent) dollars. The process converts all dollars to a common measure, 1961 year-end dollars, thereby correcting for the 5 percent decrease [(84% − 80%)/80%] in the dollar's purchasing power during the year. It should be noted that cash, the only monetary item, was not adjusted because it is a **fixed claim to dollars.** The ending balance of $20,000 can only command $20,000 of goods and services and is not influenced by whether the dollars came from the beginning, middle, or end of 1961.

Measuring nonmonetary effects Note that all nonmonetary items for 1962 in Exhibit 6–5 are factored by the same amount, 90/80, in order to restate them to 1962 year-end (90 percent) index dollars. Also note that the Accumulated Depreciation

EXHIBIT 6-5

	AS OF THE END OF 1961			AS OF THE END OF 1962		
ITEM	**HISTORICAL-COST BALANCE**	**PLA × FACTOR**	**= GPLA BALANCE**	**HISTORICAL-COST BALANCE**	**PLA × FACTOR**	**= GPLA BALANCE**
Cash	$ 20,000	M.A.ᵃ	$ 20,000	$ 60,000	M.A.ᵃ	$ 60,000
Equipment	100,000	84/80	105,000	100,000	90/80	112,500
Accumulated depreciation	(20,000)	84/80	(21,000)	(60,000)	90/80	(67,500)
Land	25,000	84/80	26,250	25,000	90/80	28,125
Total assets	$125,000		$130,250	$125,000		$133,125
Owners' capital	$125,000	84/80	$131,250	$125,000	90/80	$140,625
Retained earnings (deficit)	0	(forced)	(1,000)	0	(forced)	(7,500)
Total equities	$125,000		$130,250	$125,000		$133,125

TOM DOOLEY'S CAR WASH
Balance Sheets for the Periods Ended December 31

ᵃ M.A. = monetary asset, not GPLA adjusted.

account is considered to have been recorded at index-80 dollars (January 1, 1961, dollars) for *both* the 1961 and the 1962 balance sheets. Why is depreciation at index-80 dollars when the depreciation process has taken place continuously throughout the entire 2-year period? The answer is, Because the dollars that are being used as the basis for measuring depreciation are from the beginning of 1961 when the equipment was purchased. As a result, accumulated depreciation, depletion, and amortization are always adjusted using the same factor used to adjust the asset to which they relate.

Income and retained earnings Exhibit 6–6 illustrates both the historical-cost and the GPLA income statement and retained earnings statement for 1961 and 1962. Since the income measurement is based on changes in the balance sheets from the

EXHIBIT 6–6

TOM DOOLEY'S CAR WASH

Income Statements for the Periods Ended December 31
Historical-Cost and General-Price-Level-Adjusted

	AS OF THE END OF 1961			AS OF THE END OF 1962		
ITEM	HISTORICAL-COST BALANCE	PLA × FACTOR	GPLA = BALANCE	HISTORICAL-COST BALANCE	PLA × FACTOR	GPLA = BALANCE
Revenues						
Operations	$25,500	84/82	$26,122	$59,500	90/87	$61,552
Interest	500	84/84	500	4,000	90/90	4,000
Total	$26,000		$26,622	$63,500		$65,552
Expenses						
Depreciation	$20,000	84/80	$21,000	$40,000	90/80	$45,000
Miscellaneous expenses	2,000	84/82	2,049	7,000	90/87	7,241
Income taxes	2,000	84/84	2,000	8,250	90/90	8,250
Total	$24,000		$25,049	$55,250		$60,491
Net income from operations	$ 2,000		$ 1,573	$ 8,250		$ 5,061
Monetary holding loss	0		(573)	0		(3,240)
Net income (loss)	$ 2,000		$ 1,000	$ 8,250		$ 1,821

TOM DOOLEY'S CAR WASH

Statement of Retained Earnings for the Years 1961 and 1962
Historical-Cost and General-Price-Level-Adjusted

	as of the end of 1961			as of the end of 1962		
	HISTORICAL-COST BALANCE	PLA × FACTOR	GPLA = BALANCE	HISTORICAL-COST BALANCE	PLA × FACTOR	GPLA = BALANCE
Retained earnings (deficit), 1/1	$ 0	(See income	$ 0	$ 0	(See income	$(1,071)[a]
Net income	2,000	statement)	1,000	8,250	statement)	1,821
Less dividends	(2,000)	84/84	(2,000)	(8,250)	90/90	(8,250)
Retained earnings (deficit), 12/31	0		$(1,000)	$ 0		$(7,500)

[a] The $(1,000) beginning retained earnings balance for 1962 is the 1961 ending balance price level adjusted as follows: $(1,000) × 90/84 = $(1,071).

beginning to the end of an accounting period, we should be able to reconcile our income statement with our balance sheet through the retained earnings statement.

From Exhibit 6–5 we know that GPLA retained earnings (deficit) was $(1,000) at the end of 1961. We also know that we started 1961 with a zero balance in retained earnings, that we declared and paid $2,000 in dividends at the end of 1961, and that there were no other transactions affecting retained earnings. Given this information, what was GPLA net income for 1961? If we put the information into a retained earnings statement format, we can solve for net income. First we assume that dividends declared are a given piece of information and that the beginning and ending retained earnings are known from the balance sheet data (Exhibit 6–5). Now determine what income must be, given the dividend and retained earnings data:

	GPLA BALANCES
Retained earnings, 1/1/61	$ 0
Plus net income for 1961	Unknown
Less dividends for 1961	(2,000)
Retained earnings, 12/31/61	$(1,000)

As a result of this analysis, we know that GPLA net income for 1961 must have been $1,000.

In Exhibit 6–6 each income statement item is multiplied by the appropriate PLA factor. In the case of revenues, it is normally assumed that the inflows were recorded evenly throughout the period, therefore the average index for 1961 ($=82$ percent) is used to represent the price index at the date the revenues were recorded. If such an assumption were too unrealistic, we might go to monthly sales figures and calculate their GPLA value using the average index from each month. In the extreme, we could adjust sales on a daily basis using a daily index.

Revenues from operations and miscellaneous expenses were both assumed to have been recorded evenly throughout the period and were, therefore, factored by 84/82 in 1961 and 90/87 in 1962. Interest was paid at year-end, as were income taxes. As a result, they are stated at year-end dollars in both the historical-cost and the GPLA model for both 1961 and 1962. Depreciation expense is compatible with accumulated depreciation in the balance sheet and references dollars from the date the depreciable equipment was acquired, *not* the period during which it was depreciated.

Note that the retained earnings statement for 1962 starts with an opening balance other than the closing balance from 1961. The opening balance for 1962 is computed by restating the 1961 ending balance in terms of 1962 year-end dollars. This is simply a shortcut to restating the entire 1961 balance sheet in terms of 1962 dollars and then measuring the change in wealth position (balance sheets) from 1961 to 1962. If the entire 1961 balance sheet were restated as of the end of 1962 in 1962 year-end dollars, the ending 1961 deficit would equal $1,071.

Computing monetary gains and losses The GPLA statement for Dooley includes an item that the historical-cost model does not include: **monetary holding loss.** Where did the monetary loss come from? Monetary losses result from holding cash, a monetary asset, during a period in which the general price level increased. The monetary loss represents a loss in general purchasing power. Exhibit 6–7 illustrates how the monetary loss from holding cash during a period of inflation can be calcu-

EXHIBIT 6–7

		RUNNING CASH BALANCE ×	PLA FACTOR FOR FLOW =	BALANCE ASSUMING CASH IS
DATE	ITEM			NONMONETARY
		1961		
1/1/61	Opening balance	0		
1/1/61–12/31/61	Operating revenues	$ 25,500	84/82	$ 26,122
1/1/61–12/31/61	Operating expenses	(2,000)	84/82	(2,049)
12/31/61	Interest income	500	84/84	500
12/31/61	Income taxes	(2,000)	84/84	(2,000)
12/31/61	Dividends	(2,000)	84/84	(2,000)
Ending balance		$ 20,000		$ 20,573
				– 20,000
	1961 Monetary holding loss			$ 573
		1962		
1/1/62	Opening balance	$ 20,000	90/84	$ 21,429
1/1/62–12/31/62	Operating revenues	59,500	90/87	61,552
1/1/62–12/31/62	Operating expenses	(7,000)	90/87	(7,241)
12/31/62	Interest income	4,000	90/90	4,000
12/31/62	Income taxes	(8,250)	90/90	(8,250)
12/31/62	Dividends	(8,250)	90/90	(8,250)
Ending balance		$ 60,000		$ 63,240
				– 60,000
	1962 Monetary holding loss			$ 3,240

TOM DOOLEY'S CAR WASH

Monetary Holding Loss Calculation—1961 and 1962

lated. The calculation adjusts the monetary account balance **"as if"** it were a non-**monetary account.** However, the balance in the monetary account is not altered. The difference between the actual balance in the monetary account and the "as if" GPLA balance is a monetary holding gain or loss.

Cash is the only monetary item in our example, and therefore the entire monetary holding loss is attributable to holding cash. In more complex cases, the monetary gain or loss is computed for each monetary account, with the net total gain or loss reported in the GPLA income statement. Just as holding cash during a period of inflation results in a purchasing power loss, holding monetary liabilities such as notes or bonds payable will result in gains in general purchasing power. That is, the dollars used to repay the liabilities will be worth less in terms of general purchasing power.

Application of the GPLA Model

The GPLA model illustrated in Exhibits 6–5 and 6–6 provides statements for 1961 and 1962 based on the set of facts in the historical-cost statements. In other words, *all decisions are already made* on the basis of the historical-cost data, and the illustrations simply convert the statements to common dollars. However, to evaluate the results from a GPLA model, income measured per the GPLA model must be treated as disposable wealth (as in Exhibits 6–3 and 6–4) and used as the basis for decisions.

Exhibit 6–8 provides the general-price-level-adjusted income and retained earnings statement for the years 1961–1963 for the Dooley case. The statements assume that interest revenue has increased over that reported in Exhibit 6–4. This increase results from the fact that additional cash is retained in the business when GPLA income is the measure of disposable wealth (see Exhibit 6–9 and page 198 for a calculation and explanation of cash flows and resulting cash balances). In other words, the GPLA measure of income becomes the basis for the dividend distribution decision. The additional cash retained in the business is assumed to earn roughly the same interest rate as that reported in the Exhibit 6–4 data.

The income statements in Exhibit 6–8 also assume that taxes are equal to 50 percent of GPLA net income before tax (but after net monetary losses). This latter assumption is not critical—a change in taxes will change income and dividends by an equal amount in the opposite direction, **leaving the balance sheets the same.** The tax amount and the dividend amount are the two economic decisions that are based on GPLA wealth measurement, explaining the change in real economic (cash) flows between the first GPLA examples (in Exhibits 6–5 to 6–7) and the second GPLA examples (Exhibits 6–8 and 6–9). Keep in mind that the actual tax laws are based on the conventional accounting model.

Note that the retained earnings balance is zero because net income from the GPLA model is being used as the basis for the dividend decision (how much to distribute), as it was in the earlier historical-cost example. The ending cash bal-

EXHIBIT 6–8

TOM DOOLEY'S CAR WASH

Comparative Income Statement for the Periods
Ended December 31
(General-Price-Level-Adjusted)

	1963	1962	1961	TOTAL 1961–1963
Revenues:				
Operations	$77,935	$61,552	$26,122	$165,609
Interest[a]	8,400	4,050	500	12,950
Total revenues	$86,335	$65,602	$26,622	$178,559
Expenses:				
Depreciation	$48,000	$45,000	$21,000	$114,000
Miscellaneous	11,355	7,241	2,049	20,645
Net monetary loss	6,580	3,311	573	10,464
Income tax	10,200	5,025	1,500	16,725
Total expenses	$76,135	$60,577	$25,122	$161,834
Net income	$10,200	$ 5,025	$ 1,500	$ 16,725

[a] Note that interest has increased over previous example because of the increased cash retention.

TOM DOOLEY'S CAR WASH

Comparative Retained Earnings Statement
For the Periods Ended December 31
(General-Price-Level-Adjusted)

	1963	1962	1961
Beginning retained earnings	$ 0	$ 0	$ 0
Plus net income	10,200	5,025	1,500
Less dividends	(10,200)	(5,025)	(1,500)
Ending retained earnings	$ 0	$ 0	$ 0

Note that these are all single-period statements, *not* comparative statements of 1963. When comparative GPLA statements are prepared, the prior years comparative GPLA data are restated in current-year GPLA dollars.

EXHIBIT 6–9

TOM DOOLEY'S CAR WASH

Balance Sheets as of December 31
(General-Price Level-Adjusted)

	1963	1962	1961
Assets			
Cash	$ 120,000	$ 67,500	$ 21,000
Equipment	120,000	112,500	105,000
Accumulated depreciation	(120,000)	(67,500)	(21,000)
Land	30,000	28,125	26,250
Total assets	$ 150,000	$ 140,625	$ 131,250
Equities			
Owners' equity	$ 150,000	$ 140,625	$ 131,250
Retained earnings	0	0	0
Total equities	$ 150,000	$ 140,625	$ 131,250

TOM DOOLEY'S CAR WASH

Statement of Changes in Financial Position
For the Periods Ended December 31
(General-Price-Level-Adjusted)

	1963	1962	1961	TOTAL 1961–1963
Sources of cash				
Operations	$75,500	$59,500	$25,500	$160,500
Interest	8,400	4,050	500	12,950
	$83,900	$63,550	$26,000	$173,450
Uses of cash				
Miscellaneous expense	$11,000	$ 7,000	$ 2,000	$ 20,000
Income taxes	10,200	5,025	1,500	16,725
Dividends	10,200	5,025	1,500	16,725
	$31,400	$17,050	$ 5,000	$ 53,450
Net cash flow	$52,500	$46,500	$21,000	$120,000

Note that these are all single-period statements, *not* comparative statements of 1963.
When comparative GPLA statements are prepared, the prior years' comparative GPLA
data are restated in current-year GPLA dollars.

ance in the GPLA model ($120,000) is higher than in the historical-cost model because less cash was taken out of the business in the form of dividends. In general, the GPLA model illustrates that the changing price level has affected the measure of net income over the 1961–1963 period ($16,725 versus $26,500), which has affected the amount of dividends paid ($16,725 versus $26,500), which has affected the amount of cash retained in the business ($120,000 versus $100,000), which affects the ending wealth position of the entity ($150,000 versus $125,000).

These changes have had a cumulative effect over the 3-year period. In 1961 the only real difference was the decision to pay dividends of $1,500 after paying taxes of $1,500 (see Exhibit 6–8) instead of paying dividends of $2,000 after paying taxes of $2,000. Since dividends and taxes both call for end-of-period cash flows, the monetary loss is the same as in Exhibit 6–6. In the subsequent years, however, the higher cash balances actually resulted in greater total cash inflows from interest ($12,950 in Exhibit 6–8 versus $12,500 in Exhibit 6–3). These changes in subsequent years affect the amount of the monetary loss since the cash balance is different. For instance, the 1962 monetary loss increase from $3,240 in Exhibit 6–6 to $3,311 in Exhibit 6–8 is due to the real changes in the cash balance that occur when GPLA is used as a basis for decisions. The GPLA restatement of revenues and expenses resulted in *lower* pretax income and, therefore, *lower* cash outflows for taxes and dividends.

The total impact of these differences results in an ending wealth position under GPLA that is $25,000 greater than under the historical-cost model when the net income numbers of both models are used as a measure of disposable wealth. The $25,000 difference is attributable to $20,000 more cash under GPLA and a $5,000 greater recorded amount for land. The cash increase, representing a real economic change in the two models, is reconciled as follows:

Net cash flow, historical-cost model	$100,000
+ Increase in cash interest using GPLA model ($12,950 − 12,500)	450
+ Decrease in taxes paid using GPLA model ($26,500 − 16,725)	9,775
+ Decrease in dividends paid using GPLA model ($26,500 − 16,725)	9,775
Net cash flow, GPLA model	$120,000

Evaluation of the GPLA model The combined statements in Exhibits 6–8 and 6–9 demonstrate several interesting points. First, note that the cash balance at the end of the 3 years is exactly $20,000 greater under GPLA than under the historical-cost model. The ending cash balance under GPLA ($120,000) is also exactly equal to the *GPLA* measurement of the equipment at the end of the 3-year period. If Dooley had taken the $100,000 that he invested in car-wash equipment in 1961 and had invested in the "package" of goods and services used to make up the price index of this case, his "package" would have been worth $120,000 by the end of 1963 ($100,000 × 96/80 = $120,000). Since Dooley's ending cash position is equal to the 1963 GPLA measurement of such a "package" of goods and services, it may be concluded that Dooley has experienced neither a gain nor a loss in **general purchasing power.**

Dooley is just as well off in 1963 as he was in 1961 in terms of **wealth position measured according to the general price index.** In addition, Dooley consumed all the income, which totaled $16,725. The GPLA net income measure is, therefore, a measure of real disposable wealth defined in terms of general purchasing power.

If financial statement users are interested in their wealth position defined in terms of general purchasing power, the GPLA model may provide the most relevant information. However, some users may be more interested in wealth maintenance defined in terms of productive capacity, and the GPLA model will not be appropriate for such a goal. Recall from the case that the replacement cost of the car-wash equipment at the end of 1963 was $125,000. Dooley's cash position under the GPLA model is only $120,000, still $5,000 short of maintaining the **operating capacity** of a car-wash business.

The primary assumption underlying the GPLA model is that the wealth measure—general purchasing power—is relevant to users of the GPLA accounting data. If this assumption holds, the GPLA, or constant-dollar, model can be said to provide useful information for economic decision making. Some of the other arguments that have been presented for and against the GPLA model are summarized in Exhibit 6–10. We should note that all of these arguments are less important than the fundamental question of how to best define wealth for the decisions at hand.

Current-Entry-Value Model

To measure wealth position in terms of the productive or operating capabilities of an entity, the accounting model must consider the change in cost of specific assets. The method of measuring changes in specific assets is very similar to the GPLA approach. Instead of using general price indexes, **specific price indexes** or other measures of specific price changes can be applied to specific assets. The major variable in this approach is the specificity of the index applied to any given asset. The more specific the index, the more precise the measure of the current-entry or replacement cost. This is tempered by the fact that as the index becomes more specific, its selection becomes more subjective.

Replacement-cost example—inventory   To illustrate the replacement-cost model as it affects inventory measurement, consider the Darren Sugar Company, a wholesaler engaged in selling sugar to retailers. Darren purchased $35,000 (wholesale) worth of sugar at the beginning of 1972. By the end of 1972, the wholesale price of this sugar was $38,000. By the end of 1973, the wholesale price of the sugar was $42,000. At the end of 1974, Darren goes out of the sugar business by selling its inventory at retail for $49,000 when the wholesale price is $47,000.

Exhibit 6–11 compares the historical-cost income statements and balance sheets with their replacement-cost counterparts over the life of the entity. Several points should be emphasized in reviewing this example:

EXHIBIT 6–10

> ### EVALUATION OF GPLA ACCOUNTING
>
> #### ADVANTAGES OF GPLA ACCOUNTING
>
> 1. The GPLA model reports all financial data in terms of uniform *constant dollars,* converting every non-monetary historical dollar to a current *constant-dollar* amount. This improves the *uniformity* of the dollars used in reporting financial data and compensates for the impact of inflation on the measurement unit.
> 2. The GPLA model is *as objective as historical cost* because it simply takes historical dollars and multiplies them by an agreed-upon measure of the change in the dollar's value. Each entity, for example, with $500 of nonmonetary assets in its financial statements from the year 1957 will have them restated to the same current-dollar value. This increases the *objectivity* of the process of compensating for inflation.
> 3. The GPLA model improves the comparability of financial statements across firms. Since all dollars are restated to a common constant-dollar unit, assuming the same index is used, the impact of inflation is eliminated. This permits a comparison of several entities net of the impact of inflation.
>
> #### DISADVANTAGES OF GPLA ACCOUNTING
>
> 1. The preparation and review of GPLA financial statements is a costly process, and the cost may exceed the benefits.
> 2. Measuring GPLA values for nonmonetary items does not measure the *real change in value* of those items. In other words, very few specific assets or liabilities change in specific price at the exact same rate as the change in a general price index.
> 3. *No one index* of general-price-level changes is appropriate for all cases. It does not, for example, seem appropriate to use an index developed from price changes in consumer goods and services for a durable (nonconsumer) goods manufacturer or a long-term construction contractor. If more than one index is permitted, the GPLA valuation is *subjective* because of the need to choose the appropriate index.

EXHIBIT 6–11

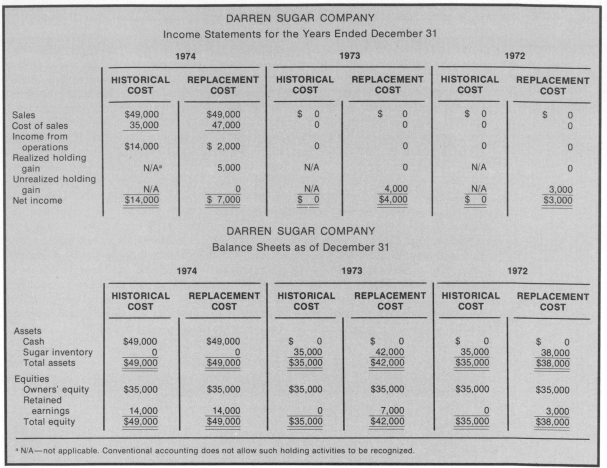

DARREN SUGAR COMPANY
Income Statements for the Years Ended December 31

	1974		1973		1972	
	HISTORICAL COST	REPLACEMENT COST	HISTORICAL COST	REPLACEMENT COST	HISTORICAL COST	REPLACEMENT COST
Sales	$49,000	$49,000	$ 0	$ 0	$ 0	$ 0
Cost of sales	35,000	47,000	0	0	0	0
Income from operations	$14,000	$ 2,000	0	0	0	0
Realized holding gain	N/Aᵃ	5,000	N/A	0	N/A	0
Unrealized holding gain	N/A	0	N/A	4,000	N/A	3,000
Net income	$14,000	$ 7,000	$ 0	$4,000	$ 0	$3,000

DARREN SUGAR COMPANY
Balance Sheets as of December 31

	1974		1973		1972	
	HISTORICAL COST	REPLACEMENT COST	HISTORICAL COST	REPLACEMENT COST	HISTORICAL COST	REPLACEMENT COST
Assets						
Cash	$49,000	$49,000	$ 0	$ 0	$ 0	$ 0
Sugar inventory	0	0	35,000	42,000	35,000	38,000
Total assets	$49,000	$49,000	$35,000	$42,000	$35,000	$38,000
Equities						
Owners' equity	$35,000	$35,000	$35,000	$35,000	$35,000	$35,000
Retained earnings	14,000	14,000	0	7,000	0	3,000
Total equity	$49,000	$49,000	$35,000	$42,000	$35,000	$38,000

ᵃ N/A—not applicable. Conventional accounting does not allow such holding activities to be recognized.

1. Total income over the life of the firm is the same for historical-cost accounting and replacement-cost accounting.
2. Revenues are *not* adjusted from their transacted values in the replacement-cost model.
3. In the replacement-cost model, the income due to the actual operating activities of the firm is separated from the impact of "holding activities."

EQUAL TOTAL INCOME   The first point in the above list is demonstrated by the fact that the ending cash position is the same, $49,000 for both models (see Exhibit 6–11). Although the replacement-cost model recognized part of the income sooner than did the historical-cost model, this is simply the result of a different allocation of profits to the three report periods. The allocation of profits in the replacement-cost model permits recognition of gains and losses due to "holding activities." The holding activities in this case stem from Darren's decision to hold on to its sugar and *not* sell sugar to retailers until 1974.

As a result of measuring changes in asset prices due to holding activities, the replacement-cost model differentiates between *holding* gains or losses and gains or losses that result from actual *transacted* activities. Over the 3-year period, most ($12,000) of Darren's profits were attributable to its holding sugar during a period of rising prices. This had nothing to do with efficient or inefficient operations because the purpose of the business was to make a profit by selling sugar to retailers. The holding gains are also separated into realized and unrealized components. In our examples, the **realized holding gain** is defined as the change in the replacement-cost measurement of any revenue or expense item attributable to price changes in the current period *only*. The **unrealized holding gain** (or yet to be realized holding gain) is defined as the change in the replacement-cost measurement of any end-of-period balance sheet item attributable to price changes in the current period *only*. The holding gains or losses reflect the changes in both income statement items (items consumed during the period) and balance sheet items that are attributable to the price changes occurring in the *current* year alone. Price changes of prior years are not reported in the current year's replacement-cost measures of holding gains.

Both the realized and unrealized holding gain (loss) accounts are income statement accounts, and like all other income statement accounts they are closed to retained earnings (owner's equity in our example because no separate equity accounts are given) at the end of each period. This process reinforces the annual nature of the holding gains. Note that the above definitions *do not* require all holding gains or losses of the current period to be reported as "realized" in the income statements of current and future periods. They *do* require the total impact of any given period's price changes to be reported as realized and unrealized holding gains only in the period in which the price changes occur. In a year when no specific price changes occur, no realized or unrealized holding gains would be reported for that year. As a result, the annual income measurement on a replacement-cost basis consists of two major components: (1) revenues at their actual recorded amounts less expenses measured in terms of their current replacement cost, resulting in replacement-cost operating income; and (2) the realized and unrealized holding gains or losses *attributable to that period's price changes alone*.

We should note at this point that at least two other alternatives to our approach for measuring holding activities exist. Alternative 2 is a simplification of alternative 1 (illustrated in Exhibit 6–11) that ignores the breakdown of the holding gain into realized and unrealized portions. Using this approach, all holding gains (or losses) from price changes during the current period would be reported as "holding gains (losses)" in the current period's income statement. For Darren Sugar Company, the "holding gain" amounts for 1972, 1973, and 1974 would be $3,000, $4,000, and $5,000, respectively. As is the case in alternative 1, the annual amount of "holding gain" would be closed to retained earnings (owner's equity) at the end of each period.

Alternative 3, which is the least desirable in our opinion, defines "realized holding gains" as the sum of the differences between the replacement-cost measurement of an income statement account and its historical-cost measurement. When "realized holding gains" are defined in this way, the sum of replacement-cost operating income and "realized holding gains (losses)" will always equal historical-cost net income (by definition). The "unrealized holding gain (loss)" is, therefore, best defined as the remaining amount of holding gain or loss needed to make the replacement-cost income number equal to the change in the replacement-cost balance sheets. In the Darren Sugar Company example, 1972 and 1973 would be the same as in Exhibit 6–11 because there are no operating income account activities. In 1974 however, a "realized holding gain" of $12,000 would be reported for the total (*3-year*) difference between the historical cost of the inventory ($35,000) and its current replacement cost of $47,000 (at current wholesale prices). Also, a $7,000 "unrealized holding loss" would be necessary so that the replacement-cost net income will equal $7,000 ($2,000 operating income plus $12,000 realized gain less $7,000 unrealized loss), which is equal to the change in the balance sheets between 1973 and 1974 on a replacement-cost basis. Most illustrations of alternative 3 treat the unrealized and realized gain (loss) accounts as balance sheet accounts that are *not* closed to retained earnings at the end of each period, which we believe to be less desirable. We also find the unrealized holding loss of $7,000 (described above) to be an undesirable side effect of the way the realized holding gain is defined (as a *multiple-period* measure of price change within a *single-period* measure of income). Therefore, we prefer either alternative 1 (as in Exhibit 6–11) or the elimination of the distinction between realized and unrealized holding gains or losses as in alternative 2.

Keep in mind that whatever method is used to disclose holding activities, the "bottom line" net income number *must be* consistent with the change in balance sheets for the model to be internally consistent. The three different ways to report holding gains discussed above may be summarized by illustrating the 1974 replacement-cost income statement for the Darren Sugar Company example using the three alternative methods:

DARREN SUGAR COMPANY 1974 Net Income per the Replacement-Cost Model: Alternative Disclosures of Holding Gains			
	ALTERNATIVE 1	ALTERNATIVE 2	ALTERNATIVE 3
Sales	$49,000	$49,000	$49,000
Cost of sales	47,000	47,000	47,000
Income from operations	$ 2,000	$ 2,000	$ 2,000
Realized holding gains	5,000	N/A	12,000
Unrealized holding gains (losses)	0	N/A	(7,000)
Holding gains	N/A[a]	5,000	N/A
Net income	$ 7,000	$ 7,000	$ 7,000

[a] Not applicable.

REVENUES BASED ON TRANSACTED AMOUNTS   The second point, that total revenues are the same, is related to the fact that the total income, over the life of the firm under the two models, is the same. In the long run, over the entity's entire life, only the transacted amounts of revenues and expense are allowed to affect income. Revenue is always recorded at the transacted amounts that represent current prices at the time of sale. However, expenses are allowed to vary in such a way as to permit the recognition of their changing prices. In 1972 the wholesale price of sugar increased $3,000, and the replacement-cost model recognized an increase in the *cost* of the asset, resulting in a holding gain. Of course, in 1974, when the sugar was sold, the higher replacement cost was matched against the transacted revenue, offsetting the previously recognized holding gains.

In terms of total lifetime income, replacement-cost accounting is not a departure from historical-cost accounting but is simply a reallocation of the total income of the firm to different time periods, as reflected by the following time lines:

INCOME—HISTORICAL-COST ACCOUNTING

	$ 0	$ 0	$14,000	Total = $14,000
Time line				
1/1/72	12/31/72	12/31/73	12/31/74	

INCOME—REPLACEMENT-COST ACCOUNTING

	$3,000	$4,000	$ 7,000	Total = $14,000
Time line				
1/1/72	12/31/72	12/31/73	12/31/74	

SEPARATION OF PROFIT SOURCES The final point is important from both an internal and an external information-seeking point of view. **Separation** of the income resulting from operations from that due to nonoperating activities is an important aspect of the replacement-cost accounting model. In the long run, the ability of the operating activities to generate cash will determine the success or failure of the business. The gains and losses attributable to holding activities may be, for many entities, relatively uncontrollable. Sometimes these holding gains and losses are referred to as **windfall gains and losses** to imply that they are not controllable. This does not mean that management or external users should ignore holding gains or losses. However, it is difficult to determine whether such holding activities are attributable to good management or sheer luck. Therefore, separating the holding activities from the operating activities prevents the *potentially* uncontrollable aspects of running the business (holding activities) from being mixed in with the controllable aspects (operating activities). Separating the holding activities from the **operations** of the firm enables financial statement users to evaluate these two different aspects of profit independently.

Replacement-cost example—depreciable assets The sugar example discussed earlier was sufficient to illustrate the key points of replacement-cost accounting. The depreciable asset example below presents some additional aspects of replacement-cost accounting that are worth noting.

Catherine's Flying Service is in the business of providing air transportation to individuals. The only asset owned by Catherine is a Lear Jet that was acquired on January 1, 1987, has an expected useful life of 3 years, and originally cost Catherine $900,000. The following data are available for the period 1987 to 1989:

YEAR	NET SERVICE REVENUES FOR THE YEAR	REPLACEMENT COST OF JET AT YEAR-END
1987	$525,000	$1,050,000
1988	630,000	1,200,000
1989	745,000	1,500,000

Exhibit 6–12 provides the summary of both the historical-cost and the replacement-cost annual statements (income and balance sheet) for each of the 3 years. The state-

ments show that Catherine has consumed all of the historical-cost income each year (through dividends) and is left with an ending cash position equal to the original cost of the Lear Jet, $900,000.

The major difference between the depreciable asset example and the (nonde-preciable) inventory example is in the notion of **catch-up depreciation,** which is required when accounting for depreciable assets. Note that the annual income statements for 1987 and 1988 recorded a total of $750,000 in depreciation expense on a year-end replacement-cost basis. The balance sheet as of 1988 shows a total of $800,000 accumulated depreciation, however, which is $50,000 greater than the sum of the replacement-cost income statement amounts. This catch-up depreciation affects the amount of the unrealized holding gain and may be reconciled with the income statement as follows:

COMPUTATION OF HOLDING GAINS			
	1989	1988	1987
Replacement-cost price change during period	$300,000	$150,000	$150,000
Less realized holding gain from current years' depreciation expense (one-third of asset used)	100,000	50,000	50,000
Remaining portion of price change *before* the adjustment for catch-up depreciation	$200,000	$100,000	$100,000
Less catch-up depreciation to account for the effect of this year's price change on portion of the asset depreciated in prior years	200,000	50,000	0
Unrealized holding gain	$ 0	$ 50,000	$100,000

These computations show how the realized and unrealized holding gains reported in the income statements are related to the change in the replacement price of the asset. The entries necessary to account for the price changes for 1987 and 1988 in a replacement-cost system could be recorded as follows:

		1989		1988		1987	
12/31	Airplane	300,000		150,000		150,000	
	Unrealized holding gain		300,000		150,000		150,000
	(To record price change)						
12/31	Depreciation expense	500,000		400,000		350,000	
	Accumulated depreciation		500,000		400,000		350,000
	(To record use of one-third of the airplane's value)						
12/31	Unrealized holding gain	100,000		50,000		50,000	
	Realized holding gain		100,000		50,000		50,000
	(To record realized portion of current price change)						
12/31	Unrealized holding gain	200,000		50,000		0	
	Accumulated depreciation		200,000		50,000		0
	(To record catch-up depreciation)						

The catch-up depreciation is essentially the portion of the current year's change in replacement cost that would have been expensed in previous years had the current replacement prices been used. In 1988, *based on the 1988 year-end replacement price* of $1,200,000, the balance in accumulated depreciation at January 1,

EXHIBIT 6-12

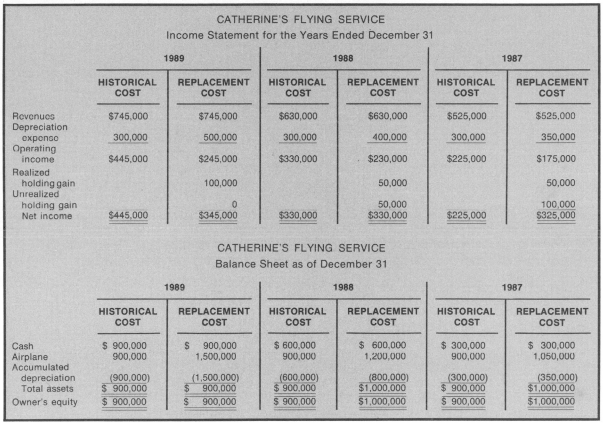

CATHERINE'S FLYING SERVICE
Income Statement for the Years Ended December 31

	1989		1988		1987	
	HISTORICAL COST	REPLACEMENT COST	HISTORICAL COST	REPLACEMENT COST	HISTORICAL COST	REPLACEMENT COST
Revenues	$745,000	$745,000	$630,000	$630,000	$525,000	$525,000
Depreciation expense	300,000	500,000	300,000	400,000	300,000	350,000
Operating income	$445,000	$245,000	$330,000	$230,000	$225,000	$175,000
Realized holding gain		100,000		50,000		50,000
Unrealized holding gain		0		50,000		100,000
Net income	$445,000	$345,000	$330,000	$330,000	$225,000	$325,000

CATHERINE'S FLYING SERVICE
Balance Sheet as of December 31

	1989		1988		1987	
	HISTORICAL COST	REPLACEMENT COST	HISTORICAL COST	REPLACEMENT COST	HISTORICAL COST	REPLACEMENT COST
Cash	$ 900,000	$ 900,000	$ 600,000	$ 600,000	$ 300,000	$ 300,000
Airplane	900,000	1,500,000	900,000	1,200,000	900,000	1,050,000
Accumulated depreciation	(900,000)	(1,500,000)	(600,000)	(800,000)	(300,000)	(350,000)
Total assets	$ 900,000	$ 900,000	$ 900,000	$1,000,000	$ 900,000	$1,000,000
Owner's equity	$ 900,000	$ 900,000	$ 900,000	$1,000,000	$ 900,000	$1,000,000

1988, would have been $400,000 instead of the actual opening replacement-cost balance of $350,000. As a result, the 1988 catch-up depreciation amount would be $50,000. The 1989 amount is $200,000, or two-thirds of the total $300,000 price increase experienced in 1989 since two-thirds of the airplane's value had been consumed as of January 1, 1989.

We should point out that if Catherine had paid dividends each year equal to replacement-cost operating income less the catch-up depreciation amount (1987 = $175,000; 1988 = $180,000; and 1989 = $145,000) *instead* of historical-cost net income, the ending cash balance would have been $1,500,000. This would have enabled Catherine to replace the jet needed to stay in business.

Evaluation of the current-entry-value model The current-entry-value (replacement-cost) model provides information that will generally prove useful to those who are committed to staying in a particular line of business. The operating-income measure of the replacement-cost model pinpoints the change in "well-offness" attributable to operations. In the sugar case, Darren could consume $2,000 in 1974 and still be able to replace the productive assets (inventory) with the $47,000 cash balance. Some accountants feel that the operating-profit measure is the best estimate of an

EXHIBIT
6–13

ADVANTAGES AND DISADVANTAGES OF THE CURRENT-ENTRY-VALUE MODEL

ADVANTAGES OF THE CURRENT-ENTRY-VALUE MODEL

1. It *separates holding activities from operating activities,* with replacement-cost operating income providing a good estimate of the long-term cash-generating ability of the entity.
2. Using specific price indexes, it facilitates the maintenance of the productive capacity of the entity by using the replacement-cost accounting data.
3. It is as objective as the historical-cost model, given the specific index chosen.
4. It increases the comparability of the accounting information across firms.

DISADVANTAGES OF THE CURRENT-ENTRY-VALUE MODEL

1. Information regarding specific price indexes may be *too* costly to obtain.
2. Replacement costs do not necessarily represent the net present value of the net assets of the entity.
3. The construction (selection) of specific price indexes is a more subjective process than that of general-price-level indexes.
4. It fails to measure the impact of changes in general purchasing power.

entity's long-run cash-generating ability, and sustained operating losses may indicate to users of financial statements that the replacement of the productive assets of the business will not be economically feasible. Exhibit 6–13 summarizes some of the commonly identified advantages and disadvantages of the current-entry-value model.

Current-Exit-Value Model

Objective of the exit-value model The **exit-value model,** or **market-value model,** is similar to the entry-value model in that it attempts to measure the value of specific assets, often by using specific price indexes. The exit-value model differs from the entry-value model in two ways: (1) the specific price indexes are used to measure selling prices, and (2) the model has no concern for breaking down income in any way. The exit-value model, however, like the entry-value model, results in the same total income as the historical-cost model over the life of the entity.

Exit prices To illustrate the first difference between the exit-value and the entry-value models, consider the Darren Sugar Company example once again. Assume that the sugar inventory was purchased at the beginning of 1972 for $35,000 and that its *retail value* increased to $39,000 by the end of 1972, $43,500 by the end of 1973, and $49,000 by the end of 1974. The exit-value model would record income for the 3-year period based on the change in the market (retail) value from period to period. The 1972 income would be $4,000 ($39,000 − $35,000); the 1973 income would be $4,500 ($43,500 − $39,000); and the 1974 income would be $5,500 ($49,000 − $43,500). The total income over the life of the entity would be $14,000 ($4,000 + $4,500 + $5,500), just as in the historical-cost model and the current-entry-value model. However, the amount of income allocated to each of the three accounting periods would differ from amounts allocated in the other two models.

Composition of exit-value income The exit-value model as normally applied to accounting data does not generate any income statement detail but simply recognizes income as the change in the market value of the net assets of the entity from the beginning to the end of the accounting period.[15] One of the most widely cited versions of the exit-value model contends that the income-generating process is a "black box" of unknown elements that cannot be meaningfully broken down into such subcomponents as "operating profits" and "holding profits."[16]

The primary objective of this model is to measure wealth in terms of a liquid or cash-equivalent value. This cash-equivalent model is said to facilitate the adaptability of the accounting information in that it continuously provides data on net assets (or investments) in a way that permits their cash yield to be computed and compared with all other net asset (investment) alternatives. The following performance measure is relevant for evaluation purposes:

$$\frac{NA_t - NA_{t-1}}{NA_{t-1}} = \text{Cash-equivalent yield}$$

where NA_t is the market (exit) value of net assets at time t, the end of the period, and NA_{t-1} is the market value of net assets at the beginning of the period. This measure is relevant for evaluation purposes both within a given set of net assets and across different sets of net assets.

Evaluation of the current-exit-value model   The market-value, or exit-value, model has many forms, some of which were noted earlier. It has historically been the least attractive alternative model for accounting policy makers and has not been seriously considered as a source of supplementary data, as have the GPLA and entry-value models. However, in some decision-making situations, the exit-value

EXHIBIT
6–14

ADVANTAGES AND DISADVANTAGES OF THE CURRENT-EXIT-VALUE MODEL
ADVANTAGES OF THE CURRENT-EXIT-VALUE MODEL
1. It calculates wealth and disposable wealth in terms of a cash-equivalent measure that is more universally relevant for comparisons within and among firms than past or present purchase prices or general-price-level adjusted prices.
2. By using specific price indexes, it facilitates the measurement of change in cash position (income) without regard to the source of the change, thereby recognizing the futility of breaking down income into separate categories.
3. It is as objective as the historical-cost model, given the specific price index chosen.
DISADVANTAGES OF THE CURRENT-EXIT-VALUE MODEL
1. Information regarding specific price indexes may be *too* costly to obtain.
2. Market values do not necessarily represent the net present value of the entity's net assets.
3. The construction (selection) of specific price indexes is a more subjective process than that of general-price-level indexes.
4. It fails to account for changes in general purchasing power.

[15] For an example of an income statement that might be used with the exit-value model, see Lawrence Friedman, "An Exit-Price Income Statement," *The Accounting Review*, January 1978, pp. 28–30.

[16] For a detailed discussion of this "black box" concept, see Raymond J. Chambers, *Accounting, Evaluation and Economic Behavior* (Englewood Cliffs, NJ: Prentice-Hall, 1966).

model can definitely provide relevant information. If the purpose of a business is to buy and sell plots of land for speculation, the current-exit value of the company's holdings may be the most useful way for the owners to determine the performance of the land speculation activities from one period to the next. The market values and changes therein may also provide the most relevant input to decision concerning the purchases or sales of land holdings. Exhibit 6–14 lists the advantages and disadvantages of the current-exit-value model.

SUMMARY

Some of the key elements of alternative models discussed and illustrated in this chapter are summarized in Table 6–5. Models that provide alternatives to the conventional accounting model are becoming more popular with decision makers who use financial accounting data. Understanding the nature of each of these alternatives, along with their respective strengths and weaknesses, will aid decision makers in selecting the most relevant accounting information for their needs.

No single model can be identified as being the most relevant for all decision-making needs. In fact, the limitations of each of the four basic models described in this chapter have led some accountants to combine models. For example, some accoun-

TABLE 6–5

KEY ELEMENTS OF ALTERNATIVE MODELS

BASIC MODEL	ALTERNATIVE TERMS USED TO IDENTIFY MODELS	BASIC WEALTH CONCEPT OF THE MODEL	METHOD OF APPLYING MODEL IN PRACTICE	OTHER KEY COMMENTS ABOUT THE MODEL
Historical-cost model	Conventional model Mixed-dollar model Original entry-value model	Wealth defined in terms of original transaction values	Original cost measurement	Historical-cost model is the *basis* of generally accepted accounting as currently practiced.
General-price-level model	Constant-dollar model Purchasing-power model General-inflation-adjusted model	Wealth defined in terms of general purchasing units	General price index applied to original costs	Basic premise is that purchasing power is wealth measure of interest. Total income not the same as in historical-cost model.
Current-entry-value model	Current-cost model Replacement-cost model Input-value model	Wealth defined in terms of current replacement cost of productive capacity	Specific price indexes applied to original costs	Basic premise is that current productive assets will be replaced with similar productive assets. Total income the same as in historical-cost model. Operating profit separated from holding profits.
Current-exit-value model	Market-value model Net-realizable-value model Current-cash-equivalent model Opportunity-cost model	Wealth defined in terms of current selling prices	Specific price indexes applied to original costs	Basic premise is that user wants to evaluate possible liquidation of investment at all times as one possible alternative. Total income the same as in historical-cost model. Income statement typically does not provide performance details.

tants have suggested combining replacement cost with general price adjustments. Certainly, the mixing of alternative valuation models is not new to accounting. As we shall see in Parts II and III of this book, the conventional or generally accepted accounting model is far from a pure historical model. In numerous instances GAAP call for deviations from historical cost.

The discussion of the alternative accounting models considered in this chapter, along with the framework of the generally accepted accounting model outlined in Chapter 2 and described in Chapters 3, 4, and 5, should enable the student to understand the details of the conventional accounting model and to evaluate the conventional model critically. Part I has provided the necessary background for understanding the remaining three parts of this text in both a practical and a conceptual sense.

QUESTIONS

Q6-1   What definition of *wealth* is employed in the historical-cost (conventional) accounting model?

Q6-2   What definition of *wealth* is employed in the general-price-level-adjusted (constant-dollar) model?

Q6-3   How does a current entry-value-based balance sheet measure (define) *wealth*?

Q6-4   How does an exit-value-based balance sheet measure (define) *wealth*?

Q6-5   What is the eventual impact of using historical-cost accounting income measures as a measure of disposable wealth during periods of steadily increasing prices?

Q6-6   What are some criteria for evaluating the alternative accounting models? How do these criteria affect decision making?

Q6-7   Identify the kinds of decisions that investors and creditors might wish to make, then identify what accounting-oriented information you believe would help them make such decisions.

Q6-8   What types of management decisions call for an understanding of the disposable wealth of the entity?

Q6-9   When would management try to obtain "new" equity or debt capital, and how does this decision relate to measurement of disposable income?

Q6-10   When might managers wish to use current-cost information for *internal* management decisions?

Q6-11   What is the fundamental difference between the current-cost model and the *GPLA* model?

Q6-12   What is the difference between *monetary* and *nonmonetary* items?

Q6-13   What is the economic impact on a corporation that has long-term bonds payable outstanding during periods of inflation?

Q6-14   What is the economic impact on a corporation that has held large amounts of cash during a period of deflation?

Q6-15   Do monetary gains or losses apply only to the GPLA model? Explain your answer.

CASES

C6-1   The historical-cost accounting model has always been used for financial reporting. Most companies that pay dividends to shareholders do not pay dividends at the same rate as income is earned. Instead, most companies pay some portion of their income to shareholders in the form of cash dividends and "retain" some of the income in the business. If net income were a true measure of change in wealth, it could all be paid out to the shareholders in the form of dividends, and the position of the entity would remain constant. What would eventually happen to an entity that paid out all of its net income to shareholders in the form of dividends?

REQUIRED Consider the above question by assuming one assumption from each of the following:

1. Inflation versus deflation
2. Growth company versus declining industry company
3. Only long-term assets used in production versus only material and labor used in production

C6–2 In her accounting class, Marge Memorex learned that holding monetary assets during inflation results in a purchasing power loss, whereas holding monetary liabilities results in a purchasing power gain. After thinking this over for some time, she concluded that better management of the company where she worked could lead to more profit (and a promotion for her as well). She requested an interview with her boss, Mr. Contemplater, so that she could tell him how the company could borrow more money and make money. Marge prepared very detailed examples that assumed very conservative rates of inflation, less than the expected inflation everyone was predicting for the next 15 years. These illustrations showed how the loans could be paid back with "cheaper" dollars at the end of 15 years, which would result in sizable monetary gains in purchasing power throughout the 15-year period. It was obvious to Marge that the company needed more debt, since this not only would result in purchasing power gains but would permit Mr. Contemplater to explore some of the new projects he had been thinking about lately. Mr. Contemplater listened to Marge and was impressed with her presentation. There was only one drawback, he said: "I can't figure out why the bank would be so stupid as to give us money so we can make more money *and* have a purchasing power gain! Seems to me the bank will have a purchasing power loss exactly equal to our gain. If you can explain this paradox to me, Marge, I might go along with your idea. But right now, you're basically telling me to take on as much debt as I can in order to make money, and that just doesn't make sense."

REQUIRED Help Marge answer the boss's question. Is the boss correct? Is Marge correct?

C6–3 A recent *Wall Street Journal* article about the steel industry has made you somewhat uneasy about your future as a salesperson for one of the major U.S. steel companies. The article said that, due to the high ratio of general inflation in recent years, profits of U.S. steel companies have been significantly overstated. Because of this overstatement of profits, the tax rates paid by the steel companies have been much higher than they appear to be and are considered to be (at least in part) a tax on assets.

The overstatement of income is said to result from unrealistically low charges for depreciation expense due to the fact that plant assets are undervalued in terms of their current values. Because of these low depreciation charges, income before tax is said to be overstated in "real" terms, with the resulting taxes also overstated. The article predicted that unless the industry could receive greater tax breaks or find new sources of capital to replace aging plant assets, or both, the outlook for the future was very poor for U.S. steel companies. Foreign steel has gained a greater share of the market in recent years, and the trend is expected to continue.

REQUIRED Evaluate the article's outlook. Is the situation described accurate? Does it apply to the steel industry alone? Why should the steel industry be more affected or less affected than other industries? What is the impact of general inflation on the problems cited?

C6–4 In 1969 a professor and 20 accounting students decided to try their luck at making a fortune in the oil industry. They each invested $10,000 and leased the oil rights to a piece of property in Western Texas. The joint venture they formed, called Wildcat #1, had a life that was limited to the oil recovery operations on the single piece of leased property (4,000 acres). The oil exploration began right away (in 1969) and went on for 15 years before the recovery operation ended. During this 15-year period, the total net income reported by Wildcat #1 amounted to $850,000. This included two major nonoperating items: (1) a loss of $130,000 (net of tax) from an explosion that destroyed an oil rig and (2) a loss of $65,000 (net of tax) due to a change in accounting method. During the 15-year period a total of $1,500,000 in salaries was paid to the 20 students. Also, dividends were paid out in the amount of $630,000. During the 15-year period the income statement reported 5 years of net losses (total = $473,000) and 10 years of net income ($1,323,000). In 1984, the end of the 15-year period, all assets were sold for $860,000, and liabilities of $440,000 were paid off.

REQUIRED In evaluating the life of the joint venture, determine the amount of "wealth improvement" that occurred over the 15-year period. In other words, how much better off was the entity at the end than at the beginning? What is the impact of the extraordinary loss on your answer? What is the impact of the accounting change on your answer? What kinds of data do you need to answer the questions?

C6–5 (CPA ADAPTED)   The objective of accounting is to provide useful information to investors and creditors for decision making. *FASB Statement No. 33* requires large publicly traded corporations to provide current-cost and constant-dollar data to external users on a supplementary disclosure basis.

REQUIRED

1. Describe how current-cost and constant-dollar data are generated from the historical financial statements.
2. Identify any advantages or disadvantages of constant-dollar data.
3. Identify any advantages or disadvantages of current-cost data.
4. How would depreciation expense differ under the three methods (historical cost, current cost, and constant dollar) in periods of inflation?
5. Is current-cost information of use to internal users as well as external users? Explain.

C6–6 (CPA ADAPTED)   Valuation of assets is an important topic in accounting theory. Suggested valuation methods include the following:

1. Historical cost (past purchase prices)
2. Historical cost adjusted to reflect general price-level changes
3. Discounted cash flow (future exchange prices)
4. Replacement cost (current purchase prices)

REQUIRED

1. Why is the valuation of assets a significant issue?
2. Explain the basic theory underlying each of the valuation methods cited above. Discuss advantages and disadvantages of each method.

EXERCISES

E6–1   The Patton Company reported the following account balances in its conventional balance sheet at December 31, 1983:

ACCOUNT	HISTORICAL-COST BALANCES
Cash	$10,000
Marketable securities—bonds	$20,000
Marketable securities—stocks	$30,000
Accounts receivable	$40,000
Accounts payable	$50,000

The stocks were purchased on January 1, 1982, when the general price level was 100. The bonds, which are being held as a temporary investment of idle cash, were purchased on June 30, 1983, when the general price level was 120. The payables and receivables had a zero balance on January 1, 1982, but have increased steadily since then, both doubling in amount during 1983. The level of cash has remained fairly stable since January 1, 1982.

REQUIRED   Compute the amounts to be reported in the December 31, 1983, general-price-level-adjusted balance sheet for the accounts listed above. The general price index at the end of 1983 is 132. Use year-end price levels.

E6–2   In 1984 the Mount Wheel Tire Company purchased a machine that cost $15,000 and had an expected life of 10 years and no salvage value. Straight-line depreciation is used to account for the machine. Mount Wheel prepares general price level adjusted (GPLA) data for all long-term assets, using the following general price index for the 1984–1988 period. The price index on the date of purchase, January 1, was 175.

END OF YEAR	INDEX (1968 = 100)
1984	187.5
1985	200.0
1986	215.5
1987	232.0
1988	250.0

REQUIRED

1. Compute the amount of depreciation expense in the GPLA income statement for 1988.
2. Illustrate how the machine would appear in the December 31, 1988, balance sheet.

E6–3 The following Accounts Payable account detail of the Speedo Corporation is for 1987:

TRADE ACCOUNTS PAYABLE				
DATE	ITEM	DEBIT	CREDIT	BALANCE
1/1/87	Opening balance			$200,000
1/31/87	Purchases on account		$20,000	
3/31/87	Payment on account	$40,000		180,000
4/1/87	Purchases on account		30,000	210,000
6/30/87	Payment on account	60,000		150,000
8/31/87	Purchases on account		55,000	205,000
9/30/87	Payment on account	65,000		140,000
12/1/87	Purchases on account		20,000	160,000
12/31/87	Balance			160,000

The general-price-index measurements for 1987 are as follows:

DATE	GPLA INDEX
1/1/87	225
1/31/87	228
3/31/87	230
4/1/87	230
6/30/87	235
8/31/87	230
9/30/87	235
12/1/87	240
12/31/87	240

REQUIRED

1. Compute the monetary gain or loss on the Accounts Payable account for 1987.
2. Explain why a gain or a loss resulted even though payments exceeded purchases.
3. Why isn't it necessary to know the price index for the purchases that make up the opening balance of $200,000?

E6–4 (CPA ADAPTED) The historical-cost balance sheet of Severance, Inc., reported $1,500,000 in depreciable assets at original cost before deducting depreciation on December 31, 1983. By the end of the next year the depreciable asset account balance was $1,650,000. All of Severance's assets are depreciated over a 10-year life with no salvage value using straight-line depreciation. The $150,000 of equipment purchased on July 1, 1984, was depreciated for half a year.

Severance prepared GPLA financial data for supplementary information. The December 31, 1983, GPLA value of the depreciable assets was $2,550,000. The general price index was 180 at the beginning of 1984, and 198 at the end of 1984.

REQUIRED

1. What would be the GPLA depreciation expense for 1984?
2. What would be the GPLA balance sheet values for depreciable assets at the end of 1984?

E6-5 The details of the cash receipts and disbursements journal of the Mercer Corporation for the first two months of 1984 are as follows:

CASH RECEIPTS AND DISBURSEMENTS				
DATE	ITEM	DEBIT	CREDIT	BALANCE
1/1/84	Opening balance			$ 95,600
1/1/84	Paid bills—utilities		$ 2,300	93,300
1/15/84	Deposited checks and cash	$56,000		149,300
1/15/04	Payroll checks issued		22,000	127,300
1/15/84	Payment on open accounts		17,500	109,800
1/30/84	Deposited checks and cash	78,000		187,800
1/30/84	Payroll checks issued		38,000	149,800
1/30/84	Payment on open accounts		28,000	121,800
2/15/84	Paid bills—utilities		3,100	118,700
2/15/84	Deposited checks and cash	59,000		177,700
2/15/84	Payroll checks issued		23,000	154,700
2/29/84	Deposited checks	68,000		222,700
2/29/84	Payment on open accounts		45,000	177,700
2/29/84	Payroll checks issued		40,000	137,700

During this 2-month period the general price index increased at a steady rate of 5 percent per month, from 100 to 110.

REQUIRED Compute the monetary gain or loss for the period.

E6-6 Dial-A-Ride, Inc., has acquired the following vehicles over its first 3 years of operations:

VEHICLE	ORIGINAL COST	ESTIMATED USEFUL LIFE IN YEARS	DATE OBTAINED	SPECIFIC PRICE INDEX AT DATE OBTAINED
1984 Chevy Van	$15,860	6	1/19/84	275
1983 Corvette	18,200	10	6/20/83	235
1983 Seville	19,750	8	7/13/83	240
1983 Ford Wagon	9,335	5	9/30/83	240
1982 Ford Van	11,640	6	11/30/81	205

Dial-A-Ride, Inc., has a policy of taking half a year's depreciation in the year an asset is acquired if it is purchased in the second half of a calendar year, and a full year's depreciation if it is acquired in the first 6 months of the year. Dial-A-Ride, Inc., has a December 31 year end.

REQUIRED Compute the 1984 current cost balance in the net asset account for these vehicles at year-end price levels assuming that Dial-A-Ride uses straight-line depreciation and that the vehicles each have an estimated salvage value of $1,000. The specific price index at December 31, 1984, is 300 percent of the base year for each of the vehicles identified above. Discuss the limitations of the specific price index.

E6-7 The G. J. Siedel Lumber Company purchased 10,000 sheets of 4' × 8' CDX plywood on June 30, 1983, for $2.00 each. On December 31, 1983, Siedel sold 5,000 sheets for $3.50 each and immediately placed an order with its supplier for another 10,000 sheets at the current cost of $2.50 per sheet. On January 19, 1984, the remaining 5,000 sheets were sold at $3.75 per sheet. The shipment ordered on December 31, 1983, arrived on January 21, 1984, at a total price of $25,000. The cost to reorder a sheet of 4' × 8' CDX plywood had increased to $2.75 per sheet on January 21, 1984, and was up to $3.00 per unit by the end of 1984. No other sales of this item took place in 1984. Other expenses, including taxes, amounted to $2,300 in 1983 and $3,400 in 1984.

REQUIRED Compute the replacement-cost (current-cost) net income for 1983 and 1984. Be sure to identify the operating income as well as the realized and unrealized holding gains.

E6–8 B. Neubig Network Services developed a replacement-cost (current-cost) information system for use by Bob Neubig in managing the business. At the end of 1984, the first year of operations, Neubig's supplies inventory, which it had acquired at the start of the year, was at 30 percent of its original quantity and had a remaining historical book value of $6,000. The replacement cost of the supplies inventory had doubled in price during 1984. Neubig had Network Service revenues of $45,000 during 1984 and paid rent on equipment and facilities of $13,000 during 1984. The rent for the equipment and facilities was not scheduled to increase during 1985 based on the annual renewal contract signed on December 31, 1984. Neubig withdrew $4,000 in "dividends" from the business during 1984 for distribution to his wife and his son, the other two shareholders in the corporation. Neubig's only asset is the supplies inventory; everything else is rented on a year-to-year basis. The tax rate is 50 percent.

REQUIRED Prepare historical cost and current cost income and retained earnings statements and a balance sheet for B. Neubig Network Services for the year 1984.

E6–9 (CPA ADAPTED) Asset measurement is a concept that involves the valuation or pricing of the future service of an asset. Receivables are particular assets that represent future claims to fixed amounts of monies.

REQUIRED

1. Discuss how the asset measurement concept is applied to receivables (short term and long term).
2. Describe how a company that has a significant amount of receivables during an inflationary period sustains a "general price-level loss." Include in your answer an example of how such a "loss" would be computed when a $100,000 receivable exists at the beginning and end of a year that had an inflation rate of 10 percent.

E6–10

——— 1. The constant-dollar model (GPLA) defines wealth and disposable wealth in terms of
   a. General purchasing power
   b. The value of a general market basket of goods and services as measured by a general price index such as the CPI
   c. A general price index that includes various goods and services being adjusted
   d. Dollars that have been adjusted for general inflationary effects
   e. All of the above

——— 2. The GPLA model
   a. Is just as objective as the conventional model, given the general price index
   b. Reports the assets and liabilities of the entity at their current costs
   c. Does not result in holding gains or losses
   d. Always results in more relevant financial statement information
   e. None of the above

——— 3. The replacement-cost model defines wealth in terms of
   a. Dollars that have been adjusted for general inflationary effects
   b. Constant dollars
   c. Current productive capacity
   d. Original transaction values
   e. None of the above

4. The replacement-cost model
   a. Measures holding gains and losses based on the changes in specific prices during the current accounting period only.
   b. Generates a measure of operating income that excludes the effects of holding profits and losses.
   c. Results in a net income measure that can be disposed of, leaving the entity as well off at the end of the period as it was at the beginning of the period.
   d. Only items a and b are true.
   e. Items a, b, and c are all true.

5. The president of a conglomerate holding company is interested in using an accounting model that will enable her to evaluate the relative performance of each of the diversified companies owned by the parent holding company. The holding company makes decisions concerning whether to hold, invest more in, or sell each of the companies with the aid of the accounting data. Which do you suggest?
   a. Historical-cost model
   b. General-price-level-adjusted model
   c. Current-entry-value model
   d. Current-exit-value model (cash-value model)
   e. Lower-of-cost-or-market-value model

PROBLEMS

P6-1 The following balance sheet information is from the conventional accounting records of the Max Corporation as of December 31, 1983.

MAX CORPORATION
Balance Sheet
December 31, 1983

Cash	$ 58,000
Inventory (FIFO cost)	20,000
Plant and equipment	60,000
Accumulated depreciation	(12,000)
Total assets	$ 126,000
Owners' equity	$ 126,000

During 1984 the following activities took place:

1. Purchased inventory on January 1, 1984, for $40,000 cash. Price index was 80 percent at this date.
2. Recorded cash sales of $65,000 evenly throughout 1984.
3. Recorded cost of sales of $32,000 for inventory used evenly throughout 1984.
4. Paid $15,000 cash for wages for the year evenly distributed throughout 1984.
5. Recorded the consumption of 20 percent of the Plant and Equipment account at the end of 1984.
6. The average price index for 1984 was 90 percent, with the year-end index at 100 percent.
7. Beginning balances in inventory and plant and equipment were stated at index values of 75 percent and 70 percent, respectively.

REQUIRED

1. What is the price-level-adjusted cash balance as of December 31, 1984?
2. What is the price-level-adjusted Plant and Equipment account as of December 31, 1984?
3. What is the net monetary gain or loss for 1984?
4. What is the price-level-adjusted net income for 1984?
5. What is the price-level-adjusted balance in owners' equity at December 31, 1984?

P6–2 Assume that the ending inventory of the H. & Betty Corporation at December 31, 1987, consisted of the following layers:

FROM	GPLA INDEX	HISTORICAL COST
1982	215	$15,000
1985	286	7,000
1986	301	2,000
		$24,000

During 1988, the following purchases of inventory were made:

January 1, 1988: $15,000 (index = 325)
June 30, 1988: $15,000 (index = 330)
December 31, 1988: $15,000 (index = 335)

Assume that 330 was the average GPLA index for 1988. Answer the following questions, which should be considered *independently* of one another.

REQUIRED

1. Assume that the conventional LIFO ending inventory at December 31, 1988, was $23,000 and the cost of goods sold was $46,000 for 1988. What are the GPLA values for ending inventory and cost of goods sold using the average GPLA index for 1988 as a basis for computation?
2. Repeat requirement 1 using the 1988 *end-of-period* GPLA index as a basis for computations.

P6–3 Refer to the facts in Problem 6–2, and answer the following independent questions. Assume that the GPLA measure uses the end-of-period index for adjusting the conventional balances.

REQUIRED

1. Assume that the FIFO cost-flow assumption was used during 1988 and that it resulted in an ending inventory value of $23,000 under the conventional accounting model. What are the corresponding GPLA measures of 1988 ending inventory and cost of goods sold?
2. Assume that the FIFO cost-flow assumption was used during 1988 and resulted in an ending inventory value of $15,000 under the conventional accounting model. What are the corresponding GPLA measures of 1988 ending inventory and cost of goods sold?
3. Repeat requirement 1 using the average GPLA index for 1988 as the basis for computations.

P6–4 Mandy's Magical Mysterious Mannequin Company reported ending finished-goods inventory of $24,000 as of December 31, 1983. The details of the inventory are as follows:

ENDING INVENTORY, 1983			
DATE OF MANUFACTURE	NUMBER OF UNITS	COST PER UNIT	COST OF INVENTORY
1978	450	$20	$ 9,000
1981	300	$25	$ 7,500
1983	250	$30	$ 7,500
	1,000		$24,000

During 1984 a total of 2,000 mannequins were manufactured at a total cost of $64,000. The average cost was $32 per unit. The beginning-of-the-year cost per unit was about $30; the year-end cost per unit was about $34.

REQUIRED

1. Prepare a specific-price-level index for mannequins for the period 1978–1984. Let 1978 be the base year (index = 100% in 1978).
2. Assume that 2,100 mannequins were sold during 1984. Under the conventional model using the LIFO cost-flow assumption, compute ending inventory and cost of goods sold.
3. Assume that your answer in requirement 2 was: ending inventory = $21,000, and cost of goods sold = $67,000. Using current costs based on average-of-the-period costs, what are the corresponding values for ending inventory and cost of goods sold for 1984?
4. Repeat requirement 3 using end-of-period current costs.

P6–5 Details of the Plant and Equipment account for the Arrow Manufacturing Company as of December 31, 1984, are as follows:

ASSET ACCOUNT BALANCE	
DATE OF ACQUISITION	**COST AT ACQUISITION**
1/1/74	$650,000
1/1/76	100,000
12/31/79	70,000
6/30/82	80,000
	$900,000

ACCUMULATED DEPRECIATION ACCOUNT BALANCE	
DATE OF ACQUISITION	**ACCUMULATED DEPRECIATION**
1/1/74	$170,000
1/1/76	75,000
12/31/79	35,000
6/30/82	20,000
	$300,000

Arrow uses the straight-line depreciation method for all depreciable assets. The company began its operations in 1974 when the general price index was 110% (on January 1, 1974). The general price index at subsequent dates is as follows:

DATE	GPLA INDEX
1/1/74	110
1/1/76	125
12/31/79	165
6/30/82	200
1/1/84	210
12/31/84	220

The current (replacement) cost index during the life of the entity for its specific assets at various dates is as follows:

DATE	SPLA INDEX
1/1/74	100
1/1/76	120
12/31/79	140
6/30/82	175
1/1/84	210
12/31/84	230

REQUIRED

1. Compute the constant-dollar (GPLA) measurement of plant and equipment and of accumulated depreciation as of December 31, 1984.
2. Repeat requirement 1 using current-cost (SPLA) measurements.
3. Compute depreciation expense for 1983 for the constant-dollar model.
4. Repeat requirement 3 using current costs.

P6–6   You have just been hired as a consultant by Tom Dooley. Tom owns a car-wash business and wants to know what his *real income* was for the first year (1983) of operations. You have gathered the following information:

TOM DOOLEY'S CAR WASH
Balance Sheet
December 31, 1983

Assets		*Owners' equity*	
Cash	$ 55,000	Common stock	$220,000
Equipment	180,000	Retained earnings	25,000
Accumulated depreciation—equipment	(30,000)		$245,000
Land	40,000		
	$245,000		

During 1983 Tom collected $105,000 in revenues and incurred $25,000 of operating expenses. Taxes for 1983 came to $25,000. Both revenues and expenses occurred evenly throughout 1983. The general-price-level index steadily increased during 1983, *ending at 120% of the first-of-the-year price level.* The car-wash equipment, which Tom paid $180,000 for, was selling for $205,000 by the end of 1983. On January 1, 1984, Tom's real estate agent told him that his car-wash business was worth $275,000 and could probably be sold for that price in a relatively short time.

REQUIRED

1. Assume that Tom defines *real income* in terms of original transaction capital amounts. What is Tom's real income for 1983? How much can Tom receive in dividends and remain as "well off" (in terms of original transaction capital) at the end of 1983 as he was at the beginning of 1983?
2. Assume that Tom defines *real income* in terms of his general purchasing power. What is Tom's real income for 1983? How much can Tom receive in dividends and remain as well off (in terms of general purchasing power) at the end of 1983 as he was at the beginning of 1983?
3. Assume that Tom tells you he would like to view the car-wash business as an investment (like a security that is only a part of a total portfolio of securities). Tom has many other investments like the car wash, and each year he evaluates each investment to decide whether to sell it, hold it, or buy more of it (for example, expand the car wash or perhaps buy another one). He asks you to tell him which accounting valuation model would be most appropriate for his needs. (1) Select from the following list of alternatives the model you feel would be most useful for Tom. (2) Explain briefly why you selected the model chosen. (3) Indicate how you would define *real income* for the model selected.
   a. Historical-cost model   c. General-price-level-adjusted model
   b. Entry-value model   d. Exit-value model

P6–7 Dr. Dopuch publishes a scientific news magazine in Chicago. This magazine, called the *Jar Full of Ideas,* is devoted to explaining new applications of old inventions. Dr. Dopuch receives manuscripts from his friends and edits every article several times before publishing it in the magazine. The conventional accounting balance sheet for the business at the beginning of 1984 was as follows:

DR. D's JAR				
Balance Sheet				
December 31, 1983				
Assets		*Liabilities*		
Cash	$18,000	Accounts payable	$ 1,400	
Accounts receivable	3,500	Wages payable	6,500	
Inventory	4,100	*Owners' equity:*		
Equipment	89,700	Stock	37,500	
Accumulated depreciation	(17,350)	Retained earnings	52,550	
	$97,950		$97,950	

During 1984 the following activities took place:

1. Billed customers $125,000.
2. Received $122,000 cash and checks from customers.
3. Purchased inventory on account, $57,300.
4. Made payments on account, $55,850.
5. Paid wages of $42,480.
6. Wages payable at year-end totaled $5,725.
7. Inventory at year-end (on a FIFO basis) was valued at $7,000.
8. The depreciation taken during 1984 was equal to 10 percent of the gross asset balance of $89,700.
9. Tax expense for the year was $8,000, which was paid in cash at year-end.

REQUIRED

1. Prepare the 1984 income statement.
2. Prepare the December 31, 1984, balance sheet.
3. Compute the return on assets, using the following formula: Net income for the period/Net assets at the beginning of the period.
4. Evaluate Dr. D's performance for 1984 and indicate how much in dividends should be paid to the share holders.

P6–8 Refer to the historical data in Problem 6–7 (Dr. D's Jar). Assume that the December 31, 1983, GPLA balance sheet was as follows:

DR. D's JAR				
GPLA Balance Sheet				
December 31, 1983				
Assets		*Liabilities*		
Cash	$ 18,000	Accounts payable	$ 1,400	
Accounts receivable	3,500	Wages payable	6,500	
Inventory	4,500	*Owners' equity:*		
Equipment	179,400	Stock	150,000	
Accumulated depreciation	(31,700)	Retained earnings	12,800	
	$170,700		$170,700	

In addition, assume the following activities for 1984:

1. The general price index increased evenly throughout the year by 14 percent.
2. Revenues and cash inflow occurred evenly throughout the year.
3. Inventory and wages were incurred evenly throughout the year.
4. *Before* considering the 1984 general-price-level increase, the depreciation expense would have been 10 percent of $179,400 ($17,940). After considering the 1984 price-level increase, GPLA depreciation expense for 1984 should equal 10 percent of the 1984 year-end balance in the Equipment account.
5. The ending inventory equals $7,000 *before* being adjusted for the 1984 general-price-level increase. Inventory is accounted for on a FIFO basis.

REQUIRED

1. Prepare the 1984 income statement.
2. Prepare the December 31, 1984, balance sheet.
3. What is the return on net assets for 1984?
4. Evaluate Dr. D's performance and indicate how much should be distributed in dividends.

(*Hint:* (1) Treat all the December 31, 1983, GPLA values above as though they are stated at index 100 dollars; (2) prepare ending balances based on the transaction data in Problem 6–7 and above; and then (3) convert the ending position to index-114 dollars.)

P6–9   Refer again to the historical data in Problem 6–7 (Dr. D's Jar). Assume that the current-entry-value balance sheet was as follows:

DR. D's JAR			
Current-Entry-Value Balance Sheet			
December 31, 1983			
Assets		*Liabilities*	
Cash	$ 18,000	Accounts payable	$ 1,400
Accounts receivable	3,500	Wages payable	6,500
Inventory	4,100	*Owners' equity*	
Equipment	250,000	Stock	200,000
Accumulated depreciation	(48,356)	Retained earnings	19,344
	$227,244		$227,244

Assume that the activities listed in Problem 6–7 took place during 1984. In addition, assume that the current cost of all items remains the same during 1984 (unchanged) *except* for the equipment, which increases in cost by 10 percent. Once again, the equipment is assumed to be 10 percent consumed during 1984.

REQUIRED

1. Prepare the current-entry-value balance sheet as of December 31, 1984.
2. Prepare the current-entry-value income statement for 1984. (*Hint:* The realized holding gain will equal the difference in depreciation expense with and without the 1984 price change. The unrealized holding gain will be the difference in the December 31, 1984, net book value of the equipment with and without the 1984 price change.)
3. Compute the return on net assets for 1984.
4. Evaluate Dr. D's performance for 1984 and decide on how much to pay out in dividends for 1984.

P6–10   Refer again to the historical data in problem 6–7 (Dr. D's Jar). Assume that the following current-exit values were obtained at the end of 1983 and 1984, respectively:

	DR. D's JAR					
	Current-Exit-Value Balance Sheets					
	December 31					
	1984	**1983**			**1984**	**1983**
Assets			*Liabilities*			
Cash	$ 23,670	$ 18,000	Accounts payable		$ 2,850	$ 1,400
Accounts receivable	6,500	3,500	Wages payable		5,725	6,500
Inventory	2,800	2,000	*Owners' equity*		229,395	195,600
Equipment (net)	205,000	180,000			$237,970	$203,500
	$237,970	$203,500				

Assume the same events and transactions as in problem 6–7.

REQUIRED

1. Compute the 1984 income (no income statement is necessary).
2. Compute the return on net assets for 1984.
3. Evaluate Dr. D's performance and decide how much to pay out in dividends.

P6–11 The following comparative historical-cost balance sheet data are available for Horngren Corp. (the price index at which each item is stated is noted in parentheses alongside the dollar amount):

	($000)	
	12/31/84	**12/31/83**
Assets		
Cash	$ 184 (120)	$ 127 (100)
Accounts receivable	269 (120)	183 (100)
Inventory	430 (85)	440 (85)
Plant and equipment	2,863 (80)	2,863 (80)
Accumulated depreciation	(1,400)(80)	(1,250)(80)
Land	800 (70)	800 (70)
	$ 3,146	$ 3,163
Liabilities and owners' equities		
Accounts payable	$ 207 (120)	$ 220 (100)
Wages payable	86 (120)	103 (100)
Notes payable (due 1990)	1,000 (80)	1,000 (80)
Common stock	800 (70)	800 (70)
Retained earnings	1,053	1,040
	$ 3,146	$ 3,163

During 1984 Horngren declared and paid $100,000 in dividends.

REQUIRED

1. Compute historical-cost net income (loss) for 1984.
2. Compute general-price-level-adjusted net income (loss) for 1984.
3. If we are willing to define wealth in terms of general purchasing power, how would you describe the dividends issued by Horngren?
4. Assume that all changes in monetary accounts took place evenly throughout 1984 at average 1984 price levels (=110). What is the net monetary gain or loss for 1984 for Horngren Corp.?
5. Based on your answers to requirements 2 and 4, what was the GPLA operating income of Horngren Corp. for 1984?

ASSETS

OVERVIEW

PART 2

In Part 1 **assets** were defined as "probable future economic benefits obtained or controlled by a particular entity as a result of past transactions or events," and the basic techniques of asset accounting at their acquisition and during their use were introduced. Accounting provides information to many decision makers interested in the states and flows of assets. Entity managers are concerned with efficient utilization of assets under their control; taxing authorities often base tax levies on accounting asset balances; creditors rely on accounting records as indicators of a debtor's liquidity; and equity investors may use asset information to evaluate future investment risk and return potentials.

Asset accounting, along with all accounting, has evolved in an atmosphere of the varying demands of many different users of accounting information. The concepts, procedures, and formats used in asset accounting have been molded by informational needs, and their evolution continues. Because of the ongoing adaptation of asset accounting to the needs of decision makers, it is difficult to determine whether each new permutation in practice will result in im-

proved information, for such an evaluation can often be done only in retrospect.

Fortunately for students of accounting, the resulting system of asset accounting has remained within the confines of a conceptual structure that provides a fairly stable frame of reference. A thorough grasp of the underlying concepts provides a necessary foundation for understanding and evaluating asset accounting.

The chapters of Part 2 focus on the following major asset categories: cash and temporary investments; accounts and notes receivable; inventories; plant, property, and equipment; intangibles; long-term investments; and leased assets. Each category is unique, with conventional accounting practices having evolved over time. And each category has promulgated rules that apply specifically to it or to its subclassifications. How accountants handle the differences in these promulgated rules is an important element of the chapters of Part 2. At the same time, *there are conceptual commonalities that link all assets*, and this overview emphasizes those commonalities.

ATTRIBUTES OF ASSETS

Future Economic Potential

Assets embody anticipated economic potential for the entity in question, and it is their future economic potential rather than their specific physical form that makes them assets. Whether the asset is cash, a machine, or a copyright, it must be expected to generate some future benefit to the entity in order to be classified as an asset. This often means that in the absence of the particular asset, the entity would have to expend other assets in the future. For instance, one asset frequently found on balance sheets is prepaid insurance. If we assume that the insurance coverage will be maintained, the prepayment for a given amount of coverage entitles the entity to that coverage without making a future cash expenditure that would be necessary in the absence of the prepayment.

Ability to Utilize Economic Potential

If an asset is to be recognized by an entity, the entity must have the right to utilize the asset's economic potential. This does not mean that "legal" ownership is required, but it does mean that there is a reasonable expectation that the entity will be able to control and/or consume the asset for its intended purpose. For example, in some cases, a leased building that is not legally owned by the entity is recognized as an asset if certain attributes of control and utilization rights exist. In other cases, assets are owned outright, but ownership alone is not sufficient for asset recognition. For instance, consider an entity that purchases a tract of land for $100,000 with the intention of mineral development. Subsequent to the purchase, the land is partially flooded. The mining potential and resale value of the land fall to zero. Notwithstanding the legal ownership, this land would not be recognized as an asset for accounting purposes. Legal ownership, in the absence of the ability to utilize economic potential, is not sufficient for accounting recognition of an asset. In the example given, a loss for the difference between the purchase price and the resale value would be recognized.

Objective Measurement in Monetary Terms

Another requirement for accounting recognition of an asset is objective measurement. This requirement leads to many complexities. The numerous rules and conventions that have evolved to govern asset measurement will be discussed in detail in the subsequent chapters. The fundamental concept here is that, at the time of acquisition, a specific money amount must be objectively assigned to the asset as a measurement of its future economic potential. An entity, for instance, could acquire patent rights to a process from an inventor for $150,000 cash. If the entity had been willing to pay up to $250,000 for the process but was able to purchase it for $150,000,

the lower amount would be assigned to the asset because it was objectively determinable in an arm's-length transaction. The $250,000, on the other hand, is hypothetical because there is no objective evidence that the transaction would have occurred at that price.

Measurement of the money amount to be assigned to an asset at acquisition follows **the general rule that the appropriate amount is the cash-equivalent price** to place the asset into its intended state at date of acquisition. When cash is paid at date of acquisition, this amount is usually easy to determine. When another means of acquisition is used, the determination of the cash-equivalent price becomes more difficult. In general, however, cash-equivalent price is the amount of cash at acquisition that would have been acceptable to the buyer and seller in an arm's-length transaction. We shall see in subsequent chapters that this determination sometimes involves computing present values of future cash flows, gathering evidence as to relative sales prices of comparable assets, making appraisals of unique assets, or using other techniques. Sometimes promulgated rules restrict the value of acquired assets to amounts other than cash-equivalent price; for instance, in certain trades of similar assets.

Occasionally an asset is recognized even though an arm's-length transaction has not taken place. Consider the case where a municipality donates a plant site to an entity. If the plant site has future economic potential, the entity has the ability to utilize that potential, and an objective measurement in monetary terms can be made, then the donated plant site would be recognized as an asset by the entity. Objective measurement in monetary terms in this case could be evidenced by sales amounts for comparable plant sites in that locality. Other sources of evidence for an objective measurement could be appraisals, tax assessments, and the like.

ACCOUNTING FOR ASSETS AT ACQUISITION

If a transaction results in an asset's acquisition, the accountant records the transaction in the accounting records of the entity at the asset's cash-equivalent price at date of acquisition. After determining that the attributes discussed above are present, the accountant measures the money amount to be assigned to the asset and determines the proper balance sheet classification and specific account title to be used. A major objective in accounting for assets at acquisition is the comprehensive identification and recording of all relevant expenditures. In general, all costs incurred in order to acquire an asset are accumulated in the one asset account. These would include such costs as the transporting, testing, and modifying of the acquired asset. Such costs are added to the basic invoice price of an asset to determine its total initial accounting balance.

We described balance sheet classifications in Part 1 of this text, and the discussions there are applicable to the chapters that follow. Issues such as choice of account titles, location of accounts on balance sheets, and current or noncurrent classification may be reviewed by reference to Chapter 4.

ACCOUNTING FOR ASSETS AFTER ACQUISITION

Changes in Economic Potential

As mentioned above, an asset is initially recorded at the date of acquisition, at which time an account title, a balance sheet classification, and a money amount are determined. From that point on, the asset is maintained without change unless some event warrants a change in the money amount or the classification.

The economic potential of any asset can vary after acquisition. Because of conservatism, accounting usually ignores increases in economic potential, whereas decreases in the economic potential of assets are usually matched with revenues in the accounting period in which the reduction takes place. If this occurs, the initial money amount is reduced in proportion to the amount of lost potential, with several different techniques being used for recording such reductions. If the economic potential is lost without any discernible benefit to the entity, then the asset amount is reduced and a loss is recognized. If the asset is used up in the production of another asset, such as raw material added to a production process that results in finished goods inventory, the new asset is increased and the old asset is reduced by equal amounts. If the asset is used up in the pursuit of current-year revenues, an expense account is increased by the amount of the asset reduction. Standardized depreciation, depletion, and amortization techniques are used to add consistency to the process of recording expenses that reduce assets.

A common aspect of the asset-allocation techniques is the use of contra accounts such as Accumulated Depreciation, Allowance for Uncollectibles, Allowance to Reduce Inventory to Market, and so on. This permits the disclosure of both the initial acquisition costs and the amounts charged off to date. These contra accounts are viewed as "valuation accounts" in the sense that they reduce the original cost of the asset account for a variety of reasons in an effort to achieve asset measurement and matching within GAAP.

Other changes in the initial recording of assets would occur when their account title or balance sheet classification changes. For instance, if an entity manufactures inventory, a current asset would be created for a specific money amount. If the entity subsequently decides that this inventory will be held for several periods as an investment, the inventory account would be eliminated and a new account that had a long-term classification would be created. Other reasons for changes in account titles and classification may occur. For instance, if an entity has a long-term receivable on its balance sheet for several periods, it would reclassify the receivable as a current asset when the receipt of cash is expected within the next year or operating cycle, whichever is longer. A long-term asset such as factory machinery is, in essence, converted into a current asset, inventory, through the manufacturing process. As the service potential of the machinery is being used up, inventory is created whose cost is eventually matched with revenues during the period in which the inventory is sold. The cost initially recorded for one asset, therefore, may flow into another asset category before it is matched with revenue.

Disposals and Retirements

Most assets of an entity are eventually disposed of through complete consumption, sale, abandonment, or trade, although a relatively few, whose economic potential remains intact, may be retained for the entire duration of the entity. In keeping with the matching principle, the dollar amounts initially assigned to a particular asset are charged against revenue as economic potential is being consumed. The allocation processes used in such matchings are imprecise, involving many estimates. If the estimates were accurate, the remaining book value of an asset at its disposition date would equal its disposition value (market value minus cost to dismantle and remove). In practice, estimates are seldom perfectly accurate, necessitating certain accounting adjustments upon disposition.

At the time of disposition all account balances relating to the asset in question are eliminated, including any contra account balances. Often the disposition value does not equal the book value, creating gains or losses that are usually recognized in the period of disposition.

Note that the date of *physical* disposition is not the critical point in time for the elimination of an asset balance from accounting recognition. Rather, it is the point at which the economic potential is, for all practical purposes, completely consumed. Assets that exist physically and are owned by an entity are not recognized as accounting assets in cases where no significant economic potential remains. For instance, an abandoned mine shaft owned by a mining company would physically exist long after it has been removed as an asset.

DISTINGUISHING BETWEEN ASSETS AND EXPENSES

Given the preceding discussion, it would seem that all expenditures other than losses could be initially classified as assets for at least some amount of time. Why, other than in anticipation of future economic benefit, would rational people ever give up resources? Many costs, however, are immediately classified as expenses. For instance, payments for services of managers are almost always recorded as expenses. Would it not be conceptually sound to record such payments as assets and amortize them as their economic potential is used up? Although such a procedure would have conceptual support, from a practical point of view it would be very inefficient.

When it is definitely known that certain types of expenditures will have short-lived economic benefits, it is common practice to recognize them as expenses immediately. This leads to the concepts of period, prepayment, product, and capital expenditures, which can be diagramed as follows:

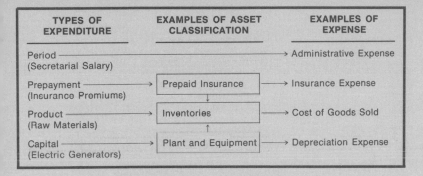

TYPES OF EXPENDITURE	EXAMPLES OF ASSET CLASSIFICATION	EXAMPLES OF EXPENSE
Period (Secretarial Salary)		→ Administrative Expense
Prepayment (Insurance Premiums)	→ Prepaid Insurance	→ Insurance Expense
Product (Raw Materials)	→ Inventories	→ Cost of Goods Sold
Capital (Electric Generators)	→ Plant and Equipment	→ Depreciation Expense

Note that period expenditures are not classified as assets, but all three other types are initially classified as assets. All assets can eventually be converted to expenses (or losses), and they often flow into another classification before becoming an expense item. Depreciation on plant and equipment can become part of inventories if the depreciable item is part of the manufacturing process. If it is not, the depreciation charge will flow directly to an expense account.

SUMMARY

In the following chapters, specific categories of assets will be examined. Each asset will be dis-cussed in terms of the basic attributes of future economic potential and objective measurement. It will be shown that accounting techniques used at acquisition of an asset, during its use, and at disposition are usually linked to the conceptual structure developed in Part 1 of the text. When currently promulgated GAAP require a material departure from this conceptual approach, the rationale for such a departure and the specific techniques involved will be given.

7

Cash and Temporary Investments

OVERVIEW   In this chapter we consider the accounting issues involved in measuring and recording cash and marketable securities. Cash is perhaps the most objectively verifiable asset, but determining the cash amount to be reported in the balance sheet involves much more than physically counting bills and coins. The determination of the amount of cash held at a point in time calls for both a clear definition of cash and well defined cutoff and verification procedures. The many dimensions of accounting for cash make it more challenging than it might at first appear. Changes in the ability of cash (the monetary measurement unit) to command goods and services is also an important dimension (see Chapter 6). Because cash may be an idle resource—that is, it doesn't earn a return—cash management aimed at minimizing idle cash is quite important. Information regarding cash and cash flow is relevant for many decisions made by internal and external users of financial statements.

Measuring and recording investments in marketable securities is also more complex than simply determining the original cost or market value at the balance sheet date. We shall see that **conservatism** has a major impact on the measuring and recording procedures used to account for temporary investments in marketable securities. Measuring and recording marketable securities frequently calls for the use of a contra asset account to adjust the original cost of marketable securities. This **contra asset valuation method,** also known as the **allowance method,** will be encountered in other assets discussed throughout this section of the text.

Although the **cash-equivalent** value is obviously a guiding concept in accounting for cash, the chapter will show that marketable equity securities provide an example of an asset whose valuation may deviate from the "cash equivalent," or "fair-value," measurement rule.

CASH

Nature of Cash
Because it is the accepted medium of exchange, **cash** is the most versatile asset. Cash can be used to purchase any other asset that the entity needs in its business operations. Its liquidity and flexibility are unparalleled by other assets. The liquid nature of cash makes a good control system necessary if management is to safeguard it properly and ensure that it is being used for legitimate purposes.

Normally the investment in the asset "cash" is not large in relation to the other assets on the balance sheet, and the amount of cash actually held in the form of currency (bills and coins) is often minimal. Most of the assets identified as cash are actually represented by such things as checking accounts, checks issued by other parties, bank drafts, certified or "cashier's" checks, and unrestricted savings accounts. The common attribute that permits these items to be classified as cash is that they can all be converted to cash (bills and coins) upon the request of their holders (owners). Note that **near-cash assets**—certificates of deposit, legally restricted deposits, sinking funds, and other similar assets that have limitations concerning their convertibility to cash—may not be classified as cash. These assets are usually reported as "investments" or "other assets."

In recent years many financial institutions have offered lines of credit, free checking, and other services to companies and individuals who maintain minimum balances in checking or savings accounts. According to SEC disclosure guidelines, these required minimum balances should not be reported as cash.[1] **Minimum balances,** sometimes termed **compensating balances,** which are called for because of loan agreements, should also be reported as investments or other assets. This is consistent with the concept that the asset must be readily convertible into cash upon the holder's demand without limitations (such as service charge penalties) in order to be classified as cash.

As we noted in Chapter 6, holding cash during periods of inflation has a "cost" attached to it in terms of lost purchasing power. Because corporate executives have become more conscious of this loss, there has been a steady decline in cash and near-cash assets as a percentage of liabilities since World War II. Evidence of this decline is provided by recent changes in the ratio between certain current assets (cash, marketable securities, and net receivables) and current liabilities:

$$\frac{\text{Cash + Marketable securities + Net receivables}}{\text{Current liabilities}}$$

Data on this ratio since 1947 are given in Table 7–1.

[1] *Accounting Series Release No. 148,* "Amendments to Regulation S–X and Related Interpretations and Guidelines Regarding the Disclosure of Compensating Balances and Short-Term Borrowing Arrangements" (Washington, DC: SEC, November 1973), deals with this subject.

TABLE 7-1

AVERAGE ANNUAL RATIOS FOR ALL U.S. MANUFACTURING COMPANIES	
PERIOD	**RATIO**
1947–1950	.88
1951–1955	.68
1956–1960	.56
1961–1965	.45
1966–1970	.26
1971–1975	.26

Source: Data from an NAA Research Report by Morton Backer and Martin Gosman titled *Financial Reporting and Business Liquidity* (copyright 1978).

Petty Cash   Although only a small part of the cash balance reported in the financial statements of most entities is actually represented by coins and currency on hand, most companies do have a custodian or cashier who handles a **petty cash fund** for day-to-day activities that require small amounts of cash. Examples of such cash needs might include providing cab fares for customers or clients, paying for postage, purchasing minor office supplies, or simply making change for employees.

Most companies with petty cash on hand use an imprest cash fund system of accounting for the cash balance. An **imprest fund** is technically an advance made by the company to an employee custodian. The custodian acts on behalf of the company and its employees, using petty cash to pay the company's minor bills, to sell stamps to employees, and so on. At any given time, the imprest fund should be accounted for through cash on hand or receipts (invoices), the total of which should add to the amount of the advance made to the custodian. The imprest method initially establishes the fund by issuing a company check to the fund custodian for the desired amount of the fund. The custodian then uses the petty cash fund for whatever needs the company may have in accordance with the guidelines or rules established by that company.

Let us assume that the desired amount of a petty cash fund is $100. The receipts for cash spent plus the remaining cash should always sum to the "opening" fund balance, $100. When the fund needs to be replenished, a check is issued to the custodian for an amount equal to the sum of the receipts. When the custodian cashes this check and adds the proceeds to the fund, it should bring the cash balance back to the original sum, $100 in this example. The following entries would be made to establish the fund, account for the fund, and replenish the fund:

6/13	Petty cash (or advance to cash custodian)	100	
	Cash (National Bank & Trust)		100
	(To establish petty cash fund)		
6/13–6/30	(To account for the activities of the fund, some system is generally needed to classify disbursements into several commonly used categories. Invoices are then filed by these categories, and the total cash outflow for each category is computed periodically by totaling the invoices		

in each category. The total invoices for all categories plus the remaining cash should always equal the fund balance, $100 in this case. No formal journal entries are necessary.)

6/30	Office supplies expense	15.25	
	Postage expense	17.50	
	Office party expense	28.95	
	Miscellaneous expense	23.00	
	Cash (National Bank & Trust)		84.70
	(To record the replenishing of petty cash and to recognize the outflow of cash by invoice category to the appropriate expense account)		

If the cash on hand plus invoices do not sum to the original balance, the difference is accounted for in an **Over and Short account**. When cash plus invoices are less than the fund balance, a debit to the Over and Short account is made as follows:

6/30	Office supplies expense	15.25	
	Postage expense	17.50	
	Office party expense	28.95	
	Miscellaneous expense	23.00	
	Over and short	5.00	
	Cash (National Bank & Trust)		89.70

Alternatively, an excess of cash plus invoices over the original balance would be credited to the Over and Short account. The Over and Short account is closed to the income statement at the end of each accounting period as miscellaneous expense or miscellaneous revenue.

Offsetting Cash Balances

Many companies have multiple checking accounts with one or more financial institutions. This policy may exist for several reasons, including maintaining business relationships with important current and potential creditors. Companies often maintain separate checking accounts for payroll checks. If a company has operations in different locations it may have a separate payroll account at each location, thereby dealing with many separate financial institutions.

It is generally acceptable to offset an overdraft or a credit cash balance in one account with a positive cash balance in another account *if* both accounts are with the *same* financial institution. However, such offsetting is not acceptable if the accounts are with different banks. When different banks are involved or when there is only one account, the credit balances, or overdrafts, should be reported as current liabilities.

Control of Cash

To the management of a company and to the auditor who is reviewing the records of management, an important aspect of cash is the **control system** that has been installed by management to safeguard its most liquid asset. Because cash is a medium that can readily be exchanged for other assets, and because it is easy to conceal and to move large amounts of cash from one place to another, management's control system must be carefully designed to safeguard cash and near-cash assets. The amount of work required to audit the Cash account will vary depending on the quality of the controls.

The key to effective cash control is a system of accounting that carefully distributes the authority and responsibility for physically handling the company's cash receipts and payments and the accounting for receipts and payments. The cash inflows may be viewed as having three phases: (1) receipt of cash (or checks), (2) recording cash inflows on the books, and (3) depositing cash receipts with the bank. All three of these phases should actually be handled by different individuals, but at a minimum, the recording of cash (phase 2) and the handling of the cash (phases 1 and 3) should be separated.

Effective cash control can also be accomplished if care is taken in delegating other noncash responsibilities to the individuals involved in these three phases. Since any one or all three phases may take very little time or effort within a given company, other duties would undoubtedly be assigned to those employees involved in one of the three phases of cash inflow control. As a result, the design of the control system must consider all employee positions that might create cash control problems. In addition to separating the various aspects of cash receipts, it is both good business practice and good control practice to deposit cash on a **timely basis.** If there is enough cash activity, someone should compute the totals of daily cash receipts and prepare deposits on a daily basis. Depositing cash on a daily basis provides more efficient use of cash because cash can be used to cover checks written by the company, can earn interest, or can be invested in some short-term activity only if it has been deposited. Also, daily deposits of cash reduce the period of time available for something to go wrong, such as theft or misplacement, and therefore the possibility of someone "lapping" with company funds is much less likely.[2]

Control of cash disbursements is as important as the control of cash receipts. The disbursement process may also be viewed as a three-phase process: (1) identifying evidence (such as invoices) that requires cash payment and preparation of the check; (2) verification of the evidence requiring payment and signing the check (may require more than one signature for this phase); and (3) sending the check and recording the payment on the books. These three phases should be divided among three or more individuals. The actual facts of a situation, such as number of employees, will usually dictate how much control is feasible. As an extreme example, the division of duties in a sole proprietorship may be impossible.

A cash-control problem   In many small companies, the delegation of various phases of cash receipts, cash disbursements, and other recording activities is simply not feasible. The risks in such cases may be quite high. The following example is based on an actual case and illustrates how inadequate cash control can lead to problems.

MS. JONES AND THE T COMPANY

Ms. Jones had worked for the T Company for many years as an office manager. She did most of the office work, and the two company owners considered her a loyal and trusted employee. After 20 years of service with the company, Ms. Jones found that she needed money for her children's education. Her husband had died and had left very little insurance for her and their three children. After some time, Ms. Jones devised a clever scheme to steal cash. She was responsible for most of the cash-disbursement activities except for signing the checks. She was also responsible for opening all the incoming mail. Her cash-disbursement duties included typing the invoices to be paid, preparing the checks for the owners' signatures, taking the signed checks and mailing them, and

---

[2] *Lapping* is a practice in which the receipt of funds from one day is not recorded until the next, permitting someone to have the use of one or more days' receipts continuously.

recording the activities in the Accounts Payable account. To help solve her financial problems, Ms. Jones would take checks that had cleared the bank and would enter a new amount on the cleared check. For example, she would change a check originally written for $100 to $1,100. (She used a check protector machine and had a method of preventing the protecting marks—***—from printing as far to the right as they should have.) She would then take the invoice for $100, being careful to select only those invoices that had been typed on a machine like her own, and would change the invoice to also read $1,100. She would then write a check to herself for $1,000, forge the owner's signature, and cash the check. When the bank returned her cleared check for $1,000 she would destroy it, marking it as a voided check in the check register. She had a canceled check for $1,100, an invoice for $1,100, and a $1,000 "scholarship" for her children courtesy of the T Company.

The activities described in this case went on for several years until Ms. Jones had the misfortune of having a check made out to herself returned with the bank statement directly to the auditors before she had a chance to destroy the check. The procedure whereby the auditor receives the bank statement directly from the bank, known as a bank cutoff statement, is an audit procedure designed to uncover such irregularities but is sometimes conducted only at year-end.

Many other control procedures could have been implemented to safeguard the T Company's cash. First, Ms. Jones was obviously involved in too many disbursement activities. Some of these activities should have been delegated to other office employees. Having someone else handle either the bank reconciliations or the preparation of checks or the handling of vendor invoices would have prevented or reduced the probability of theft. Sometimes there are so few employees that separation of duties is not economically feasible. In the case described above, however, even if Ms. Jones had been the only office employee, the simple practice of using prenumbered checks and having an owner verify that all checks were accounted for might have prevented the theft.

Bank Reconciliations

The cash-flow activities in bank accounts are periodically reported to account owners by means of a bank statement listing the deposits, withdrawals, and other account transactions that the bank has recorded during the period. The same cash-flow transactions reported in the bank statement are also recorded in the Cash account on the books of the company as the cash transactions take place. As a result, both the bank and the company maintain a record of the cash-flow activities for each bank account. However, the book balance and the bank balance in an account on any given date are not likely to be equal, because the cash-flow activities recorded by the bank and the company are generally recorded at different times. For example, a company might record an increase in its Cash account balance on the date that it makes a deposit, but the bank might not record the deposit until the following day. A difference between the book balance and the bank balance can also arise when a customer's check deposited by the company is returned by the bank because the balance in the customer's account was not sufficient to cover the check and the customer's bank would not honor it. Such returned checks, which are usually marked NSF ("not sufficient funds"), serve to notify the company that its deposit was overstated by the amount of the check.

It is customary for companies to reconcile any differences between their records and the bank's records each time a bank statement is received. The general format of a company's reconciliation process is shown in Exhibit 7–1. The reconciliation format illustrated provides a convenient framework. It focuses on an ending

EXHIBIT 7-1

GENERAL FORM OF A BANK RECONCILIATION

SILVERTRAIN LTD.
General Cash Account #001
November 30, 1984
BANK RECONCILIATION

Balance per bank statement dated 11/30/84	$5,000	Balance per General Cash Account #001 *as of* 11/30/84		$4,079
Plus:		*Plus:*		
Increases to Account #001 recorded on the books but not yet included in the bank balance per the bank statement		Items included as account balance increases per the bank statement *but not yet* included as increases on the books for Account #001		
Example:		*Examples:*		
Deposit in transit	+ 500	Interest on Account #001		+ 80
	$5,500	Collections of notes or drafts paid by creditors directly to our bank		+ 120
				$4,279
Less:		*Less:*		
Decrease to Account #001 recorded on the books but not yet included in the bank balance per the bank statement		Items included as account balance decreases per the bank statement but not yet included as decreases on the books for Account #001		
Example:		*Examples:*		
Outstanding checks	−1,800	Service charges		− 75
		NSF checks		− 504
Corrected balance as of 11/30/84	$3,700	Corrected balance as of 11/30/84		$3,700

value ($3,700) that is useful in preparing the necessary adjusting entries because it arrives at the correct cash balance that should be in the company's records. Some companies and auditors prefer to use a **four-column bank reconciliation,** which is actually a number of reconciliations in one. The four-column approach, also known as a **proof of cash,** is most useful as an audit tool (for both internal and external audit) and is discussed in Appendix C at the end of this chapter.

In addition to the types of discrepancies between the book balance and the bank balance illustrated in Exhibit 7-1, other **errors** and **adjustments** might require additions or deductions from the book or bank balances. Exhibit 7-2 summarizes the types of *errors* and their impact on the bank reconciliation. Errors made by the bank would be added or subtracted from the balance per the bank statement. An example of a bank error that might be discovered during reconciliation is a charge to the account for the check made by another company. In the case of bank errors, the company should promptly notify the bank so that the correction can be made. Naturally, bank errors do not require adjustment on the company's books.

Errors that are made by the company are often discovered during the reconciliation process. A common error is the incorrect totaling and recording of a group of checks that were deposited with the bank. Transposition errors such as transcribing a customer's check for $435 as a deposit of $453 are not uncommon when recording transactions. Note that transposition errors are always evenly divisible by 9 (that is, $453 − $435 = $18/9 = 2$); therefore, when unexplained differences are evenly divisible by 9, it is possible that a transposition error has been made. Errors that are made by the company as well as *all* other adjustments to the "book balance" side of the reconciliation require correcting journal entries to the Cash account. All correcting journal entries for additions to the book balance will debit Cash in the bank

EXHIBIT 7–2

TREATMENT OF ERRORS IN RECONCILIATIONS

SILVERTRAIN LTD.
General Cash Account #001
September 30, 1984
BANK RECONCILIATION

Balance per bank statement dated 9/30/84	$5,000	Balance per General Cash Account #001 *as of 9/30/84*	$4,079
Plus:		*Plus:*	
Bank error in favor of Silvertrain (adds to Silvertrain's balance according to the bank statement)		Silvertrain error in favor of Silvertrain (adds to cash balance on Silvertrain's books)	
Example: Silvertrain *Ltd.* charged $420 for check written by Silvertrain *Co.*	+ 420 $5,420	*Example:* Silvertrain recorded customer's check of $500 as a $50 check in making one of its deposits	+ 450 $4,529
Less:		*Less:*	
Bank error in favor of the bank (reduces Silvertrain's balance according to bank statement)		Silvertrain error in favor of the bank (reduces the cash balance on Silvertrain's books)	
Example: Bank reduced balance by only $100 for a $1,000 check written by Silvertrain to a vendor	− 900	*Example:* Silvertrain wrote check to vendor for $465 but deducted only $456 from cash balance on books	− 9
Corrected 9/30/84 balance	$4,520	Corrected 9/30/84 balance	$4,520
Action (left-side adjustments): Notify the bank of its error.		*Action (right-side adjustments):* Record adjusting entry to Cash account on Silvertrain's books	

and credit some other account (such as Interest Income, Notes Receivable, or Accounts Receivable), whereas reductions in cash will always require a credit to Cash in the bank along with some debit entry (such as Service Charge Expense or Accounts Receivable).

Example of bank reconciliation The following figures are a partial reproduction of the cash records (a checkbook) of Dr. P. Yamen, a local dentist:

	PAYMENTS			RECEIPTS		
CHECK NO.	DATE	PAID TO	AMOUNT	DATE OF DEPOSIT	DEPOSIT AMOUNT	ACCOUNT BALANCE
						$ 775.00
325	11/21	Case Crowns, Inc.	$ 25.00			750.00
326	11/26	Dental Equipment Co.	50.00			700.00
327	11/27	Al's Copper and Enamel Supplies	30.00			670.00
328	11/29	Dental Equipment Co.	17.00			653.00
				11/30	$1,500.00	2,153.00
329	12/2	National Bank & Trust Co.	100.00			2,053.00

On December 5 Dr. Yamen receives his bank statement, which shows a balance of $1,050 as of November 30. Checks returned with the bank statement account for all checks written prior to November plus all checks written *in* November except check No. 321, which was written for $80, and check No. 327. Bank service charges for the month were $3 for check-cashing fees *plus* $10 for collection fees from a $300 note due Dr. Yamen collected by the bank during November. The $300 note had been received in exchange for a $275 customer balance some time in September. The bank statement did not include the $1,500 deposit made on November 30.

If all this information is taken into account, the *corrected* book and bank balances for November 30 would be as follows:

DR. PETER YAMEN			
BANK RECONCILIATION			
Bank balance 11/30	$1,050.00	Book balance 11/30	$2,153.00
Plus:		Plus:	
Deposit-in-transit	+1,500.00	Note collection	+ 300.00
	$2,550.00		$2,453.00
Less:		Less:	
Outstanding checks	− 110.00	Collection fees	− 10.00
		Service charge	− 3.00
Corrected 11/30 balance	$2,440.00	Corrected 11/30 balance	$2,440.00

Note that the reconciliation is dated November 30, even though the reconciliation is actually prepared some time during December. To arrive at a "correct" balance as of November 30, it is necessary that the company know the disposition of November transactions from both the company's and the bank's perspective. The following adjusting entries would be recorded by Dr. Yamen:

12/5	Cash		300	
	Notes receivable			275
	Interest income			25
	(To eliminate note receivable recorded in September at book value of $275 and to record interest earned of $25 at the time of the cash payment of $300 for the maturity value of the note)			
12/5	Collection fee expense		10	
	Cash			10
	(To record collector's fee charged by the bank in conjunction with the note above. These two entries could be consolidated if desired.)			
12/5	Service charge expense		3	
	Cash			3
	(To record service charge for check fees on Yamen's account)			

In these entries, note that the items affecting the balance per books as of November 30, and only those items, have resulted in correcting entries. Note also that the correcting journal entries made to cash in conjunction with the bank reconciliation are normally the only cases of the Cash account's being part of an adjusting entry. Once cash is reconciled, other adjusting and correcting journal entries will not involve cash as either a debit or a credit entry because increases and decreases to cash are associated with actual events and transactions rather than with adjusting journal entries. The inflow or outflow of cash is related to real economic events that are transactions recorded in journal entries during a period. We should be reluctant to use cash as a part of an adjusting journal entry unless the entry is part of the cash reconciliation process or unless a clerical error is discovered independently of the reconciliation process.

TEMPORARY INVESTMENTS

Nature
of Temporary
Investments

Temporary investments in marketable securities are usually of small total value in comparison with the other current assets or the total assets of a company. Companies often make short-term investments to obtain some return on cash that is temporarily idle. At the same time, since the cash will be needed in a relatively short time for operations, these current assets will usually consist of low-risk securities such as short-term government securities where there is little risk of loss of principal or of equity securities that have a ready market.

To qualify as a current asset, the temporary investment (1) must be a security that is readily marketable, and (2) the company's management must intend to convert the investment back to cash within 1 year or the normal operating cycle of the company, whichever is longer. The first condition is fairly straightforward. We can easily verify the fact that a security has a market by observing publicly available information concerning the bid-and-ask prices or the closing selling price and the volume of shares traded.

The second condition, however, is more difficult to determine, particularly from an auditor's point of view. It is difficult to obtain reliable measures of management's intentions, and subsequent actions do not necessarily support or refute management's stated intentions. To illustrate, suppose the Nob Hill Corporation, which is in the business of managing a ski resort during the winter season, invests its idle cash in securities during the summer months and then sells the securities in the fall to buy inventories and supplies for the ski season. During the 1984 ski season there is so little snow that the ski resort never opens and the temporary investments are not converted to cash or inventories. Should the investments be reclassified as long term in the 1984 financial statements? Is it management's intention to convert these investments to cash during 1985? In this case, it seems clear that management's intention is to convert the temporary investments to cash each year. Uncontrollable factors, such as the lack of normal snowfall in this case, may prevent the intended action from being carried out as expected. Such factors do not necessarily undermine the reliability of management's expressed intentions. In some cases, however, management's intentions may not be as clear. It is necessary to evaluate management's intentions because investments need not be actually converted to cash within a cycle in order to qualify as temporary. Indeed, the same group of marketable securities could remain as a temporary investment for a number of years as long as management's intention, as of the balance sheet date, is to convert them to cash during the next accounting period.

Temporary investments might consist of either equity securities (such as certain preferred stocks or common stocks) or debt securities (such as bonds, treasury bills, or notes). These two types of securities are different in that equity or ownership interests are normally riskier than debt securities. Holders of equity securities are the last to receive funds in the event of a liquidation, and they may be entitled to dividends only after the payment of interest on the debt securities. The accounting rules that govern financial statement disclosure of temporary investments are different for equity and debt securities. Marketable equity securities will be considered first, and debt securities will be discussed in a subsequent section.

Accounting
for Marketable
Equity
Securities

Several factors have influenced the promulgation of **FASB Statement No. 12,** which prescribes GAAP for temporary equity security investments.[3] Until this statement was issued, there had been a great deal of inconsistency in the way companies reported temporary investments. Some companies reported temporary investments at cost, others measured such investments at market value on the balance sheet date with reference made to their original cost, and still others reported these investments at lower-of-cost-or-market. These inconsistencies were compounded by the tremendous fluctuations in the security markets during the early 1970s, which created significant differences in the results reported from these three valuation methods. From 1972 to 1975, for example, the Dow Jones Industrials Index, an index of 30 "blue chip" industrial stocks, went from over 1,000 (for the first time) to below 600. As a result of such wide fluctuations in well-established security markets, the FASB felt compelled to investigate the inconsistencies in the accounting treatment of marketable securities.

The initial thinking of the FASB was to move toward a market-value basis for valuing temporary investments. Market value was considered to be attractive because measurements of marketable securities on a market-value basis reflect the important qualities of relevant and reliable information. However, net income would be affected by holding gains or losses from securities valued at market, a point that the affected entities argued would be inconsistent with general principles of revenue recognition. The final pronouncement was a compromise that required the lower-of-cost-or-market (LCM) valuation approach. The major exception to LCM occurs when a decline in the market value of a temporary investment is judged to be permanent. In this case, the amount of the decline judged to be unrecoverable could be recorded as a *realized* loss, and the original cost of the investment could be written down to a new adjusted cost basis by an amount equal to the loss.

FASB Statement No. 12 requires that the market value of marketable equity securities, measured on a **total portfolio** basis, be compared with the original cost of the *total portfolio* of the temporary investment in marketable equity securities at the date of the financial statements. If the total market value is *less than* the total cost of the entire portfolio of temporary investments in marketable equity securities, an Allowance (contra asset) account should be established to reflect the difference between the total cost and the total market. For temporary investments, the credit entry to the Allowance account would be offset by an Unrealized Holding Loss account that would be reported in the income statement. If the total market value of the securities were *greater than* the total cost at the date of the financial statements, the Allowance account should have a zero balance, and the net book value of the temporary investment account should be reported at original cost.

Unrealized gains or losses resulting from adjusting entries that increase or decrease the Allowance account should be reported in the income statement for the period covered by the statement. This procedure calls for the Allowance account to be affected *only* at the time adjusting journal entries are being recorded for financial statement purposes. Note that the actual *events* that affect the Temporary Investments account (purchases and sales of marketable securities) do *not* change the bal-

---

[3] *Statement of Financial Accounting Standards No. 12,* "Accounting for Certain Marketable Securities" (Stamford, CT: FASB, December 1975).

EXHIBIT 7–3

ACCOUNTING FOR TEMPORARY INVESTMENTS PER FASB STATEMENT NO. 12

DATE	EVENT OR ACTIVITY	JOURNAL ENTRY	DEBIT	CREDIT
7/7/85	Purchase Veeco stock for $100 Purchase Atlas stock for $500	Temporary investments Cash	600	600
12/31/85	Prepare financial statements. To adjust, look at following data: **STOCK** / **ORIGINAL COST** / **12/31/83 MARKET** Veeco $100 $120 Atlas 500 450 Total $600 $570 Need $30 balance in "allowance to reduce temporary investments to market"	Unrealized loss on temporary investments Allowance	30	30
2/10/86	Sell Veeco for $130 (original cost $100)	Cash Temporary investments Realized gain on sale of temporary investments	130	100 30
3/23/86	Purchase Georgia Pacific for $200	Temporary investments Cash	200	200
6/30/86	Prepare financial statements. To adjust, look at following data: **STOCK** / **ORIGINAL COST** / **6/3/86 MARKET** Atlas $500 $510 Georgia Pacific 200 180 Total $700 $690 Current balance in Allowance account = $30 from 12/31/85. New balance required at 6/30/86 = $10. Reduce Allowance account by $20 for "unrealized gain on recovery of market decline in temporary investment."	Allowance Unrealized gain	20	20

ance in the Allowance account. Other examples of the *allowance method* of valuation will be observed in the accounting treatment for inventories, accounts receivable, estimated warranty obligations, certain long-term investments, and various other assets and liabilities.

Example of accounting for temporary investments Exhibits 7–3 and 7–4 illustrate the allowance method as it applies to the recording of temporary investments in marketable equity securities according to FASB Statement No. 12. The example in Exhibit 7–3 includes the entry to record the purchase of temporary investments on July 7, 1985, and the subsequent adjusting entries required on December 31, 1985, and again on June 30, 1986, under the *assumption* that financial statements are prepared twice a year (June 30 and December 31). Included in the example are an adjustment to reduce the investments to LCM (December 31); a sale of one of the two investments (February 10); a purchase of a third security (March 23), and an adjustment of a previously recognized loss.

It might be noted that the entry to record the "unrealized gain" on June 30,

EXHIBIT 7–4

STATEMENT PRESENTATION FOR EXAMPLE ILLUSTRATED IN EXHIBIT 7–3

Partial Balance Sheets

	JUNE 30, 1986	DECEMBER 31, 1985
Temporary investments	$700	$600
Less allowance to reduce temporary investments to market	10	30
Net temporary investments	$690	$570

Partial Income Statements

	JUNE 30, 1986	DECEMBER 31,1985
Unrealized holding loss		$30 (Debit)
Unrealized holding gain	$20 (Credit)	
Realized gain based on sale	$30 (Credit)	

1986, is essentially recording a recovery of a previously recognized loss. The Allowance account balance prior to the June 30 entry is a $30 credit. Based on the portfolio data given on June 30, only a $10 credit balance in the Allowance account is necessary to state the investments at LCM. As a result, a $20 unrealized gain must be recorded to offset the debit needed to decrease the Allowance balance from $30 to $10.

The Allowance account at the balance sheet date must always have either a credit balance or no balance. If a debit were allowed, it would be added to the original cost recorded in the Temporary Investments account, making the total or net value greater than cost, thereby violating the LCM rule.

The acquisition of Veeco stock on July 7, 1985, is recorded in the asset account at cost and remains in the asset account at cost until sold on February 10, 1986. Note that at the point of sale, the asset account is reduced by the *original cost* of the Veeco stock, and the actual (or *realized*) gain or loss is recorded just as though no Allowance account existed. No entries are made to the Allowance account at the point of acquisition or the point of sale. The Allowance account is updated when adjusting entries are recorded at the close of an accounting period.

Cost-flow assumptions   When multiple purchases of a marketable security are made at different purchase prices, we must determine the cost of the securities at the time of sale. Assume, for example, that the Stanley Vemco Corporation purchased shares of the Texas Air Corporation on three separate occasions:

PURCHASES OF TEXAS AIR CORPORATION COMMON

1. 100 shares on 3/31/83 at $13 per share
2. 200 shares on 7/26/83 at $15 per share
3. 100 shares on 9/10/83 at $16 per share

If Stanley sells 100 shares on November 20, 1983, for $17 per share, the question becomes, What is the *cost* of the 100 shares sold? For financial-reporting purposes, three assumptions regarding cost flows of securities are acceptable:

1. Specific identification—the securities sold are identified by their serial number and are costed on an actual cost basis.
2. Average cost— all the purchases are pooled together and the weighted-average cost is assigned to each ($14.75 per share in this case for Texas Air Corporation stock).
3. FIFO cost—the sale is presumed to consist of the oldest securities at their respective cost ($13 per share in this case).

The entries to record the sale will recognize a "realized" gain of anywhere from $400 ($17 − $13 = $4; $4 × 100 = $400) to $100 ($17 − $16 = $1; $1 × 100 = $100), depending on which cost-flow assumption Stanley uses. Only the first and third methods (specific identification and FIFO) are allowed for tax purposes, with FIFO permitted only when specific identification is impractical.

Transaction costs   The cost of any asset includes all the costs necessary to obtain the asset and place it into a useful state. For temporary investments, brokerage fees, taxes, and perhaps legal fees would be added to measure the total cost to be recorded. In the example given, these fees would be included in the cost of the three stocks at the time of purchase. At the time of sale, brokerage fees are netted out against the proceeds. For example, on February 10, 1986, Veeco is sold for a *net* of $130. This price may have actually been determined by taking a market value of $140 less a $10 brokerage fee for the transaction. Note that brokerage fees are *not* considered in determining the "market" value of temporary investments for application of the lower-of-cost-or-market method on the date of financial statements. Only the quoted market value of the securities at the date of the financial statements (excluding unpaid brokerage fees) is used to determine the necessary LCM adjustment, if any, to the allowance account.

Reclassification of Temporary Investments

Although the thrust of **FASB Statement No. 12** is to increase the uniformity of the treatment of temporary investments among firms, some flexibility remains available to companies concerning the managing of their portfolios. This is particularly true of companies that hold securities as both temporary and long-term investments. Frequently, the major factor that separates the classification of marketable securities between current and noncurrent assets is the time horizon of management's intended conversion of these investments back to cash. It is possible that the portfolios of securities being held for long-term and for short-term purposes could be identical in every respect, with management's intention to convert the short-term portfolio within a year as the sole basis for the classification difference.

If a security is reclassified from current to noncurrent (or from noncurrent to current), the value of the security must be the lower-of-cost-or-market value at the date of transfer to or from the current asset, Temporary Investments. Consider the example in Exhibit 7–5 for the Switch Company. This company has two securities in its short-term investments portfolio and two securities in its long-term portfolio as of December 6, 1984. While the market value of the short-term portfolio is below cost on this date, the market value of the long-term portfolio is above cost. Note that **FASB Statement No. 12** calls for unrealized gains and losses on short-term investments in marketable securities to be reported in the income statement, as illustrated in Exhibit 7–4. However, unrealized gains and losses on long-term invest-

EXHIBIT 7–5

SWITCH COMPANY
Data on Securities Held as
Temporary Investments, December 6, 1984

SECURITY	COST	MARKET	UNREALIZED GAIN (LOSS)	VALUE AT LCM	ALLOWANCE BALANCE
GM	$10,000	$ 9,900	$(100)	—	
Ford	8,000	7,700	(300)	—	
	$18,000	$17,600	$(400)	$17,600	$400 Credit

Data on Securities Held as Long-Term
Investments, December 6, 1984

SECURITY	COST	MARKET	UNREALIZED GAIN (LOSS)	VALUE AT LCM	ALLOWANCE BALANCE
Gulf	$20,000	$20,000	0	—	
Texaco	15,000	16,000	1,000	—	
	$35,000	$36,000	$1,000	$35,000	0 Credit

ments in marketable securities *do not* affect income and are *not* reported in the income statement.

Assume that on December 6, 1984, Switch transfers its Ford stock from a current-asset to a noncurrent-asset account. The transfer would be recorded at the LCM value with losses (if any) reported as *realized* losses in the income statement, as follows:

12/6/84	Long-term investment	7,700	
	Realized loss on investments	300	
	Temporary investments		8,000

The new cost basis for the Ford stock would become $7,700, with the $300 realized loss reported in income for the period.

Now consider the additional data in Exhibit 7–6 for Switch Company for the year ended December 31, 1984. Assuming that the Allowance to Reduce Temporary Investments to Market account had a $400 credit balance prior to the December 31, 1984, year-end adjusting entry, the necessary adjusting entry would be:

12/31/84	Allowance to reduce temporary investments to market	300	
	Unrealized gain on temporary investment		300
	(To record recovery of difference between cost and market values of temporary investments)		

If the Allowance to Reduce *Long-Term* Investments to Market account had no balance prior to the December 31, 1984, adjusting entries (because market value was more than cost), no adjusting entry would be required or permitted for the *long-term* investment. Chapter 14 discusses *long-term* investments in greater detail and explains why *unrealized* gains and losses on *long-term* investments do *not* affect current

EXHIBIT 7–6

SWITCH COMPANY

Data on Securities Held as
Temporary Investments, December 31, 1984

SECURITY	COST	MARKET	UNREALIZED GAIN (LOSS)	VALUE AT LCM	ALLOWANCE BALANCE
GM	$10,000	$ 9,900	$(100)	—	
	$10,000	$ 9,900	$(100)	$ 9,900	$100 Credit

Data on Securities Held as Long-Term
Investments, December 31, 1984

SECURITY	COST	MARKET	UNREALIZED GAIN (LOSS)	VALUE AT LCM	ALLOWANCE BALANCE
Ford	$ 7,700	$ 6,750	$ (950)	—	
Gulf	20,000	19,900	(100)	—	
Texaco	15,000	16,500	1,500	—	
	$42,700	$43,150	$ 450	$42,700	$0 Credit

income. Unrealized gains and losses on temporary investments *do* affect current income, however, as illustrated in Exhibits 7–3 and 7–4.

The fact that income is affected by temporary investments but not by long-term investments makes the transfer from current to noncurrent, or vice versa, an interesting internally determined entry to consider. Although the entries recorded for the data presented in the Switch Company example seem to be straightforward, proper identification of the **date of transfer** is important. If it were not learned until December 31 that the transfer had been made as of December 6, we could argue that the $950 decline in the value of the Ford stock between December 6 and December 31 should be treated as an unrealized loss in the current income statement instead of as an offset to the $1,500 unrealized gain on the Texaco stock in the long-term portfolio. Auditors must be aware of the potential implications of these internally determined entries recording the transfers and the problems of verifying the date of such transfers after the fact. The same procedures are used for transfers *from* the Long-Term Investments accounts *to* the Current Investments account. Transfers are recorded at the LCM value of the security at the date of transfer, and where market value is below cost at that date a *realized* loss is recorded for the transferred security. Note that no entry is necessary to adjust the short-term asset's or the long-term asset's Allowance account in recording such transfers.

In companies using "unclassified" balance sheets, all marketable securities are considered to be long-term assets. This eliminates the need for accounting for transfers as a result of a change in management's intended holding period. Accounting for long-term investments will be covered in more detail in Chapter 14.

Accounting for Marketable Nonequity Securities

Although **FASB Statement No. 12** does not specifically address nonequity securities, most companies are complying with the lower-of-cost-or-market spirit of the statement for nonequity securities as well. Technically, a company has the option of using lower-of-cost-or-market or cost adjusted only for market *declines* that are believed to be permanent. In this latter case, permanent declines in temporary nonequity securities should be charged against income with a direct reduction in the asset value. To illustrate, assume that Exert Corporation purchased as a temporary investment $1,500 of TRX Corporation bonds on July 18, 1983. On August 21, 1983, TRX announced its loss of a government contract, which had accounted for 30 percent of its business. The market value of Exert's investment in TRX fell to $800 and remained at about that level until year-end when it closed at $825. If this loss is viewed as a permanent decline, Exert would record a *realized* loss and a *direct* reduction in the asset account by way of the following year-end adjustment:

12/31/83	Loss on temporary investment	675	
	Temporary investment		675
	(To record permanent decline in TRX bonds)		

Alternatively, under the LCM method required in **FASB Statement No. 12** for marketable equity securities, Exert could have recorded an *unrealized* loss and an *indirect* reduction in the asset account through the following adjusting entry, whether or not the loss were expected to be permanent:

12/31/83	Unrealized loss	675	
	Allowance to reduce temporary investments		675
	(To adjust temporary investments to LCM)		

Under either of these alternatives, the bond interest should be accrued and recorded as being earned just like any other interest-bearing investment or obligation. The entries recorded in the examples above *exclude* any accrued interest because the market price of bonds is always presumed to be a quote of the price excluding accrued interest. It should be noted that the valuation of temporary investments in bonds or notes ignores the fact that they may have been purchased at a discount (below maturity value) or at a premium (above maturity value). While these discounts and premiums are amortized over the life of the securities in the case of long-term investments, **temporary investments do not amortize discounts or premiums** because the securities are to be held for such a short period of time.

When referring to marketable securities in their published financial statements, most companies will indicate the relationship of the value of their securities to market value. Of the 600 companies surveyed by *Accounting Trends and Techniques* in recent years, almost two-thirds reported marketable securities in their financial statements.[4] Of those who reported marketable securities, about 65 percent indicated that the cost reported in the statements approximated market value; another 7 percent had written down to market under LCM procedures; and less than 1 percent reported the cost alone with no reference to market. About 20 percent of the companies surveyed failed to disclose the valuation basis of their marketable securities. This evidence might suggest that the cost method is not used very often and that **FASB Statement No. 12** has resulted in more uniform reporting of the cost of marketable securities relative to their market value at the financial report date. Exhibit 7–7 illustrates how cash and temporary investments are currently being reported.

[4] American Institute of CPAs, *"Accounting Trends and Techniques"* (New York: AICPA, 1981).

FUNDS FLOW EFFECTS

Cash and temporary investments in marketable equity securities have a direct impact on funds flow because both are a part of the working capital of the entity. Increases and decreases in cash and temporary investments directly increase and decrease working capital. There is also an interrelationship between these two current assets in that they tend to be substitutes for one another. Temporary investments are the most common use of idle cash, thereby consuming cash when they increase, and providing cash when sold.

The relationship between cash and temporary investments becomes clearer when cash is used as the basis for defining funds, as discussed in Chapters 4 and 25. The uses of cash and the sources of cash for purchases and sales of temporary investments are not as prominently disclosed when funds are defined as working capital, because these purchases and sales are essentially changes that take place *within* the working capital accounts. This difference becomes most important, and is somewhat complex, when converting the entity's "net income" to a measure of "working capital from operations" when there are gains or losses from temporary investments. Because these gains and losses are normally considered nonoperating, it seems as though they should be backed out of "net income" to arrive at "working capital

EXHIBIT 7–7

REPORTING CASH AND TEMPORARY INVESTMENTS IN FINANCIAL STATEMENTS

Iowa Beef Processors, Inc. and Subsidiaries

Consolidated Balance Sheets

Assets	November 1, 1980	November 3, 1979
CURRENT ASSETS:		
Cash, including certificates of deposit of $5,450,000 and $11,850,000 (Note C)	$ 23,334,000	$ 27,138,000
Marketable debt securities, at cost	4,000,000	—
Accounts receivable, less allowance for doubtful accounts of $2,867,000 and $2,260,000	170,941,000	155,107,000
Inventories (Note D)	97,113,000	80,164,000
Deferred tax benefit	3,419,000	3,557,000
Prepaid expenses	1,891,000	1,135,000
TOTAL CURRENT ASSETS	300,698,000	267,101,000
PROPERTY, PLANT AND EQUIPMENT, at cost (Note E):		
Land and land improvements	22,058,000	17,051,000
Buildings and stockyards	62,665,000	56,188,000
Equipment	140,462,000	128,166,000
	225,185,000	201,405,000
Less accumulated depreciation	74,228,000	62,085,000
	150,957,000	139,320,000
Construction in progress	55,699,000	7,593,000
	206,656,000	146,913,000
OTHER ASSETS	2,138,000	2,775,000
	$509,492,000	$416,789,000

EXHIBIT 7–7 (continued)

Morrison Knudsen

CONSOLIDATED BALANCE SHEET

December 31,	1980	1979*
ASSETS (Thousands of dollars)		
Current assets		
Cash	$ 7,124	$ 10,089
Short-term investments, at cost which approximates market	43,897	82,726
Accounts receivable including retentions $65,574, and $61,633	183,528	159,533
Costs and earnings in excess of billings on uncompleted contracts	128,945	134,182
Equity in and advances to joint ventures	41,151	29,295
Real property held for development and sale at the lower of cost or market	25,750	14,105
Other	6,145	3,277
Total current assets	436,540	433,207
Investments and other assets		
Equity in affiliated enterprises	17,381	17,477
Marketable securities, at cost, market $9,422, and $9,691	259	259
Other investments, at cost which approximates market	10,233	7,839
Notes receivable and other assets	8,008	11,467
Total investments and other assets	35,881	37,042
Property and equipment, at cost		
Land	5,183	1,986
Buildings, ways and wharves	107,382	102,211
Construction and other equipment	178,296	155,157
Total property and equipment	290,861	259,354
Less accumulated depreciation	112,542	103,453
Property and equipment — net	178,319	155,901
Total assets	$650,740	$626,150

*The 1979 amounts have been reclassified to conform to 1980 financial statement presentation.
The accompanying notes are an integral part of the financial statements.

from operations." However, because the effect of the sale of temporary investments is contained *within* the working capital accounts, no adjustment is made to net income in computing "working capital from operations." Instead, the gain or loss affects the measurement of the net change in working capital directly and is effectively ignored in the body of the statement of changes in financial position (SCFP).

Both cash and temporary investments are key components of the SCFP. In some cases entities have used cash and near-cash current assets (such as temporary investments) as the definition of funds in the SCFP. While many users would prefer to see cash or near-cash assets as the basis for the SCFP, most reports continue to use working capital as the basis for this statement.

SUMMARY

Cash and temporary investments are important resources for the effective operations of a business entity. Cash and near-cash assets are necessary in day-to-day operations for liquidating short-term obligations of the firm as they become due. The outflows for obligations such as trade accounts payable, wages, and salaries are nearly continuous, and the management of the cash inflows from receivables and cash sales must be carefully monitored to ensure that these routine inflows and outflows are properly balanced.

In addition to current cash needs, long-range cash planning for retirement of debt issues or replacement of plant assets must also be considered in accounting for cash and near-cash resources. In subsequent chapters we shall also examine the cash implications of methods employed in accounting for accounts receivable (Chapter 8), current liabilities (Chapter 16), and long-term obligations (Chapter 18).

Efficient financial management calls for cash being available when necessary to permit smooth operations, but idle cash should be invested in assets that will generate additional resources. Holding cash that is not currently needed for operations, particularly in inflationary periods, is an inefficient strategy that may result in an economic cost to the company. Temporary investments can provide an efficient use of cash that is not required for short periods. Of course, short-term liquidity needs must be considered in developing a sound strategy.

APPENDIX C
Four-Column Proof of Cash

The **four-column proof of cash** is a sophisticated form of **bank reconciliation.** In addition to reconciling bank and book balances, the four-column proof of cash reconciles receipts and disbursements as recorded by the bank with those recorded in the books of the company. It is this reconciliation of cash receipts and disbursements for the current month, in conjunction with the reconciliation of ending balances for the current and prior months, that gives rise to the title *proof of cash.* A four-column proof of cash is frequently used by external auditors to help determine whether a company follows its stated cash procedures and acceptable accounting and bookkeeping practices. Occasionally a proof of cash is performed for an entire year. Normally, however, a proof of cash is for a 1-month period.

The following ten steps are used in preparing a four-column proof of cash. These steps are illustrated in Exhibit C–1.

Step 1. Note that the far-left column in Exhibit C–1 is for the prior month, whereas the other columns are for the reconciliations of receipts, disbursements, and ending balance of the current month. It is necessary to include the prior month in the first column because reconciling items of the prior month will affect the reconciliation of the current month's receipts and disbursements.

Step 2. The balances for monthly receipts and disbursements, along with the

EXHIBIT
C–1

FOUR-COLUMN PROOF OF CASH

ROCK RITE RADIO—WAVO AM/FM

June 1984

	MAY 31, 1984	JUNE CASH		JUNE 30, 1984
		RECEIPTS	DISBURSEMENTS	
Balances per bank statement	39,372.25	48,281.88	46,191.09	41,463.04
Deposits in transit:				
May	510.00	(510.00) H		
June		1,050.00		1,050.00
NSF check received and redeposited in June		(26.16) S	(26.16) S	
Outstanding checks:				
May	(15,172.23)		(15,172.23) O	
June			11,303.50	(11,303.50)
Service charges:				
May	15.00		15.00 L	
June			(20.00)	20.00
Bank error—subtracted $1,000 charge from account in error; corrected in June	1,000.00	(1,000.00) T		
General ledger balances	$25,725.02	$47,795.72	$42,276.20 CD	$31,229.54
		D	15.00 GJ	
			$42,291.20	

( ) indicates subtraction;
CD is from the cash-disbursements journal; *GJ* is from the general journal.

ending balance from the current month's bank statement, provide the starting point. The beginning balance per bank statement should agree with the ending balance on the prior month's bank statement. The balances should add and subtract across, or "crossfoot."

Step 3. The balances from the general ledger (book balances) should be recorded at the bottom of the cash proof. Cash receipts should equal the June debits to cash in the general ledger and cash disbursements should be the total credits to the general ledger for the current month. The general ledger balance for receipts should be matched with, or "traced" to, the supporting detail in the cash-receipts journal. Likewise, the general ledger balance for disbursements should be traced to the cash-disbursements journal. Occasionally debits or credits to cash in the general ledger may come from general journal entries in addition to the cash receipts and disbursements journals, such as when a service charge deducted by the bank is recorded by a general journal entry. When this occurs, the elements constituting the total should be separately noted (see *D*). Once again, the balances per books should crossfoot.

Step 4. Copy the prior month's reconciliation into column 1. Add or "foot" to the general ledger balance to ensure that the reconciliation was copied correctly. Reoccurring reconciling items, such as outstanding checks, are usually presented with a common heading for both months, and space should be allowed for other entries in preparing the outline of the format for steps 1–4.

Observe that the format but not the substance of the reconciliation has changed for the proof of cash in comparison with the format illustrated earlier in this chapter. Rather than reconciling bank and book balances separately to "adjusted" or "corrected" cash balances, this format **begins with the bank balances and reconciles to the book or general ledger balances.**

Step 5. Reconcile the current month's bank balance to the *book balance* in column 4. Note that the reconciliation format is as described in step 4. To accomplish this reconciliation, ask the question, Does this reconciling item make the bank balance higher or lower than the book balance? If higher, subtract; if lower, add. Examples from Exhibit C–1 follow:

1. Deposit in transit—A deposit in transit has been recorded on the books, but not by the bank. Therefore, the bank is lower than the books, and the item must be added in order to reconcile bank balance to book balance.
2. Outstanding checks—Outstanding checks have been subtracted on the books, but not by the bank. Therefore, the bank is higher than the books and the item must be subtracted in order to reconcile to the book balance.
3. Service charge—The service charge has been subtracted by the bank, but not on the books. Therefore, the bank is lower than the books, and the item must be added in order to reconcile.

Step 6. Begin reconciling receipts and disbursements by considering the **prior month's reconciling items.** All reconciling items represent timing differences. Either the natural course of time will eliminate the difference (as with deposits in transit) or an adjustment will be made to eliminate the difference (as with the service charges). In the rare event of a bank error, the bank will make a correcting entry on the bank's records. Reconciling items that were eliminated during the current month must be reconciling items for either receipts or disbursements, but not both. If the reconciling item has not been eliminated by the end of the current month, it is carried over as a reconciling item to the current month's reconciliation —for example, a service charge for the prior month for which an adjustment was inadvertently omitted during the current month. In these instances, receipts and disbursements for the current month are not affected.

For each reconciling item, first determine whether it is cash receipts or cash disbursements that were affected. Then determine whether the item should be added to or subtracted from the bank's balance **to arrive at the general ledger balance.** Examples from Exhibit C–1 follow:

1. Deposit in transit (see *H*)—The prior month's deposit in transit ($510.00) was recorded as a receipt on the books in the prior month, but by the bank in the current month. Therefore, the bank's cash receipts in the current month are higher than the receipts recorded on the books, and the item must be subtracted in order to reconcile to the book receipts.
2. Outstanding checks (see *O*)—The prior month's outstanding checks ($15,172.23) were recorded as disbursements by the bank in the current month, but on the books in the prior month. Therefore, the bank's disbursements for the current

month are higher than the disbursements recorded on the books, and the item must be subtracted in order to reconcile to book disbursements.

3. Service charges (see *L*)—Service charges were subtracted in the prior month by the bank but were not recorded on the books until the current month. Therefore, cash disbursements are affected. The bank is lower than the books for the current month, and the amount must be added to reconcile to book disbursements.

4. Bank error (see *T*)—In the prior month the bank erroneously subtracted $1,000 from the company's account. The bank corrected its mistake in the current month by adding the $1,000 back into the company's account as a receipt. The company did not make a correcting entry for the $1,000. Therefore, the bank's cash receipts are higher than the book receipts, and the item must be subtracted to reconcile to book receipts.

Step 7. Continue reconciling receipts and disbursements by considering the **current month's reconciling items.** The procedures and logic used here are identical to those used in step 6. Once again, all reconciling items are timing differences that will be eliminated either by the natural course of time or by adjusting entries. Each reconciling item affects either cash receipts or disbursements, but not both.

First determine whether it is cash receipts or cash disbursements that were affected. Then determine whether the item must be added to or subtracted from the bank balance to reconcile with the book balance. Examples from Exhibit C–1 follow:

1. Deposit in transit—The $1,050.00 deposit in transit for the current month has been recorded in cash receipts on the books, but not by the bank. Cash receipts are affected and the item must be added in order to reconcile to book receipts.

2. Outstanding checks—$11,303.50 in outstanding checks for the current month have been recorded in the books, but not by the bank. Therefore, disbursements are affected, and the item must be added in order to reconcile to book disbursements.

3. Service charge—The current month's service charge of $20.00 has been subtracted by the bank but has not been recorded on the books. The item must be subtracted from the bank's disbursements in order to reconcile to book disbursements.

Step 8. Review the current month's bank statement, the cash-receipts journal, the cash-disbursements journal, and the general ledger for items that will cause differences between the receipts and disbursements recorded by the bank and on the books but that *are not* reconciling items at either the current or the prior month-end.

The example given in Exhibit C–1 (see *S*) is a $26.16 NSF check. The check was deposited routinely by the company. However, the check was returned to the company's bank marked NSF. The bank then subtracted the $26.16 as a disbursement from the company's account and returned the check to the company. The company successfully deposited the check. The redeposit was recorded by the bank.

The company made no entry for either the return of the check by the bank or its redeposit. The bank, however, recorded a disbursement and a deposit in addition to the original deposit. Therefore, the item must be subtracted from both the bank's receipts and the bank's disbursements in order to reconcile to book receipts and disbursements. This is a very common sequence of transactions.

Step 9. Foot the receipts and disbursements columns to ensure that they reconcile. Double-underline a general ledger balance only when the reconciliation for the column is complete.

If difficulties are encountered in reconciling, the following procedures are often helpful:

1. Make certain that each month-end reconciling item is recorded in receipts or disbursements only once.
2. Use mathematical logic to double-check your accounting logic. For example, a reconciling item of the prior month that is an addition *must* be either a subtraction in receipts or an addition in disbursements.
3. If receipts and disbursements are "off" by the same amount, look for additional items that affect receipts and disbursements but not month-end balances. If they are both "off" by an amount equal to a reconciling item, check to see if a receipt is recorded as a disbursement, or vice versa.
4. A difference equal to double the amount of a reconciling item may indicate a subtraction that should be an addition, or vice versa.
5. A difference evenly divisible by 9 usually represents a transposition error (for example, 569 rather than 659).

Step 10. Record any necessary adjustments to the books. In Exhibit C-1 only the $20 service charge requires an adjustment.

QUESTIONS

Q7-1   What is cash? What items are included in the asset *cash?*

Q7-2   What is the correct procedure for handling cash overdrafts as of a report date when more than one bank is involved?

Q7-3   How should compensating balances be reported?

Q7-4   What is a petty cash fund and how does it work?

Q7-5   Outline some basic control procedures for the handling of cash inflows.

Q7-6   Outline some basic control procedures for the handling of cash outflows.

Q7-7   In reconciling a bank checking account, what is the final reconciliation amount of the reconciled account? What does it represent and how is it useful?

Q7-8   What is the impact of an NSF check on the reconciliation?

Q7-9   What is the best way to identify a transposition error?

Q7-10   What are the key attributes of those securities that are classified as temporary investments?

Q7-11   How are the bond discounts or premiums of temporary investments in bonds handled?

Q7-12   What is the required accounting treatment for temporary investments in nonmarketable securities?

Q7-13   What is the required accounting method for temporary investments in marketable equity securities?

Q7-14   When a number of different securities are included in the Temporary Investments account, how is their market value measured for LCM purposes?

Q7-15   When multiple purchases have been made at different prices for stock held as a temporary investment, which purchase price is used when part of the investment is sold in order to measure the gain or loss?

Q7-16   What is the correct method of reclassifying a temporary investment to a long-term investment?

Q7-17   Why is the LCM method internally inconsistent?

Q7-18   What does the "cost" of a temporary investment include?

Q7-19 What is the basis of measuring the outflow of a temporary investment when it is sold? (That is, what is the role of the Allowance account at time of sale?)

Q-20 What is the nature of an "unrealized gain on temporary investments" within the LCM paradigm?

CASES

C7-1 Assume that you are about to establish your own professional accounting consulting firm. You need to set up a petty cash fund of $1,000.

REQUIRED Explain how you would go about doing so, what types of applications you might have for petty cash, and how you would keep track of the use of petty cash and the replenishing of the petty cash fund. Also, explain how you would control the petty cash fund.

C7-2 As internal auditor of the KCG Corporation, you are reviewing the bank cutoff statement for one of the KCG divisions and you discover a $15,800 discrepancy between the deposits per bank statement and the deposits per books. In preparing the June 18, 1984, reconciliation, you record the $15,800 deposit, which was recorded per books on June 18, 1984, as a deposit in transit. On your next visit to this particular KCG division, you refer back to the June 18, 1984, bank statement and note that the $15,800 deposit was not recorded by the bank until Friday, June 20, 1984. The policy for all KCG divisions is to deposit all receipts on a daily basis.

REQUIRED What potential cash-control problem is suggested by these facts, and what might you do to investigate any other potential control problems?

C7-3 (CPA ADAPTED) The FASB issued *Statement No. 12,* "Accounting for Certain Marketable Securities," to clarify the accounting procedures for investments in marketable equity securities. An important part of the statement involves the distinction between the current and noncurrent classification of marketable equity securities.

REQUIRED

1. Why would a company have current and noncurrent investments in the securities of other entities?
2. What factors should be considered in determining whether investments in marketable equity securities should be classified as current or noncurrent, and how can this decision affect the financial reports of the entity?

C7-4 (CPA ADAPTED) The following four unrelated situations involve marketable equity securities.

SITUATION 1

A current portfolio with an aggregate market value in excess of cost includes one particular security whose market value has declined to less than one-half of the original cost. The decline in value is considered to be other than temporary.

SITUATION 2

The statement of financial position of a company does not classify assets and liabilities as current and noncurrent. The portfolio of marketable equity securities includes securities normally considered current that have a net cost in excess of market value of $2,000. The remainder of the portfolio has a net market value in excess of cost of $5,000.

SITUATION 3

A marketable equity security, whose market value is currently less than cost, is classified as noncurrent but is to be reclassified as current.

SITUATION 4

A company's noncurrent portfolio of marketable equity securities consists of the common stock of one company. At the end of the preceding year the market value of the security was 50 percent of original cost, and this effect was properly reflected in a Valuation Allowance account. However, at the end of the current year the market value of the security had appreciated to twice the original cost. The security is still considered noncurrent at year-end.

REQUIRED   What effect would each of the above situations have on classification, carrying value, and earnings?

C7–5   In 1985, while buying a six-pack of beer with your friend, Bob Colson, you purchased a New York State lottery ticket, which turned out to be a $1,000,000 winner. As a result of your good fortune, you decide to drop out of your last semester in SUNY Albany's accounting program and travel for a few years. Your friend Bob, who was a finance major at Wharton, has agreed to manage your $1,000,000 winnings for you by investing in stocks and bonds. He has your travel itinerary and has agreed to send you money from your investments along with periodic reports on your holdings. By January 19, 1986, you have received about $100,000 from Bob and have traveled extensively. You are basking in the sun in the Tobago Islands when you receive a cable telling you the net book value of your securities on December 31, 1986, was $900,000. You note that all four of the quarterly cables received from Bob have reported approximately the same thing, recalling Bob's promise to report to you in conformance with GAAP. For some reason, you feel uneasy about your agreement with Bob and the safety of your winnings.

REQUIRED   Is Bob managing your investments well? Should you trust your friend or place the investment responsibilities with someone else? What information would you like to have that you are not already receiving concerning your new-found wealth?

C7–6 (CMA ADAPTED)   The Pantex Corporation has gone through a period of rapid expansion to reach its present size. It now has seven divisions, but the expansion program has placed a strain on its cash resources. Therefore, the need for better cash planning at the corporate level has become very important.

At the present time, each division is responsible for the collection of receivables and the disbursement for all operating expenses and approved capital projects. The corporation does exercise control over division activities and has attempted to coordinate the cash needs of the divisions and the corporation. However, it has not yet developed effective division cash reports from which it can determine the needs and availability of cash in the next budgetary year. As a result of inadequate information, the corporation permitted some divisions to make expenditures for goods and services that need not have been made or could have been postponed until a later time, whereas other divisions had to delay expenditures that should have had a greater priority.

The accompanying table shows the 1984 cash receipts and disbursements plan prepared by the Tapon division for submission to the corporate office.

TAPON DIVISION Budgeted Cash Receipts and Disbursements For the Year Ended December 31, 1984	
	(000 OMITTED)
Receipts	
Collections on accounts	$9,320
Miscellaneous	36
	$9,356
Disbursements	
Production	
Raw materials	2,240
Labor and fringe benefits	2,076
Overhead	2,100
Sales	
Commissions	395
Travel and entertainment	600
Other	200
Administrative	
Accounting	80
Personnel	110
General management	350
Capital expenditures	1,240
	$9,391
Excess of receipts over (under) disbursements	$ (36)

The following additional information was used by the Tapon division to develop the cash receipts and disbursements budget:

1. Receipts—Miscellaneous receipts are estimated proceeds from the sales of unneeded equipment.
2. Sales—Travel and entertainment represents the costs required to produce the sales volume projected for the year. The other sales costs consist of $50,000 for training new sales personnel, $25,000 for attendance by sales personnel at association meetings (not sales shows), and $125,000 for sales management salaries.
3. Administration—Personnel costs include $50,000 for salary and department operating costs, $20,000 for training new personnel, and $40,000 for management training courses for current employees. The general management costs include salaries and office costs for the division management, $310,000; plus $10,000 for officials' travel to Pantex Corporation meetings and $30,000 for industry and association conferences.
4. Capital expenditures—Planned expenditures for capital items during 1984 are as follows:

Capital programs approved by the corporation:	
Items ordered for delivery in 1984	$300,000
Items to be ordered in 1984 for delivery in 1984	700,000
New programs to be submitted to corporation during 1984	240,000

REQUIRED Present a revised budgeted cash receipts and disbursements statement for the Tapon division. Design the format of the revised statement to include adequate detail so as to improve the corporation's ability to judge the urgency of the cash needs. Such a statement would be submitted by all divisions to provide the basis for overall corporation cash planning.

EXERCISES

E7–1 Your examination of the $1,000 petty cash fund of Betty's Fabrics, Inc., has revealed the following data:

RECEIPTS	AMOUNT
13—Cab fares	$ 253
18—Postage charges	115
1—Umbrella	13
21—UPS bills	385
1—Pocket calculator	42
14—Batteries for warehouse lights	10
2—Adding-machine tapes	18
	$ 836
Over and short	(36)
Cash and bills	200
	$1,000

It is the company's policy that items costing less than $100 are not capitalized.

REQUIRED Record the entry or entries necessary to replenish the petty cash fund.

E7–2 Each item in a bank reconciliation is included in one of the following four types of adjustments:

1. Added to bank balance
2. Deducted from bank balance
3. Added to book balance
4. Deducted from book balance

REQUIRED Identify which type of an adjustment each of the following items would be in a bank reconciliation:

BB - Bank books

1. Bank service charge   *OUR -BR*
2. Deposit in transit   *+BB*
3. Collection of note from customer by bank   *+OUR BR*
4. Checks that have been written but have yet to clear the bank   *+ BB*
5. Interest on checking account balance   *+BR*
6. Error in the total on our deposit ticket noted by the bank in favor of the bank (for example, total was overstated)   *- OUR BR*
7. NSF checks

E7-3   Indicate how each of the following items identified at year-end would be classified in the year-end financial statements:

1. A daily passbook savings account   *C*
2. Cash IOU from a corporate employee   *L*
3. A traveler's check   *cash*
4. A 26-week money market certificate   *ST in.*
5. A 30-month certificate of deposit   *LT in*
6. Postage stamps   *prepaid supplies*
7. Petty cash on hand   *cash*
8. Overdraft in a checking account   *L*
9. Undistributed payroll checks from most recent pay period held by issuing foreman   *Nothing*
10. Bond sinking fund represented by cash on deposit in unrestricted savings account   *cash Not L/current asset*

E7-4   Prepare the June 30, 1984, bank reconciliation and adjusting journal entries for VF Corporation based on the following data:

Balance per bank statement, 6/30/84	$18,629
Balance per books, 6/30/84	17,163
Note collected by bank	877
Interest posted by bank to account	190
Bank fee	63
NSF check returned with statement	602
Deposit of 7/1/84 not recorded by bank	1,011
Checks written before 7/1/84 but not received by bank	1,064

E7-5   The Temporary Investments in Stock accounts consist of the following recent acquisitions:

STOCK	COST	MARKET VALUE AT 12/31/84
General Motors	$3,000	$2,700
Control Data	2,000	2,200
Shakespear Corporation	6,000	5,800

Assume that the Allowance to Reduce Temporary Investments to Market account has a $500 credit balance *before* year-end adjustment.

REQUIRED

1. Record any necessary adjusting entry.
2. Indicate the impact of the adjustment on net income.

E7-6   On January 15 Dukes Corporation acquired marketable securities as a temporary investment for $80,000. The market values of the securities at the end of each quarter are as follows:

QUARTER ENDING	MARKET PRICE
Mar. 31	$70,000
June 30	86,000
Sept. 30	65,000

Dukes uses GAAP to value its investments in its quarterly reports.

REQUIRED

1. Record the journal entries required at June 30 and September 30.
2. Indicate how the asset would be reported in the balance sheet on September 30.
3. Record the entry to account for the sale of one-half of the securities on October 10 for $35,000.

E7-7   Baker owns 1,800 shares of Taker, which were purchased at $35 per share as the sole temporary investment held by Baker at the beginning of 1984. After adjusting entries but before the books are closed on December 31, 1984, Baker's *long-term* portfolio has the following balances:

Long-term investments	$312,000
Allowance to reduce investments to market	(57,000)
	$255,000

The market value of Taker had increased to $49.50 per share at December 31, 1984.

REQUIRED

1. Record the transfer of Taker to the Long-Term Investments account on December 31, 1984.
2. Prepare a summary of Baker's total assets with and without the transfer, assuming all other assets equal $3,000,000. What is the impact of the transfer of Taker?

E7-8   Foresythe, Inc., holds marketable equity securities as a temporary investment. The balance in the contra asset account Allowance to Reduce Temporary Investments to Lower-of-Cost-or-Market has a $10,000 credit balance as of December 31, 1986. The portfolio of equity securities at that date consisted of the following items:

	NUMBER OF SHARES	TOTAL COST	TOTAL MARKET VALUE
Gibbons Corporation common	100	$18,000	$15,000
Telex, Inc., common	150	7,500	8,000
Fastex Company common	200	15,800	16,000
		$41,300	$39,000

REQUIRED

1. Record the necessary adjusting entry, if any, as of December 31, 1986.
2. Assume that Foresythe sold 100 shares of Fastex on January 31, 1987, for $85 per share (net of commissions). Record the sale of Fastex using the average cost flow assumption.

E7-9   On November 1 Parrot Corporation purchased as a temporary investment 30 IBM 6 percent bonds (maturity value, $1,000 each), which pay interest on January 1 and July 1 each year. The bonds were selling for 105 percent of maturity value plus accrued interest on November 1. Brokerage fees are $50. Two-thirds of the IBM bonds were sold on March 31 at a loss of $220. Parrot has a December 31 year-end and accounts for nonequity securities at cost.

REQUIRED   Record *all* necessary entries for the IBM bonds from November 1 to the following July 1.

E7–10   On January 15, 1980, Bourne Corporation acquired 100 shares of Generous Motors for $80 per share plus a $50 brokerage fee as its only temporary investment. Bourne prepared quarterly financial statements. Selected market prices of Generous Motors for 1980 are as follows:

QUARTER ENDING	MARKET PRICE
Mar. 31	$70
June 30	85
Sept. 30	90
Dec. 31	75

REQUIRED

1. Record the purchase of January 15, assuming Bourne values its temporary investment by using the "market" method.
2. Record the necessary adjusting entries for September 30 and December 31, assuming the lower-of-cost-or-market (LCM) method is used.
3. Ignore your answers to requirements 1 and 2. Assume that the LCM method is used and that on May 15 Bourne sells one-half (50 shares) of its investment for $82 per share. Record the March 31 adjusting entry *and* the May 15 entry to record the sale.

PROBLEMS

P7–1   The Short-Term Investments account of Gerhardt-Mathews Publishers, Inc., consists of the following securities at the end of 1983:

	COST	12/31/83 MARKET	12/31/82 MARKET
American Motors Corporation	$ 6,737	$ 6,218	$ 6,530
AMF, Inc.	1,922	1,818	1,927
AT&T	7,142	7,022	7,102
Arrow	976	3,256	1,327
Baxter Labs	2,400	1,927	2,035
	$19,177	$20,241	$18,921

No sales or purchases have taken place during 1983.

REQUIRED

1. Record any necessary entries at 1983 year-end using the LCM method *applied on an individual security basis.*
2. Record any necessary entries at 1983 year-end using the LCM method applied per *FASB Statement No. 12,* "Accounting for Certain Marketable Securities."
3. Record any necessary entries at 1983 year-end using the market value method.
4. Evaluate the relevance, comparability, and conservatism of the three methods recorded above.

P7–2   Record the necessary entries for the information given below. Show all computations and indicate which entries belong to parts 1, 2, 3, and 4. Assume that bonds accounted for as a temporary investment are recorded at cost (no bond discount or bond premium is either recorded or amortized) and that the LCM valuation method as outlined in *FASB Statement No. 12*, "Accounting for Certain Marketable Securities," is used.

1. On April 1, 1980, you purchased bonds, par $24,000, stated interest rate of 10 percent for $21,400 including accrued interest. Interest on these bonds is paid on June 1 and December 1 annually.

2. Prepare year-end adjusting entries for your April 30, 1980, year-end. The market price of the bonds on April 30 is 85 percent plus accrued interest.

3. Record the sale of $12,000 par value of bonds on May 15, 1980, for $10,600 total consideration in cash.

4. Record interest on June 1, 1980.

P7–3   On June 12, 1984, you received the following information from the bank where your company maintains its checking account:

Balance May 3, 1984	$ 67,140
Deposits, May 4, 1984, to June 3, 1984	488,236
Collections of notes from customers, no interest included	31,450
Deposits returned NSF	13,122
Bank service charge	180
Canceled checks	510,709
Balance June 3, 1984	62,815

Included with the canceled checks was a $583 check drawn on the account of another company. The $583 was included in the $510,709 total for canceled checks. Your ledger shows deposits made on June 3 and June 4 of $17,200 and $21,000, respectively, which are *not* included in the deposits of $488,236 per bank statement. Also, checks written and mailed but not returned with the bank statement were summarized as follows:

PER CHECK REGISTER		
DATE CHECKS ISSUED	NUMBER OF CHECKS	TOTAL AMOUNT
Apr. 13	1	$ 150
May 1	1	76
May 18	2	105
May 24	1	1,200
May 29	4	3,407
May 30	3	1,621
June 1	7	11,420
June 2	8	426
June 4	10	11,826
June 6	15	14,392
June 10	26	26,174
June 11	11	21,105
		$91,902

REQUIRED

1. Prepare the bank reconciliation as of June 3, 1984, based on the above data. Note: It is necessary to determine what the general ledger balance must be.

2. Prepare any adjusting entries required by the bank reconciliation.

P7–4   The following information is taken from the cash ledger of the Ritts Corporation:

| | AMOUNT | | |
DATE	DEBIT	CREDIT	BALANCE
			$1,500
May 13 Check #187		$100	1,400
May 16 Check #188		50	1,350
May 17 Deposit	$1,000		2,350
May 17 Check #189		200	2,150
May 19 Check #190		45	2,105
May 21 Check #191		105	2,000
May 23 Check #192		40	1,960
May 23 Check #193		50	1,910
May 24 Deposit	1,200		3,110
May 26 Check #194		50	3,060
May 28 Check #195		60	3,000
May 31 Check #196		100	2,900
May 31 Deposit	400		3,300

ADDITIONAL DATA

1. On June 5 Ritts received its bank statement indicating that its bank account had a balance of $1,365 on May 24.
2. According to the bank statement, the last deposit made by Ritts was on May 17.
3. According to the bank statement, the following checks had *not* cleared the bank: 190, 191, 193, 194, 195, 196.
4. Included in the bank balance in item 1 above was $320 from the collection of a note from one of the Ritts Corporation's customers. The note receivable was interest bearing and was recorded on the Ritts's books at its face value of $300.
5. Included in the bank statement was a charge of $50 for an NSF check that Ritts deposited on May 17.
6. The bank statement indicated that a deduction of $15 from the Ritts account was made for bank services.
7. Included in the bank statement was a deduction of $100 for a check written by the Pitts Corporation, payable to Meddaugh, Inc.
8. Check #187 written by Ritts to Dean Allan on account cleared the bank for $1,000, the amount written on the check. The Ritts accountant realized he had only deducted $100 from his ledger by mistake.

REQUIRED

1. Prepare a Ritts Corporation bank reconciliation that arrives at *corrected* balances as of May 24.
2. Record the necessary journal entries to correct the Ritts Corporation's books.

P7–5 In your year-end review of the position of the McGarret Company, you are asked to reconcile the bank statement as of December 31, 1984. The following data are available to you:

Summary of check numbers of checks clearing the bank with the statement at the top of p. 260:

15808 to 15874	15965 to 15983
15876 to 15927	15986 to 15992
15929 to 15963	15994 to 16000
	182736

Bank Statement

DATE	NUMBER OF CHECKS	NUMBER OF DEPOSITS	AMOUNT	ACCOUNT BALANCE
12/18/84	15		$ 8,761	$193,104
12/20/84	16		9,432	183,672
12/21/84	10		4,861	178,811
12/21/84		1	65,803	244,614
12/22/84	2		1,915	242,699
12/26/84	15		18,605	224,094
12/27/84	21		46,109	177,985
12/27/84		1	51,207	229,192
12/29/84	22		20,018	209,174
1/2/85		2	43,806	252,980
1/3/85	30		45,610	207,370
1/4/85	29		67,108	140,262
1/5/85	28		59,215	81,047
1/5/85		1	77,106	158,153
	188	5		

Other data per bank statement:

Beginning balance	$201,865
Summary of deposits	237,922
Summary of checks cleared	281,634
Bank service fee ($1 per check)	188
Deposited December checks returned NSF	1,735
Credit memo—collection of customer note by bank, no interest included	6,000
Debit memo—automatic mortgage principal payment deduction	2,875
Ending balance	159,355

The company records for receipts and deposits provide you with the following data:

Books—Receipts

DATE OF DEPOSIT	AMOUNT OF DEPOSIT
12/14/84	$ 28,365
12/21/84	65,803
12/27/84	51,207
12/30/84	23,806
1/2/85	20,000
1/4/85	77,106
	$266,287

Books—Check Register Summary

DATE	NUMBER OF CHECKS ISSUED	CHECK NUMBERS	AMOUNT
12/3/84	71	15,861 to 15,931	$ 6,207
12/10/84	26	15,932 to 15,957	2,807
12/30/84	13	15,958 to 15,970	1,506
12/31/84	36	15,971 to 16,006	70,877
1/8/85	42	16,007 to 16,048	46,921
	188		$128,318

The following checks have not been returned by the bank as of the most recent bank statement:

DATE	CHECK NUMBERS	AMOUNT
11/10/84	15,701	$ 187
11/30/84	15,806	63
12/3/84	15,875 and 15,928	2,105
12/20/84	15,964	173
12/31/84	15,984, 15,985, 15,993,	
	and 16,001 to 16,006	16,937
1/8/85	16,007 to 16,048	46,921
		$66,386

Also, check #182,736 in the amount of $1,873 was returned with the other canceled checks. It is written on the Garret Company account (not McGarret).

REQUIRED

1. Prepare the bank reconciliation for McGarret as of December 31, 1984.
2. Record any necessary adjusting entries.

P7-6   Nucorp Energy, Inc., maintains a single bank account through which all receipts and payments are made. The bank reconciliation for November 1983 included the following data:

Balance per bank, 11/30/83	$ 17,430
Deposits in transit	1,000
	$ 18,430
Outstanding checks	(1,906)
Bank error in favor of bank	(37)
	$ 16,487

The December 1983 records and bank statement provided the following additional information:

	PER BANK STATEMENT	PER LEDGER
December checks paid	$ 4,865	$ 1,000
December service charge	85	—
December NSF checks	731	—
December deposits	5,304	5,620
December error in favor of Nucorp	18	—
December error in favor of bank	—	27
December interest on account	165	—
December 31, 1983, balance	17,136	17,587

REQUIRED

1. Prepare a bank reconciliation that arrives at the corrected balance per books for year-end financial statement purposes.
2. Record any necessary entries to state the year-end bank balance properly in the financial statements.

P7-7   The following data are available regarding the Temporary Investments account of the Swieringa Corporation as of the December 31, 1985, year-end.

STOCK	MARKET VALUES			
	PRICE AT PURCHASE DATE	PRICE AT SALE DATE	PRICE AT YEAR-END	
			1985	1984
Ford Motor	$ 4,885	—	$ 4,327	$ 4,106
Redman Ind.	7,426	$6,837	—	6,632
Armco Steel	2,860	—	3,874	3,433
Federal Mogul	5,568	6,348	—	6,061
Brunswick	2,976	—	2,743	2,637
	$23,715	$13,185	$10,944	$22,869

Swieringa decided to transfer the Armco Steel stock to the long-term investment portfolio at December 31, 1985, due to reduced expected cash-flow needs for 1986. The sale of Redman occurred on June 30, 1985, and Federal Mogul was sold on December 30, 1985.

REQUIRED

1. Record the sales of stock that occurred during 1985.
2. Record the transfer and any December 31, 1985, adjusting entries required by the data.
3. Prepare a partial balance sheet and income statement for 1985 to reflect the impact of the above entries.

P7–8 Dennison Manufacturing began operations in 1984. The following events relate to its investing activity with temporarily idle cash during the first year:

Mar. 23	Purchased 200 shares of Gearhart Industries common at $22.50 per share.
June 1	Purchased 180 shares of Marion Labs common at $40.75 per share. Purchased 10 Standard Oil $1,000, 10 percent bonds for 98 percent plus accrued interest. Interest on the bonds is paid July 1 and January 1 each year.
July 3	Received semiannual dividends of $.20 per share on Gearhart Industries common and $.35 per share on Marion Labs common, plus semiannual interest on Standard Oil bonds.
Aug. 8	Sold 90 shares of Marion Labs for $43 per share (net of commissions).
Sept. 4	Purchased 150 shares of IC Industries at $75 per share.
Nov. 18	Sold 100 shares of Gearhart Industries for $21 per share.
Dec. 13	Exchanged 50 shares of IC Industries for 100 shares of Southern Leasing, Inc. Southern Leasing is not publicly traded. IC Industries was selling for $77 per share at the date of exchange.
Dec. 28	The following dividend announcements were made in December:

SECURITY	DIVIDEND	DECLARED	RECORD DATE
Gearhart	$ .25	12/18	12/28
Marion	.35	12/15	12/31
IC	1.10	12/10	12/15
Southern	2.00	12/18	12/31

Dec. 31   The following market prices were quoted in the *New York Times* at the close of business, December 31, 1984:

	QUOTE AT CLOSE
Gearhart	$20
Marion	42
IC	74
Standard	97%

REQUIRED

1. Prepare the necessary entries to record the events listed above.
2. Record any necessary adjusting entries. Dennison uses the *FASB Statement No. 12* method of recording all temporary investments.
3. Indicate the impact of the above activity on the 1984 income statement.

P7–9 The Temporary Investments account of Jacobson's Stores, Inc., at December 31, 1983, consisted of the following items listed in the order purchased:

SECURITY	NUMBER OF SECURITIES	ORIGINAL COST PER UNIT	ORIGINAL COST TOTAL	TOTAL MARKET, 12/31/83
Zenith, Inc., 8% bonds	20(face $1,000)	$1,015	$20,300	$18,750
General Electric preferred	500	42	21,000	19,630
Detroit Edison common	360	28	10,080	10,096
Olympia common	80	61	4,880	4,960
Olympia common	100	63	6,300	6,200
Hoover Universal common	100	18	1,800	2,500
Hoover Universal common	350	21	7,350	8,750
			$71,710	$70,886

During 1984 the following transactions involving Jacobson's temporary investments took place:

DATE	EVENT
1/1/84	Received $800 bond interest.
2/1/84	Received $485 dividend on Edison common which had been declared on December 18, 1983.
2/8/84	Received $1,000 dividend on General Electric preferred.
3/18/84	Sold 150 shares of Hoover Universal for $3,900.
4/27/84	Purchased 1,000 shares of Tenneco common for $3,750.
5/30/84	Sold 500 shares of General Electric preferred for $20,000.
5/31/84	Purchased 30 AMTEK 13 percent bonds ($1,000 par) at 100 percent plus accrued interest. Interest is paid semiannually on January 1 and July 1 each year.
6/30/84	Sold 10 Zenith, Inc., bonds for 94 percent plus 6 months' accrued interest.
7/1/84	Received semiannual bond interest on AMTEK and Zenith bonds.
10/4/84	Sold 100 shares of Olympia common for $6,000.
11/21/84	Sold remaining Zenith, Inc., bonds for 95 percent plus accrued interest from July 1.
12/18/84	The following stock dividends were declared to shareholders of record December 25: Detroit Edison, $1.50 per share; and Hoover Universal, $.50 per share.
12/26/84	Sold 50 shares of Hoover Universal for $1,400.

On December 31, 1984, the following market prices were quoted in *The Wall Street Journal:*

	MARKET QUOTE 12/31/84		
	OPEN	CLOSE	CHANGE
Tenneco	3 ¾	4	+ ¼
Detroit Edison	30	31	+1
Olympia	58 ½	57	1 ½
Hoover Universal	28 ½	29	+ ½
AMTEK	99	100	+1

Jacobson's uses the FIFO cost-flow assumption and the LCM method in accounting for all temporary investments.

REQUIRED

1. Record all journal entries required for the events described above.
2. Record any necessary adjusting entries at December 31, 1984.
3. Indicate how the activity above would be disclosed in the December 31, 1984, balance sheet and income statement of Jacobson's Stores, Inc.

P7–10* The following data are taken from the records of the McKenzel Corporation for the month ending September 30, 1984.

ITEM	AMOUNT
1. Deposit made by McKenzel on September 30, received by bank on October 1	$ 1,877
2. Cash and checks deposited during September per bank statement	27,640
3. Note collected by bank from McKenzel customer including $100 interest and net of $10 collection fee	2,000
4. Deposit made by McKenzel August 31, received by bank September 3	984
5. Balance per bank, September 30	13,606
6. Balance per books, September 30	9,868
7. NSF checks returned with bank statement	387
8. Bank services charges not included elsewhere	37
9. Outstanding checks	

```
AUGUST 31
─────────
 #4875        $   47
 #4897           113
 #4930–33      1,870
 #4950–51        431    2,461

SEPTEMBER 30
────────────
 #4875            47
 #4951           113
 #5068         2,200
 #5070–74      1,733    4,093
```

10. Bank error in recording deposit of $497 as $479	—
11. Canceled checks returned with the September bank statement	26,760
12. Cash and checks on hand, September 30	491
13. Check to vendor recorded in check register as $748, check issued for correct amount of $784	—
14. Cash and checks received during September	29,024
15. Checks issued during September	28,392
16. Balance per bank, August 31	11,150
17. Balance per books, August 31	10,500

REQUIRED Prepare a four-column bank reconciliation as illustrated in Appendix C.

P7–11* As the sole bookkeeper of Michael's Computing Service, you like to "prove" your cash balances each month by preparing a four-column proof of cash. It is time to prepare the proof for May 1984. Spread before you on your desk are the following items:

1. The bank statement dated May 31, 1984. The statement lists receipts of $58,792.40, disbursements of $57,581.21, a beginning balance of $1,296.38, and an ending balance of $2,507.57.
2. The April 30, 1984, proof of cash, which shows reconciling items as follows:

Deposits in transit	$1,525.00
Outstanding checks	456.23
Interest added to your account by the bank	15.00

3. The general ledger, which shows an April 30, 1984, balance of $2,350.15, May receipts of $59,507.40, May disbursements of $56,014.43, and a May 31, 1984, balance of $5,843.12.

Upon reviewing the May bank statement you notice the following additional items.

1. You cleverly switched your company's account last January to a bank offering NOW accounts. This means that you receive interest on your deposits and do not pay service charges. May's interest deposited into your account by the bank was $25. This is your first notification of your May interest earnings.
2. The bank collected a $1,000 note for you on May 31, 1984. You are delighted to learn that this customer remitted directly to the bank.
3. A check for $653 was returned to your bank on May 30, 1984, marked NSF. You sigh deeply because you realize that the customer who wrote this check has left town and you will never collect the $653. The check was received for a cash sale of spare computer parts. The parts cannot be recovered.
4. The bank has not recorded your May 31, 1984, deposit of $4,500 in May. You assume that it will be recorded by the bank as of June 1, 1984.
5. On May 10, 1984, the bank added $1,250 to your account in error. The bank noticed the error and corrected it on May 12, 1984.

You list the outstanding checks as of May 31, 1984, and note that they total $792.45.

REQUIRED

1. Prepare the May four-column proof of cash.
2. Record any necessary adjusting entries.

P7–12* As controller of Howard Telescopes Unlimited you are used to solving problems. Therefore, upon discovering on February 8, 1984, that the general ledger has been inadvertently destroyed, you do not panic. Calmly you inform your staff that the general ledger can be reconstructed, and that you will begin that reconstruction with a four-column proof of cash for January 1984. You are delighted by the foresight that caused you to retire the old general ledger as of December 31, 1983. As a result, only general ledger postings and totals for January 1984 have been lost.

From the January 31, 1984, bank statement you extract the following information:

1. The beginning balance was $9,673.20, the ending balance was $5,499.26, receipts were $153,789.20, and disbursements were $157,963.14.
2. Service charges of $13 were deducted by the bank during January.
3. The bank had collected a $1,500 note receivable on behalf of the company and had deposited the proceeds directly into the company's account.
4. An NSF check for $775 was returned to the company and was successfully redeposited during January.

Using the cash receipts and disbursements registers as a guide, you list outstanding checks totaling $10,989.13 and calculate deposits in transit to total $9,871.22.

Although the December 31, 1983, proof of cash was destroyed with the general ledger, you located a list of reconciling items for December 31, 1983, that contains the following items:

1. Deposits in transit totaled $53,261.25.
2. Service charges deducted by the bank were $75.

3. Outstanding checks totaled $49,723.74.
4. The bank remitted a note payable for $10,000 directly to a vendor, subtracting that amount from the company's account.

   The old general ledger shows a December 31, 1983, cash balance of $23,285.71.

REQUIRED Prepare the four-column proof of cash for January 1984. This proof will verify the reconstructed general ledger balances for cash receipts and cash disbursements as well as the January 31, 1984, balance. Note that it will be necessary to determine those balances independently.

P7–13 On December 31, 1985, Martin Enterprises had the following short- and long-term investments:

SHORT-TERM PORTFOLIO				
DATE OF PURCHASE	SECURITY	ORIGINAL COST	CURRENT MARKET VALUE	12/31/84 MARKET VALUE
9/84	ABBA, Inc.	$ 4,380	$ 7,324	$ 5,043
10/84	AMF Co.	2,125	1,210	1,180
3/84	JCT Corp.	6,937	5,735	6,150
5/84	USS	5,429	6,320	6,063
6/85	ABBA, Inc.	3,721	2,947	—
9/85	JCT Corp.	9,270	11,340	—
		$31,862	$34,876	$18,436
LONG-TERM PORTFOLIO				
10/80	Willey, Inc.	$ 7,385	$ 8,240	$ 9,107
5/82	J&L Co.	6,384	10,921	8,140
7/82	Irvin	4,380	2,847	3,520
8/82	McCraw	5,439	3,108	4,607
3/83	Willey, Inc.	10,970	8,385	9,630
		$34,558	$33,501	$35,004

There were no sales of securities during 1985.

REQUIRED

1. Assume that Martin wishes to maximize the reported income from short- and long-term investments. What is the maximum profit that Martin could report in 1985? Consider transfers to or from the short-term portfolio as of December 31, 1985.
2. Assume that Martin wishes to maximize the loss from short- and long-term investments. What is the maximum possible loss for 1985?
3. Ignore requirements 1 and 2. Record any necessary entries as of December 31, 1985.

Current Receivables

8

OVERVIEW

Receivables represent an entity's claims on assets and/or services to be delivered to it by other parties at future points in time. The attributes of (1) possessing future economic benefits, (2) being under the entity's control, (3) being the results of past transactions or events, and (4) being sufficiently measurable apply to receivables as well as to all other assets. For example, a note due in 90 days has economic potential in that cash is expected to be collected. It is controlled by the payee in the sense that the payee has legal possession and usually can use it in a number of ways, such as discounting and selling and as collateral. It is objectively measureable in that a specific money amount was established usually in an arm's-length transaction. The objectivity can sometimes be lessened when a future amount must be recorded at its present value, necessitating the determination of an interest rate applicable to the transaction. When interest rates are not specified or known with reasonable certainty, an imputed, or assumed, interest rate may be used.

Current receivables can be determining factors in an entity's financial flexibility. These receivables are usually within 1 year of being converted into cash, with the bulk of trade receivables being less than 60 days from collection of cash. In the operating cycle, the receivable phase of eventual cash flows from outside parties can be crucial to an entity's liquidity. The amount of working capital in the form of current receivables depends on many factors, such as the norms of an industry, the credit policies of an entity itself, and perhaps even the economic status of an entity's customers. For instance, growing current receivables on the balance sheet of housing-industry suppliers in periods of low housing starts may indicate something very important about the entity's customers. Are they sound credit risks? When will they pay their debts? What implications are there for the entity's economic well-being?

This chapter focuses on two major current receivables, **accounts receivable** and **notes receivable,** but the main concepts developed for these two specific assets are applicable to other current receivables such as deposits, loans to officers, current portions of bond receivables, and many other miscellaneous claims. Certain specific procedures and rules are more narrowly applicable, however, and these will be discussed.

APB Opinion No. 21 established the general rule requiring the use of the time value of money in the measurement and disclosure of future cash flows.[1] This standard has exceptions, the major ones being receivables and payables created in **normal operating transactions.** An entity can *elect* to ignore the time value of money in disclosing current receivables or payables that come due within a year.

Other transactions not covered by **APB Opinion No. 21** include

1. Amounts that do not require repayment but that will be applied to the purchase price of a product or service (for example, deposits and progress payments)
2. Security deposits
3. Warranty obligations on products or services
4. Income tax settlements and financial institutions' demand deposits
5. Receivables and payables between related entities (for example, between a parent corporation and its subsidiary)

These exceptions were adopted for practical reasons. The cost of keeping track of the present value and interest charges for short periods is likely to exceed the potential benefits of such efforts. It must be emphasized, however, that the use of the time value of money in valuing current receivables and payables is neither required nor prohibited for the "exception" cases discussed above.

Because of materiality considerations, trade accounts receivable are *normally* carried on the books at the absolute money amount expected to be collected from customers without consideration of interest charges. In contrast, notes receivable, including those due within a year, normally fall into the category of contractual financial arrangements for which interest effects must be recognized. Notes are stated at the present value of future cash flows even when they are short term and trade related.

In addition to trade accounts receivable and notes receivable, the accountant must deal with many other short-term receivables, such as various advances made to customers, deposits to parties outside the entity, claims for payments from government units, insurance companies, and suppliers. Other short-term receivables are created when interest or dividends are receivable and when there are litigation claims to which the entity is entitled. The general principles relating to the measurement and classification of short-term receivables are illustrated by analyzing typical transaction situations for both accounts receivable and notes receivable.

[1] *Accounting Principles Board Opinion No. 21,* "Interest on Receivables and Payables" (New York: AICPA, August 1971).

TRADE ACCOUNTS RECEIVABLE

Valuation
Procedures
for Accounts
Receivable

Accounts receivable is the most commonly used term for outstanding receivables from trade customers. Usually the balance in the asset account labeled Accounts Receivable is equal to the sum of all unpaid invoices. The major measurement problem is related to the fact that a percentage of these unpaid invoices may not be collected; therefore, at any balance sheet date, a percentage of the total economic potential probably will not be realized. To demonstrate how accountants deal with this measurement problem, we shall analyze three procedures: (1) The direct write-off method, (2) the estimation of bad debts by aging accounts receivable, and (3) the estimation of bad debts by an analysis of sales. These are not listed in order of their conceptual support; in fact, the first method is rarely used because of its weak conceptual foundation.

The direct write-off method   The **direct write-off method** is a simplistic approach in which no **estimates** of existing receivables that will not be collected in the future are attempted. The accountant merely awaits a default by a customer on a specific invoice and then records an expense in the following manner:

Bad debt expense	XX,XXX	
Accounts receivable		XX,XXX

This approach is flawed because the expense is matched to the period in which the default occurs, which may *not* be the same period in which the revenue relating to the receivable in question was recognized. To the extent that systematic procedures for estimating future bad debts are available, a better matching of revenues and expenses is achieved with the two procedures described below. Another deficiency of the direct write-off method is that it results in balance sheet disclosure of accounts receivable for amounts that are known to be too high.

Estimating uncollectibles by aging accounts receivable   The **allowance method** of accounting for uncertainties in the collection of receivables uses a valuation or contra asset account such as Allowance for Uncollectibles to reduce the receivables disclosed to an estimate of the amount expected to be collected on outstanding invoices, and it uses an income statement account such as Bad Debt Expense to reduce net income.

Exhibit 8-1 shows an "aging of accounts receivable" as of December 31, 1984, for Mast Company. In our example, 1984 is Mast Company's first year of operations, and, therefore, the company has no basis in its own experience for establishing the "probabilities of collection" necessary in aging schedules. In such cases, industry averages may be relied upon.

The Accounts Receivable ledger account has a $42,700 balance at December 31, 1984, which is the total of all outstanding invoices. In estimating uncollectibles the company is unsure as to which receivables will not be collected; however, **the estimation process does not require specific customer identification.** We might ask, Why not wait until the accounts actually prove to be uncollectible before writing them off? This latter suggestion implies the use of the **direct write-off method** described previously, and it can legitimately be used only by companies with immaterial levels of uncollectibles. To achieve proper matching of revenues and expenses, the estimated total amount of uncollectible accounts must be charged

EXHIBIT 8–1

AGING OF ACCOUNTS RECEIVABLE

MAST COMPANY

Analysis of Outstanding Invoices at 12/31/84

INVOICE NUMBER	DATE	INVOICE AMOUNT	AGE CATEGORY[a]	PROBABILITY OF COLLECTION[a]	AMOUNT ESTIMATED TO BE UNCOLLECTIBLE
102	10/31	$ 1,000	3	.50	$ 500
108	11/2	2,000	2	.75	500
109	11/2	3,200	2	.75	800
130	12/15	3,000	1	.98	60
135	12/16	6,000	1	.98	120
142	12/20	6,500	1	.98	130
143	12/21	3,000	1	.98	60
146	12/22	1,000	1	.98	20
149	12/27	8,000	1	.98	160
150	12/30	9,000	1	.98	180
		$42,700			$2,530

[a] The probability of collecting an outstanding invoice generally becomes smaller as time passes. Mast has adopted the following schedule for estimating the probability of collection:

	Invoice Age	Probability of Collection
1.	Less than 20 days	.98
2.	21 to 60 days	.75
3.	Over 60 days	.50

to the income statement in the same period in which the revenue that generated the accounts receivable is recognized.

The following journal entry would record the uncollectibles estimated in the Exhibit 8–1 aging-of-receivables example:

12/31/84	Bad debt expense	2,530	
	Allowance for uncollectibles		2,530

Bad debt expense would be disclosed as an operating expense on Mast Company's 1984 income statement.[2] The Allowance for Uncollectibles account[3] is shown as a contra asset of accounts receivable on the firm's balance sheet as follows:

MAST COMPANY

Partial Balance Sheet
December 31, 1984

ASSETS

Current assets		
Cash		$XX,XXX
Accounts receivable	$42,700	
Less: Allowance for uncollectibles	2,530	
Net accounts receivable		$40,170
Inventories		X,XXX
Total current assets		$XX,XXX

[2] An alternative approach is to debit a contra sales account, Sales Uncollectible, in which case the reported sales would be reduced and no expense for bad debts would be disclosed. Net income and balance sheet disclosures are the same under both techniques.

[3] Common alternative titles for this account are Allowance for Doubtful Accounts, Allowance for Bad Debts, or Allowance for Uncollectible Credit Sales.

EXHIBIT 8-2

				MAST COMPANY		
				Analysis of Outstanding Invoices at 12/31/85		
INVOICE NUMBER	DATE	INVOICE AMOUNT	AGE CATEGORY	PROBABILITY OF COLLECTION		AMOUNT ESTIMATED TO BE UNCOLLECTIBLE
384	6/20	$ 6,100	3	.50		$ 3,050
389	8/1	3,900	3	.50		1,950
520	9/5	10,000	3	.50		5,000
590	11/3	7,500	2	.75		1,875
550	11/15	9,000	2	.75		2,250
561	12/8	3,200	2	.75		800
568	12/9	2,500	2	.75		625
570	12/12	5,600	1	.98		112
572	12/15	8,000	1	.98		160
573	12/24	3,000	1	.98		60
574	12/26	2,500	1	.98		50
578	12/28	7,000	1	.98		140
579	12/28	5,300	1	.98		106
580	12/29	3,000	1	.98		60
		$76,600				$16,238

The allowance method of valuing assets will normally follow two practical guides: (1) keep the primary account (in this case, Accounts Receivable) at the original transacted amount, and (2) reduce the primary account to its expected net realizable value by using a contra asset (Allowance for Uncollectibles) that is subtracted from the primary account.

To understand the allowance method, it is necessary to follow the subsequent impact of the collection and noncollection of invoices. Assume that during 1985, Mast Company has the following experience:

1. Sales (all credit), $1,500,000
2. Collections from customers, $1,446,700
3. An aging analysis of outstanding invoices at December 31, 1985 (see Exhibit 8-2)
4. Invoices determined to be uncollectible and written off during 1985 (see Exhibit 8-3)

EXHIBIT 8-3

	MAST COMPANY		
	Uncollectible Invoices		
DATE OF DETERMINATION OF UNCOLLECTIBILITY	INVOICE NUMBER	INVOICE DATE	AMOUNT
2/10/85	102	10/31/84	$ 1,000
3/15/85	135	12/16/84	6,000
6/30/85	150	12/30/84	9,000
12/20/85	387	6/20/85	3,400
			$10,400

The following journal entries would be recorded upon determination of the uncollectibility of specific invoices:

Date	Entry	Debit	Credit
2/10/85	Allowance for uncollectibles	1,000	
	Accounts receivable		1,000
	(To write off invoice #102)		
3/15/85	Allowance for uncollectibles	6,000	
	Accounts receivable		6,000
	(To write off invoice #135)		
6/30/85	Allowance for uncollectibles	9,000	
	Accounts receivable		9,000
	(To write off invoice #150		
12/20/85	Allowance for uncollectibles	3,400	
	Accounts receivable		3,400
	(To write off invoice #387)		

Note that the write-off of an invoice found to be uncollectible has no *direct* effect on the income statement. It simply reduces the allowance account and the accounts receivable by equal amounts. Although the two balance sheet accounts are affected, **the net receivable remains the same after the write-off as before the write-off.** The write-off entry is viewed as "using up" the allowance and canceling the receivable rather than reducing net assets.

Before adjusting entries are made on December 31, 1985, the relevant ledger accounts for the Mast Company would appear as follows:

ACCOUNTS RECEIVABLE				
1/1/85 Balance	42,700	Cash collections	1,446,700
Sales	1,500,000	Write-offs	19,400
12/31/85 Balance	76,600		

ALLOWANCE FOR UNCOLLECTIBLES			
Write-offs	19,400	1/1/85 Balance	2,530
Before adjusting balance	16,870		

Consider how the "before adjusting balances" in the relevant ledger accounts were determined. Accounts Receivable started 1985 with a $42,700 balance, which was the total of all outstanding invoices on January 1, 1985. During the year, credit sales to customers increased accounts receivable by $1,500,000 and cash collected from customers reduced it by $1,446,700. In addition, four invoices totaling $19,400 were written off. These transactions result in a December 31, 1985, balance of $76,600. The contra account had a January 1, 1985, credit balance of $2,530 and was reduced to the December 31, 1985, debit balance of $16,870 by the writing off of four invoices during the year.

Referring back to the aging schedule in Exhibit 8–2, we see that the estimated uncollectibles remaining in Accounts Receivable as of the end of 1985 total $16,238; therefore, the required adjusting entry necessary to result in a $16,238 credit balance in the contra asset account to state net accounts receivable properly at year-end would be:

12/31/85	Bad debt expense	33,108	
	Allowance for uncollectibles		33,108

The ending ledger account, balance sheet, and income statement disclosures related to accounts receivable would appear as follows:

ALLOWANCE FOR UNCOLLECTIBLES

Write-offs 19,400	1/1/85 Balance	2,530
	Period-end adjustment	33,108
	13/31/85 Balance	16,238

MAST COMPANY

Partial Balance Sheet
December 31, 1985

ASSETS

Current assets
Cash		$XX,XXX
Accounts receivable	$76,600	
Less: Allowance for uncollectibles	16,238	
Net accounts receivable		$60,362
Inventories		X,XXX
Total current assets		$XX,XXX

MAST COMPANY

Partial Income Statement
1985

EXPENSES

.	.
.	.
.	.
Bad debt expense	33,108
.	.
.	.
.	.

A troublesome point for accounting students is the difference between the $16,238 that is the desired balance in the Allowance account based on the aging technique at December 31, 1985, and the $33,108 that is the Bad Debt Expense recorded for 1985. This difference stems from the fact that the balance in the Allowance account at the end of any given year is normally different from the total amount of write-offs made during the following year. As a result, to achieve the desired credit balance in the Allowance account at the end of any period normally requires a debit to Bad Debt Expense for the amount of the estimate *plus* the amount of the debit (or *minus* the credit) balance in the Allowance account prior to the adjusting entry. Keep in mind that for the **aging method,** the estimate arrived at is the **desired credit balance in the Allowance account** that is required to state net accounts receivable properly.

The objective of the aging method is to represent accounts receivable consistent with the best estimate of collectibility. The entries to Bad Debt Expense, while "forced" and not necessarily representative of actual uncollectibles in any one period, over the entire life of the entity will equal the total actual bad debts. These procedures give the most accurate period-by-period picture of the asset Accounts Receivable in the balance sheet but may not result in the most accurate reflection of any one period's bad debt experience. This discrepancy becomes smaller as the accuracy of the entity's estimates of future bad debts improves.

Estimating uncollectibles by an analysis of sales   Another approach to the estimation of receivables is the use of a percentage of credit sales as the amount to be debited to expense and credited to the Allowance account in the period-end adjusting entry. The percentage used could be based on a combination of industry and company experience. This approach **focuses on the accurate representation of Bad Debt Expense in the income statement rather than net receivables on the balance sheet.**

As an example of the analysis of sales method, assume that Aqua, Inc., has credit sales of $2,000,000 in 1984, its first year of operations. Industry statistics indicate that approximately 2 percent of all credit sales are not collected, resulting in estimated bad debts of $40,000 on 1984 sales ($2,000,000 × .02). The following journal entry would record the estimated bad debts:

Bad debt expense	40,000	
Allowance for uncollectibles		40,000

Note that this entry was made *without* consideration or knowledge of the balance in either Accounts Receivable or Allowance for Uncollectibles. All disclosures for the allowance method illustrated above would be appropriate here as well. At the end of the subsequent year a percentage would again be applied to credit sales, and the entry would be repeated for the resulting amount. The major difference between this method and the aging of receivables method is that no specific analysis of details of the outstanding invoices is necessary. Although the analysis of sales method is simple and may result in a more "accurate" charge to income, it may also lead to an unrealistic net accounts receivable amount on the balance sheet.

For example, assume that Aqua, Inc., has the following history of credit sales, collections, and write-offs for its first 3 years of operations while maintaining a 2 percent of credit sales estimate for bad debt expense:

YEAR	CREDIT SALES	CASH COLLECTIONS	WRITE-OFFS OF BAD DEBTS	BAD DEBT EXPENSE
1984	$2,000,000	$1,600,000	None	$40,000
1985	2,500,000	2,100,000	$24,000	50,000
1986	3,500,000	2,900,000	30,000	70,000

The Accounts Receivable and Allowance for Uncollectibles accounts would have the following activity and balances for the 3 years:

YEAR	ACCOUNTS RECEIVABLE	
1984	$2,000,000	$1,600,000
1985	2,500,000	2,100,000
		24,000
1986	3,500,000	2,900,000
		30,000
Balance at end of 1986	$1,346,000	

YEAR	ALLOWANCE FOR UNCOLLECTIBLES	
1984		$ 40,000
1985	$ 24,000	50,000
1986	30,000	70,000
Balance at end of 1986		$ 106,000

The $106,000 balance in Allowance for Uncollectibles represents 3 percent (not 2 percent) of 1986 sales because of the lower than estimated write-offs during the first 3 years. In such a case, the company may determine a target number for the Allowance account by aging of accounts receivable or some other method that gives a "best" estimate of uncollectibles. The adjusting entry then is of an appropriate money amount to result in the target credit balance in the Allowance account. In our example, if an aging of invoices at the end of 1986 results in an estimate that $70,000 will probably not be collected, the adjusting entry would be reduced from $70,000 to $34,000:

Bad debt expense	34,000	
Allowance for uncollectibles		34,000

This would result in an account balance of $70,000 as follows:

YEAR	ALLOWANCE FOR UNCOLLECTIBLES	
1984		$40,000
1985	$24,000	50,000
1986	30,000	34,000
Balance at end of 1986		$70,000

It would be possible for Aqua to resume using the 2 percent of credit sales estimate for Bad Debt Expense in 1987 if that was considered a reasonable basis for estimating uncollectibles. Of course, adjustments of the sort shown above may again become necessary in the future.

In some cases, companies using the analysis of sales method have a good reason to change the percentage estimates. For example, assume the write-off percentage of 2 percent is considered to be excessive at the end of 1986 and the percentage is changed to 1 percent of credit sales *before* the year-end entry is recorded. The 1986 entry would be recorded as follows:

12/31/86	Bad debt expense	35,000	
	Allowance for uncollectibles		35,000
	(To record estimated uncollectibes re-		
	lated to 1986 credit sales)		

This entry would leave a $71,000 credit balance in the Allowance account. The new estimation rate of 1 percent of credit sales would be used in future periods until further evidence suggested a need for another adjustment in the estimated rate of uncollectibles.

COLLECTION OF ACCOUNTS PREVIOUSLY WRITTEN OFF If collection is made on an invoice that was previously written off, the most orderly procedure is to (1) reverse the write-off entry and (2) record the collection of cash as if no write-off had taken place. For example, assume that an invoice for $5,000 was written off in 1985 and was collected on January 3, 1986. If a check for $5,000 from the customer is received on January 3, 1986, the following entries would be recorded:

1/3/86	Accounts receivable	5,000	
	Allowance for uncollectibles		5,000
1/3/86	Cash	5,000	
	Accounts receivable		5,000

In this way the customer's individual receivable records reflect a normal collection, and the orderliness of the accounts receivable records is maintained.

THE EFFECT OF THE ALLOWANCE ACCOUNT ON BOOK VALUES AND EXPENSE AMOUNTS Let us review the effects of the valuation procedures for accounts receivable by means of the following three generalizations:

1. Net assets and net income are both reduced by the entry to record *estimated* bad debts. The debit to Bad Debt Expense reduces net income and the credit to Allowance for Uncollectibles reduces net assets. The effect takes place at the time of the periodic adjusting entry, normally at the end of the accounting period.
2. Net assets and net income are not reduced or affected by the actual write-off of an individual invoice. The debit to the Allowance account is offset by the credit to the Accounts Receivable account, both of which are current assets, and no income statement account is affected.
3. Recoveries of previously written off accounts do not affect net assets or net income. As illustrated in the January 3, 1986, journal entries at the end of the preceding section, all the debits and credits are to current asset accounts, and there is no effect on the net assets or net income.

OTHER VALUATION ALLOWANCES FOR ACCOUNTS RECEIVABLE: SALES RETURNS AND ALLOWANCES The general philosophy expressed in the preceding section was that accounts receivable should be disclosed on the balance sheet at an amount equal to the sum of outstanding invoices minus an allowance for estimated uncollectibles. Other potential reductions in the amounts collectible might also exist. If deemed material they should be estimated and accounted for, just as the allowance method was used for estimated uncollectibles. For instance, firms often give full or partial credit for returned or damaged merchandise. If, at the end of an accounting period, material amounts of sales returns or sales allowances can be expected on outstanding receivables, an adjusting entry would be necessary to reduce the carrying value of accounts receivable and recognize an expense. Referring back to our Mast Company example in Exhibit 8–1, recall that on December 31, 1984, the total Accounts Receivable balance was $42,700 and the Allowance for Uncollectibles was $2,530. Assume now that it is estimated on December 31, 1984, that $2,000 of sales returns and allowances would occur relative to the outstanding receivables. The following adjusting entry would be required:

12/31/84	Sales returns and allowances	2,000	
	Allowance for returned and damaged items		2,000
	(To record estimated sales returns and allowances on year-end receivables)		

The resulting balance sheet and income statement items are shown in Exhibit 8–4.

The accounting for subsequent years would follow the same procedures illustrated above for estimated uncollectibles; that is, the Allowance account would be debited and the Accounts Receivable account would be credited for the amounts of actual returns of merchandise. The generalizations about the effects of such transactions would be the same as those described on page 276.

Discounts   The difference between the "list" price and the actual invoice price charged to a customer is sometimes called a **trade discount**. For instance, a retailer may have a

EXHIBIT 8–4

MAST COMPANY

Partial Balance Sheet
December 31, 1984

ASSETS

Current Assets		
Cash		$XX,XXX
Accounts receivable	$42,700	
Less: Allowance for uncollectibles	2,530	
Allowance for returned and damaged items	2,000	
Net accounts receivable		38,170
Inventories		XX,XXX
Other current assets		XX,XXX
Total current assets		$ XX,XXX

MAST COMPANY

Partial Income Statement
1984

Revenues		
Sales	$XX,XXX	
Sales returns and allowances[a]	(2,000)	
Net sales	$XX,XXX	
Expenses		
Cost of goods sold	$XX,XXX	
Marketing	XX,XXX	
Bad debts	2,530	
Other expense	X,XXX	
Total expenses		XX,XXX

[a] "Sales returns and allowances" is shown here as a contra sales item. It could also be shown as an expense item comparable with bad debt expense.

catalog in which a toaster is listed at $50, but customers actually pay $35. If the $35 is the actual selling price, it is used in the recording of sales and receivables. Trade discounts, therefore, are used in marketing strategies and have no real status in the accounting records.

Cash discounts, however, require more attention from an accounting perspective. Often a company will allow its commercial customers to reduce the actual invoice price by a specified percentage if payment is received before a certain date. Any payment after the stated discount period would require the full invoice price. For example, assume that a company allows a 2 percent discount on the invoice amounts if payment is received within 20 days of the invoice date (the date of sale). This is noted 2/20, net/30 (or 2/20, n/30); that is, a 2 percent cash discount can be deducted from the invoice amount if paid within 20 days or else the total invoice amount is due no later than 30 days after the invoice date. (The word "net" as used here does not imply "net of discount" but is a conventional term that means that the total amount is due.) Such discounts are offered to motivate customers to pay for their purchases on a timely basis.

Two alternative, but quite similar, recording procedures are used in practice: the **net method** and the **gross method.** The methods differ in the determination of the initial sales and receivable amounts, with the net method anticipating the discount and the gross method initially ignoring the discount. We shall use two cases to demonstrate how these two methods are applied:

Case 1. An invoice of $1,000 dated February 2 with the discount notation 2/10, net/30 is collected within the discount period. The following journal entries would be made for the two methods:

NET METHOD

2/2	Accounts receivable	980	
	Sales		980
2/8	Cash	980	
	Accounts receivable		980

GROSS METHOD

2/2	Accounts receivable	1,000	
	Sales		1,000
2/8	Cash	980	
	Cash discount	20	
	Accounts receivable		1,000

The Cash Discount account of $20 under the gross method would be disclosed as a contra sales account on the income statement. Note that under both methods, net revenue from this sale would be $980.

Case 2. The same facts apply as in case 1, except that cash is received after the 10-day discount period has elapsed. The following journal entries would be made for the two methods:

NET METHOD

2/2	Accounts receivable	980	
	Sales		980
2/28	Cash	1,000	
	Accounts receivable		980
	Discounts forfeited		20

GROSS METHOD

2/2	Accounts receivable	1,000	
	Sales		1,000
2/28	Cash	1,000	
	Accounts receivable		1,000

In this case, the Discounts Forfeited under the net method would be disclosed as an addition to Sales or as miscellaneous revenue. In both cases, the total revenue from the invoice would be $1,000.

How do accountants decide as to the appropriate method? If adjustments are made at the end of each period to estimate the future discounts to be taken on outstanding invoices, both the net and gross methods result in the same net assets and net income. In such cases, the allowance techniques we have already described could be utilized. The choice of one cash discount method over the other should be based on the method's usefulness as an internal management tool. If management would like to see an analysis of discounts forfeited, the net method would facilitate this. If, however, management would like to have data regarding discounts taken, the gross method may prove more effective.

The Use of Accounts Receivable to Facilitate Financing

An outstanding invoice is an asset as long as it is expected to generate cash, and the net accounts receivable balance disclosed on a balance sheet represents the expected cash flow at some future point in time. Businesses often have immediate cash needs and seek to speed up the cash flow by using accounts receivable to acquire cash from financial institutions. Various arrangements are possible, including pledging, assigning, and factoring (the selling of accounts receivable). No matter what the specific arrangement, all of these financing activities involve the use of the value of the expected cash flow from customers to generate immediate cash flow from another entity.

The major accounting problems related to such financing activities revolve around the determination of the rights and obligations of the business entity and the financial institutions involved. The following questions must be answered to solve those problems:

1. Is there collateral for the financing?
2. What happens if the invoice in question is not paid by the customer?
3. Who receives the customer's payment?

For simplicity, let us use the following facts as an example of the use of accounts receivable to facilitate financing:

1. On January 14, 1984, Needco sells merchandise to a customer for an invoice amount of $50,000.

2. On January 15, 1984, the Mellon Bank lends the company $40,000.

3. On January 30, 1984, the customer pays the invoice amount.

The following sections show how these facts are applied to pledging and assigning.

Pledging   After the sale of the goods and the issuance of the invoice, Needco borrows $40,000 from the Mellon Bank and signs a note that has the following terms:

Date of note	1/15/84
Due date	1/30/84, or upon receipt by Needco of the invoice payment, whichever comes first
Note amount	$40,000
Interest rate	10% per annum
Collateral	Receivable from the customer; Needco must pay the note when due on 1/30, whether or not it receives payment from the customer

This type of arrangement is sometimes called a **pledging** of accounts receivable. The accounts receivable of $50,000 becomes security on the outstanding note. The customer will usually be unaware of the arrangement and will make its payment on the invoice to Needco in the normal manner.

No special journal entries would be required, but if Needco's financial statements are issued before the note is paid off, some form of footnote disclosure would be appropriate to explain the relationship between the accounts receivable and the notes payable. Assuming that the customer pays Needco the invoice amount on January 30, 1984, the following journal entries would be recorded:

1/14/84	Accounts receivable	50,000	
	Sales		50,000
1/15/84	Cash	40,000	
	Notes payable		40,000
1/30/84	Cash	50,000	
	Accounts receivable		50,000
1/30/84	Notes payable	40,000	
	Interest expense[a]	167	
	Cash		40,167

[a] Interest expense = [$40,000][.10][15/360] = $167.

Assigning   In another similar arrangement, the financing entity is assigned the specific proceeds of one or more invoices and usually collects a fee. Let us look at the case using the same facts as above except that Needco's invoice is **assigned** to the Mellon Bank, for which in addition to the interest charge, a fee of $1,100 is charged.

1/14/84	Accounts receivable	50,000	
	Sales		50,000
1/15/84	Accounts receivable—assigned	50,000	
	Accounts receivable		50,000

1/15/84	Cash		38,900	
	Commission expense		1,100	
	Notes payable			40,000
1/30/84	Cash		50,000	
	Accounts receivable—assigned			50,000
1/30/84	Notes payable		40,000	
	Interest expense		167	
	Cash			40,167

If Needco's financial statements are issued before the liquidation of the debt, the following disclosure would be appropriate:

ASSETS

Current Assets			
Cash			$XXX,XXX
Accounts receivable			
Accounts receivable—unassigned		$XX,XXX	
Accounts receivable—assigned	$50,000		
Less notes payable	40,000	10,000	XX,XXX
Inventories			$ XX,XXX

This presentation communicates the special relationship between the assigned accounts receivable and the notes payable. Such offsetting of an asset and a liability is not generally allowed, but an exception is permitted because of the contractual link between assigned accounts receivable and their related notes payable.

Factoring   Another technique that a business could use to generate immediate cash flow would be to **sell,** or **factor,** its accounts receivable. In such cases, all the risks and rights related to the receivables may be taken over by the financing entity. Returning to our example, assume that Needco sells the receivable to the Mellon Bank for $45,000 in cash and that Mellon takes on all the risks of collecting the receivable. The following journal entries on Needco's books would be appropriate:

1/14/84	Accounts receivable	50,000	
	Sales		50,000
1/15/84	Cash	45,000	
	Financing expense	5,000	
	Accounts receivable		50,000

Note that the financing charge reflects the fact that the financing entity may be taking on all the risks of collection. The company, however, had no residual liability in these "**without recourse**" contracts, and no special disclosure is required. It is possible for factoring to be "with recourse," in which case any defaulted receivable must be made good by the original owner of the receivable. In such cases, there exists a contingent liability that is disclosed in a footnote to the balance sheet of the original owner of the receivable.

The main pitfall for students in dealing with these types of financing arrangements is that they might become overly concerned about such terms as *pledging, as-*

signing, and *factoring.* When accounts receivable are used to facilitate the early receipt of cash, many types of contracts can be drawn up, and there may be little uniformity among them. Therefore, the accountant must appropriately account for such financing agreements **according to the specific terms of each contract.** What the contract is called is not important. The main issues are those of ownership, recourse, responsibility for collection, the amount of cash proceeds, and customer notification. Various types of footnotes and balance sheet formats are used to communicate all the material aspects of the different types of contractual arrangements encountered in practice.

NOTES RECEIVABLE

Valuation and Interest Considerations

A **note** is a formal financing instrument that a debtor makes payable to a creditor. Its legal status differs little from an accounts receivable other than in its degree of legal formality. Because notes typically have an explicit interest charge, interest is accounted for even in the case of short-term notes. Notes receivable may result from such business transactions as the following: (1) A business may lend money to other businesses or individuals; (2) a business may accept a note receivable upon making a sale; and (3) a business may accept a note to replace an ordinary accounts receivable if the debtor is unable to pay the invoice in a timely fashion.

Let us consider the third situation. Assume that Bates Corporation purchases machinery from AC Industries, with an invoice for $10,000 issued on December 1, 1983. On January 1, 1984, Bates signs a 1-year 8 percent note to replace the invoice. Bates promises to pay AC Industries $10,000 plus 8 percent interest at December 31, 1984.

The present value of future cash flows becomes the book value of the receivable or payable, and the interest charge is based on the book value of the receivable or payable outstanding during the accounting period. In this case, the maturity value of the 1-year note (the total amount to be paid including interest) is $10,800, and the interest charge for 1984 is $800. The present value of $10,800 in 1 year is computed using compound-interest Table H–2 in Appendix H at the back of the book:[4]

$$(P/F,\ 1,\ .08)(\$10,800) = (.9259)(10,800) = \$10,000$$

Assuming Bates pays the note at maturity, AC Industries would record the following journal entries for the entire series of transactions:

12/1/83	Accounts receivable		10,000	
	Sales			10,000
1/1/84	Notes receivable		10,000	
	Accounts receivable			10,000
12/31/84	Cash		10,800	
	Interest income			800
	Notes receivable			10,000

[4] Chapter 5 introduces the compound interest notations and amortization schedules used in this chapter.

The maturity value of the note is $10,800, which could be recorded as Notes Receivable, along with a contra account, Notes Receivable Discount, for $800. APB Opinion No. 21 requires that the amount of the discount be disclosed either as a contra account or in a footnote to the financial statements. In our example, we recorded the net present value of the note, and a footnote would therefore be required.

The preceding is an example of an **interest-bearing** note because the interest rate is specifically stated in the terms of the note. A **non-interest-bearing** note for the same set of facts could have the following terminology on its face: "Bates Corporation promises to pay AC Industries $10,800 on December 31, 1984." Although the note says nothing about an 8 percent interest rate, if the accounts receivable given up on January 1, 1984, have a cash-equivalent value of $10,000, then the implicit interest rate is 8 percent, and the accountant records the transaction in exactly the same way as for the interest-bearing note.

As long as we know the cash-equivalent value of the asset at the inception of a note and the cash flow during the term of the note, the interest charge can be computed. Sometimes, however, the values of the asset and the note are open to question. For example, assume that Creditor Corporation sells a plot of land to Debtor Corporation on January 1, 1984, and accepts a note with the following terms: "Debtor promises to pay Creditor $20,500 on January 1, 1987." Assume also that the land had a $10,000 book value on Creditor Corporation's books. In such a case, the accountant would have to either determine the fair value of the land at the date of sale or impute a fair value by choosing an appropriate interest rate to use in determining the present value of the note. The current applicable rules state that a rate at least equal to the rate that Debtor would have to pay for a similar "loan" at the time the land is purchased must be applied in determining the present value of both the note and the land. For the example above, if 8 percent is an appropriate rate, the following amortization schedule (rounded to the nearest dollar) would be applicable to the note receivable on Creditor Corporation's books:

DATE	TRANSACTION	INTEREST INCOME	INCREASE (REDUCTION) IN CARRYING VALUE	BOOK VALUE OF NOTE AND INTEREST RECEIVABLE
1/1/84	Sale		$16,273	$16,273
12/31/84	Interest accrual	$1,302	1,302	17,575
12/31/85	Interest accrual	1,406	1,406	18,981
12/31/86	Interest accrual	1,510[a]	1,519	20,500
1/1/87	Receipt of maturity amount		(20,500)	0

[a] Rounding error.

The present value of the maturity amount at the date of sale is computed using Table II−2 in Appendix H as follows:

$$(P/F, 3, .08)(\$20,500) = (.7938)(\$20,500) = \$16,273$$

Debtor Corporation and Creditor Corporation would record the following journal entries during the life of the note:

	CREDITOR CORPORATION			DEBTOR CORPORATION		
DATE		DEBIT	CREDIT		DEBIT	CREDIT
1/1/84	Notes receivable	16,273		Land	16,273	
	Land		10,000	Notes payable		16,273
	Gain on sale of land		6,273			
12/31/84	Interest receivable	1,302		Interest expense	1,302	
	Interest income		1,302	Interest payable		1,302
12/31/85	Interest receivable	1,406		Interest expense	1,406	
	Interest income		1,406	Interest payable		1,406
12/31/86	Interest receivable	1,519		Interest expense	1,519	
	Interest income		1,519	Interest payable		1,519
1/1/87	Cash	20,500		Notes payable	16,273	
	Notes receivable		16,273	Interest payable	4,227	
	Interest receivable		4,227	Cash		20,500

These journal entries demonstrate the symmetry of the accounting for the creditor and debtor when the same interest rate is used by each. Also note that the gain on the sale of land on the creditor's books and the book value of the asset acquired on the debtor's books are determined by applying the applicable interest rate to the maturity value of the note.

Whether notes receivable and interest receivable are separated into two accounts as shown above is a matter of choice. The major conceptual point is that the total asset balance related to the notes receivable disclosed on a balance sheet is the present value of future cash flows on the balance sheet date—in this case, the sum of the two accounts, Notes Receivable and Interest Receivable.

Discounting Notes Receivable

Those who hold notes receivable can use them to finance immediate cash flows in much the same manner as that used for accounts receivable. The specific technique that we shall discuss here is termed **discounting of a note.** It involves the transfer to a bank of the right to the cash receipt at maturity, including both principal and interest. The bank, of course, charges interest for the period between the discounting and the maturity.

To illustrate, assume that Merkel, Inc., holds a $10,000, 1-year, 12 percent note receivable from Conline Travel. The note was received on January 10, 1983, and matures on January 9, 1984. At maturity Merkel will receive $11,200 and will accrue $100 interest receivable on the note for each month it is held. The present value of $11,200 in 1 year discounted at 12 percent is

$$(P/F, \ 1, \ .12)(\$11,200) = (.8929)(\$11,200) = \$10,000 \quad \text{(rounded)}$$

the book value of the note on January 10, 1983.

Because of a need for cash, Merkel decides to **discount** the Conline note at the Colspring Bank at 12 percent on July 10, 1983. If "discount rate" meant the same as "effective interest rate," Merkel would receive $10,600 ($10,000 plus 6 months' interest at $100 per month). However, a "discount rate" computes interest based on the future (maturity) value of the note, and hence a discount rate of 12 percent will translate to an effective interest rate **greater than** 12 percent. The discount on a note is computed by using the following formula:[5]

$$\text{Discount} = \text{Maturity value} \times \text{Discount rate} \times \frac{\text{Number of days to maturity}}{365}$$

In our case, the 12 percent discount charged by Colspring Bank on the note would be:

$$\$11,200 \times .12 \times \left(\frac{183}{365}\right) = \$674 \text{ (rounded)}$$

The proceeds that Merkel received on July 10, 1983, would be $11,200 − $674 = $10,526. Assuming Merkel had *not* recorded any interest on the Conline note, the following entry would record the discounting of the note:

7/10/83	Cash	10,526	
	Notes receivable discounted		10,000
	Interest income		526

The $526 interest is less than the $600 that might have been recorded for the 6-month period January 10 to July 10 because the interest computed using a discount rate procedure is not the same as effective interest. The **effective** interest charged by Colspring Bank is in excess of 12 percent. The effective interest charged for discounting will always be greater than the stated discount rate.

    Unless otherwise stated across the face of the note, notes are all written with recourse. This means that anyone who holds the note as a result of a fair transaction has the right to try to collect the maturity value of the note from anyone else who owned the note *if* the maker (Conline in this case) fails to pay the note at maturity. Therefore, anyone who has held (owned) the note during its legal life is contingently liable for the note. To emphasize the contingent liability related to a note discounted with recourse, companies will often credit Notes Receivable Discounted rather than Notes Receivable, as illustrated in the above entry. This contra account is disclosed as follows on the balance sheet:

Notes receivable	$XXX	
Less notes receivable discounted		
(see Note X to financial statements)	XX	
Net notes receivable		$XXX

The net notes receivable amount is the same whether or not the contra account is used. But this technique highlights the fact that a contingent liability exists on the balance sheet date. A footnote would still be necessary.

    Upon payment by Conline to Colspring Bank at maturity, Merkel would re-

---

[5] Note that in some cases months are used instead of days—that is, 1/12 instead of 31/365. Another simplifying assumption is that each month has 30 days and each year has 360 days. This text will specify which assumption is being made.

cord the following entry:

1/9/84	Notes receivable discounted	10,000	
	Notes receivable		10,000

This would eliminate any amount related to the Conline note from Merkel's books. If Conline failed to pay Colspring the $11,200 on January 9, 1984, Colspring Bank would collect from Merkel, who would then try to collect from Conline. Merkel would record the following in the event of Conline's default:

1/9/84	Notes receivable discounted	10,000	
	Notes receivable		10,000
1/9/84	Defaulted notes receivable	11,200	
	Cash		11,200

Note that the $1,200 of interest has been recorded as an asset and not expensed. In addition to the maturity value of $11,200, Colspring Bank might also ask Merkel for a service charge, or **protest fee.** If a protest fee of $15 were charged for the inconvenience to the bank, the debit and credit in the second entry above would be for $11,215. Merkel would probably send the defaulted note to the credit department for further handling. If, after further investigation by Merkel's credit department, it is determined that Conline will not be able to pay the note (or some portion of it), a write-off to the Allowance account would be recorded:

1/20/84	Allowance for uncollectibles	11,215	
	Defaulted notes receivable		11,215

Normally, a single Allowance account would be used for both notes and accounts receivable.

Return to the entry recorded by Merkel on July 10, 1983, at the time the note was discounted with Colspring Bank. What would have been recorded on July 10 if Merkel had recorded interest income of $566—(172/365) × $1,200—to June 30, 1983? The proceeds of $10,526 are less than the book value of the notes receivable ($10,000) plus the accrued interest receivable ($566). As a result, a **discount fee,** or interest expense, would be recorded by Merkel:

7/10/83	Cash	10,526	
	Interest expense	40	
	Notes receivable discounted		10,000
	Interest receivable		566

Although we consider such an entry to be less appropriate, some entities might record the entry for this situation as follows:

7/10/83	Cash	10,526	
	Interest expense	674	
	Notes receivable discounted		10,000
	Interest receivable		566
	Interest income		634

This last approach seems to overstate interest income and interest expense; however, the *net* impact on Merkel's financial statement position is the same in either case.

It is important to differentiate between discounting rates and effective interest rates. Although effective interest rates are increasingly being used in practice because of the various truth-in-lending laws in most states, the use of interest rates other than effective (or true) interest rates may still be encountered. Whenever possible, interest charges should be converted to their effective rates for comparison with other rates.

As with accounts receivable, many different contracts can be written with a financial institution in a discounting situation. In addition to the recourse issue men-

EXAMPLES OF FINANCIAL STATEMENT DISCLOSURE OF ACCOUNTS AND NOTES RECEIVABLE

EXCERPT FROM
W. R. GRACE & CO. AND SUBSIDIARY COMPANIES
Consolidated Balance Sheet (In Millions)

DECEMBER 31,	1980	1979
Assets Current Assets		
Cash	$ 78.6	$ 149.5
Marketable securities	46.3	7.7
Notes and accounts receivable, less allowances of $25.9 (1979—$25.8)	743.5	737.5
Inventories	812.5	769.5
Other current assets	38.5	34.5
Total Current Assets	$1,719.4	$1,698.7

Note 2—Notes and Accounts Receivable

Notes and accounts receivable consist of:

	1980	1979
Trade, less allowances of $19.1 (1979—$15.8)	$ 687.9	$ 652.3
Other, less allowances of $6.8 (1979—$10.0)	55.6	85.2
	$ 743.5	$ 737.5

EXCERPT FROM
UNITED TECHNOLOGIES CORPORATION
Consolidated Balance Sheet

DECEMBER 31, 1980 AND 1979	IN THOUSANDS OF DOLLARS	
ASSETS	1980	1979
Current Assets:		
Cash and short-term cash investments	$ 147,028	$ 168,943
Accounts receivable	1,585,580	1,322,431
Future income tax benefits	—	115,148
Inventories and contracts in progress	4,345,982	3,654,129
Less—Progress payments and billings on contracts in progress	(1,567,489)	(1,293,359)
Prepaid expenses	66,230	61,468
Total Current Assets	$4,577,337	$4,020,760
Accounts and Notes Receivable due after one year	$ 58,995	$ 55,360

Note 6—Accounts Receivable:
Allowances for doubtful accounts of $51,896,000 and $47,249,000 have been applied as a reduction of current accounts receivable at December 31, 1980 and 1979, respectively.

Current accounts receivable include amounts which represent retainage under contract provisions and amounts which are not presently billable because of lack of funding or final prices or contractual documents under government contracts or for other reasons. These items are not material in amount and are expected to be collected in the normal course of business.

tioned above, other contractual terms can require the payment of the amount outstanding if certain events take place, such as the bankruptcy of the maker of the note and the deterioration of the liquidity position of one or more parties to the agreement.

FINANCIAL STATEMENT DISCLOSURES

Financial statement disclosure of current receivables does not usually report the techniques used to establish the allowances. The typical pattern found in annual reports is shown in Exhibit 8–5, which lists the accounts and notes receivable net of allowances on the balance sheet with a footnote containing more detail. On income statements, bad debt expense is usually included in a general expense category, such as Other Operating Expenses, or it may be netted out against sales without separate disclosure.

FUNDS FLOW EFFECTS

Current receivables are important elements in determining an entity's liquidity and financial flexibility. They are components of working capital and can be important indicators of near-term future cash flows.

As discussed in detail in Chapters 4 and 25, collections of current receivables do not affect working capital flow, but they do affect cash flow. Reclassification of receivables from long-term to short-term, on the other hand, will increase working capital but have no affect on cash.

Therefore, in a statement of changes in financial position using a working capital definition of funds, there usually will be no mention of current receivable changes except for balance sheet reclassifications from long-term to short-term, which would be shown as a source of working capital. A reclassification in the other direction is possible (though unusual), and it would be shown as a use of working capital. Statements of changes in financial position constructed on a cash basis would show an analysis of changes in receivable balances. For example, an increase in the balance in accounts receivable during a period would show up as a reconciling item between net income and cash from operations, with the increase in accounts receivable being subtracted from net income to arrive at cash from operations.

SUMMARY All current receivables that appear on balance sheets have certain common attributes. First, they are all assets and therefore must represent future economic potential that is expected to be realized within a year or the operating cycle, whichever is longer, and they must possess the other attributes common to all assets. They represent claims to assets that will be paid at some future date. This fact presents two interesting challenges: (1) How is the uncertainty about future collectibility handled? and (2) How is the difference between the present value of the expected payment and the amount to be paid handled? We have reviewed several approaches that address these issues. Receivables, in many cases, are material elements in the liquidity position of an enterprise and, as we have seen, can sometimes be used to generate immediate cash. In addition, they represent amounts and conditions that are capable of reasonably objective confirmation. A thorough understanding of the concepts, rules, and techniques of receivable accounting is necessary, therefore, for an informed evaluation of an entity's financial status.

QUESTIONS

Q8-1   Accounts and notes receivable are similar in many ways. What is the major difference in their accounting treatment, and why does this difference exist?

Q8-2   What elements of basic accounting theory support the recording of estimated bad debts?

Q8-3   Contrast the allowance and direct write-off methods of accounting for bad debts in terms of the matching principle.

Q8-4   Why is interest not usually considered in accounting for accounts receivable? (Address practical, theoretical, and promulgated GAAP considerations.)

Q8-5   Explain why an accounting period's bad debt expense does not usually equal the amount of bad debt write-offs when the allowance method is being used.

Q8-6   What are the similarities in accounting treatment among estimated bad debts, estimated returns of damaged merchandise, and estimated future cash discounts?

Q8-7   Under what circumstances can the selection of an interest rate for a customer's non-interest-bearing note affect the amount of sales revenue recognized?

Q8-8   What are the similarities and differences in the pledging, assigning, and factoring of accounts receivable?

Q8-9   Describe how a bank discount rate is used to determine the proceeds of a notes receivable discounting transaction.

Q8-10   Why are accountants concerned about the "recourse" stipulations in notes receivable discounting and accounts receivable factoring situations?

CASES

C8-1   Ms. Connelly owns a small publishing house that normally has between $50,000 and $100,000 in accounts and notes receivable from its distributors. She is currently close to signing a contract with an author, which will require a large advance payment.

REQUIRED   Explain to her how receivables can be used to help facilitate the borrowing of the necessary amount.

C8-2   Consider the following assertion: "No matter if receivables are recorded 'gross' or 'net' in terms of cash discounts, the balance sheet and income statement effects are the same."

REQUIRED   Is this a true statement? Why would certain decision makers prefer one technique to the other?

C8-3   The direct write-off method of accounting for bad debts is easy to apply and relies on very objective data. The allowance method, however, is more difficult to apply and relies on estimates.

REQUIRED   Give the theoretical support for the widespread use of the latter.

C8-4   Mr. Black and Ms. White are at odds about an accounting issue. Mr. Black states that a company should assess past bad debt experience as a percentage of credit sales and should record a bad debt expense each year based on that percentage applied to the current year's credit sales. Ms. White argues that an aging of accounts receivable should provide the estimated uncollectibles at the end of an accounting period.

REQUIRED Give the advantages and disadvantages of the two approaches, and state which you feel is better and why.

C8–5 Specific accounts receivable that have been written off are sometimes collected in part or in full.

REQUIRED Give a justification for the practice of reestablishing the specific accounts receivable and recording the cash collections by a credit to Accounts Receivable. Would net income be affected differently if the cash collection in such a case were recorded by merely debiting Cash and crediting Bad Debt Expense?

C8–6 Sales Uncollectible or Bad Debt Expense can be debited upon the establishment of the Allowance for Bad Debts balance at the end of an accounting period.

REQUIRED What theoretical arguments support each? How is the income statement affected by each?

C8–7 Mortel, Inc., has a great volume of credit sales. Mack Mortel, the president, wants you to develop a rationale for the establishment of a cash discount policy. He asks specifically: "If the company can earn an average of 20 percent on all investments, what is the maximum discount percentage we should allow for prompt payment, say within 15 days of the invoice date?"

REQUIRED Answer Mr. Mortel's question.

C8–8 Consider the following statement: "Short-term notes receivable and accounts receivable are not recorded at the present value of their maturity amounts because interest is not usually a factor when such business arrangements are made."

REQUIRED Do you agree with this statement? Can you develop an argument that gives another reason why interest often is not considered for short-term receivable transactions?

C8–9 Mondone County State Bank has always quoted its interest charge for discounting notes in terms of discount rates. In describing the cost of discounting notes to its customers, the bank wants to compose a paragraph to append to its note discount contracts. The paragraph would explain the effective annual interest rate charged for the discounting service. You are to compose such a paragraph for the following note that is being discounted at the bank:

Bank's client	Diamond Net & Sail Shop
Type of note	Interest bearing
Interest rate on note	14%
Origination date	1/1/83
Date of discounting	2/1/83
Maturity date	7/1/83
Face value of note	$20,000
Bank discount rate	16%

C8–10 Anowa Deep Sea Contractors, Inc., conducts operations throughout the world and sells offshore vessels in many countries. In the past year, Anowa has constructed 50 special-purpose vessels with long-term financing agreements in the form of notes whose effective interest rates have varied from 12 to 20 percent depending on the customer, locale, and type of vessel. Several of these sales were financed directly by Anowa by means of non-interest-bearing notes as follows:

VESSEL NUMBER	DATE OF ACQUISITION	TERM OF NOTE	MATURITY VALUE OF NOTE
180	3/15/83	4 years	$ 2,500,000
194	8/13/83	3 years	10,700,000
201	8/31/83	6 years	24,000,000
261	9/15/83	2 years	1,700,000

REQUIRED Anowa's controller asks you to analyze all the accounting effects of assigning specific interest rates to these receivables. He particularly wants to know about the impact on the company's receivables and revenues and the net effect on Anowa's income. He also wants to know if accounting theory is of any help in determining which interest rate or rates are appropriate.

C8–11 (CPA ADAPTED) When a company has a policy of making sales for which credit is extended, it is reasonable to expect a portion of those sales to be uncollectible. As a result, a company must recognize bad debt expense. There are basically two methods of recognizing bad debt expense: (1) the direct write-off method and (2) the allowance method.

REQUIRED

1. Describe both the direct write-off method and the allowance method of recognizing bad debt expense.
2. Discuss the reasons why one of the above methods is preferable to the other and the reasons why the other method is not usually in accordance with generally accepted accounting principles.

EXERCISES

E8–1 Pan Pools has an invoice outstanding with Mr. J. Boyle for a swimming pool as follows:

INVOICE NUMBER	DATE OF SALE	INVOICE AMOUNT	DOWN PAYMENT	TOTAL SALES AMOUNT
2078	6/10/83	$7,500	$2,500	$10,000

On December 31, 1983, long after the invoice is due, Pan Pools learns that Mr. Boyle is in prison and is very unlikely to pay the invoice amount.

REQUIRED Record all the 1983 journal entries related to Pan Pools' invoice #2078, assuming the allowance method is being used.

E8–2 Refer to Exercise 8–1.

REQUIRED What journal entry would be necessary if on March 1, 1984, a check for $7,500 were received from J. Boyle?

E8–3 Srillwell, Inc., has one major supplier, Apple Valley, Inc., to whom it owes $150,000 in outstanding invoices on December 1, 1983. Apple Valley agrees to substitute a note for the accounts receivable. The note has the following terms:

Due date	6/1/84
Annual interest rate	14%
Principal	$150,000

REQUIRED If the note is paid on time, show all journal entries for both companies for December 1, 1983, and June 1, 1984. Both companies have December 31 year-ends. Let each month equal 1/12 of a year.

E8–4 On July 1, 1984, Prescott Company lends $10,000 to its marketing vice-president to be paid back in five equal payments on December 31, 1984, June 30, 1985, December 31, 1985, June 30, 1986, and December 31, 1986.

REQUIRED Make up an amortization schedule for this note and show all computations; a 12 percent annual interest charge is applied to the loan.

E8-5   Jaymond Corporation had always used the direct write-off method for its accounts receivable until 1983, the current year, when it greatly expanded its credit sales. The following account information is available:

Credit sales (1983)	$2,800,000 credit balance (before closing)
Accounts receivable at 1/1/83	$400,500 debit balance
Accounts receivable at 12/31/83	$605,300 debit balance
Allowance for bad debts at 12/31/83	$25,900 debit balance
Bad debt expense	No entries

REQUIRED   Reconstruct journal entries relating to accounts receivable during 1983. Show necessary adjusting entries at December 31, 1983, assuming the ending Allowance account balance is to be 4 percent of the ending balance in accounts receivable.

E8-6   At the end of an accounting period (after adjusting entries) a company has a preclosing trial balance containing a Sales Returns and Allowances account with a $5,500 debit balance and also an Allowance for Returned and Damaged Items account with a $4,000 credit balance.

REQUIRED   What is the estimated damaged merchandise to be returned by customers at the end of the accounting period? Show computations.

E8-7   Cotton Mills Company has experienced a 5 percent return rate on its fabrics sold to fabric outlets. In the past, the company merely debited Sales and credited Accounts Receivable for the invoice price of returned merchandise. In the current year, sales were $2,800,000, returns of current year sales were $100,000, and the year-end accounts receivable balance is $560,000.

REQUIRED   If no adjustments for returns have been made for returned merchandise at year-end, what adjusting entries would be required to institute an allowance method for returned merchandise? List your assumptions.

E8-8   Karry-Off Hardware Suppliers, Inc., gives a 2 percent cash discount for payment of invoices within 15 days of the invoice date. The following data apply to invoice #8782:

Invoice number	8782
Date	9/22/83
Amount	$1,030
Date paid	10/2/83
Amount paid	$1,030 less applicable discount

REQUIRED   Give the necessary journal entries for the described invoice if (1) the net method is used and (2) the gross method is used.

E8-9   Binkey Contractors borrows $10,000 from a bank and pledges accounts receivable of an equivalent amount. The note has the following terms:

Date of note	12/1/83
Due date	1/31/84, or upon receipt of payment on pledged accounts receivable
Interest rate	15% per annum

REQUIRED   Record all necessary entries assuming the collection of cash on the pledged accounts receivable is as follows:

12/31/83	$5,000
1/15/84	$5,000

Assume that interest is paid with the final payment and that Binkey has a December 31 year-end. Let each month equal 1/12 of a year.

E8–10 A postclosing trial balance has the following accounts listed:

Accounts receivable—unassigned	$337,800
Accounts receivable—assigned	$ 31,500
Notes payable (collateralized by accounts receivable assigned)	$ (24,000)

REQUIRED Show how these accounts would appear on a balance sheet, and indicate how they should be classified.

E8–11 Mamou TV Mart sells various types of television sets and stereo equipment on long-term payment plans. Whenever large amounts of cash are needed, Mamou factors some of its receivables with Basille Factors, Inc., under a nonrecourse contract. On April 30, 1984, invoices with $12,000 total unpaid balances were factored, and Mamou received 80 percent of the invoice balance.

REQUIRED Record the journal entry to indicate the factoring, and describe how the factored invoices would be shown on a balance sheet.

E8–12 Vick's Seafood City holds the following note:

Face amount	$1,000
Annual interest rate	12%
Term	90 days
Date of note	3/10/83

On April 1, 1984, Vick's discounts the note at a bank at a discount rate of 10 percent. The discounting contract is "with recourse."

REQUIRED Compute Vick's proceeds from the bank. Assume each month has 30 days.

E8–13 Refer to Exercise 8–12.

REQUIRED What journal entries will be recorded by Vick's if the note is paid on time?

E8–14 The following information is taken from the records of the Acme Sales Company for the most recent accounting period:

Beginning balance, accounts receivable	$10,000
Beginning balance, allowance for bad debts	$ 1,000
Credit sales during the period	$50,000
Accounts written off during the period as uncollectible	$ 4,800
Recoveries of accounts written off during the period	$ 200
Total sales during the period	$80,000
Total cash received from cash sales and accounts receivables during the period	$70,600

It is estimated that 10 percent of the balance in accounts receivable at year-end will not be collected.

REQUIRED Give *only* the necessary journal entries and adjusting entries to record all changes in the Accounts Receivable account and the Allowance for Bad Debts account based on the above information.

P8–1 Diamond Hardware Supply is a distributor of hand tools and offers the following terms to its customers: 3/10, net/30. Diamond's accountant is having difficulty with the following invoices and asks your advice:

INVOICE NUMBER	DATE OF ISSUANCE	INVOICE AMOUNT	DATE OF PAYMENT	AMOUNT PAID
1087	11/15/82	$8,800	12/10/82	$8,800
1521	12/1/82	7,000	12/9/82	6,790
1777	12/16/82	2,000	12/20/82	1,940
2050	12/28/82	4,400	—[a]	—[a]

[a] Replaced by a 60-day, 12 percent note on 12/31/82 due on 2/28/83.

REQUIRED Show all 1982 journal entries necessary for the recording of sales, the collection of cash, and the receipt of the note using (1) the gross method of recording invoices and (2) the net method of recording invoices.

P8–2 Prepare the necessary journal entries to record the following (assume a 365-day year):

DATE	EVENT
May 1	Received a $1,000, 60-day, 6 percent interest-bearing note from customer X as settlement of his overdue account receivable.
May 30	Discounted X's note at the bank at 12 percent.
June 1	Received a 1-year non-interest-bearing note from customer Y in settlement of a $2,000 account receivable. The implied interest rate was 6 percent.
June 30	Received notice from the bank that X failed to pay the note. We pay the bank the necessary amount plus a $5 protest fee.
June 30	Financial statements are to be prepared at June 30. Show adjusting entries necessary from the data given above.

P8–3 Precision Electronics manufactures components for electronic toys and sells in large lots to many toy manufacturers. The following is a schedule of outstanding invoices as of December 31, 1983:

INVOICE NUMBER	DATE OF ISSUANCE	INVOICE AMOUNT	ESTIMATED PROBABILITY OF COLLECTION
8821	4/7/83	$ 85,000	.50
8978	6/20/83	60,000	.60
9006	9/1/83	100,500	.70
9777	10/15/83	200,000	.80
10101	11/20/83	45,000	.90
All others	12/1/83 to 12/31/83	1,500,000	.98
		$1,990,500	

Precision's Allowance for Uncollectibles account has a $5,000 debit balance at December 31, 1983.

REQUIRED Assuming that the aging of accounts receivable method is used to estimate bad debts, show the necessary adjusting journal entry and all computations relating to the Allowance for Uncollectibles account.

P8–4 Webster Bookbinders' major customer, Auto Publications, is in financial trouble. To keep Auto from bankruptcy, Webster has agreed to accept an interest-bearing note on several outstanding invoices as follows:

INVOICE NUMBER	DATE OF ISSUANCE	INVOICE AMOUNT
808	1/15/82	$150,000
991	6/1/82	60,000
1124	10/1/82	300,000

On November 1, 1982, Webster accepted a 1-year note with a face value of $510,000 and an interest rate of 15 percent when it became obvious that the invoices could not be paid in a timely manner. On January 1, 1983, Webster discounted the note at Jefferson National Bank at a discount rate of 18 percent. In the event of a default by Auto, the discounting agreement requires that Webster pay the full face value plus interest and 5 percent of face value penalty. The bank uses a 365-day year to compute the discounting, and Webster assumes that each month equals 1/12 of a year.

REQUIRED Assuming that Webster has a December 31 year-end and that there is reasonable assurance on December 31, 1982, that Auto will not default: (1) What journal entries are necessary at November 1, 1982, December 31, 1982, January 1, 1983, and at the maturity date if Auto pays the note? (2) What journal entries are necessary at the maturity date if Auto defaults?

P8–5 Prepare the necessary journal entries to record the following, assuming that a 365-day year is used for computing the proceeds of the discounting and that each month equals 1/12 of a year for other purposes:

DATE	EVENT
June 1	Received a $10,000, 120-day, 9 percent note from Zeta Company in settlement for an overdue account receivable.
June 15	Received a $2,000 1-year non-interest-bearing note from Beta as settlement of an account receivable in the amount of $1,760.
June 30	Closed books for the year ended June 30, 1984.
July 30	Discounted the Zeta note at the bank at 12 percent 60 days before maturity.
Aug. 15	Discounted the Beta note at the bank at 24 percent 10 months before maturity.
Oct. 1	Received notice from the bank that Zeta had failed to pay the note. The protest fee is $15.

P8–6 Alaska Fish Company cans and freezes fish for shipment to distributors throughout the United States. The company has always had a very liberal customer credit policy, but that has changed because of high interest rates and an increase in bad debts. Starting in 1983, the company instituted procedures designed to speed collection and to earn a return on unpaid amounts. In essence, the contractural terms governing credit sales now have three phases: (1) 2/10—2 percent discount off invoice amount if paid within 10 days of invoice date; (2) n/30—invoices are due between 11 and 30 days at the invoice amount; and (3) after 30 days, a 20 percent per annum interest charge is due with payment required 90 days after the invoice date. At 12/31/83, Alaska Fish Company has the following invoices outstanding:

INVOICE NUMBER	INVOICE DATE	AMOUNT
7621	6/30/83	$ 12,670
7946	8/14/83	42,500
8633	10/11/83	24,660
9001	10/24/83	10,080
9084	10/31/83	17,870
9775	11/7/83	20,430
9790	11/14/83	5,050
9801	11/21/83	11,120
Several	12/1/83	100,500
Several	12/7/83	110,600
Several	12/14/83	201,230
Several	12/21/83	310,190
Several	12/28/83	399,000

REQUIRED

1. Without considering the problem of bad debts estimation, what journal entry would be necessary to record estimated cash discounts and accrued interest on the outstanding invoices? Assume a 365-day year.
2. The Allowance for Bad Debts account has a preadjusting credit balance of $15,500 and the following probabilities of collection are made:

TIME OUTSTANDING	PROBABILITY OF COLLECTION
0–15 days	.99
16–30 days	.95
31–60 days	.90
Over 60 days	.80

Disregarding the discount and transaction in requirement 1, what journal entry would be necessary to record bad debt expense at December 31, 1983?

P8–7 Island Suppliers, Inc., sells fresh produce on credit to restaurants on several Caribbean islands. The company has used the allowance method based on a percentage of sales to account for bad debts. The bad debt experience rate has jumped dramatically due to the closing of several restaurants. The underlying causes for the business failures were felt to be the uncertainty created by the threat of strikes in the airline industry and an extremely active storm season, which kept tourism below normal. Selected information from Island's accounting statements follows:

	1984 (PRECLOSING)	1983
Sales (all credit)	$16,500,000	$17,800,000
Accounts receivable (year-end balance)	4,010,000	3,700,000
Allowance for bad debts (year-end balance)	80,200	74,000
Bad debt expense	0	82,000
Extraordinary loss (before tax effect), bad debts due to customer bankruptcy	280,000	0

At December 31, 1984, it is expected that bad debt experience will return to normal and that 2 percent of outstanding accounts receivable at year-end is an appropriate estimate.

REQUIRED Discuss the accounting disclosure that Island Suppliers has made for bad debt experience. Show the necessary adjusting entries to bring the statements in conformance with GAAP.

P8–8 Apex Finance Associates (AFA) is an agency that will attempt to collect overdue accounts receivable for a percentage of the amount collected. AFA also purchases accounts receivable on a nonrecourse basis. At December 31, 1983, (the end of its fiscal year) AFA owns uncollected invoices amounting to $1,540,000 in original invoice amounts for which AFA paid $860,000. Collection experience has averaged 60 percent on such invoices. In addition, AFA is working on client-owned receivables amounting to $10,100,000, of which 70 percent are estimated to be collected. AFA charges a flat 20 percent on all successful collections on client-owned receivables.

REQUIRED How should AFA account for the purchased invoices owned at December 31, 1983, and the collection services in process at December 31, 1983?

P8–9 Because of a recession in its industry, Horton Industries has been forced to explore every possible source of cash. On May 1, 1983, Horton takes the following steps, which will generate immediate cash:

1. Factor invoices with a face amount of $6,400,000. The financing charge is 10 percent of face value.
2. Discount with recourse two interest-bearing notes receivable as follows:

ORIGINAL DATE	FACE AMOUNT	ANNUAL INTEREST	DUE DATE	MATURITY VALUE
4/1/83	$200,000	14%	7/1/83	$207,000
3/1/83	500,000	18	9/1/83	545,000

The bank used a discount rate of 15 percent.

REQUIRED

1. Show all journal entries at May 1, 1983, to record transactions 1 and 2 above, assuming no interest had been accrued as of May 1. Assume a 365-day year.

2. Show all journal entries necessary at the date of collection of accounts and notes receivable assuming no defaults.

3. What impact did the above transactions have on Horton's net income for the period, assuming that all transactions take place within one accounting period? (Ignore tax considerations.)

P8–10   Renfer Products has a major customer that consistently defers the payment of outstanding invoices. Because this customer accounts for 21 percent of Renfer's sales and no defaults have been incurred, the company has taken a very lenient attitude. In addition, although no formal contract exists, Renfer has asked that 15 percent annual interest be paid on all invoices outstanding beyond 30 days. The customer has not as yet responded to the request. At the end of Renfer's 1983 accounting year, the following invoices with the major customer are outstanding:

INVOICE NUMBER	DATE	AMOUNT
1172	11/15/82	$135,500
1312	4/1/83	227,000
1410	9/2/83	144,000
1444	11/15/83	58,000
1499	12/12/83	98,000

REQUIRED

1. How should the potential interest on unpaid invoices be reflected on Renfer's financial statements?

2. What impact does such a situation have on the classification of the accounts receivable of the major customer?

P8–11 (CPA ADAPTED)   At January 1, 1984, the credit balance in the allowance for doubtful accounts of the Master Company was $400,000. For 1984, the provision for doubtful accounts is based on a percentage of net sales. Net sales for 1984 were $50,000,000. Based on the latest available facts, the 1984 provision for doubtful accounts is estimated to be 0.7 percent of net sales. During 1984, uncollectible receivables amounting to $410,000 were written off against the allowance for doubtful accounts.

REQUIRED   Prepare a schedule computing the balance in Master's allowance for doubtful accounts at December 31, 1984. Show supporting computations in good form.

P8–12 (CPA ADAPTED)   The Guide Company requires additional cash for its business. Guide has decided to use its accounts receivable to raise the additional cash as follows:

1. On July 1, 1984, Guide assigned $200,000 of accounts receivable to the Cell Finance Company. Guide received an advance from Cell of 85 percent of the assigned accounts receivable less a commission on the advance of 3 percent. Prior to December 31, 1984, Guide collected $150,000 on the assigned accounts receivable and remitted $160,000 to Cell, $10,000 of which represented interest on the advance from Cell.

2. On December 1, 1984, Guide sold $300,000 of net accounts receivable to the Factoring Company for $260,000. The receivables were sold outright on a nonrecourse basis.

3. On December 31, 1984, an advance of $100,000 was received from the Domestic Bank on pledging $120,000 of Guide's accounts receivable. Guide's first payment to Domestic is due on January 30, 1985.

REQUIRED   Prepare a schedule showing the income statement effect for the year ended December 31, 1984, as a result of the above facts. Show supporting computations in good form.

P8–13 (CPA ADAPTED)   On January 1, 1983, the Lock Company sold some property, which originally cost Lock $600,000, to the Key Company. Key gave Lock a $900,000 non-interest-bearing note payable in six equal annual installments of $150,000, with the first payment due and paid on January 1, 1983. There was no established exchange price for the property, and the note has no ready market. The prevailing rate of interest for a note of this type is 12 percent. The present value of an annuity of $1 in advance (an annuity due) for 6 periods at 12 percent is 4.605.

REQUIRED

1. Prepare a schedule computing the balance in Lock's net receivables from Key at December 31, 1984, based on the above facts. Show supporting computations in good form.
2. Prepare a schedule showing the income or loss before income taxes for the years ended December 31, 1983 and 1984, that Lock should record as a result of the above facts.

P8–14   The Bender Company is short of cash and has decided to assign accounts receivable to a finance company. On July 1, 1985, Bender assigned to the finance company $50,000 of its accounts receivable as collateral for a short-term loan of $35,000. The finance company charged Bender a commission of 2 percent of the total accounts assigned as of July 1, 1985, and 2 percent of the balance in the assigned receivables each month-end thereafter. Bender collected $30,000 of the assigned receivable during July and $15,000 during August.

REQUIRED   Record the necessary entries for July 1, 1985, July 31, 1985, and August 31, 1985, to account for the collections of assigned receivables and the cash received from and paid to the finance company.

P8–15   The following data are taken from the records of the Joyce Corporation on January 2, 1984. Joyce has a December 31 year-end.

ACCOUNT	BALANCE DEBIT	BALANCE CREDIT
Temporary investment	$18,000	
Allowance to reduce investment to market		$ 500
Accounts receivable	25,000	
Allowance for bad debts		3,000
Notes receivable	44,000	
Notes receivable discounted		4,000
Machinery	175,000	
Building	800,000	
Accumulated depreciation—building		450,000
Land	48,000	
Accrued interest receivable	2,000	

1. On January 15, 1984, a $500 account receivable was written off as uncollectible.
2. On January 31, 1984, Joyce discounted one of its notes receivable at Marine Midland Bank at 12 percent. The note from Turkey, Inc., had a face value of $20,000 and a stated interest rate of 6 percent. Joyce received the 120-day note on December 1, 1983, and recorded 1 month's accrued interest on December 31, 1983.
3. On February 29, 1984, a $6,600, 1-year, non-interest-bearing note receivable from Maker Corporation came due. Maker paid Joyce the full $6,600 on that date. The accrued interest on this note at December 31, 1983, was $600.
4. Joyce received notice from Merchants Bank on March 10 that A Company had failed to pay the $4,000 note

that was discounted by Joyce at Merchants Bank in 1983. Joyce paid Merchants the $4,000 principal plus $150 interest due plus a $15 protest fee.

REQUIRED   Record all necessary 1984 journal entries for the above. Joyce assumes that each month has 30 days, and the bank uses a 365-day year for discounting computations.

P8-16   The following information is taken from the trial balance (unadjusted) of the Karrott Corporation on December 31, 1984:

	TRIAL BALANCE	
	DEBIT	CREDIT
Sales (all credit sales)		$254,000
Sales returns	$ 8,200	
Sales discounts	1,900	
Accounts receivable	37,000	
Allowance for uncollectible accounts	800	
Notes receivable	15,000	
Notes discounted		6,000

The notes receivable consist of the following:

1. Six-month 10 percent note from Landry dated October 1, 1984	$ 9,000
2. Three-month 12 percent note from Germain dated November 1, 1984. Maturity value is $6,180. This note was discounted at Lincoln Bank on November 20, 1984	6,000
	$15,000

REQUIRED   (Karrott assumes that each month has 30 days and the bank uses a 365-day year for discounting computations.)

1. Record the entry necessary to adjust 1984 income for uncollectibles assuming Karrott's estimate is 1 percent of net sales.
2. Record the entry necessary to adjust 1984 income for uncollectibles assuming Karrott's estimate is 2 percent of accounts receivable.
3. Record all necessary adjusting entries relating to the notes on December 31, 1984.
4. On February 1, 1985, Lincoln Bank notified Karrott that Germain had failed to pay the note. The bank charged Karrott the full amount plus a $50 protest fee. Record the necessary entry or entries.
5. On February 1, 1985, Karrott discounted the Landry note at Syracuse Savings Bank at 12 percent. Considering the entry or entries made in requirement 4, record the discount. Assume that the remaining life of the note is exactly 60 days.
6. A $450 account with the Turkey Company was written off by Karrott as uncollectible as of February 2, 1985. Give the necessary entry, if any.

P8-17 (CPA ADAPTED)   At January 1, 1984, the credit balance in the allowance for doubtful accounts of the Master Company was $400,000. For 1984, the provision for doubtful accounts is based on a percentage of net sales. Net sales for 1984 were $50,000,000. Based on the latest available facts, the 1984 provision for doubtful accounts is estimated to be 0.7 percent of net sales. During 1984, uncollectible receivables amounting to $410,000 were written off against the allowance for doubtful accounts.

REQUIRED   Prepare a schedule computing the balance in Master's allowance for doubtful accounts at December 31, 1984. Show supporting computations in good form.

P8–18 (CPA ADAPTED) On January 1, 1983, the Pitt Company sold a patent to Chatham, Inc., which had a net carrying value on Pitt's books of $10,000. Chatham gave Pitt an $80,000 non-interest-bearing note payable in five equal annual installments of $16,000, with the first payment due and paid on January 1, 1984. There was no established exchange price for the patent, and the note has no ready market. The prevailing rate of interest for a note of this type at January 1, 1983, was 12 percent. Information on present value and future amount factors is as follows:

	PERIOD				
	1	2	3	4	5
Present value of $1 at 12%	0.89	0.80	0.71	0.64	0.57
Present value of an annuity of $1 at 12%	0.89	1.69	2.40	3.04	3.60
Future amount of $1 at 12%	1.12	1.25	1.40	1.57	1.76
Future amount of an annuity of $1 at 12%	1.00	2.12	3.37	4.78	6.35

REQUIRED Prepare a schedule showing the income or loss before income taxes (rounded to the nearest dollar) that Pitt should record for the years ended December 31, 1983 and 1984, as a result of the above facts. Show supporting computations in good form.

P8–19 (CPA ADAPTED) From the inception of its operations in 1980, Summit carried no allowance for doubtful accounts. Uncollectible receivables were expensed as written off, and recoveries were credited to income as collected. On March 1, 1984 (after the 1983 financial statements had been issued), management recognized that Summit's accounting policy with respect to doubtful accounts was not correct, and it determined that an allowance for doubtful accounts was necessary. A policy was established to maintain an allowance for doubtful accounts based on Summit's historical bad debt loss percentage applied to year-end accounts receivable. The historical bad debt loss percentage is to be recomputed each year based on all available past years up to a maximum of 5 years.

Information from Summit's records for 5 years is as follows:

YEAR	CREDIT SALES	ACCOUNTS WRITTEN OFF	RECOVERIES
1980	$1,500,000	$15,000	$ 0
1981	2,250,000	38,000	2,700
1982	2,950,000	52,000	2,500
1983	3,300,000	65,000	4,800
1984	4,000,000	83,000	5,000

Accounts receivable balances were $1,250,000 and $1,460,000 at December 31, 1983, and December 31, 1984, respectively. The bad debt loss percentage is net bad debt losses divided by credit sales.

REQUIRED

1. Prepare the journal entry, with appropriate explanation, to set up the allowance for doubtful accounts as of January 1, 1984. Show supporting computations in good form.
2. Prepare a schedule analyzing the changes in the Allowance for Doubtful Accounts account for the year ended December 31, 1984. Show supporting computations in good form.

Inventories—
Basic Concepts
and Measurement
Procedures
9

OVERVIEW   This is the first of two chapters on inventory measurement. The fact that we devote two chapters to inventory indicates the topic's relative importance and complexity. Inventory is an important asset because it represents one of the major resource commitments of most business entities. Frequently as much as 30 percent or more of an entity's assets may be invested in inventory. Because of its relative importance as a use of a company's resources, and because of the many alternative ways of measuring the inventory on hand and the cost of inventory sold, it is important for users of financial accounting data to have a thorough understanding of the accounting procedures that pertain to inventory.

This chapter outlines the basic concepts of inventory measurement procedures and reviews the sequence of decision alternatives available to management in formulating an inventory measurement policy. The alternatives considered include those related to the purchase cost identification, systems for costing inventory, cost-flow assumptions, and methods of applying the lower-of-cost-or-market rule. These alternatives are covered in a logical sequence designed to enhance one's appreciation of their ramifications for financial reporting.

In considering the alternative measurement procedures available to management, you should evaluate carefully the qualitative characteristics of the resulting accounting information. The relevance of the alternative measurement procedures is related to the economic differences associated with each alternative, which in turn is related to funds flow effects of the alternatives. The reliability of the inventory measurements will vary widely from alternative to alternative, with the objectivity of the measurements affected by virtually all dimensions of the inventory measurement alternatives. The comparability of the measurement alternatives will depend on how specifically the financial statements reveal the alternatives that were selected and what their impact is relative to other alternatives.

THE NATURE OF INVENTORY

Inventory items are assets held for direct sale to customers in the ordinary course of business or assets that will be consumed in the production of goods to be sold (for example, raw materials and manufacturing supplies). Inventory represents one of the most significant assets in most businesses, larger in many cases than total investment in plant, property, and equipment. Also, the sale of inventory is the major source of revenue for most nonservice businesses. Consequently, the items included in inventory and their measurement have a direct and substantial impact upon income determination and the financial position of a firm.

Inventory Classification

Whether or not an item should be classified as inventory depends in large part on the nature of the particular business and its economic goals and objectives. In some service industries, such as a dry-cleaning shop, there may be no inventories to speak of. An automobile may be classified as equipment to a retailer whose salespersons use it to call on customers, and as inventory to a car dealership holding it for sale to customers. The point is that few items are properly classified as inventory simply because of their basic nature. We cannot say that a given item should always be classified as inventory. It depends on intentions regarding its use; its use in turn depends primarily upon the nature of the firm involved and its economic goals and objectives.

Form, Place, and Time Utility of Inventory

Inventories are often changed in some way by businesses. Using human resources and capital (machinery, equipment, buildings, display counters, and so on), managers of businesses attempt to add utility for which customers are willing to pay. Three basic types of utility might be added; these are form, place, and time utility. **Form utility** is added when raw materials are converted to a different form. **Place utility** is added when the products or services are made available at locations that are convenient for customers. **Time utility** is added when products and services are made available at the time customers want them. Retailers and wholesalers are concerned primarily with adding place and time utility. Manufacturers are concerned with adding all three.

Inventory Accounting in Merchandising Entities

In retailing or wholesaling businesses, there is normally a need for only one major class of inventory because **merchandising entities** usually buy their goods in a form ready for sale to customers. Their economic contribution is derived from adding place and time utility—having the goods on hand in a place and at a time convenient for their customers. Their success or failure in doing so is measured by their net income or net loss for the period. Exhibit 9–1 illustrates the type of operating

EXHIBIT 9–1

RETAIL OPERATING PROFIT		
	($000)	
Sales	$18,750	
Less: Sales returns and allowances	(175)	
Sales discounts	(130)	
Net sales		$18,445
Cost of goods sold		
Beginning merchandise inventories	435	
Merchandise purchases	9,550	
Purchase returns and allowances	(135)	
Purchase discounts	(85)	
Freight-in	77	
Cost of merchandise available for sale	$ 9,842	
Ending merchandise inventory	(620)	
Cost of goods sold		(9,222)
Gross profit on sales		$ 9,223
Depreciation expense		(920)
Advertising expense		(2,050)
Salespersons' salaries and commissions		(4,105)
Administrative expenses		(630)
Net operating income before taxes		$ 1,518

income measurement that might be used by a retailer. As shown in this exhibit, the primary components involve computing net sales and cost of sales. The cost of goods sold account is based on the cost of purchased products only. Labor costs for sales and management personnel, along with depreciation, are not included in cost of goods sold for merchandising entities.

The primary measurement is "net purchases," which consists of Purchases plus Freight-in less Purchase Discounts less Purchase Returns and Allowances. The net purchases are added to the beginning inventory to compute cost of goods available for sale. Deducting the ending inventory balance from the goods available for sale provides the measurement of cost of goods sold. An abbreviated form of the gross profit measurement in Exhibit 9–1 would be:

	($000)	
Net sales	$18,445	
Cost of goods sold		
Beginning inventory	435	
Plus net purchases	9,407	
Cost of goods available for sale	$ 9,842	
Less ending inventory	620	
Cost of goods sold		9,222
Gross profit on sales		$9,223

The net purchases of $9,407,000 is the sum of $9,550,000 plus $77,000 less $135,000 and less $85,000.

Inventory Accounting in Manufacturing Entities

Inventory accounting is more complex in the case of **manufacturing entities**. A manufacturer's primary function is to add form utility by converting raw materials into finished products through the application of labor and capital. Many types of raw materials, millions of dollars of investment in machinery and equipment, and thousands of production workers might be necessary to manufacture a finished product. In addition to the complexities in accounting for the acquisition and use of diverse raw materials, labor, and capital investment, the completion of goods being produced does not usually coincide with the end of the accounting periods. Production cycles often overlap two or more accounting periods. Consequently, a number of different types of inventory accounts are necessary for manufacturing firms.

A manufacturer needs three basic classes of inventories: raw materials, work-in-process, and finished goods. **Raw materials** are those items acquired for conversion to finished goods on which no work has been performed at the balance sheet date. **Finished goods** are those items on which *all* necessary work has been performed to get them into the form necessary for sale to customers. **Work-in-process** inventory includes all those items at some point between raw materials and finished goods.

The equivalent of the "net purchases" amount for the retailer is computed in a "cost of goods manufactured" schedule for manufacturing firms, such as the one illustrated in Exhibit 9–2. This schedule considers changes in both the raw-materials inventory and the work-in-process inventory, as well as the addition of labor and overhead costs incurred during production for the current period.

The overhead costs are considered **product costs,** and they include a number of cost elements that are considered **period costs** in nonmanufacturing entities. Product costs are all the costs that are necessarily incurred as a part of the manufacturing process. These product costs are sometimes broken down into **direct** costs

EXHIBIT 9–2

SCHEDULE OF COST OF GOODS MANUFACTURED			
Beginning work-in-process-inventories			$ 271
Raw materials—beginning of period	$ 35		
Plus raw-material purchases (net)	420		
Raw materials available	$455		
Less raw materials—end of period	40		
Raw materials used		$ 415	
Plus direct labor		2,365	
Total prime cost for period		$2,780	
Plus overhead			
Indirect materials			
Factory supplies	$ 15		
Lubricants	13		
Indirect labor			
Janitorial	119		
Supervisor	172		
Inspection	113		
Factory clerks	16		
Other			
Fire and liability insurance	28		
Depreciation	697		
Taxes (real and personal property)	235		
Heat	186		
Light	113		
Power	92		
Maintenance and repairs	150		
Total overhead for period		$1,949	
Total production costs for period			4,729
Total production costs available			$5,000
Less ending work-in-process inventories			300
Total cost of goods manufactured during period			$4,700

EXHIBIT 9–3

PARTIAL FINANCIAL STATEMENTS—MANUFACTURER		
Partial Income Statement		
Sales (net)		$6,980
Cost of goods sold		
Beginning finished-goods inventory	$ 185	
+ Cost of goods manufactured during period	4,700	
Cost of goods available	4,885	
− Ending finished-goods inventory	140	
Cost of goods sold		4,745
Gross profit		$2,235
Partial Balance Sheet		
Accounts receivable		$ XXX
Ending inventories		
Raw materials	$ 40	
Work-in-process	300	
Finished goods	140	480

and **indirect** costs. GAAP require that both direct and indirect product costs be included in the cost-of-manufacturing inventories (for example, work-in-process and finished-goods inventories.)[1] Therefore, all costs incurred as a result of the manufacturing process are viewed as attaching themselves as "product costs" to the manufacturing inventories and are expensed as a part of "cost of goods sold" when the inventory is sold. Period costs, however, are expensed in the period incurred and consist of expenses unrelated to the manufacturing process. Depreciation expense on factory buildings and equipment is a product cost, whereas administrative salaries and depreciation expense on office buildings are considered to be period costs.

Exhibit 9–3 illustrates the partial income statement and balance sheet disclosures that would be used by a manufacturing entity. Most of the examples in this text, however, will deal with retail or wholesale types of operations. To make the application to manufacturers, the reader should remember that the retailer's or wholesaler's net purchases are equivalent to cost of goods manufactured (Exhibit 9–2) for a manufacturing entity. The similarities are apparent from a comparison of Exhibits 9–1 and 9–3.

General
Principles
of Measurement
and Disclosure

Keeping accurate records regarding the *physical* quantities of inventories is often a difficult problem in itself. An additional problem in measuring inventories and cost of goods sold expense results from changing prices. If prices stayed constant, most of the problems regarding inventory measurement would be eliminated. However, because changing prices can be expected and periodic reports are required, inventory measurement remains a difficult and controversial subject.

The following example will describe some of the problems. Assume that a retail clothing store began business on January 1, 1983. During 1983, the firm purchased two identical men's suits for $100 and $150. During 1983, the store sold one of the suits for $175. During 1984, the store did not buy any more suits, sold the one it had on hand for $130, and went out of business on December 31, 1984. The

---

[1] Note that manufacturing firms often use only direct, or variable, costs for inventory measurement used in internal decision making. When both direct and indirect costs are used to cost inventory, it is often called "full absorption costing."

accounting year runs from January 1 through December 31. Assume that the only decision is to charge either $100 (alternative 1) or $150 (alternative 2) to cost of goods sold expense in 1983, with the suit not sold in 1983 becoming the cost of goods sold expense in 1984. The following figures would result for 1983, for 1984, and for both years combined under the two alternatives.

	ALTERNATIVE 1			ALTERNATIVE 2		
	1983	1984	TOTAL	1983	1984	TOTAL
Sales	$175	$130	$305	$175	$130	$305
Cost of goods sold	100	150	250	150	100	250
Gross profit (loss)	$ 75	$(20)	$ 55	$ 25	$ 30	$ 55

Considering 1983 and 1984 together, the *total* results are the same. Total sales equals $305; total cost of goods sold equals $250; total gross profit equals $55. Consequently, changing inventory prices have no effect on total gross profit (and, therefore, net income) **over the life of the entity.** Because businesses seldom allow inventory levels to fall to zero, and because periodic financial statements are prepared, the inventory price changes do affect cost of goods sold expense measurement and reported income often by substantial amounts. Under alternative 1, the firm showed a big profit in 1983 and a loss in 1984; under alternative 2, the firm showed a profit in both years. The inventory costing method chosen can also have a material effect on the balance sheet figure for inventory. In our example, inventory at December 31, 1983, would be either $100 or $150, depending on the method selected.

INVENTORY MEASUREMENT PROCESS

The measurement of inventory can be viewed as a four-step process requiring the following separate tasks:

1. Measurement of purchase cost
2. Selection of a measurement system
3. Selection of a cost-flow assumption
4. Application of the lower-of-cost-or-market test

The order of these four steps is important because each step depends partly on the results from the preceding step.

Measurement of Purchase Cost
The general principle guiding the selection of items to be included in any asset is as follows: **All expenditures necessary to place the asset into its intended useful state are properly capitalized as part of the cost of that asset.** This principle is applicable to merchandise inventory and raw materials acquired, and it would include the ordering costs, the basic invoice price for the goods, the sales tax, the transportation and insurance costs to get the goods to the place of business, the hauling charges to get them from the truck or railway siding, the storage costs while in transit, various handling costs, and any other necessary costs incurred prior to the item's sale or use in production. All expenditures necessary to obtain the future service utility of the inventory are part of the purchase cost; one expenditure is no more or no less critical than any of the others in that regard. Tied closely to this line of reasoning is the **matching concept.** All of these costs should be carried forward

as assets until the year of sale and should then be matched against sales revenue as part of cost of goods sold expense in order to measure income properly.

Because of the difficulties in measuring and allocating some of these costs, as well as their relatively immaterial amount, in many cases some or all of the noninvoice costs are expensed instead of capitalized. The basic concept of acquisition cost is straightforward, but application to some assets in certain situations may be difficult to achieve or simply too costly.

Measurement of expenditures to be included in purchase cost How should items to be included in purchase cost be measured? The general principle for measuring any and all items capitalized as part of the cost of any and all assets is the following: **Measure all items at the cash-equivalent price at the date of acquisition.** The **cash-equivalent price** is the price that would result in the immediate settlement of any obligation arising upon acquisition, assuming an arm's-length transaction between the buyer and the seller.

As an example of the cash-equivalent concept, assume that the invoice price for the purchase of merchandise inventory was $10,000 with terms of 2/10, n/30 ("net/30") (meaning a 2 percent discount if paid within 10 days or the total payable within 30 days). How much should be reported in the balance sheet for this inventory if not sold or for cost of goods sold expense if the item has been sold? The answer is $9,800 regardless of when the invoice is paid, because the cash-equivalent price is $9,800. If the invoice is paid after 10 days, resulting in an actual cash outflow of $10,000, the $200 difference is the price paid for tying up the seller's capital for more than 10 days. Some businesses consider the $200 an interest expense and would debit the Interest Expense account, whereas others prefer to use a Discounts Lost account for the $200 and include it as a part of cost of goods sold.

Gross and net methods for recording purchases Two techniques are employed in recording inventory acquisitions and treating purchase discounts: the gross method and the net method. Under the **gross method,** "purchases" is debited for the *gross* invoice price. Under the **net method,** "purchases" is debited for the gross invoice price *less* any discounts available.

Regardless of which method is used for record-keeping purposes, both the gross and net methods should result in ending inventories measured at the "net" price, and accounts payable measured at the actual amount owed at the balance sheet date. Consider the following example. Assume that inventory is acquired on December 26, 1984, with a gross invoice price of $100,000, terms 2/10, n/30. On December 29, $40,000 (gross) of invoices are paid for with a $39,200 check. The accounting year ends on December 31, 1984. The following entries would be appropriate for the acquisition and payment under two methods:

	GROSS METHOD			NET METHOD		
12/26/84	Purchases	100,000		Purchases	98,000	
	Accounts payable		100,000	Purchase discounts available	2,000	
				Accounts payable		100,000
12/29/84	Accounts payable	40,000		Accounts payable	40,000	
	Cash in bank		39,200	Cash in bank		39,200
	Purchase discounts		800	Purchase discounts available		800

Must any adjusting entries be made on December 31, 1984? Assume that this firm has always paid its bills within the discount period and will probably continue to do so. Under this assumption, the liability for accounts payable that should be reflected in the balance sheet on December 31, 1984, is $60,000 minus 2 percent of $60,000, or $58,800. The cash-equivalent price of the inventory on hand that should be reflected as a current asset is $98,000. Under the net method, "purchases" is stated in the records at $98,000 and "accounts payable" is stated at $58,800 net (balance in accounts payable of $60,000 less the balance in the contra account, Purchase Discounts Available, of $1,200). Thus no adjusting entries are necessary under the net method with regard to the discounts.

Under the gross method, accounts payable is stated at $60,000 and purchases at $99,200 ($100,000 minus $800) in the accounts. If the remaining $60,000 in invoices is expected to be paid within the 10-day discount period, the following adjusting entry would be required:

Purchase discounts available	1,200	
Purchase discounts		1,200

In practice, for financial reporting purposes, it is not necessary to forecast whether a discount will be taken. Because the discount period is typically short (10 days), and because the financial reports are not usually finalized until a month or more after the end of an accounting period, the accountant usually knows which discounts were taken and which were not and can record end-of-period adjusting entries accordingly.

In addition to the above, assume that we also have inventory on hand on December 31, 1984, purchased on December 15, 1984, for $12,000, 2/10, n/30, for which payment has not been made. The following account balances would exist before adjustments under the gross and net methods:

	GROSS METHOD	NET METHOD
Purchases	$12,000 Debit	$11,760[a] Debit
Accounts payable	$12,000 Credit	$12,000 Credit
Purchase discounts available (contra accounts payable account)	0 Debit	$ 240 Debit

[a] 12,000 − (.02 × 12,000)

Under the cash-equivalent price concept, inventory should be stated in the balance sheet at $11,760. Accounts payable should be stated at $12,000, the amount actually owed on December 31, 1984, because the 10-day discount period has passed. Therefore, the following adjusting entries would be recorded:

GROSS METHOD

12/31/84	Purchase discounts lost (or Interest expense)	240	
	Purchases		240
	(To reclassify a portion of purchases.)		

NET METHOD

12/31/84	Purchase discounts lost (or Interest expense)	240	
	Purchase discounts available		240

Whichever method is used, the end result should have the same impact on cost of goods sold, and ending inventory should be valued at its cash-equivalent price. Both methods result in the same *net* purchases figure as well, with discounts lost added to the Purchases account (the net method), and discounts taken deducted from the Purchases account (the gross method).

Selection of a Measurement System

Two basic alternatives are available in selecting a measurement system: (1) periodic inventory systems and (2) perpetual systems. Recall from introductory accounting that **periodic systems** measure inventory only at the end of report periods, and they therefore do not provide information about inventory on hand and cost of goods sold on a continuous basis. **Perpetual systems** continually update both inventory and cost of goods sold after each purchase or sale of inventory. The differences and similarities encountered in recording events under these two systems are illustrated in Exhibit 9–4.

Numerous variations of these two alternatives are used in practice, but the basic attributes of the two systems noted above are constant throughout most, if not all, applications of these two systems. A periodic system has advantages as well as disadvantages. Periodic systems tend to be simple and easy to maintain and are relatively inexpensive. The following calculation is made periodically to compute cost of sales:

Beginning inventory	$ 37,000
Plus purchases (net)	981,220
Cost of goods available for sale	1,018,220
Less ending inventory	(53,450)
Cost of goods sold	$ 964,770

The ending inventory measurement (which is the next period's beginning inventory) is arrived at in periodic systems by taking a physical count of the units on hand at the end of an accounting period and pricing them out (sometimes called "extending," or making the extensions). The pricing may be done in various ways, depending on which cost-flow assumption is used in combination with the periodic system. For example, the prices assigned to the ending units may be taken from the most recent invoices.

The only records involved in the periodic system are those used to keep track of the purchases of the period. This might be nothing more than a set of invoices in some cases. Alternatively, it might consist of a number of ledger accounts that are combined to make up "net purchases," such as the following:

BALANCES IN "PURCHASES" ACCOUNTS	
Purchases	$980,000 Debit
Plus purchase discounts lost	4,180 Debit
Less purchase returns	10,250 Credit
Less purchase allowances on damaged goods	8,780 Credit
Plus freight on purchases	22,070 Debit
Net purchases	$981,220

The details of these accounts may be useful information for management to consider in evaluating operations. For example, an analysis of the details of the Purchase Returns account might identify suppliers who are sending inferior merchandise and

EXHIBIT 9-4

COMPARISON OF PERPETUAL AND PERIODIC INVENTORY SYSTEMS

EVENT	PERPETUAL SYSTEM			PERIODIC SYSTEM		
		DEBIT	CREDIT		DEBIT	CREDIT
Purchase goods on account (2/10, n/30)	Inventory	X		Purchases	X	
				Freight-in	X	
	Accounts payable		X	Accounts payable		X
Pay for freight	Accounts payable	X		Accounts payable	X	
	Cash		X	Cash		X
Return some goods	Accounts payable	X		Accounts payable	X	
	Inventory		X	Purchase returns		X
Pay for goods within 10 days	Accounts payable	X		Accounts payable	X	
	Inventory		X	Purchase discounts		X
	Cash		X	Cash		X
Sell goods on account (2/10, n/30)	Accounts receivable (or cash)	X		Accounts receivable (or cash)	X	
	Sales		X	Sales		X
	Cost of goods sold	X				
	Inventory		X			
Goods returned	Sales returns	X		Sales returns	X	
	Accounts receivable (or cash)		X	Accounts receivable (or cash)		X
	Inventory	X				
	Cost of goods sold		X			
Collected for sales within 10 days	Cash	X		Cash	X	
	Sales discounts	X		Sales discounts	X	
	Accounts receivable		X	Accounts receivable		X
End of period	None			Inventory (ending)	X	
				Cost of goods sold	X	
				Purchase returns	X	
				Purchase discounts	X	
				Purchases		X
				Freight-in		X
				Inventory (beginning)		X

would thereby signal the purchasing agent to consider other suppliers. Also, the Purchase Discounts Lost account should provide some input to evaluating the effectiveness of cash management for the period.

The periodic system requires you to know (1) your starting position (beginning inventory), (2) your acquisition costs of the period (purchases), and (3) your ending position. The simplicity and low cost of the periodic system are positive attributes that must be balanced against its drawbacks. These drawbacks include an absence of a running inventory count and a running cost of goods sold measure, both of which are required to answer the question, Has business been profitable this week or this month or this quarter? These missing information items are not provided by a periodic system. However, in the next chapter we discuss a number of estimation methods that can be used to approximate such information in a periodic system.

Periodic inventory systems tend to be cost beneficial in businesses where inventory consists of major items, such as a retailer of television sets or refrigerators or washers or dryers or stoves or microwave ovens. These businesses typically know what they have on hand without keeping detailed records and may avoid shortages because the highly visible nature of the inventory items makes it unlikely that an item will suddenly run out of stock. The periodic method is also used frequently by businesses that carry many low-cost items in inventory, such as a drugstore or a toyshop. Because of the large volume of sales and the great number of inventory items involved, it is normally too expensive to maintain a complete perpetual system.

A periodic inventory system is sometimes used in conjunction with a perpetual unit counting scheme. Although maintaining a complete perpetual system is often not economically feasible, a perpetual unit count is sometimes maintained to avoid running out of stock. The perpetual unit information, however, is nearly as complex as a complete perpetual system and is sometimes applied to a particular subset of key inventory items.

A perpetual inventory system is typically more costly and complex than a periodic system. Perpetual systems become increasingly complex as the number of items to be accounted for increases. In many cases, the cost of maintaining a perpetual record of inventory makes it impractical. A single-location hardware store may have hundreds of different-sized nuts and bolts, chains, copper wires, nails, and so on, which would be extremely costly and time consuming to inventory on a perpetual basis. In such a situation, it might be cheaper to use a periodic system and overstock small low-cost items to prevent running out of stock (and a loss of sales) than to maintain a perpetual record.

The advantages of knowing what you have on hand at any point in time, when to reorder, what cost of sales and profits are, and what items are selling well are offset primarily by the cost of perpetual systems. However, given the increasing number of multioutlet retail chains (such as True Value Hardware) in conjunction with declining costs in the computer industry, computerized perpetual systems are becoming more cost beneficial even for retailers with hundreds of inventory items. J. C. Penney, for example, has installed regional perpetual systems that record increases from purchases and decreases from sales of each item at each regional location and for the region as a whole on a continuous basis. This is made possible by sales tags that are read by registers hooked up to a central computer system, making each cash register a link (or remote terminal) in a data-processing network. The cost of such systems is offset in part by the cost savings from reduced inventory levels that are made possible by having a perpetual system.

Physical inventory Taking a physical inventory periodically is not unique to the periodic inventory system. Both perpetual and periodic systems require a physical inventory. Although the periodic system uses the physical count as a measure of ending inventory and cost of goods sold, these measures are already available in the perpetual system, and the physical count is used as a check on the accuracy of the perpetual records. It is not unusual to have a difference between the units counted and the units listed as being on hand in the perpetual records. Such differences may be attributable to clerical errors, employee or customer theft, lost or damaged merchandise, and so on. The perpetual records may therefore require adjustment based upon the physical count. Consider the following example:

| ITEM | QUANTITY | | UNIT COST |
	PER PERPETUAL RECORD	PER COUNT	
Hoover Vacuum Cleaner, #8763	78 units	76 units	$43.50

The following end-of-period adjusting entry would be recorded:

| 12/31/84 | Cost of goods sold | 87 | |
| | Inventory | | 87 |

If the actual count is greater than the count per the perpetual records, the entry would increase the Inventory account and decrease the Cost of Goods Sold account. Minor differences between counts and records are not uncommon in practice.

In-transit inventory Several aspects of the inventory count can add to the difficulties of taking physical inventory. One potential problem area is **inventory in transit.** Goods shipped to customers with terms **F.O.B. destination** (meaning "free on board to destination") are the seller's responsibility because title to the goods does not pass until the goods are received by the customer.[2] Goods in transit at year-end that have been sold on F.O.B. destination terms are to be included in the seller's ending inventory, and of course the sale is also not recorded because legal title has not yet passed to the customer. Alternatively, goods in transit on terms **F.O.B. shipping point,** or shipped on a carrier belonging to the customer or some private concern (railroad, UPS, and so forth), are not normally considered part of the seller's inventory.

Shipping documents and sales contracts provide the necessary information for classifying goods in transit as inventory or cost of goods sold. Contracts may, of course, be written in such a way that title to the inventory in question can pass to the purchaser **at any mutually agreeable point in time.** Therefore, it is difficult to generalize concerning the passage of title for goods in transit, and each situation should be considered separately. Most entities have policies on goods in transit which they apply consistently over time.

---

[2] Other invoice terminology that students might encounter includes "C.O.D." (cash on delivery); "F.A.S." (free alongside ship, where the seller pays freight to seaport vessel); "C + F" (invoice includes cost of merchandise *plus* freight costs to be paid by purchaser but incurred by seller); and "C + F + I" (where both freight and insurance are included in invoice to be paid by purchaser).

Consignment items A second potential problem involved in taking physical inventory is created by consigned goods. When companies market their products through multiple outlets, it is not uncommon to have some outlets owned by independent entities, some by the company, and some by independent entities with the help of the company. This last case often involves the source company's providing partial or complete financing of inventories for sale by the independent outlet. A common example of such a **consignment** arrangement would be a local distributor of tractors and farming equipment, which would normally not own the inventory but would act as a sales agency for one or more manufacturers. The situation where a manufacturer places its inventory in the possession of independent distributors without a transfer of title is sometimes referred to as a **floor plan** arrangement. The independent distributor usually has no ownership interest in the inventory but is responsible for taking care of the inventory until it is sold, at which time the distributor receives a commission.

Numerous contractual variations are possible in consignment agreements, and these contracts must be examined on a case-by-case basis in order to determine ownership of the inventory in question. As with goods in transit, the accountant's objective is to determine at what point title passes and a sale has taken place.

Selection of a Cost-Flow Assumption

In addition to identifying what constitutes the initial purchase cost of an item and the selection of a measurement system, a cost-flow assumption must be selected before inventory measurement can take place. Exhibit 9–5 lists some commonly used alternative cost-flow assumptions and their approximate frequency of use over the past several years. Although FIFO is now the most popular method, its popularity is decreasing, whereas the use of LIFO is increasing.

Note that **cost-flow assumptions** are just that—**assumptions** about the pattern of how **costs** flow from the asset account (Inventory) to the expense account (Cost of Goods Sold). There is no reason to believe that these cost-flow assumptions are consistent with the **actual physical flow** of inventory. The actual flow of goods may be much different from the flow assumed for **costing** purposes.

What are the basic features of the various cost-flow assumptions? Management must select from the alternatives, but how does it make such decisions? Let us examine various aspects of the inventory measurement decision by comparing some of

EXHIBIT 9–5

ALTERNATIVE INVENTORY COST-FLOW ASSUMPTIONS

TYPE OF SYSTEM		
PERPETUAL SYSTEM	**PERIODIC SYSTEM**	**APPROXIMATE PERCENTAGE OF PUBLICLY TRADED COMPANIES USING METHOD**
FIFO	FIFO	36%
LIFO	LIFO	31
Moving average	Weighted average	22
Standard costs	Standard costs	2
—	Retail methods	2
Other	Other	7
		100%

the alternatives and evaluating the basis for the differences. First we shall review some of the basic features of the principal cost-flow assumptions.

First-in, first-out The assumption when using **FIFO** is that the costs of the first items added to inventory are the costs to be assigned to the first items sold. Consequently, the costs of the last items added to inventory are assumed to be the appropriate costs to assign to ending inventory. The FIFO cost-flow assumption is one of the easiest to use because it requires only a recent invoice price and a physical count at the end of an accounting period in order to measure ending inventory and cost of goods sold. Note that this is the case for *both* perpetual *and* periodic systems because FIFO will always provide the same results when used with either system. The popularity of the FIFO method is undoubtedly related to its simplicity and the relatively low cost involved.

Last-in, first-out In a **LIFO** system, the assumption is that the most recent costs of the items acquired are the first costs to be charged to cost of goods sold, whereas the costs of the first items acquired remain in ending inventories. The LIFO method charges current costs to the income statement, and in periods of changing prices it is said to do a better job of matching costs with benefits than FIFO or other methods. It's important to note that LIFO does generate different ending inventory and cost of goods sold measurements for the periodic and perpetual systems. This fact will be illustrated in the examples that will be presented shortly.

Average cost When an average-cost method is used, all costs, including those in beginning inventory, are added together and divided by an appropriate number of units. The resulting value is used to measure both the cost of goods sold expense and ending inventory.

Standard cost Standard-cost systems, which are used in some manufacturing situations, measure the inventory and cost of goods sold based on some predetermined cost estimate. Although deviations from the estimated costs are measured and recorded, the deviations (variances) from standard are not necessarily used to measure ending inventory. Standard-cost systems, although simple in concept, are difficult to work with. The actual mechanics of such systems is one of the major subjects of most cost accounting texts, which deal extensively with manufacturing inventory cost measurement problems and alternatives.[3]

Retail methods Retail methods provide a means of measuring inventory by using estimation techniques that are in accordance with GAAP. These retail estimation procedures are examined in Chapter 10, along with other acceptable techniques for estimating inventory.

Specific identification Specific identification requires that raw materials and finished goods be tagged or numbered in such a way that each item sold or used can readily be matched with a specific invoice. In specific identification, the cost-flow assumption actually follows the physical flow of goods, which is a unique feature of this method. Some accountants have pointed out that it is the only cost-flow method that is *not* based on an assumption.

[3] For a good reference, see Charles T. Horngren, *Cost Accounting: A Managerial Emphasis,* 5th ed. (Englewood Cliffs, NJ: Prentice-Hall, 1982).

The specific identification method is normally used where a relatively small number of costly items are involved, although computerized systems are making specific identification feasible in various situations. Specific identification might be used by firms dealing in expensive jewelry, furs, and automobiles. It could also be used by manufactuers producing equipment and machinery for special customer orders. It would not be practical for retailers and wholesalers dealing in high-volume products that are not somehow unique or distinguishable from one another. Specific identification generates measurements for ending inventory and cost of goods sold that would be the same under either a perpetual or a periodic measurement system.

Other methods Many other methods and variations of methods are used to measure inventory in certain situations. None of these variations is used frequently and is not so different as to require detailed study. For instance, one variation is the **base stock method** in which inventory is viewed as being made up of some base stock quantity with additional layers added on a FIFO, LIFO, or some other basis. In most variations of the base stock method the "base" is typically made up of the minimum acceptable quantity of each item to have on hand. This base is often priced out at a LIFO cost of a previous period, providing a very conservative measure of the value of the base quantity. When layers are added on a LIFO basis, this method approximates a LIFO periodic (LIFO cost flow measured in a periodic system) inventory measurement. When base stock with FIFO layers is used, it is like a combination of a LIFO base (made up of old prices) with FIFO layers (made up of current prices).

Comparison of Cost-Flow Assumptions —Periodic System

To compare the different inventory cost-flow assumptions within a periodic inventory system, consider the following data for the Sunder Corporation:

	COST PER UNIT	NUMBER OF UNITS	TOTAL COST
Beginning inventory	$16	175	$ 2,800
Purchases (net):			
Jan. 3	18	150	2,700
Jan. 19	21	75	1,575
Feb. 6	20	300	6,000
Feb. 21	22	40	880
Mar. 8	25	85	2,125
Mar. 23	26	70	1,820
Total available		895	$17,900

On March 31 Sunder has an ending inventory of 190 units on hand. The value of ending inventory under three of the cost-flow assumptions would be computed as follows:

WEIGHTED-AVERAGE PERIODIC

$\dfrac{\text{Total cost}}{\text{Total units}}$ = Weighted-average cost per unit

$\dfrac{\$17,900}{895 \text{ units}}$ = $20 per unit

Ending inventory ($20 × 190 units) = $ 3,800

Cost of goods sold ($17,900 − $3,800) — 14,100
Total available $17,900

FIFO PERIODIC			
PURCHASE DATE	UNITS	UNIT PRICE	TOTAL COST
Mar. 23	70	$26	$ 1,820
Mar. 8	85	25	2,125
Feb. 21	35	22	770
Ending inventory	190		$ 4,715
Cost of goods sold ($17,900 − $4,715)			13,185
Total available			$17,900

LIFO PERIODIC			
PURCHASE DATE	UNITS	UNIT PRICE	TOTAL COST
Beginning inventory	175	$16	$ 2,800
Jan. 3	15	$18	270
Ending inventory	190		$ 3,070
Cost of goods sold ($17,900 − $3,070)			14,830
Total available			$17,900

If we also assume (1) that the 705 sold units generated $39,480 in revenues based on an average selling price of $56, (2) that other expenses for depreciation, salaries, and so on, came to $18,800, and (3) that the tax rate is 50 percent, the following comparative statement would result:

SUNDER CORPORATION			
Net Income under Alternative Cost-Flow Assumptions			
	PERIODIC WEIGHTED AVERAGE	PERIODIC FIFO	PERIODIC LIFO
Sales	$39,480	$39,480	$39,480
Cost of goods sold	(14,100)	(13,185)	(14,830)
Other expenses	(18,800)	(18,800)	(18,800)
Income tax expense	(3,290)	(3,747)	(2,925)
Net income	$ 3,290	$ 3,748	$ 2,925

Several points should be noted regarding the Sunder example. First, the example presents data that are consistent with rising prices in inventory costs. Second, the three methods were all based on the same set of inventory transactions, but each resulted in a different net income measurement. Third, the only real economic difference *given no other information* is the tax effect of the three alternatives. Since there are no beneficial effects in an economic sense to reporting a higher income because of the cost-flow assumption used, and because higher income results in higher taxes, the selection of a cost-flow method creates a paradox. The method that generates the highest net income also provides the worst cash flow. FIFO gives Sunder the highest income, but it results in taxes that are $457 higher than those in the average-cost method and $822 higher than those in the LIFO method. Given no other information, Sunder might select the LIFO method because it minimizes taxes without having any other apparent economic consequences (costs or benefits).

Several potential complications must be considered in conducting the type of comparative analysis illustrated above. First, the tax laws are written in such a way that a taxpayer is not allowed to use LIFO for tax purposes only. In order to use

LIFO for tax purposes, it must also be used for financial reporting. There are no stipulations about the other methods, however, and a taxpayer could use FIFO for financial reporting and the weighted-average method for tax purposes.[4]

Another complication involves the indirect effects of financial statement data. For example, the bonus that Sunder's controller expects to receive may be based on reported net income, which may provide some incentive for the controller to use FIFO even if it means paying more taxes. Still another complication involves the indirect effects of maintaining certain stipulated levels of working capital. In the early 1970s, the Chrysler Corporation was required by its bankers to switch from LIFO to FIFO. The switch was required in order to increase the recorded amount for inventory so that a condition of the banks' loans (which called for a specified level of working capital) would not be violated. The move to FIFO increased not only the inventory amount (which taken alone has a noneconomic impact) but also the automaker's income, which eventually resulted in more taxes (cash outflow) because of the switch to FIFO. Analysis of which method to select is not as simple as it might seem, and the indirect effects should be carefully studied before decisions on changes are made.

Comparison of Cost-Flow Assumptions —Perpetual System

The Sunder example will require the following additional assumptions about the pattern of sales before the effects of various cost-flow assumptions under a perpetual system can be compared:

DATES OF SALES	UNITS	TOTAL SALES REVENUE
Jan. 4–Jan. 18	140	$ 7,000
Jan. 20–Feb. 5	160	8,320
Feb. 7–Feb. 20	110	6,160
Feb. 22–Mar. 7	115	6,900
Mar. 9–Mar. 22	100	6,200
Mar. 24–Mar. 31	80	4,900
	705	$39,480

These sales data, in conjunction with the purchases reported earlier, provide the following pattern of inventory *unit* flows:

Perpetual Inventory Unit Flows

DATES	EVENT	CHANGE	UNIT BALANCE
Open	Beginning inventory		175
Jan. 3	Purchases	+150	325
Jan. 4–18	Sales	−140	185
Jan. 19	Purchases	+75	260
Jan. 20–Feb. 5	Sales	−160	100
Feb. 6	Purchases	+300	400
Feb. 7–20	Sales	−110	290
Feb. 21	Purchases	+40	330
Feb. 22–Mar. 7	Sales	−115	215
Mar. 8	Purchases	+85	300
Mar. 9–22	Sales	−100	200
Mar. 23	Purchases	+70	270
Mar. 24–31	Sales	−80	190

[4] When such differences exist between pretax net income for tax purposes and pretax net income for book purposes, accountants must use interperiod tax-allocation procedures. These procedures are explained in Chapter 17.

The perpetual records would ordinarily enter sales on a more frequent basis (for example, each day or at each sale). However, the summarized perpetual unit flow provided above will be sufficient for illustration purposes.

Moving average—perpetual   The moving-average method computes a new weighted-average unit cost after each purchase. The following computations would be made to compute the weighted-average ending inventory measurement:

			Inventory—Moving Average		
DATE	UNIT BALANCE	DOLLAR BALANCE	COSTS IN AND OUT	COMPUTATION	MOVING AVERAGE
Jan. 1	175	$2,800	+$2,800		$16.00
Jan. 3	325	5,500	+$2,700	$5,500/325	$16.92
Jan. 4–18	185	3,131	−$2,369	$16.92 × 140	
Jan. 19	260	4,706	+$1,575	$4,706/260	$18.10
Jan. 20–Feb. 5	100	1,810	−$2,896	$18.10 × 160	
Feb. 6	400	7,810	+$6,000	$7,810/400	$19.53
Feb. 7–20	290	5,662	−$2,148	$19.53 × 110	
Feb. 21	330	6,542	+$ 880	$6,542/330	$19.82
Feb. 22–Mar. 7	215	4,262	−$2,280	$19.82 × 115	
Mar. 8	300	6,387	+$2,125	$6,387/300	$21.29
Mar. 9–22	200	4,258	−$2,129	$21.29 × 100	
Mar. 23	270	6,078	+$1,820	$6,078/270	$22.51
Mar. 24–31	190	4,277	−$1,801	$22.51 × 80	

The ending inventory would be $4,277, and cost of goods sold would be $13,623 ($17,900 cost of goods available for sale less $4,277 ending inventory).

FIFO—perpetual   FIFO will result in the same measurement for ending inventory and cost of goods sold when used with either perpetual or periodic systems. This result is based on the fact that a firm cannot sell what it does not have in inventory, and therefore cost of goods sold is based on the same set of earliest purchases in either system. The following **scratch pad T** system for keeping track of perpetual records might be useful for solving perpetual inventory measurement problems. It is used first with the FIFO cost flow.
Beginning inventory:

	INVENTORY—FIFO	
DATE	UNITS	UNIT COST
Jan. 1	175	$16

Record the January 3 purchase of 150 units:

	INVENTORY—FIFO	
DATE	UNITS	UNIT COST
Jan. 1	175	$16
Jan. 3	150	18

Record the January 4–January 18 sales of 140 units—FIFO (subtracted from the beginning balance):

INVENTORY—FIFO		
DATE	UNITS	UNIT COST
Jan. 1	35	$16
Jan. 3	150	18

Record the January 19 purchase of 75 units:

INVENTORY—FIFO		
DATE	UNITS	UNIT COST
Jan. 1	35	$16
Jan. 3	150	18
Jan. 19	75	21

Record the January 20–February 5 sales of 160 units—FIFO (subtracted from beginning balance and January 3 purchase):

INVENTORY—FIFO		
DATE	UNITS	UNIT COST
Jan. 1	0	$16
Jan. 3	25	18
Jan. 19	75	21

Continuing with this approach yields the following results at March 31:

INVENTORY—FIFO			
DATE	UNITS	UNIT COST	ENDING VALUE—EXTENDED
Jan. 1	0	$16	$ 0
Jan. 3	0	18	0
Jan. 19	0	21	0
Feb. 6	0	20	0
Feb. 21	35	22	770
Mar. 8	85	25	2,125
Mar. 23	70	26	1,820
	190		$4,715

Note that this is the same ending inventory composition as the FIFO cost flow in the periodic system illustrated on page 316. The cost of goods sold would once again be $17,900 − $4,715 = $13,185.

LIFO—perpetual The LIFO cost flow in a perpetual system provides entities that have good control over inventory quantities and time requirements for restocking with a great deal of flexibility in the resulting ending inventory and cost of goods sold measurements. By carefully monitoring inventory levels and sales, purchases of inventory items can be timed in such a way that any desired quantity of beginning inventory units (and costs) flow into the cost of goods sold measurement. At one extreme, LIFO perpetual can approximate the same result as with FIFO if all beginning inventory units are permitted to flow through to cost of goods sold. Alternatively, if all beginning inventory remains in inventory due to the timing of purchases, the LIFO perpetual results will approximate the LIFO periodic results.

In the Sunder case, the LIFO perpetual results would appear as follows after the January 3 purchase:

INVENTORY—LIFO		
DATE	UNITS	UNIT COST
Jan. 1	175	$16
Jan. 3	150	18

After the January 4–January 18 sales of 140 units—LIFO:

INVENTORY—LIFO		
DATE	UNITS	UNIT COST
Jan. 1	175	$16
Jan. 3	10	18

After the January 19 purchase:

INVENTORY—LIFO		
DATE	UNITS	UNIT COST
Jan. 1	175	$16
Jan. 3	10	18
Jan. 19	75	21

After the January 20–February 5 sales of 160 units—LIFO:

INVENTORY—LIFO		
DATE	UNITS	UNIT COST
Jan. 1	100	$16
Jan. 3	0	18
Jan. 19	0	21

Continuing with this approach yields the following results at March 31:

INVENTORY—LIFO			
DATE	UNITS	UNIT COST	ENDING VALUE—EXTENDED
Jan. 1	100	$16	$1,600
Jan. 3	0	18	0
Jan. 19	0	21	0
Feb. 6	90	20	1,800
Feb. 21	0	22	0
Mar. 8	0	25	0
Mar. 23	0	26	0
	190		$3,400

The $3,400 ending inventory measurement, computed on the LIFO perpetual basis, would result in cost of goods sold of $17,900 − $3,400 − $14,500. Note that the ending LIFO perpetual inventory value of $3,400 is different from the LIFO periodic inventory measurement of $3,070. The comparative results for the three methods under both the perpetual and the periodic system are summarized in Exhibit 9–6.

EXHIBIT 9–6

		SUNDER CORPORATION		
		Comparative Results		
		COST-FLOW ASSUMPTION		
SYSTEM	INFORMATION ITEM	AVERAGE	FIFO	LIFO
Periodic	Ending inventory	$ 3,800	$ 4,715	$ 3,070
	Cost of goods sold	14,100	13,185	14,830
	Net income	3,290	3,748	2,925
Perpetual	Ending inventory	4,277	4,715	3,400
	Cost of goods sold	13,623	13,185	14,500
	Net income	3,529	3,748	3,090

In considering these results, you should be careful not to generalize them to other cases. These results are all based on the same set of facts (transactions). The differences are attributable to (1) differences in systems and (2) differences in the cost-flow assumption, which, in turn, resulted in (3) different income tax and different net income. Of all these differences, income taxes represent the only economic variable that changes from one example to the next. The other, noneconomic effects due to different cost-flow assumptions are referred to as **paper changes,** suggesting that there is no direct economic cost or benefit. In evaluating the performance of an entity over time or comparing one entity with another, it is important to distinguish between those differences or changes that are noneconomic and those that have a real economic impact on the entity. Such an objective may not be easy to pursue in analyzing published financial statements, but it is certainly worth the effort wherever possible. As we shall see in Chapter 17 on income taxes, even the tax consequences of financial accounting alternatives, which represent the real economic effects, might not be readily determinable.

**Application
of the
Lower-of-Cost-
or-Market Test**

The techniques described in the preceding sections determine the "cost" of inventory. Once cost is determined, the lower-of-cost-or-market test is normally required in setting an inventory value for balance sheet and income statement purposes. The following rule applies to inventory measurement:

> A departure from the cost basis of pricing inventory is required when the utility of the goods is no longer as great as its cost. When there is evidence that the utility of goods, at their disposal in the ordinary course of business, will be less than cost, whether due to physical deterioration, obsolescence, changes in price levels, or other causes, the difference should be recognized as a loss of the current period. This is generally accomplished by stating such goods at a lower level commonly designated as market.[5]

Because of this accounting rule, the last step in the measurement of inventories involves a test of the inventory cost to determine whether it is greater than the market value of the inventory. Under the LCM procedures, if cost is *below* market value, no adjustment is required. However, if cost is *greater* than market value, ending inventory must be reduced to market value by way of an adjusting entry.[6]

The meaning of market **Market** means the replacement cost of inventories at the end of the period, based on the quantities normally dealt in by the entity. The LCM rule is applicable to manufacturers as well as to retailers and wholesalers. As such, **market value** means the price at which an item can be purchased or produced at the end of an accounting period, not what it might be sold for. The quantities the firm deals in must also be considered in determining market. Because of **quantity discounts,** 10,000 units might cost $1.10 per unit to replace, whereas 8,000 units might cost $1.15 per unit due to larger discounts allowed for larger orders. If the entity normally buys the inventory item in lots of 8,000 units, then $1.15 per unit would be the appropriate **replacement cost** to use for application of the LCM rule.

Measuring market value Market value is measured at year-end *after* an inventory cost has been determined from the application of a cost-flow assumption and a system. As a result, the LCM method compares *market* with some specific cost, such as "LIFO perpetual cost or market." Note from the Sunder case that the "cost" being compared with "market" may vary depending on the cost-flow assumption used, and therefore the LCM results illustrated below will be affected by the cost method.

The "market" value used to compare with "cost" in the LCM method is selected from one of the following three alternative market measures:

1. *Replacement cost* (based on vendor price quotations or recent invoice prices)
2. *Floor value* (selling price of inventory less cost to sell and less a normal profit)
3. *Ceiling value* (selling price of inventory less cost to sell)

The **ceiling value** is sometimes called **net realizable value** and represents the maximum value that inventory cost can be before a loss on the sale is expected. If

[5] *Accounting Research Bulletin No. 43,* "Restatement and Revisions of Accounting Research Bulletins" (New York: AICPA, June 1953), chap. 4, par. 8.

[6] The tax code does *not* allow the lower-of LIFO cost-or-market method (LIFO with the LCM method) to be used for tax purposes. To do so would result in taxable income lower than other inventory methods in periods of rising prices (due to LIFO cost) and taxable income less than or equal to other methods in periods of falling prices (due to "market" measurement under the LCM method).

inventory cost equaled the ceiling value, selling the inventory would not result in a profit. To illustrate, assume that an inventory item normally sells for $30 per unit and that costs to complete the sale (packaging, salespersons' commissions, freight out, and so on) amount to $3.50 per unit. The ceiling value of $26.50 is the inventory cost where no operating profit will be realized.

The **floor value** is sometimes called **net realizable value less a normal profit** and represents the estimated inventory cost under normal conditions. If normal profit is 10 percent of the selling price, and the selling price and cost to sell are as before ($30.00 and $3.50, respectively), the "floor" value of the inventory would be $23.50 per unit. At a cost of $23.50 per unit and a selling price of $30 per unit, inventory will generate a "normal" profit of $3.00 per unit, or 10 percent.

The floor and ceiling measures are generated from internal historical data and are somewhat subjective in that the measurement of such terms as "normal profit" and "costs to sell" frequently requires some judgment.[7] The floor and ceiling values are intended to be used to test the reasonableness of the replacement-cost value, which is also subject to judgment and measurement error. It is expected that in many cases, replacement cost will fall somewhere between the floor value and the ceiling value because the floor and ceiling were designed to test the reasonableness of the replacement cost and thereby act as a check on the expected future costs.

Of the three market values that are computed in applying the LCM method, which one represents "market"? The answer is, **The middle value in every case.** Of the three values—floor, ceiling, and replacement—the highest and lowest dollar amounts are eliminated, and the middle value is used to represent "market" for comparison with some "cost" value. This evaluation process is also illustrated in the flow chart in Figure 9–1. To illustrate the LCM method, consider the following inventory data for the Gramen Corporation:

STEEL STOCK	COST WEIGHTED-AVERAGE COST PER POUND	MARKET			LCM VALUE PER POUND	NUMBER OF POUNDS	TOTAL LCM VALUE
		FLOOR	REPLACEMENT COST	CEILING			
$1/8"$ CRS	$7.50	$7.70	**$8.00**	$8.50	$7.50	4,000	$30,000
$1/16"$ CRS	8.74	**8.64**	8.54	8.84	8.64	1,500	12,960
$1/4"$ FS	6.80	6.30	8.00	**6.70**	6.70	2,000	13,400
							$56,360

Note that the "market" value of the $1/8"$ CRS (cold rolled sheet) is the replacement cost; of $1/16"$ CRS, the floor; and of $1/4"$ FS (flat sheet), the ceiling. For the $1/8"$ CRS stock, $8.00 per pound is the middle value (between $7.70 and $8.50), representing "market" in the LCM comparison. Because the cost of $7.50 is less than market, the $1/8"$ CRS is valued at $7.50 per pound (cost). For the $1/16"$ CRS, the $8.74 cost is compared with the $8.64 market value (floor), with market used to measure the inventory item. For the $1/4"$ FS, the market (ceiling) value of $6.70, which is less than the cost of $6.80, is used to value inventory. In each case, the **middle value** is used to represent market.

---

[7] For example, what is normal profit? Is it measured for each item of inventory? What time period is used to measure it? How are such questions resolved without involving judgment?

FIGURE 9-1

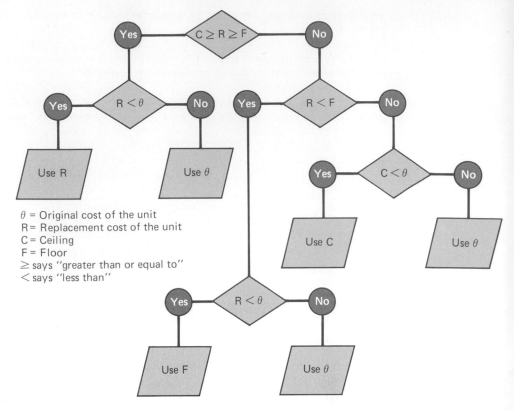

θ = Original cost of the unit
R = Replacement cost of the unit
C = Ceiling
F = Floor
$\geq$ says "greater than or equal to"
$<$ says "less than"

Application of LCM In the preceding example, LCM was applied on an item-by-item basis to Gramen Corporation's three steel products. There are three acceptable alternatives for applying LCM:

1. Item-by-item basis
2. Group basis
3. Total inventory basis

To illustrate, assume that Gramen's inventory consists of the stock listed in Exhibit 9–7. Note that all three alternative applications of the LCM method generate different ending inventory results. It is up to management to decide how the LCM method will be applied to its own entity.

Recording LCM write-downs There are several ways to report the effects of a write-down to market in the financial statements. The two statements affected are the balance sheet and the income statement, with the following optional disclosures in each:

	MAXIMUM DISCLOSURE	MINIMUM DISCLOSURE
Balance sheet	*Inventory:* Disclose the difference between cost and market in a valuation account Allowance to Reduce Inventory to Market.	*Inventory:* Directly reduce (credit) inventory for the amount of the write-down when market is less than cost.
Income statement	*Loss:* Report the loss as a separate income statement item, such as "loss due to write-down of inventory," in the "regular" section of the income statement below gross profit.	*Loss:* Include the loss in "cost of goods sold" by increasing cost of goods sold (debit) for the amount of the write-down, thereby not disclosing how much income is reduced by for the write-down to market.

The maximum disclosure case is sometimes called the **allowance method,** and the minimum disclosure case is often called the **direct write-down method.** To illustrate how these various levels of disclosure can be recorded, assume the following data for the Mikol Corporation which began operations in 1982:

	ENDING INVENTORY			
YEAR-END	NET PURCHASES FOR YEAR	AT FIFO COST	AT MARKET VALUE	AT LCM VALUE
1982	$300,000	$14,800	$15,000	$14,800
1983	300,000	18,350	17,500	17,500
1984	300,000	19,200	19,000	19,000

EXHIBIT 9–7

LCM APPLICATIONS

	NUMBER OF UNITS (POUNDS)	PER UNIT		TOTAL		LCM		
		COST	MARKET	COST	MARKET	PER UNIT	PER GROUP	IN TOTAL
Steel Stock								
1/8" CRS	4,000	$ 7.50	$ 8.00	$ 30,000	$ 32,000	$ 30,000		
1/16" CRS	1,500	8.74	8.64	13,110	12,960	12,960		
1/4" FS	2,000	6.80	6.70	13,600	13,400	13,400		
Subtotal				$ 56,710	$ 58,360	$ 56,360	$ 56,710	
Aluminum Stock								
1/32" CRS	3,000	$15.25	$15.60	$ 45,750	$ 46,800	$ 45,750		
1/16" CRS	2,000	13.40	14.00	26,800	28,000	26,800		
1/8" FS	4,000	11.85	10.50	47,400	42,000	42,000		
Subtotal				$119,950	$116,800	$114,550	116,800	
Nickel Alloy Stock								
1/32" CRS	500	$27.80	$28.00	$ 13,900	$ 14,000	$ 13,900		
1/8" CRS	620	23.15	24.40	14,353	15,128	14,353		
1/4" FS	300	20.25	20.00	6,075	6,000	6,000		
Subtotal				$ 34,328	$ 35,128	$ 34,253	34,328	
Total				$210,988	$210,288	$205,163	$207,838	$210,288

SUMMARY—LCM VALUE	
On item-by-item basis	$205,163
On group basis	207,838
On total inventory basis	210,288

The adjusting journal entries for 1982–1984, assuming either a periodic or a perpetual system, to record the write-downs to market using the maximum disclosure (allowance) approach are illustrated in Exhibit 9–8. Note that with the exception of the adjusting entry to record ending inventory, the two systems record the same LCM adjusting entries for 1983 and 1984. No adjustment is required for 1982 because market is greater than cost. Also, note that the "gain" in 1984 is not really a gain per se, but rather a reduction in a previously recognized loss. This "gain" is determined in a way that is similar to other valuation accounts (for example, Allowance for Bad Debts). The Allowance account is a balance sheet account that is only changed by way of the year-end adjustments. Therefore, at the end of 1984, before the LCM adjustment, the following balance sheet accounts are present:

Inventory (at cost)	$19,200
Allowance to reduce inventory to LCM	(850)
Net inventory (before LCM adjustment)	$18,350

However, the LCM value should be $19,000 ($19,200 cost, less a $200 "allowance"). To correct the Allowance account, and to record the reduction in the difference between cost and market (in other words, the "gain") between the 1983 year-end and the 1984 year-end, the following entry is required:

Allowance to reduce inventory to LCM	650	
Gain on recovery of LCM write-down		650

The following partial balance sheets and income statements for 1983 and 1984 would be used:

Partial Balance Sheets As of 12/31		
	1984	**1983**
Inventory (at cost)	$19,200	$18,350
Allowance to reduce inventory to LCM	(200)	(850)
Net inventory (at LCM)	$19,000	$17,500

Partial Income Statements Years Ended 12/31		
	1984	**1983**
Sales (net)	$686,400	$657,450
Cost of goods sold	299,150	296,450
Gross profit on sales	$387,250	$361,000
Gain (loss) from LCM inventory adjustment	650	(850)
Net income from operations	$387,900	$360,150

The entries for *minimum disclosure* are illustrated in Exhibit 9–9. Note that there is no formal disclosure of the write-down of $850 in 1983 and of $200 in 1984 in either the balance sheet accounts or the income statement accounts. However, the footnotes to the financial statements would indicate that "lower-of-FIFO-cost-or-market" was the basis for inventory measurement. The difference between cost and market would also be disclosed if this difference were material in amount.

The maximum disclosure provides more information for financial statement

EXHIBIT 9-8

LCM ADJUSTING ENTRIES

MAXIMUM DISCLOSURE

YEAR-END	PERIODIC SYSTEM			PERPETUAL SYSTEM
1982	Inventory (ending) Cost of goods sold Purchases	14,800 285,200	300,000	(No adjusting entry required; balance in ending inventory is already $14,800, and cost of goods sold is $285,200)

1983	Inventory (ending)
	Cost of goods sold
	   Inventory (beginning)
	   Purchases
		18,350
		296,450
			14,800
			300,000
				(No adjusting entry required; inventory is $18,350, and cost of goods sold is $296,450)

	Loss on write-down to LCM
	   Allowance to reduce inventory to LCM
		850	850	Loss on write-down to LCM 850
				   Allowance to reduce inventory to LCM 850

1984	Inventory (ending)
	Cost of goods sold
	   Inventory (beginning)
	   Purchases
		19,200
		299,150
			18,350
			300,000
				(No adjusting entry required; inventory is $19,200, and cost of goods sold is $299,150)

	Allowance to reduce inventory to LCM
	   Gain on recovery of LCM write-down
		650	650	Allowance to reduce inventory to LCM 650
				   Gain on recovery of LCM write-down 650

users, but it results in the same "bottom line" effect as the following minimum disclosure case:

Partial Income Statements
Years Ended 12/31

	1984	1983
Sales (net)	$686,400	$657,450
Cost of goods sold	298,500	297,300
Net income from operations	$387,900	$360,150

EXHIBIT 9-9

LCM ADJUSTING ENTRIES

MINIMUM DISCLOSURE

YEAR-END	PERIODIC SYSTEM			PERPETUAL SYSTEM
1982	Inventory (ending) Cost of goods sold Purchases	14,800 285,200	300,000	(No entries required)

1983	Inventory (ending)
	Cost of goods sold
	   Inventory (beginning)
	   Purchases
		17,500
		297,300
			14,800
			300,000
				Cost of goods sold 850
				   Inventory (ending) 850

1984	Inventory (ending)
	Cost of goods sold
	   Inventory (beginning)
	   Purchases
		19,000
		298,500
			17,500
			300,000
				Cost of goods sold 200
				   Inventory (ending) 200

The only difference between the two is the actual financial statement presentation. The authors suggest that maximum disclosure be used when the difference between cost and market is material in amount, otherwise no separate disclosure of the write-down should be required.

EXHIBIT 9–10

INVENTORY DISCLOSURES: POLICIES AND FOOTNOTES

EATON CORPORATION AND SUBSIDIARIES

Policy Excerpt:

Inventories

Inventories are carried at the lower of cost or market. Most domestic inventories are accounted for using the LIFO method, and all other inventories using the FIFO method.

Footnote Disclosures:

Inventories

Inventories at December 31, 1980 and 1979 consist of the following:

DECEMBER 31	1980	1979
	(MILLIONS OF DOLLARS)	
Raw materials and supplies	$136.3	$160.9
Work in process and finished goods	582.6	621.9
Totals	$718.9	$782.8

The Company believes the LIFO method more fairly presents its results of operations by reducing the effect of inflationary cost increases in inventory and thus matches current costs with current revenues. Accordingly, the LIFO method of determining cost was adopted in 1978 as to certain domestic inventories and extended in 1979 to certain additional domestic inventories, for which the FIFO method was previously used. The effect of the extension of LIFO in 1979 was to reduce net income for 1979 by approximately $10.1 million ($.39 per Common Share).

The total impact of LIFO on net income and net income per Common Share is shown in the following supplementary table.

	1980		1979		1978	
	AMOUNT	PER COMMON SHARE	AMOUNT	PER COMMON SHARE	AMOUNT	PER COMMON SHARE
YEARS ENDED DECEMBER 31	(MILLIONS OF DOLLARS EXCEPT FOR PER SHARE AMOUNTS)					
Gross LIFO effect	$20.7	$.78	$20.1	$.78	$4.2	$.16
Less increase in net income related to reduction of inventory quantities and costs valued using LIFO method	7.4	.28	0	0	0	0
Decrease in net income	$13.3	$.50	$20.1	$.78	$4.2	$.16

If the FIFO method had been used exclusively, inventories would have been $70.0 million and $45.3 million higher at December 31, 1980 and 1979, respectively.

EXHIBIT 9–10 (continued)

NATIONAL DISTILLERS AND CHEMICAL CORPORATION AND SUBSIDIARY COMPANIES
Policy Excerpt:

Inventories

Inventories are valued at the lower of cost or market. Cost is determined for the various categories of inventory using the first-in, first-out; last-in, first-out; or average cost method as deemed appropriate. Whiskey in storage for aging over a number of years is included in current assets in accordance with the general practice in the distilling industry.

Footnote Disclosure:

Note 5—Inventories

	DECEMBER 31	
	1980	1979
Finished goods	$144,790	$164,017
Work in process	31,121	34,118
Raw materials and supplies	96,416	87,566
Bulk whiskey, other spirits and wines	152,786	150,969
	$425,113	$436,670

Inventory costs of $148,566 at December 31, 1980, and $159,776 at December 31, 1979, were determined under the last-in, first-out method (LIFO). The remaining inventory costs were determined under either the first-in, first-out or average cost methods. If inventories valued under the LIFO method had been determined under the first-in, first-out or average cost methods, total inventory value would have been increased by approximately $158,000 at December 31, 1980, and $153,000 at December 31, 1979.

At December 31, 1980, inventories accounted for under the LIFO method are stated at $8,394 in excess of the amount used for federal income tax purposes.

Financial statement disclosures   In addition to reporting inventories in the balance sheet, most corporations include two other inventory disclosures in their annual reports. The first footnote to the financial statements usually describes the significant accounting policies used by the entity as the basis for preparing the statements. This "policy" footnote will normally include a description of the accounting method used to measure inventory. A separate footnote on inventory is also frequently included in the notes to the financial statements. It has become popular for companies using LIFO to explain in these supplementary footnote disclosures what inventory and income would have been reported had FIFO been used. Examples of policy notes and other footnote data for Eaton and for National Distillers and Chemical Corporation are given in Exhibit 9–10.

Exceptions to lower of cost or market   Certain exceptions to the lower-of-cost-or-market principle are allowed where inventories may be valued at higher than cost. Under such conditions, net realizable value (anticipated selling price less all expenditures to be incurred in the completion and disposal of the items) should be used. Exceptions are allowed for those products that have an immediate marketability at quoted prices and for which costs may be difficult to ascertain, such as agricultural and mineral products and others that were mentioned in Chapter 3. Note that using an amount higher than cost does not alter **total** profit for that item but does alter the **timing** of profit recognition. The following example illustrates this

YEAR	SALES	DISCOVERY COSTS	ESTIMATED VALUE	ESTIMATED COSTS TO COMPLETE AND SELL	OTHER EXPENSES
1983	0	$2,000	$3,300	$400	$500
1984	$3,000	0	0	0	$600

INCOME STATEMENT

	COST		NET REALIZABLE VALUE	
	1983	1984	1983	1984
Revenue	$ 0	$3,000	$ 900[a]	$3,000
Cost of goods sold expense	0	(2,000)	0	(2,900)
Expenses	(500)	(600)	(500)	(600)
Profit (loss)	$ (500)	$ 400	$ 400	$ (500)
Balance sheet inventory	$2,000	$ 0	$2,900	$ 0

[a] $3,300 − $400 = Net realizable value of $2,900 − $2,000 = $900.

The holding gain of $900 reported as revenue in 1983 on the net realizable value basis is offset by stating the ending inventory at $900 more on the balance sheet than it would be on the cost basis, or $2,900 instead of $2,000. Although a net loss in total of $100 (both years combined) is reflected under both the cost and net realizable value bases, the income or loss per year varies considerably.

Evaluation of LCM   The LCM inventory valuation method has been criticized because of its lack of consistency. It recognizes market values as a basis for measurement, but only when market values are *less than* costs. The question is, If market values are useful for inventory measurement, why are they not equally useful when market values are *greater than* cost? The internal inconsistency of the LCM method has been justified on the grounds of **conservatism.** However, policy makers have given some indication that the LCM method may be less acceptable in the future. Also, the courts have ruled against the use of LCM for certain parts suppliers and book publishers as a result of the *Thor Power Tool* case.[8]

We consider the additional flexibility provided by LCM to be its most impressive attribute. Given the dollar value of resources frequently involved in inventory measurement, the determination of an LCM value adds to the number of alternative measurements of inventory and cost of goods sold that could be reported based on the same set of economic facts. Three aspects of LCM add to the measurement flexibility:

1. Identification of "market" calls for judgments regarding floor, ceiling, and replacement costs.
2. Application of market may be in one of three ways (items, groups, total inventory).
3. Recording of market write-downs may be disclosed in different ways.

Given that these three choices are in *addition* to the choices of inventory system and cost-flow assumption, the number of possible financial report results that might be

[8] For a discussion, see "Effects of the Supreme Court's Thor Power Tool Decision on the Balance of Tax Accounting Power," *Journal of the American Taxation Association,* Winter 1980, pp. 5–9.

generated from any set of inventory-related transactions is extremely large. Although some judgment is required given the nature of the inventory measurement task, it is not clear that the theoretical framework, and specifically the qualitative characteristics identified and discussed in Chapter 2, can justify or are consistent with the present set of measurement alternatives.

FUNDS FLOW EFFECT

Because inventory is a current asset, any increase or decrease in its balance from period to period has a direct impact on the change in working capital. Changes in the inventory balance are also considered to have a direct impact on cash-flow measurement. From a cash-flow point of view, however, not all changes in inventory have a cash consequence. Lower-of-cost-or-market adjustments, for example, have no direct impact on cash flows. Also, various application changes, such as from a periodic to a perpetual system, or from one cost-flow assumption to another, have no direct impact on cash flows even though inventory (and working capital) may be significantly affected by such changes. The economic interpretation of inventory is enhanced when all of the various elections from among alternative measurement procedures are maintained on a consistent basis from period to period. Changes in any of these elections may have a significant negative effect on the ability to interpret the economic performance of the entity.

SUMMARY
Measurement of inventory is a complex multiple-selection process. Choices of alternative systems and/or cost-flow assumptions can significantly affect the financial results. Evaluating inventory measurement alternatives in the context of relevance, reliability, and comparability does not lead to clear choices in most cases. One method may provide more relevant information in the inventory (balance sheet) measurement at the expense of the lack of relevance in cost of goods sold measurement. Another method may be more relevant for cost of goods sold measurement at the expense of inventory measurement. Studying the alternatives will help us to understand the nature of the inventory measurement choice problem. However, understanding the nature of the desirable qualities of relevance, reliability, and comparability may not be helpful in making that choice.

In this chapter, we have reviewed the alternatives from the four-step selection process that is required for measuring and recording inventory. First a way of measuring the purchase cost is identified, then the system is selected, and then a cost-flow assumption is chosen. These three steps generate an inventory cost, which is then tested for reasonableness using the LCM method in one of its various forms. A great number of different ending inventory and cost of goods sold measurements are possible within the basic measurement framework for any given set of inventory transactions (purchases and sales). It is important to realize that the numerous different possible measurements for any set of facts are attributable to the many measurement system alternatives and are not economic in nature. Disclosures that permit financial statement users to observe separately the economic and noneconomic effects on the firm of the firm's inventory activities should be encouraged in order to enhance the relevance and comparability of inventory data.

QUESTIONS

Q9–1   What is *inventory?*

Q9–2   What types of cost may be assigned to inventory items?

Q9–3   How may purchase discounts on inventory be handled?

Q9–4   What accounts are used to compute net purchases?

Q9–5   Explain how cost of goods manufactured is computed for manufacturing firms.

Q9–6   What are *product* costs? *Period* costs?

Q9–7   What types of costs are included in product costs?

Q9–8   How is manufacturing overhead accounted for in inventory measurement?

Q9–9   What is the difference between a *periodic* system and a *perpetual* system?

Q9–10   What are the advantages and disadvantages of a periodic inventory system?

Q9–11   What are the advantages and disadvantages of a perpetual inventory system?

Q9–12   When must a physical inventory count take place?

Q9–13   What types of in-transit purchases are included in ending inventory?

Q9–14   When are consigned goods included in inventory?

Q9–15   Why are the FIFO and LIFO methods called cost-flow *assumptions?*

Q9–16   Which inventory-costing method is relatively free of assumptions? Explain.

Q9–17   For the moving average cost-flow assumption, when is it necessary to compute a revised average cost?

Q9–18   In periods of rising prices, which periodic cost-flow method will tend to result in the highest profits?

Q9–19   In applying the LCM method, how are "ceiling" and "floor" measured, and what are these measures supposed to represent?

Q9–20   What is a normal profit, and how is it used in the LCM measurement method?

Q9–21   When are market values allowed for inventory measurement?

Q9–22   When should LCM be applied?

Q9–23   Why is market value used only when it is below cost for LCM measurement?

Q9–24   Why is LCM said to be internally inconsistent?

Q9–25   Which inventory method has a real economic impact on the entity? Why?

Q9–26   Which inventory measurement procedure is said to provide maximum flexibility as far as the manipulation of inventory profits is concerned? Explain.

CASES

C9–1 (CPA ADAPTED)   In October 1984 the Alcare Corporation contracted to purchase 1,000,000 gallons of cyanide at a fixed contract price of $1.85 per gallon for gold recovery operations in the Cripple Creek, Colorado, mining area. Due to a methodological breakthrough in the gold recovery process (made public in late November 1984), the market price of cyanide (which had been stable for some time) fell to $1.30 per gallon by the end of 1984.

REQUIRED   What effect, if any, does this contract have on Alcare's 1984 financial statements? How should the contract be accounted for?

C9–2   Corporations normally *sell* inventory for more than what it cost to make (in the case of a manufacturer) or to obtain (in the case of a retailer), whereas they normally *buy* long-term assets that enable them to produce or sell goods or services for more than what they cost to make.

REQUIRED   Explain why, in the case of inventory, entities are normally able to receive more than they paid for the inventory. Consider the case of (1) a manufacturer, (2) a wholesaler, and (3) a retailer.

C9–3 Your client, Abdul Ben Shaheni, Inc., has been talking with some fellow business owners about "inventory profits." Abdul comes to you for the straight story on what exactly is meant by the term *inventory profits*. He has an oil recovery and refining business and uses the FIFO cost-flow assumption for inventories that have averaged 10,000,000 barrels of crude oil and 8,000,000 barrels of refined product over the past several years. Business has been good and profits have been high, but Abdul doesn't want to miss out on a good thing.

REQUIRED Explain to Abdul what inventory profits are and what effect, if any, they have on each of the financial statements.

C9–4 (CPA ADAPTED) Cost for inventory purposes should be determined by the inventory cost-flow method most clearly reflecting periodic income.

REQUIRED

1. Describe the fundamental cost-flow assumptions of the average-cost, FIFO, and LIFO inventory cost-flow methods.
2. Discuss the reasons for using LIFO in an inflationary economy.
3. Where there is evidence that the utility of goods, in their disposal in the ordinary course of business, will be less than cost, what is the proper accounting treatment and under what concept is that treatment justified?

C9–5 (CPA ADAPTED) Companies using LIFO inventory sometimes establish a Reserve for the Replacement of LIFO Inventory account.

REQUIRED Explain why and how this Reserve account is established and where it should be shown on the statement of financial position.

C9–6 (CPA ADAPTED) Inventory may be computed under one of various cost-flow assumptions. Among these assumptions are first-in, first-out (FIFO) and last-in, first-out (LIFO). In the past, some companies have changed from FIFO to LIFO for computing portions or all of their inventory.

REQUIRED

1. Ignoring income tax, what effect does a change from FIFO to LIFO have on net earnings and working capital? Explain.
2. Explain the difference between the FIFO assumption of earnings and operating cycle and the LIFO assumption of earnings and operating cycle.

C9–7 The lower-of-cost-or-market method of inventory valuation is to be applied in all cases where it is appropriate—that is, where market value is below cost. One of your clients, who has been using a very basic FIFO periodic system for years, would like to know how to apply the LCM method and asks your advice. This client has heard other business owners say that LCM allows a certain degree of profit manipulation by way of adjusting "floors," "ceilings," and the number of inventory "pools." These terms mean nothing to your client.

REQUIRED Explain to your client exactly what is called for in applying the LCM method and how it might be used to manipulate inventory value.

EXERCISES

E9–1 (CPA ADAPTED)

_____ 1. The acquisition cost of a heavily used raw material changes frequently. The book value of the inventory of this material at year-end will be the same if perpetual records are kept as it will be under a periodic inventory method only if the book value is computed under the

    a. Weighted-average method
    b. First-in, first-out method

    c. Last-in, first-out method
    d. Base-stock method

_____ 2. Jamison Corporation's inventory cost on its statement of financial position would have been lower using first-in, first-out than if last-in, first-out had been used. Assuming no beginning inventory, in what direction did the cost of purchases move during the period?

  a. Up
  b. Down
  c. Steady
  d. Cannot be determined

_____ 3. When using the periodic inventory method, which of the following generally would not be separately accounted for in the computation of cost of goods sold?

  a. Freight charges on the sale of inventory
  b. Cash (purchase) discounts taken during the period
  c. Purchase returns and allowances on merchandise acquired during the period
  d. Cost of transportation-in for merchandise purchased during the period

_____ 4. Which method of inventory pricing best approximates specific identification of the actual flow of costs and units in most perishable goods manufacturing situations?

  a. Average cost
  b. First-in, first-out
  c. Last-in, first-out
  d. Base stock

_____ 5. Certain information relative to the 1983 operations of Foley Company follows:

Accounts receivable, January 1, 1983	$ 8,000
Accounts receivable collected during 1983	26,000
Cash sales during 1983	5,000
Inventory, Jan. 1, 1983	12,000
Inventory, Dec. 31, 1983	11,000
Purchases of inventory during 1983	20,000
Gross profit on sales (gross margin)	9,000

What is Foley's accounts receivable balance at December 31, 1983?

  a. $7,000
  b. $12,000
  c. $17,000
  d. $13,000

E9–2 (CPA ADAPTED) The following information was available from the inventory records of the Alexander Company for January 1984:

	UNITS	UNIT COST	TOTAL COST
Balance at 1/1/84	2,000	$ 9.775	$19,550
Purchases			
1/6/84	1,500	10.300	15,450
1/26/84	3,400	10.750	36,550
Sales			
1/7/84	1,800		
1/31/84	3,200		
Balance at 1/31/84	1,900		

REQUIRED

1. Assuming that Alexander maintains perpetual inventory records, what should the inventory be at January 31, 1984, using the moving-average inventory method, rounded to the nearest dollar?

2. Assuming that Alexander does not maintain perpetual inventory records, what should the inventory be at January 31, 1984, using the weighted-average inventory method, rounded to the nearest dollar?

E9–3 The inventory activity for South American Rockwell consisted of the following changes for one of its key products:

DATE	ACTIVITY	UNITS	COST PER UNIT
1/1/84	Beginning balance	100	$1,325
1/7/84	Manufactured	50	1,830
1/9/84	Sold	(75)	—
1/14/84	Manufactured	100	1,700
1/17/84	Sold	(60)	—
1/19/84	Sold	(80)	—
1/21/84	Manufactured	120	1,680
1/26/84	Sold	(85)	—
1/28/84	Manufactured	80	1,800
1/31/84	Ending balance	150	—

REQUIRED

1. Compute the ending inventory and cost of goods sold using a periodic LIFO cost-flow assumption.
2. Repeat requirement 1, assuming perpetual LIFO.

E9–4 (CPA ADAPTED)

_____ 1. The primary basis of accounting for inventory is cost. A departure from the cost basis of pricing the inventory is required only if there is evidence that when the goods are sold in the ordinary course of business their
   a. Selling prices will be less than their replacement cost
   b. Utility will be less than their cost
   c. Replacement cost will be more than their net realizable value
   d. Replacement cost will be less than their cost

_____ 2. When valuing raw-materials inventory at lower-of-cost-or-market, what is the meaning of the term _market?_
   a. Net realizable value
   b. Net realizable value less a normal profit margin
   c. Current replacement cost
   d. Possibly any one of the above

_____ 3. If a unit of inventory has declined in value below original cost but the replacement cost exceeds the ceiling value, the amount to be used to represent the inventory value at LCM is
   a. Net realizable value
   b. Original cost
   c. Market value
   d. Net realizable value less a normal profit margin

_____ 4. Moore Corporation has two products in its ending inventory, each accounted for at the lower-of-cost-or-market. A profit margin of 30 percent on selling price is considered normal for each product. Specific data with respect to each product follow:

	PRODUCT 1	PRODUCT 2
Historical cost	$17	$ 45
Replacement cost	15	46
Estimated cost to sell	5	26
Estimated selling price	30	100

   In pricing its ending inventory using the lower-of-cost-or-market, what unit values should Moore use for products 1 and 2, respectively?
   a. $15 and $44
   b. $16 and $44
   c. $16 and $45
   d. $17 and $46

_____ 5. In pricing inventories at the lower-of-cost-or-market, a method of determining cost that cannot be used for both financial and federal income tax reporting is
   a. FIFO
   b. LIFO
   c. Weighted average
   d. Specific identification

E9–5 The Jarvis-Epoch (J–E) Pizza Shop serves hot pizza to SU students. J–E buys the pizzas frozen, heats them, and delivers them. At December 31, 1984, J–E has 200 frozen pizzas on hand at a total LIFO cost of $500. The pizzas sell for $3.50 each. The delivery persons receive a commission of $.35 per pizza. The boxes that the hot pizzas are delivered in cost $.05 each. The normal profit per pizza has been about $.70. The current wholesale price for frozen pizza is $2.30 each.

REQUIRED (show all computations):

1. What is the ceiling value?
2. What is the floor value?
3. What is the replacement value?
4. What is the cost?
5. What is the *total* value of ending inventory using lower-of-LIFO-cost-or-market?

E9–6 Records of the G. Liddy Company provide the following data relating to inventories for the year 1986:

	1/1/86	12/31/86
Inventory values at cost	$30,000	$ 30,000
Inventory values at LCM	23,000	24,000
Purchases of inventory	0	$250,000

Assume that the company values its inventories at lower-of-cost-or-market.

REQUIRED

1. Give the journal entry or entries to apply lower-of-cost-or-market (through the inventory allowance method where the inventory holding losses are reported separately) for *1986,* assuming the company uses periodic inventory procedures. This is the maximum disclosure case.
2. Give the journal entry or entries to apply lower-of-cost-or-market (through the direct inventory reduction method where the inventory holding losses are not reported separately) for *1986,* assuming the company uses perpetual inventory procedures. This is the minimum disclosure case.

E9–7

_____ 1. The concept of conservatism
    a. Results in accounting policies that are internally inconsistent.
    b. Is the basis for the lower-of-cost-or-market inventory measurement method.
    c. Is the basis for the lower-of-cost-or-market measurement method applied to temporary investments in marketable securities.
    d. Is not considered a requirement in inventory measurement.
    e. Items a, b, and c are all true statements.

_____ 2. Which of the following items is not a product cost?
    a. Glue used in assembling products.
    b. Interest on money borrowed to buy raw materials.
    c. Supplies used by a factory janitor.
    d. Lubricants for factory machines.
    e. All of the above items are product costs.

_____ 3. Battle Company had "cost of goods sold" of $43,000 during the period. The balance in the accounts payable for merchandise *increased* $5,000 during the period. Inventory, all of which is acquired on account, had an ending balance of $60,000. Cash payments for inventory acquired on account totaled $50,000 during the period. What was the beginning balance in inventory?
    a. $72,000   d. $43,000
    b. $53,000   e. $67,000
    c. $48,000

_____ 4. Suppose that Delta Corporation purchased 400 units of inventory on January 1, 1985, for $700 per unit. The ending inventory consisted of 150 units, and sales for the period amounted to 410 units. If Delta uses FIFO perpetual and the ending inventory value is equal to the beginning inventory value, what is "cost of goods sold" for the period?

a. $280,000
b. $385,000
c. $175,000

d. Cannot be determined based on above data
e. None of the above

_____ 5. An understatement of $3,500 in inventory at the end of year 3 would

a. Have no effect on net income of year 3
b. Overstate the beginning inventory of year 4
c. Overstate net income in year 3

d. Overstate cost of goods sold for year 4
e. Produce none of the effects in items a–d

E9–8

_____ 1. If year 5's ending inventory is overstated, then year 5's net income will

a. Be overstated
b. Be understated
c. Not be affected

d. Offset the error
e. Produce none of the effects in items a–d

_____ 2. The inventory of gas bag plugs of the Acme Hot Air Balloon and Wicker Basket Works at September 30 is of some concern to the president. An examination of the firm's records reveals the following:

Sept. 12 purchases	200 units @ $2.80	$ 560
Sept. 18 purchases	200 units @ $2.70	540
Sept. 26 purchases	300 units @ $2.60	780
		$1,880

The inventory on hand at the beginning of the period was 300 units at a unit cost of $3.00. The inventory on hand at the end of the period was 400 units. Based on this information, the inventory value at September 30, using the periodic LIFO cost-flow assumption, would be

a. $1,100
b. $1,180
c. $1,050

d. $1,200
e. $1,040

_____ 3. If perpetual LIFO had been applied rather than periodic LIFO, your answer to question 2 would

a. Be the same in *all* cases where sales occur evenly during the month
b. Differ in *all* cases where sales occur evenly during the month
c. Differ in *some* cases where sales occur evenly during the month
d. None of the above

_____ 4. If perpetual FIFO had been applied rather than periodic LIFO, your answer to question 2 would be

a. $1,100
b. $1,180
c. $1,050

d. $1,200
e. $1,040

_____ 5. If periodic FIFO has been applied rather than perpetual FIFO, your answer to question 4 would

a. Be the same in *all* cases
b. Differ in *all* cases

c. Differ in *some* cases
d. None of the above

E9–9 (CPA ADAPTED) The controller of the Investor Corporation, a retail business, made three different schedules of gross margin for the first quarter ended September 30, 1984:

	SALES ($10 PER UNIT)	COST OF GOODS SOLD	GROSS MARGIN
Schedule A	$280,000	$118,550	$161,450
Schedule B	280,000	116,900	163,100
Schedule C	280,000	115,750	164,250

The computation of cost of goods sold in each schedule is based on the following data:

	UNITS	COST PER UNIT	TOTAL COST
Beginning inventory, July 1	10,000	$4.00	$40,000
Purchases, July 25	8,000	4.20	33,600
Purchases, Aug. 15	5,000	4.13	20,650
Purchases, Sept. 5	7,000	4.30	30,100
Purchases, Sept. 25	12,000	4.25	51,000

The president of the corporation cannot understand how three different gross margins can be computed from the same set of data. As controller, you have explained to him that the three schedules are based on three different assumptions concerning the flow of inventory costs: FIFO, LIFO, and weighted average. Schedules A, B, and C were not necessarily prepared in this sequence of cost-flow assumptions.

REQUIRED Prepare three separate schedules computing cost of goods sold and supporting schedules showing the composition of the ending inventory under each of the three cost-flow assumptions.

E9–10 (CPA ADAPTED) The inventory account of Benson Company at December 31, 1986, included the following items:

	INVENTORY AMOUNT
Merchandise out on consignment at sales price (including markup of 40% in selling price)	$7,000
Goods purchased, in transit (shipped F.O.B. shipping point)	6,000
Goods held on consignment by Benson	4,000
Goods out on approval (sales price $2,500, cost $2,000)	2,500

REQUIRED Based on the above information, by how much should the inventory account at December 31, 1986, be reduced?

E9–11 (CPA ADAPTED) The following information is available for the Gant Company for 1986:

Freight-in	$ 20,000
Purchase returns	80,000
Selling expenses	200,000
Ending inventory	90,000

The cost of goods sold is equal to 700 percent of selling expenses.

REQUIRED What is the cost of goods available for sale?

PROBLEMS

P9–1 The following information is taken from the records of the Inventory Company for the month of January 1984:

Jan. 1	Beginning inventory: 150 units at $20 per unit, totaling $3,000	
Jan. 5	Purchased 2,000 units at $18 per unit, total cost $36,000	
Jan. 19	Sold 1,800 units	
Jan. 25	Purchased 500 units at $22.70 per unit, total cost $11,350	
Jan. 30	Sold 450 units	
Jan. 31	400 units on hand in ending inventory	

REQUIRED Compute the ending inventory under the following alternatives. Whenever calculations are necessary to compute ending inventory, be certain to show your calculations:

1. LIFO, assuming a periodic inventory method
2. FIFO, assuming a perpetual inventory method
3. Moving average, assuming a perpetual inventory method
4. LIFO, assuming a perpetual inventory method, costed *during* the period
5. Weighted average, assuming a periodic inventory method
6. LIFO, assuming a perpetual inventory method, costed at the *end* of the period
7. Base stock, assuming a perpetual inventory method, with incremental layers added on a LIFO basis
8. Base stock, assuming a periodic inventory method, with incremental layers added on a LIFO basis
9. LIFO, assuming a perpetual inventory basis, costed at the end of the period with incremental layers costed on a weighted-average basis
10. Base stock, assuming a periodic inventory basis, with incremental layers costed on a weighted-average basis

P9–2 Destruction Company prices its inventory at cost or market, whichever is lower. It uses an individual-item basis.

	ITEM NUMBER							
	890	**896**	**901**	**907**	**1,046**	**1,084**	**1,240**	**1,310**
Quantity on hand	500	800	1,100	450	375	2,500	740	630
Cost per unit	$2.70	$2.25	$3.60	$3.29	$2.02	$2.70	$1.44	$4.05
Replacement cost	2.75	2.37	3.37	2.79	1.80	2.24	1.35	4.72
Estimated selling price	4.05	3.15	4.50	2.70	2.92	3.15	2.25	5.40
Cost of completion and disposal	.32	.45	.36	.22	.63	.37	.67	.45
Normal profit	1.24	.45	.90	.81	.54	.31	.45	.91

REQUIRED Based on the information given above, determine the amount of Destruction Company's inventory.

P9–3 The Quick-Deal Company had the following transactions during 1984:

Jan. 1	Beginning inventory: 300 units at $6 per unit	
Jan. 15	Purchased 500 units at $4 per unit	
Feb. 10	Sold 200 units at $8 per unit	
June 20	Purchased 400 units at $3 per unit	
July 15	Sold 500 units at $6 per unit	
Oct. 17	Sold 200 units at $5 per unit	
Nov. 14	Purchased 700 units at $8 per unit	
Dec. 10	Sold 800 units at $10 per unit	
Dec. 27	Purchased 200 units at $7 per unit	

REQUIRED Compute ending inventory and cost of goods sold expense under each of the following assumptions:

1. Periodic FIFO
2. Periodic LIFO

3. Periodic average cost
4. Perpetual FIFO
5. Perpetual LIFO
6. Perpetual, average cost

P9-4 (CPA ADAPTED) The Frate Company was established on December 1, 1984. The following information is available from Frate's inventory records for Product Ply:

	UNITS	UNIT COST
January 1, 1985 (beginning inventory)	800	$ 9.00
Purchases		
Jan. 5, 1985	1,500	10.00
Jan. 25, 1985	1,200	10.50
Feb. 16, 1985	600	11.00
Mar. 26, 1985	900	11.50

A physical inventory on March 31, 1984, shows 1,600 units on hand.

REQUIRED Prepare schedules to compute the ending inventory at March 31, 1985, under each of the following inventory methods (show supporting computations):

1. FIFO
2. LIFO
3. Weighted average

P9-5 The Mason Corporation recently acquired 10 units of inventory consisting of small single-engine airplanes. Analysis of the inventory account revealed the following costs:

DATE	ITEM	COST
4/1/84	10 aircraft at invoice price	$586,000
6/1/84	Transportation costs paid on delivery	16,830
6/1/84	Insurance costs from date of shipment (4/1/84 to 12/31/84)	3,140
7/1/84	Cost of preparing aircraft for flight—labor	2,975
7/1/84	Cost of preparing aircraft for flight—materials	1,343
8/1/84	Cost of hangar rentals to store aircraft (6/1/84 to 12/31/84)	7,000
8/15/84	Cost of repairing wing damage incurred during test flight	3,875
8/31/84	Cost of runway fees from testing of aircraft	1,800
8/31/84	Allocation of salespersons' commissions	13,650
8/31/84	Potential customer flight costs	3,873
8/31/84	Potential customer entertainment costs	2,145

REQUIRED Prepare any adjusting entries necessary to state inventory properly as of August 31, 1984.

P9-6 The Braindrain Company records provide the following data relating to inventories for the years 1984 and 1985.

INVENTORY DATE	AT COST	AT LOWER-OF-COST-OR-MARKET
Jan. 1, 1984	$35,000	$35,000
Dec. 31, 1984	$28,000	22,000
Dec. 31, 1985	$34,000	31,000

The following data are also available:

	1985	1984
Sales	$600,000	$700,000
Purchases	350,000	300,000
Other expenses	250,000	250,000

Assume that the company values its inventories at lower-of-cost-or-market.

REQUIRED

1. Give the journal entry or entries to apply lower-of-cost-or-market (through the direct inventory reduction method where the inventory holding losses are *not* reported separately) for *1985* only, assuming the company uses periodic inventory procedures.
2. Give the journal entry or entries to apply lower-of-cost-or-market (through the inventory allowance method where the inventory holding losses are reported separately) for *1985*, assuming the company uses perpetual inventory procedures.
3. Give the journal entry or entries to apply lower-of-cost-or-market (through the direct inventory reduction method where the inventory holding losses are reported separately) for *1985*, assuming the company uses perpetual inventory procedures.

P9–7 The records of Nancy's Exterior Decorating, Inc., provide the following data relating to inventories for the years 1983 and 1984.

	INVENTORY ($000)		
	DEC. 31, 1984	DEC. 31, 1983	JAN. 1, 1983
At average cost	$145	$123	$112
At lower-of-average-cost-or-market	135	110	112

Net purchases for 1983 totaled $380,000 and for 1984 totaled $400,000. Nancy values inventories at the lower-of-average-cost-or-market.

REQUIRED Give the journal entry or entries to apply the lower-of-average-cost-or-market valuation method for 1984 assuming that (1) the holding loss is not reported separately; (2) inventory is directly reduced; and (3) periodic inventory procedures are used.

P9–8 The following data relate to the ending inventory of the Sebastian Clothing Store:

		PER UNIT	
INVENTORY CLASSIFICATION	QUANTITY	COST	MARKET
Men's suits			
Dress	100	$150	$175
Sport	200	125	110
Women's suits			
Dress	75	80	75
Leisure	50	50	60
Children's wear			
Dress	30	25	28
Play	20	10	8

REQUIRED

1. Determine ending inventory cost or market, whichever is lower:
   a. On an individual item basis
   b. By major classification of inventory
   c. On a total inventory basis
2. Give the necessary entry or entries to set up ending inventory and cost of goods sold expense for each of the above, assuming any necessary reduction from cost to market is to be reflected separately in the income statement. Assume that only one general ledger account is maintained for inventory.

P9–9 (CPA ADAPTED) The Allen Company is a wholesale distributor of automotive replacement parts. Initial amounts taken from Allen's accounting records are as follows:

Inventory at Dec. 31, 1984 (based on physical count of goods in Allen's warehouse on Dec. 31, 1984)	$1,250,000

Accounts payable at December 31, 1984:

VENDOR	TERMS	AMOUNT
Baker Company	2%, 10 days, net 30	$ 265,000
Charlie Company	Net 30	210,000
Dolly Company	Net 30	300,000
Eager Company	Net 30	225,000
Full Company	Net 30	—
Greg Company	Net 30	$1,000,000
Sales in 1984		$9,000,000

ADDITIONAL INFORMATION

1. Parts held on consignment from Charlie to Allen, the consignee, amounting to $155,000, were included in the physical count of goods in Allen's warehouse on December 31, 1984, and in accounts payable on December 31, 1984.
2. In the last week of 1984, $22,000 of parts that had been purchased from Full and paid for in December 1984 were sold and were appropriately recorded as sales of $28,000. The parts were included in the physical count of goods in Allen's warehouse on December 31, 1984, because the parts were on the loading dock waiting to be picked up by customers.
3. Parts in transit on December 31, 1984, to customers, shipped F.O.B. shipping point, on December 28, 1984, amounted to $34,000. The customers received the parts on January 6, 1985. Sales of $40,000 to the customers for the parts were recorded by Allen on January 2, 1985.
4. Retailers were holding $210,000 at cost ($250,000 at retail), of goods on consignment from Allen, the consignor, at their stores on December 31, 1984.
5. Goods were in transit from Greg to Allen on December 31, 1984. The cost of the goods was $25,000, and they were shipped F.O.B. shipping point on December 29, 1984.
6. A quarterly freight bill in the amount of $2,000 specifically relating to merchandise purchases in December 1984, all of which was still in the inventory at December 31, 1984, was received on January 3, 1985. The freight bill was not included in either the inventory or accounts payable on December 31, 1984.
7. All of the purchases from Baker occurred during the last 7 days of the year. These items have been recorded in accounts payable and accounted for in the physical inventory at cost before discount. Allen's policy is to pay invoices in time to take advantage of all cash discounts, adjust inventory accordingly, and record accounts payable, net of cash discounts.

REQUIRED Prepare a schedule of adjustments to the initial amounts using the following format. Show the effect, if any, of each of the transactions separately, and if the transactions would have no effect on the amount shown, state "none."

	INVENTORY	ACCOUNTS PAYABLE	SALES
Initial amount	$1,250,000	$1,000,000	$9,000,000
Adjustments—increase (decrease)			
1			
2			
3			
4			
5			
6			
7			
Total adjustments	_____	_____	_____
Adjusted amounts	$_____	_____	_____

P9–10 Stay-Right Corporation's accounting year ended on December 31, 1984. All revenue and expense accounts have been closed to the Revenue and Expense (Income) Summary account, but the latter account has not been closed, pending an examination of the accuracy of the accounts.

An examination of the corporation's records for 1984 led to discovery of the following facts:

1. Merchandise costing $970.46 was excluded from the December 31, 1984, inventory. The goods had been transferred to the shipping department for crating on December 30 to fill an order for goods to be shipped on January 2, 1985. The goods will be shipped F.O.B. destination.

2. Merchandise costing $450.67 was ordered on December 31, 1984, and was included in the December 31, 1984, inventory, although not received until January 3, 1985. The inventory was recorded in the corporation's records when received. This merchandise was shipped by the seller on December 30, 1984, F.O.B. shipping point.

3. Merchandise with an invoice price of $800.50 was received on December 27, 1984, and this amount was included in the ending inventory. As of January 3, 1985, $800.50 was credited to Purchase Returns and Allowances, and the merchandise was returned to the seller on this date.

4. On December 30, 1984, merchandise costing $545.87 was shipped by the seller, F.O.B. destination, and was received by Carbo Corporation on December 31. This merchandise was not included in the ending inventory because no invoice had been received from the seller.

5. Merchandise with an invoice price of $609.15 was received on December 31, 1984, with no entries being made until the condition of the merchandise could be determined, although these goods were included in the ending inventory. During the course of the examination, these goods were found to be undamaged and in accord with Stay-Right Corporation's order.

REQUIRED Prepare the journal entries that should be made as of December 31, 1984, as a result of the information above. If no entry is necessary, specify by indicating "none."

P9–11 The following data are taken from the records of the Chan Company:

YEAR-END	INVENTORY AT LIFO COST	INVENTORY AT MARKET	PURCHASES (NET) AT COST
1984	$15,000	$12,000	$100,000
1985	16,000	17,000	100,000
1986	14,000	11,000	100,000
1987	15,000	13,000	100,000

In the text we illustrated two different methods of recording inventory when the lower-of-cost-or-market (LCM) method is applied.

REQUIRED

1. Identify both methods of recording inventory at LCM and give an example using the data above for the year 1987.
2. Explain the procedure used to compute the "per unit" *market value* of any single *item* of inventory for LCM measurement purposes.
3. Explain the alternative ways of aggregating the individual inventory items once the LCM values are computed.
4. Briefly evaluate the objectivity of the LCM procedure.
5. Explain why, using generally accepted accounting principles, we use "market" values when they are less than "cost" but ignore them when market exceeds cost.

P9–12 The Quick and Easy Corporation has been in existence for 5 years. The merchandise cost data on a FIFO basis were as follows:

YEAR	BEGINNING INVENTORY	PURCHASES	ENDING INVENTORY	COST OF GOODS SOLD EXPENSE
1981	$ —	$190,000	$30,000	$160,000
1982	30,000	210,000	40,000	200,000
1983	40,000	240,000	50,000	230,000
1984	50,000	290,000	70,000	270,000
1985	70,000	250,000	60,000	260,000

A review was made of the 5-year period to determine what the results would have been using (1) the lower-of-cost-or-market procedure (with cost measured on a FIFO basis), and (2) the replacement-cost procedure (consistent use of year-end buying price as a basis for measuring inventory). The ending inventory amounts for the 5-year period, on a year-end replacement-cost basis, were as follows:

YEAR	AMOUNT
1981	$35,000
1982	38,000
1983	55,000
1984	60,000
1985	58,000

REQUIRED

1. Prepare calculations and tabulations to reflect the effects of the two alternative procedures mentioned.
2. Comment on each of the two procedures, indicating the arguments for and against each.

P9–13 (CMA ADAPTED) Kenny Company, a food wholesaler, supplies independent grocery stores in the immediate region. The company has a perpetual inventory system for all of its food products. The first-in, first-out (FIFO) method of inventory valuation is used to determine the cost of the inventory at the end of each month. Transactions for October 1984, the last month of Kenny's fiscal year, and other related information regarding two of the items (instant coffee, sugar) carried by Kenny are as follows:

	INSTANT COFFEE	SUGAR
Standard unit of packaging	Case containing 24 one-pound jars	Baler containing 12 five-pound bags
Inventory, 10/1/84	1,200 cases @ $53.22 per case	600 balers @ $6.50 per baler
Purchases	10/10/84—1,600 cases @ $56.40 per case plus freight of $480	10/5/84—640 balers @ $5.76 per baler plus freight of $320
	10/20/84—1,600 cases @ $57.00 per case plus freight of $480	10/16/84—640 balers @ $5.40 per baler plus freight of $320
		10/24/84—640 balers @ $5.04 per baler plus freight of $320
Purchase terms	2/10, n/30, F.O.B. shipping point	Net 30 days, F.O.B. shipping point
October sales	3,400 cases @ $76.00 per case	2,200 balers @ $7.80 per baler
Returns and allowances	A customer returned 50 cases that had been shipped in error. The customer's account was credited for $3,800.	As the 10/16/84 purchase was being unloaded, it was discovered that 20 balers were damaged. A representative of the trucking firm confirmed the damage and the balers were discarded. Kenny received credit of $108 for the merchandise and $10 for the freight.
Inventory values including freight and net of purchase discounts, 10/31/84		
Most recent quoted price	$56.65 per case	$5.30 per baler
Net realizable value	$60.80 per case	$5.20 per baler
Net realizable value less a normal markup of 12.5%	$53.20 per case	$4.55 per baler

Kenny's sales terms are 1/10, n/30, F.O.B. shipping point. Kenny records all purchases net of purchase discounts and takes all purchase discounts.

REQUIRED

1. Calculate the number of units in inventory and the related unit cost for instant coffee and sugar as of October 31, 1984.
2. Kenny Company applies the lower-of-cost-or-market rule in valuing its year-end inventory. Calculate the total dollar amount of the inventory for instant coffee and sugar applying the lower-of-cost-or-market rule on an individual product basis.
3. Could Kenny Company apply the lower-of-cost-or-market rule to groups of products or the inventory as a whole rather than on an individual product basis? Explain your answer.

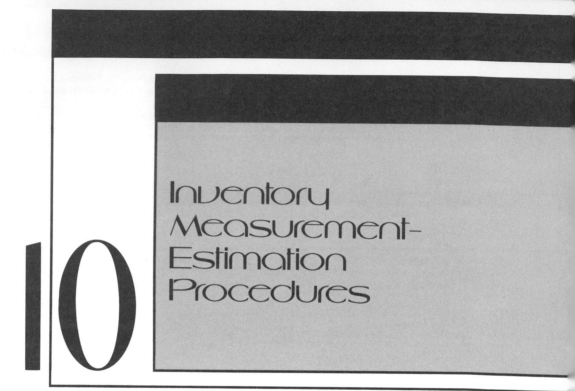

Inventory Measurement-Estimation Procedures

OVERVIEW

In Chapter 9 we covered the basic inventory measurement procedures applied in most financial reports. Each method required a physical inventory count and invoice costs. These requirements, combined with the absence of continuous information in periodic inventory systems regarding inventory value and cost of sales to date, are limitations of accounting systems that may impede the timeliness (relevance) of information. One way to view this information problem is that every entity would like to have all the information that a perpetual inventory system provides, but the incremental cost of going from a periodic system to a pure perpetual system is either impractical or otherwise unjustifiable. As a result of the significant information flow and cost differences between these two forms of **discrete inventory measurement systems,** several variations of **inventory estimation systems** that have been developed can provide many of the same advantages of the perpetual inventory system at a lower cost. Inventory estimation systems, the subject of this chapter, are not only useful to internal users of accounting data in managing and controlling the entity but are also permissible for external financial reporting *and* for income measurement for tax purposes in certain instances.

The decision to use or not to use one of the estimation methods discussed here instead of one of the discrete methods discussed in Chapter 9 will frequently involve an evaluation of the trade-offs in the qualities of relevance and reliability. The need for timely (relevant) information must be evaluated with due consideration given to the reliability (representativeness and precision) of the information within a cost-benefit framework. Careful examination of estimation methods by managers who design accounting information systems may well explain the recent increase in the use of inventory estimation systems. It is likely that inventory estimation systems will become increasingly important unless major changes occur in the tax laws, the rate of inflation, or the cost of perpetual systems.

THE BASIS FOR ESTIMATION SYSTEMS

An entity might have any number of reasons for wanting to use inventory estimation systems. **Cost** and **complexity** are two major considerations. To better understand the incremental cost of many of the estimation methods discussed in this chapter, let us first examine a very basic low-cost system that is used by many entities.

Consider the case of a retail automobile-parts supplier that carries thousands of small and large parts in inventory. This supplier makes frequent use of customer special orders from wholesalers for the many thousands of less common parts not carried in inventory. The business is run by Mr. Maxwell and his two children. All three are unfamiliar with accounting techniques. Sales of any given inventory item are inconsistent, and some inventory might not sell for a long time and then suddenly "turn over" several times in a single accounting period. It is almost impossible to forecast the demand for many of the inventory items that are carried in stock.

Mr. Maxwell does not keep detailed records but does take a physical inventory once a year, which enables him to measure ending (and, therefore, beginning) inventory. To price out the thousands of items in stock, Maxwell uses the price books he receives from the vendors of the various inventory items. The price books, which are updated on an irregular basis, quote the wholesale price that Maxwell pays for each item, and the suggested retail price. This pricing system assumes that whatever Maxwell has in ending inventory was purchased at the wholesale price quoted in the most recent price book.

Essentially the procedures that Maxwell uses represent a FIFO cost-flow assumption applied to a periodic system. Net purchases are measured by totaling the cash and checks paid to vendors and couriers, and adding the increase (or deducting the decrease) in the "unpaid invoices" liability balance from the beginning of the period to the end of the period. Once invoices are paid, they are not retained by Maxwell. The cost of actually operating this system is fairly low. However, the cost in terms of lost sales, excessive order costs, excessive inventory carrying costs, unnecessarily high income taxes, and less efficient planning and control due to a lack of *timely* information regarding inventories and cost of sales might be very high.

Many companies of various sizes and purposes incur some or all of the costs mentioned above without realizing it. These costs are not "out-of-pocket" or incremental costs that can easily be measured. Such costs are measurable only in the sense of measuring *cost savings* that result *after* efforts to improve the inventory system have been made. We shall first discuss some rather simple and low-cost estimation procedures designed to address *some* of the inefficiencies noted above in the Maxwell case and then progress to the more complex and somewhat more costly methods. Note that the following illustrations will deal with procedures typically suited for entities with relatively unsophisticated periodic inventory systems that provide managers or owners with information about purchases for a period. These procedures are able to provide reliable measures regarding inventory and cost of goods sold only when a physical inventory is taken.

Gross Margin Estimation Method

A very simple way to estimate inventory and cost of goods sold for interim purposes is by a systematic evaluation of the relationship between costs and selling prices. Consider a case where selling prices are always determined by taking the cost of merchandise and adding 100 percent, so that selling prices are 200 percent of cost. If such a pricing system were always employed, the following relationship would hold:

Sales		1.00$
Beginning inventory	X	
Purchases (net)	Y	
Cost of goods available	Z	
Ending inventory	W	
Cost of goods sold		.50$
Gross margin		.50$

where $ = sales dollars
     X = known from last physical inventory
     Y = known from invoices totaled for current period
     $Z = X + Y$
     $W = Z - .5$$

For most companies, it is probably unrealistic to assume that *all* inventory is priced at the same rate of "markup" on cost. However, the **gross margin estimation method** might still be applicable in certain cases. Assume that an entity has many different markup rates. If the sales register (or cash register) and the price tags on merchandise are designed properly, sales may be accumulated for each rate of markup. This would enable the entity to use the gross margin method when more than one margin rate is present.

Multimargin example To illustrate the **multimargin** application, assume that Maxwell sells motor oil that is marked up 10 percent over cost. A price tag on the oil

EXHIBIT
10–1

ESTIMATING COST OF GOODS SOLD—GROSS MARGIN METHOD

(1) MARKUP DESIGNATION	(2) SALES PRICE AS A PERCENT OF COST	(3) TOTAL SALES FOR PERIOD	(4) ESTIMATED COST OF SALES FOR PERIOD (COL. 3 ÷ COL. 2)
A	110%	$ 6,843	$ 6,221
B	120	927	773
F	150	3,450	2,300
G	160	3,260	2,037
K	180	1,400	778
M	200	884	442
		$16,764	$12,551

$16,764/$12,551 = 133.567% overall markup.
$12,551/$16.764 = 74.88 costs as a percent of sales overall.

might have, in addition to the price, a letter or a number that would identify the oil as a 10 percent markup item. Cash register records (tapes, printouts, and so on) identify each sale by its markup rate, and each register provides total sales by each markup category. At the end of 1 month, Maxwell has a sales summary from his registers and estimated cost analysis as illustrated in Exhibit 10–1. Assume that Maxwell started the month with no inventory and purchased $16,500 worth of merchandise (including freight-in, and so on) during the month. How profitable were operations and how much inventory is on hand? The gross margin method may be used to let Maxwell know that gross profit for the month was about $4,213 and that about $3,949 of inventory is on hand:

Partial Income Statement		
	DOLLARS	**AS A %** **OF SALES**
Sales	$16,764	100.00%
Beginning inventory	$ 0	
Purchases (net)	16,500	
Cost of goods available	16,500	
Ending inventory[a]	3,949	
Cost of goods sold[b]	12,551	(74.88%)
Gross margin[c]	$ 4,213	(25.12%)

[a] $16,500 − $12,551.
[b] Estimated per Exhibit 10–1.
[c] $16,764 − $12,551.

The gross margin method provides a relatively low-cost means of estimating inventory and cost of goods sold for interim periods with relatively little information and few requirements in terms of pricing procedures or accounting records. Note that the overall gross margin relationship from Exhibit 10–1 indicated a (weighted-average) markup of about 133 percent. If this overall relationship generated by the sales mix seems to hold true throughout the year, it may not be necessary to compute the weighted-average margin each subperiod. Also, for a seasonal business with fluctuations in sales and product mix, if the overall margin is relatively constant from year to year for a specific season, it may not be necessary to compute the weighted-average margin each subperiod.

The Retail Method

The instability of the pricing system is one of the principal limitations of the gross margin approach to measuring inventory and cost of goods sold, **particularly for retailers** who frequently have sales that temporarily alter selling prices. To compensate for the probable fluctuations in selling prices, the retail inventory procedure was developed as a method for retailers to *estimate* inventory and cost of sales. Once again, the relationship between selling prices and costs is the basis for the estimation procedure. The following additional details are required of the record-keeping system:

1. *Additional markups.* A system must be maintained so that markups greater than the normal amount are accounted for in a total sales-dollars measure. For example, if a shoe department normally adds 30 percent to cost to obtain selling price but carries one line of shoes where the markup is 50 percent of selling price, the total value of

the 20 percent additional markup (in terms of selling prices) must be accounted for. Also, sales price increases may result in additional markups.

2. *Markup cancellations.* A system must be maintained to account for cancellations of additional markups, if any. These first two items combined enable the retailer to measure **net additional markups,** which adds to the normal markup percentage.

3. *Markdowns.* A system must be maintained to measure markdowns from normal selling prices due to sales or downward price adjustments.

4. *Markdown cancellations.* These cancellations of markdowns must also be measured.

5. *Employee discounts.* These represent a special category of markdowns that are normally accounted for in order to measure total employee compensation for internal purposes.

Basic retail inventory framework With these additional details, the format illustrated in Exhibit 10–2 may be used to compute the two most common estimation measures for the retail inventory method. Note that the "cost" column measures cost of goods available for sale ($CAS) as reviewed in Chapters 3 and 9. This measure is simply beginning inventory *plus* net purchases. The "retail" column measures the beginning inventory and net purchases at their selling price, and therefore net additional markups, net markdowns, and employee discounts (all stated in terms of selling prices) are used to determine the "retail value of goods available for sale." Note also that certain items used to compute *cost* of goods available do *not* have a

EXHIBIT
10–2

FRAMEWORK OF RETAIL INVENTORY ESTIMATION PROCEDURES

	COST	RETAIL	
Beginning inventory	$ C	$ R	
+ Purchases	$ C	$ R	
+ Freight-in	$ C		
+ Additional markups		$ R	
− Markup cancellations		$ R	
− Purchase returns	$ C	$ R	
− Purchase allowances	$ C		
− Purchase discounts	$ C		
	$CAS	$RAG	The conventional retail ratio (or LCM ratio) is computed at this point: $CAS ÷ $RAG = LCM%
− Markdowns		$ R	
+ Markdown cancellations		$ R	
− Employee discounts		$ R	
	$CAS	$RAN	The cost ratio is computed at this point: $CAS ÷ $RAN = C%
− Net sales		−$ R	
Ending inventory at retail (EIR)		$EIR	

($EIR) × (LCM%) = Ending inventory at "LCM" (estimate)
($EIR) × (C%) = Ending inventory at "Cost" (estimate)

Note: $CAS less ending inventory = Cost of goods sold

Key: C = "Cost" dollar measure
R = Retail dollar measure
CAS = Cost of goods available for sale
RAG = Retail goods available—gross selling prices
RAN = Retail goods available—net selling prices

retail value counterpart. Although such things as freight-in are considered in establishing a normal markup percentage, they do not have a retail value in and of themselves.

The retail method may measure the ratio (relationship) between cost and retail values in several different ways. The two most common ratios—the **conventional retail ratio,** which is sometimes referred to as the **LCM ratio,** and the **cost ratio**—are illustrated in Exhibit 10–2. The estimate of ending inventory under the LCM method is found by taking ending inventory at retail prices (EIR) and multiplying it by the *LCM ratio.* The estimate of ending inventory under the cost method is found by multiplying ending inventory at retail by the *cost ratio.*

Comparison of LCM and cost ratios The LCM ratio is always lower than the cost ratio by design, because (as illustrated) the net markdowns and employee discounts are omitted from the retail subtotal ($RAG) used in the ratio. Therefore, the de nominator in the LCM ratio ($RAG) will always be greater than the denominator in the cost ratio ($RAN), and the numerator ($CAS) will always be the same in both ratios. Hence, **LCM is a more conservative estimate** of the cost of ending inventory by design. The conservatism is often warranted in retail businesses because of inventory losses caused by theft or damaged goods. The cost ratio, however, provides a *best estimate* of what the cost of ending inventory *should be* at the end of an accounting period, since it considers all aspects of the cost to retail relationship.

To estimate the inventory lost during a period, most retailers would compare the ending inventory based on the physical count with the ending inventory based on the retail inventory estimate by using a cost ratio, with the difference between the two being the lost inventory due to damage, theft, and so on.

To illustrate, consider the following Manegold Ski Shop data for the quarter ending March 31, 1984:

	3/31/84 LEDGER BALANCES
Accounts:	
Inventory (1/1/84)	$ 45,320 Debit
Purchases	389,657 Debit
Freight-in	15,422 Debit
Purchase discounts lost	1,481 Debit
Purchase returns	3,560 Credit
Sales	704,106 Credit
Sales returns and allowances	18,701 Debit
Additional data:	
Additional markups	$ 4,835
Additional markup cancellations	1,600
Markdowns	35,705
Markdown cancellations	10,798
Employee discounts taken	10,674
Inventory (1/1/84) at retail value	78,400
Purchases at retail	671,505
Purchase returns at retail	6,000

The multiple solution shown in Exhibit 10–3 computes both the conventional, or LCM estimate, and the cost ratio estimate of ending inventory. Following are the partial income statements under both alternatives:

```
                    Partial Income Statements
                    Quarter Ended March 31, 1984

                              LCM BASIS          COST BASIS

Sales (net)                        $685,405          $685,405
Beginning inventory    $ 45,320           $ 45,320
Purchases (net)         403,000            403,000
Goods available         448,320            448,320
Ending inventory (estimated) 15,728         16,515
  Cost of goods sold              432,592           431,805
  Gross margin                   $252,813          $253,600
```

Both of the retail methods illustrated are used primarily to provide information on ending inventory and cost of goods sold when the pricing system is subject to frequent changes due to special sales, price changes, and so on. Like the gross margin method, the retail method does require some common markup basis as a starting point. Large retailers frequently apply the retail method on a department-by-department basis because a home furnishings department, for example, may have a different basic markup rate than women's fashions or some other department. The principal difference between the gross margin and the retail method lies in the additional precision and pricing flexibility provided by the net additional markup and net markdown data of the retail method.

Retail cost-flow assumption What basic cost-flow assumption is employed in the retail methods illustrated above? This complex question must be answered in two parts. The *retail* dollars are on a FIFO basis in that the ending inventory value at retail is stated at current (end-of-period) prices. The markup and markdown data permit the retail values to change in such a way that the inventories are at their current retail prices. The *cost* values, however, are *average costs,* including historical purchase prices from prior years as well as the current year's purchase prices. The ratios are, therefore, a mixture of average costs and FIFO retail measurements. For conve-

EXHIBIT 10–3

```
                    MANEGOLD SKI SHOP
                  Estimating 3/31/84 Inventory

                            COST        RETAIL

Inventory (1/1/84)        $ 45,320     $ 78,400
Purchases                  389,657      671,565
Freight-in                  15,422
Purchase discount lost       1,481
Purchase returns            (3,560)      (6,000)
Net additional markups                    3,235
                          $448,320     $747,200      LCM RATIO:
                                                     $448,320/$747,200 = .60
Net markdowns                           (24,907)
Employee discounts                      (10,674)
Total available           $448,320     $711,619      COST RATIO:
                                                     $448,320/$711,619 = .63
Net sales                              (685,405)
Ending inventory at retail             $ 26,214

LCM estimate of ending inventory:  (.6) × (26,214) = $15,728
Cost estimate of ending inventory: (.63) × (26,214) = $16,515
```

nience, we shall refer to both of the estimates illustrated above as FIFO approximations of ending inventory.[1]

Variations of retail inventory method   Some variations in the two primary retail inventory methods illustrated above may be found in practice. One common variation actually estimates the dollar value of the "shrinkage" in inventory due to theft and damaged goods. To illustrate, refer to the Manegold Ski Shop data and further assume that Manegold estimates shrinkage at 0.3 percent (.003) of net sales dollars each period based on historical data. Using this estimate in combination with the cost ratio, Manegold would use the following estimate of ending inventory at March 31, 1984:

	COST	RETAIL
Beginning inventory	$ 45,320	$ 78,400
Net purchases	403,000	665,565
Net markups		3,235
Net markdowns		(24,907)
Employee discounts		(10,674)
	$448,320	$711,619 ←——Cost ratio = .63
Net sales		(685,405)
Estimated shrinkage		(2,056)
Ending inventory at retail		$ 24,158
Cost estimate of ending inventory – .63 × ($24,158) – $15,220		

Other common variations involve taking a cost-to-retail ratio using subtotals different from those illustrated in Exhibit 10–2. These variations may be based on circumstances that are peculiar to the operations of a given retailer.

LIFO COST-FLOW ESTIMATION PROCEDURES

The gross margin and retail inventory estimation procedures solve some of the deficiencies identified earlier for periodic inventory systems. However, these two estimation systems still have the disadvantage of not applying a LIFO cost-flow approximation in their estimation of ending inventory. Because of the lower income that results from LIFO cost flows in periods of rising prices and because of the tax advantages that result from using LIFO for tax purposes, several *LIFO estimation procedures that are acceptable for tax purposes* have been developed. The two primary LIFO estimation methods are (1) dollar-value LIFO and (2) LIFO retail. Both of these LIFO estimation methods make use of price-level information to determine the estimated LIFO value of ending inventory.[2] The two procedures are very similar, employing the same concept of identifying inventory layers by using price levels. The following example of dollar-value LIFO will be used to illustrate the similarity between the two LIFO estimation methods.

---

[1] Some might argue that both sides of the ratio represent averages, and that the retail cost flow is best classified as an average cost-flow method. The important point is that it is *not* the same as either average cost or FIFO costing as illustrated in Chapter 9. It is probably most appropriate, therefore, to use a different name, such as the "pox flow"!

[2] The price level index data may be obtained a number of ways. Methods of index development are covered in Appendix D. LIFO retail may also be applied, ignoring price-level changes.

Dollar-value LIFO is a procedure that employs the concept of constant-dollar accounting (see Chapter 6) with the concept of LIFO cost flows (see Chapter 9) in a periodic inventory system. The Internal Revenue Service first recognized the dollar-value concept as being relevant to certain industries for tax purposes in the 1930s, and by 1949 the dollar-value LIFO method was available to all taxpaying entities.

The following eight steps illustrate the procedural aspects of the dollar-value LIFO estimation process.

STEP 1 Consider the following year-end inventory values for a 5-year period:

END OF YEAR	ENDING INVENTORY AT YEAR-END PRICES	PRICE LEVEL
1980	$ 72,000	1.00
1981	100,000	1.25
1982	175,000	1.40
1983	110,400	1.15
1984	90,000	1.20

STEP 2 For illustration purposes, assume that the base layer of the first year (1980) is represented as follows:

LAYER	BY$	
1980	$72,000	
	$72,000	1980 layer in terms of index 1.00 dollars

This box represents the 1980 base layer of inventory stated in 1980 (index 1.00) dollars, or 1980 inventory at "base-year dollars" (BY$).

Common-dollar measures The 1981 ending inventory is initially measured at $100,000 based on 1981 year-end prices. At this point we wish to apply the LIFO concept to restate the $100,000 measurement, which is a FIFO valuation, to a LIFO measurement. To do so, we need to ask the question, How much more inventory is there (if any) in the $100,000 1981 dollar measurement than in the $72,000 1980 dollar measurement that we started the year (1981) with? To answer this question requires a restatement of one or both of the ending inventory values to **common-dollar,** or equal-dollar, measures. For consistency with actual practice, we shall convert both dollar measures to **base-year (index 1.00) common dollars.** The 1980 ending inventory measure of $72,000 is already stated in index 1.00 dollars and, therefore, needs no restatement in this case. The 1981 ending inventory value of $100,000 *restated* in terms of index 1.00 dollars or base-year dollars (BY$) would be $80,000. This is computed by dividing $100,000 by the 1981 price index of 1.25 ($100,000/1.25 = $80,000).

STEP 3 Now it is possible to answer the question, How much more inventory is there at the end of 1981? The increase in 1981 inventory of $8,000 base-year dollars ($80,000 BY$ − $72,000 BY$) may be represented as follows:

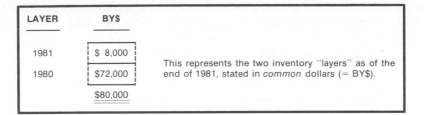

LAYER	BY$	
1981	$ 8,000	This represents the two inventory "layers" as of the
1980	$72,000	end of 1981, stated in *common* dollars (= BY$).
	$80,000	

Note that using index 1.00 as the common-dollar measure is *not* necessary but is generally accepted in practice. Any common-dollar measure would enable us to determine the real change in inventory. For example, converting both 1980 and 1981 inventory measures to 1981 dollars would result in the following:

$$1981 \quad \$100,000 \times \frac{1.25}{1.25} = \$100,000$$

$$1980 \quad \$ 72,000 \times \frac{1.25}{1.00} = \underline{-\ 90,000}$$

$$\underline{\$\ 10,000} \quad \text{1981 increase in terms of } \underline{\text{1981 dollars}}$$

The remainder of this chapter will use index 1.00 (base-year) dollars as the common-dollar measure in order to avoid confusion and to be consistent with practice. Keep in mind, however, that the common-dollar measure used is *not* relevant in and of itself. It simply allows us to measure real changes in inventory in order to layer the ending FIFO inventory measurement ($100,000 for 1981 in this example) in such a way that a LIFO estimate of ending inventory may be made.

Pricing LIFO layers

STEP 4 To restate the two inventory layers as measured in base-year dollars ($8,000 and $72,000) to their appropriate LIFO values, we next multiply each layer by the appropriate price level in effect for the year that it was added to inventory, as follows:

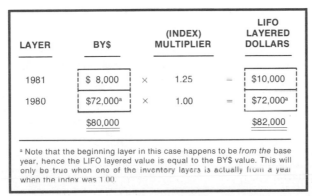

LAYER	BY$	(INDEX) MULTIPLIER	LIFO LAYERED DOLLARS
1981	$ 8,000	× 1.25 =	$10,000
1980	$72,000ᵃ	× 1.00 =	$72,000ᵃ
	$80,000		$82,000

ᵃ Note that the beginning layer in this case happens to be *from the* base year, hence the LIFO layered value is equal to the BY$ value. This will only be true when one of the inventory layers is actually from a year when the index was 1.00.

STEP 5 In step 1 we started with a 1981 ending inventory value of $100,000, and from the results in step 4 we have converted to an $82,000 LIFO estimation measure of ending inventory. This $18,000 decrease would result in $9,000 in tax savings assuming a 50 percent tax rate, which makes the dollar-value LIFO method attractive to many businesses with periodic FIFO systems. The $18,000 difference between FIFO and dollar-value LIFO may be reconciled as follows:

$72,000	1980 layer at 1980 prices
× 1.25	Index change from 1980 to 1981
$90,000	1980 layer at 1981 year-end index

Therefore:

$90,000	
−72,000	
$18,000	Difference between inventory as stated in step 1 and as restated in step 4

When compared with FIFO the dollar-value LIFO method would thus result in lower measures of ending inventory, higher measures of cost of goods sold, and lower measures of net income when applied to inventories that have increasing costs.

Additional LIFO layer

STEP 6 Continuing with the 1982 year-end computation of dollar-value LIFO inventory measurement, begin with the BY$ value of the 1982 *beginning* inventory:

LAYER	BY$	
1981	$ 8,000	
1980	$72,000	
	$80,000	BY$ for 1982 beginning inventory

To compute the value of the 1982 ending inventory at BY$, we again divide the **year-end value** at year-end (1982) prices by the year-end index which restates the ending inventory in BY$: ($175,000 ÷ 1.40 = $125,000). In terms of base-year dollars, we have added $45,000 to our inventory during 1982 ($125,000 − $80,000). We can now illustrate the 1982 ending inventory at base-year values and at LIFO layered values as follows:

LAYER	BY$	(INDEX) MULTIPLIER			LIFO LAYERED DOLLARS
1982	$ 45,000	×	1.40	=	$ 63,000
1981	$ 8,000	×	1.25	=	$ 10,000
1980	$ 72,000	×	1.00	=	$ 72,000
	$125,000				$145,000

STEP 7 To reconcile the $30,000 difference between the 1982 inventory at year-end prices in step 1 ($175,000) and the dollar-value LIFO layered value ($145,000) computed in step 6:

$ 72,000	1980 layer at 1980 prices
× 1.40	Index change from 1980 to 1982
$100,800	1980 layer at 1982 prices
− 72,000	
$ 28,800	Increase in price of 1980 layer
10,000	1981 layer at 1981 prices
× 1.12	Index change from 1981 to 1982 (1.40/1.25)
$ 11,200	1981 layer at 1982 prices
− 10,000	
$ 1,200	Increase in price of 1981 layer
$ 1,200	Increase in price of 1981 layer due to price-level change
+ 28,800	Increase in price of 1980 layer due to price-level change
$ 30,000	Total increase due to price change

Decrease in LIFO layer The dollar-value LIFO procedure illustrated above builds inventory layers on a LIFO basis. When there is a real decline in inventory, the layers are dissolved on a LIFO basis as well. Consider the decline that occurs during 1983.

STEP 8 The 1983 ending inventory at 1983 year-end (FIFO) prices is converted to BY$ as follows: ($110,400 ÷ 1.15 = $96,000). Thus the base-year dollar value of the 1983 ending inventory is $96,000. Recall that the *beginning* inventory stated in base-year dollars *was* as follows:

LAYER	BY$
1982	$ 45,000
1981	$ 8,000
1980	$ 72,000
	$125,000

To arrive at the 1983 ending inventory at base-year dollars, we would add the $72,000 BY$ from 1980, the $8,000 BY$ from 1981, and $16,000 of the $45,000 BY$ from 1982 (total = $96,000):

LAYER	BY$ 1/1/83	LAYER	BY$ 12/31/83
1982	$ 29,000	1982	$ 16,000
	$ 16,000		
1981	$ 8,000	1981	$ 8,000
1980	$ 72,000	1980	$ 72,000
	$125,000		$ 96,000

To compute the LIFO layered value for the 1983 ending inventory, we again multiply each BY$ layer by the appropriate index:

LAYER	BY$	(INDEX) MULTIPLIER			LIFO LAYERED DOLLARS
1982	$ 16,000	×	1.40	=	$ 22,400
1981	$ 8,000	×	1.25	=	$ 10,000
1980	$ 72,000	×	1.00	=	$ 72,000
	$ 96,000				$104,400

The 1983 ending LIFO layered inventory value is $104,400.

The 1983 price index of 1.15 is not used to measure the dollar-value LIFO inventory because there is no 1983 layer in 1983 ending inventory. For the example illustrated, there will never be a 1983 inventory layer under the dollar-value LIFO approach. The same will be true of other years when there is a *real* decline in inventory. Note, however, that a real decline *cannot* be determined by looking at FIFO values such as those in step 1 but must be determined only after converting to common-dollar values.

LIFO Retail   The LIFO retail method enables retailers to estimate LIFO values within the basic retail inventory framework considered in Exhibit 10–2. LIFO retail is basically a combination of procedures used in the retail method and the dollar-value LIFO method, with slight modification.

Modified cost ratio   The retail aspect of LIFO retail involves the same process illustrated earlier except that the ratio calculation is different. Instead of a cost ratio or an LCM ratio, a **modified cost ratio** is computed in the LIFO retail method. This modified cost ratio is computed by taking the ratio of the current-year (*only*) cost dollars to the current-year (only) retail dollars. Using the same data as in Exhibit 10–3, the modified cost ratio (MCR) would be:

	COST	RETAIL	
Total available	$448,320	$711,619	
Less beginning inventory	45,320	78,400	
Current-year dollars	$403,000	$633,219 ←	MCR = $403,000/$633,219 = .6364

This ratio represents the relationship between cost measures and retail measures for a specific year and does not mix in the beginning inventory dollars, which are stated in dollar measures of prior years. The **MCR is an annual ratio,** associated with a particular year only, and is useful for applying the LIFO layered concept to inventory. This ratio may also be used without price index data to estimate inventory.

Application of LIFO retail   Given an understanding of the modified cost ratio measurement illustrated above, the combining of retail inventory and the dollar-

EXHIBIT
10–4

	IDENTICAL CORPORATION					
	LIFO Retail					
	For the Years Ended December 31					
	1988		**1989**		**1990**	
	COST	RETAIL	COST	RETAIL	COST	RETAIL
Beginning inventory	$ 0	$ 0	$?	$ 72,000	$?	$100,000
Purchases (net)	247,000	385,000	329,000	516,000	423,040	697,000
Net added markups		20,000		18,000		26,000
Net markdowns		(25,000)		(49,000)		(62,000)
	$247,000	$380,000		$557,000		$761,000
Net sales		−308,000		−457,000		−586,000
Ending inventory at retail		$ 72,000		$100,000		$175,000

value method is relatively straightforward. To illustrate, consider the retail data for the Identical Corporation in Exhibit 10–4. Identical has prepared computations of the ending inventory at retail for the years 1988–1990 but has yet to measure ending inventory at cost. The following table of ending inventory at retail values for the 1988–1990 period, along with some retail price index data, is provided for the same period:

YEAR	ENDING INVENTORY AT YEAR-END PRICES	RETAIL PRICE INDEX
1988	$ 72,000	1.00
1989	100,000	1.25
1990	175,000	1.40

You may have noticed that these data are virtually the same as the data in step 1 of the dollar-value LIFO example on page 354 for the years 1980–1982. In the earlier dollar-value LIFO example, the tabled values were **dollars of cost measured on a FIFO basis**. In the LIFO retail example above, the tabled values are **retail dollars measured on a FIFO basis**.[3]

Measuring LIFO retail layers The same price-level adjustment procedure illustrated for the dollar-value method is used for the LIFO retail inventory method, with one *additional step* required to convert from LIFO layered **retail** dollars to LIFO layered **cost** dollars, using the appropriate annual modified cost ratios. For 1988, this process may be illustrated as follows:

LAYER	BY$	(RETAIL INDEX) MULTIPLIER	LIFO LAYERED RETAIL DOLLARS	MCR	LIFO LAYERED COST DOLLARS
1988	$72,000	× 1.00	$72,000	× .65	$46,800
	$72,000				$46,800

[3] Given the assumption that the retail system of measuring all net additional markups, net markdowns, and so on, is working perfectly, the total sales price of the goods on hand at year-end should equal the "ending inventory at retail." Hence, ending inventory at retail is based on current selling prices providing a FIFO flow of retail dollars.

The MCR of .65 can be computed from the data in Exhibit 10–4 as follows:

$$\boxed{1988}\quad \$247,000/\$380,000 = .65$$

The MCRs for 1989 and 1990 are:

$$\boxed{1989}\quad \$329,000/(\$557,000 - \$72,000) = .68$$
$$\boxed{1990}\quad \$423,040/(\$761,000 - \$100,000) = .64$$

To complete the analysis of the Identical example, consider the following computations as of 1989 and 1990:

Computation for 1989

LAYER	BY$	RETAIL INDEX	LIFO LAYERED RETAIL DOLLARS	MCRs	LIFO LAYERED COST DOLLARS
1989	$ 8,000	× 1.25	$10,000	× .68	$ 6,800
1988	$72,000	× 1.00	$72,000	× .65	$46,800
	$80,000[a]				$53,600

[a] $80,000 BY$ = $100,000/1.25.

Computation for 1990

LAYER	BY$	RETAIL INDEX	LIFO LAYERED RETAIL DOLLARS	MCRs	LIFO LAYERED COST DOLLARS
1990	$ 45,000	× 1.40	$63,000	× .64	$40,320
1989	$ 8,000	× 1.25	$10,000	× .68	$ 6,800
1988	$ 72,000	× 1.00	$72,000	× .65	$46,800
	$125,000[a]				$93,920

[a] $125,000 BY$ = $175,000/1.40

To summarize, the partial income statements for 1988–1990 are as follows:

IDENTICAL CORPORATION
Partial Income Statements
For the Years Ended December 31

	1988		1989		1990	
Sales (net)		$308,000		$457,000		$586,000
Beginning inventory	$ 0		$ 46,800		$ 53,600	
Purchases	247,000		329,800		423,040	
Available	247,000		376,600		476,640	
Ending inventory	46,800		53,600		93,920	
Cost of sales		200,200		323,000		382,720
Gross margin		$107,800		$134,000		$203,280

Analysis of LIFO estimation methods The dollar-value LIFO and the LIFO retail methods both take advantage of the concept of price-level adjustments to convert from a natural FIFO cost flow to a LIFO cost flow for periodic inventory systems. These methods, although somewhat complex, are relatively low cost ways of obtaining the tax benefits of LIFO without a sophisticated inventory costing system. The complexity of these two LIFO estimation procedures has probably prevented many small businesses that have no technical accounting expertise from taking advantage of the tax savings provided by such estimation procedures.

Converting from Retail to LIFO Retail

To convert from a regular retail inventory method to a LIFO retail inventory method, the cost ratio or LCM ratio used in regular retail inventory procedures must be replaced by the MCR ratio used in the LIFO retail procedures for the beginning inventory measurement in the year of the change. To illustrate, assume that the conventional (LCM) retail inventory method was used to measure inventory for the Waxing Company for 1983:

	COST	RETAIL	
Beginning inventory	$ 55,000	$ 150,000	
Purchases (net)	520,000	940,000	
Net additional markups		60,000	
	$575,000	$1,150,000 ←	LCM ratio = $575,000/$1,150,000 = .50
Net markdowns		(25,000)	
Available	$575,000	$1,125,000	
Sales		(840,000)	
Ending inventory—at retail		$ 285,000	
		× .5	
Ending inventory—at LCM		$ 142,500	

To convert to the LIFO retail method in 1984, it is first necessary to recompute the $142,500 ending 1983 inventory measure to a new ending measurement by using an MCR for 1983. This computation is made as follows:

1983 MCR	COST	RETAIL	
Available	$575,000	$1,125,000	
Less beginning inventory	− 55,000	− 150,000	1983 MCR:
1983 dollars	$520,000	$ 975,000 ←	$520,000/$975,000 = .5333

1983 RESTATED ENDING INVENTORY		
Ending inventory at retail		$285,000
MCR		× .5333
Ending inventory at cost (revised)		$152,000

Note that the use of the MCR instead of the LCM ratio *increases* 1983 ending inventory by $9,500 ($152,000 − $142,500).

Next assume that the following data were available for Waxing for 1984 *before* the change to LIFO retail:

	COST	RETAIL
Beginning inventory	$142,500	$ 285,000
Purchases (net)	603,200	1,080,000
Net additional markups		80,000
Net markdowns		(35,000)
Sales (net)		1,000,000
Additional data:		
Retail price index 1/1/84 = 1.00		
Retail price index 12/31/84 = 1.15		

To account for the change to LIFO retail, the 1984 beginning inventory of $142,500 must be adjusted, and then the LIFO retail procedure illustrated earlier is applied. For Waxing, the following entry would be recorded:

12/31/84	Inventory (1/1/84)	9,500	
	Effect of change to LIFO		9,500

This adjustment step might be viewed as an additional cost of switching to LIFO retail because it will normally *increase* beginning inventory in the year of the switch. Also, the conversion to LIFO normally brings the book income measurement and the tax income measurement in line with one another. If different inventory measurements were being used for book and for tax purposes prior to the switch to LIFO, there may be some tax consequences that need to be accounted for as well. Note that the Effect of Change to LIFO account in the above entry is an income statement account. It does *not* require separate disclosure as does the cumulative catch-up effect from accounting changes, which appears separately below extraordinary items. The computation of the LIFO retail ending inventory at LIFO layered cost would be made as shown at the top of page 363.

EXHIBIT 10-5

WAXING CORPORATION

Comparative Income Statement
For the Year Ended December 31, 1984

	ASSUMING CHANGE TO LIFO RETAIL		ASSUMING NO CHANGE FROM LCM RETAIL	
Net sales		$1,000,000		$1,000,000
Cost of goods sold:				
Beginning inventory	$152,000		$142,500	
Net purchases	603,200		603,200	
Goods available	755,200		745,700	
Ending inventory	196,100	559,100	211,583[a]	534,117
Gross margin		$ 440,900		$ 465,883
Other costs and expenses		(200,000)		(200,000)
Effect of change to LIFO		9,500		
Income tax expense (40%)		(100,160)		(106,353)
Net income		$ 150,240		$ 159,530
Liability balance:				
Total taxes payable		$ 100,160		$ 106,353

[a] Computed as follows:

Ending inventory at retail	$410,000	
1984 LCM ratio	× .51605	← LCM ratio = $745,700/$1,445,000
Ending inventory at LCM cost	$211,583	

	COST	RETAIL	
Beginning inventory	$152,000	$ 285,000	
Purchases (net)	603,200	1,080,000	
Net additional markups		80,000	
Net markdowns		(35,000)	
Available	$755,200	$1,410,000	
Net sales		−1,000,000	
		$ 410,000	Ending inventory at FIFO retail
		÷ 1.15	
		$ 356,522	Ending inventory at base-year retail prices

1984 MCR	COST	RETAIL	
Available	$755,200	$1,410,000	
Beginning inventory	152,000	285,000	MCR:
1984 dollars	$603,200	$1,125,000 ←	$603,200/$1,125,000 = .5362

1984 Ending Inventory at LIFO

LAYER	BY$	RETAIL INDEX	LIFO LAYERED RETAIL DOLLARS	MCRs	LIFO LAYERED COST DOLLARS
1984	$ 71,522	× 1.15	$ 82,250	× .5362	$ 44,100
1983	$285,000	× 1.00	$285,000	× .5333	$152,000
	$356,522				$196,100

Exhibit 10–5 compares the results of Waxing's operations for 1984 with and without the switch to LIFO retail.

Analysis Although LIFO retail reports less income for 1984, it also results in over $6,000 less taxes than does the conventional retail method. This net tax savings occurs even though the adjusting entry to 1984 beginning inventory required by the switch resulted in a $9,500 increase to the beginning inventory balance. It is possible that additional taxes payable may sometimes be required in the year of the change to the LIFO cost-flow assumption. However, future years will normally result in substantial tax savings if inventory costs continue to increase.

LIFO disclosures Most changes to the LIFO method of inventory do not result in a cumulative prior years' effect because such an effect is often not measurable. This is also the case with LIFO estimation, as indicated in the following Lance, Inc., footnote:

Lance, Inc., December 27, 1980, Annual Report Note 2.

In December 1980 the Company and one of its subsidiaries adopted the dollar value LIFO method of determining the cost of substantially all of their inventories. The change, which was made to provide better matching of current costs with current revenues, reduced inventories at December 27, 1980, by $3,214,000 and net income and net income per share for the year by $1,649,000 and $ .20, respectively. The change has no cumulative effect on prior periods since such effects cannot be determined.

The retail inventory method, dollar-value LIFO, and LIFO retail are all used in practice by entities of all sizes. Exhibit 10–6 provides several examples of footnote disclosures that indicate the use of these estimation techniques.

Additional Inventory Cost Estimation Methods

Cost estimation is not confined to the inventories of retail and wholesale operations. In fact, the measurement of manufacturing inventories involves many instances where inventory costs must be estimated. The most common inventory estimation problems for manufacturers concern the allocation of common costs to units of product. Numerous allocations are required to assign overhead costs, such as depreciation on factory plant and equipment, to the units of inventory in order to arrive at the total product cost.

One of the more interesting cost estimation problems involves the allocation of material, labor, and overhead costs to products that are jointly produced. Figure 10–1 illustrates the joint-product manufacturing process for a cereal manufacturer. The estimation problem here addresses the question, How should the joint-process costs of departments 1 and 2 be assigned to the two separate cereals? A number of different estimation methods might be used to solve this problem, but all answers are only estimates because no exact measurements of joint costs exist, since *joint products* are those that are not distinguishable from one another.

The following additional data for the Smack Cereal Corporation illustrate some of the more common solutions to this estimation problem:

| | IN 000 POUNDS | | IN UNITS | IN $000 | |
DEPARTMENT	POUNDS STARTED	POUNDS COMPLETED	FINISHED BOXES OF OUTPUT	TOTAL DEPARTMENT COSTS	TOTAL SALES VOLUME
1	1,000	1,000	/	$163	/
2	1,000	1,000	/	281	/
			Split-off subtotal	$444	
3 and 5	400	500	800,000	150	$ 700
4 and 6	600	900	1,440,000	300	1,800
				$894	$2,500

The costs, which include material, labor, and overhead, may be assigned to the two products on the basis of (1) physical measurement (weight at split-off), (2) relative sales value at completion, or (3) relative sales value at split-off. The alternative assignments of the $444,000 joint-process costs from departments 1 and 2 are illustrated in Exhibit 10–7.

FIGURE 10-1

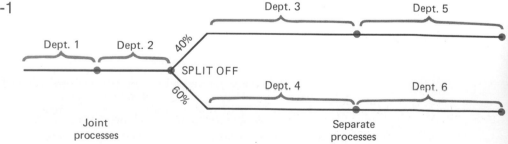

Dept. 3   Dept. 5

Dept. 1   Dept. 2   40%

SPLIT OFF

60%   Dept. 4   Dept. 6

Joint processes   Separate processes

EXHIBIT
10–6

DISCLOSURES OF INVENTORY ESTIMATION METHODS

DUPLEX PRODUCTS, INC.
October 15, 1980, Annual Report

Note B: Inventories

If the company had used the first-in, first-out (FIFO) method of inventory accounting instead of the last-in, first-out (LIFO) method, inventories would have been $7,065,000 and $4,875,000 higher at October 25, 1980, and October 27, 1979, respectively.

Charges to earnings before income taxes related to the LIFO provision were $2,190,000 in 1980 and $1,824,000 in 1979.

It is not practicable to separate the LIFO inventory into its components (raw materials, work in process, and finished goods) because the dollar value LIFO method is used.

JACOBSON STORES, INC.
July 26, 1980, Annual Report

Note 10: Inventories

All merchandise inventories are valued by the retail method and stated on the last in, first-out (LIFO) basis. At year-end, merchandise inventories were as follows:

(IN THOUSANDS)	JULY 12, 1980	JULY 28, 1979
Inventories at first-in, first-out (FIFO) cost	$32,792	$30,853
Less LIFO reserves	6,422	4,507
	$26,370	$26,346

The provisions for LIFO were $1,915,000 in 1980 and $374,000 in 1979. After consideration of the effect of income taxes, these provisions reduced earnings per common share by $1.05 in 1980 and 20 cents in 1979 from amounts which would have been reported using the first-in, first-out (FIFO) basis.

OLIN CORPORATION
December 31, 1980, Annual Report

Note 1: Inventories

If the first-in, first-out (FIFO) method of inventory accounting had beed used, inventories would have been approximately $177,000,000 and $152,000,000 higher than that reported at December 31, 1980, and December 31, 1979, respectively. FIFO values approximate replacement costs.

Because inventory costs are determined principally by the use of the dollar value LIFO method, it is not practicable to separate the inventory into its components (raw materials, work in process, and finished goods).

AMERICAN CYANAMID COMPANY
December 31, 1980, Annual Report

Note 3:

Inventories—At December 31, 1980, estimated current cost exceeded the LIFO value of the inventories by approximately $165,900 (1979—$137,500). It is not practicable to determine the major components of inventory under the dollar value LIFO inventory method.

These alternative estimation methods all result in different product costs, and, therefore, they have an impact on the measurement of ending inventory and cost of goods sold. The same estimation procedures are used in many other manufacturing situations, such as those involving chemical processes, cosmetics, lumber mills, meat-packing processes, and crude oil processing.

EXHIBIT 10–7

COST ESTIMATION METHODS

Physical Measure

PRODUCT	PERCENTAGE WEIGHT AT SPLIT-OFF	×	JOINT COST	=	ALLOCATED JOINT COST	+	SEPARATE COSTS FROM FURTHER PROCESSING	=	TOTAL COSTS	TOTAL REVENUE	TOTAL MARGIN
Sugar	60%	×	$444	=	$266.4	+	$300	=	$566.4	$1,800	$1,233.6
Plain	40	×	444	=	177.6	+	150	=	327.6	700	372.4
	100%				$444		$450		$894	$2,500	$1,606.0

Relative Sales Value

PRODUCT	TOTAL SALES VALUE	RELATIVE SALES VALUE	×	JOINT COST	=	ALLOCATED JOINT COST	+	SEPARATE COSTS FROM FURTHER PROCESSING	=	TOTAL COSTS	TOTAL REVENUE	TOTAL MARGIN
Sugar	$1,800	1,800/2,500 = .72	×	$444	=	$320	+	$300	=	$620	$1,800	$1,180
Plain	700	700/2,500 = .28	×	444	=	124	+	150	=	274	700	426
	$2,500	1.00				$444		$450		$894	$2,500	$1,606

Relative Sales Value at Split-Off

PRODUCT	TOTAL SALES VALUE	–	SEPARATE PROCESSING COSTS	=	ESTIMATED SALES VALUE AT SPLIT-OFF	RELATIVE SALES VALUE AT SPLIT-OFF	ALLOCATED JOINT COST	+	SEPARATE COSTS FROM FURTHER PROCESSING	=	TOTAL COSTS	TOTAL MARGIN
Sugar	$1,800	–	$300	=	$1,500	73%	$324	+	$300	=	$624	$1,176
Plain	700	–	150	=	550	27	120	+	150	=	270	430
	$2,500		$450		$2,050	100%	$444		$450		$894	$1,606

Retail and wholesale applications The three cost estimation procedures illustrated in Exhibit 10–7 may also be applied to various wholesale and retail situations. For example, a fabric store might purchase 500 bolts of cloth at a lump-sum price of $4,000 and then classify the bolts into "fine," "average," and "flawed" grades to be sold at three different prices. The $4,000 must be allocated to the three grades, and the relative sales value method might be useful here. In other situations where wholesalers and retailers purchase a quantity of mixed merchandise for lump-sum prices and need to assign the total price to the individual items, these estimation methods might be applied. For such items as produce, meat, fish, and poultry, however, a physical measure such as weight might be used in place of relative sales value.

FUNDS FLOW EFFECTS

The impact of the inventory estimation methods considered in this chapter on the flow of funds is no different from the effects discussed in the previous inventory chapter. The increase in working capital resulting from purchases or manufacturing of inventory generally results in an offsetting reduction in working capital from the increases in payables and other obligations, and eventually will require decreases in cash. The outflow of inventory resulting from sales is the key business activity of most firms. This activity normally generates a net increase in working capital (due to the related increase in receivables or cash or both) and an eventual net inflow of cash. The estimation procedures themselves have nothing to do with the economic flows of the entity beyond those effects that result from the use of discrete methods reviewed in Chapter 9.

The primary benefit of the estimation techniques related to fund flows is their ability to generate LIFO inventory measurements that are acceptable for tax purposes and, therefore, useful in reducing the cash flows required for taxes in entities that are experiencing rising inventory costs. These estimation methods help entities manage their working capital position in the sense that they provide managers with the information needed to control the buying, manufacturing, and selling activities of the entity and the resulting impact of these activities on the financial statements.

SUMMARY

The estimation methods illustrated in this chapter are useful for both internal and external reporting purposes. For internal purposes, management must consider the concepts of relevance and reliability as the basis for deciding how to measure ending inventory and cost of goods sold not otherwise measured by the periodic accounting information system. The relevance and reliability of the alternative estimation procedures must be constrained by the perceived additional costs and benefits from their use.

In many instances, entities might decide to use different methods for internal and external reports, or possibly different methods for different external reports. For example, management often elects to use a LIFO estimation procedure for financial reports and income tax reports but continues to use FIFO for internal reports.[4] In such cases, a special valuation account (Allowance to Reduce Inventory to LIFO Value) is used to carry forward the difference between the two methods from period to period. This valuation account is typically referred to as a *LIFO reserve* and can be a very significant dollar amount after only a few years' use.

It is difficult to generalize about superior or inferior estimation methods without considering the facts and constraints of each situation. In other words, there is no single best method for most situations. All of the estimation procedures do solve the basic problem of a periodic system in that they provide interim measures of ending inventory and cost of goods sold without the need for a physical count. Aside from this one common benefit derived from the estimation methods considered here, they are all useful to varying degrees depending on the particular situation.

---

[4] Many reasons might be given to explain the use of FIFO for internal purposes while using LIFO for external reporting. FIFO may be considered more reliable or may better reflect the actual flow of goods. Also, managers' bonuses may be based on income, which would generally be greater under a FIFO method in periods of rising prices.

APPENDIX D
Developing Price Indexes
for LIFO Estimation Methods

There are numerous ways in which a firm might obtain the price index data needed to apply the dollar value LIFO and the LIFO retail estimation procedures. The two most common index methods used are the **double-extension method** and the **link chain method.**[5] Both of these methods yield internally generated indexes based on corporate records.

DOUBLE-EXTENSION INDEX METHOD

The **double-extension method** measures the ratio of year-end cost over original cost for each inventory item. The year-end quantity is multiplied (extended) by both costs (hence, "double extension"), and the ratio results in the index. To illustrate, consider the following data:

LOCKHORN CORPORATION

INVENTORY ITEM	ORIGINAL COST	CURRENT COST (FIFO) 12/31/83
X13	$10	$15
X14	12	18
.	.	.
.	.	.
.	.	.
Z83	5	9

12/31/83 Physical Inventory

INVENTORY ITEM	UNITS	TOTAL ORIGINAL COST	TOTAL CURRENT COSTS (FIFO)
X13	1,500	$ 15,000	$ 22,500
X14	3,600	43,200	64,800
.	.	.	.
.	.	.	.
.	.	.	.
Z83	4,200	21,000	37,800
		$9,853,000	$13,794,200

Double-extension index, 1983: $\dfrac{\$13{,}794{,}200}{\$9{,}853{,}000} = 1.40$

The major drawback with the double-extension method is the need to keep track of the original cost of every inventory item used in the index, plus the fact that new inventory items can complicate matters. Consequently, double extension may be difficult to apply in some situations.

[5] See M. Stark, "A Survey of LIFO Inventory Application Techniques," *The Accounting Review* January 1978, pp. 182–186.

THE LINK CHAIN INDEX METHOD

The **link chain method,** an alternative to double extension, focuses on the year-to-year price changes. The link chain index computes an index to measure price change for the current year and then multiples the current-year price change by the cumulative prior years' index. Exhibit D–1 illustrates the link chain method. Note that in the initial year (1983), the link chain method and the double-extension method involve the exact same index measurement process since there is no prior year's index to "link" to in the link chain method. As a result, a second year's index measurement must be illustrated to show the difference between the double-extension and link chain indexes. In 1985 the "cumulative prior years' index" will be 1.256.

EXHIBIT D–1

LINK CHAIN INDEX METHOD

1983 (Year 1)

(1) ITEM	(2) BEGINNING-OF-YEAR PRICE PER UNIT	(3) ENDING INVENTORY UNITS	(4) ENDING INVENTORY AT BEGINNING-OF-YEAR PRICE	(5) END-OF-YEAR PRICE PER UNIT	(6) ENDING INVENTORY AT YEAR-END PRICE
A	$ 7	1,000	$ 7,000	$ 8	$ 8,000
B	15	4,000	60,000	18	72,000
C	20	2,500	50,000	23	57,500
			$117,000		$137,500

First year's link chain index $= \dfrac{\$137,500}{\$117,000} = 1.175$

1.175 = 1983 Index—No prior year available

1984 (Year 2)

(1) ITEM	(2) BEGINNING-OF-YEAR PRICE PER UNIT	(3) ENDING INVENTORY UNITS	(4) ENDING INVENTORY AT BEGINNING-OF-YEAR PRICE	(5) END-OF-YEAR PRICE PER UNIT	(6) ENDING INVENTORY AT YEAR-END PRICE
A	$ 8	600	$ 4,800	$ 7	$ 4,200
B	18	3,000	54,000	19	57,000
C	23	4,000	92,000	25	100,000
			$150,800		$161,200

1984 index $= \dfrac{\$161,200}{\$150,800} = 1.0689$

Second and subsequent years' link chain method

CUMULATIVE PRIOR YEARS' INDEX	×	CURRENT YEAR'S INDEX	=	CURRENT LINK CHAIN INDEX
1.175	×	1.0689	=	1.256

Index Variations In both the double-extension and the link chain methods illustrated above, year-end price indexes were used in the calculations. Some firms employing these index methods use **average of the period index values** as an alternative. Incremental layers of inventory may also be added on the basis of beginning-of-the-year prices.[6]

In addition to the double-extension and link chain indexes developed internally, numerous published indexes may be used where appropriate. The Bureau of Labor Statistics publishes many specialized retail price indexes semiannually, and the use of these indexes is permissible for tax purposes where an appropriate index is available.[7]

Measurement Pools The index computation illustrated above may be computed a number of ways. First, note that seldom, if ever, is an entire inventory used to develop the index. Normally, a *sample* of items is used to develop this index. Given that sampling is used, the next issue is how to subdivide inventory, if at all. A separate index can be developed for each subdivision, or "pool," of inventory items. The inventory pool concept permits inventory items to be grouped together by pools in order to consider together items that are subject to similar price fluctuations. It is up to management to elect a single- or multiple-pool approach to dollar-value LIFO or LIFO retail. If a multiple-pool approach is elected, the identification of pools should remain constant from year to year.

In summary, various methods of obtaining price indexes can be used with the dollar-value LIFO and LIFO retail methods illustrated earlier:

1. Double-extension method
2. Link chain method
3. Published indexes
4. Some combination of the first three where multiple pools are used

The inventory may be viewed as either a single pool of items or multiple pools of similar items. The index will normally be computed by sampling items from each pool and then applying one of the index methods. The double-extension method is said to be more costly because it requires record keeping for the original cost of inventory items, and it presents problems when new inventory items are introduced.[8]

[6] For a breakdown of the frequency with which these alternatives are used, see ibid., p. 184.

[7] In 1982 the U.S. Treasury adopted simplified LIFO rules enabling small companies to use an index that is equal to 80 percent of any appropriate published Bureau of Labor Statistics index without special petition.

[8] To address the problem of new products, various backward forecasting methods to determine what the original cost would have been had the new products been available in the base year are often used in practice.

QUESTIONS

Q10–1 Why are inventory estimation methods used primarily with the periodic inventory system?

Q10–2 What information can estimation procedures provide that is not available in a periodic inventory system?

Q10–3   What is the underlying assumption of the gross margin estimation method? What sort of situations can make this assumption unrealistic?

Q10–4   What are the underlying assumptions upon which the accuracy of the retail inventory method is based?

Q10–5   What is the implied cost-flow assumption in the conventional retail method?

Q10–6   Why is the term *additional* used in conjunction with markups but not markdowns?

Q10–7   What is the impact of an employee discount on the cost-to-retail ratio? Why are employee discounts omitted in computing the LCM ratio for the retail method?

Q10–8   The cost ratio and the LCM ratio are both used for retail inventory estimation. Which ratio will provide the better estimate of what *should be* in ending inventory? Why?

Q10–9   Identify two ways that retailers might allow for theft in their inventory estimation methods.

Q10–10   What are some of the advantages of dollar-value LIFO? What types of entities could use dollar-value LIFO?

Q10–11   Is dollar-value LIFO an estimation method? If so, in what sense is it an estimate?

Q10–12   Why are inventory values converted to base-year dollars in the dollar value LIFO method?

Q10–13   What price index is assigned to a layer of inventory added during the current period under the dollar-value LIFO method?

Q10–14   What is the primary difference between dollar-value LIFO and LIFO retail?

Q10–15   Can LIFO retail be applied in a year where there is no change in the price index? Explain.

Q10–16   What is a modified cost ratio and why is it useful in a LIFO context?

Q10–17   What is the role of the current year's modified cost ratio when there is a real decline in inventory quantity during the year?

Q10–18   What happens to the beginning inventory value in a year where a change is made from the retail method to the LIFO retail method?

Q10–19   What normal disclosure is made during a year when a change is made to the dollar-value LIFO inventory method?

Q10–20   What are the two most common methods of assigning joint costs to joint products?

Q10–21   How can you determine the most appropriate allocation method to use in the case of joint costs?

Q10–22*   How are price indexes developed for dollar-value LIFO and LIFO retail?

CASES

C10–1   Identify some common limitations of a periodic inventory system and explain how inventory estimation procedures can eliminate or reduce these problems. Consider this question in the context of a large single-location retail store that does about $3,000,000 in sales each year and is currently using a periodic system. Be sure to discuss both the costs and the benefits of the alternative estimation systems.

C10–2   In March 1984 a fire destroyed the Well-To-Do Department Store. The only data that could be found on the company's position at the date of the fire were in a partly burned general ledger. You have been sent out by the insurance company to estimate the inventory at the date of the fire because your company had issued a policy covering the inventory.

REQUIRED   Explain how you would go about estimating the inventory. Well-To-Do had prepared quarterly statements and annual reports, with the last of these dated December 31, 1983. What information would you try to obtain, and how would you use it to estimate the inventory?

C10–3   The Mautz Sales & Service Company has recently acquired the inventory of the Buckmaster/Markell Ford Dealership, which went out of business. The inventory consisted of 45 units:

	NUMBER OF UNITS	TOTAL LIST PRICE	TOTAL DEALER COST
Fiestas	3	$ 30,200	$ 28,690
Escorts	10	96,420	91,599
Pintos	5	35,196	32,732
Fairmonts	6	49,807	44,826
LTDs	7	97,683	83,031
Trucks	7	59,281	50,389
Vans	7	73,426	60,209
	45	$442,013	$391,476

Mautz paid $320,000 for the entire inventory. Mautz has sold two Escorts since acquiring the inventory and is in the process of preparing annual financial statements.

REQUIRED What cost should Mautz assign to the two sold units? What is the value of the remaining eight Escorts?

C10–4 In 1983 ACE Studios produced a movie at a total cost of $14,386,940. The movie is expected to be a blockbuster that will be shown in theaters for about 6 months, after which it will be converted to videotape sales and then sold to television for several years after video sales slow down. The movie is released just before the holidays in December 1983, with gross rentals of about $10,000,000 by December 31.

REQUIRED How much of the $14,386,940 should be charged to expense for 1983? What additional data would you like to have, and how would you use these data to answer this question?

C10–5 In November 1983 a client of yours asks you for some information about the use of LIFO inventory in retail firms like his own, a large hardware and garden store. He would like you to tell him *all the advantages and disadvantages of LIFO in comparison with the conventional retail system* now being used. Also, he has heard that changing to LIFO might have the effect of *increasing* taxes in the year of change. He does not understand how this is possible—he has read the annual reports of some companies that have switched to LIFO and they state that income is lower under the LIFO method.

REQUIRED What do you have to tell your client about LIFO, his fear of higher taxes, and other factors?

C10–6 Meddley Meat Packing has just purchased 40,000 pounds of cattle (standing weight) from Kinney Ranch. The 40,000 pounds, after slaughter, will yield 26,000 pounds of usable beef of the following cuts:

	BY WEIGHT	BY SELLING PRICE
Steaks	10%	20%
Roasts	25	35
Loins	5	10
Ribs	10	10
Hamburger	45	24
Other	5	1
	100%	100%

Meddley paid Kinney $42,000 for the cattle.

REQUIRED How should the cost be assigned to the products? How would you decide which cost-allocation method is the *most correct* in this case?

E10–1 (CPA ADAPTED) On November 21, 1984, a fire at Hodge Company's warehouse caused severe damage to its entire inventory of Product Tex. Hodge estimates that all usable damaged goods can be sold for $10,000. The following information was available from Hodge's accounting records for Product Tex:

Inventory, Nov. 1, 1984	$100,000
Purchases, Nov. 1, 1984, to date of fire	140,000
Net sales, Nov. 1, 1984, to date of fire	220,000

Based on recent history, Hodge had a gross margin (profit) on Product Tex of 30 percent of net sales.

REQUIRED Prepare a schedule to calculate the estimated loss on the inventory in the fire, using the gross margin (profit) method. Show supporting computations in good form.

E10–2 (CPA ADAPTED) The Barometer Company manufactures one product. On December 31, 1984, Barometer adopted the dollar value LIFO inventory method. The inventory on that date using the dollar value LIFO inventory method was $200,000.
  Inventory data are as follows:

YEAR	INVENTORY AT RESPECTIVE YEAR-END PRICES	PRICE INDEX (BASE YEAR 1984)
1985	$231,000	1.05
1986	299,000	1.15
1987	300,000	1.20

REQUIRED Compute the inventory at December 31, 1985, 1986, and 1987, using the dollar value LIFO method for each year.

E10–3 (CPA ADAPTED) The Jericho Variety Store uses the LIFO retail inventory method. Information relating to the computation of the inventory at December 31, 1985, follows:

	COST	RETAIL
Inventory, Jan. 1, 1985	$ 29,000	$ 45,000
Purchases	120,000	172,000
Freight-in	20,000	
Sales		190,000
Net additional markups		40,000
Net markdowns		12,000

REQUIRED Assuming that there was no change in the price index during the year, compute the inventory at December 31, 1985, using the LIFO retail inventory method.

E10–4 (CPA ADAPTED) The Supreme Clothing Store values its inventory under the retail inventory method at the lower-of-cost-or-market. The following data are available for November 1984:

	COST	SELLING PRICE
Inventory, Nov. 1	$ 53,800	$ 80,000
Markdowns		21,000
Additional markups		29,000
Markdown cancellations		13,000
Markup cancellations		9,000
Purchases	173,200	223,600
Sales		244,000
Purchase returns and allowances	3,000	3,600
Sales returns and allowances		12,000

REQUIRED   Based upon the data presented above, prepare a schedule in good form to compute the estimated inventory at November 30, 1984, at lower-of-cost-or-market under the retail inventory method.

E10-5 (CPA ADAPTED)   The Acute Company manufactures a single product. On December 31, 1985, Acute adopted the dollar-value LIFO inventory method. The inventory on that date using the dollar-value LIFO inventory method was determined to be $300,000. Inventory data for the succeeding years are as follows:

YEAR ENDED DECEMBER 31	INVENTORY AT RESPECTIVE YEAR-END PRICES	RELEVANT PRICE INDEX (BASE YEAR 1985)
1986	$363,000	1.10
1987	420,000	1.20
1988	430,000	1.25

REQUIRED   Compute the inventory amounts at December 31, 1986, 1987, and 1988, using the dollar-value LIFO inventory method for each year.

E10-6 (CPA ADAPTED)   The Red Department Store uses the retail inventory method. Information relating to the computation of the inventory at December 31, 1984, is as follows:

	COST	RETAIL
Inventory at Jan. 1, 1984	$ 32,000	$ 80,000
Sales		600,000
Purchases	270,000	590,000
Freight-in	7,600	
Additional markups		60,000
Markup cancellations		10,000
Markdowns		25,000
Markdown cancellations		5,000

Estimated normal shrinkage is 2 percent of sales.

REQUIRED   Prepare a schedule to calculate the estimated ending inventory at the lower-of-cost-or-market at December 31, 1984, using the retail inventory method. Show supporting computations in good form.

E10-7   The following data are taken from the records of Lange's Appliances, Inc., which began operations in 1982.

YEAR ENDED DECEMBER 31	ENDING INVENTORY AT LOWER-OF-FIFO-COST-OR-MARKET
1982	$76,000
1983	83,600
1984	93,600

Each year Lange has had the same units of ending inventory on hand at December 31 (5 GE washers, 5 Maytag washers, and so on). The difference in ending inventory values is strictly the result of price increases.

REQUIRED Compute the 1984 ending inventory using the dollar-value LIFO method.

E10–8 (CPA ADAPTED) The Grand Department Store, Inc., uses the retail inventory method to estimate ending inventory for its monthly financial statements. The following data pertain to a single department for October 1984:

Inventory, Oct. 1, 1984	
At cost	$ 20,000
At retail	40,000
Purchases (exclusive of freight and returns)	
At cost	100,151
At retail	146,495
Freight-in	5,100
Purchase returns	
At cost	2,100
At retail	2,800
Additional markups	2,500
Markup cancellations	265
Markdowns (net)	800
Normal spoilage and breakage	4,500
Sales	135,730

REQUIRED

1. Using the conventional retail method, prepare a schedule computing estimated lower-of-cost-or-market inventory for October 31, 1984.
2. A department store using the conventional retail inventory method estimates the cost of its ending inventory as $29,000. An accurate physical count reveals only $22,000 of inventory. List the factors that may have caused the difference between the computed inventory and the physical count.

E10–9 (CPA ADAPTED) On June 30, 1984, a flash flood damaged the warehouse and factory of Padway Corporation, completely destroying the work-in-process inventory. There was no damage to either the raw-materials inventory or the finished-goods inventory. A physical inventory taken after the flood revealed the following valuations:

Raw materials	$ 62,000
Work-in-process	0
Finished goods	119,000

The inventory on January 1, 1984, consisted of the following:

Raw materials	$ 30,000
Work-in-process	100,000
Finished goods	140,000
	$270,000

A review of the books and records disclosed that the gross profit margin historically approximated 25 percent of sales. The sales for the first 6 months of 1984 were $340,000. Raw-material purchases were $115,000. Direct-labor costs for this period were $80,000, and manufacturing overhead has historically been applied at an amount equal to 50 percent of direct-labor dollars.

REQUIRED Compute the value of the work-in-process inventory lost on June 30, 1984. Show supporting computations in good form.

E10–10 From the following information, compute the *cost* of ending inventory using LIFO retail procedures:

1986 Beginning inventory *at cost*	$ 55,000
1986 Beginning inventory, *base year* retail value	80,000
1986 Ending inventory, at 1986 retail value	125,000
1986 Ending inventory, *base year* retail value	100,000
1986 Cost-retail ratio	.60
1985 Cost-retail ratio	.50
LCM Cost-retail ratio	.65

E10–11 Central States Meats assigns the cost of beef to its various cuts of meat on a relative sales value at split-off basis. During the month of August 1984, beef costing $68,000 was processed and packaged, as summarized below:

CLASS OF CUT	SEPARATE PROCESSING AND PACKAGING COSTS—AUGUST	POUNDS OF OUTPUT	SELLING PRICE PER POUND
L	$ 3,800	19,000	$1.65
M	8,400	24,000	2.25
N	4,300	14,300	2.00
O	8,100	21,000	2.50
	$24,600	78,300	

The total joint-processing cost, including the $68,000, amounted to $92,394.

REQUIRED Determine the joint cost to be assigned to L, M, N, and O for August using the relative sales value at split-off method.

E10–12 Consider the data in Exercise 10–11.

REQUIRED Determine the joint cost and the total cost of L, M, N, and O using the physical unit of measure (weight) method of assigning joint costs.

E10–13 (CPA ADAPTED)

1. On June 10, 1985, a fire destroyed the inventory of the Tarter Corporation. The following data were discovered after the fire:

Sales, January 1 through June 10, 1985	$360,000
Inventory, January 1, 1985	80,000
Merchandise purchases, January 1 through June 10, 1985 (including $40,000 of goods in transit on June 10, 1985, F.O.B. shipping point)	330,000
Markup percentage on cost	20%

What is your estimate of the inventory on hand at June 10, 1985?
a. $70,000
b. $82,000
c. $110,000
d. $122,000

2. On April 15, 1985, a fire destroyed the entire merchandise inventory of John Anderson's retail store.

The following data are available:

Sales, January 1 through April 15	$72,000
Inventory, January 1	10,000
Purchases, January 1 through April 15	70,000
Markup on cost	20%

The amount of the loss is estimated to be

a. $24,000

b. $20,000

c. $22,400

d. $8,000

3. The following data concerning the retail inventory method are taken from the financial records of the Bandit Company:

	COST	RETAIL
Beginning inventory	$18,600	$ 30,000
Purchases	91,000	154,000
Freight-in	1,400	
Net markups		1,000
Net markdowns		1,740
Sales		156,760

The ending inventory at retail should be

a. $28,240

b. $27,980

c. $27,240

d. $26,500

4. Based on the data in Question 3, if the ending inventory is to be valued at approximately the lower-of-cost-or-market, the calculation of the cost-to-retail ratio should be based on goods available for sale at (1) cost and (2) retail, respectively, of

a. $111,000 and $186,740

b. $111,000 and $185,000

c. $111,000 and $182,260

d. $109,600 and $184,000

E10-14 (CPA ADAPTED)

1. For 1984, the cost of goods available for sale for Red Corporation was $400,000. The gross margin was 25 percent of sales. Sales for the year were $480,000. What was the amount of the ending inventory?

a. $20,000

b. $40,000

c. $16,000

d. $80,000

2. The Topper Department Store uses the retail inventory method to approximate cost. For department 302 for January 1985, cost of goods available for sale was $60,000 at cost and $75,000 at retail before considering net markups of $5,000 and net markdowns of $8,000. If sales were $66,000, how much was the inventory approximating lower-of-cost-or-market at the end of January 1985?

a. $4,500

b. $4,800

c. $5,000

d. $6,000

3. The Quick Sales Company uses the retail inventory method to value its merchandise inventory. The following information is available:

	COST	RETAIL
Beginning inventory	$ 40,000	$ 70,000
Purchases	290,000	400,000
Freight-in	2,000	
Markups (net)		3,000
Markdowns (net)		5,000
Employee discounts		1,000
Sales		390,000

What is the ending inventory at retail?
a. $71,000
b. $72,000
c. $77,000
d. $78,000

4. Based on the data in Question 3, if the ending inventory is to be valued at the lower-of-cost-or-market, what is the cost-to-retail ratio?
a. $332,000/$468,000
b. $332,000/$472,000
c. $332,000/$473,000
d. $332,000/$474,000

5. The Blue Department Store uses the retail inventory method. Information relating to the computation of the inventory at December 31, 1986, is as follows:

	COST	RETAIL
Inventory at Jan. 1, 1986	$ 16,000	$ 40,000
Sales		290,000
Purchases	135,000	300,000
Freight-in	3,800	
Net markups		20,000
Net markdowns		10,000

What should be the ending inventory at LCM cost at December 31, 1986, using the LCM retail inventory method?
a. $21,500
b. $22,500
c. $25,800
d. $27,000

PROBLEMS

P10-1   On July 31, 1984, the Borrower Company suffered a severe fire that destroyed all the inventory on hand at that time. The accounting records had been placed in a fireproof safe, however, and survived. The company needs to make a fire loss claim against its insurance company. The accounting records provide the following data:

Inventory, Jan. 1, 1984	$ 113,750
Sales through July 31, 1984	1,092,000
Purchases through July 31, 1984	877,500
Sales returns and allowances through July 31, 1984	52,400
Purchase returns and allowances through July 31, 1984	41,600

Gross profit as a percentage of cost has averaged about 28 percent for the past few years, and that percentage is considered reasonable for 1984 operations.

REQUIRED   Estimate inventory at the date of the fire.

P10-2   The following data are taken from the records of Jeannette Interiors, Inc., a retail furniture store:

| | BALANCES AS OF FEBRUARY 28, 1986 | |
	COST	RETAIL
Purchase discounts	$ 2,000	
Net markups		$ 4,000
Purchase returns	10,000	16,000
Salespersons' commissions	12,000	
Salespersons' special discounts		2,000
Net markdowns		8,000
Purchases	62,000	88,000
Bad debt expense	4,000	
Gross sales		70,000
Sales returns		2,000
Beginning inventory, 1/1/84	10,000	14,000

REQUIRED

1. Compute the ending inventory and gross margin for the 2 months ending February 28 using the retail inventory method that approximates cost.
2. Compute the ending inventory and gross margin for the 2 months ending February 28 using the retail inventory method that approximates lower-of-cost-or-market.

P10–3 The following data are taken from the records of the Winterview Corporation at December 31, 1983:

	COST	RETAIL
Beginning inventory	$16,000	$ 23,000
Purchases	75,000	100,000
Net sales		88,000

ADDITIONAL DATA

1. The retail value of beginning inventory at base-year prices = $20,000.
2. The price index at the end of 1983 = 125%.
3. The price index at the beginning of 1983 = 115%.
4. The price index at the beginning of 1982 = 100%.

REQUIRED

1. Compute the *cost* of the ending inventory at December 31, 1983, using the LIFO retail method. Show all computations.
2. Assuming the beginning inventory from 1983 was composed of only one layer from the year 1982, what was the ratio of cost to retail values for 1982?

P10–4 Charlie Company has been using FIFO for external-reporting purposes. At the beginning of 1985, the company adopted dollar-value LIFO. Following are the figures for one inventory pool under FIFO:

	PRICE INDEX	FIFO ENDING INVENTORY
1982	100%	$150,000
1983	115	180,000
1984	125	195,000
1985	132	202,500

REQUIRED Convert ending inventory on a FIFO basis to dollar-value LIFO for 1985.

P10-5 The Wolverine Metal Products Company has asked for your advice in valuing its inventory. The company, which was established in 1980, has been using the FIFO cost-flow assumption with its periodic inventory system. In November 1984 you collected the following information from the past 4 years:

YEAR-END	FIFO ENDING INVENTORY VALUE	PRICE-LEVEL INDEX AT YEAR-END
1980	$ 93,600	120%
1981	113,900	134
1982	115,200	144
1983	142,800	168

REQUIRED

1. Prepare a schedule for 1980–1983 that shows the calculated value of Wolverine's inventory at LIFO cost using the dollar value LIFO measurement method.
2. Indicate as many *sound economic* reasons as you can that might support the use of the FIFO inventory method. (This need not relate to the case above.)

P10-6 The following data are taken from the records of Gerry Salamon's, Inc., as of June 20, 1983:

ACCOUNT	BALANCE
Sales	$14,000 Credit
Employee discount	500 Debit
Markdowns	500 Debit
Markups	700 Credit
Purchases (net)	11,000 Debit
Inventory	3,000 Debit

The retail value of the beginning inventory was $5,000, and the normal selling price of the goods purchased during the period was $15,300.

REQUIRED

1. Estimate the inventory cost of June 30 and the gross profit to date using the LCM ratio.
2. Repeat requirement 1 using the cost ratio.
3. Indicate why such estimation procedures exist.
4. Which method would you use for comparison with your physical inventory to estimate "shrinkage" and why?

P10-7 The following data are taken from the records of the Cut-Throat Discount Store for the year ending May 31, 1984:

	AT COST	AT RETAIL
Sales returns		$ 2,000
Employee discounts		1,750
Freight-in	$ 4,800	
Net markdowns		2,000
Purchase returns	2,400	4,000
Purchase discounts	2,400	
Commissions	2,000	
Net markups		6,000
Purchases	38,000	48,000
Gross sales		42,750
Beginning inventory	7,000	10,000
Advertising	1,000	

REQUIRED

1. Compute the ending inventory and cost of goods sold under the retail inventory method that approximates *lower-of-cost-or-market*.
2. Compute the ending inventory and cost of goods sold under the retail inventory method that approximates *cost*.
3. The Cut-Throat Store has what it believes to be a serious problem involving loss due to theft. Because the store was designed to guard against customer theft, the owner has become suspicious of Mrs. I. Heistem, his sole cashier. The owner has taken a physical count as of May 31, 1984, and tells you that the *cost* of goods on hand at that date is actually $11,000. Assuming that any loss incurred is actually due to theft *only* (no damaged goods, and so on), what do you believe should be the amount reported for "loss due to theft"? Is the amount indicated an exact amount?

P10-8 You have the following data from the records of the Mini Tax Corporation, which started operations in 1983 and uses the LIFO retail inventory method:

	ENDING INVENTORY AT YEAR-END RETAIL PRICES	BASE YEAR $	ENDING INVENTORY AT LIFO COST	YEAR-END RETAIL PRICE INDEX
1983	$44,000	$40,000	$26,400	110%
1984	60,000	50,000	33,840	120
1985	56,250	45,000	30,120	125
1986	71,500	55,000	38,570	130

REQUIRED

1. What was the 1986 ending inventory at base-year (index = 100) *retail* price?
2. What was the base-year *retail* value of the layer added to inventory in 1986?
3. What was the LIFO *cost* value of the 1986 layer?
4. What was the decrease in inventory during *1985* at base-year *retail* dollars?
5. What was the 1984 cost-to-retail ratio?
6. What was the 1985 cost-to-retail ratio?

P10-9 The following data are taken from the records of the Lane Daley Corporation at December 31, 1985:

	COST	RETAIL
Beginning Inventory	?	$ 30,000
Purchases (net)	$190,400	280,000
Sales		276,000

ADDITIONAL DATA The $30,000 beginning inventory (at retail) is made up of the following layers:

From 1980	$12,000
From 1982	15,000
From 1983	3,000
	$30,000 from 1984 ending inventory at 1984 year-end retail prices

The following data are available for the past 6 years:

	YEAR-END PRICE INDEX	MODIFIED COST RATIO
For 1980	80%	.75
1981	90	.73
1982	100	.70
1983	125	.72
1984	150	.71
1985	200	.68

REQUIRED

1. Compute the *cost* of the 1985 ending inventory using the LIFO retail method. Show *all* computations.
2. What is the *retail* value of the 1980 inventory layer in *beginning* inventory in terms of 1980 *retail* dollars?
3. What was the *cost* of the 1985 beginning inventory?

P10–10   In January 1983 the Always Fair Real Estate Company was organized and started operations. The company is engaged in acquiring unimproved land and dividing it into lots for sale as home sites. The transactions for 1983 were as follows:

1. Purchased 200 acres of land for subdivision at a cost of $70,000. Divided the land into lots, obtaining a total of 500 lots. The remaining area was used for streets and parks. The lots were priced according to location as follows: The class A lots were listed to sell for $2,500 each, class B lots for $1,600 each, and class C lots for $1,000 each. There were 100 class A lots, 160 class B lots, and the remainder were class C lots.
2. Costs and expenses incurred in 1983 were as follows:

Legal fees for purchasing land, survey fees, etc.	$ 8,000
Grading contract	29,500
Water and sewerage system contract	24,800
Paving contract	35,640
Building model home (to be offered for sale)	87,500
Advertising and publicity	9,300
General office expenses, of which one-third is considered applicable to the period after the development of the lots	30,600
Sales manager's salary	12,000
Sales commissions	2,910

REQUIRED   Prepare a schedule in good form showing the total inventoriable costs for all the lots and the amount that should be allocated in total to each type of lot (A, B, and C).

P10–11   The following data pertain to the Crusher Company for the year 1985:

Beginning inventory at cost	$ 500
Beginning inventory at retail	800
Purchases, net invoice cost	2,800
Freight-in	200
Net sales	3,600
Selling price of purchases	4,000
1984 price index	125%

If the ending inventory for 1985 had been equal (in terms of units) to the 1985 beginning inventory, its value would have been $500 (cost) and $1,000 (retail).

REQUIRED   Compute the *cost* of the 1985 ending inventory using the LIFO retail method.

P10-12 Up until 1984 the Coffey and Schier Department Stores had been using the conventional retail inventory method. The 1983 computation of ending inventory is as follows:

| | DECEMBER 31, 1983 | |
	COST	RETAIL
Beginning inventory	$ 67,500	$ 114,650
Net purchases	607,860	876,030
Net additional markups		17,320
(LCM ratio = $675,360/$1,008,000)	$675,360	$1,008,000
Less: Net markdowns		26,830
Employee discounts		10,379
Net sales		850,291
Ending inventory at retail		$ 120,500
× LCM ratio		.67
Ending inventory at cost		$ 80,735

Data available for 1984 are as follows:

Net purchases at cost	$ 743,120
Net purchases at retail	1,050,270
Net additional markups	41,890
Net markdowns	19,420
Employee discounts	11,140
Net sales	1,026,935
Retail price index: 1/1/83	100.00%
1/1/84	105.00
1/1/85	120.75

During 1984 you have been a consultant for Coffey and Schier and they have asked you about their inventory procedures. They would like to take advantage of LIFO if possible because they are in a 50 percent tax bracket but do not know how to apply LIFO in conjunction with their retail inventory system. You agree to help them with the conversion.

REQUIRED

1. Prepare a revised schedule to compute the 1984 beginning inventory value in order to apply the LIFO method for 1984. Record any necessary entries.
2. Prepare a schedule to compute ending inventory for 1984 using the LIFO retail method.
3. Prepare a comparative schedule to illustrate 1984 net income from operations with and without the switch to LIFO. What is the tax saving attributable to this change?

P10-13 During 1983 the Dowell Department Store had record profits using the conventional retail inventory method. Dowell also paid record taxes during 1983. Following are the data necessary to compute the cost of inventory for 1983–1984 based on the previous use of the conventional retail method:

| | 12/31/84 | | 12/31/83 | |
	COST	RETAIL	COST	RETAIL
Beginning Inventory	$?	$?	$ 30,708	$ 45,160
Net purchases	312,100	432,190	256,570	367,230
Net additional markups		41,620		22,880
Net markdowns		24,838		10,628
Shrinkage		3,115		2,173
Net sales		418,635		369,769

The retail price index that is relevant for Dowell's operations increased by 14 percent during 1984.

REQUIRED

1. Compute the 1984 ending inventory on a LIFO retail basis after first converting the 1984 beginning inventory measure from the conventional LCM value by way of an appropriate journal entry.
2. Compute the 1984 tax savings, if any, attributable to Dowell's change to LIFO.

P10–14* The following data are available regarding the products of the Bleaker Corporation:

	PER UNIT			
ITEM	ORIGINAL COST OF ITEM	COST OF ITEM AT 1/1/85	COST OF ITEM AT 12/31/85	UNITS ON HAND AT 12/31/85
X246	$18.75	$27.50	$28.25	1,460
X893	7.25	16.80	17.00	5,104
KL47	2.10	18.40	19.00	3,109
BM22	18.07	14.50	14.25	2,946
BAF2	19.00	10.80	11.50	3,215

REQUIRED

1. Compute the 1985 price index using the link chain method.
2. Compute the 1985 price index using the double-extension method.

P10–15* The Goodpenny Lumber Company uses the LIFO retail inventory method for valuing its retail lumber inventory. Inventory consists of two separate "pools" of items: (1) wood products and (2) all other products (stain, hardware, paint, and so on). The two pools are sampled at the end of 1984, with the following results reported for the sample of wood products:

SAMPLED INVENTORY ITEMS	12/31/84 PHYSICAL COUNT	12/31/84 UNIT COST	1984 PRICE (COST) CHANGE	TOTAL PRICE (COST) CHANGE FROM ORIGINAL COST
Grade A pine sheet	1,800 sheets	$3.80	+12%	+180%
Grade B 2″ × 4″ studs	18,660 units	.95	+15	+210
Grade XX joints	9,750 units	4.20	+18	+200
Construction grade 2″ × 8″	4,243 units	1.86	+20	+220

This sample represents 10 percent of the total 1984 year-end cost of the wood products' "pool."

REQUIRED

1. Compute the 1984 index using the double-extension method.
2. Compute the 1984 index using the link chain method.
3. Estimate the dollar-value LIFO measure of 1984 ending inventory using the double-extension method. Assume that the beginning inventory as of January 1, 1984, had a base-year (index 1.00) value of $230,000 and a dollar value LIFO cost of $595,000.

Plant, Property, and Equipment

OVERVIEW

Long-term assets can be divided into three major categories: (1) plant, property, and equipment, which includes assets that have physical characteristics and are used in the major revenue-generating activities of the entity, (2) investments, and (3) intangibles and other assets. In this and the next chapter we cover accounting for the first category. Intangibles are covered in Chapter 13, and long-term investments in Chapter 14.

We shall trace three stages of the life cycle of plant, property, and equipment in this chapter, starting with measurement problems regarding the original acquisition cost, followed by costs incurred subsequent to acquisition, and ending with the retirement or exchange of plant assets. At all three stages the initial fair value, or cash-equivalent value, is the guiding measurement concept. Major measurement problems involving plant, property, and equipment usually center on the difficulties involved in objectively determining the fair value of the assets given up or received. The important process of allocating costs of plant, property, and equipment to years of use is covered in the next chapter.

Much of the capital supplied to a business enterprise by stockholders and creditors is used primarily for inventory and plant, property, and equipment. Investment in inventory, discussed in Chapters 9 and 10, is usually short-lived, with a turnover of specific units of inventory taking place with each sale. A primary business objective with regard to inventory should be to maintain the minimum levels consistent with current and near-term demand levels. However, plant, property, and equipment are more long term in nature. These assets represent investments in relatively fixed productive capacity. Achieving the optimum investment in plant, property, and equipment is a complex task that requires long-term planning for asset replacement and acquisition. The turnover rate is slow relative to that of inventories, and often the depreciation charge on such facilities is considered a fixed cost of operations.

THE NATURE OF PLANT, PROPERTY, AND EQUIPMENT

Plant, property, and equipment frequently represent a significant investment of an entity's capital. Many other names are used to identify these long-term assets, such as "fixed assets," "capital assets," "durable assets," "land, buildings, and machinery," and "facilities." Exhibit 11–1 shows the terms used in the notes to a published annual report. The balance sheet in this case had the major classification "Property, Plant, and Equipment," with the amount reported being the net of costs and accumulated depreciation. No matter what name is applied to these assets, they all have long-term periods of service utility, they are all important to the productive activities of the firm, and they all have physical substance. These assets are not the only asset group that is long term in nature, but they are in the only balance sheet category with all three of the above characteristics. For example, land held for investment purposes would be classified under "Long-Term Investments" or "Temporary Investments." Machinery held for resale would be classified under "Inventory" or "Other Assets." Rights to use a patent may be necessary for operations, but the right has no physical substance and the item would be classified as an "Intangible."

Within the category of plant, property, and equipment, a distinction is drawn between **wasting assets,** whose economic utility is consumed with use, and assets that are virtually nonconsumable. An example of a wasting asset would be an automobile, whose economic potential is consumed. In contrast, land, is a relatively permanent asset in that its utility as land is usually not consumed. Some would argue

EXHIBIT
11–1

DISCLOSURES OF PLANT, PROPERTY, AND EQUIPMENT BY WESTON COMPANY

Property, Plant, and Equipment (Note #6)

Property, plant, and equipment at cost for the year ended December 31, 1980, consisted of the following (in thousands):

	BALANCE AT BEGINNING OF YEAR	ADDITIONS AT COST	RETIREMENTS OR SALES	BALANCE AT END OF YEAR
Land and land improvements	$ 13,520	$ 3,312	$ 123	$ 16,709
Building	140,932	20,444	931	160,445
Machinery and equipment	327,258	76,440	6,721	396,977
Construction in process	30,073	10,633	8,063	32,643
	$511,783	$110,829	$15,838	$606,774

that this distinction is somewhat artificial and that all assets are potentially consumable. However, many companies differentiate between land and plant and equipment in their balance sheets. We shall see that segregation of plant, property, and equipment items into classes with similar useful lives is important in accounting for depreciation on such items.

MEASUREMENT OF PLANT, PROPERTY, AND EQUIPMENT AT ACQUISITION

The basic measure used in the recording of the acquisitions of plant, property, and equipment is **market price** or **cash-equivalent price.** These measures are expected to indicate the **fair value at the date of acquisition.** If we assume that the buyer and seller of plant, property, or equipment enter into an arm's-length agreement in a free market setting, it follows that at the time of the agreement the cash-equivalent price agreed upon equals the present value of the required payments. When this amount is recorded in the accounting records, it is referred to as **historical cost.** The historical cost, therefore, is the cash-equivalent price at the date of acquisition. In certain limited situations we may observe that the cash-equivalent-value or fair-value principle may not seem to be exactly the same as the present value of the payment for an asset. In such instances, specific rules may become applicable in the determination of the measured or recorded amount for a capital asset. These cases involve uncertainties as to actual values and discount rates. Some of these situations will be discussed later in the chapter.

The main justifications for the use of cash-equivalent price at the date of acquisition are that (1) it tends to be objectively measurable, (2) it tends to be readily verifiable, and (3) it is usually the result of a free-market negotiation process conducted at arm's-length with an independent entity. The market price is objectively measurable in the sense that several other entities or persons attempting to acquire the same assets in a competitive market would pay approximately the same cash price. The market price is verifiable in the sense that documentation is usually available in the form of a canceled check and a bill of sale or invoice that reports the value transferred between the buyer and the seller. If evidence exists that the acquisition is not the result of an arm's-length transaction, then additional evidence such as appraisals may be needed.

Much of the complexity in the measurement and subsequent recording of plant, property, and equipment is the result of breakdowns in these three supporting concepts. For example, sometimes cash is not the basis for the exchange agreement and some method of assigning a dollar amount to the transaction becomes necessary. Most asset acquisitions, however, are relatively straightforward, and the market-value or cash-equivalent price is used to record the acquisition. *Fair value* is the *dominant concept,* and if the cash transfer or list price does not equal the market price, other measures must be employed as a basis for recording the assets. For example, if $100,000 cash is paid for land that has a firmly established fair value of only $75,000, this indicates that something besides land is being paid for. The accountant would have to investigate the transaction carefully to determine the appropriate accounting treatment of the extra $25,000. Land would be recorded at $75,000.

When plant, property, or equipment is acquired, the acquisition cost is often something more than the invoice price alone. Many other costs related to the acquisition of an asset are often included in the acquisition cost of the asset. For example, legal fees, transportation costs, insurance, and other costs incidental to the acquisition of an asset are included, or "capitalized," in the recorded amount of the asset. The general rule in determining what should be capitalized is: **All costs incurred that are necessary to obtain the asset and place it into a useful state should be included in the cost of the asset.**

Determining
Acquisition
Costs:
An Example

Consider the following case:

> University Microcopy (UM) paid $59,000 to purchase a parcel of land just west of Ann Arbor for its new headquarters. The lot was heavily wooded and also had an old barn standing near the site of the proposed building. To prepare the land for its intended use, UM paid $5,000 to have some trees removed so that a road could be constructed to the building site. A local lumber mill paid UM $1,500 for the felled trees. UM had to pay $2,900 to have the old barn torn down, and it sold the wood from the barn for $3,500 to the same lumber mill, which used the wood for paneling. The legal costs and survey costs incurred in conjunction with the land purchase were $2,000. After a grading company had prepared the land for construction (cost of grading the land was $1,500), a building was constructed for $350,000 and a road was paved for $15,000. Landscaping was done the following year for a total of $2,500.

How would these costs be recorded? What accounts should be established? What should be the recorded amount for the land and the other assets acquired? The UM case actually describes the acquisition of three types of assets: (1) land, (2) land improvements, and (3) building. For reasons discussed below, the following summarizes the entries to record the events described in the UM case:

Land	65,400	
Land improvements	17,500	
Building	350,000	
Cash, payables, and so on		432,900

The basic factor that should determine the number of accounts to be used in recording the events in this case is the number of different **patterns of future benefits** represented by the events. Three patterns of future benefits may be identified here. The building cost is tied to the life of the building. In this case, only the $350,000 can be identified as specifically related to the cost of the building. In other cases, however, many separately billed costs could be included with the building costs. For example, air-conditioning or heating systems may be included as a cost of the building even though they may be acquired in separate transactions. Also, the fees paid to an architect for designing a building, building permit costs, legal costs, and interest charges during the construction period would be included as the costs of a building. In this case, we assume that all such costs are included in the $350,000 amount.

The Land account is separate from Land Improvements on the basis of the time period of future benefits. The Land Improvements account includes the cost of the road ($15,000) and the cost of landscaping ($2,500). Although these costs will provide benefits over a long period of time, they will not outlive the usefulness of the land itself but will eventually need to be replaced or renewed. As a result, depreciation is appropriate for the land improvements. If these two elements of land improvements had different useful lives, they would usually be recorded as separate accounts.

The Land account, because of its many components, illustrates the general rule of cost determination. In the UM case, the Land account would include the following items:

Purchase price of land	$59,000
Cost to clear the land of trees	5,000
Less proceeds from felled trees	(1,500)
Cost to tear down barn	2,900
Less proceeds from barn's wood	(3,500)
Legal and survey costs	2,000
Cost to grade construction site	1,500
	$65,400

These cost elements in the Land account are considered to be costs incurred in the process of acquiring land and preparing it for its intended use—a site upon which an office building is to be constructed. The periods of benefit of these cost elements are all considered to be the same as for the land itself. On the basis of their similarity in terms of benefit period, these costs are all capitalized as a part of the Land account. The purpose of the cost in conjunction with the benefit period provides the basis of cost determination.

Assets Acquired for Monetary Consideration

As mentioned above, the basic measurement principle for plant, property, and equipment is to record the assets acquired at their fair value. When assets are acquired in exchange for monetary considerations, the measurement of fair value is relatively straightforward because the cash equivalent of monetary items is usually readily determinable.

When cash is the basis for the exchange, fair value is considered to be the cash given up. Because cash is the principal medium of exchange, the cash equivalent is considered to be the best approximation of fair value. In addition to cash, such monetary items as debt instruments are also frequently involved in asset acquisitions. In cases where short- or long-term obligations are all or part of the consideration given in exchange for an asset, the present-value concept discussed in Chapter 5 should be employed in measuring the recorded value of the asset.

Assume that on January 1, 1984, UM paid cash of $50,000 and also borrowed $300,000 on a mortgage from the Chelsea State Bank for the building acquisition. If the mortgage called for payments of $30,542 per year for 25 years, the total mortgage payments made by UM would equal $763,550. Assuming the implied interest rate was a reasonable one in the circumstances, only $300,000 of the $763,550 would be included in the cost of the building. The $463,550 difference would be recorded as interest expense over the life of the mortgage. The financing cost is not related to the amount of future benefits provided by the building and would not be included in the recorded amount of the building. The implicit interest rate here is 9 percent, and the building acquisition at the beginning of the year along with the first payment on the borrowed amount at the end of the first year would be recorded as follows:

1/1/84	Building	350,000	
	Cash		50,000
	Mortgage payable		300,000
12/31/84	Mortgage payable	3,542	
	Interest expense	27,000	
	Cash		30,542

When monetary items other than cash are involved in the acquisition of an asset, the principal variable to be considered in cost determination is the interest rate to apply in computing the present value of the cash flows. In most instances, the interest rate is stated in the terms of the mortgage contract or other document supporting the basis of the monetary commitment. When the interest rate is stated, it should still be tested for reasonableness.

Acquisitions involving uncertain interest factors As pointed out in Chapter 5, which discusses present values, the cash-equivalent value of an acquired asset may be obscured by an uncertain interest rate when assets are paid for by means of loans or mortgages. Overstatement of the interest rate will understate the asset's value and overstate the amount of interest paid. Understating the interest rate will overstate the asset's value and understate the amount of interest paid. Because the period of the monetary obligation (that is, the mortgage or note) may differ significantly from the life of the asset being acquired, it is important to test the reasonableness of the interest rate to ensure proper asset measurement initially and proper matching of revenues with depreciation expense and interest subsequent to acquisition.[1]

The incremental interest rate that is assumed in some cases could be tested by comparing it with other interest rates being charged to the same or similar entities for similar types of obligations or similar transactions. Such tests of reasonableness normally require the professional judgment of the accountant because each major financing transaction involving a capital asset acquisition is unique to some extent. At the same time, the interest factor is usually important for the proper recording of such transactions.

When monetary instruments that are not interest bearing are given in exchange for the assets acquired, measurement of fair value may be difficult. If neither cash nor the present value of cash flows is available as a basis for measurement, fair value should be determined by measuring the market price (cash equivalent) of the assets given or received, whichever is the most readily determinable and objectively measurable. For example, if a non-interest-bearing mortgage calling for annual payments of $33,050 for 25 years plus a $50,000 cash down payment were given in exchange for the building in the UM case, the objective would be to determine either the fair market value of the building or the fair rate of interest implicit in the mortgage. If the contract for the construction of the building called for a fixed contract price of $350,000, then the contract would provide the objective evidence that the fair value of the building is $350,000. The implicit interest rate in the mortgage could be determined by first computing the table factor for the present value of an ordinary annuity (Table H–3, Appendix H) as follows:

$$\$50,000 + \$33,050(P/A, 25, i) = \$350,000$$
$$\$33,050(P/A, 25, i) = \$350,000 - \$50,000$$
$$\$33,050(P/A, 25, i) = \$300,000$$
$$(P/A, 25, i) = \$300,000/\$33,050$$
$$(P/A, 25, i) = 9.077$$

The present-value factor 9.077 in Table H–3 for $n = 25$ is found to represent

---

[1] *Accounting Principles Board Opinion No. 21,* "Interest on Receivables and Payables" (New York: AICPA, August 1971), addresses this question in detail.

a 10 percent implicit interest rate for the mortgage (see Appendix H, Table H–3, at the back of the book for $n = 25$ periods). This rate would be used to record the amount of principal and interest for each of the $33,050 payments.

Assets Acquired for Nonmonetary Consideration

Nonmonetary assets may occasionally be involved in the acquisition of plant, property, and equipment. In such instances, the general rule of fair value discussed above is applied once again. The principle is to use fair value of the asset or assets given or received, whichever is more readily and objectively determinable. These judgments, although difficult, can be important to the proper recording of the long-term productive assets of the entity. Such instances are not common, but they sometimes do require relatively subjective estimates of fair value. For example, if UM acquired the building in exchange for stock in a closely held corporation—that is, one whose stock is not publicly traded—the recorded amount of the building might be difficult to determine. To the extent that the building was unique and not comparable with other assets, or to the extent that the recent market price of the stock was unavailable due to lack of public trading activity, the recording of the building might have to be based on rather subjective evidence.

Unfortunately, no clear answers are available in some instances, and the accountant must simply rely on professional judgment plus whatever evidence regarding market values is available. In certain cases where assets are given up in exchange for other assets, special measurement rules must be applied. These cases are covered in the "Retirements and Exchanges of Assets" section of this chapter. With few exceptions, however, the fair-value concept prevails as the dominant measurement concept.

Self-Constructed Assets

Assets acquired through an entity's own construction efforts can present some unique accounting problems. The amount of self-construction may vary widely from entity to entity. A utility may, for example, undertake a construction project to build a new hydroelectric plant that could double its capacity to generate electricity. An automobile parts manufacturer could decide to construct a new warehouse for storage, or a plant nursery could use its employees to construct an addition to its greenhouse. In these three examples an entity that is not in the construction business has decided to undertake a self-construction project. The major measurement problem in such cases is the **allocation of the entity's costs and expenses** to its operations on the one hand and its nonoperating construction efforts on the other. Although such allocation problems are not uncommon in accounting—for example, they occur in most systems for determining inventory cost—the impact of allocation methods on the measurement of major capital assets deserves special emphasis because of its potential materiality.

The elements of cost involved in self-constructed assets are (1) the prime or direct costs (direct material and direct labor); (2) the indirect variable-overhead costs (the construction supervisor's wages, indirect materials, power, fringe benefits, and so on); (3) the indirect fixed-overhead costs (machinery, equipment, salaried personnel, and so on); and (4) interest costs incurred during the construction process. There is not complete agreement as to which overhead elements are to be included in the recorded cost of self-constructed assets. Prime costs must be included in the cost of self-constructed assets. Also, as a result of **FASB Statement No. 34**, corporations constructing their own assets are required to capitalize interest costs incurred during the construction period when they are material in amount.[2] In a recent financial statement, Georgia Pacific Corporation described its policy of capitalizing interest in the following way:

> The corporation capitalizes interest on borrowed funds during construction periods. Such interest is charged to the property, plant, and equipment accounts and amortized over the approximate life of the related assets in order to properly match expenses with revenues resulting from the facilities. Capitalized interest, less related amortization and income taxes, amounted to $32,000, $14,000, and $9,000 for the years ended December 31, 1980, 1979, and 1978, respectively.

The objective in determining the amount of overhead to be allocated to the self-constructed asset is twofold: (1) Do *not* distort normal operating costs with overhead generated by construction activity, and (2) do *not* charge construction with overhead generated by operations. If more overhead is charged to a self-constructed asset than the incremental overhead costs that resulted from the construction, the operating expenses for that period will be understated and operating profits will be overstated. However, if no overhead is charged to the constructed asset and incremental overhead costs were actually incurred as a result of the construction, the operating expenses will be overstated and operating profits understated for that period. Because it is not possible to measure the incremental overhead costs with precision, even after the construction is completed, professional judgment is required in measuring the relevant cost of self-constructed assets. This judgment process might be helped by asking the following questions:

1. Were profit margins on operating activities normal during the construction period?
2. What would outside contractors have bid for the construction?
3. What financing was required to undertake the construction?
4. What is the insured value of the constructed asset?
5. Can overhead allocated to the self-constructed asset be explained by incremental costs that would have been avoided without the construction activity?

Answers to these questions will help test the reasonableness of the recorded cost of the self-constructed asset. If evidence exists that the fair or cash-equivalent value of the constructed asset is *below* the recorded cost, a loss should be recognized by crediting the asset account and debiting Loss on Self-Constructed Asset. However, due to the pervasiveness of conservatism, assets constructed at a cost below fair value would not result in the recognition of a gain. Such assets would be re-

---

[2] *Statement of Financial Accounting Standards No. 34,* "Capitalization of Interest Cost" (Stamford, CT: FASB, October 1979). Interest rates were singled out from other overhead costs due to their material amount in many instances. Prior to 1970, few companies other than utilities "capitalized" their interest costs as a part of self-constructed assets. During the early 1970s, however, some companies started to follow the utilities by capitalizing their interest costs during construction. In 1974 the SEC issued *Accounting Series Release No. 163,* requiring nonutility companies to stop interest capitalization until an investigation had been conducted. Finally, in late 1979, the FASB called for uniform capitalization of interest during construction of self-constructed assets for most firms. The basic objective was to permit capitalization of the incremental interest costs that resulted from the self-construction efforts. The details of *FASB Statement No. 34* allow the capitalization of interest only if the company has debt outstanding during the construction period. Also, *FASB Statement No. 34* does not require a direct relationship between the debt of a company and its self-construction efforts. As a result of these and other specific aspects of *FASB Statement No. 34,* the pronouncement has been somewhat controversial due to its inability to resolve all uncertainties in this subjective measurement area.

corded at the cost amount and the higher market value would be ignored for recording purposes.

Assets Acquired Through Donations

Occasionally an asset is acquired in a transaction that amounts to a **transfer in one direction.** Such "exchanges" are called **nonreciprocal transfers** because one of the parties involved is viewed as not reciprocating (a one-way exchange). Such transfers are not limited to plant, property, or equipment, but they are discussed here because they do occur at times and they often involve such assets.

Measurement problems can be difficult in some cases of nonreciprocal transfers. In virtually every case, some exchange is actually taking place, although one side of the exchange may be too obscure or too subtle to permit its measurement. For example, a community may donate land to a corporation to get it to build a plant in the area. This "gift" will, of course, benefit the community by increasing the property tax base, increasing employment, and providing other related economic activities. **APB Opinion No. 29** addresses the issue of nonmonetary assets that are received by an entity in a nonreciprocal transfer, and it states that the fair value should be recorded.[3] What should be credited? In the case of the donated land, the following journal entry would be appropriate:

Land	X,XXX	
Donated capital		X,XXX

The Donated Capital account would be classified as an element of owners' equity.

The value used for both parties as a basis for recording nonreciprocal transfers should be the fair market value of the asset at date of exchange, and its determination would be based on the measurement techniques discussed in the preceding sections. To illustrate, assume that the Unified Computer Company (UCC) donated a Series IV Computer to the Paton Research Center, Inc. (PRC). UCC's net book value for the computer at the date of donation was $8,000. The fair market value of the computer at the date of donation was $10,000. The following entries would record this nonreciprocal transfer on the books of both the donor and the donee:

UCC			PRC		
Expense of contributions and gifts	10,000		Computer equipment	10,000	
Series IV Computer—equipment (net)		8,000	Donated capital		10,000
Gain on equipment		2,000			

The expense and the gain would be reported in UCC's income statement, whereas the credit to the asset account would eliminate the computer from its books. Acquisition of assets in a nonreciprocal transaction does not affect subsequent accounting for the asset. Normal accounting procedures would apply to donated assets. The Donated Capital account is a permanent owners' equity account.

Lump-Sum Acquisitions

Assets that would normally be assigned to different balance sheet classifications are sometimes acquired for a lump-sum consideration. In such cases evidence as to the

---

[3] *Accounting Principles Board Opinion No. 29,* "Accounting for Nonmonetary Transactions" (New York: AICPA, 1973), par. 18.

relative cash-equivalent values must be used to allocate the cost. For instance, if both a parcel of land and a building are acquired for a single payment of $1,000,000, evidence such as the appraisal value of each item or the recent selling prices of similar items could be used to determine the appropriate book values to be assigned as follows:

	INDEPENDENT APPRAISAL VALUES	ALLOCATION RATIO	COST ALLOCATION
Land	$ 200,000	2/14 × $1,000,000	$ 142,857
Building	1,200,000	12/14 × $1,000,000	857,143
	$1,400,000		$1,000,000

COSTS SUBSEQUENT TO ACQUISITION

General
Principle

Additional costs relating to long-term productive assets are frequently incurred subsequent to their acquisition. The question that must be asked in recording such subsequent costs is, Should they be capitalized as assets or expensed? This question turns on the accountant's judgment as to whether an asset has been created by the additional costs. Because assets are defined as costs that will produce future economic benefits, the benefit period is the focal point in accounting for such costs. If future benefits will result, future periods should be charged with a portion of the costs in order that a proper matching of expenses and benefits be made.

Many different types of costs may be incurred subsequent to acquisition, all of which must be evaluated to determine whether they do in fact provide future benefits. Our discussion of subsequent costs will consider three major categories: (1) additions, betterments, and improvements; (2) maintenance; and (3) repairs, replacements, and renewals. This discussion will outline the general types of subsequent costs and the common aspects of their accounting treatment. As we shall see, professional judgment is definitely involved in accounting for expenditures on property, plant, and equipment beyond the point of their original acquisition.

Additions,
Betterments,
and
Improvements

The common thread running through additions, betterments, and improvements is that these costs provide benefits beyond the period of expenditure. The future benefits might be represented by an increase in the **productive efficiency** and/or an extension of the original **productive life** of an asset, in which cases these costs are examples of expenditures that should be capitalized as part of long-term productive assets. Costs that would normally be called *additions* or *betterments* or *improvements* are material dollar outlays incurred to facilitate the production or revenue-generating process of current and future years. If this criterion is not met, some term other than *additions* or *betterments* or *improvements* should be used to classify the cost outlay.

Once a cost has been identified as an addition, a betterment, or an improvement, a determination must be made as to what existing or new account should be used to record the cost. Consider an example where a betterment is made to a building owned by the Garden Gate Nursery. Should the betterment be added to the Building account or should it be added to a separate account, a Betterments account? This question, and others like it, are resolved by considering the period of benefit. If the betterment is a new side entrance to the building to facilitate customer traffic flow, the life of the betterment is considered to be tied to that of the building. In such a case, it would be convenient to add the cost of the betterment to the Building account and depreciate it (along with the other costs for the building) over the remaining useful life of the building.

Sometimes the life of a capitalizable cost is different from the life of the asset to which it relates. In such cases, the cost should be classified as a separate item and depreciated over its useful life. Professional judgment and an assessment of the materiality of differences resulting from alternative treatments are important factors in determining proper accounting for additions, betterments, and improvements.

Maintenance

Maintenance usually represents regular ongoing costs required to keep the plant and equipment in a normally functioning productive state. Because of their regular and nearly continual nature and their relatively short-term benefit period, maintenance costs are typically expensed as incurred.

It is sometimes not clear whether a subsequent cost is best classified as maintenance or some other type of cost such as a betterment or an improvement. Consider the cost of painting a building. This type of expenditure may occur only once every 5 years or so and may represent a significant amount of money. Because the cost does not increase the **productive efficiency** of the building or extend its original expected **productive life,** it would not be capitalized as part of the Building account. Instead, it would be viewed as a necessary cost of the ordinary operations of the business. This is interesting because the original cost of painting the building is depreciated along with the other original costs over the life of the asset. Cleaning, painting, adjusting, and lubricating are examples of normal ongoing activities whose costs are typically classified as maintenance expense.

Repairs, Replacements, and Renewals

The question of capitalization versus expensing is most challenging in the case of costs for repairs, replacements, or renewals. Answering the question of whether there has been an increase in the **productive efficiency** or an extension of the **productive life** is not sufficient to resolve the issue. For example, the spark plugs of a piston engine must be changed every so often if the engine is to function. Replacing spark plugs might be viewed as increasing both the productive efficiency and the useful life of the engine. Should the spark plugs be capitalized? To answer the question, an additional condition must be evaluated by asking another question: **Could the cost of the repair, replacement, or renewal have been reasonably expected to occur?** If the answer is yes, as in the case of the spark plugs, then the repair, replacement, or renewal should be treated as maintenance and expensed in the period incurred.

If, however, the cost could not have been reasonably expected to occur, the capitalization of the repair, replacement, or renewal is normally called for if the cost is of a material amount. Also, the original cost of the item unexpectedly being repaired, replaced, or renewed should be written off, and a loss should be recorded for the unexpected decline in utility.

Consider, for example, the case of the Godfrey Trucking Company. One of the company's trucks blows an engine after only 10,000 miles of use. The truck (and engine) was expected to be serviceable for 100,000 miles. Furthermore, assume that the engine cost was estimated to represent 10 percent of the original $50,000 cost of the truck. The truck was being depreciated on a per-mile basis. The new engine costs $6,000 including installation, because the warranty expired after the first 5,000 miles. Was the replacement expected to occur? The answer is no, and therefore the cost of the replacement should be capitalized and the remaining book value of the replaced item should be written off as a loss. The following entries would be appropriate:

Truck #857	6,000	
Cash		6,000
(To record the replacement of the engine in truck #857)		
Accumulated depreciation—truck #857	500	
Loss on engine from truck #857	4,500	
Truck #857		5,000
(To record the loss on blown engine)		

The balance in the Truck #857 account would now be $51,000 and the accumulated depreciation balance would be $4,500:

$$(\$50,000 \times [\$10,000/\$100,000]) - \$500 =$$
$$\$5,000 - \$500 = \$4,500$$

The new depreciation rate would be $.5167 per mile:

$$\$51,000 - \$4,500 = \$46,500/90,000 \text{ miles}$$

The assumption in the Godfrey Trucking example is that the life of the engine is tied to that of the truck. If this were not the case, the same procedures discussed for the capitalization of additions, betterments, and improvements would apply. The engine would be considered a separate asset and would be depreciated over its useful life.

RETIREMENTS AND EXCHANGES OF ASSETS

Sale of Plant,
Property,
and Equipment

The disposal of productive assets calls for the elimination of the balance in both the asset account and the accumulated depreciation account and the recording of any value received in exchange. The depreciation on the asset being sold should be recorded up to the date the asset is taken out of use as a productive element of plant, property, and equipment.

Assume that the Dukes Corporation has an injection-molding machine that originally cost $28,000. The machine is being depreciated at the rate of $4,000 per year. On December 31, 1983, the preceding year-end, the balance in the Accumulated Depreciation account was $23,000. On April 1, 1984, Dukes sells the machine for $6,000 cash. The following entries would record this sale:

4/1/84	Depreciation expense	1,000	
	Accumulated depreciation		1,000
	(To record 1984 depreciation on machine)		
4/1/84	Cash	6,000	
	Accumulated depreciation	24,000	
	Machinery		28,000
	Gain on sale of equipment		2,000
	(To record the sale of equipment)		

The gain on the sale of equipment, according to current disclosure rules in **APB**

Opinion No. 30, would be reported in the income statement above the subtotal "income from continuing operations."[4]

The entries shown above were based on the assumption that the machine was in use until sold. If a machine or other plant asset is no longer being used in a productive capacity, then the asset should be reclassified as "other assets" until it is sold or otherwise disposed of. At the time of the reclassification, the "other asset" should be recorded at its fair or cash-equivalent value, but not to exceed book value. Since the fair value is usually uncertain, the book value at the time of reclassification is often used.

Suppose an entity discontinues activities at a location and immediately sells all the related assets except for a truck that has a fair value of $3,000 and book value of $4,700 (cost of $10,100 minus accumulated depreciation of $5,400) and a computer with undetermined fair value and book value of $12,500 (cost of $27,000 minus accumulated depreciation of $14,500). The appropriate journal entries for the reclassifications would be as follows:

TRUCK—DETERMINABLE FAIR VALUE

Other assets—truck	3,000	
Accumulated depreciation—truck	5,400	
Loss on reclassification of truck	1,700	
Truck		10,100

COMPUTER—UNDETERMINABLE FAIR VALUE

Other assets—computer	12,500	
Accumulated depreciation—computer	14,500	
Computer		27,000

The reclassifications are necessary so that the assets will not only be removed from the property, plant, and equipment designation that is reserved for operating assets but also be placed in a classification more descriptive of their status until they are disposed of or put back into operation.

Exchanges Involving Productive Assets

The general case Exchanges of plant assets are basically the same as other types of exchange transactions. The cash-equivalent value of the "pool" of assets given or received is the basis for recording the exchange. In dealing with exchanges of capital assets, however, the cash-equivalent value may often be obscured by information that seems relevant but simply distorts the economic substance of the exchange. Consider the following case:

The IXL Glass Company has a fleet of four trucks. On June 1, 1984, John Bohn, the owner, decided to trade in one of the trucks on a new model. The old truck was a 1981 model that originally cost $7,500. The accumulated depreciation on the old truck at June 1, 1984, was $4,900. The list price on the new truck was $9,800. To encourage Bohn to buy the new truck, the dealer offered him a $2,500 trade-in allowance on the old truck, bringing the out-of-pocket (cash) cost of the 1984 model to $7,300 ($9,800 − $2,500). Bohn took his old truck to several used-truck lots and also placed a "For Sale" sign on the truck for a few weeks. As a result of these efforts to sell the 1981

---

[4] *Accounting Principles Board Opinion No. 30,* "Reporting the Results of Operations" (New York: AICPA, 1973).

truck, the best offer he received was $2,000. The lowest offer was $1,400, and the average offer was $1,800. Because the dealer's $2,500 trade-in allowance seemed to be the best deal, Bohn traded in the 1981 model, acquiring the new truck for $7,300 in cash plus the old truck.

How should the glass company's exchange be recorded? The old asset has a number of possible values:

Net book value	$2,600
Trade-in value	2,500
Highest cash value	2,000
Lowest cash value	1,400
Average cash value	1,800

The pool of assets given up in exchange would include $7,300 cash plus the fair value of the old truck. However, the fair value of the old asset is not clear. What about the new asset's fair value? The pool of assets acquired is represented by the new truck's having a list price of $9,800. Is $9,800 the fair value received?

Using the fair-value or cash-equivalent value concept, the best estimate of the value given in this exchange based on the facts of the case would be $9,300. This value is based on the cash given up, $7,300, plus the cash forgone by trading in the old truck instead of selling it outright for $2,000. Also, the $9,300 value is supported by the knowledge that new trucks typically sell for something less than their list prices.

Three different methods may be used to record the trade-in described above: (1) fair value, (2) list price, and (3) book value. These three methods can be illustrated as follows:

	FAIR-VALUE METHOD		LIST-PRICE METHOD		BOOK-VALUE METHOD	
Truck (new)	9,300		9,800		9,900	
Accumulated depreciation (old truck)	4,900		4,900		4,900	
Loss on exchange	600		100		0	
Truck (old)		7,500		7,500		7,500
Cash		7,300		7,300		7,300

The list-price method should not be used unless the list price of the new asset is the best estimate of cash-equivalent value of the assets received. Note that for assets that do sell at list price, the fair-value method will be the same as the list-price method. The book-value method, used for recording the exchange of similar assets for tax purposes, forces the gain or loss on exchange to equal zero. The tax regulations thereby avoid the measurement problems of determining fair value in cases of asset exchange. Any gain or loss that would otherwise be recorded by using an alternative method is forced into the recorded value of the new asset.

Note that the recording of assets given up in the case above is constant. The cash outflow and the elimination of the book value of the old asset are not subject to alternative methods. Only the recorded amount of the new asset and the gain or loss are subject to change. Also, observe that the gain or loss will always be the difference between the book value of the old asset and the value assigned to the old asset in the exchange. This last point is not always easy to understand, but keep in mind that a gain or loss does not result from the acquisition of an asset. The recorded gain or loss is simply the difference between the book value of the old asset and the value assigned to it at the time of transfer. In the example above, the fair-value method assigns a $2,000 value to the old asset. The loss is the difference between the book value and the assigned value ($2,600 − $2,000). If book value had been less than fair value, a gain would have been indicated.

The fair-value method is considered the only theoretically sound basis for recording the exchange of productive assets when fair values can be determined. If the fair value of neither the asset received nor the asset given up can be determined with reasonable confidence, then the book-value method is used. However, because many entities find it convenient to maintain conformance between tax records and accounting records, and because the differences between the book-value method and the fair-value method are not always material, it is not uncommon to find applications of the book-value method for financial reporting purposes as well as for tax purposes.

The special case   There is one other major exception to the fair-value method of recording the exchange of productive assets for financial accounting purposes. This exception to the general rule contained in **APB Opinion No. 29** is for specific limited types of exchanges.[5] The rule was adopted to curtail certain gain-recognition practices and has little to offer in the way of purely conceptual underpinnings. As we shall see, the approach prescribed for certain exchanges is a modified book-value approach in which gains on trades are sometimes prohibited or limited to a specific amount.

APB Opinion No. 29 discusses various types of nonmonetary exchanges,[6] most of which are recorded using the fair-value method. However, in exchanges involving (1) **"similar" productive assets** where (2) **the earnings process is not culminated** and (3) **a gain would ordinarily be recognized using the fair-value method,** a special valuation method is required. If any one of the three conditions identified above is not present, the fair-value method should be used. The rule therefore allows all losses to be recognized whether or not **boot** (a monetary consideration involved in an exchange) is received. Gains on similar productive assets for which the earnings process is not complete are recognized only if boot is received and then there is the following limitation on the amount recognized:

$$\text{Gain recognized is limited to} \left(\frac{\text{Boot received}}{\text{Total consideration received}} \right) \times \left(\begin{array}{c} \text{Gain computed with} \\ \text{the fair value method} \end{array} \right)$$

The assets being exchanged must be similar. If timberland is being exchanged for minerals, the exchange would not qualify for special treatment. If an earnings process *is* culminated as a result of the exchange, no special treatment is allowed. For example, the exchange of finished-goods inventory between competitors and the exchange of similar productive assets with remaining useful lives do not culminate earnings processes. To illustrate the special valuation method, consider the following situation:

> Firm A and firm B enter into an exchange of *similar* machinery. Firm A is going to exchange equipment with a fair value of $4,700 for firm B's equipment, which has a fair value of $2,900. In addition, firm B pays firm A $1,800 *cash* (boot). The net book value

[5] *Accounting Principles Board Opinion No. 29*, "Accounting for Nonmonetary Transactions, par. 26.

[6] Ibid., par. 18.

of firm A's asset is $3,900 at the date of exchange, whereas firm B's asset has a net book value of $2,600.

The case described above is accorded special treatment because (1) the assets are similar, (2) an earnings process is not culminated, and (3) a gain results. The "normal" gain to firm A of $800 is the difference between the fair value of A's asset ($4,700) and its book value ($3,900). The "normal" gain to firm B of $300 is the difference between the fair value of B's asset ($2,900) and its book value ($2,600). The special rule required by **APB Opinion No. 29** calls for recognition of only a part of this gain on the books of firm A and none on the books of firm B. The partial gain for firm A is computed using the following formula:[7]

$$\text{(Total gain per the fair-value method)} \times \left(\frac{\text{Cash received}}{\text{Cash received + Fair value of asset received}} \right)$$

In the case described above, firm A's recorded gain would be computed as follows:

$$\$800 \times \frac{\$1,800}{\$1,800 + \$2,900} =$$

$$\$800 \times .3829787 = \underline{\underline{\$306}}$$

Firm B recognizes none of its $300 gain because no boot is received, resulting in the following analysis:

$$\left(\begin{array}{c} \text{Total gain per the} \\ \text{fair-value method} \end{array} \right) \times \left(\frac{\text{Cash received}}{\text{Cash received + fair value of other asset received}} \right)$$

$$\$300 \times \left(\frac{0}{0 + 4,700} \right) =$$

$$\$300 \times 0 = 0$$

The following entry would record the exchange for firm A:

FIRM A (SPECIAL METHOD)

Cash	1,800	
Machinery (from firm B)	2,406[a]	
Machinery (old)		3,900
Gain on exchange		306

[a] This amount is equal to the book value of the old asset ($3,900) minus the cash received ($1,800) plus the gain recognized ($306).

Firm B recognizes no gain according to **APB Opinion No. 29** and should record the new asset at the amount of cash paid plus the book value of the asset given up (the book-value method).[8] The entry at the top of p. 401 records the exchange.

[7] Ibid., par. 22.

[8] Ibid., par. 22.

Machinery (from firm A)	4,400	
Cash		1,800
Machinery (old)		2,600

FUNDS FLOW EFFECTS

The acquisition of plant and equipment can be financed by means of transfers of working capital, other assets, or securities or by long-term borrowing. Funds statements emphasizing cash would disclose cash expenditures for any asset acquisition as a use of funds. Working capital analyses would disclose a use of funds for any reduction in current assets or increases in current liabilities associated with long-term asset acquisitions. As is discussed in detail in Chapters 4 and 25, all significant financing activities must be disclosed in statements of changes in financial position, even those that represent transfers of noncash items (for a cash analysis) and non-working capital items (for a working capital analysis). Therefore the acquisition of land by means of long-term borrowing would be disclosed on a statement of changes in financial position even though funds are not affected by such a transaction.

Disposition of assets may affect funds when assets are sold. For instance a long-term asset with a book value of $25,000 may be sold as scrap for $10,000. The resulting loss of $15,000 is captured in net income but the positive funds flow is $10,000. As explained in Chapters 4 and 25, such transactions call for a specific kind of disclosure pattern in order to ensure that funds from operations and other sources are properly disclosed.

SUMMARY

The recording of plant, property, and equipment follows the general principle of measuring the fair value or cash-equivalent value of the assets at date of acquisition. When cash is not the basis for the arm's-length transaction, the accountant must attempt to measure the fair value of the asset(s) given or received, whichever is most objectively determinable. When the measurement calls for imputing an interest rate for a financial contract or estimating the fair value of a unique asset or one with no known market value, the accountant must rely on his or her judgment and recognize that some uncertainty will exist regarding the resulting measurement.

Costs subsequent to acquisition require classification judgments on the accountant's part. To the extent that future benefits will result from an expenditure, an asset will generally be recorded. If the future benefits are short-lived, or if the expenditure flow is fairly continuous, or if the amount of the expenditure is relatively immaterial, an expense account will generally be charged. The major measurement problems regarding costs subsequent to acquisition are resolved by applying the "future benefits" criterion.

The retirement, sale, or exchange of productive assets is usually handled in a manner similar to that used for other assets. The asset leaving the entity is eliminated from the accounts, any assets received by the entity are recorded (for example, cash from salvage value), and the difference between these inflows and outflows is recognized as either a gain or a loss. This general rule applies except for the special cases noted in the chapter.

Q11–1   What is the cash-equivalent price of an acquired asset?

Q11–2   What are the major differences between the plant, property, and equipment category and other long-term asset categories?

Q11–3   What principle determines which costs related to an acquired asset are to be capitalized?

Q11–4   Why do you think the issue of capitalizing interest on self-constructed assets has created controversy in the past, and how was the controversy "resolved" by the FASB?

Q11–5   Describe a situation in which the distinction between *maintenance* and *betterments* becomes blurred. Why is this distinction important in accounting?

Q11–6   What is the major uncertainty in accounting for self-constructed assets, and how is it resolved?

Q11–7   Contrast the accounting treatment of land used as a building site and land held for resale.

Q11–8   Under what conditions is the fair-value method not used to determine the gain on the disposition of an asset?

Q11–9   What do you think motivated current promulgated GAAP on trades of similar assets?

Q11–10   What conceptual arguments can you think of *in favor of* and *against* the capitalization of donated assets?

CASES

C11–1   Holstrum Perfumes Ltd. acquired the assets of Dubin, Inc., a small perfume manufacturer, during the current fiscal year. At year-end Holstrum is trying to determine which costs to include as property, plant, and equipment. The following accounts appear in the preadjusting trial balance:

Dubin buildings and equipment	$800,000
Dubin land	10,000
Dubin inventories	45,000
Legal fees for the Dubin acquisition	12,000
Holstrum's president's salary assigned to the Dubin acquisition	14,000
Interest on bank loan used in the Dubin acquisition	9,000
Repairs on Dubin equipment	17,500
Insurance premium on Dubin plant and equipment	6,600

REQUIRED   Discuss each of the above items and decide which should appear as part of property, plant, and equipment on Holstrum's balance sheet.

C11–2   Penelope Springer owns a winery, as does her sister, Nicole. The vineyards from which the grapes are harvested for both wineries were originally owned by their father. When their father died, each of the sisters inherited half of the 1,000 acres for her winery pursuant to a clause in the father's will that called for a payment of $100,000 to his wife. The sisters must now decide on the appropriate asset value for their accounting records.

REQUIRED   Discuss the factors to be considered in establishing the book value for the vineyards on each set of books.

C11–3   Ranchhouse Resorts operates a dude ranch in Montana. All the structures (cabins, restaurants, and other buildings) are constructed by employees during the off-season. To this point, only the cost of construction materials has been capitalized. The owner gives the following rationale for this policy: "Our staff has to be paid on a year-round basis. During the off-season, they have a lot of free time, and the wages we pay for constructing buildings cannot be separated from the wages relating to other work. There is no incremental cost to us for their labor."

REQUIRED   Write a memorandum to the owner explaining why the buildings are not properly valued on the balance sheet.

C11–4 Denmark Liners Ltd. operates 20 excursion ships in several parts of the world. Its modernization plan is to refurbish older ships every 10 years at a cost that has averaged 50 percent of the original acquisition price. The company's controller argues that because these alterations come very regularly, the balance sheet and income statement are not materially affected by the company's policy of expensing all refurbishing costs as incurred.

REQUIRED Discuss the validity of the controller's assertion, and give your opinion as to the appropriateness of this policy.

C11–5 Companies sometimes record sales of equipment in such a way that the difference between book value and sales price is debited or credited to Accumulated Depreciation.

REQUIRED When would such a procedure be justified?

C11–6 A company installed a new central computer system. The old computer, although completely depreciated for book purposes, was moved to a branch office where it was estimated that it could be used indefinitely. The original depreciation schedule was based on use at the central location.

REQUIRED Give arguments supporting the recording of the fair value of the computer at the date of transfer, and explain why such a practice is not normal.

C11–7 Princeport, Inc., manufactures chemicals for shipment throughout the world. The company's management has been attempting to sell an old loading and storage facility in Europe so that the company can concentrate its activities in the Americas. During the current year there has been a serious decline in net income, but the vice-president of finance has an idea that he thinks will both dispose of the European facility and boost net income. He would like to trade the European facility for a newer but smaller facility in Mexico. The two facilities have approximately the same fair values, which far exceed the book value of the old facility.

REQUIRED Consider the vice-president's idea and explain why the plan may be faulty.

C11–8 Continental Rentals has switched from a decentralized automobile-purchasing system to a centralized one in order to reap the benefits of volume discounts. The new automobiles are delivered through local dealerships of one automobile manufacturer, and the list price is paid by Continental's local offices. At the end of each month the manufacturer mails a check to Continental's main office for 10 percent of the total companywide purchases for that month. Each local office maintains a complete set of books that are consolidated quarterly and at year-end.

REQUIRED How should the 10 percent discount be recorded on Continental's books? Give reasons for your answer.

C11–9 Louisiana Sugar Refiners, Inc., suffered severe damage as the result of a hurricane, but the aggregate amount of insurance claims far exceeds the book value of the damaged structures. All the proceeds from insurance payments will be used to rebuild the old structures.

REQUIRED Describe the appropriate accounting for such a circumstance.

C11–10 For 20 years Pyramid Electronics has operated in a factory building that was donated to it by the city of Seattle. The agreement requires that upon relocation, the factory building's ownership reverts to the city. The building has been depreciated down to a $100,000 book value, and the company is planning to relocate to a suburb.

REQUIRED Describe the journal entries, if any, that would be necessary upon relocation.

C11–11 Consider the following opposing statements concerning the trading of assets:

1. All assets that are disposed of should first be brought to fair value, with the appropriate gain or loss recorded, and then written off. The same procedure is applicable to cash and trade transactions.
2. When no cash changes hands, trade transactions do not create gains and losses if the assets traded are similar. This rule is necessary to control manipulation of net income.

REQUIRED Compose a short statement on exchanges of assets that summarizes current GAAP and compare it with the above statements.

C11–12 Azales Trails, Inc., purchased the buildings and grounds of an old plantation site and opened it to the public on February 28, 1983. The company has a 10-year plan to restore the site to its original condition. It is estimated that $100,000 per year will be spent on renovations to the buildings. The landscaping will require $50,000 per year of normal upkeep and $60,000 per year for 10 years for new shrubs, trees, walkways, and the like.

REQUIRED Explain the proper accounting treatment of the planned expenditures and the effect they would have on the company's income statements in the first 5 years.

C11–13 During the last decade Bromo Pizza, Inc., has expanded rapidly by purchasing small buildings in surrounding suburbs from a real estate broker and converting them to pizza outlets. Financing has been arranged by means of 4-year non-interest-bearing notes with the real estate firm. It has been discovered that throughout this period the company's accountant has used a constant interest rate (8 percent) to discount the notes and to value the acquired assets. Actual interest rates have risen steadily from the 8 percent level in 1973 to 18 percent in the current year (1982). On the average, $500,000 per year has been borrowed through the non-interest-bearing notes for the period 1973 through 1982.

REQUIRED Discuss the accounting effects of using the 8 percent interest rate to discount the notes.

C11–14 (CPA ADAPTED) The methods by which a company may acquire plant assets include cash, a deferred-payment plan, the exchanging of other assets, or a combination of these methods.

REQUIRED

1. Identify five costs that should be capitalized as the cost of land. For your answer, assume that land with an existing building is acquired for cash and that the existing building is to be removed in the immediate future so that a new building can be constructed on that site.
2. At what amount should a company record a plant asset acquired on a deferred-payment plan?
3. In general, at what amount should plant assets received in exchange for other nonmonetary assets be recorded? Specifically, at what amount should a company record a new machine acquired by exchanging an older, similar machine and paying cash?

C11–15 (CPA ADAPTED) Among the principal topics related to the accounting for the property, plant, and equipment of a company are acquisition and retirement.

REQUIRED

1. What expenditures should be capitalized when equipment is acquired for cash?
2. Assume that the market value of equipment acquired is not determinable by reference to a similar purchase for cash. Describe how the acquiring company should determine the capitalizable cost of equipment purchased by exchanging it for each of the following:
   a. Bonds having an established market price
   b. Common stock not having an established market price
   c. Similar equipment having a determinable market value
3. Describe the factors that determine whether expenditures relating to property, plant, and equipment already in use should be capitalized.
4. Describe how you would account for the gain or loss on the sale of property, plant, and equipment for cash.

EXERCISES

E11–1 On October 14, 1981, a company purchased a five acre building site for $66,000 and held it until July 15, 1983, at which time 2½ acres were sold for $100,000 and a warehouse building was constructed on the remainder.

REQUIRED Record all journal entries related to the above transactions, assuming that the intent on October 14, 1981, was to sell the 2½-acre parcel. How would the land be disclosed on balance sheets before and after the July 15, 1983, sale? State your assumptions.

E11–2 Apco, Inc., has decided to locate in the city of Franklin, Alabama. It plans to construct an office building next to a municipal parking lot, which the city council has agreed to lease to Apco for $1 per year for as long as the office building is occupied. A comparable parking facility would lease for $50,000 per year. Apco plans to depreciate the building over 40 years.

REQUIRED

1. Should the parking lot be reflected in Apco's accounting records?
2. Without prejudice to your answer to requirement 1, show which ledger accounts would be debited and credited if the parking lot were considered donated capital, and discuss how the money amount could be established.

E11–3 A regional fast-foods chain acquired a restaurant building by signing a non-interest-bearing note with a maturity value of $310,000 due in 5 years. The company borrowed money from a bank within a month of the above transaction at an annual interest rate of 14 percent.

REQUIRED

1. What information would you need to determine the capitalized value of the building?
2. Using only the information given, what journal entry would be required to record the acquisition of the building? Show computations.

E11–4 Joplin Corporation converted all of its warehouse equipment from gasoline to butane. The conversion cost $42,500 and is expected to save Joplin $30,000 per year in fuel and maintenance over the remaining life of the equipment. The equipment's estimated useful life did not change because of the conversion.

REQUIRED How should the conversion costs be recorded on Joplin's books? Explain.

E11–5 Oakland Shopping Center, Inc., owns all the structures in a 20-year-old complex. In order to increase traffic, and thereby rents, Oakland has given the entire complex a major face-lifting during the current fiscal period. The following expenditures were incurred:

	COST	REPLACEMENT SCHEDULE
Painting of interiors	$88,600	5 years
New landscaping	48,000	20 years
Electronic sign	28,600	20 years
Resurfacing of parking lot	60,500	10 years
Replacement of exterior lighting with high-intensity bulbs	13,400	9 months

REQUIRED How should each of the above items be reflected on the company's financial statements? Give reasons for your answer.

E11–6 Universal Air purchased two aircraft for its freight-delivery service. The initial cost was $8,420,000 each. In addition, the company signed a service contract calling for $600,000 per year to be paid to the manufacturer of the aircraft for the 10-year expected life. To operate the new craft, Universal's pilots required special training at a total cost of $28,000.

REQUIRED Record each of the above expenditures on Universal's books and give explanations for your entries.

E11–7 Northwest Gas is a member of a consortium that financed the construction of a pipeline traversing five states. The pipeline crosses state-owned land, and the states are the legal owners of the land with exclusive use granted to the gas companies. The company plans to use the pipeline for 20 years, although its estimated physical life is 40 years.

REQUIRED How should the company record its $290,000,000 contribution to the consortium that financed construction of the line?

E11–8 A corporation used its own workers to construct an emissions-control addition to its chemical plant. The construction took place entirely within one fiscal period. At the inception of the construction, a 6-month note was signed to finance a major part of the materials acquisition for the project. The note bore interest at 12 percent per annum and had an initial value of $378,000. The proceeds from this loan were used entirely for materials acquisition. Costs related to the project included the following:

Materials acquisition	$620,000
Labor	94,000
Direct overhead	130,000
Supervision of construction	9,600
Engineering plans	25,400
	$879,000

REQUIRED What is the total cost of the addition to be included in long-term assets? Show computations.

E11–9 On July 1, 1983, McRowen Corporation, a calender-year company, discontinued operations in one of its department stores and put the building and all equipment on sale. Operations had continued through June 30, 1983, and depreciation was recorded as of June 30, 1983. The assets at June 30, 1983, had the following book values and estimated disposal values and disposal costs:

	BOOK VALUE	DISPOSAL VALUE	COSTS ASSOCIATED WITH DISPOSAL
Building	$250,000	$300,000	$25,000
Equipment	150,000	90,000	10,000

REQUIRED For purposes of the December 31, 1983, balance sheet show adjusting entries, if any, that are necessary and how these costs should be disclosed, assuming the assets are scheduled to be sold on February 1, 1984.

E11–10 Matlack Company wants to dispose of two lathes. One has a book value of $21,500 and a fair value of $25,000 and is to be traded for a new lathe with a fair value of $100,000. The other has been fully depreciated and is being sold as scrap for $5,000 cash.

REQUIRED What journal entries would be necessary for the two transactions, assuming the new lathe is paid for by the trade-in of the first plus cash of $75,000?

PROBLEMS

P11–1 The Wolverine Breakage and Honors Company has a rather unsophisticated accounting system that records no transactions until you, the company's part-time accountant, have looked them over. During the first week of March 1984 (right after your midterm exam in accounting) you stop by to record the company's recent activities. In looking through the invoices, you observe the following items:

1. A bill from Big Wally Window Company for cleaning windows in the showroom, $50.
2. A bill from Ready Roofing for repair work done on the roof. During a recent snowstorm, the roof, which is only 5 years old (expected life of the roof was 15 years), began to leak badly, causing $600 worth of damage to the merchandise inventory. Ready Roofing had originally installed the roof at a cost of $28,000, and although they felt the roof should not have leaked after only 5 years, they did not guarantee their work and insisted on

payment in advance. For $2,500, Ready put down some fresh tar and stones over the place where the roof was leaking and replaced some of the caulking material around the skylight in the roof.

3. Wolverine also had an invoice for some concrete, some brick, and some framing material. As usual, the company was running out of space in which to put all of its inventory, and so the owner was expanding the storage area out toward the rear part of the building. This work was being done by the regular employees in their "spare" time. They were working an extra day occasionally (Saturday), working a full day at "time and one-half" pay rates, making a 48-hour-work week on those weeks. The materials invoices came to $949. Because these invoices were a few months old, some had accrued finance charges that amounted to $30. The wages for the five employees, which are due for the 8 weeks since you last paid them, came to 1,840 hours work for total wages of $16,170.

4. On February 14 a university student came to the company store to pick up an item he had ordered several weeks earlier and accidentally walked through the front doors without opening them, totally destroying the doors. The doors had originally cost $1,750 when purchased and installed 3 years earlier. The bill for the replacement of the doors came to $2,800, with installation costs of $250. The replacement was not too difficult because the identical type of door was still available at the same place where the original doors were purchased. Upon replacing the doors, the company installing them noted that the doors would last 10 years under normal use, which of course did not include walking through them.

5. A bill for $300 for painting the one side of the building where students had painted obscene expressions. This was the third time in the last 6 years that Wolverine's owners had had to have the same side of the building painted. The last time was 2 years ago and the cost had been $200.

REQUIRED   Record the information summarized above.

P11–2   On July 1, 1980, Onsi Company acquired an automobile for $5,200. At that time the automobile was estimated to have a 4-year life and a salvage value of $400. Straight-line depreciation has been recorded through December 31, 1982. On July 1, 1983, the above-mentioned automobile is traded in for a new one having a list price of $6,000. The dealer allows a $2,000 trade-in allowance for the old automobile, and Onsi pays the $4,000 difference in cash. The old automobile has a cash value of not more than $1,000 or less than $900, according to a number of quotes from local used-car dealers.

REQUIRED

1. Three possible methods can be used to record trade-in allowances on the books of the Onsi Company. Show entries for all three methods, label which method is which, and indicate the reasoning behind each method.

2. What would the purchase price have been if Onsi had decided to keep the old automobile *and* buy the new one without a trade-in?

P11–3   Company Z has constructed an asset for its own use. A breakdown of costs directly related to construction follows:

ITEM	DESCRIPTION	COST
1	Raw materials and direct labor	$ 500,000
2	Variable overhead, including special tools and construction supervisors' salaries	200,000
3	General overhead, including fixed-factory-overhead costs	200,000
4	*Total* interest on debt used to finance construction, one-half of which was incurred before construction was completed	100,000
		$1,000,000

_____ 1. The maximum possible value to be recorded in the asset account would be
  a. $950,000   c. $900,000
  b. $1,000,000   d. $700,000

_____ 2. Item 3 could be included in the asset account

a. If it does not make the cost of the asset higher than the market value or distort profit from normal operations
b. As long as it does not distort the profit from normal operations
c. Only when the factory is operating at full capacity
d. If it would result in a higher net income for the period

_____ 3. An outside construction company had originally offered to construct the asset for Z at a fixed contract price of $880,000. Z has accumulated total construction costs of $900,000 in the asset account at the completion date. Z should
a. Transfer all $900,000 to the completed asset account
b. Transfer $880,000 to the completed asset account and $20,000 to an intangible asset account
c. Transfer $880,000 to the completed asset account and $20,000 to a Loss on Self-Constructed Assets account
d. Transfer $900,000 to the completed asset account and disclose the $20,000 difference in a footnote

_____ 4. Assume the same data as part 3 above *except* that the outside contractor's fixed contract price was $920,000 instead of $880,000. Z should
a. Transfer $900,000 to the completed asset account
b. Transfer $920,000 to the completed asset account and report a "gain on self-constructed assets" of $20,000
c. Transfer $920,000 to the completed asset account and $20,000 to an unearned revenue account
d. Transfer $920,000 to the completed asset account and disclose the $20,000 difference in a footnote

P11–4 Several types of costs subsequent to acquisition were discussed in the text: (1) betterments, (2) repairs, (3) improvements, (4) maintenance, (5) renewals, (6) additions, and (7) replacements.

REQUIRED Which of these seven costs should be capitalized (=assets) and which should be expensed? If you need additional information, explain what that information is and how it will affect your decision. You may discuss the items in groups or separately, whichever you prefer.

P11–5 You are in the process of obtaining some new car-wash equipment. The old equipment has a *net* book value of $7,000, an original cost of $50,000 and accumulated depreciation of $43,000, on July 1, 1989, the date of acquisition. Consider the following information concerning the purchase:

1. List price of new equipment, $75,000.
2. Cash given in addition to old equipment, $65,000.
3. Trade-in allowed for old equipment, $8,000.
4. Bids received from other local car-wash businesses on old equipment:
   a. $5,000
   b. $5,500
   c. $6,000
5. According to a recent industry publication, the "Blue Book" value of the old equipment is $5,700.
6. The transaction is deemed to have culminated in an earnings process.

REQUIRED Record the exchange of the old asset for the new.

P11–6

_____ 1. If a discount is available on a newly acquired long-term asset, the discount should be
a. Deducted from the value of the asset only if the asset is paid for within the discount period
b. Deducted from the value of the asset even if it is lost
c. Ignored in determining the asset value to be recorded
d. None of the above

2. Major costs incurred subsequent to the acquisition of an asset for replacements or renewals should be capitalized if

a. They are normally expected to occur
b. They are due to poor maintenance
c. They are unusual and unexpected

d. All of the above
e. None of the above

_____ 3. The best general criterion for deciding whether a cost should be included in the value of a new asset is to determine
a. If the cost was necessarily incurred in the process of getting the asset to a usable state
b. If the cost was optional or a part of the base model price
c. If the cost was incurred before or after the asset arrived at the ultimate place of use
d. All of the above

_____ 4. The cost of disposing of fully depreciated equipment that is being replaced by new equipment
a. Should be added to the cost of the New Equipment asset account
b. Should be charged to depreciation expense in the period of disposal
c. Should have been considered in estimating the "scrap value" of the old equipment
d. None of the above

P11–7 Upon opening a new shop, Applerose Boutique purchased all of its displays, counters, racks, and cash register equipment from a defunct department store for a lump-sum price of $44,000. Additional expenditures re lated to the acquisition include transportation to the shop, $1,500; installation charges from an outside contractor, $2,100; increased insurance expense, $400 per year; increased annual property taxes, $1,100; employee wages to stock the display counters and racks, $4,000; and payment to a general contractor for certain electrical modifications in the building because of the new equipment, $3,500.

REQUIRED

1. Show the journal entries required for the above expenditures, and give explanations for the selected accounting treatment.
2. Explain why it might be desirable to attempt to allocate the above costs to more than one account, and explain what possible techniques could be used to do this.

P11–8 Oxy Hex Rustproofing, Inc., has purchased a site for a new shop and warehouse on the border between residential and commercial areas. The site has 4 undeveloped acres, but only 1 acre is to be used for the buildings. The other 3 acres are to be divided up and sold as commercial sites. Several unresolved issues relating to the accounting for this property remain at the December 31, 1983, year-end.

1. The previous owner insisted on selling the entire site, although only 1 acre was zoned for commercial use. The price paid was $200,000, and this amount was debited to the Land account on June 1, 1983. Real estate appraisers claimed that the one commercial acre had a fair value of about $140,000 while the residentially zoned portion was valued at about $60,000.
2. Subsequent to the purchase, the company made an effort to have the 3 residential acres rezoned to commercial and it was successful. Total cost involved in the rezoning effort amounted to $30,000, mostly in outside attorneys' fees. This amount was debited to Administrative Expense.
3. On December 31, 1983, the three rezoned acres are on sale at an asking price of $100,000 each, the price recommended by real estate appraisers.

REQUIRED

1. Explain how the Land account balance should be adjusted in light of the above transactions. What implications do you see for balance sheet classifications?
2. Show all necessary journal entries to accomplish the adjustment described in requirement 1.

P11–9 Platte Engines Corporation, a U.S. company, started constructing a plant in Belgium in 1982 and completed it on September 15, 1983. The following ledger accounts were used to record the expenditures during construction:

DATE	NATURE OF EXPENDITURE	AMOUNT	ACCOUNTING TREATMENT
7/1/82	Bank loan to finance construction	$12,600,000	Long-term notes payable, due 12/31/85
During 1982	Payments to general contractors	6,000,000	Building—Belgium plant
During 1982	Interest on loan	630,000	Interest expense—1982
During 1982	Payments to company personnel assigned to construction supervision	210,000	Administrative expense—1982
During 1983	Payments to general contractors	6,800,000	Building—Belgium plant
During 1983	Interest on loan	1,260,000	Interest expense—1983
During 1983	Payments to company personnel assigned to construction supervision	400,000	Administrative expense—1983

In addition, used equipment was transported from a U.S. plant to the Belgium facility during February 1983. The equipment had a book value of $480,000 and a fair value of $600,000. Platte recognized a gain of $120,000 and debited the Equipment—Belgium Plant account for $600,000. Transportation cost of $150,000 was debited to Miscellaneous Expense. Platte has a December 31 year-end.

REQUIRED Show all necessary journal entries to adjust Platte's books at December 31, 1982, and December 31, 1983. Assume that books are still open on each date.

P11–10 Because of the high cost of gasoline, Syvander Cartage Company decided to trade four of its light-duty gasoline-powered vans for four diesel-powered vans. The following schedules give details of the transactions:

VAN NUMBER	OLD VANS AT DATE OF TRADE		NEW VANS AT DATE OF TRADE	
	BOOK VALUE	FAIR VALUE	LIST PRICE	CASH PAID (RECEIVED)
165	$ 5,500	$ 6,000	$10,000	$3,000
184	8,900	7,000	10,000	2,500
171	13,000	10,500	10,000	(1,500)
88	4,400	3,000	10,000	6,000

REQUIRED

1. Using the book-value method, show journal entries to record the trade-in transactions for each truck.
2. Using the fair-value method, show journal entries to record the trade-in transactions for each truck.

P11–11 During 1983 Matthews Pharmacy expended considerable sums on modifications to its major store, including the following:

ITEM	DESCRIPTION	COST
1	Addition of fire protection system pursuant to a fire marshall's order.	$24,500
2	Rearrangement of check-out lines. (No new equipment was involved.)	10,500
3	Replacement of roof damaged in a windstorm. (The old roof, which was estimated to have cost $5,000 when the building was constructed at 12/31/69, was not written off.)	18,800
4	Painting of entire interior. (Painting takes place at 5-year intervals.)	15,000
5	Blacktopping of parking lot. (The cost of the original surface was $10,000 and is in the Land account. The old surface provided the base for the new surface.)	22,000

At the time the above modifications were complete (December 31, 1983), the building was one-half depreciated on a straight-line basis with zero estimated residual value.

REQUIRED Show all necessary journal entries related to the above transactions and give explanations.

P11-12

_____ 1. In accounting for all the various types of expenditures subsequent to acquisition for plant and equipment, the most *fundamental* question addressed is:
a. Was the cost expected or unexpected?
b. Does the cost represent an asset?
c. Will the benefit period of the expenditure exceed the benefit period of the asset that it pertains to?
d. How much better off are we as a result of the expenditure?

Use the following information for questions 2 and 3:

In 1985 Paré Enterprises acquired a farm outside Quebec for $85,000. The land had once been used for farming, but Paré intended to convert it to a complex of office buildings. The farmhouse and barn on the land were both removed at a cost of $8,000, and their contents were auctioned off for $5,000. Other costs incurred by Paré during 1985 in the process of constructing the first office building, a 20-story structure, were as follows:

Survey of land	$ 750
Abstract and title to farmland and structures on land	1,160
Legal fees at date of purchase	2,505
Real estate fees	4,220
Costs of grading building site on northwest corner of land	1,838
Cost of concrete footings for foundation of office building	18,000
Cost of material, labor, and overhead billed by general contractor in conjunction with office building construction to date	215,000
Profit billed to Paré by general contractor to date	67,000

The total cash payments made by Paré for the above during 1985 came to $195,000.

_____ 2. What is the recorded book value of the land as of 1985 year-end?
a. $103,473   d. $98,473
b. $94,253   e. $101,635
c. $96,635

_____ 3. What would be the balance in the Office Building under Construction account on Paré's books?
a. $300,000   d. $233,000
b. $195,000   e. $234,838
c. $301,838

P11-13 (CPA ADAPTED) Selected accounts included in the property, plant, and equipment section of the Kingston Corporation's balance sheet at December 31, 1983, had the following balances:

Land	$175,000
Land improvements	90,000
Buildings	900,000
Machinery and equipment	850,000

During 1984 the following transactions occurred:

1. A tract of land was acquired for $125,000 as a potential future building site.
2. A plant facility consisting of land and building was acquired from the Nostrand Company in exchange for

10,000 shares of Kingston's common stock. On the acquisition data, Kingston's stock had a closing market price of $45 per share on a national stock exchange. The plant facility was carried on Nostrand's books at $89,000. The appraisal values for the land and building, respectively, are $120,000 and $240,000.

3. Items of machinery and equipment were purchased at a total cost of $300,000. Additional costs were incurred as follows:

Freight and unloading	$ 5,000
Sales tax	12,000
Installation	25,000

4. Expenditures totaling $75,000 were made for new parking lots, streets, and sidewalks at the corporation's various plant locations. These expenditures had an estimated useful life of 15 years.

5. A machine costing $50,000 on January 1, 1970, was scrapped on June 30, 1984. Double-declining balance depreciation has been recorded on the basis of a 10-year life.

6. On July 1, 1984, a machine was sold for $20,000. Original cost of the machine was $36,000 on January 1, 1981, and it was depreciated on the straight-line basis over an estimated useful life of 7 years and a salvage value of $1,000.

REQUIRED

1. Prepare a detailed analysis of the changes in each of the following balance sheet accounts for 1984: Land, Land Improvements, Buildings, Machinery and Equipment. Disregard the related accumulated depreciation accounts.

2. List the items in the fact situation that were not used to determine the answer to requirement 1. Show the pertinent amounts and supporting computations in good form for each item. In addition, indicate where, or if, these items should be included in Kingston's financial statements.

P11–14 (CPA ADAPTED) At December 31, 1983, certain accounts included in the property, plant, and equipment section of the Townsand Company's balance sheet had the following balances:

Land	$100,000
Buildings	800,000
Leasehold improvements	500,000
Machinery and equipment	700,000

During 1984 the following transactions occurred:

1. Land site number 621 was acquired for $1,000,000. Additionally, to acquire the land Townsand paid a $60,000 commission to a real estate agent. Costs of $15,000 were incurred to clear the land. During the course of clearing the land, timber and gravel were recovered and sold for $5,000.

2. A second tract of land (site number 622) with a building was acquired for $300,000. The closing statement indicated that the land value was $200,000 and the building value was $100,000. Shortly after acquisition, the building was demolished at a cost of $30,000. A new building was constructed for $150,000 plus the following costs:

Excavation fees	$11,000
Architectural design fees	8,000
Building permit fee	1,000
Imputed interest on funds used during construction	6,000

The building was completed and occupied on September 30, 1984.

3. A third tract of land (site number 623) was acquired for $600,000 and was put on the market for resale.
4. Extensive work was done to a building occupied by Townsand under a lease agreement that expires on December 31, 1993. The total cost of the work was $125,000:

Painting of ceilings	$ 10,000	estimated useful life is 1 year
Electrical work	35,000	estimated useful life is 10 years
Construction of extension to current working area	80,000 $125,000	estimated useful life is 30 years

The lessor paid one-half of the costs incurred in connection with the extension to the current working area.
5. During December 1984 costs of $65,000 were incurred to improve leased office space. The related lease will terminate on December 31, 1986, and is not expected to be renewed.
6. A group of new machines was purchased under a royalty agreement that provides for payment of royalties based on units of production for the machines. The invoice price of the machines was $75,000, freight costs were $2,000, unloading charges were $1,500, and royalty payments for 1984 were $13,000.

REQUIRED

1. Prepare a detailed analysis of the changes in each of the following balance sheet accounts for 1984: Land, Buildings, Leasehold Improvements, Machinery and Equipment. Disregard the related accumulated depreciation accounts.
2. List the items in the fact situation that were not used to determine the answer to requirement 1 and indicate where, or if, these items should be included in Townsand's financial statements.

12

Depreciation and Depletion

OVERVIEW   In the preceding chapter we discussed the concepts and techniques used to capitalize the costs of plant, property, and equipment. In this chapter we discuss the concepts and techniques related to the assigning of costs of capitalized assets to periods that benefit from their use. The process of assigning capitalized asset costs to periods of benefit is referred to as **cost allocation.** The terms *depreciation, depletion,* and *amortization* are all used to describe cost allocation for various types of capitalized assets. **Depreciation** is typically used in conjunction with allocations for plant and equipment; **depletion** describes the allocation of the cost of natural resources; and **amortization** describes the allocation of the cost of intangibles.

These terms are sometimes used interchangeably, however, and their similarities far outweigh their differences. They all relate to the process of assigning asset costs to periods in which some or all of the asset is consumed. Assets are consumed in the sense that they have experienced a decline in service potential.

414

THE BASIC MEASUREMENT PROBLEM

The use of capital assets in the revenue-generating process results in the production of goods and services as well as a decline in the expected future service potential of the capital assets. Based on the **matching concept,** the accountant's measurement objective in recording the depreciation, amortization, or depletion of an asset is to determine the amount of service potential consumed for a specified period in terms of a portion of the original cost of that asset.

A major challenge to the accountant, then, is the ascertaining of the productive asset's service potential and the amount of service potential consumed in a specific period of time. Unfortunately, it is almost impossible to clearly specify these critical attributes. For example, we can measure the number of miles a truck travels during a time interval, but we do not know exactly how many miles of service potential are available. Similarly, we may be able to measure the number of hours an injection-molding machine has been used or the number of units produced by the machine, but we cannot be sure how many hours or units are available in total.

Industrial engineers are often relied upon to provide estimates of the measurement units used in determining potential utility, such as machine-hours or units of output. However, because the estimates of service life are generally not precise, the consumption measurements used may not be ideal for determining the decline in service potential during a period of time. Furthermore, certain assets, such as buildings and desks, seem to lack any obvious consumption measure to apply to their usage.

Indeed, the accountant faces a difficult assignment in attempting to measure the decline in the service potential of productive capital assets. It is an assignment that, by its very nature, cannot be accomplished with precision. This is a common problem in all situations involving cost allocation. In one sense, this problem is caused by the need to have fixed reporting periods with the report date cutting across numerous incomplete production cycles. Consider a business venture that has no reporting requirements prior to the end of the venture. Virtually all cost-allocation problems, including depreciation, are eliminated in such a case. Upon the liquidation of the venture, what is essentially a measurement of ending cash less beginning cash is used to determine position and change in position. However, in most other cases, the need for information regarding an entity's position and performance prior to the final liquidation of the business requires that periodic reports be prepared. These reports, whether on an annual, a quarterly, or a monthly basis, all require the allocation of costs to time periods of concern to decision makers.

In addition to the goal of assigning the appropriate cost to each period benefited, accountants also strive to recognize an accurate gain or loss upon the ultimate disposal of an asset. Of course, the limitations of depreciation techniques create problems for both the determination of periodic depreciation charges and the resulting book values upon which gains and losses on disposition are based.

The cost-allocation problems involved in measuring the decline in service potential of plant and equipment, natural resources, and intangible assets are all resolved in essentially the same way. Although accountants cannot be expected to measure the decline in service potential *with absolute accuracy,* they can *systematically approximate* this decline. The methods of systematically approximating the decline in service potential all rely in part on the principles of consistency and comparability for their conceptual underpinnings. In this chapter we shall illustrate systematic methods used to determine depreciation and depletion. The systematic amortization methods for intangibles, which involve the same basic measurement concepts, are discussed in Chapter 13.

In critically evaluating the different methods of depreciation and depletion, two things should be kept in mind: (1) the dollar amounts involved in these measurements are typically very significant; and (2) the measurement of decline in service potential over various time periods is only an approximation.

ALTERNATIVE DEPRECIATION METHODS

Estimates Required for Allocation

Because the decline in the service potential of plant and equipment cannot usually be accurately measured, the allocation process involves a somewhat arbitrary partitioning of cost with no clear criterion available to test for "correctness." However, to the extent that we have a "general sense" of the actual decline in service potential, we may be able, by application of professional judgment, to identify preferred allocation methods as those that result in cost allocations that are similar to our expectations. In addition, GAAP call for systematic and rational techniques of cost allocation. Although the choice of a technique may be characterized as somewhat arbitrary or at least subjective, once it is chosen, the pattern of allocation should be systematic. The accountant, then, has a loose framework for the task of measuring depreciation. However, the key elements in all depreciation techniques are estimates, all of which are subject to estimation errors.

Consider the following information items used to allocate systematically the cost of an asset to the periods of benefit:

1. The estimated service life (for example, time or units of output)
2. The expected pattern of service (for example, increasing utility or decreasing utility)
3. The estimated net residual or salvage value at the end of the service life

Note that these three estimates required in the process of depreciation (as well as depletion and amortization) in effect define the process as being subjective. At the date of acquisition, the asset's cost may be objectively measurable. However, once an asset is placed into production and this uncertain process of measuring and recording its decline in service potential begins, the objectivity of the remaining historical cost (original cost minus depreciation to date) is reduced because of the subjectivity of depreciation techniques. That is, although original historical cost is relatively objectively determinable, the book values of productive assets become more arbitrary as imprecise methods of cost allocation are applied to them during their service lives. This limitation cannot be overcome by application of other valuation models, including the current-cost and constant-dollar models discussed in Chapter 6, because they also have subjective elements. Due to the subjective nature of such processes, the resulting net book values of virtually all productive assets are *estimates* of their remaining service potential. The subjective nature of the depreciation techniques should be kept in mind as the different depreciation methods are being reviewed, inasmuch as the mechanical nature of these methods sometimes leads us to believe that the depreciation measurement process is more precise than it actually is.

Units-of-Output Depreciation

The **units-of-output depreciation method** is any method that bases the first of the three unknowns identified above, the estimated service life, on some output unit measurement. Figure 12–1 shows that the units-of-output method results in a constant depreciation amount being associated with each unit of output; in this case, for each unit produced, $1 of depreciation results.

FIGURE 12-1

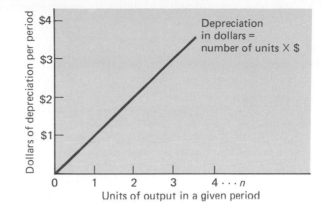

For example, assume that a forklift truck has an estimated service life of 25,000 hours of use. A timer could be connected to the forklift and could be used to calculate depreciation. Assume further that the forklift, which cost $88,000, was expected to be equally useful during each of the 25,000 hours of use, and that the net salvage value was expected to be $13,000 at the end of the 25,000 hours of use. The truck was used 1,500 hours in 1984 and 3,000 hours in 1985. Depreciation on the truck would be computed as follows:

$$1984: \quad (1{,}500 \text{ hr}) \times \frac{\$88{,}000 - \$13{,}000}{25{,}000 \text{ hr}} = \$4{,}500$$

$$1985: \quad (3{,}000 \text{ hr}) \times \frac{\$88{,}000 - \$13{,}000}{25{,}000 \text{ hr}} = \$9{,}000$$

The $3 rate per service hour [($88,000 − $13,000)/25,000 hr] is multiplied by the hours of use in any given period to estimate the amount of service potential expended in terms of the original cost of the truck. The depreciation would be recorded as follows:

	1984		1985	
	DEBIT	CREDIT	DEBIT	CREDIT
Depreciation expense (or manufacturing overhead control)	4,500		9,000	
Accumulated depreciation		4,500		9,000
(To record decline in service potential of forklift truck)				

Note that the scrap value of $13,000 was deducted from the original cost of $88,000 in order to arrive at the $75,000 amount to be depreciated. The $75,000 is spread over 25,000 service hours, after which time the net book value of the asset would be $13,000 ($88,000 asset less $75,000 accumulated depreciation), the **estimated** net residual value of the forklift. The debit part of the entry will typically go to a Manufacturing Overhead Control account if the asset being depreciated is related to a manufacturing process. From this account, it will be systematically allocated to work-in-process inventory, finished-goods inventory, and cost of goods sold. In nonmanufacturing entities or for nonmanufacturing-related assets, the debit will be charged directly to depreciation expense that will be charged against revenue of the period.

Depreciation Based on Time

It is very common for depreciation schedules to be based on time periods rather than units of output. This necessitates estimating the service life in years or months. How does an entity determine the service life of an asset? This question may be difficult to answer. Sometimes a company may have had experience with a type of asset that will help it estimate the economic service life. However, with unique assets such as buildings or assets that embody new technological improvements—electric steel furnaces (instead of coal), solar heating systems (instead of gas), and so on—these estimates are more difficult to make. Keep in mind that service life is not necessarily equivalent to physical life. An asset may remain in existence long after its service potential is used up. The depreciation schedules described in this text are based on estimates of service life. For instance, a computer may have a very long physical life, but technological advances may cause it to be considered obsolete within only a few years of acquisition, thereby reducing its service life to that shorter period.

One source often used for estimating the useful life of an asset is the Internal Revenue Code. In 1962 the IRS set up a guideline life system to help taxpaying entities in selecting asset lives. A heavy truck was classified as an asset with a 6-year life, whereas an automobile was assigned a 3-year life, and a factory building, a 45-year life. The asset-life guidelines, which serve primarily as a lower limit on the depreciation time period, were relaxed somewhat in a 1972 change in the code, and it was generally accepted that if it could be demonstrated that shorter or longer lives were appropriate, they may be used. The Economic Recovery Tax Act of 1981 allows much more liberal write-off schedules: autos, 3 years; most other equipment, 5 years; and most buildings, 15 years. The tax rules do not require conformance between financial accounting and tax accounting for asset lives. However, many companies have used the same estimated service life for both purposes, another example of the influence of tax laws on financial accounting. Whether this will continue under the 1981 tax law is unknown at this time.

Straight-line depreciation The **straight-line (SL) depreciation method,** and all the other methods of depreciation considered below, are based on estimates of the expected service life (the first of the three unknowns) in terms of time. The straight-line, increasing-rate, and decreasing-rate methods, some possible patterns for which are illustrated in Figure 12–2, all estimate service life in terms of years or months.

FIGURE 12–2

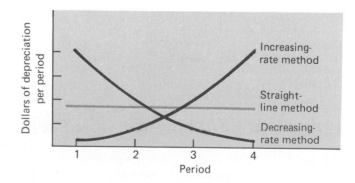

Although it would also be possible to develop a combination of units and time system, this is rarely encountered in practice.

The first estimate required under the straight-line method is the expected useful life in terms of the time period in which the asset will be used, such as 10 years. The second unknown, the pattern of service, is considered to be equal for each unit of **time** (that is, each year) under the straight-line method. The estimate of residual value should be independent of the method of depreciation. Assume that the forklift truck described earlier is expected to last 10 years. The straight-line depreciation of the truck for 1984 and 1985, the first two years of operation, would be computed by multiplying the cost minus estimated salvage value by $^1/_{10}$ as follows:

$$1984: \quad \frac{1}{10} \times (\$88,000 - \$13,000) = \underline{\underline{\$7,500}}$$

$$1985: \quad \frac{1}{10} \times (\$88,000 - \$13,000) = \underline{\underline{\$7,500}}$$

For each of the 10 years, $7,500 would be recorded for depreciation, or one-tenth of the original cost to be depreciated of $75,000, which is often referred to as the **depreciation base.**

Straight-line depreciation is not only the most simple method but also the most commonly used method. According to recent issues of *Accounting Trends and Techniques,* which surveys 600 major companies each year, about 75 percent of the companies surveyed use straight-line depreciation for financial-reporting purposes.

Decreasing-rate depreciation Two primary methods of depreciation result in decreasing depreciation expense amounts each period: the sum-of-the-years'-digits method and the declining-balance method.

SUM-OF-THE-YEARS'-DIGITS METHOD The **sum-of-the-years'-digits (SYD) method** results in depreciation of a decreasing fraction of the depreciation base each year. The denominator is the sum of the years from 1 to the number of years (n) of expected service $(1 + 2 + \ldots + n)$, and the numerator is the number of years' service remaining as of the beginning of the computation year. For an asset with a 3-year life, the SYD fraction in the first year would be $3/(1 + 2 + 3)$, or $^3/_6$, or $^1/_2$. A quick formula to sum a series of numbers from 1 to n is

$$\frac{(n)(n + 1)}{2} = \text{The sum of 1 to } n$$

For the forklift truck discussed above, the 10-year life calls for the summation of the numbers 1 through 10, which is calculated by the formula

$$[(10)(11)]/2 = {}^{110}/_2 = 55$$

In the first 2 years the SYD depreciation for the lifttruck would be:

$$1984: \quad \frac{10}{55} \times (\$88,000 - \$13,000) = \underline{\underline{\$13,636}}$$

$$1985: \quad \frac{9}{55} \times (\$88,000 - \$13,000) = \underline{\underline{\$12,273}}$$

TABLE 12–1

DECLINING-BALANCE METHOD

	(1) ×	(2) =	(3)	(4)	(5)
YEAR	DEPRECIATION RATE PER YEAR	BOOK VALUE: BEGINNING OF YEAR	DEPRECIATION EXPENSE FOR THE YEAR	TOTAL ACCUMULATED DEPRECIATION END OF YEAR	NET BOOK VALUE END OF YEAR
1984	.17406	$88,000ª	$15,317	$15,317	$72,683
1985	.17406	72,683	12,651	27,968	60,032
1986	.17406	60,032	10,449	38,417	49,583
1987	.17406	49,583	8,630	47,047	40,953
1988	.17406	40,953	7,128	54,175	33,825
1989	.17406	33,825	5,888	60,063	27,937
1990	.17406	27,937	4,863	64,926	23,074
1991	.17406	23,074	4,016	68,942	19,058
1992	.17406	19,058	3,317	72,259	15,741
1993	.17406	15,741	2,741ᵇ	75,000	13,000

ª Note that estimated residual is not used in these computations.
ᵇ $1 rounding error forced into 1993 depreciation expense.

The depreciation expense would decrease by $1,363 per year ($= \frac{1}{55} \times$ $75,000$), and the total depreciation over the life of the asset would equal $\frac{55}{55} \times$ $75,000 = $75,000, leaving a net book value of $13,000 after 10 years.

DECLINING-BALANCE METHOD Another decreasing-rate method that is frequently used is the **declining balance (DB) method.** This system of computing depreciation takes a *fixed rate* times the *net book value* of the asset at the beginning of the period. To leave the correct net book value (= the estimated residual value) at the end of the estimated useful life, the following formula is used to determine the appropriate rate:

$$\text{Fixed rate} = 1 - \sqrt[n]{\frac{\text{Residual value}}{\text{Original cost}}}$$

where n is number of years expected service life.

For the forklift truck, the rate would be

$$1 - \sqrt[10]{\frac{\$13,000}{\$88,000}} = 1 - \sqrt[10]{.1477273} = .17406$$

Table 12–1 shows how this rate does yield the desired residual value.

DOUBLE-DECLINING-BALANCE METHOD In practice, the declining balance method is most often used by fixing a rate that is double that of straight-line depreciation and is called the **double-declining-balance (DDB) method.**[1] Double the straight-line rate for an asset with a 10-year life would yield a fixed rate of 20 percent per year, which would be applied to the declining book value each year. Table 12–2 shows how the 1984–1986 and 1993 (year 10) depreciation expense would be computed for the forklift truck. When the rate of depreciation is arbitrarily set, such as at 200 percent of the straight-line rate in Table 12–2, the book value at the end of

---

[1] The federal tax laws permit the fixed depreciation rate to be as much as 200 percent (double) that of the straight-line rate for assets that qualify (principally new assets).

TABLE 12-2

	(1)	×	(2)	=	(3)		(4) TOTAL	(5)
YEAR	DDB RATE PER YEAR		BOOK VALUE: BEGINNING OF YEAR		DEPRECIATION EXPENSE FOR THE YEAR		ACCUMULATED DEPRECIATION END OF YEAR	NET BOOK VALUE END OF YEAR
1984	.20		$88,000		$17,600		$17,600	$70,400
1985	.20		70,400		14,080		31,680	56,320
1986	.20		56,320		11,264		42,944	45,056
·	·		·		·		·	·
·	·		·		·		·	·
1993	.20		11,811		2,362		78,551	9,449

DOUBLE-DECLINING-BALANCE METHOD

the asset's service life will normally differ from the expected salvage value. At the same time, the DDB method in Table 12-2 does illustrate a rapid depreciation pattern that many companies are attracted to for tax purposes.[2]

Companies often use a combination of the declining-balance and straight-line methods in order to arrive at a net book value equal to the residual value at the end of the asset's service life. To accomplish this, companies use the declining-balance method during the early years and switch to the straight-line method before the net book value falls below the expected residual value. The rate determined by the formula above seems to be a more appropriate and internally consistent way to use declining-balance depreciation. However, the tax benefits of the double-declining-balance method combined with the unwillingness of many companies to use different methods for book and tax purposes, have resulted in the frequent use of the double-declining-balance and straight-line methods in combination.

The declining-balance methods illustrated in Tables 12-1 and 12-2 are appropriate for assets that are more useful (provide more service) in the early years of their useful life. In fact, many assets are equally useful over their service life. As assets age, however, they may require more maintenance to remain serviceable, a fact that is often used to justify decreasing-charge methods. In other words, the periodic utility provided by an asset is viewed as a combination of its decreasing output minus the increasing outflow for periodic maintenance cost. Figure 12-3 shows that the total utility is relatively constant and is made up of the depreciation charge (which is decreasing over time) plus the maintenance charge (which is increasing over time). Although this notion may be roughly accurate in some cases and gives conceptual support for accelerated depreciation, it is not used in practice to establish depreciation rates.

Increasing-rate depreciation The **increasing-rate method,** also known as the **present-value method** or **annuity method,** views the cost of the asset minus the present value of its estimated residual value as being equal to the discounted present value of an annuity of future benefits. Implicit interest rate information is needed,

[2] Prior to 1981, tax rules allowed a maximum 200 percent of the straight-line rate for new equipment and 150 percent for used equipment. For the period 1981 to 1984, both new and used equipment acquisitions can be depreciated at a maximum of 150 percent of the straight-line rate. In 1985 the maximum goes up to 175 percent and in 1986 to 200 percent. Buildings acquired before 1981 are depreciated at a maximum of 150 percent of the straight-line rate, and those acquired in 1981 and later can use the 175 percent rate.

FIGURE 12-3

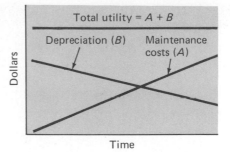

and this might be considered a disadvantage. However, detailed analysis of capital budgeting in basic managerial finance courses or managerial accounting courses has demonstrated the importance of interest and the time-value effect on cash flows and asset values. (We have made the same point in Chapter 5 and in several other chapters of this text). We are reasonably safe in assuming that most capital assets have been acquired after some consideration of their discounted present value.

PRESENT-VALUE METHOD   The following example describes the **present-value (PV) method** of depreciation. Assume that Big Lakes Dredge Company purchases a barge for $2,000,000. The barge is expected to generate an **even cash flow** to be received at the end of each year over its useful life of 5 years. Also, the investment in this barge is expected to generate a 10 percent return. What is the 5-year annuity that will earn 10 percent per year on the $2,000,000 investment? To answer this question requires knowledge of the remaining principal value of the investment (= the undepreciated asset) each period for 5 years. The annuity calculation takes this declining principal into consideration, computing an annuity that over 5 years will return 10 percent each year and cover the cost of the declining investment value as well. The annuity is computed as follows:

$$(P/A,\ 5,\ 10\%)\ x = \$2,000,000$$
$$(3.7908)\ x = \$2,000,000$$
$$x = \$2,000,000/3.7908$$
$$x = \$527,593$$

In other words, by using Table H–3 in Appendix H at the back of the book, we see that 3.7908 is the factor that determines that an annuity of $527,593 per year for 5 years will earn 10 percent on our investment, which will be fully depreciated at the end of 5 years (no residual value). Table 12–3 is an amortization table that computes the net revenue (interest) and repayment of principal under the *assumption* that a cash flow equal to the annuity actually takes place. The present-value depreciation method takes the capital recovery figures in column 3 as the depreciation charge, which is an increasing amount from year 1 to year 5, and column 3 sums to the original cost of $2,000,000. Columns 1 and 2 represent expectations and may or may not ever come about.[3] This does not prevent the use of column 3 as the annual

---

[3] Note that if the cash flows originally expected (column 1) do occur at the even rate of $527,595 per year, the return on the net asset (Column 4) will be exactly 10 percent per year! If the cash flows in column 1 occurred in conjunction with either straight-line or decreasing-rate depreciation methods, the annual return on the net asset would begin below 10 percent and would increase to well above 10 percent by year 5. In the latter case, the even cash flow results in significant growth in terms of its return-on-investment percentage. Which is more relevant?

TABLE 12–3

		PRESENT-VALUE DEPRECIATION METHOD		
END OF YEAR	(1) GROSS REVENUE (ASSUMED CASH INFLOW FROM BARGE)	(2) 10% NET REVENUE (INTEREST ON INVESTMENT BALANCE, COL. 4)	(3) RECOVERY OF COST OF BARGE (DEPRECIATION)	(4) BALANCE OF INVESTMENT IN BARGE
0				$2,000,000
1	$ 527,593	$200,000	$ 327,593	1,672,407
2	527,593	167,241	360,352	1,312,055
3	527,593	131,206	396,387	915,668
4	527,593	91,567	436,026	479,642
5	527,593	47,951 (rounded)	479,642	0
Total	$2,637,965	$637,965	$2,000,000	

depreciation expense, however, and column 4 would then represent the net book value of the asset at the end of the year indicated.

Because of its consistency with the well-established present value model, the present-value depreciation method has some conceptual merit. Understanding the present-value depreciation method will help you to understand bonds, leases, and pensions, all of which also deal with basic present-value techniques. At the same time, the use of present-value depreciation is limited in practice and has little *direct* practical application in financial accounting.

Partial-year depreciation **Partial-year depreciation** calls for an additional calculation under both the increasing-rate and decreasing-rate methods. For example, in the present-value depreciation in column 3 of Table 12–3, assume that the barge was purchased and placed into use on July 1, 1985, and that Big Lakes Dredge has a December 31 year-end for reporting purposes. Depreciation expense for 1985 and 1986 would be computed as shown in Table 12–4.

The same type of partitioning is applied to other methods as well, leaving the *yearly* calculation the same for a given asset with a given expected life, cost, depreciation method, and salvage regardless of the date of the entity's year-end.

For *tax purposes,* most assets are depreciated either a full year or a half year in the year of acquisition. If a company purchases an asset during the first half of its fiscal year, it may elect to take either half or one full year's depreciation. For assets

TABLE 12–4

	BARGE DEPRECIATION SCHEDULE		
YEARLY DEPRECIATION	1985	1986	1987
1 $327,593	= $163,796.50[a]	$163,796.50[a]	
2 360,352	=	180,176.00[b]	$180,176.00[b]
3	=		
Annual depreciation expense	$163,796.50	$343,972.50	

[a] Half the first year's depreciation.
[b] Half the second year's depreciation.

purchased during the last half of the fiscal year, it may elect a half year or no depreciation. This practice frequently carries over to depreciation expense for financial-reporting purposes, making daily or monthly depreciation rates somewhat uncommon.

Group
Depreciation
and
Composite
Depreciation

Depreciation is sometimes calculated for a number of assets simultaneously rather than on an individual asset basis. When the assets are similar, it is called **group depreciation,** and when they are a mixture of unlike assets, it is called **composite depreciation.** Both of these methods are basically the same, although there are slight variations. They all involved systematically calculated depreciation rates per year by taking some type of average of the asset lives involved.

To illustrate one common form of composite depreciation, consider the motor pool at University Delivery, Inc. The pool consists of buses, trucks, vans, and automobiles, which are being depreciated on a composite basis. The composite depreciation rate, as computed in Table 12–5, is 18.4049 percent of the total original cost of $1,630,000. Depreciation will be recorded at this composite rate for a period of 4.393333 years. After that period, with depreciation taken at $300,000 per year (.184049 × $1,630,000 = $300,000), the book value of this collection of motor pool vehicles will be the expected residual value of $312,000:

$$\$1,630,000 - (4.393333 \times \$300,000) = \$312,000$$

In considering the composite or group methods, certain anomalies emerge. For example, after 4.39 years, although fully depreciated, the heavy trucks and buses have a considerable remaining service life. The greater the variance in the expected service life (column 5), the greater the incidence of fully depreciating assets well before or after their service life expires. The composite rate of 18.4049 percent is also an average, with the actual rates (assuming straight-line depreciation as in Col-

TABLE 12–5

COMPOSITE DEPRECIATION SCHEDULE

ASSETS	(1) UNITS	(2) TOTAL ORIGINAL COST	−	(3) TOTAL ESTIMATED RESIDUAL VALUE	=	(4) TOTAL AMOUNT TO BE DEPRECIATED	÷	(5) ESTIMATED USEFUL LIFE IN YEARS	=	(6) TOTAL DEPRECIATION PER YEAR
Buses	15	$ 460,000		$ 45,000		$ 415,000		10		$ 41,500
Heavy trucks	20	440,000		20,000		420,000		8		52,500
Light trucks and vans	35	280,000		67,000		213,000		3		71,000
Automobiles	60	450,000		180,000		270,000		2		135,000
Total		$1,630,000		$312,000		$1,318,000				$300,000

$$\text{Composite rate of depreciation} = \frac{\text{Column 6 total}}{\text{Column 2 total}}$$

$$= \frac{\$\ 300,000}{\$1,630,000} = 18.4049\%$$

$$\text{Composite life} = \frac{\text{Column 4 total}}{\text{Column 6 total}}$$

$$= \frac{\$1,318,000}{\$\ 300,000} = 4.39 \text{ years}$$

umn 6) varying between 10 percent for the buses and 50 percent for the automobiles. Greater variance in the individual rates also contributes to the lack of precision.

The most serious estimation problem and the biggest advantage in terms of saved clerical effort with the pooled methods occur when assets are retired or replaced prior to the end of their expected service life. Because, under these pooled depreciation methods, no record is maintained for depreciation accumulated per asset, it is difficult to determine the net book value on a specific asset at a specific point in time. Therefore, gains and losses on the early retirement or sale of these assets are not recorded.

To illustrate, assume that after using the buses for 3 years, University Delivery, Inc., sells all 15 of them to Eastern Michigan University for $293,000. **If the buses had been accounted for as a separate asset** on a straight-line basis, they would have accumulated 3 years' depreciation at $41,500 per year (3 × $41,500 = $124,500) and would have had a net book value of $335,500 ($460,000 − $124,500) after 3 years. The following entry would have recorded the sale and the loss of $42,500 ($335,500 − $293,000):

Cash	293,000	
Accumulated depreciation—buses	124,500	
Loss on sale of buses	42,500	
Buses		460,000
(To record sale of 15 buses to Eastern		
Michigan University after 3 full years		
of use)		

Under the composite depreciation system, the sale of the buses, given the same facts as above, would have been recorded as follows:

Cash	293,000	
Accumulated depreciation	167,000	
Buses		460,000
(To record sale of assets in motor pool		
composite asset group)		

The entry of $167,000 to Accumulated Depreciation is a forced number, and any gain or loss that would otherwise have been recorded is absorbed in the Accumulated Depreciation account, with no reconciliation and no gain or loss recorded until the end of the composite life. Major additions and deletions that leave the old composite rate and life materially misspecified would require the computation of a new composite rate and life.

In general, the composite or group methods may be useful in dealing with large numbers of durable productive assets with similar useful lives (such as power hand tools), but problems may result when they are used for major capital assets, as in the illustration above. The variance in asset life and depreciation rate for material capital assets permits gains or losses to go unrecorded under the group or composite depreciation systems.

Comparison of Basic Depreciation Methods

The calculation of depreciation is a subjective process that typically involves material dollar amounts. The estimates required in recording depreciation are often difficult to verify independently, and differences in estimates can create significant differences in depreciation results. Consider the cases involving the forklift truck

TABLE 12-6

COMPARISON OF ALTERNATIVE DEPRECIATION RESULTS FOR FORKLIFT TRUCK EXAMPLE

	(1) UNITS-OF- OUTPUT METHOD	(2) STRAIGHT- LINE METHOD	(3) SUM-OF- THE-YEARS'- DIGITS METHOD	(4) DOUBLE- DECLINING- BALANCE METHOD	COMMENTS
Expected service life	25,000 hours	10 years	10 years	10 years	This estimate is specified in units (column 1) and time (columns 2, 3, and 4).
Expected residual value	$13,000	$13,000	$13,000	$13,000	This estimate is constant.
Original cost	$88,000	$88,000	$88,000	$88,000	This amount is constant.
First year (1984) depreciation expense	$ 4,500	$ 7,500	$13,636	$17,600	A $10,100 difference between columns 2 and 4.
Second year (1985) depreciation expense	$ 9,000	$ 7,500	$12,273	$14,080	A $6,580 difference between columns 2 and 4.
Net book value at the end of year 2 (1985)	$74,500	$73,000	$62,091	$56,320	A $16,680 difference between columns 2 and 4.

from pages 417 to 421. In each case it was assumed that the estimated life of the forklift truck (25,000 hours for the units-of-output method and 10 years for the other method) and the estimated residual value ($13,000) were unchanged throughout its useful life. The only one of the three unknowns that varied significantly was the pattern of consumption.

If the estimated service life in hours is considered reasonably accurate, then it would seem that the units-of-output method would best represent the actual pattern of consumption. In some cases, however, the total time period of service life is more relevant than is the total number of units of service. For instance, a special-purpose machine used to manufacture one automobile model may be considered obsolete because of market conditions long before it has produced the maximum number of units of which the machine is capable.

Table 12-6 summarizes the different results obtained from the four most common methods of depreciation when applied to the forklift truck example. This schedule demonstrates the impact of these alternative methods on both income determination and asset valuation. Of course, the total amount to be depreciated is $75,000 in every case, but the *timing* of the $75,000 *allocation* between income statement (depreciation expense) and balance sheet (undepreciated asset balance in Forklift Truck account) varies widely in the 10-year interim. Therefore, we should attempt to select a method that best approximates the actual decline in the asset's service potential. At the same time, we should not be overly concerned about a lack of precision because the process, by definition, is subjective and simply cannot be measured with precision.

Published annual reports usually include a short discussion of depreciation policy in their notes to the financial statements (see Exhibit 12-1).

EXHIBIT
12-1

FINANCIAL STATEMENT NOTES ON DEPRECIATION POLICY

NUCORP ENERGY, INC.

Property and Equipment

The Company depreciates its property and equipment, other than oil and gas properties, using the straight line method at rates calculated to amortize the cost of assets over their estimated useful lives. The lives used in computing property and equipment depreciation are as follows:

ASSET CLASSIFICATION	ESTIMATED USEFUL LIFE
Buildings and facilities	10–40
Equipment and related facilities	3–27
Transportation equipment	2–7

Expenditures for maintenance, repairs, and minor renewals are charged to operations as incurred. Expenditures for additions, improvements, replacements and major renewals are capitalized in the property accounts. The cost and accumulated depreciation of assets retired, or otherwise disposed of, are eliminated from the accounts and any resulting gain or loss from these disposals is included in operations.

LONG ISLAND LIGHTING CO.

Depreciation

The provisions for depreciation result from the application of straight-line rates to the original cost, by groups, of depreciable properties in service. The rates are determined by annual age-life studies of depreciable properties. Depreciation accruals were equivalent to 3% of average depreciable plant cost for each of the years 1976 through 1980.

MASCO CORPORATION

Depreciation and Amortization

Depreciation is computed using the straight-line method over the estimated useful lives of the assets. Annual depreciation rates are as follows: land improvements, 4 to 10 percent; building including fixtures, 2-1/2 to 10 percent; and machinery and equipment, 10 to 33-2/3 percent. Depreciation was $24,381,000, $19,435,000 and $15,630,000 in 1980, 1979 and 1978, respectively.

CANADIAN NATIONAL

The cost of depreciable assets retired or disposed of, less salvage, is charged to accumulated depreciation, in accordance with the group plan of depreciation except for CN Trucking and CN Hotels and Tower divisions which follow the unit plan whereby gains or losses are taken into income as they occur.

Depreciation is calculated at rates sufficient to write off properties over their estimated useful lives, generally on a straight-line basis. For railway and telecommunications properties, certain rates are authorized by the Canadian Transport Commission, the Canadian Radio-television and Telecommunications Commission and the Interstate Commerce Commission. The rates for significant classes of assets are as follows:

	ANNUAL RATE
Ties	3.25%
Rails	1.15%
Other track material	1.90%
Ballast	4.00%
Road locomotives	4.60%
Freight cars	2.97%
Commercial communications systems	4.37%

Hotel properties are depreciated at annual rates of 2% to 10% and vessels at 5%.

DEPRECIATION, PRICE CHANGE, AND CAPITAL INVESTMENT

Impact of
Price Changes

There has recently been much discussion regarding the failure of the conventional accounting model to reflect the consumption of capital accurately. This has been identified as one of the reasons for the so-called erosion in the productive capital of the American economy. Indeed the misuse and misunderstanding of the accounting model may be partly to blame for the erosion of the corporate productive capital base.

Understanding this problem is directly related to understanding the limitations of the conventional historical-cost-based accounting model. In Chapter 6 we saw that in periods of changing prices, the historical-cost model does not reflect a depreciation charge equal to the **current cost** of the capital asset consumed in the revenue-generating process. This was attributed primarily to the fact that the historical-cost model assigns asset values in terms of **original transaction values.** In periods of increasing prices, the historical-cost model allocates the **original cost** of a capital asset to the periods in which the asset is consumed. No matter which depreciation method is applied, the amount to be charged to income over the service life of the productive capital asset is *limited* to the original transaction cost under the conventional model.

To see how this may result in an erosion of capital, consider the case of the Harper Independent Salesman Company, Inc. Mr. Harper, the sole proprietor, is a free-lance manufacturer's representative for a number of small tool and die companies in the area, selling to various businesses on a commission basis. Harper has but one capital asset, a 1985 Wingnut, which he drives when carrying samples and delivering orders to customers. The car, which is expected to last 2 years and have no residual value, cost Harper $8,500 at the beginning of 1985. In preparing his tax returns, Harper has declared depreciation expense, revenue, and other miscellaneous expenses for 1985–1986 as follows:

	1986	1985
Revenues—commission	$34,000	$30,000
Depreciation expense	(4,250)	(4,250)
Other business expenses	(19,500)	(17,000)
Taxable income	$10,250	$ 8,750
Income taxes (25%)	(2,562)	(2,187)
After-tax income	$ 7,688	$ 6,563

As the table indicates, Harper has been a modestly successful salesman who has not been able to avoid paying taxes.

Harper learns that a new Wingnut, which he needs to purchase at the end of 1986 to replace his 1985 model, costs a lot more than he paid for the old one. The new 1987 model is identical to the one he purchased in 1985 for $8,500 but is much more expensive because of inflation. The price of the 1986 model was $12,500, and the 1987 model is now selling for $15,600. After studying his tax returns and the data on the current cost of the Wingnut, Harper concludes that he paid too much in income tax because he was not able to depreciate the fair value consumed in using the Wingnut.

He observes that a friend who bought his Wingnut for $12,500 in 1986 was able to deduct $6,250 depreciation expense for tax purposes for 1986. Because Harper paid a lower price for the same type of automobile, he was able to deduct only $4,250 in 1986 for virtually the same amount of consumed service utility. This fact cost Harper $500 in taxes [($6,250 − $4,250) × .25]. It is this type of analysis that leads to the notion of "paying taxes on capital." Because Harper had to pay more taxes than his friend even though he consumed an equal amount of an almost identical asset, he is considered to be paying taxes on his capital assets as well as on his income.

Tax is not the only consideration. We have seen that during inflationary or deflationary times, the conventional model is unable to measure wealth (= capital) and change in wealth (= disposable income) in terms of current costs or current productive capacity. The conventional model maintains the **original transaction value** without regard to changing prices. If Harper consumed the after-tax income amounts for 1985–1986, he would be left with $8,500, his originally transacted capital investment. What will happen to Harper's ability to stay in business if he spends all of his after-tax income each year (that is, pays "dividends" to himself equal to net income)? If prices increase, Harper may have to go into debt to stay in business. The only alternative is to not spend all of the net income but to **retain earnings** in the business to maintain capital in terms of productive capacity.

If we extrapolate this situation to the capital-intensive industries in the United States since World War II and particularly over the past decade, we can begin to see why the accounting treatment accorded major capital assets, such as plant and equipment, has come under attack by many critics of accounting information. The steel industry and the railroad industry are good examples of the negative long-term effects resulting from inaccurate information regarding the economic value of durable assets consumed in the production process. Accounting income in these industries has been illusory in part, and dividends paid have actually been liquidating dividends to a certain degree.

The Investment Tax Credit

The problems of taxing capital have not gone unnoticed by federal taxing agencies. The Treasury, the IRS, and the House Ways and Means Committee have all considered this problem. Instead of any permanent or long-range solution, the government has used tax incentives to stimulate economic activity and make it easier (cheaper) for companies to acquire capital assets.

The **investment tax credit** is, perhaps, the most significant tax incentive employed by the federal government. This tax credit allows corporations that purchase durable capital assets that qualify to deduct up to 10 percent of the cost of the asset from the current income tax liability.[4] In addition, the full cost of the asset is deductible as depreciation expense over the asset's life.

Flow-through versus deferral There are two alternative methods of accounting for the beneficial effects of the investment tax credit. These two methods—the **flow-through method** and the **deferral method**—result in potentially significant differences in their financial statement impacts. At the same time, we should recognize that their financial statement differences, illustrated below, are not economic in nature and represent different accounting treatments of the same basic economic

[4] The amount of the credit varies between 4 and 10 percent depending on the life of the asset.

event. Consider the following data regarding the Westgate Nursery's acquisition of a new backhoe-grader:

DATA FOR 1984	
Income before depreciation and tax	$45,000
Tax rate	25%
Cost of new backhoe-grader acquired on 1/1/84	$25,000
Investment credit allowed	10%
Depreciation method	Straight-line
Estimated service life	10 years
Estimated salvage value	None

The following journal entries record the facts for 1984 under the two alternative accounting treatments:

ENTRY EXPLANATION	FLOW-THROUGH METHOD		DEFERRAL METHOD	
Acquire asset	Backhoe-grader 25,000 Cash	25,000	Backhoe-grader 25,000 Cash	25,000
Recording 1984 depreciation—$^{1}/_{10}$ of asset cost	Depreciation expense 2,500 Accumulated depreciation	2,500	Depreciation expense 2,500 Accumulated depreciation	2,500
Recording tax obligation—before considering tax credit	Income tax expense 10,625 Income tax payable	10,625	Income tax expense 10,625 Income tax payable	10,625
Recording tax credit	Income tax payable 2,500 Income tax expense	2,500	Income tax payable 2,500 Deferred investment tax credit	2,500
Amortization of $^{1}/_{10}$ portion of deferred tax credit for 1984	No entry under flow-through method		Deferred investment tax credit 250 Income tax expense	250

As indicated, the tax credit under the deferral method is spread out *over the life of the asset* to which it pertains. The income tax *expense* for 1984 is $8,125 under the flow-through method and $10,375 under the deferral method. The $2,250 difference will be spread out over the remaining life of the backhoe, reducing income tax expense each year for the next 9 years by $250 per year. Note that the income tax payable for 1984 is $8,125 for *both* methods. This current liability will require an outflow of cash in the near future.

Why have two alternatives for the impact on income tax expense? The deferral method assumes that there is some "benefit" in reducing the "tax expense" part of the entry by the $2,500 credit, and it argues that this benefit should be spread out over the life of the asset that generated the tax credit. To accomplish this, it establishes a nonliability credit balance account, Deferred Investment Tax Credit, which is amortized by reducing Income Tax Expense by $250 each year over the 10-year life of the asset.

The flow-through method, which according to *Accounting Trends and Techniques* is used by over 80 percent of the reporting entities, takes the entire "benefit" in the period in which the credit is received. The Income Tax Expense and the Income Tax Payable accounts are *both* reduced by the full amount of the tax credit. Some policy makers have argued that a major impact on the Income Tax Expense account (which is reported in the income statement) might distort the relationship between the pretax income reported in the published financial statements and the income tax expense figure reported. It is inevitable that the tax credit must affect the amount of income tax expense reported—the question is, How much and how fast? These problems of maintaining the relationship between pretax income and income tax expense are rather extensive, and the policy that governs this problem will be examined in Chapter 17, "Accounting for Income Taxes."

Promulgated GAAP do not resolve this issue. As a result of heavy pressure from the business sector, the APB reversed its requirement, **APB Opinion No. 2,** that the deferral method be used.[5] Currently **APB Opinion No. 4** governs, and it allows either method, although it states that deferral is preferable.[6]

In evaluating these and other alternative accounting methods, the economic aspect of the differences between methods can be important. In the investment tax credit, there are no apparent real economic consequences to the entity of selecting one method or the other. However, managers may prefer one method to another for their own economic reasons. For example, if a manager's salary or bonus is based on net income, it may be beneficial for that manager to use the flow-through method of accounting for the investment tax credit in the sense that the manager's current compensation would be more if the flow-through method were used, holding everything else constant. Although, on the surface, it might not seem as though the accounting method should matter, the fact that over 80 percent of the firms surveyed used the flow-through method suggests that it does matter to the managers who select accounting methods.

ACCOUNTING CHANGES AND DEPRECIATION

The process of measuring and recording depreciation is based on several estimates. Given the fact that these estimated data are not known with certainty, it may sometimes be necessary for them to be revised prior to the end of an asset's service life. Consider two basic types of changes covered by **APB Opinion No. 20,** which are discussed in Chapters 3 and 24: (1) changes in estimates and (2) changes in principle (method). Changes involving the estimated service life or the estimated salvage value of an asset are considered to be changes in estimates. Changes involving the assumed pattern of service utility (depreciation method) are considered to be changes in principle.[7]

Assume that on January 1, 1987, the Redman Corporation acquires metal-cutting machinery used in the production of recreational vehicles. The assets cost $25,000, have an estimated life of 4 years, and have an estimated scrap value of $5,000 at the end of 4 years. Redman uses straight-line depreciation. Let us take this

[5] *Accounting Principles Board Opinion No. 2,* "Accounting for the 'Investment Credit'" (New York: AICPA, December 1962).

[6] *Accounting Principles Board Opinion No. 4,* "Accounting for the 'Investment Credit'" (amending No. 2) (New York: AICPA, March 1964).

[7] The term *principle,* as used in *Accounting Principles Board Opinion No. 20,* "Accounting Changes" (New York: AICPA, July 1971), considers all alternative accounting methods as principles. This is a broader definition than that used in Chapter 2 of this book and in other APB official pronouncements.

set of base data to illustrate the following *independent* changes:

Change 1: Assume that during the third year it becomes apparent that the assets will last 5 years and their scrap value is reestimated at $3,600.

Change 2: Assume that during year 3, Redman decides to switch to SYD depreciation.

The following entry would record change 1, which is an example of two changes in estimates taking place at the same time (both life and salvage value):

Computations

1. Book value of the asset at the *beginning* of the period of change in estimate	Cost	$25,000
	− Accumulated depreciation	10,000
	Net book value	$15,000
2. *Revised* balance to be depreciated	Net book value	$15,000
	− Salvage value	3,600
	Net to be depreciated	$11,400
3. *Revised* remaining service life		3 years
4. *Revised* depreciation for 1989, 1990, and 1991 under straight-line depreciation method	$\dfrac{\$11,400}{3} = \$3,800$	

Entry

12/31/89	Depreciation expense or manufacturing overhead control	3,800	
	Accumulated depreciation		3,800

The change in estimate is always recorded in such a way that only the year of the change and future years are affected. No changes in the amounts recorded in prior years take place.

The following entries would record change 2, an example of a change in accounting principle:

Computations

1. Book value of the asset at the *beginning* of the period of the change in principle	Cost	$25,000
	− Accumulated depreciation	10,000
	Net book value	$15,000
2. Book value at the *beginning* of the period of change in principle assuming the new method (SYD) has been used ($^4/_{10} + {}^3/_{10} = {}^7/_{10} \times \$20,000 = \$14,000$)	Cost	$25,000
	− Accumulated depreciation	14,000
	Net book value	$11,000
3. Difference in book value		$4,000

Entries

?/?/89	Cumulative effect of a change in accounting principle	4,000	
	Accumulated depreciation		4,000
	(To record change to SYD depreciation method)		
12/31/89	Depreciation expense or manufacturing overhead control	4,000	
	Accumulated depreciation		4,000
	(To record year 3 depreciation using the SYD method)		

The first $4,000 entry above, which could be recorded at any point during the year that the decision to change is made, is sometimes referred to as the **catch-up entry.** This entry records the cumulative difference between the new method and the old method, $4,000 in this case as of the start of the year of change. The Accumulated Depreciation account is adjusted (either increased or decreased), and the offsetting entry to the Cumulative Effect account is reported in the income statement as a separate item just above the final net income number and below extraordinary items (if any). In this case, the catch-up entry will reduce net income by $4,000 (not considering tax effects). Changes in depreciation methods may have a significant impact on net income, and the disclosure of the methods used is a reporting requirement of **APB Opinion No. 22.**[8] Also, the periodic depreciation expense and the accumulated depreciation must be reported in the financial statements or the notes thereto. Details of reporting for accounting changes will be covered in Chapter 24.

DEPLETION OF NATURAL RESOURCES

Valuation of
Resources

Accounting for natural resources is similar to accounting for other productive assets. The cost of natural resources includes any necessary and reasonable cost required to place the resource into a productive state. This would include (1) any **price paid to acquire the resources** (or the rights to extract the resources), (2) the **costs to explore** for reserves, and (3) any **development costs** incurred in the process of preparing for the extraction of the resources. This might include the costs of erecting temporary buildings or sheds, the costs of stripping the land, the costs of locating the resources, and so on. These costs form the depletable base of the natural resources. The depletion expenses from these resource costs, in combination with the materials, labor, and other overhead costs incurred in the extracting, processing, transporting, and storing of the natural resources, all become a part of the product (resource) cost, which is inventoried until sold. Cost of assets that are separable from the resource reserve, such as buildings and equipment, are not included in the depletion base, but are depreciated by means of an appropriate depreciation technique.

Depletion of
Resources

The measurement of depletion cost is not unlike the measurement of depreciation. Although there are fewer unknowns in depletion cost measurement, there is usually as much or more uncertainty. To measure depletion cost, the following data are required:

1. The total amount of resources to be extracted
2. The total amount of resources extracted in a given period of time
3. The total cost of obtaining the resources
4. The expected net residual value of item 3

These items parallel those on page 415, which identify the unknowns required for depreciation. However, although the pattern of use must be estimated for depletable assets, the amount of resources actually produced in a period is known with relative certainty. The total amount of resources available (item 1 above) and the net

[8] *Accounting Principles Board Opinion No. 22,* "Disclosure of Accounting Policies" (New York: AICPA, April 1972).

residual value of the total cost of the resources both involve a degree of uncertainty, as did their counterparts for depreciable assets.

The periodic depletion charge would be calculated as follows:

$$\left(\frac{\text{Resources extracted during current period}}{\text{Estimated total resources to be extracted}} \right) \times \left(\begin{array}{c} \text{Cost of} \\ \text{natural resources} \end{array} \right) = \begin{array}{c} \text{Depletion cost} \\ \text{for current period} \end{array}$$

The following entry would record the depletion:

Inventory of minerals (or cost of goods sold if no inventory balances are maintained)	XXX	
Natural resources or accumulated depletion		XXX
(To record periodic depletion)		

The depletion charge becomes part of the product cost, and the asset account, Natural Resources is either directly or indirectly reduced. The indirect reduction of the asset, through the use of a contra asset account such as Accumulated Depletion, is preferred because it provides information that enables financial statement users to determine the ratio of extracted to unextracted resources.

Successful-Efforts and Full-Costing Methods

Many nonrenewable resources, such as diamonds, oil, gold, and gas, require certain exploration efforts before discovery. The costs of these exploration efforts are often substantial, and there has been some controversy about the way these costs should be treated when the exploration results in no resources being discovered. This controversy reached its peak in the early 1970s when the costs of oil and gas began to soar and Congress started to investigate oil company profits.

The two basic methods of accounting for exploration costs and other costs associated with the discovery of natural resources, the **full-costing method** and the **successful-efforts method,** can yield significantly different results. The difference between these two methods is basically their treatment of the costs of unsuccessful exploration. The **full-costing** method considers unsuccessful exploration costs to be a necessary cost of the successful efforts (the you-can't-win-all-the-time concept) and therefore capitalizes all exploration costs within a specific cost center as part of the asset "natural resources."[9] The **successful-efforts** method treats the cost of unsuccessful efforts as expenses of the period incurred. Exhibit 12–2 shows the depletion footnote disclosures from two companies' published financial statements.

To illustrate, consider the following data from the Bourne Extraction Company, which has drilled three exploratory oil wells during 1987. To simplify the example, assume that the only costs related to the oil reserve are the exploration costs. In practice, of course, there are costs related to the land itself and development costs.

[9] *Cost center* is defined in SEC Release No. 33-5968 and *Accounting Series Release No. 258* as a county-by-county location within which the full-costing method may be applied. Capitalized costs are limited to the net expected value of the future benefits to be derived from the successful discoveries on a "cost-center-by-cost-center" basis.

SITE	COSTS ACCUMULATED IN THE "EXPLORATION IN PROCESS" ACCOUNT
Well 1—Wyoming County, Texas	$1,300,000
Well 2—Wyoming County, Texas	1,400,000
Well 3—Wyoming County, Texas	1,200,000
	$3,900,000

Only well 3 was successful, resulting in a discovery of oil estimated at 15,000,000 barrels. The following entries illustrate the two alternative accounting methods, assuming 2,000,000 barrels of crude oil are extracted in 1987 and are sold to a processor for $4,000,000.

SUCCESSFUL EFFORTS

	DEBIT	CREDIT
1. Exploration expense	2,700,000	
Natural resources	1,200,000	
Exploration in process		3,900,000
2. Cost of resources sold to processor[a]	160,000	
Accumulated depletion		160,000
3. Cash (accounts receivable)	4,000,000	
Sales		4,000,000

FULL COSTING

	DEBIT	CREDIT
1. Natural resources	3,900,000	
Exploration in process		3,900,000
2. Cost of resources sold to processor[b]	520,000	
Accumulated depletion		520,000
3. Cash (accounts receivable)	4,000,000	
Sales		4,000,000

[a] Depletion computation:

$$\frac{2,000,000 \text{ barrels}}{15,000,000 \text{ barrels}} \times \$1,200,000 = \$ \ 160,000$$

Resulting net profit, 1987 $1,140,000 ($4,000,000 − $2,700,000 − $160,000)

[b] Depletion computation:

$$\frac{2,000,000 \text{ barrels}}{15,000,000 \text{ barrels}} \times \$3,900,000 = \$ \ 520,000$$

Resulting net profit, 1987 $3,480,000 ($4,000,000 − $520,000)

As illustrated, the successful-efforts method is more conservative in that it immediately expenses unsuccessful efforts and, as a result, generally reports lower assets and lower profits than does the full costing method.

Changes in the estimated total recoverable resources may occur over the life of the extraction process. These changes are treated just like a change in the estimated life or salvage value of a depreciable asset. A change in an estimate results in a change in the cost of depletion for each unit of production. For example, if Bourne Extraction Company determined in 1988 that (based on a new seismic analysis) the total recoverable resources were expected to be 12,000,000 barrels instead of 15,000,000 barrels and then went on to extract another 2,000,000 barrels in 1988, the 1988 de-

EXHIBIT
12–2

DEPLETION FOOTNOTE DISCLOSURES

NUCORP ENERGY, INC.

Oil and Gas Properties

The Company capitalizes all exploration and development costs (full cost accounting) incurred for the purpose of finding oil and gas reserves. These amounts include the costs of drilling and equipping productive wells, dry hole costs, lease acquisition costs, delay rentals, and administrative expenses related to exploration and development activities. Such costs are amortized using the future gross revenue method on a company-wide basis whereby the annual provision for depreciation, depletion and amortization is computed by dividing the costs of the oil and gas properties, including estimated future development costs, by estimated future gross revenues from proved oil and gas reserves and applying the resulting rate to revenue produced during the period. The depreciation, depletion and amortization rate was 41% for 1978, 30% for 1979, and 20% for 1980 of oil and gas gross revenues. Transactions involving sales of reserves in place, unless extraordinarily large reserves are involved, are recognized as adjustments to the costs of total oil and gas properties and accumulated depreciation, depletion and amortization, and no gain or loss is recognized.

NICOR, INC.

Oil and Gas Exploration and Development Costs

The oil and gas companies follow the full-cost method of accounting whereby substantially all acquisition, exploration and development costs are capitalized and depleted.

pletion would be computed as follows:

1. Original estimate of remaining barrels, 1/1/88	13,000,000	(15,000,000 − 2,000,000 of 1987 production)
2. New estimate of remaining barrels, 1/1/88	10,000,000	(12,000,000 − 2,000,000 of 1987 production)
3. Net book value of remaining barrels, 1/1/88		
Assuming full costing	$ 3,380,000	($3,900,000 − $520,000)
Assuming successful efforts	$ 1,040,000	($1,200,000 − $160,000)

1988 DEPLETION

SUCCESSFUL EFFORTS:	FULL COSTING
$\frac{2,000,000 \text{ barrels}}{10,000,000 \text{ barrels}} \times \$1,040,000 = \underline{\$208,000}$	$\frac{2,000,000 \text{ barrels}}{10,000,000 \text{ barrels}} \times \$3,380,000 = \underline{\$676,000}$

This method of accounting for the change in the estimated reserves is conceptually the same as that for changes in the estimated life of depreciable assets covered previously in this chapter.

Both the successful-efforts method and the full-costing method are currently acceptable, although the history of how this current status evolved is much more complex than it would appear. At one point, the FASB had ruled in **FASB Statement No. 19** in favor of requiring all oil and gas producers to use the successful-efforts method.[10] This position was overruled by the SEC and was later suspended

[10] *Statement of Financial Accounting Standards No. 19,* "Financial Accounting by Oil and Gas Producing Companies" (Stamford, CT: FASB, December 1977).

by the FASB in its **Statement No. 25.**[11] The SEC ruled in favor of allowing either method, but, more importantly, it also favored a new valuation method called reserve recognition accounting, which was aimed at valuing the current worth of the proved quantity of oil and gas that had been discovered but was still unrecovered.

Reserve Recognition Accounting for Oil and Gas Producers

The historical-cost-based methods of accounting for exploration costs illustrated above are currently acceptable for financial-reporting purposes. However, the SEC now requires supplementary disclosure by certain oil and gas companies in the form of **reserve recognition accounting (RRA).** The RRA method proposed by the SEC called for measuring the oil or gas at something approximating its **fair market value at the wellhead** instead of the **cost** incurred. RRA is an application of discovery value accounting that is quite different from conventional historical-cost-based accounting. As a general example, if a firm discovered that one of its office paintings was an original Bergan, valued at $1,000,000 more than what it had originally paid, it could record this as follows:

Paintings (asset)	1,000,000	
Appraised capital (owners' equity)		1,000,000
(To record discovery of valuable painting)		

As an alternative, it would also be possible to report this discovery value in the income statement by expanding the recording to the following two entries:

Paintings (asset)	1,000,000	
Gain on discovery of asset (income statement)		1,000,000
(To record gain on discovery of asset)		
Gain on discovery of asset (income statement)	1,000,000	
Appraisal capital (owners' equity)		1,000,000
(To close gain reported in the income statement to owners' equity)		

Estimating the fair market value of the oil or gas at the wellhead (which is required for current supplementary RRA disclosures as well as formal recording procedures illustrated for the painting) is a very subjective process, and, for the time being at least, the SEC has abandoned its plan to require that the RRA method be adopted for general reporting purposes. The RRA valuation of the resource would require the following:

1. An estimate of the amount of resources discovered
2. An estimate of the selling price of the processed product
3. An estimate of the future production costs between wellhead and point of final sale
4. The expected period of sale
5. The appropriate rate to use in discounting future amounts of inflows and outflows (revenues and expenses) to their present value
6. The expensing of all exploration and acquisition costs as they are being incurred

[11] *Statement of Financial Accounting Standards No. 25*, "Suspension of Certain Accounting Requirements for Oil and Gas Companies" (Stamford, CT: FASB, February 1979).

The SEC RRA reporting requirements resulted in the disclosure as exemplified in Exhibit 12–3. At this time both the SEC and the FASB are reconsidering their disclosure requirements. The SEC now has given the FASB the green light to develop the *disclosure* requirements of oil and gas producers. The FASB is proposing the following general disclosures:[12]

1. All oil and gas producers must report their accounting methods.
2. All publicly held companies must disclose the following about their oil and gas operations:
   a. Proved reserves
   b. Capitalized costs
   c. Costs incurred
   d. Results of operations
   e. Discounted future net cash flows

Statutory
Depletion
Allowances

The Internal Revenue Service (IRS) uses the term *depletion* in a way that does not exactly correspond to our definitions above. The IRS allows a deduction for the greater of (1) the **cost depletion** (determined by either the successful-efforts method or the full-costing method) or (2) the **statutory "depletion" percentage.** The statutory percentage varies from 5 to 22 percent, depending on the resource involved, and is multiplied by the gross income received during the period. A depletion expense deduction based on the statutory rate for income tax purposes has nothing to do with the *cost* of the resource, and the total depletion taken for tax purposes from any reserve of resources may exceed the total cost being depleted for financial reporting. This difference between book and tax expense is accounted for by using the tax-allocation procedures discussed in Chapter 17, "Accounting for Income Taxes." Also, **FASB Statement No. 9** deals with special tax-allocation procedures for oil and gas companies.[13]

FUNDS FLOW EFFECTS

The acquisitions of property, plant, and equipment may affect funds (cash and/or working capital) in the period of acquisition, and in the case of long-term credit arrangements, funds in future periods are affected. The acquisition transactions, however, have no direct effect on net income. Depreciation and depletion charges do not reduce funds but do reduce net income. It is important therefore to fully understand that fund flows from operations are not *reduced* or affected in any way by such cost allocations. As discussed fully in Chapters 4 and 25, a reconciliation of net income and funds from operations does entail an "add back" for depreciation and depletion charges. If net income is $800,000 and that amount includes a depreciation charge of $250,000, then, holding everything else constant, funds from operations would be $1,050,000.

[12] Proposed Statement of Financial Accounting Standards, "Disclosure of Oil and Gas Producing Activities" (Stamford, CT: FASB, April 15, 1982).

[13] *Statement of Financial Accounting Standards No. 9*, "Accounting for Income Taxes—Oil and Gas Producing Companies" (Stamford, CT: FASB, October 1975).

EXHIBIT 12–3

Set forth below is an unaudited supplemental summary of activities for United's investment in oil and gas operations. This summary has been prepared on the basis of Reserve Recognition Accounting (RRA) as required by the Securities and Exchange Commission (SEC). (All data expressed in thousands of dollars.)

Summary of Oil and Gas Operations Prepared on the Basis of RRA—

	YEAR ENDED DECEMBER 31		
	1980	1979	1978
Additions and revisions to proved reserves:			
Additions to estimated proved reserves	$114,433	$112,110	$80,245
Revisions to reserves proved in prior years—			
Increase in prices of oil and gas	61,137	21,224	7,060
Interest factor—accretion of discount	26,454	16,554	9,519
Other	(36,274)	(20,210)	(5,512)
Total revisions to estimated proved reserves	51,317	17,568	11,067
Total additions and revisions to proved reserves	165,750	129,678	91,312
Related exploration and development costs:			
Costs incurred during the year—			
Acquisitions of unproved properties	28,374	21,243	14,579
Exploration	44,636	39,140	43,788
Development	53,919	28,988	25,492
	126,929	89,371	83,859
Changes in deferred costs	(29,347)	(20,760)	(15,740)
Development costs incurred, previously considered in valuation of proved reserves	(2,985)	(2,812)	(1,771)
Total related exploration and development costs	94,597	65,799	66,348
RRA income before other expenses and income taxes	71,153	63,879	24,964
Operation, maintenance and other expenses—including salaries, wages and other general and administrative expenses	7,917	5,480	2,732
RRA income before interest and income taxes*	63,236	58,399	22,232
Provision for income taxes	26,897	22,846	5,993
Income, before interest, from oil and gas producing activities on the basis of RRA	$ 36,339	$ 35,553	$16,239

* Comparable income before interest and taxes for oil and gas producing activities under generally accepted accounting principles was $20,250,000 in 1980, $8,775,000 in 1979 and $8,443,000 in 1978.

Analysis of changes in RRA Valuation of Proved Reserves—

	TOTAL			UNITED STATES			CANADA		
	1980	1979	1978	1980	1979	1978	1980	1979	1978
Present value at beginning of year	$264,536	$165,540	$ 95,188	$263,069	$164,595	$ 94,295	$1,467	$ 945	$893
Revisions to reserves proved in prior years	51,317	17,568	11,067	50,694	17,585	10,963	623	(17)	104
	315,853	183,108	106,255	313,763	182,180	105,258	2,090	928	997
New field discoveries and extensions	114,433	112,110	80,245	107,526	111,511	80,245	6,907	599	—
Purchase of reserves	421	1,510	1,243	421	1,510	1,243	—	—	—
Projected development costs incurred	2,985	2,812	1,771	2,820	2,812	1,771	165	—	—
Production, net of lifting costs	(58,100)	(35,004)	(23,974)	(58,058)	(34,944)	(23,922)	(42)	(60)	(52)
Present value at end of year	$375,592	$264,536	$165,540	$366,472	$263,069	$164,595	$9,120	$1,467	$945

* Based on the method of providing income taxes prescribed by the SEC, the year-end tax liability associated with the RRA valuation of proved reserves would be $147,231,000, $98,270,000 and $59,279,000 in 1980, 1979 and 1978.

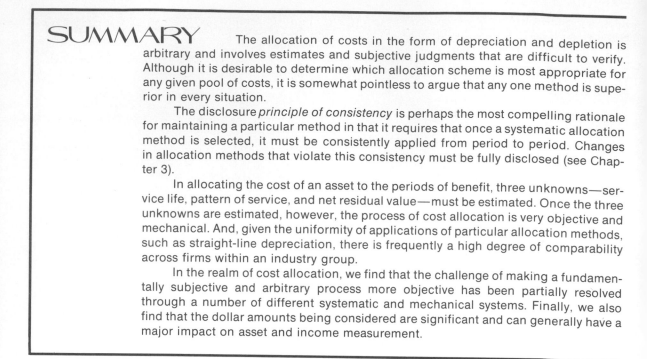

SUMMARY

The allocation of costs in the form of depreciation and depletion is arbitrary and involves estimates and subjective judgments that are difficult to verify. Although it is desirable to determine which allocation scheme is most appropriate for any given pool of costs, it is somewhat pointless to argue that any one method is superior in every situation.

The disclosure *principle of consistency* is perhaps the most compelling rationale for maintaining a particular method in that it requires that once a systematic allocation method is selected, it must be consistently applied from period to period. Changes in allocation methods that violate this consistency must be fully disclosed (see Chapter 3).

In allocating the cost of an asset to the periods of benefit, three unknowns—service life, pattern of service, and net residual value—must be estimated. Once the three unknowns are estimated, however, the process of cost allocation is very objective and mechanical. And, given the uniformity of applications of particular allocation methods, such as straight-line depreciation, there is frequently a high degree of comparability across firms within an industry group.

In the realm of cost allocation, we find that the challenge of making a fundamentally subjective and arbitrary process more objective has been partially resolved through a number of different systematic and mechanical systems. Finally, we also find that the dollar amounts being considered are significant and can generally have a major impact on asset and income measurement.

QUESTIONS

Q12–1   What basic accounting concepts support the allocation of capitalized costs to different periods?

Q12–2   Cost allocation in the form of depreciation, depletion, and amortization has been characterized as arbitrary. In what sense is this characterization correct? Incorrect?

Q12–3   What key estimates are needed for depreciation determination, and how do they affect the depreciable base?

Q12–4   What is the relationship between the *fair value* and the *book value* of a depreciable asset over its useful life?

Q12–5   "In the year of disposal of a depreciable asset, net income would not change whether or not depreciation is recorded on the disposed asset." In what sense is this statement true? Does it represent good accounting policy? Why?

Q12–6   Discuss the advantages of group depreciation. How are gains and losses on disposal of a specific asset accounted for under this method?

Q12–7   What effect does the expected pattern of service life utilization have on the selection of a depreciation method?

Q12–8   What role does estimated salvage value play in the declining-balance and sum-of-the-years'-digits depreciation methods?

Q12–9   In what sense is the units-of-production method of depreciation a "straight-line" method?

Q12–10   What basic accounting question lies at the heart of the successful efforts versus full-costing controversy, and how have promulgated GAAP "resolved" this question?

C12–1 Consider the following statement: "Any asset whose estimated salvage value is less than its original cost must be depreciated, depleted, or amortized."

REQUIRED Do you agree with this statement? Can you think of any exceptions?

C12–2 McFarland Company has purchased a new generator for its plant at a cost of $210,000. The generator is expected to be in constant use, to have a useful life of 5 years, and to have a $50,000 salvage value. Total electrical generation is expected to decline at a rate of 3 percent of the original capacity each year. The production engineer states: "According to my knowledge of accounting, the depreciation of the generator must reflect the fact that total benefits to the company are steadily decreasing throughout its life."

REQUIRED Explain to the engineer what options are available for depreciation of the generator based on theoretical and practical considerations.

C12–3 MetroLand Developers buys large tracts of land and develops them into residential sites. One such site, located 40 miles northwest of Houston, required an expenditure of $520,000 for an access road that will eventually be replaced by a state-owned road. The road is expected to be used for 4 years, during which time the sites are to be developed and sold. Metro's accountant must decide on the proper accounting for the cost of the access road. She has devised five alternatives:

1. Write off the cost as incurred.
2. Capitalize the cost and amortize it on a straight-line basis for 4 years.
3. Capitalize the cost and amortize it on the proportion of current year's sales to total estimated sales.
4. Capitalize the cost and amortize it on the proportion of the number of sites sold in the current year to the total estimated number of sites to be sold.
5. Capitalize the cost and write it off when all sales are completed.

REQUIRED Give your opinion of each of these alternatives. Which alternative would you recommend and why?

C12–4 Breaker Radio Corporation has an individualistic approach to accounting for the investment tax credit. It defers the effect of the credit by reducing the book value of the depreciable asset, and it depreciates the reduced book value using the straight-line basis. The controller justifies this procedure as follows: "The investment credit is, in essence, a reduction of asset cost. As such, it should directly affect depreciation charges."

REQUIRED Discuss the validity of the controller's statement.

C12–5 In auditing a client's asset records, you discover that depreciation expense has increased considerably during the current year. Upon further investigation you find that the depreciation method was changed (from straight-line to double-declining balance) for one group of assets, and the estimated remaining life was considerably shortened for another group of assets.

The entire "catch-up" amount as of the beginning of the current year caused by the method change was debited to depreciation expense, and the difference between the prior years' depreciation charges for the new useful life versus the old useful life was also charged to depreciation expense.

REQUIRED Write a memorandum to the controller to explain the appropriate accounting for such changes, and describe what adjustments (if any) are necessary.

C12–6 Consider the following pattern of fair values and book values for a depreciable asset:

	1/1/78	12/31/78	12/31/79	12/31/80	12/31/81	12/31/82
Book value	$100,000	$82,000	$64,000	$46,000	$28,000	$10,000
Fair value	100,000	90,000	60,000	40,000	15,000	10,000

REQUIRED Explain why such book values may be perfectly appropriate given the series of fair values shown. At what point or points in time are book values and fair values the same? Why is this so?

C12–7 The president of Merkel Toys, Inc., is asked to give her final approval of the company's annual financial statements before they are distributed to stockholders. In examining the preliminary December 31, 1983, balance sheet, she finds two curious items marked by asterisks:

			($000)
Current assets			
Cash			$ 305
Accounts receivable			1,201
Inventory			800
Marketable securities			12
Portions of long-term assets to be depreciated in 1984*			412
Total current assets			$2,730
Long-term assets			
Plant and equipment			
Building (net of accumulated depreciation)	$1,508		
Land	667		
Equipment (net of accumulated depreciation)	2,505		
		$4,680	
Less cost reclassified as current*		412	$4,268

At first the reclassification seems to make sense, but upon reflection the president calls on you, as the company's CPA, to give your opinion.

REQUIRED Draft a memorandum explaining the incidence of such reclassifications in practice.

C12–8 Utah Coal Processors has just completed a plant that will convert coal to a liquid fuel that has almost the same properties as crude oil. The conversion process uses coal as both a heat source and a raw material. It is estimated that of the 500,000 tons of exploitable coal in reserve, 90,000 tons will be used as a heat source for the conversion process, 300,000 tons will be converted to fuel oil, 100,000 tons will be mined and sold in the conventional manner, and 10,000 tons will be used as energy for conventional mining. The following schedule gives some additional information:

Cost of coal-mining rights	$5,000,000
Production schedule	1. 50,000 tons per year to be used as raw material in the conversion process
	2. 15,000 tons per year to be used as a heat source in the conversion process
	3. 16,666 tons per year to be sold as solid coal
	4. 1,666 tons per year to be used as an energy source for conventional mining

It is expected that the gross-profit margin on the liquid fuel will be twice as much as that on the solid coal.

REQUIRED Describe a rational depletion policy for this project.

C12–9 Your company uses group depreciation for all machinery and equipment on a plant-by-plant basis; that is, each plant's machinery and equipment are pooled separately. During the current fiscal year a renovation in one plant resulted in the scrapping of several machines. Upon reviewing the preliminary income statement for the current year, the president of your company is surprised that a loss on disposition of the equipment is not reported, noting that the amounts involved must have been material.

REQUIRED Explain how losses on disposition of assets under the group depreciation method can affect the income statement.

C12–10 The presidents of two oil exploration companies are discussing the pros and cons of the successful-efforts and full-costing methods of accounting. One company has, on average, 20 exploration teams at locations throughout the world, whereas the other, a much smaller company, usually has two such teams. The president of the smaller company argues that successful-efforts accounting would force his company to show a very irregular stream of annual earnings, which would be misleading to outsiders. The other president argues that the long-run reported income would be the same under either method.

REQUIRED Discuss the logic of each argument, and describe conditions under which each would be (1) valid and (2) invalid.

C12–11 (CPA ADAPTED) Property, plant, and equipment (plant assets) generally represent a large percentage of the total assets of most companies. Accounting for the acquisition and usage of such assets is, therefore, an important part of the financial-reporting process.

REQUIRED

1. Distinguish between *revenue* and *capital expenditures,* and explain why this distinction is important.
2. Briefly define *depreciation* as used in accounting.
3. Identify the relevant factors in determining the annual depreciation. Are these factors determined objectively or are they based on judgment?
4. Explain why depreciation is usually shown in the "sources of funds" section of the statement of changes in financial position.

EXERCISES

E12–1 A company purchased a remote site for oil and gas development for $1,660,000. After exploiting about one-half of the reserves, it decided to sell half the site to a resort developer and deplete the remaining reserve through wells on the remaining land.

REQUIRED If the selling price of the land is $300,000, what journal entry would be appropriate to record the sale of the land? State your assumptions.

E12–2 On January 1, 1965, an office building was purchased for $18,800,000 and was depreciated on a straight-line basis ($1,000,000 estimated salvage and 25-year estimated useful life) until December 31, 1983, the end of the fiscal period. On October 1, 1984, the remaining useful life was felt to be 15 years with a salvage value of $3,500,000.

REQUIRED What effect would these changes in estimates have on the January 1, 1984, and December 31, 1984, retained earnings balances? Explain.

E12–3 On June 30, 1983, Mainline Railroad, a calendar-year company, installed a new computer at a total cost of $4,330,000. This computer has an estimated useful life of 5 years and an estimated salvage value of $1,500,000. Although straight-line depreciation is to be used, the computer's first 6 months of operation are considered a break-in period in which only one-half of its capacity will be utilized.

REQUIRED Construct a depreciation schedule that reflects this pattern of usage. Explain.

E12–4 Construct a schedule to show what the depreciation charge would be each year for equipment that cost $150,000 in 1984 and has a 6-year estimated useful life with zero estimated salvage value. Assume that the company depreciates equipment a half a year in the year of acquisition and a half a year in the year of disposal. The sum-of-the-years'-digits method is used.

E12–5 Anthro Insecticides, Inc., depreciates its buildings by means of the double-declining-balance method. On August 15, 1983, the company purchases a building that costs $6,600,000 and has an estimated useful life of 20 years with a $2,000,000 estimated salvage value.

REQUIRED If the company depreciates its buildings for a full month in the month of acquisition, how much total depreciation would be charged for 1983 and 1984?

E12–6 A large manufacturer uses the composite depreciation method for depreciating tools. If a new plant is opened on January 1, 1983, with the following tools, what is the depreciation charge for 1983?

	TOTAL PURCHASE PRICE	AVERAGE ESTIMATED USEFUL LIFE	ESTIMATED SALVAGE VALUE
10 drill presses	$ 88,000	15 years	$ 500 each
5 lathes	140,500	10 years	2,500 each
Miscellaneous	30,000	6 years	0

E12–7 On July 1, 1983, Hodiac, Inc., a calendar-year company, added equipment to its film-processing plant at a cost of $10,100,000. The equipment has an estimated useful life of 10 years.

REQUIRED What is the relative impact of the flow-through and deferral methods of accounting for the 10 percent investment credit on 1983 net income?

E12–8 Refer to exercise 12–7.

REQUIRED If Hodiac, Inc., had federal income tax expense of $8,800,000 for 1983 before considering the investment credit, what journal entries would record the tax effects of the two methods of accounting for the investment credit?

E12–9 During 1983 Imperial Oil and Gas spent $82,500,000 in exploration costs and estimated that 25 percent of its efforts resulted in the discovery of exploitable reserves. Imperial uses the successful-efforts method of accounting for exploration costs.

REQUIRED What is the difference between the company's year-end 1983 balance sheet as presented and what it would have been if the full-costing method had been used, assuming that 10 percent of the discovered reserve had been produced and sold?

PROBLEMS

P12–1 At the beginning of year 1, a firm acquired a new machine having an invoice price of $10,000. The net cost of moving an old machine to make way for the new one was $800. The old machine remained in use at a different site. Installation of the new machine cost $400. Costs of testing the new machine were $150 for the operators' time and $100 in wasted materials before the machine was properly adjusted. The new machine had an expected useful life of 8 years and a net estimated salvage value of $450.

REQUIRED

1. For accounting purposes, what is the cost of the new machine?
2. What is the depreciation expense to be recorded in year 2 assuming the sum-of-the-years'-digits method is used?
3. What is the depreciation expense to be recorded in year 2 assuming the double-declining-balance method is used?

P12–2   At the beginning of its current fiscal year, Freedom Corporation acquires a fixed asset for $100,000. The estimated life is 4 years, and there is no estimated salvage value. Assume a relevant interest rate of 8 percent and an income tax rate of 40 percent.

REQUIRED   What is the present value at date of acquisition of the tax benefits resulting from using sum-of-the-years'-digits depreciation as opposed to straight-line depreciation for tax purposes on this asset? Show a schedule to support your answer.

P12–3   On January 1, 1985, Janell Corporation purchased a forklift truck to be used in its warehouse for finished-goods inventory. The list, or advertised, price was $22,000, but Janell paid only $20,000 in cash. The estimated useful life at the purchase date was 10 years or 24,000 hours of use, and the estimated salvage value was $1,000.

The following table shows the actual use of the forklift truck for 3 years and certain other transactions for those years:

	HOURS OF USE	WAGES OF FORKLIFT OPERATORS	REPAIRS ON FORKLIFT TRUCK PAID TO OUTSIDE SHOP	MAINTENANCE PERFORMED BY CORPORATION PERSONNEL	COST OF ENGINE REPLACEMENT
1985	2,000	$11,000	$ 500	$ 0	$ 0
1986	1,000	6,500	700	200	0
1987	3,000	14,000	1,200	100	4,000

REQUIRED

1. Assume that the engine replacement, which took place on January 1, 1987, extended the estimated useful life of the forklift truck by 2 years or 4,800 hours of use but did not change the estimated salvage value. The cost of the old engine accounted for $2,000 of the original cost of the forklift truck. Compute depreciation for 1985, 1986, and 1987, using both the straight-line and units-of-output methods.
2. Assume that the forklift truck was sold on December 31, 1986, for $15,000. Show all necessary journal entries relating to the forklift truck for the year 1986. Use the straight-line method of depreciation.

P12–4   A company spent $430,000 for a mine estimated to contain 2,000,000 tons of ore. It was expected that after the ore had been completely extracted, the land would be worth $30,000. Building and equipment, used exclusively for mining purposes, cost $420,000 when installed on the mine site, and they will have no residual value when the ore is exhausted. During the first year 200,000 tons of ore were mined, and $118,000 was spent for labor and operating costs. Also during the year 150,000 tons were sold and shipped to customers.

REQUIRED

1. Compute cost of goods sold for the first year. Clearly show all components of the cost of goods sold.
2. Record all journal entries relating to inventory and cost of goods sold during the first year except for closing entries.

P12–5   Alpha Corporation owns a machine that cost $30,000 (no residual value) and is being depreciated on a straight-line basis over 10 years. Early in the seventh year, based on new information from recent experience, the corporation decided that the total life of this machine should have been 15 years.

REQUIRED

1. What type of "accounting change" is involved in the year 7?
2. Give the entry, if any, to record the change in year 7 (show all computations).
3. Give the depreciation entry for year 7.
4. Explain *where* the entries made in requirements 2 and 3 would affect the financial statements (regular income, extraordinary income, retained earnings adjustment, and so on).

P12–6 Prior to 1986 Darren Corporation had never had an audit. At the end of 1986, before the arrival of the auditor, the company accountant prepared comparative financial statements for 1985 and 1986. According to these statements, Darren had income of $44,000 in 1985 and $46,000 in 1986, and retained earnings of $180,000 at the end of 1985 and $205,000 at the end of 1986.

During the audit it was discovered that an invoice dated January 1982 for $10,000 (paid in cash at that time) had been charged to "operating expense," although it was for the purchase of Machine X. Machine X has an estimated life of 10 years and no residual value. Darren uses straight-line depreciation.

REQUIRED

1. What type of accounting change is involved?
2. Prepare the necessary entry or entries for 1986.
3. Illustrate how the change would be reflected in the comparative financial statements. Use the income and retained earnings figures, but ignore any tax effect.

P12–7 Early in 1982 Topeka Mining Company opened a copper mine in Southeast Asia under a 10-year lease with a local government. The ore body and facilities had the following characteristics:

Initial payment for mining rights	$ 4,500,000
Cost of roads and ground clearing	$10,200,000
Cost of equipment and buildings	$18,880,000
Estimated tons of ore reserve	20,000,000
Estimated physical life of equipment and buildings	15 years
Planned ore extraction rate	1,500,000 tons per year

Because of the remote location of the mine, all facilities must be abandoned upon termination of mining. The government has made it known that the 10-year lease will not be renewed.

REQUIRED Construct depreciation schedules for buildings and equipment based on the straight-line method and depletion schedules based on the units-of-output method assuming that all estimates are accurate.

P12–8 Assume the facts given in the preceding problem and the following production and sales experience for 1982 and 1983 (assume production cost expenditures for labor and materials of $1 per ton):

	1983	1982
Production in tons	1,100,000	2,000,000
Sales in tons @ $4/ton	1,200,000	1,500,000

REQUIRED Show all the necessary journal entries related to production and sales for those 2 years. Use a LIFO cost-flow assumption for valuing inventory.

P12–9 On January 1, 1983, Western Life Insurance Company purchased 2,000 typewriters at an average cost of $1,350 each. Each typewriter was expected to last 4 years and had a $400 salvage value. During 1984, Western had the following additional activity related to typewriters:

	1984
Acquisitions	40 @ $1,500
Disposals	30 @ $1,100

REQUIRED If the group depreciation method is used, show all journal entries concerning typewriters for 1983 and 1984.

P12–10 On June 30, 1980, Oahu Pineapple Growers, Inc., purchased a harvesting machine for $450,000. The machine had an estimated useful life of 8 years and an estimated salvage value of $25,000. During 1982 the total useful life and salvage value estimates were changed to 7 years and $50,000, respectively. As of January 1, 1983, the company switched from straight-line to double-declining-balance depreciation. On June 1, 1984, the company traded in the harvester for a new model. The new model had a fair value of $800,000 and was paid for by $600,000 cash plus the trade-in. Oahu charges one full year of depreciation for the year of acquisition and no depreciation for the year of disposal.

REQUIRED Record all journal entries related to the harvester from June 30, 1980, through its disposal.

P12–11 On January 1, 1983, Anchorage Timber Company purchased seven trucks at a total cost of $1,800,000 on which a 10 percent investment tax credit was allowed. The controller wants an analysis comparing the following two alternative treatments of the investment credit and depreciation:

ALTERNATIVE 1	ALTERNATIVE 2
Deferral method	Flow-through method
Sum-of-the-year's-digits depreciation used for accounting and tax purposes	Straight-line depreciation used for accounting and tax purposes
Four-year useful life	Four-year useful life
Salvage value, $20,000 each	Salvage value, $20,000 each

REQUIRED Construct a schedule showing the total effect on net income of the two alternatives for each year of useful life, and show all computations. The company has a 40 percent average tax rate.

P12–12 Texon, Inc., a large oil and gas producer, engages in a comprehensive program of exploration and development. During 1983 Texon spent $200,800,000 in drilling exploratory wells, 10 percent of which were successful in that they resulted in exploitable reserves. Texon estimated that proved reserves from these wells would include 10,000,000 barrels of oil.

REQUIRED

1. Show journal entries to record the exploration cost for 1983 under the successful-efforts method and the full-costing method.
2. Assume the facts given above. Assume also that production commenced in 1984 and that the following information is available:

Production	1,000,000 barrels
Sales	900,000 barrels @ $85 per barrel
Production cost	$5 per barrel
Royalties	$2 per barrel paid upon extraction

   Show all necessary journal entries for 1984 under both the successful-efforts method and the full cost method.

P12–13 Worldwide Mining, Inc., started extraction of an ore body in 1984. Total cost of mining rights was $500,000, and total reserves were estimated to be 4,000,000 tons. The company incurred $2,000,000 of expenditures to drill shafts and ready the mine for extraction. The selling price of the ore was $10 per ton, and all the ore produced was shipped from the mining site at the customer's expense. Statutory depletion allowed by the IRS was 10 percent of gross revenues.

REQUIRED Compute the accounting depletion charge and statutory depletion allowance for 1984 if 500,000 tons are extracted and sold.

P12–14 On January 1, 1983, Redbone Transport Company replaced its fleet for $27,000,000. The new equipment is estimated to have a 4-year useful life and a 10 percent salvage value.

REQUIRED

1. Make up a schedule that shows the fiscal year in which straight-line depreciation will exceed double-declining-balance depreciation.
2. If the equipment is used for the full 4 years and the estimated residual value turns out to be accurate, show the journal entry for the disposal of the equipment at December 31, 1986, under both straight-line and double-declining-balance depreciation.

P12–15 In May 1985 Great Flats Mining, a division of U.S. Industries, discovered copper in northern California. It was estimated that the deposit would produce 8,000 tons of copper ore. The land had been purchased in 1984 at a cost of $6,950,000. The expected resale value of the land after mining operations for the copper discovery was $4,500,000. The $60,000 in costs of exploration and discovery for 1985 was *not* expensed during 1985. The following costs were incurred during 1985 (after the discovery) to facilitate mining operations:

	ECONOMIC LIFE	COST
Mine buildings and sheds	20 years	$300,000
Track and rail cars	25 years	250,000
Power hoist and equipment	15 years	300,000

The buildings, tracks, and rail cars are not expected to be reused after the 8,000 tons are mined. The hoist and other equipment will be used elsewhere. Operations began on January 3, 1986, and the results of the first year's efforts can be summarized as follows:

Tons of ore mined	1,800 tons
Tons of ore sold @ $1,500 per ton	1,200 tons
Direct-labor costs	$500,000
Other operating costs (excluding depreciation and depletion)	$40,000

REQUIRED (assume that *all* amounts are material)

1. Compute the gross profit from operations for the year 1986.
2. Assume that in 1987, 2,000 tons were mined and 2,000 tons were sold. What would be the amount of depletion charged to 1987 cost of sales if the estimate of the remaining copper deposit were increased to 6,700 tons on December 31, 1987?

P12–16 (CPA ADAPTED) On January 1, 1985, Barth Company, a small machine-tool manufacturer, acquired some new industrial equipment for $1,000,000. The new equipment was eligible for investment tax credit, and Barth took full advantage of the credit and accounted for the amount by using the flow-through method. The new equipment had a useful life of 5 years, and the salvage value was estimated to be $100,000. Barth estimated that the new equipment would produce 10,000 machine tools during its first year and that production would then decline by 1,000 units per year over the remaining useful life of the equipment.

The following depreciation methods may be used: double-declining-balance, straight-line, sum-of-the-years'-digits, units-of-output.

REQUIRED

1. Which depreciation method would result in the maximization of profits for financial statement reporting for the 3-year period ending December 31, 1987? Prepare a schedule showing the amount of accumulated depre-

ciation at December 31, 1987, under the method selected. Show supporting computations in good form. Ignore present-value, income tax, and deferred income tax considerations in your answer.

2. Which depreciation method would result in the minimization of profits for income tax reporting for the 3-year period ending December 31, 1987? Prepare a schedule showing the amount of accumulated depreciation at December 31, 1987, under the method selected. Show supporting computations in good form. Ignore present-value considerations in your answer.

13

Intangibles, Insurance, and Other Assets

OVERVIEW   Intangibles, insurance, and other assets are relatively immaterial in amount in most entities. They are interesting assets to study, however, in that they draw upon basic accounting concepts to measure and record their impact on the entity. They also present some conceptually challenging situations in addressing such basic questions as the following: Does this item represent an asset? If so, what is the benefit period of the asset? What revenues should the asset's cost be matched against? As we shall see, reference to economic theory will help explain the nature of the most common intangibles found in the financial reports of publicly traded companies.

The definition of assets (covered in Chapter 2 in the discussion of elements of financial statements) and the application of the definition are perhaps the most important theoretical concepts applied to the material in this chapter. Determining whether an item meets the conditions of providing future benefits that are both controllable by the entity and objectively measurable presents the most difficult challenge to accountants in the area of intangible assets.

INTANGIBLES

<table>
<tr><td>Intangibles
Defined</td><td>An **intangible** is generally defined as "something without physical substance." In an accounting context, intangibles *could* include all the items that have value to the company because of what they represent but that do not have physical substance in themselves. Such a definition would normally encompass short-term assets such as cash, marketable securities, notes and accounts receivable, and prepaid expenses. This definition might also apply to long-term assets such as leased plant and equipment, long-term investments in securities, and long-term contractual arrangements that entitle the company to various goods or services in the future. Strictly speaking, all of these items and many others are intangibles; however, the accounting use of the term is much more restricted.</td></tr>
</table>

Intangibles
Defined

An **intangible** is generally defined as "something without physical substance." In an accounting context, intangibles *could* include all the items that have value to the company because of what they represent but that do not have physical substance in themselves. Such a definition would normally encompass short-term assets such as cash, marketable securities, notes and accounts receivable, and prepaid expenses. This definition might also apply to long-term assets such as leased plant and equipment, long-term investments in securities, and long-term contractual arrangements that entitle the company to various goods or services in the future. Strictly speaking, all of these items and many others are intangibles; however, the accounting use of the term is much more restricted.

Conventional accounting practice applies the word *intangible* to certain assets that are long-lived and provide some legal rights to the company. The rights are often in terms of some exclusive arrangement, possibly for a specified time period, that gives the company a competitive advantage. The intangibles may be purchased or developed internally, with internally developed intangibles often being assigned relatively small dollar values in the accounting records even though they might represent very valuable assets. Still, not all accounting intangibles fit this latter description. The initial description of an intangible given above was too broad to represent practice, and the latter definition is too narrow. Perhaps a more pragmatic definition would be to define **accounting intangibles** as **assets that have no physical substance, that convey certain legal and economic rights, and that are not dealt with separately elsewhere in the financial statements.** In other words, the classification "intangibles" might include any intangible item not otherwise measured and reported in some other asset classification.

Identifiable
Intangibles

Several important attributes can differentiate intangible assets from one another. These attributes include (1) whether or not the asset is specifically identifiable, (2) whether or not the life of the asset is determinable, (3) the method by which the asset was acquired, and (4) whether or not the asset would be of value to another entity.

The first attribute forms the basis for dividing intangibles into two separate categories, with identifiable intangibles as the most common type. Examples of identifiable intangibles include copyrights, patents, trademarks, trade names, franchise fees, and research and development costs. We shall consider the accounting for identifiable intangibles first, with an emphasis on the common aspects of their proper accounting treatment. Then we shall discuss in detail the principal unidentifiable intangible, *goodwill*.

General treatment The general accounting treatment for intangible assets is to record them at the original acquisition cost and to amortize the cost over the expected useful life on a straight-line basis. The original cost is measured the same way as all other assets and is one of the common features of accounting for assets mentioned in the "Overview" to Part II. The cash-equivalent price of the intangibles, measured by considering the assets given or received, whichever is more objectively measurable, is the basis for measuring the cost of intangibles. Also, any element of cost that is incurred in the process of getting the asset to its intended useful state may be capitalized as part of the cost of the intangible. Although these overall guiding concepts are straightforward enough, their application to intangibles calls for the same degree of professional judgment required in measuring other assets. Application of these concepts will not always be a simple matter in measuring intangibles.

The amortization method is straight-line for most intangibles, as stipulated in **APB Opinion No. 17.**[1] This opinion also stipulated that the overall maximum amortization period for intangible assets should be no more than 40 years.[2] The actual maximum amortization period used in any given case should be the lesser of 40 years, the legal life of the asset, or the useful life of the asset. For example, **patents** are granted for a 17-year period, which would be the maximum useful life. In addition, we might find that the useful life of the patent is fewer than 17 years due to rapidly changing technology, in which case the useful life would be used as the amortization period.

The **copyright** for an intermediate accounting text is a good example of an intangible with a useful revenue-generating life well within its legal life. Copyrights granted by the federal government after January 1, 1978, are for the life of the author plus 50 years, whereas previously issued copyrights were granted for 28 years with a possible 47-year renewal. Because of the rapidly changing nature of accounting, an intermediate text, for example, will normally have a useful life of about 3 to 5 years, making the legal life unimportant for amortization purposes.

A potentially important intangible that may have a nominal recorded value is a **trademark** or a **trade name,** which provides the right to prohibit competitors from using the symbol or name, respectively. The federal government registers these rights for 20 years, with renewals available as long as the symbols or names are in use. The amount recorded in accounting for a trademark or trade name is limited to the amount actually paid for the registration of the name or symbol, plus any legal costs involved in acquiring it and successfully defending its ownership. These actual costs are usually small. However, after some period of successful operations a trademark or a trade name may have a value in the marketplace much greater than its recorded value. Some firms attempt to capitalize on their trade names or symbols by selling or renting franchises.

In a **franchise agreement,** one party, the **franchisor,** grants to another, the **franchisee,** the right to market a certain line of products or services under the franchisor's name. In return for this right, the franchisee pays a stipulated fee. Examples of franchised trade names would be McDonald's hamburger chain or Midas Muffler outlets. A franchise agreement often contains certain restrictive stipulations that control the operations of the franchisee. For example, the building style, products carried, and suppliers used might be restricted by the franchise agreement. The uniformity of operations often required by such agreements is usually of benefit to both parties. The amortization of the intangible aspects of **franchise fees** should be spread evenly over their expected useful lives but not in excess of 40 years. Amortization of trademarks or trade names also should be on a straight-line basis over the expected useful life, but not in excess of 40 years.

The method by which the intangible asset is acquired does not influence the accounting treatment, but it will usually influence the recorded amount. In general, internally developed intangibles have lower recorded amounts than externally acquired intangibles that are similar. Assume that a new automobile fuel is developed and that it is more efficient than gas and costs much less to produce. The internal

---

[1] *Accounting Principles Board Opinion No. 17,* "Intangible Assets" (New York: AICPA, August 1970), par. 30.

[2] Ibid., par. 29.

development costs might be minimal compared with the price that an outside entity would have to pay to acquire the rights to such a process once it has been developed. In either case, however, the accounting treatment calls for recording the asset at acquisition cost or development cost. The actual development costs, which can be capitalized as an asset cost (discussed below under "Research and Development Costs"), may be relatively minor when compared with their market value.

Whether or not an intangible is of use to outsiders varies greatly among intangibles and entities. An innovation in fuels may be of use to nearly every firm or individual, whereas an innovation in injection-molding equipment may only be of interest to those industries that use such equipment. Moreover, an innovation in a special chemical blending formula may only be of value to a single company that has designed its production process around that secret blending formula. In the latter case, would the rights to the formula have any value to competitors with similar or substitute products? Would the formula rights have any asset value? It is possible that even unique intangibles that can be implemented by only one company may have value outside that company. For example, a competitor may be willing to pay for the secret blending formula rights to reduce competition and increase its own profit, even though it may never use the formula. Although even unique intangibles may have a "market" value to outside entities, those intangibles that are of greater use to a larger interest group tend to have a greater value to those who own them.

Research and development costs **Research and development** are terms used to describe investigative activities (research) that are undertaken in hope of gaining new insight and knowledge that can be applied by an entity to create (develop) new products or services. **Research and development (R&D) costs** often relate to some of the more important processes that create identifiable intangibles. In industries that experience significant technological changes, such as the aerospace and the computer industries, research and development is a crucial activity. It seems clear that at least *some* of the research and development activities of firms in highly technical industries will provide future benefits and will qualify as assets.[3] At the same time, it is not always clear to management or to the researchers themselves which research projects will provide future benefits and which will prove to be worthless prior to (or perhaps even after) their completion. Periodic financial disclosure requirements, however, call for classification of all costs as either assets or expenses; therefore, some sort of judgment must be made regarding the expected future benefits of all projects regardless of their stage of completion. Although this judgment may be viewed as a difficult process for management, it is even more difficult for independent auditors, who tend to know somewhat less about the technical aspects of an industry's specific research efforts. Because of the tremendous amount of uncertainty and subjectivity involved in measuring the asset value of R&D activities, **FASB Statement No. 2** was issued.[4] It called for across-the-board **expensing of all research and development costs in the period incurred.**

The impact of the FASB's requirement calling for the expensing of all research and development costs may not be as significant as it would at first seem. If we assume (1) an even amount of annual expenditures that have future benefits and (2) a

[3] For a good discussion of this issue, see Harold Bierman, Jr., and Roland E. Dukes, "Accounting for Research and Development Costs" *Journal of Accountancy,* April 1975, pp. 48–55.

[4] *Statement of Financial Accounting Standards No. 2,* "Accounting for Research and Development Costs" (Stamford, CT: FASB, October 1974).

uniform future benefit period from any given year's research activities, we can observe that the long-range effect on the **income statement** of immediate expensing is not much different from the previously accepted alternative of capitalizing and amortizing over an extended period some or all of a given period's research and development costs. Consider the following example:

> Delta Corporation has incurred $10,000 in expenditures for research in each of the past 5 years. All $10,000 of the research costs is expected to have future benefits for 5 years, and so these costs would ordinarily qualify for capitalization as assets. The data in Table 13–1 show the impact on the financial statements over a 5-year period, assuming first that all costs are expensed per **FASB Statement No. 2** and second that the company uses the previously acceptable alternative of capitalizing and amortizing over a 5-year period on a straight-line basis.

TABLE 13–1

		PER FASB STATEMENT NO. 2		ASSUMING CAPITALIZATION		
YEAR	**EXPENDITURES FOR R&D**	**ASSET**	**R & D EXPENSES**	**GROSS ASSET**	**NET ASSET**	**AMORTIZATION EXPENSE**
1981	$10,000	0	$10,000	$10,000	$ 8,000	$ 2,000
1982	10,000	0	10,000	20,000	14,000	4,000
1983	10,000	0	10,000	30,000	18,000	6,000
1984	10,000	0	10,000	40,000	20,000	8,000
1985	10,000	0	10,000	50,000	20,000	10,000

ALTERNATIVE METHODS OF R&D ACCOUNTING

From the Delta example, we see that if the two assumptions hold (uniform future benefits = $10,000 and uniform benefit period = 5 years), after 1984 there is no difference in income. There is, however, a "permanent" balance sheet difference of $20,000 between the two methods. Note that there might also be additional research and development expenditures that have no expected future benefit. This additional amount would be added to the "expense" figures on *both* sides of the above analysis and would not affect the analysis.

The balance sheet difference resulting from **FASB Statement No. 2** affects several key financial statement ratios, including return-on-assets ratios, which would be higher due to the lower asset base.[5] In addition to the uncertainty problem, another argument that has been suggested in support of **FASB Statement No. 2** is that the benefit period is relatively short, and, therefore, the "asset" value does not exist for any material time period. This argument is more or less appealing depending on the specific situation. To the extent that future benefits exist, **FASB Statement No. 2** will undoubtedly cause the assets of the firm to be understated. Also, to the extent that the amount of research and development costs that have future benefits and the benefit periods are *not* uniform from year to year, the applications of **FASB Statement No. 2** will adversely affect the matching process in income determination.

As discussed previously, the advantage of **FASB Statement No. 2** is that it facilitates the objectivity and comparability of accounting for R&D costs. In this case, it appears as though the comparability and objectivity considerations domi-

---

[5] See Chapter 27 for a description of these ratios. The return-on-asset ratio (income over assets) would look better (higher) because income would be the same in the long run, and assets would be less under *FASB Statement No. 2,* hence the higher ratio.

EXHIBIT
13–1

RESEARCH AND DEVELOPMENT INCOME STATEMENT DISCLOSURE			
EATON CORPORATION AND SUBSIDIARIES Statements of Consolidated Income			
	1980	1979	1978
YEAR ENDED DECEMBER 31	(THOUSANDS OF DOLLARS)		
Net sales	$3,176,466	$3,359,914	$2,790,521
Interest income	5,546	8,052	10,445
Excess of insurance settlement over book value	25,360	0	0
Other income—net	37,172	26,353	14,255
	3,244,544	3,394,319	2,815,221
Costs and expenses:			
Cost of products sold	2,392,355	2,487,770	2,067,228
Selling and administrative expenses	482,753	453,300	357,962
Research and development expenses	74,328	67,582	47,202
Interest expense	89,179	86,925	67,202
Exchange loss—net	3,897	3,935	15,957
	3,042,512	3,099,512	2,555,551
Income before income taxes and extraordinary credit	202,032	294,807	259,670
Income taxes	86,248	141,543	140,378
Income before extraordinary credit	115,784	153,264	119,292
Extraordinary credit	0	0	11,584
Net income	$ 115,784	$ 153,264	$ 130,876
Per common share:			
Net income:			
Primary:			
Income before extraordinary credit	$4.35	$5.86	$4.55
Extraordinary credit	0	0	.45
Net income	$4.35	$5.86	$5.00
Fully diluted:			
Income before extraordinary credit	$4.18	$5.56	$4.33
Extraordinary credit	0	0	.42
Net income	$4.18	$5.56	$4.75
Dividends	$1.72	$1.61	$1.50
Average number of common shares outstanding	26,377,422	25,925,648	25,842,855

The Financial Review on pages 24 to 31 is an integral part of the Consolidated Financial Statements.

nated the matching and asset recognition considerations in the formulation of accounting policy.

Most entities do not report R&D costs as a separate component in their income statement and do not discuss R&D activities in the notes to financial statements since R&D costs tend to be immaterial for most entities. However, companies that do engage heavily in R&D activities will tend to report R&D as a separate component of income, as is done in the Eaton Corporation statements illustrated in Exhibit 13–1. The relative importance of R&D will tend to determine the level of disclosure.

CAPITALIZABLE RESEARCH AND DEVELOPMENT COSTS There are some instances where the research and development costs of an entity may be capitalized according to several FASB interpretations.[6] In cases where an entity incurs research

---

[6] See, for example, *Financial Accounting Standards Board Interpretation No. 6,* "Applicability of FASB Statement No. 2 to Computer Software" (Stamford, CT: FASB, 1975) par. 4, as well as *FASB Interpretations No. 4 and No. 5.*

and development costs according to the conditions of a contract with an outside entity, such R&D costs may be added to the cost of the products or services or both that the outside entity is acquiring. (Inventory costs are handled in a similar way when the inventory is being developed according to the specifications of and for the sole benefit of an outside entity.) R&D costs that have been incurred in order to produce unique benefits to a customer in accordance with a purchase contract are to be treated like assets of the entity doing the R&D work until the products or services are sold, at which point the R&D should be matched with the revenues received.

Cases of capitalizable R&D are most common in the computer industry for software development and in the extractive industries where prospecting, drilling, and other exploration costs are capitalizable as a cost of the minerals or other natural resources. Also, when an entity incurs R&D costs in developing assets for use in its own selling and administrative activities, such system development costs may be

EXHIBIT 13–2

GOODWILL

FERRO CORPORATION AND SUBSIDIARIES
Consolidated Balance Sheets
December 31, 1980 and 1979

	(DOLLARS IN THOUSANDS)	
ASSETS	**1980**	**1979**
Current Assets:		
Cash and short-term securities of $16,406,000 in 1980 and $18,815,000 in 1979 at cost (approximate market)	$ 30,291	$ 24,831
Trade notes and accounts receivable, after deduction of $4,790,000 in 1980 and $4,956,000 in 1979 for possible losses in collection	122,317	111,721
Inventories (note 2)	110,921	103,547
Other current assets	18,879	21,773
Total current assets	$282,408	$261,872
Other Assets:		
Investments in affiliated companies, at approximate equity	$ 5,573	$ 2,213
Unamortized excess of cost over net assets acquired	3,138	2,934
Sundry other assets	7,928	7,787
Total other assets	$ 16,639	$ 12,934
Plant and Equipment, at cost:		
Land	$ 7,494	$ 7,050
Buildings	67,305	60,409
Machinery and equipment	152,722	130,212
	227,521	197,671
Less accumulated depreciation and amortization	92,958	81,840
Net plant and equipment	134,563	115,831
Total Assets	$433,610	$390,637

Notes to Consolidated Financial Statements

From the summary of significant accounting policies footnote:

Financial results for acquisitions accounted for as purchases are included in the consolidated financial statements from the date of acquisition. The excess of cost over equity in net assets of acquired companies is being amortized over periods benefited, with the most extended period being 20 years.

EXHIBIT
13–2
(cont.)

NATIONAL DISTILLERS AND CHEMICAL CORPORATION AND SUBSIDIARY COMPANIES
Consolidated Balance Sheet

ASSETS	(DOLLAR AMOUNTS IN THOUSANDS)	
	1980	1979
Current assets		
Cash	$ 43,079	$ 45,066
Short-term investments—at lower of cost or market	24,825	3,693
Accounts and notes receivable—less allowance for doubtful accounts		
1980—$4,103; 1979—$3,781	293,096	308,930
Inventories (Note 5)	425,113	436,670
Prepaid expenses and other assets (Note 3)	53,594	22,965
Total current assets	839,707	817,324
Investments in insurance subsidiaries (Note 8)	108,426	93,976
Investments in associated companies (Note 9)	146,964	146,028
Miscellaneous investments and other receivables	26,004	15,158
Deferred charges and other assets	8,414	8,276
Property, plant and equipment—less accumulated depreciation		
1980—$394,965, 1979—$410,859 (Note 6)	487,131	520,748
Goodwill—net of amortization (Note 7)	61,841	62,997
	$1,678,487	$1,664,507

From Footnote 1—Accounting Policies

Goodwill
    The excess of the cost of acquired businesses over values assigned to net assets is classified as goodwill, and with respect to acquisitions made after 1970 is being amortized to income for a period of not more than 40 years. In the opinion of management, goodwill which arose from acquisitions made prior to 1970 has not diminished in value and is not being amortized.

Footnote 7

    Unamortized goodwill applicable to acquisitions made after 1970 was $46,642 at December 31, 1980 and $47,798 at December 31, 1979. Amortization of such goodwill charged to income amounted to $1,161, $1,106, and $868 in the years ended December 31, 1980, 1979, and 1978, respectively. Goodwill arising from acquisitions made prior to 1970 in the amount of $15,199 is not being amortized.

capitalized as an asset. Of course, the cost of assets that are used in the process of conducting R&D activities, such as facilities and equipment, should be capitalized as assets and depreciated or amortized over their benefit period.

Unidentifiable Intangibles— Goodwill

A firm may have any number of unidentifiable assets that do not appear on its books. The human resources of the firm, management's experience and expertise in running the firm, management's personality, customer relationships, superior locations for conducting certain types of business activities, and various other elements go into the making of a business whose "whole" value may be greater than the sum of its separately valued identifiable parts. These unidentifiable intangibles are generally grouped together and referred to as **goodwill,** one of the most complicated concepts in accounting, and perhaps the most controversial. Exhibit 13–2 gives two examples of how goodwill is reported in practice. Note that goodwill is sometimes called "unamortized excess of cost over net assets acquired," as in the Ferro Corporation report. Titles such as this are becoming more common than the term "goodwill," which is still being used by the National Distillers and Chemical Corporation.
    One way to define **goodwill** is to say that recorded goodwill **represents the**

EXHIBIT
13–3

Acquisition Information for Fox Company as of December 31, 1991	HISTORICAL BOOK VALUE	ESTIMATED FAIR MARKET VALUE
Assets		
Cash and receivables	$ 75,000	$ 75,000
Inventory	89,000	105,000
Plant and equipment	421,000	600,000
Total assets	$585,000	$780,000
Liabilities		
Current payables	$ 60,000	$ 60,000
Long-term notes	100,000	100,000
Total liabilities	$160,000	$160,000
Net assets	$425,000	$620,000

otherwise unrecorded assets of the firm. That is, it is something of value, an asset, for which the entity has no explicit recorded cost. Goodwill cannot be separated from the firm. It has no value in and of itself, and its value is measurable only in the context of the firm to which it pertains.

Measurement of Goodwill

Upon purchase of the entire outstanding common stock of an entity or a "significant interest" in an entity's common stock, accountants measure the value of goodwill by taking the price paid for the specifically identifiable net assets acquired less the fair market value of those net assets acquired.[7] This is the **only way goodwill is measured and recorded in the accounting records** under current generally accepted accounting principles.

Consider the situation where Parent Corporation acquires Fox Company for $800,000 cash on December 31, 1991. Exhibit 13–3 lists the information that Parent obtains about Fox as of the date of the acquisition. According to Exhibit 13–3, the fair market value of the Fox Company's net assets is $620,000. However, because of the existence of Fox's unrecorded assets (goodwill), Parent is willing to pay $800,000 to acquire a 100 percent interest in Fox. The value of the goodwill in this case is $180,000, the difference between the price paid ($800,000) and the fair market value of the *recorded* net assets ($620,000). The asset *goodwill* would be recorded by Parent at the time of acquisition and amortized on a straight-line basis over its estimated economic life, but not in excess of 40 years.[8] The entries for December 31, 1991, the date of acquisition, and December 31, 1992, the first annual amortization adjustment (assuming Parent has a December 31 year-end and uses a 30-year useful life for amortizing goodwill), would appear on Parent Company's books as follows:

12/31/91	Cash and receivables	75,000
	Inventory	105,000
	Plant and equipment	600,000
	Goodwill	180,000

[7] *Significant interest* refers to *Accounting Principles Board Opinion No. 18,* "The Equity Method of Accounting for Investments in Common Stock" (New York: AICPA, March 1971), par. 17. See Chapter 14 on the equity method of accounting for long-term investments.

[8] *Accounting Principles Board Opinion No. 17,* "Intangible Assets," par. 29.

	Current payables		60,000
	Long-term notes		100,000
	Cash		800,000
	(To record the acquisition of the assets and liabilities of Fox Company for cash)		
12/31/92	Goodwill amortization expense	6,000	
	Goodwill		6,000
	(To amortize goodwill for 1 year)		

Goodwill can also be computed in a situation where a firm buys a significant interest in another company. Assume the same facts as those presented above except that Parent wants to acquire only 40 percent of the common stock of Fox for $280,000. How much goodwill is being acquired by Parent, and what is Fox's implied total goodwill? The computation of both the goodwill acquired by Parent and Fox's implied total goodwill are as follows:

1. Estimated market value of Fox's net assets — $620,000
   % of Fox being acquired — $\times$ 40%
   40% of market value of Fox's recorded assets — $248,000

2. Price paid — $280,000
   40% of the market value of recorded assets being acquired — 248,000
   40% of unrecorded assets (goodwill) being acquired — $ 32,000

3. Total goodwill
   $32,000 = 40\%$ of Fox's goodwill
   $.4x = \$32,000$
   $x = \$32,000 \div .4$
   $x = \$80,000$ total goodwill of Fox Company

Since Parent is acquiring a 40 percent interest, $32,000 of the total purchase price of $280,000 is attributable to goodwill, and the $32,000 amount is 40 percent of the total $80,000 Fox Company goodwill implied by the purchase. The following entry would record the purchase of 40 percent of Fox Company on Parent's books:

12/31/91	Long-term equity investment in Fox Company	280,000	
	Cash		280,000
	(To record acquisition of a 40% interest in Fox Company common stock)		

When less than 50 percent of a company is being acquired, all of the net assets being acquired (including goodwill) are included in one account on the books of the acquiring company. The entries for amortizing goodwill in such cases are also somewhat more complex. The details of such acquisitions are examined in Chapter 14.

In the above case, note that even though $32,000 of the $280,000 paid by Parent for a 40 percent interest in Fox is objective evidence that Fox's *total* goodwill is $80,000, goodwill could *not* be recorded by Fox as a result of the transaction. Because Fox did not purchase the goodwill, and because **goodwill must be purchased to be recorded,** Fox cannot record its own implied goodwill on its books.

Methods of Estimating Goodwill

Accountants have traditionally attributed the willingness of one firm to pay more than the fair market value of the assets of another firm to the expectation of superior **earnings** on the part of the firm being acquired. There are many approaches to estimating goodwill before an acquisition, most of which involve attempts to estimate a superior earnings number. Three common methods are used to estimate the amount to be paid for goodwill *before* a purchase:

1. Discounted present-value method
2. Payback method
3. Number of years of superior earnings method

These three methods are discussed in the following sections.

Discounted present-value method The **discounted present-value method** of estimating how much goodwill is worth is tied to the concept of superior earnings. Basically, this method seeks to take the discounted present value of a series of superior earnings estimates for a given number of years into the future. The following example illustrates both the estimation of superior earnings and the estimation of what might be paid for goodwill *assuming* goodwill is worth 5 years' superior earnings discounted at an 8 percent implied interest rate.

Assume that Air Production Company is about to acquire Gas Bag, Inc. The average return on assets in the gas bag industry is 5 percent. Gas Bag, Inc., has the following historical data:

YEAR	NET INCOME (BEFORE EXTRAORDINARY ITEMS)	BOOK VALUE OF RECORDED NET ASSETS	MARKET VALUE OF RECORDED NET ASSETS
1983	$ 400,000	$ 4,000,000	$ 4,500,000
1984	500,000	5,000,000	5,500,000
1985	600,000	6,000,000	6,500,000
1986	500,000	6,000,000	6,500,000
1987	400,000	6,000,000	6,500,000
Total	$2,400,000	$27,000,000	$29,500,000
Average for 1983–1987	$ 480,000	$ 5,400,000	$ 5,900,000

The average return for the past 5 years has been about 8.9 percent on recorded net assets ($480,000/$5,400,000) for Gas Bag, Inc., compared with the industry average of 5.0 percent. As a result, Gas Bag, Inc., is said to have superior earnings of $210,000 per year [(8.9% − 5.0%) × ($5,400,000)]. Let us assume that Air Production is willing to purchase 5 years' worth of superior earnings, discounted at 8 percent, based on the belief that the next 5 years will be like the last 5 (that is, our averages above are also our expected future values). Air Production might then compute goodwill as follows:

Gas Bag's return ($5,400,000 × 8.9%)	= $480,000
Industry average ($5,400,000 × 5.0%)	= 270,000
Annual expected superior earnings	= $210,000
$(P/A, 5, .08) \times \$210,000 =$	
$3.9927 \times \$210,000$	= $838,470

Based on these assumptions, Air Production would be willing to pay $838,470 for the goodwill, or excess superior earnings capacity, of Gas Bag, Inc.

Some accountants believe that the method illustrated above is the most sound basis for estimating goodwill, primarily because of its consideration of the present-value concept.

Payback method Another way to estimate goodwill before a purchase is the **payback method.** This method is also based on the concept of superior earnings. Using the example above, assume that Air Production is willing to pay for goodwill in Gas Bag, Inc., but requires a payback of 15 years on all investments. In other words, all such investments are expected to "pay back" their cost in 15 years or less. If we assume that Gas Bag will continue to report $480,000 income for the next 15 years, Air Production would be willing to pay $7,200,000 (15 years × $480,000 income per year), and goodwill would be the difference between this price and the fair market value of Gas Bag's net assets, or $700,000 ($7,200,000 − $6,500,000). This approach might be used to set an upper limit on the purchase price for Air Production.

Number of years of superior earnings The **number of years of superior earnings method** is fairly straightforward in that it simply multiplies the superior earnings figure (as calculated above) by some specified number of years that the purchasing company is willing to pay for. There is really no difference between this method and the first method illustrated except that this method ignores present values. In the case illustrated, 5 years' superior earnings at $210,000 per year would make goodwill worth $1,050,000 over and above the value assigned to the *recorded* net assets.

Evaluation of Goodwill Estimation Methods

The methods of computing goodwill described above are becoming less popular and are of questionable value to accountants for the following reasons:

1. Recorded goodwill for accounting purposes **can only be measured by taking the difference between the price actually paid after a purchase and the fair value of the net assets acquired.**
2. The concept of superior earnings is inconsistent with currently accepted financial theory because it fails to consider the uncertainty or variability of the expected future earnings estimates.
3. There is no real evidence to support any one method of estimating the goodwill of the firm either in theory or in practice.

The first point simply reminds us that, for financial accounting purposes, we do not need to know how the goodwill value was derived. We merely have to compare the total purchase price actually transacted with the current value of all identifiable net assets acquired in the purchase. The second point is that the expected rate of return is not the sole basis for valuing the firm. At least two factors—the mean or average (expected) return *and* the variance of the expected return—are important in assessing the value of an asset or group of assets.[9]

This point may be illustrated by looking at a simple example. Suppose there are three companies in an industry and the probability distribution (or density func-

[9] For a more elaborate discussion of this "two-parameter" view of the firm, see William Beaver, *Financial Reporting: An Accounting Revolution* (Englewood Cliffs, NJ: Prentice-Hall, 1981), chap. 2.

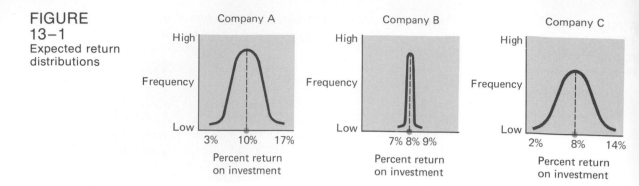

FIGURE
13–1
Expected return
distributions

Company A

High

Frequency

Low

3%   10%   17%

Percent return
on investment

Company B

High

Frequency

Low

7% 8% 9%

Percent return
on investment

Company C

High

Frequency

Low

2%   8%   14%

Percent return
on investment

tion) of their expected returns is represented by the three distributions given in Figure 13–1. The average "expected" return on investment (income over fair value of net assets) for these three companies (assuming the future will be like the past) would be: Company A = 10 percent; Company B = 8 percent; and Company C = 8 percent. Based on these averages *only,* we would probably all prefer Company A, and we would be indifferent between B and C. Let us now consider the risk or the uncertainty of the returns from these three companies, which may be represented by the variance of the past returns.

As illustrated in Figure 13–1, Company B has very little variation, with the complete range of past returns falling between 7 percent and 9 percent for the most part. Company A has the widest range, with past returns falling between 3 percent and 17 percent, whereas Company C returns have been between 2 percent and 14 percent. Company A has the largest variance, or risk, and Company B has the smallest variance, or risk. According to the traditional analysis of goodwill, Company A would have "superior returns" because its average return is above the industry average of 8.67 percent [(10% + 8% + 8%) ÷ 3 = 8.67%], whereas the returns for Companies B and C are below industry average. Yet we might prefer acquiring Company B because of the greater certainty that we will get at least a 7 percent return. It is not clear that Company A would be preferred by all interested parties, and it is not clear that Company A is the only company with goodwill.

Asset pricing theory   In the context of basic economic theories, we would say that Company A must offer investors more than an 8 percent expected return to compensate them for the additional risk they are taking (the chance of getting as low as a 3 percent return in the short run). Using the same reasoning, we can argue that no one will invest in C, since it has the same "expected" (average) return as B but *more risk* (the chance of getting as low as a 2 percent return). This relationship between risk and expected return is illustrated graphically in Figure 13–2.

The only assets that one would be willing to purchase are those assets on the "efficient assets" curve. Assets below the curve (Company C) are inefficient in one of two ways: The investor can earn either (1) a higher expected return for the same risk (or less risk such as Company A) or (2) the same expected return for less risk (Company B). If one assumes that risk and expected return are the only important variables, no one would be interested in investing in Company C.

Other deficiencies of the "superior earnings" methods   There are other reasons to doubt the validity of the traditional "superior earnings" measures. For example, "return" ratios will be distorted to the extent that the book value of assets will not be

FIGURE
13–2
Risk-expected
return tradeoff

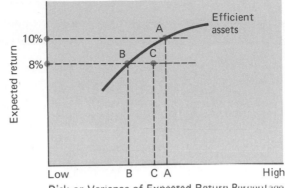

comparable across firms. If Company A is a new firm with nearly all of its assets valued in relatively current dollars and companies B and C are old firms with relatively noncurrent dollars for asset values, what does that do to the analysis? It would be necessary for all firms to use relatively uniform measures, such as the current market value of assets, to make a satisfactory comparison of returns across firms. Of course, income measurement would also have to be adjusted for this inconsistency. To the extent that accounting measures of net assets and earnings are useful for measuring return on investment, the measurement of expected earnings alone, without consideration of the variance in earnings, is probably an incomplete measure of the basis for goodwill to be purchased by an investing entity.

There is no generally accepted method for establishing the acquisition prices and the resulting goodwill measurement. The current market value of the stock of the firm to be acquired is undoubtedly an important piece of information and one that is normally easy to determine. To get all (or even a large percentage) of the existing owners to "tender" their shares of stock, however, the acquiring firm generally offers them a price substantially above the "going" market price. Exhibit 13–4 provides two examples of tender offers for the common stock of Conoco, Inc., made by Du Pont and Mobil in July 1981 when both companies were bidding to gain control of Conoco. The tender offer price is what actually determines the amount of goodwill involved in purchases of significant interests in other entities. It is this actual transacted price that accountants use to measure and record goodwill. How the tender price is actually determined is something that is now known and not readily determinable by parties outside the entity making the offer. It is possible that any one or all of the estimation procedures illustrated above have been used in practice. However, estimation procedures based on the notion of excess or superior earnings have little justification in theory.

Goodwill is an interesting and complex asset. The question, How can we best *estimate* the value of goodwill? still cannot be answered in any generalizable way, and it is not likely that any generalizable method exists in practice. The beneficial effects arising from the combination or merger of any two firms may be unique in each case, and the unrecorded assets are not apt to be the same in any two cases. Fortunately, accountants do not have to know what goodwill consists of specifically or how the acquisition price of an entity is determined. Given the purchase price and the fair value of the (net) assets acquired, goodwill can be measured and recorded with little difficulty.

EXHIBIT 13-4

TENDER OFFER

This announcement is not an offer to purchase or a solicitation of an offer to sell these securities. The Offer is made only by the Offer to Purchase dated July 17, 1981 and the related Letter of Transmittal and it is not being made to, nor will tenders be accepted from or on behalf of, holders of Shares residing in any jurisdiction in which the making of the Offer or acceptance thereof would not be in compliance with the law. In those jurisdictions whose securities laws require the Offer to be made by a licensed broker or dealer, the Offer is being made on behalf of the Purchaser by one or more registered brokers or dealers licensed under the laws of such jurisdictions.

Notice of Offer to Purchase for Cash

43,500,000 Shares of Common Stock

of

Conoco Inc.

at

$90 Net Per Share

by

Mobil Corporation

Mobil Corporation, a Delaware corporation (the "Purchaser"), is offering to purchase 43,500,000 shares of Common Stock, par value $5.00 per share (the "Shares"), of Conoco Inc., a Delaware corporation (the "Company"), at $90 net per Share to the selling stockholder, in cash, upon the terms and subject to the conditions set forth in the Offer to Purchase dated July 17, 1981 (the "Offer to Purchase") and the related Letter of Transmittal (which together constitute the "Offer"). The purpose of the Offer is to enable the Purchaser to acquire control of the Company, as the first step in acquiring the entire equity interest of the Company.

The Proration Date is 12:00 Midnight, New York City Time, on Sunday, July 26, 1981. The Withdrawal Deadline is 12:00 Midnight, New York City Time, on Thursday, August 6, 1981. The Offer Expires on Thursday, August 13, 1981 at 12:00 Midnight, New York City Time, Unless Extended.

The Offer is conditioned upon a minimum of 43,500,000 Shares being properly tendered and not withdrawn prior to the expiration of the Offer.

Upon the terms and subject to the conditions of the Offer, Shares will be deemed to have been accepted for payment and purchased when, as and if the Purchaser gives oral or written notice to the Depositary of such acceptance. The expiration date for the Offer may be extended from time to time by oral or written notice to the Depositary of such extension, followed by a public announcement of such extension prior to 9:00 A.M., New York City Time, on the next business day after the previously scheduled expiration date.

EXHIBIT 13–4 (cont.)

Tenders of Shares will be irrevocable, except that Shares may be withdrawn prior to 12:00 Midnight, New York City Time, on August 6, 1981, and, unless theretofore accepted for payment as provided in the Offer, may also be withdrawn after September 14, 1981. In addition, if another tender offer for some or all of the Shares is made by another bidder (other than the Company), Shares not yet accepted for payment may be withdrawn on the date of, and for ten business days after, the commencement (other than by public announcement) of such competing offer, provided the Purchaser has notice or otherwise has knowledge of such competing offer. To be effective, a written, telegraphic, telex or facsimile notice of withdrawal must be timely received by the Depositary and must specify the name of the tendering stockholder, the number of Shares to be withdrawn and the names in which the certificates are registered, if different from that of the tendering stockholder. If certificates have been delivered, the serial numbers shown on certificates to be withdrawn must be submitted and the signatures on the notice of withdrawal guaranteed.

Upon the terms and subject to the conditions set forth in the Offer, the Purchaser will accept for payment 43,500,000 Shares properly tendered prior to 12:00 Midnight, New York City Time, on August 13, 1981 (or, if the Offer is extended, by the time specified in such extension) and not withdrawn as permitted by the Offer. If prior to 12:00 Midnight, New York City Time, on July 26, 1981, more than 43,500,000 Shares are properly tendered and not so withdrawn, Shares will be accepted for payment on a *pro rata* basis (with appropriate adjustments to avoid acceptance of fractional Shares). If less than 43,500,000 Shares are tendered by such time and not withdrawn, all of such Shares will be accepted for payment and Shares tendered thereafter will be accepted for payment in the order tendered, subject to the condition that a minimum of 43,500,000 Shares are properly tendered and not withdrawn. Payment for all Shares purchased pursuant to the Offer will be made in all cases only after receipt by the Depositary or the Forwarding Agent of certificates therefor, a properly completed, duly executed Letter of Transmittal and any other required documents.

The information required to be disclosed by Rule 14d-6(e)(1)(vii) of the General Rules and Regulations under the Securities Exchange Act of 1934 is contained in the Offer and is incorporated herein by reference.

Requests for copies of the Offer to Purchase and the Letter of Transmittal may be directed to the Information Agent or the Dealer Manager as set forth below, and will be furnished promptly at the Purchaser's expense.

The Information Agent is:

GEORGESON & CO. INC.

20 North Clark Street	Wall Street Plaza	606 South Olive Street
Chicago, Illinois 60602	New York, New York 10005	Los Angeles, California 90014
(312) 346-7161 (collect)	(212) 440-9800 (collect)	(213) 489-7000 (collect)

The Dealer Manager for the Offer is:

Merrill Lynch White Weld Capital Markets Group

Merrill Lynch, Pierce, Fenner & Smith Incorporated

One Liberty Plaza
165 Broadway
New York, New York 10080
(212) 637-7152 or
(212) 637-7678
(collect)

July 17, 1981

EXHIBIT 13-4 (cont.)

Notice of Offer for
All Outstanding Shares of Common Stock

of

Conoco Inc.

at

$95 Per Share Net in Cash for
34,400,000 Conoco Shares

and

1.7 Shares of Du Pont Common Stock for
Each Remaining Conoco Share

by

Du Pont Holdings, Inc.

A Wholly Owned Subsidiary of

E. I. du Pont de Nemours and Company

Du Pont Holdings, Inc. (the "Purchaser"), a wholly owned subsidiary of E. I. du Pont de Nemours and Company ("Du Pont"), is offering, upon the terms and subject to the conditions set forth in the Prospectus dated July 15, 1981 and in the related Letter of Transmittal (collectively, the "Offer"), to exchange either (a) $95 net to the seller in cash or (b) 1.7 shares of Du Pont Common Stock ("Du Pont Shares"), for each outstanding share of Conoco Inc. ("Conoco") Common Stock ("Conoco Shares"). A tendering stockholder may specify the number of Conoco Shares which he desires to exchange for cash or for Du Pont Shares, but the Purchaser shall not be obligated to accept more than 34,400,000 Conoco Shares (representing approximately 40% of the presently outstanding Conoco Shares) for cash or to accept more than 52,425,275 Conoco Shares (representing approximately 60% of the presently outstanding Conoco Shares) for exchange for Du Pont Shares. However, the Purchaser may elect (but shall not be obligated) to accept for cash or for Du Pont Shares all or any additional Conoco Shares so tendered, except that the Purchaser will not in any event accept for cash more than 43,500,000 Conoco Shares (representing approximately 51% of the presently outstanding Conoco Shares).

If more Conoco Shares are tendered for cash or Du Pont Shares than the Purchaser is obligated to accept for either form of consideration, tendering stockholders may receive

EXHIBIT 13–4 (cont.)

consideration all or partly in a form (Du Pont Shares or cash) other than the form they have elected. The extent to which tendering stockholder elections for cash or Du Pont Shares will be followed will depend on the number of Conoco Shares validly tendered prior to 12:00 Midnight, New York City Time, on Friday, July 24, 1981 (the "Proration Date") and not withdrawn and on the number of such Conoco Shares for which elections to receive cash or Du Pont Shares are made on or prior to the Proration Date. Stockholders whose tenders are made after the Proration Date may not receive the form of consideration elected by them. Information concerning the manner of selecting Conoco Shares for exchange for cash or Du Pont Shares is set forth in the Prospectus.

> THE OFFER IS CONDITIONED UPON A MINIMUM OF 43,500,000 CONOCO SHARES (REPRESENTING APPROXIMATELY 51% OF THE PRESENTLY OUTSTANDING CONOCO SHARES) BEING VALIDLY TENDERED AND NOT WITHDRAWN ON OR PRIOR TO THE EXPIRATION DATE OF THE OFFER. THE PRORATION DATE IS 12:00 MIDNIGHT, NEW YORK CITY TIME, ON FRIDAY, JULY 24, 1981. THE OFFER WILL EXPIRE AT 5:00 P.M., NEW YORK CITY TIME, ON MONDAY, AUGUST 17, 1981, UNLESS EXTENDED.

The Purchaser reserves the right, at any time or from time to time, to extend the period of time during which the Offer is to remain open by giving oral or written notice of such extension to the Exchange Agent.

All tenders of Conoco Shares are irrevocable, except that Conoco Shares tendered pursuant to the Offer may be withdrawn at any time prior to 12:00 Midnight, New York City Time, on Tuesday, August 4, 1981, and, unless theretofore accepted for exchange as provided in the Offer, may also be withdrawn after September 12, 1981. In addition, if another bidder commences a tender offer for Conoco Shares, Conoco Shares not yet accepted for exchange may be withdrawn on the date of, and for ten business days after, the commencement (other than by press release) of such competing offer, provided the Purchaser has received notice or otherwise has knowledge of the commencement of such competing offer. To be effective, a written, telegraphic, telex or facsimile transmission notice of withdrawal must be timely received by the Exchange Agent. Any such notice of withdrawal must specify the name of the person having deposited the Conoco Shares to be withdrawn, the number of Conoco Shares tendered for cash that are to be withdrawn, if any, and the number of Conoco Shares tendered for Du Pont Shares that are to be withdrawn, if any. If the certificates for Conoco Shares have been delivered or otherwise identified to the Exchange Agent, the name of the registered holder and the serial numbers shown on the particular certificates evidencing the Conoco Shares withdrawn must also be furnished to the Exchange Agent prior to the release of withdrawn Conoco Shares.

The Purchaser's obligation to accept for exchange Conoco Shares tendered pursuant to the Offer is subject to the condition, among others, that the stockholders of Du Pont approve a proposal to amend the Certificate of Incorporation of Du Pont to increase the authorized number of Du Pont Shares and to approve the issuance of Du Pont Shares in connection with the acquisition of Conoco. A special meeting of Du Pont stockholders to consider such proposal has been called for August 17, 1981.

On July 6, 1981, Du Pont and Conoco entered into an agreement (the "Agreement"), which has been approved by the Boards of Directors of Du Pont and Conoco, pursuant to which, following the consummation of the Offer, Conoco will be merged into the Purchaser (the "Merger"). Pursuant to the Merger each Conoco Share will be converted into cash or Du Pont Shares and, depending upon the results of the Offer, stockholders of Conoco may be permitted to elect to receive cash or Du Pont Shares, subject to certain proration provisions, as described in the Prospectus.

EXHIBIT 13–4 (cont.)

The information required to be disclosed by Rule 14d-6(e) (1) (vii) of the General Rules and Regulations under the Securities Exchange Act of 1934 is contained in the Prospectus and is incorporated herein by reference.

The Prospectus and Letter of Transmittal contain important information which should be read before any action is taken by holders. Any tender may be made only by a duly executed Letter of Transmittal.

Copies of the Prospectus and the Letter of Transmittal are being mailed to record holders of Conoco Shares and are available, at the Purchaser's expense, from the Information Agent or the Dealer Manager at the addresses set forth below.

The Information Agent

MORROW & CO.

345 Hudson Street	39 South LaSalle Street
New York, New York 10014	Chicago, Illinois 60603
(212) 255-7400 (Collect)	(312) 236-8600 (Collect)

The Dealer Manager

The First Boston Corporation

20 Exchange Place
New York, New York 10005
(212) 825-2000 (Collect)

July 15, 1981

INSURANCE

Insurance agreements affect many accounting decisions. Prepaid insurance premiums represent the right to receive future benefits. Receivables from loss claims are assets as well, and various insurance claims may affect income determination. Insurance is an important part of running a business because it allows a company to reduce various types of risk. Certain types of insurance are deemed necessary by virtually all businesses, whereas others are considered optional. Three types of insurance and their accounting implications will be discussed in the following sections: (1) liability insurance, (2) casualty insurance, and (3) life insurance.

Liability Insurance

Businesses have dealings with their customers, employees, and society and are generally held to the same potential liabilities and obligations as are individuals. When customers or employees incur some injury or damage on company premises, the company may become liable to pay damages. For instance, when an accident occurs in a place of business that results in pollution to waterways, or when an accident at a nuclear power plant results in possible exposure to radiation, the company involved is potentially liable to those who are adversely affected. A contract between a company and a third party, the insurance firm, enables the company to pass some or all of the various potential liabilities on to the insurance company for a price, called a **premium.** Most **liability insurance** calls for a prepayment of the insurance premium, which is recorded as a prepaid asset. The following journal entry shows how a 1-year insurance prepayment would be recorded:

6/1/91	Prepaid insurance	28,000	
	Cash		28,000
	(To record annual insurance premium)		

The prepaid asset would be amortized throughout the coverage period, normally on a straight-line basis, as a charge to income. For example, the first-quarter charge for the above annual premium prepayment would be amortized as follows:

9/1/91	Insurance expense	7,000	
	Prepaid insurance		7,000
	(To record expired insurance for one-quarter of the year)		

When liability insurance is prepaid for longer than 1 year, present-value amortization will more accurately reflect the annual expense and should be used. The total amount of the prepayment, say $28,000, for a 5-year policy would equal the present value of an annuity for 5 years at the appropriate interest rate for the company seeking coverage [28,000 ÷ (P/A, 5 years, x%)]. Also, the balance in the prepaid insurance account should be broken down into current and long-term portions. For example, suppose that a company prepays $28,000 for a 5-year liability policy and that an 8 percent interest rate is appropriate. A 5-year future annuity that equals $28,000 today can be calculated as follows, assuming an 8 percent interest rate:

$$\frac{\$28,000}{(P/A, 5, 8\%)} = \frac{\$28,000}{3.9927} = \underline{\$7,013}$$

The appropriate journal entries for the first year would be as follows:

6/1/91	Prepaid insurance	28,000	
	Cash		28,000
5/31/92	Insurance expense	7,013	
	Interest income[a]		2,240
	Prepaid insurance[b]		4,773

[a] .08 × $28,000.
[b] $7,013 − $2,240.

The interest income is not usually shown separately.[10] It is netted out against the insurance expense which is equivalent to the following more conventional presentation:

5/31/92	Insurance expense	4,773	
	Prepaid insurance		4,773[a]

[a] 7,013 − (28,000 × .08%) = 4,773.

[10] *Accounting Principles Board Opinion No. 21*, "Interest on Receivables and Payables" (New York: AICPA, August 1971), explicitly excludes such prepayments from the *requirement* that compound interest be considered. Therefore, it would be in accordance with GAAP merely to allocate $5,600 ($28,000 ÷ 5) per year to insurance expense.

The partial balance sheet and income statement at the end of the first year would be as follows:

PARTIAL BALANCE SHEET, 5/31/92		PARTIAL INCOME STATEMENT, 5/31/92	
Current assets		Insurance expense	$4,773
Prepaid insurance	$ 5,155[a]		
Noncurrent assets			
Prepaid insurance	18,072		
	$23,277		

[a] $7,013 − [($28,000 − $4,773) × .08] = $5,155.

The entry for year 2 of the 5 years' prepayment would be recorded as follows:

5/31/93	Insurance expense	5,155	
	Prepaid insurance		5,155[a]

[a] 7,013 − [(28,000 − 4,773) × .08] = 5,155.

If insurance payments do not coincide with the end of an accounting period, the premium is prorated to the periods involved on a straight-line basis. In the example above, the insurance expense for the period June 1, 1991, to December 31, 1991, would be $2,784 for 7 months' coverage (7/12 × $4,773 = $2,784). Note that this present value amortization of the prepaid insurance is equivalent to the present value depreciation illustrated in Chapter 12.

Casualty Insurance

Casualty insurance involves a contract by which the insurance company, in exchange for an annual premium payment, agrees to pay the insured entity for casualty losses suffered by that entity. Normal types of casualty losses would include losses due to fire, theft, water damage, wind damage, and so on. The accounting entries to record the payments of these casualty insurance premiums are equivalent to those illustrated above for liability insurance. Usually, the amount of casualty insurance coverage suggested by the insurance company is the **fair value** of the property to be insured, which may be substantially different from the historical cost or net book value of the insured assets.

Coinsurance

Sometimes a company has an insurance policy wherein it participates in the risk taken, along with the insurance firm. This **coinsurance clause** allows the entity seeking insurance to insure for less than the total fair value of the insured property and to share in casualty losses in some cases. The accounting aspect of the coinsurance problem stems from the accountant's need to determine the proceeds receivable ("claim") from the insurance company and the appropriate gain or loss. The insured party in a coinsurance arrangement will receive the lowest of the following three values in a casualty loss situation:

1. The face amount on the insurance policy
2. The fair market value of the loss
3. An indemnity amount computed from the following coinsurance formula:

$$\text{Indemnity amount} = \text{Face value of policy} \times \frac{\text{Fair market value of loss} \div \text{Total fair market value of assets involved in claim}}{\text{Percent of coinsurance}}$$

EXHIBIT 13–5

DATA FOR COINSURANCE EXAMPLES

	COMPANY A	COMPANY B	COMPANY C
Data Items Needed			
1. Fair market value of loss	$ 9,000	$ 9,000	$14,000
2. Total fair market value of assets involved in loss	12,000	12,000	20,000
3. Face value of policy	8,000	8,000	20,000
4. % coinsurance	80%	60%	80%
Three Values Considered for Reimbursement			
Face value of policy (item 3 above)	$ 8,000	$ 8,000	$20,000
Fair market value of loss (item 1 above)	9,000	9,000	14,000
Indemnity $\left(\text{item 3} \times \dfrac{\text{item 1} \div \text{item 2}}{\text{item 4}}\right)$	7,500	10,000	17,500
Proceeds (lowest value)	$ 7,500 (Indemnity)	$ 8,000 (Face value of policy)	$14,000 (Market value of loss)

Note that the *percentage of loss* using fair market values is determined by dividing the fair market value of the loss by the *total* fair market value of the assets involved in the claim. Also note that if the percentage of loss using market values divided by the percentage of coinsurance results in a number *greater than one*, there is no need to compute the indemnity because the indemnity will be *more* than the face value of the policy and will, therefore, not be the amount received.

To see how these calculations work, consider the coinsurance examples in Exhibit 13–5. The indemnity calculations for the three companies illustrated in Exhibit 13–5 are given in Exhibit 13–6.

From an accounting standpoint, the most important elements of information derived from the above computations are (1) the proceeds receivable from the insurance company and (2) the percentage loss using fair market values. Assume that the assets for Company A were machinery with an original cost of $5,000 and accumulated depreciation of $3,000 at the date of the casualty loss. Also, for Company C assume that the assets were inventory with an original cost of $18,000. The entries

EXHIBIT
13–6

INDEMNITY CALCULATIONS

Company A
$$\$8,000 \times \frac{\$ 9,000 \div \$12,000}{.80} = \$ 8,000 \times \frac{.75}{.80} = \underline{\$ 7,500}$$

Company B
$$\$8,000 \times \frac{\$ 9,000 \div \$12,000}{.60} = \$ 8,000 \times \frac{.75^a}{.60} = \underline{\$10,000}$$

Company C
$$\$20,000 \times \frac{\$14,000 \div \$20,000}{.80} = \$20,000 \times \frac{.70}{.80} = \underline{\$17,500}$$

 ᵃ Since .75/.00 is greater than 1.0, it was not necessary to compute this value.

for Company A and Company C are given below, using the following steps:

1. Eliminate the percentage of assets lost from *all* related accounts.
2. Record the receipt of proceeds (or proceeds claim) from insurance company.
3. Force gain or loss. The gain or loss may also be computed by taking the difference between the proceeds and the net book value of the eliminated asset or assets.

COMPANY A

Cash (or insurance proceeds receivable)	$ 7,500	
Accumulated depreciation—machinery (75%)	2,250	
Machinery (75%)		$ 3,750
Gain on casualty loss		6,000

COMPANY C

Cash (or receivable)	14,000	
Inventory (70%)		12,600
Gain on casualty loss		1,400

The gain or loss recorded as a result of a claim is the difference between the net book value of the assets lost (or the percentage of the loss based on fair market values times the total net book value) and the value received from the insurance company. If the insured party receives more than the value recorded on the books, a gain takes place; whereas a loss results when the proceeds received are less than the book value. Because it is possible to insure assets for more than their original cost when they have increased in value, and because many insured assets, such as plant and equipment, tend to increase in cost over time, it is not uncommon to find gains resulting from casualty claims.

Life Insurance

Life insurance is occasionally purchased by a company to insure itself against losses of its key managers and officers. Such insurance policies are evidence that the human assets of the firm have some value and that a loss to the firm would result if the services of certain key people were lost. There are basically two types of life insurance: ordinary life and term insurance. An **ordinary life policy** requires the payment of premiums until the death of the insured or until the policy is canceled. Such a policy will, after a stipulated period of time (usually 3 years), have some cash value to the entity paying the premiums. This value, called the **cash-surrender value,** is an amount that the entity is entitled to receive as a repayment of premiums paid should it decide to cancel the insurance contract. The cash-surrender value of life insurance policies is similar to a savings account in the sense that a portion of the premium is available for the company to receive in cash if desired, and as a result it represents an asset to the company.

A **term insurance policy** requires that premiums be paid for a set number of periods or until the death of the insured, should this occur before the set number of periods pass. A death benefit is paid only if the insured dies during the term of the policy. Once the set number of periods stipulated in the policy passes, the policy expires unless it is renewed. Term insurance policies have no cash-surrender value; therefore, no asset needs to be accounted for except when the insured dies during the term of the policy.

Most ordinary life policies require standard premium payments to the insur-

EXHIBIT
13–7

TERMS OF AN ORDINARY LIFE INSURANCE POLICY		
YEAR	BEGINNING-OF-YEAR PREMIUM PAYMENT	CASH-SURRENDER VALUE OF POLICY AT YEAR-END
1991	$600	0
1992	600	0
1993	600	$ 630
1994	600	900
1995	600	1,300

ance company each year. As mentioned above, the resulting cash-surrender value begins usually at the *end* of the *third* year of the policy and grows by a prescribed amount each year thereafter. Exhibit 13–7 illustrates the payments and cash-surrender value schedule for a $25,000 life insurance policy over its first 5 years.

The accounting problem presented by life insurance that has cash-surrender values is, How should the premium payments be treated during the first 3 years? The answer is, Assign the asset value of $630 that exists after 3 years as follows:

1/1/91	Prepaid life insurance		600	
	Cash			600
12/31/91	Life insurance expense		600	
	Prepaid life insurance			600
1/1/92	Prepaid life insurance		600	
	Cash			600
12/31/92	Life insurance expense		600	
	Prepaid life Insurance			600
1/1/93	Prepaid life insurance		600	
	Cash			600
12/31/93	Life insurance expense		600	
	Prepaid life insurance			600
12/31/93	Cash value of life insurance		630	
	Life insurance expense			210
	Gain on life insurance			420

After 1993 the annual increase in cash-surrender value is offset against the annual premium at the end of each year. Note that the *annual increase* in cash-surrender value will not necessarily accrue throughout the year but may often take place on the very last day of the policy year. As a result, interim adjustments for cash-surrender value would not be recorded in those cases. Each specific policy will indicate whether or not increases in cash value accrue to the policyholder. In the case being discussed here, the journal entries, using increases in cash-surrender value from Exhibit 13–7, would be as follows:

1/1/94	Prepaid life insurance		600	
	Cash			600
12/31/94	Insurance expense		330	
	Cash value of life insurance		270	
	Prepaid insurance			600
1/1/95	Prepaid life insurance		600	
	Cash			600

12/31/95	Insurance expense	200	
	Cash value of life insurance	400	
	Prepaid insurance		600

Assuming that halfway through the fifth year the insured officer dies, the company would record the proceeds as follows:

6/30/95	Cash	$25,000	
	Insurance expense	300	
	Prepaid insurance		300
	Cash value of life insurance		900
	Gain on life insurance		24,100

Life insurance is rarely a significant component of either income statement or balance sheet presentations and will seldom be reported as a separate component of any financial statement.

OTHER ASSETS

Deferred
Charges

Deferred charges (that is, "delayed expenses") are often listed among the assets of a firm. These charges are usually noncurrent assets, but there are exceptions. It seems that most assets might fall under the heading of a "delayed expense" as the cycle of cash to goods to cash is completed. Since many assets are normally charged to expense when their benefits expire, they might all be considered delayed expenses. Therefore, there is really no unique meaning to the term "deferred charges." In practice, the term serves either as a catchall for minor assets of the firm or as a way of listing assets without describing their nature to statement readers. Assets sometimes found under this heading include long-term prepaid expenses, bond issue costs, leasehold costs, interperiod tax allocations where tax payments precede revenue recognition, other prepaid taxes, rearrangement or reorganization costs, and initial organization costs. These more descriptive terms should be used on the balance sheet to identify such assets instead of the more ambiguous "deferred charges" whenever it is practical to do so.

Organization
Costs

Organization costs are those costs that are reasonable and necessary to incorporate or establish the entity. These costs would consist primarily of legal costs, various application fees, costs for underwriting the issuance of stock, and temporary rental costs and services paid to facilitate the organization of the firm.[11] The cost of establishing a business entity is viewed as an asset having benefit over the life of the firm, which accountants assume to be long-term.[12] Some argue that these costs do not represent an asset and therefore should be expensed immediately; however, most agree to the asset status. We agree with the latter, and therefore our examples classify organization costs as a long-term asset, which is consistent with the going-concern principle. For tax purposes, businesses are permitted to amortize organization costs over a period greater than or equal to 5 years. As a result, we find that most firms in practice amortize this asset over a 5-year period for both financial and tax reporting purposes. This seems to be conceptually inconsistent and somewhat diffi-

[11] Underwriting costs might also be directly offset against the Paid-in-Capital account in the owners' equity accounts.

[12] This refers to the "going-concern" assumption discussed in Chapter 2.

cult to justify under generally accepted principles. Yet it is the most commonly used method of handling these transactions. The only justification for this treatment is its relatively immaterial nature in most instances.

Leaseholds

Leaseholds are essentially the rights to use of property. They are usually represented by a long-term partial prepayment of rent for operating-type leases (discussed in more detail in Chapter 15, "Leased Assets"). Short-term prepaid rent is usually amortized or written off on a straight-line basis. Long-term prepaid rents should be amortized using present-values over the rental period.

In the long-term case, the prepayment of "leasehold" is only part of the rental cost. For example, assume that Libby, Inc., wants to rent a hot-dog stand from Vendor Corporation for 5 years. Vendor wants some of the rent payment immediately and some over the 5-year rental period. The part of the rent paid initially, say 30 percent of the total present value of the payments, would be termed *leasehold*. This prepayment would be amortized over the next 5 years as follows:

| 12/31/84 | Rent expense | XX[a] | |
| | Leasehold (asset) | | XX |

[a] This expense would increase over the 5-year period using present-value amortization.

The periodic additional rent payments would be recorded as follows:

| 12/31/84 | Rent expense | YY | |
| | Cash | | YY |

Total rent expense for the period would consist of the cash rental payments ($YY) *plus* the portion of the prepaid rent ($XX) amortized each year.

Companies in the Development Stage

Businesses that begin operations without having any financial or managerial assistance from a parent company or related entity usually incur an operating loss during the start-up period when they are in the **development stage.** During the early development of the firm, it is sometimes uncertain whether the firm will survive and turn into a profitable entity or perish. If it is virtually certain that the firm will survive, we might argue that the early development costs (and losses) will have future benefit to the firm and should, therefore, be capitalized and amortized over some useful life. The arguments here are parallel to those regarding organization costs. When there is not a high degree of certainty, however, we might argue that these development costs and losses should be recognized in the income statement in the period incurred.

Because the degree of certainty regarding future events is a function of individual expectations, it is difficult to judge in any uniform or consistent way. To eliminate this problem, the FASB promulgated **FASB Statement No. 7,** which eliminated the judgment factor, just as **FASB Statement No. 2** had done in the case of research and development costs.[19] The inconsistencies in treating companies in the development stage were eliminated by requiring all of these companies to report their costs, expenses, and losses just as any well-established firm would. In short, no special treatment is permitted simply because a firm is in the start-up stages of its

---

[19] *Statement of Financial Accounting Standards No. 7,* "Accounting and Reporting by Development Stage Enterprises" (Stamford, CT: FASB, June 1975).

operations. Also, **FASB Statement No. 7** explicitly stipulated that the financial statements, ordinarily required, clearly include the following information:[14]

1. The total "accumulated deficit from development stage" as an element of owners' equity.
2. Income statements showing the revenues and expenses for each year reported *as well as* the cumulative revenues and expenses for the entire development stage period.
3. The statement of changes in financial position should show the sources and uses of funds for both the current period *and* the entire development stage period including the current period.
4. A statement of stockholders equity showing the total cumulative data since inception for stock issue: (a) the date and number of shares issued and the value received for their issuance; (b) if value received for stock was not cash, a description of the assets received (i.e., other stock, legal services, etc.) and the value assigned to them.
5. The first year that the firm is no longer in the development stage, it should clearly indicate that data from prior periods were on a development stage basis. Also, the cumulative data requirements regarding income (2 above) and changes in financial position (3 above) are no longer needed even though comparative prior years' data are reported.

The major feature of **FASB Statement No. 7** is that it reduces the need for judgments, and the auditing of such judgments, regarding the expected future performance of development stage firms.

FUNDS FLOW EFFECTS

This discussion of intangibles, insurance, and other assets was devoted primarily to measurement issues, which tends to be the major concern in accounting for these assets. We should also point out, however, that all of these assets are long-term in nature, and increases and decreases due to acquisitions or amortization will normally have an impact on the measurement of both working capital flows and cash flows. The acquisition of intangibles will normally result in use of cash and/or working capital that does not affect income measurement and, therefore, does not impact on "funds provided by operations" under either the cash or working capital concept of "funds." Alternatively, the systematic assignment of the cost of these assets to income tends to represent expenses (such as amortization expense) that do not consume cash or working capital. As a result, the expensing or writing off of intangibles and other assets will normally call for an adjustment to the net income number during the process of converting "net income" to a measure of the "funds provided by operations."

The amount of resources invested in intangibles, insurance, and other assets tends to be relatively minor in amount. As a result, sources and uses of funds from the operating and nonoperating activities do not normally play a major role in the actual measurement and reporting of the funds flow activities of the entity. However, as noted in this chapter, the actual benefit to be received from certain intangibles and other assets may be much greater than their recorded values, and this tendency to understate their economic significance should be taken into consideration in evaluating the funds flow activities of the entity.

[14] Ibid., par. 11.

SUMMARY

Intangibles generally do not represent major dollar amounts when compared with the other resources of most firms. Intangibles, however, may be as important to the future earning power of a firm as any major productive asset category.

The most commonly reported intangible is goodwill, followed in terms of frequency of reported instances by patents, trade names, and copyrights. Goodwill disclosures are by far the most common of all intangibles, with about one-third of all companies surveyed by *Accounting Trends and Techniques* reporting goodwill, largely as a result of business combinations. Less than 10 percent of the companies included in recent surveys reported disclosures of other classes of intangibles. Exhibit 13–8 illustrates the relative importance of such assets for SCOA Industries, an entity that did elect to disclose its intangibles in the balance sheet.

The concepts applied in accounting for intangibles are the same as those used for other assets, as are the measurement issues and problems encountered. We have noted that the determination of which intangibles meet the definition of an asset and, for those that do, what their recorded value should be are key conceptual issues for many intangibles. In the case of research and development costs, we observed that although future benefits often exist, the measurability of those costs that will result in future benefits were so uncertain that all R&D costs are required to be expensed.

In addition to questions of asset status and measurability, the life of intangibles also presented problems due to the nebulous nature of many intangibles. As a result of the problems associated with uncertain useful lives, an arbitrary limit of 40 years has been established for all intangibles.

The concept of goodwill discussed in this chapter will provide a useful basis for dealing with the equity method of accounting for long-term investments considered in Chapter 14. Also, the discussion of leaseholds will serve as a brief introduction to a major category of intangibles, leased assets, which is the subject of Chapter 15.

EXHIBIT
13–8

INTANGIBLES—SCOA INDUSTRIES Partial Consolidated Balance Sheets		
	($000)	
	JANUARY 31, 1981	JANUARY 31, 1980
Total Current Assets	$241,174	$213,416
Depreciable Assets (net)	42,944	33,761
Leased Assets (net)	52,193	49,778
Intangibles	665	780
Other	5,499	5,932
Total Assets	$342,475	$303,667

QUESTIONS

Q13-1 What is the most practical definition of *intangibles* as used in accounting?

Q13-2 What are some examples of identifiable intangibles?

Q13–3   What are the most prominent attributes of the following intangibles: research and development, trademarks, copyrights?

Q13–4   What are *unidentifiable intangibles*?

Q13–5   How is the life of a patent determined for accounting purposes?

Q13–6   How are intangibles amortized?

Q13–7   How can intangibles that can only be used by a single entity have a market value?

Q13–8   Why do firms engage in R&D activities if R&D has no future benefit (since it is not an asset)?

Q13–9   What is the long-run effect of *FASB Statement No. 2,* "Accounting for Research and Development Costs," on the financial statements of entities with a relatively constant amount of successful (beneficial) R&D activity?

Q13–10   How do accountants measure goodwill?

Q13–11   What are *excess earnings*?

Q13–12   Why do some entities earn a higher return on assets than other entities in the same industry?

Q13–13   Why should an entity pay for liability insurance?

Q13–14   Why would an entity buy life insurance? Whose life would a corporation insure?

Q13–15   What is the purpose of a coinsurance clause?

Q13–16   What values are most relevant for determining the insurance needs for an entity's plant and equipment? Where do these values come from?

Q13–17   What is the difference between *ordinary life insurance* and *term insurance*?

Q13–18   What three possible values are considered by coinsurance clauses for payment of claims? Which value is received by the claimant?

Q13–19   What are *deferred charges*? Give several examples.

Q13–20   What types of costs would be included in organization costs?

Q13–21   What is a *leasehold*? How does it differ from *prepaid rent*? From *leases*?

Q13–22   Explain the differences in GAAP for development stage companies versus other companies per *FASB Statement No. 7,* "Accounting and Reporting by Development Stage Enterprises."

CASES

C13–1   The Biggs Company purchased the net assets of the Tin Company for $10,000,000. The book value of the Tin Company at that time was $8,000,000. The $2,000,000 difference was said to represent "goodwill."

REQUIRED   What is goodwill? Why would Biggs Company pay more than $8 million for Tin Company?

C13–2   T. Campbell and J. Butt are competitors. Butt has a patent with a remaining legal life of 10 years, which it uses as the basis of a major product—Targo. Campbell has just obtained a new patent that will enable it to produce a product that will directly compete with the market for Targo. Butt purchased Campbell's new patent for $2,000,000 but is not planning to use it to produce the new product. The management of Butt Corporation has recorded the $2,000,000 patent as an expense for the period.

REQUIRED   What is the appropriate accounting treatment in this case? What additional data would make you more certain of your answer?

C13–3   In 1981 Seagram's, Mobil, and Du Pont all began bidding through tender offers for Conoco common stock. Before the bidding began, Conoco was selling in the market at about $50 per share. Within weeks, the three investor entities had bid the price up to $120 per share.

REQUIRED   What do you believe would be a rational economic explanation for such an extreme change in the market value of Conoco common stock? What role, if any, does the chapter material have in explaining such a phenomenon?

C13–4 In July 1985 Kaybee Toys, Inc., received an offer from ICI, an investment group, to acquire a 50 percent interest in Kaybee for $15,000,000. The book value of Kaybee's net assets at the date of the offer was $20,500,000 but was considered to be worth $25,000,000. The directors of Kaybee were pleased to have such an offer but turned it down.

Business continued to be good for Kaybee, and in December 1985 the directors asked the bank for a $10,000,000 loan to acquire new facilities. The bank, however, told them that their net assets were not large enough to warrant such a loan. To justify the loan, Kaybee's directors now want the accountants to record goodwill of the company based on ICI's offer.

REQUIRED Explain what the implied goodwill is in the ICI offer. Assuming you are the bank lending officer how should the request from Kaybee's directors be treated?

C13–5 On January 19, 1985, the Baimen Corporation developed a cure for chicken pox. Baimen had been a medical research firm up until then, but after the discovery it became the sole producer of the serum to prevent chicken pox. Baimen had spent a total of $10,000,000 on the development of the serum over a number of years. The actual cost of the mixture that proved to be the appropriate serum was $115 (including labor). The total cost of filing for the patent was $2,876. A number of drug and chemical companies had offered Baimen between $300,000,000 and $500,000,000 for the patent on the serum. Baimen's net assets prior to the discovery were $6,000,000. To produce and distribute the serum, Baimen will need equipment and facilities costing $12,000,000.

REQUIRED How should this discovery be accounted for on Baimen's books? What problems do you foresee for Baimen before it can begin to take advantage of its discovery? How much better off is Baimen as a result of this discovery?

C13–6 The Scientific Systems Corporation has been developing specialized computer programs for the NASA Space Shuttle project during the past year. At year-end, the balance in the account that has been used to accumulate all costs associated with the research and development of these specialized software programs is $4,867,500. The total revenues of Scientific Systems for the past year were $10,000,000. Other costs besides the above that were expenses of the period totaled $7,586,000. The NASA project is still in process at year-end.

REQUIRED How should the cost of the NASA project be reported in Scientific System's financial statements?

EXERCISES

E13–1 (CPA ADAPTED) The general ledger of the Elvik Corporation as of December 31, 1986, includes the following accounts:

Organization costs	$ 5,000
Deposits with advertising agency (will be used to promote goodwill)	8,000
Discount on bonds payable	15,000
Excess of cost over book value of net assets of acquired subsidiary	70,000
Trademarks	12,000

REQUIRED In the preparation of Elvik's balance sheet as of December 31, 1986, what should be reported as total intangible assets?

E13–2 (CPA ADAPTED)

_____ 1. If a company constructs a laboratory building to be used as a research and development facility, the cost of the laboratory building is matched against earnings as
   a. Research and development expense in the period or periods of construction
   b. Depreciation deducted as part of research and development costs

    c. Depreciation or immediate write-off depending on company policy

    d. An expense at such time as productive research and development has been obtained from the facility

_____ 2. In accordance with generally accepted accounting principles, which of the following methods of amortization is normally recommended for intangible assets?

    a. Sum-of-the-years'-digits   c. Units-of-production

    b. Straight-line   d. Double-declining balance

_____ 3. In 1985 the MSA Corporation incurred research and development costs as follows:

Materials and equipment	$100,000
Personnel	100,000
Indirect costs	50,000
	$250,000

These costs relate to a product that will be marketed in 1986. It is estimated that these costs will be recouped by December 31, 1989. What amount of research and development costs should be charged to income in 1985?

    a. $0   c. $200,000

    b. $50,000   d. $250,000

_____ 4. How should goodwill be written off?

    a. As soon as possible to retained earnings

    b. By systematic charges to retained earnings over the period benefited, but not in excess of 40 years

    c. As soon as possible as a one-time charge to expense and reported as an extraordinary item

    d. By systematic charges to an operating expense over the period benefited, but not in excess of 40 years

_____ 5. On May 15, year 1, a company acquired a patent on a new product. This patent is being amortized over a 17-year economic life. On May 10, year 10, to protect its patent, the company purchased a patent on a competing product that was originally issued on May 20, year 6. Because of its unique plant, the company does not feel that the patent can be used in producing the competing product. The cost of the patent should be

    a. Amortized over a period of 17 years   c. Amortized over a period of 8 years

    b. Amortized over a period of 13 years   d. Charged to expense in year 10

E13–3 (CPA ADAPTED) Howard, Inc., incurred research and development costs in 1984 as follows:

Materials used in research and development projects	$ 400,000
Equipment acquired that will have alternative future uses in future research and development projects	2,000,000
Depreciation for 1984 on above equipment	500,000
Personnel costs of employees involved in research and development projects	1,000,000
Consulting fees paid to outsiders for research and development projects	100,000
Indirect costs reasonably allocable to research and development projects	200,000
	$4,200,000

REQUIRED What is the correct amount of research and development costs to be charged to Howard's 1984 income statement?

E13–4 (CPA ADAPTED) Oval Company was organized in late 1984 and began operations on January 1, 1985. The company conducts market research studies on behalf of manufacturers. Prior to the start of operations, the following costs were incurred:

Attorney's fees in connection with organization of company	$19,000
Improvements to leased offices prior to occupancy	16,000
Meetings of incorporators, state filing fees, and other organization expenses	15,000
	$50,000

The company has decided to record the amortization of organization costs over the maximum period allowable under generally accepted accounting principles.

REQUIRED What should be the amount of organization costs amortized for 1985?

E13-5 The Frecka Corporation has agreed to purchase the Student Company. The net book value of the Student Company is $25,000. Over the past several years Student Company has had an average net income of $5,000 per year. The current market value of Student's net assets is $30,000. A normal rate of return on appraised net assets is considered to be 12 percent. Frecka requires a 12 percent return.

REQUIRED Assume that Frecka computes goodwill by estimating the discounted present values of 8 years' superior earnings. How much will Frecka pay for the *goodwill* of Student, and what is the total price that Frecka will pay?

E13-6 Ace Company is considering the acquisition of Spade, Inc. Using a discounted present-value approach to estimate goodwill, determine the amount that Ace would be willing to pay for Spade's goodwill as of January 1984. Assume that Ace is willing to purchase 5 years of superior earnings discounted at 10 percent. The industry average return on net assets is 8 percent. The historical data for Spade are:

YEAR	NET INCOME	BOOK VALUE OF NET ASSETS	MARKET VALUE OF NET ASSETS
1981	$682	$5,600	$6,300
1982	529	5,900	6,700
1983	718	6,500	7,000

E13-7 Carson, Inc., suffered a casualty loss this year when a fire damaged its office building. A great deal of inventory was also lost. Fortunately, Carson carried casualty insurance. Terms of the policy and data on the loss of assets are given below.

REQUIRED What gain or loss would be recorded by Carson as a result of the fire? Record the entry.

Fair value of loss	$39,750
Total value of assets involved in loss	$45,000
Face value of policy	$30,000
Coinsurance	80%
Total book value of assets damaged before the fire	$35,000

E13-8 Record the loss incurred for each of the following assets, which are covered by separate policies that all contain 80 percent coinsurance clauses. Round your answers to the nearest dollar.

ASSET	HISTORICAL COST	ACCUMULATED DEPRECIATION	MARKET VALUE BEFORE LOSS	MARKET VALUE OF LOSS	FACE VALUE OF INSURANCE POLICY
Building	$800,000	$200,000	$1,600,000	$840,000	$1,300,000
Equipment	180,000	10,000	200,000	100,000	150,000

E13–9   Delta Company is about to enter into an "operating lease" (rental) arrangement for some equipment owned by XYZ Company. The following options are available to Delta:

OPTION 1	OPTION 2
Pay $33,000 each year-end for 10 years	Pay $22,080 at the beginning of year 1 and then $30,000 each year-end for 10 years

Delta selects option 2.

REQUIRED

1. What is the implied interest rate on the leasehold payment?
2. Record the necessary journal entries for the leasehold and the first annual payment on Delta's books.

E13–10

_____ 1. Patents have a 17-year legal life, and the *legal* costs involved
    a. Must be amortized over 17 years on a straight-line basis
    b. May be amortized over a longer period if the benefit exceeds 17 years
    c. Are frequently amortized over a shorter period because the useful life often is less than the legal life
    d. Should be written off in the period the patent is granted

_____ 2. The cost of research and new-product development
    a. Must be expensed in the period incurred
    b. Should be amortized over a period of not more than 40 years
    c. Can be expensed or capitalized depending on the period of benefit
    d. None of the above

_____ 3. The text indicates that the straight-line method of amortization is normally used for intangibles unless management presents a convincing case that another method is appropriate. Which of the following best illustrates a case for accelerated amortization?
    a. Copyright for an intermediate accounting text expected to generate sales over a 5-year period
    b. Patent acquired on a product expected to sell 1,000 units in each of the next 10 years
    c. Franchise fee for a McDonald's hamburger outlet
    d. Organization costs to be amortized over a 5-year period

_____ 4. In *practice,* the best way to *measure* goodwill that will be reported as an asset is
    a. To capitalize the excess earnings potential at the normal rate of return
    b. To measure the excess of the price paid over the net market value of the assets acquired
    c. To find the discounted present value of the future superior earnings for a limited number of years
    d. All of the above are acceptable for measuring the asset value of goodwill to be reported in the financial statements.

_____ 5. In January 1986 Ingram Company purchased a patent for a new consumer product for $170,000. At the time of purchase, the patent was valid for 17 years. Due to the competitive nature of the product, the patent was estimated to have an economic life of 10 years. In January 1990 the product was removed from the market under governmental order because of a potential health hazard involved. What amount should Ingram write off during 1990, assuming no amortization has been recorded in 1990?
    a. $10,000   **c.** $102,000
    b. $17,000   **d.** $130,000

PROBLEMS

P13–1 (CPA ADAPTED)   The Ziti Company followed a policy of deferring all research and development costs and amortizing them over a 5-year period with a full year's amortization taken in the year of the expenditure. Commencing January 1, 1975, Ziti changed its policy in accordance with *FASB Statement No. 2*, "Accounting for Research and Development Costs," to one of expensing all research and development costs as incurred. At December 31, 1974, deferred research and development costs of $3,500,000 appeared on Ziti's balance sheet. Research and development expenditures in 1975 amounted to $800,000.

REQUIRED

1. What amount of research and development costs should be charged to the income statement for the year ended December 31, 1975?
2. What amount of deferred research and development costs should appear in Ziti's balance sheet at December 31, 1975?

P13–2   On January 1, 1983, the following data were available regarding the Norgaard Company:

Average net earnings, past 4 years	$ 10,200,000
Average net assets, past 4 years	$ 85,000,000
Net assets, 1/1/83	$100,000,000
Industry average return on net assets over past 4 years	10%
Market value of net assets, 1/1/83	$140,000,000

REQUIRED

1. Estimate Norgaard's goodwill assuming you will pay for 5 years' superior earnings.
2. Assume that you require all investments to pay back in 12 years. You estimate that Norgaard's past earnings are likely to continue at the same *rate* over the next 20 years. How much are you willing to pay for Norgaard, and what portion of that price represents goodwill? (*Hint:* Assume that the book value of Norgaard's net assets will remain constant over the next 20 years.)
3. Estimate Norgaard's goodwill assuming you are willing to pay for superior earnings for 8 years. Your time preference rate for funds is such that you are willing to pay 15 percent more for $1 today than $1 one year from today.

P13–3   The Heitger Company carried life insurance policies on its key executive officers. Details of these officers' policies are as follows:

				CASH-SURRENDER VALUE		
OFFICE	DATE OF POLICY	FACE OF POLICY	ANNUAL PREMIUMS	3 YEARS AFTER ISSUANCE OF POLICY	12/31/83	12/31/84
Ogan	1/1/72	$400,000	$1,500	$2,000	$6,000	$6,500
Heintz	6/30/81	400,000	2,500	3,600	0	3,600
Groomer	1/1/83	400,000	3,500	5,000	0	0
Chook	7/1/68	200,000	1,800	1,200	7,000	7,300

The life insurance policies held by Heitger do not permit cash-surrender values to increase on an accrual basis. Instead, increases take place only on the anniversary date of the policy. Premiums are also paid on anniversary dates.

On December 18, 1984 Heitger learned that Mr. Chook (age 79), one of its key founding executives who was still active in company management, had accidentally drowned in a water-skiing accident while honeymooning with his fifth wife (age 19) in the Virgin Islands. A claim was filed with the insurance company.

REQUIRED   Record on Heitger's books all of the activity related to the insurance policies described above for the year 1984.

P13–4   On September 30, 1984, the MFC Corporation entered into a lease with the Sony Leasco Corporation for the installation of a sound system in a 50-story office building being managed by MFC. (MFC is leasing the office building from the lessor-owner on a 20-year lease.) The following options were made available by Sony Leasco for acquiring the sound system:

Option 1:	$150,000 on 10/1/84
	$40,000 per year for next 5 years starting 10/1/85
	option to renew for 10 additional years at $40,000 per year
Option 2:	$0 on 10/1/84
	$40,000 per year for next 5 years starting 10/1/85
	$79,315 per year for 10 additional years starting 10/1/95

The sound system is expected to be of equal benefit to the lessor (Sony Leasco) over its entire useful life, which is 30 years. MFC Corporation signs a lease in accordance with option 1 above.

REQUIRED

1. What is the implicit term of the lease?
2. What is the implicit interest rate?
3. Record the leasehold and any other entries required on MFC's books through October 1, 1985, assuming option 1 is selected and that MFC has a December 31 year-end.
4. Prepare an amortization table that shows the balance in the Leasehold account as of October 2, 1989.

P13–5 Zero Corporation had a fire that damaged its plant and its inventory during the period. The loss was insured by two separate policies, each with an 80 percent coinsurance clause. Data concerning the fire are as follows:

ASSET	FACE OF POLICY	NET BOOK VALUE	TOTAL MARKET VALUE	MARKET VALUE OF LOSS
Inventory	$ 80,000	$ 95,000	$110,000	$ 66,000
Plant	525,000	350,000	650,000	487,500

REQUIRED

1. Compute the amount to be received from the insurance company on the two separate assets.
2. Assume depreciation on the plant totaled $100,000 at the date of the fire. Record the fire loss for both inventory and plant.

P13–6 The net tangible assets on the *books* of EZ Company total $500,000, and *total* earnings for the past 5 years were $280,000. Included in the $280,000 were some extraordinary gains totaling $50,000, and a loss (which is never expected to occur again) amounting to $35,000. An 8 percent return on *appraised* net assets is considered normal for the industry.

Collins Company decided to buy EZ and is willing to pay net book value, *plus* $50,000 for the difference between book and market values, *plus* some amount for goodwill. To arrive at a dollar value for the goodwill, Collins decides to measure the discounted present value of above-average earnings over the next 5 years (based on the assumption that the next 5 years will be just like the last 5 years).

REQUIRED

1. Compute goodwill and the total purchase price, assuming Collins Company uses a 10 percent discount rate.
2. List the factors that might represent goodwill.
3. How do accountants actually measure goodwill?

P13–7 The Horrigan Corporation is considering the purchase of all 100,000 shares of Beckett, Inc., stock. Beckett has recorded profits of about $1,000,000 per year (average) over the past 5 years on assets of $8,000,000. The industry average return on assets is only 8 percent. Included in Beckett's profits and losses over the past 5 years have been the following unusual events:

1. A $500,000 gain on a fire in the warehouse
2. A $180,000 gain on a life insurance claim for an insured officer of the corporation
3. A $250,000 gain on the sale of partly used assets
4. A $400,000 gain on the early retirement of long-term bonds payable
5. A $330,000 loss due to a change in the method of accounting for depreciable assets

The Horrigan Corporation expects to pay a price for Beckett's net assets in excess of their fair market value estimated at $10,000,000. Horrigan estimates that goodwill is the present value of 10 years of "superior earnings" discounted at 10 percent. Beckett's stock is selling at $110 per share.

REQUIRED

1. What is Horrigan's estimate of Beckett's goodwill?
2. Explain why Horrigan might be willing to pay more than $10,000,000 for Beckett.
3. Will Horrigan's estimate of Beckett's goodwill be useful in preparing an offering price for Beckett's board of directors? Explain.

P13-8 The Merit Corporation began its manufacturing operations in 1984. During the year the following costs were incurred:

```
$108,000  —  placement costs of machinery and equipment
  18,730  —  cost of operators' salary during machinery adjustment period
  19,620  —  cost of wasted materials during machinery break-in period
  65,960  —  general overhead on factory during setup stage
  40,000  —  depreciation of factory assets during start-up stage
 185,200  —  cost of consultants and outside engineers during setup and start-up stages
$437,510  —  total costs
```

Merit's management has capitalized these costs in the asset account Organization Costs. The costs are being amortized over a period of 30 years.

REQUIRED

1. Indicate the appropriate disposition of each of the costs identified in the problem.
2. Record any correcting entries required.
3. Explain the relevant promulgations on development stage companies.

P13-9 There are five companies operating in an industry in which you wish to invest. You have collected the following information on these five companies:

	COMPANY 1	COMPANY 2	COMPANY 3	COMPANY 4	COMPANY 5
Book value of net assets	$4,000,000	$7,000,000	$ 6,000,000	$6,000,000	$5,000,000
Expected future return on book value	10%	11%	12%	8%	15%
Market value of net assets	$5,000,000	$6,000,000	$10,000,000	$4,000,000	$8,000,000
Expected future return on market value	8%	13%	7%	12%	10%
95% confidence interval[a]— book value return measure	7%–13%	8%–14%	3%–23%	7.5%–8.5%	2%–21%
95% confidence interval[a]— market value return measure	3%–13%	0%–26%	6.5%–7.5%	3%–21%	5%–15%
Market value of outstanding stock	$4,800,000	$6,800,000	$11,000,000	$5,000,000	$8,000,000

[a] This means that you expect the return to be in this range 95 percent of the time.

REQUIRED

1. Are book values *more* or *less* relevant, reliable, and comparable than market values in evaluating these five companies? Explain.
2. Assume that you may use book values *only*. Which of the five companies would you most prefer to invest in? Explain your choice.
3. Is there a systematic relationship between book values and market values of corporate assets in real entities? Explain.
4. Assume that you may use market values *and* book values to make your investment. Which company would you prefer to invest in? Explain your choice.
5. Are any of these companies unreal in the sense that theory tells us they could not exist because no one would invest in them? Explain.
6. Of the five companies, what is your estimate of the amount of goodwill for each? What is your estimate of the cost to acquire each?

P13–10 The following activities occurred during 1984 concerning the Comiskey Corporation:

1/1/84	On 1/1/81 a $1,000,000 insurance policy was taken out on Chairman Callaway, paying a $1,000 annual premium on that date. This life insurance policy has no cash-surrender value until 1/1/84, at which time it has a value of $2,500. The annual premium is fixed at $1,000 per year and is paid on 1/1 each year.
2/29/84	A fire in the warehouse resulted in the loss of inventory and damage to the building, which had a net book value of $450,000 on the date of the fire. Inventory with a book value of $400,000 was in the warehouse on the date of the fire. Both the building and the inventory were covered by 80 percent coinsurance policies. The face value of the "contents" policy was $1,000,000, and the face value of the building policy was $1,500,000. These face values were also the estimated market values of the inventory and building on the date of the fire. The estimated market value of the loss was $30,000 in inventory and $450,000 for the warehouse.
3/31/84	Purchased 30 percent of the net assets of the Nichols Company for $400,000 cash. The net assets of Nichols had a book value equal to $1,000,000. The difference between the price paid and the book value of the assets acquired is attributable to an undervalued patent with a remaining life of 10 years. Nichols had reported earnings of $45,000 for the quarter ending 3/31/84.
6/30/84	Signed a lease with Collins, Inc., for the use of office space over the next 10 years. The operating lease called for an initial payment on 6/30 of $250,000 and 19 semiannual rental payments of $50,000 for the next 10 years starting 12/31/84. Comiskey had the option of paying 20 semiannual payments of $77,785 starting 6/30/84 but turned this option down.
7/1/84	Construction on a new research facility was completed, and research in the $3,000,000 facility began on 7/1/84. The building is expected to be used over the next 4 years for designing the new Mars Probe, after which it will be torn down and replaced.
7/2/84	Acquired office fixtures that had an estimated useful life of 15 years for $90,000. The fixtures consisted of walls, stairways, lighting, and doors for the facility being leased from Collins. These leasehold improvements are to be amortized on a straight-line basis, with the residual value expected to be zero.
9/30/84	Acquired a patent on a tool used for construction of space probes. The research that went into the development of this tool had cost $150,000 in 1984, and a total of $400,000 over the past 2 years. The construction of the prototype of the tool cost $250. The patent application costs and other legal costs were $1,300.
12/30/84	Received word that Chairman Callaway had died at his winter resort in St. Croix.
12/31/84	Annual earnings reported by Nichols for 1984 were $180,000. Dividends received by Comiskey amounted to $10,000. On this date Nichols declared dividends totaling $25,000 to shareholders of record 12/31/84.
12/31/84	Research and development expenses incurred for salaries of research scientists, components of the Mars Probe, and tools used in constructing the probe since 7/1/84 totaled $3,587,000.
12/31/84	Prepared adjusting entries for 1984 year-end statement preparation.

REQUIRED Record the events and any necessary adjusting entries for the information given in the problem.

P13–11 The Christman Company has asked you to help it measure the amount of goodwill, if any, for an acquisition it is about to make. The company intends to acquire the net assets of the Mensching Corporation as of January 1, 1984. The following data are available regarding Mensching on that date:

Net assets, 1/1/84	$2,500,000	Number of shares of common stock	100,000
Average net assets, past 5 years	$2,200,000	Expected average net earnings, next 5 years	$378,000
Average net earnings, past 5 years	$264,000	Expected average net assets, next 5 years	$2,700,000
Estimated market value of net assets, 1/1/84	$3,000,000	Industry average return on assets, past 5 years	10%
Closing price of common stock, 12/31/83	$35	Industry average return on assets expected, next 5 years	12%

REQUIRED

1. Assuming Christman is willing to pay for 5 years' excess earnings, how much is Mensching's goodwill worth?
2. Assuming Christman plans to estimate goodwill as the present value of 5 years' superior earnings discounted at 10 percent, what is Mensching's estimated goodwill?
3. Assume that Christman requires that one-half (50 percent) of the total purchase price of all investments be paid back in 5 years. What is the maximum purchase price and the implied goodwill of Mensching included in that price?
4. In estimating Mensching's goodwill, is the historical earnings record or the expected future earnings more important? Evaluate the relevance, reliability, and comparability of these two earnings measures. Which did you use in requirements 1 and 2? Why?
5. What is the relevance of the market value of the Mensching stock in your analysis of goodwill and the total purchase price of Mensching's net assets? If the $35 security price of December 31, 1983, represented a price that all investors believed to be the only relevant measure of the stock's value, what would Christman have to pay for Mensching's net assets, and what portion of the price would be goodwill?
6. What limitations should we be aware of in measuring the return on assets (for example, net earnings/net assets) and industry average return on assets? Discuss the relevance, reliability, and comparability of this "return" measure.

P13–12 (CPA ADAPTED) The Thomas Company is in the process of developing a revolutionary new product. A new division of the company has been formed to manufacture and market this product. As of year-end (December 31, 1983) the new product has not yet been manufactured for resale; however, a prototype unit was built and is in operation.

Throughout 1983 the new division incurred certain costs. These costs include design and engineering studies, prototype manufacturing costs, administrative expenses (including salaries of administrative personnel), and market research costs. In addition, approximately $500,000 in equipment (estimated useful life—10 years) was purchased for developing and manufacturing the new product. Approximately $200,000 of this equipment was built specifically for the design development of the new product; the remaining $300,000 of the equipment was used to manufacture the preproduction prototype and will be used to manufacture the new product once it is in commercial production.

REQUIRED

1. How are *research* and *development* defined in *FASB Statement No. 2,* "Accounting for Research and Development Costs"?
2. Briefly indicate the practical and conceptual reasons for the conclusion reached by the FASB on accounting and reporting practices for research and development costs.
3. In accordance with *FASB Statement No. 2,* how should the Thomas Company's various costs described above be recorded on its financial statements for the year ended December 31, 1983?

P13–13 (CPA ADAPTED) The Barb Company has provided information on intangible assets as follows:

1. A patent was purchased from the Lou Company for $1,500,000 on January 1, 1984. Barb estimated the remaining useful life of the patent to be 10 years. The patent was carried in Lou's accounting records at a net book value of $1,250,000 when Lou sold it to Barb.
2. During 1985 a franchise was purchased from the Rink Company for $500,000. In addition, 5 percent of revenue from the franchise must be paid to Rink. Revenue from the franchise for 1985 was $2,000,000. Barb estimates the useful life of the franchise to be 10 years and takes a full year's amortization in the year of purchase.

3. Barb incurred research and developments costs in 1985 as follows:

Materials and equipment	$120,000
Personnel	140,000
Indirect costs	60,000
	$320,000

Barb estimates that these costs will be recouped by December 31, 1988.

4. On January 1, 1985, Barb, based on new events that have occurred in the field, estimates that the remaining life of the patent purchased on January 1, 1984, is only 5 years from January 1, 1985.

REQUIRED

1. Prepare a schedule showing the intangibles section of Barb's balance sheet at December 31, 1985. Show supporting computations in good form.
2. Prepare a schedule showing the income statement effect for the year ended December 31, 1985, as a result of the above facts. Show supporting computations in good form.

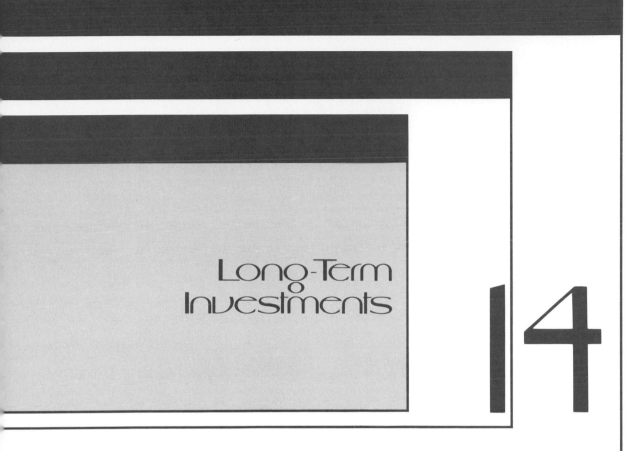

Long-Term Investments

14

OVERVIEW

In this chapter we discuss acounting for long-term investments of a business entity. Investments of one entity in another may be made to achieve controlling or noncontrolling interests in either a related or a nonrelated entity. These differences have important implications for the alternative accounting methods considered in this chapter.

A fundamental difference in accounting for the various types of investments is the degree of certainty with which their value may be measured. Bonds and notes are generally more objectively measurable because of their known cash flows to maturity. The contractual cash flows are all defined in advance.

The measurement of long-term investments in bonds and notes calls for application of the present-value concepts illustrated in Chapter 5. The measurement of these assets is equal to the discounted present value of the cash flows that are stipulated in the terms of the bond or note. Although the interest rate is normally specified in the terms of the instrument, it is sometimes necessary to impute the interest rate when it is not specifically stated. Once the interest rate is identified and the cash flows are known, accounting for bonds and notes is a relatively straightforward process. Their measurement is reliable because of the objective and unbiased data upon which they are based.

Long-term investments in marketable equity securities are different from those in bonds and notes in the sense that the cash flows to be derived from common stocks are much less certain. The accounting procedures for marketable equity securities are also somewhat more complex. The amount of ownership interest involved in equity securities determines which accounting procedures should be used to record long-term investments in stocks. Because of the more uncertain cash flows, the measurement and recording of long-term investments in stocks is a less reliable process than it is for bonds and notes. Several alternative valuation methods are applied in an effort to obtain relevant information for different types of long-term stock investments.

In the first part of this chapter we focus on long-term investments in bonds and notes. The accounting procedures for these assets are mirror images of the accounting procedures for long-term bonds and notes that are liabilities of the firm. We discuss the liability side of these instruments in Chapter 18. In the second part of the chapter we focus on equity securities. As you study the accounting procedures involved in long-term equity investments, you will gain some insight into the issues that are dealt with in the advanced accounting topics of consolidations, mergers, and acquisitions. For those who are interested, the fundamental nature of consolidations is considered in Appendix E of this chapter.

INVESTMENT IN BONDS

The recorded value of investments in bonds or notes on the books of the investing company should be accounted for by using present-value techniques in order to be consistent with the basis for their initial valuation. Applying the present-value concept to investments in bonds is somewhat more complex than it is for leases (see Chapter 15) because bonds and certain types of notes are made up of *two* cash-flow elements: (1) a stream of payments (an annuity) over the life of the bond and (2) a lump-sum payment at maturity. (Leases normally involve only a series of equal payments.) The price of a bond at any point is equal to the present value of these two cash flows **discounted at the effective interest rate.** Assume that a $100,000 bond having a stated interest rate of 8 percent with interest payable semiannually will mature in 5½ years. A yield, or effective interest rate, of 10 percent is desired. The market price that would yield a 10 percent return and the entry to record the purchase of the bond in such a case are as follows:[1]

1/1/90	Bond investment	91,696	
	Cash		91,696

The appropriate computations are as follows:

Value = (1) PV of 11 payments, $4,000 semiannual interest ($100,000 × .08 × ½ year) at 5%, plus
      (2) PV of $100,000 maturity value at the end of 11 semiannual periods at 5%.
   = ($4,000) (P/A, 11, 5%) Appendix H, Table H–3 + ($100,000) (P/F, 11, 5%) Appendix H, Table H–2
   = [($4,000)(8.3064)] + [($100,000)(.5847)]
   = $33,226 + $58,470
   = $91,696

[1] Recall that interest rates are always stated at an annual rate and need to be adjusted for semiannual or quarterly interest payments. Therefore, we use 11 periods at 5 percent effective interest instead of 5½ periods at 10 percent effective interest for valuation purposes.

This market price would be quoted in the financial press at "91.696 +" with a yield of 10 percent. The 91.696 + indicates that the bond is selling for 91.696 percent of its maturity value, with "+" indicating "plus accrued interest" since the last interest payment date. Rather than computing interest each day and adding it to the bonds price, the quoted percentage of the maturity value is always stated *without* including accrued interest to date (called "ex interest"), hence the need for the "+" designation.

This measurement procedure permits the computation of the market price when the market interest rate and the cash flows are known. In the case illustrated above, 10 percent is assumed to be the market rate of interest required at the date of purchase, and $4,000 and $100,000 are the annuity cash flow and maturity cash flow, respectively. One might ask, Why does the market rate of interest (10 percent) differ from the stated rate of interest (8 percent)? and Why doesn't the bond sell for $100,000? There is one answer to both of these questions. Generally, at the date a bond issue is originally sold, the stated rate of interest and the market rate of interest are the same or very similar. As a result, bond issues will initially be sold at or near their maturity value. However, due to continuous changes in interest rates caused by the changes in the supply and demand for short- and long-term cash, the stated and market rates of interest may differ subsequent to the original issuance and before the maturity of the bonds. It is not uncommon to find market interest rates during the life of a bond that are above or below the stated or "nominal" interest rates. Exhibit 14–1 illustrates a typical *Wall Street Journal* bond issue announcement made by various brokers.

Because the cash flows stipulated in any given bond issue are fixed the market price of the bond adjusts to reflect the current market rate of interest. Bonds may be selling at a "discount," a "premium," or at "par" subsequent to their original issuance but before maturity. These terms can be explained in the context of stated and market rates of interest:

1. **Discount:** When the interest rate required by investors is greater than the stated interest rate on the bonds, the market (investors) will bid the price of the bond down below its maturity value in order to allow the fixed cash payments stipulated in the bond to yield an interest rate that is higher than the stated rate. When the market rate exceeds the stated rate, bonds sell below maturity value.
2. **Premium:** When the interest rate required by investors is less than the stated interest rate on the bonds, the market (investors) will bid the price of the bond up above its maturity value in order to allow the fixed cash payments stipulated in the bond to yield an interest rate that is lower than the stated rate. When the market rate is less than the stated rate, bonds sell above maturity value.
3. **Par:** When the market interest rate required by investors is equal to the stated interest rate on the bonds, the bonds will sell at their maturity value. Par value is the same as maturity value.

In the case discussed above, the bonds sold at a discount because the market rate (10 percent) was greater than the stated rate (8 percent) of interest. The difference between the par value ($100,000) and the market value ($91,696) of the bond is called the **bond discount.** This discount, in the case of long-term investments in bonds, is systematically amortized over the life of the bond.

Effective Interest Amortization Method

The **effective interest method** of amortizing the discount is consistent with the basis of valuation. Because the bond will return $100,000 after 5½ years and is purchased for only $91,696, a "gain" of $8,304 would be recognized at maturity unless

EXHIBIT 14–1

BOND ISSUE ANNOUNCEMENT

In the opinion of Messrs. Ice Miller Donadio & Ryan. Indianapolis. Indiana, Bond Counsel. under existing statutes. regulations. proposed regulations, rulings and judicial decisions. interest on the Bonds is exempt from present Federal income tax except when held by a person who is a "substantial user" or a "related person" as explained under "Tax Exemption" in the Official Statement. and the principal of and interest on the Bonds are exempt from all taxes in the State of Indiana. except the state inheritance tax.

NEW ISSUE

$40,000,000

City of Petersburg, Indiana

Pollution Control Revenue Bonds, 1981 Series
(Indianapolis Power & Light Company Project)

The Bonds will be issued to provide funds for the acquisition, construction, installation and equipping of certain air and water pollution control, and sewage and solid waste disposal facilities at the Petersburg Generating Station Units 1, 2. 3 and 4 of Indianapolis Power & Light Company. The Bonds, except to the extent payable from bond proceeds and investments, will be payable solely from revenues received by the Trustee from payments under a Loan Agreement with respect to a loan evidenced by First Mortgage Bonds of

Indianapolis Power & Light Company

Dated: August 1, 1981   Due: August 1, 2011

The Bonds will be issuable as coupon Bonds in the denomination of $5,000 each, registrable as to principal only, or as fully registered Bonds in the denomination of $5,000 or any whole multiple thereof. Coupon Bonds and fully registered Bonds will be interchangeable. Principal and semi-annual interest (February 1 and August 1, first payment February 1, 1982) will be payable at the principal corporate trust office of the Trustee, Merchants National Bank & Trust Company of Indianapolis. Indianapolis, Indiana. The Bonds will be subject to redemption prior to maturity as described in the Official Statement.

12% Bonds due August 1, 2011
Price 100%
(Plus accrued interest from August 1, 1981)

The Bonds may or may not be available for sale from the syndicate at the above price on and after the date of this announcement.

The Bonds are offered when, as and if issued and received by the Underwriters and subject to the approval of legality by Messrs. Ice Miller Donadio & Ryan. Indianapolis. Indiana. Bond Counsel, and certain other conditions. Certain legal matters will be passed upon by Messrs. Peck. Shaffer & Williams.Cincinnati. Ohio. Special Tax Counsel. Certain legal matters will be passed upon for the Underwriters by Messrs. Simpson Thacher & Bartlett. New York. New York. Delivery of the Bonds in New York, New York is expected on or about August 6. 1981.

the value of investment were somehow increased by $8,304 between the date of purchase and the maturity date. This "gain," or discount, is actually attributable to the fact that the market rate of interest is greater than the stated rate of interest and, therefore, should be allocated to the interest effect in the income statement over the life of the bond. Because the interest received on the bond is based on the **par value** and the bond was purchased for something less than the par value, the purchaser is effectively receiving something more than the stated 8 percent interest. The effective, or true, rate of interest is the basis used to account for the interest income. For any given interest period, the difference between the interest income based on the effective interest rate and the cash received, which is based on the nominal interest rate, represents the amortization of some portion of the $8,304 bond discount. On the first interest payment date, the following entry would be made:

7/1/90	Cash	4,000[a]	
	Bond investment	585[c]	
	Bond interest income		4,585[b]

[a] .04 × $100,000 = $4,000 (constant for each interest payment)
[b] .05 × $91,696 = $4,585 (an increasing amount)
[c] An increasing amount

The second payment would result in interest income recognition of $4,614 [.05 × ($91,696 + $585)] and a discount amortization of $614 ($4,614 − $4,000). The entries that record the interest income and amortization of the bond discount or premium are frequently illustrated using an amortization table, which may be prepared at the date of purchase for the entire life of the bond. Table 14–1 shows the amortization schedule for the example described above over the 5½-year remaining life of the bond.

When bonds are sold at a premium, the same type of amortization schedule would be appropriate except that the effective interest (interest income) in column 2 would be less than the cash payment (column 1), and therefore the amortized pre-

TABLE 14–1

BOND AMORTIZATION SCHEDULE

Facts: $100,000 par value
8% stated semiannual interest rate
10% effective market interest rate compounded semiannually
5½ years remaining life of bond

DATE	(1) CASH INTEREST − PAYMENT	(2) EFFECTIVE INTEREST = INCOME	(3) AMORTIZATION OF BOND DISCOUNT	(4) BALANCE IN BOND INVESTMENT ACCOUNT
1/1/90	$ 0	$ 0	$ 0	$ 91,696
7/1/90	4,000	4,585	585	92,281
1/1/91	4,000	4,614	614	92,895
7/1/91	4,000	4,645	645	93,540
1/1/92	4,000	4,677	677	94,217
7/1/92	4,000	4,711	711	94,928
1/1/93	4,000	4,746	746	95,674
7/1/93	4,000	4,783	783	96,457
1/1/94	4,000	4,822	822	97,279
7/1/94	4,000	4,863	863	98,142
1/1/95	4,000	4,907	907	99,049
7/1/95	4,000	4,951[a]	951[a]	100,000
Total	$44,000	$52,304	$8,304	

Column 1 represents the *debit* to cash.
Column 2 represents the *credit* to interest income.
Column 3 represents the *debit* to the Bond Investment account.
Column 4 gives the balance in the asset account Bond Investment immediately after the amortization entry is recorded.
[a] Rounding error of $1 in last computation is forced.

mium (column 3) would be a credit that would reduce the Bond Investment account.

Alternative amortization method   Another way to account for an investment in bonds purchased at a price other than par is to amortize the discount or premium on a **straight-line basis.** This will also allow the value at maturity to equal $100,000, so that no gain or loss will be recognized at the point of maturity. However, the straight-line method evenly spreads out the effect of the discount or premium on interest income over the remaining life of the bond. Although less appropriate in theory, this method is easier to use and is justifiable in practice on the grounds that the differences between the straight-line method and the effective interest method are not material in amount. In the example above, the $8,304 discount would be amortized by the following entry:

7/1/90	Cash	4,000[a]	
	Bond investment	755[b]	
	Bond interest income		4,755[c]

[a] .04 × $100,000 = $4,000 (constant)
[b] $8,304 ÷ 11 = $755 (constant)
[c] $4,000 + $755 = $4,755

This same entry would be made for each of the 11 interest payments. The maximum difference between the straight-line method and the effective interest method can be found in the first (or the last) interest payment period; in this case, $755 − $585 = $170. If $170 is not a material amount, then the use of the straight-line method might be permitted. Although other methods of allocating the bond discount or premium might be equally acceptable in some instances, the present-value method and the straight-line method are the only systematic allocation methods for bond valuation normally found in practice. No lower-of-cost-or-market adjustments are necessary for bonds, and no other adjustments are required once management's intention to hold the bonds as a long-term investment has been established.

Recording interest and amortization on bonds   The example illustrated above assumed that the year-end of the investing firm did not fall between the date of purchase and the date of interest payment. It is fairly common to have adjusting entries for statement preparation fall between interest payment dates. In the example above, assume that the investing firm wanted to prepare quarterly statements as of March 31, 1990, and June 30, 1990. The most convenient way to record interest and amortization is to record *both* at the time interest income is *recognized*. The following entries show the two quarterly adjustments for both the present-value method and the straight-line method of amortization:

		PRESENT-VALUE		STRAIGHT-LINE	
3/31/90	Interest receivable	2,000.00		2,000.00	
	Bond investment	292.50[a]		377.50[a]	
	Bond interest income		2,292.50		2,377.50
6/30/90	Interest receivable	2,000.00		2,000.00	
	Bond investment	292.50[a]		377.50[a]	
	Bond interest income		2,292.50		2,377.50

[a] This is simply one-half of the first 6 months' amortization amount. A separate present-value amortization amount would only be necessary in those cases where quarterly interest payments are actually made.

The entry to record the actual receipt of the semiannual interest payment on July 1, 1990, would have no effect on the income for the period or the balance sheet totals but would simply decrease interest receivable and increase cash:

		STRAIGHT-LINE AND PRESENT-VALUE	
7/1/90	Cash	4,000	
	Interest receivable		4,000

The present-value method presented above is consistent with proper asset valuation and should be encouraged. When material differences result from the use of alternative methods, the present-value method is to be used.

Acquisition of Bonds Between Interest Dates

In accounting for bonds, perhaps the most difficult concept to understand is the recording of the purchase between interest payment dates. Assume that Atlantic Corporation buys $10,000 of face value 6 percent bonds on May 1, 1985, for $9,700. The bonds pay interest on January 1 and July 1 of each year. To record the purchase, we must recognize that the purchase price *includes* 4 months' accrued interest as of May 1 for the period January 1 to May 1. In theory, the market value should increase by $50 each month for the additional interest accruing to the bondholder.[2] In practice, to enable bond traders to assess the changing value of the bond separate from the accrued interest effects, bonds are traded at some percentage of face value *plus* accrued interest. In the case above, what was the quoted market price of the bond (assuming no brokerage fee was paid)? Four months' accrued interest equals $200, so the bond quoted in the market at the time of purchase was 95 + (95 percent of face value plus $200 accrued interest). A purchase at 95 + would be recorded as follows:

5/1/85	Bond investment	9,500	
	Interest receivable	200	
	Cash		9,700
7/1/85	Bond investment	20	
	Cash	300	
	Interest receivable		200
	Interest income		120

The July 1 entry records the receipt of 6 months' interest ($300) by Atlantic Corporation, which represents 2 months' earned interest income (the length of time Atlantic held the interest-bearing investment) plus 4 months' interest paid by Atlantic at the date of purchase. The 4 months' interest ($200) purchased on May 1, 1985, might be viewed as prepaid interest, with the entry of July 1, 1985, recording the repayment of this prepaid interest. Such a trading procedure makes payment of interest by the company that issued the bond much easier. If the interest were not included in the purchase price, separate interest payments would have to be made to Atlantic ($200) and to the company from which Atlantic purchased the bond ($400). Because bonds may be exchanged many times during any interest payment period, making separate interest payments to each holder of the bonds would be inefficient.

The July 1, 1985, entry also recorded $20 as the two months' (May and June) amortization of the total $500 bond discount. If we assume that straight-line amorti-

[2] $10,000 × .06 = $600 ÷ 12 months = $50 per month.

zation is used, what is the maturity date of the bonds? A rate of $10 per month would put maturity at 50 months from May 1, 1985 (that, is June 30, 1989). Although formulas are available to determine the effective interest (yield) in the situation above, accountants and investors seldom need to compute this information. The yield is generally provided in the market price information quoted in most financial news sources, and bond yield tables are also available to assist in determining the effective interest. Note that the issue date of the bond above was never mentioned and was not needed to record the purchase or for recording the interest and amortization. This highlights the fact that the value of the bond or note at any point in time is strictly a function of the *remaining* cash flows, along with the stated and effective interest rates.

Financial
Statement
Measurement

Most long-term investments in bonds and notes are recorded at cost, with discounts or premiums amortized over the remaining time to maturity. Because bonds and notes tend to be considered relatively low risk investments in comparison with preferred or common stocks, they are popular investments for financial institutions such as banks and insurance companies, which need to invest capital but do not wish to take on the risk of loss in principal. By holding debt to maturity, there is a high probability that the principal (or par) amount will be returned, along with interest. Still, between the date of purchase and the date of maturity, market values may be substantially below cost, and the sale of a bond under such circumstances would result in realized losses. The difference between cost and market is normally noted on the face of the balance sheet and/or in the footnotes (see the Alabama Bancorporation annual report in Exhibit 14–2).

EXHIBIT
14–2

ALABAMA BANCORPORATION AND SUBSIDIARIES
Excerpts from Consolidated Statement of Condition and
Notes Investments

	DECEMBER 31 1980
Assets	
Net Loans	$1,575,305
Investment Securities*	
Taxable securities	221,149
Tax-free securities	387,136
Total investment securities (market value of $523,859)	608,285
Total Assets	$2,738,570

* *Note E (Details)–Investment Securities*
The amounts at which investment securities are carried and their approximate fair market values are summarized as follows:

	DECEMBER 31, 1980	
	MARKET VALUE	CARRYING AMOUNT
U.S. Treasury and Federal agency securities	$191,948	$210,869
State, county, and municipal obligations	321,636	387,136
Other securities	10,275	10,280
	$523,859	$608,285

EXHIBIT
14–3

AMICA MUTUAL INSURANCE COMPANY				
	PAR VALUE	STATEMENT VALUE	COST VALUE	MARKET VALUE
Total Bonds	$248,765,000	$240,353,094	$238,220,151	$215,520,891
Total Stocks		$136,262,377	$ 48,701,576	$136,817,956
Grand Total		$376,615,471	$286,921,727	$352,338,847

Insurance companies typically provide a great deal of detail about their investments, with the number of shares of each security held, its cost, and its current market value normally disclosed in the annual report. Exhibit 14–3 illustrates a *summary* of such detail from an annual report of AMICA, a life insurance company. Note that the difference between the cost of bonds ($238,220,151) and their statement value ($240,353,094) is the *net* result of the amortization of discounts and premiums since acquisition. AMICA apparently purchased the bonds in total at a net discount because the current book value is greater than cost.

INVESTMENT IN STOCKS

The basis for recording stock acquisitions is the market price at the time of exchange plus any transaction costs (such as brokerage fees). Stock investments, like inventory, must be identified as having specific costs for specific lots, and, therefore, some of the same measurement problems will occur. What happens if we buy a package of three securities for a given price and there is no current market value for one of them? In this case, we would assign the security without a market price the difference between the total cost less the market price of the other two securities. In some cases, the market price of two or more securities may be unknown, and it may be necessary to wait until one or more are sold in order to make a specific allocation of the original cost. There is no clear solution to stock valuation in such cases, and the accountant must concentrate on the value of the package of securities until objective information about the value of the subcomponents can be obtained.

Multiple investments in the stock of the same company might also be made at different prices. With most securities, it is possible to use specific identification for valuation purposes at the time of sale because securities are usually numbered. For financial-reporting purposes, however, both the average cost and the first-in, first-out cost-flow assumptions are permitted for recording the securities at the time of sale when multiple purchases have occurred at different prices. For tax purposes, the average-cost method is not permitted but the other two methods are.

Valuation
Methods
for Stocks

Several security measurement methods are permitted for investments in stocks. All stocks may be classified as either **voting** or **nonvoting.** Voting stock is commonly referred to as **common stock;** nonvoting stock, as **preferred stock.**[3] The ownership of the voting stock of another entity, when the interest in the other entity is signifi-

---

[3] For example, see *Accounting Principles Board Opinion No. 18,* "The Equity Method of Accounting for Investments in Common Stock" (New York: AICPA, March 1971), par. 1.

TABLE
14-2

STOCK VALUATION METHODS	
SITUATION	**APPROPRIATE METHOD**
1. Nonvoting stock	Lower-of-cost-or-market
2. Voting stock, not a significant interest in investee (under 20%)	Lower-of-cost-or-market
3. Voting stock, can influence investee but not control (between 20% and 50%)	Equity method
4. Voting stock, controlling interest (over 50%) in an entity whose operations are not related to the investor company's primary operations	Equity method
5. Voting stock, controlling interest (over 50%) and whose operations are compatible with those of the investor company	Consolidation method

cant, may affect the method of accounting for such long-term investments. The key attribute that must be determined is the extent of one company's investment interest in the other. Table 14-2 summarizes the methods required by GAAP in various situations.[4]

Of the three methods identified, we shall consider the lower-of-cost-or-market method and the equity method in the following sections. The market-value method, which is not acceptable according to GAAP in most situations, will also be illustrated for comparison purposes. Consolidation methods, which are considered in detail in advanced accounting texts, are introduced in Appendix E of this chapter. Understanding the equity method will help the student understand consolidations when they are discussed.

Lower-of-Cost-or-Market Valuation Method

The **lower-of-cost-or-market (LCM) method** is required for long-term investments in marketable equity securities that do not qualify for the equity method.[5] If voting (or nonvoting) stock is *not* considered to be marketable, the cost method should be used in place of the LCM method. The LCM method for long-term investments is similar to the treatment of *temporary* investments in marketable securities discussed in Chapter 7 (see pages 237-244). As with temporary investments, the long-term investments to be accounted for by the lower-of-cost-or-market method must be valued as a total portfolio of securities, with the total cost being compared with the total market value. The account Long-Term Investments will remain at cost, and when the total market value falls below cost, a contra asset account, Allowance to Reduce Long-Term Investments to Market, is established to adjust the net asset value of the investments. In the LCM method, of course, the net asset value may not exceed the cost.

At the end of each accounting period, or whenever the financial statements are to be prepared, the **allowance method** is used to adjust the net asset to the lower-of-cost-or-market value at the date of the statements.[6] In adjusting the Allowance

---

[4] Ibid.

[5] *Statement of Financial Accounting Standards No. 12*, "Accounting for Certain Marketable Securities" (Stamford, CT: FASB, December 1975).

[6] The allowance method was discussed in the Part II "Overview" and has been applied in several previous chapters, including Chapter 7 (marketable securities); Chapter 8 (accounts receivable); and Chapter 9 (inventory).

account *in the case of temporary investments,* the offsetting account that was debited (for a loss) or credited (for a gain) was an income statement account called Unrealized Gain (or Loss) on Investments. However, *in the case of long-term investments,* the offsetting account is an owners' equity account (not a retained earnings account) called Unrealized Loss on Long-Term Investments. Thus, the routine adjustments to the Long-Term Investments account will not affect income but will directly affect owners' equity.

Consider the following sequence of events:

1. On June 13, 1986, the Skadden Corporation purchased $1,400 of AAA stock and $2,300 of AICPA stock as a long-term investment.
2. At the end of 1986, the market value of the two stocks according to their closing prices quoted in the financial press was $1,500 and $1,900, respectively, for a total of $3,400.
3. On January 19, 1987, AAA was sold for $1,500.
4. On May 24, 1987, Ergo is purchased for $1,700.
5. On December 31, 1987, the market value of the stocks was $2,075 for AICPA and $1,725 for Ergo for a total of $3,800.

These events would be recorded as follows:

Event 1

6/13/86	Long-term investments	3,700	
	Cash		3,700
	(To record initial purchase)		

Event 2

DECEMBER 31, 1986			
	COST	MARKET	UNREALIZED GAIN OR LOSS
AAA	$1,400	$1,500	$100
AICPA	2,300	1,900	(400)
	$3,700	$3,400	$(300)

Desired balance in Allowance account = $300 Credit
Current balance in Allowance account = 0
Necessary adjustment to Allowance account = $300 Credit

12/31/86	Unrealized loss on investments	300	
	Allowance to reduce long-term investments to market		300
	(To adjust to LCM)		

Event 3 (Ignore the Allowance account when recording the sale of long-term investments.)

1/19/87	Cash	1,500	
	Long-term investments (original cost)		1,400
	Gain on sale of investments		100
	(To record sale of AAA stock)		

Event 4

5/24/87	Long-term investments	1,700	
	Cash		1,700
	(To record purchase of Ergo stock)		

Event 5

DECEMBER 31, 1987			
	COST	MARKET	UNREALIZED GAIN OR LOSS
AICPA	$2,300	$2,075	$(225)
Ergo	1,700	1,725	25
	$4,000	$3,800	$(200)

Desired balance in Allowance account = 200 Credit
Current balance in Allowance account = 300 Credit
Necessary adjustment to Allowance = 100 Debit

12/31/87	Allowance to reduce long-term invest- ments to market	100	
	Unrealized loss on investments		100
	(To adjust to LCM)		

Account Balances as of 12/31/87

(Asset)	Long-term investments	$4,000 Debit
(Contra asset)	Allowance to reduce long-term investments to market	200 Credit
(Owners' equity)	Unrealized loss on investments	200 Debit
(Income statement)	*No effect*	0

A few points in the example above should be stressed. First, the Allowance method is being applied here because adjustments are made to the Allowance (contra asset) account at year-end only, and sales or purchases of additional long-term investments do not affect the balance in the Allowance account balance directly. Also, we should note that the last adjusting entry on December 31, 1987, credits an account titled Unrealized *Loss* on Investments for the recovery of $100 in the market value of the portfolio from the preceding year-end. Since this owners' equity account will always have either a debit balance or no balance, it will never represent an unrealized *gain,* which is consistent with the LCM rule.

The rationale behind the LCM method of recording holding gains and losses for long-term investments suggests that in the long run the holding gains and losses will approximately offset one another; therefore, there is no reason to permit changes in value to affect short-run (annual or quarterly) income. The LCM method requires balance sheet disclosure of the cumulative short-run downward fluctuations without any effect on income determination.[7] If, at some point, it becomes clear that the declines may be permanent (or as long-term as the time horizon for holding the

[7] *Statement of Financial Accounting Standards No. 12,* "Accounting for Certain Marketable Securities."

investments), an adjustment may be made to write down the investment account.[8] To illustrate, assume the following balances at the end of year 1983:

Account	
Asset: Long-term investments	$200,000 Debit
Contra asset: Allowance to reduce long-term investments	50,000 Credit
Owners' equity: Unrealized loss on long-term investments	50,000 Debit

Assume that on January 10, 1984, $35,000 of the total decline in market value is considered permanent. The following entries would be recorded:

1/10/84	Allowance to reduce long-term invest- ments	35,000	
	Long-term investments		35,000
1/10/84	Loss on decline in market value of long- term investments	35,000	
	Unrealized loss on long-term invest- ments		35,000

This would leave the net book value of the asset as before, $150,000, but it would reduce the Unrealized Loss account and reduce retained earnings (by way of reducing net income). The tax implications of this adjustment are not clear-cut, but in most cases the loss would not be permitted for tax purposes until the time the investment is actually sold.[9]

Equity Valuation Method

The **equity method** is based on the assumption that the investor can exercise *significant influence* over the firm that it is investing in because of the magnitude of its investment. Although anything greater than a 50 percent ownership interest in voting shares would obviously enable the investor firm to *control* the investee, something less than a 50 percent ownership interest might also enable the investor to have a significant *influence* on the investee in such matters as dividend policy. As a result of its concern over investor firms' "using" investees as a means of increasing or decreasing investor income by influencing the investee's dividend policy, the APB issued **Opinion No. 18,** which prescribes the equity method in situations where the investor could significantly influence the investee firm.[10] In the examples that follow, the equity method requires the investor firm to record income from the investee in such a way that the amount of dividends declared or paid by the investee will not affect the reported income of the investor.

The guidelines established by **APB Opinion No. 18** call for the use of the equity method when an investor owns between 20 and 50 percent of the investee firm's stock. The key condition, however, is the investor's ability to *significantly influence* the investee. It is possible that a 10 percent interest in a firm with widely dispersed ownership could represent significant influence. Alternatively, a 30 percent interest in a firm whose other major active shareholder owns 51% may not

---

[8] Ibid.

[9] Because of this difference for book and tax purposes, an adjustment such as the one illustrated would create a timing difference in accounting for income taxes. These differences are explained in Chapter 17.

[10] *Accounting Principles Board Opinion No. 18,* "The Equity Method of Accounting for Investments in Common Stock," par. 17.

have much influence on the firm's policies or management. In practice it is often difficult to determine exactly when an investor has the ability to influence the investee, and the management's and the auditors' judgment becomes important.[11]

Once the initial investment is recorded, the equity method attempts to track and record the changes in the net assets (owners' equity) of the investee firm on the books of the investor. The net assets of the investee may be completely different from the market value of the stock at any point in time. Therefore, determining the carrying value of the investment does not consider the market value of the investment, as does the LCM method. Also, since the initial investment is based on the market value of the stock (not the net assets of the investee) at the time of purchase, tracking the book value requires some rather peculiar and unique adjustments. The essence of the equity method is to record the investor's share of the investee's net income for any period (after acquisition) as an increase in the investor's assets and an increase in the investor's income.

To illustrate the equity method, consider the following example in which a parent firm (P Company) acquires voting common stock that gives it a significant influence in an unconsolidated subsidiary (S Company). Assume that the following historical-cost (book values) and appraisal-value (market-value) information concerning S Company is available on July 1, 1986, the date of acquisition:

ITEM	BOOK VALUE	FAIR MARKET VALUE	DIFFERENCES— MARKET VALUE OVER BOOK VALUE
Nondepreciable assets	$300,000	$ 350,000	$ 50,000
Depreciable assets	600,000	850,000	250,000
Total assets	$900,000	$1,200,000	$300,000
Liabilities	300,000	300,000	0
Net assets	$600,000	$ 900,000	$300,000

Furthermore, assume that P Company acquires a 30 percent interest in the 100,000 outstanding shares of S Company's common stock on July 1, 1986, for $10 per share. The following data are also provided:

a. At the date of acquisition, S Company's depreciable assets have an estimated remaining life of 25 years—straight-line depreciation is being used.

b. S Company reported net income of $50,000 for the year ended June 30, 1987.

c. S Company paid $10,000 in dividends during the year ended June 30, 1987.

d. P Company amortizes all intangible assets over 20 years.

The entry to record the initial investment in S Company is the same under all methods of valuing the long-term investment, simply recording the investment at cost. After the recording of the investment, several items will systematically affect the asset value. The following T-account summarizes the activity that will be re-

[11] In 1976 the SEC filed a legal suit against a company that was using the cost method to account for a 19.87 percent investment in another company. The SEC argued the company was able to exercise a significant influence over the investee's operations, and, therefore, the equity method should have been used. The company agreed to switch to the equity method, which caused pretax earnings to increase by 22 percent in 1976 and 55 percent in 1975 (reported for comparison purposes). See *Interpretation No. 35,* "Criteria for Applying the Equity Method of Accounting for Investments in Common Stock" (Stamford, CT: FASB, May 1981); and Deloitte, Haskins, and Sells, *This Week in Review,* June 26, 1981, p. 2.

corded periodically in the Long-Term Investment in S Company asset account:

LONG-TERM INVESTMENT IN S COMPANY		
DEBIT—INCREASE		**CREDIT—DECREASE**
(1) Initial cost	XXX	(3) Dividends of S	XXX
(2) P's share of S's net income	XXX	(4) Amortization of S's goodwill	XXX
		(5) Amortization of "excess depreciation" from appraisal value of S's depreciable assets	XXX

For the example above, we can compute the information for items 1–5 as illustrated in Exhibit 14–4 and then record the relevant journal entries.

Computations 1, 2, and 3 in Exhibit 14–4 are used for recording the first three entries in the T-account and are relatively straightforward. Computation 4 required that we define *goodwill* (see Chapter 13). *Goodwill* here is defined as the difference between the price paid for the 30 percent interest in S Company ($300,000) and the fair market value of 30 percent of its identifiable net assets (.30 × $900,000 = $270,000). In this case, P Company paid $300,000 for $270,000 worth of identifiable net assets, which were recorded by S Company, and $30,000 in unidentifiable assets (= goodwill), which are expected to have a remaining life of 20 years based on the stated assumptions in this case (P Company amortizes intangibles over 20 years). These facts suggest that S's *total* goodwill is $100,000 because $30,000 is paid for a

EXHIBIT
14–4

COMPUTATIONS—ITEMS AFFECTING P COMPANY'S
INVESTMENT IN S COMPANY

(1) Initial cost of P's investment in S
  30,000 shares at $10 per share = $300,000
  total cost of 30% investment in S

(2) P's share of S's net income for the year ended June 30, 1987
  $50,000   (From item *b* in data list)
  ×   .30   (P's % ownership)
  $15,000   (P's share of S's net income)

(3) Dividends of S received by P for year ended June 30, 1987
  $10,000   (Dividends paid by S per item *c* in data list)
  ×   .30   (P's % ownership of S)
  $ 3,000   (P's share of S's dividends)

(4) Amortization of goodwill in S
  $300,000   (Price paid for S)
  −270,000   (30% of the market value of S = .3 × $900,000)
  $ 30,000   Goodwill acquired by P, included in purchase price
  ÷   20 years
  $ 1,500   Annual amortization of P's share of goodwill

(5) Amortization of excess depreciation
  $850,000   Market value of depreciable assets—S
  −600,000   Net book value of depreciable assets—S
  $250,000   Excess value of depreciable assets not recorded on S's books but used by P to value S
  ×   .30   (P's % ownership of S)
  $ 75,000   Amount of excess value of depreciable assets included in P's $300,000 investment in S but not recorded or depreciated by S after P's acquisition of S
  ÷   25 years   (Remaining life of S's assets)
  $ 3,000   Annual excess depreciation to be recorded by P as a write-down in its asset "Investment in S Company"

30 percent share of S's goodwill. The only goodwill to be accounted for, however, is the $30,000 of goodwill in S acquired by P because goodwill must be purchased to be recorded. The S goodwill is amortized by P over a 20-year period by systematic charges to "income from unconsolidated equity investment."

Computation 5 in Exhibit 14–4 is also somewhat complicated in its assumptions. The thrust of this adjustment is to suggest that P paid $300,000 for the net assets of S, which included (1) 30 percent of their recorded values (.3 × $600,000 net assets at book value = $180,000); (2) 30 percent of the appraisal increase in the recorded assets [.3 × ($900,000 − $600,000) = $90,000]; and (3) 30 percent of the "unrecorded assets" represented by total goodwill (.3 × $100,000 = $30,000). The total appraisal increase of $300,000 is largely attributable to the differences between book value and market value of the depreciable assets ($250,000 appraisal increase for all depreciable assets times 30 percent, or $75,000 for P's 30 percent share), which is *not* being depreciated on S's books (and, therefore, does not affect S's net income). This excess value ($75,000) acquired by P and included in its Long-Term Investment in S Company account must be written off over the next 25 years, the remaining life of S's depreciable assets.

The journal entries in Exhibit 14–5 record all the activities in the Long-Term Investment in S Company account for the year ended June 30, 1987. The logic of these adjustments for goodwill and the excess depreciation is very similar. It is based on the assumption that adding S's income, which is based on S's *book* values, to the initial investment in S, which was based on *market* values for S's assets, is inconsistent. Therefore, certain "adjustments" to P's share of S's net income are necessary to account for the differences between the book values used by S and the market values of those S assets being used by P. The differences attributable to goodwill and depreciable assets are systematically written off against income from S on P's books.

EXHIBIT 14–5

JOURNAL ENTRIES TO ACCOUNT FOR P COMPANY'S INVESTMENT IN S COMPANY		
July 1, 1986	Long-term investment in S Company	300,000	
	Cash		300,000
	(To record initial investment, item 1 above)		
July 1, 1986–	Long-term investment in S Company	15,000	
June 30, 1987	Income from unconsolidated equity investment		15,000
	(To record P's share of S's net income, item 2 above)		
	Cash	3,000	
	Long-term investment in S Company		3,000
	(To record receipt of dividends, item 3 above)		
June 30, 1987	Income from unconsolidated equity investment	1,500	
Adjustments	Long-term investment in S Company		1,500
	(To amortize P's share of S's goodwill, item 4 above)		
	Income from unconsolidated equity investment	3,000	
	Long-term investment in S Company		3,000
	(To amortize P's share of S's excess depreciation, item 5 above)		

Disclosure of equity investments The equity method is sometimes referred to as "one-line consolidation." Note that in Exhibit 14–5 the entries to record P's investment in S result in changes to one balance sheet account and one income statement account. The asset Long-Term Investment in S Company is increased for purchases and P's share of net income in S, and it is decreased for dividends and the write-off of goodwill and excess depreciation. The activity in the asset account affecting income (items 2, 4, and 5 in the T-account) is reported in a single income statement account, Income from Unconsolidated Equity Investment. This one-line disclosure is by design.[12]

There are several exceptions to this one-line effect in the income statement. For example, some companies might record the **undistributed income** from S Company and the **distributed income** (or dividend income) in separate accounts to differentiate between income from subsidiaries that did not generate an inflow of funds (an economic flow) and income that did generate funds. Also, there are different accounting treatments accorded undistributed income for book and tax purposes which would call for separation of these two amounts.[13] In the P Company case, the undistributed income and dividend income could, for example, be jointly recorded as follows at the end of the accounting period:

6/30/87	Cash	3,000	
	Long-term investment in S Company	12,000	
	Undistributed income from unconsolidated equity investment		12,000
	Dividend income—equity investments		3,000
	(To record P's share of S income and the receipt of dividends from S)		

Although there are relatively few details regarding equity investments in the financial statements, the footnotes often provide extensive information on equity investments, particularly those investments that are controlled by the parent company but are being accounted for on an equity basis due to the nature of the business (situation 4 in Table 14–2). For example, in Exhibit 14–6 the General Electric Company's investments are disclosed in a rather detailed footnote and include comparative financial statement data for the wholly owned credit company, General Electric Credit Corporation, which is accounted for by the parent company on the equity basis.

To be consistent with other pronouncements such as APB Opinion No. 30 and **FASB Statement No. 4,** P Company might sometimes report more than one income statement account to reflect the change in the S Company investment.[14] This would occur in those instances where S reports material income statement items that require separate disclosure, such as accounting principle changes, prior period adjustments, extraordinary items, and discontinued segments. However, the net im-

[12] *Accounting Principles Board Opinion No. 18,* "The Equity Method of Accounting for Investments in Common Stock," par. 19c.

[13] For a discussion of this difference, see *Accounting Principles Board Opinion No. 24,* "Accounting for Income Taxes—Equity Method Investments" (New York: AICPA, April 1972); and Chapter 17, "Accounting for Income Taxes."

[14] *Accounting Principles Board Opinion No. 30,* "Reporting the Results of Operations" (New York: AICPA, June 1973), and *Statement of Financial Accounting Standards No. 4,* "Reporting Gains and Losses from Extinguishment of Debt" (Stamford, CT: FASB, March 1975)

EXHIBIT 14–6

GENERAL ELECTRIC COMPANY
Investments: Footnote Disclosure

12. Investments

(In millions) December 31	1979	1978
Nonconsolidated finance affiliates	$ 824.0	$ 683.6
Nonconsolidated uranium mining affiliate	157.5	86.7
Miscellaneous investments (at cost):		
Government and government-guaranteed securities	233.1	241.4
Other	147.5	119.1
	380.6	360.5
Marketable equity securities	44.0	37.4
Associated companies	301.3	257.1
Less allowance for losses	(15.9)	(14.8)
	$1,691.5	$1,410.5

Current and retained earnings

(In millions) For the year	1979	1978
Earned income	$1,102.4	$ 813.6
Expenses:		
Interest and discount	528.2	336.7
Operating and administrative	395.6	315.1
Provision for losses — receivables	69.4	56.4
— other assets	(1.8)	8.0
Provision for income taxes	21.1	20.1
	1,012.5	736.3
Net earnings	89.9	77.3
Less dividends	(72.7)	(61.8)
Retained earnings at January 1	221.3	205.8
Retained earnings at December 31	$ 238.5	$ 221.3

Condensed consolidated financial statements for the General Electric Credit Corporation (the principal nonconsolidated finance affiliate) are shown below. More detailed information is available in General Electric Credit Corporation's 1979 Annual Report, copies of which may be obtained by writing to: General Electric Credit Corporation, P.O. Box 8300, Stamford, Connecticut 06904.

General Electric Credit Corporation
Financial position

(In millions) December 31	1979	1978
Cash and marketable securities	$ 373.8	$ 367.5
Receivables:		
Time sales and loans	7,480.3	6,052.7
Deferred income	(1,124.1)	(843.9)
	6,356.2	5,208.8
Investment in leases	1,207.1	1,031.7
Sundry receivables	140.6	78.1
Total receivables	7,703.9	6,318.6
Allowance for losses	(231.2)	(199.3)
Net receivables	7,472.7	6,119.3
Other assets	321.3	171.9
Total assets	$8,167.8	$6,658.7
Notes payable:		
Due within one year	$3,921.0	$2,953.0
Long-term — senior	1,743.0	1,571.1
— subordinated	324.8	325.5
Other liabilities	631.3	513.7
Total liabilities	6,620.1	5,363.3
Deferred income taxes	718.0	615.7
Deferred investment tax credit	13.3	3.2
Capital stock	566.4	443.7
Additional paid-in capital	11.5	11.5
Retained earnings	238.5	221.3
Equity	816.4	676.5
Total liabilities, deferred tax items and equity	$8,167.8	$6,658.7

Investment in the nonconsolidated uranium mining affiliate consists of investment in a wholly owned affiliate (established in the course of obtaining a U.S. Department of Justice Business Advisory Clearance Procedure Letter in connection with the 1976 Utah merger) to which all of the then existing uranium business of Utah has been transferred. All common stock of this affiliate has been placed in a voting trust controlled by independent voting trustees. Prior to the year 2000, General Electric and its affiliates may not withdraw the common stock from the voting trust except for sale to unaffiliated third parties. Directors and officers of the affiliate may not be directors, officers, or employees of General Electric, Utah or of any of their affiliates. Uranium may not be sold by this affiliate, in any state or form, to, or at the direction of, General Electric or its affiliates.

All outstanding shares of preferred stock of the uranium affiliate are retained by Utah as an affiliate of General Electric. Payment of cumulative quarterly dividends out of legally available funds on this preferred stock is mandatory in amounts equal to 85% of the affiliate's net after-tax income for the previous quarter (without taking account of any deduction for exploration expense as defined). Utah, as holder of the preferred stock, must make loans with up to ten-year maturities when requested by the affiliate, although the aggregate amount of such loans need not at any time exceed preferred dividend payments for the immediately preceding two calendar years.

The estimated realizable value of miscellaneous investments was $350 million at December 31, 1979 and 1978.

Marketable equity securities are valued at the lower of cost or market. Aggregate market value of marketable equity securities was $181 million and $173 million at year-end 1979 and 1978, respectively. At December 31, 1979, gross unrealized gains on marketable equity securities were $137 million.

Investments in nonconsolidated affiliates and associated companies included advances of $122.6 million at December 31, 1979 ($51.0 million at December 31, 1978).

pact of S's ongoing operations would normally appear as a single-line item in P's income statement as illustrated in Exhibit 14–7 for the Ferro Corporation ("equity in net earnings of affiliated companies") or as a footnote explanation of the details making up the Net Revenue or Net Sales account.

A caution regarding the equity method The equity method procedures considered in the P Company example are not complete in the sense that not all of the adjustments that *might* need to be recorded have been illustrated. As with the pro-

EXHIBIT 14–7

FERRO CORPORATION
Income Statement Disclosure of Investments

FERRO CORPORATION and Subsidiaries

Consolidated Statements of Income
Years ended December 31, 1980, 1979 and 1978

	1980	1979	1978
	(Dollars in Thousands)		
Net Sales	$695,580	591,930	494,414
Cost of Sales	523,206	435,806	352,463
Selling, Administrative and General Expenses (note 8)	114,843	99,619	91,557
	638,049	535,425	444,020
Operating Income	57,531	56,505	50,394
Other Income:			
Interest earned	2,880	2,464	1,899
Royalties	1,191	834	615
Equity in net earnings of affiliated companies	1,165	940	221
Miscellaneous	3,783	2,711	1,846
	9,019	6,949	4,581
Other Charges:			
Interest expense	13,345	8,547	4,948
Foreign currency loss (gain):			
Realized	5,465	3,087	881
Unrealized	(4,607)	(624)	(568)
Net foreign currency loss	858	2,463	313
Miscellaneous	3,038	2,067	1,557
	17,241	13,077	6,818
Income Before Taxes	49,309	50,377	48,157
United States and Foreign Income Taxes, including deferred taxes of $754,000 in 1980, $1,370,000 in 1979 and $1,040,000 in 1978 (note 6)	20,290	19,465	20,500
Net Income	$ 29,019	30,912	27,657
Per Share Net Income	$ 3.77	4.07	3.67

cedures required for preparing consolidated statements, the equity method should record adjustments to eliminate (fractionally based on the percentage ownership) the intercompany activities (if any) from the financial statements of P and S *prior to* adding P's share of S's net income.[15] These complexities, which are considered in detail in advanced accounting texts, are often not material in cases where the parent and the subsidiary are not major customers of one another.

Equity Method
Accounting
Change

Because the ownership interest in an investee may change periodically due to activities of the investor (such as buying or selling the investee's stock) or the investee (such as when the investee repurchases and retires outstanding common stock), the investee should be evaluated periodically. In some cases, a change to or from the equity method might be warranted.

Change to the equity method To illustrate a change *to* the equity method, assume that Karras Enterprises owns a 15 percent interest (15,000 shares) in the Lindell A. C., which was acquired on January 1, 1983, at a cost of $300,000 and has been accounted for on the LCM basis. On January 2, 1985, Karras purchased an additional 15 percent ownership (15,000 shares) in Lindell for $315,000 and was required to switch from the LCM method to the equity method because of the ability of the 30 percent interest to influence Lindell's operations. To account for a change to the equity method, the investor (Karras) should determine the book value of the investment that would have been reported as of the date of the change (January 2, 1985) had the equity method been applied from the date of the initial purchase (January 1, 1983). The difference between the old method (LCM) and the equity method **should be accounted for retroactively** by way of an adjustment to the beginning retained earnings balance in the year of the change. The information required to record such a change is not always readily available and may even require calculating what the market value of the investee was as of the date of the investor's initial purchase of the investee's stock.

In the Karras case, assume that the book value of Lindell's net assets on January 1, 1983, was $1,500,000. The difference between a 15 percent interest in the book value (.15 × $1,500,000 = $225,000) and the price paid ($300,000 is $75,000 and is attributable to goodwill and the market value of depreciable assets having an estimated remaining useful life of 25 years as of January 1, 1983. During the period January 1983 to December 1985, data for Lindell were as follows:

DATE	NET INCOME	DIVIDENDS	NET BOOK VALUE	MARKET VALUE OF STOCK
1/1/83	$ 0	$ 0	$1,500,000	$20
12/31/83	300,000	100,000	1,700,000	22
12/31/84	310,000	100,000	1,910,000	21
12/31/85	330,000	100,000	2,140,000	23

The Long-Term Investment in Lindell A. C. account on the books of Karras Enterprises as of January 1, 1985, would have been $300,000 under the LCM method of accounting. If the equity method had been used between January 1, 1983, and January 1, 1985, Karras would have recorded the following activity:

---

[15] *Accounting Principles Board Opinion No. 18,* "The Equity Method of Accounting for Investments in Common Stock," par. 19.

LONG-TERM INVESTMENT IN LINDELL A.C.

DEBIT—INCREASE			CREDIT—DECREASE		
1/1/83	Initial cost	$300,000	12/31/83	15% share of Lindell's dividend distribution	$15,000
12/31/83	15% share of Lindell's net income	45,000	12/31/83	Amortization of difference between price paid and book value[a]	3,000
12/31/84	15% share of Lindell's net income	46,500	12/31/84	15% share of Lindell's dividend distribution	15,000
			12/31/84	Amortization of difference between price paid and book value	3,000
1/1/85	Balance	$355,500			

[a] Amortization of $75,000 excess of price paid over net book value over 25 years expected life on a straight-line basis.

The $55,500 difference between the LCM method and the equity method would be treated as a retroactive adjustment to retained earnings and would be recorded along with the additional 15 percent purchase through the following entries:

1/2/85	Long-term investment in Lindell A. C.	55,500	
	Retained earnings		55,500
	(To record change to equity method)		
1/2/85	Long-term investment in Lindell A. C.	315,000	
	Cash		315,000
	(To record additional purchase of Lindell stock at $21 per share market price)		

The equity method would be applied for 1985 and future years. In 1985 Karras would recognize 30 percent of Lindell's income and dividends and would amortize the initial excess of cost over book value ($75,000) as well as the additional excess of cost over book value ($315,000 − [.15 × $1,910,000] = $28,500), which is assumed to be amortized over a 20-year period. These entries would be recorded as follows:

12/31/85	Long-term investment in Lindell A. C.	99,000	
	Income from unconsolidated subsidiary		99,000
	(To record 30% of Lindell's net income)		
12/31/85	Cash	30,000	
	Long-term investment in Lindell A. C.		30,000
	(To record receipt of dividends)		
12/31/85	Income from unconsolidated subsidiary	4,425[a]	
	Long-term investment in Lindell A. C.		4,425
	(To amortize excess of price paid over book value of assets acquired)		

[a] $[(1/25) \times (\$75,000)] + [(1/20) \times (\$28,500)]$

The accounting for changes to the equity method is treated retroactively as required in **APB Opinion No. 18.**[16] These changes are technically considered to be changes in the reporting entity, which are to be treated retroactively *like* a prior-period adjustment. The nature of this accounting change and its treatment will be reviewed in Chapter 24.

Change from the equity method   To change from the equity method to the LCM method because of a decline in the investor's influence over the investee does not require any specific adjustment. The new method is applied to current and future periods. Under the new method (LCM), no adjustments would be made to the asset Long-Term Investments for the investor's share of the investee's net income or dividends or difference between book value and cost. However, in certain infrequent situations where the cost method is used (because of the nonmarketability of the investee's common stock), a dividend from the investee which is liquidating from the investor's position will require a downward adjustment to the Long-Term Investment account.

To illustrate how this write-down would apply, assume that Peterson, Inc., had a long-term investment in Salamon. This investment in Salamon was previously accounted for on the equity basis, but in 1981 Peterson sold shares in Salamon equal to 20 percent of Salamon's stock, leaving Peterson with a 10 percent interest. During 1982 and 1983 Salamon issued $100,000 in dividends on total reported net income of $150,000, and Peterson simply recorded its $10,000 as dividend income. However, at the end of 1984 Salamon paid Peterson $5,000 in dividends even though a net loss of $40,000 was reported. The total net income from 1982 to 1984 of $110,000 would have provided only $11,000 as Peterson's share of Salamon's earnings. As a result, only $1,000 of the 1984 dividends ($11,000 from Peterson's 10 percent share of Salamon's earnings for the 3 years less the $10,000 dividends already reported) are reported as dividend income by Peterson, with the other $4,000 reducing Peterson's investment in Salamon. This would be recorded as follows on Peterson's books:

12/31/84	Cash	5,000	
	Dividend income		1,000
	Investment in Salamon		4,000

When the cumulative amount of dividends received (or receivable) by Peterson (after changing from the equity method) exceed the cumulative amount of Peterson's share of Salamon's net income, the excess amount is to be treated as a liquidating dividend by Peterson (the investor). In this case, the $15,000 in dividends exceeded the $11,000 (10 percent) share of Salamon's earnings by $4,000.

Financial Statement Disclosures—Equity Method

Supplementary disclosures that are generally appropriate for equity investments that are material in amount relative to the investor's position include the following:

1. Summarized information on assets, liabilities, and operating income
2. The name of each investee and the percentage of ownership
3. The identification of those investees in which the investor owns 20 percent or more of the common stock but is not being accounted for on the equity method basis, along with an explanation

[16] Ibid.

An example of such footnote disclosure for the National Distillers and Chemical Corporation is given in Exhibit 14–8.

EXHIBIT 14–8

NATIONAL DISTILLERS AND CHEMICAL CORPORATION
Equity Investment Footnote

Note 9 — Investments in Associated Companies

Summary financial information for associated companies as a group is as follows:

Balance sheet data	December 31 1980	1979
Current assets	$286,394	$287,453
Property, plant and equipment — net	258,204	248,221
Other assets	89,835	60,515
	$634,433	$596,189
Current liabilities	$132,570	$106,963
Long-term debt	80,311	67,530
Other liabilities	60,770	61,430
Shareholders' equity	360,782	360,266
	$634,433	$596,189
National's share of shareholders' equity	$146,964	$146,028

At December 31, 1980, the Company's share of the undistributed earnings of corporate associated companies was $30,909.

Investments in associated companies consist of interests in:

	% Owned 1980	1979
National Petro Chemicals Corporation, a domestic corporation	50	50
National Helium Corporation, a domestic corporation	50	50
U.S.I. Far East Corporation, a Taiwanese corporation	43	50
Unilever Emery N.V., a Dutch corporation	—	50
Quimic S.A. de C.V., a Mexican corporation	49	49
Poliolefinas, S.A., a Brazilian corporation	28	28
United Polymers Corporation, a Taiwanese corporation	—	20
RMI Company, a domestic partnership	50	50
Syngas Company, a domestic partnership	33.6	33.3

As a result of the merger of United Polymers Corporation into U.S.I. Far East Corporation in June 1980, the Company's percentage investment in U.S.I. Far East was reduced from 50 to 43 per cent.

In December 1980, the Company sold its investment in Unilever-Emery N.V. to the other 50 per cent stockholder.

Income statement data	Year Ended December 31 1980	1979	1978
Revenues	$740,015	$619,228	$477,471
Net earnings	113,910	47,874	55,388
Distributions	74,262	55,781	36,709
National's share of earnings	39,381	25,744	26,075
National's share of distributions	34,910	24,901	15,450

Prior to 1980 the Syngas Company was in the formative stage and had no revenues. In 1980 Syngas became operational, supplying synthesis gas to the partner owners. Since the production of Syngas is purchased by the partner owners, the above income statement data for the year 1980 do not include any amounts with respect to Syngas. The Company's share of the 1980 results of operations of Syngas is included with costs and expenses in determining profits of the Chemical Division.

The Company includes its share of the income or loss and investment tax credits of the domestic partnerships, RMI Company and Syngas Company, in computing its taxable income. The resulting tax (expense) or benefit (except with respect to Syngas in 1980) is included in share of earnings of associated companies. Such (expense) benefit was ($15,272) in 1980, $1,337 in 1979 and $4,064 in 1978.

The Company is contingently liable in respect of indebtedness of certain of the associated companies for moneys borrowed. At December 31, 1980, the maximum amount of the Company's contingent liability was estimated at $30,350, assuming the other investor in one of the associated companies makes its required contribution should the liability arise.

EXHIBIT 14–9

Comparison of Methods of Accounting for Long-Term Investments

EQUITY METHOD

DATE	ACCOUNT	DEBIT	CREDIT
7/1/87	Investment in S Company Cash	300,000	300,000
7/1/87–6/30/88	Investment in S Company Income from S Company	15,000	15,000
7/1/87–6/30/88	Cash Investment in S Company	3,000	3,000
6/30/88	Income from S Company Investment in S Company	1,500	1,500
6/30/88	Income from S Company Investment in S Company	3,000	3,000

LCM METHOD

ACCOUNT	DEBIT	CREDIT
Same		
No entry		
Cash Dividend income	3,000	3,000
No entry		
Unrealized loss Allowance to reduce long-term investments to market	10,000	10,000

MARKET-VALUE METHOD

ACCOUNT	DEBIT	CREDIT
Same		
No entry		
Same as LCM		
No entry		
Realized loss Investment in S Company	10,000	10,000

Comparative Financial Statement Data
June 30, 1987

EQUITY METHOD

BALANCE SHEET	DEBIT	CREDIT
Cash	$ 3,000	
Investment in S Company	307,500	
INCOME STATEMENT		
Income from S Company		$10,500

LCM METHOD

BALANCE SHEET	DEBIT	CREDIT
Cash	$ 3,000	
Investment in S Company	300,000	
Allowance to reduce long-term investments to market		10,000
Unrealized loss	10,000	
INCOME STATEMENT		
Dividend income		3,000

MARKET-VALUE METHOD

BALANCE SHEET	DEBIT	CREDIT
Cash	$ 3,000	
Investment in S Company	290,000	
INCOME STATEMENT		
Realized loss	$ 10,000	
Dividend income		$3,000

| Market-Value Method | The **market-value method** of accounting for marketable securities may sometimes be an acceptable valuation method for those firms that have a significant amount of long-term investments in marketable securities, such as mutual funds, insurance companies, pension funds, and certain savings institutions.[17] The market-value method is straightforward, and many consider it the most relevant valuation method for marketable securities. In the equity example given above, assume that the market value of S Company falls to $9 per share on June 30, 1987. Exhibit 14–9 compares the market-value method with both the LCM method and the equity method for P's investment in S. |

The market-value method records the purchase and the receipt of dividends from S Company just as the LCM method does. However, the adjusting entry made at the end of the period records any actual change in the market value of S Company's stock. In the above example, note that although both the equity method and the LCM method report *income* from S Company, the market-value method shows the net effect to be a *loss*. Some have argued that the market-value method is the most appropriate valuation method for marketable securities because of its superior relevance, reliability of measurement, and comparability across entities. Having carefully considered the complexities of both the LCM method and the equity method, such arguments seem to have a certain appeal.

FUNDS FLOW EFFECTS

Long-term investments are generally acquired by consuming cash or working capital, resulting in a use of funds. There are some cases where long-term investments are acquired without the use of funds. For example, one entity might trade its own stock or debt or convertible debt for an interest in another entity. This is not uncommon in mergers or in acquisitions of a significant equity interest in another entity. It is also possible to exchange one long-term investment for another in those cases where a takeover bid fails. For example, both Seagram and Du Pont were acquiring Conoco stock in a bid to gain control of Conoco. When Seagram decided to pull out of the bidding, it sold its share of Conoco to Du Pont in exchange for Du Pont's stock, which resulted in Seagram's gaining an equity level investment in Du Pont. While the majority of acquisitions of long-term investments require the use of cash or working capital, some very large transactions involving increases in long-term investments do not have an effect on funds flows.

The reduction of long-term investments normally provides a source of working capital. To the extent that the sale of long-term investments results in a gain or loss, it will also affect net income and, therefore, the measurement of "funds provided by operations." An adjustment to the Long-Term Investments that are being accounted for on the LCM basis does not affect funds flows or net income but represents a change in long-term assets and owners' equity that does not provide or use funds. An analysis of the journal entry used to record any change in long-term investments is usually the best way to determine how changes in long-term investments affect cash and working capital.

[17] Industry practices, which are guided by AICPA industry guides, as well as state and federal regulations for banks, insurance companies, and thrift institutions should be considered before market values are used for measuring such assets.

SUMMARY

The accounting procedures for long-term investments examined in this chapter are not of major importance to firms that do not have significant long-term investments in the operations of other firms. However, for entities with material investments in other entities, these accounting procedures may be crucial for the appropriate measurement of the financial statements. It is important for users of financial statements to have a basic understanding of how such entities account for their unconsolidated subsidiaries; without such knowledge, users will have difficulty in evaluating reported financial results. Investments accounted for under the equity method are particularly important in this regard. The financial statements of firms that have material investments that are being accounted for using the equity method report only the net result of such investments in the formal financial statements, which may not reveal as much information as necessary to evaluate the performance of such investments. As a result, investors need to consider the supplementary footnote disclosures in order to evaluate the performance and contribution of such equity investments.

APPENDIX E
Introduction to the Concepts and Techniques of Consolidation

It is not unusual for one corporation to own the voting stock of another coporation. When this occurs, the definition of the *entity* being accounted for becomes complex. An important question is the degree of control. Does one entity have control over the actions of another? That is, are the relations between two entities at arm's length? If entity A sells a tract of land to entity B and a gain of $2,000,000 is recorded, we might assume that the selling price was at market value if A and B were unaffiliated. But the knowledge that A owns a substantial percentage of B's voting stock might make the arm's-length assumption suspect. If entity A owns 100 shares of Texaco stock, accounted for as a marketable security, the dividends received on that investment would be recorded as income and the security would be carried at lower-of-cost-or-market in conformance with GAAP for such investments. But if entity A owns 51 percent of the voting shares of entity B, of what significance are dividend payments by B? Can they be viewed as economic events independent of the will of entity A's management?

To address the issues related to entity definition, accountants have developed consolidation techniques that are used in certain cases where one company owns majority voting shares of another. Consolidation techniques take the financial statements of two legally distinct entities and combine them in such a way that the resulting consolidated statements show an "as if merged" picture. A true merger means that the acquiring entity purchases the voting stock of the entity being acquired, which subsequently goes out of existence, leaving the assets and liabilities on the books of the acquiror. However, keep in mind that consolidation accomplishes only an "*as if* merged" result. The entities do not merge in a legal sense. They both remain in existence and maintain separate accounting records.

COMPARISON OF A MERGER AND A CONSOLIDATION

Assume that entities A and B have the following summarized trial balances:

	PREMERGER TRIAL BALANCES	
	A	B
Assets	$1,000	$400
Liabilities	800	100
Common stock	200	300

Entity A then purchases 100 percent of entity B's common stock for $300 cash, and entity B ceases to be a separate entity. The merged trial balance would appear as follows:

	POSTMERGER TRIAL BALANCE
Assets	$1,100
Liabilities	900
Common stock	200

The postmerger entity A trial balance reflects the fact that $400 of assets and $100 of liabilities were purchased at a cost of $300.

If, on the other hand, the stock acquisition does not affect entity B's separate company status, entity A would debit an Investment account and credit Cash, and entity B would make no entry because the transaction was between entity B stockholders and entity A. The postacquisition trial balances would appear as follows:

	POSTACQUISITION TRIAL BALANCES	
	A	B
Investment	$300	$—
Other assets	700	400
Liabilities	800	100
Common stock	200	300

Consolidation procedures would be required to show an "as if merged" status. This involves, in this simple case, the elimination of the Investment account appearing on A's trial balance and the Common Stock appearing on B's trial balance. This is usually done by means of a consolidation worksheet, which takes the form shown in Table E-1.

TABLE E-1

CONSOLIDATION WORKSHEET

	A	B	ELIMINATIONS DEBIT	ELIMINATIONS CREDIT	CONSOLIDATED TRIAL BALANCE
Investments	300	—		300	—
Other assets	700	400			1,100
Liabilities	800	100			900
Common stock	200	300	300		200

Note that the consolidated trial balance is identical to the postmerger trial balance for entity A shown above, thus emphasizing the "as if merged" effect of the consolidation procedures. In our simple example, the consolidated entity's financial statements would report the assets held by the two entities (except for the Investment account), the liabilities owed by the two entities, and the owners' equity of the acquiror only.

CONSOLIDATION AT DATE OF ACQUISITION— WORKSHEET TECHNIQUES

On January 1, 1984, Parent Corporation purchases 100 percent of the voting stock of Subsidiary Corporation for $4,000,000 cash. Their post-acquisition summarized trial balances are as follows:

	PARENT	SUBSIDIARY
Cash	$ 150,000	$ 60,000
Accounts receivable	2,500,000	850,000
Inventories	1,100,000	660,000
Investment in Subsidiary	4,000,000	—
Depreciable assets	8,500,000	3,200,000
	$16,250,000	$4,770,000
Accounts payable	$ 560,000	$ 330,000
Long-term liabilities	1,500,000	700,000
Common stock	11,400,000	3,000,000
Retained earnings	2,790,000	740,000
	$16,250,000	$4,770,000

Note that Parent Corporation has an Investment in Subsidiary account with a balance of $4,000,000, which is the cash paid for the subsidiary's stock to the former stockholders of the subsidiary. Subsidiary Corporation, therefore, does not reflect on its books the fact that its stock is owned by Parent Corporation. How do we combine these two trial balances to achieve a single-entity perspective? Exhibit E-1 shows the consolidation worksheet used to accomplish this.

The "excess of cost over book value" is shown in the asset section of the consolidated trial balance. This amount represents (1) goodwill and/or (2) an understatement or overstatement of net assets in terms of their fair values on Subsidiary

EXHIBIT E-1

Consolidation Worksheet at Date of Acquisition

| | COMPANY TRIAL BALANCES | | ELIMINATIONS | | |
	PARENT COMPANY	SUBSIDIARY COMPANY	DEBIT	CREDIT	CONSOLIDATED TRIAL BALANCE
Cash	150,000	60,000			210,000
Accounts receivable	2,500,000	850,000			3,350,000
Inventories	1,100,000	660,000			1,760,000
Investment in Subsidiary	4,000,000	—		4,000,000	—
Excess of cost over book value			260,000		260,000
Plant, property, and equipment	8,500,000	3,200,000			11,700,000
Total assets	$16,250,000	$4,770,000			$17,280,000
Accounts payable	$ 560,000	$ 330,000			$ 890,000
Noncurrent liabilities	1,500,000	700,000			2,200,000
Common stock	11,400,000	3,000,000	3,000,000		11,400,000
Retained earnings	2,790,000	740,000	740,000		2,790,000
	$16,250,000	$4,770,000			$17,280,000

Corporation's trial balance. A determination must be made as to the nature of this excess. For instance, if it were known that Subsidiary's inventories were understated by $100,000 and all its other assets and liabilities were stated at fair values, then the consolidated balance sheet at date of acquisition would appear as follows:

Cash	$ 210,000
Accounts receivable	3,350,000
Inventories	1,860,000[a]
Goodwill	160,000[b]
Plant, property, and equipment	11,700,000
Total assets	$17,280,000
Accounts payable	$ 890,000
Noncurrent liabilities	2,200,000
Common stock	11,400,000
Retained earnings	2,790,000
Total liabilities and owners' equity	$17,280,000

[a] $1,760,000 + $100,000 (understatement) = $1,860,000.
[b] $160,000 = the cost of intangibles labeled "goodwill."

CONSOLIDATION AT A DATE SUBSEQUENT TO ACQUISITION

The principle of presenting the consolidated entity as if only one entity existed is applied to subsequent periods as well. During 1984 both Parent Corporation and Subsidiary Corporation have normal operations resulting in changes in their accounts, and all such transactions are handled on the separate books without reference to the fact that one company is owned by the other. Assume that the before-closing trial balances of each company at December 31, 1984, are as follows:

	PRECLOSING TRIAL BALANCES	
	PARENT COMPANY	SUBSIDIARY COMPANY
Cash	$ 230,000	$ 75,000
Accounts receivable	2,800,000	805,000
Receivable from Subsidiary	200,000	—
Inventories	2,900,000	700,000
Investment in Subsidiary	4,000,000	—
Plant, property, and equipment	10,300,000	4,500,000
Total assets	$20,430,000	$6,080,000
Accounts payable	$ 700,000	$ 300,000
Payable to Parent	—	200,000
Noncurrent liabilities	1,650,000	205,000
Common stock	11,400,000	3,000,000
Retained earnings	2,790,000	740,000
Sales	10,500,000	3,700,000
Cost of goods sold	(5,650,000)	(1,350,000)
Other expenses	(960,000)	(715,000)
	$20,430,000	$6,080,000

In consolidation procedures, it is crucial that we understand that the account balances shown above were not affected at all by the worksheet "entries" shown in Exhibit E–1 at January 1, 1984. A new worksheet must be constructed, and all appropriate eliminations and adjustments must be made at the end of each accounting period.

To consolidate the corporations' balance sheets and income statements, the following adjustments and eliminations are necessary:

1. The "receivable from Subsidiary" of $200,000 and the "payable to Parent" of $200,000 must be eliminated. This receivable and payable reside completely within one economic entity and have no external consequence.

2. The "investment in Subsidiary" amount must be eliminated, as was the case at the date of acquisition shown above, as well as Subsidiary's owners' equity balances. Again, this will create an "excess of cost over book value" amount, which we determined to be partly goodwill and partly a revaluation of Subsidiary's beginning inventory.

3. The $260,000 excess of cost over book value included $160,000 of goodwill at January 1, 1984. If we assume that the goodwill is amortized for consolidation purposes over 20 years, the following worksheet entry would be necessary:

Goodwill amortization expense	8,000	
Excess of cost over book value		8,000

4. If we assume that all the beginning inventory was sold during 1984, the $100,000 of beginning inventory excess of cost over book value assigned to inventory would have to be added to consolidated "cost of goods sold," resulting in the following worksheet entry:

Cost of goods sold	100,000	
Excess of cost over book value		100,000

EXHIBIT E-2

Consolidation Worksheet at December 31, 1984

	PRECLOSING TRIAL BALANCES		ELIMINATIONS		
	PARENT COMPANY	SUBSIDIARY COMPANY	DEBIT	CREDIT	CONSOLIDATED TRIAL BALANCE
Cash	$ 230,000	$ 75,000			$ 305,000
Accounts receivable	2,800,000	805,000			3,605,000
Receivable from Subsidiary	200,000	—		$ 200,000 (1)	—
Inventories	2,900,000	700,000			3,600,000
Investment in Subsidiary	4,000,000	—		4,000,000 (2)	—
Excess of cost over book value			$ 260,000 (2)	8,000 (3)	152,000
				100,000 (4)	
Plant, property, and equipment	10,300,000	4,500,000			14,800,000
Total assets	$20,430,000	$6,080,000			$22,462,000
Accounts payable	$ 700,000	$ 300,000			$ 1,000,000
Payable to Parent	—	200,000	200,000 (1)		—
Noncurrent liabilities	1,650,000	205,000			1,855,000
Common stock	11,400,000	3,000,000	3,000,000 (2)		11,400,000
Retained earnings	2,790,000	740,000	740,000 (2)		2,790,000
Sales	10,500,000	3,700,000			14,200,000
Cost of goods sold	(5,650,000)	(1,350,000)	100,000 (4)		(7,100,000)
Other expenses	(960,000)	(715,000)			(1,675,000)
Amortization of goodwill expense			8,000 (3)		(8,000)
	$20,430,000	$6,080,000			$22,462,000

Exhibit E-2 shows the consolidation worksheet at December 31, 1984, which incorporates the worksheet entries shown above (numbers in parentheses correspond to numbers in above list). Exhibit E-3 shows the consolidated balance sheet and income statement.

COMPLEXITIES IN CONSOLIDATION TECHNIQUES

To emphasize the major objectives of consolidation, the preceding discussion has been kept simple. Many events and situations can create complexities that must be handled by consolidation techniques. Intercompany sales must be eliminated against the related intercompany purchases. This creates problems because of potential carryover effects to subsequent years. Also, the parent company may own less than 100 percent of the voting shares of the subsidiary. This creates the need to report minority interests.

As examples of these two additional complexities, assume that in our previous example, Parent Company on January 1, 1984, paid $3,200,000 (instead of $4,000,000) for 80 percent (instead of 100 percent) of the common stock of Subsidiary Company. During 1984 transactions are the same as in our previous example, except that Parent sells merchandise to Subsidiary. The merchandise had a cost to Parent of $50,000 and was sold to Subsidiary for $90,000. Subsidiary sold the merchandise to a customer for $120,000. The preclosing trial balances for Parent and Subsidiary are as shown at the top of page 521.

PARENT COMPANY AND SUBSIDIARY

Consolidated Balance Sheet
December 31, 1984

Cash	$ 305,000
Accounts receivable	3,605,000
Inventories	3,600,000[a]
Goodwill	152,000[b]
Plant, property, and equipment	14,800,000
Total assets	$22,462,000
Accounts payable	$ 1,000,000
Noncurrent liabilities	1,855,000
Common stock	11,400,000
Retained earnings	8,207,000[c]
Total liability and owners's equity	$22,462,000

PARENT COMPANY AND SUBSIDIARY

Consolidated Income Statement
for the Year Ended December 31, 1984

Sales	$14,200,000
Cost of goods sold	7,100,000
Other expenses	1,675,000
Goodwill amortization	8,000[d]
Net income	$ 5,417,000

[a] Consolidated inventories at 12/31/84 equal the book value from each company's books. The excess of cost over book value in inventory is assigned to the cost of goods sold at 12/31/84. In 1985 and in the future, the worksheet adjustment to the "excess of cost over book value" will be accompanied by a debit to consolidated retained earnings.
[b] Consolidated goodwill at 12/31/84 is the original $160,000 minus one year's amortization of $8,000.
[c] Consolidated retained earnings equals Parent's retained earnings (1/1/84) balance plus the consolidated net income for 1984.
[d] Goodwill amortization expense will be $8,000 per year for 20 years. Current GAAP require that goodwill be amortized over a period of not more than 40 years (see Chapter 13, page 458 for a discussion of this policy).

To construct a consolidated income statement and balance sheet, adjustments and eliminations are necessary. Again we see that the worksheet is a convenient format with which to organize the consolidation process. The worksheet entries shown in Exhibit E–4 are described as follows:

1. Elimination of interentity receivables and payables
2. The elimination of the investment account against 80 percent of Subsidiary's owners' equity and the establishment of the initial "excess of cost over book value"
3. Amortization of one-twentieth of goodwill
4. The charge to cost of goods sold for the initial market value adjustment to inventory
5. The elimination of interentity sales and purchases

The worksheet shown in Exhibit E–4 is used to construct the formal income statement and balance sheet shown in Exhibit E–5.

	PRECLOSING TRIAL BALANCES	
	PARENT COMPANY	SUBSIDIARY COMPANY
Cash	$ 1,030,000	$ 75,000
Accounts receivable	2,800,000	805,000
Receivable from Subsidiary	200,000	—
Inventories	2,900,000	700,000
Investment in Subsidiary	3,200,000	—
Plant, property, and equipment	10,300,000	4,500,000
Total assets	$20,430,000	$6,080,000
Accounts payable	$ 700,000	$ 300,000
Payable to Parent	—	200,000
Noncurrent liabilities	1,650,000	205,000
Common stock	11,400,000	3,000,000
Retained earnings	2,790,000	740,000
Sales	10,500,000	3,700,000
Cost of goods sold	(5,650,000)	(1,350,000)
Other expenses	(960,000)	(715,000)
	$20,430,000	$6,080,000

EXHIBIT E-4

Consolidated Worksheet at 12/31/84
(With Minority Interest and Interentity Sales)

	PRECLOSING TRIAL BALANCES		ELIMINATIONS		CONSOLIDATED TRIAL BALANCE
	PARENT COMPANY	SUBSIDIARY COMPANY	DEBIT	CREDIT	
Cash	$ 1,030,000	$ 75,000			$ 1,105,000
Accounts receivable	2,800,000	805,000			3,605,000
Receivable from Subsidiary	200,000	—		$ 200,000 (1)	—
Inventories	2,900,000	700,000			3,600,000
Investment in Subsidiary	3,200,000	—		3,200,000 (2)	—
Excess of cost over book value	—	—	$ 208,000 (2)	5,400 (3) 100,000 (4)	102,000
Plant, property, and equipment	10,300,000	4,500,000			14,800,000
Total assets	$20,430,000	$6,080,000			$23,212,600
Accounts payable	$ 700,000	$ 300,000			$ 1,000,000
Payable to Parent	—	200,000	200,000 (1)		—
Noncurrent liabilities	1,650,000	205,000			1,855,000
Common stock	11,400,000	3,000,000	2,400,000 (2)		11,400,000 600,000[a]
Retained earnings	2,790,000	740,000	502,000 (2)		2,790,000 148,000[a]
Sales	10,500,000	3,700,000	90,000 (5)		14,110,000
Cost of goods sold	(5,650,000)	(1,350,000)	100,000 (4)	90,000 (5)	(7,010,000)
Other expenses	(960,000)	(715,000)			(1,675,000)
Amortization of goodwill expense	—	—	5,400 (3)		(5,400)
	$20,430,000	$6,080,000			$23,212,600

[a] Minority interest.

EXHIBIT
E–5

PARENT COMPANY AND SUBSIDIARY
Consolidated Income Statement
1984

Sales	$14,110,000[a]
Cost of goods sold	7,010,000[b]
Other expenses	1,675,000
Goodwill amortization	5,400[c]
Total net income	$ 5,419,600
Less minority interest	327,000[d]
Consolidated net income	$ 5,092,600

[a] Consolidated sales = (Total separate sales of $14,200,000 minus interentity sale of $90,000) = $14,110,000.
[b] Consolidated cost of goods sold = (Total separate cost of goods sold of $7,000,000 plus the market-value adjustment of $100,000 minus the interentity purchase of $90,000) = $7,010,000.
[c] Goodwill amortization = (1/20)($108,000) = $5,400.
[d] Minority interest in net income = (20% of Subsidiary's separate net income of $1,635,000) = $327,000.

PARENT COMPANY AND SUBSIDIARY
Consolidated Balance Sheet
December 31, 1984

Cash	$ 1,105,000
Accounts receivable	3,605,000
Inventories	3,600,000
Goodwill	102,600[a]
Plant, property, and equipment	14,800,000
Total assets	$23,212,600
Accounts payable	1,000,000
Noncurrent liabilities	1,855,000
Common stock	11,400,000
Retained earnings	7,882,600[b]
Minority interest	1,075,000[c]
	$23,212,600

[a] Goodwill = ($108,000)(19/20) = $102,600.
[b] Retained earnings -(Parent's 1/1/84 balance of $2,790,000 plus consolidated net income of $5,092,600) = $7,882,600.
[c] Minority interest = (20% of Subsidiary's 1/1/84 owners' equity of $3,740,000 plus 20% of Subsidiary's separate net income of $1,635,000) = ($748,000 + 327,000) = $1,075,000.

The parent-subsidiary examples shown in this appendix introduce the worksheet approach to consolidation procedures. The concept that motivates these techniques is the entity concept. In real-world settings, many additional difficulties face the accountant who attempts to consolidate separate legal entities in one reporting economic entity. One source of complexity is the treatment of income taxes. Income taxes are extremely complex for single entities, and that complexity escalates for consolidated entities. For instance, although the entity consolidates for financial accounting purposes, it may elect to file separate returns for income tax purposes, creating extreme complexity for consolidations.

In summary, the consolidation procedures are very important in accounting for certain affiliated entities. The subject is immensely complex and requires a tremendous effort to master. Advanced accounting texts cover this subject in detail.

Q14-1   When is the cost method appropriate for long-term investments?

Q14-2   When is the LCM method appropriate for long-term investments?

Q14-3   When is the equity method appropriate for long-term investments?

Q14-4   When is the present-value method appropriate for long-term investments?

Q14-5   When is the market-value method appropriate for long-term investments?

Q14-6   How is the interest on bonds purchased between interest payment dates handled by the party investing in the bonds?

Q14-7   What two economic flows are provided by bonds?

Q14-8   What is a bond discount? A bond premium?

Q14-9   What is the impact on interest income when a bond discount is amortized?

Q14-10   What is the impact on "working capital from operations" when a bond discount is amortized? A bond premium is amortized?

Q14-11   When is straight-line amortization of a bond discount or a bond premium appropriate?

Q14-12   How might one determine whether an investor company can exercise a significant influence over an investee?

Q14-13   What is the difference between the LCM method for long-term investments and the LCM method for short-term investments?

Q14-14   Why are bonds generally considered to be less risky than common stock?

Q14-15   Why do some accountants believe that the LCM method of accounting for investments is internally inconsistent?

Q14-16   When is the equity method permitted for investees that are more than 50 percent owned by the investor entity?

Q14-17   What is the title of the owners' equity account used in the LCM method?

Q14-18   What is the objective of the equity method accounting procedures?

CASES

C14-1   You have recently been hired by a national CPA firm, and on your second assignment in January 1985 you are reviewing the short-term and long-term investments of the Warren Corporation. Warren has a significant amount of resources tied up in investments. Because of Warren's liquid position, the investment community is expecting it to become involved in merger activity. In reviewing the activity in the Long-Term Investments account, you note that 50,000 shares of Duo Tex stock that were purchased in 1982 for $10 per share were transferred to the Long-Term Investments account (from the Temporary Investments account) on December 15, 1984, when the market price was $8 per share. The following entry was recorded:

12/15/84	Long-term investments	400,000	
	Retained earnings	100,000	
	Temporary investments		500,000

On December 15, 1984, Warren Corporation purchased 50,000 additional shares of Duo Tex for $8 per share as a temporary investment.

REQUIRED

1. Discuss the propriety of these entries. Was the accounting treatment correctly handled?
2. Would your judgment regarding the propriety of Warren's accounting treatment have been different if $400,000 had been invested in some other stock (besides Duo Tex) on December 20, 1984?

C14–2 Mr. C. J. Bartley, the president of Bartley, Inc., is on the board of directors of ten other corporations. Mr. Bartley is not only a director of the Jayson Corporation but also a member of its "audit committee," to whom Jayson's auditors must report. Bartley, Inc., has owned a 19.85 percent interest in Jayson Corporation as a long-term investment since 1965, long before Mr. Bartley became a member of the Jayson board. Bartley, Inc., in accordance with *APB Opinion No. 18,* "The Equity Method of Accounting for Investments in Common Stock," has always accounted for the investment in Jayson at lower-of-cost-or-market. Jayson's net income and dividends over the past 6 years have been somewhat unusual:

	NET INCOME	DIVIDENDS
1986	$5,736,000	$2,500,000
1985	5,420,000	1,100,000
1984	5,180,000	4,600,000
1983	4,960,000	3,840,000
1982	5,020,000	500,000
1981	4,813,000	2,100,000

REQUIRED

1. Given *no* additional information, how should Bartley, Inc., be accounting for its investment in Jayson Corporation? Explain your answer.
2. What additional information about Bartley, Inc., or Jayson Corporation might influence your answer to requirement 1?
3. If Mr. R. D. Jayson owned 35 percent of Jayson Corporation's stock, how would your answer to requirement 1 be affected?

C14–3 Sorter Corporation owned 50 percent of the voting stock of Ronen Corporation. Ronen Corporation owned 50 percent of the voting stock of Sorter Corporation.

REQUIRED Explain how these investments would be accounted for on the books of both Sorter and Ronen.

C14–4 (CPA ADAPTED) The most common method of accounting for unconsolidated subsidiaries is the equity method.

REQUIRED

1. Under what circumstances should the equity method be applied?
2. At what amount should the initial investment be recorded, and what events subsequent to the initial investment (if any) would change this amount?
3. How are investment earnings recognized under the equity method, and how is the amount determined?

C14–5 The long-term investments portfolio of Ng, Inc., consists of the following items as of the end of 1984:

SECURITY	ORIGINAL COST	MARKET 12/31/84	MARKET 12/31/83	NUMBER OF YEARS HELD
A	$ 37,600	$ 41,220	$ 41,250	9
B	65,731	21,725	21,430	10
C	53,608	64,230	63,900	7
D	28,145	36,590	36,380	5
	$185,084	$163,765	$162,960	

Eight years ago the market value of security B fell to $19,000. It has continued to increase steadily in value since that time. On December 31, 1984, Ng, Inc., recorded the following entry:

| Realized loss on investments | 43,000 | |
| Investment in security B | | 43,000 |

Ng, Inc., had also realized a gain on the sale of used equipment during 1984 in the amount of $45,000. Ng proposed to report a single item, "other gains and loss," at $2,000 in the 1984 income statement.

REQUIRED Discuss the propriety of the entry recorded by Ng for $43,000 and the proposed disclosure in the context of GAAP. In your discussion consider the relevance, reliability, and comparability aspects of accounting for investments, and illustrate what you believe would be the best financial statement presentation for Ng.

EXERCISES

E14-1 On January 2, 1984, a calendar–year-end entity purchased some bonds as a long-term investment. These bonds cost $95,735 and had a face (par) value of $100,000 and a stated interest rate of 5 percent. The bonds mature in 5 years. Interest payments on the bonds are made on January 1 and July 1 of each year. The effective yield on the bonds on January 2, 1984, was 6 percent.

REQUIRED

1. Using the effective interest method to account for the bonds, how much interest income would be recorded for 1984?
2. What is the net book value of the bonds on December 31, 1984?

E14-2 In January 1985 the Harold Corporation acquired 20 percent of the outstanding common stock of Chan Company for $400,000. This investment gave Harold the ability to influence, but not control, Chan. The book value of these shares was $300,000. The excess of cost over book value was attributed to an identifiable *intangible* asset that was undervalued on Chan's balance sheet and had a remaining useful life of 10 years. For the year ended December 31, 1985, Chan reported net income of $90,000 and paid cash dividends of $20,000 on its common stock.

REQUIRED What is the carrying value of Harold's investment in Chan Company at December 31, 1985?

E14-3 On December 31, 1984, Bentenhaus Corporation acquired a 40 percent interest in Otis for $215,000 cash. The following data pertain to Otis at the date of acquisition:

| | DECEMBER 31, 1984 | |
	BOOK VALUE	APPRAISAL VALUE
Nondepreciable assets	$120,000	$125,000
Depreciable assets—net	480,000	555,000
Total assets	$600,000	$680,000
Liabilities	200,000	200,000
Net assets (100%)	$400,000	$480,000

For the year ending December 31, 1985, Otis reported net income of $100,000 and declared cash dividends of $10,000 payable on January 1, 1986.

REQUIRED

1. What is the amount of goodwill purchased by Bentenhaus?
2. The depreciable equipment has an expected remaining life of 30 years on a straight-line basis. Bentenhaus amortized all intangible assets over a 10-year life. What is the net change in the Investment in Otis account for the year ending December 31, 1985?

3. What is the *net* income statement impact on Bentenhaus's investment in Otis for the year ending December 31, 1985?

E14–4 Zero company is accounting for its long-term investments in marketable equity securities by using the lower-of-cost-or-market method. At the end of 1987, Zero Company's investments were as follows:

	DECEMBER 31, 1987	
	COST	MARKET
Security X	$1,000	$ 700
Security Y	2,000	2,400
Security Z	3,000	2,500
Total	$6,000	$5,600

The Allowance to Reduce Investments to Market account had a credit balance of $500, which was established in 1986. There were no sales or purchases during 1987.

REQUIRED

1. Prepare any adjusting entries required as of December 31, 1987.

2. Illustrate the way long-term investments would appear in the 1986–1987 comparative balance sheets.

E14–5 The following data pertain to Punk Rock, Inc., as of December 31, 1984:

	BOOK VALUE	MARKET VALUE
Nondepreciable assets	$ 620,000	$ 750,000
Depreciable assets	730,000	1,000,000
Total assets	$1,350,000	$1,750,000
Liabilities	450,000	450,000
Net assets	$ 900,000	$1,300,000
Common stock outstanding—100,000 shares		

On January 1, 1985, Disco Ltd. buys 25 percent of Punk's outstanding stocks at $19 per share. At the date of acquisition, the composite life of Punk's depreciable assets is 22½ years. Punk paid dividends of $120,000 during 1985 and reported net income of $680,000. Assume that Disco amortizes all intangible assets over a 20-year period.

REQUIRED What is the value of the asset Long-Term Investment in Punk Rock, on Disco's books as of January 1, 1986?

E14–6 (CPA ADAPTED)

_____ 1. Drab, Inc., owns 40 percent of the outstanding stock of Gloom Company. During 1985 Drab received a $4,000 cash dividend from Gloom. What effect did this dividend have on Drab's 1985 financial statements?
   a. Increased total assets   c. Increased income
   b. Decreased total assets   d. Decreased the investment account

_____ 2. Investor, Inc., owns a 40 percent interest in Alpha Corporation. During the calendar year 1985, Alpha had net income of $100,000 and paid dividends of $10,000. Investor mistakenly recorded these transactions using the *cost method* rather than the *equity method* of accounting. What effect would this have on (1) the Long-Term Investment in Alpha account, (2) net income, and (3) retained earnings, respectively?
   a. Understate 1, overstate 2, overstate 3   c. Overstate 1, overstate 2, overstate 3
   b. Overstate 1, understate 2, understate 3   d. Understate 1, understate 2, understate 3

_____ 3. How should the goodwill of a 40 percent owned subsidiary be written off?
   a. As soon as possible to retained earnings
   b. By systematic charges to retained earnings over the period benefited, but not in excess of 40 years
   c. By systematic charges to "earnings from unconsolidated subsidiaries" over the period benefited, but not in excess of 40 years
   d. Should not be written off until the "investment in subsidiary" is sold

_____ 4. A parent corporation that uses the equity method of accounting for its investment in a 40 percent owned subsidiary, which earned $20,000 and paid $5,000 in dividends, made the following entries:

Investment in subsidiary	8,000	
Earnings in unconsolidated subsidiary		8,000
Cash	2,000	
Dividend revenue		2,000

What effect will these entries have on the parent's statement of financial position?
   a. Financial position will be fairly stated.
   b. Investment in subsidiary will be overstated; retained earnings, understated.
   c. Investment in subsidiary will be understated; retained earnings, understated.
   d. Investment in subsidiary will be overstated; retained earnings, overstated.

_____ 5. On January 1, 1986, Brevity Corporation acquired, as a long-term investment, a 40 percent common stock interest in Astute Company for $130,000. On that date, Astute had net assets of $300,000. During 1986 Astute reported net income of $60,000 and declared and paid cash dividends of $15,000. What is the maximum amount of income that Brevity can report from this investment for the calendar year 1986?
   a. $ 6,000   c. $23,750
   b. $18,000   d. $24,000

E14-7 The long-term investment portfolio of the Takem Corporation, accounted for on an LCM basis, consisted of the following items as of the end of 1984:

	12/31/84	AS OF 12/31/83	
SECURITY	MARKET	COST	MARKET
Alpha	$ 6,910	$ 7,350	$ 6,520
Beta	6,415	6,100	4,800
Gamma	10,100	9,840	11,580
	$23,425	$23,290	$22,900

During January 1984 Takem purchased 100 shares of Delta as a *short-term* investment for $18 per share. The market price of Delta (the only short-term investment ever purchased by Takem) was $16.75 per share by December 31, 1984. During December 1984 Takem reclassified one-half of the Gamma stock to its short term portfolio (entry has not been recorded as yet).

REQUIRED

1. Prepare the necessary entries to record Takem's investment activities and adjustments for 1984.
2. Discuss the impact on Takem's financial position at December 31, 1984, with and without the transfer of Gamma.

E14-8 On July 1, 1983, a company purchases one hundred, $1,000 par value bonds for $1,114.69 each. Each bond pays interest of $70 on June 30 and December 31 of each year until maturity on July 1, 1993.

REQUIRED What is the approximate effective interest rate related to the acquisition? Show computations. (*Hint:* Use the tables in Appendix H at the back of the book.)

E14–9 On October 11, 1983, Master Security Company pays $1,000,000 for bonds of GMA, Inc., that pay interest semiannually on June 30 and December 31. On December 31, 1983, the end of Master's fiscal year, the following adjusting entry is made:

Bond investment	3,333	
Interest receivable	16,667	
Bond interest revenue		20,000

REQUIRED Is the effective interest rate on this investment less than or greater than the stated interest rate on the bonds? What are the nominal and effective interest rates for this investment? Explain.

E14–10 (CPA ADAPTED)*

_____ 1. The Nugget Company's balance sheet on December 31, 1986, is as follows:

ASSETS	
Cash	$ 100,000
Accounts receivable	200,000
Inventories	500,000
Property, plant, and equipment	900,000
	$1,700,000
LIABILITIES AND STOCKHOLDERS' EQUITY	
Current liabilities	$ 300,000
Long-term debt	500,000
Common stock (par $1 per share)	100,000
Additional paid-in capital	200,000
Retained earnings	600,000
	$1,700,000

On December 31, 1986, the Bronc Company purchased all of Nugget's outstanding common stock for $1,500,000 cash. On that date, the fair (market) value of Nugget's inventories was $450,000, and the fair value of Nugget's property, plant, and equipment was $1,000,000. The fair values of all of Nugget's other assets and liabilities were equal to their book values. As a result of Bronc's acquisition of Nugget, the consolidated balance sheet of Bronc and Nugget should reflect goodwill in the amount of
a. $500,000
b. $550,000
c. $600,000
d. $650,000

_____ 2. Assuming (1) all the information in the preceding question and (2) that Bronc's balance sheet (unconsolidated) at December 31, 1986, reflected retained earnings of $2,000,000, what amount of retained earnings should be shown in the December 31, 1986, consolidated balance sheet of Bronc and its new subsidiary, Nugget?
a. $2,000,000
b. $2,600,000
c. $2,800,000
d. $3,150,000

_____ 3. On January 1, 1986, Tom Kat, Inc., purchased 25 percent of Carmel's outstanding shares of stock for $115,000 cash. The investment will be accounted for by the equity method. On that date, Carmel's net assets (book and fair value) were $300,000. Tom Kat has determined that the excess of the cost of its investment in Carmel over its share of Carmel's net assets has an indeterminate life.
Carmel's net income for the year ended December 31, 1986, was $50,000. During 1986 Tom Kat received $5,000 cash dividends from Carmel. There were no other transactions between the two companies. On January 1, 1986, the investment in Carmel would be recorded on Tom Kat's books at
a. $75,000
b. $85,000
c. $115,000
d. $155,000

_____ 4. Assuming all the information in the preceding question and *ignoring income taxes,* Tom Kat's income statement for the year ended December 31, 1986, should include "equity in 1986 net income of Carmel" in the amount of

a. $7,500
b. $11,500

c. $12,500
d. $6,500

_____ 5. On January 1, 1984, the Pint Corporation paid $400,000 for 10,000 shares of Quart Company's common stock, which represents a 10 percent long term investment in Quart. Pint received dividends of $1 per share from Quart in 1984. Quart reported net income of $150,000 for the year ended December 31, 1984. The market value of Quart's common stock on December 31, 1984, was $39 per share. *Ignoring income taxes,* the amount reported in Pint's 1984 income statement as a result of Pint's investment in Quart was

a. $10,000
b. $15,000

c. $30,000
d. 0

E14–11 Assume that Masco has net income of $14,500,000 from operations for 1984. Included in arriving at the net income figure was the following:

Cash	300,000	
Bond investment		20,000
Bond interest income		280,000
(To record interest income and amortize bond discount for year)		

REQUIRED Given no other information, compute "working capital from operations" for Masco for 1984. (Ignore taxes).

E14–12* Ace company discloses the following items on its consolidated income statement:

Total net income	$12,889,000
Less minority interest	480,000
Consolidated net income	$12,409,000

REQUIRED

1. If the percentage of ownership by Ace is 60 percent, what was the subsidiary's separate net income? Show computations.
2. What reference to minority interest would you expect to see on Ace's consolidated balance sheet?

PROBLEMS

P14–1 Northwest Resources, Inc., purchased 20 Fleming, Inc., $1,000 par bonds on April 1, 1983 as a long-term investment. The bonds had a stated interest rate of 10 percent and paid interest semiannually on April 1 and October 1 of each year. The effective interest rate was 12 percent, and the maturity date was April 1, 2003.

REQUIRED

1. Record Northwest's journal entry on the date of acquisition. Show computations.
2. If Northwest sells 10 of the bonds on April 1, 1984, for $10,500, what journal entry is required? Show computations.

P14–2 On September 1, 1985, the Consul Company acquired $10,000 face value 8 percent bonds of Envoy Corporation at 104. The bonds were dated May 1, 1985, and they mature on April 30, 1990, with interest payable each October 31 and April 30.

REQUIRED

1. What entry should Consul make to record the purchase of the bonds on September 1, 1985?
2. What entry should Consul make to record the receipt of interest on October 31, 1985?
3. What entries should Consul make to adjust its investment at December 31, 1985, the year-end of the company, assuming the cost method is used to record the investment?
4. Prepare an amortization table pertaining to the investment in Envoy Corporation bonds.

P14–3 Marian Research, Inc., acquires the following long-term investments in bonds on January 1, 1984:

Number of bonds	10
Par value	$1,000
Stated interest rate	13%
Effective interest rate	14%
Interest payment schedule	Semiannually on 6/30 and 12/31
Maturity date	1/1/99

REQUIRED Construct an amortization schedule for the above investment assuming that Marian has a December 31 fiscal year-end.

P14–4 Assume all the information given in the preceding problem.

REQUIRED If Marian has a March 31 fiscal year-end, record all the journal entries related to the investment in bonds for 1984 and 1985.

P14–5 On June 30, 1985, Arizona, Inc., acquired a 30 percent interest in Safeway's stock for $76,000 cash. The following data are available for Safeway at June 30:

Assets, nondepreciable—book value	$ 80,000
Assets, nondepreciable—market value	100,000
Assets, depreciable (10-year remaining life)—book value	100,000
Assets, depreciable (10-year remaining life)—market value	150,000
Liabilities—book value	60,000
Liabilities—market value	50,000
Net income—year to date	48,000
Dividends declared and paid—year to date	30,000

Both Arizona and Safeway have December 31 year-ends. At year-end, Safeway reported total net income of $100,000 and dividends declared and paid of $60,000. The net income included an extraordinary loss of $20,000 from flood damages that occurred in September. Safeway and Arizona use straight-line depreciation. Arizona amortizes intangible assets over a 40-year period.

REQUIRED

1. Record the acquisition of Safeway stock on June 30, 1985.
2. Record any necessary entries to account for the investment in Safeway at December 31, 1985.
3. Record the sale of 10 percent of Arizona's investment in Safeway (3 percent of Safeway's total stock) on January 1, 1986, for $8,200 cash.

P14–6 The following activities occurred in the Long-Term Investments account of the Neritz Corporation during 1984:

DATE	EVENT
1/19	Sold 25 shares of Maxin for $900 net.
2/28	Acquired debentures of Arren, Inc., for 89.2156 percent plus accrued interest since September 1. These 8 percent bonds mature to $80,000 in 6 years and pay interest semiannually.
3/23	Sold 100 shares of Loredo for $4,750 net.
3/23	Reclassified 100 shares of Loredo from long-term to short-term.
4/24	Purchased 150 shares of Silverton for $5,700.
5/25	Sold 300 shares of Bolder for $7,500 net.
8/28	Acquired 200 shares of Maxin for $32 per share net.
9/29	Sold 150 shares of Silverton for $37 per share.
10/20	Purchased 500 shares of Mimi Heat for $10.50 per share.
10/30	Sold 75 shares of Maxin for $35 per share.

The long-term investment portfolio contained the following additional data at year-end:

	As of 12/31/83		MARKET VALUE PER SHARE	
	NUMBER OF SHARES	COST PER SHARE	12/31/83	12/31/84
Maxin	150	$15	$35	$36
Loredo	200	55	46	45
Silverton	200	28	32	40
Bolder	300	35	27	20
Arren debentures	—	—	—	88%+
Mimi Heat	—	—	—	10.75

REQUIRED

1. Record the activities for 1984 and all necessary adjusting entries, assuming Neritz uses a FIFO flow assumption for all marketable securities.

2. Repeat requirement 1, assuming Neritz uses an average flow assumption for securities.

3. Evaluate the performance of Neritz Corporation's long-term investments during 1984.

P14–7 On January 2, 1990, the Pie Company acquired a 40 percent interest (4,000 shares) in the Cherry Company for $84,000. At the date of acquisition, the following information related to Cherry Company was available:

	BOOK VALUE	MARKET VALUE
Current assets	$ 80,000	$100,000
Long-term depreciable assets (10-year remaining life)	100,000	140,000
	$180,000	
Current and long-term liabilities	40,000	40,000
Common stock (at par)	100,000	
Capital in excess of par	20,000	
Retained earnings	20,000	
	$180,000	

At December 31, 1990, Cherry Company reported $20,000 net income (including a $5,000 extraordinary loss). During the year, Cherry declared several cash dividends totaling $6,000, but as of year-end it had only paid $4,000 in dividends.

Pie Company amortizes any purchased goodwill over a 20-year life. The market price of Cherry's stock has increased steadily since Pie's purchase.

REQUIRED

1. Record the journal entry or entries to record the acquisition of Cherry, assuming (a) the equity method was used and (b) the LCM method was used.

2. Record the journal entry or entries to record the dividends of Cherry, assuming (a) the equity method was used and (b) the LCM method was used.

3. Record all the other entries necessary to record the above information on Pie Company's books using (a) the equity method and (b) the LCM method. Show and clearly label all computations, and briefly explain the purpose of any necessary entries.

P14–8 Investing, Inc., owned a 10 percent interest in the net assets of Divided Company, which it acquired on July 1, 1982, for $500,000, and which has been accounted for on an LCM basis since then. It was estimated that the total fair market value of Divided exceeded the book value of the net assets by $2,000,000 as of June 30, 1982, with 60 percent of this difference attributable to undervalued depreciable assets with a remaining life of 15 years and 25 percent of the difference attributable to goodwill. The earnings and dividend history of Divided for the period January 1, 1982, to December 31, 1983, were as follows:

QUARTER ENDING	NET EARNINGS	CASH DIVIDENDS	NET BOOK VALUE
3/31/82	$110,000	$50,000	$2,970,000
6/30/82	80,000	50,000	3,000,000
9/30/82	70,000	50,000	3,020,000
12/31/82	130,000	65,000	3,085,000
3/31/83	150,000	60,000	3,175,000
6/30/83	95,000	60,000	3,210,000
9/30/83	87,000	60,000	3,237,000
12/31/83	165,000	75,000	3,327,000

On October 1, 1983, Investing acquired an additional 20 percent interest in Divided for $1,100,000, making Investing the largest shareholder of Divided common stock. Both Divided and Investing are December 31 year-end companies. The excess of the price paid for the additional 20 percent interest over the net book value of Divided's net assets is attributable in part to goodwill (30 percent of the difference) and undervalued depreciable assets (50 percent of the difference) that have a remaining expected life of 15 years.

Investing's accounting policies include amortization of all intangibles over the maximum allowable period, and depreciation on a straight-line basis. Investing has not had any business activity with Divided except for the above-mentioned purchases, and it has not had any Investing, Inc., corporate officers on Divided's board of directors as of December 31, 1983.

REQUIRED Record all of the necessary journal entries to account for Investing's interest in Divided Company for 1982 and 1983.

P14–9 On April 1, 1990, Meddaugh Corporation purchased a 30 percent interest in the common stock of Beta Company, whose total outstanding shares equal 100,000. Beta depreciates its assets over a 20-year life, and the average remaining life at this date is 10 years. Meddaugh has used present-value computations to determine that Beta's *total* goodwill is $24,000. Meddaugh, whose report period ends December 31 each year, amortizes all intangibles over the maximum allowable period. Data for Beta Company at April 1, 1990, are as follows:

	BOOK VALUE	MARKET VALUE
Nondepreciable assets	$ 60,000	$ 70,000
Depreciable assets—net	80,000	100,000
Total assets	$140,000	$170,000
Liabilities	50,000	50,000

REQUIRED

1. Record the purchase of Beta on the books of the Meddaugh Corporation.

2. Assume that Beta reports net income for 1990 and cash dividends as follows:

QUARTER ENDED	REPORTED NET INCOME	DIVIDENDS
Mar. 31	$10,000	$ 5,000
June 30	12,000	6,000
Sept. 30	13,000	7,000
Dec. 31	15,000	7,000
	$50,000	$25,000

Record any entries necessary to state the balance properly in the Investment in Beta account at December 31, 1990. Clearly label all computations and entries.

3. On January 1, 1991, Meddaugh sold 10 percent of its investment in Beta (3,000 shares) for $2 per share. Record the sale on Meddaugh's books.

4. If, after some years passed, you discovered that Beta Company was 51 percent owned by an individual who was also chairman of the board and president of the company, would it influence your method of accounting for Beta on Meddaugh's books? Explain briefly the alternative methods of accounting for long-term investments in stock and when they should be used.

P14–10 On June 30, 1984, the Easy River Corporation purchased a 10 percent interest in the 100,000 outstanding shares of Golden Mills, Inc., for $1,500,000. Because of Golden's performance and outlook, Easy River acquired an additional 20 percent interest (20,000 shares) on January 3, 1986, for $3,000,000. The following data are available as of December 31, 1986, for Golden Mills, Inc.:

DATE	BOOK VALUE OF NET ASSETS	ESTIMATED REMAINING LIFE OF DEPRECIABLE ASSETS	NET INCOME FOR YEAR (OR YEAR TO DATE)	DIVIDENDS PAID FOR YEAR (OR YEAR TO DATE)	STOCK PRICE	MARKET VALUE OF IDENTIFIABLE NET ASSETS
1/1/84	$10,000,000	24	—	—	—	$11,000,000
6/30/84	10,400,000	24	$ 500,000	$100,000	$150	12,000,000
12/31/84	10,700,000	23	1,000,000	300,000	145	13,000,000
12/31/85	11,500,000	23	1,200,000	400,000	150	14,000,000
12/31/86	12,400,000	24	1,500,000	600,000	156	15,000,000

Both Golden Mills and Easy River are December 31 year-end companies. Both companies use straight-line depreciation for all depreciable assets, and they amortize all intangibles over a 10-year life on a straight-line basis. The differences between the book and market values of the identifiable net assets are attributable to valuation differences in both depreciable assets (75 percent of all differences) and nondepreciable assets and liabilities (25 percent of all differences) over the period 1984 to 1986.

REQUIRED

1. Record the investment in Golden Mills from June 1984 to the end of 1986 assuming the LCM method is used.

2. Record the investment in Golden Mills from June 1984 to the end of 1986 assuming the market-value method is used.

3. Record the investment in Golden Mills from June 1984 to the end of 1986 assuming the equity method is used.

4. Discuss the reliability and comparability of these three measurement methods.

P14–11 Assume the information given in the preceding problem. Assume also that Easy River used the LCM method to record its investment in Golden Mills from June 1984 to January 1986. On January 3, 1986, due to the additional purchase of Golden Mills stock, Easy River changes to the equity method of accounting.

REQUIRED

1. Record the change to the equity method on January 3, 1986.
2. Record any necessary entries to account for Easy River's investment in Golden Mills for the remainder of 1986.

P14–12 (CPA ADAPTED) The North Salem Company has supplied you with the following information regarding two investments made during 1985:

1. On January 1, 1985, North Salem purchased 40 percent of the 500,000 shares of the voting common stock of the Yorktown Company for $2,400,000 cash, representing 40 percent of Yorktown's net worth. Yorktown's net income for the year ended Dcember 31, 1985, was $750,000. Yorktown paid dividends of $.50 per share in 1985. The market value of Yorktown's common stock was $14 per share on December 31, 1985. North Salem exercised significant influence over Yorktown's operating and financial policies.
2. On July 1, 1985, North Salem purchased 15,000 shares representing 5 percent of the voting common stock of the Mahopac Company for $450,000 cash. Mahopac's net income for the 6 months ended December 31, 1985, was $350,000 and for the year ended December 31, 1985, was $600,000. Mahopac paid dividends of $.30 per share each quarter during 1985 to stockholders of record on the last day of each quarter. The market value of Mahopac's common stock was $32 per share on January 1, 1985, and $34 per share on December 31, 1985.

REQUIRED

1. As a result of these two investments, what balance should be in North Salem's Investments account at December 31, 1985? Show supporting computations in good form.
2. As a result of these two investments, what income should North Salem report for the year ended December 31, 1985? Show supporting computations in good form.

P14–13 (CPA ADAPTED) On September 1, 1977, the Horn Company used cash to purchase 200,000 shares representing 45 percent of Mat Company's outstanding stock. As a result of the purchase, Horn is able to exercise significant influence over Mat's operating and financial policies. Goodwill of $500,000 was appropriately recognized by Horn at the date of the purchase.

On December 1, 1978, Horn purchased 300,000 shares representing 30 percent of Simon Company's outstanding stock for $2,500,000 cash. The stockholders' equity section of Simon's balance sheet at the date of the acquisition was as follows:

Common stock, par value $2 per share	$2,000,000
Additional paid-in capital	1,000,000
Retained earnings	4,000,000
	$7,000,000

Furthermore, at the date of acquisition, the fair value of Simon's property, plant, and equipment, net, was $3,800,000, whereas the book value was $3,500,000. For all of Simon's other assets and liabilities, the fair value and book value were equal. As a result of the transaction, Horn is able to exercise significant influence over Simon's operating and financial policies.

Assume that Horn amortizes goodwill over the maximum period allowed and takes a full year's amortization in the year of purchase.

REQUIRED Prepare a schedule computing the amount of goodwill and accumulated amortization at December 31, 1978, and the goodwill amortization for the year ended December 31, 1978. Show supporting computations in good form.

P14–14 (CPA ADAPTED) For the past 5 years Herbert has maintained an investment (properly accounted for and reported upon) in Broome amounting to a 10 percent interest in Broome's voting common stock. The purchase price was $700,000, and the underlying net equity in Broome at the date of purchase was $620,000. On January 2 of the current year, Herbert purchased an additional 15 percent of Broome's voting common stock for $1,200,000;

the underlying net equity of the additional investment at January 2 was $1,000,000. Broome has been profitable and has paid dividends annually since Herbert's initial acquisition.

REQUIRED Discuss how this increase in ownership affects the accounting for, and reporting upon, the investment in Broome. Include in your discussion adjustments, if any, to the amount shown prior to the increase in investment to bring the amount into conformity with generally accepted accounting principles. Also describe how current and subsequent periods would be reported upon.

P14–15 On December 30, 1984, the Icerman Corporation (a calendar-year company) sold one-half of its 26,000 shares of stock in the Fordham Corporation, recording the following entry:

12/30/84	Cash	468,000	
	Loss on sale of stock	78,000	
	Equity investment in subsidiary		546,000

On December 31, 1984, Fordham Corporation paid a $.25-per-share cash dividend to shareholders of record as of December 31, 1984. The market value of Fordham stock closed at $36.50 per share on December 31, 1984.

Icerman had been accounting for the investment in Fordham on an equity basis but sold half of its stock because of Fordham's poor earnings record. A dispute between Icerman and Fordham over the way Fordham management was handling the situation preceded the sale. Fordham reported a net loss for 1984.

Icerman has been using the LCM method to account for its other long-term stock investments, which consisted of the following securities:

STOCK	COST	MARKET 12/31/83	12/31/84
Jaenicke Co.	$15,000	$16,000	$15,000
Mastro, Inc.	31,000	19,000	31,500
Luoma Ltd.	27,000	30,000	28,000
	$73,000	$65,000	$74,500

REQUIRED Record any entries necessary to account for Icerman's long-term investments as of December 31, 1984, for the year then ended.

P14–16* Merit Contractors owns 100 percent of the common stock of Bates, Inc. During the year, Merit purchased supplies from Bates at a price of $60,000. The supplies had an initial purchase price of $50,000. The supplies remain in Merit's inventory of supplies at year-end.

REQUIRED How would the intercompany sale affect Merit's consolidated financial statements?

15

Leased Assets

OVERVIEW

Acquisition of productive resources can be accomplished through immediate cash payment, deferred cash payments, exchanges of assets, payment in equity securities, donations by outside parties, and so on. In this chapter we analyze in detail various types of deferred cash payment acquisitions referred to as *leasing.* We view the leasing process from several points of view. On the one hand, the user of the leased assets, termed the *lessee,* though not the legal owner, may have all the normal property rights associated with ownership. On the other hand, the legal owner of the leased assets, the *lessor,* may in some instances merely be involved as financing agent whose primary goal is to generate interest revenue, with no intention of owning the leased asset in the long run. The manufacturer, or other initial owner of the leased asset, may be involved in a leasing transaction that generates both an initial gross profit on the sale and interest revenue from payments made by the lessee on the unpaid balance in the long-term lease receivable.

Accountants must determine the economic substance of leasing transactions in order that the financial statements of the parties to those agreements properly report their assets, liabilities, and owners' equity. For this reason, policies have been developed that attempt to see through the legal form of lease contracts to the economic substance. If the entity that utilizes a resource is merely renting it, it would not be appropriate for the entity to recognize it as an asset. If, on the other hand, the lessee has the normal ownership property rights, its accounting records should reflect an asset for the acquisition price, a liability for any unpaid balance, and periodic depreciation of the asset.

An analogous situation exists in evaluating the lessor's position regarding leased resources. If the lessor retains ownership property rights, then its accounting reports must show the resource as a productive asset, with depreciation shown as an expense and rents shown as revenues. If the lessor is operating merely as a financing agent, then the lessor's statements will reflect a receivable and interest revenue.

This chapter covers accounting concepts, techniques, and rules that are relevant to current practices related to lease accounting. We will concentrate on a lease's contractual terms as the primary element for analysis, thereby emphasizing the symmetry of accounting for both the lessor and lessee, the two parties to the agreement. We shall see that accountants are guided by the basic notion that accounting statements should be governed by the *substance* rather than the *form* of transactions. An extension of this basic premise is that the method of financing an asset acquisition is irrelevant to the subsequent accounting for that asset.

ASSET VALUATION AND FINANCING ALTERNATIVES

Regardless of methods of financing, assets should be initially recorded at their cash-equivalent prices resulting from arm's-length transactions. An asset can be paid for (financed) in many ways, but the initial recorded amount of the asset will be the same in all cases, if everything but the method of financing is held constant. Amortization of the acquired asset is also not affected by the means of financing; that is, amortization, depreciation, or depletion for an asset is computed independently of the financing method used to acquire the asset.

An asset can be paid for in cash at the date of purchase, in cash at a subsequent date, in common stock, in assets other than cash, or under any other terms agreed on by the participating parties. If all parties to an acquisition transaction are participating at arm's-length (according to their independent interests), the **value received** (the cash-equivalent price of the new asset) will be equal to the **value given up** (the present value of the item given up or to be given up) no matter what the form of payment. Once an asset is recorded, the schedule for amortization is developed based on the initial cash-equivalent price and estimates of the useful life and salvage value of the asset. The strict separation of initial cost determination and subsequent financing applies to both the seller and the buyer of assets. For example, suppose that on January 1, 1983, a manufacturer of equipment sells an item for $50,000. No matter what financing arrangement the buyer has made, the initial amount recorded as the asset cost and the subsequent accounting for that cost are the same, as illustrated in Exhibit 15–1.

Note that in part A of Exhibit 15–1 the means of payment has no effect on the initial value of assets received by the buyer and given up by the seller, on the subsequent accounting for the cost of goods sold by the seller, or on the amortization of the asset cost by the buyer as shown in part B. However, the means of financing does determine the accounting for subsequent finance-related transactions, which includes interest and reduction of principal payments, as is evident in alternative 2 in Part C.

EXHIBIT 15–1

ASSET ACQUISITION UNDER THREE FINANCING ALTERNATIVES

A. RECORDING OF INITIAL TRANSACTION AT 1/1/83

ALTERNATIVE MEANS OF PAYMENT	SELLER		BUYER	
1. Immediate cash payment	Cash	50,000	Equipment	50,000
	Sales	50,000	Cash	50,000
2. Subsequent cash payment plus interest at 10% on 12/31/83	Receivable	50,000	Equipment	50,000
	Sales	50,000	Payable	50,000
3. Payment in buyer's common stock	Investment in common stock	50,000	Equipment	50,000
	Sales	50,000	Common stock	50,000

B. SUBSEQUENT ACCOUNTING FOR ASSET COST AT 12/31/83

ALTERNATIVE MEANS OF PAYMENT	SELLER		BUYER	
1. Immediate cash payment	Cost of goods sold	35,000	Depreciation expense	5,000[a]
	Inventory	35,000	Accumulated depreciation	5,000
2. Subsequent cash payment plus interest at 10% on 12/31/83	Cost of goods sold	35,000	Depreciation expense	5,000
	Inventory	35,000	Accumulated depreciation	5,000
3. Payment in buyer's common stock	Cost of goods sold	35,000	Depreciation expense	5,000
	Inventory	35,000	Accumulated depreciation	5,000

C. ENTRIES TO RECORD FINANCING ACTIVITIES AT 12/31/83

ALTERNATIVE MEANS OF PAYMENT	SELLER		BUYER	
1. Immediate cash payment	None		None	
2. Subsequent cash payment plus interest at 10% on 12/31/83	Cash	55,000	Interest expense	5,000
	Receivable	50,000	Payable	50,000
	Interest revenue	5,000	Cash	55,000
3. Payment in buyer's common stock	None		None	

[a] Depreciation is based on straight-line depreciation on a 10-year life with no salvage value.

This chapter is concerned with leases, a particular method of long-term financing. Many leasing transactions follow a variation of the pattern shown in alternative 2 of Exhibit 15–1; but, because of the many variations in this method of financing assets, a separate discussion highlighting the unique aspects of financing through leasing is needed. First, key elements of lease agreements will be defined. Then the general conceptual issues will be presented, followed by specific promulgated rules. Discussion of the rules is separated into those governing (1) the initial classification of leases into ordinary rental types and sales/purchases types and (2) the accounting for subsequent financing-related transactions.

ACCOUNTING FOR LEASE TRANSACTIONS— THE GENERAL APPROACH

Leasing Terminology Before we begin our discussion of accounting for lease transactions, we first need to introduce some of the specialized terminology commonly used in lease agreements.

The following list contains short definitions of the basic vocabulary.[1] We'll expand upon these terms in later sections and will introduce other terms as some of the more detailed rules are covered.

1. **Lease:** An agreement by which one party (**lessor**) conveys to another party (**lessee**) the right to use property, plant, or equipment (land and/or depreciable assets), usually for a stated period of time and for a stated price.

2. **Inception of the lease:** The date of the lease agreement or the date of commitment, if earlier.

3. **Lease term:** The probable period of time during which the lease agreement will remain in force.

4. **Fair value of leased property:** The price for which the property could be sold in an arm's-length transaction between unrelated parties.

5. **Fair rental of leased property:** The rental rate that would normally be charged for similar property under similar terms and conditions.

6. **Executory costs:** The cost of such things as insurance, maintenance, and taxes paid in connection with the leased property, including any other costs normally associated with ownership.

7. **Bargain purchase option:** A lessee's option to purchase the leased property at a price sufficiently below its expected fair value to make the exercise of the option almost certain.

8. **Bargain renewal option:** A lessee's option to renew the lease at a rental price sufficiently below its expected fair value to make the exercise of the option almost certain.

9. **Estimated economic life:** The estimated remaining useful life of the property for the purpose for which it was intended, regardless of the lease term.

10. **Estimated residual value:** The estimated fair value of the leased property at the end of the lease term.

11. **Unguaranteed residual value:** The expected fair value of the leased property at the end of the lease term that is not guaranteed by the lessee or a third party unrelated to the lessor.

12. **Lessee's incremental borrowing rate:** The rate of interest that the lessee would have had to pay at the inception of the lease to borrow the funds, on similar terms, to purchase the leased property.

13. **Lessee's minimum lease payment:** Those lease payments that can be reasonably expected to be paid by the lessee.

14. **Lessor's minimum lease payment:** The sum of the lessee's minimum lease payments and any residual guaranteed by a third party.

15. **Capital lease:** A lease that transfers substantially all the benefits and risks inherent in the ownership of the property to the lessee, who accounts for the lease as an acquisition of an asset and the incurrence of a liability.

16. **Sales-type lease:** A lease that usually results in a manufacturer's or dealer's profit or loss to the lessor and transfers substantially all the benefits and risks inherent in the ownership of the leased property to the lessee; in addition, (1) the collection of the minimum lease payments is reasonably predictable, and (2) no important uncertainties exist regarding costs to be incurred by the lessor under the terms of the lease.

17. **Direct financing lease:** A lease that does not result in a manufacturer's or dealer's profit or loss to the lessor but does transfer substantially all the benefits and risks inherent in the ownership of the leased property to the lessee; in addition, (1) the

[1] These definitions are consistent with those in promulgated GAAP, which we shall discuss in detail later in this chapter.

collection of the minimum lease payments is reasonably predictable, and (2) no important uncertainties exist regarding costs to be incurred by the lessor under the terms of the lease.

18. **Operating lease:** A lease that is essentially a rental agreement, with no ownership rights being passed on to the lessee.

The
Conceptual
Issues

The fundamental issue that makes accounting for leases an interesting and complex process is the fact that lease agreements convey to the lessee the rights to use an asset, but they do not necessarily convey the legal title to the asset. Accountants attempt to "see through" the legal form of these agreements to determine their economic substance. In some cases the contractual terms indicate that the lease is merely a rental (an operating lease); in other cases the contractual terms indicate that in substance the lessee has assumed an ownership interest in the asset. Because lease contracts have an almost infinite number of variations regarding how much money is to be paid, how and if legal ownership is transferred, who has responsibility for normal operating expenditures, and many others, determining substance over form can be difficult.

A major problem for accountants is determining which contractual terms signify a sale with long-term financing and which signify a rental. As in many accounting decisions, the accountant is faced with a continuum of possibilities, which in the case of leases ranges from clear-cut rentals to clear-cut sales, with a large gray area between the two extremes. Exhibit 15-2 illustrates the range of possibilities and shows some examples of leasing arrangements along the continuum.

From the lessee's perspective, cash is being paid out for certain rights in regard to an asset. Are the rights acquired such that an asset can be recorded on the books of the lessee or do the rights signify a temporary rental to be recorded as a period expense? Are the payments reductions of a long-term liability created when an asset was acquired? If they are a period expense, no asset or liability is recorded. If they are liability reductions, the lessee must record and amortize the initial purchase price of the asset as well as the related liability. By the same token, the lessor receives cash payments that must be classified either as rental income or as reductions in a long-term receivable. The lessor's and lessee's decisions affect their balance sheet and income statement categories.

In the cases depicted in Exhibit 15-2 the entity has control over the asset in question for at least some period of time ranging from a small percentage of total service life in situation 1 to 100% in situation 5. As we move from situation 2 to situation 4, the percentage of useful life during which the lessee has control over the

EXHIBIT
15-2

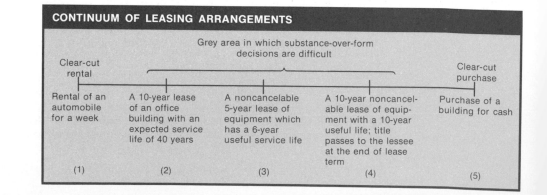

CONTINUUM OF LEASING ARRANGEMENTS

Grey area in which substance-over-form decisions are difficult

Clear-cut rental				Clear-cut purchase
Rental of an automobile for a week	A 10-year lease of an office building with an expected service life of 40 years	A noncancelable 5-year lease of equipment which has a 6-year useful service life	A 10-year noncancelable lease of equipment with a 10-year useful life; title passes to the lessee at the end of lease term	Purchase of a building for cash
(1)	(2)	(3)	(4)	(5)

leased asset increases, but even in situation 4, the legal ownership is not transferred until the end of the lease term.

Consider the following example which illustrates recording alternatives. Lessor signs a lease agreement with Lessee, giving Lessee the right to use an asset for several years in return for specified payments to Lessor. The key question is, In substance did Lessee purchase an asset and did Lessor sell an asset? If the answer is yes, then the normal entries related to the sale and acquisition of an asset using long-term financing are made in the first accounting period by Lessee and Lessor as follows:

LESSEE			**LESSOR**		
Asset	XX		Receivable	XX	
Liability		XX	Sales		XX
Amortization expense	XX		Cost of Goods sold	XX	
Accumulated amortization		XX	Inventory		XX
Interest expense	XX		Cash	XX	
Liability	XX		Interest revenue		XX
Cash		XX	Receivable		XX

If the answer is no, which means that in substance the asset has not been sold, then the required accounting entries for the first year are simply as follows:

LESSEE			**LESSOR**		
Rent Expense	XX		Cash	XX	
Cash		XX	Rent revenue		XX
			Depreciation Expense	XX	
			Accumulated depreciation		XX

Note that the lessee terms the allocation of the capitalized lease "amortization" rather than "depreciation." This is often done in practice, but remember that "amortization" and "depreciation" are simply different names for the same basic process.

The factors affecting the decisions concerning the initial classification of, and subsequent accounting for, leases are *fundamentally* the same as those used for the classification of assets, liabilities, revenues, and expenses. But the complexities of the contractual terms encountered in leasing arrangements make the classification question quite difficult to resolve in many real-world situations.

When an asset is acquired for cash, several factors are usually known with a reasonable degree of certainty: (1) a purchase transaction has occurred; (2) the cash-equivalent price is the amount of the cash payment; (3) the buying entity has legal ownership of the asset and use of it for the entire service life (if the entity so desires). In lease situations there can be, and often is, uncertainty on all three points. How should such ambiguities be handled? Professional judgment in conjunction with guidance from the conventional accounting model is one possibility. This is feasible in the case of leases, just as in other accounting situations, but this approach is likely to yield inconsistent treatments across similar leasing situations. This potential for inconsistent treatment of similar lease transactions and the claim that lessees resist showing large lease liabilities on their balance sheets resulted in a series of standards that govern lease accounting. From 1949 to the present more than fifteen separate pronouncements and interpretations of pronouncements have been issued related to the lease question, and we will analyze the currently applicable rules later in this chapter. Before we discuss promulgated GAAP and the many specific requirements and tests included in them, we need to describe the general accounting procedures used for leases.

General Measurement and Recording Techniques

Lessors who hold the legal title to leased assets may be banks, manufacturers, real estate landlords, retailers, and others. In all cases, it can be safely assumed that the lessor desires a return on investment in the leased asset. In the case of a bank, the return usually is in the form of interest on an unpaid receivable, and the lease is called a **direct financing lease.** For a manufacturer or retailer, the initial sale usually creates a gross profit and the subsequent payments include an element of interest income, and the lease is called a **sales-type lease.** An apartment house landlord views the rental payments on short-term leases as rent revenue, and the lease is called an **operating lease.**

Lessees can include any entity that needs to utilize an asset but, for any of a number of reasons, does not choose to be the legal owner of the asset. From the point of view of the lessee, if the lease is a mere rental, it is termed an **operating lease,** just as it is in the case of a lessor. A lease that in substance is a purchase by the lessee includes those that from the lessor's perspective are called direct financing and sales-type leases. From the point of view of the lessee, these are termed **capital leases.**

We will introduce the accounting for lease transactions by constructing a general case that includes a manufacturer, a financial institution, and an asset user in order to demonstrate how the different parties account for asset-acquisition transactions under varying contractual terms. The following entities are parties in our examples:

1. Kirk Farms, which needs a Model 10 tractor for its operations. Model 10 tractors have an expected useful life of 6 years with no salvage value.
2. First Bank, which currently receives 10 percent interest on long-term loans.
3. Rut Tractors, Inc., which manufactures Model 10 tractors at an inventoried cost per unit of $12,000 and sells them to farms for $18,000 or rents them for $100 per week.

An operating lease Kirk rents the Model 10 tractor for 1 week, and the cash flow is as follows:

Journal entries for such a rental would follow the normal pattern:

RUT				KIRK		
Cash	100			Rent Expense	100	
Rent revenue		100		Cash		100
Depreciation expense	38[a]					
Accumulated deprecia-						
tion		38				

[a] $12,000/312 weeks = $38.46.

Purchase with long-term financing (*bank loan*) Kirk borrows $18,000 from the bank by signing a 2-year note at 10 percent annual interest and purchases the tractor for cash with the following pattern of initial cash flows:

| Rut Tractors, Inc. (seller) | ←$18,000 (purchase price)— | Kirk Farms (buyer-debtor) | ←$18,000 (loan)— | First Bank (creditor) |

Each party's journal entries for the year of the transactions are as follows:

RUT			KIRK			FIRST BANK		
			Cash	18,000		Notes receivable	18,000	
			Notes payable		18,000	Cash		18,000
Cash	18,000		Tractor	18,000				
Sales		18,000	Cash		18,000			
Cost of goods sold	12,000		Interest expense	1,800		Interest receivable	1,800	
Inventory		12,000	Interest payable		1,800	Interest income		1,800
			Depreciation expense	3,000				
			Accumulated depreciation		3,000			

A *direct financing lease* First Bank purchases the tractor for cash and leases it to Kirk Farms under a 6-year noncancelable lease that calls for ownership to be transferred to Kirk Farms at the end of the lease term. The lease payments have a present value of $18,000 using a 10 percent interest rate. Payments are in the form of an ordinary annuity for 6 years. The following pattern depicts the cash flows required:

| Rut Tractors, Inc. (seller) | ←$18,000 (purchase price)— | First Bank (lessor) | ←$4,133 (annual lease payments)— | Kirk Farms (lessee) |

Journal entries related to the lease for the first year are shown below:

RUT			FIRST BANK			KIRK		
Cash	18,000		Tractor	18,000		Leased tractor	18,000	
Sales		18,000	Cash		18,000	Lease liability		18,000
Cost of goods sold	12,000		Lease receivable	18,000				
Inventory		12,000	Tractor		18,000			
			Cash	4,133		Lease liability	2,333	
			Lease receivable		2,333	Interest expense	1,800	
			Interest income		1,800	Cash		4,133
						Amortization expense	3,000	
						Accumulated amortization		3,000

Lease receivables and liabilities follow the same valuation principles as do all long-term receivables and payables. Amortization schedules, therefore, follow the standard formats. The following amortization schedule would be appropriate for First Bank and Kirk Farms:

DATE	PAYMENT	INTEREST	REDUCTION IN LEASE RECEIVABLE/LIABILITY	LEASE RECEIVABLE/LIABILITY
1/1/81				$18,000
12/31/81	$ 4,133	$1,800	$ 2,333	15,667
12/31/82	4,133	1,567	2,566	13,101
12/31/83	4,133	1,310	2,823	10,278
12/31/84	4,133	1,028	3,105	7,173
12/31/85	4,133	717	3,416	3,757
12/31/86	4,133	376	3,757	0
	$24,798	$6,798	$18,000	

The periodic payments of $4,133 can be computed based on the assumptions that the lessor earns 10 percent on the unpaid balance and that the lease payments are in the form of an ordinary annuity for 6 years. The annuity payment is computed by using the appropriate factor in Table H–3 in Appendix H at the back of the book. The calculation is as follows:

$$[1/(P/A, 6, .10)] \times \$18,000 =$$
$$(1/4.3553) \times \$18,000 =$$
$$.2296 \times \$18,000 = \$4,133 \text{ (rounded)}$$

A sales-type lease Kirk Farms leases the tractor directly from Rut Tractors with the same contractual terms as above, except that First Bank is not a party to the transaction.

Rut Tractors, Inc. (lessor) ←— $4,133 (annual lease payment) — Kirk Farms (lessee)

Journal entries for the first year of this sales-type lease are:

	RUT				KIRK		
Lease receivable	18,000			Leased tractor	$18,000	
Sales		18,000		Lease liability		$18,000
Cost of goods sold	12,000					
Inventory		12,000				
Cash	4,133			Lease liability	2,333	
Lease receivable		2,333		Interest expense	1,800	
Interest income		1,800		Cash		4,133
				Amortization expense	3,000	
				Accumulated amortization		3,000

The summary presented in Exhibit 15–3 emphasizes the critical similarities and symmetries among the four transactions. It is important to realize that the legal

EXHIBIT 15–3

COMPARATIVE FINANCIAL STATEMENT EFFECTS OF VARIOUS LEASE CLASSIFICATIONS AND BANK LOAN

RUT TRACTORS, INC.

RUT'S INITIAL BALANCE SHEET ACCOUNTS / RUT'S INCOME STATEMENT

SITUATIONS	LEGAL OWNERSHIP	TRACTOR	RECEIVABLE	LIABILITY	RENT REVENUE	SALES REVENUE	INTEREST REVENUE	COST OF GOODS SOLD	RENT EXPENSE	INTEREST EXPENSE	DEPRECIATION EXPENSE
1. Operating lease[a]	Yes	12,000			100/week						2,000
2. Bank loan	No					18,000		12,000			
3. Direct financing lease[b]	No					18,000	1,800	12,000			
4. Sales-type lease[a]	Yes		18,000			18,000		12,000			

KIRK FARMS

KIRK'S INITIAL BALANCE SHEET ACCOUNTS / KIRK'S INCOME STATEMENT

SITUATIONS	LEGAL OWNERSHIP	TRACTOR	RECEIVABLE	LIABILITY	RENT REVENUE	SALES REVENUE	INTEREST REVENUE	COST OF GOODS SOLD	RENT EXPENSE	INTEREST EXPENSE	DEPRECIATION EXPENSE
1. Operating lease[a]	No								100/week		
2. Bank loan	Yes	18,000		18,000						1,800	3,000
3. Direct financing lease[b]	No	18,000		18,000						1,800	3,000
4. Sales-type lease[a]	No	18,000		18,000						1,800	3,000

FIRST BANK

FIRST BANK'S INITIAL BALANCE SHEET ACCOUNTS / FIRST BANK'S INCOME STATEMENT

SITUATIONS	LEGAL OWNERSHIP	TRACTOR	RECEIVABLE	LIABILITY	RENT REVENUE	SALES REVENUE	INTEREST REVENUE	COST OF GOODS SOLD	RENT EXPENSE	INTEREST EXPENSE	DEPRECIATION EXPENSE
1. Operating lease[a]	No										
2. Bank loan	No		18,000				1,800				
3. Direct financing lease[b]	Yes		18,000				1,800				
4. Sales-type lease[a]	No										

[a] Rut is lessor.
[b] First Bank is lessor.

ownership of the tractor does not necessarily lead to its recognition as an asset on the balance sheet of the owner. For instance, Kirk is legal owner in situation 2 only, but the tractor is recognized on Kirk's balance sheet in situations 2, 3, and 4. Depreciation or amortization is recorded on the books of the entity that recognizes the tractor as an asset: Rut in situation 1 (for $^1/_6$ of Rut's cost of $12,000) and Kirk in situations 2, 3, and 4 (for $^1/_6$ of Kirk's cost of $18,000). Also, note that the first-year interest expense and interest income are the same amount ($1,800) in all situations involving long-term financing, that the entities with long-term receivables have interest income, and that Kirk, the lessee, records a long-term liability and shows interest expense in those cases.

First Bank's financial statements are interesting in that they show only long-term receivables and interest revenues in situations 2 and 3. This is consistent with their status as a financial institution whose goal is to participate in such lease arrangements to earn interest revenue on the unpaid balance of the receivable.

Account Titles Used in Practice The journal entries shown to this point are simplified in order to communicate the essence of the accounting treatment. The actual account titles used in practice vary significantly. For lessee accounting for capital leases, we shall use the account *Lease Liability* to record the present value of minimum lease payments. Other account titles common in practice are *Lease Payable* and *Obligations Under Capital Leases.* The capitalized leased asset also receives several titles: *Leased Equipment, Leased Property, Leased Property Under Capital Leases,* and others.

The lessors' account titles also vary in practice. We shall use two accounts, one primary and one contra, to capture the net receivable for direct financing and sales-type lessors. The two accounts are *Gross Investment in Direct Financing (or Sales-type) Leases,* which includes the minimum lease payments to be received, and *Unearned Interest,* which includes the interest to be earned on future payments. Balance sheet presentations show the primary and contra accounts as follows:

Gross investment in direct financing (or sales-type) leases	$XX
Less: Unearned interest	(X)
Net lease payments receivable	$XX

Other account titles—for example, *Minimum Lease Payments Receivable*—are often used in practice. If only the net amount is shown on a balance sheet, a footnote is required for communication of the gross amount and the unearned interest amount. These and other disclosure patterns are discussed later in this chapter.

ACCOUNTING FOR LEASE TRANSACTIONS— PROMULGATED GAAP

Classification of Leases As mentioned earlier, the desire for consistency in the accounting for leases with similar contractual terms has precipitated a great volume of promulgated GAAP. Currently, **FASB Statement No. 13,** "Accounting for Leases," issued in 1976 is the major governing document.[2] It is supplemented and interpreted in several other FASB standards and interpretations issued since that time.[3]

In general, the standards regulating the accounting for lease transactions have become increasingly rigorous and detailed. The spirit of all these promulgations has remained constant, however. Simply stated, the goal has been to ensure that the accounting for leasing arrangements that are in substance sales of "leased" property by lessors to lessees should be consistent with the economic substance of the transactions rather than with the legal form of the lease contracts. Translation of this rather straightforward goal to rules that are effective for the many detailed and complex contractual terms has proved difficult for accounting policy makers and for those who must comply with the rules.

We shall discuss the major rules governing the initial classification of leases and then explore the accounting for certain specific contractual terms that have a significant impact on account balances for both the lessee and lessor.

In applying promulgated GAAP to lease situations, the principle question is, What is the economic substance of the lease agreement? **FASB Statement No. 13** lists four criteria to be used by the lessee in making the initial classification decision.[4] If *any one* of the following criteria is met, the lease must be recognized as a **capital lease** in the financial statements of the lessee:

1. **Ownership transfer**   If, by the end of the lease term, the ownership (title) of the leased property is transferred to the lessee, then the lease is a capital lease.
2. **Probable ownership transfer**   If the lease contains a bargain purchase option that makes it probable that the lessee will purchase the leased asset during or at the end of the lease term because the option allows purchase below the expected market value, then the lease is a capital lease.
3. **Percentage of estimated economic life of the leased asset covered by the lease term**   If the lease term is for 75 percent or more of the estimated remaining useful life of the leased asset, then the lease is a capital lease. (This criterion is not applicable if the inception of the lease is within the last 25 percent of the total economic life of the leased asset).
4. **Percentage of initial fair value accounted for by the lessee's minimum lease payments**   If the present value of the minimum lease payments is 90 percent or more of the fair value of the leased property, then the lease is a capital lease. (This criterion is not applicable if inception of the lease is within the last 25 percent of the total economic life of the leased asset.)

The lessor, likewise, must decide if a lease is an operating lease or not and the above four criteria are also used in making that judgment. In addition to meeting

[2] *Statement of Financial Accounting Standards No. 13,* "Accounting for Leases" (Stamford, CT: FASB, November 1976).

[3] As of the date of this writing, FASB No. 13 had been augmented by FASB statements No. 17, "Accounting for Leases—Initial Direct Costs" (1977), No. 22, "Changes in the Provisions of Lease Agreements Resulting from Refundings of Tax-Exempt Debt" (1978), No. 23, "Inception of the Lease" (1978), No. 26, "Profit Recognition on Sales-Type Leases of Real Estate" (1979), No. 27, "Classification of Renewals or Extensions of Existing Sales-Type or Direct Financing Leases" (1979), No. 28, "Accounting for Sales with Leasebacks" (1979), and No. 29, "Determining Contingent Rentals" (1979) and by FASB interpretations No. 19, "Lessee Guarantee of the Residual Value of Leased Property" (1977), No. 24, "Leases Involving Only Part of a Building" (1978), and No. 26, "Accounting for Purchase of a Leased Asset by the Lessee During the Term of the Lease" (1978).

[4] *Statement of Financial Accounting Standards No. 13,* "Accounting for Leases," par. 7.

any one of the above, a lease, in order to be classified as a direct financing or sales-type lease by the lessor, must meet two additional criteria.[5]

1. Collection of the minimum lease payments is reasonably predictable.
2. No important uncertainties exist for unreimbursable costs yet to be incurred by the lessor under the lease.

These criteria parallel those included in the revenue-recognition discussion in Chapters 2 and 3 and are necessary to ensure that the receivables and/or sales revenues recognized by the lessor at the inception of the lease have in fact been realized.

Taken as a whole, these six criteria are designed to standardize the substance-over-form decisions that accountants face in lease situations. Some argue that such a "laundry list" of criteria takes away professional judgment in this area, while others feel that the cost in terms of reduced latitude of judgment is justified by the increased consistency that they feel is achieved. As we have seen and will continue to see, promulgated GAAP are often rationalized along such lines.

As an example of the application of the above criteria, consider the following simple lease agreement.

On January 1, 1984, a lessee enters into a 4-year noncancelable lease with year-end payments of $100,000 per year. The leased property, which has a fair value of $320,000 at January 1, 1984, reverts to the lessor at the termination of the lease, and the property has a 5-year estimated economic life. Executory costs (insurance, repairs, and taxes), which are estimated at $12,000 per year, are to be paid by the lessee. The annual lease payments were computed in contemplation of a 15 percent return for the lessor, and 15 percent is the lessee's incremental borrowing rate at January 1, 1984.

Criteria 1 and 2 are not met because the ownership does not transfer to the lessee and there is no mention of a bargain purchase option. Criterion 3 is met because the lease term covers 80 percent of the economic life of the asset. Criterion 4 is not met because the present value of the lease payments is less than 90 percent of the fair value of the leased asset—that is, $(P/A, 4, .15)(\$100,000) = \$285,500$, which is less than $(.90)(320,000) = \$288,000$.

Because one of the four criteria is met, the lessee would classify this lease as a capital lease. The lessor would have to test the two additional criteria. If both are met, the lessor would classify the lease as either a direct financing or sales-type lease. Otherwise, the lessor would classify the lease as an operating lease.

Note that executory costs are not included in the computation. They would merely be expensed as paid by the lessee. If in our example the lessor retained the responsibility to make the cash payments for executory costs but wanted to earn the same rate of return (15 percent), the annual payments would be increased to $112,000, with the present value being computed as follows: $(P/A, 4, .15)(\$112,000 - \$12,000) = \$285,500$, which is the same amount as when executory costs were paid directly by the lessee.

Often leases are structured to include beginning-of-the-period payments. For instance in our example assume that the same lessee payments were made at the beginning of the period:

[5] Ibid., par. 9.

$100,000	$100,000	$100,000	$100,000	Termination of the lease
1/1/84	1/1/85	1/1/86	1/1/87	12/31/87

Because the lessor gets an immediate cash payment of $100,000 at the inception of the lease, the present value increases as shown in the following computation for an annuity due:

$$[(P/A, 3, .15) + 1](\$100,000) =$$
$$(2.2832 + 1)(\$100,000) = \$328,200$$

Under this revised payment schedule, criterion 4 is met because the present value of minimum lease payments exceeds 90 percent of the fair value of the leased property.

Lease terms   Two crucial areas relating to the criteria listed earlier must be explored more closely: (1) the lease term and (2) the present value of minimum lease payments.

First, the lease term can extend to periods beyond the fixed noncancelable portion to include additional periods during which one could reasonably expect that the leasing agreement will remain in effect. We may have, therefore, two major time elements in the lease term:

Fixed noncancelable period	Expected extension period
Lease term = Total time lease is expected to remain in effect	

The **fixed noncancelable period** is that period during which a lease is cancelable only upon (1) occurrence of a remote contingency, (2) permission of the lessor, (3) entering a new lease, or (4) payment of a penalty.[6] The **expected extension period** can be governed by many possible contractual arrangements. For example, the lessor might have the option of automatically requiring renewal of the lease for several years in addition to a fixed noncancelable period. Similarly, the lease terms might give the lessor the right to receive a penalty payment if the lessee does not renew the lease after the fixed noncancelable period.

Some agreements that extend the lease term beyond this fixed noncancelable period include a **bargain renewal option.** Bargain options come after some period over which lease payments are made. For instance, if a leased asset with a fixed noncancelable period of 5 years is expected to have a fair rental value of $10,000 per year for years 6, 7, and 8 and the lease contract allows the lessee to renew the lease at the end of year 5 for $5,000 per year, the term would probably be extended to 8 years.

Fixed noncancelable period = 5 years	Bargain renewal period = 3 years
Term = 8 years	

[6] Ibid., par 5f.

In such cases the payments made during the noncancelable period would have to be high enough to allow the lessor to be satisfied with *bargain* payments in the last 3 years. As we shall see more clearly when the present-value computations are discussed in detail, the present value of all minimum lease payments becomes the initial lease liability for the lessee. This value in turn is the market value of the resources expected to be consumed during the lease term. Therefore, there are no "bargains" when the lease term is looked at in its entirety. If one portion is a "bargain" (years 6, 7, and 8 in our example) then the other portion of the lease term (years 1–5) must be something less than a bargain.

There are many other contractual stipulations that could cause a reasonable person to believe that a lease term should be extended beyond the fixed noncancelable period. For instance, a lease with a 5-year fixed noncancelable period having a normal renewal option for years 6 and 7 and then a bargain option (either extension of the rental agreement or purchase) at the beginning of year 8 could be depicted in the following ways:

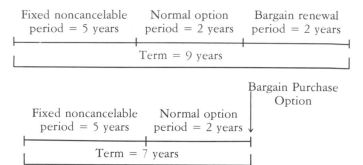

Another stipulation that would cause an extension of a lease term would be if the lessee guarantees the lessor's debt throughout a rental period. The following depicts a guarantee of debt extended beyond the noncancellable period, thereby increasing the term:

Fixed noncancelable period = 5 years   Renewable period over which lessee guarantees lessor's debt = 2 years

Term = 7 years

The above examples demonstrate that *professional judgment* is paramount in decisions regarding lease terms. Decision on the materiality of bargains, penalties, and debt guarantees all ultimately require judgment. It is obvious therefore, that the promulgation of GAAP does not completely eliminate professional judgment.

To summarize then, the lease term is the sum of several possible periods of time that can be specified in lease contracts.[7] Included are:

1. The fixed noncancelable period
2. Periods covered by bargain renewal options
3. Penalty periods, that is, periods over which material penalties must be paid for nonrenewals

[7] Ibid., par. 5f.

4. Periods during which the lessee guarantees the lessor's debt related to the leased property
5. Periods covered by ordinary renewal options prior to the date of a bargain purchase option
6. Periods representing renewal or extension of the lease at the lessor's option, not extending beyond the date of a bargain purchase option

Minimum lease payments   Another major issue, in addition to determining the lease term, is the computation of money amounts to be used in the accounting records. The pivotal phrase here is "minimum lease payments." **Minimum lease payments** for the *lessee* are those payments that can be reasonably expected to be paid, with the exception of (1) those payments that can be expected because of a guarantee of the lessor's debt and (2) executory costs.[8] This reasonable expectation of payment is determined in a manner that closely parallels the determination of lease term. For instance, if the lease has a bargain renewal option that extends the lease term, then, of course, the payments required during the bargain renewal period must be included in the minimum lease payments along with those necessary under the fixed noncancelable period. In addition, if the lessee guarantees a residual value to the lessor, this also becomes a component of the minimum lease payment.

To summarize, the lessee's minimum lease payments can be depicted as follows:

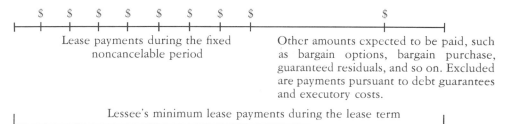

The lessor's minimum lease payments, depicted below, are those receipts that can be reasonably expected from the lease arrangement. Included would be the lessee's minimum lease payments plus payments from third parties who guarantee a residual amount.[9]

Lessee's minimum lease payments	+	Guaranteed residual to be paid by a third party

Lessor's minimum lease payments

FASB Interpretation No. 19[10] clarified certain aspects of residual guarantees. First it sharpened the definitions by excluding guarantees for damage or unusual wear. It also addressed the problem of third-party guarantors of residual value. In cases where insurance companies or other third parties are engaged to guarantee

---

[8] Ibid., par. 5j.

[9] Ibid., par. 5j.

[10] *FASB Interpretation No. 19*, "Lessee Guarantee of the Residual Value of Leased Property" (Stamford, CT: FASB, October 1977).

residual value of leased assets, the lessee's minimum lease payments are not reduced unless the lessor explicitly releases the lessee from its obligation for residual value.

Computation of present value of minimum lease payments Normally leases call for payments that are in the form of an annuity, either an ordinary annuity or an annuity due. In situations such as the tractor example discussed earlier, a straightforward computation is appropriate. But in the real world, complexities such as bargain purchase options and uncertainty about the appropriate interest rate to be used in the present-value computations may exist. An important goal of the various accounting pronouncements is to require that the amounts expected to be paid (or received) over the life of a lease should be reflected in the accounting records if a lease is deemed to be other than an operating lease.

BARGAIN PURCHASE OPTION Let us consider certain of these complexities by examining variations on our tractor leasing example. Assume the following contractual stipulations:

1. Inception date: 1/1/81
2. Kirk Farms is the lessee.
3. Rut Tractors, Inc., is the lessor.
4. Fixed noncancelable period is 6 years.
5. Fair value of the tractor at 1/1/81 is $18,000.
6. Option to buy at the end of the lease term for $2,000.
7. Estimated fair value at the end of the lease is $4,000.
8. Estimated useful life of the tractor is 10 years.

How much should the minimum lease payments be if we assume that a 10% interest rate is appropriate for the lessor and the lessee? As stated earlier, the lessor can reasonably expect the lessee to exercise the $2,000 bargain purchase option at December 31, 1986. Therefore, the lessee's minimum lease payments would include the six annual annuity payments plus the $2,000 option payment. If we assume a 10 percent annual interest rate, we can compute the annuity payment as follows, using appropriate tables in Appendix H at the back of the book. First, we subtract the present value of the option payment of $2,000 from the original $18,000 value of the tractor to get the amount that must be recouped through the annuity payments:

$$\$18,000 - [(P/F, 6, .10)(\$2,000)] =$$
$$\$18,000 - [(.5645)(\$2,000)] =$$
$$\$18,000 - \$1,129 = \$16,871$$

Next, we multiply the $16,871 by the factor for an annuity equal to a present value in order to determine the annuity payment:

$$[1/(P/A, 6, .10)][\$16,871] =$$
$$(.2296)(\$16,871) = \$3,874$$

Payments would thus have the following pattern:

Payments		$3,874	$3,874	$3,874	$3,874	$3,874	$2,000 $3,874
Date	1/1/81	13/31/81	12/31/82	12/31/83	12/31/84	12/31/85	12/31/86

The amortization schedule for these payments is as follows:

DATE	PAYMENT	INTEREST	REDUCTION IN LEASE RECEIVABLE/LIABILITY	LEASE RECEIVABLE/LIABILITY
1/1/81				$18,000
12/31/81	$ 3,874	$1,800	$ 2,074	15,926
12/31/82	3,874	1,593	2,281	13,645
12/31/83	3,874	1,365	2,509	11,136
12/31/84	3,874	1,114	2,760	8,376
12/31/85	3,874	838	3,036	5,340
12/31/86	3,874	534	3,340	2,000
12/31/86	2,000	—	2,000	0
	$25,244	$7,244	$18,000	

The lessee is legally obliged to pay six payments of $3,874, and it is assumed that the purchase option of $2,000 will be exercised, thus summing to a minimum lease payment of $25,244, which has a present value at January 1, 1981, of $18,000. This present value is calculated as follows:

$$\text{Present value of annuity} + \text{present value of future amount} =$$
$$[(P/A, 6, .10)(\$3,874)] + [(P/F, 6, .10)(\$2,000)] =$$
$$[(4.3553)(\$3,874)] + [(.5645)(\$2,000)] -$$
$$\$16,872 + \$1,129 = \$18,000(\text{rounded})$$

BARGAIN RENTAL OPTION   In the case of a bargain rental option, the contractual terms would allow the lessee to lease the tractor for some period beyond December 31, 1986, for rental payments that would be significantly less than the fair rental expected to be in effect at that time. The lease term, in such cases, is extended to include the bargain rental period and the minimum lease payments would include the present value of those payments. The computation of present values would follow the same steps as previously shown.

GUARANTEED RESIDUAL VALUE   Bargain options, of course, are not always features of lease agreements. In some cases, the lessee may agree to return the asset with or without a guarantee of residual value. If, for instance, in our tractor-leasing example, we change the terms so that the lessee guaranteed a $1,000 residual value and expected about $1,000 in actual residual value at December 31, 1986, then the $1,000 to be paid would be included in the lessee's minimum lease payments. Remember that the fair value of the tractor at January 1, 1981, was $18,000. It is expected that the lessor will receive a total of $1,000 at 12/31/86 for residual value. The annuity necessary to equate the present value of all payments to $18,000 is computed as follows:

1. $\$18,000 - [(P/F, 6, .10)(\$1,000)] =$
$\$18,000 - [(.5645)(\$1,000)] -$
$\$18,000 - \$564 = \$17,436$

2. $[1/(P/A, 6, .10)](\$17,436) =$
$(.2296)(\$17,436) = \$4,003$

The lessee is obliged to pay a $4,003 annuity for 6 years plus $1,000 at the end of the lease term resulting in the following amortization schedule:

DATE	PAYMENT	INTEREST	REDUCTION IN LEASE RECEIVABLE/LIABILITY	LEASE RECEIVABLE/LIABILITY
1/1/81				$18,000
12/31/81	$ 4,003	$1,800	$ 2,203	15,797
12/31/82	4,003	1,580	2,423	13,374
12/31/83	4,003	1,337	2,666	10,708
12/31/84	4,003	1,071	2,932	7,776
12/31/85	4,003	778	3,225	4,551
12/31/86	4,003	452[a]	3,551	1,000
12/31/86	1,000	—	1,000	0
	$25,018	$7,018	$18,000	

[a] Rounding error.

INTEREST RATE DETERMINATION   Determination of the appropriate interest rate is important in the measurement of lease effects. In all of our examples so far, it was assumed that at January 1, 1981, the lessee and lessor have the same interest rates for borrowing and lending. We must show what interest rate to use if the two parties to a lease indicate different rates. In the tractor leasing example it was assumed that 10 percent was the appropriate interest rate. This example illustrated that the minimum lease payments did indeed have a present value that equaled the fair value of the tractor. In some situations the interest rates are open to question and their determination will greatly affect accounting balances. For instance, if we had used a 12 percent interest rate to compute present value of the minimum lease payments stated above, the initial capitalized amount would have been reduced from $18,000 to $16,965 computed as follows:

$$[(P/A \ 6, \ .12)(\$4,003)] + [(P/F, \ 6, \ .12)(\$1,000)] =$$
$$[(4.1114)(\$4,003)] + [(.5066)(\$1,000)] =$$
$$\$16,458 + \$507 = \$16,965$$

Note that the lower the interest rate, given a stated payment schedule, the higher the capitalized value and liability, and vice versa. Holding everything else constant, the "90 percent fair value" criterion is more likely to be met with a lower interest rate.

Promulgated GAAP speak to this issue by requiring that if both the lessee's incremental borrowing rate (the rate the lessee would have paid to buy the leased asset at the inception of the lease under a secured loan with terms similar to those of the lease)[11] and the rate implicit in the lease[12] (the rate of interest the lessor used to establish the lease payments) are known by the lessee, then the lower of the two is used by the lessee. However, the capitalized value of the leased property cannot exceed its fair value at the inception of the lease. Therefore, the fair value of the leased property at the inception date is the maximum capitalized value for the leased asset.[13] The lessor uses the interest rate implicit in the lease for all present-value computations.

Lessee Journal Entries   As was stated previously, the lessee first classifies the lease as operating or capital, and if a capital lease is indicated, the present value of minimum lease payments is computed. In the lessee's case the following journal entries would be appropriate

[11] *Statement of Financial Accounting Standards No. 13,* "Accounting for Leases," par. 5l.

[12] Ibid., par. 5k.

[13] Ibid., par. 10.

for both the bargain purchase option (see amortization schedule on p. 553) and the guaranteed residual (see amortization schedule on p. 554) examples discussed earlier:

Inception of the lease		BARGAIN PURCHASE OPTION		GUARANTEED RESIDUAL	
		DEBIT	CREDIT	DEBIT	CREDIT
1/1/81	Leased equipment	18,000		18,000	
	Lease liability		18,000		18,000
Normal lease payments[a]					
12/31/81	Interest expense	1,800		1,800	
	Lease liability	2,074		2,203	
	Cash		3,874		4,003

[a] Normal lease payments from 12/31/82 through 12/31/86 would be recorded in the same way, except for the effects of the changing interest amounts.

Amortization of a capital lease is computed according to the lessee's normal depreciation method for depreciable assets of a similar nature. The depreciable life used in the amortization computation is the economic life of the leased asset if the lease transfers ownership or contains a bargain purchase option. In other cases, the depreciable life is the lease term.[14] If the lessee expects to receive any estimated residual value at the end of the asset's depreciable life, that amount is deducted from the capitalized amount of the lease to establish the amortizable base. The amortization and termination entries in our examples would be as follows:

Normal amortization		BARGAIN PURCHASE OPTION		GUARANTEED RESIDUAL	
		DEBIT	CREDIT	DEBIT	CREDIT
12/31/81	Lease amortization expense	1,800		2,833	
	Accumulated amortization		1,800		2,833
		($18,000 ÷ 10 yrs. = $1,800 through 12/31/90)		($17,000 ÷ 6 = $2,833 through 12/31/86)	

Termination of the lease

		BARGAIN PURCHASE OPTION		GUARANTEED RESIDUAL	
12/31/86	Lease liability	2,000			
	Cash		2,000		
	Lease liability			1,000	
	Accumulated amortization			17,000	
	Leased equipment				18,000
	(If transfer of equipment is made)				
	OR				
	Cash			1,000	
	Accumulated amortization			17,000	
	Leased equipment				18,000
	Lease liability			1,000	
	Cash				1,000
	(If transfer of cash is made, assuming the lessee sells the asset for $1,000)				

[14] Ibid., par. 11.

Lessor Journal Entries

We have discussed the general approach lessors take in accounting for leases, the criteria they use for classifying leases, and some examples of how they compute the necessary lease payments. Recall that for lessors, three types of leases were discussed: (1) operating, (2) direct financing, and (3) sales-type.

We first became familiar with lessor accounting terminology by examining the simple cases of direct financing and sales-type leases when there are no bargain options or residual values involved. We will first show journal entries for the simple cases, followed by the more complex.

Lessor Accounting for a simple direct financing lease In our tractor example let us first assume that First Bank is the lessor for Kirk Farms (see p. 543). Based on the data presented earlier, the following amortization schedule is appropriate for First Bank who is a direct financing lessor:

DATE	PAYMENT	INTEREST INCOME	REDUCTION IN LEASE RECEIVABLE	LEASE RECEIVABLE
1/1/81				$18,000
12/31/81	$ 4,133	$1,800	$ 2,333	15,667
12/31/82	4,133	1,567	2,566	13,101
12/31/83	4,133	1,310	2,823	10,278
12/31/84	4,133	1,028	3,105	7,173
12/31/85	4,133	717	3,416	3,757
12/31/86	4,133	376	3,757	0
	$24,798	$6,798	$18,000	

The sum of the payment amounts ($24,798) is entered at the inception of the lease by the lessor as follows:

1/1/81	Gross Investment in direct financing lease	24,798	
	Equipment		18,000
	Unearned interest		6,798

The net lease receivable, sometimes termed "net investment," at January 1, 1981, is $24,798 − $6,798 = 18,000. Note once again that there is no profit on the initial transaction for the direct financing lessor.

As is normally true when contra accounts are used, the lessor balance sheet presentations of leases contain a certain amount of variation depending on the detail desired. The net receivable is the present value of future payments, in our case $18,000 at January 1, 1981, but the balance sheet disclosure may show both the gross investment and contra amounts or merely the net amount alone. We shall see later that certain footnote disclosures are mandatory for lessors and lessees.

Normal lease payment journal entries are made for each annuity payment as follows:

12/31/81	Cash	4,133	
	Unearned interest	1,800	
	Gross investment in direct financing lease		4,133
	Interest Revenue		1,800

From December 31, 1982, through December 31, 1986, the same entry would be made except for the effects of the changing interest factor.

Lessor accounting for a simple sales-type lease   In this example Rut Tractors (the manufacturer) is the lessor (see p. 544). The accounting procedures are the same as in the preceding example, except in the initial year of the lease. At the inception a sales transaction is recorded, and it is followed by a cost of goods sold entry:

1/1/81	Gross investment in sales-type lease		24,798	
	Sales			18,000
	Unearned interest			6,798
	Cost of goods sold		12,000	
	Inventory of tractors			12,000

Note that a gross profit of $6,000 is recognized by Rut in the first year of the lease (sales of $18,000 less cost of goods sold of $12,000). This is exactly the same gross profit which would have been recorded if the sale had been for $18,000 cash.

If we assume the same contractual terms for a financing lease and for a sales-type lease, the differences in lessor accounting exist only in the first year in terms of the initial entry and the cost of goods sold and inventory entries. All other entries would be identical.

Lessor accounting for bargain purchase option   Return to the example starting on p. 552, where the contractual terms were such that a reasonable assumption could be made that the lessee would exercise the $2,000 bargain purchase option. What implications does this payment of $2,000 at the termination of the lease have on the lessor's accounting for the lease?

The minimum lease payments include the six annuity payments of $3,874 and the final bargain purchase option payment of $2,000 (see the amortization schedule on p. 553). The following journal entries would be appropriate for direct-financing and sales-types lessors:

DIRECT FINANCING

Inception of the lease

1/1/81	Gross investment in direct financing lease	25,244	
	Equipment		18,000
	Unearned interest		7,244

Normal lease payments[a]

12/31/81	Cash	3,874	
	Unearned interest	1,800	
	Gross investment in direct financing lease		3,874
	Interest revenue		1,800

SALES-TYPE

Inception of the lease

1/1/81	Gross investment in sales-type lease	25,244	
	Sales		18,000
	Unearned interest		7,244

Recording of cost of goods sold

1/1/81	Cost of goods sold	12,000	
	Inventory of tractor		12,000

Normal lease payments

12/31/81	Cash	3,874	
	Unearned interest	1,800	
	Gross investment in sales-type lease		3,874
	Interest revenue		1,800

---

[a] Normal lease payments for 12/31/82 through 12/31/86 would be recorded in the same way, except for the effect of the changing interest amounts.

Termination of the lease

12/31/86	Cash	2,000	
	Gross investment in direct financing lease		2,000

Termination of the lease

12/31/86	Cash	2,000	
	Gross investment in sales-type lease		2,000

Lessor accounting for residual values Contractual terms vary when it comes to the residual value at the termination of a lease. In some cases, the lessee or a third party guarantees a certain amount of residual value to the lessor. In other cases no guarantee is made, and the lessor merely takes possession of the equipment. Again, the lessor must record an initial amount that includes (1) all cash that it is reasonable to assume the lessee or another will pay plus (2) an amount equal to the unguaranteed portion of the residual value. Let us examine two examples in which the leased equipment reverts to the lessor. In one case, a guaranteed residual equal to expected fair value of the equipment is to be paid at the termination date; in the other, the guaranteed residual is less than the expected fair value of the equipment at termination.

GUARANTEED RESIDUAL EQUALS EXPECTED FAIR VALUE Using our tractor example, assume the same facts as in the example starting on p. 553, which calls for a guaranteed residual of $1,000 and an estimated fair value at termination of $1,000. The lessee's minimum lease payments are as follows:

	$4,003	$4,003	$4,003	$4,003	$4,003	$1,000 (guaranteed $4,003 residual)
1/1/81	12/31/81	12/31/82	12/31/83	12/31/84	12/31/85	12/31/86

The lessor's gross investment in leased equipment is $25,018 and its net investment (the present value of the minimum lease payment) is $18,000. The journal entries throughout the lease term would follow the normal patterns, and the entry to record the residual transfer at termination would be as follows:

IF CASH IS TRANSFERRED

12/31/86	Cash	1,000	
	Gross investment in direct financing lease		1,000

IF THE EQUIPMENT IS TRANSFERRED

12/31/86	Used equipment	1,000	
	Gross investment in direct financing lease		1,000

GUARANTEED RESIDUAL IS LESS THAN EXPECTED FAIR VALUE—DIRECT FINANCING LEASE Let us modify the above example in one way only: The residual value is now expected to be $2,000 at the termination date. This has implications for the actual lease payments in that the lessor now, in order to earn 10 percent on the initial desired present value of $18,000, can accept smaller annuity payments since the lessor will be left with an asset worth twice as much as before—that is, $2,000 instead of $1,000. The lessor now expects to receive, in addition to amounts payable by the lessee, $1,000 of unguaranteed residual. The desired lease payments would be computed by first subtracting the present value of the $2,000 expected residual from the $18,000: $18,000 − (P/F, 6, .10) $2,000 = $16,871; and then by computing an annuity equal to that amount: [1/(P/A, 6, .10)$16,871 = $3,874. The lessee's minimum lease payments would then be:

$1,000 (guaranteed

$3,874	$3,874	$3,874	$3,874	$3,874	$3,874	residual)
1/1/81	12/31/81	12/31/82	12/31/83	12/31/84	12/31/85	12/31/86

The lessor's gross investment is the sum of the lessee's minimum lease payments ($24,244) plus the $1,000 unguaranteed residual for a total of $25,244 as depicted

DATE	PERIODIC PAYMENTS AND RESIDUAL	INTEREST INCOME	REDUCTION IN LEASE RECEIVABLE	LEASE RECEIVABLE
1/1/81	—	—	—	18,000
12/31/81	$ 3,874	$1,800	$ 2,074	15,926
12/31/82	3,874	1,593	2,281	13,645
12/31/83	3,874	1,365	2,509	11,136
12/31/84	3,874	1,114	2,760	8,376
12/31/85	3,874	838	3,036	5,340
12/31/86	3,874	534	3,340	2,000
12/31/86	2,000	—	2,000	—
	$25,244	$7,244	$18,000	

The journal entries throughout the lease term would follow the standard pattern for lessor accounting, and the entry to record the residual transfer would be as follows if the equipment in fact has a $2,000 residual value at 12/31/86:

12/31/86	Used equipment	2,000	
	Gross investment in direct financing		
	lease		2,000

The estimated residual values should be reviewed throughout the lease term. If a permanent decline in that estimated amount is felt to have occurred, the lessor must revise the recorded receivable accounts downward and a loss is recorded. No gains on increases in estimated residual values are allowed by GAAP.[15]

SALES-TYPE LEASE In a sales-type lease, the lessor recognizes an initial profit, which reflects the fact that the unguaranteed residual is expected to be received at the termination of the lease. In the determination of cost of goods sold, GAAP call for the present value of the unguaranteed residual to be deducted from the cost (book value) of the leased asset at the inception of the lease. Using the facts reflected in the amortization schedule above, the following initial journal entry would be appropriate for a sales-type lessor (Rut Tractors whose manufacturing cost is $12,000):

[15] Ibid., par. 17d.

1/1/81	Gross investment in sales-type lease	25,244	
	Cost of goods sold	11,435	
	Sales		17,435
	Inventory of tractors		12,000
	Unearned interest		7,244

Gross investment in sales-type lease is recorded at the sum of the minimum lease payments ($24,244) and the unguaranteed residual ($1,000). Cost of goods sold is recorded at the inventory cost on the books of the lessor ($12,000) minus the present value of the unguaranteed residual ($565). Sales is recorded at the present value of minimum lease payments $[(P/A, 6, .10)($3874)] + [(P/F, 6, .10)($1,000)] = $17,435$ (rounding error of $2). Inventory of tractors is reduced by the book value of the leased item ($12,000). Unearned interest is recorded at the gross investment in sales-type lease minus the sum of (1) the present value of minimum lease payments and (2) the present value of the unguaranteed residual $[$25,244 − ($17,435 + $565) = $7,244]$.

Lessor accounting for initial direct costs   Lessors often incur costs that are directly related to the negotiating and finalizing of lease contracts. Included in this category of costs are commissions, legal fees, credit investigations, and so forth. **FASB Statement No. 17** refers to these as **initial direct costs.**[16] **FASB Statement No. 13** requires that such costs be deferred and amortized over the lease term for operating leases and charged to income (expensed) in the period the lease agreement is initiated for sales-type leases.[17]

As an example of the accounting for deferred initial direct costs, assume that Baxter, Inc., owns rental property that had an initial book value of $300,000 and an estimated useful life of 30 years starting on July 1, 1984, with zero estimated salvage value. Baxter incurs $15,000 in initial direct costs for a 3-year operating lease that commences on July 1, 1984. If Baxter uses straight-line depreciation for the building, the following entries would be necessary for 1984, assuming a December 31, 1984, year-end.

7/1/84	Deferred initial direct costs	15,000	
	Cash		15,000
12/31/84	Amortization expense[a]	2,500	
	Deferred initial direct costs		2,500
12/31/84	Depreciation expense	5,000	
	Accumulated depreciation building		5,000

[a] $15,000 × (6/36) = $2,500.

For direct financing leases, the lessor first expenses the initial direct costs as follows:

Initial direct costs	XX	
Cash (and so on)		XX

[16] *Financial Accounting Standards No. 17,* "Accounting for Leases—Initial Direct Costs" (Stamford, CT: FASB, November 1977).

[17] *Statement of Financial Accounting Standards No. 13,* "Accounting for Leases," pars. 17c, 18b, 19c.

A portion of the unearned income equal to the initial direct costs is then recognized as follows:

Unearned interest—lease	XX	
Interest revenue—lease		XX

The balance of the unearned interest is recognized as income over the lease term. A new implicit interest rate would be computed, which when used to discount the lessor's expected receipts would equal the lessor's net investment. Initial direct costs thereby increase the lessor's net investment in the lease (that is, gross investment minus unearned interest) and reduce future interest revenue.

A rationale for the different treatment of initial direct costs for direct financing and sales-type leases is that for direct financing lessors, the costs are related to future revenue to be earned as interest income. For sales type lessors, the initial direct costs are associated with the sales revenue generated at the inception of the lease.

Lessee and Lessor Disclosure

Currently promulgated GAAP call for extensive disclosure of lease agreements in the financial reports of both lesseees and lessors.

Lessee disclosures For lessees, the required disclosure includes several major items.[18] First, lessees must disclose the general nature of their leasing arrangements. For their operating leases, lessees must disclose rental expense with separate amounts for minimum, contingent (those based on sales level or some other basis), and sublease rentals. If the lessee has operating leases with initial or noncancelable portions that extend beyond 1 year, they must disclose total minimum lease payments for each of the next 5 years. For their capital leases, lessees must disclose (1) gross amounts of capitalized leased assets by major categories, (2) total minimum lease payments for each of the next 5 years, and (3) information on certain sublease rentals and contingent rentals.

In addition to these footnote narratives, GAAP call for (1) a separate disclosure of the current amortization of capitalized leases or a statement of the amount included in depreciation expense, (2) disclosure of the capitalized leased assets and their accumulated amortization, and (3) disclosure of the capitalized lease liabilities classified in the same manner as ordinary liabilities.[19] All of these disclosures are felt to be necessary in order to give the readers of financial statements a complete picture of the lessee's obligations for leased property. Exhibit 15–4 shows the footnote disclosure for operating leases made by Varlen Corporation in a recent annual report. Exhibit 15–5 shows the footnote disclosure for capital leases made by Tiger International in another recent annual report.

EXHIBIT 15–4

VARLEN CORPORATION'S DISCLOSURE OF OPERATING LEASES

The Company and its subsidiaries occupy various manufacturing plants and office facilities under noncancelable operating leases which generally require payment of taxes and insurance. At January 31, 1981, the aggregate minimum future rental commitments under such leases was approximately $3,500,000. Amounts due annually in each of the next five years range from $290,000 to $600,000.

Total rental expense amounted to approximately $1,214,000 in fiscal 1981 ($1,268,000 in 1980 and $923,000 in 1979).

[18] Ibid., par. 16.

[19] Ibid., par. 13.

EXHIBIT
15–5

TIGER INTERNATIONAL'S FOOTNOTE DISCLOSURE FOR CAPITAL LEASES

At December 31, 1980, the Company was lessee under long-term leases on aircraft and engines, railcar equipment, facilities and other equipment. These leases extend for varying periods through 2019. There are renewal and fair market value purchase options on the leased equipment and facilities. Rentals during the renewal option periods are generally at rates that are as favorable as for the initial lease periods. Under most equipment leases, the Company is obligated to bear the cost of maintaining and operating the equipment.

Capital Leases

Property, plant, and equipment recorded as assets under capital leases at December 31, are as follows (in thousands):

	1980	1979
Equipment used in operations:		
Equipment for lease or under lease	$173,401	$167,407
Equipment used in air cargo operations	383,991	118,541
Building and leasehold improvements	3,464	1,801
	560,856	287,749
Less accumulated amortization	(128,672)	(107,968)
	$432,184	$179,781

Lessor disclosures When a lessor earns a significant portion of its revenue from lease activities, certain disclosures are required.[20] They include: (1) a general description of the lessor's leasing activity; (2) in the case of direct financing and sales-type leases, a disclosure of net investment in leases broken down into current and noncurrent portions, future minimum lease payments, unguaranteed residual and unearned income components of the net investment, and minimum lease payments for each of the next 5 years; (3) in the case of operating leases, a disclosure, by major category, of the cost or book value of property held for operating leases, total accumulated depreciation on such property and other miscellaneous disclosures. Exhibit 15–6 shows Rockaway Corporation's lease disclosure in a recent report.

Current and Noncurrent Balance Sheet Classifications

Lessors and lessees must classify their lease liabilities and net lease receivables into the current and noncurrent portions. For instance, consider the following amortization schedule:

DATE	PAYMENT	INTEREST	REDUCTION IN LEASE RECEIVABLE/PAYABLE	LEASE RECEIVABLE/PAYABLE
1/1/84				$100,000
12/31/84	$ 40,211	$10,000	$ 30,211	69,789
12/31/85	40,211	6,979	33,232	36,557
12/31/86	40,211	3,654[a]	36,557	0
	$120,633	$20,633	$100,000	

[a] Rounding error.

Given this schedule, the following balance sheet categories would be appropriate at 12/31/84:

[20] Ibid., par. 23.

LESSEE BALANCE SHEET 12/31/84		LESSOR BALANCE SHEET 12/31/84	
Current Liabilities		*Current Assets*	
Lease liability	$33,232	Gross investment in sales-type lease	$40,211
		Less unearned interest	6,979
		Net investment in sales-type lease	$33,232
Noncurrent Liabilities		*Noncurrent Assets*	
Lease liability	$36,557	Gross investment in sales-type lease	$40,211
		Less unearned interest	3,654
		Net investment in sales-type lease	$36,557

Note that the current and noncurrent amounts equal the reductions in the lease payable and receivable for the appropriate years on the amortization schedule.

Sale-Leaseback Transactions In some cases an entity owns an asset outright but would like to reap the possible tax benefits of a leasing arrangement.[21] In addition, the entity may need to improve its cash position by an immediate sale of the asset while retaining use of the asset. In such cases an entity can sell the asset to another party, say a bank, and then immediately lease it back as depicted below:

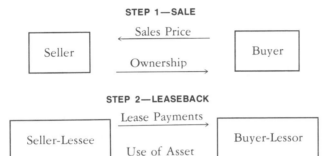

STEP 1—SALE

Seller → Sales Price ← Buyer
Seller → Ownership → Buyer

STEP 2—LEASEBACK

Seller-Lessee → Lease Payments → Buyer-Lessor
Seller-Lessee ← Use of Asset ← Buyer-Lessor

EXHIBIT 15–6

> **ROCKAWAY CORPORATION'S DISCLOSURE AS LESSOR FOR OPERATING LEASES**
>
> *Accounting for Box-making Machinery*
>
> Part of the Corporation's business is the manufacture of box-making machinery for lease. For the initial right to possess such machinery, substantially all lessees pay an amount which approximates the cost of manufacture. The Corporation retains legal title to the machines and leases them to box manufacturers. Repossession of the machinery is rarely required. For accounting purposes, the cost of these machines is charged to expense and the payment for the initial right to possess is included in revenues at the time of shipment. Rents and royalties relating to the use of these machines are based upon the value of the boxes produced and sold and are included in revenues as earned.
>
> In 1980 and 1979, the Corporation entered into agreements which, for accounting purposes, have been treated as operating leases. The carrying value of the leased assets, $724,000 and $638,000 in 1980 and 1979, respectively, has been included in machinery and equipment.

[21] The potential tax benefits of leasing assets rather than purchasing them outright involve the ability to deduct lease payments as current deductions for tax purposes rather than depreciation deductions, which may be lower. Furthermore, lease payments for rented land may be deducted for tax purposes, whereas owned land cannot be depreciated.

The accountant again is confronted with a "substance-over-form" determination. Should the "sale" be recorded in the normal way, with any gain or loss recognized? Should the lease be handled according to the GAAP governing leasing arrangements? The answers to such questions could be based on purely conceptual considerations, but it was felt by policy makers that this would lead to much variation in practice. **FASB Statement No. 13,**[22] as amended by **FASB Statement No. 28,**[23] therefore, prescribes the treatment of sale-leaseback transactions in order to limit inconsistencies. The main features of the rules can be summarized as follows:

1. First, recognize as an immediate loss any excess of book value over fair value at the time of the sale-leaseback transaction. Defer any difference (gain or loss) between the sale-leaseback "selling" price and the book value (after adjustment to fair value, if necessary).

   For instance, a ship that originally cost $15,000,000 and had accumulated depreciation of $7,000,000 is the object of a sale-leaseback transaction. The sale-leaseback "selling," price is $6,500,000 and the fair market value is $6,000,000. The following seller-lessee journal entries would be necessary to recognize the loss and the "sale" transactions:

Loss on write-down of ship to fair value	2,000,000	
Ship		2,000,000
(To write a ship down to fair market value		
as part of a sales-leaseback transaction)		
Cash	6,500,000	
Accumulated Depreciation	7,000,000	
Ship		$13,000,000
Deferred Gain		500,000
(To record the sale of a ship in a		
sale-leaseback transaction.)		

2. The lease payments are accounted for by the lessee and lessor in the manner—and according to the criteria—discussed for leases in general. If one of the four classification criteria (p. 547) is met, the leaseback is classified as a capital lease by the lessee. If none of the criteria is met, the lease is an operating lease. The purchaser-lessor also applies the applicable criteria for lessors to determine the proper lease classification.

3. If the lease is a capital lease, the gain is recognized in proportion to the amortization of the leased asset (for all but land leases, which are recognized on a straight-line basis over the lease term). For operating leases, deferred gains are recognized in income in the proportion that current rental expense bears to total rental payments over the lease term.

The following example demonstrates the accounting for a sale and leaseback transaction between Texas Manufacturing (the seller-lessee) and Houston Bank (the buyer-lessor). On January 1, 1983, Texas Manufacturing purchased equipment for $700,000. After 1 year's use the book value was $560,000. The asset at January 1, 1984, has an estimated remaining life of 4 years with no salvage value expected. Texas Manufacturing, on January 1, 1984, sells the equipment at fair value to Hous-

---

[22] Ibid., par. 32–34.

[23] *Statement of Financial Accounting Standards No. 28,* "Accounting for Sales with Leasebacks" (Stamford, CT: FASB, May 1979).

ton Bank for $600,000 cash and leases it back immediately under a 4-year, noncancelable lease with no residual guarantee or bargain options. The following amortization schedule is applicable for the lease if a 15 percent interest rate is used:

DATE	PAYMENTS	INTEREST	REDUCTION IN PRINCIPAL	NET RECEIVABLE OR PAYABLE
1/1/84				$600,000
12/31/84	$210,158	$ 90,000	$120,158	479,842
12/31/85	210,158	71,976	138,182	341,660
12/31/86	210,158	51,249	158,909	182,751
12/31/87	210,158	27,407[a]	182,751	0
	$840,632	$240,632	$600,000	

[a] Rounding error.

The 1984 journal entries for lessee and lessor for the lease arrangement would be as follows:

TEXAS MANUFACTURING (SELLER-LESSEE)

1/1/84	Cash	600,000	
	Accumulated depreciation	140,000	
	Deferred gain		40,000
	Equipment		700,000
	Leased equipment	600,000	
	Lease liability		600,000
12/31/84	Interest expense	90,000	
	Lease liability	120,158	
	Cash		210,158
	Depreciation expense	150,000[a]	
	Accumulated depreciation		150,000
	Deferred gain	10,000[b]	
	Recognized gain on sale-leaseback		10,000

HOUSTON BANK (BUYER-LESSOR)

	Equipment	600,000	
	Cash		600,000
	Gross investment in direct financing lease	840,632	
	Equipment		600,000
	Unearned interest		240,632
	Cash	210,158	
	Unearned interest	90,000	
	Gross investment in direct financing lease		210,158
	Interest revenue		90,000

[a] $600,000/4 = $150,000.

[b] ($150,000/$600,000) × $40,000 = $10,000.

Note that over the course of the entire life of the asset, the original cost of the equipment will be charged to Texas Manufacturing's income:

1983 Depreciation expense		$140,000
1984–1987 Depreciation expense	$150,000	
Gain recognition	(10,000)	
Net charge	$140,000 × 4 =	560,000
Total charge to income		$700,000

This method of deferring gains on the initial sale transaction allows the effect of the gain to be netted out and therefore eliminated as a factor that affects net income.

<h2>Real Estate Leases</h2>

Real estate leases often involve both land and buildings, and the land normally has an unlimited useful life. Land, therefore, poses special classification problems when it is included in a lease. Recall the lease classification criteria listed on pp. 547 and 548, which can be summarized as follows:

Applicable to both lessee and lessor
1. Ownership transfer
2. Bargain purchase option
3. Lease term 75 percent or more of economic life
4. Present value 90 percent or more of fair value

Applicable to lessor
5. Collectibility
6. Known costs

The FASB sought to modify the application of these criteria in light of the special characteristics of land.[24] Three major real estate leasing situations will be discussed: (1) land alone, (2) land and building, and (3) real estate and equipment.

Land alone The classification of land leases is based on above-listed criteria 1 and 2 for lessees and 1,2,5, and 6 for lessors. Therefore if ownership is transferred or a bargain purchase option exists (as described in the standard), the lessee would account for the land lease as a capital lease; otherwise, the lease would be an operating lease. If the applicable criteria are met, the lessor would account for the leased land as a direct financing or sales-type lease.

Land and building For a lease of land and building that meets criteria 1 or 2 for the lessee, the capital lease classification is made, with the relative fair values of land and building used to allocate minimum lease payments. The lessee would not amortize the lease of land. If criteria 1 or 2 and both 5 and 6 are met for the lessor, the lease is accounted for as a single unit as either a direct financing or a sales-type lease.

For a lease of land and building that does not meet criteria 1 or 2, the relative value of the land and building governs the classification process: (1) If land is less than 25 percent of the total fair value of all property covered by the lease, both parties consider the lease as a single unit for application of criteria 3 and 4. Note that for criterion 3, the building's estimated life is used. If either criterion 3 or 4 is met, the lessee accounts for the lease as a capital lease, and the lessor, assuming criteria 5 and 6 are met, accounts for the lease as either a direct financing or a sales-type lease. (2) If the fair value of the land is 25 percent or more of the total fair value of the leased property, criteria 3, 4, 5, and 6 are applied as applicable to the building as a separate unit. If the building portion does not meet the appropriate criteria, land and building combined are treated as a single operating lease. If the building meets the appropriate criteria, the building is treated as a capital lease by the lessee and a direct financing or sales-type lease by the lessor, with the land portion treated as a separate operating lease by both parties.

[24] *Statement of Financial Accounting Standards No. 13,* "Accounting for Leases," par. 24–28.

Real estate and equipment If a real estate lease involves equipment, the portion of the minimum lease payments associated with the equipment is estimated by an appropriate technique—for example, relative fair value—and the equipment is treated as a separate lease for application of classification criteria.

FUNDS FLOW EFFECTS

Leasing arrangements may have significant effects on an entity's funds flow. In the case of an operating lease, the lessee and the lessor have cash inflows and outflows, respectively, equal to the actual rent payments made in a period.

Nonoperating leases have more complex implications for an entity's funds flow. Because such leases defer significant portions of initial acquisition value, they affect statements of changes in financial position in much the same manner as would the purchase or sale of property under a long-term financing agreement. A lessee's cash is decreased by lease payments but working capital is decreased only upon the reclassification of a portion of the lease liability from long-term to short-term. A lessee must also consider the nonfund aspect of depreciation charges on leased property when reconciling net income and funds from operations.

Effects of leasing agreements on lessor's funds flow is symmetrical to that of lessees. However, under sales-type leases, any profit or loss on the initial "sales" transaction is not associated with an equal flow of funds and therefore must be treated as an adjustment when reconciling net income and funds from operations. Similarly, amortization of capitalized leased assets is treated in the same manner as depreciation in the reconciliation of net income and funds from operations.

An important consideration in determining an entity's current liquidity position is the fact that the portion of any lease liability or receivable classified as current is only the principal-reduction portion. This amount may be far less than the actual cash flow in the next period. This flow includes both the principal and the possibly very large interest portion.

SUMMARY

Lease accounting follows the general pattern of accounting for asset acquisitions and sales with long-term financing. Initial book values, amortization of asset values, and principal and interest payments related to leases are governed by the underlying concepts for those types of transactions. It is in the area of deciding what the economic substance of a transaction is, as opposed to its legal form, that the impact of detailed promulgated GAAP is most strongly felt. Promulgated GAAP are designed to lend consistency of accounting treatment to the many possible contractual patterns found in lease arrangements.

Specific criteria have been developed to govern the "substance-over-form" determination. Lessees account for leased equipment as either operating leases, which are handled as rentals, or capital leases, which involve the recognition of assets and liabilities. Lessors account for leases either as operating (rental) agreements or, when certain criteria are met, as direct financing or sales-type agreements. In the latter two cases, receivables are recorded and the leased asset's book value is eliminated. For sales-type leases the lessor recognizes profit or loss on the initial transaction with the lessee. When leases are classified as other than operating on the books of either the lessee or the lessor, appropriate interest factors must be considered for determining the present values of payables and receivables, and interest expense and interest income as applicable must be computed.

APPENDIX F
Leveraged Leases

Leveraged leases are certain direct financing type leases where the lessor does not provide all of the capital to finance the leased asset but rather borrows some funds from another party. In other words, the owner of the asset being leased (the lessor) has borrowed from some financial institution in order to buy the asset, which is then leased to a lessee who will ultimately use it.

A diagram of a typical leveraged lease arrangement may be illustrated as follows:

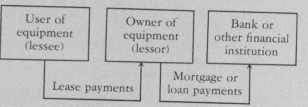

To explain the advantages and disadvantages of leveraged leases to the various parties involved, consider the following case.

In September 1984, Margolas Garden Gate Nursery (MGGN) began to consider construction of a new greenhouse. The greenhouse they wanted to acquire would cost $1,500,000 and would be depreciated over 6 years for book and tax purposes on a double-declining-balance basis.[25] Since MGGN did not have the capital for the desired greenhouse, they sought external funding. One of the family members who owned MGGN also was a part owner in the investment firm of Major Capital Finance, Inc. (MCFI). MCFI invests in leveraged leases and has agreed to put up $300,000 in investment capital, borrow $1,200,000 from First National Bank of Manchester on a 12 percent first-mortgage basis, and acquire the greenhouse for $1,500,000[26] Then, MCFI would act as a lessor and lease the greenhouse to the nursery at an interest rate of 14 percent.

In order to consider the impact of the leverage obtained by MCFI from the bank on the financing lease, it is *not* necessary to focus on whether the lease is an

---

[25] The double-declining-balance method is changed to straight-line over the last 3 years in order to fully depreciate the asset.

[26] The $1,200,000 of debt obtained by the lessor must be nonrecourse to the lessor. The bank may, however, have recourse to the leased assets and/or the remaining lease payments from the lessee. See *FASB Statement No. 13*, par. 42c.

operating or a capital lease since it doesn't necessarily have any effect on the leverage aspect, which is what is of interest to us here. First we shall assume that the lessor treats the lease as an operating lease. It is the impact on the lessor that we are interested in evaluating, since *the effect of a leveraged financing lease on the lessee is no different than it is in the case of a nonleveraged financing lease.* Based on the data in the case, the 6-year annuity payments from MCFI to the bank (for the $1,200,000, 12 percent mortgage) and the 6-year annuity payments from MGGN to MCFI for the $1,500,000 greenhouse would be computed as follows:

PAYMENT FROM THE MCFI TO BANK

$$(P/A, 6, .12)x = \$1,200,000$$
$$4.1114x = \$1,200,000$$
$$x = \$\ 291,871$$

PAYMENT FROM MGGN TO MCFI

$$(P/A, 6, .14)x = \$1,500,000$$
$$3.8887x = \$1,500,000$$
$$x = \$\ 385,733$$

IMPACT OF A LEVERAGED LEASE ON THE LESSOR

Assume that the greenhouse is in place by January 1, 1985, and that the lease begins on that date, with payments to the lessor and to the bank taking place each December 31. The following entries reflect the impact of the leveraged lease on the lessor for income tax purposes *only* during the first year, assuming the asset is eligible for a 10 percent investment tax credit on December 31, 1984, the date the lessor takes title to the greenhouse.[27]

12/31/84	Greenhouse (or Leased assets)	1,500,000	
	Cash		300,000
	Mortgage payable (12%)		1,200,000
	(To acquire greenhouse from builder)		
12/31/84	Income taxes payable	150,000	
	Income tax expense		150,000
	(To record 10 percent tax credit on purchase of greenhouse)		
1/1/85	Memo: Enter into 6-year lease with MGGN for greenhouse.		
12/31/85	Mortgage payable (12%)	147,871	
	Interest expense	144,000[a]	
	Cash		291,871
	(To record first payment on mortgage, including interest expense, for 1985)		
12/31/85	Depreciation expense—greenhouse	500,000	
	Accumulated depreciation		500,000
	(To record 1 year's depreciation expense for tax purposes)		
12/31/85	Cash	385,733	
	Rent Revenue		385,733
	(To record receipt of rent from MGGN)		

[a] $1,200,000 × .12 = $144,000.

[27] Note that these entries are not necessarily those that would be recorded for financial reporting purposes. They are intended simply to illustrate the tax impact on the lessor.

Several points might be mentioned regarding the leveraged lease. First, the 10-percent investment credit entry of December 31, 1984, is assumed to reduce the existing balance in MCFI's 1984 income tax payable.[28] Second, the lessor is treating the lease as an operating lease for tax purposes and is depreciating the asset over its 6-year life. We assume that the only statements that MCFI prepares are for tax purposes, that MCFI is in a 50-percent tax bracket, and that MCFI has other profitable activities against which it can apply the tax credits and operating losses of the MGGN lease agreement.

TAXABLE INCOME AND CASH FLOW EFFECTS

What is the impact on taxable income and cash flow of the MGGN lease during the first year? The following analysis demonstrates the positive effects of the leveraged lease for MCFI during the first year of the lease:

TAXABLE INCOME EFFECT (TAX PURPOSES ONLY)		
1984:	Reduction in tax payable	$ 150,000
1985:	Rent revenue	$ 385,733
	Interest expense	(144,000)
	Depreciation expense	(500,000)
	Operating loss from MGGN lease	$(258,267)
	Income tax reduction at 50% rate	$(129,134)
CASH FLOW EFFECT		
December 31, 1984:	Cash payment to bank	$(300,000)
	Cash savings from tax credit	150,000
	Net initial cash inflow (outflow)	$(150,000)
December 31, 1985:	Cash rent payment from MGGN	$ 385,733
	Cash mortgage payment to bank	(291,871)
	Cash inflow	93,862
	Cash savings from taxes	129,134
	Net cash inflow	$ 222,996

The initial outlay of $150,000 is fully recovered in 1 year, with an additional return of over $70,000 (about 49 percent). This first year's effect is very attractive to the lessor, however it should be noted that for the analysis to be relevant, the lessor must have at least $258,267 in taxable income in 1985 from other sources to be able to take advantage of the $129,134 in tax savings. Exhibit F–1 provides the taxable income and cash-flow data for the entire 6-year lease period. Considering the time value of money, the cash flow effects and the opportunity for MCFI to explore other such leases, the economic feasibility of leveraged leases to both the lessor and the lessee makes them attractive.

ANALYSIS OF LEVERAGED LEASES

Many of the variables such as interest rate, life of asset, amount of investment tax credit, amount of down payment required of lessee (none in this case), amount of

[28] For a detailed discussion of accounting methods for the investment tax credit, see Chapter 17.

EXHIBIT F-1

INCOME STATEMENT DATA FOR LESSOR (MCFI)

YEAR-END	RENT RECEIVED	LESSOR'S MORTGAGE			DEPRECIATION EXPENSE	TAXABLE INCOME (LOSS)	TAX PAYABLE (50%) INCREASE (DECREASE)	NET CASH FLOW
		12% INTEREST	PRINCIPLE	TOTAL PAYMENT				
1984	0	0	0	0	0	0	0	$(150,000)
1985	$ 385,733	$144,000	$ 147,871	$ 291,871	$ 500,000	$(258,267)	$(129,134)	222,996
1986	385,733	126,255	165,616	291,871	333,333	(73,855)	(36,928)	130,790
1987	385,733	106,382	185,489	291,871	222,222	57,129	28,565	65,298
1988	385,733	84,123	207,748	291,871	148,148	153,462	76,731	17,131
1989	385,733	59,193	232,678	291,871	148,148	178,392	89,196	4,666
1990	385,733	31,273	260,598	291,871	148,140	206,311	103,156	(9,294)
	$2,314,398	$551,226	$1,200,000	$1,751,226	$1,500,000	$ 263,172	$ 131,586	$ 281,587

down payment required by lessor (usually 20 to 50 percent) will affect the economic feasibility of a leveraged lease. The example given is not meant to be typical but is merely designed to demonstrate the potentially beneficial effects on the lessor when the lessor borrows to finance a leased asset. It might be noted that certain tax benefits, such as who will depreciate the leased asset and who will take the investment tax credit, are also negotiable elements of a leveraged lease agreement. In the case illustrated, it is possible that MGGN is accounting for the greenhouse as a capital lease for financial reporting purposes but has passed on the right to depreciate the greenhouse for tax purposes to MCFI. Why would MGGN agree to such an arrangement? Two commonly observable facts would justify such a clause in a leveraged lease agreement: (1) the lessee (MGGN) is in need of the leased asset but is not profitable for tax purposes and is not currently paying taxes (or is not paying significant amounts of taxes over a period of several years) and therefore cannot benefit from the depreciation expense on the leased asset for tax purposes; and (2) the lessee needs the asset for operations but will not have cash with which to acquire the asset until sometime in the future and therefore must accept the lessor's suggestion that it forgo the depreciation for tax purposes in order to obtain the desired asset. New businesses or closely held corporations that operate at close to zero taxable income are among the entities who often enter into such an arrangement. However, established publicly held entities have also been involved in leveraged leases as well from the position of both lessor and lessee.

Actual instances of leveraged leasing activities are not commonly observable in published financial reports of publicly held companies because the relationship between a lessor's debt and assets owned for leasing purposes is not direct. Lessors may simply have long-term leases receivable. For example, a recent balance sheet of General Electric Credit Corporation, the finance affiliate of General Electric, reported $1,207,100,000 of investments in leases, along with long-term notes payable of $1,743,000 (senior debt) and $324,800,000 (subordinate debt).[29] While General Electric Credit has both lease receivables and long-term debt, it is not clear from the balance sheet data that any of the leases are leveraged leases by de-

[20] For details, see Exhibit 14-6 in Chapter 14.

ANNOUNCEMENT OF LEASE COMMITMENT

NUGGET OIL CORPORATION

$15,680,000
(Maximum Equipment Cost)

*Lease Financing Commitment for Three Land
Drilling Rigs provided by*

General Electric Credit
CORPORATION

*The undersigned initiated this transaction and
assisted in the negotiations.*

Prescott, Ball & Turben

Members New York Stock Exchange. Inc./Member SIPC

Cleveland   New York

sign. Announcements made in the financial press, such as the one in Exhibit F-2, serve to notify shareholders that General Electric Credit Corporation is involved in these activities, as well as to suggest to potential lessees that the company may be a source of investment capital.

LESSOR ACCOUNTING FOR LEVERAGED LEASES PER GAAP

The financial accounting method for lessors required for leveraged leases is *not* the same as the cash-flow effects illustrated above. For financial reporting, lessors are required to use an accounting method that to some extent smooths out the earnings from the leveraged lease over the life of the lease. Leveraged leases are characterized by an initial outflow of cash, followed by a period of declining inflows that turn negative in the final stage of the lease (see Exhibit F-1, last column). Since the flows are very uneven but are predictable once the lease is signed, the smoothing procedure allocates the earnings to the periods covered by the lease on a more uniform basis.[30]

[30] For details, see *Statement of Financial Accounting Standards No. 13*, "Accounting for Leases" (Stamford, CT:FASB, November) pars. 41–47.

Q15-1 Why is the determination of substance over form important and difficult in leasing situations?

Q15-2 How would you characterize the "spirit" of current GAAP relating to lease accounting?

Q15-3 Describe in your own words the criteria used to classify leases as operating and capital from the lessee's point of view? Evaluate the criteria as a whole in terms of their usefulness in determining substance over form.

Q15-4 From the lessor's point of view, leases are classified as operating, direct financing, or sales-type leases. What are major differences in the lessor's objectives for engaging in a lease transaction for each classification?

Q15-5 What differences exist in lease classification criteria between lessors and lessees? Why are such differences necessary?

Q15-6 How is an interest rate determined for lessee accounting for capitalized leases? Why do you think promulgated GAAP address this issue in particular?

Q15-7 When can the lessor's and lessee's minimum lease payments be different?

Q15-8 What contractual provisions extend a lease term beyond the fixed noncancelable term? In general, what accounting effects does such an extension create?

Q15-9 Contrast the substance and the form of sales-leaseback agreements. How do promulgated GAAP respond to this distinction?

Q15-10 "Off-balance-sheet" financing has been cited as one problem solved by current GAAP for leases. If "off-balance-sheet" financing is defined as the nondisclosure of what is in substance a long-term lease liability, how would you evaluate the effectiveness of current GAAP in solving this problem?

Q15-11* What is a leveraged lease?

Q15-12* Is there differential effect on lessee accounting procedures for a leverages lease as opposed to a non-leveraged lease?

C15-1 Coral Dredging, Inc., has signed a 5-year contract to maintain a ship channel. In order to perform the required service it must either buy, rent, or lease a dredging vessel. Coral's management is very concerned about its financial position because of covenants in an existing bond contract, which call for the maintenance of a certain debt-to-equity ratio (that is, total debt to total stockholders' equity).

REQUIRED Discuss the initial effects on Coral's debt-to-equity ratio of each of the following courses of action: (1) purchasing the vessel with a long-term mortgage note, (2) renting the vessel on a monthly basis, (3) acquiring the vessel through a capital lease, and (4) the issuing of common stock whose proceeds would be used to purchase the equipment for cash.

C15-2 McMann Company constructs communications satellites that it sells to major companies and governments throughout the world. To date all sales have been on a cash basis, but that policy is being reconsidered because major competitors have started allowing various forms of long-term purchases and leasing plans. McMann's president calls upon you to explain why a major competitor, whom he knows leases its products, shows no lease revenue on its published income statement. The competitor's income statements show all its revenues in the form of sales and interest income.

REQUIRED Draft a reply to the president's inquiry.

C15-3 DoNuts Are Us has outlets in many major cities nationwide. Each outlet is owned by a manager under a franchising contract that calls for a franchise fee and a percentage of total sales to be remitted to the company. In return the company provides advertising and sells operating equipment, ingredients, and supplies to outlets at cost. Max Weber, a prospective manager needs $150,000 to purchase the necessary building and equipment. His bank is willing to provide the capital under a 10-year leasing arrangement.

REQUIRED Explain to Mr. Weber, what contractual terms are necessary if *his* accounting records are to show the building and equipment as assets.

C15-4 Recognized revenue of manufacturer-lessors is very sensitive to interest rates used in valuing lease receivables.

REQUIRED Describe a rational policy for establishing revenue to be recognized by a company that engages in sales-type leases with a wide variety of customers who are charged different interest rates.

C15-5 Penn National Railroad is considering the acquisition of rolling stock. The company's treasurer insists that an operating lease is most desirable for a variety of reasons. Operating personnel argue that any leasing agreement must contain an option to purchase the equipment.

REQUIRED Explain the accounting effects of purchase options in leasing agreements with particular attention being paid to maintaining an operating lease classification.

C15-6 Marathon Inns operates several resort hotels. The one hotel that is not owned was put into operation on March 1, 1983, the beginning of the fiscal period, under a lease agreement. The hotel is expected to have a 40-year useful life, with a $1,000,000 residual value. Straight-line depreciation is used on all hotels. The lessor is National Life Insurance and the terms of lease are as follows:

Term	20 years, noncancellable
Applicable interest rate	15%
Ownership	Transfers to Marathon at the termination date upon final required payment
Fiscal-year-end lease payments	$1,500,000 due on 2/28 of each year
Termination payment	$5,000,000

REQUIRED Compose a footnote that contains the required disclosure for the above lease as of February 29, 1984 (leap year). Dollar amounts need not be shown.

C15-7 Redford Mills has been advised that considerable tax savings could be earned and working capital could be increased by selling its factory building to a bank at its fair value and then leasing it back over the building's estimated useful life.

REQUIRED Explain in general terms how the gain or loss on the sale of the buildings would be handled for accounting purposes.

C15-8 Assume that you are going into the deep-sea-fishing charter business. You estimate revenues and costs for your first year of operations as follows:

Revenues	200 days at $400 per day
Variable expenses	60% of revenues

The only fixed expense is expected to be related to the boat, which must be rented, purchased, or leased. Several boats are available:

Rental	Minimum rental is for 250 days a year at $150 per day. The contract calls for a 1-year rental.
Purchase	$80,000 to be paid back by five equal year-end payments with a 19 percent annual interest charge.
Lease	Seven year-end payments of $23,500. Title is transferred at termination.

REQUIRED Discuss the advantages and disadvantages of each alternative.

C15–9 Arkansas Investment, Inc., is planning to open a leasing service group that would engage primarily in direct financing leases. The vice-president who is to head up the new group gives you the following hypothetical situation: Arkansas Investment, Inc., purchases a shopping center complex and leases it to an operating company under a 20-year lease with no transfer of title.

REQUIRED Explain the significance of the transfer of title clause in this situation. What potential impact does it have on accounting for the leases?

C15–10 Consider the following statement: "Current accounting rules are such that leased equipment can appear as a long-term asset on the books of both the lessee and the lessor."

REQUIRED Is this in conformity with the spirit of accounting standards? Can you formulate a lease contract that would make such a statement at least plausible?

C15–11 During 1981 and 1982 there was a great deal of leasing activity that was essentially designed to shift the tax benefits of property from companies that could not take advantage of the benefits due to operating losses, and so on, to companies that could take advantage of the benefits. One means of shifting these benefits from one company to another is through sale-leaseback activities.

REQUIRED Assume that the U.S. Car Company is going to acquire equipment costing $4,000,000 with an expected economic life of 5 years. Because of operating losses, U.S. Car is unable to benefit from the investment credit or the depreciation on the equipment. How can U.S. Car benefit indirectly from the tax advantages by a sale-leaseback arrangement with Interstate Business Machines (IBM)? IBM has no interest in owning the equipment but is interested in reducing its income taxes, which are in excess of $3,000,000 annually. Explain how a sale-leaseback arrangement could benefit both parties.

C15–12 (CPA ADAPTED) Milton Corporation entered into a lease arrangement with James Leasing Corporation for a certain machine. James's primary business is leasing, and it is not a manufacturer or dealer. Milton will lease the machine for a period of 3 years, which is 50 percent of the machine's economic life. James will take possession of the machine at the end of the initial 3-year lease and lease it to another smaller company that does not need the most current version of the machine. Milton does not guarantee any residual value for the machine and will not purchase the machine at the end of the lease term.

Milton's incremental borrowing rate is 10 percent, and the implicit rate in the lease is $8^{1}/_{2}$ percent. Milton has no way of knowing the implicit rate used by James. Using either rate, the present value of the minimum lease payments is between 90 and 100 percent of the fair value of the machine at the date of the lease agreement. Milton has agreed to pay all executory costs directly, and no allowance for these costs is included in the lease payments. James is reasonably certain that Milton will make all lease payments, and, because Milton has agreed to pay all executory costs, there are no important uncertainties regarding costs to be incurred by James.

REQUIRED With respect to Milton (the lessee) answer the following:

1. What type of lease has been entered into? Explain the reason for your answer.
2. How should Milton compute the appropriate amount to be recorded for the lease or asset acquired.
3. What accounts will be created or affected by this transaction and how will the costs related to the transaction be matched with earnings?
4. What disclosures must Milton make regarding this lease or asset?

With respect to James (the lessor) answer the following:

1. What type of leasing arrangement has been entered into? Explain the reason for your answer.
2. How should this lease be recorded by James and how are the appropriate amounts determined?

3. How should James determine the appropriate amount of earnings to be recognized from each lease payment?
4. What disclosures must James make regarding this lease?

C15–13 (CPA ADAPTED) Capital leases and operating leases are the two classifications of leases described in FASB pronouncements from the standpoint of the lessee.

REQUIRED

1. Describe how a capital lease would be accounted for by the lessee, both at the inception of the lease and during the first year of the lease, assuming the lease transfers ownership of the property to the lessee by the end of the lease.
2. Describe how an operating lease would be accounted for by the lessee, both at the inception of the lease and during the first year of the lease, assuming equal monthly payments are made by the lessee at the beginning of each month. Describe the change in accounting, if any, when rental payments are not made on a straight-line basis.

Note: Do not discuss the criteria for distinguishing between capital leases and operating leases.

C15–14 (CPA ADAPTED) Sales-type leases and direct financing leases are two of the classifications of leases described in FASB pronouncements from the standpoint of the lessor.

REQUIRED Compare and contrast a sales-type lease with a direct financing lease regarding the following:

1. Gross investment in the lease
2. Amortization of unearned interest income
3. Manufacturer's or dealer's profit

Note: Do not discuss the criteria for distinguishing between the leases described above and operating leases.

EXERCISES

E15–1 A company has the following alternatives: (1) leasing equipment for $2,035.08 per month under an operating lease or (2) leasing the same equipment for year-end lease payments of $24,421, including $21,000 in interest in the first year under a capital lease. The leased property has a fair value of $150,000 and a 10-year estimated useful life, with no estimated salvage value.

REQUIRED Show the journal entries necessary to record payments under each leasing agreement for the first year.

E15–2 Consider the following facts related to a lease contract:

Original fair value of leased asset	$100,000
Lease term and estimated useful life of leased asset	4 years
Effective interest rate	10%
Estimated residual value	None

Compute the lease payments required for the above if (1) an ordinary annuity of four payments is applicable and (2) if an annuity due of four payments is appliable.

E15–3 A lease contract calls for seven equal year-end payments of $20,000 each and applies an effective interest rate of 14 percent. In addition, there is a bargain purchase option of $10,000 at the end of the seventh year. Compute the initial lease liability for the lessee.

E15–4 On January 1, 1983, a bank purchases an apartment house and immediately leases it to a small corporation. The lease is noncancelable for 10 years and calls for ten year-end payments of $100,000 per year through December 31, 1992, followed by a renewable option period of five year-end payments of $10,000 per year and then a transfer of ownership. The $10,000 payments are estimated to be well below the expected fair rental value for that period. The building has an expected useful life of 40 years. A 10-percent interest rate is applicable.

REQUIRED What is the lessor's net lease receivable at the inception of the lease?

E15–5 Consider the following lease agreement:

Inception of lease	1/1/84
Estimated executory cost	$5,000 per year paid by lessee
Fixed noncancelable lease term	5 years (ownership remains with lessor after lease term)
Estimated economic life	6 years
Lessee's minimum lease payments	$80,000 per year (year-end payments)
Estimated unguaranteed residual at 12/31/88	$30,000
Effective interest rate	12%

REQUIRED Compute (1) the lessor's net lease receivable at January 1, 1984, and (2) the lessee's 1984 interest expense.

E15–6 A truck rental agency has two surplus heavy-duty vehicles that it wants to dispose of. Each truck has a book value of $164,000. On January 1, 1984, two agreements are made for their disposition as follows:

> Truck 1: Sold for Cash of $147,500.
>
> Truck 2: Leased under a 4-year noncancelable lease contract that calls for four year-end payments of $51,664. The interest rate implicit in the lease is 15 percent. Ownership does not transfer, and the truck has a remaining useful life of 4 years.

REQUIRED Show the January 1, 1984, journal entries for each transaction and give the rationale for the lease entry.

E15–7 A lessee acquires an asset through a capitalizable lease with the following terms:

Inception of lease	7/1/83
Lease payment amounts and due dates	$10,000 on 6/30/84, 6/30/85, and 6/30/86
Bargain purchase option at 6/30/86	$4,500
Effective interest rate	12%

REQUIRED Construct an amortization schedule and 1983 journal entries for the above lease assuming a December 31 year-end.

E15–8 Consider the following amortization schedule for a capitalized lease.

DATE	PAYMENT	INTEREST[a]	REDUCTION IN LEASE PAYABLE	LEASE LIABILITY
1/1/84				94,328[b]
12/31/84	$ 42,000	$15,092	$26,908	67,420
12/31/85	42,000	10,787	31,213	36,207
12/31/86	42,000	5,793	36,207	
	$126,000	$31,672	$94,328	

[a] Interest rate applicable to the lease is 16%.

[b] (P/A, 3, .16) ($42,000) = $94,328.

REQUIRED Indicate the current/noncurrent classification on the lessee's 12/31/84 balance sheet.

E15–9* You have just inherited $1,000,000 from your uncle and are interested in investing your fortune. A local business, Fellingham and Wolfson Corporation, is about to expand and needs $3,000,000 for its new facilities. You decide it is a sound business with good future prospects and decide to purchase the facilities with $750,000 in cash plus a $2,250,000 mortgage note from the Oceanside State Bank. The mortgage is to be repaid in year-end annual installments over a 15-year period with interest of 14 percent. After purchasing the facilities on December 31, 1983, you lease them to the Fellingham and Wolfson Corporation over a 20-year period, with annual payments beginning December 31, 1984, to include 18 percent interest on any unpaid principal amount. Fellingham and Wolfson Corporation will take title to the facilities at the end of the 20-year period. You will depreciate the facilities on a straight-line basis for tax purposes over the 20-year lease term.

REQUIRED

1. What is the annual lease payment amount to be paid by Fellingham and Wolfson?
2. What is the impact on your net cash flow for 1983 and 1984 assuming: (a) a 10 percent investment tax credit; (b) a 40 percent tax rate; and (c) $800,000 and $600,000 in other taxable income for 1983 and 1984, respectively?

PROBLEMS

P15–1 Delta Jewelry Stores, Inc., has 20 retail outlets in the Southeast, mostly in shopping centers. Until December 31, 1983, each outlet was rented by way of short-term (less than 1 year) renewable rental agreements. Rental payments charged to the Rent Expense account in 1983 totaled $1,500,000. Delta has plans to add one major new location on January 1, 1984, and is currently evaluating three alternatives: (1) A 6-month rental contract with one 6-month renewal option for $10,000 per month. (2) A 20-year noncancelable lease, with no transfer of ownership at the end of the period. Year-end lease payments are $100,000 per year, and the leased property has a fair value of $500,000. (3) A purchase of land and a building for $1,400,000 with long-term bank financing. The building has a fair value of $500,000 and a useful life of 20 years. The bank loan would require $300,000 down plus four equal year-end installments. Delta's incremental borrowing rate is 20 percent. Use 20 percent for all computations.

REQUIRED

1. Discuss the effects of each alternative on Delta's December 31, 1984, financial statements under current GAAP.
2. Discuss the pros and cons of each method of financing the retail outlet from a management perspective.

P15–2 Midwest Coastal, Inc., owns heavy dredging equipment used in harbor maintenance, channel construction, and other maritime applications. In addition to bidding on projects that require company-manned equipment, Midwest also leases some of its equipment with no crews, in which case the lessee has all operating control. Midwest is about to sign such a contract for a dredge with the Army Corps of Engineers with the following stipulations:

1. A 5-year noncancelable lease with annual year-end payments of $2,000,000 per year. The interest rate implicit in the lease is 13 percent.
2. The Corps of Engineers has full responsibility for manning, maintenance, and operation.
3. The remaining useful life of the dredge is estimated to be 7 years, and the dredge's value on Midwest's books is $5,500,000. The dredge's current fair value is $8,000,000.

4. The Corps of Engineers guarantees an $800,000 residual, which is equal to the estimated fair value at the termination of the lease.

REQUIRED

1. From Midwest's perspective, what is the substance of this transaction? What accounting rules apply?
2. Without prejudice to your answers above, what journal entries are necessary for Midwest at the inception of the lease and at the first lease payment date if this lease is determined to be a sales-type lease?

P15-3 Joskie Industries has owned an office building in downtown Cleveland for 5 years. The building, which was purchased on January 1, 1979, has the following history:

Purchase price	$20,000,000
Accumulated depreciation[a]	4,500,000
Net book value at 12/31/83	$15,500,000

[a] The building, which had an initial estimated useful life of 20 years and a $2,000,000 estimated salvage vaue, has been depreciated on a straight-line basis for 5 years.

At December 31, 1983, Joskie is in desperate need of cash and has the opportunity to sell the office building to Clevestate, Inc., for $17,000,000 in cash, with an agreement to lease it back from Clevestate for 20 payments of $2,400,000 each, starting January 1, 1984, as part of a 20-year noncancelable lease. An interest rate of 15 percent is applicable to this lease transaction. The building has a fair value of about $17,500,000.

REQUIRED

1. How would such a transaction affect the liquid position of Joskie Industries?
2. What is the accounting treatment for such a transaction? Show all journal entries and computations at January 1, 1984.

P15-4 You are the auditor for Sea Transport, a major shipping company. In reviewing various obligations outstanding, you come across a 10-year rental contract with Nola Shipyards relating to two oil tankers. These oil tankers are not capitalized by Sea Transport, and the rental payments are recorded as operating lease payments. Your scrutiny of the contracts reveals the following:

1. The rental agreement can be canceled by Nola only.
2. The agreement contains a clause that allows Sea Transport to purchase the oil tankers for $500,000 each at the end of the lease term.

You analyze all aspects of the contract and determine that none of the criteria for capitalizing a lease are met, except for the purchase option, about which you are uncertain.

REQUIRED

1. Discuss why the issue of purchase options is important.
2. How would you determine if a bargain purchase option exists in the Sea Transport case?

P15-5 Chattanooga Locomotive Manufacturing Company manufactures locomotives at a cost of $2,000,000 each. They offer customers two plans for payment. One is a single cash payment of $3,000,000. The other is a 10-year "lease" plan that transfers title at the end of the noncancelable lease term for a $1 additional payment. On the lease plan, Chattanooga earns an effective 10 percent rate.

REQUIRED

1. Show the journal entry to record a sale of one locomotive under the cash plan and show the journal entry to record cost of goods sold.
2. If Chattanooga leases a locomotive on January 1, 1985, with payments due on December 31 of each year, show all journal entries relating to the lease on January 1, 1985, and December 31, 1985.
3. B&O Railroad is trying to decide whether to acquire a locomotive under the cash plan or lease plan described above. Under the cash plan, the purchase price would be borrowed and repaid with one payment in 2 years plus interest at 10 percent per annum. The locomotive has a 20-year useful life and would be depreciated on a straight-line basis with no estimated salvage value. If the lease plan is accepted, the same depreciation plan would be applicable and B&O would capitalize the lease. The lease is effective January 1, 1985.
   a. What is the liability book value relating to the locomotive transaction under each of the plans on December 31, 1986?
   b. What is the book value of the locomotive on December 31, 1986, under each plan?
   c. What is the interest expense for 1986 under each plan?

P15-6 The leasing department of First National Bank is considering a financing arrangement for new medical equipment. The proposed scheme would have the bank pay for the equipment and then lease it to a consortium of doctors under the following contractual terms:

Inception of the lease	1/1/84
Total initial purchase cost	$8,500,000
Estimated economic life	10 years
Executory costs	Paid by lessee
Noncancelable lease term	6 years
Estimated unguaranteed residual value at the end of the sixth year	$1,000,000—ownership remains with lessor
Renewal option	The lessee has the right to rent the equipment for a 4-year period starting at the end of the lease term for $200,000 per year, which is the estimated fair value of such a rental for years 7 through 10

REQUIRED If 15 percent is the interest rate used by the bank, determine the lease payments and the accounting status of the above lease for the lessor and the lessee. Show all computations.

P15-7 Superior Products, Inc., intends to purchase a building for $3,500,000, sell it to a financial institution for $3,981,650 and then lease it back under a 20-year noncancelable lease with ownership transferring to Superior Products, Inc., at the termination of the lease. Additional facts about the lease contract and the company's operations are as follows:

Purchase and sale date of building	12/29/83
Inception of lease	1/1/84
Required lease payments	A year-end annuity of $500,000 per year for 20 years.
Lessee's incremental borrowing rate	11%
Facts about the lessee's depreciation schedule	Straight-line depreciation over an estimated useful life of 40 years. Estimated residual value, $1,000,000.

REQUIRED Show all journal entries relating to the building for 1983 and 1984 on the books of the lessee.

P15-8 On January 1, 1984, Circle Earthmovers began offering its customers alternative financing arrangements for the acquisition of its equipment. In the past it sold equipment for cash, usually relying on the customers' banks for financing. A 5-year sales-type lease is now being offered in which ownership would be transferred to the lessee at the termination of the lease. The following facts relate to equipment under consideration:

	COST TO MANUFACTURE	NORMAL SELLING PRICE
Model 84	$110,000	$192,500
Model 110	640,000	960,000

Lease payments commence 1 year after initiation of the lease. The interest rate implicit in the lease payments is to be 14 percent.

REQUIRED If during 1984 Circle sells ten Model 84 and five Model 110 earthmovers for cash and identical numbers under the leasing arrangement, what journal entries would be necessary to record the initial transactions? Show all computations.

P15-9 Consider the leasing arrangement described in the preceding problem. Assume that Washtenaw Contractors, Inc., acquires a Model 110 earthmover on June 30, 1985, under the lease contract described. The fair value of the equipment is approximately $985,000 on June 30, 1985, and Circle is demanding annuity payments of $280,000. Circle's contract shows a selling price of $961,268 and an interest rate of 14 percent. Useful life is estimated to be 7 years, with no estimated residual value, and double-declining-balance depreciation is used. The company's incremental borrowing rate at the date of signing the lease is 13 percent.

REQUIRED Assume that Washtenaw has a December 31 year-end. What journal entries related to the lease are necessary for 1985 for Washtenaw?

P15-10 Follett Company is considering leasing a drilling rig under an arrangement that has a noncancelable term followed by an option to rent at fair rental prices and finally an option to purchase as diagramed below:

```
1/1/84                          12/31/87                          12/31/89
     Noncancelable lease term        Rental option period with
  |                              |                              |
     with year-end payments           $1,000,000 annual
     of $3,410,000                     year-end payments
Inception                                            Purchase option
of lease                                             Price = $200,000
```

On January 1, 1984, the leased equipment has a fair value of approximately $12,200,000 and an estimated useful life of 10 years, with no estimated residual value. The estimated residual value at December 31, 1989, is $1,000,000, and the purchase option price at that time is $200,000. Assume that 10 percent is an appropriate interest rate.

REQUIRED

1. Is this a capitalizable lease for Follett? Give arguments to support your answer.
2. Without prejudice to your answer in requirement 1, compute Follett's booked asset value on January 1, 1984, for the rig under the assumption that it is capitalized.
3. Record the lease transaction on Jan. 1, 1984.

P15-11 (CMA ADAPTED) The Davids Corporation is a diversified company with nationwide interests in commercial real estate developments, banking, copper mining, and metal fabrication. The company has offices and operating locations in major cities throughout the United States. Corporate headquarters for Davids Corporation is located in a metropolitan area of a midwestern state, and executives connected with various phases of company operations travel extensively. Corporate management is presently evaluating the feasibility of acquiring a business aircraft that can be used by company executives to expedite business travel to areas not adequately served by commercial airlines. Proposals for either leasing or purchasing a suitable aircraft have been analyzed, and the leasing proposal was considered to be more desirable.

The proposed lease agreement involves a twin-engine turboprop Viking that has a fair market value of $900,000. This plane would be leased for a period of 10 years beginning January 1, 1984. The lease agreement is cancelable only upon accidental destruction of the plane. An annual lease payment is to be made on January 1, 1984. Maintenance operations are strictly scheduled by the lessor, and Davids Corporation will pay for these services as they are performed. Estimated annual maintenance costs are $6,200. The lessor will pay all insurance premiums and local property taxes, which amount to a combined total of $3,600 annually and are included in the annual lease payment of $127,600. Upon expiration of the 10-year lease, Davids Corporation can purchase the Viking for $40,000. The estimated useful life of the plane is 15 years, and its salvage value in the used-plane market is estimated to be $100,000 after 10 years. The salvage value probably will never be less than $75,000 if the engines are overhauled and maintained as prescribed by the manufacturer. If the purchase option is not exercised, possession of the plane will revert to the lessor, and there is no provision for renewing the lease agreement beyond its termination on December 31, 1993.

Davids Corporation can borrow $900,000 under a 10-year term loan agreement at an annual interest rate of 12 percent. The lessor's implicit interest rate is not expressly stated in the lease agreement, but this rate appears to be approximately 8 percent on ten net rental payments of $124,000 per year and the initial market value of $900,000 for the plane. On January 1, 1984, the present value of all net rental payments and the purchase option of $40,000 is $796,880 using the 12-percent interest rate. The present value of all net rental payments and the $40,000 purchase option on January 1, 1984, is $917,144 using the 8-percent interest rate implicit in the lease agreement. The financial vice-president of Davids Corporation has established that this lease agreement is a capital lease as defined in *Statement of Financial Accounting Standards No. 13,* "Accounting for Leases."

REQUIRED

1. What is the appropriate amount that Davids Corporation should recognize for the leased aircraft on its statement of financial position (balance sheet) after the lease is signed?

2. Without prejudice to your answer in requirement 1, assume that the annual lease payment is as stated in the question, that the appropriate capitalized amount for the leased aircraft is $884,313 on January 1, 1984, and that the appropriate interest rate is 9 percent. How will the lease be reported in the December 31, 1984, statement of financial position (balance sheet) and related income statement? (Ignore any income tax implications.)

3. Identify and explain the four factors that differentiate a capital lease from an operating lease.

P15–12 Derrick Company leased equipment with an estimated economic life of 12 years to User Company for a lease period of 10 years. The normal selling price of the equipment was $288,256, and the unguaranteed residual value at the end of the lease term was estimated to be $20,000. User Company agreed to pay an annual rental of $40,000 at the beginning of each year and was responsible for all maintenance, insurance, and property taxes. Derrick Company incurred costs of $205,000 in manufacturing the equipment and $4,000 in negotiating and closing the lease. The collectibility of the lease payments was reasonably assured, and no additional costs were expected to be incurred by Derrick Company. The implicit interest rate for Derrick Company was 9 percent per year, and this rate was known to User Company.

REQUIRED

1. How should this lease be classified by Derrick Company? Explain.

2. Assuming that Derrick Company classified this lease as a sales-type lease, compute the following at the inception of the lease:
   a. Gross investment in the lease

b. Net investment in the lease
c. Unearned interest revenue
d. Selling price of the equipment
e. Cost of goods sold

3. Prepare a table summarizing the amortization of the net investment in the lease and the recognition of interest revenue over the lease term for Derrick Company assuming the lease was signed on January 1, 1984.

4. Prepare the journal entries for the first year of the lease in the accounts of Derrick Company.

P15–13 (CPA ADAPTED)

_____ 1. To improve its cash position, R-K Industries entered into a sale and leaseback agreement with Sunco, Inc. R-K sells its office building to Sunco for $36,600,000 and leases it back under a 25-year noncancelable lease. Sunco makes no profit on the initial transaction. Payments of $2,000,000 are to be made semiannually over the term of the lease. What is the implicit interest on this agreement?

a. 5.1%   d. 10%
b. 6.0%   e. None of the above
c. 7.08%

_____ 2. On January 1, 1980, the No Asset Company leased 20 tractor trailers from the Money Company. The total fair market value of the trailers was $8,000,000, and the expected useful life of each trailer was 20 years. No Asset agreed to pay Money Company $861,000 on January 1, 1980, and $1,000,000 each subsequent January 1 for the next 11 years. The appropriate interest rate for both the lessor and lessee is 10 percent. No Asset Company must also pay all maintenance and insurance costs on the trailers, an amount estimated to be $60,000 per year. What is the interest expense on the books of No Asset Company for the year ended June 30, 1980?

a. None—this is an operating lease   d. $324,755
b. $430,500   e. $400,000
c. $286,950

_____ 3. On January 1, 1975, the Green Company entered into a noncancelable lease agreement with the Blatt Company for a machine that was carried on the accounting records of Green at $2,000,000. Total payments under the lease agreement, which expires on December 31, 1984, are $3,550,800, of which $2,400,000 represents the price of the machine to Blatt. Payments of $355,080 are due each January 1. The first payment was made on January 1, 1975, when the lease agreement was finalized. The interest rate of 10 percent, which was stipulated in the lease agreement, is considered fair and adequate compensation to Green for the use of its funds. Blatt expects the machine to have a 10-year life with no salvage value and will depreciate it on a straight-line basis. The lease agreement should be accounted for by Green as a lease equivalent to a sale and by Blatt as a lease that is, in substance, a purchase.

What should be the revenue derived by Green from this lease for the year ended December 31, 1975?

a. $204,492   c. $604,492
b. $355,080   d. $755,080

_____ 4. Assuming all information presented in the preceding problem and ignoring income taxes, what should be the expenses incurred by Blatt from this lease for the year ended December 31, 1975?

a. $204,492   c. $444,492
b. $355,080   d. $595,080

_____ 5. When the lessor's balance sheet indicates that a portion of plant assets and of the related accumulated depreciation pertains to equipment leased to customers, it is evident that:

a. The lessor used the operating method of accounting for these leases
b. The lessor has violated generally accepted accounting principles
c. These leases are "leveraged" leases as defined by FASB Statement No. 13, "Accounting for Leases"
d. The lessor classified these leases as capital leases

6. Your client constructed an office building at a cost of $500,000. The client sold the building to Q Company at a material gain and then leased it back from Q Company for a fixed annual rental. The lease is classified as an operating lease. How should the gain be treated?

    a. Recognize the gain in full as an ordinary item in the year of the transaction

    b. Recognize the gain in full as an extraordinary item in the year of the transaction

    c. Defer the gain and recognize it over the lease term

    d. Defer the gain until the end of the lease term

P15–14 (CPA ADAPTED) The Jackson Company manufactured a piece of equipment at a cost of $7,000,000 and held it for resale from January 1, 1984, to June 30, 1984, at a price of $8,000,000. On July 1, 1984, Jackson leased the equipment to the Crystal Company. The lease is appropriately recorded as an operating lease for accounting purposes. The lease is for a 3-year period expiring June 30, 1987. Equal monthly payments under the lease are $115,000 and are due on the first of the month. The first payment was made on July 1, 1984. The equipment is being depreciated on a straight-line basis over an 8-year period with no residual value expected.

REQUIRED

1. What expense should Crystal appropriately record as a result of the above facts for the year ended December 31, 1984? Show supporting computations in good form.

2. What income or loss before income taxes should Jackson appropriately record as a result of the above facts for the year ended December 31, 1984? Show supporting computations in good form.

P15–15 (CPA ADAPTED) The Truman Company leased equipment from the Roosevelt Company on October 1, 1984. The lease is appropriately recorded as a purchase for accounting purposes for Truman and as a sale for accounting purposes for Roosevelt. The lease is an 8-year period expiring September 30, 1992. Equal annual payments under the lease are $600,000 and are due on October 1 of each year. The first payment was made on October 1, 1984. The cost of the equipment on Roosevelt's accounting records was $3,000,000. The equipment has an estimated useful life of 8 years, with no residual value expected. Truman uses straight-line depreciation and takes a full year's depreciation in the year of purchase. The rate of interest contemplated by Truman and Roosevelt is 10 percent.

REQUIRED

1. What expense should Truman appropriately record as a result of the above facts for the year ended December 31, 1984? Show supporting computations in good form.

2. What income or loss before income taxes should Roosevelt appropriately record as a result of the above facts for the year ended December 31, 1984? Show supporting computations in good form.

P15–16* Merkel Furniture and Carpet Center, Inc., is a well-established local retailer of furniture and carpets. It was planning to expand its business by opening a second store in the spring of 1984. The second location was to be housed in a single building that would serve as both a showroom and a warehouse. The building cost $2,000,000 to construct. Two local businesspeople, plus one of the Merkel brothers, had formed an investment firm called DIME, Inc., which put up $200,000. DIME borrowed the remaining $1,800,000 from the Chelsea State Bank on April 1, 1984, on a 12 percent 10-year first mortgage basis with annual payments each March 31. On April 2, 1984, DIME then leased the facility to Merkel over a 10-year period with annual lease payments of $368,582 starting March 31, 1985. DIME was to receive a 10 percent investment tax credit on the building and was to receive a depreciation deduction for tax purposes over the 10-year period on a straight-line basis. Merkel was to receive title to the building on March 31, 1994, the end of the lease period. DIME also earned $700,000 in other taxable income during each of the first 2 years of the lease, which was taxable at a 45 percent rate.

REQUIRED

1. What is the implicit rate of interest charged by DIME, Inc., in the lease agreement?
2. What is DIME's net cash flow effect from the lease agreement for each of the first 2 years of the lease?
3. If Merkel treats the lease as a capital lease with the economic life of the building equal to 40 years and uses straight-line depreciation, record any necessary entries for Merkel for the years ending December 31, 1984 and 1985.
4. Explain how the answer to 3 above was affected by the fact that this is a leveraged lease.

EQUITIES

OVERVIEW

PART 3

Here we use the term **equities** to encompass all the elements disclosed on the right-hand side of a balance sheet (when presented in the account format). Some accountants refer to these elements as **liabilities and stockholders' equity,** certainly an acceptable practice. For this overview section, however, we prefer *equities* for one major reason—it emphasizes the similarities among the specific items making up the equity category, our main objective in the overview section. There are differences between these items, important differences of course, and these will be briefly mentioned here. They will become more apparent as specific topics are covered in the chapters in Part 3.

Such a thread of similarity must exist, or accountants could not logically add all the elements together and call the result "total equities" or "total liabilities and stockholders' equity." Without such a thread of similarity, that total could not be used in analyzing financial statements.

But what is it that makes liabilities similar to stockholders' equity? More specifically, what is it that makes, say, bonds payable similar to retained earnings or accounts payable similar to preferred stock or any other element properly listed as part of total equities similar to any other? If these questions are to be answered, we must search for a pattern. Whatever the pattern, it must be derived from the nature of accounting and the underlying concepts and principles we have emphasized throughout this book. Remember that accounting communicates. The external financial reports tell stories about the entity, conveying information that helps the user make rational decisions. Specifically, the balance sheet portrays the financial position of a firm at an instant in time as accurately as the accountant can reflect it, based on all the underlying assumptions and principles that we study in this text. These underlying concepts are not immutable. Instead they are subject to change as conditions change and as knowledge improves regarding those conditions. And a great deal of judgment is necessary in interpreting and applying them in the setting of a given entity.

CONCEPTUAL UNDERPINNINGS

The conceptual nature of equities can be determined in part by a broad review of the nature of assets. Assets are at the very heart of business endeavor and, consequently, at the very heart of accounting. Managers must work hard to optimize the amounts and types of assets utilized in their businesses. Certainly the corner drugstore's amounts and types of assets differ from those of large manufacturing firms. Given a firm's objectives, the effective acquisition, utilization, and disposition of assets are at the very heart of operations. Such handling of assets is generally considered to be the primary function of management. Consequently, one of the basic messages conveyed by financial statements is how successfully or unsuccessfully management has handled the asset stream.

Sources of Assets

Another function of management is to determine how and where to obtain the assets. One basic message presented by the equity side of the balance sheet is where the resources utilized to acquire the assets came from. **Equities can be viewed as sources of assets,** and that is one thread of similarity running through them.

In a broad sense, total equities are a consequence of total asset needs. Based on such factors as the anticipated demand for the entity's goods or services, management decides the optimum amount of total asset needs, asset needs by category (current and noncurrent), and specific asset element needs (cash, buildings, land, and so forth). The relationships within and between specific categories of assets (current versus noncurrent, for example) have an impact on the relationships that exist between various categories of equities (current liabilities versus long-term liabilities, for example). This is not to say, of course, that a given source of funds can necessarily be traced to the acquisition of a given asset or assets.

Claims Against the Entity

As is true of most generalizations, there are exceptions to the statement that equities are sources of assets. In Chapter 16, "Current Liabilities," we shall see that loss contingencies meeting the requirements of certain criteria are recorded as liabilities. Certainly such liabilities are not sources of assets. And this leads us to the second thread of similarity running through equities: **Equities represent claims against the entity.**

The word "claims," as used in this context, must be clearly understood. Here it is used in a very broad sense to mean that the equities have certain rights according to the terms in their contracts with the entity. The variety in these contractual agreements is almost limitless. The interpretation of them, often a difficult and judgmental process, is basic to the reasonable accounting for, and classification of, equities as short-term liabilities, long-term liabilities, stockholder equity items, or some combination of these possibilities.

Common stockholders, for example, have certain rights, such as the right to vote on a number of issues (for candidates for the board of directors, on the issuance of additional shares of common stock or bonds), the right to receive a pro rata share of any common stock dividends declared, and the right to share in the distribution of assets in the event of the firm's liquidation. However, common stockholders cannot force dividend declarations except under unusual circumstances, and if they wish to disinvest in the firm, they cannot force the firm to buy back their stock. Their claims are residual, and, these contractual terms have an impact on the manner in which accountants disclose stockholder elements in the balance sheet. Creditors, on the other hand, have specific claims to resources, and their claims generally take precedence over stockholders' claims.

Measurement of Equities

The basic measurement concept for initially recording equities is the same as that used for assets: **All equities should be measured and initially recorded at their cash-equivalent amount.** Remember that "cash equivalent" means the amount of cash necessary to settle the claim, assuming an arm's-length transaction between the parties involved. The words "initially recorded" are important. For example, 20-year bonds with a par value of $1,000,000, issued at $900,000, would be recorded as follows:

Cash	900,000	
Unamortized discount	100,000	
Bonds payable		1,000,000

Conceptually, the $900,000 is the cash-equivalent price to retire the bonds immediately after issuance. However, what if $30,000 is the unamortized discount after 10 years? The carrying value (book value) of the bonds would be $970,000 ($1,000,000 − $30,000) at that time. The $30,000 would be the result of following generally accepted accounting principles for amortization of the discount during the intervening 10 years. The $970,000 would not necessarily be (and usually would not be) the market value of the bonds at that date because the market rate of interest at that date might not be the same as the market rate at the date of issuance. Thus, the $970,000 is not the cash-equivalent price of the bonds at that date. It is the "claim" of the bondholders at that date based on having followed generally accepted accounting principles during the 10 years since issuance. We follow the "cost concept" in accounting and do not adjust equities for changes in fair market values. Thus, like assets, equities are necessarily reflected at their cash-equivalent amount *only* at the date on which they are initially recorded.

The cash-equivalent amount is not necessarily obvious, however, and must frequently be estimated. Sometimes this is best achieved using present-value concepts. This is frequently done in the case of long-term bonds and notes payable, lease obligations, and pension liabilities. Often objectively established market values are best, such as when common or preferred stock is issued for an asset. The fair market value of the stock would be used if more easily and objectively ascertainable. If not, the fair market

value of the asset would be used as a surrogate measure of the cash-equivalent price for the exchange. Other possibilities will be covered in the following chapters, but, again, the accountant must use considerable judgment in making such determinations.

INTERRELATIONSHIPS WITH THE INCOME STATEMENT

In considering equities in general, it is important to keep in mind the interrelationships between the nature and measurement of these equities and fundamental accounting concepts and generally accepted accounting principles, mainly those related to the income statement.

Accounting is evolutionary. It changes over periods of time (1) as the business, economic, and political environments change and (2) as accountants alter and adjust the generally accepted accounting principles that guide what they do. Since the mid-1930s, the main emphasis in the development of GAAP has been directed at the income statement, often with a corresponding impact on the balance sheet.

For instance, consider the bonds payable example mentioned earlier. The accounting principle (use of the effective interest method) related to amortization of discount is directed primarily at determination of the appropriate interest expense to be matched against revenues for income-determination purposes. Principles related to the deferral of taxes were also developed primarily to bring about what is considered to be a better matching of expenses and revenues. Such emphasis on the income statement, with the resulting balance sheet effects, has made it difficult at times to properly classify specific elements in the balance sheet. In any case, the interpretation and application of the matching concept during the past 50 years have perhaps had the greatest influence on the types and amounts of equities reflected in the balance sheet.

SUMMARY AND CONCLUSIONS

Despite a substantial increase in the number of promulgated standards and rules for the measurement and presentation of equities issued over the past 20 years or so, accountants must still exercise professional judgment in this area. With the advent of convertible and callable bonds and preferred stocks and the variability in contractual terms with suppliers of capital, the distinctions between various types of debt and between debt and common stockholders' equity have become blurred. Such distinctions, however, must be made if the balance sheet is to reflect the firm's financial condition as well as possible and act as a foundation for making reasonable and rational decisions about the entity. Observing the similarities between equity elements is of at least equal importance in understanding the firm's financial position and in determining how that position has changed over the years and is likely to change in the future.

Current Liabilities

16

OVERVIEW   Accounting liabilities are claims against the resources of an entity that have the following characteristics: (1) the entity to whom a payment is expected to be made is known,[1] (2) the maturity amount of the payment is known or can reasonably be estimated, and (3) the date of payment is known or can reasonably be estimated. Payment can be in the form of assets, services, forgiveness of debt, and many other transfers of value. As we shall discuss later, an obligation can be an *accounting* liability and yet not be considered a *legal* liability at the balance sheet date, or vice versa. Accountants look to the substance of the economic situation rather than to its legal form in judging whether an accounting liability exists. Sometimes commitments call for a future exchange of resources, and until one party to the agreement performs all or a part of the agreement, no liability is recorded. Such **executory contracts** could include the promise to pay for an asset upon future delivery.

Although liabilities are balance sheet items, the effects that certain liabilities have on the income statement can be quite significant. For instance, the accruing of

---

[1] In some cases the specific potential payee cannot be identified, but a unique class of entities from which the payees may emerge is known. For example, warranty liabilities are recorded, although it is not known with certainty which specific customers from the class of all customers will make claims.

unpaid wages at period-end is motivated as much by the matching principle as by the objective of disclosing all accounting liabilities on the balance sheet. The same point can be made for the recording of a liability for unearned income, such as customer advance payments. Normally, as long as the products or services for which the advance is made are not delivered, an accounting liability exists for the advance. In general, then, we must view the recording of liabilities as complementary elements of transactions that can also affect either other balance sheet items or income statement items.

As with accounts receivable, the time value of money is usually considered in the measurement of the money amount assigned to liabilities. Exceptions occur when the differences between present and future values are immaterial or when specific rules prescribe a different treatment. We shall note these exceptions in our discussions.

Current liabilities are liabilities that are expected to require the expending of a current asset or the incurring of another liability within 1 year of the balance sheet date or within the period of the entity's operating cycle, if longer. Current liabilities are important in the determination of an entity's liquidity position. The evaluation of an entity's liquidity influences the decisions of bankers, suppliers, employees, and many others who are affected by an entity's ability to pay its short-term obligations. Even those parties whose interests are often viewed as more long-term, such as bondholders and stockholders, must necessarily be concerned with the entity's short-term liquidity status. Usually both bond interest and dividend payments use up current assets and are dependent on the entity's liquidity. All such concerns translate into a need for complete accounting disclosure of short-term obligations based on objective evidence and acceptable measurement techniques.

Exhibit 16–1 shows a typical disclosure pattern in published annual reports. Note how the "commitments and contingent liabilities" are shown "short" (that is, no money amounts are given), with reference to footnotes for explanation. The commitments could refer to certain executory contracts that are not recorded but that require narrative explanation. Contingencies, as we shall discuss in detail later, are certain potential obligations that may or may not result in the recording of a liability and the eventual payment to a creditor.

EXHIBIT 16–1

DISCLOSURE OF CURRENT LIABILITIES

GEARHART INDUSTRIES, INC.
Excerpt from Balance Sheet

	JANUARY 31, 1981	1980
	(IN THOUSANDS)	
Current liabilities		
Notes payable (Note 7)	$12,370	$ 1,295
Accounts payable	17,948	9,174
Income taxes payable (Note 6)	10,132	1,902
Accrued liabilities (Note 5)	11,766	7,014
Current maturities of long-term debt (Note 8)	1,524	314
Total current liabilities	$53,740	$19,699
Commitments and contingent liabilities (Notes 12, 13 and 14)		

In this chapter we discuss the accounting concepts and techniques applicable to current and contingent liabilities (such as those in Exhibit 16–1), along with the footnotes that are often used to augment the balance sheet descriptions. The chapter focuses on three major types of liabilities: (1) current liabilities with fixed maturity values, (2) current liabilities with estimated maturity values, and (3) potential liabilities that are contingent on some future event.

CURRENT LIABILITIES WITH FIXED MATURITY VALUES

If a liability amount is to be disclosed on a balance sheet, its maturity amount and anticipated payment date must either be known or able to be reasonably estimated. Most liabilities are based on contractual agreements that fix maturity amounts, the amount of assets to be paid in order to eliminate the claim against the entity. In some cases, no such explicit agreement exists, and estimates of maturity amounts are required.

This section deals with liabilities whose future maturity amounts are known. This does not mean that judgment is not required in accounting for such liabilities. Knowledge of maturity amounts does not eliminate the need for judgment regarding interest rates and classifications. Questions of *when* and *how* interest factors are to be used in accounting for short-term liabilities require accounting judgments. Uncertainty is often encountered in distinguishing between short-term and long-term liabilities. Here, the accountant must judge whether working capital will be used up in the liquidation of a liability in order to classify the liability properly as current or noncurrent.

Accounts Payable

Accounts payable are trade obligations that arise from the acquisition of merchandise and services. The accounts payable of one entity are reflected as accounts receivable of other entities. The accounting for accounts payable, however, is not a mirror image of the accounting for accounts receivable. For example, it is usually assumed that an entity will pay all of its accounts payable. Recall that for accounts receivable, it is normal to estimate bad debts even when the creditor does not know exactly which customers will default. This is so because experience indicates that *some* defaults will occur. Debtors—in that they are assumed to be going concerns—are expected to pay all legitimate debts.

Valuation factors found in accounts receivable accounting, such as cash discounts and returns and allowances, are less troublesome in accounts payable accounting because management's intention at the balance sheet date is known. Should the gross method or net method be used to record merchandise purchases? As in accounts receivable accounting, the technique used for recording the initial transaction is not crucial because adjusting entries can always be made to achieve a period-end liability balance that is the best estimate of amounts expected to be paid. (See Chapter 9 for a discussion of the acquisition of merchandise.) If management intends to take a 2 percent discount and is able to pay within the discount period, then the liability is disclosed at 98 percent of the invoice price. The same is true of anticipated returns of unsatisfactory merchandise. If damaged merchandise is detected or can be estimated at period-end, a journal entry would be made to reduce the liability and other affected accounts by the purchase price of the goods expected to be returned.

The general rule for valuation of liabilities is the complement of the general asset valuation rule.[2] That is, the cash-equivalent value at the initial transaction date of the asset to be given up is the appropriate valuation. Because of the short period of time that normally elapses between purchase and payment, present-value computations are not required for accounts payable. This relaxation of the general rule for valuation of future asset flows is justifiable on practical grounds only. The more theoretically sound practice of always taking interest factors into consideration is not prohibited, but the cost of keeping track of the minor interest factors may outweigh the benefits of more precise financial disclosure.

Advances and Commitments on Unexecuted Contracts

Vendors sometimes receive cash from purchasers before performing the service or shipping the product. In other vendor-purchaser relationships, although no assets are transferred in advance, the purchaser may be committed to buy at specific prices during periods in which prices fluctuate. These situations may create current liabilities for parties to the unexecuted contracts, as shown in the following examples.

Advance payments   In the case of the **advance payment,** the key question is, How much is the liability? For instance, Vendor, Inc., receives $10,000 in cash from a customer as an advance payment for a truck trailer. The truck trailer will cost Vendor $7,000 to construct. What does Vendor owe the customer? If we assume that the contract calls for delivery of the trailer within 2 months of the advance payment, then it can safely be said that Vendor owes the customer the delivery of a trailer that will cost $7,000 to construct. Should the liability be recorded at $7,000 or $10,000? If the liability were to be recorded at $7,000, then revenue would have to be recognized for $3,000 in advance of delivery or even construction of the trailer in this case. The realization principle therefore suggests that a $10,000 liability should be recorded by Vendor, Inc. Delaying revenue recognition can be justified also by noting that if the delivery is not made, then $10,000 would have to be paid back to the customer. Recording of the transaction, excluding those entries related to construction of the trailer, would be as follows:

7/1/83	Cash	10,000	
	Customer advances		10,000
8/2/83	Customer advances	10,000	
	Sales		10,000

Customer advances would be disclosed as a current liability on any balance sheet dated from July 1, 1983, to August 1, 1983.

Losses on contractual commitments   In the case of a definite commitment to purchase items during a time of fluctuating prices, the purchaser sometimes finds that such a fixed commitment was unwise because prices for the item have decreased. For instance, on November 1, 1982, Brown Ice Cream Company contracted to purchase 20,000 gallons of cream per month from a dairy cooperative for all of 1983 at $2.50 per gallon. This was done in anticipation of steadily increasing prices. On De-

---

[2] Refer to the discussion of *Accounting Principles Board Opinion No. 21,* "Interest on Receivables and Payables" (New York: AICPA, August 1971) in Chapters 5 and 8. The rule states that ordinary customer receivables and supplier payables due within 1 year under customary trade terms are not required to be shown at their present values. This means that no interest factors need be applied to most accounts receivable and accounts payable.

cember 31, 1982, the end of Brown's fiscal year, the market price for cream is $1.40 per gallon and the price is expected to be at least that low for all of 1983. Brown does have an obligation to purchase the 240,000 gallons at $2.50, but is it an accounting liability? Such unexecuted contracts usually are not recorded, and the liability is not recorded until delivery has been made. Is there a liability for the $1.10 per gallon differential between the contract price and the market price at December 31, 1982? Viewed purely as an unexecuted contract, there is no liability, but one would be recorded here in order to recognize a loss on the fixed-price contract:

12/31/82	Loss on contractual commitment	264,000	
	Accrued loss on contractual commitment		264,000

In this case, the account Accrued Loss on Contractual Commitment is classified as a current liability on Brown's December 31, 1982, balance sheet. When an actual delivery is made in 1983, the following entry would be appropriate:

1/31/83	Purchases (20,000 gallons @$1.40)	28,000	
	Accrued loss on contractual commitment	22,000	
	Accounts payable (20,000 gallons @$2.50)		50,000
	(To record delivery of 20,000 gallons)		

The accounting motivation here is to have 1982 absorb the loss on the commitment to purchase cream at $2.50 per gallon. This allows the cost of the bad decision to be matched with the results of operations in the year in which the decision was made. This recognition of the loss in the commitment year is in keeping with the principle of conservatism, which suggests that all known losses are to be recognized when they become apparent.

Notes Payable and Interest Payable

The accounting issues related to **notes payable** and **interest payable** are similar to the issues discussed in Chapter 8 concerning notes and interest receivable. Determining the present value of all future cash flows necessary to liquidate the note is the major measurement problem. Usually a promissory note is interest bearing; that is, it has specific terms, such as interest rate, maturity date, and amount, which make such computations straightforward. In a non-interest-bearing note, there is no explicit interest rate, but the implicit interest rate can be computed if the present value is known. Take the situation where on January 1, 1983, Roundtree, Inc., borrows $20,000 by signing a 2-year, $24,200 maturity value note. In such a case the $20,000 of cash received is the present value, and the implicit interest rate can be computed by using the Table H–2 factors in Appendix H at the back of the book:

$$(P/F,2, i)(\$24,200) = \$20,000$$
$$(P/F,2, i) = \$20,000 \div \$24,200$$
$$(P/F,2, i) = .8264$$

The .8264 factor in Table H–2 is for a 10 percent interest rate.

There are two methods of recording notes, the net method and the gross method, which result in the same net amounts disclosed. Assume that Roundtree, Inc., ends its fiscal year on December 31. Either of the following recording patterns could be used:

GROSS METHOD					NET METHOD		
1/1/83	Cash	20,000			Cash	20,000	
	Notes payable discount	4,200					
	Notes payable		24,200		Notes payable		20,000
12/31/83	Interest expense	2,000			Interest expense	2,000	
	Notes payable discount		2,000		Notes payable		2,000
12/31/84	Notes payable	24,200			Notes payable	22,000	
	Interest expense	2,200			Interest expense	2,200	
	Notes payable discount		2,200		Cash		24,200
	Cash		24,200				

The balance sheet disclosure at December 31, 1983, for each method would appear as follows:

GROSS METHOD ROUNDTREE, INC. PARTIAL BALANCE SHEET, 12/31/83			NET METHOD ROUNDTREE, INC. PARTIAL BALANCE SHEET, 12/31/83		
Current liabilities			*Current liabilities*		
Accounts payable		$ XXX	Accounts payable		$ XXX
Notes payable (see Note X)	$24,200		Notes payable (see Note X)		22,000
Less discount	2,200	22,000			

As is true of many alternative recording techniques, the alternative technique for notes payable gives the same net balance in slightly different words. In the Roundtree case, the December 31, 1983, book value of $22,000 is the present value of $24,200 at 10 percent in 1 year:

$$(P/F, \ 1, \ .10)(\$24,200) =$$
$$(.9091)(\$24,200) = \$22,000$$

In the Roundtree case, if the liquidation of the liability will definitely require $24,200 within 12 months of the balance sheet date, why is the liability only $22,000? As with all accruals of expenses, one justification can be found in the matching principle. The benefits derived from the loan and the cost of the loan are matched. In our example, only 1 year had elapsed at December 31, 1983, and, therefore, only 1 year's interest charge should have been expensed in the fiscal year ending December 31, 1983. Although the *discount* on a note payable is defined as the difference between the present value and the maturity value, it is actually composed of a mixture of principal and interest elements. Roundtree's discount account at December 31, 1983, can be analyzed as follows:

	PRESENT VALUE AT 12/31/83	+	DISCOUNT AT 12/31/83	=	MATURITY VALUE AT 12/31/84
Principal	$18,182[a]	+	$1,818	=	$20,000
Interest	3,818[b]	+	382	=	4,200
Total	$22,000	+	$2,200	=	$24,200

[a] $18,182 = (P/F,1,.10)($20,000).

[b] $3,818 = (P/F,1,.10)($4,200).

EXHIBIT
16–2

FOOTNOTE DISCLOSURE FOR NOTES PAYABLE

GEARHART INDUSTRIES, INC.
Excerpt from Note on Short-term Borrowings

A summary of notes payable to banks primarily for foreign borrowings during fiscal years 1981, 1980, and 1979 is as follows:

	1981	1980	1979
	(DOLLAR AMOUNTS IN THOUSANDS)		
End of period:			
Balance	$12,370	$ 1,295	$ 253
Average interest rate	26.0%	24.0%	32.0%
During the period:			
Average outstanding monthly balance	$ 2,090	$ 8,700	$1,019
Weighted average interest rate	20.5%	17.1%	11.1%
Maximum month-end balance	$12,370	$16,100	$6,000

The average outstanding monthly balance for each period was computed by averaging the month-end balances during the year. The weighted average interest rate for each period was computed by dividing the interest expense by the average amount outstanding.

The relatively high average interest rates on foreign loans reflect the cost of borrowing in certain foreign countries which presently have significantly higher inflation rates than the United States.

Interest expense on short-term borrowings for fiscal years 1981, 1980, and 1979 was $709,000, $1,481,000 and $114,000, respectively.

The above analysis is applicable to many discount and premium situations in accounting. It points out that the disclosure of the present value of future cash flows is the principle governing notes payable accounting.

Annual reports should show notes payable at their net present value with sufficient disclosure so that readers can determine the effective interest rate and the maturity values.[3] Exhibit 16–2 shows how Gearhart Industries, Inc., disclosed its notes payable in a recent annual report. (See Exhibit 16–1 for the corresponding balance sheet.)

The Interaction of Long-term and Short-term Debt Classifications

As of each balance sheet date, accountants must decide on the classification of items into **long-term** and **short-term** categories. The criteria for such classifications (see Chapters 2, 4, and 5 for a discussion of the general principles involved) can usually be applied in a straightforward way, but sometimes circumstances can lead to uncertainties. Several common patterns are discussed in turn: (1) debt previously classified as long-term being reclassified as short-term, (2) debt previously classified as long-term that is maturing but is not being reclassified in anticipation of further long-term financing, and (3) debt previously classified as short-term being reclassified as long-term in anticipation of long-term financing.

All long-term liabilities are expected to be paid off eventually or refinanced, and, of course, reclassification to short-term occurs for any balance sheet dated within 1 year (or operating cycle, if longer) of the anticipated payment date. This is accomplished by direct adjustment to the balance sheet, usually with no journal entries being necessary. Having current maturities of long-term debt being reclassified is necessary if a clear picture of the entity's liquidity position is to be reported. In some cases, management may expect to pay the currently maturing long-term debt

[3] Ibid., par. 15.

EXHIBIT 16–3

DISCLOSURE OF RECLASSIFICATIONS OF DEBT FROM SHORT-TERM TO LONG-TERM

McCORMICK & COMPANY, INCORPORATED
Excerpt from Notes

Long-term Debt

On January 12, 1981, the Company negotiated a $25,000,000 credit agreement with four domestic banks providing for revolving credit and term loans maturing in installments from 1985 to 1991 . . . .

In addition, the Company has entered into multicurrency credit facilities aggregating $12,000,000 with two foreign banks . . . .

Because of the availability of long-term financing under the terms of these agreements and the Company's intent to refinance a portion of its short-term commercial paper and bank borrowings on a long-term basis, $30,000,000 of short-term borrowings has been reclassified as long-term debt at November 30, 1980.

MEASUREX CORPORATION
Excerpt from Notes

Long-term Debt

On February 13, 1980, the Company entered into an agreement, effective November 30, 1979, with a group of four banks for a five-year unsecured revolving $25.0 million term loan. At November 30, 1980 and 1979, $2.8 million and $19.9 million, respectively, of notes payable has been reclassified to long-term debt under this agreement.

with funds that have been accumulated for the purpose of retiring the debt (for example, a bond sinking fund). In such cases where no working capital is expected to be consumed, it is not necessary to recognize a current liability for the maturing debt as of the balance sheet date.

The distinction between short-term and long-term also becomes blurred when debt that is currently maturing is expected to be refinanced on a long-term basis. Management may expect to pay off the current maturity of a long-term debt with the proceeds of long-term financing. Alternatively, management may expect to restructure a short-term loan into a long-term debt. The critical accounting judgment is, What are the chances of management's expectation actually occurring? **FASB Statement No. 6** guides accounting judgment on this issue by giving the conditions necessary for the exclusion of debt that would normally be classified as a short-term liability from the current liability classification.[4] The entity must both intend to refinance the obligation on a long-term basis and be able to consummate the refinancing. The ability to refinance can be demonstrated either by actual refinancing between the balance sheet date and the date on which financial statements are issued or by the existence by the statement date of a definite agreement permitting the debtor to refinance on a long-term basis. Footnote disclosure of any such agreement is required, and the excerpts in Exhibit 16–3 exemplify the typical disclosure. Note that in the case of McCormick & Company, the balance sheet would show $30,000,000 as long-term, although that amount matures within a year of the balance sheet date. In the case of Measurex Corporation, the availability of the revolving 5-year term loan allowed for reclassification of short-term maturities.

Obligations Related to Employee Compensation

Business entities frequently pay employees on schedules that do not exactly correspond to accounting periods. For instance, if a company's payday for hourly workers is always on Friday, most accounting periods will end on a day other than a payday. This creates the need for accrual entries to record expenses and current liabilities

[4] *Statement of Financial Accounting Standards No. 6,* "Classification of Short-Term Obligations Expected to Be Refinanced" (Stamford, CT: FASB, May 1975).

related to the unpaid employee compensation at the end of most accounting periods.

In addition to liabilities created by accrued wages, liabilities are created each payday or period-end because of such withholdings as income tax, Social Security tax, union dues, and insurance premiums. Liabilities are also created for the employer's contribution to unemployment compensation programs, pension plans, and insurance plans. These liabilities related to payroll expense are normally paid to outside entities within a short time after the period-end.

The following example illustrates the computation of, and the accounting for, several of the above items. Pipen Company has ten hourly workers who are paid weekly on Friday. As of December 31, 1984, a Monday, the workers have earned $3,600 gross pay for which no payment has been made. The following withholdings are applicable to the unpaid compensation at December 31, 1984:

ITEMS WITHHELD FROM EMPLOYEES' GROSS PAY		
	AMOUNT	PAYEE
1. Income tax	$ 756	U.S. government
2. FICA (employee contribution)	216	U.S. government
3. Union dues	90	United Auto Workers
4. Life insurance	110	American Assurance Co.
5. Employee pension contribution	144	National Life Corp.
6. Charitable contributions	40	United Way
	$1,356	

In addition to the $1,356 withheld from the gross pay, the employer must pay the following amounts:

ITEMS TO BE PAID FOR BY PIPEN COMPANY		
	AMOUNT	PAYEE
1. Unemployment compensation	$ 24	U.S. government
2. Unemployment compensation	36	State of Michigan
3. FICA (company contribution)	216	U.S. government
4. Company pension contribution	144	National Life Corp.
	$420	

To record the unpaid wages and all resulting obligations, the following journal entry would be made on December 31, 1984:

12/31/84	Wages expense	3,600	
	Payroll expense	420	
	Wages payable		2,244
	FICA payable		432
	Union dues payable		90
	Employee income tax payable		756
	Employee life insurance payable		110
	Pension payable		288
	Federal unemployment tax payable		24
	State unemployment tax payable		36
	Miscellaneous payable		40

Note that the Wages Payable account is credited for the *net* amount to be paid to employees for 1984 unpaid wages on the next payday. This $2,244 is equal to

EXHIBIT
16–4

DISCLOSURE OF COMPENSATED ABSENCES

RIBLET PRODUCTS CORPORATION
Excerpt from Notes

Compensated Absences

The Company accrues a liability for employees' compensation for vacations if rights to such vacation pay have vested. In 1981 the Company will also accrue a liability for vacations being earned which may not vest until a future date. This change is to comply with a new pronouncement by the Financial Accounting Standards Board. The new method will be applied retroactively and is not expected to have a material effect on the financial statements.

TEXFIL INDUSTRIES, INC.
Excerpt from Notes

Subsequent to October 31, 1980, Statement No. 43, Accounting for Compensated Absences, was issued by the Financial Accounting Standards Board. As a result, effective in fiscal 1982 the Company will begin accruing a liability for the cost of vacation benefits that employees have earned but not yet taken . . . .

$3,600 minus the withholding of $1,356. Payroll expense is debited for the company's contribution to unemployment compensation, FICA, and pensions. All the liability accounts will remain on the books until payments are made to the various entities concerned.

Another employee-related liability must often be recognized when it is expected that workers will be paid for absences related to vacations, holidays, illnesses, and the like. Again, the matching principle suggests that all necessary costs of operations should be matched with revenues in the periods that benefit from the costs. **FASB Statement No. 43** codifies this conceptual point in the area of compensated absences of employees.[5] If (1) the employer's obligation is related to services rendered, (2) the amount to be paid is reasonably estimable, (3) the actual payment is probable, and (4) the employees' rights vest (stay in effect even upon employee termination) or accumulate (carry over to subsequent periods), then a liability and an expense must be accrued for the estimated amount of compensated absences outstanding as of the end of an accounting period. Footnote disclosure is required in the event that all the above criteria are met except that the amount is not reasonably estimable. Exhibit 16–4 shows the footnote disclosure related to compensated absences in two companies' annual reports.

Obligations
Related to
Customers

Sales tax   In the normal course of business, an entity may incur liabilities to its customers and to other parties as the result of sales. **Sales tax,** for instance, is collected from customers and is subsequently paid to state and local governments. For example, Big 8 Party Store collects $15,000 in sales tax from customers during January on sales of $375,000. The state allows vendors to retain 2 percent of sales tax collected as compensation for the collection service and requires monthly payments no later than the twenty-first of the subsequent month. Journal entries to record the sales tax collection obligation and compensation can be summarized as follows:

[5] *Statement of Financial Accounting Standards No. 43,* "Accounting for Compensated Absences" (New York: FASB, November 1980).

Cash	390,000	
Sales		375,000
Sales tax payable		14,700
Sales tax compensation		300

Note that Big 8 has a current liability of $14,700 at month-end and records revenue for the commissions earned for the amount allowed to be retained by the vendor.

Customer deposits   Another common liability related to sales occurs when a customer deposits money as a form of security, as occurs in some rental contracts. Such deposits are to be returned at a future period if contractual terms are met by the depositor. In practice, the amount of the deposit remains constant until a determination is made as to the refund. **APB Opinion No. 21** states that security deposits are excluded from its requirement that interest factors be accounted for.[6] Conceptually, there is no reason why interest could not be taken into consideration.

In the rental of an office building, for example, a deposit, or some portion thereof, may be retained by the landlord in the event of damages. A liability equal to the retained amount would remain on the books until either it is returned or a determination is made that damage has taken place. In the latter case, the liability account would be reduced by the amount of the damage. The following journal entries are based on a short-term lease requiring a deposit:

6/28/81	Cash	20,000	
	Deposits		20,000
	(Deposit collected from tenant on a 6-month rental agreement for a warehouse)		
10/2/81	Repair expense	15,500	
	Cash		15,500
	(To repair damages caused by tenant's truck.)		
12/28/81	Deposits	20,000	
	Repair expense		15,500
	Cash		4,500
	(To pay the tenant for the deposited amount minus the retainage for damage)		

Deposits liabilities should be classified as noncurrent if repayment is not expected within a year of the current balance sheet date or within the operating cycle if longer than a year.

Advance ticket sales   Advance ticket sales create current liabilities for the unearned revenue. Although cash is received in advance, revenue is not recognized until the service has been performed. Exhibit 16–5 shows how American Airlines described its accounting for advance payment for airline tickets.

Tickets for sports and entertainment events are often sold in advance. The following example deals with this situation. Assume that the production company for "Stoned," a rock group, sells 20,000 tickets at $15 each in advance of a performance. The following journal entry would record the initial sale and subsequent revenue recognition:

---

[6] *Accounting Principles Board Opinion No. 21,* "Interest on Receivables and Payables," par. 3.

EXHIBIT
16–5

DISCLOSURE OF ADVANCE TICKET SALES

AMERICAN AIRLINES, INC.
Excerpt from Notes

Note 1:

Passenger Revenues. Passenger ticket sales are initially recorded as a current liability. Revenue derived from the sale is recognized at the time transportation is provided.

Date of sale	Cash	300,000	
	Unearned revenue		300,000
Date of performance	Unearned revenue	300,000	
	Sales		300,000

Unearned revenue would be disclosed as a current liability on any balance sheet issued between the advance sale date and the performance date. Note that no costs are estimated and that the liability equals the total ticket receipts, as in the customer advance situation described earlier. The revenue-recognition principle that governs this and similar transactions, such as magazine subscriptions, is rather conservative and calls for the delay of any revenue recognition until after the service has been performed. A rationalization for recognizing a liability in such cases is the fact that if the performance is canceled, the purchase price of the tickets must be returned to the customers.

Obligations to Stockholders and Other Parties

As with other liabilities, the payment of dividends does not normally coincide with the end of an accounting period. When cash or property dividends have been declared and remain unpaid at a balance sheet date, the dividend obligation is disclosed as a current liability. Chapter 21 examines the nature of dividends and explains why dividends in arrears on preferred stock and declared dividends to be paid in the form of capital stock are not disclosed as liabilities.

Many other miscellaneous classes of short-term creditors can exist for any business. A bank overdraft creates a liability to the bank. It should not be disclosed as "negative cash" but as a current liability. Property taxes, excise taxes, penalties, fines, and many other levies create obligations to governmental units and are normally classified as current. Many parties in the business environment can potentially have claims against the entities' assets. In most cases, when a miscellaneous expense or loss account is debited and a miscellaneous liability account is credited, the amount is immaterial. Of course, if the amount is material, disclosure in the financial statements and/or the notes must be sufficiently clear so that financial statement users will not be misled.

ESTIMATED AND CONTINGENT CURRENT LIABILITIES

Unlike the liabilities discussed in the preceding sections, the maturity values of some current liabilities are not known with certainty. The accountant may know that a liability exists, but the amount expected to be paid may have to be estimated. This may result from an obligation with a single payee, such as the year-end federal income tax obligation, where the amount of that liability may have to be estimated due to lack of complete information. In other instances, several parties are potential payees, but it is not known exactly which will be paid, as when a department store has gift certificates outstanding. The amounts for individual certificate holders are known, but the number of those who will exercise their privilege must be estimated. A closely related but slightly more complex estimation problem is created when a company has product warranties outstanding. For instance, if a company sells 100,000 refrigerators and guarantees them for parts and service for 1 year, it is highly probable that some percentage will require expenditures in the future. The total amount of the obligation, however, is dependent on two unknown variables: the number of units returned for service and the dollar amount per unit.

All the above examples are normally termed **estimated liabilities** because a future payment is highly probable, but the amount must be estimated. Another common thread running through many estimated liabilities is that they are the result of applying the revenue recognition and matching principles. Recording of the income tax obligation at period-end is the complement of the income tax expense charge for the current year. The gift certificate obligation is recorded in cases where the earnings process related to the future redemption of the unredeemed certificates is considered incomplete at year-end. In warranty obligations, the year of sales normally absorbs all determinable expense, and the estimated warranty expense and its complementary liability are recorded in conformance with the matching principle.

Accountants must also deal with a related class of situations, **contingent liabilities,** which involve potential claims. If a claim is heavily dependent on a future event's occurring and that event has less than a high probability of occurring, then the liability is only potential and is termed *contingent.* It is not recorded on the books but is disclosed by a footnote if certain conditions are met. For instance, a lawsuit against a company may potentially require a cash payment to the claimant. However, the outcome is not known until the case has been decided by the judge or jury. The lawsuit case is helpful in distinguishing between estimated and contingent liabilities. Until the verdict has been rendered or an out-of-court settlement has been achieved, only a potential liability exists. After a settlement has been determined, but before the amount of damages has been set, an estimated liability may be called for if a reasonable estimate of the money amount can be made. The concepts, rules, and conventions that dictate just what monetary and other forms of disclosure are necessary in specific cases of estimated and contingent liabilities are discussed in the following sections.

Current Liabilities Normally Termed *Estimated*

Income taxes payable   The income tax status of corporations is similar to that of individuals. They must usually file income tax returns and make payments to federal and other governmental authorities. In this section we focus on the most material source of income tax obligations, the federal income tax. However, the concepts developed here are applicable as well to state and local income taxes.

Let us assume that a corporation has estimated its taxable income at the end of its fiscal year, December 31, 1983, to be $10,000,000. The following schedule shows the applicable tax rates for this corporation:

TAXABLE INCOME ($)	TAX RATE	TAX OBLIGATION
$ 0 to 24,999	17%	$ 4,250
25,000 to 49,999	20	5,000
50,000 to 74,999	30	7,500
75,000 to 99,999	40	10,000
100,000 to 10,000,000	46	4,554,000
		$4,580,750

Total payments to the IRS for 1983 would be $4,580,750 if the estimate for taxable income at December 31, 1983, is correct. Quarterly payments are made during the taxable year based on estimates of taxable income.

Assume that the following schedule of payments applies to 1983:

PAYMENT DATE	PAYMENT AMOUNT
April 15	$1,000,000
July 15	1,000,000
September 15	1,000,000
December 15	1,000,000
	$4,000,000

At each payment date, federal income tax (FIT) expense was debited and cash was credited. As we see by comparing cash payments with estimated total income tax obligations, $580,750 remains to be accrued at December 31, 1983:

| 12/31/83 | FIT expense | 580,750 | |
| | FIT payable | | 580,750 |

Why is the $580,750 considered an estimated liability? For most corporations, the amount booked as of year-end is based on estimates that will be modified by the tax return deadline of March 15, and extensions on that deadline are often requested and granted because of the complexity of many corporate tax returns. Note that in our example, the income statement could show FIT expense of $4,580,750 while the balance sheet would show a current liability, FIT payable, of only $580,750. This result occurs because of the quarterly payments that must be made to the IRS. The quarterly payments could even exceed the total tax obligation, thus creating a current receivable for the difference.

Warranties The estimated costs of warranty obligations should be matched with sales revenues in the period in which the sales are made.[7] Warranty accounting is an application of the matching principle that creates a current liability based on estimated future costs.

At the end of each accounting period, an estimate is made of the cost of servicing all outstanding warranty commitments. The estimating procedure must consider the probability of claims as well as the probable cost of servicing those claims. This estimate could be based on a percentage of sales or an aging analysis comparable with those discussed in accounts receivable accounting (see Chapter 8).

General Electronics, Inc., guarantees its microwave ovens for 1 year for parts and labor. During 1984, the company sells 50,000 ovens for $375 each. If the track record for warranty cost indicates that an amount equal to 1 percent of total sales is

---

[7] Warranty obligations are discussed in this text as estimated liabilities, but this classification is open to question because of the overlap between estimated and contingent liabilities. In its *Statement of Financial Accounting Standards No. 5,* "Accounting for Contingencies" (Stamford, CT: FASB, March 1975), the FASB classifies warranty obligations as contingencies because of the uncertainty of claims. Justification for categorizing warranty obligations as estimated liabilities is based on the fact that in most cases, companies know, with a great deal of certainty, that claims will occur, and they usually have a routine estimation procedure that is quite accurate.

normally paid for repairs, and the company uses a percentage-of-sales approach for estimating sales, the following journal entry would be made at year-end:

12/31/84	Warranty expense	187,500	
	Warranty liability		187,500

By this technique, a "best estimate" for the warranty expense is matched with the current-year sales. The drawback to this approach is that any year-end balance in the Warranty Liability account can be distorted if the estimates made from year to year are not accurate. The aging approach emphasizes the balance sheet but has the drawback of distorting the current charge. Assume that General Electronics uses the following aging schedule to estimate its warranty obligation:

DATE OF SALE	PROBABLE NUMBER OF CLAIMS	PROBABLE COST PER CLAIM	TOTAL ESTIMATED COST
0–60 days before year end	2,000	$60	$120,000
61–120 days before year-end	1,000	60	60,000
121–365 days before year-end	500	60	30,000
			$210,000

This schedule is based on the fact that the claims tend to come early in the ovens' useful lives and that the cost per repair does not vary significantly across age groups. This does not mean, of course, that every repair is expected to cost the same amount. It simply means that the average cost per repair is constant for all age groups.

Whenever estimates of payables are made in conjunction with accruing expenses, the before-adjusting balance in the liability account must be considered. General Electronics has the following history in its Warranty Liability account:

1/1/84	Balance	$200,000	credit
1984	Payments (actual costs)	180,000	debit
12/31/84	Before-adjustment balance	$ 20,000	credit

The necessary adjusting entry brings the Warranty Liability account up to the estimated $210,000 amount:

12/31/84	Warranty expense	190,000	
	Warranty liability		190,000

Warranty liability, then, has an ending balance of $210,000, which is the best estimate of probable claims; and warranty expense for 1984 is $190,000, which is the $210,000 minus the overestimate of $20,000 made at December 31, 1983.

Note that certain "warranty" contracts are net revenue generators. For instance, assume that General Electronics in our example offers its customers 1-year warranty contracts for $30 each for year 2 and beyond. If 10,000 such contracts are sold during December 1984 to become effective January 1, 1985, what accounting is necessary for the $300,000 cash received and for the estimated cost of servicing the ovens? Contracts of this type are accounted for as sales and, therefore, are made to conform to normal revenue recognition and matching principles. If revenue of $300,000 is recognized, the matching estimated cost of providing the services must be estimated and recorded as a liability. Again, several approaches can be followed for estimating probable cost. The following table shows the results of an aging schedule that can be used to estimate probable cost to be matched with the revenue from the service contracts:

YEAR OF ORIGINAL SALE	NUMBER OF CONTRACTS SOLD IN 1984	PROBABLE NUMBER OF CLAIMS PER THOUSAND CONTRACTS	PROBABLE COST PER CLAIM	TOTAL ESTIMATED COST
1983	5,000	50	$65	$16,250 (5 × 50 × $65)
1982	3,000	60	70	12,600 (3 × 60 × $70)
1981	1,500	70	75	7,875 (1.5 × 70 × $75)
Before 1981	500	80	85	3,400 (.5 × 80 × $85)
	10,000			$40,125

The journal entries at the date of sale, assuming all sales are made at December 31, 1984, would be as follows:

EXHIBIT
16–6

DISCLOSURE OF WARRANTY OBLIGATION

RANCO INCORPORATED

Excerpt from Note

Product Warranty:

Generally, the Company and its subsidiaries accrue product warranty costs based upon sales levels, warranty terms, and actual return experience. Product warranty expense was $465,000 in 1980 and $2,114,000 in 1979. Accrued product warranty costs were $1,080,000 and $2,067,000 at September 30, 1980 and 1979, respectively.

TOKHEIM CORPORATION

Excerpt from Balance Sheet

	$000	
	1980	1979
Current Liabilities:		
Current maturities of term debt and notes payable, banks (Notes 4 and 5)	$ 7,749	$ 4,697
Accounts payable	10,222	8,583
Accrued expenses:		
Salaries, wages and commissions	1,927	1,273
Retirement plan contributions (Note 9)	1,230	1,134
Taxes, other than United States and foreign income taxes	1,116	835
Sales incentive plans	1,074	802
Warranty expense	2,010	1,064
Other	2,370	2,114
Total accrued expenses	9,727	7,222
United States and foreign income taxes (Note 7):		
Currently payable	2,748	1,320
Deferred	(1,417)	(876)
Total income taxes	1,331	444
Total current liabilities	29,029	20,946

12/31/84	Cash	300,000	
	Sales of service contracts		300,000
12/31/84	Service contract expense	40,125	
	Service contract liability		40,125

As in the "pure" warranty situation, the service contracts create a current liability, and the follow-up procedures in subsequent years are very similar in terms of estimating and adjusting the liability account. Companies disclose warranty obligations and expense in a number of ways. Exhibit 16–6 shows how two companies disclose warranty items. One describes its warranty costs in a footnote, whereas the other lists its warranty liability in a separate element of the current liabilities on the balance sheet. Warranty expense and liability are often not large enough for separate designations on financial statements.

Other estimated payables **Premiums, deposits,** and **trading stamps** give customers the right to products and services or refunds. For instance, a cereal company may insert coupons in its product, entitling each holder to a free premium. As we shall see, the principles guiding accounting practice are the same here as in previous cases of estimated liabilities. Assume that, in the first year of the premium offer, 500,000 boxes of Sugar Bombs cereal each contain one coupon for a free toothbrush and are sold with the expectation that 50 percent of the coupons will be redeemed. Each toothbrush costs $.15 to purchase and $.35 to process and mail. If 250,000 toothbrushes are purchased and 125,000 are mailed by the end of the first year, the journal entries would be as follows:

During year	Premium inventory	37,500	
	Cash		37,500
	(To record purchase of premiums)		
During year	Premium expense	62,500	
	Premium inventory		18,750
	Cash		43,750
	(To record the mailing of premiums)		
Year-end	Premium expense	62,500	
	Premium liability		62,500
	(To record estimated liability as of year-end)		

The year-end balance in the Premium Liability account would then be $62,500, which is $.50 (total cost to purchase and mail a toothbrush) multiplied by 125,000 (estimated number of premiums yet to be mailed).

The concepts illustrated above apply to companies issuing trading stamps except that the issuing of trading stamps is a revenue-generating event. When trading stamps are sold to retail outlets, the issuer records a sale for the cash received. In addition, a liability account is credited and an expense account is debited for the total estimated cost of redemption of stamps. As stamps are being redeemed, the liability account, the inventory of premiums account, and other asset accounts are reduced.

Consider the accounting judgments needed in the following case. A & B Trading Stamps, Inc., sells 200,000,000 stamps to a nationwide food store chain for $200,000. A & B's obligation is to redeem the stamps for premiums selected from a published premium catalog. A & B estimates that it will cost $150,000 to redeem the stamps that will be turned in. Who is A & B's customer? When is revenue earned? To whom is the obligation for redemption owed? How much is the liability? The rationale for current practice gives the following answers. A & B's customer is the food store chain, and, therefore, the point of sale is the point at which the stamps were sold to the food store chain. This is based on the notion that the critical event in the earnings process is the closing of the sale with the food store chain. The obligation for redemptions is to the holders of the stamps, and that obligation is for the estimated cost of probable redemptions. Once the revenue is recognized at the point of sale, all actual and estimated cost must be matched with that revenue. The following pattern of journal entries is necessary, assuming the estimate was perfect:

At point of sale	Cash	200,000	
	Sales		200,000
	Redemption expense	150,000	
	Estimated liability for redemptions		150,000
Purchase of premiums	Inventory of premiums	100,000	
	Cash		100,000
Redemption of stamps	Estimated liability for redemptions	150,000	
	Inventory of premiums		100,000
	Cash and other accounts used to record various costs of redemption, such as salaries and rent		50,000

Of course, estimates of costs are not always perfect, and adjustments from period to period would be necessary.

Potential Obligations Normally Termed *Contingencies*

Occasionally an entity is involved in a set of circumstances at a balance sheet date that may result in a gain or a loss at a future time if certain events take place. The gain or loss is said to be *contingent* on the future events' occurring. These situations involve more uncertainty than that normally associated with accounting estimates. Accountants often estimate money amounts based on estimates of a future event, but the occurrence of that future event is not in doubt. In the case of contingencies, there is uncertainty that the event will occur. As we shall see, promulgated GAAP on contingencies do give guidance, but they by no means eliminate judgment. To understand current acceptable practice, let us first analyze the general approach to contingency accounting without considering the specific rules. The accountant has to investigate the entity's environment to detect *existing* conditions that could cause gains and losses upon the occurrence or nonoccurrence of some future event or events. Each contingency would have to be evaluated as to its probability of occurrence and the financial impact if it did occur. If there were no restrictions imposed by rules, such judgments would result in decisions about the nature of accounting for such circumstances and could result in several types of disclosure including (1) recognition of contingent gains and losses and their balance sheet effects, (2) footnote disclosure, and (3) no disclosure.

FASB Statement No. 5[8] and **FASB Interpretation No. 14**[9] are attempts to standardize accounting for contingencies, and they do channel accounting practice in

[8] *Statement of Financial Accounting Standards No. 5,* "Accounting for Contingencies."

[9] *Interpretation of Financial Accounting Standards No. 14,* "Reasonable Estimation of the Amount of a Loss" (Stamford, CT: FASB, September 1976).

a particular direction. For instance, all the options discussed above are not open because of these rules. The basic approach of the rules is to give guidelines as to when and how contingent gains and losses are to be reflected in the financial statements. The general rule is that gains are to be reflected only in footnotes and that losses are to be evaluated by applying specified criteria, with accounting treatment dependent on the nature of the contingency.

The first step in the approach suggested by the FASB is to evaluate each contingency situation according to the probability that, as of the balance sheet date, an asset has been impaired (its economic potential reduced by the event) or a liability has been incurred. Three probability classes are given to guide such judgments:

1. **Probable**—likely to occur
2. **Reasonably possible**—between probable and remote
3. **Remote**—not likely to occur

The determination that an asset has been impaired or that a liability has been incurred establishes that a loss contingency exists. The assignment of one of the above probability classes to the loss contingency determines the accounting disposition of the contingency. In general, for losses, the "probable" contingencies are recorded in the accounting records, and the others may be footnoted if they are deemed "reasonably possible." Gain contingencies, on the other hand, are never recorded in the accounting records, but as we shall see, they can be footnoted.

To disclose a loss contingency, a money amount may have to be estimated. If no money amount or range is known or can be reasonably estimated, then obviously no loss contingency can be recorded no matter how probable the contingent event. In cases where only a range of potential losses is estimable and the event is probable, the rules require that the lower end of the range be accrued. If a specific money amount can be estimated and the event is probable, then that amount must be accrued.

In cases where a loss contingency is deemed "reasonably possible," footnote disclosure only is necessary, and in cases where the loss contingency is deemed "remote," no disclosure is necessary but is permissible.

Gain contingencies are never recorded, but they must be disclosed in footnotes if they are either probable or reasonably possible. If gain contingencies are deemed remote, they should not be disclosed in any fashion. Figure 16–1 summarizes the judgments necessary under **FASB Statement No. 5.**

As an exercise in making accounting judgments that are guided by promulgated GAAP, read the following examples and determine the proper accounting and disclosures. Each case is followed by discussion and real-world disclosure examples.

Recalls and litigation Jaspar, Inc., has a December 31, 1984, year-end. In late November 1984 two important items came to management's attention. *First,* the Environmental Protection Agency (EPA) indicated to Jaspar that because of alleged defects, it might have to recall 25,000 of its snowmobiles sold during the past 3 years. Jaspar has estimated that the minimum cost of adjusting each snowmobile would be $150 and that it would take at least 3 years to handle all the claims. Furthermore, the company doesn't feel that it will be able to avoid the recall, but as of December 31, 1984, no final order from the government has been received. *Second,* the company learned that it it was being sued by Lawnperson on a major patent in-

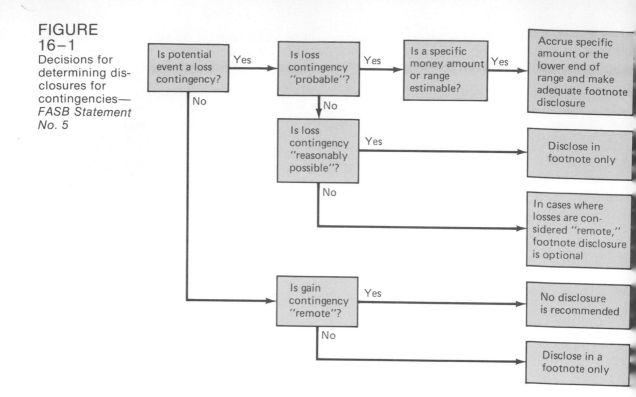

FIGURE 16–1
Decisions for determining disclosures for contingencies—*FASB Statement No. 5*

Flowchart boxes:

Is potential event a loss contingency? — Yes → Is loss contingency "probable"? — Yes → Is a specific money amount or range estimable? — Yes → Accrue specific amount or the lower end of range and make adequate footnote disclosure

No (from "Is loss contingency probable?") → Is loss contingency "reasonably possible"? — Yes → Disclose in footnote only

No (from "reasonably possible") → In cases where losses are considered "remote," footnote disclosure is optional

No (from "Is potential event a loss contingency?") → Is gain contingency "remote"? — Yes → No disclosure is recommended

No (from "Is gain contingency remote?") → Disclose in a footnote only

fringement issue. Lawnperson is suing for $25,000,000 in damages and lost income. Jaspar's management is very uncertain as to the outcome of the suit, and its lawyers are not willing to comment one way or the other. However, the lawyers and management feel that if the suit were lost, the damages would range from $10,000,000 to $25,000,000.

The EPA recall is a loss contingency. Is the loss probable? This is the crucial question in this case. Phrases such as "it might have to recall" and "the company doesn't feel that it will be able to avoid the recall" must be weighed. Money amounts per unit are given, and we can assume that they are legitimate. If we decide that the contingency event is probable, the following journal entry is necessary:

12/31/84	Loss due to EPA recall	3,750,000	
	Contingent liability—short-term		1,250,000
	Contingent liability—long-term		2,500,000

(It is assumed that a third of the repairs will be performed in 1985 and a third in each subsequent year)

The balance sheet would contain a reference to a footnote in which the nature of the contingent liability would be discussed. Is the loss extraordinary? A review of the promulgated GAAP on extraordinary items covered in Chapter 3 will show that this question also calls for a great deal of professional judgment.

The second case seems to involve more uncertainty than the first. Because the probability of the contingency event is not clear, a money amount range is given. In a case such as this one, the accountant would have to press management and the attorneys for more information, but the ultimate judgment might still rest with the accountant. The resolution would seem to be that at minimum a footnote disclosure would be necessary to explain the situation. If it turns out that the event is classified as probable, then $10,000,000, the lower end of the estimated range, would be booked.

Exhibit 16–7 shows the disclosure made by the Firestone Tire and Rubber Company for a government-mandated recall of some of its products. The analysis included in this note indicates that the situation warranted the recording of liabilities.

Expropriation Marbar International, a conglomerate with operating units throughout the world, has a December 31 year-end. In August 1983 Marbar learned that its facilities in Revoltina would probably be expropriated by the political party that would be in power after the current disturbances. The book values, fair market values, and amount of compensation expected to be received from Revoltina are listed in the following schedule (in $000):

	BOOK VALUE	FAIR VALUE OF ASSETS	COMPENSATION
Cash	$ 405	$ 405	$ 405
Accounts receivable (net)	7,946	7,946	0
Finished inventories	9,920	10,000	5,000
Land	2,000	4,500	500
Buildings	23,770	40,000	10,000
Less: Accumulated depreciation	(7,460)		
Equipment	53,891	30,000	5,000
Less: Accumulated depreciation	(17,781)		

EXHIBIT 16–7

DISCLOSURE OF PRODUCT RECALL LIABILITIES

FIRESTONE TIRE & RUBBER COMPANY
Excerpt from Note

Tire recall and related costs

In October, 1978, a provision for tire recall of $234.0 million was charged against income. The provision represented management's estimate of the cost of fulfilling the Company's obligations under an agreement with the National Highway Traffic Safety Administration and the Company's cash-refund program.

In October, 1979, based on experience to date and anticipated future charges, the 1978 provision was reduced. Management also determined that the provision should be broadened to include $60.0 million of other related costs which were not considered for inclusion in the 1978 provision. The net effect of the above was to reduce the provision by $46.9 million or $.82 per share, for which no provision for income taxes was required because of the use of 1978 foreign tax credits of $20.8 million.

In July, 1980, the 1978 recall program was extended to cover certain tires produced after the original program's cut-off date. The accrued liability at October 31, 1980, represented management's estimate of anticipated future charges.

The number of tires still to be returned and the other costs yet to be incurred may vary from management's estimates. Any additional adjustments required by such variance will be reflected in future income.

The activity in the accrued liability for tire recall and related costs for 1980 and 1979, follows:

($000)		
	1980	1979
Accrued liability at beginning of year	$56.4	$227.2
Amount credited during the year		(46.0)
Amounts charged thereto	(29.7)	(123.9)
Accrued liability at end of year	$26.7	$ 66.4

In such a case, promulgated GAAP require a determination of whether a loss contingency existed at year-end and whether assets were impaired or liabilities created by year-end. In Marbar's case, if the situation at December 31, 1984, constituted an existing condition that made it probable that expropriations would occur, then the following entry dated December 31, 1983, would be recorded:

12/31/83	Receivable from Revoltina	20,905,000	
	Extraordinary loss due to nationalization of assets	51,786,000	
	Accumulated depreciation—buildings	7,460,000	
	Accumulated depreciation—equipment	17,781,000	
	Cash		405,000
	Accounts receivable		7,946,000
	Finished inventories		9,920,000
	Land		2,000,000
	Buildings		23,770,000
	Equipment		53,891,000

Note that no liability is recorded, as this is a case of asset impairment only.

Risks from self-insurance Can a liability be recorded when a company is aware of certain risks of doing business but does not carry normal insurance coverage on such risks? Should a business record as contingent losses amounts that would have been charged as insurance expense if insurance coverage had been in effect? Another way of addressing this issue would be to answer the following question: Can a business anticipate losses that do not meet the criteria of probable asset impairment or liability incurrence merely because no insurance was carried for the events under consideration?

Consider the hypothetical case where two companies, A and B, are identical except that Company A carries property insurance, whereas Company B does not. The following analysis shows the effect of the difference in insurance coverage for 4 years of operations that, except for that difference, would have been the same for A and B:

	YEAR	NET INCOME BEFORE LOSSES AND PREMIUMS	INSURANCE PREMIUM EXPENSE	PROPERTY DAMAGE	INSURANCE CLAIM RECEIPTS	NET INCOME
Company A	1	$ 500,000	$(162,500)	$(100,000)	$100,000	$ 337,500
	2	500,000	(162,500)	(200,000)	200,000	337,500
	3	500,000	(162,500)	—	—	337,500
	4	500,000	(162,500)	(350,000)	350,000	337,500
		$2,000,000	$(650,000)	$(650,000)	$650,000	$1,350,000
Company B	1	$ 500,000	—	$(100,000)	—	$ 400,000
	2	500,000	—	(200,000)	—	300,000
	3	500,000	—	—	—	500,000
	4	500,000	—	(350,000)	—	150,000
		$2,000,000		$(650,000)		$1,350,000

For the entire 4-year period, A and B have the same total net operating results, but the timing of net income amounts is very different. Should Company B be allowed to record an expense and a liability each year based on estimates of future property damage? Current GAAP call upon several arguments to deny this option: (1) lack of insurance does not equate to asset impairment; (2) losses are random events and therefore cannot be considered probable; and (3) a company cannot have an obligation to itself, which would be the implication if a liability were recorded for future damage in a self-insurance situation.[10]

FUNDS FLOW EFFECTS

By their very nature, current liabilities have a direct impact on funds and financial flexibility. The potential importance of the impact is evidenced by the widespread use of the current ratio (current assets ÷ current liabilities) by grantors of short-term credit, as a means of evaluating ability to repay loans. Unusually large balances in current payables relative to current assets are signals to potential creditors that further investigation is warranted.

Because current liabilities are components of working capital, statements of changes in financial position on the working capital basis do not treat current liabilities separately. Cash basis statements, however, must describe the cash effects of changes in current liability balances. As an example, the "cash from operations" analysis would start with net income, and increases in accrued expenses payable would be added. This is necessary because although net income is reduced by accrued expenses, no cash is used in accruals. By the same token decreases in accrued liability balances would necessitate subtractions from net income to arrive at cash from operations.

Reclassification from long-term to short-term liabilities, and vice versa, can have material effects or working capital flows. On the balance sheet date before the payment of a long-term note, the maturity amount must be reclassified to current, thus indicating a use of working capital. Decisions about reclassifications, as discussed in this chapter; therefore may have material effects on reported funds flow.

SUMMARY

In this chapter we discussed accounting for current (short-term) liabilities. As in other areas of accounting, judgment is crucial. Accountants must decide whether an item is to be classified as current or noncurrent, whether evidence supports a particular estimate, whether a potential event is probable, and many others. Although judgment is the key to accounting choices, promulgated GAAP do guide practice in some cases and these were highlighted in the chapter.

All liability judgments contain some element of uncertainty. With accounts and notes payable, uncertainty is at a minimum. Estimated liabilities may involve uncertain money amounts, for example, estimated taxes, and/or uncertain payees, department store gift certificates being a case in point. Contingent liabilities involve great uncertainties in many cases and rules have been promulgated to guide the accountant's judgments.

Note that the distinctions made between current and noncurrent liabilities and between liabilities and owners' equity are not as clear-cut as they may appear at first. There are commonalities among all of these categories.

---

[10] *Statement of Financial Accounting Standards No. 5*, "Accounting for Contingencies," par. 28.

Q16–1   How does the determination of current assets for balance sheet disclosure affect the determination of current liabilities?

Q16–2   What are the arguments for and against disclosing current liabilities at *present values?* What are the current GAAP on this issue? Do you agree with them? Why?

Q16–3   What are the similarities and differences between *accounts receivable* accounting and *accounts payable* accounting?

Q16–4   Why are commitments on executory or unexecuted contracts not recorded as liabilities? Why are deposits on executory contracts recorded as liabilities?

Q16–5   Notes payable classified as current are disclosed at present values. Contrast this with disclosure of accounts payable, and give the rationale for the difference between the two.

Q16–6   What evidence is required to support the classification of short-term maturities of notes payable as long-term?

Q16–7   Distinguish between estimated and contingent liabilities.

Q16–8   Contingent losses and contingent gains are accounted for differently in practice. Discuss the differences, and give the rationale for them.

Q16–9   The accruing of liabilities at period-end can be justified from both a balance sheet and an income statement point of view. Briefly sketch each point of view, and give your opinion as to which is the more logical.

Q16–10   Why is unearned revenue recorded, and how is the money amount determined?

CASES

C16–1   Cramer Fabricators, Inc., has three outstanding contracts with workers, customers, and suppliers as follows:

1. At fiscal year-end, the company signed a new labor contract that will increase total labor cost by approximately $60,000 in the next period, assuming no change in output.
2. The company currently holds $205,000 in customer advances for work that is not completed at year-end.
3. The company signed a 2-year contract to purchase a fixed amount of steel plate at a fixed price per ton plus an adjustment based on an industry price index. It turns out that by year-end, the index has gone up and the price of the specific steel plate has declined.

REQUIRED   Discuss the accounting treatment for each of these contracts.

C16–2   At fiscal year-end a large corporation has several short-term loans outstanding amounting to $205,000,-000. The corporation is planning a sale of preferred stock, the proceeds of which will be used to pay off the loans. The underwriters for the preferred stock issue are confident that the market for such stock will be strong and are advising a quick issuance.

REQUIRED   Respond to management's assertion that the proposed preferred stock issuance is a sound basis for reclassifying the short-term debt to long-term on the current balance sheet.

C16–3   Broadwalk Builders, whose fiscal year-end is December 31, has a severe solvency problem. It owes a major supplier $850,000 for past-due invoices. On October 1, 1983, the supplier agreed to consolidate all the invoices into one 6-month note due on March 31, 1984. The note is non-interest-bearing and calls for a payment at maturity of $935,000. The president of the company suggests that the difference between the total invoice amounts and the maturity value of the note should be charged to the Purchases account.

REQUIRED   Explain (1) why this treatment would be wrong and (2) what the appropriate accounting should be.

C16–4   In 1978 Plato Imports purchased fruit orchards in a Mediterranean country for $8,500,000. The first crop is due in 1984. On December 31, 1983, the end of its fiscal year, Plato is informed that its fruit crop will be quarantined because of an insect infestation. No sale of quarantined fruit is allowed. The company has $1,200,000 in inventoried cost related to its first crop. The company has narrowed its alternatives to the following:

1. Sell its orchards to a domestic concern for $3,000,000. The sale date would be January 15, 1984.
2. Continue to operate the orchards. The expected cost to eradicate the infestation and dispose of the current crop is $450,000.

REQUIRED   Explain the accounting implications of each alternative.

C16–5   Amstar, Inc., manufactures compressors that are sold to industrial customers. For the past 5 years, an average of 1 percent of the compressors have proved defective, which has resulted in credits being given for the entire sales price. Amstar's policy is to allow the full credit rather than attempt repairs under the assumption that transportation and repair costs would exceed the value of the overhauled units. Whenever a customer notifies the company of a defect, Amstar merely issues a credit and records the transaction by debiting sales and crediting accounts receivable.

REQUIRED   Write a memo to management explaining the proper accounting for such a situation. Give the rationale for your suggested treatment, and explain its financial statement effects.

C16–6   You, as controller of your corporation, are asked to settle an argument between the director of insurance and a vice-president, who state, respectively: (1) "Although the company does not carry insurance for damage to property, it still incurs costs whenever damage takes place. It is appropriate, therefore, to charge each year with an estimated amount based on average damage incurred over some relevant period." (2) "Insurance premiums, property damage, and insurance claims should be accounted for on a pure cash basis. That is, when premiums are paid, charge insurance expense; when damage occurs, charge a loss; and when claims are paid by the insurance company, reduce the loss or record a gain."

REQUIRED   Write a short response to each statement.

C16–7   Evaluate the following statement: "The distinction made between contingent and estimated liabilities is artificial because all contingent liabilities require estimates and all estimated liabilities are contingent on some future event's occurring, namely, the debtor's ability and willingness to pay its debts."

C16–8 (CPA ADAPTED)   The two basic requirements for the accrual of a loss contingency are supported by several basic concepts of accounting. Three of these concepts are *periodicity* (time periods), *measurement,* and *objectivity.*

REQUIRED   Discuss how the two basic requirements for the accrual of a loss contingency relate to the three concepts listed above.

C16–9 (CPA ADAPTED)   The following three independent sets of facts relate to (1) the possible accrual or (2) the possible disclosure by other means of a loss contingency.

1. A company offers a 1-year warranty for the product it manufactures. A history of warranty claims has been compiled, and the probable amount of claims related to sales for a given period can be determined.
2. Subsequent to the date of a set of financial statements, but prior to the issuance of the financial statements, a company enters into a contract that will probably result in a significant loss to the company. The amount of the loss can reasonably be estimated.
3. A company has adopted the policy of recording self-insurance for any possible losses resulting from injury to others by the company's vehicles. The premium for an insurance company would have an annual cost of $2,000. During the period covered by the financial statements, no accidents involving the company's vehicles resulted in injury to others.

REQUIRED   Discuss the accrual and/or type of disclosure necessary (if any) and the reason or reasons why such disclosure is appropriate for each of the three independent sets of facts above. Complete your response to each situation before proceeding to the next situation.

C16–10 (CPA ADAPTED)   Loss contingencies may exist for companies.

REQUIRED

1. What conditions should be met for an estimated loss from a loss contingency to be accrued by a charge to income?
2. When is disclosure required, and what disclosure should be made, for an estimated loss from a loss contingency that need not be accrued by a charge to income?

EXERCISES

E16–1   Crimm Detective Agency has eight hourly employees who are paid each week. At the end of the current fiscal year, there are three workdays for which wages have not been paid as follows:

Unpaid gross wages	$3,100
Income tax to be withheld	620
FICA taxes to be withheld	155
Insurance premiums to be withheld	70
Pension contributions to be withheld	120
FICA taxes (company's contributions)	155
Unemployment tax (company's contributions)	60

REQUIRED   Show the journal entry (entries) necessary for wages and related items at the fiscal year-end.

E16–2   A manufacturer of custom-made machine tools requires that 20 percent of the contract price be deposited before it starts a project. On April 20, 1983, a contract is signed for a total price of $31,000. The job is completed on August 15, 1983, at which time an invoice for the full invoice price minus the deposit is sent to the customer.

REQUIRED   If the fiscal year ends on May 31, show all the journal entries necessary for the above transactions and indicate their financial statement effects on May 31, 1983. Assume that the total cost is $18,000 and that the job is one-half complete at May 31. The percentage-of-completion method is not used for such contracts.

E16–3   On December 10, 1982, Joplin Printers contracted with a paper supplier to purchase 100,000 reams of bond during 1983 for $4.00 per ream. On December 31, 1982, the year-end, Joplin determines that although 100,000 reams was a good estimate of usage for 1983, $4.00 was not a bargain. The new purchasing agent now has bids from other suppliers for similar quality paper that costs $3.80 and $3.75 per ream.

REQUIRED   How should this situation be reflected in the financial statements? Show the necessary journal entries.

E16–4   Consider the facts in the preceding question, and assume that at year-end (December 31, 1982) it was estimated that only 75,000 reams would be used in 1983 and that a contract was signed on December 31, 1982, to sell the excess 25,000 reams to a competitor for $3.60 each.

REQUIRED   Should this contract be reflected in Joplin's financial statements at December 31, 1982? If your answer is yes, what journal entry would be necessary? Assume that the $3.75 and $3.80 per ream prices are correct at December 31, 1982, and that the $3.60 per ream reflects the fact that the competitor must pay for transportation to its warehouse.

E16–5   On June 30, 1983, the end of its fiscal period, Beams Manufacturing shows the following "long-term liabilities" section on its preliminary balance sheet:

Note payable (due 12/31/83) (effective annual interest rate 12%)	$ 100,000
Serial bonds payable (due 6/1/84)	1,200,000
Serial bonds payable (due 6/1/85)	1,400,000

The note is with First Bank of Des Moines, with which the company has a formal agreement that allows the company to refinance the note at maturity with an effective interest rate of 120 percent of the then-existing prime rate. The company intends to use this contract to extend the due date to June 1, 1985. Accumulated interest must be paid on December 31, 1983, on the original note, however. How should the "long-term liabilities" section of the balance sheet be modified to reflect the above information?

E16–6   Breighton, Inc., has the following before-adjusting balances relating to warranties at the end of its fiscal period:

Warranty expense	0
Current warranties payable	$875,000

At year-end, the company estimates that the future servicing of warranties for all sales to that date will be $1,650,000. Three-quarters of the estimated cost is expected to be incurred during the next fiscal year, with the remainder being incurred in the subsequent fiscal year. Show all necessary adjusting entries and the balance sheet disclosure necessary for the warranty information given.

E16–7   At its fiscal year end, Mackeral Trucks, Inc., has discovered a defect in the transmissions used in its heavy-duty tractors. The transmissions are manufactured by another company using Mackeral's specifications. Management has decided that it is *probable* that 10,000 trucks will have to be recalled and repaired at a total cost of $250 per truck. It has also decided that it is reasonably possible that the supplier will contribute one-half of the repair cost to Mackeral.

REQUIRED   Record the journal entry (if any) for the recall, and state why you think this entry is or is not necessary.

E16–8   A hotel operator has paid claims amounting to $8,750,000 to guests who were injured in a fire. The company is in the process of suing the hotel building contractor, who management feels is primarily responsible for the fire. At the end of the current fiscal period, management feels that it is probable that $2,500,000 will be collected in an out-of-court settlement.

REQUIRED   How should such a prospect be accounted for on the hotel operator's books? Give reasons for your recommendation.

E16–9   A company has serial bonds outstanding on December 31, 1983, the end of its fiscal period. The following schedule shows the interest and principal payments that will be made during 1984 and 1985:

PAYMENT DATE	PAYMENT OF 10% NOMINAL INTEREST (ANNUAL)	PAYMENT OF PRINCIPAL	BALANCE IN BONDS PAYABLE
6/30/84	$100,000	0	$2,000,000
12/31/84	100,000	$1,000,000	1,000,000
6/30/85	50,000	0	1,000,000
12/31/85	50,000	1,000,000	0

REQUIRED   Assuming that the bond was initially sold to yield 10 percent, how should the balance sheet reflect the bond obligation on December 31, 1983?

E16–10   Consider the following sequence of events for Star Travel and Farwest Airlines. On August 15, 1983, Star Travel collected $185,000 from clients for a Chicago-to-Seattle charter flight. Star Travel sent a check to Farwest for $166,500 (total airfare less 10 percent commission) on September 13, 1983. The flight is scheduled for October 5, 1983.

REQUIRED   Record all journal entries related to the charter for both companies, assuming that Star Travel has an August 31, 1983, year-end and that Farwest Airlines has a September 30, 1983, year-end.

P16–1   Alabama Steel Fabricators (ASF) purchases all of its steel from two suppliers, A and B. Supplier A's terms are 2/10, n/20; supplier B's terms are 1/15, n/30.

REQUIRED

1. What annual interest rate would have to be available on short-term investments to make the nonexercise of such purchase discounts advantageous?
2. What are the different financial statement effects of the gross and net methods of recording purchases when discounts are available?

P16–2   Arizona Hardware Wholesalers had the following history of hand tool purchases during March 1984:

DATE OF INVOICE	DATE OF PAYMENT	MODEL NUMBER	QUANTITY	PRICE PER 100	PURCHASE TERMS
3/1/84	3/14/84	1004	200	$1,500	2/10, n/20
3/5/84	3/15/84	7761	100	850	1/15, n/30
3/10/84	Returned on 3/19/84 because of damage	1118	200	400	2/10, n/20

REQUIRED   Show all necessary journal entries for the above transactions using both the gross and the net method of recording purchases.

P16–3   You are the controller of the California Contracting Company (CCC), a constructor of commercial buildings. You have completed all the adjusting procedures except for the disposition of one item that you feel has the characteristics of a contingent liability. A building completed during August 1984 has developed cracks in the slab, and the owners have notified you that they are withholding $100,000 of their final payment until repairs have been made. Your building supervisor contends that the concrete subcontractor is responsible for the cracks and should make the repairs. After consultation with all parties concerned on December 31, it has been determined that CCC and the subcontractor will each pay half of the repair cost. The repairs will be made during January, and the total cost is estimated to be between $30,000 and $40,000.

REQUIRED

1. Is this a contingent liability at the December 31 year-end?
2. What journal entries, if any, are necessary at year-end?

P16–4   Connecticut Appliances, Inc. (CAI), is the sole distributor of a line of imported food processors. Its agreement with the manufacturer requires that all warranties be CAI's sole responsibility. CAI has sold the processors during 1982 and has given a generous guarantee on the product, including labor and parts for a 1-year period after sale. CAI also pays all the postage charges. The following schedule shows CAI's estimates for repairs during 1983 for 1982 sales:

1983	EXTIMATED COST OF LABOR AND PARTS	ESTIMATED POSTAGE
1st quarter	$5,000	$250
2nd quarter	6,000	300
3rd quarter	8,000	400
4th quarter	9,000	450

As of December 31, 1982, $1,500 total expenditures have been debited to Warranty Expense for all costs related to repairs.

REQUIRED

1. What journal entries, if any, are necessary to record the above situation at the December 31, 1982, year-end?
2. Compose a footnote to the balance sheet to explain CAI's warranty policy.

P16–5 Saline Department Store has 10,000 gift certificates outstanding at the end of its first fiscal period (December 31, 1983). The certificates are worth $25 each. Saline expects that 80 percent of the certificates will be turned in for merchandise during 1984 and 20 percent during 1985. Upon sale of the gift certificates, Cash was debited and Sales was credited. Saline marks up its merchandise 100 percent. Each certificate, therefore, will command $25 of retail price and $12.50 of cost to the company.

REQUIRED

1. Show the necessary adjusting entry on December 31, 1983 and discuss what conceptual principles guide the adjustment?
2. Indicate how the balance sheet and income statement would be affected by the above journal entry.

P16–6 The following items relate to Lane, Inc., at December 31, 1984, the end of its fiscal period:

1. Estimated warranty expenditures:

SALES MADE DURING	YEAR OF EXPENDITURE		TOTAL
	1985	1986	
1982	$ 40,000	$ 0	$ 40,000
1983	50,000	20,000	70,000
1984	105,000	60,000	165,000
Total estimated warranty liability at 12/31/84			$275,000

2. Total federal income taxes to be paid for 1984	$1,700,000
Quarterly payments made during 1984	$1,200,000
3. Face value of bank note due 6/30/85	$150,000
(refinancing is expected for one-half of the note amount, and the terms meet the criteria listed in *FASB Statement No. 6*)	
4. Gross amount of unpaid payroll at 12/31/84	$28,500
(income tax withholdings total 20 percent of the gross pay)	
5. Customer deposits expected to be applied to sales during 1985	$20,000
6. Sales tax collected in December 1984 to be paid to the state in January 1985	$17,700
7. Gross amount of invoices to be paid to suppliers on which 2 percent is expected to be deducted for discounts	$330,500
8. Face value of bonds due in 5 years (with interest of $1,725,000 to be paid in 1985)	$11,500,000

REQUIRED Show how each of the above items would appear in the liability sections of Lane's balance sheet and give a short explanation of each.

P16–7 Jackson Contractors, Inc., purchased equipment for its new facilities by means of various notes with local banks as follows:

1. Cement truck—Purchased on 1/1/84 for $120,000 by means of a 2-year installment agreement that calls for four equal payments on 6/30/84, 12/31/84, 6/30/85, and 12/31/85. The payments include principal and interest at an effective annual rate of 14 percent.

2. Small tools—Purchased on 2/1/84 by means of a 60-day non-interest-bearing note with a maturity value of $30,000. The fair value of the tools was $29,000 at the date of purchase.

3. Fabrication shop—A bank loan of $150,000 negotiated on 2/1/84 was used to pay for the shop, which cost $102,000. The balance of the cash was initially used as working capital. The bank loan was a variable-interest-rate loan due on 4/1/85 with interest paid at the end of each calendar quarter. The interest rates used in the computation were equal to the prime rate at the end of each quarter and those rates were as follows: 3/31/84, 16 percent; 6/30/84, 18 percent; 9/30/84, 20 percent; 12/31/84, 19 percent; 4/1/85, 20 percent.

REQUIRED Show all journal entries for 1984 and the liability balances that would appear at the December 31, 1984, year-end on the company's balance sheet.

P16-8 During 1983 Rolls-Cummings Ltd. produced some jet engines for a major aircraft manufacturer. Each engine was guaranteed against all defects for 1 year after sale. The company has two methods of accomplishing repairs: (1) it allows the customer to document repair costs, and the company makes direct payments for those that meet certain qualifications; (2) it performs repairs at its own facilities for major jobs, in which case transportation costs are incurred.

At the end of the 1983 fiscal year, the company's repair experience and estimates are as follows:

SALES MADE DURING		UNITS	PER UNIT REPAIR COST INCURRED	TOTAL ESTIMATED FUTURE COST
Jan.	1983	10	$ 8,000	$ 0
Feb.	1983	12	17,800	0
Mar.	1983	10	7,500	0
Apr.	1983	15	27,500	0
May	1983	18	6,000	10,000
June	1983	11	6,050	10,000
July	1983	5	5,500	20,000
Aug.	1983	17	49,600	20,000
Sept.	1983	6	5,500	30,000
Oct.	1983	7	4,000	30,000
Nov.	1983	9	64,500	40,000
Dec.	1983	10	5,000	40,000

On December 31, 1983, the company decided to discontinue making the engine because of the losses incurred due to the higher than contemplated warranty-related costs. As of December 31, 1983, no adjusting entries have been made, and the costs incurred have been debited to Warranty Expense during 1983.

REQUIRED Show the necessary entry for the above situation, and discuss the income statement and balance sheet effects.

P16-9 Maynard Mineral Resources leases a mining site that is operated by an independent contractor on a commission basis based on tons produced. The owner is paid royalties on tons sold. During the first year of operating the mines, the following production and payments took place:

TONS MINED	TONS SOLD	AVERAGE SALES PRICE PER TON	COMMISSION RATE PER TON	ROYALTY RATE
100,000	85,000	$100	$50	18% of sales

Production and sales take place uniformly throughout each year, and commissions are paid on the fifteenth of the month following production. Royalties are paid semiannually in July and January for the preceding 6 months.

REQUIRED

1. How would the year-end (12/31) balance sheet of Maynard Mineral Resources reflect its obligations at the end of year 1?
2. What journal entries would be necessary to record the amounts shown on the balance sheet in requirement 1?

P16–10 (CMA ADAPTED) The Ander Company manufactures a variety of hand tools. The company uses the calendar year for reporting purposes. Information regarding selected assets and liabilities as of December 31, 1980, before any year-end adjustments, follows:

Cash. Ander has $900,000 in various checking accounts. Of this amount, $50,000 is a compensating balance against a note with the Holly National Bank.

Securities. Ander has investments in the common stock of three companies and the bonds of one foreign government. The $100,000 investment in the bonds was made in January 1980 so that Ander could conduct business in that country. The common stock investments were made to invest excess funds temporarily. The stock investments are with heavily traded companies listed on major exchanges. Details of these three common stock investments are listed in the following schedule.

COMPANY	ACQUISITION DATE	PURCHASE PRICE	MARKET VALUE DECEMBER 31, 1980
Stan Co.	6/15/80	$180,000	$140,000
Clarmont, Inc.	9/30/80	90,000	80,000
Tra, Inc.	10/15/80	70,000	90,000

The books still contain the account Allowance for Decline in Market Value of Temporary Investments, with the $40,000 credit balance established at December 31, 1979.

Accounts Receivable. The outstanding accounts receivable as of December 31, 1980, total $400,000, including $20,000 due from officers of the company. The Allowance for Uncollectible Accounts account had a debit balance of $12,000 at December 31, 1980. An aging of the accounts receivable at year-end indicates that $10,000 of the accounts receivable will be uncollectible.

Notes Receivable. Ander holds two notes receivable. One is a $20,000 trade note receivable dated March 1, 1980. This is a 1-year note that calls for a payment of 12 percent interest at maturity. The other note is from Rexit, a company in which Ander has a 30 percent interest. This is a 1-year note for $50,000 dated July 1, 1980. The note carries a 10 percent interest rate, and the interest is due at maturity.

Inventories. Ander's inventory is costed on a moving-average basis and totals $950,000. This amount includes $100,000 of merchandise held in foreign countries in excess of normal requirements in order to meet foreign government investment requirements. The market value is $180,000 for the excess foreign inventory and $1,200,000 for the remaining inventory.

Accounts Payable. Outstanding accounts payable as of December 31, 1980, total $500,000. Included in this balance is $60,000 due to an unconsolidated joint venture.

Notes Payable. Three notes payable are outstanding at December 31, 1980, as follows:

1. Ander has a $60,000, 12-month note with CTH Finance. The note is due December 1, 1981, and carries a 15 percent interest rate with the interest due at maturity.
2. A note covering a borrowing from PNH Insurance Co. for $100,000 is due April 1, 1981, and carries a 10 percent interest rate. This note contains an agreement that permits Ander to refinance the note into a 3-year note at maturity. Interest is payable annually on the anniversary date, and the current year's interest must be paid before the note can be refinanced. Ander plans to notify the insurance company early in 1981 of its intentions to refinance the note when the note becomes due.
3. Ander's third note is with Holly National Bank for $500,000. The note is dated July 1, 1980, and is due July 1, 1985. Interest of 16 percent is payable annually on the anniversary date of the note.

Income Taxes Payable. Ander has accrued $80,000 in income taxes related to 1980 income.

Customer Advances. Customers are required to make advance payments for special orders. Special orders normally are filled within 6 weeks from the date of the order. Customer advances at December 31, 1980, total $15,000.

REQUIRED Ander Company is preparing its classified statement of financial position as of December 31, 1980, for presentation in its annual report to its shareholders.

1. For each item that should be classified as a current asset, identify the account, the appropriate amount, and any additional disclosures that would be required either in the body of the statement or in the accompanying notes.

2. For each item that should be classified as a current liability, identify the account, the amount, and any additional disclosures that would be required either in the body of the statement or in the accompanying notes.

P16–11 (CMA ADAPTED) Refer to the facts in the preceding problem. Ander Company's classified statement of financial position contains the following sections: Current Assets; Long-term Investments; Property, Plant, and Equipment; Intangible Assets; Other Assets; Current Liabilities; Long-Term Liabilities; Owners' Equity.

REQUIRED For each item that was not classified as a current asset or current liability in Ander's statement of financial position as of December 31, 1980:

1. Identify the account and amount.
2. Explain why the item is not a current asset or current liability.
3. State where, if at all, the item would be classified on Ander's statement of financial position.

P16–12 (CMA ADAPTED)

_____ 1. *FASB Statement No. 5,* "Accounting for Contingencies," defines a *contingency* as "an existing condition, situation, or set of circumstances involving uncertainty as to possible gain or loss." According to this statement, which of the following items would not be considered a loss contingency?
   a. Collectibility of receivable arising from credit sales
   b. Pending or threatened litigation
   c. Depreciation of plant and equipment
   d. Guarantees of indebtedness of others
   e. Obligations related to product warranties and product defects

_____ 2. According to *FASB Statement No. 5,* "Accounting for Contingencies," proper accounting for contingencies, assuming the probable asset or liability effect can reasonably be estimated, would result in
   a. A loss being charged to income
   b. A gain being credited to income
   c. Both losses and gains being accounted for on the income statement
   d. Losses being charged to an appropriation of retained earnings
   e. None of the above

_____ 3. A short-term obligation should be included in current liabilities if the enterprise
   a. Has signed an agreement to replace it with a long-term obligation
   b. Has renewed the current liability with short-term obligations for an uninterrupted period that extends either beyond 1 year or the operating cycle
   c. Repays it after the balance sheet date but then subsequently issues a long-term obligation whose proceeds are used to replenish current assets before the balance sheet has been issued
   d. Has issued equity securities for the purpose of refinancing the current liability on a long-term basis after the balance sheet date but before the balance sheet has been issued
   e. Replaces the current liability with an interest-bearing note due in 36 months after the balance sheet date but before the balance sheet has been issued

_____ 4. An example of a loss contingency that should be accrued for financial reporting purposes is
   a. A note receivable discounted without recourse at a bank
   b. Litigation involving patent infringement
   c. Product warranties similar to warranties the enterprise has made for several years
   d. Possible future decline in market value of inventory
   e. A dispute over additional income taxes for prior years

Accounting for Income Taxes

17

OVERVIEW   In this chapter we cover two topics: (1) interperiod tax allocation and (2) accounting for net operating losses. The first topic makes up the bulk of the chapter and explains the accounting procedures involved in reconciling differences between the income for financial accounting and external-reporting purposes (called **book income**) and the income computed per tax laws for tax-reporting purposes (called **tax income**). The second topic explains how losses are accounted for and disclosed for financial-reporting purposes given their current tax treatment.

In Chapter 3 we covered **intraperiod** ("within period") **tax allocation,** which dealt with the ways in which the income tax expense of a specific period is reported in various sections of that period's financial statements. Here we cover the allocation of tax *between periods,* or **interperiod tax allocation.** Interperiod tax allocation is a complex accounting subject from both a theoretical and a practical point of view. It is necessary to understand (or at least accept) that income for book and tax purposes need not be the same, since the objectives of financial reporting and tax reporting are not necessarily the same. Recall the discussion of alternative accounting models in Chapter 6, which illustrated how income measurement changed as the definition of wealth changed. In some respects, book and tax incomes are two variations along the same lines as the Chapter 6 alternatives.

623

For tax purposes, **change in wealth (income)** is defined by a rather complex set of rules outlined in the Tax Code established by the U.S. Congress and enforced by the Internal Revenue Service (IRS). There is no formal theoretical framework comparable to that of the FASB discussed in Chapter 2 to direct Congress in defining taxable income. However, a common thread running through much of the Tax Code tends to explain the basis for many of the tax-accounting procedures that differ from those of the accrual accounting model. **Taxable income** is defined (by the code) to represent more of a cash-based (*non*-accrual-based) measure of change in wealth than conventional financial accounting. This is logical because it would be difficult for an entity to pay taxes unless a net cash inflow took place! We frequently find that when a transaction recorded for ''book'' purposes gives rise to a revenue or a gain *without* a cash inflow, or gives rise to an expense or a loss *without* a cash outflow, its treatment for tax purposes is likely to be different. These differences between book and tax incomes form the basis for our discussion of interperiod tax allocation in this chapter.

Definitions for elements of financial statements, specifically liabilities and expenses, play a key role in providing a theoretical foundation for this subject. The controversy over the applicability of certain definitions of financial statement elements is so extreme that under some interpretations of those definitions, the bulk of the material in this chapter would be eliminated as an accounting subject. This controversy will be explained as the topic of interperiod tax allocation is presented. In addition the topics in this chapter represent applications of the matching concept as well as that of conservatism.

BASIS FOR INTERPERIOD TAX ALLOCATION

Interperiod tax allocation is required because of the differences between book income and tax income and because **APB Opinion No. 11** states that the matching concept should be maintained in measuring and reporting book income.[1] If book income and taxable income were the same, no interperiod allocation would be necessary. Assume, for example, that Penman, Inc., recorded $2,000,000 in revenues and $1,500,000 in expenses before tax during 1984. If the tax rate were 25 percent, Penman would record the following entry at the end of 1984:

12/31/84	Income tax expense	125,000	
	Income tax payable		125,000

The problem involved in interperiod tax-allocation procedures occurs when tax income differs from book income. Suppose Penman, because of various tax laws, was allowed to report only $1,750,000 of the revenues in 1984 for tax purposes and only $1,400,000 of the 1984 expenses for tax purposes. The two income measures would be computed as follows:[2]

---

[1] *Accounting Principles Board Opinion No. 11,* ''Accounting for Income Taxes'' (New York: AICPA, December 1967), par. 8.

[2] Note that the $262,500 net income measure for tax purposes is a relatively unimportant figure that is seldom reported or used. Pretax ''tax'' income is the basis for computing the tax obligation (taxes payable), $87,500 in this case.

	INCOME MEASURES—1984	
	BOOK	**TAX**
Revenues	$2,000,000	$1,750,000
Expenses	(1,500,000)	(1,400,000)
Pretax income	$ 500,000	$ 350,000
Income tax expense (25%)	(125,000)	(87,500)
Net income	$ 375,000	$ 262,500

The tax-allocation problem stems from the inequality that results when we try to record the situation illustrated. If we wish to report the $125,000 income tax expense that was computed based on the revenue and expense transactions **recorded and reported in 1984 book pretax income,** we must debit an income statement account, Income Tax Expense, for $125,000. This approach, which is currently taken by GAAP, views taxes as *an expense* related to reported income before taxes, as opposed to *a distribution* to the government based on information not reported in the "book" income statement.[3] If taxes are considered to be an expense associated with reporting $2,000,000 in (book) revenue, then it is argued that $87,500 is *not* an appropriate amount to charge to income tax expense. However, some accountants have argued that taxes should be viewed as a loss, or as a distribution having nothing to do with the reported amount of book income. In the latter case, it is argued that a tax "loss" of $87,500 should be charged against the $500,000 pretax accounting income of 1984. While GAAP call for the former viewpoint (expense of $125,000), the issue is still debated. Whether we view taxes as an expense or a loss, we recognize that we have to pay $87,500 in taxes based on the 1984 pretax income figure in the tax return ($350,000) and must, therefore, credit Cash or Income Tax Payable for that amount. The entry would be:

| 12/31/84 | Income tax expense | 125,000 | |
| | Income tax payable | | 87,500 |

This creates an inequality that is unacceptable in the conventional double-entry system. One possible solution to this problem would be to compute the tax expense and tax payable based on only one of the two pretax income numbers. Which of the two pretax income numbers above would be more appropriate? Which of the two tax measurements represents a real and essentially unavoidable economic cost to Penman, Inc.? Some have argued that the problem illustrated above might best be resolved by forcing the book "expense" to equal the "payable" because the payable represents the real economic cost to Penman for 1984 and must legally be paid. Such a solution would greatly simplify accounting for income taxes and would eliminate the need to continue with most of the remainder of this chapter. However, forcing the "tax expense" to equal the "tax payable" was considered to be unacceptable from the APB's point of view. The APB indicated that such a practice would result in an income tax expense that was based on revenues and expenses other than those being reported in the financial statements.[4] Such a method would result in a failure to match revenues and expenses in the income statement.

[3] The notion that taxes are a *distribution* of earnings to the government would be compatible with a pure equity theory of accounting (Assets = Equities) and would imply that the deferred income tax procedures illustrated here are not required for financial-reporting purposes.

[4] *Accounting Principles Board Opinion No. 11,* "Accounting for Income Taxes."

As a result of the different income measurement methods and the perceived need to maintain both methods, the APB required the **deferred income tax method** of accounting. The deferred income tax method requires the use of interperiod tax-allocation procedures that are discussed below. If you understand the reason *why* interperiod tax-allocation procedures are required, it will make most of the subissues clearer and will provide a fundamental frame of reference.

The Nature of Income Differences

The financial goals of the entity are diverse and might include examples such as maximizing net income or maximizing return on assets. Although there is no unique financial statement objective for all entities, the objective of most entities with respect to taxes tends to be much clearer. Most entities seek to minimize their tax payments within the guidelines defined in the Tax Code.[5] Minimizing taxable income is an acceptable and common practice. As a result, there is seldom complete agreement between book income and taxable income, and entities often seek out such differences whenever they may result in lower tax payments.

What kinds of differences exist between book and tax incomes? We shall consider three broad categories of differences:

1. Timing differences
2. Permanent differences
3. Other differences

Each of these categories will be described in the context of their relationship to the expense-payable inequality problem cited earlier.

Timing Differences

When a revenue or an expense amount is recognized in different periods because of differences in the recognition point for tax and book purposes, it creates what is called a **timing difference.** Timing differences will always reverse themselves in that a difference between book income and tax income originating in the current period will be offset by a difference (or differences) in the opposite direction in some future period (or periods). Over the life of the entity these timing differences will all offset one another, so that pretax book income will equal pretax taxable income despite the existence of such timing differences. To illustrate, assume that Penman, Inc., is in business for the 3-year period 1984–1986 and goes out of business at the end of 1986. Penman recognizes revenue at the point of sale for book purposes but uses the installment basis for tax purposes (thereby delaying recognition until cash from sales is received). The following revenues are reported for book and tax purposes:

REVENUE RECOGNITION METHOD	1984	1985	1986	1987	1984–1987 TOTAL
Point of Sale—Book	$200,000	$200,000	$200,000	0	$600,000
Installment Basis—Tax	$100,000	$185,000	$210,000	$105,000	$600,000

The total revenue is the same over the entire life of the business, which is 3 years for book-reporting purposes but 4 years for tax-reporting purposes. Assuming a 25 per-

[5] Given that firms have a preference for cash today versus cash next year, and so forth, and given that there are no economic side effects, entities will logically seek to minimize their taxes.

cent tax rate once again, the income tax expense (for book purposes) and the income tax payable (for tax purposes) would be measured as follows:

	1984	1985	1986	1987	TOTAL
Income tax expense—book	$50,000	$50,000	$50,000	0	$150,000
Income tax payable—tax	$25,000	$46,250	$52,500	$26,250	$150,000

To account for these year-to-year inequalities caused by timing differences, keeping in mind that over the life of the entity the Expense and Payable are equal amounts, a Deferred Income Tax account is employed, as follows:

		1984		1985		1986		1987	
DATE	ACCOUNT	DEBIT	CREDIT	DEBIT	CREDIT	DEBIT	CREDIT	DEBIT	CREDIT
12/31	Income tax expense	$50,000		$50,000		$50,000		0	
	Deferred income tax		$25,000		$ 3,750	2,500		$26,250	—
	Income tax payable		25,000		46,250		52,500		$26,250

Note that by the end of 1987, the balance in Deferred Income Tax (which would appear in the balance sheet as a liability account) would be zero:

DEFERRED INCOME TAX		YEAR-END
	25,000	12/31/84
	3,750	12/31/85
2,500		12/31/86
26,250		12/31/87
	0	12/31/87 balance

Economic basis of timing differences In the Penman example there is no tax savings in an absolute sense because total tax payments equal $150,000 for both methods of revenue recognition. Why, then, should Penman use different methods of accounting for book and tax? The answer lies in the present-value concept as it applies to cash flows. To illustrate the effective tax savings, consider the following example:

1. A machine is purchased on January 1, 1983, at a cost of $80,000.
2. Its estimated life is 4 years.
3. Its estimated salvage value is zero.
4. Straight-line depreciation is used for book purposes.
5. Double-declining-balance depreciation is used for tax purposes.
6. The tax rate equals 40 percent for each of the 4 years 1983–1986.
7. Financial pretax income and taxable income are each $100,000 *before* depreciation deduction in each of the 4 years.

The following calculations provide the data for our analysis:

	METHOD	
YEAR	STRAIGHT-LINE DEPRECIATION (FOR BOOK PURPOSES)	DOUBLE-DECLINING BALANCE DEPRECIATION (FOR TAX PURPOSES)
1983	$20,000	2 × 25% × $80,000 $40,000
1984	20,000	50% × ($80,000 − $40,000) 20,000
1985	20,000	50% × ($80,000 − $60,000) 10,000
1986	20,000	Remaining balance 10,000
Total	$80,000	$80,000

YEAR	INCOME TAX EXPENSE BASED ON STRAIGHT-LINE METHOD
1983	($100,000 − $20,000) × 40% = $ 32,000
1984	($100,000 − $20,000) × 40% = $ 32,000
1985	($100,000 − $20,000) × 40% = $ 32,000
1986	($100,000 − $20,000) × 40% = $ 32,000
Total	($400,000 − $80,000[a]) × 40% = $128,000[b]

YEAR	INCOME TAX PAYABLE BASED ON DOUBLE-DECLINING-BALANCE METHOD
1983	($100,000 − $40,000) × 40% = $ 24,000
1984	($100,000 − $20,000) × 40% = $ 32,000
1985	($100,000 − $10,000) × 40% = $ 36,000
1986	($100,000 − $10,000) × 40% = $ 36,000
Total	($400,000 − $80,000[a]) × 40% = $128,000[b]

[a] Depreciation equals $80,000 in total for the 4 years *regardless* of which depreciation method is used. The depreciation deduction in total can never exceed the total depreciable base of the asset (cost minus estimated salvage value)—in this case, $80,000.

[b] Income taxes amount to $128,000 in total for the 4-year period for both book and tax purposes.

The net present value of the tax savings that results from using the double-declining-balance method for tax purposes, which is computed in Exhibit 17–1, amounts to $1,536 in this case assuming a 10 percent time preference rate for money. The following journal entries reflect the prior calculations:

12/31/83	Income tax expense		32,000	
	Deferred income tax			8,000
	Income tax payable			24,000
12/31/84	Income tax expense		32,000	
	Income tax payable			32,000
12/31/85	Income tax expense		32,000	
	Deferred income tax		4,000	
	Income tax payable			36,000
12/31/86	Income tax expense		32,000	
	Deferred income tax		4,000	
	Income tax payable			36,000

The deferred income tax method illustrated above is required to account for all timing differences under generally accepted accounting principles. Note that the amount of the balance in the Deferred Income Tax account is based on the tax rate in effect when the timing difference originates. It is not adjusted to reflect subsequent changes in the rate or the imposition of new taxes.

EXHIBIT
17–1

NET TAX SAVINGS RESULTING FROM DIFFERENCE IN TAX PAYABLE AND TAX EXPENSE

YEAR	TAX EXPENSE	–	TAX PAYABLE	=	TAX SAVINGS (TAX INCREMENT)	×	PRESENT-VALUE FACTOR @ 10%	=	PRESENT VALUE OF TAX SAVINGS (TAX INCREMENT)
1983	$ 32,000	–	$ 24,000	=	$8,000	×	.9091		$7,273
1984	32,000	–	32,000	=	0	×	.8264		0
1985	32,000	–	36,000	=	(4,000)	×	.7513		(3,005)
1986	32,000	–	36,000	=	(4,000)	×	.6830		(2,732)
	$128,000		$128,000		$ 0				$1,536

Types of timing differences Timing differences are very common, and most publicly traded entities exhibit differences between book and tax incomes. Table 17–1 summarizes various types of accounting items that involve timing differences based on a survey reported in *Accounting Trends and Techniques*. Depreciation is clearly the most common example of timing differences and has probably generated the largest dollar difference represented by the Deferred Income Tax account as well. Because most companies use accelerated depreciation for tax-reporting purposes and straight-line depreciation for financial-reporting purposes, the balance in the Deferred Income Tax account is normally a credit. Also, due to the Economic Recovery Tax Act of 1981, the depreciable life of an asset is no longer tied to the useful (economic) life concept for tax purposes. As a result, we find common examples of timing differences where property is being depreciated over 5 or 10 years for tax purposes and 20 or 30 years for financial reporting purposes. This Tax Act has resulted in a near-term increase in the credit balance carried in the Deferred Income Tax account and will probably result in greater fluctuations in the year-to-year bal-

TABLE 17–1

ITEMS GENERATING TIMING DIFFERENCES USED BY A SAMPLE GROUP OF 600 COMPANIES

SOURCE OF TIMING DIFFERENCE	NUMBER OF TIMES DIFFERENCE WAS OBSERVED IN		
	1980	1979	1978
Depreciation	476	470	472
Unremitted earnings from subsidiaries	133	100	124
Employee benefits	84	78	72
Inventory valuation	97	81	70
Installment sales	63	59	62
Discontinued operations	49	44	57
Pensions	70	70	56
Long-term contracts	57	53	48
Intangible drilling costs	39	31	35
Leases	37	26	31
Interest and taxes during construction	45	20	21
Warranties/guarantees	26	24	26
Translation of foreign currency	26	19	22

Source: *Accounting Trends and Techniques* (New York: AICPA, 1981), p. 300.

ances because of the increased size of the differences between book and tax depreciation expense.

The items identified in Table 17–1 are those that are reported at a different time for book purposes than for tax purposes, at least in part. In some cases, the difference is the result of applying accrual accounting and matching for book purposes but not applying these accrual-based revenues or expenses for tax purposes until the cash flows actually take place. For instance, advance cash payments that are received prior to the rendering of services (for example, to rent facilities or for labor to be performed) or the providing of goods for sale are frequently recorded as income for tax purposes but are accrued liabilities ("Revenue received in advance") for book purposes.

An example of a timing difference where the revenue recognition is postponed beyond when it is reported for book purposes is in long-term construction contracts that take over a year to complete. The revenue is frequently recognized on a percentage-of-completion basis for book purposes but not reported for tax purposes until the project is completed. To illustrate, assume a new domed stadium is to be constructed by Eger Construction over a 3-year period for $3,000,000. After 1 year a third of the work is finished at a cost of $750,000. Under the percentage-of-completion method, $1,000,000 (one-third) of the total revenue could be reported, resulting in $250,000 in profit for financial reporting purposes. Using the completed contract method, no revenue would be recognized until completion. Assuming a 40 percent tax rate, the $250,000 timing difference between book and tax income before tax would result in a $100,000 credit ($250,000 × 40%) to the Deferred Income Tax account. Of course, at the completion of the project all timing differences would reverse as the entire amount of profit on the project is recognized on Eger's tax return.

Another difference is the accounting for warranty expense on an accrual basis for book purposes, whereas the actual costs incurred are the only amounts that are deductible for computing taxable income in most cases. Still another example of a timing difference is in pension accounting where the amount of the pension expense is not always equal to the cash payments to the employees' pension fund. The following entry might be recorded:

12/31/85	Pension expense	85,000	
	Unfunded pension liability		20,000
	Cash		65,000

In such a case, only $65,000 would be deductible in computing taxable income, and the *tax effect* of the $20,000 difference would be accounted for in the Deferred Income Tax account as a timing difference.

A more subtle timing difference occurs when the recorded book value of an asset acquired in an asset exchange transaction is different for book and tax purposes. As noted in Chapter 11, the book value of an asset for tax purposes is normally the amount that will result in no gain or loss being recorded, since gains or losses on exchanges are normally not allowed for tax purposes. However, since gains and losses are frequently recorded for book purposes, the resulting book value of the acquired asset will usually differ for book and tax, creating a timing difference accounted for in the Deferred Income Tax account.

Some accrual-based expenses are allowed for tax purposes, and therefore it is not accurate to suggest that taxable income is strictly a cash concept. Common examples of allowable accrued expenses are uncollectible-receivables expense, and expenses associated with the write-down to market of inventory items valued on other than a LIFO basis for book purposes. Our objective here is not to prepare an exact or exhaustive list of all timing differences. Those with an expert knowledge of tax laws realize that there is good reason to use such qualifying terms as "normally" or "frequently" in describing the tax effects discussed above. There are often exceptions or other caveats to the general tax rules that might allow alternative procedures to be used for tax purposes in special situations. We focus here on the general case so that we can explain the differences between book and tax income and how to account for them.

Permanent Differences

Permanent differences involve items that enter into the computation of book income before tax *or* taxable income, but never both. Items that affect only *one* of these two income measures present a problem different from timing differences because they will never reverse themselves. To illustrate, assume that Holt Enterprises has goodwill recorded on its books from the purchase of 100 percent of Fellingham, Inc., in a previous period. Consolidated income for Holt in 1985 is as follows:

	PRETAX BOOK INCOME—1985
Revenues	$10,000,000
Cost of sales	(6,000,000)
Selling and administrative expense	(2,000,000)
Goodwill amortization	(200,000)
Income before tax	$ 1,800,000

Assume further that Holt faces a 30 percent tax rate but that the $200,000 expense for goodwill is not deductible for tax purposes in arriving at taxable income. No other differences between book and tax exist. Holt's taxable income of $2,000,000 requires an income tax payable of $600,000 (.30 × $2,000,000), whereas pretax book income of $1,800,000 requires an income tax expense of only $540,000 (.30 × $1,800,000), resulting in the following entry:

| 12/31/85 | Income tax expense | 540,000 | |
| | Income tax payable | | 600,000 |

The Deferred Income Tax account *cannot be used* in the case of permanent differences because the difference will never be reversed (that is, the IRS will never allow goodwill to be charged against taxable income). A debit of $60,000 to any balance sheet account would result in an apparent asset with no future benefit that would never be removed. In viewing the entry above we must ask, Which of the two accounts might better be changed to conform with the other? Or, Which one *cannot* be changed because of its real economic basis? The answer to the second question is the Income Tax Payable account because the $600,000 in taxes must be paid regardless of the amount of book income. As a result of this analysis, we conclude that permanent differences must affect *both* the Income Tax Expense account and the Income Tax Payable account equally, and that the expense must equal the payable with respect to permanent differences. Holt would, therefore, record the following entry for 1985:

12/31/85	Income tax expense	600,000	
	Income tax payable		600,000

The 1985 income statement would appear as follows:

HOLT ENTERPRISES
Income Statement
Year Ended December 31, 1985

Revenues	$10,000,000
Cost of sales	(6,000,000)
Selling and administrative expense	(2,000,000)
Goodwill amortization	(200,000)
Pretax income tax	$ 1,800,000
Income tax expense	(600,000)
Net income	$ 1,200,000

Note that although the stated tax rate in the Holt Enterprises example was 30 percent, the effective tax rate for Holt for 1985 is $33^1/_3$ percent ($600,000/$1,800,000). **APB Opinion No. 11** requires the differences between book income and tax income that create "significant variations in the customary relationship between income tax expense and pretax accounting income" should be disclosed or otherwise explained in the notes to the final statements.[6] If the customary relationship (30 percent in this case) and the effective rate ($33^1/_3$ percent) are considered to be significantly different, a footnote would explain the difference as follows:

Statutory tax rate	30%
Impact of goodwill on taxable income—not deductible for tax purposes	$3^1/_3$
Effective tax rate per books	$33^1/_3$%

Such reconciliations for differences between the statutory tax rate (legal rate) and the recorded effective rate in the income statement are common footnote disclosures. It should be pointed out that timing differences did not alter the effective tax rate, and, therefore, timing differences would not ordinarily enter into the reconciliation process.

Types of permanent differences   Many differences between book income and tax income are permanent. A thorough understanding of all these permanent differences requires an understanding of many intricate tax laws as well as financial accounting procedures. Although it is not possible here to cover all permanent differences, we have compiled a list of major permanent differences in Table 17–2, which also includes a brief description of the permanent difference.

One of the items in Table 17–2, "unremitted earnings of subsidiaries," is actually capable of being either a timing difference or a permanent difference or both. According to **APB Opinions No. 23 and 24**,[7] when a corporation reports as a part of its book income the undistributed income (or income **not received in the form**

---

[6] *Accounting Principles Board Opinion No. 11*, "Accounting for Income Taxes," par. 63c.

[7] See *Accounting Principles Board Opinion No. 23*, "Accounting for Income Taxes—Special Areas" (New York: AICPA, April 1972); and *Accounting Principles Board Opinion No. 24* "Accounting for Income Taxes—Equity Method Investments" (New York: AICPA, April 1972).

TABLE 17-2

EXAMPLES OF PERMANENT DIFFERENCES

PERMANENT DIFFERENCE	DESCRIPTION
Municipal bond income	Municipal bond income is never included in computing taxable income. It is a nontaxable source of income.
Goodwill	Amortization expense for goodwill is never deducted in computing taxable income.
Depletion	Depletion for tax purposes involves a special computation based on *revenues* instead of costs. As such, total depletion for tax purposes will normally *exceed* depletion expense for book purposes. The excess of tax depletion over book depletion is considered a permanent difference.
Life insurance	Expenses for life insurance premiums are not deducted in computing taxable income. Also, gains from life insurance claims are a nontaxable source of income.
Undistributed earnings of subsidiaries	When a parent reports undistributed income from unconsolidated subsidiaries (see Chapter 14) and the parent does not expect these undistributed earnings to be paid by the subsidiaries (through dividend payments) in the future, *the portion that is not expected to be distributed in the future is a permanent difference*. However, the portion of the subsidiary income that is expected to be received in the future is treated as a timing difference.
Dividends from domestic subsidiaries	A maximum of only 15 percent of the dividends received from equity investments in domestic unconsolidated subsidiaries is taxable. The exclusion of the 85 percent of remitted earnings of subsidiaries is increased to 100% for subsidiaries that are 80 percent owned by the parent.
Fines and legal penalties	These book expenses are not deductible in computing taxable income.

of dividends) of unconsolidated subsidiaries or corporate joint ventures, management of the corporation must determine whether that undistributed income will be distributed to the corporation (in the form of dividends) at some future date. If the undistributed income is expected to be received in some future period, the difference between book (where it is reported as income) and tax (where it is *not* reported as income until dividends are received) is treated as a timing difference. If, on the other hand, management determines that some or all of the undistributed income will be permanently retained in the unconsolidated subsidiaries or corporate joint ventures, the difference between book and tax is treated as a permanent difference. The *Accounting Trends and Techniques* data in Table 17-3 reveal that both treat-

TABLE 17-3

TREATMENT OF UNDISTRIBUTED EARNINGS BY A SAMPLE GROUP OF 600 COMPANIES

TREATMENT METHOD	NUMBER OF COMPANIES USING METHOD		
	1980	1979	1978
Taxes accrued on all undistributed earnings (timing difference)	21	25	31
Taxes accrued on a portion of undistributed earnings	154	150	119
Taxes not accrued on undistributed earnings (permanent difference)	218	215	238
No mention of undistributed earnings	207	210	212
Total companies	600	600	600

Source: *Accounting Trends and Techniques* (New York: AICPA, 1981), p. 310.

ments are frequently used, with permanent differences being judged as most appropriate in most cases.

Some of the differences identified in Table 17–2 are noted elsewhere in this and other accounting texts. Providing the rationale for all of these permanent differences goes beyond the scope of this text. However, you should be able to recognize some of the more common types of permanent differences in order to properly interpret the tax implications of financial accounting.

Other Differences A number of other aspects of tax laws that might create differences between tax obligations and book income tax expense need to be considered in financial reporting. The most common example in this category is the **investment tax credit.** As indicated in Chapter 12, the investment tax credit is a credit or reduction in the dollars of **taxes payable** for a specific period but may be accounted for as an equivalent reduction in the book tax expense either in the same period (the flow-through approach) or over a number of periods (the deferral approach). Accounting for the investment tax credit differs from the timing differences and permanent differences discussed above in that it is involved with **dollars of taxes** rather than **taxable dollars.** However, there is a similarity as well in that the flow-through method treats the tax credit like a permanent difference, whereas the deferral method treats the credit like a timing difference.

To illustrate, assume that during 1985 Holt Enterprises purchased an asset with a 10-year life that resulted in an investment tax credit of $80,000 for 1985. The book and tax incomes using data in the income-statement on p. 632 and *before* considering the credit are:

	INCOME TAX EXPENSE	INCOME TAX PAYABLE
Pretax income	$1,800,000	$1,800,000
Add back permanent difference (goodwill amortization) not deductible for tax purposes	200,000	200,000
	$2,000,000	$2,000,000
Applicable tax rate	× .30	× .30
	$ 600,000	$ 600,000

This type of schedule is convenient for computing the expense and payable amounts, but remember that it is a computation schedule only. It starts with pretax book income each time and makes adjustments to pretax book income for computation purposes only. In other words, the schedule under the income tax expense column computes the $600,000 amount used to record income tax expense by making adjustments to pretax book income, but **pretax book income is not being revised for financial-reporting purposes.** In Holt's 1985 income statement illustrated earlier, pretax income was reported at $1,800,000, and it will remain at that amount.

Now that Holt's computation schedule above is dealing in dollars of tax, the investment tax credit (or any other tax credit) may be considered. The following schedule reflects treatment of the investment credit under the flow-through method:

	INCOME TAX EXPENSE	INCOME TAX PAYABLE
Pretax income	$1,800,000	$1,800,000
Add back permanent difference	200,000	200,000
	$2,000,000	$2,000,000
Applicable tax rate	× .30	× .30
	$ 600,000	$ 600,000
Less tax investment credit	80,000	80,000
	$ 520,000	$ 520,000

The journal entry would be as follows:

12/31/85	Income tax expense		520,000	
	Income tax payable			520,000

The deferral method spreads out the "benefit" of the $80,000 credit for *book* purposes over the life of the equipment (10 years) on a straight-line basis. In 1985 the tax credit reduced income tax expense from $600,000 to $592,000. The following schedule reflects treatment of the investment credit under the deferral method:

	INCOME TAX EXPENSE	INCOME TAX PAYABLE
Pretax income	$1,800,000	$1,800,000
Add back permanent difference	200,000	200,000
	$2,000,000	$2,000,000
Applicable tax rate	× .30	× .30
	$ 600,000	$ 600,000
Less tax investment credit	8,000[a]	80,000
	$ 592,000	$ 520,000

[a] $1/10 \times \$80,000$.

The journal entry would be as follows

12/31/85	Income tax expense		592,000	
	Deferred investment tax credit			72,000
	Income tax payable			520,000

From 1986 to 1994 the $72,000 Deferred Investment Tax Credit balance sheet account would be allocated to the income statement by the following entry:

12/31	Deferred investment tax credit		8,000	
	Income tax expense			8,000

Another difference between book income and tax income that is neither a timing difference nor a permanent difference occurs when a preferential tax rate is allowed for some component of taxable income. The **capital gains tax** on marketable securities is a common example. The long-term capital gains rate is a lower tax rate that applies to gains on securities that have been held for over 1 year. The preferred tax rate appears as an item in the footnote reconciliation between the statutory tax rate and the effective tax rate for book purposes just as a permanent difference would appear, although it is not a permanent difference per se. To illustrate, assume that in 1985 W. Bentz, Inc., had a long-term capital gain of $100,000 that was taxable at a 20 percent rate. Bentz also has $500,000 other income taxable at the statutory rate of 46 percent, and investment tax credits of $50,000 from 1985 capital expenditures. The following computations would apply:

	INCOME TAX EXPENSE	INCOME TAX PAYABLE
Other income	$500,000	$500,000
Tax rate	× .46	× .46
Tax on other income	$230,000	$230,000
Capital gain	$100,000	$100,000
Tax rate	× .20	× .20
Tax on capital gain	$ 20,000	$ 20,000
Total tax before credits	$250,000	$250,000
Less tax credits	50,000	50,000
Net tax expense/payable	$200,000	$200,000

The partial income statement for Bentz would be as follows:

W. BENTZ, INC.

Partial Income Statement

1985

Income before taxes	$600,000	
Income tax expense (see Note Y)	200,000	
Net income	$400,000	

Note Y:

Statutory rate	46.0%	$276,000
Less effect of tax credit	(8.4)	(50,000)
Less effect of tax preference on capital gain	(4.3)	(26,000)
Effective tax rate	33.3%	$200,000

The tax preference items will have an impact on book income tax expense that is similar to the effect of a permanent difference, as illustrated in footnote Y of the Bentz example.

Integrated Example

To illustrate the integration of accounting procedures for timing differences, permanent differences, and the investment credit, as well as intraperiod tax allocation, consider the following example:

Complete Cuisine, Inc., reported pretax book income from operations for 1984 of $495,000 and also a $100,000 extraordinary loss. Included in arriving at the $495,000 figure were the following:

1. Depreciation expense on a straight-line basis, $200,000
2. Goodwill expense, $30,000

3. Municipal bond interest income, $35,000
4. Sales of appliances sold on the installment basis but recorded as revenue at the point of sale, $800,000
5. Warranty expense, $60,000

For tax purposes, Complete Cuisine uses accelerated depreciation, which amounted to $300,000 in 1984. Also, sales on the installment basis, which is used for tax purposes, were $760,000 for 1984. Actual warranty costs allowed as expense for tax purposes totaled $48,000. The statutory tax rate is 40 percent. During 1984 Complete Cuisine purchased equipment with a 10-year life, which qualified for a $38,000 investment tax credit. The deferral method is used to account for the tax credit.

To solve this problem, we refer to the worksheet format illustrated earlier, which will help compute the "expense" and "payable" components of the income tax entry. We also need to refer to our Chapter 3 illustrations of *intra*period tax-allocation procedures to account for the extraordinary loss. Beginning with pretax book operating income, the following computation schedule would be used:

	INCOME TAX EXPENSE	INCOME TAX PAYABLE
Pretax operating income per books	$495,000	$495,000
1. Timing difference from depreciation		(100,000)
2. Permanent difference from goodwill	30,000	30,000
3. Permanent difference from bond interest	(35,000)	(35,000)
4. Timing difference from installment sales		(40,000)
5. Timing difference from warranty expense		12,000
	$490,000	$362,000
Applicable tax rate	× .40	× .40
	$196,000	$144,800
Less investment tax credit	(3,800)	(38,000)
Taxes on operations	$192,200	$106,800
Extraordinary loss	$(100,000)	$(100,000)
Applicable tax rate	× .40)	× .40
Tax credit on extraordinary loss	$ 40,000	$ 40,000

The journal entries for 1984 and the partial income statement for financial-reporting purposes would be:

12/31/84	Income tax expense		192,200	
	Deferred investment credit			34,200[a]
	Deferred income taxes			51,200[b]
	Income tax payable			106,800
12/31/84	Income tax payable		40,000	
	Extraordinary loss			40,000

[a] $38,000 − ($^1/_{10}$ × $38,000) − $34,200 unamortized credit.

[b] Forced or computed by multiplying the net timing difference by their appropriate tax rate (for example, − $100,000 − $40,000 + $12,000 = − $128,000 × .40 = $51,200 credit to deferred income taxes).

```
                    COMPLETE CUISINE, INC.
                   Partial Income Statement for the
                   Year Ended December 31, 1984

         Operating income before taxes              $495,000
         Income tax expense                          192,200
         Net income from operations                 $302,800
         Extraordinary loss (net of $40,000 tax credit)  (60,000)
         Net income                                 $242,800


    Footnote X:


         Statutory tax rate              40.0%        $158,000
         Impact of bond interest          3.0          12,000
         Impact of goodwill              (3.5)        (14,000)
         Impact of investment credit     (1.0)         (3,800)
         Effective tax rate              38.5%        $152,200
```

The net tax to be paid by Complete Cuisine for 1984 is only $66,800 ($106,800 from operations less a $40,000 credit on the extraordinary loss), whereas the net amount of tax per the income statement is $152,200 ($192,200 from operations less a $40,000 credit on the extraordinary loss). The difference between the payable and the expense of $85,400 ($152,200 − $66,800) is reported in the two deferred tax accounts ($34,200 + $51,200 = $85,400). The deferred income taxes ($51,200) represent the net timing differences at their respective tax rate. The deferred investment credit ($34,200) represents the unamortized $38,000 tax credit from 1984 capital expenditures. The $5,000 net permanent difference ($30,000 − $35,000 = − $5,000), along with the difference attributable to the investment credit ($3,800), reduced the effective tax rate as reported in the financial statements from 40 percent to 38.5 percent. This is reconciled in footnote X to the income statement.

Analysis of example Note that in the computation schedule permanent differences (items 2 and 3) have an impact on both the expense side and the payable side, whereas timing differences (items 1, 4, and 5) have an impact on the expense or the payable only. Normally, timing differences affect the payable. These effects on the computation schedule are more logical to recall if the two columns of the computation schedule are thought of in the context of the basic tax entry:

	PERMANENT DIFFERENCES				TIMING DIFFERENCES			
	DEBIT	CREDIT	DEBIT	CREDIT	DEBIT	CREDIT	DEBIT	CREDIT
Income tax expense	+		−		0		+ or −	
Income tax payable		+		−		+ or −		0

The inequality of debits and credits that results from timing differences is accounted for in the Deferred Income Tax account. Only timing differences affect the balance in Deferred Income Tax. In virtually all large business entities, the Deferred Income Tax account carries a relatively large credit balance, suggesting that more taxable income has been reported for book purposes than for tax purposes over the life of the entity. Although year-to-year fluctuations may increase or decrease the Deferred Income Tax account, its balance tends to be rather sizable and increases over time.

Financial Statement Disclosure

Proper **financial statement disclosure** should enable users to reconstruct the basic entries affecting tax expense and tax payable during the period. Consider the financial statement and footnote data from a Crown Zellerbach annual report shown in Exhibit 17–2. The first footnote schedule indicates the sources of income before tax broken down by U.S. versus foreign sources. In the second footnote schedule, the taxes payable, by source, are identified. Although there is an overall tax credit (receivable) for tax purposes of $11.6 million for 1980, foreign taxes ($10.1 million) and state taxes ($.9 million) were paid during 1980. A $22.6 million federal tax refund is indicated.

The next sections of the schedule summarize the source of timing differences between the payable (credit) of −$11.6 million and the book expense of $30.4 million reported in the income statement. Of the $42.0 million in timing differences, $25.2 million is based on U.S. federal tax differences. Most of the overall $42.0 million timing differences are attributable to U.S. ($18.1) and foreign ($15.2) depreciation differences between tax and book incomes. The entry to record taxes for 1980 could be reconstructed as follows:

Income tax expense	30.4	
Income taxes receivable—U.S.	22.6	
Income taxes payable—foreign		10.1
Income taxes payable—state		.9
Deferred income tax		42.0

The credit of $42.0 million to the Deferred Income Tax account includes all but $.3 million of the $42.3 change in the balance sheet account balance between 1980 and 1979 ($161.1 − $118.8 = $42.3). It is not uncommon to find a statement, such as that of Crown Zellerbach, in which the complete explanation for the change in the Deferred Income Tax account is not reconcilable with the footnote disclosure. There is, of course, an explanation in every case, even though the explanation may not be determinable from the financial statement data. In this case, Crown Zellerbach is accounting for a timing difference, which is related to its workmen's compensation, using what is called the **net of tax method**. This method was used prior to the issuance of **APB Opinion No. 11** and, because of certain complexities, was never changed. The Workmen's Compensation account, which is included under the title "Other Liabilities" in the balance sheet, could have been directly adjusted for timing differences by the following entry:

Other liabilities	.3	
Deferred income tax		.3

The differential effect on the financial statements of the treatment noted above is not considered to be material in these circumstances.

The final section of the income tax footnote reconciles the statutory tax rate of 46 percent with the effective tax rate per books for 1980 of 23.8 percent (=$30.4/$127.8). Note that this effective rate per books is not the same as the effective rate for tax purposes. In this case, the effective rate *payable* is zero because no net tax payable is incurred during 1980. This situation is not a rare one

EXHIBIT
17–2

ILLUSTRATION OF INCOME TAX DISCLOSURES

CROWN ZELLERBACH AND SUBSIDIARIES
Partial Income Statement Data (in Millions of Dollars)

	1980	1979	1978
Income before unusual items and income taxes	$104.7	$221.1	$149.1
Gain on disposal of investment	35.0	0	0
Share of operating earnings (losses) and writedown of investment in 50 percent owned affiliate	(31.9)	(10.0)	12.1
Gain on involuntary conversion	20.0		
Income before taxes	$127.8	$211.1	$161.2
Federal, state, and foreign taxes	30.4	77.6	49.1
Net income	$ 97.4	$133.5	$112.1

Selected Balance Sheet Data

	1980	1979
Current Liabilities		
Accrued federal, state, and foreign taxes	$ 2.6	$ 50.7
Other Liabilities		
Deferred income taxes	$161.1	$118.8

Footnote Data

Income Taxes

The components of income before income taxes were as follows:

	(IN MILLIONS OF DOLLARS)		
	1980	1979	1978
United States	$ 77.4	$156.2	$105.1
Foreign	50.4	54.9	56.1
	$127.8	$211.1	$161.2

The provision for income taxes and the deferred taxes related to specific timing differences consisted of:

	(IN MILLIONS OF DOLLARS)		
	1980	1979	1978
Current:			
U.S. federal	$ (22.6)	$ 27.1	$ 16.2
State	.9	5.6	5.0
Foreign	10.1	22.9	13.2
Total current	(11.6)	55.6	34.4
Deferred:			
U.S. federal—			
Depreciation	18.1	9.9	6.9
Foreign exchange	6.3	(.3)	—
Interest capitalized	5.6	—	—
Log inventories	(3.9)	—	(.6)
Other, net	(.9)	(1.2)	(.8)
Total U.S. federal	25.2	8.4	5.5
Foreign—			
Depreciation	15.2	11.8	9.5
Other, net	1.6	1.8	(.3)
Total foreign	16.8	13.6	9.2
Total deferred	42.0	22.0	14.7
Federal, state, and foreign taxes	$ 30.4	$ 77.6	$ 49.1

EXHIBIT 17-2 (continued)

Investment and energy tax credits included in the current U.S federal provision were $19.8 million in 1980, $16.7 million in 1979, and $12.6 million in 1978.

A reconciliation between the federal statutory tax rate and the effective tax rate follows:

	1980	1979	1978
Statutory tax rate	46.0%	46.0%	48.0%
Earnings taxed at the capital gains rate	—	(4.7)	(4.6)
Provision for state income taxes	.4	1.4	1.6
Investment and energy tax credits	(15.5)	(7.9)	(7.8)
Foreign income taxes	(12.0)	(2.0)	(4.0)
Loss (income) of 50 percent owned affiliates recorded net of income taxes	9.6	2.5	(3.9)
All other, net	(4.7)	1.5	1.2
Effective tax rate	23.8%	36.8%	30.5%

Due to reinvestment policies and available tax credits, no additional tax liability is considered necessary on approximately $208 million of undistributed earnings of 50 percent owned affiliates and foreign subsidiaries at December 31, 1980.

and is becoming increasingly common because of the more liberal depreciation policies and the investment credits available to corporations.

Other examples of footnote disclosures are illustrated in Exhibits 17-3, 17-4, and 17-5. Note that although these exhibits vary slightly from the Crown Zellerbach format shown in Exhibit 17-2, they all include essentially the same data.

Conceptual Issues

Several conceptual issues concerning interperiod tax-allocation procedures have been the source of considerable debate.[8] Most significantly, some accountants have questioned the very nature of the Deferred Income Tax (DIT) account, which is listed as a long-term liability on the balance sheet. They have questioned the propriety of such a classification, arguing that these taxes are not a liability. It has also been pointed out that, in practice, the DIT account is in effect a large permanent "liability" on the books of most entities and that there is little likelihood the account will ever reverse itself to any significant degree. Furthermore, some have argued that the book tax expense reported in the income statement has no economic basis and merely distorts the measure of a firm's performance. Of course, others have argued that DIT is a liability and that the measure of book tax expense does a superior job of matching revenues with expense in the income statement.

The key issues here are fundamental and to a large extent involve the application of elements of financial statements as defined in **SFAC No. 3**.[9] However, the reason that these issues are of interest stems from the absolute dollar size of the DIT accounts of many entities. It is not uncommon to find credit balances in DIT accounts in excess of 10 percent of the total assets of an entity. Because of the magnitude of the DIT account and the uncertainty of its nature, the debate over the propriety of current GAAP for interperiod tax allocation will probably continue.

[8] See, for example, James H. Ditkoff, "Financial Tax Accounting at the Crossroads," *Journal of Accountancy,* August 1977; and H. Herring III and Fred Jacobs, "The Expected Behavior of Deferred Tax Credits," *Journal of Accountancy,* August 1976.

[9] *Statement of Financial Accounting Concepts No. 3,* "Elements of Financial Statements of Business Enterprises" (Stamford, CT: FASB, December 1980).

EXHIBIT
17–3

CSX CORP
Footnote Disclosures

Note 4. Income Taxes. Income taxes were (in thousands of dollars):

Current	1980	1979	1978
United States	$ 27,152	$ 12,096	$ 4,249
State	15,367	4,966	2,744
Foreign	1,078	3,417	288
	43,597	20,479	7,281
Deferred			
United States	38,455	30,784	(4,025)
State	1,462	819	1,915
	39,917	31,603	(2,110)
Total	$ 83,514	$ 52,082	$ 5,171

The income tax provision reconciled to the tax computed at statutory rates is (in thousands of dollars):

	1980	1979	1978
Tax at statutory rates	$167,956	$133,034	$65,508
Investment tax credits used	(94,967)	(85,493)	(57,196)
Capital gains rate differential	(9,820)	(5,255)	(3,293)
State income taxes—net of Federal tax benefit	7,650	4,230	2,195
Effect of different tax and book bases arising from business combinations	(1,474)	(1,616)	(5,369)
Minority interest in earnings of subsidiaries	11,735	7,912	3,908
Adjustment to prior years' income taxes (net of related investment tax credits)	(8,872)	(10,119)	(120)
Other items—net	11,306	9,389	(462)
Total	$ 83,514	$ 52,082	$ 5,171

The deferred income tax provision represents the tax effect of timing differences as follows (in thousands of dollars):

	1980	1979	1978
Depreciation	$ 52,904	$ 36,990	$71,386
Investment tax credits reinstated (used)	7,345	(8,248)	(69,258)
Capitalized interest	6,917	4,048	—
Intangible drilling costs	3,471	2,346	2,438
Casualty losses	(14,761)	(8,224)	(6,848)
Gain on retirements	(7,401)	(8,069)	(7,441)
Abandonment losses	(6,536)	(1,236)	1,149
Other timing differences—net	(2,022)	13,996	6,464
Total	$ 39,917	$ 31,603	$ (2,110)

Investment tax credits of approximately $209 million are being carried forward for income tax purposes and expire in 1983 through 1987. Approximately $23 million are being carried forward for financial statement purposes and expire in 1987.

The Federal income tax returns of Chessie Industries and their subsidiaries have been examined for various prior periods and certain proposed adjustments are being contested. Management believes adequate provision has been made for any adjustments which might be assessed for all years through 1980.

EXHIBIT
17–4

HAZELTINE CORPORATION
Footnote Disclosures

Note 8. Income Taxes

Income before income taxes for 1980, 1979, and 1978 is comprised of the following components:

	1980	1979	1978
Domestic	$7,814,000	$9,555,000	$7,909,000
Foreign	1,076,000	434,000	479,000
	$8,890,000	$9,989,000	$8,388,000

The components of income tax expense for 1980, 1979, and 1978 are as follows:

	1980	1979	1978
Currently payable			
U.S. Federal Income Taxes	$ —	$ 777,000	78,000
State Income Taxes	80,000	676,000	263,000
Foreign Income Taxes	515,000	20,000	—
Deferred Income Taxes Applicable to:			
Uncompleted Contracts			
Federal Income Taxes	2,785,000	2,293,000	2,849,000
State Income Taxes	282,000	(44,000)	185,000
Other			
Federal Income Taxes	504,000	675,000	597,000
State Income Taxes	58,000	(45,000)	54,000
Foreign Income Taxes	(174,000)	280,000	—
Total	$4,050,000	$4,632,000	$4,026,000

The following table compares the Company's effective tax rates to the Federal statutory rates for 1980, 1979 and 1978.

	1980	1979	1978
Provisions at Federal Statutory Rate	46.0%	46.0%	48.0%
Tax effect of:			
Investment and foreign tax credits	(2.6)	(2.5)	(1.0)
State taxes, net of Federal benefit	2.6	3.2	3.1
Other	(.4)	(.3)	(2.1)
Actual Tax Provision	45.6%	46.4%	48.0%

The Company's Federal income tax returns have been examined by the Internal Revenue Service through the year 1975. No material charges to income are anticipated to result from any examinations of the Company's tax returns.

PRACTICAL CONSIDERATIONS IN INTERPERIOD TAX ALLOCATION

Because of the numerous timing differences that could exist over a period of time, we can easily imagine the amount of record keeping, time, and cost that would be required if an attempt were made to handle each timing difference individually. In practice, an entity will have numerous timing differences, all overlapping. In a given year, some differences are originating while others are reversing. For timing differences that are reversing, or coming due, their balance sheet classification in the Deferred Income Tax account is based on the asset to which they are related. If the

EXHIBIT
17–5

R. J. REYNOLDS INDUSTRIES, INC.

Notes to Consolidated Financial Statements *(Dollars in Millions Except Per Share Amounts)*

Note 9: Provision for Income Taxes

The provision for income taxes consists of the following:

	1980	1979	1978
Current:			
Federal	$ 278.3	$ 304.1	$284.4
State	49.3	51.0	40.7
Foreign	57.7	39.2	28.7
	385.3	394.3	353.8
Deferred:			
Federal	73.5	58.3	50.9
State	7.1	7.6	4.5
Foreign	2.9	6.1	3.2
	83.5	72.0	58.6
Provision for income taxes	$ 468.8	$ 466.3	$412.4

Deferred income tax expense results from timing differences in the recognition of revenue and expense for book and tax purposes. The sources of these differences and the tax effect of each were as follows:

	1980	1979	1978
Excess of tax over book depreciation	$ 23.3	$ 29.2	$ 27.3
Intangible drilling and development costs	21.8	36.0	29.8
Various other items	38.4	6.8	1.5
Deferred income taxes	$ 83.5	$ 72.0	$ 58.6

Pre-tax income for domestic and foreign operations is shown in the following table:

	1980	1979	1978
Domestic	$ 916.2	$ 875.4	$732.4
Foreign*	223.0	141.8	121.9
	$1,139.2	$1,017.2	$854.3

* Pre-tax income of foreign operations is earnings of all operations located outside the United States, some of which may also be currently subject to U.S. tax jurisdiction.

The differences between the effective tax rates and the statutory U.S. federal income tax rates are explained as follows:

	1980 AMOUNT	1980 % OF PRE-TAX INCOME	1979 AMOUNT	1979 % OF PRE-TAX INCOME	1978 AMOUNT	1978 % OF PRE-TAX INCOME
Income tax computed at statutory U.S. federal income tax rate	$524.0	46.0%	$467.9	46.0%	$410.1	48.0%
Taxes on foreign operations in excess of (less than) the statutory U.S. federal income tax rate	(34.8)	(3.1)	(21.9)	(2.2)	(9.6)	(1.1)
State taxes, net of federal benefit	30.5	2.7	31.7	3.1	23.5	2.8
Investment tax credit	(68.5)	(6.0)	(18.7)	(1.8)	(18.5)	(2.2)
Miscellaneous items	17.6	1.6	7.3	0.7	6.9	0.8
Provision for income taxes	$468.8	41.2%	$466.3	45.8%	$412.4	48.3%

At December 31, 1980, there were $531 million of accumulated and undistributed earnings of foreign subsidiaries and earnings of Domestic International Sales Corporations for which no provision for U.S. federal income taxes has been made. These undistributed earnings are intended to be reinvested indefinitely or received free of additional tax.

There are a number of issues pending as a result of Internal Revenue Service audits. The resolution of these issues is not expected to have a material adverse effect on the Company's financial position.

reversing difference pertains to a long-term asset, the related deferred income taxes are considered to be long-term. In general, the deferral is classified as current or long-term based on the balance sheet classification of the asset or liability giving rise to the deferral. However, when the deferral is not associated with an asset or liability, it should be classified as current or noncurrent based on when the deferral is expected to reverse.[10]

When it becomes difficult and costly to identify and account for timing differences individually, one of two approaches has been suggested to simplify the problem. One is called the *group-of-similar-items, gross change method,* and the other the *group-of-similar-items, net change method.*[11] We refer to them simply as the *gross change method* and the *net change method.*

Gross Change Method

Under the **gross change method,** similar timing differences arising from similar types of transactions (installment sales, for example) must be grouped together. For each similar group, a computation is made of the tax effects of *originating* differences using the current tax rate. A computation is also made for each similar group for *reversing* differences at the tax rates in existence when the differences originated. The difference between these two computations is the increase or decrease in the Deferred Income Tax account for the period for that particular group of differences. These three steps must be followed:

1. Group similar timing differences originating in the current period, and calculate the increase in deferred income taxes using the current tax rate.
2. Group similar timing differences that are reversing during the current period, and calculate the tax effects using the applicable prior-period tax rates.
3. Determine the difference between step 1 and step 2. This is the net change in deferred income taxes for the period.

Observe that the gross change method is like the individual item basis in that the amortization (reversal) of deferred income taxes during a period **is based on the tax rates that were in effect when the deferred taxes originated.** It simplifies the procedure mainly through the grouping of similar timing differences.

But what if the deferred tax balance has built up over a number of years when the tax rate was changing? Must you specifically identify a reversal with a specific tax rate? The answer is no, and this is another simplifying aspect of the gross change method over the individual item basis. Either a FIFO or a weighted-average measurement of the tax rate in effect in the prior periods may be used in the years of reversal. The weighted-average rate is computed by dividing the aggregate deferred income taxes at the beginning of the period for similar differences by the aggregate (pretax) timing differences at the beginning of the period.

Gross change—weighted-average rate An example will clarify these points. Assume that the firm uses the installment method for reporting gross profit on its tax return but reports gross profit in the year of sale on its books. Also assume that the firm uses accelerated depreciation on its tax return and straight-line depreciation on

---

[10] *Statement of Financial Accounting Standards No. 37,* "Balance Sheet Classification of Deferred Income Taxes" (Stamford, CT: FASB, July 1980).

[11] Donald Bevis and Raymond Perry, "Accounting for Income Taxes, An Interpretation of APB Opinion No. 11" (New York: AICPA, 1969), p. 20.

EXHIBIT 17–6

GROSS CHANGE METHOD—COMPUTATION OF WEIGHTED-AVERAGE TAX RATES

		SIMILAR GROUP 1				SIMILAR GROUP 2	
YEAR	TAX RATE ×	AGGREGATE TIMING DIFFERENCES— INSTALLMENT BASIS VS. ACCRUAL BASIS =	AGGREGATE DEFERRED TAX CREDIT	TAX RATE ×	AGGREGATE TIMING DIFFERENCES— ACCELERATED DEPRECIATION VS. STRAIGHT LINE =	AGGREGATE DEFERRED TAX CREDIT
1984	48% ×	$ 6,000 =	$ 2,880	48% ×	$ 8,000 =	$ 3,840
1985	50 ×	8,000 =	4,000	50 ×	10,000 =	5,000
1986	47 ×	4,000 =	1,880	47 ×	6,000 =	2,820
1987	40 ×	5,000 =	2,000	40 ×	0 =	0
		$23,000	$10,760		$24,000	$11,660

Aggregate weighted-average tax rate $\dfrac{\$10,760}{\$23,000} = 46.78\%$ Aggregate weighted-average tax rate $\dfrac{\$11,660}{\$24,000} = 48.58\%$

its books. The aggregate timing differences and aggregate deferred income taxes relating to these differences during the past 4 years are provided in Exhibit 17–6. Assume that during 1988 the firm reported pretax accounting income of $110,000 and taxable income of $105,000. The $5,000 difference between book income and tax income resulted because straight-line depreciation exceeded accelerated depreciation by $10,000 (a reversing difference), whereas gross profit on installment sales per books exceeded gross profit on installment sales reported on the tax return by $15,000 (an originating difference). Assume that the tax rate in 1988 was 45 percent. The following computations would be made:

	INCOME TAX PAYABLE
Pretax accounting income	$110,000
Originating difference:	
Installment sales gross profit per books in excess of tax return amount	(15,000)
Reversing difference:	
Straight-line depreciation per books in excess of accelerated depreciation per tax return	10,000
Taxable income	$105,000
Tax rate	×.45
Tax payable	$ 47,250

Calculations of tax expense and deferred tax are as follows:

Gross change—weighted-average method	
Taxes payable	$47,250
Originating difference:	
Installment sales—45% × $15,000	6,750
Reversing difference:	
Depreciation—48.48%[a] × $10,000	(4,858)
Tax expense	$49,142

[a] See computation in Exhibit 17–6.

The appropriate journal entry would be:

Income tax expense	49,142	
Deferred income tax ($6,750 − $4,858)		1,892
Income tax payable		47,250

Note that offsetting the $4,858 against the $6,750 to determine a *net* credit to deferred income taxes of $1,892 is appropriate only if deferred income taxes relating to installment sales and depreciation are either both noncurrent or both current (here we assume that both are noncurrent), since current items cannot be netted against noncurrent. Note also that if installment sales were a reversing item and depreciation an originating item in our example, the reversal would have been calculated using the weighted-average percentage (46.78 percent) applicable to installment sales, as computed in Exhibit 17–6.

Gross change—FIFO rate If a FIFO method were used rather than a weighted-average method, the only difference would be in the method of expense calculation. The resulting figures would be computed as follows:

Taxes payable (as before)		$47,250
Originating difference:		
45% × $15,000		6,750
Reversing difference:		
48% × $8,000	$3,840	
50% × $2,000	1,000	(4,840)
Income tax expense		$49,160

The appropriate journal entry would be:

Income tax expense	49,160	
Deferred income tax ($6,750 − $4,840)		1,910
Income tax payable		47,250

Note that while the payable remains the same in every case, the different measurement of the change in the deferral account ($1,910 versus $1,892 = $18) affects the book income tax expense amount. As a result, the *method* of computing the change in the deferral account may help to explain the difference between the statutory tax rate and the effective tax rate per books. This is the third type of item (along with permanent differences and tax credits or preferences) that can have an impact on the reported income tax expense of the entity for financial-reporting purposes. At the same time it might be observed that *none* of these three items has any economic effect on the entity because they have no impact on the income tax payable amount.

Net Change Method The net change method further simplifies the calculation. As long as the originating and reversing differences of similar items are either both current or both noncurrent (here we assume that both are noncurrent), the difference between them is multiplied by the *current year's tax rate,* and deferred income taxes are either increased or decreased by the resulting figure. Thus, there is no amortization of deferred taxes during periods when the aggregate timing differences increase. An amount equal to the tax effect of the aggregate increase in timing differences will be added to the Deferred Income Tax account. In years when the aggregate timing differences result in a decrease in deferred taxes, care must be taken to ensure that the decrease does not exceed amounts previously provided. This might happen because the current year's tax rate might exceed the weighted-average rate of prior years.

Using the data in the preceding examples, the following calculations would be made under the net change method:

Taxes payable (as before)	$47,250
Deferred tax change:	
($15,000 − $10,000) × 45%	2,250
Income tax expense	$49,500

The appropriate journal entry would be:

Income tax expense	49,500	
Deferred income tax		2,250
Income tax payable		47,250

There is an inherent inaccuracy in the net change method in that if all differences were reversed so that the balance should theoretically be zero, it would not equal zero unless no changes in tax rates had occurred. Fortunately, the differences do not all reverse in going concerns. Also, the statutory tax rates that affect timing differences have not fluctuated greatly over the past several decades, and therefore the effect of rate inaccuracies is usually minimal.

ACCOUNTING FOR NET OPERATING LOSSES

Even though income taxes must be calculated and paid on a yearly basis, the Internal Revenue Service recognizes that a firm's profitability is more long-term in nature and that income of one or a few years may be offset by losses of other years. It would therefore seem unfair and inequitable to tax a firm on income of one year while not allowing tax relief for loss years. To offset such an inequity, federal tax laws allow firms to balance their tax burden at least partially over periods of income and loss through tax loss carryback and carryforward provisions. A firm with a net operating loss (NOL) during the current year may elect to either (1) carry the loss back 3 years and claim refunds of taxes paid in those years and apply any remaining loss that might exceed the income of the past 3 years against the taxes on future income for the next 15 years (carryforward) or (2) *only* carry the loss forward for 15 years as a reduction of taxable income in those years. Once the total loss incurred has been utilized to offset taxable income, no further offsetting is permissible. Also, if the total NOL is not fully utilized during the 15-year carryforward period, the offsetting effect of any unused portion is lost.

For example, if a firm suffers a NOL in 1983 and elects the carryback-carryforward option (option 1 above), the loss is carried back first to 1980 and offset against taxable income for that year. Assuming it exceeds taxable income for 1980, the unused portion is carried to 1981, then 1982, then 1984, then 1985, and so on, until fully utilized *or* until the full 15 future years have expired, whichever comes first. At the end of 1983, a claim for a refund is filed with the Internal Revenue Service for taxes already paid during the period 1980–1982. For the carryforward period, the firm waits until it files its tax returns for 1984, 1985, and so on, and offsets the unused loss carryforward against income in each of those years, reducing the income taxes that would otherwise have to be paid. If the carryforward option (option 2 above) is elected, a similar procedure would be followed, except that there would not be any carryback. Once one of the NOL options is elected, it is irrevocable.

Note that to this point we have been concerned only with filing tax returns and claims for refunds. Our basic problem is what to do with NOLs from a financial accounting viewpoint.

Accounting for the Loss Carryback-Carryforward Option

If the **loss carryback-carryforward** option is elected, accountants are in nearly unanimous agreement as to how the effects of carryback losses should be handled for financial accounting purposes. The view is that the refund of prior years' tax payments should be reflected as a current receivable and as a reduction of the year's operating loss (as an ordinary item). Assume the following facts concerning the Lattimer Corporation:

YEAR	TAX RATE	TAXABLE INCOME (LOSS)	TAXES PAID
1980	40%	$ 30,000	$12,000
1981	45	45,000	20,250
1982	48	40,000	19,200
1983	—	(100,000)	0
Total		$ 15,000	$51,450

Following the *required order of offset,* Lattimer would calculate a claim for a refund as follows:

YEAR	TAX RATE	TAXABLE INCOME (LOSS)	TAXES TO BE REFUNDED
1980	40%	$ 30,000	$12,000
1981	45	45,000	20,250
1982	48	25,000	12,000
1983	—	(100,000)	0
Total		$ 0	$44,250

The appropriate journal entry would be:

12/31/83	Income tax refund receivable	44,250	
	Reduction of loss due to loss carry-back		44,250

The lower part of Lattimer's 1983 income statement would appear as follows:

	INCOME—1983
Operating loss before income tax effect	$(100,000)
Less: Reduction of loss due to carryback	44,250
Net operating loss	$ (55,750)

Because of the tax benefits of the net operating loss, Lattimer is able to receive a refund of $44,250 of the total $51,450 in taxes paid over the past 3 years, thereby reducing the 1983 loss *after taxes* to $55,750. There is no remaining loss carryforward in this case because the $100,000 loss in 1983 did not exceed the total income for the previous 3 years (1980–1982).

To illustrate the carryback-carryforward option when the loss is carried forward as well, assume that Sundem, Inc., had reported the following facts over that past several years:

YEAR	TAX RATE	TAXABLE INCOME (LOSS)	TAXES PAID (REFUNDED)
1981	40%	$180,000	$ 72,000
1982	40%	260,000	104,000
1983	40%	195,000	78,000
1984	—	(800,000)	(254,000)
1985	40%	270,000	42,000

At the end of 1984, Sundem would be able to file for a refund for the taxes paid during 1981, 1982, and 1983 ($72,000 + $104,000 + $78,000 = $254,000). Since the total net operating loss of $800,000 would not be completely used up in offsetting the incomes of 1981, 1982, and 1983 ($180,000 + $260,000 + $195,000 = $635,000), the remaining loss of $165,000 ($800,000 − $635,000) would be carried forward and offset against 1985 taxable income of $270,000. This would reduce 1985 taxable income to $105,000 ($270,000 − 165,000), resulting in taxes of only $42,000 in 1985.

It should be noted that Sundem could have also elected to have the entire $800,000 loss of 1984 carried forward to 1985 and future periods. In such an event, no refund for $254,000 would have been received for the 1984 loss, and no taxes would have been due for 1985 since the carryforward amount would have more than offset the $270,000 taxable income.

Accounting for a Loss Carryforward
The proper handling of a loss carryforward for financial accounting purposes is somewhat complex. As of the end of 1984 Sundem has incurred a net operating loss of $800,000. Assume that Sundem had elected to carry this loss forward (a decision was made not to carry the loss back). The extent to which Sundem will be able to take advantage of the loss carryforward depends on whether there will be taxable income during the next 15-year period. If realization **is assured beyond any reasonable doubt,** proper matching would dictate that the financial income effects of the carryforward should be reflected in 1984, the year the net operating loss sustained.[12] However, if realization **is not assured,** the benefits of a loss carryforward should not be recognized until the year in which they are actually realized through a reduction of taxes otherwise payable.[13]

Other important questions remain unanswered. First, what is the nature of the tax benefits from carryforwards? Does the nature change if the benefits are anticipated as opposed to actually realized? The APB answered these questions as follows. If tax benefits can reasonably be anticipated and reflected in the year of loss,

[12] *Accounting Principles Board Opinion No. 11,* "Accounting for Income Taxes," par. 47.

[13] Ibid., par. 45.

the benefits are being matched with the loss giving rise to them and are therefore considered to be ordinary in nature. Consequently, they should have an impact on income (loss) from continuing operations. However, if the tax benefits of the loss are not recognized in the financial records until some future period or periods, when they are realized they should be considered extraordinary because they resulted from losses of prior periods, not the current period or periods. Consequently, they should not have an impact on income (loss) from continuing operations.

Measuring and Recording the Carryforward Benefit

What criteria determine whether tax benefits are *assured beyond a reasonable doubt?* Two conditions must be fulfilled. First, the loss must result from an identifiable, isolated, and nonrecurring cause and the company must have been continuously profitable or, at worst, have only suffered occasional losses that were more than offset by taxable income in subsequent years. Second, future taxable income is virtually certain to be large enough to offset the loss carryforward during the carryforward period.[14]

Tax benefit recognized in current period To illustrate, assume the following facts:

1. In 1983 Fertig, Inc., suffered a net operating loss of $100,000.
2. The tax rate in 1983 is 48 percent.
3. The anticipated tax rate for the years of carryforward is 50 percent.
4. Tax benefits can be anticipated beyond any reasonable doubt.

The following journal entry for 1983 would be appropriate assuming the carryforward-only election:

| 12/31/83 | Estimated tax benefits—loss carryforward (50% × $100,000) | 50,000 | |
| | Reduction of loss due to tax carryforward | | 50,000 |

The **estimated** future tax rate is used as the basis for measuring the tax carryforward portion of the benefits. The debit entry would be to an asset account, which would be broken down between current and noncurrent depending on when it is anticipated that the actual reduction in taxes payable will take place. The credit is an ordinary income statement item, reported in 1983 as follows:

FERTIG, INC.
Partial Income Statement

	1983
Operating loss before tax effect	($100,000)
Less: Reduction due to tax carryforward	50,000
Net operating loss	$ (50,000)

[14] Ibid., par. 45.

Assume that the following results occur in 1984, 1985, and 1986:

YEAR	TAXABLE INCOME BEFORE CARRYFORWARD LOSS	TAX RATE	TAXES ON INCOME BEFORE CARRYFORWARD LOSS
1984	$ 25,000	50%	$12,500
1985	60,000	50	30,000
1986	35,000	50	17,500
Total	$120,000		$60,000

No more than the $100,000 actual net operating loss from 1983 can be used to off-set future taxes, resulting in a maximum decrease of $50,000 in taxes in this case, computed as follows:

YEAR	CARRYFORWARD LOSS OFFSET	TAX RATE	REDUCTION IN TAXES PAYABLE
1984	$ 25,000	50%	$12,500
1985	60,000	50	30,000
1986	15,000	50	7,500
Total	$100,000		$50,000

The following entries would be appropriate:

12/31/84	Income tax expense	12,500	
	Income tax payable		12,500
12/31/84	Income tax payable	12,500	
	Estimated tax benefits—loss carryforward		12,500
12/31/85	Income tax expense	30,000	
	Income tax payable		30,000
12/31/85	Income tax payable	30,000	
	Estimated tax benefits—loss carryforward		30,000
12/31/86	Income tax expense	17,500	
	Income tax payable		17,500
12/31/86	Income tax payable	7,500	
	Estimated tax benefits—loss carryforward		7,500

Note that because all $50,000 of tax benefits was reported as a reduction of the net operating loss in 1983, no income statement effects are reported in income for the years 1984, 1985, and 1986. During those years, the asset account is simply reduced (amortized) with a corresponding reduction in taxes payable. The partial income statements for 1984–1986 would appear as follows:

FERTIG, INC.			
Partial Income Statements			
	1984	1985	1986
Income before taxes	$25,000	$60,000	$35,000
Less: Income tax expense	12,500	30,000	17,500
Net income	$12,500	$30,000	$17,500

But what if the actual tax rates for the carryforward years do not turn out to be those anticipated in 1983? Assume the same facts as before except that in 1985 the actual tax rate is 45 percent. Everything else would remain the same as previously illustrated except for the following entries in 1985:

| 12/31/85 | Income tax expense (45% × $60,000) | 27,000 | |
| | Income tax payable | | 27,000 |

12/31/85	Income tax payable	27,000	
	Income tax expense	3,000	
	Estimated tax benefits—loss carryfor-		
	ward (50% × $60,000)		30,000

When the applicable future tax rates are different than the estimated rate used to measure the tax benefit at the time the asset was recognized, the effect of the rate change—in our example (50% − 45%) × $60,000, or $3,000—should be accounted for in the period of change as an adjustment to the asset account and to income tax expense. This is simply another example of a change in estimate. It is not to be considered an error, a prior period adjustment, or a change in accounting principle. Nor is it to be considered extraordinary. Note that in the entry to adjust the asset account, the amount of reduction in the payable is given in the previous entry ($27,000 in this case), and the amount of asset amortization is given by the original estimated tax rate (50 percent) and the pretax income ($60,000). The entry to the Income Tax Expense account ($3,000) is essentially a forced amount.

Tax benefit recognized in future periods Assume all of the data in the Fertig, Inc., example except that the tax benefits are *not* assured beyond a reasonable doubt. In such a case, no asset is recognized for the carryforward tax benefits, and estimating future tax rates is no longer a measurement issue. The following entries would be appropriate:

| 12/31/84 | Income tax expense | 12,500 | |
| | Income tax payable | | 12,500 |

12/31/84	Income tax payable	12,500	
	Tax reduction due to loss carryfor-		
	ward—extraordinary		12,500

| 12/31/85 | Income tax expense | 30,000 | |
| | Income tax payable | | 30,000 |

12/31/85	Income tax payable	30,000	
	Tax reduction due to loss carryfor-		
	ward—extraordinary		30,000

12/31/86	Income tax expense	17,500	
	Income tax payable		17,500
12/31/86	Income tax payable	7,500	
	Tax reduction due to loss carryfor- ward—extraordinary		7,500

The partial income statements for 1983 to 1986 would appear as follows:

FERTIG, INC.
Partial Income Statements

	1983	1984	1985	1986
Income (loss) before taxes	$(100,000)	$25,000	$60,000	$35,000
Less: Income tax expense	0	12,500	30,000	17,500
Income (loss before extraordinary item	$(100,000)	$12,500	$30,000	$17,500
Extraordinary item: Tax reduction due to loss carryfor- ward		12,500	30,000	7,500
Net income (loss)	$(100,000)	$25,000	$60,000	$25,000

Note that the impact of the loss carryforward appears as an extraordinary item in the income statements for 1984–1986. Tax loss carryforwards are the most common type of extraordinary item encountered in practice.

FUNDS FLOW EFFECTS

Accounting for income taxes has an important effect on both cash and working capital flows. The most direct impact on funds flows comes from the income tax payable aspect of tax accounting. The tax payable, which is based on tax income rather than book income, will decrease working capital by increasing current liabilities. There will also be an eventual outflow of cash as the current tax obligation is paid. While the payable side of the entry to account for taxes is not a prominent item in financial statement disclosures, it has an important impact of funds flow measurement.

The income tax expense side of the entry to account for taxes is reported in the income statement, and details are normally provided in the notes to the financial statements. Since the amount of the income tax expense does not represent a use of funds, it should be a reconciling item in the statement of changes in financial position. In a format that starts with "income from operations" and computes "funds from operations," the difference between the tax expense and the tax payable, which is the result of long-term timing differences, would be an adjusting item. If the long-term Deferred Income Tax account *increases*, the adjustment would be to *increase* income from operations to compute funds from operations. A decrease in the deferral will decrease income from operations. When the change in the deferral is small, it will normally not appear as a separate adjustment to income from operations in computing the source of funds provided by operations.

SUMMARY

In this chapter we have reviewed the accounting and reporting requirements for interperiod tax allocation and for net operating losses. Interperiod tax allocation is a complex subject that exists largely because accounting policy makers want to maintain the matching concept in the income statement. Most of the material in this chapter would be unnecessary were it not for the desire to match against the revenues and expenses reported for financial accounting purposes an income tax expense amount that *appears* to be based on reported revenues and expenses, even though the actual tax obligation for the period may be (and normally is) quite different. If the APB had considered income tax expense to be a loss or a distribution of earnings, it could have simply required the income tax expense to equal the income tax payable. This would have made most of this chapter unnecessary for financial accounting purposes. Some have argued that booking the payable amount as the expense would also be more representative of economic reality.

In using financial accounting data to evaluate the reporting entity, remember that there is a difference between the book tax expense and the actual taxes payable. For example, some have suggested that corporations using non–LIFO inventory methods are mismanaged because they could save cash (and use it for dividends) by switching to LIFO and paying less income taxes. However, even where LIFO results in lower income, it is entirely possible that the corporation in question may already be in a nontax situation for tax purposes (while reporting a positive book net income figure and, therefore, book tax expense). The Crown Zellerbach report in this chapter provides an example of such a case. Keep in mind that the taxes payable side of the entry is the economic side, affecting the statement of changes in financial position, whereas the expense side is a noneconomic variable affecting the book net income of the entity.

QUESTIONS

Q17–1   The objectives established by the federal government for determining taxable income differ from the objectives for determining accounting income in certain important ways. Discuss them.

Q17–2   What is the firm's basic objective when filing its tax return and paying taxes? In what ways might fulfilling this objective have an impact on accounting income measurements?

Q17–3   What is interperiod tax allocation, and how does it differ from intraperiod tax allocation?

Q17–4   What are timing differences, and how are they accounted for?

Q17–5   What are permanent differences, and how are they accounted for?

Q17–6   What is the proper accounting treatment for the investment tax credit?

Q17–7   What is the proper accounting treatment for tax preference items that are taxed at a favorable rate?

Q17–8   What kinds of items are able to change the book income tax expense amount from the statutory income tax rate?

Q17–9   How can financial statement readers determine the nature of the differences between the effective tax rate for book income tax expense and the statutory tax rate?

Q17–10   How can financial statement readers determine the actual effective tax rate paid by the entity during an accounting period?

Q17–11   Explain the arguments in favor of interperiod tax allocation.

Q17–12   Explain the arguments against interperiod tax allocation.

Q17–13   Explain the methodology used in the gross change method of accounting for taxes.

Q17–14   What types of differences between book and tax income are being accounted for by the gross change method? By the net change method?

Q17–15 Explain how the assumption about tax rates (FIFO versus weighted average) affects the gross change method of accounting for taxes.

Q17–16 Explain the net change method of accounting for taxes. How does it differ from the gross change method?

Q17–17 What will happen if tax rates increase over time and the net change method is used in a case where all timing differences have reversed themselves and there are no timing differences outstanding?

Q17–18 Explain the alternatives available for accounting for the tax effect of net operating losses.

Q17–19 When may the tax benefits of net operating losses to be *carried forward* be recorded as assets?

Q17–20 How are net operating losses reported in the financial statements when they are carried forward to future periods in which taxable income is earned (1) assuming they *have not* been recognized as an asset in the year of the NOL, and (2) assuming they *have* been recognized as an asset in the year of the NOL?

CASES

C17–1 (CPA ADAPTED) For accounting purposes, the investment tax credit can be accounted for by one of two "generally accepted" methods.

REQUIRED Identify and explain these two accounting methods for the investment tax credit. *Do not discuss income tax computations of the investment tax credit.*

C17–2 (CPA ADAPTED) Deferred income taxes are required under generally accepted accounting principles. *Accounting Principles Board Opinion No. 11,* "Accounting for Income Taxes," requires the use of the deferral method of comprehensive interperiod tax allocation. Under the deferred method, (1) the gross change method and (2) the net change method are used to account for timing differences.

REQUIRED

1. Describe the gross change method.
2. Describe the net change method.

C17–3 (CPA ADAPTED) Income tax allocation is an integral part of generally accepted accounting principles. The applications of intraperiod tax allocation (within a period) and interperiod tax allocation (between periods) are both required.

REQUIRED

1. Explain the need for *interperiod* tax allocation.
2. Accountants who favor *interperiod* tax allocation argue that income taxes are an expense rather than a distribution of earnings. Explain the significance of this argument. *Do not explain the definitions of expense or distribution of earnings.*
3. Indicate and explain whether each of the following *independent* situations should be treated as a timing difference or a permanent difference:
   a. Estimated warranty costs (covering a 3-year warranty) are expensed for accounting purposes at the time of sale but deducted for income tax purposes when incurred.
   b. Depreciation for accounting and income tax purposes differs because of different bases of carrying the related property. The different bases are a result of a business combination treated as a purchase for accounting purposes and as a tax-free exchange for income tax purposes.
   c. A company properly uses the equity method to account for its 30 percent investment in another company. The investee pays dividends that are about 10 percent of its annual earnings.
4. Discuss the nature of the Deferred Income Tax accounts and possible classifications in a company's balance sheet.

C17–4 Explain the nature of the difference, if any, that is normally observed between the book treatment and the tax treatment of the following items:

1. Installment sales
2. Construction contracts
3. Goodwill amortization
4. Insurance premiums on life insurance policies
5. Warranty expense
6. Municipal bond interest
7. Depreciation expense
9. Pension expense
10. Fines

Be sure to indicate the effect, if any, on the deferred income tax account for each item listed.

C17–5 (CMA ADAPTED) The Internal Revenue Code (IRC) has a significant impact on accounting-reporting practices. The accounting methods selected for reducing taxable income are often used in the measurement of financial-reporting income. If different methods are used for book and tax purposes, the provision for the income tax liability and the income tax charge must be adjusted accordingly. Therefore, the income tax laws influence reported income whether the same or different methods are used for both book and tax purposes.

REQUIRED Present a discussion supporting the conclusions of the statement above. Include in your discussion an example of

1. An accounting method that became popular for financial-reporting purposes (although not required to be used by the IRC) following its inclusion in the IRC
2. An accounting method that must be used for financial-reporting purposes if it is selected for income tax purposes

EXERCISES

E17–1 At the beginning of 1984 Fox Corporation purchased $100,000 worth of equipment that qualified for a 5 percent investment tax credit. Net income per books before tax was $40,000. The equipment has an expected useful life of 5 years. Fox reported timing differences that, in total, reduced pretax income for tax return purposes by $10,000. The effective tax rate is 40 percent. The deferral method is used to record the investment tax credit.

REQUIRED

1. Record the necessary entry for 1984.
2. Explain the impact on your answer to requirement 1 if the flow-through method had been used instead of the deferral method.

E17–2 The Lecture Company started operations in 1985 and reported the following pretax income figures.

YEAR	NET INCOME BEFORE TAXES
1985	$50,000
1986	50,000

In 1987 the president of the company suffered a nervous breakdown, and, therefore, the firm reported a pretax loss of $150,000. The president was not expected to recover, and losses are expected in the foreseeable future. Assume a 45 percent tax rate for all 3 years.

REQUIRED

1. Illustrate how the loss would be reported in 1987.
2. What conditions would make you change your answer to requirement 1? How would your answer change?

E17–3 On January 10, 1983, Joe Cheung purchased a sports car for $28,000 cash. Joe planned to use the car for his consulting business. He is writing the car off over 4 years for tax purposes using the double-declining-balance method. The straight-line method is being used for book purposes. The asset is expected to have no scrap value. Joe's appropriate tax rate is 30 percent. Joe's pretax book income was $20,000 in each of the 4 years from 1983 to 1986.

REQUIRED Prepare the appropriate journal entries for 1983 to 1986 on Joe's books.

E17–4 Refer to the data in the preceding exercise. Assume that Joe Cheung's tax rate changes from 1983 to 1986 as follows:

YEAR	RATE
1983	30%
1984	35
1985	40
1986	45

REQUIRED Repeat the requirement for exercise 17–3 using the gross change method.

E17–5 Refer to the data in exercises 17–3 and 17–4 above.

REQUIRED

1. Repeat the requirement for exercise 17–3 using the net change method.
2. Is the answer to requirement 1 in this exercise the same as that of one of the previous two exercises? Explain.

E17–6 (CPA ADAPTED) Pang Corporation has engaged you to compute its corporate federal income tax due for its calendar-year 1984 income tax return. According to Pang's records, its corporate federal taxable income for the calendar-year 1984 was $1,000,000 before considering the following additional information:

1. Estimated tax payments of $250,000 for the calendar-year 1984 were made in 1984.
2. An investment credit of $100,000 is allowable for the calendar-year 1984 for qualified property bought and placed into service in 1984.
3. Pang had a net operating loss of $300,000 for the calendar-year 1983. Of the 1983 net operating loss, $240,000 was used to offset profits of prior years, and the appropriate refunds were received in 1984.

REQUIRED Assuming a federal income tax rate of 40 percent, prepare a schedule computing Pang's 1984 corporate federal income tax due. Any possible alternative treatments should be resolved in a manner that will minimize taxable income. Show supporting computations in good form.

E17–7 The following data are available regarding the Kirkpatrick Corporation. Kirkpatrick uses accelerated depreciation for tax purposes and straight-line depreciation for accounting purposes. It recognizes gross margin on installment sales in the year of sale for accounting purposes, and on the basis of cash received for income tax purposes.

Depreciation in 1983 for tax purposes in excess of accounting depreciation	$140,000
Estimated life of all depreciable property acquired in early 1981 (year in which Kirkpatrick began operations)	8 years
Gross margin on installment sales in 1983 not collected by year-end	$240,000
Gross margin on installment sales of prior years collected in 1983	$200,000
Pretax accounting income in 1983	$400,000
Tax rate in 1983	48%
Weighted average tax rate for all prior years	42%

Assume no investment tax credit.

REQUIRED

1. Compute taxable income and income taxes payable for 1983.
2. Summarize the changes in deferred income taxes for 1983 using the weighted-average gross change method.
3. Record the tax entry for 1983.

E17-8 Assume all data provided in the preceding exercise.

REQUIRED

1. Record the tax entry for 1983 using the net change method.
2. Explain the potential problem with the net change method when tax rates change.

E17-9 The Salatka Metal Company reported the following information for 1983:

Taxable income	$120,000
Pretax accounting income	$260,000
Tax rate	45%
Interest on tax-exempt municipal bonds (included in the $260,000 above)	$ 20,000
Depreciation expense:	
Deducted in arriving at the $120,000 taxable income	$ 90,000
Deducted in arriving at the $260,000 pretax accounting income	$ 60,000
Equipment purchased during the year (qualifies for a 10 percent investment credit)	$ 40,000

The company uses the flow-through method for the investment tax credit.

REQUIRED Record the necessary journal entries to account for tax expense, taxes payable, and deferred income taxes for 1983.

E17-10

_____ 1. You are about to select a depreciation method for use in computing *taxable* income. You believe that the new company you work for will be in a 22 percent tax bracket for the first five years and a 48 percent tax bracket thereafter. The average useful life of the equipment is 10 years, with an original (current) cost of $200,000 and an estimated salvage value of $25,000. An appropriate interest rate for your company is 8 percent. Which of the following depreciation methods do you feel will result in the lowest absolute dollars of tax payments over the entire 10-year period? (Ignore the time value effects on the dollars of taxes paid.)
   a. Straight-line method
   b. Sum-of-the-years'-digits method
   c. Decelerated (present-value) method
   d. Double-declining-balance method
   e. None of the above

_____ 2. Assume all of the data in the preceding question. Assume also that you select a straight-line depreciation for book (financial-reporting) purposes and an accelerated method for tax-reporting purposes. Also assume that the company's tax rate does change from 22 percent to 48 percent after 5 years. Which of the following statements is true?
   a. The Deferred Income Tax (DIT) account will have an increasing credit balance over the first 5 years based on a 48 percent tax rate.
   b. The DIT account will have a credit balance over the first 5 years based on a 22 percent tax rate.
   c. The DIT account will require an adjustment after 5 years to correct for the change in the tax rate.
   d. The DIT account will be increased *and* decreased based on the 22 percent tax rate over the entire 10-year life of the equipment.
   e. None of the above.

3. Because of timing differences, Change-Up Company reported the following for 1982–1984:

	1982	1983	1984
Taxable income per tax return	$40,000	$60,000	$20,000
Net book income before taxes	70,000	70,000	70,000

Assume that the tax rate is 40 percent and that correct interperiod tax-allocation procedures are employed. At the end of 1984, the (1) tax expense; (2) taxes payable; and (3) *balance* in the Deferred Income Tax account should be

a. (1) $28,000; (2) $8,000; and (3) $27,000 credit
b. (1) $8,000; (2) $28,000; and (3) $36,000 debit
c. (1) $28,000; (2) $8,000; and (3) $36,000 credit
d. (1) $28,000; (2) $8,000; and (3) $20,000 credit
e. None of the above

4. The effective tax rate reported in the income statement will differ from the statutory tax rate as a result of which of the following?

a. Actual income taxes *paid* during the period exceed the liability for income taxes computed on pretax accounting income.
b. The income tax liability computed on pretax accounting income exceeds the actual income taxes *paid* during the period.
c. An expense deducted for financial reporting is not deductible for income tax purposes in any period.
d. A cost expensed this period for income tax purposes is not considered for financial reporting until a later period.
e. None of the above.

5. A corporation reports income of $225,000 before federal income taxes in its income statement, but because of timing differences, taxable income reported in the income tax return is $125,000. If the normal tax rate is 20 percent on the first $25,000, and the surtax applicable for taxable income in excess of $25,000 is 30 percent, what net income after federal taxes would the corporation report in its income statement?

a. $190,000
b. $170,000
c. $160,000
d. $120,000
e. Some other amount

E17–11 The Dietrick Corporation experienced the following sequence of incomes and losses for the first 6 years of operations:

YEAR	PRETAX INCOME (LOSS)
1978	$(20,000)
1979	30,000
1980	60,000
1981	75,000
1982	(195,000)
1983	55,000

In 1981 the tax rate increased from 35 to 40 percent. Realization of the tax benefits is uncertain.

REQUIRED

1. Record the necessary entries for 1982 and 1983 related to income taxes.
2. Illustrate the partial comparative income statements for 1981, 1982, and 1983 as they would appear in the 1983 annual report.

E17-12 McIntyre Ltd. experienced the following pretax operating results for 1981–1985:

YEAR	PRETAX INCOME (LOSS)	TAX RATE
1981	$ 25,000	40%
1982	38,000	40
1983	45,000	40
1984	50,000	45
1985	(180,000)	

At the end of 1985, McIntyre's planners are uncertain as to why profits were off in 1985 or when the market for McIntyre's products will rebound. The anticipated tax rate in 1986 and future years is 50 percent.

REQUIRED

1. Record any necessary entries for 1985 on McIntyre's books to account for the NOL.
2. Assume that McIntyre's profits rebounded in 1986 to $70,000 before taxes, and that the tax rate was 50 percent. Record any entries required to account for taxes in 1986.
3. Illustrate partial comparative income statements for McIntyre for 1984, 1985, and 1986 as they would appear in the 1986 annual report.

E17-13 On December 29, 1984, Company X purchased $100,000 worth of long-term assets that qualified for a 6 percent investment tax credit. The assets have a useful life of 6 years and a $5,000 scrap value. Straight-line depreciation will be used on the assets. The company reported profits of $500,000 before taxes in 1984. The tax rate is 50 percent. Although the tax credit is allowed in 1984, *no depreciation will be taken until 1985.*

_____ 1. If the company elects to report the full "benefit" of the tax credit in 1984, the effect on income will be to
a. Increase income over the next 6 years
b. Have no impact on 1984 income and increase income for the next 6 years
c. Increase income in 1984 and decrease depreciation expense for the next 6 years
d. None of the above

_____ 2. If the company elects to report the "benefit" of the tax credit over the life of the asset, the effect on income will be to
a. Decrease 1984 income and increase income over the next 6 years
b. Have no impact on 1984 income and increase income for the next 6 years
c. Increase income in 1984 and decrease depreciation expense for the next 6 years
d. None of the above

_____ 3. The *income tax payable* for 1984 will be
a. Higher if the flow-through method is elected
b. Higher if the deferral method is elected
c. The same for both methods
d. None of the above

_____ 4. The *income tax expense* for 1984 will be
a. Higher if the flow-through method is elected
b. Higher if the deferral method is elected
c. The same for both methods
d. None of the above

5. The *net book value* of the assets at the end of 1985 (after adjustment) will be
   a. $75,000 if the deferral method is elected
   b. $80,000 if the deferral method is elected
   c. $83,333 if the flow-through method is elected
   d. $75,000 if the flow-through method is elected
   e. Both b and c
   f. None of the above

PROBLEMS

P17-1   The following information concerns the activities of the Ballew Company for the years 1983 through 1988. The company has only one type of timing difference, only originating or reversing differences occur in any given year, and reversals always occur in the order in which they originated.

YEAR	PRETAX ACCOUNTING INCOME	TAXABLE INCOME	TAX RATE
1983	$60,000	$40,000	45%
1984	50,000	35,000	45
1985	55,000	67,000	48
1986	63,000	76,000	50
1987	45,000	38,000	35
1988	48,000	61,000	48

REQUIRED

1. Prepare the necessary journal entries to record the income tax consequences of the above data.
2. What is the method implied by the problem for dealing with changes in the DIT account?

P17-2   The following data are available regarding the activities of the Barry Lewis Corporation. During the period of time involved, Lewis did not have any timing differences.

YEAR	TAX RATE	PRETAX NET OPERATING INCOME (LOSS)
1979	20%	$10,000
1980	25	20,000
1981	20	15,000
1982	35	35,000
1983	—	(200,000)
1984	40	40,000
1985	50	60,000
1986	20	15,000

REQUIRED

1. If Lewis elects the carryback-carryforward option, record the journal entries during the period 1983 through 1986 to reflect the consequences of the 1983 pretax net operating loss. Assume that no entries have been made to reflect income tax expense for the years 1983–1986. Also assume that the tax benefits of any carry-forward loss are assured beyond a reasonable doubt and that the expected future tax rate was 25 percent in 1983.
2. Assuming everything as in requirement 1 *except* that the tax benefits of any carryforward loss are *not* assured beyond a reasonable doubt, record the journal entries for 1983 through 1986.

P17-3   The Jamis Corporation has pretax financial income of $300,000 and an income tax rate of 48 percent. The following additional information has been determined.

1. Jamis recorded $60,000 straight-line depreciation expense for financial-accounting purposes but deducted $80,000 accelerated depreciation on its tax return.

2. Jamis recorded $20,000 as product warranty expense on its books, whereas $35,000 may be deducted on its tax return. The $15,000 difference had been deducted in prior years in determining accounting income. The Estimated Product Warranty Liability account is properly classified as a current liability on the balance sheet.

3. Jamis uses the percentage-of-completion method on its books for construction contracts and the completed contract method on its tax return. On its books, Jamis recorded $75,000 of gross profit on construction contracts while reporting $45,000 on its tax return. The difference will be taxed next year when the last contract is expected to be completed.

4. Jamis received $50,000 from a life insurance company when its president died of a heart attack. The $50,000 nontaxable gain was recorded as part of the ordinary income.

5. Jamis received $100,000 rent in advance at the beginning of the year. This represents 5 years' rent of $20,000 per year. All of the $100,000 is taxable in the current year.

REQUIRED

1. Compute taxable income for the current period.
2. Prepare the journal entry or entries to record tax expense, income tax payable, and deferred tax amounts. Make a separate debit or credit for deferred taxes for each timing difference above.
3. Indicate how the deferred tax items should be reflected in a balance sheet.

P17-4 On January 1, 1984, R. Bartlett Corporation purchased all of its machinery at a cost of $300,000. The machinery was made in Japan. Income before income tax expense was $1,000,000 for the year 1984. Included in that figure were the following:

1. Expenses for goodwill amortization, $5,000
2. Depletion expense on natural resources, $10,000
3. A full year's depreciation expense on the machinery on the straight-line basis, assuming a $20,000 scrap value and a 7-year life
4. Interest revenue on New York City municipal bonds, $15,000
5. Cost of goods sold based on the weighted-average cost, $1,800,000
6. Gain on retirement of callable bonds, $10,000

A number of differences exist between the book income figure before tax (given above) and taxable income. Bartlett used sum-of-the years'-digits depreciation for tax purposes. In addition, FIFO inventory valuation is used for tax purposes, and cost of sales using FIFO was $20,000 more than reported on the books. Bartlett is taking a $30,000 deduction from taxable income for depletion expense in 1984, which is allowed for tax purposes. Also, Bartlett has operating loss carryforwards of $50,000 (the net loss before taxes) from the preceding year. The tax rate is 40 percent except for the gain on the callable bonds, which is taxed at 30 percent. Assume these tax rates have never changed, and that the tax loss carryforward was recorded as a $20,000 asset.

REQUIRED

1. Compute the income tax expense and the income tax payable for 1984. Clearly label all adjustments or computations.
2. Record the tax expense, the tax payable, and other related tax data in journal entry form. Use the proper intraperiod and interperiod tax allocation in recording the entry.
3. Illustrate Bartlett's partial income statement for 1984.

P17-5 For the year 1985 the Apple Company had book net income before taxes of $100,000. *Included* in arriving at this net income figure were the following items:

1. A $15,000 "profit" for work on a construction project *to be* completed early in 1986. The total "profit" estimated for this project is $75,000. (Apple Company uses the percentage-of-completion method of profit recognition for book purposes, and the completed contract method for tax purposes.)
2. A $1,000 loss on the final work for a 4-year construction project completed this year. "Profit" on this project for the first 3 years was as follows: 1982, $20,000; 1983, $20,000; 1984, $36,000.

3. Municipal bond interest income, $5,000.
4. Depreciation expense, $20,000.

The 1985 *depreciation expense* for tax purposes was $2,000 *less* than for book purposes. Due to the acquisition of new assets, Apple qualified for a $2,000 investment tax credit in 1985. The income tax rate has been 40 percent for the past 6 years including 1985. The flow-through method is used for the tax credit.

REQUIRED

1. Compute the *tax expense* and the *tax liability* for Apple for 1985. Show your computation.
2. Record the journal entry for Apple's 1985 income taxes.
3. Illustrate Apple's partial 1985 income statement.

P17–6 M. Gibbins, Inc., purchased heating equipment for its offices in Alberta, Canada, on January 1, 1983. The equipment cost Gibbins $1,800,000 and was being depreciated over a 4-year life for tax purposes using the sum-of-the-years'-digits method. Gibbins was writing the asset off over a 6-year life for book purposes using straight-line depreciation. The equipment was assumed to have no scrap value in either case. The tax rates have changed over the years as follows:

YEAR	RATE
1983	35%
1984	40
1985	40
1986	45
1987	45
1988	40

REQUIRED Record the entries to account for the equipment on Gibbins's books for the period 1983 to 1988 using the gross change method on a FIFO rate basis. Assume that income tax payable is $150,000 each year from 1983 to 1988.

P17–7 On January 1, 1979, the Murdock Corporation purchased a GMC semitractor trailer for $68,000. The truck had an estimated life of 10 years and no scrap value. Murdock uses straight-line depreciation for book purposes and sum-of-the-years'-digits depreciation for tax purposes. On January 1, 1984, Murdock traded the 1979 model truck in on a new one that had a manufacturer's suggested list price of $95,000. Murdock traded the old truck in on the new one, giving the dealer $60,000 in cash plus the old truck. A number of competitors had been willing to pay Murdock between $25,000 and $27,000 for the old truck that was traded in. The new truck is to be expensed over a 10-year life on a straight-line basis for book purposes but is being written off over 5 years using the sum-of-the-years'-digits method for tax purposes. Murdock has always had a 40 percent tax rate. The tax value of the new asset qualifies for a 10 percent investment credit, which is accounted for by Murdock using the deferred method over a 10-year period.

REQUIRED

1. Record the trade-in for both book and tax purposes on January 1, 1984, in accordance with GAAP and IRS, respectively. (*Hint:* Refer to Chapter 11, pp. 397–399.)
2. Record the tax effect of the loss for book purposes.
3. Measure the depreciation expense on the new asset for book and tax purposes for the period 1984 to 1989. Is this a timing difference or a permanent difference?
4. Reconcile the Deferred Income Tax account as it relates to both assets from 1979 to 1993.
5. Record the investment credit related to the purchase of the new asset.

P17–8 The New Depths Oil Company (New DOC) discovered an estimated 8,000,000 barrels of oil on leased property in the Hartwick Pines State Forest region of Michigan in 1983. The following data are available regarding New DOC's activities for the exploration of this site:

YEAR	BARRELS EXTRACTED AND PROCESSED	WHOLESALE SALES OF PROCESSED OIL	BOOK NET INCOME BEFORE DEPLETION AND TAXES
1983	1,800,000	$ 82,000,000	$30,000,000
1984	2,400,000	100,800,000	46,000,000

The total capitalized exploration costs for the discovery amounted to $48,000,000. The depletion for 1983 for book purposes was based on the original estimate of 8,000,000 total barrels of oil. However, by the end of 1984, the estimated remaining barrels are equal to the number of barrels already extracted and processed. The depletion rate for tax purposes is equal to 15 percent of the sales for any given year. Assume a 40 percent tax rate.

REQUIRED

1. Record the necessary depletion entries and their tax effects for 1983 and 1984 on New DOC's books.
2. Explain how the difference between depletion expense for book and tax purposes is accounted for using this example.
3. Prepare partial comparative income statements as they would appear in New DOC's 1984 annual report. Also prepare any necessary footnote disclosures.

P17–9 The records of the Arnett Corporation for the first 3 years of operations can be summarized as follows ($000 omitted):

	PER BOOKS			PER TAX RECORDS		
	1984	1983	1982	1984	1983	1982
Revenues	$18,160	$15,230	$ 9,468	$16,086	$12,396	$ 5,683
Cost of goods sold	(7,290)	(5,800)	(3,800)	(8,460)	(6,300)	(4,100)
Depreciation	(1,000)	(1,000)	(1,000)	(1,200)	(1,600)	(2,000)
Other	(620)	(470)	(340)	(620)	(470)	(340)
Pretax income	$ 9,250	$ 7,960	$ 4,328	$ 5,806	$ 4,026	$ (757)

During 1985 Arnett reported the following pretax book income data ($000 omitted):

	1985
Revenues	$19,360
Cost of goods sold	(8,465)
Depreciation	(1,000)
Other	(710)
Pretax book income	$ 9,185

The following differences were reported for the 1985 tax return:

1. Revenue for tax purposes was $680,000 greater than for book purposes.
2. Cost of goods sold was $9,000,000 for tax purposes.
3. Depreciation expense was $200,000 less for tax purposes than for book purposes.
4. The tax rate for 1985 is 48 percent. The tax rates for 1982–1984 were 40 percent in 1982, 46 percent in 1983, and 44 percent in 1984.

All the differences between book and tax noted above are attributable to timing differences. Each of the revenue and expense classifications identified above is considered to represent a group of similar items for accounting purposes.

1. Compute the tax liability for 1985 and record the necessary entries assuming that Arnett uses the gross change method (FIFO basis) of computation.
2. Compute the tax liability for 1985 and record the necessary entries assuming that Arnett uses the gross change method (weighted average basis).
3. What is the balance to be reported at December 31, 1985, in the Deferred Income Tax account for requirements 1 and 2?

P17–10 (CMA ADAPTED)   PSK Electronics, Inc., has a November 30 fiscal year. The corporate controller is responsible for preparing the financial statements that will be audited by PSK's independent public accountant.

PSK's pretax consolidated income for the year ended November 30, 1984, includes $80,000 from its own operations and $20,000 from its wholly owned domestic manufacturing company for a total of $100,000. The consolidated corporate income tax return for the 1983–1984 fiscal year, which has not been filed yet, reveals the following facts:

1. PSK has used the LIFO inventory method for tax purposes since the 1982–1983 fiscal year.
2. PSK uses accelerated depreciation for tax-reporting purposes and straight-line depreciation for financial-reporting purposes. Consequently, depreciation on PSK's tax return is $10,000 greater than the depreciation on its income statement.
3. PSK has a $5,000 investment credit for the current tax year; it uses the flow-through method for investment credit.
4. PSK pays the premiums on key corporate officers' life insurance policies and is the beneficiary of these policies. Premiums paid on these policies amounted to $3,000 in the current fiscal year, of which $2,000 was expensed and $1,000 represented an increase in the cash-surrender value of the policies.

The LIFO election for tax purposes has resulted in substantial tax savings, but it has also had a depressing effect on earnings per share (EPS). The president of PSK would like to use the FIFO inventory method for the 1983–1984 financial statements or at least disclose in the notes to the financial statements what the EPS would have been had the FIFO method been used. The use of FIFO would have increased PSK's book inventory by $20,000 as of November 30, 1984.

For ease in calculation, assume that PSK is subject to a federal income tax rate of 40 percent and that the provision and current liability for state income taxes is $4,000.

REQUIRED

1. For each of the four items described for PSK Electronics, explain whether the treatment used for income tax purposes can differ from the treatment used in preparing the financial statements that are to be audited.
2. Calculate the income tax provision that will be reflected on PSK's income statement prepared for the year ended November 30, 1984.
3. From the data in the problem, calculate the change in PSK's Deferred Income Tax account (or accounts) from December 1, 1983, to November 30, 1984.

P17–11 (CPA ADAPTED)   The Mikis Company has supplied you with the following information regarding its 1983 income tax expense for financial statement reporting:

1. The provision for current income taxes (exclusive of investment tax credits) was $600,000 for the year ended December 31, 1983. Mikis made estimated tax payments of $550,000 during 1983.
2. Investment tax credits of $100,000 arising from fixed assets put into service in 1983 were taken for income tax reporting in 1983. Mikis defers investment tax credits and amortizes them to income over the productive life of the related assets for financial statement reporting. Unamortized deferred investment tax credits amounted to $400,000 at December 31, 1983, and $375,000 at December 31, 1982.
3. Mikis generally depreciates fixed assets using the straight-line method for financial statement reporting and various accelerated methods for income tax reporting. During 1983, depreciation on fixed assets amounted to $900,000 for financial statement reporting and $950,000 for income tax reporting. Commitments for fixed

assets amounted to $450,000 at December 31, 1983. Such fixed assets will be subject to an investment tax credit of 10 percent.

4. For financial statement reporting, Mikis has accrued estimated losses from product warranty contracts, prior to their occurrence. For income tax reporting, no deduction is taken until payments are made. At December 31, 1982, accrued estimated losses of $200,000 were included in the liability section of Mikis's balance sheet. Based on the latest available information, Mikis estimates that this figure should be 30 percent higher at December 31, 1983. Payments of $250,000 were made in 1983.

5. In 1978 Mikis acquired another company for cash. Goodwill resulting from this transaction was $800,000 and is being amortized over a 40-year period for financial statement reporting. The amortization is not deductible for income tax reporting.

6. Mikis has a wholly owned foreign subsidiary. In 1983 this subsidiary had income of $175,000 before U.S. and foreign income taxes and a provision for taxes in its own country of $70,000. No earnings were remitted to Mikis in 1983. For U.S. income tax reporting, Mikis will receive a tax credit for $70,000 when these earnings are remitted. Mikis records taxes on the unremitted earnings of this subsidiary for financial statement reporting.

7. Premiums paid on officers' life insurance policies amounted to $80,000 in 1983. These premiums are not deductible for income tax reporting.

8. Assume that the U.S. income tax rate was 48 percent.

REQUIRED

1. What amounts should be shown for (1) provision for current income taxes, (2) provision for deferred income taxes, and (3) investment tax credits recognized in Mikis's income statement for the year ended December 31, 1983? Show supporting computations in good form.

2. Identify any information in the fact situation that was not used to determine the answer to requirement 1, and explain why this information was not used.

P17–12 (CPA ADAPTED) The Point Corporation has engaged you to compute its federal taxable income for the year ended December 31, 1984. According to Point's accounting records, the corporation's income before income taxes was $600,000. Additional information, none of which is included in the $600,000 of income before income taxes, is as follows:

1. On January 20, 1984, Point sold for $30,000 common stock of Cullen Company that was purchased for $32,000 on April 1, 1982.

2. On February 21, 1984, Point sold for $40,000 common stock of Mary Company that was purchased for $36,000 on December 3, 1982.

3. On March 15, 1984, Point sold for $53,000 preferred stock of Mealy Company that was purchased for $52,000 on December 14, 1983.

4. On May 29, 1984, Point sold for $60,500 common stock of Bin Company that was purchased for $61,000 on April 17, 1984.

5. On June 3, 1984, Point purchased for $70,000 common stock of Dorn Company. On December 31, 1984, Point still owned this common stock, but the market value of the stock had increased to $73,000.

6. During 1984 Point received dividends of $15,000 from domestic corporations and dividends of $14,000 from current earnings of a wholly owned domestic subsidiary, with which Point does not file a consolidated return.

7. During 1984 Point received interest income of $7,000 from corporate bonds and interest income of $6,500 from municipal obligations.

8. Point rents a small portion of the space in its plant. During 1984 Point received $18,000 in rental income from this space. Depreciation and other occupancy costs of this space are included in the income before income taxes of $600,000 above.

9. During 1984 Point received $23,000 in royalties from a patent on an invention.

10. On December 20, 1984, Point paid a 10 percent bonus to all of its officers because Point had record sales and earnings in 1984. The bonus amounted to a total of $20,000.

11. On December 31, 1984, Point contributed $90,000 to a qualified profit-sharing trust. The contribution represented 5 percent of each employee's salary.

12. In 1984 Point had a fire in a shed outside its plant. At the time of the fire, the shed had an adjusted basis of $16,000. The value of the shed before the fire was $18,000, but the shed was worth only $11,000 after the fire. Point's insurance policy covered $6,000 of the fire loss.

13. During 1984 Point paid finance charges of $650 on gasoline credit cards used by Point's employees for business purposes.

14. During 1984 Point contributed $11,000 to various recognized charitable organizations and $2,200 to the local tax-exempt private college.

REQUIRED   Prepare a schedule, beginning with income before income taxes of $600,000, computing Point's federal taxable income for the 1984 calendar year. Any possible alternative treatments should be resolved in a manner that will minimize taxable income. Show supporting computations in good form.

P17–13   During 1986 the Smart Corporation reported net income *before taxes* of $280,000. At year-end you sit down with the Smart managers to help them figure out the corporation's taxable income and to record the necessary information for both tax and book purposes. During your review, you discover the following information. (Assume a 40 percent tax rate.)

1. Included in the $280,000 was an $80,000 *net* profit from a construction project that is expected to be completed in 1987. The expected total *net* profit on this project is $275,000. The completed contract method is used for tax purposes.

2. Included in the $280,000 was a $75,000 deduction for pension expense. A total of $60,000 was paid to the pension fund in 1981.

3. Included in the $280,000 was a $15,000 deduction for amortization of goodwill in the investment in Winters Corporation, a 60 percent owned subsidiary.

4. Included in the $280,000 was $10,000 of interest on New York City bonds. Only $8,000 of the interest had been received; the other $2,000 was accrued at year-end.

5. Included in the $280,000 was a gain from a trade-in on a major piece of construction equipment. The following entry was used to record the trade-in:

Earth-moving equipment—new	700,000	
Accumulated depreciation, equipment—old	550,000	
Cash		600,000
Earth-moving equipment—old		600,000
Gain on equipment trade-in		50,000

6. An investment *tax credit* of $30,000 was allowed on the equipment purchased in item 5 above. The flow-through method is used to account for the credit.

7. Included in the $280,000 was a *net* loss of $25,000 on a project completed this year. The estimated total profit on the project at the end of last year had been $240,000. The actual total profit on the project was $200,000. (See item 1 above.)

8. An extraordinary loss of $50,000 was included in the $280,000 net figure.

9. A change in depreciation methods resulted in a gain of $30,000 for the cumulative prior years' effect.

10. An error in the consignment inventories resulted in a $40,000 overstatement of 1985 ending inventory.

11. Included in the $280,000 was a charge of $35,000 for depletion expense related to excavation of a limestone quarry. For tax purposes, a total of $50,000 depletion expense is permitted in 1986.

12. Inventories for book purposes were accounted for on a FIFO basis. For tax purposes, a weighted-average method is used. At December 31, 1986, ending inventory values were as follows: FIFO, $380,000; weighted average, $430,000. The 1986 beginning inventory values were the same for book and tax.

REQUIRED

1. Use the following worksheet format to evaluate items 1 through 12. For example, assume that a $10,000 expense included in the $280,000 is not allowed for tax purposes until 1987.

WORKSHEET			
ITEM	TYPE OF DIFFERENCE BETWEEN BOOK AND TAX (IF ANY)	ADJUSTMENT TO BOOK INCOME OF $280,000 NEEDED TO COMPUTE TAXABLE INCOME	TAX IMPACT OF DIFFERENCE (− = DECREASES; + = INCREASES)
Item from lot	Timing difference (TD)	+$10,000	+$4,000

2. **a.** What is the *total* tax expense reported in 1986? (Show computations.)
   b. What is the *total* tax payable reported in 1986? (Show computations.)
   c. For financial-reporting purposes, using proper intraperiod tax allocation, show how the data in the problem would be reported in the comparative 1985–1986 income and retained earnings statements. (You may use the following assumed data to help you illustrate this requirement.)

1986 DATA

Revenues	$2,000,000
Dividends—cash	15,000
Dividends—stock	25,000

1985 DATA (AS REPORTED 12/31/85)

Income Statement

Sales	$3,000,000
Less all expenses and costs	(2,000,000)
Taxes	(400,000)
Net income	$ 600,000

Retained Earnings Statement

Retained earnings, 12/01/04	$6,200,000
1985 net income	600,000
Dividends	(300,000)
Retained earnings, 12/31/85	$6,500,000

P17–14 Orion Enterprises has computed its preliminary consolidated income before taxes for 1984 at $12,876,000 but, unless otherwise indicated, has not yet included the following items. Assume that Orion's tax rate is 40 percent.

1. On December 30, 1984, Orion traded some earth-moving equipment that had cost $880,000 for a company jet valued at $750,000. The equipment had a useful life of 20 years when it was purchased 6 years ago and was being depreciated on a straight-line basis for book purposes and tax purposes. A cash payment of $160,000 was also made to complete the purchase price of the jet, which is expected to last 20 years. The trade has not been recorded.

2. Warranty costs incurred in 1984 amounted to $184,000. Warranty expense recorded in 1984 amounted to $350,000, resulting in an ending balance of $525,000 in the estimated liability account.

3. On June 30, 1984, Orion acquired a 100 percent interest in Pegasus. Pegasus had net assets that had a market value of $440,000. Orion paid $660,000 cash for Pegasus and planned to amortize goodwill over the next 10 years. Orion has not yet accounted for the goodwill but has included all other aspects of the investment in Pegasus in the preliminary income figure.

4. On June 30, 1984, Orion purchased plant assets that cost $30,000,000 and had a useful life of 15 years, with no scrap value. The assets were to be depreciated on a double-declining-balance basis for tax purposes over 10 years, and on a straight-line basis for book purposes. They qualify for a 10 percent investment tax credit to be accounted for on a flow-through basis. A full year's depreciation is taken in 1984 for tax purposes and a half year is taken for book purposes. Orion has not yet recorded these data.

5. Orion is entitled to deduct depletion expense of $1,876,000 for tax purposes but may record only $1,000,000 depletion in 1984 for book purposes. Depletion has not yet been recorded.

6. On September 10, 1984, Orion collected $1,800,000 on a life insurance policy that had a cash-surrender value of $96,000 at the time the policy was exercised. This gain, which has not yet been recorded, is considered to be extraordinary.

7. Included in Orion's long-term investments are municipal bonds, which had been in default of interest payments for the past 2 years but paid $2\frac{1}{2}$ years' interest on July 1, 1984, equal to $125,000. Interest income was *not* recognized in 1982 and 1983. No entry has been recorded for 1984.

8. A wholly owned company of Orion's uses the installment sales method of accounting for tax purposes, and the point-of-sale method of accounting for book purposes. For book purposes, sales reported during 1984 were $2,860,000. For tax purposes, sales reported during 1984 were $3,600,000. The book sales and expenses have already been recorded in the preliminary book income number.

9. On December 31, 1984, Orion prepares the following summary for its ten subsidiaries accounted for on an equity basis:

ORION'S SHARE OF 1984 REPORTED NET INCOME	DIVIDENDS DECLARED AND PAID IN 1984	GOODWILL TO BE AMORTIZED IN 1984	PORTION OF 1984 SUBSIDIARY NET INCOME TO BE PERMANENTLY RETAINED BY SUBSIDIARY
$873,240	$247,000	$83,000	$383,000

None of these items has yet been recorded. There is no excess depreciation.

REQUIRED

1. Prepare any necessary entries to record items (1) through (9) that have not yet been recorded and included in the preliminary income figure.

2. Prepare a schedule to help compute Orion's tax expense and tax payable for 1984.

P17–15 The H. Q. Langenderfer Corporation experienced the following pretax results for 1981–1984 for both book and tax purposes:

YEAR	PRETAX INCOME	TAX RATE
1981	$40,000	40%
1982	15,000	35
1983	87,000	30
1984	31,000	38

During 1985, because of a large uninsured loss on plant assets, Langenderfer incurred a pretax operating loss of $180,000. Langenderfer has recently taken out insurance to cover the plant assets and definitely expects to report profits on future operations. However, because of an anticipated change in the tax laws, Langenderfer is not certain whether to account for the loss through the carryback-carryforward option or the carryforward option only. The following forecasts have been prepared by Langenderfer's financial-planning staff:

YEAR	EXPECTED PRETAX INCOME	EXPECTED TAX RATE
1986	$ 42,000	46%
1987	27,000	48
1988	65,000	50
1989	31,000	50
1990	108,000	50

Langenderfer has an opportunity to invest all discretionary funds in a corporate joint venture with J. Reynolds, Inc. All funds invested in the joint venture at the end of each year (December 31) are expected to return 12 percent per year on the invested amount over the next several years.

REQUIRED

1. If you were advising Langenderfer, how would you suggest that the net operating loss benefits be treated?
2. Record any entries necessary for 1985 to account for the tax aspect of the net operating loss, assuming Langenderfer elects to carry the entire NOL forward.
3. Assume that the actual pretax income measures and the actual tax rate for 1986 were $30,000 and 40 percent, respectively. Prepare the necessary entries for 1986.
4. Assume that the actual pretax income measure in 1987 is $155,000 and that the tax rate is 45 percent. Record the necessary entries for 1987.
5. Ignore your answers to requirements 1–4. Assume instead, that Langenderfer elects the carryback-carryforward option for the 1985 NOL. Also assume that the expected future tax rate is 45 percent. Record the necessary entries for 1985.
6. Refer to the assumptions in requirement 5. Further assume that the 1986 pretax operating profit is $85,000 and the tax rate is 50 percent. Record any necessary entries for 1986.

18

Noncurrent Liabilities– Long-Term Notes and Bonds

OVERVIEW

The conceptual underpinnings developed in the "Overview" to Part III, in Chapter 15 on lease accounting, and in Chapter 16 on current liabilities hold with full force in the present chapter. Noncurrent, or long-term, liabilities are conceptually very similar to current liabilities except for the time element. Because long-term liabilities are normally governed by formal contracts between debtor and creditor, the specific terms of such contracts are crucial in making accounting decisions. For instance, we saw in our discussion of long-term leases that although capital leases follow a rather standard pattern of repayment, the contractual terms are varied, necessitating many accounting judgments. The need for accounting judgments based on specific contractual terms is also a feature of the accounting for bond and note contracts discussed in this chapter. The accountant strives to determine the economic substance of the contractual terms. The terms themselves are important in the sense that they govern the amount and timing of cash (or other value) flows.

In judging the various contractual terms found in noncurrent debt arrangements, the accountant is guided by the general rules that apply to all receivables and payables:

1. The net book value of the receivable or payable appearing on a balance sheet must be equal to the present value of the anticipated future cash flow.
2. The interest income or expense appearing on the income statement must be based on the effective interest rate applied to the net book value of the receivable or payable during the accounting period.

Promulgated GAAP require that virtually *all* noncurrent liabilities be valued according to the above rules even in cases where interest rates are not specifically stated in the debt instrument.[1]

Long-term liability accounting is greatly affected by the principles of revenue recognition and matching. One motivation for measuring liabilities in terms of present values by means of effective interest rates is to achieve an appropriate matching of the costs and benefits of debt. The income statement effects and the balance sheet effects of debt are tightly interrelated.

The disclosure of long-term debt in financial statement footnotes is complex and usually comprehensive. Exhibit 18–1 shows the "long-term debt" footnote that appeared in a company's annual report, and the balance sheet items to which the note refers. Most footnotes on long-term debt include descriptions of the type of debt instrument, maturity dates, interest rates, redemption terms, conversion terms, contractual restrictions (covenants) on the debtor, and more. We shall discuss these and other important issues related to notes and bonds. The detail shown in Exhibit 18–1 is not unusual because current GAAP require the disclosure of principal amounts and effective interest rates for each major debt instrument.[2] In Exhibit 18–1 the interest-bearing notes and bonds have face value amounts equal to their present values. Later in the chapter we shall discuss the required disclosure for the premiums and discounts that result when face values of debt instruments do not equal present values.

LONG-TERM NOTES

Contractual Terms of Notes

Rather than issuing securities to the general public as with stocks and bonds, companies often borrow from such financial institutions as insurance companies and banks. In this case, the debt instrument is usually called a **note,** which is a formal agreement to pay specified cash flows to a creditor. Although the general accounting rules listed above govern the computing of the net liabilities and the interest charges, the particulars of recording and disclosing notes must be in conformance with their **contractual terms.** Notes can include virtually any contractual terms that the creditor and debtor agree to, and, therefore, complete standardization of accounting disclosure across all forms of notes cannot be achieved.

To demonstrate the many possible contractual patterns, assume that Notemaker Corporation borrows $75,000 from a bank on January 1, 1983, under three different schemes of repayment:

Repayment Scheme I: Pay 10 percent annual interest on the principal on December 31 in 1983, 1984, and 1985 and pay the principal on December 31, 1985.

[1] *Accounting Principles Board Opinion No. 21,* "Interest on Receivables and Payables" (New York: AICPA, August 1971).

[2] Ibid.

EXHIBIT
18–1

DISCLOSURE OF LONG-TERM DEBT

MASCO CORPORATION
Excerpt from Balance Sheet

	1980	1979
Liabilities		
Notes payable	$ 28,629,000	$ 13,647,000
Accounts payable	30,656,000	30,386,000
Income taxes	20,320,000	13,767,000
Accrued and other liabilities	38,245,000	34,085,000
Total current liabilities	$117,850,000	$ 91,885,000
Other Liabilities		
Long-term debt, excluding current portion	$328,401,000	$315,826,000
Deferred income taxes, noncurrent	10,545,000	7,803,000
Total liabilities	$456,796,000	$415,514,000

Excerpt from Note

Long-term Debt

Long-term debt, excluding current portion, consists of the following at December 31:

	(IN THOUSANDS)	
	1980	1979
Notes, 12¼%, due 1985	$100,000	—
Notes payable to banks under revolving credit agreements	75,000	—
Bank term loans, due 1981–86	—	$175,000
Debentures, 8⅞%, due 2001	75,000	75,000
Convertible Subordinated Debentures, 4½%, due 1988	29,512	30,000
Other	48,889	35,826
	$328,401	$315,826

In May, 1980, the Company sold $100,000,000 of 12¼ percent notes due 1985 and applied the proceeds to reduce bank term loans. The remaining bank term loans of $75,000,000 were refunded in August, 1980, as the Company entered into revolving credit and term loan agreements with the same banks. Under the new bank agreements, the revolving credits run to June 30, 1985, at which time they can be converted to term loans payable semi-annually in eight equal installments beginning December 31, 1985; interest is charged at the Company's option at either the floating prime rate or the sum of the London Inter-bank Offered Rate plus ½ percent with increasing rates during the repayment period of the term loans.

The Debentures may be redeemed at the Company's option in whole or in part, at a declining premium which approximates 7 percent in 1981. The Debentures are subject to mandatory annual sinking fund payments in the amount of $4,875,000 beginning in 1987.

The convertible Subordinated Debentures are convertible prior to maturity, unless previously redeemed, into common stock at $32¼ per share.

At December 31, 1980, other long-term debt consists of obligations incurred primarily for acquisitions, principally payable through 1984 with varying interest rates.

As to the above obligations, certain agreements contain limitations on additional borrowings and restrictions on cash dividend payments. At December 31, 1980, the amount of retained earnings not restricted for cash dividends approximated $86,000,000 under these provisions.

The aggregate maturities of long-term debt, including current portion, during the next five years are approximately as follows: 1981—$28,600,000, 1982—$10,400,000, 1983—$12,600,000, 1984—$8,500,000 and 1985—$112,400,000.

Repayment Scheme 2: Pay $25,000 of the principal on December 31 in 1983, 1984, and 1985 plus 10 percent annual interest on the unpaid principal on the same dates.

Repayment Scheme 3: Pay $99,825 on December 31, 1985.

What is the payment schedule for Repayment Scheme 1?

Payment		$7,500[a]	$7,500[a]	$82,500[b]
Time line	└───────	──┴─────	──┴─────	──┘
Date	1/1/83	12/31/83	12/31/84	12/31/85

[a] Interest for 1983 and 1984 is computed as follows:
($75,000)(1)(.10) = $7,500

[b] Interest for 1985 plus principal payment is computed as follows:
($75,000)(1)(.10) + $75,000 = $82,500

If we assume a December 31 fiscal year-end, the balance sheet on December 31, 1983, would show a noncurrent liability "notes payable" of $75,000. This represents the present value of future cash payments (P/F factors are from Table II–2 in Appendix H at the back of the book):

$$(P/F, 1, .10)\$7,500 + (P/F, 2, .10)\$82,500 =$$
$$(.9091)\$7,500 + (.8264)\$82,500 = \$75,000 \text{ (rounded)}$$

The income statements would show interest expense of $7,500 for the years 1983, 1984, and 1985. The following amortization schedule summarizes the accounting for the note over its life:

DATE	CASH PAYMENT	INTEREST EXPENSE	REDUCTION OF LIABILITY	CARRYING VALUE OF LIABILITY
1/1/83	0	0		$75,000
12/31/83	$ 7,500	$7,500	0	75,000
12/31/84	7,500	7,500	0	75,000
12/31/85	82,500	7,500	$75,000	0

What is the payment schedule for Repayment Scheme 2?

Payment		$32,500[a]	$30,000[b]	$27,500[c]
Time line	└───────	──┴─────	──┴─────	──┘
Date	1/1/83	12/31/83	12/31/84	12/31/85

[a] Interest for 1983 plus $25,000 of principal
($75,000)(1)(.10) + $25,000 = $32,500

[b] Interest for 1984 plus $25,000 of principal
($50,000)(1)(.10) + $25,000 = $30,000

[c] Interest for 1985 plus $25,000 of principal
($25,000)(1)(.10) + $25,000 = $27,500

In this case, the balance sheets for each year show reducing balances in the noncurrent liability account. Interest expense in the income statements represents 10 percent interest on the outstanding liability balance during the period covered by the income statement, as summarized in the following amortization schedule:

DATE	CASH PAYMENT	INTEREST EXPENSE	REDUCTION OF LIABILITY	CARRYING VALUE OF LIABILITY
1/1/83	0	0	0	$75,000
12/31/83	$32,500	$7,500	$25,000	50,000
12/31/84	30,000	5,000	25,000	25,000
12/31/85	27,500	2,500	25,000	0

Remember that the carrying value in the Notes Payable account is always the present value of *all* future cash payments related to the note or notes. For instance, on December 31, 1984, the $25,000 book value is computed as follows:

$$(P/F, 1, .10)\$27,500 =$$
$$(.9091)(\$27,500) = \$25,000 \text{ (rounded)}$$

Repayment Scheme 3 is an example of contractual terms that apply to what are sometimes called **non-interest-bearing notes,** although interest is as much a factor here as it is in the other repayment schemes. Non-interest-bearing notes, however, require the imputation of an interest rate. What interest rate equates $75,000 on January 1, 1983, with $99,825 3 years later? The formula for such a computation requires that it be determined in the following relationship:

$$\text{Principal} \times (1 + i)^n = \text{Maturity payment}$$

where i is the interest rate and n is the number of interest periods. In our example, the terms take on the following numbers:

$$\$75,000 \times (1 + i)^3 = \$99,825$$
$$(1 + i)^3 = \frac{\$99,825}{\$75,000}$$
$$(1 + i)^3 = 1.331$$
$$1 + i = \sqrt[3]{1.331}$$
$$1 + i = 1.10$$
$$i = 1.10 - 1$$
$$i = .10$$

Given the following repayment schedule and the imputed 10 percent interest rate, an amortization schedule can be constructed summarizing the accounting treatment:

```
Payment              $0        $0      $99,825
Time line      |       |         |         |
Date         1/1/83  12/31/83  12/31/84  12/31/85
```

DATE	CASH PAYMENT	INTEREST EXPENSE	CHANGE IN LIABILITY	CARRYING VALUE OF LIABILITY
1/1/83	0	0	0	$75,000
12/31/83	0	$7,500	+ $ 7,500	82,500
12/31/84	0	8,250	+ 8,250	90,750
12/31/85	$99,825	9,075	− 90,750	0

Again, the carrying value of the liability can be computed as the present value of future payments. The $75,000 at January 1, 1983, is computed as follows:

$$(P/F, 3, .10)\$99,825 = (.7513)\$99,825 = \$75,000 \text{ (rounded)}$$

Exhibit 18–2 compares the journal entries required to record the accounting effects of these three repayment patterns for the $75,000 loan.

Looked at from one point of view, the three notes analyzed above can all be described as $75,000 face value, 3-year notes with 10 percent effective annual interest rates. But the differences in contractual terms actually result in differences in cash flows, interest charges, and book values. The general accounting rules for long-term receivables and payables allow for a consistent and rational accounting for any variation in contractual terms.

Mortgages and Other Secured Notes

When assets are pledged as security for a loan, the creditor will have certain rights to the property until the note is paid in full. The contract governing secured loans can relate to new property being acquired or old property that the debtor has owned for some time. *Mortgages* and other forms of collateral provide security to the creditor through the pledging of particular assets. This additional security should translate into a lower interest charge than would be possible if no asset were used as security for the loan.

As one example of a collateralized note, consider the case where on January 1, 1983, Star Cartage, Inc., buys a building site for $60,000, pays $20,000 as a down payment, and signs a mortgage loan with a bank for the $40,000 balance. The loan agreement calls for two payments, on December 31, 1983, and December 31, 1984, of $20,000 plus interest of 12 percent on the unpaid balance. Legally, the title to the land passes to Star Cartage, but the title is encumbered by the mortgage. As is the case when contractual form contradicts economic reality, accountants would ignore

EXHIBIT 18–2

		JOURNAL ENTRIES FOR THREE REPAYMENT SCHEMES					
		REPAYMENT SCHEME 1		REPAYMENT SCHEME 2		REPAYMENT SCHEME 3	
		DEBIT	CREDIT	DEBIT	CREDIT	DEBIT	CREDIT
1/1/83	Cash	75,000		75,000		75,000	
	Notes payable		75,000		75,000		75,000
12/31/83	Interest expense	7,500		7,500		7,500	
	Notes payable			25,000			
	Cash		7,500		32,500		
	Interest payable						7,500
12/31/84	Interest expense	7,500		5,000		8,250	
	Notes payable			25,000			
	Interest payable						8,250
	Cash		7,500		30,000		
12/31/85	Interest expense	7,500		2,500		9,075	
	Notes payable	75,000		25,000		75,000	
	Interest payable					15,750	
	Cash		82,500		27,500		99,825

this legal technicality for disclosure purposes and record the asset and liability as follows:

1/1/83	Land		60,000	
	Notes payable			40,000
	Cash			20,000
12/31/83	Interest expense		4,800	
	Notes payable		20,000	
	Cash			24,800
12/31/84	Interest expense		2,400	
	Notes payable		20,000	
	Cash			22,400

The fact that a mortgage exists on the land need not be formally reflected in the account titles. Accounting for notes with mortgage terms follows the same pattern as that for notes without mortgage terms. The title of the liability account could be Mortgage Payable in order to be more informative.

Regardless of the account title, there should be a balance sheet footnote disclosure describing any mortgage or other collateral terms related to liabilities. The footnote in Exhibit 18–3 explains that certain assets are collateral for portions of long-term debt. Both the assets and the long-term debt on the balance sheet are cross-referenced to the footnote in this case. Exhibit 18–3 and several of the other exhibits in this chapter contain specialized terms that will be defined and discussed throughout the chapter.

BONDS

Bonds are debt securities that are issued by a company to creditors called **bond-holders.** Each bond is a legal contract with at least the following characteristics:

1. **A maturity obligation amount.** This is a money amount per bond that is to be paid at the end of the bond term. Often called **face value** or **par value,** this amount is *not* the principal or the cash received upon issuance.
2. **Inception and maturity dates.** These two dates define the term of the bond. Although a 20-year bond has exactly 20 years between inception and maturity, it may be sold after the inception date. Differences in bond terms and periods outstanding are not uncommon, and the accounting procedures are capable of handling many such possible variations.
3. **An annuity obligation amount.** This is a periodic payment that is based on a fixed percentage of the maturity amount. A $1,000 maturity amount bond with a $100 yearly annuity obligation amount is called a *10 percent bond,* or a bond with a 10 percent *nominal* or *stated* interest rate.
4. **An annuity payment date.** The annuity payments are usually made semiannually. Annual and quarterly payments are also possible.

Because contractual terms are so pivotal in accounting for long-term debt, an understanding of common terms used in such agreements is necessary. The following definitions are stated in terms of debt instruments and will be supplemented throughout the chapter as specific topics are covered:

1. **Debenture.** A security (bond) that is backed by the general credit of the issuer without specific collateralized assets.

EXHIBIT
18–3

DISCLOSURE OF MORTGAGE NOTES

NORDSON CORPORATION
Excerpt from Notes

8. Long-term debt

Long-term debt at November 2, 1980, and October 28, 1979, consisted of the following:

	1980	1979
Note to Prudential Insurance Company (A)	$ 2,200,000	$3,300,000
Industrial Revenue Bonds—City of New Richmond, Wisconsin (B)	775,000	850,000
Industrial Revenue Bonds—Gwinnett County, Georgia (C)	2,000,000	2,000,000
Industrial Revenue Bonds—Anderson County, South Carolina (D)	6,000,000	—
Note to foreign bank (E)	930,498	1,063,657
	11,905,498	7,213,657
Less amounts due within one year	(722,901)	(726,512)
Total	$11,182,597	$6,487,145

(A) *Note to Prudential Insurance Company*—this unsecured 10.5% note is payable in annual installments of $550,000 until 1983. The loan agreement has various restrictive covenants none of which, in the opinion of management, will adversely affect operations. Annually the Company is entitled to prepay an amount equal to the required annual installment at a 2% penalty. In addition, the Company may make additional prepayments, the amounts of which are subject to a prepayment penalty of 6% in 1980 declining to 3% in 1983.

(B) *Industrial Revenue Bonds—City of New Richmond, Wisconsin*—issued in connection with a packaging machinery manufacturing plant expansion, located in New Richmond, Wisconsin, including equipment and fixtures. Due in annual installments ranging from $75,000 to $100,000 plus interest ranging from 5% to 6% until November 1989. The plant, equipment, and fixtures having an original cost of $1,331,000 are assigned as collateral.

(C) *Industrial Revenue Bonds—Gwinnett County, Georgia*—issued in connection with the construction of an office and laboratory building located in Gwinnett County, Georgia. Due in annual installments, ranging from $40,000 to $275,000 beginning in 1989, plus semiannual interest ranging from 7.50% to 7.70% until 2003. The land, building and appurtenant structures having an original cost of $2,018,000 are assigned as collateral.

(D) *Industrial Revenue Bonds—Anderson County, South Carolina*—issued in connection with the construction of a manufacturing facility located in Anderson County, South Carolina. The bonds bear an interest rate equal to 60% of the prime interest rate charged by the First National Bank of Atlanta ("FNBA") until May 1, 1983. Effective May 1, 1983, FNBA has two options as to repayment as defined in the Bond Indenture Agreement.

The options are: 1) quarterly interest payments at 65% of FNBA's prime rate through May 1, 1985, at which time the entire principal of $6,000,000 is payable, or 2) quarterly principal payments and interest at 65% of FNBA's prime rate through May 1, 1985, followed by quarterly principal payments and interest at 65% of FNBA's prime rate plus one quarter percent through May 1, 1990. A first mortgage on the real and personal property with an original cost of $5,325,000 is assigned as collateral under the Bond Indenture Agreement which includes various restrictive covenants, none of which, in the opinion of management, will adversely affect operations.

(E) *Note to foreign bank*—a 6.25% note which is payable in quarterly installments of DM44,300 ($24,500) until March 15, 1990. Land and other assets with an original cost of approximately $1,772,000 which are part of the Company's German operations are assigned as collateral.

The maximum (see Item D above) aggregate annual maturities of long-term debt for each of the five years subsequent to November 2, 1980, are as follows: 1981—$723,000, 1982—$723,000, 1983—$1,152,000, 1984—$1,030,000 and 1985—$6,173,000.

2. **Covenant.** A particular clause of a debt contract that is incidental to the main purpose of the contract and that describes the rights and obligations of the parties if certain actions are taken or certain states occur.

3. **Indenture.** The contract that specifies the rights and obligations of debtors and creditors.

4. **Senior debt.** A debt that takes precedence over other debts or has a prior claim on the assets of the debtor in the event of liquidation or foreclosure.

5. **Subordinate debt.** A debt of an entity that has other senior debt outstanding.

Determination
of Bond
Selling Price

The value of the contractual rights described above depends on the individual and collective judgments of those who make up the market for bonds. Each bond issue is valued by the market, and the effective interest rate to the issuer is the one associated with the sale transaction between the issuer and the original bondholder.

Assume that Issuer, Inc., issues 10,000 bonds on February 1, 1984. Each bond has a $1,000 maturity amount to be paid on January 31, 1989, the maturity date. The annuity amount is $80 per bond to be paid on January 31 of each year starting on January 31, 1985. This represents an 8 percent nominal interest rate. Issuer, then, is promising to pay the following cash flows per bond:

Amount		$80	$80	$80	$80	$1,080
Time line						
Date	2/1/84	1/31/85	1/31/86	1/31/87	1/31/88	1/31/89

How much would an investor be willing to pay for one bond on February 1, 1984? If we assume that an investor can earn 10 percent on comparable investments and that this investor subscribes to the present-value theory, he or she would make the following computation:

$$A(P/A, n, i) + F(P/F, n, i) =$$
$$\$80(P/A, 5, .10) + \$1,000(P/F, 5, .10) =$$
$$\$80(3.7908) + \$1,000(.6209) =$$
$$\$303.26 + \$620.90 = \$924.16$$

Because the desired interest rate is 10 percent and the nominal rate is only 8 percent the investor pays less than the maturity value of the bond. Accountants term the difference between the selling price and the maturity value a **discount** when the selling price is less than the maturity value or a **premium** when the selling price is greater than the maturity value. In the example above, there is a discount of $75.84. The concepts of discounts and premiums and the accounting for them will be examined later in this chapter.

Debtor
and Creditor
Amortization
Schedules:
A Basic
Symmetry

The investor, then, would be willing to pay $924.16 for one Issuer, Inc., bond on February 1, 1984. The bond will yield 10 percent, as shown in the amortization schedule for the one investor in Exhibit 18–4.

Note that in Exhibit 18–4 interest income is always 10 percent of the previous net book value of the investment. For instance, the interest income of $96.53 on January 31, 1988, is 10 percent of the net investment of $965.26 on January 31, 1987. The interest income for the entire 5-year period equals the net positive cash flow of $475.84.

The amortization schedule for the debtor (bond issuer) is symmetrical with that of the creditor (bondholder). Let us assume that on February 1, 1984, Issuer, Inc., sells all of its 10,000 bonds to yield 10 percent. Issuer's amortization schedule (Exhibit 18–5) for the entire liability would be similar to the one shown in Exhibit 18–4 except that it is presented from the debtor's point of view and is for the entire bond issue. It is critical that the Net Liability column be completely understood.

EXHIBIT
18–4

BONDHOLDER'S AMORTIZATION SCHEDULE

DATE	CASH FLOW IN (OUT)	INTEREST INCOME	INCREASE (DECREASE) IN INVESTMENT	NET INVESTMENT
2/1/84	$ (924.16)	—	$ 924.16	$ 924.16
1/31/85	80.00	92.42	12.42	936.58
1/31/86	80.00	93.66	13.66	950.24
1/31/87	80.00	95.02	15.02	965.26
1/31/88	80.00	96.53	16.53	981.79
1/31/89	80.00	98.21[a]	18.21	1,000.00
1/31/89	1,000.00	—	(1,000.00)	—
	$ 475.84	475.84	0	

[a] Rounding error of $.03.

Each of the numbers appearing in that column can be computed independently, as demonstrated in the lower part of Exhibit 18–5.

Recording Bond Transactions

Bonds with annual interest payment dates

DISCOUNTS   Accountants have a special way of recording bonds. Instead of having one ledger account with, in our example, a balance of $9,241,640 on February 1, 1984, they typically use two ledger accounts, Bonds Payable (the primary account) and Discount (a contra account) or Premium (an adjunct account).

BONDS PAYABLE	**DISCOUNT ON BONDS PAYABLE**
$10,000,000	$758,360

EXHIBIT
18–5

BOND ISSUER'S AMORTIZATION SCHEDULE FOR BONDS SOLD AT A DISCOUNT

DATE	CASH FLOW IN (OUT)	INTEREST EXPENSE	INCREASE (DECREASE) IN NET LIABILITY	NET LIABILITY
2/1/84	$ 9,241,640	—	$ 9,241,640	$ 9,241,640
1/31/85	(800,000)	$ 924,164	124,164	9,365,804
1/31/86	(800,000)	936,580	136,580	9,502,384
1/31/87	(800,000)	950,238	150,238	9,652,622
1/31/88	(800,000)	965,262	165,262	9,817,884
1/31/89	(800,000)	982,116[a]	182,116	10,000,000
1/31/89	(10,000,000)	—	(10,000,000)	—
	$ (4,758,360)	$4,758,360	0	

2/1/84	$800,000 (*P/A*, 5, .10) + $10,000,000 (*P/F*, 5, .10) = $ 9,241,640
1/31/85	$800,000 (*P/A*, 4, .10) + $10,000,000 (*P/F*, 4, .10) = $ 9,365,804[b]
1/31/86	$800,000 (*P/A*, 3, .10) + $10,000,000 (*P/F*, 3, .10) = $ 9,502,384[b]
1/31/87	$800,000 (*P/A*, 2, .10) + $10,000,000 (*P/F*, 2, .10) = $ 9,652,622[b]
1/31/88	$800,000 (*P/A*, 1, .10) + $10,000,000 (*P/F*, 1, .10) = $ 9,817,884[b]
1/31/89	$10,000,000 (*P/F*, 0, .10) = $10,000,000

[a] Rounding error of $328.
[b] Rounded.

To demonstrate the required journal entries, let us assume that Issuer, Inc., has a January 31 year-end and that all the facts in our example remain the same:

2/1/84	Cash	9,241,640	
	Discount on bonds payable	758,360	
	Bonds payable		10,000,000
	(To record the issuance of 10,000 5-year, $1,000 maturity value, 8 percent nominal interest rate bonds at an effective yield rate of 10 percent)		
1/31/85	Interest expense	924,164	
	Discount on bonds payable		124,164
	Cash		800,000
	(To record the payment of the nominal interest and the amortization of bond discount)		

The income statement for the year ending January 31, 1985, would include interest expense of $924,164. Balance sheet disclosure at the end of the accounting period would be the maturity value in the Bonds Payable account less the Discount on Bonds Payable account, which has been reduced by the amount of the amortization:

ISSUER, INC.
(Partial) Balance Sheet
January 31, 1985

Noncurrent liabilities
Bonds payable	$10,000,000	
Less discount	634,196	$9,365,804

The rationale for using two accounts is that the maturity value of the bond should be communicated to financial statement readers. In practice, the balance sheet often shows only the net liability. In such cases, GAAP require that a footnote contain information about the face and discount and/or premium amounts.[3] Exhibit 18–6 illustrates two common disclosure patterns. Rochester Gas and Electric Corporation shows its net amount of "long-term debt" on the balance sheet and provides for a reconciliation of that amount in the analysis in the footnote. Note that the balance sheet amount of $381,172,000 for 1979 is equal to the total maturity value for long-term debt of $381,667,000 *minus* the net discount of $495,372. The $384,303,000 balance for 1978 is the total maturity value plus the net premium of $635,667. The Tannetics, Inc., footnote gives information on discounts related to each bond issue.

Consider once again Exhibit 18–5. Several points should be emphasized to indicate the relationship between the general rules and the accounting techniques used:

1. The initial net liability of $9,241,640 is the present value of future cash flows on February 1, 1984, and the balance of $9,365,804 is the present value of future cash flows on January 31, 1985. This pattern holds for all amounts in the Net Liability column.

[3] Ibid.

EXHIBIT
18–6

DISCLOSURE OF BOND PREMIUMS AND DISCOUNTS

ROCHESTER GAS AND ELECTRIC COMPANY
Excerpt from Balance Sheet

	(THOUSANDS)	
	1979	1978
Long-term debt	$381,172	$384,303

Excerpt from Notes

Long-term debt First Mortgage Bonds—Series Due	PRINCIPAL AMOUNT DECEMBER 31,	
	1979	1978
3 L Mar. 1, 1979		$ 16,677
2¾ M Aug. 15, 1980	$ 12,000	12,000
3⅜ M June 1, 1982	6,000	6,000
3⅜ O Mar. 1, 1985	10,000	10,000
4⅞ R July 1, 1987	15,000	15,000
5 S Oct. 15, 1989	12,000	12,000
4½ T Nov. 15, 1991	15,000	15,000
4⅝ U Sept. 15, 1994	16,000	16,000
5.8 V May 1, 1996	18,000	18,000
6¼ W Sept. 15, 1997	20,000	20,000
6.7 W July 1, 1998	30,000	30,000
8 Y Aug. 15, 1999	30,000	30,000
9⅛ Z Sept. 1, 2000	30,000	30,000
10¾ AA Aug. 1, 1983	29,667	29,667
9¼ BB June 15, 2006	50,000	50,000
8⅜ CC Sept. 15, 2007	50,000	50,000
9½ DD Dec. 1, 2003	40,000	40,000
6½ EE Aug. 1, 2009	10,000	
	$393,667	$400,344
Less: Due within one year	12,000	16,677
Total long-term debt	$381,667	$383,667

Bond discount and premium applicable to the years 1979 and 1978 is $495,372 and $635,667, respectively.

TANNETICS, INC.
Excerpt from Notes

4 Notes and loans payable

Notes and loans payable consist of the following:

	JULY 31, 1979	JULY 31, 1978
10½% Senior sinking fund debentures, due 1992, net of unamortized discount of $636,360 and $704,544, respectively	$11,863,640	$11,795,456
10% subordinated debentures due 1989, net of unamortized discount of $379,692 and $307,040, respectively	540,674	513,326
.	.	.
.	.	.
Long-term Indebtedness	$14,007,994	$14,071,950

2. The interest expense recognized on the January 31, 1985, income statement is for *past* interest charges, not for any future amounts of interest. This is consistent with the matching concept, which requires that an expense be matched with the benefit derived. The benefit from the use of the bond proceeds during the period February 1, 1985, through January 31, 1986, has not yet been received on January 31, 1985, and, therefore, no expense is recognized for that period on January 31, 1985. Likewise, the liability for nominal interest payments accrues to bondholders as time passes. Therefore, on January 31, 1985, no current liability is shown for the next nominal interest payment.

3. The difference between the initial present value and the total actual cash flows is the total interest charge.

In addition to the first-period entries shown on page 682, Issuer, Inc., would record the following additional journal entries through the remaining life of the bonds:

1/31/86	Interest expense	936,580	
	Discount on bonds payable		136,580
	Cash		800,000
1/31/87	Interest expense	950,238	
	Discount on bonds payable		150,238
	Cash		800,000
1/31/88	Interest expense	965,262	
	Discount on bonds payable		165,262
	Cash		800,000
1/31/89	Interest expense	982,116	
	Discount on bonds payable		182,116
	Cash		800,000
1/31/89	Bonds payable	10,000,000	
	Cash		10,000,000
	(To record the payment of the maturity value of the bonds)		

This method of reducing the original discount or premium by applying the effective interest rate to the carrying value of the bond is sometimes referred to as the **effective interest method** of amortization. It is often compared with the straight-line method, which entails a constant discount or premium amortization. In our example, straight-line amortization would result in $151,672 being credited to Discount on Bonds Payable each year (the original discount of $758,360 divided by 5 years). Such a procedure also results in a constant annual interest expense charge of $951,672—$151,672 + $800,000. In general, the effective interest method is considered to be generally accepted except in cases where there is no material difference between the two methods.

PREMIUMS   Up to this point we have discussed issuing bonds at a discount, that is, at an amount less than the bond's face or maturity value. Bonds may also be issued at a premium, at an amount that is greater than face or maturity value. Accounting procedures for a bond issued at a premium are parallel to those shown above for discounts.

A bond contract obliges the issuer to two streams of cash:

1. The maturity amount.

2. An annuity called the nominal interest payment, which is paid on an annual or semi-annual basis.

These two streams of cash are fixed by contract and are constant regardless of what the bonds actually sell for. Whether a discount or a premium will result depends on the cash yield demanded by investors. This varies continuously, and changes will take place between the time the bond contracts are printed and the time they are sold. Hence, a company could go through all the legal and regulatory steps necessary to issue bonds with an 8 percent nominal interest rate in mind, and by the time the bonds were actually sold, the market interest rate could be 10 or 6 percent. The investors would then decide how much to pay for the fixed cash flows by applying the 10 or 6 percent in a present-value computation.

Let us now analyze the issuance of a bond at a premium. Assume that Issuer, Inc., sells 10,000 of its 8 percent, $1,000 maturity value bonds on February 1, 1984, when the market will settle for an interest rate (yield) of 6 percent. The computation of the total selling price for all the bonds would be as follows:

$$\$800,000(P/A, 5, .06) + \$10,000,000(P/F, 5, .06) =$$
$$\$800,000(4.2124) + \$10,000,000(.7473) =$$
$$\$3,369,920 + \$7,473,000 - \$10,842,920$$

The premium of $842,920 equals the proceeds of the sale minus the maturity value. An amortization schedule for bonds issued at a premium has the same characteristics as one for a discount issuance (see Exhibit 18–7). Note that the total nominal interest payment of $4,000,000($800,000 × 5) is more than the total interest expense of $3,157,080. The difference is the amount of the premium at date of issuance, $842,920. Amortization of the initial premium amount reduces the interest expense each year. The journal entries for all bond transactions are as follows:

2/1/84	Cash	10,842,920	
	Premium on bonds payable		842,920
	Bonds payable		10,000,000
1/31/85	Interest expense	650,575	
	Premium on bonds payable	149,425	
	Cash		800,000
1/31/86	Interest expense	641,610	
	Premium on bonds payable	158,390	
	Cash		800,000
1/31/87	Interest expense	632,106	
	Premium on bonds payable	167,894	
	Cash		800,000
1/31/88	Interest expense	622,033	
	Premium on bonds payable	177,967	
	Cash		800,000
1/31/89	Interest expense	610,756	
	Premium on bonds payable	189,244	
	Cash		800,000
1/31/89	Bonds payable	10,000,000	
	Cash		10,000,000

In comparing the journal entries with those on pages 682 and 684 for the discount example, note that the premium has the opposite effect on the interest expense amounts.

Balance sheet presentation highlights the fact that the Premium on Bonds Pay-

EXHIBIT
18–7

		BOND ISSUER'S AMORTIZATION SCHEDULE FOR BONDS SOLD AT A PREMIUM		
DATE	**CASH FLOW IN (OUT)**	**INTEREST EXPENSE**	**INCREASE (DECREASE) IN NET LIABILITY**	**NET LIABILITY**[a]
2/1/84	$10,842,920	—	10,842,920	10,842,920
1/31/85	(800,000)	650,575	(149,425)	10,693,495
1/31/86	(800,000)	641,610	(158,390)	10,535,105
1/31/87	(800,000)	632,106	(167,894)	10,367,211
1/31/88	(800,000)	622,033	(177,967)	10,189,244
1/31/89	(800,000)	610,756[a]	(189,244)	10,000,000
1/31/89	(10,000,000)	—	(10,000,000)	—
	$ (3,157,080)	3,157,080	0	

[a] Rounded.

able is an adjunct account to the primary account, Bonds Payable. The net liability to be reported for bonds is computed by adding the primary account balance and the adjunct account balance. For instance, on January 31, 1985, Issuer's balance sheet would show the following:

```
                    ISSUER, INC.
               (Partial) Balance Sheet
                  January 31, 1985

Noncurrent liabilities
Bonds payable          $10,000,000
Premium                    693,495    $10,693,495
```

Bonds with semiannual interest payment dates Bonds often have terms that require interest payments at intervals of less than a year; the most common period is 6 months. The differences between these semiannual payments and annual payments can be illustrated by comparing two bond issues that are identical in every respect *except* for the different interest payment schedules. The following example demonstrates that the interest payment schedule will affect the value of the bond, all else being equal.

	ANNUAL PAYMENTS	**SEMIANNUAL PAYMENTS**
Maturity value	$10,000,000	$10,000,000
Nominal interest rate	6%	6%
Nominal interest payments	$600,000 annually	$300,000 semiannually
Effective interest rate	8%	8%
Computation of sales price	$600,000(P/A, 5, .08) + $10,000,000(P/F, 5, .08) = $600,000(3.9927) + $10,000,000(.6806) = $2,395,620 + $6,806,000 = $9,201,620	$300,000(P/A, 10, .04) + $10,000,000(P/F, 10, .04) = $300,000(8.1109) + $10,000,000(.6756) = $2,433,270 + $6,756,000 = $9,189,270

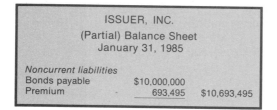

EXHIBIT
18–8

COMPARATIVE AMORTIZATION SCHEDULES FOR THE ANNUAL AND SEMIANNUAL PAYMENTS CASES						
	ANNUAL			SEMIANNUAL		
DATE	CASH RECEIPT (PAYMENT)	INTEREST EXPENSE	BOOK VALUE LIABILITY	CASH RECEIPT (PAYMENT)	INTEREST EXPENSE	BOOK VALUE LIABILITY
1/1/1	$ 9,201,620		$ 9,201,620	$ 9,189,270	$ —	$ 9,189,270
7/1/1				(300,000)	367,571	9,256,841
1/1/2	(600,000)	$ 736,130	9,337,750	(300,000)	370,274	9,327,115
7/1/2				(300,000)	373,085	9,400,200
1/1/3	(600,000)	747,020	9,484,770	(300,000)	376,008	9,476,208
7/1/3				(300,000)	379,048	9,555,256
1/1/4	(600,000)	758,782	9,643,552	(300,000)	382,210	9,637,466
7/1/4				(300,000)	385,499	9,722,965
1/1/5	(600,000)	771,484	9,815,036	(300,000)	388,919	9,811,884
7/1/5				(300,000)	392,475	9,904,359
1/1/6	(600,000)	784,964[a]	10,000,000	(300,000)	395,641[a]	10,000,000
1/1/6	(10,000,000)	—	0	(10,000,000)		0
	$ (3,798,380)	$3,798,380		$ (3,810,730)	$3,810,730	

[a] Rounded.

The comparative amortization tables for these two alternatives in Exhibit 18–8 demonstrate the impact of the different interest payment schedules on interest expense. Note that because of the initial difference in selling price, the interest expense is different for each period and in total. The accounting journal entries and disclosures would follow the same patterns for semiannual payments as those discussed for annual payments.

Bonds sold between interest payment dates Market conditions often dictate that the issuance date of a bond be a date other than the inception date on the face of the bond. Assume that 1,000 bonds with face value of $1,000 and nominal interest of 10 percent are dated January 1, 1984. They are not issued, however, until March 1, 1984, when the market interest rate on such bonds is 10 percent. The bond contract calls for the payment of $100,000 nominal interest on December 31 of each year. How much would the purchaser of the bonds pay on March 1, 1984, two months after the inception date? Ordinarily we would sum the present value of the annuity and the present value of the maturity payment: $A(P/A, n, i) + F(P/F, n, i)$. In this case, however, because the nominal interest rate equals the market rate, we know that the bonds would sell for face value, or a total of $1,000,000, except for the fact that 2 months of the first interest period have passed without the issuing company's having use of the borrowed funds. In such cases, the purchaser pays the normal purchase price plus a prorated portion of the first period's interest payment. Proceeds from the sale on March 1, 1984, would be $1,000,000 plus $16,667, which is two-twelfths of the $100,000 annual interest amount. The issuing company would therefore make the following journal entries to record the first year's transactions:

3/1/84	Cash	1,016,667	
	Bonds payable		1,000,000
	Interest payable		16,667

12/31/84	Interest payable	16,667	
	Interest expense	83,333	
	Cash		100,000

The December 31, 1984, cash payment includes interest expense for the 10 months from issuance to the end of the accounting period plus the January and February interest that was paid for by the bondholder. The procedure of having the purchaser pay for an accrued interest at a date of issuance between interest payment dates makes the bond issuer's record keeping simpler. It permits the issuer to pay a uniform nominal interest amount on each payment date without regard to the actual issuance dates.

Expenses of issuing debt instruments   Whenever a business raises capital, costs are incurred. Many of the costs are expensed immediately; such expenses include, for example, the cost of corporate officers, corporate attorneys, and corporate accountants who hold meetings and perform analyses. These internal costs are not usually accumulated separately and segregated in the accounting records. Bond issue costs and issue cost for debt instruments paid to outsiders such as consultants, underwriters, brokers, independent accountants, and printers, however, are usually segregated and reported on the balance sheet as a noncurrent asset such as "unamortized bond issue costs." As with all noncurrent assets, amortization is required when an asset has a limited useful life. In this case, the life of the bond issue is the amortization period for the bond issue costs.

The amortization of bond issue costs can be viewed as an annuity equal to the present value of the issue costs. For instance, assume that on January 1, 1981, a $10,000,000 face value bond issue is sold to yield 12 percent. The bonds mature in 10 years, and the bond issue cost is $300,000. The annual issue cost amortization would be computed using the inverse of the factor for the present value of an ordinary annuity as follows:

$$[1/(P/A, 10, .12)][\$300,000] =$$
$$(.17698)(\$300,000) = \$53,094$$

An amortization schedule that gives the amortization expense for each year is shown in Exhibit 18–9. Journal entries for the first year would be as follows:

1/1/81	Unamortized bond issue costs	300,000	
	Cash		300,000
12/31/81	Bond issue expense	17,094	
	Unamortized bond issue costs		17,094

In Exhibit 18–9 bond issue expense is handled in a manner consistent with that of bond premium and discount. A much simpler technique employs the straight-line amortization method. However, **APB Opinion 21,** which addresses this issue, specifically calls for the use of the interest factor in the amortization procedure unless the results of other methods are not materially different from those of the "interest" method.[4]

Fiscal period considerations   Although bonds have fixed periodic payment schedules, their schedules will not normally coincide with the fiscal period used for ac-

[4] Ibid., par. 14.

EXHIBIT
18–9

BOND ISSUE COSTS AMORTIZATION SCHEDULE

DATE	ANNUITY	INTEREST FACTOR	BOND ISSUE EXPENSE	BOND ISSUE COST UNAMORTIZED BALANCE
1/1/81	—	—	—	$300,000
12/31/81	$53,094	$36,000	$ 17,094	282,906
12/31/82	53,094	33,949	19,145	263,761
12/31/83	53,094	31,651	21,443	242,318
12/31/84	53,094	29,078	24,016	218,302
12/31/85	53,094	26,196	26,898	191,404
12/31/86	53,094	22,969	30,125	161,279
12/31/87	53,094	19,353	33,741	127,538
12/31/88	53,094	15,305	37,789	89,749
12/31/89	53,094	10,770	42,324	47,425
12/31/90	53,094	5,669[a]	47,425	0
			$300,000	

[a] Rounded.

counting statements. Amortization schedules that show interest expense, net bond liability balances, and issue-cost expense, therefore, do not mesh with the fiscal periods, necessitating adjusting journal entries in most cases. The simplest and most commonly used technique for measuring money amounts for the required adjusting entries is to apportion amortization schedule amounts on the basis of time elapsed between the last interest payment date and the balance sheet date. Refer to the amortization schedule in Exhibit 18–7. The interest expense and the premium amortization for the interest period February 1, 1984, to January 31, 1985, are $650,575 and $149,425, respectively. If we assume that the fiscal period ends on March 31, 1985, what amounts are to be recorded for interest expense and premium amortization in the period-end adjustment process? The following schedule aids in the discussion:

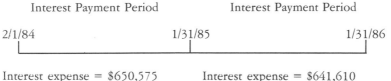

Interest Payment Period   Interest Payment Period

2/1/84   1/31/85   1/31/86

Interest expense = $650,575   Interest expense = $641,610
Premium amortization = $149,425   Premium amortization = $158,390

As of March 31, 1984, two months have elapsed during the first interest period and the apportionments are simply (2/12)($650,575) and (2/12)($149,425), or $108,429 and $24,904, respectively. For the period February 1, 1985, to March 31, 1985, the apportionments for interest expense and premium amortization are: interest expense (2/12)($641,610) = $106,935, and premium amortization (2/12)($158,390) = $26,398.

Adjusting journal entries and the cash payment entry would be made as follows:

3/31/84	Interest expense	108,429	
	Premium on bonds payable	24,904	
	Interest payable		133,333

1/31/85	Interest payable	133,333	
	Interest expense	542,146[a]	
	Premium on bonds payable	124,521[b]	
	Cash		800,000
3/31/85	Interest expense	106,935	
	Premium on bonds payable	26,398	
	Interest payable		133,333
1/31/86	Interest payable	133,333	
	Interest expense	534,675[c]	
	Premium on bonds payable	131,992[d]	
	Cash		800,000

[a] $650,575 − $108,429.
[b] $149,425 − $24,904.
[c] $641,610 − $106,935.
[d] $158,390 − $26,398.

Note that the interest payable amounts are two-twelfths of $800,000 on March 31, 1984, and March 31, 1985. These amounts would be reported as current liabilities on the balance sheets for those dates. The same apportionment procedures would be used for the computation of bond-issue expense.

Early Extinguishment and Conversion of Debt

Not all obligations with fixed maturity dates such as notes and bonds remain outstanding for their full lives. Contractual terms often allow for an **early extinguishment** of the debt or a **conversion** of the debt into equity securities. In certain instances, a subsequent mutual agreement between the debtor and the creditor allows for an early retirement of the debt. Bonds can also be purchased in the open market and canceled or held by the issuer as treasury bonds.

In all cases where the debt is eliminated before the initially scheduled maturity date, the accountant must record the transaction by eliminating all account balances related to the obligation, including the primary liability account, the interest payable account, any premium or discount account, and any debt issue cost account. This usually results in a gain or a loss being recorded on the debt extinguishment.

We shall discuss three different types of early extinguishments:

1. Retirement of bonds pursuant to a call provision
2. Retirement of bonds by open market purchases
3. Retirement of bonds pursuant to a conversion feature

Retirement of bonds pursuant to a call provision The issuing company may often retire bonds before their maturity date by paying the investor a fixed amount per bond. In the case of Issuer, Inc. (see Exhibit 18–5), 10,000, 8 percent bonds were originally issued on February 1, 1984, to yield 10 percent. Assume that a clause (a **call provision**) in the bond agreement allows the issuer to purchase bonds from the holders on or after January 31, 1986, at 103 percent of maturity value plus any unpaid interest. Issuer, Inc., then would have a choice of either allowing the bonds to remain outstanding until maturity on January 31, 1989, or exercising its option to retire (call) the bonds by paying bondholders $1,030 per bond on or after January 31, 1986.

Many factors affect the decision to retire bonds, such as the issuer's current and future cash positions and interest rates. Let us assume that on January 31, 1986,

Issuer, Inc., can borrow the $10,300,000 at 6 percent interest compounded annually to be paid back on January 31, 1988. If all other things were held constant and management wanted to base its decision concerning the retirement solely on the time value of cash flows, the following analysis would be appropriate:

Alternative 1 — Do Not Retire Bonds

	CASH INFLOW (OUTFLOW)	
Net cash outflow from 1/31/86 through 1/31/89 is $2,400,000 (nominal interest) plus $10,000,000 (maturity value) =	$(12,400,000)	Cash flow
Present value at 1/31/86 of cash flows at the then current interest rate: (P/A, 3, .06)($800,000) + (P/F, 3, .06)($10,000,000)	$(10,534,400)	Present value of cash flow

Alternative 2 — Retire Bonds

Borrow on 1/31/86	$10,300,000	
Buy back bonds on 1/31/86	(10,300,000)	
Pay off loan on 1/31/88: $10,300,000 (F/P, 2, .06)	(11,573,080)	
	$(11,573,080)	Cash flow
Present value at 1/31/86 of the cash flow at the then current interest rate: (P/F, 2, .06)($11,573,080)	$(10,300,000)	Present value of cash flow

Given this set of facts and assumptions, Issuer, Inc., would retire the bonds on January 31, 1986, because that alternative is a less costly way of paying for the borrowed funds. Issuer, Inc., would be $234,400 better off by retiring the bonds. In light of this analysis, it is interesting that the accounting for this retirement results in a *loss* being recognized. Refer to Exhibit 18–5 for the book values used to record the retirement in the following journal entries:

1/31/86	Interest expense	936,580	
	Discount on bonds payable		136,580
	Cash		800,000
	(To record nominal interest payment and discount amortization)		
1/31/86	Cash	10,300,000	
	Notes payable		10,300,000
	(To record the loan from the bank)		
1/31/86	Bonds payable	10,000,000	
	Extraordinary loss on retirement of bonds	797,616	
	Discount on bonds payable		497,616
	Cash		10,300,000
	(To record the retirement of bonds)		

Even though a loss is recorded in the above example, our computations that show that in terms of the present value of cash flows, the company is better off to retire the bonds. Let us analyze the relationship of "book" loss to "real" loss.

EXHIBIT
18-10

DISCLOSURE OF EXTINGUISHMENT OF DEBT AS AN EXTRAORDINARY ITEM

GREATER JERSEY BANCORP.
Excerpt from Income Statement

	($000)		
	1980	**1979**	**1978**
Income before extraordinary item	$7,014	$6,173	$3,914
Extraordinary item—gain on extinguishment of debt after applicable income tax effect	450		
Net income	$7,464	$6,173	$3,914

Excerpt from Notes

Note 8: Long-term debt

Long-term debt is comprised of the following:

	DECEMBER 31	
	1980	**1979**
7¾% Debentures	$17,306,000	$19,900,000
5½% Convertible capital notes	6,454,900	6,654,100
Liability for participations sold under repurchase agreements	3,590,068	4,008,876
Mortgage notes payable	2,998,084	3,259,206
	$30,349,052	$33,822,182

The extraordinary item represents a gain of $833,661 less related income tax effect from the retirement of $2,594,000 of the 7¾% debentures due March 1, 1998.

The *book loss* of $797,616 is the amount paid to bondholders ($10,300,000) less the book value of the bonds on January 31, 1986 ($9,502,384). Again, the *economic benefit* of retirement as computed above is the difference in present values of the alternatives, $10,534,400 for alternative 1 and $10,300,000 for alternative 2. That is, the issuer is $234,400 better off in terms of present value of future cash flows if retirement is selected.

The key point is that the book value of the bonds upon which the book loss is based is computed using the interest rate in effect at the date of issuance, 10 percent, whereas the computation of the "real" gain on January 31, 1986, was based on a 6 percent interest rate. When making financing decisions, management typically uses the current interest rate for comparing alternatives. Accountants, however, must allocate the total interest charge for the life of the bonds in an orderly and consistent manner; and as seen in this chapter, amortization schedules can be drawn up upon the issuance of bonds, disregarding fluctuations in interest rates from that point on.

Current GAAP require that all gains and losses from the extinguishment of debt be aggregated and, if the total is material in an accounting period, be reported on the income statement as an extraordinary item.[5] This rule is applied irrespective

[5] *Statement of Financial Accounting Standards No. 4,* "Reporting Gains and Losses from Extinguishment of Debt" (Stamford, CT: FASB, March 1975).

of the criteria established for the identification of extraordinary items in other standards. Exhibit 18–10 shows how Greater Jersey Bancorp. disclosed such an extraordinary item in an annual report.

Retirement of bonds by open market purchases   Corporations can purchase their own bonds on the **open market.** The computations and accounting practices described above for call provisions are used here as well, except that the price paid for bonds depends on the market price and not the call provision price. Upon purchase of its own bond, the issuing company can officially cancel the bond or hold it in the treasury. In the latter case, the bonds are carried at par value in a contra account to bonds payable. Again taking the facts from Issuer, Inc. (Exhibit 18–5), assume that rather than calling all the bonds, the company purchases 500 bonds on the open market for $1,020 each on January 31, 1986, and pays a $7,500 commission on the transaction. The following journal entry and balance sheet disclosure would be necessary (assuming the normal interest payment entry has already been made):

1/31/86	Treasury bonds	500,000	
	Extraordinary loss on purchase of treasury bonds	42,381	
	Discount on bonds payable		24,881
	Cash		517,500

Balance Sheet Disclosure at 1/31/86		
Long-term debt		
Bonds payable	$10,000,000	
Treasury bonds	(500,000)	
Discount	(472,735)	$9,027,265

The carrying value per bond is the same before and after the bond purchase because of the reduction of proportionate amounts of both discount and maturity value. Before the purchase, the book value per bond was $9,502,384 ÷ 10,000 = $950.24. After the purchase of the treasury bonds, the book value per bond is still $950.24 = ($9,027,265 ÷ 9,500). The computation for the reduction of the discount account is:

$$\frac{500}{10,000} (\$497,616) = \$24,881$$

The reduction in maturity value is:

$$\frac{500}{10,000} (\$10,000,000) = \$500,000$$

Early retirement of debt can generate gains as well as losses. In periods of rising interest rates, debtors can sometimes purchase their bonds in the open market at amounts considerably lower than book values. For instance, in our previous example, Issuer, Inc., purchased 500 bonds with a book value of $475,119 for $517,500 in cash under the assumption that the interest rates had decreased since issuance. If we assume that the interest rate on January 31, 1986, is 16 percent, a completely different outcome results. Individual bondholders would, with a 16 percent market interest rate, value the future cash flow for each bond outstanding as follows:

$$(P/A, 3, .16)(\$80) + (P/F, 3, .16)(\$1,000) = \$820.37$$

Each bond purchased at $820.37 by Issuer, Inc., would generate a gain of $129.8 before considering the commission of $7,500. (Book value of $950.24 minus purchase price of $820.37 = $129.87.) If 500 bonds are purchased and a commission of $7,500 is paid, the following journal entry would be made:

1/31/86	Treasury bonds	500,000	
	Discount on bonds payable		24,881
	Cash		417,685
	Extraordinary gain		57,434[a]

[a] ($129.87 × 500) − $7,500 = $57,435 with a $1 rounding error.

Retirement of bonds pursuant to a conversion feature Management has a clear incentive to raise capital at the lowest possible cost. One technique used to accomplish this objective is to include a convertibility feature in a bond contract. **Convertibility** allows a bondholder to convert a bond into a specified number of shares of stock of the issuing company. Exhibit 18–11 includes typical descriptive language used in notes to annual reports to describe the convertibility feature of outstanding bonds.

Although the time period in which conversion can take place is specified in these contracts, a convertibility feature usually allows the bondholder some latitude in choosing the time at which conversion will be most advantageous. The exact point cannot be predicted, because it depends on the interaction of each bondholder's risk-and-return preferences and the estimates of future market conditions for bonds and stocks. Convertible bonds are usually sold such that on the issuance date (1) the

EXHIBIT 18–11

DISCLOSURE OF CONVERTIBILITY FEATURE

ROHR INDUSTRIES INC.

Excerpt from Notes

Note 6–Convertible Subordinated Debentures

The 5¼% debentures due in 1986 are convertible into common stock of the Corporation at $23.04 a share, which price is subject to adjustment under certain circumstances. Annual sinking fund requirements of $1,500,000 are due December 1, 1980, through 1986. In fiscal 1980, the Corporation acquired $483,000 of the debentures through open market purchases to apply to the 1980 sinking fund requirement. The debentures are redeemable at 101.35% declining annually to par in 1985. The debentures are subordinated to all indebtedness for borrowed money. The Corporation is in compliance with the terms of the indenture.

ALEXANDER'S, INC.

Excerpt from Notes

The 5½% Convertible Subordinated Debentures are convertible into shares of the Company's common stock at $32.25 per share, at any time through January 1, 1996. At July 26, 1980, 558,140 shares of common stock were reserved for conversion. The debentures are subordinated to all existing and future "senior indebtedness" and are redeemable by the Company at any time at prices ranging from $102.894 in 1980 to par in 1990 and thereafter. The Company is required to make mandatory annual sinking fund payments sufficient to redeem $1,000,000 in principal amount beginning January 1, 1982. The Company may apply to sinking fund payments $2,000,000 in principal amount of previously reacquired debentures.

selling price of the bond exceeds the aggregate market value of the number of shares into which it may be converted, and (2) the effective interest rate on the bonds is lower than it would have been without the convertibility feature.

Accounting for the issuance of convertible bonds is identical to that for bonds issued without a convertibility feature. Promulgated GAAP require that no portion of the proceeds from the sale of convertible debt be associated with the conversion feature.[6] Premiums and discounts are handled just as in the nonconvertibility case. Retirement of convertible bonds either at maturity or earlier also follows the normal pattern, with extraordinary gains and losses being recorded in the case of an early extinguishment of material amounts.

Upon conversion, however, accountants must choose one of two alternatives. In the first alternative, a gain or loss can be recognized for the difference between the bond-carrying value and the current fair market value of the stock. In this case, the stock is recorded as if it were issued to the open market. For instance, if a $1,000 par value bond with book value of $1,050 is converted into five no-par common shares whose market value per share is currently $220, the following entry would be made:

Bonds payable	1,000	
Premium on bonds payable	50	
Extraordinary loss on conversion of bonds	50	
Common stock (no par)		1,100

In the second alternative, no gain or loss is recorded. The book value of the bond at the date of conversion is merely assigned to the newly issued stock as follows:

Bonds payable	1,000	
Premium on bonds payable	50	
Common stock (no par)		1,050

Promulgated GAAP do not specify which alternative is to be used, and conversion is not considered to be early extinguishment of debt because the bondholder initiates the transaction.

Bonds Issued with Stock Warrants Convertibility features are not the only method used to make a bond issue more attractive to investors and thereby achieve lower financing costs. Bonds are sometimes issued with **stock warrants** attached. These warrants allow the owner to purchase a share of stock in the issuing company for a fixed dollar amount within a specified period of time. Warrants are different from conversion features in that the bond itself is not turned in to acquire the stock. Such warrants are detachable from the bonds and often trade in the open market.

The accountant must decide on the appropriate allocation of the sales price of the bonds and warrants combined. Accountants are guided in their decision by **APB Opinion No. 14,** which states that any conversion feature that is separable from the debt security should have a value assigned to it on the basis of the relative fair values of the debt and the detachable warrant at the time of issuance.[7] The value assigned

---

[6] *Accounting Principles Board Opinion No. 14,* "Accounting for Convertible Debt and Debt Issued with Stock Purchase Warrants" (New York: AICPA, March 1969), par. 10.

[7] Ibid., pars. 14 and 15.

EXHIBIT
18–12

to a detachable warrant is credited to a paid-in capital account such as Warrants Outstanding. This Warrants Outstanding account will remain on the books until exercised or until the time limitation runs out. Exhibit 18–12 shows how outstanding warrants related to debt were disclosed in a published annual report.

Assume that a $1,000 face value bond is issued at $1,080 and that it has two detachable warrants, each of which allows the holder to purchase one share of common stock at $220 anytime during the next 5 years. The common stock is selling for $180 per share at date of issuance; the warrants are selling for $25 each; and the bonds without warrants are selling for $1,020. The following allocations would be made:

	INDIVIDUAL MARKET VALUE	PROPORTION	ALLOCATION OF SELLING PRICE
Bonds	$1,020	$1,020/$1,070 = .953	(.953)($1,080) = $1,029.24
Warrants	50	$ 50/$1,070 = .047	(.047)($1,080) = $ 50.76
	$1,070		$1,080.00

The following journal entry would record this transaction:

Date of issuance	Cash	1,080.00	
	Bonds payable		1,000.00
	Premium on bonds payable		29.24
	Warrants outstanding		50.76

Assume further that one warrant was exercised when the stock price reached its highest point in the fourth year after issuance, and the other was allowed to lapse at the end of the fifth year:

Date of exercise	Cash	220.00	
	Warrants outstanding	25.38	
	Common stock—par of $50		50.00
	Additional paid-in capital		195.38
Date of expiration	Warrants outstanding	25.38	
	Additional paid-in capital		25.38

Several points deserve emphasis. First, the initial selling price is allocated between a liability account and an owners' equity account. A gain or a loss is never recorded on exercise or expiration of the warrant. The expired warrants simply create a credit to owners' equity, as illustrated above. The market price at the exercise date does not affect the cash flow, although usually the market price is greater than, or equal to, the exercise price before exercise takes place.

Serial Bonds Bonds are contracts between debtors and creditors and, as such, can take on a wide variety of contractual terms. To this point, we have discussed bond issues with one maturity date. **Serial bonds,** as the name implies, have several sequential maturity dates usually separated by uniform intervals of time. For instance, a bond contract may call for one-third of the bonds outstanding to be retired every 2 years starting at the end of year 20. It would not be appropriate to call such an issue a 20-year bond. It would be, for all practical purposes, three different bond issues—one for 20 years, one for 22 years, and one for 24 years.

Accounting for serial bonds is identical to accounting for ordinary single maturity bonds. More computations and amortization schedules are needed, however. If the serial bonds described above have a 10 percent nominal interest rate and $1,000,000 in total face value for each maturity date and are issued to yield 12 percent, the following computations would be necessary to determine selling price:

First series due in 20 years
$(P/A, 20, .12)(\$100,000) + (P/F, 20, .12)(\$1,000,000) =$
$\qquad (7.4694)(\$100,000) + (.1037)(\$1,000,000) =$
$\qquad\qquad \$746,940 + \$103,700 = \$\ \ 850,640$

Second series due in 22 years
$(P/A, 22, .12)(\$100,000) + (P/F, 22, .12)(\$1,000,000) =$
$\qquad (7.6446)(\$100,000) + (.0826)(\$1,000,000) =$
$\qquad\qquad \$764,460 + \$82,600 = \$\ \ 847,060$

Third series due in 24 years
$(P/A, 24, .12)(\$100,000) + (P/F, 24, .12)(\$1,000,000) =$
$\qquad (7.7843)(\$100,000) + (.0659)(\$1,000,000) =$
$\qquad\qquad \$778,430 + \$65,900 = \$\ \ 844,330$

Total selling price $\qquad\qquad\qquad\qquad\qquad\quad \underline{\underline{\$2,542,030}}$

A separate amortization schedule is constructed for each, starting with beginning book values of $850,640, $847,060 and $844,330, respectively. Combined journal entries would be appropriate to accumulate the interest expense and discount amortization for each period. At the end of year 20, the first issue matures, and, of course, bonds payable of $1,000,000 would be eliminated by a payment of cash for the maturity value. In years 21 and 22, interest and amortization entries would be made for the two remaining issues. In years 23 and 24, only the last issue remains to be accounted for.

When serial bonds are sold for a lump sum to an underwriter, the individual effective interest rate for each maturity group may not be known. In such circumstances a variation on the straight-line amortization of premium or discount may be used. For instance, assume that three $10,000 bonds are sold for $31,200 on 1/1/84 with maturities on 12/31/88, 12/31/89, and 12/31/90. The following schedule shows how the premium could be assigned.

	(1)	(2)	(3)
	FACE VALUE OUTSTANDING	**RATIO OF FACE VALUE OUTSTANDING TO TOTAL OF COLUMN 1**	**PREMIUM AMORTIZATION**[a]
1984	$ 30,000	30/180	$ 200
1985	30,000	30/180	200
1986	30,000	30/180	200
1987	30,000	30/180	200
1988	30,000	30/180	200
1989	20,000	20/180	133
1990	10,000	10/180	67
Total	$180,000	180/180	$1,200

[a] Column 2 ratio × Total Premium.

Serial bonds, therefore, entail no unique concepts or rules. They are treated according to their contractual terms. For the most part, the accounting is not unique, but special disclosure is often necessary to explain the nature of the bond obligations and the timing of the maturities. Exhibit 18–13 gives two examples of the disclosure of serial bonds in published annual reports.

EXHIBIT 18–13

DISCLOSURE OF SERIAL BONDS

MOORE McCORMACK RESOURCES, INC.
Excerpt from Notes

Note 8:
Long-Term Debt
(Dollars in Thousands)

	DECEMBER 31,	
	1980	1979
U.S. government-guaranteed ship financing bonds, secured by first preferred ship mortgages on two Great Lakes vessels, consisting of $4,335 of serial bonds (at rates from 7.95 percent to 8.15 percent and repayable annually through 1983) and $62,672 of sinking fund bonds (at a rate of 8.875 percent and subject to increasing semiannual redemptions beginning in 1984 and ending in 2001)	$67,007	$68,227

ATWOOD OCEANICS, INC.
Excerpt from Notes

	1980	1979
Financing bonds, secured by drilling vessels: 7.90–8.25 percent serial bonds due in semiannual installments	$1,946,000	$3,694,000

The serial bonds outstanding as of September 30, 1980, are due in two semiannual installments of $874,000 in 1981 and two semiannual installments of $99,000 in 1982. The sinking fund bonds require mandatory semiannual sinking fund payments commencing February 15, 1982. As long as the government guarantees are in effect, the Company must obtain advance permission before disposing of any vessels or entering into certain types of business mergers or consolidations. Further, the Company must deposit a portion of the income from secured drilling vessels into a Reserve Fund account if it does not maintain a specified (1) ratio of working capital to annual lease hire and other lease obligations, (2) ratio of long-term debt to net worth, and (3) net worth. At September 30, 1980, the Company was in compliance with the specified requirements; therefore, was not subject to the reserve fund deposit.

Sinking
Fund Bonds
and Bonds
with Other
Restrictive
Terms

As already mentioned in this chapter, bond contracts can have an almost infinite variety of terms. Debtors want to borrow money at the lowest possible interest rates and with the fewest imposed restrictions. Creditors, however, want the highest possible interest rate and assurance of payments. The debtor will often agree to certain terms (**covenants**) in the contract that are advantageous to the creditors in order to keep the interest rates low.

One contractual term that may accomplish this is the mandatory payment into a sinking fund. **Sinking fund bonds** call for specific periodic payments into a fund that will ultimately be used to pay off the maturity value. This, in essence, converts a one-time maturity payment into a series of payments. The payments are not to creditors, but to a fund. Assume that a 5-year, $10,000,000 maturity value bond issue calls for five year-end payments into a sinking fund. The payments are to be computed as an annuity whose future value will be $10,000,000 at the maturity date. Also assume that a trustee is paid 3 percent of the beginning balance in the fund as a commission. How much must be paid into the fund each year? The answer depends on the return expected on fund investments net of the trustee's commissions. Such a computation can be made by means of the inverse of Table H–4 (Appendix H) factors for our example. If we assume a 13 percent expected return reduced to 10 percent by the trustee's commission:

$$[1/(F/A, 5, .10)]\$10,000,000 = \$1,637,975$$

The bond contract, therefore, would call for five year-end payments of $1,637,975 each. These payments become a legal obligation of the debtor, and any missed payments may give the creditors the right to take legal action to collect all amounts owed to them.

The Sinking Fund account that is debited for each payment amount is also increased by the return earned on the investments purchased with fund assets. Trustee fees are subtracted from the earnings of the fund. If the fund actually earns an 8 percent return in the second year and subsequent years, the following summary journal entries would be necessary:

12/31/1	Sinking fund	1,637,975	
	Cash		1,637,975
12/31/2	Sinking fund	1,719,874	
	Sinking fund income		81,899
	Cash		1,637,975
	[(8% − 3%)($1,637,975) = $81,899]		
12/31/3	Sinking fund	1,805,867	
	Sinking fund income		167,892
	Cash		1,637,975
	[(8% − 3%)($3,357,849) = $167,892]		
12/31/4	Sinking fund	1,896,161	
	Sinking fund income		258,186
	Cash		1,637,975
	[(8% − 3%)($5,163,716) = $258,186]		
12/31/5	Sinking fund	1,990,969	
	Sinking fund income		352,994
	Cash		1,637,975
	[(8% − 3%)($7,059,877) = $352,994]		
12/31/5	Cash	9,050,040	
	Sinking fund		9,050,846
	Bonds payable	10,000,000	
	Cash		10,000,000

EXHIBIT
18–14

DISCLOSURE OF DEBT COVENANTS

ATWOOD OCEANICS, INC.
Excerpt from Notes

Notes payable to banks and a leasing corporation

In October 1980, the Company received a commitment from a bank group to provide the Company a secured Revolving Credit, Term Loan facility in the principal amount of $48,600,000. This facility will be used to refinance the existing notes payable to banks ($20,000,000 as of November 12, 1980), to finance construction of a submersible rig and to provide for a standby letter of credit required to finance the purchase of a drilling tender. The Revolving Credit will be converted to a term loan at September 30, 1983, and will be repaid in twenty equal quarterly installments commencing December 31, 1983.

Under the most restrictive terms of the commitment agreement, the Company has agreed, among other things, to maintain defined (1) working capital of $5,000,000 and (2) net worth of at least $30,000,000. The Company is also restricted, among other things, (1) from paying cash dividends in excess of ten percent of aggregate consolidated income for any period from September 30, 1979, and (2) from incurring new debt other than to reduce bank debt until receipt of a commitment for long-term financing for the submersible rig which is acceptable to the banks or until the outstanding commitment under the loan facility has been reduced to $28,000,000 or less and, if after giving effect to any additional debt, the ratio of total debt to net worth does not exceed 2 to 1.

At September 30, 1980, the note payable to a leasing corporation required monthly principal payments of $95,000 increasing monthly with the final installment due in July, 1983.

TANNETICS, INC.
Excerpt from Notes

The Company is required to provide for the mandatory redemption of $1,111,000 aggregate principal amount of the 10½% Debentures on December 1, 1983, and on each December 1, thereafter through December 1, 1991, to retire 80% of the issue one year prior to maturity, through the operation of a sinking fund.

The indenture under which the 10½% Debentures were issued provides, among other things, for restrictions upon incurring additional indebtedness, creation of encumbrances, sale of substantial amount of assets, making certain investments, payments of cash dividends and maintenance of working capital. Approximately $2,472,000 of retained earnings as of July 31, 1979, is available under the terms of indenture, for payment of cash dividends.

GELCO CORPORATION
Excerpt from Notes

Note 7:
G. Subordinated Debentures:
Subordinated debentures are as follows (dollars in thousands):

	1980	1979
9¾%, due 1993	$ 16,000	$16,000
14⅝% due 1999	85,000	
	$101,000	
Unamortized discount	(611)	
	$100,389	$16,000

The 9¾ percent debentures were issued in July 1978 and require annual payments of $2,000,000 from July 1986 to 1993. Interest is payable semiannually. The debentures may be redeemed in whole or in part at 109.05 percent of principal in 1980, decreasing to 100 percent in 1993. The 14⅝ percent debentures were issued in December 1979 and require annual sinking fund payments of $6,375,000 from December 1989 to 1998. Interest is payable semiannually. The debentures may be redeemed in whole or part at 106.9375.

Note that the sinking fund was short by $949,154 because it earned 5 percent after commissions rather than 10 percent. This shortfall must be made up by the debtor. Another important point is that ordinary bonds payable accounting and disclosure are unaffected by sinking fund accounting and disclosure except that bonds payable amounts that are to be paid off within the next accounting period with sinking fund assets need not be reclassified as short-term liabilities to the extent of the anticipated sinking fund balance at maturity.

Other covenants may also require special accounting. In some cases, in an attempt to limit dividends, the bond contract calls for appropriation of retained earnings. (This method of segregating retained earnings will be discussed in Chapter 21.) In other cases, the bond or note contract calls for a certain liquidity status for the debtor. If for instance, working capital falls below a specified amount, the creditors may demand immediate payment. These types of restrictive covenants are disclosed in notes to financial statements (see Exhibit 18–14).

DISCLOSURE RULES FOR CERTAIN LONG-TERM OBLIGATIONS

The preceding sections have analyzed the principles and techniques covering many noncurrent obligations. As an indication of the importance to decision makers of an entity's future commitments, the FASB has specified footnote disclosure for certain long-term obligations. **FASB Statement No.** 47 specifies disclosure requirements for two classes of long-term obligations: (1) maturities and sinking fund requirements of all long-term borrowings and redemption requirements of redeemable preferred stock; and (2) required payments pursuant to an entity's unconditional purchase obligations related to project financing where the entity is obliged to either purchase certain quantities of products or services at fixed prices or make specified payments related to a supplier's facilities.[8]

Disclosure of Long-term Borrowings and Mandatory Redemptions

FASB Statement No. 47 requires that the next 5 years' payments called for by contracts for long-term borrowings including sinking fund requirements be disclosed. The same is true of mandatory preferred stock redemptions. Exhibit 18–15 shows the FASB's suggested disclosure format for a company that has (1) a debenture calling for $10,000,000 of annual sinking payments in 19X2, 19X3, and 19X4, $15,000,000 in 19X5, and $20,000,000 in 19X6; (2) a $50,000,000 note due in 19X5; and (3) a $32,000,000 preferred stock issue calling for sinking fund payments of $1,500,000 per year until retirement.

Disclosure of Unconditional Purchase Obligations

As we discussed in Chapter 15 on leases, there are many ways of acquiring the use of plant and equipment. In some cases, the asset and obligation are recorded on the entity's books; in others, the asset and obligation are not capitalized and are merely discussed in notes. **FASB Statement No.** 47 does not add new measurement rules (rules related to the capitalization and therefore booking of money amounts). It

---

[8] *Statement of Financial Accounting Standards No. 47,* "Disclosure of Long-Term Obligations" (Stamford, CT: FASB, March 1981).

EXHIBIT
18–15

DISCLOSURE OF LONG-TERM BORROWINGS AND MANDATORY PREFERRED STOCK REDEMPTIONS

Illustrative Footnote[a]

Maturities and sinking fund requirements on long-term debt and sinking fund requirements on preferred stock subject to mandatory redemption are as follows (in thousands):

	LONG-TERM DEBT	PREFERRED STOCK
19X2	$10,000	$1,500
19X3	10,000	1,500
19X4	10,000	1,500
19X5	65,000	1,500
19X6	20,000	1,500

[a] *Statement of Financial Accounting Standards No. 47,* "Disclosure of Long-Term Obligation," Appendix C.

does, however, prescribe footnote disclosures for certain interesting financing arrangements. The kinds of arrangements covered are termed **unconditional purchase obligations,** and their nature can perhaps best be described by an example.[9] Chemical Manufactures, Inc. (CMI), builds a plant to process a chemical under an agreement with National Chemical Company (NCC) in which NCC agrees to submit 100,000 tons for processing for each of 20 years. NCC agrees to pay a fixed price per ton for processing and agrees to advance funds to CMI if CMI cannot meet its financial obligations. In such a case, the FASB requires the 5-year disclosure pattern shown in Exhibit 18–16. Note that **FASB Statement No. 47** *recommends but does not require* the interest and present-value disclosures at the bottom of the schedule.

TROUBLED DEBT RESTRUCTURING

Not all debt is paid off according to the original contractual terms. In some cases, the debtor's financial status deteriorates to a point that necessitates either a change in terms or the forcing of a reduced payment (or payments) involving a monetary loss to the creditor. In such cases, it may be deemed advantageous for the creditor to change the terms of the contract in order to avoid or reduce the loss. This is called **troubled debt restructuring** and is different from **refinancing,** which is usually the term used for an ordinary extension of debt with no loss contemplated. We shall first survey the accounting for troubled debt restructuring as if no promulgated GAAP related to this issue, and we shall then analyze how **FASB Statement No. 15** guides accounting practice.[10]

Assume that Bad News, Inc., has a note due to First Bank on December 31, 1984. (The note is a 1-year note initiated on January 1, 1984, with principal of $10,000 and an interest rate of 10 percent. The total maturity amount is therefore

[9] Adapted from *Statement of Financial Accounting Standards No. 47,* "Disclosure of Long-Term Obligation," Appendix C.

[10] *Statement of Financial Accounting Standards No. 15,* "Accounting by Debtors and Creditors for Troubled Debt Restructuring" (Stamford, CT: FASB, June 1977).

EXHIBIT
18–16

DISCLOSURE OF UNCONDITIONAL PURCHASE OBLIGATIONS

Illustrative Footnote[a]

To secure access to facilities to process chemical X, the company (NCC) has signed a processing agreement with a chemical company allowing NCC to submit 100,000 tons for processing annually for 20 years. Under the terms of the agreement, NCC may be required to advance funds against future processing charges if the chemical company is unable to meet its financial obligations. The aggregate amount of required payments at December 31, 19X1, is as follows (in thousands):

19X2	$ 10,000
19X3	10,000
19X4	9,000
19X5	8,000
19X6	8,000
Later years	100,000
Total	$145,000
Less: Amount representing interest	(45,000)
Total at present value	$100,000

In addition, the company is required to pay a proportional share of the variable operating expenses of the plant. The company's total processing charges under the agreement in each of the past 3 years have been $12 million.

[a] *Statement of Financial Accounting Standards No. 47*, "Disclosure of Long-Term Obligation," Appendix C.

$11,000.) Bad News asks the bank to extend the note for 4 years, at which time it feels it could pay $12,000. First Bank decides that it would be better to comply with the request than to force payment and, therefore, revises the contract to the terms requested. 12 percent annual interest is an appropriate interest rate for such a loan. Does this mean that First Bank has a loss and that Bad News has a gain? The book value of the note on both parties' books is $11,000 ($10,000 principal plus $1,000 accrued interest) on December 31, 1984. The present value of the $12,000 payment 4 years hence is only $7,626, computed as follows:

$$(P/F, 4, .12)\$12,000 =$$
$$(.6355)\$12,000 = \$7,626$$

If no promulgated rule existed to govern accounting for this situation, the following journal entries would be made:

	DEBTOR'S BOOKS				CREDITOR'S BOOKS		
	ACCOUNT	**DEBIT**	**CREDIT**		**ACCOUNT**	**DEBIT**	**CREDIT**
12/31/84	Notes payable (old)	11,000			Notes receivable (new)	7,626	
	Gain		3,374		Loss	3,374	
	Notes payable (new)		7,626		Notes receivable (old)		11,000
End of years 1985–1988	Interest expense	XX			Notes receivable	XX	
	Notes payable		XX		Interest revenue		XX
	(.12 × beginning notes payable)				(.12 × Beginning notes receivable)		
12/31/88	Notes payable	12,000			Cash	12,000	
	Cash		12,000		Notes receivable		12,000

FASB Statement No. 15 does not allow the gains and losses to be recognized in the above situation. In essence, as long as the total cash to be paid at the new maturity exceeds the book value of the note on December 31, 1984, no book value change is made because of the change in terms. The effect of the change in terms is handled prospectively through a reduced interest factor that is computed by equating the future value to the present book value. In this case, an interest factor of only .021989 would be used:

$$\$11,000\ (1 + i)^4 = \$12,000$$
$$(1 + i)^4 = \frac{\$12,000}{\$11,000}$$
$$1 + i = \sqrt[4]{1.0909}$$
$$1 + i = 1.021989$$
$$i = 1.021989 - 1$$
$$i = .021989$$

The comparative amortization schedules for **FASB Statement No. 15** requirements and "conceptually correct" accounting are as follows:

	FASB STATEMENT NO. 15				"CONCEPTUALLY CORRECT"		
DATE	PAYMENT	INTEREST	BOOK VALUE	DATE	PAYMENT	INTEREST	BOOK VALUE
12/31/84	—	—	$11,000.00	12/31/84	—	—	$ 7,626.00
12/31/85	—	$241.88	11,241.88	12/31/85	—	$ 915.12	8,541.12
12/31/86	—	247.20	11,489.08	12/31/86	—	1,024.93	9,566.05
12/31/87	—	252.63	11,741.71	12/31/87	—	1,147.93	10,713.98
12/31/88	—	258.29[a]	12,000.00	12/31/88	—	1,286.02[a]	12,000.00
12/31/88	$12,000	—	—	12/31/88	$12,000	—	—

[a] Rounded.

FASB Statement No. 15, therefore, obscures the fact that such restructuring usually involves economic gains and losses. In our example, no journal entry would be necessary as of the date of restructuring. The debt would of course be classified as noncurrent for the three balance sheet dates starting December 31, 1984.

The basic philosophy of **FASB Statement No. 15** is that no recognition of gains and losses on troubled debt restructuring is allowed if the *total cash flow* anticipated equals or exceeds the book value of the obligation at the date of restructuring. **Total cash flow** is the absolute amount to be received, *not* the discounted (present value) amount. In our example, the book value on December 31, 1984, was $11,000, and the total cash flow was $12,000; therefore, no gain or loss was recorded. However, gains (for debtors) and losses (for creditors) must be recognized if the restructuring results in total cash flows that are *less than* the book value of the debt at the date of restructuring. If First Bank had agreed to accept a promise to pay $10,500 on December 31, 1985, one year after the original note was due, it would have required recognition of a $500 gain for Bad News and a $500 loss for First Bank at December 31, 1984, which would be recorded as follows:

	DEBTOR'S BOOKS				CREDITOR'S BOOKS		
DATE	ACCOUNT	DEBIT	CREDIT		ACCOUNT	DEBIT	CREDIT
12/31/84	Notes payable (old)	11,000			Notes receivable (new)	10,500	
	Gain		500		Loss	500	
	Notes payable		10,500		Notes receivable		11,000

In cases where the total cash flow is less than the book value of the debt at re structuring, a gain or loss must be recognized, and the restructured loan is treated as interest-free debt by both debtor and creditor. No interest expense or interest income is recorded thereafter by either party.

FASB Statement No. 15 distinguishes between the possible kinds of debt restructuring. First, the rules are applicable only in those cases where concessions are made to the debtor. Within that class of events, two means of restructuring are discussed: (1) continuation of the debt with modified terms and (2) settlement of the debt at less than the recorded amount. We have already seen an example of the required accounting for the first case. In the second case, which involves the payment of the debt in cash, assets, or securities, gain and loss recognition is allowed. For instance, if A owes B $15,000 on June 1, 1985, and transfers a parcel of land with book value of $20,000 and fair value of $10,000 in payments pursuant to a troubled debt restructuring, the following journal entries are allowed under **FASB Statement No. 15**:

	A (DEBTOR)				B (CREDITOR)		
6/1/85	Notes payable	15,000		6/1/85	Land	10,000	
	Ordinary loss	10,000			Ordinary loss	5,000	
	Land		20,000		Notes receivable		15,000
	Extraordinary gain		5,000				

A's gain is extraordinary because of the **FASB Statement No. 4** rule on the retirement of debt.[11] A's loss of $10,000 reflects the difference between book value and fair value and A's gain reflects the fact that land worth $10,000 retired a $15,000 debt.

Stock issuance on payment of debt in transactions covered by **FASB Statement No. 15** would also result in gain and loss recognition. In the above case, if B accepted 500 shares of $10 par value stock with a current fair value of $14, the following journal entries would be appropriate:

	A (DEBTOR)				B (CREDITOR)		
6/1/85	Notes payable	15,000		6/1/85	Stock	7,000	
	Common stock— par		5,000		Ordinary loss	8,000	
	Additional paid-in capital		2,000		Notes receivable		15,000
	Extraordinary gain		8,000				

[11] *Statement of Financial Accounting Standards No. 4*, "Reporting Gains and Losses from Extinguishment of Debt."

FIGURE
18–1
Summary of
provision of
*FASB Statement
No. 15*

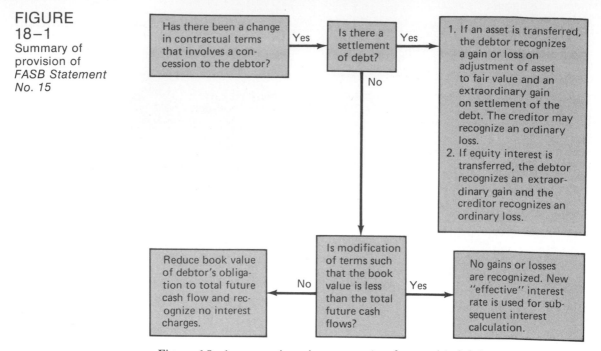

Figure 18–1 summarizes the accounting for troubled debt restructuring under **FASB Statement No. 15.**

FASB Statement No. 15 calls for specific footnote disclosures on the part of debtors and creditors who have been involved in troubled debt restructuring as follows:

DEBTORS	CREDITORS
1. For each restructuring, disclose the principal changes in terms and/or the major features of settlement.	1. For modified receivables, disclose by major category (a) the aggregate recorded investment, (b) the gross interest that would have been earned given no restructuring, and (c) the interest income recognized on restructured debt.
2. For all the restructurings, disclose the aggregate gains, tax effects, and net of tax-per-share effects.	2. If commitments exist to lend more to debtors whose debt was restructured and remains outstanding, disclose the total amount of commitments.
3. For all transfers of assets, disclose the aggregate net gain or loss.	

**EXHIBIT
18–17**

DISCLOSURE OF RESTRUCTURED DEBT

CERTRON CORPORATION
Excerpt from Notes

Note 4—1978 Restructure of debt:

On October 31, 1978, the Company obtained a new source of financing and restructured its bank debt by exchanging cash, preferred stock and warrants to purchase common stock in satisfaction of all existing bank debt.

In accordance with *Financial Accounting Standards Board Statement No. 15*, the Company estimated the fair value of the preferred stock and warrants and recorded an extraordinary gain on restructure of debt of $3,497,000.

Exhibit 18–17 shows how Certron Corporation disclosed a restructuring of debt in a published annual report.

FUNDS FLOW EFFECTS

Noncurrent notes and bonds are major sources of funds for many enterprises. The balance between long-term debt and owner's equity is considered a key indicator of an entity's financial flexibility, because it may signal the potential for future long-term borrowing. Managing the funds flow from and to creditors has taken on added importance in an era of high interest rates and depressed equity markets.

Working capital is decreased by the reclassification of long-term debt to short-term. When a sinking fund sufficient to liquidate the debt has been accumulated, no reclassification is required and therefore no working capital is consumed.

The difference between bond interest expense and nominal bond interest amounts, the amount of amortization of bond discount and premium, requires special treatment on a funds statement. Net income is reduced by interest expense, including the amortization of any discounts and premiums that are nonfund balances. For instance, interest expense for a period may be $102,000 including cash flow of $100,000 and discount amortization of $2,000. The $2,000 would have to be added back to net income to arrive at "funds from operations." The same logic holds for premium amortization, which calls for a subtraction from net income.

Interest accruals at period end reduce working capital but have no effect on cash. Payments of previous period's interest accruals have the opposite impact on working capital and cash.

SUMMARY   Business entities have obligations to many parties. Generally, if an obligation is such that a money amount and a payment date can be assigned to it with reasonable confidence, accountants will record a liability in the accounting records. All liabilities have the common attribute of being obligations that are expected to be liquidated by a transfer of something of value at a future point (or points) in time. The payment can take many forms, but one basic guiding principle underlies the measurement of that anticipated transfer: The time value of money is to be reflected in the measurement of liabilities.

In the preceding two chapters we saw that when accountants measure liabilities, they normally ignore interest factors for such short-term debt as accounts payable and taxes payable. Interest factors, however, are considered when measuring most other liabilities, especially those involving formal debt instruments.

Another guideline for liability accounting is that the substance of the contractual terms that define the relationship between the debtor and the creditor must be reflected. For instance, many of the accounting conventions that exist concerning bonds have evolved because of the unique payment schedules that distinguish bond contracts. Accounting reflects certain aspects of the formal contractual terms. At the same time, the difference between effective yield and nominal interest is not ignored.

Although all long-term liabilities are quite similar, accounting conventions and promulgated GAAP may create the impression of differences in basic approach. For instance, a simple note payable is accounted for in much the same way as is a serial bond. The accounting convention of premium and discount amortization makes the two cases seem different when, in fact, the same fundamental measurement and disclosure principles apply to both. As we have seen throughout this text, promulgated GAAP sometimes call for a departure from conceptual principles. This is certainly the case in accounting for restructured debt where "real" gains and losses are ignored. In defense of the rule makers, there are usually economic and social reasons for such departures. This merely demonstrates that accounting rule making is part of a social mechanism. Policy makers must respond to many different pressures because accounting is an important function in our society, and accounting policy affects many constituencies.

QUESTIONS

Q18-1 What distinguishes a liability involving a note from other liabilities such as accounts payable and wages payable?

Q18-2 Three of the columns from a typical note payable amortization schedule might have the following headings: "Cash Payment," "Interest Expense," and "Carrying Value." Describe how the money amount in each column is computed.

Q18-3 How do mortgage notes differ from notes without mortgages, and how do such differences affect accounting disclosure?

Q18-4 Differentiate the *principal amounts* of notes payable from the *face values* of bonds payable.

Q18-5 When would a bond probably sell at a discount? At a premium?

Q18-6 In a typical amortization schedule for a bond issue, what is the relationship between total interest expense and the net cash flows for the life of the bond?

Q18-7 Why is debt issue cost deferred and amortized instead of being treated as a period expense?

Q18-8 How is an "economic gain" on early retirement of debt shown on the income statement?

Q18-9 Name three methods of extinguishing bond debt before retirement, and briefly describe the accounting for gains and losses on such transactions.

Q18-10 What are the major differences and similarities between sinking fund bonds and serial bonds?

Q18-11 What is the major conceptual difficulty with *FASB Statement No. 15*'s prescriptions concerning accounting for troubled debt restructuring? Why do you think such a rule was promulgated?

CASES

C18-1 Royal Hawaiian Air Freight is negotiating for the purchase of five used airplanes. The alternative financing arrangements include the issuance of (1) debentures at an effective interest rate of 15 percent, (2) notes payable with the equipment used as collateral at $13^1/2$ percent, and (3) preferred stock with a cumulative dividend rate of 18 percent. The effective rate is expected to be 18 percent for the sale of preferred stock.

REQUIRED Explain why the interest rates differ across alternatives.

C18-2 Leslie Books has a 20-year bond issue outstanding with the following disclosure on its December 31, 1983, balance sheet and notes:

Noncurrent Liabilities
  Bonds Payable (Note 6) $1,118,602

Note 6
Long-term debt. The company issued 10,000, $100, 18 percent, bonds on June 30, 1983, for an effective yield of 16 percent. There were no charges to income for 1983 because the first interest payment is scheduled for July 1, 1984.

REQUIRED As Leslie's auditor, write a memorandum explaining why the accounting treatment described is wrong and indicate what it should be.

C18–3 Country Cooking, Inc., has an aggressive financial management team that is continually seeking cost savings. In the past, substantial savings have resulted from improved credit and collection procedures and the taking of all discounts offered by suppliers. The cost of borrowed funds is now being investigated. The company has two long-term debts outstanding on July 1, 1983: (1) a 14 percent, annual interest bond that matures on June 30, 1988, was initially issued at par, and is being carried at $10,000,000; and (2) a non-interest-bearing note payable to a bank that has a maturity amount of $2,832,000, a maturity date of June 30, 1985, and book value of $2,000,000 on July 1, 1983.

Both debt instruments contain clauses that allow for retirement. The bond can be called on July 1, 1983, at 102 percent of par value, and the note can be paid off on July 1, 1983, by payment of $2,000,000 plus a 2 percent of maturity value penalty. The company can currently borrow funds at an effective rate of 16 percent by means of 5-year non-interest-bearing mortgage notes.

REQUIRED As the company's chief financial analyst, describe the analysis necessary to determine whether retirement is cost effective.

C18–4 Farm Implements Corporation is in deep financial trouble and is now negotiating with its major creditor, the National Bank, for relief. Farm has suggested that it could avert bankruptcy by converting the $1,850,000 currently maturing note to an annuity obligation of $195,327 per year for 10 years, the first installment of which would be paid 1 year hence.

REQUIRED Explain to the bank and to the corporation what the accounting implications of such a restructuring would be.

C18–5 Kinner Corporation has serial bonds that will come due over the next 5 years. In addition, Kinner has a sinking fund into which a fixed amount has been deposited over the life of the bond issue. The major assumption governing the amount of the sinking fund deposits was that the fund would earn the same effective interest rate as that implicit in the initial selling price of the bond.

REQUIRED Discuss the reasons why the fund may be "short" or "over" at the maturity dates, and give the accounting treatment that will be necessary under each scenario.

C18–6 On April 1, 1984, C. E. Smith Company issued 20-year bonds having a par value of $15,000,000 at a significant discount. The company has a December 31 year-end and pays interest on the bonds on March 1 and September 1 of each year. The president of the company is concerned about the amount of the current year's net income and requests an analysis of the impact that the following accounting alternatives will have on net income:

1. Amortization of discount
   a. Effective interest method
   b. Straight-line method
2. Issue cost
   a. Immediate write-off
   b. Straight-line amortization
   c. Effective interest amortization
3. Interest accrual
   a. Allocation of interest expense to the current year according to the time the bonds are outstanding
   b. Charging interest expense on the basis of cash payments

REQUIRED What kind of impact would each alternative have on net income? Indicate the GAAP for each alternative.

C18–7 Consider the following statement: *"FASB Statement No. 15 is a significant break with good accounting judgment. It allows losses and gains to go unrecorded and results in a significant misstatement of balance sheet accounts. It is an indication of the dangers inherent in allowing input from interested parties to influence accounting policy."*

REQUIRED Evaluate this statement in terms of the conceptual question involved, that is, does *FASB Statement No. 15* violate the conceptual structure of accounting? Also, discuss the societal and political pressures that affect accounting policy formation, and give your appraisal of what legitimate level of influence the affected parties should have on policy decisions.

C18–8 (CPA ADAPTED) The appropriate method of amortizing a premium or discount on the issuance of bonds is the effective interest method.

REQUIRED

1. What is the effective interest method of amortization, and how is it different from and similar to the straight-line method of amortization?
2. How is amortization computed using the effective interest method, and why and how do amounts obtained using the effective interest method differ from amounts computed under the straight-line method?

C18–9 (CPA ADAPTED) Gains or losses from the early extinguishment of debt that is refunded can theoretically be accounted for in the following ways:

1. Amortized over the remaining life of the old debt
2. Amortized over the life of the new debt issue
3. Recognized in the period of extinguishment

REQUIRED

1. Discuss the supporting arguments for each of the three theoretical methods of accounting for gains and losses from the early extinguishment of debt.
2. Which of the three methods is generally accepted, and how should the appropriate amount of gain or loss be shown in a company's financial statements?

C18–10 (CPA ADAPTED) One way for a corporation to accomplish long-term financing is through the issuance of long-term debt instruments in the form of bonds.

REQUIRED

1. Describe how you would account for the proceeds from bonds issued with detachable stock purchase warrants.
2. Contrast a serial bond with a term (straight) bond.
3. For a 5-year (nonserial) bond issued at a premium, why would the amortization in the first year of the life of the bond differ using the interest method of amortization instead of the straight-line method? In your discussion, explain whether the amount of amortization in the first year of the life of the bond would be higher or lower using the interest method instead of the straight-line method.
4. When a bond issue is sold between interest dates at a discount, what journal entry is made and how is the subsequent amortization of bond discount affected? In your discussion, explain how the amounts of each debit and credit are determined.
5. Describe how you would account for and classify the gain or loss from the reacquisition of a long-term bond prior to its maturity.

EXERCISES

E18–1 On August 1, 1983, a company signs a non-interest-bearing note that calls for one payment of $120,000 on August 1, 1984.

REQUIRED Compute the amount of cash received if the effective annual interest rate for the loan is 14 percent.

E18-2 Your company has two alternative methods of financing an equipment purchase:

1. Borrow $28,000 to be paid back in three equal year-end annual installments that include interest and principal
2. Borrow $28,000 to be paid back by means of one lump-sum payment at the end of 3 years

REQUIRED Construct an amortization schedule for each alternative assuming a 16 percent effective annual interest rate for both, and compare the cash flows. Which is more desirable?

E18-3 On June 30, 1984, Bali Industries recorded the following journal entry upon issuance of 1,000, 10-year, 15 percent bonds having a face value of $100:

Cash	86,522	
Bonds payable		86,522

REQUIRED How should these bonds be presented on a balance sheet at the date of issuance? What can be said about the relationship of the effective and the nominal interest rates?

E18-4 Show the proper journal entry for the issuance of $1,000,000 face value, 13 percent bonds issued at par 3 months after their initial issuance date.

E18-5 What income statement effect would result in the year of issuance from the incurrence of $700,000 of issue cost on a 20-year bond that was sold at an effective interest rate of 18 percent midway in the fiscal year? Show the computations.

E18-6 On November 30, 1984, Brandywine Produce has a bond issue outstanding that has a face value and a book value of $1,800,000. Pursuant to a call provision, the company buys back all of the bonds at $104^{1}/_{2}$ percent of face value.

REQUIRED

1. Ignoring interest payments, record the appropriate journal entry for the retirement of the bonds.
2. What journal entry would be necessary if unpaid interest was $126,000 at the date of retirement?

E18-7 On December 31, 1984, Reliance Group, Inc., has 10,000, $1,000 face value bonds outstanding with a book value of $998 per bond. Each bond is convertible into 50 shares of no-par common stock that is currently selling for $22 per share.

REQUIRED Assuming all interest has been paid to date, show the different journal entries possible to record the conversion of one bond.

E18-8 A company has a bond issue outstanding that requires annual year-end sinking fund contributions of $500,000.

REQUIRED What would the balance in the sinking fund be at the end of 3 years if the fund earned an average of 11 percent on the beginning fund balance? Show the appropriate journal entries to record the sinking fund activity for the 3 years.

E18-9 (CPA ADAPTED) On January 1, 1979, the Hopewell Company sold its 8 percent bonds that had a face value of $1,000,000. Interest is payable on December 31 of each year. The bonds mature on January 1, 1989. The bonds were sold to yield a rate of 10 percent. The present value of an ordinary annuity of $1 for ten periods at 10 percent is 6.1446. The present value of $1 for ten periods at 10 percent is 0.3855.

REQUIRED Prepare a schedule to compute the total amount received from the sale of the bonds. Show the computations.

E18–10 (CPA ADAPTED) On July 1, 1978, Salem Corporation issued $2,000,000 of 7 percent bonds payable in 10 years. The bonds pay interest semiannually. The bonds include detachable warrants giving the bondholder the right to purchase, for $30, one share of $1 par value common stock anytime during the next 10 years. The bonds were sold for $2,000,000. The value of the warrants at the time of issuance was $100,000.

REQUIRED Prepare in general journal format the entry to record the issuance of the bonds.

PROBLEMS

P18–1 Granger, Inc., sells 15,000, $1,000 maturity value bonds on January 1, 1983. The nominal interest rate is 10 percent and the yield is 12 percent. The maturity dates are as follows: one-third of the issue at January 1, 1988, one-third at January 1, 1993, and one-third at January 1, 1998. Interest payments are made annually.

REQUIRED

1. Show the computations of selling prices for each group of bonds.
2. Show the necessary journal entry on the issuance date.

P18–2 On August 1, 1984, Roller Bearings, Inc., issues 20,000, $100 face value bonds dated July 1, 1984, at 100 plus accrued interest. The bonds have a nominal interest rate of 10 percent, and the interest payment dates are December 31 and July 1 of each year. Roller Bearings has an October 31 year-end.

REQUIRED Record all the journal entries necessary for this bond issue through the first interest payment.

P18–3 Zantu International intends to sell 10,000, 20-year, 10 percent, $1,000 face value convertible bonds on January 1, 1984. The president of Zantu asks you to compare the accounting for bonds that have detachable warrants with bonds that are convertible, using the following assumptions (assume independent cases):

BONDS WITH DETACHABLE WARRANTS

1. On January 1, 1984, 10,000 bonds are sold for $1,100 each.
2. Each bond has ten warrants allowing the holder to purchase one share of no-par common stock for each warrant at $25 per share anytime after December 31, 1984.
3. On January 1, 1984, the fair value of each warrant is $10 and the fair value of each bond without warrants is $1,000.

CONVERTIBLE BONDS

1. On January 1, 1984, 10,000 bonds are sold for $1,000 each.
2. Each bond is convertible into 40 shares of no-par common stock anytime after December 31, 1984.
3. On January 1, 1984, bonds without convertibility features are selling for $950.

REQUIRED

1. Give all journal entries necessary for the issuance of the bonds for each alternative.
2. Give all journal entries necessary for the conversion of one-half of the bond issue on January 1, 1985 and exercise of one-half of the warrants on January 1, 1985. Assume that all interest journal entries have been properly recorded and that the common shares are selling for $27 each on January 1, 1985.

P18–4 Selected accounts of the R. E. Cycle Company are presented in comparative form:

	ADJUSTED TRIAL BALANCE DATA	
	12/31/91	12/31/90
Bond interest expense	$ 6,600	$ 550
Bond interest payable	2,000	2,000
Bonds payable—issued 12/1/90	100,000	100,000
Bond discount	8,200	8,800

The data in the adjusted trial balance columns are correct. The bonds were issued between interest payment dates at 91.15 percent of maturity value plus accrued interest, and the straight-line method is used.

REQUIRED

1. Answer the following questions. (They do not necessarily have to be answered in this order.)
   a. What is the monthly straight-line amortization rate on the bonds?
   b. For how many months after December 31, 1991, will the bonds be outstanding?
   c. What is the *stated* rate of interest on the bonds?
   d. If interest is paid semiannually, what are the two interest payment dates?
2. Give the journal entry to record the bond issue.
3. Give the year-end accrual entry for bonds for both years.

P18–5 The Bionca Corporation issued $100,000 face value, 5-year bonds with a nominal interest rate of 8 percent payable semiannually on June 30 and December 31 of each year. The bonds were sold on January 1, 1981, and they mature on December 31, 1985. The effective interest rate to Bionca, based on the proceeds from the issuance, was 10 percent. The amortization of the bond premium or discount is recorded when interest payments are made using the present-value (effective interest) method.

REQUIRED

1. Record the bond issuance on January 1, 1981.
2. Record the necessary entries for the following dates: June 30, 1981, and December 31, 1981.
3. Record the retirement on June 29, 1982, of one-half of these bonds, assuming Bionca purchased them in the market at 94 percent plus accrued interest for one-half of 1982.

P18–6 The Monroe Corporation issued 4-year, 14 percent bonds having a face value of $100,000. Interest is payable semiannually on December 31 and June 30 of each year. The bonds were sold on January 1, 1983, for an effective interest rate of 12 percent per year. The amortization of premium is recorded, using the *effective yield* method, when semiannual interest is paid. The bonds were retired on December 31, 1984, by payment of $105,000 plus interest for the period July 1 to December 31, 1984.

REQUIRED

1. What journal entry is necessary on December 31, 1983, to record the payment of interest and amortization of premium?
2. What journal entries are necessary on December 31, 1984?

P18–7 The balance sheet of Electronics, Inc., shows the following on December 31, 1980:

8% bonds payable, maturing on June 30, 1988	$600,000
Unamortized premium on bonds payable	21,000
Unamortized bond issue costs	1,620

Interest is payable semiannually on June 30 and December 31, at which time amortization of premium and issue costs is also recorded, using the straight-line method. On April 1, 1982, Electronics purchases and retires $100,000 face value of bonds for $101\frac{1}{2}$ plus accrued interest.

REQUIRED Prepare all the journal entries necessary to reflect the purchase and retirement of the bonds on April 1, 1982.

P18-8 The following information is available on the Wilson Corporation's 12 percent bonds as of January 1, 1981:

Bonds payable, maturing on December 31, 1988	$200,000
Unamortized premium on bonds payable	7,680
Unamortized bond issue costs	480

Interest is payable annually on December 31. Straight-line amortization of bond premium and issue costs is used. On May 1, 1984, the Wilson Corporation purchases and retires $20,000 face value of bonds for a total of $21,500 *including* accrued interest.

REQUIRED Compute the amount of gain or loss associated with the retirement of these bonds. *Show all calculations.* Make any necessary journal entries on May 1, 1984.

P18-9

_____ 1. On January 1, 1976, the X Company sold $100,000,000 of 6 percent bonds at a yield rate of 8 percent. Upon issuance, the X Company paid $150,000 to lawyers, accountants, and so on, for fees related to the issuance. Interest is payable semiannually on July 1 and January 1. The bonds will mature in 20 years on January 1, 1996. The X Company adjusts and closes its books annually on December 31. The entry to record the issuance of the bonds on X's books would be:

	DEBIT	CREDIT
a. Bond issue costs	150,000	
Cash		150,000
Cash	80,363,900	
Discount on bonds payable	19,636,100	
Bonds payable		100,000,000
b. Bond issue costs	150,000	
Cash		150,000
Cash	80,208,400	
Discount on bonds payable	19,791,600	
Bonds payable		100,000,000
c. Bond issue costs expense	150,000	
Cash		150,000
Cash	80,363,900	
Discount on bonds payable	19,636,100	
Bonds payable		100,000,000
d. Bond issue costs expense	150,000	
Cash		150,000
Cash	80,208,400	
Discount on bonds payable	19,791,600	
Bonds payable		100,000,000

_____ 2. Refer to part 1. What entry would be required on December 31, 1990, to record the bond interest expense and related amortization? (Ignore bond issue costs entries.)

    a. Bond interest expense
        Discount on bonds payable
        Cash

    b. Bond interest expense
       Discount on bonds payable
       Bond interest payable

    c. Bond interest expense
       Bond interest payable

    d. No entry required

3. Refer to part 1. What is the total net book value of bonds payable ("bonds payable" less the unamortized balance in "discount on bonds payable") on the December 31, 1990, balance sheet?
    a. $(P/A, 11, .04)\$3,000,000 + (P/F, 11, .04)\$100,000,000$
    b. $(P/A, 10, .03)\$3,000,000 + (P/F, 10, .03)\$100,000,000$
    c. $(P/A, 10, .04)\$3,000,000 + (P/F, 10, .04)\$100,000,000$
    d. $(P/A, 11, .03)\$3,000,000 + (P/F, 11, .03)\$100,000,000$
    e. $(P/A, 10, .04)\$3,000,000 + (P/F, 5, .08)\$100,000,000$

4. One aspect of *FASB Statement No. 15* on troubled debt restructuring is:
    a. No gains or losses are permitted
    b. Gains are permitted only if cash flows are unchanged after restructuring
    c. Only when the expected future total cash flows in the future are more than the book value of the debt at date of restructuring can a gain or loss be recognized
    d. If the cash payments called for by the restructuring will result in a change in the implicit interest rate, a gain or loss must be recognized
    e. None of the above

5. When bonds outstanding are retired prior to their maturity with the proceeds (cash) from a new bond issue
    a. No gains or losses are reported on the retirement of the old bonds
    b. Gains or losses on the old bonds will alter the book value of the new bond issue
    c. Gains or losses on the retired bonds do not alter the book value of the new bond issue but are reported in ordinary income in the period in which retirement occurs
    d. Gains and losses must be reported as extraordinary items in the period in which retirement occurs whether or not a new bond issue is used to finance retirement
    e. None of the above

6. Convertible bonds have been used in the past as an alternative to issuing common stock to obtain capital. The investor is willing to accept a lower interest rate on a convertible bond than on a "straight" bond because
    a. The investor believes that interest rates in the future will decline on long-term debt
    b. The investor is certain that the price of common stock to which the bond is convertible will increase very rapidly
    c. The investor is reducing the risk of buying common stock outright because if the stock declines in value, the investor will still receive interest and principal at maturity on the debt
    d. The investor is uncertain whether to buy stock or bonds, and therefore the convertible bond gives the desired amount of flexibility and return comparable to the going rate on treasury bills.
    e. The investor is willing to take a higher risk than that associated with an outright purchase of stock

7. On January 1, 1987, Debt Company sold 30-year, 6 percent bonds having a face value of $10,000,000 at an effective interest rate of 8 percent. The bonds pay interest semiannually on June 30 and December 31. Debt Company has a June 30 year-end. What interest expense should be recorded on Debt Company's books for December 31, 2006 (exactly 10 years prior to maturity)?
    a. $346,320
    b. $343,870
    c. $256,132
    d. $253,680
    e. $300,000

P18–10 (CMA ADAPTED)

_____ 1. During 1968 the Luccy Corporation issued $1,000,000 of 20-year, 6 percent bonds at par. During 1976 Luccy reacquired all of those bonds for $925,000 and canceled them. The difference between the face amount of the bonds and the redemption amount ($75,000) is material. How would this transaction be reflected in the 1976 financial statements of Luccy Corporation?

    a. The $75,000 gain should be reported as a separate line item on the income statement.

    b. The $75,000 gain, net of the related tax effect, should be shown as an extraordinary item on the income statement.

    c. The $75,000 gain should be classified as a deferred income item on the balance sheet and taken into income over the remainder of the original 20-year life of the bonds.

    d. The difference of $75,000 is a reduction of the interest paid in the period from 1968 until the year the bonds were reacquired and, as a result, should be considered a "prior period adjustment" and added directly to retained earnings.

    e. The transaction should be shown in the financial statements in some manner other than that described above.

_____ 2. When detachable warrants to buy common stock are part of an issue of long-term bonds payable

    a. The issuance price must be allocated between the bonds and the warrants, with the amount allocated to the warrants reflected in the stockholders' equity section until the warrants are utilized to acquire common stock

    b. The issuance price must be allocated between the bonds and the warrants, with the amount allocated to the warrants reflected as part of long-term liabilities

    c. The issuance price may or may not be allocated between the bonds and the warrants, depending upon whether in the judgment of the accountant the warrants had any value at the date the bonds were issued

    d. No allocation is made to the warrants until it is first determined whether they will be utilized to acquire common stock; if management believes they will be utilized, an amount equal to their fair market value at that time is allocated to them

    e. The issuance price should not be allocated between the bonds and the warrants

_____ 3. In a situation where the proceeds of a new debt instrument are used to call an old debt instrument, _FASB Statement No. 4,_ "Reporting Gains and Losses from Extinguishment of Debt," requires that any gain or loss on the early extinguishment of debt

    a. Be amortized over what would have been the life of the old debt and treated as an extraordinary item on the income statement

    b. Be amortized over what would have been the life of the old debt and treated as an ordinary item on the income statement

    c. Be reported on the income statement as an extraordinary item in the period of refinancing

    d. Be reported on the income statement as an ordinary item in the period of financing

    e. Be reported as an "unrealized gain or loss" and shown as a deferred item on the balance sheet

_____ 4. The preliminary balance sheet of Equity, Inc., prepared on December 31, 1978, included a $3,000,000 note payable due April 20, 1979. On January 10, 1979, the company issued additional shares of its common stock for cash proceeds of $4,800,000 and used $2,300,000 of these proceeds to reduce the note payable. Audited financial statements were to be released on March 15, 1979, while management was still in the process of negotiating a line of credit that would be used to expand operations and to eliminate the remaining balance of the $3,000,000 note payable. In the audited December 31, 1978, balance sheet, the required presentation regarding the $3,000,000 note payable is to report a

    a. $3,000,000 current liability because the debt was not paid before December 31, 1978

    b. $3,000,000 long-term liability because current assets will not be used to liquidate the debt

    c. $3,000,000 long-term liability because the debt was, or will be, refinanced on a long-term basis

    d. $3,000,000 current liability described as "notes payable expected to be refinanced"

    e. $700,000 current liability and a $2,300,000 noncurrent liability because only a portion of the debt was refinanced on a long-term basis

5. Sealo Company has recently experienced declining profits, liquidity problems, and an unfavorable trend in its debt-to-equity relationship. In 1978 the company completed negotiations whereby a creditor agreed to accept 100,000 shares of Sealo common stock in settlement of a note payable for $500,000. Market value of the shares was $300,000. In accounting for this troubled debt restructuring, the appropriate treatment for Sealo is to
   a. Reduce liabilities and increase paid-in capital by $500,000
   b. Reduce liabilities by $500,000, increase paid-in capital by $300,000, and recognize interest income of $200,000
   c. Reduce liabilities by $500,000, increase paid-in capital by $300,000, and recognize an extraordinary gain of $200,000
   d. Reduce liabilities by $500,000 and create a separate paid-in capital section entitled "equity of former creditors—$500,000"
   e. Reduce liabilities by $500,000, increase paid-in capital by $300,000, and increase retained earnings directly for $200,000

6. ERON Corporation sold an issue of 8 percent convertible bonds at a premium in 1978. Each $1,000 face value bond included a detachable warrant to purchase one share of ERON common stock at $3.25. The required accounting procedure for the issuance of these securities is to
   a. Credit the entire proceeds to paid-in capital if the bonds are common stock equivalents
   b. Account for the entire proceeds as long-term debt because of the inseparability of the debt and conversion feature
   c. Recognize as paid-in capital an appropriate portion of the proceeds attributable to the detachable warrants
   d. Ignore any portion of the total proceeds that is attributable to the market value of the warrants
   e. Recognize paid-in capital attributable to the warrants only to the extent that the proceeds exceed the face value of the bonds

7. The December 31, 1978, balance sheet of Silvaso Enterprises reported a $5,000,000 face value issue of bonds payable. The bonds have an 8 percent interest coupon payable semiannually and were sold to yield 7 percent to investors. The balance of unamortized bond premium at the beginning of 1978 was $300,000, with a remaining amortization period of 15 years. Under the compound interest (or effective interest) method of amortizing the premium, the annual effect of premium amortization on the 1978 financial statements is
   a. To decrease total liabilities by $29,000
   b. To decrease interest expense by $20,000
   c. To increase interest expense by $29,000
   d. To decrease interest expense by $9,000
   e. Not given above

8. When bonds payable are retired before maturity through a refunding transaction, any material excess of payments to bondholders upon retirement over the net carrying value of the retired bonds should be
   a. Amortized over the remaining life of the retired bonds
   b. Recognized as an extraordinary loss net of related income taxes
   c. Amortized over the life of the new bond issue
   d. Deducted from the carrying value of the new bonds
   e. Disclosed separately in computing income from continuing operations

P18–11 (CPA ADAPTED) On September 1, 1978, the Junction Company sold at 104 (plus accrued interest) 4,000 of its 10-year, 9 percent, $1,000 face value, nonconvertible bonds with detachable stock warrants. Each bond carried two detachable warrants; each warrant was for one share of common stock, at a specified option price of $15 per share. Shortly after issuance, the warrants were quoted on the market at $3 each. No market value can be determined for the bonds described above. Interest is payable on December 1 and June 1. Bond issue costs of $40,000 were incurred.

REQUIRED Prepare in general journal format the entry to record the issuance of the bonds. Show supporting computations.

P18 12 (CPA ADAPTED) On December 1, 1976, the Cone Company issued its 7 percent, $2,000,000 face value bonds for $2,200,000, plus accrued interest. Interest is payable on November 1 and May 1. On December 31,

1978, the book value of the bonds, inclusive of the unamortized premium, was $2,100,000. On July 1, 1979, Cone reacquired the bonds at 98, plus accrued interest. Cone appropriately uses the straight-line method for the amortization of bond premium because the results do not materially differ from those using the interest method.

REQUIRED Prepare a schedule to compute the gain or loss on this early extinguishment of debt. Show supporting computations in good form.

P18–13 (CPA ADAPTED) On January 1, 1978, MyKoo Corporation issued $1,000,000 of 5-year, 5 percent serial bonds to be repaid in the amount of $200,000 on January 1 of 1979, 1980, 1981, 1982, and 1983. Interest is payable at the end of each year. The bonds were sold to yield a rate of 6 percent. Information on present-value and future-value factors is as follows:

PRESENT VALUE OF AN ORDINARY ANNUITY OF $1 FOR 5 YEARS		FUTURE VALUE OF AN ORDINARY ANNUITY OF $1 FOR 5 YEARS	
5%	6%	5%	6%
4.3295	4.2124	5.5256	5.6371

NUMBER OF YEARS	PRESENT VALUE OF $1		FUTURE VALUE OF $1	
	5%	6%	5%	6%
1	.9524	.9434	1.0500	1.0600
2	.9070	.8900	1.1025	1.1236
3	.8638	.8396	1.1576	1.1910
4	.8227	.7921	1.2155	1.2625
5	.7835	.7473	1.2763	1.3382

REQUIRED

1. Prepare a schedule showing the computation of the total amount received from the issuance of the serial bonds. Show supporting computations.
2. Assume that the bonds were originally sold at a discount of $26,247. Prepare a schedule of amortization of the bond discount for the first 2-years after issuance, using the interest (effective rate) method. Show supporting computations.

P18–14 (CPA ADAPTED) On January 1, 1976, when its $30 par value common stock was selling for $80 per share, a corporation issued $10,000,000 of 4 percent convertible debentures due in 10 years. The conversion option allowed the holder of each $1,000 bond to convert the bond into 5 shares of the corporation's $30 par value common stock. The debentures were issued for $11,000,000. The present value of the bond payments at the time of issuance was $8,500,000, and the corporation believes that the difference between the present value and the amount paid is attributable to the conversion feature. On January 1, 1977, the corporation's $30 par value common stock was split 3 for 1. On January 1, 1978, when the corporation's $10 par value common stock was selling for $90 per share, holders of 40 percent of the convertible debentures exercised their conversion options. The corporation uses the straight-line method for amortizing any bond discounts or premiums.

REQUIRED

1. Prepare in general journal format the entry to record the original issuance of the convertible debentures.
2. Prepare in general journal format the entry to record the exercise of the conversion option, using the book value method. Show supporting computations.

P18–15 (CMA ADAPTED)

_____ 1. The unamortized discount on bonds payable
   a. Should be shown as an asset on the balance sheet

b. Should be expensed immediately
c. Should be shown as a liability on the balance sheet
d. Should be shown as a deduction from the maturity value of the bonds on the balance sheet
e. Should be reported as a loss on issuance of bonds

_____ 2. Bond issue costs
a. Should be charged as an expense when incurred
b. Should be charged against retained earnings when incurred
c. Should be amortized over the life of the bonds to which they apply
d. Should be included in organization costs
e. Should be charged to interest expense when incurred

_____ 3. On December 31, 1974, a company refinanced a $10,000,000, 11 percent bond issue due December 31, 1979, by a direct exchange of $10,000,000 of 10 percent bonds due December 31, 1984. Costs to issue the new bonds amounted to $200,000. The total present value of the new securities is $9,000,000. Unamortized discount on the 11 percent bonds amounted to $100,000 at the date of exchange. How should this transaction be accounted for?
a. Write off the issue costs immediately and amortize the gain over 10 years
b. Amortize the gain over 5 years and include the costs in the carrying value of the new issue
c. Amortize the gain over 10 years net of issue costs on new bonds
d. Recognize the loss on exchange immediately and write off the issue costs to expense over the next 10 years
e. Recognize the gain on exchange immediately, treating the issue costs as part of the reacquisition price

19 Pensions

OVERVIEW

Accounting for pensions is a controversial subject and is going through a period of change. The central issues in the pension-accounting controversy involve the application of the basic definitions of *assets, liabilities,* and *expenses* to pension arrangements of business entities. Although the review and restatement of these elements of financial statements (assets, liabilities, and expenses) in the **Statement of Financial Accounting Concepts No. 3** drew some attention to pension-accounting issues, the main concern with existing accounting practices focused on the increasing number of pension commitments that were not being recorded or reported in financial statements.[1] Many financial analysts believed that these "off-balance-sheet" effects were undermining the financial statements.[2] Part of the increase in pension commitments was attributable to the passage by Congress of the Pension Reform Act of 1974, known more commonly as the Employee Retirement Income Security Act (ERISA), which called for more benefits to employees, and part was attribut-

---

[1] *Statement of Financial Accounting Concepts No. 3,* "Elements of Financial Statements" (Stamford, CT: FASB, December 1980).

[2] See, for example, "The Market Has Spotted Those Pension Problems," *Fortune,* December 1, 1980, pp. 143–146.

able to effective bargaining by labor unions for increased pension benefits. The result has been a review of pension-accounting practices by the FASB. The focus of this review has been the nature, timing, measurement, and reporting of financial statement elements involved in pension contracts.[3] Pensions will probably represent the first major accounting issue to test the strength of direction provided by **SFAC No. 3.**

Understanding the accounting procedures for pensions also draws extensively on the use of present-value concepts, for pensions represent another long-term obligation (or asset) of the firm that is measured primarily on the basis of discounting future economic flows. There is a similarity between accounting for pensions and accounting for leases, bonds, notes, and other instruments that specify the timing of the economic flows. If you understand these similarities, you will see that pension accounting is another logical application of discounted present-value measurement in accounting.

THE NATURE OF PENSIONS

Pensions are contractual agreements between a company and its employees that specify (1) **what benefits will be available to the employee** upon retirement or upon termination of employment for other reasons (such as death or job transfer) and (2) **how these benefits will accrue to the employee.** Pension costs are expenses to the company, and in theory the commitment made by the company to its employees through pension contracts represents current or future obligations of the company. Once the employer has made payments on its commitment to the employees, the accounting for pension payments by the employer is normally complete. The managing of the pension fund assets and payments from the pension fund to the employees are activities that are not accounted for on the employer's books but are the responsibility of the pension fund itself, which is usually viewed as a separate entity. Figure 19–1 explains the typical relationship between the funding company, the pension fund, and the employees covered by the pension plan.

The employer makes payments to the pension fund, which in turn invests the cash or other assets to earn additional funds. Ultimately the pension fund makes

FIGURE
19–1
Parties to pension plan

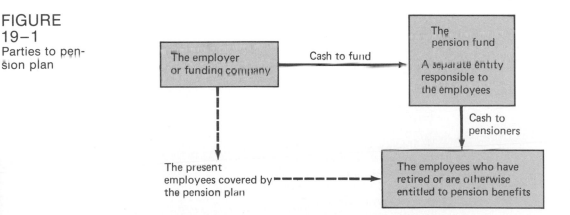

[3] See the FASB discussion memo "Employers Accounting for Pensions" (Stamford, CT: FASB, May 1980), p. 211.

payments to the employees based on the benefits stipulated in their pension contract. When a pension fund is established for a large group of employees the fund is normally managed by someone hired by the employees, such as the trust department of a bank, which will invest the pension fund's assets (cash received from the funding company) in bonds, equity securities, treasury notes, land, and other business ventures, depending on the contractual restrictions placed on the fund managers by the employees. In some cases, the employees will hire a fund manager to represent them independently and to manage pension fund assets. In other cases, the fund may simply be a series of insurance policies being purchased by the funding company for its individual employees.

The exact nature of the fund and when and how it makes payments to the covered employees is determined by the terms of the contract negotiated between the employer and its employees and may vary considerably from firm to firm. Most of the details negotiated as a part of pension contracts *do not* involve the employer's accounting system except that the amount and the timing of the employer's payments to the pension fund will have to be recorded properly on the employer's books.

In this chapter we focus on the accounting for pension plans on the books of the employer, not the pension fund. We begin by defining some of the key terms used in pension accounting. We then use a conceptual example to illustrate some of the principal controversial pension-accounting issues. After these conceptual examples, labeled non-GAAP, we shall discuss current GAAP for pension fund accounting by employers.

In addition to these sections that consider the basic pension-accounting procedures, we shall illustrate disclosures required for the pension fund, and also some of the accepted actuarial methods used to estimate the required payments from the employer to the fund. We shall then take a brief look at the role that Congress played in the 1974 Pension Reform Act.

Definition of Key Terms

The key terms relevant to pension fund accounting can be divided into (1) those describing the general nature of pension plans; (2) those describing the process of measuring pension obligations; and (3) those describing the recording of pension-related transactions. The following list summarizes these key terms:

1. *Description of Plans*
   a. Defined benefit plans
   b. Funded and unfunded plans
   c. Contributory and noncontributory plans
2. *Pension Obligations Measurement*
   a. Actuary
   b. Actuarial cost methods
   c. Actuarial assumptions
   d. Implicit earnings (interest)
   e. Actuarial gains and losses
3. *Types of Pension Costs*
   a. Normal costs
   b. Past service costs
   c. Prior service costs
   d. Vested benefit costs

Description of plans Pension plans are normally based on contractual arrangements that have been negotiated between the employer and the employees to provide retirement benefits to the employees based on their period of service. A pension plan is essentially a deferral of wages in that the employee generally must work to earn pension benefits but will not get paid until retirement for a portion of the earnings. When the actual benefits earned by the employees are described in the pension contract, such contracts are called **defined benefit pension plans.** By defining the benefits earned, the employer and employee are able to measure their respective costs and benefits for a specific period of employment.

Most plans call for payments by the employer to a pension fund that is an independent entity separate from the employer. Such plans are called **funded plans,** and these plans are now required, to a minimum extent, as a result of ERISA. **Unfunded plans** are those for which no separate assets are accumulated. Unfunded plans are much less common than funded plans and are permitted only as voluntary supplements to the requirements for minimally funded plans under the provisions of ERISA.

Many pension plans are **noncontributory plans** in which the employer contributes 100 percent of the amounts that are contractually due. In **contributory plans,** the employee pays at least part of the periodic payments to the pension fund, usually through a payroll deduction plan. In these contributory plans the employee has the option of paying taxes on his or her contribution at the time at which it is contributed to the pension fund or paying taxes upon receipt of the pension payment (or payments) from the pension fund. Employees usually elect to defer paying taxes until they receive payments from the pension fund.

Measuring pension obligations The process of measuring the specific dollar amounts of the pension obligation is generally performed by an **actuary,** who is a specialist in forecasting certain factors needed to estimate the cost of a pension plan. To illustrate, consider a group of employees who are expected to work for 30 years and then retire at age 62. Under the agreement stipulated in the employees' pension plan they will receive a specified amount of pension benefits, say $700 per employee, each month after retirement for the rest of their lives. The employer has paid into the pension fund an amount of cash based on the length of time worked, say $2,000 for each full year of work provided by each employee. The actuary will determine the amount to be funded each year ($2,000 per employee in this example) by taking the contractual benefit amount ($700 per employee per month) and answering the following questions:

1. How long will the employees (on average) live beyond age 62?
2. What will be the pension fund earnings on payments made to the fund by the employer prior to retirement?
3. What will be the employee turnover in the company?
4. How many employees will make it to retirement age?
5. What will be the real purchasing power of the pension benefits when they are received after retirement?

By using various systematic allocation techniques called **actuarial cost methods,** the actuary is able to determine the total present value of the employer's contractual obligation for the benefits identified in the plan (for example, $700 per month after age 62 until death).

Some of the actuarial cost methods used by actuaries will be illustrated later in this chapter. All of the actuarial cost methods are based, in part, on **actuarial assumptions,** or estimates concerning the information pertaining to the questions listed above. These assumptions or estimates are subject to revision. For example, the actuary must assume some rate of return, or **implicit earnings,** for the pension fund assets between the time the assets are paid to the fund and the time the fund makes the payments to its pensioners. Sometimes, based on the actual results that occur subsequent to the initial actuarial estimates, these estimates need to be revised or adjusted. These revisions typically result in **actuarial gains or losses,** sometimes called **experience gains or losses.** If the actuary originally assumed that fund assets would earn 7 percent per year, and experience demonstrated that a better estimate would be 8 percent per year, an actuarial gain would result. In recording the pension-related activities on the funding company's books, the accountant depends in part on the information provided by the actuary.

Types of pension costs   Although the actuarial cost methods and assumptions are somewhat complex, the recording of pension activity by using the actuarial information is relatively straightforward. The funding company may be obligated to pay three types of costs that are measured by the actuary. The most fundamental of these three costs is the **normal cost,** which is the amount of pension obligation earned by the funding company's employees during the current accounting period.

Employees usually earn a certain amount of pension benefits for each year of their employment in accordance with their particular labor agreement. For example, an employee may earn an additional $1,000 in pension benefits to be paid at the date of retirement for each full year of employment. The present value of these normal costs is measured annually based on the actuarial assumptions and the actuarial cost methods employed for each specific pension plan. In most corporations, normal costs are funded annually as they are being incurred.

In addition to normal costs, most pension plans of publicly traded U.S. corporations involve other pension costs. These costs present some of the more difficult accounting problems related to pensions. The two other major types of pension costs are **past service costs** and **prior service costs,** both of which are measures of costs that must be paid for by the employer for past employees' services. **Past service costs** are those costs that, according to the pension agreement, the employer must pay for in recognition of the services provided by the employees **before the inception of the pension plan.** This recognition of past employee service to the company as of the beginning of the pension plan is something for which employee representatives will aggressively bargain. Having the employer recognize and fund these past services will help to ensure that the pension fund will be able to provide adequate retirement benefits to employees who are nearing retirement age at the inception of the plan. The time line in Figure 19–2 shows the relationship between past service costs and normal costs for a pension plan that is established on January 1, 1973. Both costs are to be paid for by the employer on behalf of the employees through periodic payments to the pension fund beginning in 1973.

When the pension benefits of an existing pension plan are amended to provide increased retirement benefits to employees, the employees' representatives will normally seek retroactive recognition so that the increased benefits will apply to the prior services of the employees as well as their future services. Amendments to pen-

FIGURE
19-2
Past service
cost/normal cost

Earliest date
pension plan
recognizes
benefits

Date pension
plan is
initiated

1/1/64

1/1/73

Past service cost period

Normal cost period

sion plans frequently call for increased benefits for employee services resulting in adjustments (increases) to **normal costs** in the current and future periods, and also resulting in increased **prior service costs** to the extent that they pertain to services already provided by the employees. The time line in Figure 19-3 shows the relationship between the terms used to identify pension costs associated with plans that have been amended to increase retroactive benefits for service periods prior to the amendment. Note that the amendment to the plan on January 1, 1984, provides for additional retroactive pension benefits. The term *prior service costs* is used to identify *all* the remaining retroactive benefits yet to be funded by the employer and would encompass past service costs yet to be funded (if any) as of the date of the amendment. When the term *prior service costs* is used, it signifies that the pension plan has been amended, that the amendment has provided for a change in the retroactive benefits, and that the amount stated as prior service costs includes *both* the new (additional) retroactive benefits *and* the remaining unfunded original past service costs recognized at the inception of the plan. In short, the measurement of prior service costs includes all the retroactive benefits that remain to be paid by the employer. For convenience, we sometimes use PSC to represent past service cost or prior service cost or both. Because accounting rarely differentiates between the treatment afforded these two retroactive benefits, the abbreviation PSC can be used to represent all retroactive benefits to be paid by the employer.

Although the employer has certain contractual commitments to the pension fund, the employee also has certain obligations that must be fulfilled before a claim to receive pension fund assets can be recognized. This claim is against the fund, which is not our focal point in this chapter, but it does affect the employer's accounting and recording procedures. When an employee has earned pension benefits and has a legal right to receive benefits even if he or she leaves the employer or the pension plan is terminated, these earned benefits are called vested benefits. The vested portion of pension benefits at any point in time do not necessarily equal the total defined benefits earned by an employee who will remain with the employer until retirement. In other words, the vested benefit amount at any point in time

FIGURE
19-3
Prior service
cost/past service
cost/normal cost

Earliest date
pension plan
recognizes
benefits

Date pension
plan is
initiated

Date pension
plan is amended
to increase past
benefits

1/1/64

1/1/73

1/1/84

Past service cost period

Prior service cost period

Normal cost period

EXHIBIT
19-1

VESTED BENEFITS AND PENSION FUND ASSETS

UTAH POWER & LIGHT COMPANY
Excerpt from Notes to Financial Statements

6. Retirement Plan

The company has a trusteed, funded, noncontributory retirement income plan for employees. Total cost for contributions to the plan was $6,732,000 in 1980, $5,741,000 in 1979, and $4,976,000 in 1978. The company accrues the cost of the plan using the aggregate cost funding method and makes contributions to the plan equal to the amounts accrued.

The actuarially computed present value of vested and nonvested benefits of the plan as of January 1, 1980 (the date of the most recent actuarial valuation), was $53,145,000 and $18,175,000, respectively. Net assets available for benefits at January 1, 1980, were $42,948,000. Earnings on net assets and actuarially determined future contributions to the plan are expected to provide full funding for all vested and nonvested benefits.

The weighted average assumed rate of return used in determining the actuarial present value of accumulated plan benefits was 5.9% for the January 1, 1980, valuation.

might be less than (or equal to) the employee's total defined benefits based on his or her total service to date. However, vested benefits represent the current minimum benefits to which the employee is legally entitled should employment be terminated. As a result, vested benefits have major implications for both the employer and the pension fund. Specifically, it is desirable to have the pension fund assets greater than or equal to the employees' collective vested benefits. If an employer went bankrupt and the pension fund had fewer assets than the sum of the employees' vested benefits, the employees might not receive their entitled vested amounts. Despite this fact, the net assets of pension funds are often insufficient to cover all vested benefits. A footnote disclosure providing information on net fund assets and vested and nonvested benefits is illustrated in Exhibit 19–1. Note that the $42,948,000 in fund assets is *less* than the $53,145,000 vested benefits. The implied interest rate in this case is 5.9 percent. The exact meaning of this disclosure will become clearer as we go through the chapter.

ACCOUNTING FOR NORMAL COSTS

Normal costs are based on a combination of actuarial assumptions and the employee pension benefits contracted for in the labor agreement. Note that the actuary will *assume* that the employer will pay the normal cost into the fund each year as this cost is being incurred. Because of the time value of money that is implicit in the actuary's estimates of the annual normal cost amount, normal costs not paid as incurred would require an interest penalty component for delayed payment. The employer will often be required to pay the normal cost to the pension fund each year. The following entry would record a $38,000 annual normal cost (NC) payment:

12/31/83	Pension expense (NC)	38,000	
	Cash		38,000

The employer may sometimes be able to defer or prepay the annual normal cost according to the terms of the pension contract.[4] First consider the case where

---

[4] See *Accounting Principles Board Opinion No. 8,* "Accounting for the Cost of Pension Plans" (New York: AICPA, November 1966), par. 43.

the employer is able to pay only $33,000 of the full $38,000 annual normal cost pension expense for the year 1983. Further assume that the employer is able to pay the 1984 normal cost of $40,000 at the end of 1984 as well as the unpaid normal cost from 1983. In addition, assume that the actuary has based the normal cost calculation on the assumption that the employer will pay the normal cost to the pension fund each year-end and that the pension fund will earn 10 percent per year on its assets. The following entries would be recorded for 1983 and 1984:

12/31/83	Pension expense (NC)	38,000	
	Cash		33,000
	Pension liability		5,000
12/31/84	Pension expense (NC)	40,000	
	Pension expense (interest)	500	
	Pension liability	5,000	
	Cash		45,500

Note that the employer must pay the pension fund $500 more than the unpaid $5,000 normal cost from 1983. This $500 is like an interest expense, and it must be paid to the pension fund because the fund was prevented from earning an additional $500 in interest (assumed by the actuary to have been earned) for 1984 due to the employer's failure to pay the full $38,000 normal cost in 1983. This interest cost would normally be recorded as a part of the December 31, 1984, pension expense entry as follows:

12/31/84	Pension expense	40,500	
	Pension liability	5,000	
	Cash		45,500

What if the employer decides to prepay some part of the normal cost for future years in addition to the current year's normal cost? Assume once again that the annual normal cost is $38,000 for 1983 and $40,000 for 1984 and that the fund is expected to earn 10 percent. If the employer pays $50,000 to the fund in 1983, the following entries would be recorded:

12/31/83	Pension expense (NC)	38,000	
	Prepaid pension costs	12,000	
	Cash		50,000
12/31/84	Pension expense	38,800	
	Prepaid pension costs		12,000
	Cash		26,800

The cash payment for 1984 normal cost is reduced by $12,000 from the 1983 prepayment *and* $1,200 for the assumed additional 1984 earnings of the pension fund generated by the prepayment of $12,000 into the fund in 1983. The 1984 entry might also be recorded as follows:

12/31/84	Prepaid pension costs	1,200	
	Pension expense		1,200
	(To recognize implicit interest on prepaid pension asset)		
12/31/84	Pension expense	40,000	
	Prepaid pension costs		13,200
	Cash		26,800

In both sets of entries, the 1984 Pension Expense account will be $38,800, and the balance in the asset Prepaid Pension Costs will be zero at the end of 1984. The second set of entries illustrates how the employer will receive credit for prepayments into the fund. If the employer has an excess of cash that might be expected to earn less than 10 percent if invested in temporary investments, prepaying pension costs might be a reasonable "investment" alternative.

THE NATURE OF PAST AND PRIOR SERVICE COSTS

Perhaps the most fundamental controversy concerning pension accounting in recent years has been the nature of past and prior service costs. What do these costs represent? Are they elements of the financial statements or not? If they are elements, are they assets or liabilities or expenses? These questions have been extensively debated over the past several years by policy makers, practitioners, and reporting entities. From the authors' point of view, we feel that there is conceptual merit in considering past and prior service costs to be both assets and liabilities of the employer. The following discussion considers some of the rationale. However, even though these arguments may not be universally accepted, examining the implications of treating past and prior service costs as assets and liabilities will be useful in explaining the proper accounting treatment for pensions according to **APB Opinion No. 8,** "Accounting for the Cost of Pension Plans."

Liability Argument

Past and prior service pension benefits are negotiated between the employees and the entity. In most instances, the entity will incur some **contractual obligation** to pay the pension fund a specified amount for employees' services that have already been consumed by the entity. Typically, the entity will resist paying more for work already performed unless the employees force it to do so by threatening a strike or using other means. The employment contract that results may provide the employees with some legal rights to receive these retroactive benefits, requiring the entity (employer) to pay such past or prior service cost benefits in accordance with the contract.

The retroactive benefits contracted for by the employees for services already performed might be viewed as a liability of the employer. They may be viewed as legal commitments for future outflows of the entity's resources similar to deferred income taxes or estimated warranty obligations. In considering the definition of liabilities per **SFAC No. 3,** it would seem that past or prior service costs normally represent "probable future sacrifices of economic benefits arising from present obligations. . . . " The main argument against considering these costs to be liabilities at the date of the contract is the argument that the rendering of *future* services by employees is the *critical event* giving rise to the obligation. This line of argument suggests that the legal contractual commitment to provide increased retroactive benefits is not sufficient to record a liability, but that the future efforts of employees would result in a more relevant event upon which to base recognition.

Asset or Expense

The debit side of the liability entry, assuming the liability is recognized at the time retroactive plan benefits are established or increased, also presents a problem. Is the debit an expense or an asset? If it is an asset, what is the expected benefit period and how should matching take place? The argument that contracts or contract amendments providing retroactive benefits have some measurable asset characteristics is appealing. The employees' attitude, and performance are likely to be better with

TABLE 19-1

EXAMPLES OF UNFUNDED PRIOR SERVICE COSTS

COMPANY	FISCAL YEAR-END	UNFUNDED PRIOR SERVICE COSTS		FISCAL 1977 OR 1978 PENSION & RETIREMENT EXPENSE	
		MILLIONS OF DOLLARS	AS PERCENT OF 3-YEAR AVERAGE PRETAX PROFIT	MILLIONS OF DOLLARS	AS PERCENT OF LABOR EXPENSE
Ford Motor	12	$3,400.0	198.5	$ 624.4	5.8
General Electric	12	820.0	55.1	319.2	4.9
General Foods	3	235.7	69.5	51.4	6.8
General Motors	12	7,300.0	155.2	1,207.7	6.6
Bendix	9	508.2	280.1	69.0	6.9
Bethlehem Steel	12	1,120.0	(deficit)	272.1	11.5
Chrysler	12	2,055.5	1,066.3	296.8	7.2
Du Pont	12	1,288.1	171.4	260.2	9.0
Lockheed	12	821.0	822.6	103.0	6.9
U.S. Steel	12	1,200.0	249.3	234.5	6.0

Source. *Business Week*, August 14, 1978, pp. 60-61, with permission.

such increased benefits than without them, suggesting that future benefits will accrue to the employer. One could argue that the performance of the overall production or service functions of the entity will be indirectly enhanced by the increased recognition granted to employees for their services, that such benefit is controlled by the employers alone, and that the event giving rise to the benefit (the contract) has already occurred. As a result the criteria for asset recognition appear to have been met. The alternative argument—to expense these increased costs at the time they are contracted for—suggests that the managers (employers) of the business entity have legally committed the entity to an economic loss. In our view, this argument is less logical but has some support. Note that the question of asset or expense is relevant only if one feels that a liability should be recognized at the time the contract is agreed upon.[5]

If accountants were to recognize retroactive benefits as assets (or expenses) and liabilities, they would very likely have a major impact on the balance sheets of many U.S. corporations. Table 19-1 gives some idea of the size of the unfunded prior service costs for certain publicly traded companies.

APB Opinion No. 8 decided that **a liability would not be recognized** for all unfunded prior service costs. Only a portion of unfunded past and prior service costs may appear as liabilities on the books of the employer corporations. This chapter shows how we measure the portion of unfunded prior service costs actually reported in the financial statements per **APB Opinion No. 8.** To illustrate the measurement problems, the following section describes a **non-GAAP** recording procedure in that it will record all past and prior service costs as both an asset (or expense) and a liability. Following this discussion, we'll examine accounting for past and prior service costs according to established GAAP.

[5] In the following illustrations (pp. 730–733), the hypothetical *non*-GAAP examples that record these pension obligations for PSC as a liability use an *asset* account as the offsetting debit. These examples could be made even less complex by immediately expensing the PSC benefits when recognized as liabilities. Conceptually, the representation of the PSC benefits as an asset has some advantages for the following illustrations.

ACCOUNTING FOR PAST AND PRIOR SERVICE COSTS

A Conceptual
Non–GAAP
Approach

The purpose of providing a non–GAAP illustration is twofold: (1) to demonstrate that pension accounting is, conceptually, a fairly straightforward topic; and (2) to describe some of the alternatives considered in the process of revising pension-accounting procedures. For both GAAP and non–GAAP illustrations, we focus on accounting for the past and prior service costs (PSC) portion of the pension costs. To remove any complexity of normal cost in the following illustrations, assume that normal cost is a constant $20,000 per year, and that at the end of each year the employer pays normal costs to the pension fund in cash.

Assume that PSC contracted for by the employees with their employer represents both an asset and a liability for the employer, Arrow Corporation. Assume that Arrow Corporation's initial pension plan agreement as a result of recent labor negotiations requires Arrow to pay normal cost benefits continuously into the future and also obligates Arrow to pay $316,990 in past service cost benefits as of December 31, 1985. According to its contract with the labor union, Arrow must pay this past service cost amount to the pension fund over the next 4 years, in four equal installments, with interest of 10 percent per year on the unpaid balance. The annuity required to pay off this PSC obligation is determined as follows, using Table H-3 in Appendix H:

$$\$x \ (P/A, \ 4, \ .10) = \$316,990$$
$$\$x \ (3.1699) = \$316,990$$
$$\$x = \frac{\$316,990}{3.1699}$$
$$\$x = \$100,000$$

The amortization amounts necessary to pay off Arrow's PSC obligation are shown in Table 19–2. Further assume that the asset for recognizing past service costs is going to be amortized over a 6-year period, the expected useful life of the PSC asset. For reasons that will become apparent later, we shall amortize the PSC asset over the 6-year life using present-value amortization (see Chapter 12, pp. 422–423. The theory for this example is that future benefits will result from the employer's willingness to recognize PSC benefits. The amortization amounts necessary to write off the PSC asset over a 6-year life at an implicit interest rate of 10 percent are shown in Table 19–3.

TABLE 19–2

ARROW CORPORATION
AMORTIZATION OF PSC LIABILITY (A NON–GAAP EXAMPLE)

DATE	CASH PAYMENTS	10% INTEREST COMPONENT	PRINCIPAL COMPONENT	PRINCIPAL BALANCE IN PSC LIABILITY AT YEAR-END
12/31/85	—	—		$316,990
12/31/86	$100,000	$31,699	$ 68,301	248,689
12/31/87	100,000	24,869	75,131	173,558
12/31/88	100,000	17,356	82,644	90,914
12/31/89	100,000	9,086[a]	90,914	0
Total	$400,000	$83,010	$316,990	

[a] Rounded.

TABLE 19-3

			ARROW CORPORATION AMORTIZATION OF PSC ASSET (A NON–GAAP EXAMPLE)	
DATE	GROSS EXPENSE – ANNUITY	10% IMPLICIT INTEREST	= NET PSC EXPENSE	BALANCE IN PSC ASSET AT YEAR-END
12/31/85	—	—	—	$316,990
12/31/86	$ 72,783	$ 31,699	$ 41,084	275,906
12/31/87	72,783	27,591	45,192	230,714
12/31/88	72,783	23,071	49,712	181,002
12/31/89	72,783	18,100	54,683	126,319
12/31/90	72,783	12,632	60,151	66,168
12/31/91	72,784	6,616[a]	66,168	0
Total	$436,699	$119,709	$316,990	

[a] Rounded.

The amortization expense, *before* consideration of the offsetting implicit interest on the PSC asset (gross expense annuity), is computed as follows:

$$\$x \ (P/A, \ 6, \ 10\%) = \$316,990$$
$$\$x \ (4.3553) = \$316,990$$
$$\$x = \frac{\$316,990}{4.3553}$$
$$\$x = \$72,783$$

Note that, in theory, there is no reason to expect that the life of the PSC asset will be the same as the time period over which the PSC liability will be paid. The Arrow example described above is similar to the case of a company buying a $316,990 asset with a 6-year life by using 100 percent debt financing and paying off the debt over a 4-year period. The entries recorded in Exhibit 19–2 would reflect the accounting required by Arrow over the life of the PSC asset[6] and liability assuming the $100,000 payments on the liability were made as scheduled.

Financial statement impact—non–GAAP example Exhibit 19–3 summarizes the total impact of the PSC on the balance sheets and income statements over the period 1985–1991. The total effect of the labor agreement calling for recognition of $316,990 in retroactive benefits was to reduce net income by $400,000. The impact on income is made up of the $316,990 original obligation (which was capitalized and expensed as "PSC expense"), plus $83,010 in interest expense.

Arrow is required to pay more than $316,990 because the $316,990 represents the present value (December 31, 1985) of the value of the retroactive benefits. The interest of 10 percent in this example is equal to the **implicit earnings** rate for the pension fund and represents the estimated amount that the pension fund would earn per year on the $316,990 of retroactive benefits if paid by Arrow to the pension fund on December 31, 1985. Because Arrow did not pay the entire $316,990 as of December 31, 1985, it must pay interest to the pension fund on the unpaid

[6] Some would argue that no asset (no future benefits) exist for Arrow as a result of the recognition of PSC benefits, in which case this account could be PSC Expense, and the entries to amortize the PSC asset would be omitted.

EXHIBIT 19–2

NON–GAAP ACCOUNTING EXAMPLE

Year Ended December 31

	1985		1986		1987		1988	
	DEBIT	CREDIT	DEBIT	CREDIT	DEBIT	CREDIT	DEBIT	CREDIT
PSC Asset	316,990							
PSC Liability		316,990						
(To record asset and obligation per labor contract agreement)								
PSC Liability			68,301		75,131		82,644	
Interest Expense			31,699		24,869		17,356	
Cash				100,000		100,000		100,000
(To record payment on PSC obligation per labor contract agreement)								
PSC Expense			41,084		45,192		49,712	
PSC Asset				41,084		45,192		49,712
(To amortize PSC asset)								
Pension Expense (Normal Cost)			20,000		20,000		20,000	
Cash				20,000		20,000		20,000

amount to compensate the fund for lost (implicit) earnings. If Arrow had paid the entire $316,990 on December 31, 1985, no interest would have been required. If Arrow had paid over a period longer than 4 years, more interest would have been required. What would the total interest have been if Arrow had paid the $316,990 PSC obligation in six equal annual payments? (The necessary information for a 6-year annuity is already available in Table 19–3.) A total of $119,709 in interest expense would have been paid, with the *total* income statement effect from the PSC obligation increasing to $436,699. Hence, total expense equals total cash outflow.

The illustration for the Arrow Company is not radically different from GAAP

EXHIBIT 19–3

ARROW CORPORATION
Analysis of Pension Impact on Financial Statements (Non–GAAP Example)

BALANCE SHEET IMPACT

DATE	(1) ASSET BALANCE	(2) LIABILITY BALANCE	(3) COL. (1) – (2)	NET INCOME STATEMENT IMPACT[a]
12/31/85	$316,990	$316,990 Credit	0	0
12/31/86	275,906 Debit	248,689 Credit	$ 27,217 Debit	$72,783 Debit
12/31/87	230,714 Debit	173,558 Credit	57,156 Debit	70,061 Debit
12/31/88	181,002 Debit	90,914 Credit	90,088 Debit	67,068 Debit
12/31/89	126,319 Debit	0	126,319 Debit	63,769 Debit
12/31/90	66,168 Debit	0	66,168 Debit	60,151 Debit
12/31/91	0	0	0	66,168 Debit

[a] This net impact on the income statement is the sum of (1) the Interest Expense amount from each of the $100,000 annual payments on the liability plus (2) the amortization expense from writing off the asset. For example, in 1988 these two components are $17,356 interest plus $49,712 amortization (see entries in Exhibit 19–2).

EXHIBIT 19-2 (continued)

	1989 DEBIT	1989 CREDIT	1990 DEBIT	1990 CREDIT	1991 DEBIT	1991 CREDIT	Totals DEBIT	Totals CREDIT
PSC Asset							316,990	
PSC Liability								316,990
(To record asset and obligation per labor contract agreement)								
PSC Liability	90,914						316,990	
Interest Expense	9,086						83,010	
Cash		100,000						400,000
(To record payment on PSC obligation per labor contract agreement)	54,683		60,151		66,168		316,990	
PSC Expense								
PSC Asset		54,683		60,151		66,168		316,990
(To amortize PSC asset)								
Pension Expense (Normal Cost)	20,000		20,000		20,000		120,000	
Cash		20,000		20,000		20,000		120,000

Year Ended December 31

and will provide a good conceptual basis for understanding GAAP accounting procedures. The principal difference between GAAP and the illustrations in the Arrow example stems from the fact that GAAP do not recognize an asset or a liability for the PSC benefits.

Procedures for PSC Accounting According to GAAP

To illustrate procedures that are consistent with generally accepted accounting principles,[7] assume the Max Corporation incurred a PSC obligation of $316,990 as a result of a recent labor contract settlement of December 31, 1985. Max must also pay the pension fund normal costs of $20,000 per year. The pension fund is expected to earn 10 percent on fund assets. Without recognizing either an asset or a

TABLE 19-4

AMORTIZATION TABLE FOR MAX CORPORATION—AMORTIZATION PERIOD AND FUNDING PERIOD BOTH 4 YEARS

DATE	AMORTIZATION OF PSC — ANNUITY AMOUNT	10% INTEREST ON BALANCE SHEET ACCOUNT BALANCE	PSC PENSION EXPENSE (DEBIT)	FUNDING PSC — CASH PAYMENT (CREDIT)	BALANCE SHEET ACCOUNT — CHANGE—DEBIT (CREDIT)	ACCOUNT BALANCE—DEBIT (CREDIT)
12/31/85	0	0	0	0	0	0
12/31/86	$100,000	0	$100,000	$100,000	0	0
12/31/87	100,000	0	100,000	100,000	0	0
12/31/88	100,000	0	100,000	100,000	0	0
12/31/89	100,000	0	100,000	100,000	0	0
Total	$400,000		$400,000	$400,000		

[7] *Accounting Principles Board Opinion No. 8,* "Accounting for the Cost of Pension Plans."

liability, Max will begin paying off the PSC obligation and amortizing (expensing) the PSC benefits. In doing so, Max may elect to amortize (expense) over a period that is longer, shorter, or equal to the period of funding. Let us illustrate all three possible cases, starting with the one where the amortization period for the PSC benefits equals the funding period, which is assumed to be 4 years.

Amortization period equal to funding period   The amortization schedule in Table 19–4 would be used as the basis for the following entries on December 31, 1986–1989 (in $000):

	1986		1987		1988		1989	
	DEBIT	CREDIT	DEBIT	CREDIT	DEBIT	CREDIT	DEBIT	CREDIT
Pension expense (PSC)	100		100		100		100	
Cash		100		100		100		100
(To record PSC expense)								
Pension expense (NC)	20		20		20		20	
Cash		20		20		20		20
(To record normal cost expense)								

When the period (or the amount) of funding is equal to the period (or the amount) of amortization, the recording process is quite simple. The decrease in cash is equal to the pension expense for the PSC benefits. The debit side of the entry to record the payment on the unrecorded liability for the PSC obligation (both interest and principal) is equal to the credit side of the entry to reduce the unrecorded asset for the PSC benefits.

Amortization period shorter than funding period   Accounting for PSC becomes more complex when the period (or the amount) of funding is different from the amortization period. Table 19–5 illustrates the necessary calculations to support the entries required for a 4-year amortization period and a 6-year funding period for Max Corporation's $316,990 PSC obligation. The entries to record *only the PSC amounts* would be as follows, with the amounts taken directly from Table 19–5:

	1986		1987		1988	
	DEBIT	CREDIT	DEBIT	CREDIT	DEBIT	CREDIT
Pension expense (PSC)	100,000		102,722		105,715	
Pension liability		27,217		29,939		32,932
Cash		72,783		72,783		72,783

	1989		1990		1991	
	DEBIT	CREDIT	DEBIT	CREDIT	DEBIT	CREDIT
Pension expense (PSC)	109,014		12,632		6,616	
Pension liability		36,231	60,151		66,168	
Cash		72,783		72,783		72,784

TABLE 19-5

AMORTIZATION TABLE FOR MAX CORPORATION—AMORTIZATION PERIOD SHORTER (4 YEARS) THAN FUNDING PERIOD (6 YEARS)						
		AMORTIZATION OF PSC		FUNDING PSC	BALANCE SHEET ACCOUNT	
DATE	ANNUITY AMOUNT (4 YEARS)	10% INTEREST ON BALANCE SHEET ACCOUNT BALANCE	PSC PENSION EXPENSE (DEBIT)	CASH PAYMENT (CREDIT)	CHANGE— DEBIT (CREDIT)	ACCOUNT BALANCE— DEBIT (CREDIT)
12/31/85	0	0	0	0	0	0
12/31/86	$100,000	0	$100,000	$ 72,783	$(27,217)	$ (27,217)
12/31/87	100,000	$ 2,722	102,722	72,783	(29,939)	(57,156)
12/31/88	100,000	5,715a	105,715	72,783	(32,932)	(90,088)
12/31/89	100,000	9,014a	109,014	72,783	(36,231)	(126,319)
12/31/90	—	12,632	12,632	72,783	60,151	(66,168)
12/31/91	—	6,616a	6,616	72,784	66,168	0
Total	$400,000	$36,699	$436,699	$436,699		

a Rounded.

The data in Table 19-5 should be viewed as a table that provides the amortization expense amount (= pension expense for PSC) that is based upon a given cash payment for PSC ($72,783 per year) and **a balance sheet account (Pension Liability) representing the cumulative difference between the cash flow and the expense.** Note that the total pension expense is equal to the total cash payments, as in Table 19-4. However, unlike Table 19-4, a balance sheet account is necessary in Table 19-5 to record the **difference between the cash flow and the pension expense amount.** The basic purpose of this balance sheet account is to enable the entry to balance. Without the balance sheet account, the entry would look like two one-sided unequal entries, such as the following:

12/31/86   Pension expense   100,000
                  Cash   72,783

The $27,217 difference between the 1986 cash payment and the pension expense ($100,000 − $72,783) is called a **pension liability,** but is it really a liability? Conceptually, this pension liability account is the difference between the remaining net book value of the *unrecorded* PSC asset and the *unrecorded* PSC obligation. Some have argued that the entire PSC obligation for $316,990 either is a liability or is not a liability. Furthermore, because the generally accepted accounting method does *not* permit recognizing the entire PSC as a liability, the recognizing of part of the PSC as a liability might be considered to be internally inconsistent.

Amortization period longer than funding period To further illustrate the fundamental difference between the generally accepted method of accounting for pensions and the conceptual approach shown earlier in the Arrow Corporation example, consider the case where the period of amortization (6 years) is longer than the period of funding (4 years). Note that this third of three possible cases is the one that is parallel to the Arrow Corporation case illustrated earlier. The computations to support the journal entries are listed in Table 19-6. The following entries would record the tabular data for the PSC alone:

	1986		1987		1988	
	DEBIT	**CREDIT**	**DEBIT**	**CREDIT**	**DEBIT**	**CREDIT**
Pension expense	72,783		70,061		67,068	
Prepaid pension	27,217		29,939		32,932	
Cash		100,000		100,000		100,000

	1989		1990		1991	
	DEBIT	**CREDIT**	**DEBIT**	**CREDIT**	**DEBIT**	**CREDIT**
Pension expense	63,769		60,151		66,168	
Prepaid pension	36,231			60,151		66,168
Cash		100,000				

Comparison of Conceptual and GAAP Approaches

If the the data in Table 19–6 are compared with the data in Exhibit 19–3, the similarities between the Max case and the Arrow case become apparent. The *net* balance sheet effect for Arrow (column 3 in Exhibit 19–3) is identical to the single balance sheet account balance for Max (Table 19–6) at December 31 of each year. As a result, an appropriate definition for the balance sheet account in the Max (GAAP) case is that it **represents the difference between the unrecorded PSC asset and the unrecorded PSC liability.**

In terms of the relationship between the expenses of Max Corporation and Arrow Corporation, we observe that the *total* pension expense is the same for both companies each year (1986–1991). However, Arrow's expenses were broken down into an interest expense component and an amortization of the PSC expense portion. The Max illustration did not differentiate between interest expense and amortization expense but instead referred to both components as pension expense.

Note that in the Arrow case, the total amount charged to *PSC expense* was limited to the *initial* obligation for past service costs ($316,990). The remainder of the expense was called *interest expense* because it was attributable to the fact that Arrow

TABLE 19–6

AMORTIZATION TABLE FOR MAX CORPORATION—AMORTIZATION PERIOD LONGER (6 YEARS) THAN FUNDING PERIOD (4 YEARS)

	AMORTIZATION OF PSC			FUNDING PSC	BALANCE SHEET ACCOUNT	
DATE	**ANNUITY AMOUNT (6 YEARS)**	**10% INTEREST ON BALANCE SHEET ACCOUNT BALANCE**	**PSC PENSION EXPENSE (DEBIT)**	**CASH PAYMENT (CREDIT)**	**CHANGE— DEBIT (CREDIT)**	**ACCOUNT BALANCE— DEBIT (CREDIT)**
12/31/85	0	0	0	0	0	0
12/31/86	$ 72,783	0	$ 72,783	$100,000	$27,217	$ 27,217
12/31/87	72,783	$ 2,722	70,061	100,000	29,939	57,156
12/31/88	72,783	5,715[a]	67,068	100,000	32,932	90,088
12/31/89	72,783	9,014[a]	63,769	100,000	36,231	126,319
12/31/90	72,783	12,632	60,151	0	(60,151)	66,168
12/31/91	72,784	6,616[a]	66,168	0	(66,168)	0
Total	$436,699	$36,699	$400,000	$400,000		

[a] Rounded.

was not able (or willing) to pay off the obligation immediately. The faster the funding of PSC, the lower the amount of interest expense for the employer, and the lower the total charge to income resulting from the PSC obligation.

Departures from Schedules

Several other points should be noted in comparing the Max and Arrow cases. Note that Arrow elected to amortize the PSC asset over 6 years using **present-value amortization methods.** Present-value amortization is also the implicit amortization method in the Max case. This is a *necessary condition* if the two cases are to be comparable as to their income statement effects.

In addition to changes in the rate of amortization, change may also be made in the schedule of cash payments to the pension fund. Suppose that Max (or Arrow) was unable to pay the entire $100,000 payment in 1988. What impact would this have on the schedules? In measuring the impact on the income statement due to changes in either the funding or the amortization schedules, it may be much easier to refer to the Arrow illustrations. In the context of the Arrow case, such changes are fairly straightforward. Amortization and changes in amortization for the PSC asset are no different than they would be for any other asset; and payments on the PSC debt as well as changes from intended payment schedules are not different than for any other type of debt. In pension accounting, however, it is generally more difficult to see these underlying concepts by examining computations such as those in Tables 19–4, 19–5, and 19–6. It is even more difficult to understand or to define the balance sheet account reported under GAAP (Prepaid Pension or Pension Liability) by examining the traditional amortization schedules (see Tables 19–5 and 19–6) and journal entries. As a result of the non–GAAP Arrow Corporation example, we are able to show that the balance sheet account for PSC reported under GAAP is simply the difference between the unrecorded PSC asset balance and the unrecorded PSC liability balance at any point in the life of the PSC obligation.

LIMITATIONS ON PENSION EXPENSE

The generally accepted principles for pension accounting outlined in **APB Opinion No. 8** set forth both minimum and maximum values for pension expense to be reported in the income statement in any given year.[8] **Minimum pension expense** is the total of the following three elements:

1. Normal cost
2. Interest on any unfunded past or prior service cost obligation (whether or not it is recorded)
3. A provision for vested benefits

Maximum pension expense, on the other hand, is the total of the following three elements:

1. Normal cost
2. Ten percent (one-tenth) of past or prior service costs until fully amortized
3. An implicit interest charge (or credit) on the *balance* in the *recorded* pension liability (or asset).

[8] Ibid., par. 17.

The **minimum pension expense** allowed is based in part on implicit interest rates. This implied rate of return established by the actuary times the unpaid balance in the entire past or prior service cost obligation is the second element of the minimum. Remember that the entire past or prior service obligation is *not* the *recorded* pension liability amount (as in the Max case, Table 19–5), but rather the entire unrecorded balance (as in the Arrow case, Table 19–2).

The minimum expense must also include another amount for situations where the total vested benefits to date are in *excess* of the total payments to the pension fund plus the *recorded* (recognized) pension liability. Assume that the total amount of vested employee benefits is $500,000 and that the current value of the pension fund assets is $300,000. Further, assume that the liability recorded on the books of the employer has a $120,000 balance. Vested benefits would exceed fund assets plus pension liability by $80,000 [$500,000 − ($300,000 + 120,000)]. This $80,000 would generally not be expensed immediately but would be charged to pension expense by means of a complex allocation formula. This minimum formula per **APB Opinion No. 8** has been indirectly affected by a different set of minimum conditions spelled out in ERISA. The ERISA requirements, which generally provide for a more rigid set of minimum conditions, are reviewed later in this chapter.

**EXHIBIT
19–4**

ILLUSTRATION OF MINIMUM PENSION EXPENSE CALCULATIONS

Variation 1 (Table 19–4)

	1987	1986
1. Normal cost	$20,000	$20,000
2. 10% of past service cost balance	24,869[a]	31,699[b]
3. Provision for vested benefits	0	0
	$44,869	$51,699

Variation 2 (Table 19–5)

	1987	1986
1. Normal cost	$20,000	$20,000
2. 10% of past service cost balance	27,591[c]	31,699[d]
3. Provision for vested benefits	0	0
	$47,591	$51,699

Variation 3 (Table 19–6)

Same as Variation 1 because minimum is dependent on actual funding and total PSC obligation balance, which are the same in Variations 1 and 3.

[a] 10% of [$100,000 (*P/A*, 3, .10)].
[b] 10% of [$100,000 (*P/A*, 4, .10)].
[c] 10% of [$72,783 (*P/A* 5, .10)].
[d] 10% of [*P/A*, 6, .10)].
Note: The 10% rate for item 2 above will vary from example to example, depending on the actuarial implicit interest rates.

Maximum
Pension
Expense

The **maximum pension expense** is based on an arbitrary fixed 10 percent (one-tenth) of the past or prior service cost amount (until fully amortized), plus normal cost and an interest charge. The implicit interest charge is based on the balance in the balance sheet account (Pension Liability or Prepaid Pension) before the pension expense is recorded for that period.

To illustrate the maximum and minimum expenses, consider the three variations of the Max case illustrated in Tables 19–4, 19–5, and 19–6. Exhibit 19–4 computes the minimum for the three variations **assuming that vested benefits do not exceed funding.** Note that the second item, interest on the unfunded PSC, cannot be determined from the conventional accounting amortization schedules. These figures are more easily identified in Tables 19–2 and 19–3 where the total liability was treated as a separate account.

The maximum pension expense calculations for these three variations are illustrated in Exhibit 19–5. Note that the "pension expense" recorded in all three variations of the Max case exceeds the maximum allowed per **APB Opinion No. 8.** The amortization period would have to be extended in each variation to meet the maximum allowable expense. The illustrations were for an unacceptably short time pe-

EXHIBIT
19–5

ILLUSTRATION OF MAXIMUM PENSION EXPENSE CALCULATIONS		
Variation 1 (Table 19–4)		
	1987	**1986**
1. Normal cost	$20,000	$20,000
2. 10% of past service cost obligation	31,699[a]	31,699[a]
3. Implicit interest of 10% on pension asset or liability	0	0
	$51,699	$51,699
Variation 2 (Table 19–5)		
	1987	**1986**
1. Normal cost	$20,000	$20,000
2. 10% of past service cost obligation	31,699[a]	31,699[a]
3. Plus implicit interest of 10% on pension liability	2,722[b]	0[b]
	$54,421	$51,699
Variation 3 (Table 19–6)		
	1987	**1986**
1. Normal cost	$20,000	$20,000
2. 10% of past service cost obligation	31,699[a]	31,699[a]
3. Less implicit interest of 10% on pension asset	(2,722)[c]	(0)[c]
	$48,977	$51,699

[a] 10% of $316,990 original PSC until fully amortized.
[b] See Table 19–5, "10% Interest on Balance Sheet Account Balance."
[c] See Table 19–6, "10% Interest on Balance Sheet Account Balance."
Note: The 10% rate in item 2 for the examples above is *fixed* and will *not* change from example to example. However, the 10% interest factor in item 3 is specific to this case and will vary depending on the implicit interest rate used by the actuary for return on pension fund assets.

EXHIBIT
19–6

PENSION FOOTNOTE, PSC AMORTIZATION PERIOD

AMP INCORPORATED AND PAMCOR, INC., AND THEIR SUBSIDIARIES
Footnote to Financial Statements, December 31, 1980

8. Employee Retirement Plans

The Company has a pension plan covering substantially all domestic employees. Certain international subsidiaries also have pension plans. Total pension expense was $12,112,000 in 1980, $12,157,000 in 1979, and $9,793,000 in 1978 which includes, as to certain defined benefit plans, amortization of past service cost over 10 years. The Company's policy is to fund pension costs currently.

At January 1, 1980, accumulated plan benefits and plan net assets for the United States defined benefit plan were:

Actuarial present value of accumulated plan benefits:	
Vested	$ 69,108,000
Nonvested	7,766,000
	$ 76,874,000
Net assets available for plan benefits	$104,414,000

The assumed rate of return used in determining the actuarial present value of accumulated plan benefits was 7½%.

A change during 1980 in the actuarial cost method used and in actuarial assumptions relative to rate of return, salary increases, and turnover for the United States employees' plan had the effect of reducing net income by approximately 1¢ per share.

The Company's international pension plans are not required to report to certain governmental agencies pursuant to ERISA and do not otherwise determine the actuarial value of accumulated benefits or net assets available for benefits as calculated and disclosed above. At December 31, 1980, the net assets of those plans exceeded the present value of vested benefits.

---

riod in order to simplify the illustrations and the amortization schedules. Actual amortization periods for PSC benefits are often disclosed in the footnotes to the employer's financial statements, such as the footnote shown in Exhibit 19–6.

The maximum and minimum are established as tests of the amount of pension expense and are not intended to prescribe a particular method of accounting for past or prior service costs. Any systematic method of expensing past or prior service costs that falls within the maximum and minimum computations is permissible under **APB Opinion No. 8.**[9]

ACTUARIAL COST METHODS

Actuaries use various cost methods and assumptions to determine the amount of pension cost obligations for normal cost and past and prior service cost. Although it is not the intention of this text to explain all the various **actuarial cost methods,** the examples will provide an understanding of how pension costs are measured.

Two actuarial cost methods will be illustrated below. The first, called the **unit credit method,** is the currently acceptable method for certain disclosures called for by **FASB Statement No. 35** and **FASB Statement No. 36** for employee pension fund and employer financial statements.[10] The unit credit method is *one* of several

[9] Ibid., par. 23.

[10] *Statement of Financial Accounting Standards No. 35,* "Accounting and Reporting by Defined Benefit Pension Plans," and *Statement of Financial Accounting Standards No. 36,* "Disclosure of Pension Information" (Stamford, CT: FASB, March and May 1980).

methods under the **accumulated benefits approach** required by the FASB and is based on historical service and pay data that do not anticipate future pension cost increases attributable to pay raises. The unit credit method results in increasing pension costs over time, with earlier years' pension expense lower and later years' expense higher than many of the other actuarial cost methods.

The second method is called the **entry-age normal method** and is one of the most widely used methods in practice. This method charges each period with a pension expense that is either a *constant absolute amount* (a fixed number of dollars) or a *constant relative amount* of total compensation (such as a constant percentage of total pay benefits). We illustrate the constant absolute amount to provide the sharpest contrast with the unit credit method.

Unit Credit Method

To illustrate the **unit credit method** of cost estimation, assume that the Dowd Chemical Company has entered into a defined benefit pension agreement with its 100 employees whereby each employee will receive $1,000 *per year* after retirement for each year he or she has worked for Dowd. If an employee works 35 years for the company, he or she will receive $35,000 per year following retirement. This benefit provided by Dowd is based on each employee's entire period of employment, even though some work has been performed *prior* to the original pension agreement. (In other words, each employee receives past service cost benefits for work performed prior to the pension agreement.) The actuary has provided Dowd and the trustee of the pension fund hired by the employees with the following data:

1. The average age of the Dowd labor force is 40 years.
2. The average employee has been with the company 15 years.
3. The retirement age is 60 years.
4. Turnover at Dowd is nonexistent.
5. The average life expectancy of Dowd employees is 75 years.
6. The pension fund assets will earn 8 percent per year.

The following time line represents the current position of the Dowd labor force as of December 31, 1985:

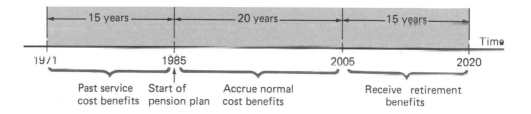

PSC amount Based on the data provided by the actuary, the past service cost benefits as of the inception of the plan are equal to the present value of 15 years' benefits at $1,000 per year for 100 employees due in 20 years. In other words, by the year 2005 the pension fund must have assets equal to the present value of $15,000 per year for the next 15 years (2006–2020) for each of the 100 employees. What amount must be available in 2005 to cover this past service cost benefit? The value of this annuity as of 2005 would be computed as follows:

$$100[\$15,000 \ (P/A, \ 15, \ 8\%)] =$$
$$100[\$15,000 \ (8.5595)] =$$
$$100(\$128,392.50) = \$12,839,250$$

Because the $12,839,250 is the value of the annuity at date of (average) retirement (2005), how much would Dowd have to pay the pension fund trustee today (1985) to satisfy this obligation 20 years from now? This amount is computed as follows:

$$\$12,839,250 \ (P/F, \ 20, \ 8\%) =$$
$$\$12,839,250 \ (.2145) = \$2,754,019$$

On December 31, 1985, the present value of the past service cost obligation for Dowd is $2,754,019. If Dowd paid the pension fund this amount today and the fund earned 8 percent per year on its assets, the amount would be enough to pay each employee $15,000 per year each year from 2006 to 2020. If Dowd pays the PSC obligation over some future period from December 31, 1985, the total payments to the fund will exceed the $2,754,019 present value of the PSC obligation because of interest factors. This was illustrated earlier in the several variations of the Max Corporation case where payment of the PSC obligation took place over 4 or 6 years.

Normal cost amount Referring again to the time line, we see that 20 years of normal costs remain to be earned by the employees. By the end of 1986, each of the 100 employees will have earned another $1,000 per year to be paid in an annuity over the period 2006–2020. What is the cost to the employer of this 15-year annuity for the 100 employees at December 31, 1986? The present value of a 15-year annuity of $1,000 each per year for 100 employees at 2005 is

$$100[\$1,000 \ (P/A, \ 15, \ 8\%)] =$$
$$100[\$1,000 \ (8.5595)] =$$
$$100[\$8,559.50] = \$855,950 \text{ at } 12/31/05$$

The present value of this amount as of December 31, 1986 is

$$\$855,950 \ (P/F, \ 19, \ 8\%) =$$
$$\$855,950 \ (.2317) = \$198,324 \text{ at } 12/31/86$$

Normal cost expense for 1986 would be $198,324. Note that from 1986 to 2005 the normal cost for the unit credit method will increase each year. The 1987 normal cost, assuming no changes in the actuarial assumptions, would be

$$\$855,950 \ (P/F, \ 18, \ 8\%) =$$
$$\$855,950 \ (.2502) = \$214,159 \text{ at } 12/31/87$$

Entry-Age Normal Method

The **entry-age normal method** tends to normalize or smooth out the pension expense to a greater extent than do most other actuarial methods. The Dowd data summarized above can be used to illustrate this alternative.

To measure pension costs under the entry-age normal method, first determine the total value of *all retirement benefits* (PSC and normal costs) as of the date of retirement, 2005 in the Dowd case. At the date of retirement, the pension fund should have assets equal to the present value of a 15-year annuity of $35,000 per year for each of the 100 employees. This amount, at 2005, would be

$$100[\$35,000 \ (P/A, 15, 8\%)] =$$
$$100[\$35,000 \ (8.5595)] =$$
$$100[\$299,582.50] = \$29,958,250$$

Next, determine the annuity amount that, over **the entire benefit period** (both the PSC period and the normal cost period), 1971–2005, or 35 years in the Dowd case, would accumulate to $29,958,250 by 2005. The 35-year annuity that would result in a fund balance of $29,958,250 by 2005 is

$$\$x \ (F/A, 35, 8\%) = \$29,958,250$$
$$\$x \ (172.3168) = \$29,958,250$$
$$\$x = \frac{\$29,958,250}{172.3168}$$
$$\$x = \$173,856 \ (\text{rounded})$$

If $173,856 were paid into the fund each year-end from 1971 through 2005 and the fund earned 8 percent each year on its assets, the balance in the fund would be $29,958,250 at the end of 2005, and each of the 100 employees could receive a $35,000 per year annuity for the period 2006–2020.

PSC amount The $173,856 annuity represents a uniform pension cost amount that would satisfy the pension PSC and normal cost obligation **assuming it began at the end of 1971.** Because the plan is not started until 1985, the past service cost obligation at the beginning of the plan would equal the future value of the 15-year annuity of $173,856 per year for the period 1971–1985, or

$$\$173,856 \ (F/A, 15, 8\%) = \$173,856 \ (27.1521) =$$
$$= \$4,720,555 \text{ at } 12/31/85$$

Normal cost amount The normal cost from 1986 through 2005 would remain $173,856 per year each year. The total of the $4,720,555 PSC at December 31, 1985, plus the $173,856 per year normal cost would accumulate to $29,958,250 by the end of 2005.

Table 19–7 compares the unit credit and the entry-age normal methods. Note that as of December 31, 1985, the entry-age normal method measures the past service cost benefits at about $2,000,000 more than the unit credit method, a significant difference. Variations of the entry-age normal method that measure pension benefits based on salary (rather than years of service, as in these examples) and that

TABLE 19–7

DOWD CHEMICAL COMPANY PENSION PLAN—COMPARISON OF ACTUARIAL COST METHODS

ACTUARIAL COST METHOD	PAST SERVICE COST AT 12/31/85	NORMAL COST		
		1986	1987	1988
Unit credit method	$2,754,019	$198,324	$214,159	$231,363
Entry-age normal method	4,720,555	173,856	173,856	173,856

anticipate future salary increases might generate annual normal cost measures that are greater than the comparable normal cost measures under the unit credit method in some situations. The most important point is simply to observe that both PSC and normal costs will vary depending on which actuarial cost method is used.

Changes in Actuarial Estimates

Occasionally, new evidence emerges that requires the actuary to revise the estimated pension cost obligations. These revisions result in **actuarial gains or losses,** referred to as **experience gains or losses** in ERISA, which may affect current and future normal cost expense. **APB Opinion No. 8** suggests two methods of accounting for the effect of year-to-year gains and losses in order to minimize or reduce wide fluctuations in normal cost expense.[11] The **spreading method** spreads the annual gain or loss over a period of 10 to 15 years, with the specific period to be elected by each employer.[12] The normal cost for each year would be adjusted for between one-tenth and one-fifteenth of the actuarial gains and losses from the last 10 to 15 years, respectively.

A second alternative, the **averaging method,** computes the average of past annual actuarial gains and losses and adjusts the current normal cost expense accordingly. Consider the following data from the Great Lakes Dairy's pension plan:

YEAR	PRIMARY REASON FOR GAIN OR LOSS	ACTUARIAL GAIN (LOSS) FOR YEAR
1979	Increase in employee life expectancy	$(48,000)
1980	Higher than expected return on fund assets	88,000
1981	Higher than expected employee turnover	76,000
1982	Change in estimated retirement rate	(37,000)
1983	Lower than expected return on fund assets	(24,000)
1984	Higher than expected return on fund assets	35,000
		$ 90,000

The average gain over the period 1979–1984 was $15,000 per year ($90,000/6 years). The averaging method would reduce 1984 normal cost by $15,000 as a result of experience gains.

Under the spreading method, the annual gains and losses would be spread out over a period of 10 to 15 years (20 years is permitted for multi-employer plans) on a straight-line basis. Assume Great Lakes Dairy decides to spread the gains and losses over a 10-year period. The pension plan started in 1979, and therefore the 1984 adjustment would be $9,000, computed as follows:

YEAR	GAIN (LOSS)	ANNUAL ADJUSTMENT AMOUNT
1979	$(48,000)	$(4,800)
1980	88,000	8,800
1981	76,000	7,600
1982	(37,000)	(3,700)
1983	(24,000)	(2,400)
1984	35,000	3,500
	$ 90,000	$ 9,000

[11] *Accounting Principles Board Opinion No. 8,* "Accounting for the Cost of Pension Plans," par. 30.

[12] The 15-year limit is for single-employer pension plans and is the result of the 1974 Pension Reform Act. Prior to 1974, *APB Opinion No. 8* permitted a 20-year spread. A 20-year spread is now permitted for multiemployer plans.

Each year until 1989 the additional gain or loss would be added in to the $9,000. If the 1985 actuarial gain were $19,000, the 1985 adjustment would be $10,900—$9,000 + (.10 × $19,000). In 1989, the $48,000 actuarial loss from 1979 would have been fully spread over the period 1979 to 1988, and it would be deleted from the total, such that the 1989 adjustment would begin with one-tenth of the $88,000 gain from 1980 and continue to add one-tenth of each subsequent year's gain or loss up to and including one-tenth of 1989's gain or loss.

The spreading method, unlike the averaging method, accurately accounts for the actual gains and losses by fully amortizing each year's gain or loss. The averaging method simply adds in historical results each year and then computes a new average that represents a best estimate of what a typical gain or loss might be in the long run. The averaging method may also consider expected future gains or losses in its computation. The $48,000 loss from 1979 in our example might remain in the averaging computation indefinitely, or it might be dropped after 10, 15, or 20 years depending on how management feels the average is best computed. There is no strict formula for applying the averaging method.

It should be noted here that under either of these two approaches, any gain or loss resulting from a single event that is not likely to occur again or is somehow unique and not related to the operation of the pension plan should *not* be included as an actuarial gain or loss but should be reported as a gain or loss of the period in which the event took place. Examples of such events would include plant closings or mergers, which could, as a side effect, have a substantial impact on pension costs by way of affecting the number of employees covered, and so on.

Changes in Actuarial Cost Methods

Changes in actuarial cost methods are treated as changes in estimates rather than changes in principles. The new cost method being adapted is applied prospectively to the pension plan as of the beginning of the period of the change.[13] Pension costs reported in prior years *should not be retroactively adjusted.* The effect of these changes should be disclosed in the notes to the financial statement.

THE IMPACT OF ERISA

The **Employee Retirement Income Security Act (ERISA),** passed by Congress in 1974, has had a significant impact on private pension plans. The essence of the act was to reduce the uncertainty that pension benefits promised by employers would be provided. The act virtually did away with unfunded pension plans, requiring employers to fund employee benefits by using an acceptable actuarial cost method that will ensure that payments will be sufficient to cover all pension obligations according to the plan. The government's own Social Security system is perhaps the only remaining example of a major pay-as-you-go retirement system still in force after the enactment of ERISA.

The act also required a significant increase in the vested benefits for most plans, requiring vesting of all benefits described in the plan by the fifteenth year of employment, and fractional vesting for shorter periods. Although not all plans were affected by this requirement, it eliminated situations where no vesting occurred until after 15 to 25 years of employment, a practice that was considered to be unfair to employees.

Under the present law, three possible vesting patterns are allowable. The first calls for no vesting until the end of 10 years, after which all benefits earned by an

---

[13] *Accounting Principles Board Opinion No. 8,* "Accounting for the Cost of Pension Plans," par. 47.

employee become 100 percent vested. The second calls for no vesting until the fifth year of employment, after which the employee's benefits are 25 percent vested. The percentage of earned benefits that are vested then increases by 5 percent per year for years 6–10, and 10 percent per year for years 11–15, so that after 15 years the employee's benefits are 100 percent vested. A third pattern, called the **rule of 45,** provides a vesting formula based on the sum of the age of the employee plus the years of employment. The employee is 50 percent vested when the sum reaches 45, and 100 percent vested when the sum reaches 55, so long as at least 10 years of service have been provided. Table 19–8 provides an illustration of how these three vesting patterns would appear in one example.

ERISA also called for an organization (the **Pension Benefit Guarantee Corporation,** or **PBGC**) to be established to take over the management of private pension plans that have been terminated. The PBGC has authority to impose a lien of up to 30 percent of an employer's net assets for certain unfunded pension obligations. A number of pension plans have been terminated since 1974 due to their failure to comply with ERISA's terms. Over 400 private pension plans have been unable to meet the funding requirements under ERISA, and the PBGC has taken over as the trustee of these funds.

FINANCIAL STATEMENT DISCLOSURES

Employer Disclosures

Disclosures regarding pensions have been expanded as a result of **FASB Statement No. 36.**[14] Employers are now required to disclose the nature of the pension plan and to present some statement of the employer's accounting and funding policies. In addition, the employer is required to report

1. The actuarially determined present value of the *vested* benefits
2. The actuarially determined present value of the *nonvested* benefits
3. The net assets of the pension fund available for benefits
4. The implied rates of return used to measure items 1 and 2

Examples of these disclosures from two corporate annual reports are given in Exhibit 19–7. The pension disclosures are typically made in two of the footnotes to the financial statements. The policy footnote will usually describe the accounting or funding methods, and another footnote will usually describe both the vested and the nonvested portion of the accumulated plan benefits. The difference between the total vested and nonvested plan benefits and the fund's assets would represent the pension benefits that have been earned but are yet to be funded by the employer. Most companies tend to follow a policy of funding all benefits as incurred on an annual basis. Therefore any difference between *total* accumulated plan benefits and fund assets would normally represent the employer's unfunded past or prior service cost obligations.

Pension Fund Disclosures

The employees' pension fund, which is normally a separate entity owned by the employees, is obliged to report to the employees on fund operations. **FASB Statement No. 35** established certain reporting requirements designed to enable users to evaluate the fund's ability to provide current and future benefits to employees.[15] These

[14] *Statement of Financial Accounting Standards No. 36,* "Disclosure of Pension Information."

[15] *Statement of Financial Accounting Standards No. 35,* "Accounting and Reporting by Defined Benefit Pension Plans."

TABLE 19-8

ACCEPTABLE VESTING PATTERNS

Assume retirement benefits provide a $1,000 per year annuity for life after retirement for each additional year of service.

		VESTING PATTERN						
		FULL VESTING AFTER TENTH YEAR	VESTING BEGINS IN FIFTH YEAR		RULE OF 45			
YEARS OF SERVICE	DEFINED RETIREMENT BENEFITS (ANNUAL ANNUITY AMOUNT)	VESTED BENEFITS	VESTED BENEFITS	PERCENT VESTED	EMPLOYEE'S AGE	VESTED BENEFITS	PERCENT VESTED
1	$ 1,000	$ 0	$ 0	0	30	$ 0	0
2	2,000	0	0	0	31	0	0
3	3,000	0	0	0	32	0	0
4	4,000	0	0	0	33	0	0
5	5,000	0	1,250	25	34	0	0
6	6,000	0	1,800	30	35	0	0
7	7,000	0	2,450	35	36	0	0
8	8,000	0	3,200	40	37	4,000	50
9	9,000	0	4,050	45	38	5,400	60
10	10,000	10,000	5,000	50	39	7,000	70
11	11,000	11,000	6,600	60	40	8,800	80
12	12,000	12,000	8,400	70	41	10,800	90
13	13,000	13,000	10,400	80	42	13,000	100
14	14,000	14,000	12,600	90	43	14,000	100
15	15,000	15,000	15,000	100	44	15,000	100
16	16,000	16,000	16,000	100	45	16,000	100

disclosures are similar to those noted above for employers and include information concerning

1. The present value of the accumulated pension plan benefits that are vested and also the present value of nonvested benefits
2. The amount of vested benefits of participants currently receiving benefits and the vested benefits of those *not* currently receiving benefits
3. Pension fund assets at their fair market value and annual changes in assets available for benefits
4. The impact, in terms of present values, of changes resulting from plan amendments, changes in actuarial assumptions or methods, and other changes that affect the nature of the pension plan

The financial statements are not covered by **FASB Statement No. 35,** and although they are not required by the FASB, they are normally provided by the pension plan to the employee covered by the plan.

FUNDS FLOW EFFECTS

Pensions are a significant element of labor costs and tend to have a major role in fund flows as a result. The pension expense that is charged to operations is not always representative of the amount of funds consumed for the pension plan in any given period, however, and as a result pension expense may have a nonfund element

EXHIBIT
19–7

PENSION DISCLOSURES—EMPLOYERS

R. J. REYNOLDS INDUSTRIES, INC.
Notes to Consolidated Financial Statements
(Dollars in Millions Except Per Share Amounts)

Note 15
Pension Plans
The Company provides retirement benefits for substantially all of its regular full-time employees, including certain employees in foreign countries, through Company-administered plans and plans administered under collective bargaining agreements.

Pension expense for 1980, 1979, and 1978 was $84 million, $75 million, and $58 million, respectively. The increase in 1979 compared to 1978 resulted largely from the Del Monte merger. The Company's policy with respect to Company-administered plans is to fund pension costs accrued. Past service costs are amortized over a 30-year period.

The following table presents information regarding the financial condition of the Company's domestic defined benefit plans, as estimated by the Company's consulting actuary, as of the most recent valuation date, December 31, 1979:

	CALCULATED BASED ON CURRENT SALARY LEVELS OF PLAN PARTICIPANTS	CALCULATED BASED ON ACTUARIAL PROJECTIONS OF FUTURE SALARY INCREASES
Actuarial present value of accumulated plan benefits[a]		
Vested	$431.5	$567.1
Non-vested	94.6	171.4
	$526.1	$738.5
Net assets available for benefits (at market value)	$567.7	$567.7

[a] The assumed rate of return used in determining the actuarial present value of accumulated plan benefits was 8 percent.

The Company's foreign pension plans are not required to report to certain U.S. government agencies pursuant to ERISA and do not otherwise determine the actuarial value of accumulated benefits in the same manner as those calculated and disclosed above. For those plans, the value of vested benefits does not differ materially from the total assets and balance sheet accruals related to those plans.

In addition, the Company makes payments under the terms of various collective bargaining agreements to provide welfare benefits, including pension benefits, for covered employees. It is not practical at this time to determine the amount of these payments ultimately used to fund pension benefit plans or the current financial condition of these plans.

GENERAL TELEPHONE & ELECTRONICS CORPORATION AND SUBSIDIARIES
Excerpts from Notes

7 Pension Plans
Most subsidiaries have trusteed pension plans which are maintained without cost to the employees. These subsidiaries generally fund pension costs as accrued. The actuarially determined aggregate costs of all plans, including amortization of unfunded liability over periods not exceeding 30 years, was $294 million, $265 million, and $226 million for 1980–1978, respectively.

For domestic pension plans, the actuarially computed present value of accumulated plan benefits, based on an assumed rate of return of 6%, totaled $2.2 billion, including $400 million applicable to non-vested plan benefits. Net assets of these plans totaled $2.5 billion at December 31, 1980. The Company's foreign pension plans are not required to report to certain governmental agencies pursuant to ERISA and therefore similar information has not been determined for these plans. However, the market value of the assets of the plans was in excess of the actuarially computed value of accumulated benefits at December 31, 1980.

included. As we noted in this chapter, only in those instances where the amount of funding equals the amount of expense is there a direct relationship between fund flows and pension expense. Whenever an asset such as Prepaid Pension Costs or a liability such as Unfunded Pension Costs is reported in the balance sheet, it signals the reader that there has been a cumulative differential between funding and expensing of pension costs. An asset would signal that the use of funds exceeded the cumulative amount of pension expense, while a liability would signal that the cumulative pension expense has exceeded the actual use of funds. Similarly, year to year changes in balance sheet accounts tend to signal what the relationship between funding and expense was in the most recent income statement. An increase in the Unfunded Pension Liability account would signal that the pension expense was greater than the funds paid to the pension plan during the past year, which would require an addition to the net income figure in converting it to "funds provided by operations." Since the differences between the pension expense and the funds paid to the pension plan may be significant in any given period, pensions may represent a significant factor in converting net income to a "funds from operations" figure.

SUMMARY

From a conceptual point of view, accounting for pensions is not significantly different from accounting for leased assets, and there are conceptual similarities with accounting for mortgages and other debt instruments as well. The major difference stems from the fact that, for generally accepted accounting purposes, no asset or liability is recorded on the firm's books to reflect past or prior service cost obligations. The key issues in pension accounting involve the application of the elements defined in **SFAC No. 3** to employee pension plans, with assets and liabilities being the critical elements of concern. The special terminology and accounting rules for such things as actuarial gains and losses or maximum and minimum expense calculations tend to make pension accounting somewhat more procedural and difficult than other topics. However, pensions are fundamentally similar to other long-term obligations of the firm.

QUESTIONS

Q19-1   Define the following terms: (a) unfunded pension plans, (b) noncontributory pension plans, and (c) defined benefit pension plans.

Q19-2   Define the following terms: (a) normal costs, (b) past service costs, (c) prior service costs, and (d) vested benefits.

Q19-3   What is an *actuary*, and what types of factors do actuaries use to measure pension costs?

Q19-4   Explain the following statement: "The assets of a pension fund are sometimes less than the actuarial vested benefits of the employees covered by the fund."

Q19-5   Evaluate the implications of the pay-as-you-go type of pension system used by the U.S. government on U.S. employees who make payments to the U.S. Social Security system.

Q19-6   In accounting for pension plans according to GAAP, corporations sometimes report assets identified as "prepaid pension costs" or some similar title. Explain how these "assets" are generated. Discuss whether they are consistent with the general definition of *asset*.

Q19–7 In accounting for pension plans according to GAAP, employers sometimes report Pension Liability accounts in their balance sheets. Explain the relationship between these reported liabilities and the total contractual obligations yet to be funded by the employer corporations.

Q19–8 Describe the impact of the Pension Reform Act of 1974 (ERISA) on GAAP for employers' pension plans.

Q19–9 What are the components of the minimum pension expense that can be reported by an employer in any given year?

Q19–10 What are the components of the maximum pension expense that can be reported by an employer in any given year?

Q19–11 How are changes in actuarial estimates treated from an accounting standpoint?

Q19–12 How are changes in actuarial cost methods accounted for?

Q19–13 Does the actuarial cost method used by an entity affect the measurement of the present value of the past service cost? Explain.

Q19–14 Is the annual normal cost measurement different for each actuarial cost method? Explain.

Q19–15 What is the impact on the estimated past service cost when the estimate of employee turnover rate is increased because of recent experience?

Q19–16 What is the impact on employees' vested benefits when the plant where they work is permanently closed down by the parent corporation because of inefficiencies and the employees are laid off?

Q19–17 Under what conditions will an employer who is recognizing both past service cost benefits and normal cost benefits in a defined benefit contributory pension plan report no balance sheet accounts related to the pension plan in the annual report?

Q19–18 Discuss the comparability of pension costs among entities under GAAP pension methods.

CASES

C19–1 Provide *brief* answers to the following questions related to pensions.

1. What were the major accounting implications of the 1974 Pension Reform Act?
2. How does the actuary know what the annual pension plan costs are to the company? (That is, what sort of things does the actuary consider in making these estimates?)
3. If I work for my firm for 8 years and then change jobs, will I be guaranteed any rights under its pension plan? How much and why?

C19–2 (CPA ADAPTED) Generally accepted accounting principles require that pension costs be accounted for on the accrual basis. The various components of pension expense include (but are not limited to) (1) normal cost, (2) past service cost, (3) prior service cost, and (4) interest.

REQUIRED Define each of the four terms above, and discuss how each of the costs is accounted for under generally accepted accounting principles.

C19–3 (CPA ADAPTED) The accounting for past service cost has been a controversial issue. Some members of the profession advocate the accrual of past service cost only to the extent funded, whereas others advocate the accrual of past service cost regardless of the amount funded.

REQUIRED

1. What are the arguments in favor of accruing past service cost only to the extent funded?
2. What are the arguments in favor of accruing past service cost regardless of the amount funded?

C19–4 Parrott Construction Company instituted a funded pension plan for its employees. Included in the plan was recognition of $48,000,000 of actuarially determined present value of past service cost benefits as of January 1, 1975. Parrott has been funding and amortizing these past service costs over a 30-year period based on an assumed interest rate of 9 percent on fund assets. In 1983 the actuary informs Parrott that because the pension fund has experienced a return on fund assets well in excess of the assumed return, the balance in the pension fund assets is much greater than anticipated. In fact, based on the 30-year funding period, the current pension fund assets are greater than the planned fund assets for 1985—over 2 years ahead of schedule. Parrott is experiencing some cash-flow problems because of a decline in new construction and decides to take advantage of the favorable pension fund experience by not making any payments to the pension fund in 1983 or 1984. The management asks for your advice as to how the pension expense might be handled.

REQUIRED Discuss the propriety of Parrott's plans and tell the management how to handle the expense.

C19-5 (CPA ADAPTED) Pension plans have developed in an environment characterized by a complex inter-action of social concepts, legal considerations, actuarial techniques, income tax laws, and accounting practices. *APB Opinion No. 8* delineates acceptable accounting practices for the cost of pension plans.

REQUIRED

1. The following terms are relevant to accounting for the cost of pension plans. Define or briefly explain (a) normal cost, (b) past service cost, (c) prior service cost, (d) funded plan, (e) vested benefits, (f) actuarial gains and losses, and (g) interest.
2. Identify the disclosures required in financial statements regarding a company's pension plan.

C19-6 The Elliott Corporation reported the following data in the footnote to its 1984 annual report:

> The pension expense was $76,835 for 1984 and $73,396 for 1983. The company funds all normal costs as incurred. Past service costs are being amortized over 30 years.
> The accumulated benefits and plan net assets at December 31, 1984 were as follows:

Actuarial present value of accumulated pension plan benefits:	
Vested	$6,840,000
Nonvested	3,112,000
	$9,952,000
Net assets available for plan benefits	$5,937,000

> The actuarial present values of accumulated pension plan benefits were measured based on an assumed rate of return on fund assets of 7.1 percent.

REQUIRED

1. Evaluate Elliott's pension plan.
2. Explain the meaning of each information item.
3. What is the relationship between the *vested benefits* and the *funding period?*

EXERCISES

E19-1 The C. Casey Company has a contributory pension plan for all of its employees. In 1984 a total of $400,000 was withheld from employees' salaries and deposited into a pension fund administered by an outside trustee. In addition, Casey deposited $800,000 of its own money into the fund in 1984. Based on the report of Casey's outside actuaries, which was received in December 1984, the 1984 actuarial cost of the pension plan was $1,300,000, which included $1,000,000 for normal cost and $300,000 for past service costs based on a 20-year amortization period. As a result of this report, Casey deposited $100,000 of its own money into the fund on January 12, 1985.

REQUIRED

1. What is the correct pension expense to be reported in Casey's 1984 income statement?
2. What is the impact on Casey's balance sheet at December 31, 1984?
3. Reconstruct the pension entry or entries December 31, 1984.

E19–2 Varsity, Inc., initiated a pension plan for its employees on January 1, 1986. At that time, it had 100 *former* employees who were to be covered by the plan and whose benefits had an actuarially determined present value of $983,000. These former employees would begin receiving benefits immediately. Varsity funded the entire $983,000 for the former employees on January 1, 1986. Normal costs of $200,000 for 1986 were fully funded at year end. Also, on December 31, 1986, Varsity made the first of 15 annual $750,000 payments to the fund for the past service cost benefits of the currently employed workers.

REQUIRED

1. Record these payments on Varsity's books for 1986.
2. Explain how they would be reported in the financial statements.

E19–3 In January 1985 Maize Company adopted a pension plan for its eligible employees. Unfunded past service cost was determined to be $9,000,000, and this amount will be paid for in ten annual installments of $1,464,701 to an outside funding agency administering the plan. The first payment for PSC is remitted to the fund on December 31, 1985. The following additional information is relevant:

Normal cost expense for 1985 (remitted to funding agency in 1985)	$860,000
Past service cost expense for 1985	750,000

REQUIRED

1. What is the unfunded pension cost to be reported in Maize's balance sheet for 1985?
2. What is the implicit interest on pension fund assets?

E19–4 As of December 31, 1985, the employees of T. Burns Technology, Inc., had just negotiated an initial pension contract. The following information is provided to you concerning the 50 technicians working for T. Burns:

1. The average age of the employees is 35 years.
2. The average employee has worked for Burns for 10 years.
3. The average employee will retire at age 55.
4. Burns is not expected to have any employee turnover.
5. The average life expectancy of an employee is 80 years.
6. The pension fund assets are expected to earn 12 percent per year.
7. Each employee will be credited with a $500-per-year annuity upon retirement for each year he or she has worked for Burns. All payments are assumed to be made at year-end.

REQUIRED

1. Measure the past service cost benefits of Burns's employees for December 31, 1985, using the unit credit method.
2. Measure the normal cost for December 31, 1986, and December 31, 1987, using the unit credit method.

E19–5 Assume all data listed in the preceding exercise.

REQUIRED

1. Measure the past service cost benefits of Burns's employees for December 31, 1985, using the entry-age normal method.
2. Measure the normal cost for December 31, 1986, and December 31, 1987, using the entry-age normal method.

E19–6 Assume that the accumulated benefit schedule for each employee of the Wixom Wax Works is as follows:

END OF YEAR	ACCUMULATED PENSION BENEFITS	END OF YEAR	ACCUMULATED PENSION BENEFITS	END OF YEAR	ACCUMULATED PENSION BENEFITS
1	$ 1,987	8	$22,723	15	$63,132
2	4,172	9	26,982	16	71,432
3	6,577	10	31,668	17	80,562
4	9,220	11	36,821	18	90,606
5	12,131	12	42,491	19	101,653
6	15,331	13	48,727	20	113,805
7	18,851	14	55,586		

Assume also that Wixom has adopted a plan in which vesting does not begin until the end of year 5 of employment. At the end of year 5, an employee's benefits become 25 percent vested. At the end of each of the next 5 years (years 6–10), the percentage of vesting increases by 5 percent each year (to 50 percent by the end of year 10). At the end of each of the following 5 years, the benefits increase by 10 percent per year (years 11–15) so that by the end of year 15 an employee is 100 percent vested.

REQUIRED

1. Prepare a vesting schedule.
2. What would an employee be entitled to after 12 years with Wixom Wax Works?
3. What would an employee with 10 years' experience at another company and 5 years' experience with Wixom be entitled to?
4. What are the alternative vesting schemes under ERISA?

E19–7 On January 1, 1984, Crisp, Inc., adopted a noncontributory pension plan for its employees. The actuarially determined present value of the past service cost benefits is estimated to be $1,250,000 at the inception of the plan, based on an assumed 12 percent return of pension fund assets. Crisp decided to fund the past service cost over 10 years and expense this component of pension cost over the next 25 years. Crisp also intends to fund annual normal costs of $285,000 each year.

REQUIRED Record the December 31 journal entries necessary to recognize the pension costs for 1984, 1985, and 1986. Ignore maximum and minimum limits.

E19–8 IXL Glass Company initiated a pension plan for its employees on January 1, 1983. The present value of the past service cost at that date was determined to be $875,000, based on a 10 percent return of fund assets. The management of IXL decided to fund these costs over 5 years and amortize them over 8 years.

REQUIRED

1. Prepare an amortization schedule for the past service costs.
2. Explain the balance in the balance sheet account related to past service costs at the end of year 5 (1987).

E19–9 The Whenever Corporation initiated a pension plan for its employees on January 1, 1982. The past service cost benefits were estimated to be $2,896,000 at that date, based on an assumed 12 percent return on fund assets. The management of Whenever decided to fund these costs over 15 years and amortize them over 30 years.

REQUIRED

1. Determine the balance in any balance sheet account as of the end of year 2001 (the end of the twentieth year). (*Hint:* You should *not* need to prepare an amortization table to do this.)
2. Record the past service costs for the year 1992.

E19–10

_____ 1. Which of the following is *not* likely to result in an actuarial gain?
   a. A decrease in the employee turnover rate

b. An increase in the expected return on fund assets
c. A decrease in the life expectancy of the employees
d. A plant closing
e. All the above are likely to result in an actuarial gain

_____ 2. When a company adopts a pension plan for accounting purposes, past service costs should be
a. Treated as a prior period adjustment because no future periods are benefited
b. Amortized in accordance with procedures used for income tax purposes
c. Amortized under accrual accounting to current and future periods benefited
d. Treated as an expense of the period during which the funding occurs
e. None of the above

_____ 3. In a balance sheet prepared in accordance with GAAP, what is the nature of a balance sheet account with a credit balance title "Unfunded Past Service Cost Benefits"?
a. It is the total present value of the past service cost benefits owed to the employees.
b. It is that portion of the total past service cost benefits that have vested.
c. It is the difference between the balance in the unrecorded assets and the balance in the unrecorded liabilities from the non-GAAP example in the chapter.
d. It is the sum of the past service cost benefits earned by the employees since the inception of the plan and to be paid to them upon retirement.
e. None of the above is correct.

_____ 4. What is the difference between *past service costs* and *prior service costs?*
a. *Past service costs* refer to costs applicable to periods prior to a particular date of actuarial valuation, and *prior service costs* refer to costs applicable to employee service prior to the inception of the pension plan.
b. *Past service costs* refer to employee benefits applicable to employee service prior to the inception of a pension plan, and *prior service costs* refer to all retroactive benefits applicable to periods prior to the date of a pension plan amendment.
c. *Past service costs* refer to costs applicable to a pension plan for an employee who enters the plan after the inception of the plan in order to bring his or her benefits into line with those of other participants in the plan, and *prior service costs* refer to changes in prior period pension costs that are caused by a change in actuarial valuation.
d. There is no difference between the two terms, and they can be used interchangeably.
e. None of the above is correct.

_____ 5. Employee benefits under a pension plan that are not contingent upon an employee's continuing service are referred to as
a. Defined benefits
b. Insured benefits
c. Funded benefits
d. Unfunded benefits
e. None of the above is correct.

PROBLEMS

P19–1 (CPA ADAPTED) Liberty, Inc., a calendar-year corporation, adopted a company pension plan at the beginning of 1984. This plan is to be funded and noncontributory. Liberty used an appropriate actuarial cost method to determine its normal annual pension cost for 1984 and 1985 as $15,000 and $16,000, respectively, which was paid in the same year.

Liberty's actuarially determined past service costs were funded on December 31, 1984, at an amount properly computed as $106,000. These past service costs are to be amortized at the maximum amount permitted by generally accepted accounting principles. The interest factor assumed by the actuary is 6 percent.

REQUIRED Prepare journal entries to record the funding of past service costs on December 31, 1984, and the pension expenses for the years 1984 and 1985. Under each journal entry give the reasoning to support your entry. Round to the nearest dollar.

P19–2   Aaron Hanks is employed by the A. B. Company as its sole employee covered by a pension plan started on January 1, 1983. Hanks is 35 years old and has worked for A. B. Company for 10 years. He is planning to work 25 more years and retire at age 60. He is an athlete and, according to insurance company actuaries, is expected to live to the age of 96. The company established a pension fund for Hanks crediting him for the 10 years already worked and generating retirement benefits such that he will be able to receive $130,000 per year at the end of each year from age 60 to age 89. The pension fund, which will be managed by a trustee, is expected to earn 15 percent per year on funded assets.

REQUIRED

1. Assuming the entry-age normal method is used, compute the present value of the past service cost benefits for Hanks on January 1, 1983.
2. Record any entry required to recognize the past service cost benefits at January 1, 1983.
3. Record the normal cost for 1985.
4. What should the pension fund balance be in 25 years under the entry-age normal method?

P19–3   Assume all data in the preceding problem.

REQUIRED

1. Assuming the unit credit method is used and the $130,000 retirement annuity is earned evenly over the 35 years of employment, compute the present value of the past service cost benefits for Hanks on January 1, 1983.
2. Record any entry required to recognize the past service cost benefits at January 1, 1983.
3. Record the normal cost for 1985.
4. What should the balance in the pension fund be in 25 years under the unit credit method?

P19–4   The Mt. Wheel Tool Corporation was established in 1945. In 1960 the mechanics union bargained for a pension fund, which was to be a "funded type" plan, fully funded by the corporation. At the inception of the plan it was determined that the benefit to be recognized for work *previously* performed by union members was valued at $61,446 as of January 1, 1960. Mt. Wheel Tool began funding the pension plan on December 31, 1960. The *yearly* pension benefit generated by the labor union members for work performed during the first 6 years is as follows: 1960, $29,500; 1961, $31,250; 1962, $32,740; 1963, $33,310; 1964, $34,000; 1965, $34,000.

Mt. Wheel intended to pay for the past service cost pension benefits over a 10-year period. The company also agreed to fund the annual normal cost pension benefit at the end of the period in which it was earned. For financial-reporting purposes, Mt. Wheel wished to amortize past service cost pension expense reported in the income statement over a 20-year period. The pension fund assets are assumed to earn 10 percent interest annually.

REQUIRED

1. Record the pension expense for 1961 (year 2) and 1962 (year 3) on Mt. Wheel Tool Corporation's books.
2. Assume that in 1963 Mt. Wheel discovered some estimation errors made by the actuary that resulted in an overstatement of the normal cost pension liability of $10,000 *per year* for 1960, 1961, and 1962. Also, the correct normal cost liability for 1963 is $23,310. Record the 1963 pension entry assuming the discounted present value of the errors (as of December 31, 1963) will be spread over the minimum number of periods.
3. Indicate the balance, if any, in any pension-related asset or liability account on the Mt. Wheel Tool Corporation's books as of the 1970 year-end—just *prior* to the entry to record the 1970 pension expense.

P19–5   Task Corporation initiated a pension plan for its employees on January 2, 1950. On this date, the actuary determined that the past service costs amounted to $600,000, and that the normal costs were expected to be $100,000 each year for the next 5 years. Both estimates made by the actuary were based on the assumption that the pension fund could earn a 6 percent annual return on the funded amounts. Task decided to fund the normal costs each year and to fund the past service costs over the next 5 years (1950–1954), with all payments being made to the trustee on December 31 each year.

REQUIRED

1. Given that Task intends to fund all pension costs, compute the *minimum* pension expense for 1950.
2. Given that Task intends to fund all pension costs, compute the *maximum* pension expense for 1950.
3. Assume that past service costs are amortized over a 15-year period. Record the necessary journal entry for the pension expense for 1951.
4. What is the balance in the Prepaid Pension account as of December 31, 1951?

P19-6 In 1985 Dart Corporation initiated a pension plan covering all of its employees. When the plan began, it was estimated that the past service costs for the existing labor force totaled $840,000. Dart decided to *amortize* the past service costs over a 10-year period and to fund them over a 20-year period. The pension fund is expected to earn about a 10 percent rate of return. Normal costs are expected to be $150,000 each year for the first 3 years.

REQUIRED

1. Record Dart's pension expense for the first 3 years (1985, 1986, and 1987). Ignore minimum and maximum limits.
2. Using the information from requirement 1 as a base, consider the following. In 1987 it was discovered that certain assumptions and data used by the actuary required adjustment, which resulted in "actuarial gains" of $40,000. The company decided to "spread" these gains over the maximum allowable period of years. Indicate the number of years, and record the 1987 entry to account for pension expense in light of this additional information.

P19-7 Refer to the data in problem 19–6 (but ignore the additional data in requirement 2). Consider the following additional data. In 1995 an adjustment is made to Dart's pension plan whereby the existing labor force (one-half of which is the same as in 1985) will have an additional $500,000 funded for them by Dart for their prior services. Also, the normal costs for the next few years are expected to be $200,000 per year. Dart decides to fund these prior service costs over 20 years and amortize them over a 10-year period.

REQUIRED Record Dart's pension expense for 1995, 1996, and 1997. Ignore minimum and maximum limits.

P19-8 At the beginning of 1985 the XYZ Corporation decided to *fund* its past service pension costs of $2,000,000, which stem from the work of the existing labor force before the inception of its new pension plan, over a period of 15 years. The pension fund is expected to generate a 6 percent return on funds left with the trustee. The rate of return earned by XYZ Corporation on its assets is 8 percent. The present opportunity rate for XYZ on new projects is 10 percent. The bank prime rate at the inception of the plan is 9 percent. Assume for all entries required below that the normal pension costs from the services performed *during the year* of the journal entry are $80,000 and are fully funded.

REQUIRED Answer the following *independent* questions and requirements as briefly as possible:

1. What is the shortest period over which the $2,000,000 will be expensed? (This question does *not* need to be answered in an exact way.)
2. Assume the $2,000,000 is to be amortized over 10 years. What is the pension-related entry to be recorded on XYZ's books for the second year (1986) of funding? Ignore maximum and minimum requirements.
3. Assume that in the second year of funding, a $6,000 gain was discovered in the actuary's estimations. The error is assumed to be material, and the effect is to be "spread out" over the *maximum* number of years. Indicate how this information will be reflected in the 1986 journal entry. (Amortize PSC over 10 years.)
4. Assume that XYZ has a cash shortage during the *third* year (1987) and, as a result, can only fund $100,000. Record the 1987 journal entry for the pension plan. (Amortize PSC over 10 years.)
5. Ignore requirement 4 and assume that the pension plan was funded according to the original provisions. Clearly identify the balance that would be shown in any and all balance sheet accounts related to the pension plan at the *end* of 10 years (1994). Also record the necessary journal entry on XYZ's books for 1995 (the eleventh year). (Amortize PSC over 10 years.)
6. In 1996 a total of 275 workers began to receive benefits from the retirement plan that XYZ initiated in 1985. Their total pension benefits in 1996 amounted to $275,000. Record the necessary impact on XYZ's books.

P19-9 The average employee of the Korff Corporation has worked for the company for 10 years and is 15 years away from retirement, and the expected normal cost to be funded over the next 15 years is $450,000 per year. At the end of this 15-year period the pension fund is expected to have assets valued at $25,773,750. The pension plan, initiated this year, provides past service cost benefits for the previous 5 years of employment. The assumed rate of interest on pension fund assets is 10 percent. The entry-age normal method has been used to determine the $450,000 annual normal cost amount. Korff plans to fund the past service cost benefits over 15 years and to expense (amortize) these over 10 years.

REQUIRED

1. What is the present value of the past service cost benefit at the inception of the plan?
2. What is the amount of the pension expense related to past service costs at the end of the first year of the plan? Ignore maximum and minimum limits.
3. What is the amount of the cash payment to the fund for past service costs at the end of the first year of the plan?
4. Record the entries to account for past service costs and normal costs for the first 2 years of the plan.
5. Identify the balance in the balance sheet accounts (if any) related to the pension plan at the end of the second year of the plan.

P19-10 The following table summarizes the actuarial gains and losses for the pension plan of the Outslay & Robinson Manufacturing Company as of December 31, 1984.

YEAR	MAJOR CAUSE OF GAIN OR LOSS	AMOUNT OF GAIN (LOSS) COMPUTED
1977	Estimated retirement age	$ 63,000
1978	Estimated life of employees	(21,000)
1979	No changes	0
1980	Estimated employee life expectancy	76,000
1981	No changes	0
1982	Estimated retirement age	69,000
1983	Estimated employee turnover rate	(42,000)
1984	Estimated retirement age	81,000

The 1983 and 1984 normal cost before considering actuarial gains and losses is $295,680. Outslay & Robinson has a policy of funding normal costs as incurred. Past service costs, which had a present value of $2,500,000 on January 1, 1977 (the inception of the plan), are being funded over 20 years and expensed over 15 years. The pension fund is expected to earn 12 percent on fund assets.

REQUIRED

1. Assume that Outslay & Robinson uses the spreading method for actuarial gains and losses, with a 10-year period used for amortization. Record the necessary entries for 1983 and 1984.
2. Assume that Outslay & Robinson uses the average method for actuarial gains and losses. Record the necessary entries for 1984, and present comparative balance sheet and income statement pension data for 1983 and 1984.

P19-11 On January 1, 1978, the Dave-Hollywood-Frederick Corporation initiated a pension plan for its employees. The actuarial present value of past service cost benefits, based on a return of 10 percent on fund assets, was estimated to be $1,685,000 at the inception of the plan. Frederick intended to fund these costs over 15 years and to expense (amortize) them over 20 years. In 1984 Frederick's employees negotiated an increase in their retroactive benefits. The amendment to the plan resulted in an additional retroactive benefit cost of $565,000 as of January 1, 1984, based on an assumed return of 10 percent on pension fund assets. Frederick planned to fund the prior service cost benefits over a 10-year period and amortize them over the next 15 years. Annual normal costs for 1984, 1985, and 1986 were $98,000 per year, which were funded as incurred.

REQUIRED

1. Record the entries necessary to account for Frederick's pension plan for 1984, 1985, and 1986. Ignore maximum and minimum limits.
2. What balance sheet accounts, if any, would appear in Frederick's balance sheet for the 1986 year-end?

P19–12 In the actuary's report to Rush Corporation, the funding employer, the following historical review of the actuarial gains and losses was provided. (Amounts are in thousands of dollars.)

YEAR	ANNUAL NORMAL COST CONTRIBUTION BEFORE GAIN AND LOSSES	EXPERIENCE GAIN (LOSS) PER ACTUARY	EMPLOYER'S NET ANNUAL CONTRIBUTION
1974	$ 5,867	$ (263)	$ 6,130
1975	6,425	621	5,804
1976	8,107	3,087[a] (583)	5,020
1977	9,876	(691)	10,567
1978	11,424	1,087	10,337
1979	16,947	(3,940)[b]	20,887
1980	17,865	(648)	18,513
1981	19,288	12,134[c]	7,154
1982	21,784	1,837	19,947
1983	24,969	(3,260)[d]	28,229
1984	28,743	1,846	26,897
1985	32,107	3,622	28,485

[a] Includes $3,620,000 gain from plant closing.

[b] Includes $2,969,000 loss from major change in mortality tables for all employees in Rush Corporation's industry.

[c] Includes $12,000,000 for a change in the estimated return of fund assets from $9\frac{1}{2}$ to 11 percent.

[d] Includes a $2,987,000 adjustment for the estimated turnover rate change in combination with a negotiated change in the vesting provisions of the plan.

Rush has used the spreading method to record actuarial gains and losses, using the minimum allowable allocation period for spreading.

REQUIRED

1. Considering footnotes a through d to the above table, compute Rush's pension expense for 1983, 1984, and 1985.
2. Assume that Rush uses the averaging method instead of the spreading method. Compute the pension expense for 1983, 1984, and 1985.

P19–13 On July 13, 1984, Taurus, Inc., decided to change its actuarial cost methods from the entry-age normal method to the unit credit method. The following facts were available regarding the Taurus pension plan:

1. Plan was initiated on January 1, 1975.
2. Pension benefits recognized at the inception of the plan for all covered employees require the pension fund to have assets on December 31, 2004, equal to a 15-year annuity of $35,000 per year for each of the company's 1,000 employees. These benefits are recognized as being earned evenly over a 35-year period of employment, in effect recognizing 5 years in past service cost benefits on average for each employee.
3. There is no balance in the unfunded pension cost account as of July 13, 1984, because Taurus has had fully funded pension expense each year since the plan was initiated, funding and amortizing the past service cost benefits over a 20-year period.
4. The change to the unit credit method is considered to be *a change in estimate* and is treated prospectively just as a change in the life of a depreciable asset would be treated.
5. A 10 percent interest rate is used for the return on fund assets.

REQUIRED

1. Compute the present value of the remaining unfunded pension costs (both past service costs and normal costs) as of 1984 that need to be funded between 1984 and December 31, 2004, assuming Taurus makes annual contributions to the pension fund each December 31.

2. Compute the present value of the normal cost payments for the next 21 years beginning December 31, 1984, assuming the unit credit method is used and each employee earns an additional $1,000 retirement annuity for 15 years after retirement each year between 1984 and 2004.

3. If your answer to requirement 2 is greater than your answer to requirement 1, then treat the difference like an interest-bearing *unrecorded* asset and spread the benefit of this asset out over a 20-year period using the present-value amortization as a reduction in normal cost expense each year. (Note: This situation would indicate that PSC have already been funded under the assumptions of the unit credit method.)

    If your answer to requirement 1 is greater than your answer to requirement 2, then it will be necessary to treat this difference as the remaining unfunded past service cost amount. In this case, assume that the remaining PSC will be funded and amortized over the next 5 years (1984 through 1988).

4. Record the pension expense for 1984.

5. Illustrate the partial comparative income statements for 1982, 1983, and 1984 for Taurus assuming that (1) net income before taxes and before pension expense for both book and tax purposes is $6,800,000 in each of the three years; (2) the tax rate is 25 percent and (3) only the amount of cash paid to the pension fund is allowable as an expense for tax purposes, with differences between book and tax treated as timing differences.

6. What is the impact of this change on Taurus's cash flow during 1984?

P19–14 (CMA ADAPTED) Dane Enterprises, which began operations in 1980, instituted a pension plan on January 1, 1985. The insurance company administering the pension plan has computed the present value of past service costs at $100,000 for the 5 years of operations through December 31, 1984. The pension plan provides for fully vested benefits when employees have completed 10 years of service. Therefore, there will be no vested benefits until December 31, 1989.

The insurance company proposed that Dane Enterprises fund the past service cost in equal installments over 15 years calculated by the present-value method. Using an interest rate of 5 percent, the annual payment for past service cost would be $9,634. The company's controller agreed to this payment schedule. In addition, the controller concluded that 15 years was a reasonable period for amortizing the past service costs for book purposes. Consequently, the past service costs will also be amortized at the annual rate of $9,634 for 15 years.

The normal cost of the pension fund is estimated to be $30,000 each year for the next 4 years. The annual payment to the insurance company covering the current year's normal cost and the annual installment on the past service cost is payable on December 31 each year, the end of Dane's fiscal year. On December 31, 1985, the insurance company was paid $39,634 ($30,000 + 9,634) to cover the company's pension obligations for 1985.

REQUIRED

1. Calculate and label the components that constitute the maximum and minimum 1985 financial statement pension expense limits in accordance with generally accepted accounting principles for Dane Enterprises.

2. Assume that Dane Enterprises will be unable to remit the full pension payment ($39,634) in 1986 and will only submit $30,000 (the normal cost) to the insurance company. If Dane can recognize $39,634 as pension expense in 1986, show the entry required. If Dane cannot recognize the $39,634 as pension expense in 1986, explain why not.

P19–15 (CMA ADAPTED) The CMA Corporation, which has been in operation for the past 23 years, decided late in 1982 to adopt, beginning January 1, 1983, a funded pension plan for its employees. The pension plan is to be noncontributory and will provide for vesting after 5 years of service by each eligible employee. A trust agreement has been entered into whereby a national insurance company will receive the yearly pension fund contributions and administer the fund.

Management, through extended consultation with the fund trustee, internal accountants, and independent actuaries, arrived at the following conclusions:

1. The normal pension cost for 1983 will be $30,000.

2. The present value of the past service cost at the date of inception of the pension plan (January 1, 1983) is $200,000.

3. Because of the large amount of money involved, the past service costs will be funded at the rate of $23,365 per year for the next 15 years. The first payment will not be due until January 1, 1984.

4. In accordance with *APB Opinion No. 8*, the unit credit method of accounting for the pension costs will be followed. Pension costs will be amortized over a 10-year period. The 10-year accrual factor is $29,805 per year. Neither the maximum nor the minimum amortization amounts as prescribed by *APB Opinion No. 8* will be violated.

5. Where applicable, an 8 percent interest rate is assumed.

REQUIRED

1. Define normal pension costs and past service costs.

2. What amounts (use "**XXX**" if amount can't be calculated) will be reported in the company's (1) income statement for 1983, (2) balance sheet as of December 31, 1983, and (3) notes to the statements? Give account titles with the amounts.

3. What amounts (use "**XXX**" if amount can't be calculated) will be reported in the company's (1) income statement for 1984, (2) balance sheet as of December 31, 1984, and (3) notes to the statements? Give account titles with the amounts.

Stockholders' Contributed Capital

20

OVERVIEW

Equity is the third major balance sheet classification, the others being **assets** and **liabilities.** Conceptually, equity can be viewed from several perspectives. First there is what could be called a **balance sheet structure** perspective. The money amount assigned to total equities on an entity's balance sheet is equal to its net assets (assets minus liabilities). In this sense, equity is a **residual**—a money amount representing the residual claims of owners in the assets of the entity.[1] This perspective is consistent with the fact that creditors' claims have priority over owners' claims. Decision makers are often interested in the ratio of debt to equity, and this may justify such a perspective.

Another way of viewing an entity's equity is to analyze each of its components in terms of what it indicates about the **sources of the entity's net assets.** Certain percentages of the net assets of an entity may have been **contributed** by common stockholders, preferred stockholders, and perhaps other parties. A certain percentage may have been **earned** through operations. In addition, some transactions in the entity's own securities may have had an effect on net assets. This point of view emphasizes the

[1] This is the meaning of *equity* adopted by the FASB in its conceptual framework project. See Chapter 2 of this text and *Elements of Financial Statements of Business Enterprises* (Stamford, CT: FASB, 1980).

financial evaluation of the entity. Decision makers may be interested in the proportions of capital contributed by common stockholders as opposed to preferred stockholders or in the proportions represented by retained earnings as opposed to total contributed capital.

Finally, equity can be viewed from a **legal** perspective. Each category in the equity section of a balance sheet has specific legal implications. Accountants make a concerted effort to report the status of each category in a manner consistent with the statutes that govern corporations. For instance, the distinctions made on balance sheets between common stock and preferred stock are consistent with legal distinctions. Virtually all the transactions related to equity must be accounted for and disclosures made in a manner which does not contradict the governing statutes.

As we have stated many times in this text, accountants are primarily concerned with communicating the economic substance as opposed to the legal form of transactions. In equity accounting, the legal requirements often necessitate considerable detail and fine distinctions in the accounting records and financial statements. Fortunately, there seems to be a great degree of overlap between economic substance and legal form in this area, and on balance it would seem that much of the detail shown in the equity section of accounting reports can be justified by the needs of decision makers.

All three perspectives are valid, but a thorough understanding of equity accounting is contingent on combining the elements of each into a comprehensive view. Such a view must consider the limitations of the entire accounting model. Limitations inherent in asset and liability accounting apply with equal force to equity accounting. Money amounts assigned to equity accounts are based on original transaction amounts, and this restricts their usefulness for certain decisions. For instance, there is no guarantee that the ownership interests measured and reported in balance sheets are accurate indicators of the owners' claims to resources and those who look to accounting statements for such information must understand how all of the numbers have been derived.

Figure 20–1 shows the many possible classifications used in the equity sections of balance sheets. In this chapter we concentrate primarily on the items in categories 1 and 2 in Figure 20–1, which includes equity transactions other than those affecting retained earnings. We shall see that the Figure 20–1 categorization is not completely accurate because retained earnings can be affected by some of the transactions listed under categories 1 and 2, but most equity transactions do follow this classification scheme.

Few corporations have balance sheets that include all the classifications shown in Figure 20–1. Exhibit 20–1 contains three excerpts from published annual reports in which some of the classifications appear. Each company refers the readers to several notes that give details about specific items. Several such notes will be analyzed in the remainder of this chapter. It is apparent, then, that the equity section of a balance sheet is complex and requires knowledge of many concepts, rules, statutes, and accounting procedures if a thorough understanding of it is to be achieved.

CAPITAL FORMATION

The
Advantages of
the Corporate
Form

In the United States a large percentage of all business resources is controlled by corporations. There are several basic reasons for preferring the corporate form over the partnership, proprietorship, or other forms of business. First, corporate investors are able to limit their obligation to contribute assets to the corporation without

FIGURE 20–1   Segmentation and composition of owners' equity

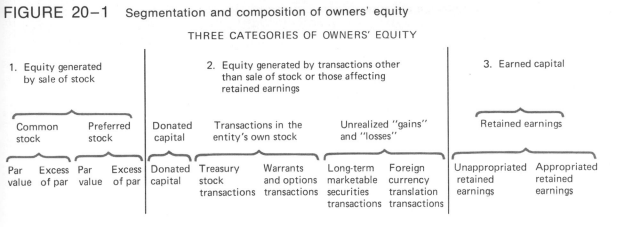

THREE CATEGORIES OF OWNERS' EQUITY

1. Equity generated by sale of stock

- Common stock
  - Par value
  - Excess of par
- Preferred stock
  - Par value
  - Excess of par

2. Equity generated by transactions other than sale of stock or those affecting retained earnings

- Donated capital
  - Donated capital
- Transactions in the entity's own stock
  - Treasury stock transactions
  - Warrants and options transactions
- Unrealized "gains" and "losses"
  - Long-term marketable securities transactions
  - Foreign currency translation transactions

3. Earned capital

- Retained earnings
  - Unappropriated retained earnings
  - Appropriated retained earnings

limiting their ability to share in corporate profits. In partnerships, however, a partner will generally have unlimited responsibility for the liabilities of the business created by any of the general partners and may be called upon to contribute additional resources to the partnership to satisfy these liabilities. Second, the corporate form has the advantage of continuity even when the composition of the individual investors changes. In partnerships, the withdrawal of any one partner may necessitate liquidation of the partnership or other formal legal action. The corporate form facilitates changes in owners by making its ownership shares negotiable, and organized stock exchanges routinely process large numbers of changes in corporate ownership interests. Finally, corporations provide a form of business that permits the accumulation of large amounts of equity investment necessary to conduct efficient operations in a modern industrial state where the **ownership** and the **management** of business resources are separated. Try to imagine, for example, the operations of IBM or General Motors being conducted as a partnership. These basic attributes of corporate ownership allow for the accumulation of the large amounts of resources often necessary in today's economy.

The corporate form also insulates the business from the different preferences of individual investors. Although those owning a majority can, through their voting rights, force dividends to be paid at times when management might not make such a decision, no one individual or group without majority control can force dividend payments. This gives the corporation flexibility to pursue actions desired by the majority of its investors. In partnerships, on the other hand, one individual in some cases can force partial or complete liquidation.

The Incorporation Process

In the United States corporations are established under the laws of specific states. State statutes vary in some respects, but there are many commonalities because of the widespread adoption of the Model Business Corporation Act (MA).[2] The MA has been adopted by more than 35 states, and its major provisions, although they are

[2] See *Model Business Corporation Act and Professional Corporations Supplement* (Philadelphia: American Bar Association, 1979).

EXHIBIT
20–1

EQUITY SECTIONS OF BALANCE SHEETS

COLT INDUSTRIES, INC.
Excerpts from Balance Sheet

	($000)	
	1980	1979

Shareholders' Equity (Notes 3, 5, and 7)

	1980	1979
Preferred stock—$1 par value, 2,077,189 and 2,246,023 shares authorized, 421,694 and 590,528 shares outstanding (involuntary liquidation value at December 31, 1980—$31,479)	$ 422	$ 590
Common stock—$1 par value, 30,000,000 shares authorized, 13,269,650 and 13,209,875 shares issued	13,270	13,210
Capital in excess of par value	149,472	160,700
Retained earnings	522,532	463,979
	685,696	638,479
Less cost of 209,525 and 420,021 shares of common stock in treasury	8,060	16,887
	$677,636	$621,592

ABE SCHRADER CORPORATION
Excerpts from Balance Sheet

	($000)	
	1979	1978

Shareholders' Equity (Notes 5 and 6)

	1979	1978
Preferred stock, $1 par; authorized and unissued 1,000,000 shares		
Common stock, $.10 par; authorized 3,000,000 shares; issued and outstanding 1,711,600 shares in 1979 and 1,694,480 shares in 1978	$ 171	$ 169
Capital in excess of par	429	393
Retained earnings	9,743	9,875
	10,343	10,438
Net unrealized loss on marketable equity securities	(158)	(115)
	$10,185	$10,322

TIDWELL INDUSTRIES, INC.

	($000)	
	1979	1978

Stockholders' Equity (Notes A, D, H, I, and M)

	1979	1978
Common stock, par value $.10 per share—authorized 3,000,000 shares	$ 171	$ 171
Additional paid-in capital	6,505	6,500
Donated capital	49	49
Retained earnings	2,437	591
Cost of shares of Common Stock in Treasury (Deduction)	(329)	(329)
	$8,833	$6,982

not always instituted uniformly, apply in many other jurisdictions for all types of corporations except those engaged in insurance or banking.

In general, the incorporation process consists of the following steps:

1. The promoters draw up articles of incorporation. This document gives details about the corporation's structure and management, such as its name, purpose, location of the corporate office, number and classes of shares of stock, consideration to be paid for shares, and the members of the initial board of directors.
2. Incorporators sign the articles of incorporation and file them with the secretary of state of the state of incorporation.
3. The secretary of state issues a certificate of incorporation or charter.
4. Shareholders pay in at least the amount specified by statute as minimum capital; for example, the MA calls for a minimum of $1,000.
5. The initial board of directors has an organization meeting at which corporate bylaws are adopted and corporate officers are elected.

Once the corporation comes into existence, the promoters lose their unique status as initiators of the new corporate venture. In some cases, they become ordinary stockholders or officers of the corporation. In other cases, their association with the corporation is limited to its initial organization. In any event, after incorporation the board of directors must develop strategies for raising the needed capital. The articles of incorporation merely specify the classes of stock and maximum number of shares that can be issued. It is up to the board and officers to attract investors.

The Marketing of Corporate Shares

Many variations in the types of ownership securities have evolved to attract investors. Corporations offer potential investors securities that are, in essence, bundles of contractual terms that specify investor rights. The investors assess these rights according to expected risks and returns, the assumption being that given a certain grouping of productive assets, securities with different rights will provide different returns and entail different risks. What are the major attributes of equity securities in terms of the rights they convey? Consider the following rights.

Rights of common stockholders If only one type of stock is issued by a corporation, the shares are termed common stock and the following rights are usually conveyed:

1. The right to vote on various corporate matters. The bylaws will normally specify the time of the annual meeting at which the stockholders' voting rights are exercised. They can elect or remove directors, change the bylaws, approve mergers, approve changes in the articles of incorporation, and perform other such actions. Not all classes of stock convey voting rights. Even stock that is termed *common* may have limited voting rights if another class has full voting rights. For example, there are sometimes two or more classes of common stock, designated Class A common, Class B common, and so on.
2. The right to share in dividends. Investors usually expect a return in the form of dividends or stock appreciation. If declared, dividends are paid to stockholders on the

basis of the number of shares held. However, the directors are not obliged to declare dividends, and no liability is created for undeclared dividends. (Chapter 21 examines the accounting for dividend declaration and payment.)

3. The right to share in the residual assets of the business in the event of corporate liquidation. One factor that makes ownership of common stock risky is that common stockholders, upon liquidation of the corporation, receive what is left over after the preferred claims of creditors and other classes of stock have been satisfied.

4. The right to acquire new shares in proportion to the stockholder's ownership of outstanding shares, termed the **preemptive right.** The MA calls for the particulars of this right to be explicitly stated in the articles of incorporation. Even in cases where the articles are silent, the courts have held that officers, directors, and majority stockholders must be "fair" and "reasonable" in the issuance of new shares so that no particular group will be favored. Courts have also held that the preemptive right is not applicable to treasury stock transactions, transactions related to mergers, and shares issued for noncash consideration.

Rights of preferred stockholders   If more than one class of equity securities is issued, some modification in the above bundle of rights is made. However, note that although the **preferred stock** of an entity confers certain "preferences," which common stock does not, the preferred stock rights usually lack at least one of the rights given to common stockholders. For example, although preferred stock usually receives preference in terms of dividends, it frequently does not confer the voting right or the preemptive right. Preferred stocks may also give the investor the right to convert the preferred stock into common stock; the reverse is never true.

Rights of owners of options   In addition to the two primary classes of equity securities, corporations may issue contracts that enable the holders to become stockholders in the issuing corporation if certain actions are taken. Options that permit the holder to purchase common stock at a fixed price some time within a specified period and are evidenced by a certificate are called **warrants.** Employees and others are sometimes given the short-term, nonnegotiable rights to purchase common stock. Such **options** are often a part of employee compensation plans and may be exercised only by the employee. Another instance of a nonnegotiable, short-term option is when current stockholders are issued such rights pursuant to preemptive rights considerations.

Warrants may be attached to a bond or preferred stock, allowing the holder to purchase common stock at a fixed price or, in the case of **nondetachable warrants,** to convert the primary security into common stock. **Detachable warrants** often trade in a market independent of the primary securities.

In summary, corporate management can choose from a variety of equity securities in its attempt to raise capital. The four basic rights listed above must be features of the common stock's contractual terms. If other classes of equity securities are issued, an almost infinite number of permutations of rights can be fashioned within the limitation of the applicable laws. Securities sold to the public must comply with state statutes ("blue-sky laws") in the state in which the securities are sold. If the securities are sold interstate or by mail, they must also comply with the federal securities laws.[3]

---

[3] Business law texts give details concerning the various statutory provisions. See J. W. Wyatt and M. B. Wyatt, *Business Law: Principles and Cases* (New York: McGraw-Hill, 1975), pp. 617–639.

SPECIFIC CHARACTERISTICS OF VARIOUS CLASSES OF EQUITY SECURITIES

Par and Stated Values

Articles of incorporation normally place a **face value** on stock, but this represents something very different from the face value of bonds and notes. The face value amount of stock is called **par value,** and, in terms of the MA it represents the money amount below which the stock cannot initially be sold.[4] In some states, it is possible for a corporation to issue stock at less than par. However, when stock is initially sold by the corporation below par value, the initial investor is contingently liable for the difference between the par value and the price paid. Once issued, the stock may be repurchased by the corporation or sold between two investors at any amount agreeable to the parties. Par value was originally intended to provide some security for investors and creditors by ensuring a known minimum capitalization per share. Par value still has that status in law, but because the par value is usually much smaller than the selling price, it is not of great economic consequence.

Par value plays a more prominent role in preferred stock than it does in common stock. Dividend payments are often determined as a percentage of par value, and liquidation preferences may also be stated in terms of par value. A $100 par value, 10 percent preferred stock must pay $10 per share to all preferred stockholders before the common stockholders receive any dividends. Upon liquidation of the corporation, the preferred stockholders would receive the $100 par value or some other stated amount per share before the common stockholders received any residual value.

Certain stocks are termed **no par** and are sold without par values. In such cases, the MA allows an amount to be fixed by the board of directors by assigning a **stated value** to the stock, and the stated value is then treated the same as par value for accounting purposes.[5]

The term **legal capital** is used for the amount of capital state statutes require to be maintained after the corporation is organized. It is usually equal to the par value (or stated value), and in theory it is supposed to give creditors a minimum amount of protection.

Features of Preferred Stock

Stock ownership does not guarantee any return to investors, which creates an inherent risk in all kinds of equity investments. There is, however, a range of riskiness depending on the terms of the equity security. Preferred stock is generally considered to be less risky than common stock because, as we have mentioned, it usually receives preferential treatment with regard to dividend payments and repayment of a specific amount per share before common stock upon liquidation. These dividend and liquidation preferences, although not providing guarantees, make a corporation's preferred stock a less risky investment than its common stock. Common stock, however, must offer certain advantages over preferred stock in order to attract investors into taking on greater risk. Perhaps the greatest advantage to common stockholders is that, in general, no fixed ceiling is placed on dividend payments to these stockholders. If the company continually prospers, common stockholders may receive increasing dividends; or in the absence of increasing dividends, the appreciation in market value may be significant. Preferred stock, however, would not

---

[4] *Model Business Corporation Act,* p. 18.

[5] Ibid.

normally be expected to appreciate in value above a certain point because of the contractual limitations normally placed on returns.

Preferred stock contracts may have any number of different provisions as to how and when dividends will be paid. Usually the preferred dividend rates are stated on the security. For a $100 par, 10 percent preferred stock, a dividend of $10 per year is paid before common stockholders receive any payment. Another way of stating the same contractual term would be to designate this preferred stock as a $10 preferred stock.

Although preferred dividends are usually limited to a fixed amount per year, in some situations the contract may call for dividends in excess of a fixed amount. For example, the contract may specify that preferred stockholders will participate in any common stock dividends, in which case the stock is called **participating preferred stock.** This participation would be over and above the fixed preferred stock dividend. As an illustration assume that Property Associates has two classes of stock outstanding as follows:

	PAR VALUE
1. 12% fully participating preferred stock, 10,000 shares of $100 par value	$1,000,000
2. Common stock, 100,000 shares of $1 par value	$ 100,000

How would the dividends be shared among common and preferred stockholders if total dividends declared were $300,000? First the preferred stockholders would be paid $120,000, assuming no past dividends were missed. Then the common stockholders would be paid an equal percentage of their par value, or $12,000 (12 percent of $100,000). The remaining $168,000 would be divided in proportion to par values of common and preferred. Common stockholders would get an additional $15,273—($100,000/$1,100,000) × $168,000—and preferred stockholders would get an additional $152,727—($1,000,000/$1,100,000) × $168,000.

Another situation that permits preferred stockholders to receive more than the fixed percentage of par value in one year may occur when the preferred stock is **cumulative.** This provision requires that if the corporation fails to pay all or part of the annual preferred dividend, then it must pay both the accumulated deficiency (dividends in arrears) and the current amount in subsequent years before common stockholders can receive any dividends. Although no guarantees are made that any dividends will ever be declared, it is not normal for financially strong corporations to omit the payment of cumulative preferred dividends. In addition, some preferred stock acquires voting rights if dividends are passed.

Convertibility features   As was mentioned earlier, another provision often found in preferred stock contracts is the right of shareholders to convert their shares into common stock. **Convertibility** allows investors to enjoy the added security of preferred stock along with the higher potential returns available to common stock. For example, assume that Robots, Inc., issues 10,000 shares of $100 par, 12 percent preferred stock that is convertible into common on a basis of five common shares to one preferred share. On January 1, 1983, the date of issuance, the preferred stock sold for $105 per share and the common stock sold for $15 per share. On December 31, 1984, the market value of the common stock has increased to $30 per share. Preferred stockholders must decide if they want to exercise their option to convert.

They may want to retain their preferred stock status, or they may want to convert and sell or hold common stock.

Call provision   Although the issuer cannot force conversion, contractual terms often give the issuer the right to **call,** or redeem, preferred stock. This means that the corporation may, at its option, pay a specified amount per share (usually over 100 percent of par value) and thereby reacquire the preferred stock. Statutes often prohibit such transactions if they would lead to insolvency of the corporation.

Redeemable preferred stock   Some preferred stock has mandatory **redemption requirements** or is **redeemable** at the stockholder's option. Are these types of securities closer to liabilities or to owners' equity? Most preferred and common stock can be distinguished from debt by at least three main factors: (1) no periodic payments can be demanded by the stockholders; (2) no specific maturity date exists; and (3) stockholders' claims upon liquidation in general are secondary to creditors' claims. However, redeemable preferred stock falls in the gray area between debt and equity because a future cash obligation may exist in the case of such securities. This distin-

EXHIBIT 20–2

EXAMPLES OF SIMPLE AND COMPLEX OWNERS' EQUITY

THE LIMITED STORES, INC.
Excerpts from Balance Sheet

	($000)	
	8/2/80	8/4/79
Shareholders' Equity (Note 7)		
Common Stock, without par value, 30,000,000 shares authorized	$ 167	$ 165
Paid-in capital	5,285	4,539
Retained earnings (Note 2)	43,855	36,694
Total shareholders' equity	$49,307	$41,398

GENESCO, INC.
Excerpts from Balance Sheet

	($000)	
	7/31/80	7/31/79
Total current liabilities	$106,575	$117,174
Long-term debt (Note 8)	78,900	92,456
Subordinated commitment to foreign finance subsidiary (Note 9)	12,200	12,383
Capitalized lease obligations (Note 11)	20,013	25,089
Provision for operations being divested (Note 10)	14,828	19,728
Deferred credits to income	2,438	2,599
Redeemable preferred stock (Note 12)	39,324	45,345
Non-redeemable preferred stock (Note 12)	55,144	55,154
Common stock (Note 12)	13,108	13,108
Additional paid-in capital	63,813	60,769
Accumulated deficit	(32,862)	(36,315)
Treasury stock, at cost	(28,681)	(28,681)
Employee stock purchase accounts (Note 16)	(18,386)	(18,682)
Total liabilities and stockholders' equity	$326,414	$360,127

guishes these securities from equity while not giving them all of the attributes of debt. The Securities and Exchange Commission (SEC) has responded to this ambiguity by requiring registrants having redeemable preferred stock to modify their balance sheet disclosures by including as many as three headings (rather than the normal general heading "Shareholders' Equity"): (1) preferred stock that is redeemable at the stockholder's option or according to mandatory redemption requirements, (2) preferred stock that is either not redeemable or redeemable only at the issuer's option, and (3) common stock.[6] No combined total for equity is allowed, and a separate footnote disclosing terms of redemptions, changes, and 5-year maturity schedules for redeemable preferred stock is required.

Disclosure of Stock Characteristics

Because of the many possible combinations of contractual terms, the reporting of the classes of stock on balance sheets requires considerable care. Capital structures range from the simple with only one class of common stock to the very complex that may include redeemable preferred stock with its ambiguous classification status. Terminology can be diverse. The term "capital stock" is often used synonymously with "common stock" and "perferred stock." "Owners' equity" is used synonymously with "shareholders' equity" and "stockholders' equity." Exhibit 20–2 shows the components of owners' equity sections of balance sheets of two corporations whose capital structure involves different levels of complexity.

ACCOUNTING PROCEDURES FOR EQUITY SECURITIES

Recording the Issuance of Equity Securities

Issuance of one class of stock for cash In many respects, accounting for the sale of stock is the same as that for any other business transaction. For example, the cash-equivalent value of the assets given or received is a guiding principle in establishing money amounts. Generally, asset or liability accounts or both are debited and owners' equity accounts are credited when stock is issued. If Tweed Mills, Inc., is incorporated and sells 10,000 shares of $1 par value common stock at $5 per share, the measurement and recording are straightforward:

Cash	50,000	
Par value common stock		10,000
Additional paid-in capital		40,000

This records the resource received (cash) and the equity created by the transaction. For no-par stock whose stated value equals the amount received, the journal entry would be the same except that only one paid-in capital account would be credited:

Cash	50,000	
Common stock		50,000

Issuance of one class of stock for noncash considerations The major difference in the accounting for cash and noncash transactions is in the measurement of the value exchanged. In the cash transaction, the value is equal to cash changing hands, but in the noncash transaction, the accountant has to look to indirect evidence of the cash-

---

[6] Securities and Exchange Commission, *Accounting Series Release No. 268,* "Presentation in Financial Statements of Redeemable Preferred Stocks" (Washington, DC: Government Printing Office, July 1979).

equivalent value of assets given or received.[7] For instance, if a new stock issue is made involving an exchange of stock for a parcel of land, the value of the land may be more objectively determinable than the stock. However, the opposite situation may exist if the stock is actively traded in the market and the land has not been exchanged recently or is somewhat unique.

If a corporation issues stock to liquidate a liability, the present value of the liability payment on the date of issuance of the stock would be considered objectively determinable, and, therefore, it would be used as the basis for recording the issue. If no reasonable basis for measuring the value of the stock issued or item received is available, then in some cases the board of directors may have the item received independently appraised or the board may set the value itself.

Issuance of more than one security for a lump-sum consideration If some combination of securities such as common stock, preferred stock, and detachable warrants is issued for one money amount, a proration of the money amount based on the relative fair values of the various securities is the preferable approach to valuation. To illustrate, assume that a plant site with an appraisal value of $100,000 is acquired by issuing the following:

TYPE OF SECURITY	NUMBER OF SHARES	PAR VALUE	FAIR VALUE PER SHARE	TOTAL FAIR VALUE	PRORATION
Common stock	1,000	$ 10	$ 54	$ 54,000	54%
Preferred stock	400	100	105	42,000	42
Detachable warrants	400	—	10	4,000	4
				$100,000	

The values assigned to each security and the journal entries to record the transactions would be as follows:

ACCOUNT	DEBIT	CREDIT
Building site	100,000	
Common stock—par		10,000
Common stock—additional paid-in capital		44,000
Preferred stock—par		10,000
Preferred stock—additional paid-in capital		2,000
Warrants outstanding		4,000

Stock subscriptions Promoters will sometimes offer stock on a **deferred payment,** or **subscription,** basis. In such cases, subscribers promise to purchase securities at a specific price, but the formal issuance of the shares takes place only after the full payment of the subscription amount. An asset, "subscriptions receivable," is recorded at the time the stock is offered, and subscribers have a legal obligation to the corporation. Should the corporation increase an owners' equity account? The con-

[7] Although this general rule is consistent with the rule found in *Accounting Principles Board Opinion No. 29,* "Accounting for Nonmonetary Transactions" (New York: AICPA, May 1973), par. 18, *APB Opinion No. 29* explicitly does not govern issuance of stock. This general rule, therefore, rests on a general principle and is not covered by a promulgation.

tractual terms of the subscription may be pivotal in making such accounting judgments. State laws governing subscriptions normally give subscribers the same rights as stockholders, including dividend and voting rights. This would imply that an owners' equity account should be recorded upon initiation of a subscription contract. If a subscriber defaults, however, the company may have to pay back any cash received to that point. This gives the transaction a liability dimension. In practice, subscriptions are normally recorded as owners' equity. The following illustrates the complete subscription cycle, including a default by one subscriber:

1. On January 1, 1985, Ms. Riff subscribes to 1,000 shares of Zeffer, Inc., $5 par common stock at $20 per share, to be paid in two payments of $10,000 each on April 1, 1985, and July 1, 1985. Mr. Berry subscribes to 100 shares of Zeffer, Inc., stock under the same terms as above; that is, two payments of $1,000 each.

2. Ms. Riff makes both payments, and Mr. Berry makes the first but defaults on the second.

Journal entries for these events would be recorded by Zeffer as follows. On January 1, 1985, Zeffer would record the subscription:

1/1/85	Subscriptions receivable	22,000[a]	
	Common stock subscribed		5,500[b]
	Additional paid-in capital		16,500[b]

[a] Balance sheet classification: asset.
[b] Balance sheet classification: owners' equity.

On July 1, 1985 1,100 shares of $5 par common stock will be issued if all payments are made. Note that "common stock subscribed" will be eliminated when the stock certificate is issued upon final payment. The receipt of the two Riff payments and the single Berry payment are recorded as follows:

4/1/85	Cash	11,000	
	Subscriptions receivable		11,000
7/1/85	Cash	10,000	
	Subscriptions receivable		10,000
	Common stock subscribed	5,000	
	Common stock par value		5,000

Ms. Riff is issued 1,000 shares of common stock. Mr. Berry has paid in $1,000 but has defaulted on the second payment. State law usually determines which of the following three alternatives applies upon default:

1. Zeffer, Inc., retains all or a portion of the cash collected. If all of the cash is retained, an entry would record the elimination of the Subscriptions Receivable and the Common Stock Subscribed balances and the reduction of Additional Paid-In Capital:

7/1/85	Common stock subscribed	500	
	Additional paid-in capital	500	
	Subscriptions receivable		1,000

2. Zeffer, Inc., must issue shares to Mr. Berry in proportion to the cash received. The appropriate entry would be as follows:

7/1/85	Common stock subscribed	500	
	Additional paid-in capital	750	
	Subscriptions receivable		1,000
	Common stock par value		250

3. Other provisions of state laws may require that Mr. Berry receive all or some portion of the amount paid in depending on the issuer's experience in selling the stock to other parties.

<table>
<tr><td style="vertical-align:top; width:20%">Recording the Reacquisition of Equity Securities</td><td>

General principles   Once issued, most stock remains outstanding for an indefinite period of time. Preferred stock, because of possible call, redemption, and conversion features, may have more follow-up transactions than does common stock. For either class of stock, however, the corporation may, within legal limits, purchase its own shares in the open market and hold them as treasury stock until subsequent sale, transfer, or cancellation. **Treasury stock,** therefore, is previously issued stock that has been reacquired by the issuer but has not yet been canceled or reissued. State statutes generally allow a corporation to purchase its own shares up to the amount of unrestricted, positive retained earnings unless the articles of incorporation specify differently. In addition, statutes usually prohibit treasury stock purchases if insolvency would result.

</td></tr>
</table>

Before discussing the specific accounting alternatives available for stock reacquisition situations, we need to discuss certain general guidelines. First, the corporation cannot be viewed as owning itself. As a result, treasury stock does not give the corporation the rights usually accompanying stock ownership. Treasury stock does not carry the voting privilege, and dividends do not apply to it. Second, dealing in one's own stock cannot lead to revenue recognition, although it may directly reduce retained earnings. As will be illustrated, the income statement is not affected by treasury stock transactions except for the effect that the reduction in the number of shares outstanding has on the earnings-per-share disclosure. Third, the number of shares authorized and issued is not affected by reacquisitions, but the number of shares outstanding is reduced when the corporation purchases treasury stock. Only if a reacquired share is formally retired (canceled) is the number of shares issued reduced. Fourth, treasury stock that has not been retired as of a balance sheet date is reported as a contra to all of owners' equity (as illustrated in Exhibits 20–1 and 20–2) and not as an asset.

Retirement of stock   Accountants view stock reacquisition from the point of view of management's intention regarding retirement. If stock is "constructively" retired in the sense that management does not intend to reissue it, the fact that it is not **legally retired** according to state statutes is not relevant for accounting. Current promulgated GAAP address the major question to be answered in the case of constructive retirement: What is the disposition of the difference between original par or stated value and the amount paid on reacquisition?[8] Consider the following set of facts with two different reacquisition prices, $90 per share and $130 per share.

Blackwell, Inc., has preferred stock outstanding and retained earnings as follows:

[8] *Accounting Principles Board Opinion No. 6, "Status of Accounting Research Bulletins"* (New York: AICPA, October 1965), par. 12a.

Preferred stock—par value (10,000 shares @ $100 per share)	$1,000,000
Preferred stock—additional paid-in capital	200,000
Retained earnings	500,000

If $90 per share is paid upon reacquisition of 10 percent of the shares outstanding for constructive retirement, GAAP call for a credit to an additional paid-in capital account as follows:

Preferred stock—par value	100,000	
Additional paid-in capital from pre-		
ferred stock reacquisition		10,000
Cash		90,000

If the amount paid upon reacquisition for constructive retirement exceeds par, or stated, value, then two alternatives are allowed for the excess: In our example of reacquisition of 1,000 shares at $130 per share, either of the following would be permitted. Alternative 1 involves charging the excess to retained earnings:

Preferred stock—par value	100,000	
Retained earnings	30,000	
Cash		130,000

Alternative 2 involves allocating the excess to additional paid-in capital and retained earnings:

Preferred stock—par value	100,000	
Retained earnings	21,429	
Preferred stock—additional paid-in		
capital	8,571	
Cash		130,000

In this case, the excess charged to "retained earnings" and "preferred stock—additional paid-in capital" is based on their proportionate book values, ($500,000/ $700,000) and ($200,000/$700,000), respectively. Although GAAP do not specify one allocation method, they do limit the charge to additional paid-in capital to the sum of the pro rata amount in that account (in our case 10 percent of $200,000 = $20,000—that is, 10 percent of the stock was retired and therefore a maximum of 10 percent of the additional paid-in capital can be eliminated), plus any previous net "gains" on treasury stock transactions for the same class of stock (in our case, we have no indication of such transactions).[9] If a class of stock is fully retired and there remains additional paid-in capital relating to it, the amount is assigned to the common stock outstanding.

Conversion of preferred stock When preferred stock is converted into common stock, all of the paid-in capital associated with the converted preferred shares is eliminated and the appropriate common stock "contributed capital" accounts are credited. For instance assume that Robots, Inc., issues 10,000 shares of $100 par, 12 percent preferred stock, at $105 per share on January 1, 1983. Each share is con-

[9] Ibid.

vertible into five shares of $10 par value common. On December 31, 1983, all shares are converted. The journal entries, ignoring dividends, would be as follows:

1/1/83	Cash	1,050,000	
	Preferred stock—par		1,000,000
	Preferred stock—additional		
	paid-in capital		50,000
12/31/83	Preferred stock—par	1,000,000	
	Preferred stock—additional		
	paid-in capital	50,000	
	Common stock—par		500,000
	Contributed capital from conversion		
	of preferred stock		550,000

If the common stock had a $25 par value, retained earnings would be reduced for the necessary balancing amount as follows:

12/31/83	Preferred stock—par	1,000,000	
	Preferred stock—additional	200,000	
	paid-in capital	50,000	
	Retained earnings		
	Common stock—par		1,250,000

Under no circumstances would conversions lead to recognition of gains and losses, and they would never result in direct credits to retained earnings.

Treasury stock transactions   Corporations may have several motives for purchasing previously issued common stock. Corporations may need relatively small numbers of shares when employees exercise options or when dividends are to be paid by issuing stock. Also, previously issued common stock is used in the acquisition of businesses, as compensation, and in many other types of business transactions. In addition, corporations may purchase their own shares merely to buy out one investor group's interest or to increase earnings per share. If a relatively small number of shares is required, it may be more practicable to acquire one's own shares and then transfer them than it would be to issue previously unissued shares. Aside from possible limitations caused by the number of authorized shares, the current stockholders' preemptive rights must be considered. In other words, all authorized shares may already be outstanding, thus barring a new issuance without a change in the articles of incorporation. In the situation where current stockholders have a preemptive right, a new issuance must be offered to them first, before new stockholders are added.

Two approaches to accounting for common stock reacquisition predominate in practice: (1) the cost method of treasury stock accounting and (2) the par value method of treasury stock accounting.

THE COST METHOD   The **cost method** is most applicable when stock is purchased with the intention of reissuance because the technique does not disturb the original equity account balances. Treasury Stock is debited and Cash is credited for the cost of the stock. The balance in the Treasury Stock account then reflects the cost of all reacquired stock still held in treasury. The following case illustrates both the reacquisition journal entries and the balance sheet disclosures.

DATE OF TRANSACTION	DESCRIPTION OF TRANSACTION
1/1/84	Bayou Drilling, Inc., incorporated and issued 100,000 shares of $1 par value common stock at $9 per share.
12/31/84	The company had $150,000 in net income during 1984.
9/10/85	The company purchased 1,000 shares of common stock on the open market at $12 per share.
12/31/85	At the end of its fiscal period in which it earned $275,000, Bayou Drilling sold 500 shares of treasury stock at $11 per share.
3/14/86	The company sold 250 shares of treasury stock at $14 per share.
10/30/86	The company sold 200 shares of treasury stock at $8 per share.
12/31/86	At the end of its fiscal period in which it earned $250,000 in net income, Bayou Drilling still held the remaining 50 shares of treasury stock.

The following journal entries would record Bayou Drilling's earnings and the issuance, reacquisition, and reissue of common stock for 1984 and 1985:

1/1/84	Cash		900,000	
	Common stock—par			100,000
	Additional paid-in capital			800,000
	(Issued 100,000 shares @ $9)			
12/31/84	Income summary		150,000	
	Retained earnings			150,000
9/10/85	Treasury stock		12,000	
	Cash			12,000
	(Purchased 1,000 shares @ $12)			
12/31/85	Cash		5,500	
	Retained earnings		500	
	Treasury stock			6,000
	(Sold 500 shares @ $11)			
12/31/85	Income summary		275,000	
	Retained earnings			275,000

The resulting owners' equity section of Bayou Drilling's December 31, 1985 balance sheet would appear as follows:

BAYOU DRILLING, INC.
Partial Balance Sheet
December 31, 1985

Owners' equity

Common stock—par $1 (authorized, 200,000; issued, 100,000; outstanding, 99,500)	$100,000	
Additional paid-in capital	800,000	$ 900,000
Retained earnings		424,500
Treasury stock (500 shares @ $12)		(6,000)
Total owners' equity		$1,318,500

Refer to the treasury stock entry of December 31, 1985. Note that retained earnings is reduced by the $500 "loss" that occurred when 500 shares of the treasury stock that cost $12 per share were sold for $11 per share. The original Additional Paid-in Capital account is not affected by this "loss" under the cost method. Treasury stock effects are apparent in several places on the December 31, 1985, balance sheet. Common stock outstanding has been reduced to 99,500, reflecting the 500 shares still in treasury. The treasury stock balance is shown as the last item that is subtracted from the entire owners' equity.

The following journal entries would be necessary for 1986:

3/14/86	Cash	3,500	
	Paid-in capital from treasury stock transactions		500
	Treasury stock		3,000
	(Sold 250 shares @ $14)		
10/30/86	Cash	1,600	
	Paid-in capital from treasury stock transactions		500
	Retained earnings	300	
	Treasury stock		2,400
	(Sold 200 shares @ $8)		
12/31/86	Income summary	250,000	
	Retained earnings		250,000

BAYOU DRILLING, INC.
Partial Balance Sheet
December 31, 1986

Owners' equity

Common stock—par $1 (authorized, 200,000; issued, 100,000; outstanding, 99,950)	$100,000	
Additional paid-in capital	800,000	$ 900,000
Retained earnings		674,200
Treasury stock (50 shares @ $12)		(600)
Total owners' equity		$1,573,600

In 1986 there are transactions creating "gains" and "losses" on treasury stock. On March 14, 1986, a new account, Paid-in Capital from Treasury Stock Transactions, is created to capture the "gain" of $500. This balance is eliminated on October 30, 1986, when a "loss" totaling $800 is incurred. Note that rather than show a negative balance in this account, retained earnings is debited for the $300 excess "loss." On December 31, 1986, the cost of the 50 remaining treasury shares remains as a contra to the entire owners' equity. Under the cost method of treasury stock accounting, the elimination of any original capital amounts awaits retirement of shares. The December 31, 1986, balance sheet, therefore, shows 100,000 shares issued and 99,950 shares outstanding with the original capital accounts unchanged.

THE PAR VALUE METHOD Whereas the cost method seems compatible with the notion that treasury stock is awaiting reissuance, the par value method seems more compatible with the assumption that treasury stock is to be retired. In general, the par value method wipes the slate clean upon reacquisition by eliminating the original pro rata capital amounts except for par value. Assuming the same facts for Bayou Drilling, Inc., the par value method would require the following journal entries and disclosures for treasury stock transactions:

9/10/85	Treasury stock	1,000	
	Additional paid-in capital	8,000	
	Retained earnings	3,000	
	Cash		12,000
	(Purchased 1,000 shares @ $12)		

12/31/85	Cash	5,500	
	Additional paid-in capital		5,000
	Treasury stock		500
	(Sold 500 shares @ $11)		

BAYOU DRILLING, INC.
Partial Balance Sheet
December 31, 1985

Owners' equity

Common stock—$1 par (authorized, 200,000; issued, 100,000; outstanding 99,500)	$100,000	
Additional paid-in capital	797,000	$ 897,000
Retained earnings		422,000
Treasury stock (500 shares @ $1)		(500)
Total owners' equity		$1,318,500

3/14/86	Cash	3,500	
	Additional paid-in capital		3,250
	Treasury stock		250
	(Sold 250 shares @ $14)		

10/30/86	Cash	1,600	
	Additional paid-in capital		1,400
	Treasury stock		200
	(Sold 200 shares @ $8)		

BAYOU DRILLING, INC.
Partial Balance Sheet
December 31, 1986

Owners' equity

Common stock—$1 par (authorized, 200,000; issued, 100,000; outstanding, 99,950)	$100,000	
Additional paid-in capital	801,650	$ 901,650
Retained earnings		672,000
Treasury stock (50 shares @ $1)		(50)
Total owners' equity		$1,573,600

Note that treasury stock was recorded at par value of $1 a share. The original additional paid-in capital—$8 a share—was eliminated upon acquisition of the treasury shares, and Retained Earnings was reduced for the excess of cost over the original issuance price. Note also that for the par-value method we did not use the account Paid-in Capital from Treasury Stock Transactions in the 3/14/86 and 10/30/86 entries. This account is merely a subset of Additional Paid-in Capital and is rarely disclosed in published statements. Its use is optional in both the par-value and cost methods.

The location of par value method treasury stock in the owners' equity section varies in practice. Some accountants prefer to show treasury stock carried at par value immediately below the stock to which it relates as follows:

```
                    BAYOU DRILLING, INC.
                    Partial Balance Sheet
                    December 31, 1986

Owners' equity
   Common stock—$1 par (authorized, 200,000; issue, 100,000; outstanding,
      99,950)                                                $100,000
      Less treasury stock, 50 @ par                              (50)
      Common stock outstanding                                 99,950    $  901,600
   Additional paid-in capital                                $801,650       672,000
   Retained earnings
      Total owners' equity                                              $1,573,600
```

Exhibit 20–3 and the following discussion of its major aspects analyze some of the similarities and differences between the cost method and the par value method of treasury stock accounting:

1. Common Stock — Par remains at the initial issuance amount until there is retirement or cancellation. This, of course, is consistent with the fact that treasury shares remain issued until retirement.

2. Additional Paid-in Capital under the cost method remains constant unless retirement takes place, in which case a proration of the original additional paid-in capital is written off. Under the par value method, the Additional Paid-in Capital account is reduced when treasury stock is purchased and may be increased or decreased when treasury stock is resold. Note that retirement would not change the Additional Paid-in Capital balance because the par value method treats the purchase of treasury stock as a retirement of part of the Additional Paid-in Capital amount.

3. The Paid-in Capital from Treasury Stock account is very similar to the Additional Paid-in Capital account, and often only the latter is used in practice.

4. Retained Earnings is never increased by treasury stock transactions, but it may be reduced under the cost method when "losses" are incurred on treasury stock transactions in excess of the net amount of "gains" on treasury stock transactions. The balance in paid-in capital from treasury stock transactions is never negative (a debit).

5. Outstanding Treasury Stock is carried at full purchase price under the cost method and at par under the par value method.

6. Total Owners' Equity is not affected by the choice of treasury stock accounting techniques.

Exhibit 20–4 shows two examples of treasury stock disclosure in annual reports. Gelco Corporation uses the cost method, which is by far the most commonly used method in practice. NCNB Corporation records its treasury stock at par. Again, analysis of the footnotes referred to on the balance sheet is necessary for a complete understanding of any equity transaction.

Other Owners' Equity Transactions

Donated capital Motives exist for encouraging individuals and organizations to donate assets and capital stock to corporations. Municipalities may attempt to lure a new business by donating a plant site. A major owner may return a portion of his or her stockholdings in the belief that a resale will improve the liquidity position of the business. To decide how these types of transactions are to be recorded in the accounting records, a series of judgments must be made. Does the transaction change

EXHIBIT 20–3

BAYOU DRILLING, INC.

Comparison of Owners' Equity Account Balances
for Cost and Par Value Methods of Treasury Stock
Accounting

DATE	TRANSACTION	COMMON STOCK—PAR		ADDITIONAL PAID-IN CAPITAL		PAID-IN CAPITAL FROM TREASURY STOCK TRANSACTIONS		RETAINED EARNINGS		TREASURY STOCK		TOTAL OWNERS' EQUITY	
		COST METHOD	PAR VALUE METHOD	COST METHOD	PAR VALUE METHOD	COST METHOD	PAR VALUE METHOD	COST METHOD	PAR VALUE METHOD	COST METHOD	PAR VALUE METHOD	COST METHOD	PAR VALUE METHOD
1/1/84	Initial issuance of common stock	$100,000	$100,000	$800,000	$800,000	—	—	—	—	—	—	$ 900,000	$ 900,000
12/31/84	Earnings = $150,000	100,000	100,000	800,000	800,000	—	—	$150,000	$150,000	—	—	1,050,000	1,050,000
9/10/85	Purchase of 1,000 treasury shares @ $12	100,000	100,000	800,000	792,000	—	—	150,000	147,000	$(12,000)	$(1,000)	1,038,000	1,038,000
12/31/85	Earnings = $275,000	100,000	100,000	800,000	792,000	—	—	425,000	422,000	(12,000)	(1,000)	1,313,000	1,313,000
12/31/85	Sale of 500 treasury shares @ $11	100,000	100,000	800,000	797,000	—	—	424,500	422,000	(6,000)	(500)	1,318,500	1,318,500
3/14/86	Sale of 250 treasury shares @ $14	100,000	100,000	800,000	800,250	$500	—	424,500	422,000	(3,000)	(250)	1,322,000	1,322,000
10/30/86	Sale of 200 treasury shares @ $8	100,000	100,000	800,000	801,650	—	—	424,200	422,000	(600)	(50)	1,323,600	1,323,600
12/31/86	Earnings = $250,000	100,000	100,000	800,000	801,650	—	—	674,200	672,000	(600)	(50)	1,573,600	1,573,600

EXHIBIT
20–4

DISCLOSURE OF TREASURY STOCK AT COST AND AT PAR

GELCO CORPORATION
Excerpts from Balance Sheet

	($000)	
	1980	1979
Redeemable preferred stock (Note H)	$ 50,000	—
Common stockholders' equity (Notes B, G, and I):		
Common stock, par value $.50 per share:		
Authorized 25,000,000 shares (1980 and 1979)		
Issued 10,191,849 shares (1980 and 1979)	5,096	$ 5,096
Additional paid-in capital	45,148	44,695
Retained earnings	100,319	59,923
Less treasury stock, 89,382 shares (1980) and 89,822 shares (1979), at cost	(1,863)	(1,647)
Total common stockholders' equity	$148,700	$108,067

NCNB CORPORATION
Excerpts from Balance Sheet

	($000)	
	1980	1979
Shareholders' Equity		
Preferred stock, $10 par value:		
authorized—2,000,000 shares; issued—none; common stock, $2.50 par value: authorized—25,000,000 shares: issued—19,269,103 and 18,160,136 shares (Notes 12, 16, and 19)	$ 48,173	$ 45,400
Surplus	90,986	77,288
Undivided profits (Notes 8 and 10)	213,116	179,467
Excess of cost over market value of marketable equity securities (Note 2)	(1,776)	(2,153)
Less: Treasury stock, at par value (8,370 shares)	(21)	
Total shareholders' equity	$350,478	$300,002

the owners' interest in the corporation? If the answer is yes, owners' equity is increased. Promulgated GAAP call for the recording of the fair value of the asset received in such transactions.[10] Regardless of the incentive for a donation, the asset or stock received is accounted for as if the corporation had made a normal payment to acquire it. Donation of a plant site or other long term asset would require all the normal accounting techniques of recording, amortizing, and retiring that a purchased asset would require. Because nothing of value would be given in return at the date of donation, some form of appraisal would be necessary to establish the asset's initial book value. The credit side of a donation entry is recorded as permanent contributed capital in an account titled Donated Capital. This account would normally remain in the accounting records for the life of the entity irrespective of the disposition of the donated asset or treasury stock.

Unrealized "gains" and "losses" Conventional accounting theory is a very flexible tool that can be applied to many different economic transactions. Certain types of transactions, however, are particularly troublesome, resulting in uncertainty as to

[10] *Accounting Principles Board Opinion No. 29*, "Accounting for Nonmonetary Transactions," par. 18.

the proper accounting treatment. When no clear-cut theoretical stance is apparent on an accounting issue that has material impact on financial statements, there tends to be a great variation in practice depending on the self-interest of the reporting entities. If a mandatory rule is suggested in such cases, the final result is necessarily arbitrary or at least not purely theoretically based.

Two such issues have resulted in promulgated GAAP that require the reporting of owners' equity accounts that are neither contributed nor earned. Accounting for long-term marketable equity securities may result in unrealized losses being recorded as the asset account is made to reflect current values.[11] These "losses," however, are not disclosed on income statements because of the long-term nature of the investment. (See Chapter 14 for a detailed discussion of the accounting for long-term marketable equity securities.) Instead, promulgated GAAP call for these periodic fluctuations to be reflected in an owners' equity account that carries a debit balance.

Another case where periodic fluctuations create "gains" and "losses" that are troublesome for accountants involves the translation of foreign financial statements. When a branch of an entity operates in a foreign country, the financial statements of the foreign component must be translated into the domestic currency. Fluctuations in exchange rates between the two currencies create exchange adjustments that must be reflected on the entity's financial statements. Do such continuous fluctuations generate income statement-type gains and losses or should they, too, be held in abeyance in the owners' equity section? The FASB has adopted a resolution similar to the one for long-term equity securities, in which certain translation adjustments are debited or credited to a stockholders' equity account and are not reflected in the income statement.[12] Advanced accounting texts cover this topic in detail.

FUNDS FLOW EFFECTS

Stockholders' contributed capital usually forms the initial capital endowment of corporations. Funds, defined as either cash or working capital, flow in upon the cash sale of stock and working capital is increased by subscriptions to stock and the sale of stock for any current asset. Statements of changes in financial position often show the sale of equity securities as "other sources" of funds.

Transactions in already issued stock can affect funds flows, with the purchase and sale of treasury stock usually involving cash. Retirement of stock can be accomplished by means of cash payments to stockholders, in which case funds are consumed, or by means of transfers of other assets, in which case the funds flow effects would depend on the nature of the transferred asset. Conversions of preferred stock into common stock have no effect on funds flows.

---

[11] *Statement of Financial Accounting Standards No. 12,* "Accounting for Certain Marketable Securities" (Stamford, CT: FASB, December 1975).

[12] *Statement of Financial Accounting Standards No. 52,* "Foreign Currency Translation" (Stamford, CT: FASB, 1981).

SUMMARY

In this chapter we have concentrated on accounting for contributed capital in corporations. Several reasons were cited for the corporate form of business, most of which revolve around the fact that corporations have a legal existence separate from that of owners. At the same time, however, the owners' rights are specified in laws and contracts. Underlying owners' equity accounting is the concept of the business entity's obligation to owners. When viewed as two separate entities, the business and its owners are seen to have rights and obligations that are governed by the laws and contracts applicable to such associations.

Because of the complexity of the laws governing equity ownership and the necessity for aggressive marketing of ownership shares, accountants must record, and provide disclosure of, many specific aspects of the relationship between the business and its owners. As in liability accounting, the contractual terms between the specific parties are of major importance in equity accounting.

Decision makers are interested in the status of a corporation's contributed capital because of what it says about the entity's current and prospective financial structure. Creditors and equity owners may evaluate investment opportunities in terms of the expected operating results, the relationship of debt to equity, and the structure of equity itself. The ultimate beneficiaries of any profitable operations are to some degree specified by the nature of their contractual relationship to the entity. Accounting's primary role in the area of equity accounting, therefore, is to supply the information necessary for informed decisions.

QUESTIONS

Q20–1   List the advantages of the corporate form of business, and describe how the entity concept is related to these characteristics.

Q20–2   If only one class of stock is issued, what rights are usually conveyed by the stock?

Q20–3   Contrast the rights conveyed by preferred stock with those conveyed by common stock.

Q20–4   What are the differences and similarities between preferred stock and debt?

Q20–5   Preferred stock can be callable, convertible, and/or redeemable. Distinguish between these features in terms of the right of the stockholders.

Q20–6   Several owners' equity sections of published balance sheets are shown in this chapter. Describe the prominent features of the formats you find in these and others you may be familiar with, such as the "normal" sequence of accounts and the types of detail presented.

Q20–7   What measurement problems do accountants face when stock is issued for noncash considerations, and how are these problems normally resolved?

Q20–8   When securities are sold by means of a subscription plan, there is no certainty that all money amounts will be collected. How is this uncertainty reflected in the accounting records?

Q20–9   List several motivations for a corporation's acquiring its own securities, and discuss the preferable accounting method for each.

Q20–10   Contrast the par value method with the cost method of accounting for treasury stock in terms of the initial recording of treasury stock acquisitions.

C20–1 Consider the following Owners' Equity section and related note from a published financial statement.

COLT INDUSTRIES AND SUBSIDIARIES
Excerpts from Balance Sheet
Shareholders' Equity (Notes 3, 5, and 7)

	(IN THOUSANDS OF DOLLARS, EXCEPT PAR VALUES)	
	1980	1979
Preferred stock— $1 par value, 2,077,189 and 2,246,023 shares authorized, 421,694 and 590,528 shares outstanding (involuntary liquidation value at December 31, 1980— $31,479)	$ 422	$ 590
Common stock— $1 par value, 30,000,000 shares authorized, 13,269,650 and 13,209,875 shares issued	13,270	13,210
Capital in excess of par value	149,472	160,700
Retained earnings	522,532	463,979
	$ 685,696	$ 638,479
Less cost of 209,525 and 420,021 shares of common stock in treasury	8,060	16,887
	$ 677,636	$ 621,592

5. Capital Stock
Changes in capital stock are shown below for 1978, 1979, and 1980:

	PREFERRED STOCK $1 PAR VALUE	COMMON STOCK $1 PAR VALUE	TREASURY STOCK	
			SHARES	COST
Balance at January 1, 1978	$1,204,981	$ 8,106,164	(116,350)	$ (6,544,000)
Conversion of preferred stock and exercise of options	(421,575)	735,783	—	—
Stock issued under three-for-two stock split	—	4,198,955	(58,175)	—
Balance at December 31, 1978	$ 783,406	$13,040,902	(174,525)	$ (6,544,000)
Purchase of treasury stock	—	—	(541,500)	(22,624,000)
Conversion and retirements of preferred stock and exercise of options	(192,878)	168,973	296,004	12,281,000
Balance at December 31, 1979	$ 590,528	$13,209,875	(420,021)	$ (16,887,000)
Purchase of treasury stock	—	—	(97,000)	(3,727,000)
Conversion and retirements of preferred stock and exercise of options	(168,834)	59,775	307,496	12,554,000
Balance at December 31, 1980	$ 421,694	$13,269,650	(209,525)	$ (8,060,000)

The authorized preferred stock is issuable in series. Outstanding preferred stock has voting rights and is entitled to cumulative dividends. At December 31, 1980, the following series were outstanding:

	ANNUAL DIVIDEND RATE	SHARES OUTSTANDING	INVOLUNTARY LIQUIDATION VALUE	REDEMPTION VALUE PER SHARE
Convertible preferred				
Series A	$1.60	135,412	$ 5,417,000	$ 41.00
Series B	4.50	10,808	1,081,000	101.00
Series D	4.25	218,449	21,845,000	101.00
		364,669	$28,343,000	
Non-convertible preferred				
Series E	2.75	57,025	3,136,000	55.00
		421,694	$31,479,000	

The payment of dividends on common stock is restricted if shareholders' equity of the company would thereby be reduced below the aggregate involuntary liquidation preference applicable to outstanding preferred stock ($31,479,000), plus the amount of capital attributable to common stock ($13,060,000). At December 31, 1980, shareholders' equity was $633,097,000 in excess of this requirement.

All series of preferred stock, except Series E, are convertible into common stock of the company: Series A at the rate of four shares of common stock for each five shares of preferred; Series B at the rate of 7.604 shares of common stock for each share of preferred; and Series D at the rate of 2.166 shares of common stock for each share of preferred, subject to certain specified adjustments.

At December 31, 1980, shares of common stock were reserved for the following purposes:

Conversion of preferred stock	663,763
Issuance under stock options	588,335

REQUIRED   How does such a presentation communicate aspects of the rights of the various classes of stockholders? What rights are not explicitly communicated?

C20–2   Par value is often considered a legal technicality with little or no economic impact. Why is this so? Can you think of cases where par value has a direct impact on accounting and on economic transactions?

C20–3   If a corporation has three classes of stock, what can generally be said about the rights of each class of stockholders?

C20–4   Preferred stockholders can be *assumed* to want certain characteristics in their investments in comparison with common stockholders and bondholders.

REQUIRED   What do you think these characteristics are? How do you think (1) convertibility features, (2) call provisions, and (3) redemption provisions affect these basic attitudes of preferred stockholders?

C20–5   Your client, Fennway Auto Parts, Inc., has the following line item on its preliminary income statement:

Extraordinary item—gain on receipt of donation of operating locations from the city of Columbus	$977,000

REQUIRED   What impact on total assets and total owners' equity would such a misclassification have? Explain the correct accounting for such a transaction.

C20–6   Prepare counterarguments for the following statement: "Treasury stock is purchased at a fair market price. It can be sold for value or reissued for services performed. It has the attributes of an asset and should therefore be disclosed as an asset on balance sheets."

C20–7 (CPA ADAPTED)   Problems may be encountered in accounting for transactions involving the stockholders' equity section of the balance sheet.

REQUIRED

1. Describe the accounting for the subscription of common stock at a price in excess of the par value of the common stock.
2. Describe the accounting for the issuance for cash of no-par value common stock at a price in excess of the stated value of the common stock.

C20–8 (CPA ADAPTED) A corporation's capital (stockholders' equity) is an important part of its statement of financial position.

REQUIRED Identify and discuss the general categories of capital (stockholders' equity) for a corporation. Be sure to enumerate specific sources included in each general category.

C20–9 (CPA ADAPTED) *Part A.* Capital stock is an important area of a corporation's equity section. Generally, the term *capital stock* embraces the common and preferred stock issued by a corporation.

REQUIRED

1. What basic rights are inherent in the ownership of common stock, and how are they exercised?
2. What is preferred stock? Discuss the various preferences afforded preferred stock.

Part B. In dealing with the various equity securities of a corporate entity, it is important to understand certain terminology.

REQUIRED Define (1) treasury stock, (2) legal capital, (3) stock right, and (4) stock warrant.

C20–10 (CPA ADAPTED) For numerous reasons, a corporation may reacquire shares of its own capital stock. When a company purchases treasury stock, it has two options as to how to account for the shares: (1) the cost method, and (2) the par value method.

REQUIRED Compare and contrast the cost method with the par value method for each of the following:

1. Purchase of shares at a price less than par value
2. Purchase of shares at a price greater than par value
3. Subsequent resale of treasury shares at a price less than purchase price but more than par value
4. Subsequent resale of treasury shares at a price greater than both purchase price and par value
5. Effect on net income

C20–11 Review the discussions of *liability* in Chapters 2 and 18. Now consider the following securities:

BONDS	PREFERRED STOCK
Term: 20 years	Redemption: At stockholders' option starting in 3 years
Interest payments: $100 annual per bond	Dividend payments: $100 annual per stock, cumulative
Maturity value: $1,000 per bond	Par value: $1,000 per stock

REQUIRED From the general creditors' point of view, which security poses the biggest threat to the liquidity of the company? Give both the short-run and the long-run perspectives and reasons for your answer.

EXERCISES

E20–1 A corporation has collected all subscriptions receivable on common stock at December 31, 1983, except for $10,000 that was owed by a subscriber who died on December 31, 1983. The subscriber had paid two-thirds of the original subscription amount of $30,000 for 3,000 shares of no-par value common stock.

REQUIRED Show the journal entry necessary under each of three different assumptions concerning the governing state law.

E20-2 Axner Corporation has the following detailed disclosure in a note to its financial statements:

Retained earnings (beginning of year)	$9,100,000
Net income	2,300,000
Dividends	(4,500,000)
Treasury stock transactions	(420,000)
Retained earnings (end of year)	$6,480,000

REQUIRED Reconstruct the journal entries that may have led to the treasury stock entry.

E20-3 A balance sheet contains the following items:

Subscriptions receivable	$ 232,400
Common stock ($10 par) issued and outstanding, 100,000 shares	1,000,000
Additional paid-in capital—common stock	412,000
Common stock subscribed	140,000

REQUIRED

1. How many shares were subscribed to, assuming no cash has yet been received?
2. If no cash has yet been received from the subscribers, what was the original subscription price per share? Show computations.
3. How was additional paid-in capital affected by the subscriptions?

E20-4 Ebberwhite, Inc., has been actively acquiring its own common shares and has the following owners' equity section on December 31, 1984:

Common stock—$1 par (authorized, 1,500,000; issued, 500,000; outstanding, 450,000)	$ 500,000
Additional paid-in capital	1,800,000
Retained earnings	8,400,000
Treasury stock	(50,000)
	$10,650,000

All the stock sold initially for $5 per share and the treasury stock was reacquired for $7 per share, none of which was reissued.

REQUIRED

1. What treasury stock method is being used?
2. How was retained earnings affected by the treasury stock transaction?
3. What journal entry would be recorded if the treasury stock were retired?

E20-5 Price Robotics, Inc., constructed a research laboratory in Oxford, Mississippi, after having received a donation of a building site from the city of Oxford. During the current fiscal period, the following journal entries were made relating to the building site:

1/1/83	Laboratory site	198,000	
	Donated capital		198,000
12/31/83	Amortization expense	9,900	
	Laboratory site		9,900

REQUIRED

1. If you assume that the above journal entries are correct, what can you deduce about the terms of the donation?

2. How is donated capital classified on Price's balance sheet, and how will this classification be affected by future events?

E20-6 Maxie Metals Corporation sold convertible preferred stock on June 30, 1984. The following information relates to the company's owners' equity on June 30, 1984:

Number of preferred shares issued	100,000
Par value of preferred stock	$100 per share
Preferred stock dividend rate	$15 per share annually
Preferred stock convertibility	10 shares of common for 1 share of preferred commencing 12/1/84
Preferred stock selling price	$108 per share at 6/30/84
Common stock par value	$10 per share
Common shares outstanding	1,000,000 issued at $10 par

REQUIRED If 50,000 shares of preferred are converted on December 1, 1984, how would the company's owners' equity section appear on December 31, 1984, assuming total retained earnings is $1,300,000 before the conversion?

E20-7 A corporation reacquired 5,000 shares of $3.50 par value common stock for $5.00 per share. The stock originally sold for $13.50 per share. Before the reacquisition at $5.00 per share, the corporation's owners' equity section was as follows:

Common stock—par value $3.50 per share	
(100,000 shares authorized, 90,000 shares issued and outstanding)	$ 315,000
Common stock—additional paid-in capital	900,000
Retained earnings	200,000
Total owners' equity	$1,415,000

REQUIRED

1. Show the journal entry for the treasury stock acquisition using the cost method.

2. Show the journal entry for the treasury stock acquisition using the par value method.

E20-8 A company has the following stock outstanding on December 31, 1983, the end of its fiscal year:

Common stock (no par):	
Authorized, issued, and outstanding, 600,000 shares	$1,200,000
Preferred stock ($100 par, 12%):	
Authorized, issued, and outstanding, 10,000 shares	1,000,000
Preferred stock—Additional paid-in capital	100,000
Retained earnings	500,000

REQUIRED If the preferred stock is cumulative and no dividends have been paid in 1982 and 1983, what is the maximum dividends per share that could be declared for common stock on December 31, 1983? Explain your answer.

E20-9 On August 15, 1983, Apex, Inc., was incorporated and issued 100,000 shares of common stock with a par value of $10 per share and 1,000 shares of preferred stock with a par value of $100 per share. The shares were purchased by the five former partners of Apex. On September 1, 1983, common and preferred stock was issued for the acquisition of property, plant, and equipment as follows:

NUMBER OF SHARES	FAIR APPRAISED VALUE OF ASSETS	
3,000 common shares	Land	$20,000
400 preferred shares	Building	35,000
	Equipment	16,000
		$71,000

The board of directors decides that the common shares have a fair value of $10 per share on September 1, 1983, and that the preferred stock has appreciated to a fair value of $102.50 per share by September 1, 1983.

REQUIRED Record the journal entry for this acquisition of property, plant, and equipment. Show computations.

PROBLEMS

P20–1 Minnesota Travel, Inc., was incorporated on August 8, 1983, at which time 50,000 shares of common stock and 2,000 shares of preferred stock were authorized. Consider the following facts and events:

1. The par value of common stock is $5 per share.
2. The par value of preferred stock is $100 per share.
3. The sale of shares was as follows:

STOCK ISSUED			ITEM(S) RECEIVED	
DATE	TYPE	NUMBER OF SHARES	DESCRIPTION	FAIR VALUE
8/8/83	Common	25,000	Cash	$250,000
8/15/83	Common	10,000	Land and office building	180,000
	Preferred[a]	1,000		
9/1/83	Common	5,000	Cash	60,000
9/1/83	Preferred	100	In payment of loan from president of corporation	Non-interest-bearing note was due on 9/1/84 and had a maturity value of $13,000 and an effective interest rate of 10%

[a] Preferred stock's market value equals its par value

REQUIRED Record all the necessary journal entries for the above transactions. Show all computations.

P20–2 Lansing Tire and Rubber, Inc., has the following owners' equity section on its balance sheet on December 31, 1984:

Contributed Capital	
Preferred stock—Par (100,000 shares authorized, issued, and outstanding; par value is $100 per share)	$10,000,000
Preferred stock—additional paid-in capital	1,100,000
Common stock—par (500,000 shares authorized, issued, and outstanding; par value is $10 per share)	5,000,000
Common stock—additional paid-in capital	15,000,000
Retained earnings	4,500,000

During 1985 Lansing Tire and Rubber has the following transactions in its own shares:

4/15/85	Purchased 10,000 shares of common stock at $20 per share
8/25/85	Purchased 5,000 shares of common stock at $22 per share
9/10/85	Purchased 1,000 shares of preferred stock at $105 per share and canceled them
12/12/85	Sold 6,000 shares of common treasury stock at $18 per share

REQUIRED

1. Prepare all journal entries for the above transactions for both the cost and par value methods.
2. Prepare the December 31, 1985, owners' equity section of the balance sheet, assuming that net income was $4,500,000, common dividends declared on Jun 1, 1985, were $1.50 per share, and preferred dividends declared on December 31, 1985, were $1,000,000. Show the results for both the par value and cost methods.

P20-3 The Gourmet Club, a regional catering service, was incorporated on January 10, 1984. Two hundred thousand shares of common stock with a par value of $1 per share were authorized and 100,000 shares were sold on January 10, 1984, at $1 per share. Each former partner subscribed to one-fourth of the remaining authorized stock and each agreed to make payments of $12,500 on June 30, 1984, and December 31, 1984. All payments were made except for one—Ms. Jane Buris failed to make the final payment. It was decided to return her initial $12,500 payment to her, as this was consistent with state laws.

REQUIRED

1. Show all journal entries necessary to record the above transactions.
2. To the extent possible, indicate the balance sheet accounts affected by the above transactions.

P20-4 University Research Labs, Inc., was incorporated on August 15, 1983. The following list describes the transactions affecting owners' equity:

1. The city of Ann Arbor gave two concessions to motivate the corporation to locate there: (1) Title to a plant site valued at $150,000 was transferred to the company and (2) an exemption from property tax for 5 years. On August 15, 1983, the present value of the exemption was at least $25,000.
2. University Research Labs issued all of its authorized stock, which included (1) 100,000 shares of no-par common at $5 per share, and (2) 1,000 shares of 14 percent preferred with a par value of $100 per share.
3. The cost of issuance included $10,500 paid to lawyers, printers, consultants, and accountants for legal and technical services related to the issuance of stock. It was also estimated that the president of the corporation spent a minimum of 300 hours on stock issuance matters. His salary would work out to an hourly rate of $85.
4. On August 20, 1983, the board of directors voted to establish a stated value for the common stock at $5 per share.

REQUIRED

1. Discuss the nature of each transaction.
2. Show all the necessary journal entries.

P20-5 Following is an excerpt from the comparative owners' equity sections of Stereo Components Corporation's balance sheets for 1983 and 1984:

	1984	1983
Owners' equity		
Preferred stock—$10 par (authorized 100,000 shares)	$1,000,000	$ 500,000
Preferred stock—additional paid-in capital	250,000	100,000
Common stock—$5 par (authorized 1,000,000 shares)	5,000,000	4,500,000
Common stock—additional paid-in capital	1,100,000	900,000
Paid-in capital from treasury stock transaction	3,750	—
Retained earnings (no dividends were declared)	600,000	550,000
Treasury stock	—	(32,500)
	$7,953,750	$6,517,500

REQUIRED   Describe the probable transaction or transactions that caused the changes in each owners' equity section account during 1984, and show the journal entries involved in each of your proposed explanations.

P20–6   Sloan Sisters, a partnership, is about to incorporate into Sloan, Inc., which will have the following authorized stock: 100,000 shares of common stock having a par value of $1.00 per share; and 1,000 shares of 14 percent, cumulative preferred stock having a par value of $100 per share.

Millie and Natalie Sloan will contribute their shares (60 percent and 40 percent, respectively) of the assets of partnership:

	BOOK VALUE	FAIR VALUE
Cash[a]	$ 10,000	$ 10,000
Accounts receivable	75,500	70,000
Inventories	85,000	90,000
Plant	150,000	175,000
Equipment	200,000	300,000
Land	50,000	400,000

[a] Cash remaining after all liabilities of the partnership have been paid off.

The preferred stock is expected to have a fair value equal to its par value. All of the authorized preferred shares and half of the authorized common shares will be issued to the sisters in payment for the contributed assets.

REQUIRED   Record the journal entries necessary for the issuance of the shares upon incorporation. How many shares of each security does each stockholder receive?

P20–7   Enterprise Shuttle Service, Inc., has 40,000 shares of $50 par value, 12 percent, cumulative preferred stock outstanding on January 1, 1983, the beginning of its fiscal year. The preferred shares, which were issued at par, are callable at 104 percent of par value anytime after July 1, 1983, and are currently convertible at the option of stockholders into 10 shares of common stock for each share of preferred. Between January 1 and June 30, 1983, 12,000 shares were converted into $2.00 par value common stock when the market price of each common share was $9.50 and the market price of each preferred share was $51. On July 1, 1983, the company calls and retires all outstanding shares by paying the call price plus dividends to date for the current year.

REQUIRED   Record all the journal entries relating to preferred stock during 1983, ignoring dividend payments, except for the dividend on the called stock.

P20–8   KJUN Broadcasting Corporation was organized in October 1984. Five hundred thousand shares of $2.00 par value common stock were authorized and subscribed to by three stockholders under the following payment schedule:

		PAYMENTS		
STOCKHOLDER	SHARES	10/1/84	6/30/85	12/31/85
Boudreaux	100,000	$100,000	$100,000	$100,000
Thibodeaux	300,000	300,000	300,000	300,000
Breaux	100,000	100,000	100,000	100,000

All payments were made on schedule except that Breaux failed to make the final payment. The 100,000 shares Breaux had subscribed to were issued to a fourth investor, N. Abshire, who paid $2.50 per share in cash. Breaux was refunded an amount equal to his actual payments minus a penalty of $.50 per share for all the shares that he had subscribed to.

REQUIRED   Record the journal entries for all the above transactions.

P20–9   Providential Finance, Inc., has the following owners' equity balances at the end of its fiscal year:

	12/31/84
Preferred stock—(par $100)	
Authorized, issued, and outstanding, 300,000 shares	$30,000,000
Preferred stock—Additional paid-in capital	3,000,000
Common stock (par $1.00)	
Authorized 5,000,000, issued and outstanding 4,000,000 shares	4,000,000
Common stock—additional paid-in capital	7,300,000
Retained earnings	6,400,000

During 1985 the company had the following transactions in its own shares:

2/14/85	Purchased 10,000 common shares at $14 per share in the open market
4/10/85	Called and retired 100,000 shares of preferred stock at 102 percent of par, plus dividends of $10 per share
8/11/85	Traded 8,000 common treasury shares for a building site that had a fair market value of $120,000
11/30/85	Sold 1,000 common treasury shares to the market for $13 per share

REQUIRED Record all the journal entries necessary for the above transactions, assuming the cost method is used for treasury stock.

P20–10 Assume all the facts in the preceding problem.

REQUIRED Record the necessary journal entries for the transactions assuming the par value method is used for treasury stock.

P20–11 Consider the following comparative owners' equity balances for Quaker State Distributors, Inc.:

	1984	1983
Preferred stock—par value		
($50 per share par, 12%, 50,000 shares authorized and 30,000 issued and outstanding at 12/31/84, and 20,000 shares issued and outstanding at 12/31/83)	$1,500,000	$1,000,000
Preferred stock—additional paid-in capital	300,000	—
Common stock—par value		
($5.00 per share par, 1,000,000 shares authorized, 400,000 shares issued, and 390,000 shares outstanding at 12/31/84, and 200,000 shares issued and outstanding at 12/31/83)	2,000,000	1,000,000
Common stock—Additional paid-in capital	4,000,000	2,400,000
Retained earnings	2,000,000	4,050,000
Treasury stock	(150,000)	—

The 10,000 treasury shares were purchased on June 1, 1984. New issuances of preferred and common stock took place on July 5, 1984.

REQUIRED

1. Compute the amount of shares issued in 1984.
2. Record all journal entries related to stock issuances during 1984.
3. What method is being used for treasury stock? Why?

P20–12 Assume all the facts in the preceding problem.

REQUIRED

1. Show the journal entries for the retirement of the treasury stock on January 1, 1985, when the fair value of a common share is $18.

2. Regardless of your answer to requirement 1, show the February 12, 1985, journal entry to record the sale of 5,000 shares of treasury stock in the open market at $12 per share and the subsequent sale on March 10, 1985, of the remaining 5,000 shares at $16 per share.

P20-13   Mr. Chips Restaurants, Inc., sells franchises throughout the northeastern United States. Currently, 50 Mr. Chips Restaurants are owned by local managers who are also owners of the corporation's stock. The company purchases the land and constructs the building, and the franchisee then subscribes to an agreed-upon amount of $10 par value common stock and is given possession of the restaurant. The subscription payments are made in five equal year-end payments plus 15 percent interest on the unpaid balance. The title passes after all payments have been made. For example, a restaurant now costs a total of $200,000 to construct. On January 1, 1983, a franchisee subscribed to 10,000 shares of common stock at an agreed-upon price of $35 per share. At that time the common shares were selling for $15 per share on the open market.

REQUIRED

1. Is the full $35 per share contributed capital? Explain.
2. Is the full $350,000 properly recorded as subscription receivable?
3. How should the above transactions be recorded?

P20-14 (CMA ADAPTED)

_____   1. Preferred stock has several features that may make it a more desirable form of financing than long-term
  E   debt. Which of the following statements concerning the advantages of preferred stock over long-term debt is generally *false?*
         a. Preferred stock dividends are a weaker legal obligation than bond interest for the issuing corporation.
         b. Preferred stock normally has no final maturity date.
         c. Preferred stock adds to the corporation's equity base.
         d. Preferred stockholders cannot force a corporation into legal bankruptcy for dividends.
         e. Preferred stock is sold on a lower-yield basis than bonds.

_____   2. The *par value* of common stock is
  D   a. The present value of the stock   d. The legal nominal value assigned to the stock
         b. The liquidation value of the stock   e. The amount received by the corporation
         c. The book value of the stock   when the stock was originally sold

_____   3. Flexall Corporation holds 10,000 shares of its $10 par value common stock as treasury stock. The trea-
  C   sury stock was acquired two years ago for $110,000. The company uses the cost method of accounting for treasury stock. If the shares are subsequently sold for $140,000, this transaction would result in
         a. A $30,000 gain on sale of investments
         b. A credit to retained earnings of $30,000
         c. Additional paid-in capital of $30,000
         d. A reduction in the balance of treasury stock by $100,000
         e. An addition of $140,000 to various paid-in capital accounts

_____   4. Which of the following would *not* be found under the heading "Capital Stock" in a company's balance
  E   sheet?
         a. Paid-in capital in excess of par value on preferred stock
         b. Common stock, $5 par value
         c. Common stock dividends payable in common stock
         d. Common stock subscribed
         e. Common stock dividends payable in cash

21

Stockholders' Earned Capital

OVERVIEW The owners' equity-related disclosures, in conjunction with other disclosures in financial statements, communicate information about how management has financed asset acquisitions in the past and about the current state of the business entity's obligations to its owners. To understand what the owners' equity disclosures mean, it is necessary to understand the rights and obligations of both the stockholder and the business entity and the kinds of transactions that affect owners' equity. The distinctions made between par value, additional paid-in capital, preferred stock, common stock, and other contributed capital classifications are required because they help portray the contractual relationship between the entity and its stockholders. Disclosures concerning earned capital (retained earnings) also communicate something about the rights and obligations of the business and its stockholders and the history of transactions that affect those rights and obligations. The full significance of owners' equity disclosures can be determined only by viewing owners' equity in relation to other disclosures. The balance between liability and owners' equity amounts as sources of assets is a major indicator of a business's financial status.

The retained earnings classification is usually more difficult to understand than any other balance sheet classification. One problem is that the retained earnings balance not only represents the net effect of all operating transactions over the life of the entity but also reflects dividend transactions and the effect of other possible transactions, such as certain dealings in an entity's own securities, errors, certain changes in accounting principles, and reorganizations. To fully comprehend the retained earnings balance, therefore, many diverse transactions over the life of the entity would have to be analyzed or at least considered.

Before getting into the complexities of retained earnings accounting, let us study an extreme simplification in order to emphasize the fundamental relationships. Assume that an entity has had only cash transactions throughout its existence and that no dividends have been declared, resulting in the following balance sheet items:

$$\frac{\text{Cash}}{\$1,000,000} = \frac{\text{Liabilities}}{\$500,000} + \frac{\text{Common stock}}{\$200,000} + \frac{\text{Retained earnings}}{\$300,000}$$

The retained earnings balance of $300,000 resulted from a series of revenue and expense transactions that generated net assets of $300,000 (Net assets = Assets − Liabilities). The entity controls $1,000,000 in cash, of which $500,000 is to be paid to creditors according to the terms of the debt agreements; $200,000 is the initial contribution made by common stockholders; and $300,000 is the amount that would normally be available for ordinary dividend payments (depending on state laws). Why is $300,000 said to be available for dividends? Review the sources of the asset controlled. The $300,000 represents the net asset generated by revenue-producing activities. Paying dividends based on this balance does not disturb the liability or paid-in capital balances. Thus, conceptually the original status of stockholders and the rights of creditors are not affected by such dividend payments.

Let us now relax the assumption that all assets are held in cash and assume that $900,000 is held in plant and equipment:

$$\frac{\text{Cash}}{\$100,000} + \frac{\text{Plant and equipment}}{\$900,000} = \frac{\text{Liabilities}}{\$500,000} + \frac{\text{Common stock}}{\$200,000} + \frac{\text{Retained earnings}}{\$300,000}$$

We see that although the Retained Earnings account has a $300,000 balance, the ability to pay a $300,000 cash dividend is no longer certain. There is no assurance that the long-term assets could be converted into cash or that a loan could be negotiated to provide sufficient cash for the same $300,000 dividend payment as before.

Although a positive retained earnings balance technically represents an excess of accumulated net income over accumulated dividends, it does not necessarily mean that the entity has the financial ability to pay dividends. The best interests of stockholders are not necessarily served by the payment of dividends in all situations, even when this payment is both legally and financially feasible. In the above example, would it actually be in the best interest of stockholders to sell some or all of the long-term assets or to borrow in order to pay dividends?

The entity has a certain amount of flexibility in formulating a dividend payment policy. The alternative chosen will have a significant impact on the nature of returns to the holders of various classes of equities. The fundamental basis of dividend policy lies in investors' risk-and-return preferences. Investors in preferred stock can be viewed as having opted for regular payments, usually with the possibility of conversion to the more risky common stock. Alternatively, investors in common stock have opted for a more uncertain return pattern that includes unspecified dividend payments and uncertain share value appreciation.

To a great extent, many corporations attempt to establish stable common stock dividend policies where a pattern of dividend payments is set and maintained. Of course, because of the different contractual terms in preferred stock contracts and the interaction of preferred and common stock dividends, preferred dividend payment patterns tend to be even more stable than those for common stock. As we discussed in Chapter 20, until preferred stock dividends have been paid in full (including any payments missed in previous periods in the case of cumulative preferred stock), no common dividends can be paid.

DIVIDENDS

Relationship Between Statutory and Accounting Terms

As is often the case across groups of professionals, accountants and attorneys use different terms to describe the same basic concept. This overlapping of terms is especially troublesome in the area of corporate dividends. In particular, the very important concept of **"surplus"** in most statutes does not coincide with any one accounting concept, and this diversity of meaning can be confusing when we are trying to understand what dividend payments are permissible. *Surplus,* when used alone in a statute, means the excess of assets over the sum of liabilities plus par value or stated capital of capital stock. Statutes often refer to **earned surplus** (which means roughly the same thing as **retained earnings**) and **paid-in surplus,** (which means roughly the same thing as **additional paid-in capital**). These distinctions are important in deciding whether dividends can be paid and in choosing an accounting treatment.

Limitations on Dividend Payments

The Model Business Corporation Act (MA) gives the board of directors the discretion to declare dividends in the form of cash, property, or the corporation's own shares subject to certain tests of validity:

1. **The surplus test.** The MA and all state statutes permit dividend declaration when a positive retained earnings balance exists. Some states allow dividend declaration in the absence of positive retained earnings when positive additional paid-in capital exists. A few states allow dividends in cases of negative "surplus" when there is current net income.[1] These statutes require that dividends be declared before the closing of the books for the fiscal period.
2. **The solvency test.** The MA allows dividends only if their payment would not render the corporation insolvent—that is, unable to pay its creditors on a timely basis.

Many statutes allow corporations that own depletable (wasting) assets to declare dividends to the extent of retained earnings ("earned surplus") *plus* the amount of the depletion allowance. Liquidating dividends, which are based on the depletion allowance, are rare in going concerns, which are assumed to continue in existence at current or greater levels of capitalization.

In some cases, certain dividends have been declared unlawful because they were unintentionally liquidating or led to insolvency. In such cases, the board of directors may be held personally liable and/or the dividends may be declared refundable from the stockholders. In such cases, reliance on accounting records has been allowed as evidence of "good faith," emphasizing the important role accounting plays in an entity's relationship with its stockholders.

[1] Significantly, one of the states that adopted this provision (termed the "nimble" dividend rule) is Delaware, which is the state of incorporation for many major companies.

To the extent that the total amount of dividends does not create a period-end debit balance in retained earnings (a deficit), the dividends are usually termed **ordinary.** The immediate accounting effect of ordinary dividend declaration is to reduce retained earnings and increase a current liability (Dividends Payable). **Liquidating** dividends on the other hand, reduce "permanent" capital accounts such as Par or Stated Value or Additional Paid-in Capital.

Liquidating
Dividends

Liquidating dividends are more common in situations involving single-purpose ventures. Mining ventures sometimes have the exploitation of a finite resource reserve as their sole objective. In such cases, the business entity may be liquidated in proportion to the exploitation of the reserve. For example, assume that Asbestos Developers, Inc., sells 1,000 shares of common stock and uses the funds to purchase and exploit an asbestos deposit. Assume also that the total reserve is estimated at 50,000 tons and that a total of $90,000 is paid for exploitation rights. The venture lasts 5 years with the following transactions:

1/1/83	Sold no-par common stock for a total of $100,000.
1/2/83	Purchased exploitation rights on 50,000 tons for $90,000.
1983–1987	Extracted and sold 10,000 tons per year at a net operating profit of $20 per ton after all costs except depletion of exploitation rights.
12/31/83–12/31/87	Management paid cash dividends equal to net cash provided by operations, and a $10,000 cash balance was maintained.

Journal entries for these transactions would follow the normal pattern except that dividends are partially ordinary and partially liquidating:

1/1/83	Cash	100,000	
	Common stock		100,000
	(Sale of stock)		
1/2/83	Asbestos exploitation rights	90,000	
	Cash		90,000
	(Purchase of mine)		
1983	Cash	200,000	
	Income summary		200,000
	(Operating profit of $20 per ton)		
1983	Income summary	18,000	
	Accumulated depletion		18,000
	(Depletion of $1.80 per ton—		
	$90,000 ÷ 50,000)		
12/31/83	Income summary	182,000	
	Retained earnings		182,000
	(Close net income to retained earnings)		
12/31/83	Dividends—ordinary	182,000	
	Dividends—liquidating	18,000	
	Cash		200,000
	(Dividend payment)		
12/31/83	Retained earnings	182,000	
	Common stock	18,000	
	Dividends—ordinary		182,000
	Dividends—liquidating		18,000
	(Close dividends accounts)		

The December 31, 1983, post-closing ledger accounts would appear as follows:

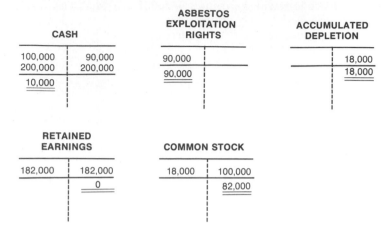

CASH		ASBESTOS EXPLOITATION RIGHTS		ACCUMULATED DEPLETION	
100,000	90,000	90,000			18,000
200,000	200,000	90,000			18,000
10,000					

RETAINED EARNINGS		COMMON STOCK	
182,000	182,000	18,000	100,000
	0		82,000

If this pattern of transactions continues over the 5-year period, we see that the Cash account is maintained at $10,000; that the net book value of the asbestos reserve is reduced to zero by the end of the fifth year; that retained earnings has a zero balance at each year-end; and that the contributed capital account, Common Stock, is reduced by the same amount as the liquidating dividends each year. At December 31, 1987, the cash balance of $10,000 is equal to the common stock balance of $10,000, and a final liquidating dividend is paid in that amount to completely liquidate the entity.

The term *liquidating dividends* is applied in cases other than those involving depletable assets. Exhibit 21–1 shows how Computer Instruments Corporation disclosed a "liquidating dividend" in relation to the sale of a portion of its business. The term *liquidating dividend* is also used when a corporation is actually going out of business and the assets are being distributed to stockholders. Exhibit 21–2 shows how Overseas National Airways, Inc., disclosed the termination of its operations.

Ordinary Cash
Dividends

The vast majority of dividends do not affect par, stated value, or additional paid-in capital accounts. In most cases, common and preferred stock dividends are paid in cash and reduce retained earnings. Because of the interaction of common and preferred stock rights, however, the determination of the permissible amount of dividends for each class can be quite complex.

Because preferred stock is usually cumulative, one year's dividend declarations can affect subsequent years' dividend payments. Remember that cumulative preferred stock always grants the right of dividend preference over common stockholders for both current dividends and any missed dividends in past periods (dividends in arrears). Accountants must be familiar with the potential interactions that can result because of this contractual stipulation. Assume that Ajax, Inc., has two classes of stock: (1) $10 par value common stock of which 100,000 shares are outstanding and (2) $100 par value, 10 percent preferred stock of which 100,000 shares are outstanding. The company's earnings and dividend experience through December 31, 1986, is summarized in Exhibit 21–3 (p. 801).

In 1983 Ajax reported net income of $1,000,000 but declared no dividends, resulting in a retained earnings balance of $1,000,000; no liability is shown at

EXHIBIT
21–1

DISCLOSURE OF LIQUIDATING DIVIDENDS UPON PARTIAL DISSOLUTION

COMPUTER INSTRUMENTS CORPORATION
Excerpts from Note, Balance Sheet, and Statement of Capital Changes

Note 2. Distribution of Partial Liquidating Dividend

On November 2, 1977, the Board of Directors authorized the distribution of a liquidating dividend of $.50 cents per share on the outstanding shares of the Company payable on December 12, 1977, to stockholders of record November 14, 1977. The distribution arises from the Company's sale of a portion of its assets and businesses to Vernitron Corporation, effected in August 1976. On the same date the Board of Directors voted to amend the Certificate of Incorporation to reduce the Par Value of Common Stock from $.25 per share to $.10 per share.

	($000)	
	1978	**1977**
Stockholders' equity:		
Preferred stock, par value $1 per share; authorized, 500,000 shares; issued, none.		
Common stock, par value $.10 per share; authorized 3,000,000 shares; 1,455,198 issued in 1978; 1,451,198 shares issued in 1977 (Notes 1, 2, and 8)	$ 145	$ 145
Capital in excess of par value (Notes 1, 2, and 8)	366	365
Retained earnings (Note 2)	144	292
Less: common stock in treasury—100 shares at cost	(3)	(3)
	$ 652	$ 799

	($000)	
Statement of Capital Changes		
Net loss	$(148)	$ (74)
Retained earnings at beginning of year	292	1,092
Distribution of partial liquidating dividend (Note 2)		(725)
Retained earnings at end of year	$ 144	$ 292

December 31, 1983, even though the preferred stock is cumulative, because there is no claim on the entity's resources for undeclared dividends. The board of directors need not declare any dividends even on cumulative preferred stock. In 1984 net income is $2,000,000, and the board of directors declares a total of $1,000,000 in preferred dividends, which leaves dividends in arrears at $1,000,000 at December 31, 1984. The declared but unpaid dividends at December 31, 1984, are classified as a current liability. The year 1985 is the first year in which common stockholders receive dividends because the total dividend declaration is more than enough to eliminate the dividends in arrears and the 1985 preferred dividend preference. In 1986 the company incurs a net loss of $500,000 but still declares preferred dividends of $1,000,000. Keep in mind that the incurrence of a loss in one year does not normally mean that ordinary dividends are prohibited by state laws. Normally, as long as no deficit is created, the dividend is considered ordinary. Journal entries for the above dividend declarations and payments would be as follows:

1983	None		
12/15/84	Dividends—preferred	1,000,000	
	Dividends payable		1,000,000
1/15/85	Dividends payable	1,000,000	
	Cash		1,000,000

12/15/85	Dividends—common	500,000	
	Dividends—preferred	2,000,000	
	Dividends payable		2,500,000
1/15/86	Dividends payable	2,500,000	
	Cash		2,500,000
12/15/86	Dividends—preferred	1,000,000	
	Dividends payable		1,000,000
1/15/87	Dividends payable	1,000,000	
	Cash		1,000,000

EXHIBIT 21–2

DISCLOSURE OF LIQUIDATING DIVIDENDS UPON DISSOLUTION

OVERSEAS NATIONAL AIRWAYS, INC. (DISSOLVED)
Excerpts from Note, Balance Sheet, and Statement Changes in Cash Balance

1. Cessation of Operations

The company discontinued flight operations in September 1978 and, pursuant to a Plan of Dissolution and Complete Liquidation (the "Plan") adopted by its shareowners, dissolved on January 15, 1979. It is currently winding up its affairs pursuant to the General Corporation Law of Delaware.

In January, 1979, the Board of Directors approved and the Company paid a liquidations dividend equivalent to $8.00 per share. Holders of warrants and stock options were paid an amount equal to the differential between $8.00 and the exercise price of the warrants or options. The total payment aggregated $34,366,587 of which $30,695,784 was paid to shareowners and $3,670,803 was paid to warrant and option holders.

OVERSEAS NATIONAL AIRWAYS, INC. (DISSOLVED)
Statement of Assets, Liabilities and Former Security Holders' Interest
December 31, 1979

	($000)
Assets	
Cash including certificates of deposit of $3,500,000	$ 3,509
Accounts receivable (net of allowance for doubtful accounts of $26,000)	1,192
Prepaid expenses and other assets	85
	$ 4,786
Liabilities and Former Security Holders' Interest	
Liabilities	
Bank overdraft	$ 168
Accounts payable and accrued expenses	391
	$ 559
Former Security Holders' Interest	
Amount due to former shareholders, warrant and option holders, subject to the effects, if any, of litigation discussed in Note 8	4,227
	$ 4,786

Statement of Changes in Cash Balance

	($000)
Excess of income over expense	$ 1,783
Less:	
Liquidating dividend	$34,366
Decrease in accounts payable and accrued expenses	2,853
Other net	20
	$37,239
Decrease in cash balance	$35,456
Cash balance at:	
Beginning of year	$38,965
End of year	$ 3,509

EXHIBIT 21-3

	EARNINGS				DIVIDENDS			
					AJAX, INC., EARNINGS AND DIVIDEND HISTORY			
YEAR	NET INCOME (NET LOSS)	DATE OF DECLARATION	AMOUNT	DATE OF PAYMENT	12/31 RETAINED EARNINGS BALANCE	12/31 DIVIDENDS PAYABLE BALANCE	AMOUNT PAYABLE TO	
							PREFERRED	COMMON
1983	$1,000,000	None	None	None	$1,000,000	None	None	None
1984	2,000,000	12/15/84	$1,000,000	1/15/85	2,000,000	$1,000,000	$1,000,000	None
1985	3,000,000	12/15/85	2,500,000	1/15/86	2,500,000	2,500,000	2,000,000	$500,000
1986	(500,000)	12/15/86	1,000,000	1/15/87	1,000,000	1,000,000	1,000,000	None

As previously stated, preferred stockholders do not have the right to dividends until the board of directors declares them. Often, however, contractual terms specify that upon certain arrearages, preferred stockholders do get the right to vote. Exhibit 21-4 shows the disclosure made by the Horn & Hardart Company in such a case.

Dates of declaration, record, and payment Another point about the dividend declaration and payment patterns in the Ajax example (Exhibit 21-3) deserves mention. Note that there is always some period between the declaration date and the payment date. This enables corporations with a large number of shareholders to revise the list of shareholders entitled to dividends. This list is assembled as of a specific interim date called the **date of record.** In our example, that date could fall sometime between December 15 and January 15 of each year. December 15 would be called the **date of declaration,** and January 15 would be the **date of payment.**

Retained earnings statement The **retained earnings statement** is simply a reconciliation of beginning and ending retained earnings balances. The Dividends accounts are closed to retained earnings at the end of each accounting period. Detailed disclosure of dividend activity in published financial reports is made in the retained earnings statement or statement of capital changes. Exhibit 21-5 shows two formats for these statements. Dana Corporation has a free-standing retained earnings statement, whereas Lightolier Incorporated combines the income statement and the retained earnings statement.

EXHIBIT 21-4

DISCLOSURE OF PREFERRED DIVIDEND ARREARAGE

THE HORN & HARDART COMPANY
Excerpt from Note

The preferred shareholders are entitled to cumulative dividends of $5 per share annually. The shares have a liquidation value of $100 each plus dividends in arrears and may be redeemed (not less than 10,000 shares at a time) at the Company's option, upon sixty days prior notice, for $107.50 per share plus dividends in arrears. No dividends have been declared or paid on the preferred stock since September, 1, 1971 (Note 5). At December 30, 1978, dividends in arrears on such stock were $36.25 per share or $838,861. Preferred shareholders are entitled to the same voting rights as common shareholders because of the dividend arrearages. No cash dividends may be paid on common stock until all dividends in arrears on the preferred stock have been paid.

EXHIBIT
21–5

DISCLOSURE OF RETAINED EARNINGS STATEMENTS

DANA CORPORATION
Statement of Retained Earnings

| | YEAR ENDED AUGUST 31 | |
	1978	1977
	(IN THOUSANDS)	
Balance at Beginning of Year	$489,364	$410,715
Net income for the year	134,225	107,787
Cash dividends declared ($1.26 per share in 1978; $.97 in 1977)	(40,226)	(29,138)
Balance at end of year	$583,363	$489,364

LIGHTOLIER INCORPORATED AND SUBSIDIARIES
Consolidated Statement of Operations and Retained Earnings

| | FISCAL YEAR ENDED | |
	JUNE 1, 1979	JUNE 2, 1978
	(IN THOUSANDS)	
Net sales	$ 86,120	$ 79,397
Royalties and other income (net) (Note B)	411	225
Total	$ 86,532	$ 79,623
Cost of sales	$ 55,990	$ 52,361
Selling and administrative expenses	24,904	23,297
Interest expense	1,211	1,305
Total	$ 82,107	$ 76,964
Earnings before income taxes	$ 4,425	$ 2,659
Income taxes (Notes A(3), A(5) and H)	2,050	1,133
Net Earnings	$ 2,375	$ 1,525
Net earnings per common share (based on average number of common shares outstanding during each year)	$1.75	$1.14
Dividends per common share	$ .22	$ .19
Net Earnings	$ 2,375	$ 1,525
Retained earnings—beginning of year	18,462	17,178
Total	$ 20,838	$ 18,704
Dividends	298	241
Retained Earnings—End of Year (To Balance Sheet)	$ 20,539	$ 18,462

Noncash Dividends

Property dividends Dividends can be paid in the form of something of value other than cash, such as ownership shares in other corporations, merchandise, services, the forgiving of debt, or even elements of property, plant, and equipment. This shows that, conceptually, the physical nature of the value transferred to stockholders makes no difference. Of course, all dividends must be paid on a pro rata basis to all stockholders of a given class of stock based on their relative ownership. Dollar amounts must be assigned to the value transferred, and this can create certain complexities. For instance, should gains and losses be recognized on the transferred items? As a case in point, assume that several parcels of land with a total current fair value of $500,000 and a book value of $50,000 are distributed to stockholders in the form of a dividend. Should the land be revalued to $500,000 on the books of the company, leading to the recognition of a $450,000 gain? The fact that stockholders do receive real value of $500,000 argues for the following journal entry:

Dividends	500,000	
Gain on land		450,000
Land		50,000

rather than:

Dividends	50,000	
Land		50,000

Note that the ending balance in retained earnings is the same no matter which alternative is used because the gain would increase retained earnings by $450,000. In general, assets involved in noncash dividends are considered at their fair values, and gains or losses are recognized. This reflects economic reality because the company could choose to sell the assets for their fair values and use the cash so generated for a cash dividend. In such cases, there would be no question about the appropriateness of recognizing gains and losses. Accountants, however, must, in the absence of a sale, make a judgment as to the validity of the evidence supporting fair values. Promulgated GAAP speak directly to this issue in **APB Opinion No. 29.**[2] It states that transfers of nonmonetary assets to investors must be at the fair value of the asset and that gains and losses are to be recognized on any required revaluation.

Scrip dividends　Corporations may declare a dividend that promises to pay an amount at some future date and may issue **dividend certificates** as evidence of the obligation. In such cases, Retained Earnings is debited for the present value of the future payment and Scrip Dividend Payable is credited. Any interest payment is charged to an expense account, which is consistent with the notion that the decision to pay dividends is separate from the financing decision. This route may be taken by a company that has positive retained earnings but is not currently able to make the cash payment.

Small stock dividends　A corporation may declare a dividend in the form of its own stock in lieu of paying cash, transferring assets, or forgiving debt. In such cases, the board of directors declares a dividend in the form of stock at one date, to stockholders of record as of a later date, to be issued at a third date. This pattern of dates is the same as that for cash or property dividends. Unlike other forms of dividends, however, no liability is recorded on the declaration date because no asset will be used up upon the issuance of stock, and most state laws allow the board to rescind declared stock dividends before stock issuance under the theory that they do not change the stockholder's interest in the corporation.

　　We shall use the following facts to introduce the accounting for stock dividends: Williams Products, Inc., has 100,000 shares of $10 par value common stock outstanding on December 10, 1983, at which time the board of directors decides that instead of paying cash to stockholders, it will issue shares to the stockholders of record at December 25, 1983, on the basis of 1 share for each 10 shares held. Cash

---

[2] *Accounting Principles Board Opinion No. 29,* "Accounting for Nonmonetary Transactions" (New York: AICPA, May 1973).

equivalent to the stock's December 10, 1983, fair value of $20 per share will be paid for fractional shares, and the stocks will be issued on December 31, 1983. For example, if Mr. Jones owns 105 shares on the date of record, he would receive 10 shares and $10 in cash rather than 10 and ½ shares.

The important question that determines the basis of the accounting treatment of stock dividends is, Does the stock dividend transfer something of immediate value to the stockholders? The recorded value of the new issue depends on its effect on the price per share of all the existing shares. If no dilution occurs, retained earnings should be reduced by the preissuance market value of the shares issued. For Williams Products, assuming no fractional shares, the following journal entry would be recorded:

12/31/83	Stock dividends (10,000 @ $20)	200,000	
	Common stock—par $10		100,000
	Additional paid-in capital—common		
	stock		100,000

The Stock Dividends account is closed to retained earnings. Note that the predividend market price is applied to all the shares issued, and retained earnings is reduced by the full amount of assumed market value.

In the absence of a promulgated rule, the accountant would have to decide whether the stock market adjusts the market price in each case. This would be difficult because of all the other factors causing changes in stock prices. To guide the accountant in making this decision, promulgated GAAP state that stock market discounting of stock dividends is unlikely when the issuance of additional shares is ". . . less than, say, 20% or 25% of the number previously outstanding . . ."[3] A distinction, therefore, is made between "small" and "large" stock dividends with the demarcation being the 20–25 percent level. The student, however, should realize that this guidance was given several decades ago and that the language is much less constraining than that in other situations. It does not actually stipulate a fixed percentage but merely suggests a range that accountants should consider. Applying straightforward logic, one could infer that if the issuer reduces retained earnings for the full market value of small stock dividends, then the recipient of the shares should recognize dividend income to be consistent. Promulgated GAAP reject this logic and prescribe that the recipient merely spread the cost of the initial shares over the new total number of shares owned and that no income be recognized. Obviously the accounting policy governing recipients of small stock dividends is inconsistent with the policy governing the issuers of such dividends. Although this situation displays a conceptual fallacy, it may be justifiable in terms of practicality.

The shares issued in a small stock dividend may be new shares or treasury shares. Remember that treasury shares do not receive dividends but may be reissued to existing stockholders to pay stock dividends. Treasury shares, reissued in a small stock dividend, reduce retained earnings by their fair value at the date of reissuance. In other respects the transactions would be accounted for as a sale of treasury stock at market value.

An important point is that stock dividends do not create liabilities. Sometimes the following entry is made on the declaration date.

Stock dividends	XX	
Stock dividend distributable		XX

[3] *Accounting Research Bulletin No. 43,* "Stock Dividends and Stock Split-Ups (New York: AICPA, 1953), chap. 7B.

Stock Dividends Distributable is not a liability account. It would be shown in paid-in capital if a balance sheet were issued before the issuance date. On the issuance date this account is closed to the permanent paid-in capital accounts.

Exhibit 21–6 shows Moog Inc.'s statement of capital changes and the equity section of its balance sheet, which discloses the effects of a 10 percent stock dividend. Note that the excess of fair value of the issued stock over the par value of $1,248,000 was credited to additional paid-in capital.

Large stock dividends and stock splits   Besides the small stock dividend situation, additonal shares are sometimes issued to existing stockholders on a pro rata basis when the assumption of no market effect is not tenable. Large stock dividend are similar to small stock dividends. The percentage of new shares issued is greater than

EXHIBIT
21–6

DISCLOSURE OF A STOCK DIVIDEND

MOOG, INC. AND SUBSIDIARIES
Excerpts from Statement of Capital Changes and Balance Sheet

	($000) YEARS ENDED SEPTEMBER 30	
	1978	1977
COMMON STOCK		
Beginning of year	$ 653	$ 653
97,294 shares issued—10% stock dividend	64	
End of year	718	653
ADDITIONAL PAID-IN CAPITAL		
Beginning of year	3,963	3,963
Excess of fair value of 10% stock dividend over par value of related shares and cash in lieu of fractional shares	1,248	
End of year	5,212	3,963
RETAINED EARNINGS		
Beginning of year: as previously reported	11,849	10,475
Adjustment for cumulative effect of change in method of accounting for capital leases (Note 1)	(115)	(36)
As restated	11,733	10,438
Net earnings	3,299	1,882
Cash dividends declared, $.391 in 1978 and $.364 in 1977 (Note 3)	(631)	(587)
Fair value of 10% stock dividend	(1,321)	
End of year	13,080	11,733
COST OF TREASURY SHARES		
Beginning and end of year	(2)	(2)
TOTAL SHAREHOLDERS' EQUITY	$19,008	$16,348

	($000) YEARS ENDED SEPTEMBER 30	
	1978	1977
SHAREHOLDERS' EQUITY		
Common stock of $ 66²/₃ par value per share (Note 14)	$ 718	$ 653
Additional paid-in capital	5,212	3,963
Retained earnings (Notes 8 and 10)	13,080	11,733
	19,011	16,350
Less cost of common shares in treasury	2	2
TOTAL SHAREHOLDERS' EQUITY	$19,008	$16,348

the 20–25 percent level. If the new shares issued have exactly the same legal form as the previously issued shares—that is, par or stated value is unchanged and shares authorized is unchanged—such a transaction is termed a **large stock dividend.** For example, if a company with 100,000 shares of $1 par value common stock issues a 40 percent stock dividend, the following entry would be appropriate at the distribution date:

Stock dividends	40,000	
Common stock—par $1		40,000

Again the Stock Dividends account would be closed to retained earnings.

If the old shares are modified or canceled, with new shares with different legal characteristics (such as new par value) being issued, the transaction is termed a **stock split,** or **stock split-up.** Because such events do not change the economic status of either the corporation or the stockholders, accounting is concerned primarily with reporting any changes in legal status. For instance, if a large stock dividend is issued for par value stock, an entry would be necessary to record the par value of the new shares issued. In the case of stock splits, it is often necessary to cancel accounts based on old par values and record the same amount of money in a new account. Such entries have no impact on total capitalization.

What motivates corporations to declare large stock dividends and stock splits? The following example may help to answer that question. Assume that Fast Growth Industries, Inc., has 250,000 shares of $1 par value common stock outstanding at July 1, 1984, with a market value of $30 per share. The board of directors has a policy of keeping the market price of its shares below $30 per share. This policy may have been adopted because the board members believe that the outstanding stock or any new issuances of the stock would find a broader market in that range. They accomplish this by issuing a 2-for-1 stock split whenever the market price reaches $30 or more per share. The history of the market price per share of Fast Growth's stock and total market value of outstanding stock for the 1981–1984 period is illustrated in Figure 21–1. Note that the *total* market value of all shares is the same before and after the stock split, whereas the per share values are reduced. In the real world, it is difficult to isolate the effects of splits. Research indicates that an adjustment approximately as shown in Figure 21–1 can be expected for all stock dividends and splits.

In summary, although stock dividends and stock splits can affect individual owners' equity accounts, they do not affect the *total* amount of owners' equity. Unlike dividends, which pay out resources, these transactions have little impact on the entity's economic status.

Exhibit 21–7 shows the disclosures made by Anixter Bros., Inc., pursuant to the declaration of a large stock dividend. Note the wording in the sentence "A two-for-one common stock split effected in the form of a 100% stock dividend . . ." This sentence seems to use the terms "stock split" and "stock dividend" synonymously. Keep in mind that in this example, par values are not changed, and retained earnings is reduced by the total par value recorded on the 3,338,099 new shares issued.

Exhibit 21–8 shows the disclosure for a stock split with the reduction of par value. Note that the statement of capital changes does not indicate a money amount effect for the stock split. This is evidence that stock splits have no effect on owners' equity except for the common stock description in the balance sheet, which in this case shows par value at $2.50 per share rather than $5.00.

FIGURE
21–1

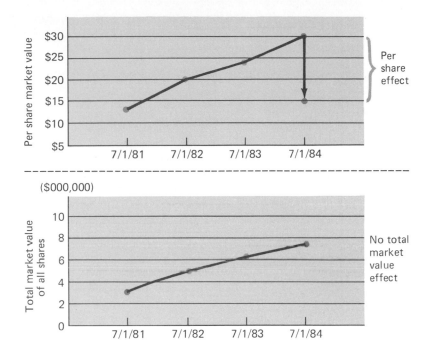

RETAINED EARNINGS APPROPRIATION

Exhibit 21–9 shows a statement of retained earnings in which retained earnings is broken down into two categories—**appropriated** and **unappropriated.** Note that the stockholders' equity section of the balance sheet contains only one amount for retained earnings and that this amount is broken down into the two categories on

EXHIBIT
21–7

DISCLOSURE OF LARGE STOCK DIVIDENDS

ANIXTER BROS., INC.

Excerpts from Note

A two-for-one common stock split effected in the form of a 100% stock dividend was declared by the Board of Directors on July 22, 1980. All of common stock and related prices, dividends and per share amounts have been restated to reflect the stock split.

Changes in common stock ($1 par value) for the two years ended July 31, 1980 are comprised of the following:

	SHARES ISSUED	
	1980	**1979**
Balance, beginning of year	3,265,863	3,237,516
Exercise of employee stock options N(1)	24,236	21,937
Conversion of 7% Convertible Subordinated Notes N(1)	48,000	6,410
Additional shares resulting from two-for-one stock split	3,338,099	
Balance, end of year	6,676,198	3,265,863

N(1) Prior to giving effect to the two-for-one stock split.

EXHIBIT
21–8

DISCLOSURE OF STOCK SPLIT WITH A CHANGE IN PAR VALUE

AUTOMATIC SWITCH COMPANY
Exerpts from Notes, Balance Sheet, and Statement of Capital Changes

On June 13, 1978, the Board of Directors of the Company declared a two-for-one common stock split to shareholders of record on June 26, 1978, and changed the par value from $5.00 to $2.50 per share. Average shares outstanding and earnings per share for prior years have been adjusted to reflect the stock split.

Balance Sheet

	($000)	
	12/31/78	12/31/77
Stockholders' Equity:		
Common stock, $2.50 par value, authorized 4,400,000 shares;		
Outstanding 1978, 4,070,120 shares; 1977, 4,054,220 shares (Note 3)	$10,175	$10,135
Paid-in surplus (Note 3)	8,009	7,726
Earned surplus	59,710	49,040
Total Stockholders' Equity	$77,895	$66,902

Statement of Capital Changes

	($000)	
	1978	1977
Net Income	$14,329	$10,190
Earned Surplus Beginning of Year	49,040	41,281
Total	$63,369	$51,472
Less Cash Dividends Declared	3,659	2,432
Earned Surplus End of Year	$59,710	$49,040

the retained earnings statement. The footnote describes the reason for appropriated retained earnings, and the statement of capital changes gives details of the transactions that affected appropriated and unappropriated retained earnings.

Segregations such as those presented in Exhibit 21–9 can be either voluntary or contractually mandated. No matter what the motivation, however, the effect of an appropriation of retained earnings is that, although positive retained earnings may exist, a certain portion of retained earnings will not be the basis for dividend payments. We shall discuss the general case first and then the more specific voluntary and contractually mandated cases in turn.

The following example demonstrates the accounting treatment of retained earnings appropriations. Assume that Alpha, Inc., earns $1,000,000 per year for its first 4 years of operations (January 1, 1983, through December 31, 1986), pays no dividends, and appropriates $500,000 in each of the first 3 years. The following annual journal entries would close net income to retained earnings and would appropriate retained earnings:

12/31/83– 12/31/85	Income summary	1,000,000	
	Retained earnings unappropriated		1,000,000
12/31/83– 12/31/85	Retained earnings unappropriated	500,000	
	Retained earnings appropriated		500,000

EXHIBIT
21-9

DISCLOSURE OF APPROPRIATED RETAINED EARNINGS

WESTCOAST TRANSMISSION COMPANY LIMITED
Excerpts from Balance Sheet, Statement of Capital Changes, and Footnote

	(IN THOUSANDS)	
	12/31/80	12/31/79
STOCKHOLDERS' EQUITY:		
Capital stock (Note 4):		
Authorized		
5,000,000 preferred shares without nominal or par value		
75,000,000 common shares without nominal or par value		
Issued		
739,322 $4.25 cumulative redeemable preferred shares Series A		
(1979—792,080 preferred shares series A)	$ 36,966	$ 39,604
36,189,581 common shares (1979—35,407,614 common shares)	189,716	182,599
Contributed Surplus	1,561	1,361
Retained Earnings	188,542	168,393
	$416,785	$391,957

Statement of Capital Changes
Consolidated Statement of Retained Earnings
For the years ended December 31

	(IN THOUSANDS)		
	1980	1979	1978
Unappropriated retained earnings:			
Balance, beginning of year as previously reported	$126,346	$111,604	$101,718
Adjusted of prior years net income (Note 9)	2,443	2,443	1,022
As restated	$128,789	$114,047	$102,740
Net income	51,826	49,870	46,359
	$180,615	$163,917	$149,099
Deduct dividends paid:			
Preferred shares	$ 3,183	$ 3,402	$ 3,400
Common shares	28,494	28,122	23,652
	$ 31,677	$ 31,524	$ 27,052
	$148,938	$132,393	$122,047
Transferred from (to) appropriated retained earnings	2,638	(3,604)	(8,000)
Balance, end of year	$151,576	$128,789	$114,047
Appropriated retained earnings (Note 5):			
Reserved for redemption of preferred shares			
Balance, beginning of year	$ 39,604	$ 36,000	$ 28,000
Transferred from unappropriated retained earnings		4,000	8,000
Transferred to unappropriated retained earnings for redemption (Note 4)	(2,638)	(000)	
Balance, end of year	$ 36,966	$ 39,604	$ 36,000
Retained earnings, end of year	$188,542	$168,393	$150,047

Note 5. Appropriated Retained Earnings:

The Company has provided a Retraction Purchase Fund which will be returned to unappropriated retained earnings as the preferred Shares Series A are redeemed.

If at the end of 1986 Alpha elects to eliminate the appropriation, a reversal of the total effects shown above would be required:

12/31/86	Retained earnings appropriated	1,500,000	
	Retained earnings unappropriated		1,500,000

Consider the following analysis for the 4-year period:

YEAR	NET INCOME	BALANCE IN RETAINED EARNINGS APPROPRIATED	BALANCE IN RETAINED EARNINGS UNAPPROPRIATED	TOTAL RETAINED EARNINGS
1983	$1,000,000	$ 500,000	$ 500,000	$1,000,000
1984	1,000,000	1,000,000	1,000,000	2,000,000
1985	1,000,000	1,500,000	1,500,000	3,000,000
1986	1,000,000	0	4,000,000	4,000,000
	4,000,000			

Remember that total retained earnings equals total undistributed net income whether or not retained earnings is appropriated.

Voluntary Appropriation

To provide for growth, companies often wish to retain working capital generated by operations. Cash dividends are a drain on working capital, and a curtailment of dividend payments has the opposite effect if everything else is held constant. Management may desire to communicate to stockholders that a curtailment of, or a restriction on, dividend payments is in effect through the formal mechanism of appropriating retained earnings. The board of directors, however, is not required to make such a decision, and dividends could be curtailed or restricted without a formal appropriation of retained earnings. Another critical point is that appropriations do not necessarily affect dividend policy. For instance, if in the Alpha, Inc., example, dividends for the period 1983 through 1986 would not have been greater than $500,000 per year in any event, the appropriation of retained earnings would have had no effect on dividend policy.

Required Appropriation

Debt instruments such as notes and bonds sometimes stipulate a fixed schedule of appropriations for the debtors' retained earnings. Such a contractual restriction on a debtor's dividend-paying practices is motivated by the creditors' hope that smaller payments to stockholders will translate into a greater ability to pay back the debt. State corporate laws also often restrict a portion of retained earnings equal to the total cost of treasury stock held by the company. As in the case of voluntary appropriations, contractually or legally mandated appropriations of retained earnings do not necessarily change dividend policies. If the amount of appropriation is small compared with total retained earnings, and if dividends would normally not be a large percentage of the retained earnings balance, appropriation of retained earnings has little actual effect.

Relationship Between Appropriations and Fund Balances

As implied in the above discussion, the appropriation of retained earnings does not create assets. Just as a corporation could have a large retained earnings balance and at the same time have no current assets with which to pay dividends, a corporation could have both a large balance in appropriated retained earnings and little working capital. This fact does not go unnoticed by creditors and management. Debt instruments, therefore, sometimes require that assets be set aside in a fund in conjunction with, or independent of, any possible retained earnings appropriations. Obviously, if assets are actually set aside and insulated from other business uses, the creditor's position is improved in real terms. Management, in some cases, voluntarily sets aside resources in separate funds for special purposes, which again may either be in conjunction with, or independent of, appropriation of retained earnings. The critical point is that the creation of separate asset funds and the appropriation of retained earnings are different events, each requiring its own accounting treatment. They may both be required by the same contract, but they are two distinct activities.

Let us review these points by reference to the Alpha, Inc., example discussed earlier. Assume that the $500,000 annual appropriation of retained earnings and an equal contribution of cash to a fund are both required by the terms of a 3-year, $1,500,000 maturity value non-interest-bearing note signed on January 1, 1983, and payable on January 1, 1986. In addition to the retained earnings appropriation schedule described in the example, the note requires the year-end payment of an annuity into a fund that will provide $1,500,000 at December 31, 1985, if a 10 percent annual earnings rate on fund assets is assumed. The payment is made to a separate fund that is restricted to the eventual payment of the maturity amount on January 1, 1986. The journal entries in Exhibit 21–10 demonstrate the independence of the two series of transactions.

Although both series of journal entries are based on the requirements of a contract, their effects on the accounting records are independent of one another. Contracts are often written with the requirement of either funding or appropriation. The preceding comparison is equally applicable to the accounting for voluntary appropriations of retained earnings. For example, change the setting to a plant expansion fund set up by management because if foresees the need for a $1,500,000 expenditure on January 1, 1986. The board of directors approves the appropriation of $500,000 per year, and management decides to establish a fund by payment of an

EXHIBIT 21–10

COMPARISON OF FUNDS AND APPROPRIATIONS OF RETAINED EARNINGS					
	JOURNAL ENTRIES TO RECORD FUND TRANSACTION			JOURNAL ENTRIES TO RECORD APPROPRIATION OF RETAINED EARNINGS TRANSACTIONS	
12/31/83, 84, and 85	Fund for the payment of note	453,172[a]		Retained earnings unappropriated	500,000	
	Cash		453,172	Retained earnings appropriated		500,000
12/31/04	Fund for the payment of note	45,317[b]				
	Interest income		45,317			
12/31/85	Fund for the payment of note	95,167[c]				
	Interest income		95,167			
1/1/86	Cash	1,500,000		Retained earnings appropriated	1,500,000	
	Fund for the payment of note		1,500,000	Retained earnings unappropriated		1,500,000
1/1/86	Notes payable	1,500,000				
	Cash		1,500,000			

[a] $(1/F/A, 3, .10) \$1,500,000 = \$453,172$.
[b] Assuming the fund actually earns 10%. $(\$453,172)(.10) = \$45,317$.
[c] $(\$453,172 + \$453,172 + \$45,317)(.10) = \$95,167$ (rounded).

annuity into a plant expansion fund. All money amounts and journal entries would be the same except that the title of the fund would be "Plant Expansion Fund" and the final entry would include a debit to a plant asset.

Another record-keeping detail often found in practice is the specific designation of the Appropriated Retained Earnings accounts. In our examples, the account titles could be **Retained Earnings Appropriated for Plant Expansion** and **Retained Earnings Appropriated for Notes Payable.**

Use of
the Term
Reserve

Instead of designating a segregation of retained earnings by the use of the term **appropriation,** the account title sometimes uses the term **reserve.** For example, it is not uncommon to see **Reserve for Plant Expansion** or **Reserve for Bond Redemption** in the owners' equity section of a balance sheet. This usage of *reserve* is permissible under GAAP but is unfortunate because it may imply that a fund is actually being created when, in fact, no segregation of assets is taking place.

Even more troublesome is the use of the term *reserve* in other parts of the balance sheet; for instance, **Reserve for Depreciation** rather than **Allowance for Depreciation.** Again, this may mislead readers into thinking that a fund to replace assets is created by depreciation. This practice has long been discouraged.[4]

Perhaps the major misuse of the term *reserve* has occurred when contingencies have been recorded by debiting an expense account and crediting a reserve account. For instance, a company is confident that it will eventually have fire damage on its uninsured property. It therefore estimates the loss for a 10-year period and allocates 10 percent to each period by means of the following entry:

Fire loss	XX	
Reserve for fire loss		XX

When damage occurs, the entry would be:

Reserve for fire loss	XX	
Building		XX

As discussed in Chapter 16, **FASB Statement No. 5** does not allow such recognition unless the event meets certain criteria that the current uninsured loss situation does not meet.[5] In no case, however, would a retained earnings "reserve" account be used to record such contingencies. A liability would be the appropriate account if the criteria were met.

In summary, appropriation of retained earnings is a communication device. It does not create funds, and it can never be used to offset revenues, expense, gains, or losses.

NEGATIVE RETAINED EARNINGS AND QUASI-REORGANIZATION

As mentioned previously, a corporation can have accumulated net losses in excess of undistributed net earnings, a deficit. In many states, ordinary dividends cannot be paid when a deficit exists, which creates the possibility of long periods of no divi-

---

[4] See *Accounting Terminology Bulletin No. 1,* pars. 57–64.

[5] *Statement of Financial Accounting Standards No. 5,* "Accounting for Contingencies" (Stanford, CT: FASB, 1975), pars. 14 and 28.

dend payments. Thus a large accumulated deficit can, in effect, make the issuance of new stock very unlikely. In some situations, businesses with deficits could be viable and could make positive contributions to the economy but for the restrictions created by their deficit positions. Some states, therefore, have a remedy that provides that reductions in asset book values and paid-in capital book values can be used to offset the elimination of **negative retained earnings,** without going through federal bankruptcy proceedings. Promulgated GAAP give the general procedures to be followed in **quasi-reorganization,** which is sometimes called **corporate readjustment.**[6]

First, assets are revalued to fair value, usually resulting in a loss, which increases the deficit further, but it may have the beneficial effect of reducing subsequent charges for depreciation and cost of goods sold. Next, the negative balance in retained earnings is eliminated by reducing (debiting) paid-in capital accounts and crediting retained earnings for an amount equal to the deficit. This is accomplished by reducing the par value or additional paid-in capital, or both.

For example, assume that Failing Company has the following book values and asset fair values on December 31, 1982. Assume also that the assets are revalued on the books to fair value and that the par value of the stock is reduced to $.50 per share:

	PRE-QUASI-REORGANIZATION BOOK VALUES	FAIR VALUES	POST-QUASI-REORGANIZATION BOOK VALUES
Cash and accounts receivable	$ 90,000	$ 90,000	$ 90,000
Plant and equipment	800,000	700,000	700,000
	$890,000		$790,000
Liabilities	$ 70,000		$ 70,000
Common stock—Par (600,000 shares @ $1.00 and @ $.50)	600,000		300,000
Common stock—additional paid-in capital	400,000		400,000
Capital from quasi-reorganization			20,000
Retained earnings	(180,000)		0
	$890,000		$790,000

The following journal entries would be needed to effect the quasi-reorganization:

12/01/82	Retained earnings	100,000	
	Plant and equipment		100,000
12/31/82	Common stock—par value	300,000	
	Capital from quasi-reorganization		300,000
12/31/82	Capital from quasi-reorganization	280,000	
	Retained earnings		280,000

In order not to mislead readers of financial statements, retained earnings affected by quasi-reorganization procedures must be clearly identified as such in post-reorganization balance sheets. Ten years is considered a long enough period for explicitly stating the date of reorganization, termed *dating of retained earnings.*[7]

[6] *Accounting Research Bulletin No 43,* "Quasi-Reorganization or Corporate Readjustment" (New York: AICPA, June 1953).

[7] *Accounting Research Bulletin No. 46,* "Discontinuance of Dating Earned Surplus" (New York, AICPA, February 1956).

FUNDS FLOW EFFECTS

Retained earnings increases with profitable operations and decreases with losses, as, in general, do funds. The net assets generated by operations are often in the form of working capital—for example, a profitable company will usually generate more cash and receivables from customers than it pays for productive inputs. The change in the Retained Earnings balance from the beginning to the end of a fiscal period mirrors, in many cases, a significant amount of the change in working capital. This is why statements of changes in financial position start their analyses with net income and show the reconciliation of net income to funds from operations. Whereas net income or loss *may* indicate the direction and amount of funds flow, cash dividend declarations *always* reduce working capital and their payment always reduces cash. Other types of dividends, such as scrip or property, may not affect working capital in the current period, if ever. Dividends payable in stock do not affect funds.

A quasi-reorganization will not generate funds directly, but it may give prospective investors who could supply funds more confidence in the dividend-paying ability of the entity. Any revaluation of current assets in a quasi-reorganization would affect working capital and future charges to income—for instance, reduction of inventory carrying values would reduce working capital and future cost of goods sold expense.

The importance of an entity's dividend-paying ability is vividly demonstrated by the existence of quasi-reorganization procedures. These are sometimes used when corporations have relatively large deficits and are therefore unable to pay dividends. Quasi-reorganization restructures the owners' equity section of the balance sheet and also revalues certain assets to fair value. The result is the elimination of the deficit, thus allowing for future profits to be a basis for dividends.

SUMMARY

Stockholders' earned capital is usually increased by profitable operations and reduced by the payment of dividends. Remember that changes in retained earnings merely *reflect* certain net asset flows, but not all asset flows. The presence of positive retained earnings balances *does not* indicate that the entity controls any specific amount of net assets. Many transactions other than those reflected in retained earnings can affect net assets.

In general, dividends reduce the retained earnings balance by an amount equal to the fair value of the asset given up by the entity. In the case of liquidating dividends, however, paid-in capital accounts are reduced. Stock dividends do not consume assets, but, depending on their size and the par or no-par status of the stock, they can affect retained earnings.

Often a portion of the retained earnings balance is segregated into an account called Retained Earnings Appropriated. The purpose of this segregation can be merely to communicate management's voluntary decision to restrict dividend payments, or it may represent a legal requirement pursuant to a loan or other agreement.

QUESTIONS

Q21-1   What is the relationship between the *legal* and the *financial* ability to pay dividends?

Q21-2   What can reasonably be hypothesized about common and preferred stockholders' preferences for regular dividends?

Q21-3 Discuss the difference between the "surplus" test found in statutes and the general accounting notion that dividends can be paid when positive retained earnings exist.

Q21-4 Why are liquidating dividends more common in certain entities engaged in natural resource production than in other industries? What other situations may entail liquidating dividends?

Q21-5 What is the nature of the "obligation" an entity has to preferred stockholders for dividends? When does such an "obligation" become an accounting liability?

Q21-6 What potential dangers can you visualize in allowing corporations to recognize gains upon the issuance of property dividends? On balance, do you agree with current GAAP on this issue?

Q21-7 Why would a company declare a small stock dividend when it could presumably sell the shares and use the cash to pay a cash dividend?

Q21-8 Contrast the legal, economic, and accounting effects of voluntary and mandated appropriations of retained earnings.

Q21-9 Describe how the improper use of "reserve" accounting could be used to artificially smooth net income over several years.

Q21-10 Would a quasi-reorganization be advantageous in a state that allows dividends to be paid out of current net income even when deficits exist? Explain.

CASES

C21-1 Overhill Bakeries, Inc., has 200,000 shares of $10 par value common stock issued and outstanding. The stock sells in the over-the-counter market at $220 per share. Management is considering the issuance of additional shares and is concerned that the high market value per share will adversely affect potential investors. One suggestion is to have a 10-for-1 split. Another suggestion is to declare a 100 percent stock dividend. A third suggestion is to merely amend the articles of incorporation so that the par value of the stock is reduced to $1 per share.

REQUIRED Discuss the probable effect of each course of action, and recommend the course that will achieve the desired results.

C21-2 As a credit analyst for an insurance company, your assignment consists of evaluating the riskiness of applicants for long-term loans. How would you rank two companies that are alike in every way except that one appropriates all retained earnings by means of an account titled Reserve for Long-Term Obligation, whereas the other does not appropriate any retained earnings but establishes a sinking fund that is to be used solely for the repayment of long-term debt? In the latter case, the fund is expected to be equivalent to about one-half the total long-term debt outstanding.

C21-3 In examining a client's financial statements dated December 31, 1983, you discover the following relationships between certain balance sheet items and the underlying ledger accounts:

BALANCE SHEET ITEMS		LEDGER ACCOUNTS	
Dividends payable	$ 1,125,000	Cash dividends payable on 1/10/84	$400,000
		Stock dividends payable on 1/10/84	500,000
		Scrip dividends payable on 1/21/85	225,000
			$1,125,000
Common stock	11,183,000	Common stock—par	$5,000,000
		Common stock—Additional paid-in capital	6,800,000
		Treasury stock (Cost)	817,000
			$10,983,000
Retained earnings	7,760,000	Unappropriated retained earnings	$6,000,000
		Accumulated depreciation of plant assets	1,760,000
			$7,760,000

REQUIRED Evaluate each balance sheet item, and suggest any changes that you feel are necessary.

C21-4 New Jersey Resorts, Inc., has had several years of depressed earnings, which has reduced retained earnings. An analysis of the fair values and book values of the company's hotels shows that book values are currently $10,000,000 below fair values. As a way of alleviating pressure from stockholders for dividends, the treasurer suggests that all the hotels be revalued to fair value and that scrip dividends be issued in an amount equal to the resulting gain. He argues that such a "reorganization" would both satisfy the stockholders and result in more realistic asset valuation on the balance sheet.

REQUIRED Write a short memo that evaluates the suggested course of action from the point of view of GAAP and sound financial management.

C21-5 Discuss the following assertion: "Large stock dividends are useful in situations where a company wants to give its stockholders a return on their investments but is not able to finance cash dividend payments."

C21-6 Emerson Corporation is considering becoming the sole owner of Trinity Electric, Inc., by means of a trade of 5,000,000 of its own unissued common shares for 5,000,000 of Trinity's common shares.

REQUIRED As the owner of 1,000,000 shares (20 percent) of Emerson's outstanding shares, how would you evaluate your own position before and after the transaction?

C21-7 Mary Bartlett, chairperson of the board of Worldwide Enterprises, Inc., is very concerned about the low dividend payments contemplated in the next fiscal period. She feels that stockholders will not appreciate the need for the company's retention of cash for expansion purposes. She asks you, as controller, to draft a strategy that would somehow communicate clearly to stockholders that although the company has strong earnings and positive retained earnings, it is in the best interests of stockholders that working capital from operations be plowed back in to plant assets.

REQUIRED Suggest how the appropriation of retained earnings on the balance sheet along with an explanatory note can be used for such purposes.

C21-8 (CPA ADAPTED) Stock splits and stock dividends may be used by a corporation to change the number of shares of its stock outstanding.

REQUIRED

1. What is meant by a large stock dividend, often termed a stock split effected in the form of a dividend?
2. From an accounting viewpoint, explain how a large stock dividend differs from an ordinary or small stock dividend.
3. How should a stock dividend that has been declared but not yet issued be classified in a statement of financial position? Why?

EXERCISES

E21-1 Delta Petroleum, Inc., was organized in 1980 to extract oil and gas from several fields in Mississippi. At the end of its fiscal year on August 31, 1984, Delta's balance sheet appears as follows:

Current assets		$2,100,000
Noncurrent assets		
Petroleum reserves	18,700,000	
Less depletion	7,220,000	
	$11,480,000	
Other assets	5,500,000	
Total assets		$19,080,000
Liabilities		$4,400,000
Owners' equity		
Common stock (no par)		$10,600,000
Retained earnings		4,080,000
Total liabilities and owners' equity		$19,080,000

REQUIRED Assuming no dividends have been paid to date, what are the maximum "normal" and "liquidating" dividends that could be paid on August 31, 1984? Explain.

E21–2 Assume all the data presented in the preceding exercise.

REQUIRED Show the journal entry necessitated by the declaration of a $6,000,000 dividend on August 31, 1984.

E21–3 On April 1, 1983, a company has 40,000 shares of $1 par value common stock outstanding. The stock has a stable market value of $4.20 per share.

REQUIRED

1. Show the journal entries necessary for the declaration on April 1, 1983, of a 15 percent dividend payable in common stock and the issuance of the stock on May 1, 1983.
2. Show the journal entries necessary for a 50 percent stock dividend declared on June 1, 1983, with issuance on July 1, 1983, assuming the event in requirement 1 has taken place.

E21–4 On December 31, 1983, Alexander's Great Greek Pizzas, Inc., has owners' equity items as follows:

	BOOK VALUES
Preferred stock—par ($100)	
(10,000 shares issued and outstanding)	$1,000,000
Common stock—par ($.50)	
(400,000 shares issued and outstanding)	200,000
Additional paid-in capital	420,000
Retained earnings	3,200,000

The above items reflect the results of a $12-per-share preferred stock dividend declaration and a 2-for-1 common stock split during 1983.

REQUIRED Reconstruct the book values of each item immediately before the dividend declaration and the stock split.

E21–5 Siedel Builders, Inc., has a policy of maintaining a balance in Appropriated Retained Earnings for amounts equal to expected capital expenditures for the next fiscal period. The following schedule shows Siedel's experience for the first 3 years of operations:

YEAR	NET INCOME	DIVIDENDS	THE FOLLOWING YEAR'S CAPITAL EXPENDITURES	
			EXPECTED	ACTUAL
1	$1,230,000	$ 400,000	$ 640,000	$ 700,000 (year 2)
2	2,200,000	1,000,000	1,300,000	1,200,000 (year 3)
3	600,000	1,200,000	1,000,000	Unknown (year 4)

REQUIRED Show all journal entries affecting retained earnings for each of the 3 years.

E21–6 A. Bailey Associates discloses the following information in the notes to its current financial statements: "The company is required under bond covenant agreements to contribute to a sinking fund an amount equal to $1/20$ of the year-end book value of bonds payable. In addition, dividends are restricted to $1/8$ of the year-end balance of total retained earnings." Each bond has a maturity value of $1,000, and each of the 10,000 bonds has an unamortized premium of $100 at year-end. The year-end retained earnings balance is $8,800,000.

REQUIRED Show all the journal entries related to the sinking fund and retained earnings appropriation for the current year, assuming the retained earnings restriction is to be communicated by appropriating retained earnings and that no appropriation has yet been made.

E21–7 Fly Airlines Corporation issued 200,000 shares of $5 par value common stock at $8 per share and currently has 5,000 shares as treasury stock purchased at a cost of $10 per share.

REQUIRED Show the journal entries necessary for the following independent events: (1) a 100 percent stock dividend and (2) a 2-for-1 stock split. How would each event affect the balance sheet items?

E21–8 Pressler, Inc., has three stockholders with the following ownership interests:

STOCKHOLDER	SHARES OF COMMON
A	50,000
B	150,000
C	300,000

Rather than paying cash dividends, the company declares a property dividend with a total market value of $1,000,000 to be paid in shares of other companies' stock that were purchased several years ago. The distribution scheme is as follows:

RECIPIENT	COMMON SHARES OF	PURCHASE PRICE AND BOOK VALUES PER SHARE	NUMBER OF SHARES DISTRIBUTED	MARKET PRICE PER SHARE	NUMBER OF SHARES OWNED
Stockholder A	AB Corp.	$10	?	$25	5,000
Stockholder B	CD Corp.	100	?	100	5,000
Stockholder C	EF Corp.	20	?	50	15,000

REQUIRED

1. How many shares should be distributed to each stockholder?
2. How would such a dividend distribution be recorded?

E21–9 United Metals Corporation has experienced several years of operating losses, which resulted in the following summarized balance sheet:

	BOOK VALUE	FAIR VALUE
Assets		
Current assets	$ 82,000	$ 80,000
Land	150,000	180,000
Plant	1,170,000	900,000
Equipment	300,000	250,000
Total assets	$1,702,000	
Liabilities		
Current liabilities	102,000	
Notes payable	300,000	
Bonds payable	1,000,000	
	$1,402,000	
Owners' equity		
Common stock—par	500,000	
Additional paid-in capital	100,000	
Retained earnings	(300,000)	
	$ 300,000	
Total liabilities and owners' equity	$1,702,000	

REQUIRED

1. Show the journal entries necessary to effect a quasi-reorganization.
2. What are the potential benefits of such a procedure?

E21-10 Dixie Bottlers, Inc., has both common and cumulative preferred stock outstanding. Because of rapid growth since its incorporation the company has not paid any dividends, although it has been profitable with the resulting December 31, 1983, retained earnings (assume cost method for treasury stock):

Retained earnings appropriated—cost of treasury stock	$ 400,000
Retained earnings appropriated—preferred dividends in arrears	1,100,000
Unappropriated retained earnings	2,000,000
	$3,500,000

REQUIRED Show the journal entries necessary if Dixie sells its treasury stock for $450,000 and declares $1,100,000 preferred dividends on January 1, 1984.

PROBLEMS

P21-1 Helen Jones and Regina Jackson are independent geologists who discovered a mineral deposit on government land that they had leased for exploration. They determined that exploitation of the deposit was feasible and formed J. Minerals, Inc., for that purpose. The following list summarizes all the transactions that occurred during the life of the project:

1/1/84	Formed J Minerals, Inc., by becoming stockholders. Each stockholder contributed $100,000 and received 10,000 shares of no-par common stock.
1/2/84	Paid $50,000 for exploitation rights of 100,000 tons of estimated reserve.
During 1984	Total expenditures for mining 50,000 tons of minerals amounted to $120,000. (All labor, materials, and equipment were provided by a contractor.) Sold 50,000 tons for $5.00 per ton. Paid cash dividends of $6.50 per share.
During 1985	Total expenditures for mining 50,000 tons of minerals amounted to $130,000. Sold 50,000 tons for $5.25 per ton. Paid cash dividends of $6.625 per share.
12/31/85	Distributed all remaining assets to the stockholders and dissolved the corporation.

REQUIRED Show all the journal entries necessary for the above transactions.

P21-2 Brownel Corporation's balance sheet has the following owner's equity section on December 31, 1982:

Capital stock, par value $2 per share (shares authorized, 200,000,000; shares issued and outstanding, 60,250,000)	$ 120,500,000
Capital in excess of par value	262,150,000
Retained earnings	4,827,700,000
Total owners' equity	$5,210,350,000

Brownel stock is selling for $8.75 per share on December 31, 1982. The board of directors intends to declare a cash dividend of $1.25 per share on January 1, 1983. In addition, the board wants to explore the effects of the following:

1. A 10 percent stock dividend on January 1, 1983
2. A 50 percent stock dividend on January 1, 1983
3. A 2-for-1 stock split on January 1, 1983

REQUIRED Consider each of the above three actions *independently*, and show how each action would affect the balance sheet. Show all the journal entries.

P21-3 After several years of profitable operations, Solid State, Inc., has had 2 years of heavy losses resulting in a deficit at the December 31, 1985, year-end. No dividends have been paid during the current year, and the management is facing a severe capital shortage. One option that seems quite attractive is a quasi-reorganization, which is permissible under state law.

The following is a summarized balance sheet at December 31, 1985, and other information concerning the fair values of assets:

	BOOK VALUE	FAIR VALUE
Assets		
Cash	$ 8,500	$ 8,500
Accounts receivable	45,000	45,000
Plant (net)	1,500,000	1,000,000
Equipment (net)	4,000,000	3,500,000
Land	500,000	800,000
Total assets	$6,053,500	$5,353,500
Liabilities		
Current liabilities	$ 80,000	
Long-term liabilities	500,000	
Common stock—par	3,000,000	
Common stock—additional paid-in		
capital	3,500,000	
Retained earnings	(1,026,500)	
	$6,053,500	

REQUIRED

1. Show all the journal entries necessary to accomplish a quasi-reorganization if par is to remain at $3,000,000.
2. Show the postreorganization balance sheet.

P21-4 The following excerpt is from the Outstanding Corporation's balance sheet dated December 31, 1985:

Owners equity	
Preferred stock—$5 par	
Dividends 30¢ per share, cumulative, fully participating (200,000 shares authorized, 80,000 shares issued, 80,000 shares outstanding)	400,000
Common stock—$5 par (200,000 shares authorized, 55,000 shares issued, 50,000 shares outstanding)	275,000
Additional paid-in capital: From common issue	100,000
From treasury stock transactions	10,000
Donated capital	100,000
Retained earnings	630,000
Less: Treasury stock (5,000 shares at cost)	(70,000)

On January 1, 1986, the market price of the common stock was $15 per share, and the market price of the preferred stock was $6 per share.

REQUIRED

1. Assume that net income from the year ending December 31, 1985, was $193,000 and that the entire amount was paid as cash dividends to both preferred and common stockholders on December 31, 1985. Assume also that cash dividends on preferred stock were 1 year in arrears prior to the dividend—that is 1984 dividends had not been paid. *Compute* the cash paid to both the preferred and the common stockholders. (Show all computations.)

2. Record a 5 percent common stock dividend issued on February 1, 1986, from treasury stock, declared on January 1, 1986.

3. Record a 40 percent common stock dividend issued on February 8, 1986, from unissued stock, declared on January 11, 1986.

P21-5 The Stereo-Type Corporation shows a preliminary owners' equity section for its balance sheet as of December 31, 1985, as follows:

Owners' equity	
Preferred stock (par value $10, 6%, nonparticipating, noncumulative, authorized 10,000 shares, issued 10,000 shares)	$100,000
Common stock (stated value $10, authorized 200,000 shares, issued 140,000 shares)	?
Capital in excess of stated value	270,000
Donated capital	80,000
Retained earnings	406,000
Total owners' equity	$?

Stereo-Type Corporation is profitable, and its stock is selling for $20 per share in the market. The corporation paid its preferred shareholders $6,000 in dividends for 1985. It also paid a total of $100,000 in cash dividends to common stockholders during 1985.

REQUIRED

1. Fill in the two missing amounts in the equity section.

2. If the board of directors issues a 10 percent stock dividend on December 31, 1985, what journal entry is necessary?

3. Determine the total owners' equity amount after the stock dividend.

4. Considering only the preliminary owners' equity section *without* the effect of requirement 2, determine what the total owners' equity amount would be if the corporation decided to buy back 10,000 shares of its own stock at the market price of $20 per share and not issue the stock dividend. Show results under both the cost and par-value methods.

5. What would the journal entry be for the transaction in requirement 4 under both the cost and par-value methods?

P21-6 Pickwick Supply, Inc., has both cumulative preferred and common stock outstanding on December 31, 1984, the end of its fiscal period. The equity section of the December 31, 1984, balance sheet is as follows:

Preferred stock—par (100,000 shares authorized, issued, and outstanding)	$10,000,000
Additional paid-in capital	2,100,000
Common stock—par (500,000 shares authorized and issued, and 490,000 outstanding)	2,000,000
Additional paid-in capital	4,440,000
Retained earnings	
Appropriated	7,000,000
Unappropriated	2,000,000
Treasury stock—common (10,000 shares)	(85,000)

REQUIRED Record the journal entries for each of the following transactions in 1985:

1. On January 15, 1985, Pickwick sells all of the treasury stock for $11.50 per share.

2. On February 1, 1985, Pickwick purchases the following treasury stock: 20,000 shares of preferred at $105 per share; and 5,000 shares of common at $12 per share. The cost method is used to record these transactions.

3. On October 1, 1985, Pickwick declares dividends of $10 per share on preferred and $1.50 per share on common to be paid on December 1, 1985.

4. Net income for 1985 is $4,300,000, $2,000,000 of which is appropriated.
5. On December 31, 1985, the company declares a 10 percent stock dividend on common stock, at which time the market value of the common stock is $14 per share.

P21–7 A corporation had a $500,000 credit balance in retained earnings at the beginning of its 1984 fiscal year. During 1984 the following operating activity took place:

Sales	$10,780,000
Expenses (other than depletion expense)	8,300,000
Depletion expense	700,000
Net income	$ 1,780,000

REQUIRED If no dividends have ever been paid and the beginning balance in Accumulated Depletion is $4,000,000, what is the maximum "normal" dividend that could be declared in 1984? What is the maximum "liquidating" dividend that could be declared in 1984? Show the journal entries for each, assuming the maximum amounts are declared, and show the effect on owners' equity.

P21–8 Preston Parts, Inc., has several classes of stock outstanding on January 1, 1983:

	ORIGINAL SELLING VALUE	PAR VALUE	CALL PRICE	CONVERTIBILITY RATIO	ANNUAL DIVIDEND RATE	DIVIDEND PAYMENT DATE	OUTSTANDING SHARES	MARKET VALUE PER SHARE
Preferred A	$ 101	$ 100.00	None	10-to-1	10%	6/30 and 12/31	100,000	$ 95
Preferred B	1,020	1,000.00	$1,050	100-to-1	12	12/31	20,000	980
Preferred C	100	100.00	None	None	14	12/31	50,000	1,025
Common	2	0.80	None	None	Variable	6/30 and 12/31	500,000	9

REQUIRED

1. Record the journal entries necessary for the following transactions:

a.	3/31/83	Called and retired all of the Class B preferred stock.
b.	5/15/83	Declared normal semiannual dividends for Class A preferred and $.50 per share for common.
c.	6/30/83	Paid all dividends payable.
d.	7/1/83	20,000 shares of Class A preferred were converted when the market value of the common was $11 per share and the market value of Class A preferred was $109 per share.
e.	10/18/83	Purchased 10,000 shares of common at $12 per share to be held in treasury. The par value method was used.
f.	11/15/83	Declared dividends as follows: Class A preferred—normal semiannual amount; Class C preferred—normal annual amount; common—$.60 per share.
g.	12/31/83	Paid all dividends payable.

2. Assuming no other transactions except for those above have affected the stock accounts, show how each security would appear in the December 31, 1983, balance sheet.

P21–9 Springer Castings, Inc., has an opportunity to become a subcontractor for a major Defense Department project. The project would last 7 years and would utilize 120 percent of Springer's current capacity. Springer's management estimates that $42,000,000 is needed to assemble the facilities necessary for the venture. Banks are willing to lend up to $20,000,000 on 5-year mortgage notes if the remaining needed capital can be raised from the sale of common stock. The banks will require year-end appropriations of retained earnings and year-end contributions to a trustee-controlled sinking fund in the amount of $3,000,000 per year starting December 31, 1984.

Springer's December 31, 1983, summarized balance sheet and asset fair values are as follows:

	BOOK VALUE	FAIR VALUE
Assets		
Current assets	$ 604,000	$ 604,000
Noncurrent assets	19,750,000	15,400,000
	$20,354,000	
Liabilities		
Current liabilities	$ 1,500,000	
Noncurrent liabilities	4,801,000	
	$ 6,301,000	
Owners' equity		
Common stock (no par)	$17,000,000	
Retained earnings	(2,947,000)	
	14,053,000	
	$20,354,000	

The management expects the following results if the project is accepted:

	1984	1985	1986	1987	1988	1989	1990
				IN THOUSANDS			
Net income[a]	$10,000	$11,000	$11,000	$12,000	$12,000	$12,000	$8,000

[a] Includes interest on proposed debt and fund.

On December 31, 1983, the management performs a quasi-reorganization in which the noncurrent assets are written down to fair market value and the retained earnings deficit is eliminated. Common stock is issued for $22,000,000, and the banks lend $20,000,000 on 5-year non-interest-bearing notes, with no payment due until January 1, 1989. The effective interest rate on the notes is 14 percent.

REQUIRED Presume that the expected operating results are realized and that the sinking fund actually earns 16 percent per year.

1. Show all the summary journal entries relating to the quasi-reorganization, the stock issuance, and the borrowing necessary at December 31, 1983.
2. For 1984 and 1985, show all entries relating to the sinking fund, the appropriation of retained earnings, and the notes payable.

P21–10 Assume all the facts in the preceding problem.

REQUIRED

1. Show the resulting owners' equity section of Springer's balance sheets on December 31, 1983, 1984, and 1988, assuming no dividends are paid.
2. What is the maximum amount of dividends that could be declared at the end of 1983, 1984, and 1988? Explain.
3. What will the sinking fund balance be before payment of the notes on December 31, 1988? How much is needed to pay off the notes on January 1, 1989?

P21–11 (CMA ADAPTED) The Shlee Company was established on July 1, 1974. It was authorized to issue 200,000 shares of $5 par value common stock and 50,000 shares of 6 percent $10 par value, cumulative, and non-participating preferred stock. Shlee Company has a July 1–June 30 fiscal year.

The following information relates to the stockholders' equity accounts of the Shlee Company:

Prior to the 1976–1977 fiscal year, Shlee Company had 105,000 shares of outstanding common stock issued as follows:

1. On July 1, 1974, 95,000 shares were issued for cash at $20 per share.
2. On July 24, 1974, 5,000 shares were exchanged for a plot of land that cost the seller $70,000 in 1968 and had an estimated market value of $130,000 on July 24, 1974.
3. On March 1, 1976, 5,000 shares were issued; the shares had been subscribed for $32 per share on October 31, 1975.

During the 1976–1977 fiscal year, the following transactions regarding common stock took place:

1. On October 1, 1976, subscriptions were received for 10,000 shares at $40 per share. Cash of $80,000 was received in full payment for 2,000 shares, and stock certificates were issued. The remaining subscriptions for 8,000 shares were to be paid in full by September 30, 1977, at which time the certificates were to be issued.
2. On November 30, 1976, Shlee purchased 2,000 shares of its own stock on the open market at $38 per share. Shlee uses the cost method for treasury stock.
3. On December 15, 1976, Shlee declared a 2 percent stock dividend for stockholders of record on January 15, 1977, to be issued on January 31, 1977. Shlee was having a liquidity problem and could not afford a cash dividend at the time. Shlee's common stock was selling at $43 per share on December 15, 1976.
4. On June 20, 1977, Shlee sold 500 shares of its own common stock that it had purchased on November 30, 1976, for $21,000.

Shlee issued 30,000 shares of preferred stock at $15 per share on July 1, 1975.

CASH DIVIDENDS

Shlee has followed a schedule of declaring cash dividends in December and June, with payment being made to stockholders of record in the following month. The cash dividends that have been declared since inception of the company through June 30, 1977, are as follows:

DECLARATION DATE	COMMON STOCK	PREFERRED STOCK
12/15/75	$.10 per share	$.30 per share
6/15/76	.10 per share	.30 per share
12/15/76	—	.30 per share

Because of the company's liquidity problems, no cash dividends were declared during June 1977.

RETAINED EARNINGS

As of June 30, 1976, Shlee's Retained Earnings account had a balance of $370,000. For the fiscal year ending June 30, 1977, Shlee reported net income of $20,000.

In March 1976, Shlee received a term loan from the Union National Bank. The bank requires Shlee to establish a sinking fund and restrict retained earnings for an amount equal to the sinking fund deposit. The annual sinking fund payment of $40,000 is due on April 30 each year; the first payment was made on schedule on April 30, 1977.

REQUIRED Prepare the stockholders' equity section of the statement of financial position, including appropriate notes, for Shlee Company as of June 30, 1977, as it should appear in its annual report to the shareholders.

P21–12 (CPA ADAPTED) Current conditions require that the Austin Company have a quasi-reorganization (corporate readjustment) at December 31, 1976. Selected balance sheet items prior to the quasi-reorganization (corporate readjustment) are as follows:

1. Inventory was recorded in the accounting records at December 31, 1976, at its market value of $3,000,000.

2. Property, plant, and equipment were recorded in the accounting records at December 31, 1976, at $6,000,000 net of accumulated depreciation.

3. Stockholders' equity consisted of the following:

Common stock, par value $10 per share (authorized, issued, and outstanding, 350,000 shares)	$3,500,000
Additional paid-in capital	800,000
Retained earnings (deficit)	(450,000)
Total stockholders' equity	$3,850,000

Additional information:

1. Inventory cost at December 31, 1976, was $3,250,000.

2. Property, plant, and equipment had a fair value of $4,000,000.

3. The par value of the common stock is to be reduced from $10 per share to $5 per share.

REQUIRED Prepare the stockholders' equity section of the Austin Company's balance sheet at December 31, 1976, as it should appear after the quasi-reorganization (corporate readjustment) has been accomplished. Show supporting computations. (Ignore income tax and deferred tax considerations.)

P21-13 (CPA ADAPTED) Howard Corporation is a publicly owned company whose shares are traded on a national stock exchange. At December 31, 1976, Howard had 25,000,000 shares of $10 par value common stock authorized, of which 15,000,000 shares were issued and 14,000,000 shares were outstanding.

The stockholders' equity accounts at December 31, 1976, had the following balances:

Common stock	$150,000,000
Additional paid-in capital	80,000,000
Retained earnings	50,000,000
Treasury stock	18,000,000

During 1977 Howard had the following transactions:

1. On February 1, 1977, a secondary distribution of 2,000,000 shares of $10 par value common stock was completed. The stock was sold to the public at $18 per share, net of offering costs.

2. On February 15, 1977, Howard issued at $110 per share, 100,000 shares of $100 par value, 8 percent cumulative preferred stock with 100,000 detachable warrants. Each warrant contained one right, which with $20 could be exchanged for one share of $10 par value common stock. On February 15, 1977, the market price for one stock right was $1.

3. On March 1, 1977, Howard reacquired 20,000 shares of its common stock for $18.50 per share. Howard uses the cost method to account for treasury stock.

4. On March 15, 1977, when the common stock was trading for $21 per share, a major stockholder donated 10,000 shares which are appropriately recorded as treasury stock.

5. On March 31, 1977, Howard declared a semiannual cash dividend on common stock of $.10 per share, payable on April 30, 1977, to stockholders of record on April 10, 1977. The appropriate state law prohibits cash dividends on treasury stock.

6. On April 15, when the market price of the stock rights was $2 each and the market price of the common stock was $22 per share, 30,000 stock rights were exercised. Howard issued new shares to settle the transaction.

7. On April 30, 1977, employees exercised 100,000 options that were granted in 1975 under a noncompensatory stock option plan. When the options were granted, each option had a preemptive right and entitled the employee to purchase one share of common stock for $20 per share. On April 30, 1977, the market price of the common stock was $23 per share. Howard issued new shares to settle the transaction.

8. On May 31, 1977, when the market price of the common stock was $20 per share, Howard declared a 5 percent stock dividend distributable on July 1, 1977. The appropriate state law prohibits stock dividends on treasury stock.

9. On June 30, 1977, Howard sold the 20,000 treasury shares reacquired on March 1, 1977, and an additional 280,000 treasury shares costing $5,600,000 that were on hand at the beginning of the year. The selling price was $25 per share.

10. On September 30, 1977, Howard declared a semiannual cash dividend on common stock of $.10 per share and the annual dividend on preferred stock, both payable on October 30, 1977, to stockholders of record on October 10, 1977. The appropriate state law prohibits cash dividends on treasury stock.

11. On December 31, 1977, the remaining outstanding rights expired.

12. Net income for 1977 was $25,000,000.

REQUIRED   Prepare a worksheet to be used to summarize, for each transaction, the changes in Howard's stockholders' equity accounts for 1977. The columns on this worksheet should have the following headings:

1. Date of transaction (or beginning date)
2. Common stock—number of shares
3. Common stock—amount
4. Preferred stock—number of shares
5. Preferred stock—amount
6. Common stock warrants—number of rights
7. Common stock warrants—amount
8. Additional paid-in capital
9. Retained earnings
10. Treasury stock—number of shares
11. Treasury stock—amount

Show supporting computations.

P21–14 (CPA ADAPTED)   Tomasco, Inc., began operations in January 1973 and had the following reported net income or loss for each of its 5 years of operations:

YEAR	NET INCOME (LOSS)
1973	$ (150,000)
1974	(130,000)
1975	(120,000)
1976	250,000
1977	1,000,000

At December 31, 1977, the Tomasco capital accounts were as follows:

Common stock, par value $10 per share (authorized, 100,000 shares; issued and outstanding, 50,000 shares)	$ 500,000
4% nonparticipating noncumulative preferred stock, par value $100 per share (authorized, issued, and outstanding, 1,000 shares)	100,000
8% fully participating cumulative preferred stock, par value $100 per share (authorized, issued, and outstanding, 10,000 shares)	1,000,000

Tomasco has never paid a cash or a stock dividend. There has been no change in the capital accounts since Tomasco began operations. The appropriate state law permits dividends only from retained earnings.

REQUIRED   Prepare a worksheet showing the maximum amount available for cash dividends on December 31, 1977, and how this amount would be distributable to the holders of the common shares and each of the preferred shares. Show supporting computations.

P21-15 (CPA ADAPTED)   During May 1977 Gilroy, Inc., was organized with 3,000,000 authorized share of $10 par value common stock, and 300,000 shares of its common stock were issued for $3,300,000. Net income through December 31, 1977, was $125,000.

On July 3, 1978, Gilroy issued 500,000 shares of its common stock for $6,250,000. A 5 percent stock dividend was declared on October 2, 1978, and issued on November 6, 1978, to stockholders of record on October 23, 1978. The market value of the common stock was $11 per share on the declaration date. Gilroy's net income for the year ended December 31, 1978, was $350,000.

During 1979 Gilroy had the following transactions:

1. In February Gilroy reacquired 30,000 shares of its common stock for $9 per share. Gilroy uses the cost method to account for treasury stock.

2. In June Gilroy sold 15,000 shares of its treasury stock for $12 per share.

3. In September each stockholder was issued (for each share held) one stock right to purchase two additional shares of common stock for $13 per share. The rights expired on December 31, 1979.

4. In October 250,000 stock rights were exercised when the market value of the common stock was $14 per share.

5. In November 400,000 stock rights were exercised when the market value of the common stock was $15 per share.

6. On December 15, 1979, Gilroy declared its first cash dividend to stockholders of $.20 per share, payable on January 10, 1980, to stockholders of record on December 31, 1979.

7. On December 21, 1979, in accordance with the applicable state law, Gilroy formally retired 10,000 shares of its treasury stock and had them revert to an unissued basis. The market value of the common stock was $16 per share on this date.

8. Net income for 1979 was $750,000.

REQUIRED   Prepare a schedule of all transactions affecting the capital stock (shares and dollar amounts), additional paid-in capital, retained earnings, and the treasury stock (shares and dollar amounts), and the amounts that would be included in Gilroy's balance sheet at December 31, 1977, 1978, and 1979, as a result of the above facts. Show supporting computations.

22

Hybrid Securities and Earnings Per Share

OVERVIEW

This is the third chapter that deals with the owners' equity section of the balance sheet. The accounting methods discussed in Chapters 20 and 21 explained how we report events that affect the owners' equity accounts. This chapter considers two additional topics that are important for understanding the *nature* of owners' equity, in addition to the actual reporting of events and transactions affecting equity accounts considered in the earlier chapters. These two topics involve an explanation of hybrid securities and a description of how various types of securities affect the computation of earnings per share. For our purposes, **hybrid securities** are defined as those securities that have the potential to be converted to some form of stock. Because hybrid securities can have a complicating effect on the calculation of earnings per share, they will be discussed first.

Hybrid securities are those securities that may complicate the measurement of **earnings per share (EPS).** EPS measurements are provided because many external users wish to have the net income of the entity reported on a per share basis. The fact that the final figures in conventional income statements are earnings per share to **common stockholders** suggests that these stockholders are considered to be the most important equity interest. The earnings-per-share calculation, therefore, focuses on the interests of the common stockholders.

In the "Overview" to Part III of this text, it was noted that in the broadest sense, all accounts on the right-hand side of the balance sheet represent equity interests. From this perspective, the balance sheet equation becomes Assets = Equities. The current and long-term creditors join with the stockholders in that they all have an interest in the assets of the entity. Yet, in the conventional financial-reporting process, the stockholder's interest are accorded special emphasis. The stockholder is the addressee of the published annual reports, and it is the common stockholder's interests that are considered in computing earnings per share.

Some have called this emphasis on the common stockholder in the conventional accounting statements the **residual equity** approach. Thus, the income statement is seen as a description of how operations resulted in a change in the residual equity interest of the stockholders. As a result, tax payments, bond interest payments, payments to vendors, and so on, are expenses in arriving at the net income number that remains for the "residual" equityholders' interests. In essence, a strict adherence to the broad equity concept (Assets = Equities) would result in few "expenses" in the income statement because all claimants (IRS, bondholders, vendors, and so on) would be viewed as having an equity interest.

Hybrid securities that affect the earnings-per-share calculation are the central topic of this chapter, which is divided into two parts. In the first part we discuss the nature and purpose of hybrid securities; in the second part we show how to calculate earnings per share in both simple and complex capital structures.

HYBRID SECURITIES

Hybrid securities are securities that have the potential to be converted to some form of stock, normally common stock. Why would a security be issued in one form with an option to convert it into another form? To explain why such conversion options may be of value to an investor, it is necessary to discuss the riskiness of various types of investments.

Investment Risk
In general, the liabilities and owners' (stockholders') equity side of the balance sheet lists the claims against the assets of the entity in the order of their riskiness, as illustrated in Exhibit 22–1. Generally, current liabilities represent the least risky claims, whereas common stocks represent the most-risky claims. In the event of liquidation of an entity, the order of payments to those with long-term claims against the entity's remaining assets will generally follow the order in which the claims on the right-hand side of the balance sheet are listed. For example, holders of bonds or notes will receive all of their claims against the company before common stockholders can receive any distribution of assets.

It would seem rational, then, for investors in a given entity to consider bonds to be less risky than preferred stock, and both bonds and preferred stock to be less risky than common stock. One reason for this risk ordering is based on the order of returns, or cash payments. The bondholders, for example, receive cash interest payments periodically according to their contractual legal claim with the entity and without regard to whether the entity is profitable. If the entity pays dividends after paying the current claims of bondholders and other expenses, the preferred stockholders will normally have the first claim to receive dividends. Other factors besides the likelihood of cash payments enter into the risk characteristics of various securi-

EXHIBIT
22-1

ORDERING OF LIABILITIES AND OWNERS' EQUITY

ROCKAWAY CORPORATION AND SUBSIDIARIES
Partial Balance Sheet

	DECEMBER 31,	
	1980	1979
Liabilities and Stockholders' Equity		
Current liabilities		
Short-term borrowings (note 5)	$ 932,000	$ 1,289,000
Current installments of long-term debt (note 7)	186,000	184,000
Accounts payable	1,461,000	1,370,000
Accrued expenses and other liabilities (note 6)	1,723,000	1,683,000
Federal income taxes	263,000	277,000
Total current liabilities	4,565,000	4,803,000
Long-term debt, less current installments (note 7)	3,537,000	2,832,000
Deferred income taxes (note 9)	123,000	103,000
Total liabilities	8,225,000	7,738,000
Stockholders' equity (notes 7 and 10)		
Senior preferred 5% cumulative non-voting stock of $100 par value per share. Authorized 5,000 shares; issued 770 shares	77,000	77,000
Common stock without par value. Authorized 2,400,000 shares; issued 1,264,498 shares at stated value in 1980 (1,147,129 in 1979)	6,058,000	4,602,000
Retained earnings	9,404,000	9,553,000
	15,539,000	14,232,000
Less cost of 26,852 shares of common stock in treasury (24,411 in 1979)	227,000	227,000
Total stockholders' equity	15,312,000	14,005,000
	$23,537,000	$21,743,000

ties. However, expected cash flows are usually considered to be most important in assessing risk.

It is now possible to evaluate the nature and purpose of hybrid securities. In essence, there are two primary reasons for the entity's establishing and using hybrid securities:

1. For capital formation
2. For incentive compensation

The remaining discussion in the first part of this chapter considers hybrid securities from these two viewpoints.

HYBRID SECURITIES FOR CAPITAL FORMATION

Various types of hybrid securities have been described in some detail in previous chapters of this text. The following list briefly summarizes those securities that are primary sources of capital for corporations:

1. *Convertible bonds.* Debt that can be converted after some specified holding period to either common or preferred stock. The conversion feature enables the investor to benefit if the stock price increases above a certain level. If the stock price does not increase, the investor retains the right to receive interest payments plus the face value of the debt at maturity. The issuing company, in turn, is able to issue debt with a lower than normal interest rate for equivalent nonconvertible debt, temporarily reducing the cost of new capital.

2. *Convertible preferred stock.* The benefits and costs of convertible preferred stock are very similar to those of convertible bonds. The major difference is that the initial investment in the convertible preferred does not have to be refunded by the issuer if conversion does not occur. The preferred shareholders have the added security of receiving a stated dividend amount before any dividends can be paid to the common shareholders.

3. *Stock warrants.* Stock warrants are the manifestation of stock rights in that they entitle the holder to acquire stock at a fixed price. They normally have a limited life of 5 years or less, although some have infinite lives. It may take one or more warrants to acquire a share of stock at some prespecified price. Warrants have a trading value of their own once issued and are sometimes issued in conjunction with other securities as a part of a package, such as bonds issued with detachable warrants. Warrants are also sometimes issued to current owners to fulfill their preemptive rights in situations where additional common stock is being offered. Warrants to acquire stock at a fixed price that is greater than the stock's current market value are currently worthless; therefore, buying warrants may result in a total loss of the invested amount.

These securities are generally considered to be an indirect means of obtaining new permanent equity capital for the corporation. Rather than directly issuing more common stock, the entity provides the investor with a less risky option that enables the potential equity investor to evaluate the stock price performance before and during the option period. The popularity of these hybrid securities has fluctuated during the past 30 years. Their popularity soared during the conglomerate merger era of the 1960s but later declined. During the late 1970s and early 1980s they have reemerged in various forms as a means of attracting investment capital.

Hybrid securities such as those listed above have been developed to facilitate **capital formation.** Companies in need of capital to expand plant assets or to replace existing assets at higher replacement costs may need more resources than their operations have been able to generate. Investors who have capital to invest are seeking the best return on investment given the risk involved. To reduce the risk to the investor, convertible securities contracts were developed. These contracts include options to convert from one security to another, frequently after a certain holding period. The following example describes the typical conversion features for a bond:

> The Demski Corporation issued $1,000,000 face value grade Aa bonds on January 1, 1985.[1] The bonds had a 10 percent stated interest rate and were sold for $1,134,198 to yield 8 percent effective interest. The typical interest rate required for grade Aa non-convertible bonds at the beginning of 1985 was about 10 percent. However, because the Demski bonds would be convertible into 10 shares of $2 par value common stock for each $1,000 face value bond on or after January 1, 1987, the investors in the market were willing to accept an 8 percent return. On January 1, 1985, Demski Corporation common stock was selling for $99 per share.

The convertible bonds described in this case offer the investor the option of holding the bond until maturity and receiving at least an 8 percent return (assuming Demski does not become bankrupt), trading the bonds in on common stock after waiting at least 2 years, or selling the bonds in the market at the current market price at any point in time. Investors are willing to pay a "premium" for the option to convert to stock at a later date because of the increased investment flexibility. This premium is

---

[1] Grade Aa is one of several bond ratings. Moody's and Standard & Poor's classification of the riskiness of bonds ranges from Aaa (best) to C (worst). These grades serve as a qualitative assessment of the credit worthiness of the issuing company for each particular bond issue.

represented by their willingness to accept an interest rate that is less than the going rate on other bonds that are similar in all respects except for the conversion feature.

Conversion
Premium
The conversion option offers the investor an unlimited "upside" return should the price of the stock increase after 2 years to more than $113.42 per share, but also provides at least an 8 percent return in this case. As a result of this flexibility, the conversion option may be attractive enough for investors to pay a premium. As already mentioned, this option is designed to be attractive to investors. The question is, How much extra will investors pay for the conversion feature? This premium is the difference between the alternatives facing the investor. One way of looking at the premium is to compute the difference between the following alternatives:

Alternative A: Convertible bond ($1,000 face, stated rate of 10%), grade Aa	$1,134.20
Alternative B: Common stock (10 shares × $99)	990.00
Premium for conversion option	$ 144.20

Some would argue that the $144.20 premium measure is not appropriate because the convertible bond cannot be converted to common until January 1, 1987. However, if the investor is considering an investment in alternative A or B and selects A, then $144.20 is the premium paid for buying debt with the right to acquire stock at a fixed price in the future (essentially $113.42 per share) instead of buying the stock immediately for $99 per share. Another pair of alternatives facing investors would be, Should they invest in the convertible debt or a "straight" grade Aa bond? This suggests a premium of only $134.20 per bond, computed as follows:

Alternative A: Convertible bond ($1,000 face, stated rate of 10%), grade Aa	$1,134.20
Alternative C: Straight bond ($1,000 face, stated rate of 10%), grade Aa	1,000.00
Premium for conversion option	$ 134.20

The important assumption stated in this example is that a bond, similar to the Demski bond in all respects except for the conversion feature, would be selling in the market to yield 10 percent. Given this assumption, the conversion feature for alternative A versus alternative C is only $134.20. Both measures of the premium paid for the conversion option are somewhat subjective. In either event, it seems clear that the investor was willing to pay some premium for the option to convert the bond to common stock after January 1, 1987.

Bond
and Stock
Pricing
If the price of Demski Corporation common stock is $110 per share on January 1, 1987, what is the conversion feature worth at that time? Once the convertibility feature can be exercised, the market price of the bond will normally be related to the market price of the security to which it can be converted. The process that makes the two securities related to one another in price is called **arbitrage.** On January 1, 1987, the convertible bond would sell for about $1,100 because it could be traded for 10 shares of stock with a market value of $110 each. If the bonds were more valuable than the stock, they would be selling at more than $1,100. However, if the stock increases in price from $110 per share, there will have to be a comparable increase in the price of the convertible bond.

Source of Capital	By giving investors the option of holding debt or common stock, the issuing company may be better able to attract capital investors. If the company uses the new capital effectively and the market price of the stock increases to reflect this successful management of capital, the bondholders may convert to common stock, eliminating the need to retire or refund the bonds. The issuance of debt that is eventually converted to stock increases the equity capital of the issuing company. Alternatively, if the stock price does not increase enough to cause conversion, the investors will receive their interest income as some compensation during the bond-holding period and will eventually receive cash upon the sale or retirement of the bonds. The latter alternative will, of course, require the use of cash on the part of the issuing company. If management does an efficient and effective job with the resources from the convertible issue, the likelihood that the capital will remain invested in the issuing company is increased, resulting in advantages for all suppliers of equity capital.

HYBRID SECURITIES FOR INCENTIVE COMPENSATION

A second reason for the development of hybrid securities involves the need for an effective **management incentive system.** Stock options are essentially the same thing as **calls,** which give the holder the right to purchase shares of stock at a fixed call (purchase) price over some specific time period. The difference is that options generally do not require an investment by the holder, whereas calls are purchased by the investor. Although potential gains on calls are unlimited, when the market price of the stock fails to go above the call price during the period in which the call may be exercised, the entire cost of the call becomes a loss. For options, the potential amount of the gain is also unlimited, but the chance of loss is zero. The tax aspects of options frequently enable the holder to control the date on which tax has to be paid, and to have the benefits taxed as capital gains rather than ordinary income.

Stock option plans are designed primarily to make the goals of management and owners more congruent. To the extent that a manager's wealth is related to stock performance, the manager should be interested in maximizing stock performance, which in turn benefits the owners.

There are many complex and unique aspects involved in describing stock option plans, making it difficult to generalize about their many alternative forms. We shall now focus on the broad accounting issues involved in measuring and reporting stock option arrangements.

Terminology and Option Features	As with most other accounting topics that are heavily dependent on the contractual terms, real-world terminology for incentive compensation plans frequently makes simple explanation difficult.[2] Many terms can be used to describe what is essentially a stock option; included are *stock purchase plans, stock thrift plans, stock compensation plans, stock award plans, stock bonus plans,* and *stock savings plans.* This text does not define all of these terms because they are *not* uniformly defined in practice. Table 22–1 summarizes the general categories of long-range incentive plans offered by

[2] Terminology is a key aspect of leases, pensions, loans contracts, factoring, or assignment of receivables, as well as many other accounting topics. Because of the many variations in terminology observed in practice, it is essential that the student focus on the basic underlying concepts so as not to be confused by the various forms.

TABLE
22-1

LONG-TERM INCENTIVE PLANS FOR THE TOP 100 CORPORATIONS (1970–1979)									
	1979	1978	1977	1976	1975	1974	1973	1972	1971	1970
Qualified options only	2	3	4	7	12	19	24	29	45	61
Nonqualified options only or both qualified and nonqualified options	82	81	82	81	75	68	60	54	44	29
Stock appreciation rights	62	56	45	33	27	20	13	8	—	—
Phantom stock	2	2	3	4	4	4	4	3	3	—
Dividend units	3	5	5	6	5	5	5	6	6	5
Restricted stock	8	7	6	6	—	—	—	—	—	—
Performance units[a]	26	23	17	10	6	3	1	—	—	—
Performance shares[a]	12	8	9	8	5	6	3	1	—	—
No plan	7	7	7	5	5	6	10	11	11	10

[a] These forms of compensation normally involve cash payouts based on the future performance of accounting performance measures such as EPS or return on assets.

Source: Towers, Perrin, Forester, and Crosby, *Top 100 Compensation Study 1979* (New York, 1979), p. 14.

major U.S. corporations and gives a historical perspective of the change in their popularity, which is partly explained by changes in tax laws. The tax laws have been responsible for the demise of qualified option plans, which are now no longer permitted. Most of the plans identified in Table 22-1 are discussed below. We use the term **stock option** throughout this section to refer to incentive compensation plans in general. No matter what the incentive plan is called, the evaluation of several common features will prove to be more important in reporting incentive plans for accounting purposes.

Perhaps the most pivotal determination for accounting is whether a plan results in compensation to the grantees. If a stock option plan is determined to be **noncompensatory,** it is viewed as giving no compensation to the employee at the date of grant and results in no expense to the employer. If a plan is **compensatory,** the employee is viewed as having received some compensation and an expense *is* recorded by the employer. From an economic point of view, the issuance of a stock option must provide some expected benefit or it would be a futile exercise. The major accounting issue then becomes one of measuring these benefits in a way that reflects the expected value of the assets to be provided by the issuing company.

Is a Plan Compensatory or Noncompensatory?

A corporation may want to reward its employees in a way that will permit the corporation to avoid recording an expense and also permit the employee to minimize personal taxes on the incentive plan's benefits. Although stock option plans are complicated by the problems involved with precisely measuring the employees' benefits, this measurement problem makes it possible for an employer to give employees something of value without recording an expense. Consider the following example:

On December 30, 1986, the Janell Corporation granted stock options to all of its employees. Each employee received one stock option for each $1,000 of salary (or fraction thereof) received during 1986. Each option entitled the holder to purchase one share of stock for $25 per share between January 1, 1989, and June 30, 1989, if he or she was still employed by Janell during that period. The market price of Janell stock on the date of grant (December 30, 1986) was $27 per share. The total number of options was 4,300.

A fundamental question that must be answered before compensation expense can be measured and recorded is, Did the employees receive anything of value on December 30, 1986, the date of the grant? The employees must work 2 additional years to be able to exercise their options. The market price must also remain above $25 per share during the option period if the options are to be of any value to the employees. Whether or not the employees received any compensation seems uncertain at December 30, 1986.

Conditions for noncompensatory plans To help resolve this uncertainty and to increase the uniformity in measuring and recording stock option plans, **APB Opinion No. 25,** issued in 1972, identified *four criteria,* all of which must be met if a plan is to qualify as a **noncompensatory stock option plan:**[3]

1. The plan must be made available to virtually all employees, with only limited qualifications or restrictions permitted. (For example, a plan *could* be limited to full-time employees and still meet this condition.)
2. The plan must offer the option benefits to all participants on an equitable basis. (For example, on the basis of salary or years of experience, and so on.)
3. The option exercise period must be limited to a reasonably brief time interval.
4. The value of the option at the issue date must be no greater than the value that would normally accrue to a stockholder receiving a stock right. (In practice, this value is typically no more than about 15 percent of the stock price at the date of grant.)

If a stock option plan meets all four of these criteria, the option would be accounted for as a noncompensatory plan. No entry for compensation expense would be required on the books of the issuing company for financial-reporting purposes. Any plan that does not meet *all four* criteria is a compensatory plan.

Is the stock option plan in the Janell Corporation example compensatory or not? Given the description of the plan and the four conditions listed above, it seems that the plan is noncompensatory. The plan is available to all employees on an equitable basis with a limited (January 1, 1989, to June 30, 1989) exercise period. Also, the value of the option at the date of grant (December 30, 1986) is only 7.4 percent of the stock price on that date [($27 − $25)/$27 = .074]. No expense is recorded, and no journal entry is actually necessary to record the granting of a noncompensatory option. Footnote disclosure of noncompensatory stock option plans is necessary, as illustrated in Exhibit 22–2.

Compensatory Plans Three major types of incentive plans can result in compensation expense being recorded. The first type of compensation to be described is in the form of a **stock**

[3] *Accounting Principles Board Opinion No. 25,* "Accounting for Stock Issued to Employees" (New York: AICPA, October 1972).

EXHIBIT
22–2

DESCRIPTION OF NONCOMPENSATORY STOCK OPTIONS IN COMPANY REPORTS

LOWE'S COMPANIES, INC.

STOCK OPTION PLANS—For a number of years qualified stock option plans have been in effect to enable management to offer stock options to key employees. The plans have been noncompensatory and have no effect on the earnings statement. The tax benefits flowing from the early disposition of stock by the optionees have been treated as an addition to capital in excess of par value.

KDI CORPORATION

STOCK OPTIONS—In accounting for noncompensatory options the Company makes no entry in its accounts until the options are exercised and the option price of the shares is paid. Upon receipt of payment, $35 per share of the amount is credited to the capital stock account and the remainder credited to the capital in excess of par value account. No charge is reflected in the income account with respect to options granted or exercised.

option, whereas the other two more recent variations of the traditional stock option plans are commonly known as **stock appreciation rights,** and **restricted stock of-ferings.**

Stock options as compensation Stock options that do not meet all four criteria of **APB Opinion No. 25** identified earlier require the recording of compensation expense by the employer. The question then becomes, **What is the amount of compensation expense and when is it recorded?** According to **APB Opinion No. 25,** the **measurement date** is the date when the number of shares an employee may acquire *and* the purchase price to the employee (if any) are both known.[4]

When measurement date is the date of grant Consider the following example, in which an employee of the Eichenseher Corporation received compensation in the form of stock options (the plan does not meet the criteria of a noncompensatory plan):

> For a Christmas bonus on December 30, 1984, Eichenseher Corporation gave Ron Hilton, the company's vice-president of finance, stock options that entitle him to purchase up to 4,000 shares of Eichenseher common stock for $15 per share. Hilton cannot exercise the options until Christmas 1986, and he must decide whether to exercise his option to buy stock at $15 per share on or before June 1, 1987. To exercise the options, he also has to remain in Eichenseher's employ. On December 30, 1984, the date of the grant, Eichenseher Corporation common stock was selling for $20 per share.

The measurement date in this case is the **date of the grant** because the key factors needed to measure compensation are all known at that date:

1. Number of shares involved in option, 4,000
2. Exercise price of the options, $15
3. Market price of the shares at measurement date (always known), $20

In the Eichenseher example, the compensation expense would be

$$\text{Number of shares} \times (\text{Market price} - \text{Option Price}) =$$

$$4,000 \times (\$20 - \$15) = \$20,000$$

[4] Ibid.

The compensation would be recorded by Eichenseher on December 30, 1984, the date of the grant, by the following entry:

| 12/30/84 | Deferred compensation expense | 20,000 | |
| | Common stock options | | 20,000 |

Both of these accounts are owners' equity accounts and would appear in the 1984 year-end balance sheet as follows:

```
                    EICHENSEHER CORPORATION
                     Partial Balance Sheet
                       December 31, 1984

Owners' Equity
  Common stock (par $10)                                    $ 5,000,000
  Capital in excess of par:
    From stock issuance                     $6,000,000
    From exercise of common stock optionsª      75,000        6,075,000

  Common stock options (4,000 shares)          20,000
  Less: Deferred compensation expense         (20,000)                0

  Retained earnings                                          10,000,000
      Total owners' equity                                 $21,075,000

ª From previous stock options.
```

The stock options appear in the balance sheet even though they have no impact on the balance sheet totals. This form of disclosure informs financial statement readers that the stock options are outstanding. The additional details in the footnotes to the financial statements will normally disclose the number of options at each option price and the option periods.

The contra equity account, Deferred Compensation Expense, would be amortized over the period of time between the date of the grant (December 30, 1984) and the earliest possible exercise date (December 25, 1986). The entry to record compensation expense for 1985 (assuming Hilton worked for Eichenseher throughout 1985) would be recorded as follows:

| 12/31/85 | Compensation expense | 10,000 | |
| | Deferred compensation expense | | 10,000 |

The $10,000 expense would be recorded in the income statement, and the contra equity account balance would be reduced by $10,000. The partial balance sheet for December 31, 1985 would appear as follows:

```
                    EICHENSEHER CORPORATION
                     Partial Balance Sheet
                       December 31, 1985

Owners' equity
  Common stock (par $10)                                    $5,000,000
  Capital in excess of par:
    From stock issuance                     $6,000,000
    From exercise of common stock options      75,000        6,075,000

  Common stock options (4,000 shares)          20,000
  Less: Deferred compensation expense         (10,000)        10,000
```

Assume that on December 31, 1986, Hilton exercised 2,000 of the stock options, purchasing 2,000 shares of Eichenseher common for $15 per share when the market price of the stock was $25 per share. The following entries would amortize the remaining deferred compensation expense and would record the issuance of 2,000 shares to Hilton:

12/31/86	Compensation expense		10,000	
	Deferred compensation expense			10,000
12/31/86	Cash		30,000	
	Common stock options		10,000	
	Common stock			20,000
	Additional paid-in capital			20,000

The partial balance sheet for 1986 would appear as follows:

EICHENSEHER CORPORATION
Partial Balance Sheet
December 31, 1986

Owners' equity		
Common stock (par $10)		$5,020,000
Capital in excess of par:		
From stock issuance	$6,000,000	
From exercise of common stock options	95,000	6,095,000
Common stock options (2,000)		10,000

The only account remaining on December 31, 1986, is Common Stock Options—$10,000 Credit, which represents the 2,000 unexercised options available to Hilton. In the case where stock options expire, the entry that records the compensation is reversed. In the example above, if Hilton had not exercised the remaining 2,000 options by June 2, 1987, the following entry would be recorded by Eichenseher:

6/2/87	Common stock options		10,000	
	Compensation expense			10,000
	(To record expired stock options)			

The credit to compensation expense would offset any compensation expense debits in arriving at the net employee compensation expense for 1987.

When measurement date is unknown at date of grant   The Eichenseher Corporation example assumed that the **measurement date** was the **date of grant** because both the number of options offered Hilton (4,000) and the exercise price ($15 per share) were known at the date of the grant. What if the number of options or the exercise price was unknown? According to **APB Opinion No. 25,** the accountant should **estimate** the number of shares and the option price (if any) at the date of the grant and should record the options just as though the estimated information (number of shares and option price) was known at the date of the grant. When the actual number of shares and option price become known, the accounts are then reconciled to reflect the actual data. When the actual data are available, they are **treated like a change in estimate,** as illustrated in Chapter 3. Consider the following example:

On December 27, 1988, Bedford Corporation issued stock options to its 25 top-level managers, which entitled each of them to receive a number of stock options equal to their annual salary for the year 1991 divided by $1,000. The option price was $30 per share. The options could not be exercised until December 27, 1990. Bedford makes annual salary decisions on December 15 of the preceding year. The **expected** average annual salary of the 25 managers for 1991 was estimated to be $175,000 as of the date of the grant (December 27, 1988). The market price of Bedford common was $29 per share at the date of the grant.

Because the market price of the stock is below the option price, no entry would be made for either deferred compensation expense or the stock options at the date of the grant. (The same would have been true of the Eichenseher example if the market price had been at or below $15 per share.) Assume that by December 31, 1989, the market price of Bedford has increased to $35 per share. Because the market price is now greater than the option price, it is reasonable to estimate a value for the stock options. In practice, the *estimated* value of the options is generally based on the actual market price less the option price (if any).[5] In this example, the options are estimated to be worth $5 each ($35 − $30) as of the end of 1989. Based on this estimate, the following entry would be recorded:

12/31/89	Deferred compensation expense	10,937.50	
	Compensation expense	10,937.50	
	Common stock options		21,875.00[a]
	(To record estimated benefits from employee stock options)		

[a] 25 × ($175,000/$1,000) = 4,375 total estimated options
4,375 × ($35 − $30) = $21,875 total expected value of options to be charged to compensation expense between 12/27/88 and 12/27/90

Assume that during the following year (1990) one of the 25 managers resigns (before December 27, 1990) and that the average salary of the remaining 24 managers for 1991 was set at $150,000 on December 15, 1990, when the market price of Bedford common had increased to $36 per share. The following entries would be required:

12/15/90	Common stock options	275.00[a]	
	Deferred compensation expense		275.00
	(To revise estimate of the value of the stock options)		
12/31/90	Compensation expense	10,662.50	
	Deferred compensation expense		10,662.50
	(To record compensation expense from stock option for 1990)		

[a] 24 × ($150,000/$1,000) = 3,600 total options
3,600 × ($36 − $30) = $21,600 total expected value of options

Previous estimated option cost	$21,875
Current estimated option cost	21,600
Correction to stock options outstanding	$ 275

Note that the illustrated entries are simply another application of the accounting procedures governing changes in accounting estimates. No retroactive adjust-

[5] The average market price of the stock over the entire accounting period is often used as a basis for this estimated option value.

EXHIBIT
22–3

STOCK OPTION PLAN DISCLOSURES IN COMPANY REPORTS

CROWN ZELLERBACH
Excerpt from Notes

Stock Option Plan

Under the Corporation's Nonqualified Stock Option Plan, options are granted for periods not exceeding ten years. They become fully exercisable after a two-year waiting period, are exercisable only while the optionee is an employee and terminate when the optionee ceases to be an employee, except in cases of death and certain retirements. At December 31, 1980, there are 1,019,782 shares of authorized and unissued common stock reserved for options of which 888,807 shares are outstanding.

Common shares under option at December 31, 1980, and activity for the year then ended were as follows:

	DEC. 31, 1979	GRANTED	EXERCISED	DEC. 31, 1980	PRICE PER SHARE
May 24, 1973	77,500		10,600	66,900	$28.00
October 25, 1973	6,100			6,100	41.88
February 1, 1974	2,000			2,000	34.75
June 3, 1974	3,500			3,500	31.88
July 25, 1974	36,925		7,350	29,575	29.50
November 20, 1975	159,200		15,500	143,700	36.38
October 28, 1976	12,000			12,000	43.13
June 9, 1977	334,200		105,168	229,032	36.00
October 12, 1977	37,000		15,000	22,000	32.38
February 9, 1978	2,200		300	1,900	30.38
June 8, 1978	2,000			2,000	33.00
November 9, 1978	3,600			3,600	30.88
January 11, 1979	500			500	32.00
June 14, 1979	161,500		4,000	157,500	35.88
June 12, 1980	—	216,500	8,000	208,500	44.75
	838,225	216,500	165,918	888,807	

At their meeting on May 8, 1980, the Corporation's shareholders authorized the issuance of stock appreciation rights (SARs) with respect to the Plan. When granted, such rights, after a six-month waiting period, offer the grantee the alternative of receiving an amount equivalent to the difference between the option price and the market value of the shares at the date of exercise, instead of exercising the option. This amount may be paid in cash or in shares at the discretion of the Corporation.

At December 31, 1980, SARs with respect to options for 100,500 shares at prices ranging from $28.00 to $41.88, which were granted on June 12, 1980, were fully exercisable.

AMP INCORPORATED AND PAMCOR, INC. & THEIR SUBSIDIARIES
Excerpt from Notes

9. Stock Plus Cash Bonus Plan and Treasury Stock

Under terms of the incentive Stock Plus Cash Bonus Plan, participating employees are credited with bonus units having a designated value of slightly more than 95% of the market price of the Company's stock on an award date. The stock bonus computation is based on the amount of the increase in the market price of the stock over the designated value on the award date. The Plan also provides that for awards made on or after October 28, 1972, the computation may be adjusted by discounting the market price of the stock on the computation date by a percentage (not to exceed 7.5% per year) to reflect the growth in earnings per share during the period. The cash bonus is a predetermined percentage (not more than 50%) of the value of the stock bonus. Charges to income before income taxes for current and future distributions under the Plan totaled $8,272,000 in 1980, $5,490,000 in 1979 and $7,397,000 in 1978.

All of the treasury shares (1980—1,444,293; 1979—1,465,553; 1978—1,271,421) are available for payment of stock bonuses under the Plan. Treasury shares were increased through the purchase of 40,000 shares in 1980, 249,600 shares in 1979 and 588,318 shares in 1978. Distributions under the Plan, on a last-in, first-out basis, were 61,260 shares in 1980, 55,468 shares in 1979 and 46,461 shares in 1978. For awards granted before and outstanding at December 31, 1980, based on the market price as of that date, approximately 255,000 shares would be distributed in the years 1981 through 1986.

Other Capital was increased $546,000 in 1980, $246,000 in 1979 and $115,000 in 1978 through gains and tax benefits on the excess of fair market value over the cost of treasury shares distributed.

EXHIBIT
22–3
(continued)

HAZELTINE CORPORATION
Excerpt from Notes

Note 11. Stock Options

At December 31, 1980, there were 8,225 shares of common stock reserved for issuance to officers and key employees under the Company's 1968 Qualified Stock Option Plan. Transactions relating to the stock options for 1980 and 1979 are as follows:

	SHARES	
	1980	1979
Options outstanding at beginning of year	15,400	23,850
Options granted	—	—
Options exercised at prices averaging $11.28 in 1980 and $3.19 in 1979	(7,175)	(8,450)
Options expired	—	—
Options outstanding at end of year prices averaging $12.52 in 1980 and $11.94 in 1979	8,225	15,400
Available at end of year for future grants	—	—

Options are exercisable after one year from date of grant and expire five years from date of grant.

ment is required or permitted for inaccuracies in the original estimates. The change is simply accounted for in the current (and possibly some future) period. Exhibit 22–3 illustrates typical financial statement disclosures of stock option plans.

Stock
Appreciation
Rights

Because of the elimination of employee tax benefits for certain qualified stock option plans in 1981, employers sought to develop new compensation schemes with different benefits. One of these schemes, called **stock appreciation rights (SARs),** was designed to permit employees to benefit from stock price appreciation without having to pay an exercise price for the option. In exercising regular stock options, the employee would normally pay cash at the date of exercise equal to the option price times the number of shares purchased, as in the Eichenseher example where Hilton paid $30,000 cash on December 31, 1986, to exercise 2,000 options. In addition, the IRS defines the difference between the option price and the market price at the date of exercise as taxable income to the employee. The combined effect of the cash exercise price and the taxable income could create a cash-flow problem for an employee when exercising stock options, making them less attractive to some extent.

To reduce this problem, SARs are designed so that employees can receive the benefits of increases in stock price between some preestablished base period market price and the market price at the date the SAR is exercised. Generally, the corporation will offer to pay this stock price appreciation in either cash or shares of stock. The objective is the same as before—to give employees an incentive to increase the market price of the stock through efficient and effective operation of the corporation. However, SARs do not require the employees to hold the corporation's stock as an investment in order to receive compensation for improvements in stock price performance, and they do not require cash outflow to exercise the SARs.

Accounting for SARs SARs may represent compensation to the employee, and if so, they must be recorded as compensation expense even before their exact value to the employee is known. Consider the following example:

Perry, Inc., offered SARs to its president, Mrs. K. Perry, for the appreciation on 20,000 shares of Perry common stock. The SARs were granted on December 31, 1982, when the stock was selling for $18 per share. Mrs. Perry was to receive all price appreciation from the date of the grant to the date of exercise. The exercise period was identified as January 1, 1985, to December 31, 1986. The SARs expired after December 31, 1986. Perry, Inc., was selling for $23 per share on December 31, 1983, $19 on December 31, 1984, and $15 on December 31, 1985. Mrs. Perry exercised all 20,000 SARs on June 30, 1986, when the stock was selling for $22 per share.

The SARs are accounted for on a prospective basis, just as options are when the number of shares or option price is unknown. For SARs, however, an income statement account, Compensation Expense, is used to account for changes in the *expected cost* of the SARs. The income statement is directly affected because no shares of stock or options to acquire shares of stock are issued and, as a result, the SARs cannot be viewed as a contra equity account like that used to account for the stock options. The expected compensation expense is based on the current market price of the stock from the date of the grant forward. Compensation expense is considered to accrue during the period before the SARs can be exercised, and expected compensation expense may fluctuate during the exercise period as well. The following entries would be recorded by Perry, Inc., over the life of the SARs described above:

DATE	PERCENT OF SARs EARNED	SAR BASE PRICE	CURRENT MARKET PRICE	TOTAL EXPECTED BENEFIT	JOURNAL ENTRY	DEBIT	CREDIT
12/31/82	0	$18	$18	0	None		
12/31/83	50	18	23	$100,000	Compensation expense	50,000	
					Compensation liability		50,000
12/31/84	100	18	19	20,000	Compensation liability	30,000	
					Compensation expense		30,000
12/31/85	100	18	15	0	Compensation liability	20,000	
					Compensation expense		20,000
6/30/86	100	18	22	80,000	Compensation expense	80,000	
					Cash		80,000

The Compensation Expense account is increased when the value of the SARs increases and is decreased when the value of the SARs decreases, but not below the $18 "base price" of the SARs. In this illustration, Compensation Expense is offset by a Compensation Liability account based on the assumption that Mrs. Perry will receive the SAR benefits in cash. If the SARs will be redeemed for stock, an owners' equity account such as SARs Outstanding would be used in place of the Compensation Liability account.

The amount of compensation expense recorded each year (1983–1986) is based on the difference between the base price and the current market price times the unexpired holding period times the number of options. For example, at December 31, 1983, 50 percent of the holding period has expired, suggesting that Mrs. Perry has earned one-half of the SAR benefits for her managerial services provided during 1983. The market price of the stock is $5 per share more than the base price ($23 − $18 = $5). Therefore, the compensation benefit for 1983 is

$$\$5 \times 50\% \times 20{,}000 \text{ shares } = \$50{,}000$$

In 1984 and 1985 the market price declines, and therefore there is no expected increase in benefits from the SARs. Instead, a **decrease** in benefits previously recognized in 1983 must be recorded. This decrease in expected benefits is recorded by reducing the liability and the expense in 1984 and 1985. Note that the credit to Compensation Expense would be offset against the other employee compensation costs, thereby reducing the expense in 1984 and 1985. The amount of the entry for 1984 is the difference between the $50,000 expected benefit as of December 31, 1983, and $20,000, the expected benefit at December 31, 1984, computed as follows:

$$(\$19 - \$18) \times 100\% \times 20{,}000 \text{ shares } = \underline{\$20{,}000}$$

At the end of 1985, there is no expected benefit because the current market price is less than the SAR base price. Therefore, the remaining $20,000 of the original $50,000 total expected benefit is eliminated.

Exhibit 22–4 illustrates the financial statement disclosure of SARs. Due to a lack of uniform accounting, the FASB addressed the issue of accounting for SARs in **Interpretation No. 28.**[6] The result was to consider compensation through SARs to accrue from the date of the grant until exercised. The SARs are valued on the basis of the difference between the current market price and the SAR base price for all financial statements prepared between grant and exercise dates. The entries illustrated in the Perry example represent yet another application of change in estimate accounting to account for changes in the value of the SARs between financial statement dates. Note that the total Compensation Expense at the expiration of the SARs will always equal the compensation actually received. In the case of Perry, Inc., this amounted to $80,000 (+$50,000 − $30,000 − $20,000 + $80,000 for 1983, 1984, 1985, and 1986, respectively).

Restricted Stock Offerings
The third form of option involves **restricted stock offerings (RSOs).** In RSOs, the employer offers stock to its employees for a specified option price, actually issuing the stock to the employee at the date of the grant and placing certain restrictions on the employee's use of the restricted stock. Typically, these restrictions require the employee to keep the stock for a specified time period and not use the restricted stock to obtain funds in any way, such as for collateral.

The RSOs are essentially the same as a straight option except that the stock is actually transferred to the employee at the date of the grant, which in turn creates a favorable tax advantage over the straight options. Due to the transfer of stock to the employee, RSOs are taxable income to the employee, but the employee may elect to pay taxes on the difference between the market price and the option price **either at the date of grant or the date of exercise.** This provides additional flexibility over straight options, making RSOs more attractive from the employee's viewpoint.

[6] *FASB Interpretation No. 28,* "Accounting for Stock Appreciation Rights and Other Variable Stock Option or Award Plans" (Stamford, CT: FASB, December 1978).

EXHIBIT
22–4

SAR DISCLOSURES IN COMPANY REPORTS

INTERLAKE, INC.
Excerpt from Notes

Note 4–Stock Incentive Plans

The Company's 1975 stock option plan provides for the granting of options for the purchase of common stock to officers and other key employees at prices equal to the fair market value at the dates of grant. A maximum of 375,000 shares may be granted under the plan until December 31, 1984. Options become exercisable one-third annually, on a cumulative basis, starting one year from the date of grant and may be exercised until ten years have elapsed from the date of grant.

The Company's 1977 Stock Incentive Program consists of a Stock Appreciation Rights Plan under which a maximum of 300,000 shares of common stock may be issued, a Stock Awards Plan and a Restricted Stock Purchase Plan. Total shares issued for the latter two plans may not exceed 100,000. Stock appreciation rights (S.A.R.'s) are issued concurrently with specific stock option grants and entitle the holders to receive the difference between option price and market price at the time of exercise of the S.A.R.'s in cash, shares of common stock, or a combination of the two at the Company's discretion. An equivalent number of shares under option are surrendered upon exercise of S.A.R.'s. Under the Stock Awards Plan, shares of common stock are issued at the date of the award and delivered to recipients 20% immediately and 20% on each of the four succeeding anniversary dates, subject to certain restrictions. The Board of Directors has not adopted a Restricted Stock Purchase Plan. Changes in common shares under option and related S.A.R.'s for the three years are summarized as follows:

	1980		1979		1978	
	OPTION SHARES	AVERAGE OPTION PRICE	OPTION SHARES	AVERAGE OPTION PRICE	OPTION SHARES	AVERAGE OPTION PRICE
Stock Options:						
Outstanding—beginning of year	247,198	$29.99	200,249	$30.77	211,900	$28.45
Granted	78,500	25.94	70,000	26.29	57,900	25.63
Exercised	(4,723)	23.75	(5,400)	18.43	(7,375)	17.61
Surrendered for exercised S.A.R.'s	(9,874)	24.19	(5,150)	22.35	(55,275)	18.15
Canceled or expired	(47,287)	31.03	(12,501)	29.86	(6,901)	31.67
Outstanding—end of year	263,814	28.93	247,198	29.99	200,249	30.77
Exercisable—end of year	140,093	31.51	128,730	33.03	91,524	31.64
Available for grant	71,339		102,552		161,176	
Stock Appreciation Rights:						
Outstanding—beginning of year	136,932		109,250		26,275	
Granted	33,250	25.94	35,650	26.21	140,050	26.94
Exercised	(9,874)		(5,150)		(55,275)	
Canceled or expired	(25,367)		(2,818)		(1,800)	
Outstanding—end of year	139,941		136,932		109,250	

Accounting for RSOs To illustrate, assume that on December 28, 1984, Ricchiute, Inc., offered RSOs to its top managers when its $1 par value common was selling for $80 per share. The RSOs could be purchased by certain employees for $20 per share before December 31, 1984, but employees were restricted from selling the stock or using it as collateral for 15 years. After holding the RSO stock for 5 years,

10 percent of these restrictions would be lifted each year for years 6 through 15 (for example, 10 percent of the shares purchased would become unrestricted each year).

By December 31, 1984, 100,000 RSOs had been purchased by Ricchiute employees. The following entry would be recorded:

12/31/84	Cash	2,000,000	
	Deferred compensation expense	6,000,000	
	Restricted stock plan		8,000,000
	(To record purchase of RSOs by employees)		

The Deferred Compensation Expense account and the Restricted Stock Plan account are both owners' equity accounts and would be adjusted over time to reflect changes in the estimated compensation expense. Assuming no change in the price of Ricchiute stock, the Deferred Compensation Expense account would be amortized at the rate of 10 percent per year beginning in 1990 (through 1999) as follows:

12/31/90	Compensation expense	600,000	
	Deferred compensation expense		600,000
12/31/00	Restricted stock plan	800,000	
	Capital in excess—from RSOs		790,000
	Common stock		10,000

Once again, the total Compensation Expense charged to income should equal the sum of the differences between the price paid ($20 per share) and the value received by the employees at the termination dates when the restrictions are lifted.

The employer's accounting for RSOs depends on the contractual restrictions placed on the stock. The accounting objective is, however, the same as that for the other forms of options. The employer attempts to measure the compensation to be received by the employee and spreads this compensation expense over the required period of service. This normally requires estimating the total compensation expense during the service period. Like so many areas where accounting depends on the contractual terms agreed to by two or more parties, there is some danger in trying to generalize the rules. The accountant must use judgment and maintain an independent attitude in evaluating and reporting on contracts between employees and employers. Exhibit 22–5 illustrates the financial statement disclosure of an RSO plan.

Conceptual Issues in Compensation Schemes

The conceptual issues underlying the various compensation schemes present difficult accounting measurement problems. Clearly, most employees who participate in an incentive plan involving stock options consider the options to be an element of their total compensation. Yet because many options are issued when the market price is less than or equal to the option price, and because the option is often contingent upon uncertain future events, measuring the expected future benefits provided by an incentive scheme is difficult. The future uncertainties raise questions as to how much compensation will be received, when compensation will be received, and under what set of possible future events would compensation not be received. All of these uncertainties pose measurement and recording problems. The timing of the recognition and the allocation of the benefits of incentive compensation arrangements represent problems that by their very nature cannot be objectively addressed. As a result, in accounting for many of these compensation schemes, the object has been to measure and record on the basis of the best estimate of compensation, given

EXHIBIT
22–5

RESTRICTED STOCK OPTION DISCLOSURE IN COMPANY REPORTS

ROHR INDUSTRIES INC.

Excerpt from Notes

The Corporation has two *restricted stock plans* authorizing the issuance of up to 350,000 shares of common stock. Rights to purchase common stock under the plans are granted to key employees of the Corporation by the Restricted Stock Plan Committee, which consists of outside directors. The Committee also determines the purchase price of the shares of the common stock which historically has been less than fair market value at the date of grant but not less than the par value of the shares sold. No rights were exercisable at July 31, 1980, and rights for 20,500 shares were exercisable at July 31, 1979, at a price of $1.00 per share. During fiscal 1980 and 1979, rights for 6,000 shares and 2,500 shares, respectively, were granted at a price of $1.00 per share.

Full cash payment of the purchase price is required at the time the shares are sold. Shares of common stock purchased by an employee are placed in escrow and are subject to restrictions as to sale or disposal. These restrictions generally lapse in installments at the rate of 20% a year commencing on the fifth anniversary from the date of purchase. If the employee fails to comply with the restrictions relating to his continued employment, the Corporation has the option, under certain circumstances, to repurchase the restricted shares at the employee's original cost.

Prior to fiscal 1980, 197,750 shares of common stock (net of shares repurchased by the Corporation) were sold under the then existing restricted stock plans and in 1980, an additional 20,500 shares of common stock were purchased by persons having rights under the plans. The Corporation repurchased 9,200 shares from terminated employees. The excess of the fair market value of such shares over the purchase price at the date of sale, which is considered to be compensation, is being amortized in the accounts ratably over a nine-year period in most cases.

At July 31, 1980, common stock was reserved for:

Restricted Stock Plans	240,750

the available information, and to treat new information as a change in estimate. The accounting procedures reviewed thus far in this chapter are considered to be consistent with this approach and with the fundamental objective of matching employee costs with benefits from employee services.

EARNINGS PER SHARE

The remainder of this chapter focuses on the accounting procedures required by **APB Opinion No. 15** for computing earnings per share.[7] The requirements have many procedural aspects. However, the objective is very straightforward: Take the income of the entity and report it to the ownership interests on a per share basis. Although the objective is straightforward, accomplishing it can be complex at times. The following illustrations will move from the simple and more general cases to the complex and less common ones.

Simple Capital Structure— Constant Number of Shares

A **simple capital structure** has only one form of voting equity capital, such as common stock, and no other forms or **potential** forms of voting equity capital, such as convertible bonds or stock warrants. Preferred stock would not normally result in a complex capital structure, unless such stock is convertible into common stock. **Constant shares outstanding** simply means that the number of equity shares does not change during the period in which income and earnings per share (EPS) are to be measured.

Assume that Newell, Inc., reported net income of $15,000,000 for the year

[7] *Accounting Principles Board Opinion No. 15,* "Earnings per Share" (New York: AICPA, May 1969).

1983. Newell has had 1,000,000 shares of no-par common issued and outstanding throughout 1983 and has no other actual or potential equity securities. The following EPS figure would be reported in Newell's 1983 income statement:

$$\frac{\text{Net income}}{\text{Number of shares of common}} = \frac{\$15,000,000}{1,000,000} = \underline{\$15.00} \text{ per share}$$

As illustrated, the EPS concept and this first example are quite simple to understand. It is not uncommon to find companies with simple capital structures. However, the number of shares of common stock outstanding will frequently change for most publicly traded stocks.

What if Newell also had 100,000 shares of $100 par, 5 percent ordinary preferred stock outstanding throughout 1983? What effect would this have on the EPS calculation? The EPS number is aimed at the common stockholder, and therefore the preferred shareholders' "interests" in earnings must be deducted from net income in order to determine the per share amount of earnings accruing to the common stockholder. In the Newell example, assuming preferred dividends had been declared *or* that the preferred stock was cumulative with respect to dividends, the following EPS would be reported:

$$\frac{\begin{array}{c}\text{Net income to}\\ \text{common stockholders}\end{array}}{\begin{array}{c}\text{Number of shares}\\ \text{of common}\end{array}} = \frac{\$15,000,000 - [\$5\ (100,000\ \text{shares})]}{1,000,000\ \text{shares}} = \underline{\$14.50} \text{ per share}$$

Note that reported earnings will remain at $15,000,000 and that the $500,000 adjustment to net income is **for computational purposes** only. If the preferred stock is *not* cumulative and no dividends have been declared, no adjustment to net income would be required for computing EPS, and it would remain at $15.00 per share.

Simple Capital Structure— Changing Number of Shares

One of the most common complexities of EPS calculations occurs when the number of common shares issued and outstanding fluctuates during the income measurement period. Assume that Danielson Corporation had reported earnings of $1,830,000 for 1984. Further assume that Table 22–2 summarizes all changes in the shares of common stock outstanding during 1984 resulting from the issuance and repurchase of shares. What should Danielson Corporation divide the $1,830,000 income by to report EPS for 1984? The answer is the weighted-average number of shares outstanding during 1984, which would be computed as follows:

BALANCE IN TOTAL SHARES ISSUED AND OUTSTANDING	×	FRACTION OF THE PERIOD (IN MONTHS) THAT BALANCE WAS MAINTAINED WITHOUT CHANGE	=	WEIGHTED-AVERAGE NUMBER OF SHARES OUTSTANDING FOR THE PERIOD
36,000 shares	×	2/12	=	6,000 shares
34,500 shares	×	4/12	=	11,500 shares
39,000 shares	×	2/12	=	6,500 shares
37,800 shares	×	4/12	=	12,600 shares
		12/12		36,600 shares

The weighted-average number of shares would be 36,600 for 1984, and Danielson would report EPS of $50 ($1,830,000/36,600 shares) for the year ending December

TABLE
22–2

SHARES OUTSTANDING—DANIELSON CORPORATION		
DATE	SHARES INCREASED (DECREASED)	TOTAL SHARES ISSUED AND OUTSTANDING
1/1/84	—	36,000
2/28/84	(1,500) Repurchase	34,500
6/30/84	4,500 Issue	39,000
9/1/84	(1,200) Repurchase	37,800
12/31/84	—	37,800

31, 1984. The weighted average number of shares can also be computed using a daily or a weekly number for shares outstanding.

The changes in the number of shares of stock outstanding resulting from issuance and repurchase of stock illustrated above are treated prospectively in computing the weighted-average number of shares outstanding during an accounting period. Changes in the number of shares that are the result of stock dividends and stock splits are given retroactive treatment, however, and are therefore treated as if they had always been outstanding. To illustrate, assume the same facts as in Table 22–2. In addition, assume that Danielson has a 2-for-1 stock split (or a 100 percent stock dividend) on March 23, 1984. In terms of the flow of events, the following time line represents this situation:

PROSPECTIVE		RETROACTIVE	PROSPECTIVE	
	REPURCHASE	SPLIT	ISSUE	REPURCHASE
1/1/84	2/28/84	3/23/84	6/30/84	9/1/84
36,000	−1,500	+34,500	+4,500	−1,200

The revised computation of weighted-average shares would be as follows:

PERIOD ENDING	BALANCE IN TOTAL SHARES ISSUED AND OUTSTANDING	×	FRACTION OF THE PERIOD (IN MONTHS) THAT BALANCE WAS MAINTAINED WITHOUT CHANGE	=	WEIGHTED-AVERAGE NUMBER OF SHARES OUTSTANDING FOR THE PERIOD
2/28/84	72,000	×	2/12	=	12,000 shares
6/30/84	69,000	×	4/12	=	23,000 shares
9/1/84	73,500	×	2/12	=	12,250 shares
12/31/84	72,300	×	4/12	=	24,100 shares
			12/12		71,350 shares

A total of 71,350 shares would be used to represent the weighted-average number of shares outstanding for 1984, resulting in EPS of $25.65.

Multiple EPS Figures and Complex Capital Structures

When corporations have securities outstanding that have the potential to be converted to common stock, the corporation is said to have a **complex capital structure.** The capital structure is complex because the measure of shares outstanding that best estimates the common shareholder interests of the corporation is unclear. Because of the potential dilution in per share earnings represented by securities that

TABLE
22–3

MULTIPLE EPS MEASURES

1. *Primary earnings per share.* Computed by dividing adjusted earnings by the weighted-average shares of common stock and common stock equivalents

$$\frac{\text{Net income} - \text{Preferred stock dividends } \textit{if} \text{ preferred stock } \textit{is not} \text{ a CSE} + \text{After-tax effect of bond interest expense } \textit{if} \text{ bonds } \textit{are} \text{ CSEs}}{\text{Weighted-average number of shares of common stock and common stock equivalents}}$$

2. *Fully diluted earnings per share.* Computed by dividing adjusted earnings by the maximum number of potential common shares, given the limitations prescribed in *APB Option No. 15.*

$$\frac{\text{Net income} - \text{Preferred stock dividends } \textit{if} \text{ preferred stock } \textit{is not} \text{ convertible to common} + \text{After-tax effect of bond interest expense on bonds convertible to common}}{\text{Weighted-average number of shares of common stock, assuming maximum dilution}}$$

have the potential to become common stock, it might be misleading to consider only the weighted-average shares of the actual common stock *outstanding* in computing EPS.[8] The accountant is faced with the problem of evaluating all the securities that have the potential to become common stock in order to estimate the probable number of shares of common by which net income should be divided.

Common stock equivalents (CSEs) are those securities that are not common stock but, in substance, are equivalent to common stock because they are likely to be converted to common stock in the future. Convertible debt, convertible preferred stock, stock rights, stock options, and stock warrants are all hybrid securities that have the ability to represent common stock equivalents and to dilute the computation of earnings per share.

Table 22–3 shows how the two EPS measures that are to be reported by firms with complex capital structures, called **primary EPS** and **fully diluted EPS,** are computed.

If all hybrid securities are considered to be dilutive common stock equivalents, then primary EPS would normally be **about the same** as fully diluted EPS. Note that only those hybrid securities that are dilutive **common stock equivalents** (CSEs) are considered in the denominator when computing **primary EPS.** All dilutive securities are considered in the denominator when computing **fully diluted EPS.** Note also that all securities that may be converted to common stock will not necessarily dilute (reduce) the EPS calculations if conversion is assumed.

Determining CSEs and Dilutive Effects

The various hybrid securities can all have somewhat different tests applied to them to help the accountant determine whether they are CSEs and whether they are dilutive. All **antidilutive securities** (those that increase EPS when conversion is assumed) are ignored in computing the shares in the denominator for both primary and fully diluted EPS calculations. All dilutive securities that are **also common stock equivalents** are considered in the denominator for both primary and fully diluted EPS calculations. All **dilutive securities** that are *not* CSEs are considered in the denominator for computing fully diluted earnings per share. The decision rule is

_____

[8] To have a dilutive effect simply means that the hybrid securities being considered will *reduce* EPS from what it would otherwise have been measured to be without (before) considering the convertible securities. As we shall see, some hybrid securities have an antidilutive effect whereby EPS is increased when the security is considered to represent common stock. Antidilutive securities are treated as not converted in computing primary and fully diluted EPS so as to present more conservative EPS measures.

FIGURE
22–1
Dilution—case
decision rule

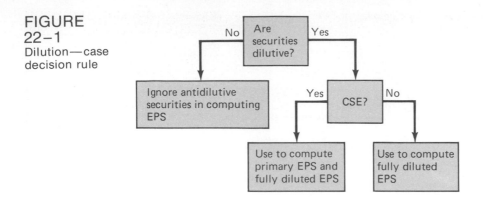

summarized in the flow chart in Figure 22–1. Bear in mind that it *is possible* (though unlikely) that a given security could be dilutive for one EPS calculation (for example, fully diluted), but *not* for the other calculation.

Test for dilution effect of rights, options, and warrants Rights, options, and warrants are always common stock equivalents but are not necessarily dilutive. The test to determine whether they are dilutive is essentially the same for all three. If the exercise price of the rights, options, or warrants is higher than the market price, the securities are antidilutive and do not enter into the EPS computation. However, if the exercise price is lower than the market price, the securities will have a dilutive effect on the EPS calculation. It should be noted that the market price used for comparison with the option price varies depending on whether primary or fully diluted EPS is being computed. The average market price for the period is used for primary EPS. Fully diluted EPS is based on the end-of-period market price or the average market price for the period, whichever yields the lowest EPS figure.[9] Also note that if the number of options is in excess of 20 percent of the issued stock, the treasury stock method (discussed below) must be used to determine whether the options are dilutive.

Test for dilution effect of convertibles Convertible preferred stock and convertible bonds are normally dilutive. To determine whether they have a dilutive effect, EPS (both primary and fully dilutive) must be computed with and without conversion assumed. If EPS is higher for either primary or fully diluted when conversion is assumed, then the convertible security is said to be **antidilutive.**

Test for common stock equivalency Table 22–4 summarizes the testing for common stock equivalency. Note that the CSE test for convertible securities is only made once, at the time the securities are issued. To illustrate, assume that Stefcik, Inc., issued $100,000 of convertible bonds with a stated interest rate of 7 percent at a premium that resulted in a cash yield of 6 percent (say $7,000/$116,666). Each $1,000 bond is convertible into 10 shares of Stefcik common. The current rate of interest on grade Aa bonds at the date the bonds are issued is 10 percent. Since two-thirds of the Aa bond rate would be $6\frac{2}{3}\%$ interest, any yield of less than $6\frac{2}{3}\%$

---

[9] *Accounting Principles Board Opinion No. 15,* "Earnings per Share," par. 36 and 42.

TABLE
22–4

TESTING FOR CSE	
TYPE OF SECURITY	**CSE TEST**
Stock options	Always a CSE; assume conversion if dilutive
Stock rights and warrants	Always a CSE; assume conversion if dilutive
Convertible preferred stock, convertible bonds, or convertible notes payable	A CSE if cash yield *at date of issuance* is less than two-thirds of the then current rate of interest on grade Aa corporate bonds.

would require the security to be considered a common stock equivalent.[10] Stefcik would add 10,000 shares of common to its denominator shares to compute EPS. To be consistent in both the numerator and the denominator, the after-tax effect of the bond interest expense would be added to net income. By adding the interest expense to income in the numerator and the equivalent shares of common to the denominator, the convertible bond is treated *as if it were converted* to common stock.

The tests discussed above outline the critical factors that accountants must consider in computing EPS for complex capital structures.[11] The following examples will illustrate these guidelines.

Computing the Dilutive Effect of Rights, Options, and Warrants

The dilutive effect of stock rights, options, and warrants can be computed by using the four-step **treasury stock measurement method** outlined in Table 22–5. To illustrate the treasury stock method for measuring dilution of rights, assume that the Keller Corporation issued 10,000 stock rights prior to January 1, 1984, and reported net income of $380,000 for the year.[12] Keller also has 100,000 shares of

TABLE
22–5

TREASURY STOCK MEASUREMENT PROCEDURE	
Step 1	*Assume* that the rights, options, and/or warrants have all been exercised, and compute the number of shares of common stock that would be issued and the cash that would be received (from the exercise price, if any).
Step 2	*Assume* that the cash (if any) from step 1 is used to repurchase treasury stock immediately at the appropriate market price (average for primary, and higher of average or year-end for fully diluted). Such assumed treasury stock purchases are limited to a maximum of 20 percent of the outstanding shares of common stock.
Step 3	Compute the *net new shares* assumed by taking the shares computed in step 1 and subtracting the shares computed in step 2, adding the *positive* number to the denominator. (Note that if the number of shares from step 2 is larger than the number from step 1, the securities are anti-dilutive.)
Step 4	(If necessary) *If* the cash from step 1 is more than enough to repurchase 20 percent of the outstanding common stock, it shall be *assumed* to be applied in order to first reduce short-term debt, then long-term debt, with the remainder *assumed* to be invested in U.S. government securities. This last step will affect the assumed income in the numerator by altering interest expense and possibly interest income.

[10] In 1982, **FASB Statement No. 55** changed the benchmark for convertibles from two-thirds of the bank prime rate to two-thirds of the Aa corporate bond rate because of wide fluctuations in the prime lending rate.

[11] For an alternative procedure for identifying the most dilutive EPS measure, see S. Davidson and R. Weil, "A Shortcut in Computing Earnings Per Share," *The Journal of Accountancy,* December 1975, pp. 45–47.

[12] If the rights are issued during the year, use the weighted-average approach to compute their equivalent shares of common (for example, 10,000 rights issued on June 30, 1984, would represent 5,000 equivalent shares for the year).

EXHIBIT 22–6

APPLICATION OF TREASURY STOCK PROCEDURE

Step 1 — 10,000 new shares of common stock assumed. $150,000 cash proceeds from rights assumed.

Step 2 — $150,000 cash can repurchase 7,500 shares ($150,000/$20) for primary EPS, and 6,000 shares ($150,000/$25) for fully diluted EPS.

Step 3 — Net new shares in denominator: 2,500 shares for primary (10,000 − 7,500), and 4,000 new shares for fully diluted (10,000 − 6,000).

Step 4 — Unnecessary in this case.

Computation:

PRIMARY EPS

$$\frac{\$380,000}{102,500 \text{ shares}} = \$3.71 \text{ per share}$$

FULLY DILUTED EPS

$$\frac{\$380,000}{104,000 \text{ shares}} = \$3.65 \text{ per share}$$

EXHIBIT 22–7

APPLICATION OF TREASURY STOCK PROCEDURE

Step 1 — 10,000 new shares of common stock assumed.
$150,000 cash proceeds from rights assumed.

Step 2 — $150,000 cash can repurchase 4,000 shares (= maximum of 20 percent of common stock outstanding for both primary and fully diluted EPS):

$$\frac{\$150,000}{\$20} = 7,500, \text{ which is greater than 4,000; therefore, use 4,000 for primary.}$$

$$\frac{\$150,000}{\$25} = 6,000, \text{ which is greater than 4,000; therefore, use 4,000 for fully diluted.}$$

Step 3 — Net new shares in denominator: 6,000 for both (10,000 − 4,000).

Step 4 — Cash remaining after step 2 would be $70,000 primary ($150,000 − $80,000) and $50,000 fully diluted ($150,000 − $100,000).

Adjusted net income for primary and fully diluted EPS would be computed as follows:

	NUMERATOR NET INCOME FOR PRIMARY	NUMERATOR NET INCOME FOR FULLY DILUTED
Net income	$380,000	$380,000
Plus interest on short-term debt	3,000[a]	3,000[a]
Plus interest on long-term debt	4,800[b]	2,400[c]
Less tax effect	(3,120)	(2,160)
Adjusted net income	$384,680	$383,240

[a] Assume that $30,000 was used to retire short-term debt.
[b] Assume that $40,000 was used to retire long-term debt.
[c] Assume that $20,000 was used to retire long-term debt.

Computation:

PRIMARY EPS

$$\frac{\$384,680}{26,000 \text{ shares}} = \$14.80 \text{ per share}$$

FULLY DILUTED EPS

$$\frac{\$383,240}{26,000 \text{ shares}} = \$14.74 \text{ per share}$$

TABLE
22–6

"AS IF CONVERTED" PROCEDURE FOR TESTING CONVERTIBLES

Step 1   Determine the number of shares of common stock to which the convertible security can be converted and add it to the shares in the denominator.

Step 2   *For convertible bonds,* determine the after-tax effect of the bond interest expense and add it to net income in the numerator. *For convertible preferred,* do not adjust net income for preferred dividends.

common stock issued and outstanding throughout 1984. Each right is convertible into one share of common at an exercise price of $15 per share. The average market price for 1984 was $20 per share and the year-end market price was $25 per share. The solution is shown in Exhibit 22–6.

Although step 4 is seldom involved in the computation, let us illustrate this step by first reducing the number of shares of Keller Corporation common stock outstanding from 100,000 shares to 20,000 shares. Further, assume that Keller had $30,000 of short-term 10 percent debt and $100,000 of long-term 12 percent debt. Keller deducted $3,000 and $12,000 in interest expense, respectively, on the short- and long-term debt in computing the $380,000 net income figure reported for 1984. Keller had an effective tax expense rate of 40 percent for 1984. Exhibit 22–7 shows how primary and fully diluted EPS would be computed.

Although the Keller Corporation examples involve stock rights, the same principles and procedures apply to stock warrants and stock options.

Computing the Dilutive Effect of Convertible Securities

The dilutive effect of convertible securities can be computed by using the two-step "as if converted" procedure outlined in Table 22–6. Note that this procedure, like that for rights, options, and warrants, attempts to measure the impact on the EPS figures *as if* the convertible securities had been converted to common stock. To illustrate, assume that Skadden, Inc., had the following capital structure as of December 31, 1984:

SKADDEN, INC.
Partial Balance Sheet
December 31, 1984

Long-term liabilities:	$10,000,000
Convertible bonds, 7% interest, $1,000 par value bonds, issued at par on 1/1/80, maturity date 12/31/99, each convertible into 10 shares of Skadden common after December 31, 1987	
Owners' equity:	
10% cumulative preferred, par $100; issued and outstanding, 25,000 shares	$ 2,500,000
6% convertible cumulative preferred, par $100, convertible into one share of common per share; issued and outstanding, 25,000 shares	2,500,000
Common stock, par $1, authorized 2,000,000 shares; issued and outstanding, 1,500,000 shares	1,500,000
Capital in excess of par	
On common	$6,000,000
On 10% preferred	275,000
On 6% preferred	250,000
Retained earnings	6,525,000
	10,850,000
Total owners' equity	$23,875,000

Additional facts for the Skadden, Inc., example:

1. Skadden's 1984 net income after tax, $9,595,000
2. Skadden's effective 1984 tax rate, 25 percent
3. Aa bond rate when bonds were issued, 14 percent
4. Aa bond rate when 6 percent preferred stock was issued, 8 percent
5. Dividend rate on 10 percent preferred stock, $10 per share per year
6. Dividend rate on 6 percent preferred stock, $6 per share per year
7. Yield on convertible debt, $70/$1,000 = 7 percent per year
8. Yield on 6% preferred stock, $6/$110 = 5.45 percent per year

Recall that to test for dilution, the EPS calculations must be made with and without conversion assumed. To test for CSE, the yield on both of the convertible issues must be compared with their respective grade Aa bond interest rates at date of issuance. In the Skadden example, the convertible bonds *are* CSEs—7% is greater than (14% × ⅔)—and their conversion is assumed in computing both primary and fully diluted EPS. The 6 percent preferred is *not* a CSE—5.45% is greater than (8% × ⅔)—and its conversion is assumed only for computing fully diluted EPS. Of course, the 10 percent preferred is *not* convertible and, therefore, not considered except as its dividends affect the numerator. The "as if converted" tests of the convertibles for the primary and fully diluted EPS computations of Skadden, Inc., are computed as follows:

CONVERTIBLE BONDS—FOR PRIMARY EPS

Step 1 $10,000,000/$1,000 = 10,000 bonds, each convertible into 10 shares of common for a total potential new shares of common = 100,000 shares

Step 2 $700,000 of 1984 bond interest expense converts to a $525,000 addition to the numerator ($700,000 × (1 − Tax rate) = $700,000 × .75 = $525,000)

CONVERTIBLE PREFERRED—FOR FULLY DILUTED EPS

Step 1 $2,500,000/$100 = 25,000 shares of 6 percent preferred, which are convertible into 25,000 shares of common

Step 2 Do not adjust numerator net income for $150,000 in 6 percent preferred dividends

---

Note that there is also $250,000 in dividends on the 10 percent preferred stock that must be deducted from the numerator net income figure in computing both EPS figures. For primary EPS, the $150,000 dividends on the 6 percent convertible preferred must be subtracted from the numerator net income because the 6 percent preferred is not a CSE. The EPS calculations would be:

PRIMARY EPS

$$\frac{\begin{matrix}\text{Net} \\ \text{income}\end{matrix} - \begin{matrix}\text{Preferred stock dividends } if \\ \text{preferred stock is } not \text{ a CSE}\end{matrix} + \begin{matrix}\text{After-tax bond interest} \\ \text{expense } if \text{ bonds } are \text{ CSEs}\end{matrix}}{\text{Weighted-average number of shares of common stock and CSEs}}$$

$$= \frac{\$9,595,000 - (\$250,000 + \$150,000) + \$525,000}{1,500,000 \text{ shares} + 100,000 \text{ CSE shares}}$$

$$= \frac{\$9,720,000}{1,600,000} = \underline{\$6.08} \text{ primary EPS}$$

$$\frac{\text{Net income} - \frac{\text{Preferred stock dividends } if}{\text{preferred stock } is \; not \text{ convertible}} + \frac{\text{After-tax bond interest}}{\text{expense on convertible bonds}}}{\substack{\text{Weighted-average number of shares of common stock} \\ \text{and potential common shares}}}$$

$$= \frac{\$9,595,000 - \$250,000 + \$525,000}{1,500,000 \text{ shares } + 25,000 \text{ shares} + 100,000 \text{ shares}}$$

$$= \frac{\$9,870,000}{1,625,000} = \underline{\$6.07} \text{ fully diluted EPS}$$

In the case of Skadden, Inc., how can we be certain that the convertible bonds or preferred stocks are dilutive? The best way to check this is to compute both primary and fully diluted EPS with and without assuming their conversion. In the Skadden example, primary EPS without assuming the bonds are converted would have been $9,195,000/1,500,000 shares = $6.13. Hence we can conclude that the bonds had a dilutive effect on EPS.

Another way of looking at this is to compute the "equivalent EPS" on the **bonds alone** by considering the bonds' impact on both the numerator and the denominator; in this case, $525,000/100,000 shares = $5.25 per share. For bonds to be dilutive, **EPS before considering the bonds (as if converted) would have to be greater than $5.25 per share.** If EPS were less than $5.25, the bonds would be antidilutive.

The fully diluted EPS without the impact of the bonds would have been $9,345,000/1,525,000 = $6.13. Without the impact of the convertible preferred, fully diluted EPS would have been $9,720,000/1,600,000 = $6.08 (the same as primary EPS). In the case illustrated, both primary and fully diluted EPS are *diluted* by the convertible securities. The difference between the two EPS numbers is so slight that Skadden would not be required to report two different and separate EPS figures. When the dilutive effect on per share computations is less than 3 percent for primary EPS or fully diluted EPS or between the two, it is not necessary to consider the dilutive effect in the computation and presentation of EPS.[13]

Reporting EPS for Unusual Events

When corporations report unusual events in their income statements, they should also report them on a per share basis.[14] Three possible unusual events could receive separate income statement disclosure and, therefore, should receive separate EPS treatment:

1. Discontinued operations
2. Extraordinary items
3. Cumulative effect of accounting changes

When any of these items appear in the income statement, their corresponding per share effect should also be reported in the EPS data. A corporation's income statement containing EPS disclosures is shown in Exhibit 22–8.

[13] *Accounting Principles Board Opinion No. 15,* "Earnings per Share," par. 15.

[14] Although separate disclosure is only *required* for Income from Continuing Operations and Net Income, *Accounting Principles Board Opinion No. 15,* "Earnings per Share," strongly encourages separate disclosure of unusual events on a per share basis as well. EPS disclosures are also required for cumulative effects of an accounting change.

EXHIBIT
22–8

EPS DISCLOSURES

EASCO CORPORATION AND SUBSIDIARY COMPANIES
Consolidated Statements of Income

(DOLLAR AMOUNTS IN THOUSANDS, EXCEPT PER SHARE DATA)

FOR THE YEARS ENDED DECEMBER 31,	1980	1979	1978
Net sales	$357,287	$351,721	$317,448
Costs and expenses			
Cost of products sold, exclusive of depreciation	299,022	288,207	254,199
Selling, general and administrative expenses	41,836	38,314	35,456
Provision for depreciation of properties	5,163	4,772	4,706
Interest expense	4,832	5,132	4,555
	350,853	336,416	298,916
Income before income taxes	6,434	15,305	18,532
Provision for federal and state income taxes			
Current (reduced by investment tax credits of $502, $448, and $1,337)	3,305	6,549	6,804
Deferred	(589)	573	1,291
	2,716	7,122	8,095
Net Income	$ 3,718	$ 8,183	$ 10,437
Per share earnings applicable to common stock			
Primary—assuming no dilution	$.97	$2.30	$3.18
Fully diluted	$.97	$2.21	$2.88

The accompanying notes are an integral part of these financial statements.

EPS Analysis

The flow chart in Figure 22–2 summarizes the measurement of EPS discussed in the last part of this chapter. As mentioned earlier, EPS is a rather simple concept but may be very difficult to operationalize. Some accountants believe that reporting income on a per share basis is important in financial reporting, whereas others believe that the per share figures may be misleading and are of relatively little significance. Certainly the accounting rules governing EPS measurement contain a number of rather arbitrary elements, such as the two-thirds of grade Aa bond interest rate criterion for the convertible bonds. Moreover, there is little or no relationship between GAAP for EPS measurement and the conceptual framework of accounting. The goal of anticipating which hybrid securities will eventually be converted to common stock may be a valid goal for accounting to pursue, but the procedures currently applied in pursuit of the goal have left the profession open to criticism.

The research that has been reported on the stock market's pricing of the common stocks of entities with complex capital structures suggests that the market treats complex securities as debt when such securities are not likely to be converted to common stock (called **overhanging issues**). In contrast, the market treats complex securities that are likely to be converted as if they were common stocks. This is consistent with finance theory, which demonstrates through the use of arbitrage proofs that there is no difference in the value of firms with simple and complex capital structures, all else being equal.[15] Since the accounting treatment of complex securities (discussed in this chapter) is not consistent with the market's identification of

[15] For a good review of this literature and some empirical evidence, see Thomas Frecka, "The Effects of Complex Capital Structures on the Market Value of Firms" (Ph.D. diss., Syracuse University, December 1977). Also, see E. Fama and M. Miller *The Theory of Finance* (Hinsdale, IL: Dryden Press, 1972).

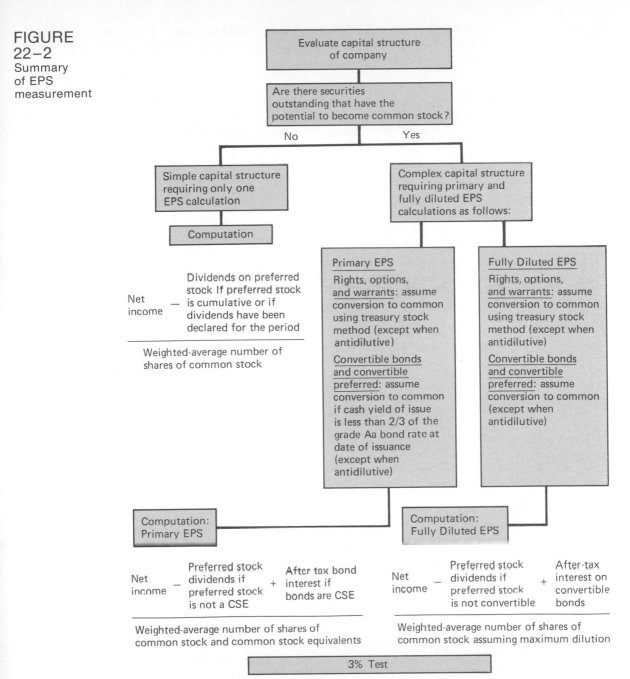

FIGURE 22–2
Summary of EPS measurement

Evaluate capital structure of company

Are there securities outstanding that have the potential to become common stock?

No — Simple capital structure requiring only one EPS calculation

Yes — Complex capital structure requiring primary and fully diluted EPS calculations as follows:

Computation

$$\frac{\text{Net income} - \text{Dividends on preferred stock If preferred stock is cumulative or if dividends have been declared for the period}}{\text{Weighted-average number of shares of common stock}}$$

Primary EPS

Rights, options, and warrants: assume conversion to common using treasury stock method (except when antidilutive)

Convertible bonds and convertible preferred: assume conversion to common if cash yield of issue is less than 2/3 of the grade Aa bond rate at date of issuance (except when antidilutive)

Fully Diluted EPS

Rights, options, and warrants: assume conversion to common using treasury stock method (except when antidilutive)

Convertible bonds and convertible preferred: assume conversion to common (except when antidilutive)

Computation: Primary EPS

$$\frac{\text{Net income} - \text{Preferred stock dividends if preferred stock is not a CSE} + \text{After tax bond interest if bonds are CSE}}{\text{Weighted-average number of shares of common stock and common stock equivalents}}$$

Computation: Fully Diluted EPS

$$\frac{\text{Net income} - \text{Preferred stock dividends if preferred stock is not convertible} + \text{After-tax interest on convertible bonds}}{\text{Weighted-average number of shares of common stock assuming maximum dilution}}$$

3% Test

If fully diluted EPS is less than 3% below primary EPS, only primary EPS need be reported which issues will or will not be converted to common stock, it suggests that the market pricing mechanism is not completely consistent with the accounting EPS measurement process.

Although some aspects of these rules may seem confusing or even somewhat inconsistent, EPS measurement will undoubtedly continue to be an extremely important measure of income from the viewpoint of many external users of financial statements. Understanding how it is computed and what variables may affect its measurement will permit a more cautious and appropriate application of the EPS figures in business decisions.

FUNDS FLOW EFFECTS

Hybrid securities are characterized by complex contracts between the entity and its employees or outside capital investors. The objective of these securities is to provide the entity with additional sources of working capital or cash in one of two ways: (1) providing new sources of cash or working capital through the issuance of hybrid securities such as convertible debt; or (2) providing a savings in cash outflow by substituting hybrid securities such as stock options for other forms of employee compensation. In the second situation, cash or working capital inflows may also accrue to the entity when certain types of options are exercised by employees.

There is only one common situation in which hybrid securities have an impact on measuring the "funds provided by operations," and the effect of this situation is the same for both cash and working capital. When stock options, stock appreciation rights, and restricted stock options are considered to represent compensation expense according to GAAP, they generally result in an expense that does not result in either a cash or a working capital outflow. As a result, compensation expense based on these securities should be added back to (or subtracted from) net income in arriving at "funds provided by operations." Also, SARs to be paid in cash would provide an example of an accrued compensation liability that would be classified as current if the exercise period were less than a period away. Such an example was illustrated earlier in the chapter in the Perry case.

SUMMARY

In this chapter we have considered the measurement problems involved with hybrid securities. These securities have been developed to facilitate corporate capital formation and to strengthen the goal congruence between employers and employees through the careful design of incentive compensation contracts. The problems involved in measuring the costs of compensation schemes and matching them with the benefits (employees' efforts) are not solvable in an objective sense because of the degree to which they are based on uncertain future events. The procedures to account for these various compensation schemes illustrated in the chapter must be evaluated with the understanding that the *relevance* of measuring employee benefits takes precedence over the *reliability* of the measurements. Conceptually, we must argue that employees are receiving something with expected future value, and that they are earning these future benefits through their current and future efforts on the entity's behalf. The *accrual model* and the *matching concept* suggest that it is relevant to measure and account for these future benefits while being earned rather than when received. We must, therefore, deal with the lack of reliable measures as best we can by applying conventional measurement procedures used for changes in accounting estimates to deal with the inherent uncertainty in such compensation schemes.

The hybrid securities considered here and in earlier chapters have a complicating effect on earnings per share measurement. The earnings per share number is probably the most widely cited, most frequently quoted element of financial accounting information. The measurement process is fairly straightforward in cases of simple capital structure. When complex capital structures are present, however, guidance for the accounting treatment of the hybrid securities is not found in the conceptual framework of accounting. The illustrations of the various securities and their appropriate accounting procedures draw heavily on the rule aspects of GAAP, with only a minor tie to the theoretical accounting framework. The material covered here focuses on common shareholders' interests and how they are accounted for through EPS measurement, as well as the employees' interests and how owners contract with employees through hybrid securities in an effort to motivate employees to set and attain goals that will be beneficial to the entity. Reporting on the nature of employee incentive contracts and reporting on the per share performance of the firm, although not always directly related to one another, have common attributes in their involvement with the accounting aspects of equity and near-equity securities. Both subjects represent important dimensions of financial reporting and are capable of having a material impact on key financial results such as net income and EPS. As a result, users of financial report information should carefully evaluate the impact of these subjects on the entity's financial statements when making business decisions concerning the entity.

QUESTIONS

22–1 Define convertible bonds, stock warrants, stock rights, stock options, and debt issued with warrants attached.

22–2 Why do corporations issue convertible bonds and convertible preferred stock instead of common stock?

22–3 Why would a corporation issue stock rights, stock warrants, and stock options?

22–4 Define the following types of compensation arrangements: compensatory stock option plans; noncompensatory stock option plans; stock appreciation rights (SARs); restricted stock offerings (RSOs).

22–5 At what date (what point in time) is the value of an employee's stock option determined according to GAAP?

22–6 Explain the similarities and differences between calls and stock options.

22–7 What is a *simple capital structure?* Give an example.

22–8 What is a *complex capital structure?* Give an example.

22–9 What is a *common stock equivalent?* Give an example.

22–10 What is the test for determining whether stock rights, stock options, or stock warrants are common stock equivalents?

22–11 What is the test for determining whether convertible bonds or convertible preferred stocks are common stock equivalents?

22–12 How large must the dilution effect (difference between primary EPS and fully diluted EPS) be before both of these EPS figures must be reported?

22–13 From the entity's point of view, what are the primary advantages, if any, of a compensatory stock option plan in lieu of a cash bonus?

22–14 From the entity's point of view, what are the primary advantages, if any, of a noncompensatory stock option plan in lieu of a cash bonus?

22–15 From the employee's perspective, what is the advantage of an SAR plan versus a stock option plan?

22–16 From the employer's perspective, what are the most attractive features of an SAR plan?

22–17 From the employee's perspective, what is the advantage of an RSO plan versus a stock option plan?

22–18 From the employee's perspective, what are the most attractive features of RSO plans?

22–19 What impact do RSO shares have on the computation of EPS during the restricted period prior to their unconditional issuance to employees?

22–20 What impact do SARs have on the computation of EPS during the period between the date of grant and the exercise date?

CASES

C22–1 (CPA ADAPTED) Jones Company has adopted a traditional stock option plan for its officers and other employees. This plan is properly considered a compensatory plan.

REQUIRED Discuss how accounting for this plan will affect net earnings and earnings per share. *Ignore income tax considerations and accounting for income tax benefits.*

C22–2 (CPA ADAPTED) Public enterprises are required to present earnings-per-share data on the face of the income statement.

REQUIRED Compare and contrast primary earnings per share with fully diluted earnings per share for each of the following:

1. The effect of common stock equivalents on the number of shares used in the computation of earnings-per-share data
2. The effect of convertible securities that are *not* common stock equivalents on the number of shares used in the computation of earnings-per-share data
3. The effect of antidilutive securities.

C22–3 Noncompensatory stock option plans are considered to be of value to some but do not appear to be of value according to their treatment under GAAP. What four conditions must these stock option plans meet? Discuss the reasoning behind each of these four conditions, and explain why someone might consider a noncompensatory option to be valuable. In light of the reasons why a noncompensatory option has some value, why doesn't accounting measure and report that value?

C22–4 On July 1, 1984, R. H. Raymond, Inc., issued 15,000 stock options to company employees as a bonus for excellent second-quarter profits. The options, issued on a pro rata basis to all employees, would be exercisable in 2 years and would expire on September 1, 1986. The exercise price was $23 per share, only $3 below the average market price during the first half of 1984. Trading in Raymond common on July 1 was brisk because of the news about the profits and the options, and Raymond closed at $22 per share on the date of the grant. The market price on December 31, 1984, was $24 per share. Mr. Raymond and his employees were all very pleased with the new plan.

REQUIRED Discuss the nature of this stock option plan and show how it would be recorded on Raymond's books during 1984. Explain the impact on Raymond's financial statements and on the employees' wealth position. Why, do you think, were the employees so happy with this plan? Why is Mr. Raymond happy? Discuss the reason for any inconsistency between the employees' feelings and the financial statements' impact of the option plan.

C22–5 (CPA ADAPTED) The earnings-per-share data required of a company depend on the nature of its capital structure. A corporation may have a simple capital structure and only compute "earnings per common share," or it may have a complex capital structure and have to compute "primary earnings per share" and "fully diluted earnings per share."

REQUIRED

1. What securities would be considered *common stock equivalents* in the computation of earnings per share?
2. What disclosures (both financial and explanatory) are necessary for earnings per share when a corporation has a *complex capital structure?*

C22–6 (CPA ADAPTED) Earnings per share (EPS) is the most featured single financial statistic about modern corporations. Daily published quotations of the stock prices of many securities have recently been expanded to include a "times earnings" (a price over earnings, or P/E, ratio) figure based on EPS. Analysts' discussions will often focus on the EPS of specific corporations.

REQUIRED

1. Explain how dividends or dividend requirements on any class of preferred stock that may be outstanding can affect the computation of EPS.
2. One of the technical procedures applicable in EPS computations is the "treasury stock method":
   a. Briefly describe the circumstances under which it might be appropriate to apply the treasury stock method.
   b. There is a limit to the extent to which the treasury stock method is applicable. Indicate what this limit is, and give a succinct indication of the procedures that should be followed beyond the treasury stock limits.
3. Under some circumstances, convertible debentures would be considered "common stock equivalents"; under other circumstances, they would not.
   a. When is it proper to treat convertible debentures as common stock equivalents? What is the effect on the computation of EPS in such cases?
   b. When convertible debentures are not considered common stock equivalents, how are they handled for purposes of EPS computations?

C22–7 (CPA ADAPTED) A corporation has a noncompensatory stock purchase plan for all of its employees and a compensatory stock option plan for some of its corporate officers.

REQUIRED

1. Compare and contrast the accounting at the date the stock is issued for the noncompensatory stock purchase plan and the compensatory stock option plan.
2. What entry should be made for the compensatory stock option plan at the date of the grant?

EXERCISES

E22–1 The Merit Company has 26,000 shares of common stock issued and outstanding at the end of 1984, 20,000 of which have been outstanding throughout the year. On May 1, 1984, Merit issued options on 4,000 shares to its employees at an exercise price of $10 per share, and it also sold an additional 6,000 shares at a market price of $9 per share. Merit reported net income for 1984 of $28,000 and paid cash dividends during 1984 to both the preferred stockholders ($4,000) and the common stockholders ($8,000).

REQUIRED Compute the primary and fully diluted EPS to be reported by Merit at the end of 1984, and the price-earnings ratio on Merit common assuming a year-end price of $8.50 per share.

E22–2 The Jessica Mowery Corporation had 4,000,000 shares of common stock outstanding at the beginning of 1985. On April 1, 1985, Jessica issued 1,000,000 shares of convertible preferred stock that were not considered to be common stock equivalents but would be convertible to 1,000,000 shares of common after 1990. On June 20, 1985, Jessica had a 2-for-1 common stock split. On July 1, 1985, Jessica issued an additional 500,000 shares of common stock for $10 per share. During 1985 Jessica paid cash dividends of $2,000,000 on preferred stock and $6,375,000 on common stock. In 1985 Jessica paid taxes of $8,000,000 resulting in net income of $16,000,000.

REQUIRED

1. Compute primary and fully diluted EPS for Jessica for 1985.
2. Assume that there was *no* activity in the preferred stock or common stock during 1984 and that at the end of 1984 Jessica had reported net income of $12,000,000 and EPS of $3 per share. Show how these 1984 data might be reported in 1985 for comparative statement purposes.

E22–3 In 1983 Great Lakes Hardware established a stock option plan for its employees. All management personnel with full-time jobs were eligible to participate in the plan. Under the conditions of the plan, every employee receives 10 options for each full year of employment with the company. The employee must remain employed by Great Lakes for 3 years beyond the date of the grant before the options can be exercised. Once the options become exercisable, they must be exercised within an 8-month period or they expire. On December 28, 1983, Great Lakes granted a total of 2,580 options to its employees at an option price of $18 per share. The market price of Great Lakes had fluctuated between $12 and $26 per share during 1983 and was selling for $20 per share on the date of the grant. The year-end closing price of Great Lakes was $21 per share.

REQUIRED

1. Record the necessary entries for the stock option plan for 1983. Fully explain the basis for your answer.
2. Show how these options would be reported in the 1983 balance sheet or in the balance sheet footnotes.

E22–4 On September 1, 1984, C. G. Carpenter, Inc., issued stock options to a few of Carpenter's key employees —Bean, Jasper, Hoyt, and Moekel. The options enabled each of the four employees to purchase up to 1,000 shares of Carpenter, Inc., stock for $28 per share between September 1, 1986, and December 31, 1986, providing they were still employed by Carpenter during the exercise period. On September 1, 1984, the closing price of Carpenter common was $30 per share. The 1984 year-end closing price was $36 per share, $6 above the average price for 1984.

REQUIRED

1. What kind of a stock option plan is involved?
2. Record any entries you think might be necessary to report these options on Carpenter's books for 1984 and 1985.

E22–5 The B. Basi Corporation has had several changes in its capital structure for the year 1985 as follows:

1/1/85	400,000 shares of common stock outstanding
2/28/85	Issued 25,000 shares of common stock
6/30/85	Issued 50,000 stock rights
9/30/85	Issued 40,000 shares of preferred stock with 40,000 common stock warrants attached

Each stock right entitled the holder to acquire one share of common stock at $15 per share. Each stock warrant entitled the holder to acquire one share of common stock at $20 per share. The average price of common stock during 1985 was $25 per share, and the year-end price was $28 per share.

REQUIRED Compute the weighted-average number of shares of common stock and common stock equivalents to be used for computing primary EPS for 1985. Also compute the weighted-average number of shares to be used for computing fully diluted EPS for 1985.

E22–6 Repeat exercise 22–5, assuming instead that the average price of common stock for 1985 was $18 per share and that the year-end price was $19 per share.

E22–7 Repeat exercise 22–5, assuming instead that the beginning number of shares of common stock outstanding is 100,000 instead of 400,000 and that the average price of common stock for 1985 was $40 per share, with the year-end price equal to $50 per share.

E22–8 On January 1, 1984, Mr. T. Burns was elected president of the Shank Corporation. As a part of his employment contract, Burns received stock options to purchase 30,000 shares of Shank common at $10 per share some time between December 31, 1986, and July 1, 1987. On the date the options were issued (January 1, 1984), Shank common was selling for $11 per share. The following stock price quotes were available for Shank common:

12/31/84	$13 per share
12/31/85	$15 per share
12/31/86	$18 per share

On December 31, 1986, Burns exercised 20,000 options.

REQUIRED

1. Is this a noncompensatory stock option plan? Explain.
2. What entries, if any, would be recorded on Shank Corporation's books between January 1, 1984, and December 31, 1986?

E22–9 On December 27, 1983, J. T. Thompson, Inc., issued stock options to Dubke, an employee of Thompson's, allowing Dubke to purchase shares of Thompson between January 1, 1986, and July 31, 1986, for 10 percent below the market value of the stock. Dubke was to receive a number of options equal to his 1986 salary (as determined on December 31, 1985) divided by $100, rounded to the nearest number of options. Dubke's expected 1986 salary was $100,000 at the date of the grant. The market price at the date of the grant was $35 per share. The market price increased to $40 per share by the end of 1984 and $45 per share by the end of 1985.

REQUIRED

1. Record the impact of these stock options, if any, on Thompson's books for the years ending December 31, 1983 and 1984.
2. Assume that Dubke's 1986 salary is set at $108,600 on December 31, 1985. Record the 1985 entry, if any, to account for the stock options.

E22–10 (CPA ADAPTED)

_____ 1. What is the inherent justification underlying the concept of common stock equivalents in an earnings-per-share computation?
   a. Form over substance
   b. Substance over form
   c. Form and substance considered equally
   d. Substance over form or form over substance, depending on the circumstances

_____ 2. In a primary earnings-per-share computation, the treasury stock method is used for options and warrants to reflect assumed reacquisition of common stock at the average market price during the period. If the exercise price of the options or warrants exceeds the average market price, the computation would
   a. Fairly present primary earnings per share on a prospective basis
   b. Fairly present the maximum potential dilution of primary earnings per share on a prospective basis
   c. Reflect the excess of the number of shares assumed issued over the number of shares assumed reacquired as the potential dilution of earnings per share
   d. Be antidilutive

_____ 3. The nature of primary earnings per share involving adjustment for stock options can be described as
   a. Historical because earnings are historical
   b. Historical because it indicates the firm's valuation
   c. Pro forma because it indicates potential changes in the number of shares
   d. Pro forma because it indicates potential changes in earnings

_____ 4. With respect to the computation of earnings per share, which of the following would be _most_ indicative of a simple capital structure?

a. Common stock, preferred stock, and convertible securities outstanding in lots of even thousands
b. Earnings derived from one primary line of business
c. Ownership interests consisting solely of common stock
d. Equity represented materially by liquid assets

_____ 5. In computing earnings per share, the equivalent number of shares of convertible preferred stock is added as an adjustment to the denominator (number of shares outstanding). If the preferred stock is preferred as to dividends, which amount should then be added as an adjustment to the numerator (net earnings)?
a. Annual preferred dividend
b. Annual preferred dividend times 1 minus the income tax rate
c. Annual preferred dividend times the income tax rate
d. Annual preferred dividend divided by the income tax rate

_____ 6. Which of the following statements best describes the effect of cash yield at issuance of convertible securities on calculating earnings per share (EPS)?
a. If less than two-thirds of the current interest rate on Aa bonds these securities are used to calculate primary EPS but *not* fully diluted EPS.
b. If less than two-thirds of the current interest rate on Aa bonds, these securities are used to calculate fully diluted EPS but *not* primary EPS.
c. If greater than two-thirds of the current interest rate on Aa bonds, these securities are used to calculate primary EPS and fully diluted EPS.
d. If greater than two-thirds of the current interest rate on Aa bonds, these securities are used to calculate fully diluted EPS but *not* primary EPS.

_____ 7. A company issued a new class of convertible preferred stock during the year. At the date of issuance, the cash yield on the stock was 60 percent of the interest rate on Aa bonds. By the end of the year, however, the cash yield was equal to 90 percent of the interest rate on Aa bonds. At the end of the year, what type of classification should this security receive for computation of earnings per share?
a. Long-term debt equivalent
b. Other potentially dilutive security
c. Convertible preferred stock
d. Common stock equivalent security

PROBLEMS

P22-1 Assume that on July 1, 1984, the P. E. Meyer Corporation issued $1,000,000 in convertible bonds that yield 10 percent. The bonds mature on June 30, 1994, and pay nominal interest of 9 percent per year. Interest is paid semiannually on June 30 and December 31. Each $1,000 bond is convertible into 20 shares of Meyer no par common stock on or after December 31, 1986. On the bond issue date, Meyer common was selling for $50 per share, and grade Aa bonds were selling in the market to yield 14 percent. On July 1, 1984, the prime lending rate was 16 percent.

REQUIRED

1. What was the issue price of the convertible bonds?
2. What premium did investors in Meyer bonds pay for the right to convert to common stock?
3. Are the Meyer bonds considered to be common stock equivalents?
4. Explain why your answers to requirements 2 and 3 are or are not consistent.
5. Record the issuance of the bonds on July 1, 1984, and the first semiannual interest payments.
6. Record conversion of the $1,000,000 of bonds on December 31, 1986. Assume that Meyer common is selling for $70 per share on this date.

P22-2 On May 1, 1985, the W. T. Granite Corporation, as a last-ditch effort to avoid bankruptcy, hired a well-known chief executive officer (CEO) to run the company. Granite agreed to pay the CEO, as part of his compensation, options to acquire 100,000 shares of Granite common at $12.50 per share. The options could be exercised between January 1, 1987, and June 30, 1988, providing the CEO was still working for Granite at the exercise date. Granite common stock was selling for $10.00 per share on the date of the grant (May 1, 1985). Granite common stock was selling for $14.00 per share on December 31, 1985, and had increased to $16.00 per share by December 31, 1986. On June 30, 1987, when Granite common was selling for $17.00 per share, the CEO exercised one-half of the options.

REQUIRED

1. Record all of the necessary entries on Granite's books to account for the stock options from May 1, 1985, to December 31, 1987. Granite has a December 31 year-end.
2. Repeat requirement 1, assuming that either the option price or the number of shares were not known until the end of 1985.
3. Explain how the December 31 year-end affects the accounting entries recorded in requirement 1.

P22–3 J. Collins Ltd. employs 2,000 managers in its consulting services business. As an incentive for its managers, Collins offers stock options to any employee who works on a consulting assignment and meets certain requirements. For each $1,000 in revenue from a consulting assignment that covers salary and computer costs by more than $30,000, the employee or employees on the assignment will receive 10 options to purchase Collins common. For example, if two employees worked on an assignment where gross billings were $85,000, and salaries for the assignment plus computer costs were $28,000, they would share 270 options:

Gross billings	$85,000
Direct costs	−28,000
Minimum contribution	−30,000
Excess contribution	$27,000 ÷ $1,000 = 27 × 10 options = 270 options

During 1983 Collins had 15 managers who collectively worked on 38 different assignments that exceeded salaries and computer costs by more than $30,000. The total of these excess contributions amounted to $487,500, with each of the managers earning 325 options on average. Employees must remain in Collins's employ for 1 year beyond the date of grant before the options can be exercised. Compensation expense is recorded in the year options are first earned.

On December 31, 1983, the first year of this plan, Collins issued 4,125 options to purchase Collins common at $40 per share to 13 of the 15 managers who remained in Collins's employ at the end of 1983. Collins common closed at $56 per share on December 31, 1983. Collins has experienced employee turnover of about 25 percent per year during the last 5 years.

REQUIRED Record any journal entries necessary to account for the stock option plan on Collins's books for 1983. Assume 50 percent of the compensation is expensed in 1983.

P22–4 Refer to the data in the preceding problem, and consider the following additional data. During 1984 Collins had 24 employees earning options that would have enabled them to collectively purchase 7,840 shares of Collins at $45 per share. Because of employee turnover, only 6,450 options were issued to 20 employees on December 31, 1984. These options were exercisable 1 year from the date of grant.

On December 31, 1984, when Collins common was selling at $58 per share, all 3,820 options issued on December 31, 1983, to the 12 managers who were still employed by Collins on December 31, 1984, were exercised.

REQUIRED

1. Record the necessary entries to account for Collins's stock options for 1984. Assume 50 percent of the options from 1984 are expensed in 1984.
2. Illustrate the footnote disclosure regarding options that would appear in the Collins 1984 annual report.

P22–5 As a Christmas bonus in 1983, B. Wolverton, Inc., issued stock options to its top ten employees. Each of the ten employees was to receive one option for each $100 of salary for 1986. Although the company's 1986 salary decision would not be made until early 1986, the following data were available early in 1984:

FOR THE YEAR	AVERAGE INDIVIDUAL SALARY OF TOP TEN EMPLOYEES	PERCENTAGE CHANGE FROM PRIOR YEAR
1982	$115,600	+13.67
1983	126,950	+ 9.82
1984	142,184	+12.00

Each of the ten employees covered by the option plan was required to remain in Wolverton's employ until December 31, 1985, when the options would become exercisable at a price equal to $6 below the December 31, 1985, market price per share. On December 25, 1983 (the date of grant), Wolverton common was selling for $68 per share. On December 31, 1983 and 1984, Wolverton common closed at $72 per share and $65 per share, respectively. The options were to expire on July 1, 1986, if not exercised.

During 1984 the company experienced poor profits and a weakening market for its products. Early in 1985, Wolverton announced a 6 percent across-the-board salary increase for 1985 for its top ten officers. One of these officers, who would have earned $185,000 in 1985, resigned and went to work for a competitor.

At the end of 1985 Wolverton common was selling at $74 per share. Early in 1986 Wolverton announced its salary increases for 1986, which consisted of an average raise of 15 percent for the nine remaining top managers. During 1986 the following options were exercised:

	NUMBER OF OPTIONS	MARKET PRICE PER SHARE AT EXERCISE DATE
1/2/86	4,380	$75
2/28/86	3,274	76
4/30/86	1,720	75
6/30/86	5,300	74

REQUIRED

1. Record the necessary journal entries, if any, for 1983 on Wolverton's books to account for these options given *only* that information which was available in 1983. Assume an expected future salary rate increase of 10 percent per year.

2. Record the necessary journal entries, if any, for 1984 and 1985 on Wolverton's books to account for these stock options given *only* the available data for 1984 and 1985, respectively. Assume that the expected future salary rate increase is 8 percent per year at the end of 1984 and 10 percent per year at the end of 1985.

3. Record the necessary journal entries, if any, to account for the exercise of these options during 1986.

4. Compute the number of options, if any, that expired unexercised. Explain why the options were or were not unexercised.

P22–6 In 1983 McKeown, Inc., established an employee compensation plan for three of its key employees by using stock appreciation rights (SARs). Each of the three employees was to receive the price appreciation on 10,000 shares of McKeown common from the date of grant (December 30, 1983) to the exercise date. The SARs were exercisable during the year 1986 only, providing the three were still employed by McKeown at that time. McKeown common was selling for $51 per share on the date of grant, $55 per share on December 31, 1984, and $53 per share on December 31, 1985.

In December 1985, shortly after raises had been announced for the coming year, one of the three employees quit McKeown and went to work for one of McKeown's competitors.

On March 30, 1986, one of the employees exercised 5,000 SARs when the market price of McKeown common was $56 per share. Another 6,000 options were exercised on July 16, 1986, when McKeown common was selling for $54 per share. The remaining SARs were exercised on December 31, 1986, when the stock was selling for $51.50 per share. On December 31, 1986, after exercising their options, the other two employees resigned from McKeown and went to work for a competitor.

REQUIRED

1. Record the journal entries necessary to account for the SARs from 1983 to 1986 assuming McKeown reports on a calendar-year basis.
2. Show how the footnotes to the McKeown, Inc., financial statements would appear at the end of 1984 and 1985.

P22–7   Bildersee, Inc., established an incentive compensation plan in 1983 using stock appreciation rights (SARs). The SARs were issued to the ten key managers of Bildersee in varying numbers, with a total of 17,850 rights on the appreciation of the common stock above a $20 per share base granted on September 1, 1983. The rights became exercisable on March 31, 1986, and expired on July 1, 1986. Bildersee common closed at $43 per share on September 1, 1983, $45 per share on December 31, 1983, $58 per share on December 31, 1984, and $62 per share on December 31, 1985. On March 31, 1986, all of the SARs were exercised when the market price of Bildersee common was trading at $55 per share. Bildersee has a December 31 year-end. SARs are paid in cash.

REQUIRED

1. Record any journal entries necessary to account for the SARs from September 1, 1983, to March 31, 1986.
2. Describe the nature of the information to be disclosed at December 31, 1985, in the notes to the financial statements.

P22–8   On December 15, 1984, P. Reckers, Inc., established an RSO plan for its key employees by offering restricted stock at a price of $10 per share when the market price was $40 per share. By December 31, 1984, the market price was $38 per share. Employees purchased 100,000 shares on December 15, 1984. On December 15, 1985, the restrictions on the stock were lifted, and 96,000 shares of Reckers $2 par value common stock were issued. Under the conditions of the plan, Reckers had repurchased the remaining 4,000 shares on July 15, 1985, when the employee holding these RSO shares resigned. The market price of Reckers common closed at $43 per share on December 15, 1985, and $42 per share on December 31, 1985. Reckers reports on a December 31 year-end basis.

REQUIRED   Record any journal entries for 1984 and 1985 on the books of Reckers, Inc., to account for the RSO plan.

P22–9   Black and Chang Ltd. established a restricted stock offering (RSO) plan for its top-level divisional managers in 1984. On December 31, 1984, the date of the offering, Black and Chang ($10 par) common was selling for $65 per share. Eligible employees purchased 200,000 shares of stock for the offering price of $30 per share. These employees were not allowed to actually receive the stock, which was being held by Black and Chang, until 2 years had passed. After 2 years, beginning on December 31, 1986, the restrictions on the use of the stock were lifted at the rate of 25 percent (50,000 shares) per year over the next 4 years. On December 31, 1989, the last 25,000 RSO shares became unrestricted. The closing prices of Black and Chang common were as follows:

DATE	CLOSING PRICE OF BLACK AND CHANG COMMON
12/31/85	$63
12/31/86	66
12/31/87	68
12/31/88	65
12/31/89	67

If the manager does not remain employed by Black and Chang throughout the RSO period, the corporation retains the right to repurchase any remaining RSOs at the original purchase price of $30 per share. Between 1984 and 1989 employee turnover affected the number of RSO shares as follows.

DATE	NUMBER OF SHARES REPURCHASED DUE TO EMPLOYEE TERMINATION
12/31/86	20,000
1/10/89	5,000

REQUIRED

1. Record any journal entries necessary to account for the compensation to Black and Chang managers between December 31, 1984, and December 31, 1989.
2. Illustrate how the financial statements would disclose the RSO plan as of the ends of 1984, 1985, and 1986.

P22–10 The stockholders' equity section of the Price Corporation as of December 31, 1980, was as follows:

Owners' equity ($000 omitted):

7% preferred, cumulative, $100 par value, convertible into 10 shares of common each (authorized, 200,000 shares; issued and outstanding, 150,000)	$ 15,000
Common stock, $1 par value (authorized, 50,000,000 shares; issued and outstanding, 10,000,000)	10,000
Capital in excess—from preferred	3,000
—from common	85,000
Retained earnings	97,000
Total owners' equity	$210,000

The preferred stock was all issued on April 1, 1980. The common stock was issued as follows: 8,000,000 shares on January 1, 1979; 2,000,000 shares on June 30, 1980.

Price also issued convertible bonds on October 1, 1979. The bonds had a face value of $20,000,000 and a stated interest rate of 7.5 percent and sold for $25 million. Each $500,000 bond was convertible into 50,000 shares of common stock.

During 1980 Price hired some top executives away from its major competitor by offering them executive stock options. The options, issued April 1, 1980, gave the executives the right to purchase 1,000,000 shares of common at a price of $10 per share anytime after December 31, 1983. Price's 1980 net income before tax was $75,000,000. The effective tax rate is 40 percent. The following data were available for 1979 and 1980:

	COMMON DIVIDENDS	MARKET PRICE	INTEREST RATE ON Aa BONDS
3/31/79	$.15	$8.25	12%
6/30/79	.15	8.30	10
9/30/79	.15	8.50	8
12/31/79	.20	8.60	8
Average, 1979	N/A	8.40	10
3/31/80	.20	8.75	9
6/30/80	.25	9.00	10
9/30/80	.30	9.50	11
12/31/80	.50	10.50	10
Average, 1980	N/A	9.50	10
Average, last 9 months	N/A	9.75	10

REQUIRED   Answer the following questions. Show all computations.

1. Prepare a schedule showing the common stock equivalency status of (a) convertible bonds, (b) convertible preferred stock, and (c) employee stock options.

2. Prepare a schedule computing the weighted-average number of shares of stock for (a) primary EPS and (b) fully diluted EPS.

3. Ignore requirements 1 and 2. Assume that on January 1, 1981, Price reacquired 1,000 shares of its own common stock at $10.50 per share. Record this information using the par value method.

4. Ignore requirements 1–3. Assume that on January 1, 1981, Price declared a 10 percent common stock dividend. Record the dividend.

5. Ignore requirements 1–4. Assume that Price declared a 50 percent common stock dividend. Record the dividend on January 1, 1981.

6. Ignore requirements 1–5. Assume that Price decided to split its common stock 2 for 1 on January 1, 1981. Record the split.

7. Give your estimate of the market price per share of Price common stock after requirement 4 above.

8. Give your estimate of the market price per share of Price common stock after requirement 6 above.

9. Give your estimate of the impact of requirement 5 on total owners' equity.

10. Critically evaluate *APB Opinion No. 15* on EPS as briefly and specifically as possible. (List points that show why it is arbitrary or inadequate.)

11. Under what conditions would you be required to report only *one* EPS figure for a firm with a *complex* capital structure?

12. Identify the major features of a *qualified stock option* plan.

P22–11 (CPA ADAPTED)   The stockholders' equity section of Lowe Company's balance sheet as of December 31, 1984, contains the following data:

$1.00 cumulative convertible preferred stock, par value $25 per share (authorized, 1,600,000 shares; issued, 1,400,000; converted to common 750,000 and outstanding, 650,000 shares); involuntary liquidation value, $30 per share, aggregating $19,500,000)	$16,250,000
Common stock, par value $.25 per share (authorized, 15,000,000 shares; issued and outstanding, 8,800,000 shares)	2,200,000
Additional paid-in capital	32,750,000
Retained earnings	40,595,000
Total stockholders' equity	$91,795,000

On April 1, 1984, Lowe Company acquired the business and assets and assumed the liabilities of Diane Corporation in a transaction accounted for as a pooling of interests. For each of Diane Corporation's 2,400,000 shares of $.25 par value common stock outstanding, the owner received one share of Lowe Company's common stock.

Included in Lowe's liabilities are 5½ percent convertible subordinated debentures issued at their face value of $20,000,000 in 1983. The debentures are due in 2003 and until then are convertible into Lowe's common stock at the rate of five shares of common stock for each $100 debenture. To date none of these have been converted.

On April 2, 1984, Lowe Company issued 1,400,000 shares of convertible preferred stock at $40 per share. Quarterly dividends to December 31, 1984, have been paid on these shares. The preferred stock is convertible into common stock at the rate of two shares of common for one share of preferred. On October 1, 1984, 150,000 shares of the preferred stock were converted into common stock, and on November 1, 1984, 600,000 shares were converted.

During January 1983 Lowe Company granted options to its officers and key employees to purchase 500,000 shares of the company's common stock at a price of $20 per share. The options do not become exercisable until 1985.

During 1984 dividend payments and average market prices of Lowe's common stock were as follows:

	DIVIDENDS PER SHARE	AVERAGE MARKET PRICE PER SHARE
First quarter	$.10	$20
Second quarter	.15	25
Third quarter	.10	30
Fourth quarter	.15	25
Average for the year		25

The December 31, 1984, closing price of the common stock was $25 per share. Assume that the interest rate on Aa bonds was 7 percent throughout 1983 and 1984. Lowe Company's consolidated net income for the year ended December 31, 1984, was $9,200,000. The provision for income taxes was computed at a rate of 48 percent.

REQUIRED

1. Prepare a schedule showing the evaluation of the common stock equivalency status of the (a) convertible debentures, (b) convertible preferred stock, and (c) employee stock options.
2. Prepare a schedule showing the weighted-average number of shares for computing
   a. Primary earnings per share for 1984
   b. Fully diluted earnings per share for 1984
3. Prepare a schedule showing the computation (to the nearest cent) of
   a. Primary earnings per share for 1984
   b. Fully diluted earnings per share for 1984

P22–12 (CPA ADAPTED)   The following schedule sets forth the short-term debt, long-term debt, and stockholders' equity of Darren Company as of December 31, 1984. The president of Darren has requested that you assist the controller in preparing figures for earnings-per-share computations.

Short-term debt	
Notes payable—banks	$ 4,000,000
Current portion of long-term debt	10,000,000
Total short-term debt	$ 14,000,000
Long-term debt	
4% convertible debentures due April 15, 1996	$ 30,000,000
Other long-term debt less current portions	20,000,000
Total long-term debt	$ 50,000,000
Stockholders' equity	
$4 cumulative, convertible preferred stock, par value $20 per share (authorized, 2,000,000 shares; issued and outstanding, 1,200,000 shares); liquidation preference $30 per share aggregating $36,000,000	$ 24,000,000
Common stock, par value $1 per share (authorized, 20,000,000 shares; issued, 7,500,000 shares including 600,000 shares held in treasury)	7,500,000
Additional paid-in capital	4,200,000
Retained earnings	76,500,000
Total	$112,200,000
Less cost of 600,000 shares of common stock held in treasury (acquired prior to 1984)	900,000
Total stockholders' equity	$111,300,000
Total long-term debt and stockholders' equity	$161,300,000

The "other long-term debt" and the related amounts due within 1 year are amounts due on unsecured promissory notes that require payments each year to maturity. The interest rates on these borrowings range from 6 to 7 percent. At the time that these monies were borrowed, Aa rated bonds were issued with an interest rate of 7 percent.

The 4 percent convertible debentures were issued at their face value of $30,000,000 in 1966 when the interest rate on Aa bonds was 5 percent. The debentures are due in 1996 and until then are convertible into Darren's common stock at the rate of 25 shares for each $1,000 debenture.

The $4 cumulative, convertible preferred stock was issued in 1983. The stock had a market value of $75 at the time of issuance when the interest rate on Aa bonds was 9 percent. On July 1, 1984, and on October 1, 1984, holders of the preferred stock converted 80,000 and 20,000 preferred shares, respectively, into common stock. Each share of preferred stock is convertible into 1.2 shares of common stock.

On April 1, 1984, Darren acquired the assets and business of Brett Industries by the issuance of 800,000 shares of Darren common stock in a transaction appropriately accounted for as a purchase.

On October 1, 1983, the company granted options to its officers and selected employees to purchase 100,000 shares of Darren's common stock for $33 per share. The options are not exercisable until 1986.

During 1984 the average and ending market prices of Darren common stock were as follows:

	AVERAGE MARKET PRICE	ENDING MARKET PRICE
First quarter	$31	$29
Second quarter	33	32
Third quarter	35	33
Fourth quarter	37	34
Average for the year	34	—
December 31, 1984	—	34

Dividends on the preferred stock have been paid through December 31, 1984. Dividends paid on the common stock were $.50 per share for each quarter.

Darren Company's net income for the year ended December 31, 1984, was $8,600,000. There were no extraordinary items. The provision for income taxes was computed at a rate of 48 percent.

REQUIRED

1. Prepare a schedule showing the adjusted number of shares for computing
   a. Primary earnings per share for 1984
   b. Fully diluted earnings per share for 1984
2. Prepare a schedule showing the adjusted net income for computing
   a. Primary earnings per share for 1984
   b. Fully diluted earnings per share for 1984. Do not compute earnings per share.

P22–13 (CMA ADAPTED) On June 1, 1983, Harden Company and Lower Company merged to form MHL, Inc. A total of 450,000 shares were issued to complete the merger. The new corporation reports on a calendar-year basis.

On April 1, 1985, the company issued an additional 200,000 shares of stock for cash. All 650,000 shares were outstanding on December 31, 1985.

MHL, Inc., also issued $500,000 of 20-year, 6 percent convertible bonds at par on July 1, 1985, when the interest rate on Aa bonds was 8 percent. Each $1,000 bond converts to 40 shares of common at any interest date. None of the bonds has been converted to date.

MHL, Inc., is preparing its annual report for the fiscal year ending December 31, 1985. The annual report will show earnings-per-share figures based upon a reported after-tax net income of $840,000 (the tax rate is 40 percent).

REQUIRED

1. Should the MHL, Inc., convertible bonds be treated as common stock equivalents for the computation of earnings per share? Explain your answer.

2. Regardless of your answer to requirement 1, assume that the convertible bonds are not to be treated as common stock equivalents. Determine for 1985

    a. The number of shares to be used for computing (1) primary earnings per share, and (2) fully diluted earnings per share.

    b. The earnings figures to be used for computing (1) primary earnings per share, and (2) fully diluted earnings per share.

P22–14 *Comprehensive Review* (*Note:* This problem should not be assigned unless Chapter 14 on long-term investments and Chapter 17 on taxes have already been completed.)

On June 30, 1986, the Gonedes Corporation acquired a 30 percent interest in Belle Labs for $400,000 cash and 500,000 shares of Gonedes common stock, which was selling for $5 per share on the date of the transaction. It is now December 31, 1986, the year-end for both Gonedes and Belle Labs. The following data have been collected by your staff auditors:

ITEM NUMBER	BELLE LABS	
1	Income reported from 1/1/86 to 6/30/86	$400,000
2	Income reported for the year 1986	850,000
3	Dividends declared and paid from 1/1/86 to 6/30/86	150,000
4	Dividends declared for the year 1986	300,000
5	*Position of Belle as of 6/30/86:*	

	BOOK VALUE	ESTIMATED MARKET VALUE
Nondepreciable assets	$ 4,000,000	$ 4,500,000
Depreciable assets[a]	6,000,000	7,500,000
Total assets	$10,000,000	$12,000,000
Liabilities	3,500,000	3,500,000
Net assets	$ 6,500,000	$ 8,500,000

[a] Estimated remaining useful life is 20 years on a straight-line basis assuming no salvage value.

ITEM NUMBER	GONEDES CORPORATION	
20	Net income for the year 1986 excluding income from Belle Labs and taxes thereon.	$6,500,000
21	10% long-term debt, convertible into 220 shares of common for each of the 5,000 $1,000 bonds on or after 1/1/87. Issued on 1/1/85 to yield 8 percent and maturing on 12/31/04, with interest paid on 6/30 and 12/31. Balance is as of 7/1/86.	5,957,198
22	Stock options were issued on 7/1/86 to certain Belle employees to purchase 45,000 shares of Gonedes common at $4 per share on or after 1/1/88.	
23	Gonedes common stock, par $1 (authorized, 10,000,000 shares; issued and outstanding as of 6/29/86, 6,000,000 shares).	6,000,000
24	The tax rate is 40 percent.	
25	Gonedes has elected to declare the undistributed income of Belle Labs (that portion of income not received in the form of dividends) to be permanently nontaxable for tax-reporting purposes.	

Gonedes issued its 10 percent convertible debt at a time when the interest rate was relatively favorable (15 percent on Aa Bonds). The current interest rate on Aa bonds is 21 percent. Gonedes common stock was selling for $4.50 per share on December 31, 1986.

REQUIRED

1. Record the issuance of the stock options on July 1, 1986, and any additional entries required for 1986.
2. Record all unrecorded entries related to the bonds for the year 1986.
3. Record all entries related to the investment in Belle Labs for the year 1986. Amortize goodwill over 20 years.
4. Compute the primary and fully diluted earnings-per-share figures that would be reported by Gonedes for the year ending December 31, 1986.

FINANCIAL

ADDITIONAL

AND

OVERVIEW

Part 4 consists of five chapters, four of which present in-depth reviews of subjects that were introduced in earlier chapters. Chapter 23 is on several different accounting situations that can present special problems involving revenue recognition. We discussed revenue recognition in a general way at several points in the text; here the discussion is more detailed and specific. Chapter 24 is on accounting changes, a subject introduced in Chapter 3 and discussed at several other points in the text. Chapter 25 presents further discussion of the statement of changes in financial position, which was introduced in Chapter 4. Accounting for price changes, covered in detail in Chapter 26, was first introduced in Chapter 6. Thus, Chapters 23, 24, 25, and 26 cover the previously introduced subjects in greater depth, with the focus here on understanding financial statement disclosures and

PART

4

REPORTING:

CONCEPTS

ISSUES

being able to evaluate financial statement data in a meaningful way. The final chapter, Chapter 27, considers disclosure issues not previously addressed in the earlier parts of the text. Interim financial reporting and SEC reporting are introduced, along with basic procedures involved in financial statement analysis. Given the increasing prominence of both SEC reporting and quarterly financial statements, these topics are considered to be necessary for rounding out the student's exposure to, and awareness of, important and common aspects of financial accounting reporting practices.

The material in Part 4 is comprehensive in the sense that it draws upon many key accounting issues presented in the previous three parts of the text, particularly parts 2 and 3. Given the detailed coverage of accounting practices and procedures in these earlier chapters, it is now possible to take a more global view of some of the overriding disclosure problems and issues that are relevant to modern financial reporting. The framework of accounting theory considered in Chapter 2 will also take on more meaning as we discuss disclosure practices. The qualities of relevance, reliability, consistency, and materiality take on a more important meaning in light of the possible alternative disclosures of a given event or situation.

The purpose of these final chapters is to review and integrate many of the accounting concepts and procedures covered in the text. In looking back at previous materials, keep in mind the strengths and weaknesses that were considered earlier and their impact on financial reports. Understanding the nature and limitations of accounting information is important to the effective use of accounting for decision-making needs.

23

Special Revenue-Recognition Problems

OVERVIEW   Revenue can be recognized at points other than the point of delivery of products or services if there are overriding considerations involving the timeliness of information or unusual uncertainties surrounding the revenue transactions. In this chapter we examine the concepts and techniques related to several types of revenue-generating events that lead to recognition of revenue either before or after the time that would normally be considered the point of sale: (1) long-term construction contracts, (2) installment sales, (3) franchise sales, (4) certain real estate sales, and (5) sales with right of return.

    The following time line diagrams the continuum of points that accountants may choose for recognition of revenue:

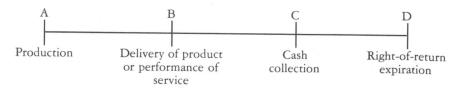

A	B	C	D
Production	Delivery of product or performance of service	Cash collection	Right-of-return expiration

As discussed in Chapter 3, the product delivery point or the service performance point (*B*) is often an appropriate time for revenue recognition **if there are no important uncertainties** concerning either the collection of the sales price or the performance of all services related to the sale. We shall see that entities engaged in long-term construction contracts often recognize revenue at point *A*, during production of the product. However, entities experiencing extreme uncertainties concerning the collectibility of receivables may recognize revenue at point *C*, after the delivery of the product or at the time the cash is collected. If a sales contract allows the buyer to return a product, point *D* could be the appropriate recognition point. Such departures from the norm are justified by practical considerations. For example, in long-term construction contracts, there is a need for timely indicators of financial performance between the signing of a contract and its completion, which often spans several years. In response to very different circumstances the installment sales technique is justified when the collection of receivables is so uncertain that objective estimates of uncollectibles are not available.

In all the special revenue-recognition situations discussed in this chapter, we observe several exceptions to the norms for the timing of revenue recognition. In each case, rules have been promulgated to guide accounting decisions in a certain direction. For instance, in the franchise and real estate cases, the rules lean toward deferral of recognition past the "normal" sales point, but in long-term construction contracts, the rules lean toward recognition of revenue before the "normal" sales point. We shall see that there are good conceptual and practical reasons for these exceptions. However, it must be emphasized that these are **exceptions** and that they involve a small percentage of all revenue-recognition transactions across the economy. Of course, they can be of material consequence for a single entity, or even for an entire industry.

LONG-TERM CONSTRUCTION CONTRACTS

The two main approaches to accounting for long-term construction contracts are the **completed contract method** and the **percentage-of-completion method**. Basically, under the completed contract method the income generated from a contract is not reported in the accounting records until the construction has been completed, whereas under the percentage-of-completion method the income effect is recognized during the construction process.

We shall use a single contract case to illustrate both methods. On January 1, 1983, Texas Contractors, Inc. (TCI), whose fiscal year ends on December 31, signs a fixed-fee contract to construct a deep-sea drilling platform at a total bid price of $300,000,000. At the date of signing the contract, TCI makes the estimates of costs, profits, and billings as shown in the table at the top of p. 878.

The degree of confidence that can be placed in the cost estimates determines whether revenue is to be recognized before the completion of a project. Basically, if the estimates are dependable, recognition during construction is in conformance with GAAP.[1]

---

[1] *Accounting Research Bulletin No. 45*, "Long-Term Construction-Type Contracts" (New York: AICPA, October 1955).

	($000,000)				
	DURING 1983	DURING 1984	12/31/84 TOTAL TO DATE	DURING 1985	12/31/85 TOTAL TO DATE
Actual costs	$ 50	$100	$150	$100	$250
Estimated costs to complete	200		100		0
Total estimated costs	$250		$250		$250
Percentage of total cost	20%	40%	60%	40%	100%
Estimated total gross profit	$ 50		$ 50		$ 50
Estimated billings to be allowed	$ 54	$108	$162	$138	$300

The Percentage-of-Completion Method

The **percentage-of-completion method** relies on estimates of cost to determine the revenue effect to be recognized each period. We examine three cases of actual cost experience: (1) **perfect initial estimates,** the unrealistic case where the estimates shown in the above table exactly equal the cost incurred; (2) **imperfect initial and interim estimates,** an example of the usual pattern where costs differ from the initial and interim estimates; and (3) **estimated loss,** an example of the case where, during production, it becomes apparent that the entire project will generate a loss.

Perfect initial estimates The accounting procedures for the percentage-of-completion method involve two steps: (1) **estimating** gross profits on a percentage-completed basis, and (2) **recording** the entity's assets and income in such a way that the partial profit is recognized in the financial reports.

The recording procedures call for the accumulation of all costs of construction in a current asset account usually labeled Construction in Process. This account is normally thought of as an inventory account. At the end of each accounting period, the estimated gross profit associated with the cost incurred is also debited to the asset account and credited to a revenue account, Construction Income.[2] Billings are recorded by debits to Construction Accounts Receivable and credits to Construction Billings. The Construction Billings account is normally treated as a contra account, offsetting the amount in the Construction in Process account. The disclosure on the balance sheets during construction shows the net of the Construction in Process and the Construction Billings accounts as a current asset or a current liability, depending on which is greater. In other words, if the asset account Construction in Process has a balance greater than the credit balance in Construction Billings, the two accounts will be offset against one another with the net reported as an asset "Excess of Construction in Process over Construction Billings."[3]

The following journal entries would record the entire construction period for the perfect-initial-estimates case:

[2] This account is referred to in practice by many different names, including Gross Profit on Incomplete Projects, Profits on Long-Term Contracts, and so forth. The important point is that it represents the *net* of revenues less costs on the contracts, or gross profit.

[3] The liability where billings exceed the asset might be shown as "Billings in Excess of Construction in Process." Also, when the net amount is reported in the balance sheet, the inventory account Construction in Process is sometimes referred to as Costs plus Profit (that is, Costs plus Profit in Excess of Billings) because it includes the costs incurred plus the profit recognized to date under the percentage-of-completion method.

		($000,000)					
DATE	ACCOUNTS, EXPLANATIONS, AND COMPUTATIONS	1983		1984		1985	
1/1 to 12/31	Construction in process	50		100		100	
	Cash and other accounts		50		100		100
	(To record costs as incurred)						
12/31	Construction in process	10		20		20	
	Construction income		10		20		20
	(To record revenue recognition on a percentage-of-completion basis)						
	Formula: (% of Total estimated cost incurred to date)(Total estimated gross profit) − (Previous gross profit recognized)						
	1983 = (20%)(Estimated gross profit) = (20%)(50,000,000) − $10,000,000						
	1984 = [(60%)($50,000,000)] − (1983 recognized) = $30,000,000 − $10,000,000 = $20,000,000						
	1985 = [(100%)($50,000,000)] − (1984 and 1983 recognized) = $50,000,000 − $30,000,000 = $20,000,000						
12/31	Construction accounts receivable	54		108		138	
	Construction billings		54		108		138
	(To record billings allowed under the contract assuming year-end billings)						
1/31	Cash			54		108	
	Construction accounts receivable				54		108
	(To record cash collections, assuming a 1-month collection period. Note that the final cash receipt would be on 1/31/86 under the assumed schedule.)						
12/31	Construction billings					300	
	Construction in process						300
	(To record the completion of the project by closing the asset and unearned revenue accounts)						

Income statement and balance sheet disclosures would be as follows on 12/31 of each year:

	($000,000)				
	1983		1984		1985
Income Statement					
Portion of total contract revenue earned		$60		$120	$120
Cost of construction		50		100	100
Gross profit		$10		$ 20	$ 20
Balance Sheet					
Current assets					
Construction accounts receivable		$54		$108	$138
Construction in process	$60		$180		
Less construction billings	54		162		
Cost plus profit in excess of billings		$ 6		$ 18	

Imperfect initial and interim estimates The events depicted above assumed perfect estimates—a most unrealistic example used to familiarize the reader with the procedures. In the real world, estimates are seldom perfect and accounting complexities are thereby created. To illustrate changing estimates, assume that billings remain the same as above but that costs and estimates have the following pattern:

	($000,000)		
	1983	**1984**	**1985**
Actual costs incurred during year	$ 45	$120	$ 95
Actual costs of prior years	0	45	165
Estimated cost to complete at 12/31[a]	205	105	0
Estimated total costs	$250	$270	$260
Estimated percentage completed (rounded)	18%	61.1%	100%
Estimated total gross profit	$ 50	$ 30	$ 40

[a] Estimates are made at the end of each year.

Note that *on December 31, 1983,* $45,000,000 has been incurred and $250,000,000 is the estimated total cost, resulting in an estimated 18 percent completion *as of that date* ($45,000,000/$250,000,000 = 18%). *On December 31, 1984,* a total of $165,000,000 has been incurred, but the total estimated cost *as of that date* is $270,000,000, resulting in an estimated 61.1 percent completion *as of that date* ($165,000,000/$270,000,000 = 61.1%). The gross profit computations for 1984 and 1985 are another application of the accounting method used for changes in estimates. The following computation schedule shows how the change in the estimated total costs from $250,000,000 to $270,000,000 in 1984, and from $270,000,000 to $260,000,000 in 1985, are accounted for:

	($000,000)		
	1983	**1984**	**1985**
Contract price	$300	$300	$300
Actual costs—current year	$ 45	$120	$ 95
Plus: Actual costs—prior years	—	45	165
Total actual costs to date	$ 45	$165	$260
Plus: Estimated costs to complete	205	105	0
Total estimated costs	$250	$270	$260
Total estimated (actual) gross profit	$ 50	$ 30	$ 40
Times percent completed ($45/$250), ($165/$270), and ($260/$260)	18%	61.1%	100%
Gross profit earned to date	$ 9	$ 18.3	$ 40
Less: Gross profit already recognized	0	9.0	18.3
Gross profit—current period	$ 9	$ 9.3	$ 21.7

The following journal entries would record this pattern of cost and estimates:

		($000,000)					
DATE	ACCOUNTS AND EXPLANATIONS	1983		1984		1985	
1/1 to 12/31	Construction in process	45		120		95	
	Cash and other accounts		45		120		95
	(To record costs as incurred)						
12/31	Construction in process	9		9.3		21.7	
	Construction income		9		9.3		21.7
	(To record revenue recognition on a percentage-of-completion basis)						
12/31	Construction accounts receivable	54		108		138	
	Construction billings		54		108		138
	(To record billings per contract)						
1/31	Cash			54		108	
	Construction accounts receivable				54		108
	(To record cash collections on billings)						
12/31	Construction billings					300	
	Construction in process						300
	(To record the completion of the project by closing the asset and unearned revenue accounts)						

If we assume that all billings and cash collections were identical to those shown in the previous example, the income statement and balance sheet disclosure would be as follows:

	($000,000)		
	1983	1984	1985
Income Statement			
Portion of total contract revenue earned	$54	$129.3	$116.7
Cost of construction	45	120.0	95.0
Gross profit	$ 9	$ 9.3	$ 21.7
Balance Sheet			
Current assets			
Construction accounts receivable	$54	$108	$138
Construction in process	$54	$100.0	
Less construction billings	54	162.0	
Cost plus profit in excess of billings		21.3	

One disclosure item requires further explanation. The "portion of total contract revenue earned" numbers reported in the partial income statements for each year can be computed by multiplying the total bid price by the estimated percentage completed as of the end of any year and subtracting the revenue recognized in all previous periods. For example:

For 1983, (18%) ($300,000,000) = $ 54,000,000

For 1984. [(61.1%) ($300,000,000)] − $54,000,000 = $129,300,000

For 1985: [(100%) ($300,000,000)] − $183,300,000 = $116,700,000

Estimated loss   Our coverage so far has considered the situations in which the total contract resulted in a net gross profit being earned. Certainly it is possible that a loss can be incurred on long-term construction contracts. In such situations, **the entire projected loss is reflected at the earliest possible reporting date.** Consider the following modifications to our previous example:

	($000,000)		
	1983	**1984**	**1985**
Actual costs incurred during year	$ 45	$205	$ 65
Actual costs of prior years	0	45	250
Estimated cost to complete at 12/31	205	60	0
Estimated total costs	$250	$310	$315
Estimated percentage completed	18%	80.6%	100%
Estimated total gross profit (loss)	$ 50	$ (10)	$ (15)

The first year would be accounted for as in the previous example. However, the higher costs experienced and projected in 1984 result in a projection of a $10,000,000 loss for the total contract ($250,000,000 actual + $60,000,000 estimated cost to complete = $310,000,000). At the end of 1985 the actual total loss finally realized amounted to $15,000,000 because total actual costs were $315,000,000. The computation schedule for the 3-year period would appear as follows:

	($000,000)		
	1983	**1984**	**1985**
Contract price	$300	$300	$300
Actual costs—current year	$ 45	$205	$ 65
Plus: Actual costs—prior years	0	45	250
Total actual costs to date	$ 45	$250	$315
Plus: Estimated costs to complete	205	60	0
Total estimated costs	$250	$310	$315
Total estimated gross profit (loss)	$ 50	$ (10)	$ (15)
Times percent complete (or 100% if a loss is projected)	18%	100%[a]	100%
Gross profit (loss) to date	$ 9	$ (10)	$ (15)
Less: Gross profit (loss) already recognized	0	9	(10)
Gross profit (loss) current period	$ 9	$ (19)	$ (5)

[a] Note that when the total estimated gross profit (loss) is negative (a loss), the percentage considered to be complete is always 100%. In other words, anytime a loss is estimated, it is recognized in full immediately.

Assuming billings and cash collections follow the same pattern as before, the following journal entries and analysis would be made:

		($000,000)					
DATE	ACCOUNTS AND EXPLANATIONS	1983		1984		1985	
During year	Construction in process	45		205		65	
	Cash and other accounts		45		205		65
	(To record costs as incurred)						
12/31	Construction in process	9					
	Construction income		9				
	(To record revenue recognition on a percentage-of-completion basis)						
12/31	Construction loss			19		5	
	Construction in process				19		5
	(To record losses)						
12/31	Construction accounts receivable	54		108		138	
	Construction billings		54		108		138
	(To record billings)						
1/31	Cash			54		108	
	Construction accounts receivable				54		108
	(To record collections)						
12/31	Construction billings					300	
	Construction in process						300
	(To record the completion of the project by closing the asset and unearned revenue accounts						

The income statement and balance sheet disclosures for the three annual reports would be as follows:

	($000,000)		
	1983	1984	1985
Income Statement			
Portion of total contract revenue earned	$54	$186[a]	$ 60[a]
Cost of construction	45	205	65
Gross profit (loss)	$ 9	$ (19)	$ (5)[b]
Balance Sheet			
Current assets			
Construction accounts receivable	$54	$108	$138
Construction in process	$54	$240	
Less construction billings	54	162	
Cost plus profit in excess of billings	0	$ 78	

[a] These revenue numbers are "forced" in an anticipated loss situation. Cost of construction is known and the loss disclosure is mandated by GAAP. The sum of the 3 years' revenue is $300,000,000.

[b] $5,000,000 is the underestimation of total cost made at 12/31/84.

Completed
Contract
Method

GAAP allow for the deferral of revenue recognition in cases where estimates are not dependable. The **completed contract method** accomplishes this by the use of accounting procedures identical to those described above for the percentage-of-completion method except that no measurement is made of estimated gross profit on construction during the construction period. As a result, the current asset account Construction in Process accumulates only those costs incurred. An end-of-the-construction-period entry is recorded to recognize the total actual gross profit earned on the entire project.

The following shows the journal entries under the completed contract method for case 2 data (imperfect estimates) except for the billings and cash collections entries, which would be the same as those in our previous examples:

		($000,000)		
DATE	ACCOUNTS	1983	1984	1985
During year	Construction in process	45	120	95
	Cash and other accounts	45	120	95
12/31	Construction billings			300
	Construction in process			260
	Construction income			40

The income statement and balance sheet disclosures would reflect those entries as follows:

	($000,000)		
	1983	1984	1985
Income Statement			
Total contract revenue earned	0	0	$300
Cost of construction	0	0	260
Gross profit	0	0	$ 40
Balance Sheet			
Current assets			
Construction accounts receivable	$54	$108	$138
Excess of construction in process over construction billings		3	
Current liability			
Excess of construction billings over construction in process	9		

Note that on December 31, 1983, billings to date of $54,000,000 exceed the accumulated cost by $9,000,000. On December 31, 1984, the opposite relationship holds, with accumulated costs exceeding billings by $3,000,000.

Under the completed contract method, foreseeable losses on all contracts should be recognized at the earliest reporting date, just as they are under the percentage-of-completion method. Returning to the TCI example involving an estimated loss, the following journal entries and disclosures would be necessary under the completed contract method:

		($000,000)		
DATE	ACCOUNTS	1983	1984	1985
During year	Construction in process	45	205	65
	Cash and other accounts	45	205	65
12/31	Construction loss		10	5
	Construction in process		10	5
12/31	Constuction billings			300
	Construction in process			300

	($000,000)		
	1983	1984	1985
Income Statement			
Portion of total contract revenue earned	0	$240	$ 60
Cost of construction	0	250	65
Gross profit (loss)	0	$ (10)	$ (5)
Balance Sheet			
Current assets			
Construction accounts receivable	$54	$108	$138
Excess of construction in process over construction billings		78	

Other considerations In practice, construction companies often have many projects under construction at one time. Some of the projects may be characterized by dependable estimates and others may not. In such cases, it is possible that both methods, percentage-of-completion and completed contract, would be used for different projects. This fact should be disclosed. It is also possible that some contracts would be expected to be profitable and others would not. It is common practice in such cases, if there are many outstanding projects, to disclose the net effect of all contracts on the income statement.

The excess of billings over related cost and the excess of cost over related billings may vary for different contracts. GAAP call for all contracts resulting in asset balances to be shown separately from all contracts resulting in liability balances. That is, the netting of resulting assets and liabilities is not allowed.

Some long-term construction contracts are "cost plus fixed fee." This means that a fixed amount in excess of cost will be received by the contractor. This assures a positive gross profit, and the percentage-of-completion method is used to allocate the gross profit to the periods of construction.

The income statement formats shown above include both the gross revenue and the gross profit. In practice, often only the gross profit is disclosed, especially if long-term construction contracts account for a relatively small amount of total business revenues. Actual balance sheet disclosure of Construction in Process is often shown under the inventory caption with footnote explanations. Exhibit 23–1 shows two examples of actual disclosures in published financial statements. Note that the inventory footnote gives details concerning long-term construction contracts.

INSTALLMENT SALES

Revenue recognition does not usually depend upon the collection of cash. Accrual-accounting techniques have been developed to reflect basic economic events that are often evidenced by the creation of receivables and payables.

It is normal in conventional accounting, therefore, to record revenue at the point of credit sales with appropriate adjustments being made for any uncertainties about collectibility. Promulgated GAAP firmly support this approach.[4] In some cases, however, although the delivery of the product or service has been accomplished, significant uncertainties remain about the ultimate collectibility of the sales

[4] *Accounting Principles Board Opinion No. 10,* "Omnibus Opinion—1966" (New York: AICPA, December 1966), par. 12.

EXHIBIT
23–1

EXAMPLES OF PERCENTAGE-OF-COMPLETION METHOD DISCLOSURES

SANDERS ASSOCIATES
Excerpt from Balance Sheet

	($000)	
	JULY 25, 1980	JULY 27, 1979 (RESTATED)
Assets		
Current assets		
Cash and short-term investments	$ 27,607	$39,698
Accounts receivable	46,633	16,304
Inventories	69,922	31,517
Other current assets	3,050	628
Total current assets	$147,212	$88,147

Excerpt from Notes

Inventories

Inventories at July 25, 1980, and July 27, 1979, are summarized as follows (in thousands):

	1980	1979
Fixed-price contracts in progress reported on percentage-of-completion method	$ 78,760	$70,562
Other fixed-price contracts and finished and in-process products	$ 44,149	$24,553
Raw materials, purchased parts, supplies, etc.	16,161	2,596
	$ 60,310	$27,149
	$139,070	$97,711
Less: Progress billings	69,148	66,194
	$ 69,922	$31,517

RECOGNITION EQUIPMENT, INC.
Excerpt from Balance Sheet

	($000)	
	1980	1979
Assets		
Current Assets		
Cash	$ 8,512	$ 8,500
Accounts receivable, less $438,000 in 1980 and $142,000 in 1979 for doubtful accounts (note 3)	25,395	20,882
Inventories (note 4)	40,638	26,362
Other current assets	1,366	1,542
Total current assets	$ 75,911	$57,286

Excerpt from Notes

Note 4: Inventories

Inventories at October 31, 1980 and 1979 comprised the following (in thousands):

	1980	1979
Raw materials and parts	$ 21,451	$10,578
Work in process	13,924	11,320
Finished goods	3,056	3,198
Long-term contract	2,207	1,266
	$ 40,638	$26,362

At October 31, 1980, inventories of $2,207,000 relating to a long-term contract accounted for under the percentage of completion method as costs are incurred consisted of costs incurred plus accrued profits of $2,374,000 less progress payments received of $167,000. Revenues which have been recorded on this contract will be billable to the customer upon shipment, which is expected to occur during 1981. At October 31, 1979, inventories of $1,266,000 relating to a long-term contract accounted for under the completed contract method consisted of costs incurred of $1,906,000 less progress payments received of $640,000.

amount. Here, both promulgated GAAP[5] and the concept of ojbective measurement allow for a deferral of gross profit recognition until cash has been collected. The **installment sales method** of revenue recognition is sometimes used to accomplish such deferrals.

Let us use the following facts about Red Star Department Stores' installment sales experience to demonstrate the unique features of installment sales accounting:

	1983 (FIRST YEAR OF OPERATIONS)	1984	1985
Installment sales	$400,000	$550,000	$600,000
Cost of installment sales	320,000	434,500	468,000
Gross profit	$ 80,000	$115,500	$132,000
Gross profit as a percentage of sales	20%	21%	22%
Collections of cash from:			
1983 Sales	$110,000	$210,000	$ 50,000
1984 Sales		220,000	200,000
1985 Sales			350,000

Under ordinary point-of-sale accounting, 1983, 1984, and 1985 revenues recognized would have been $400,000, $550,000, and $600,000, respectively; and the related cost of goods sold, estimates of bad debts, and other related effects would have been matched with the recognized revenues. Under the installment sales method, however, only $22,000 of gross profit would be recognized in 1983. This is computed by applying the **1983** gross profit percentage, 20 percent, to cash receipts (20%)($110,000) = $22,000. Subsequent years' revenue recognition would also be governed by cash flows. The following analysis compares the revenue recognized under installment sales and point-of-sale methods for all 3 years:

INSTALLMENT SALES ACCOUNTING

	1983	1984	1985
Gross profit recognized[a]	$22,000	$88,200	$129,000

[a] Computation of gross profit recognized for each year:

1983	(Collections on 1983 sales)(1983 Gross profit percentage)	
	($110,000)(20%) =	$ 22,000
1984	(Collections on 1983 sales)(1983 Gross profit percentage)	
	($210,000)(20%) =	$ 42,000
	(Collections on 1984 sales)(1984 Gross profit percentage)	
	($220,000)(21%) =	46,200
	Total	$ 88,200
1985	(Collections on 1983 sales)(1983 Gross profit percentage)	
	($50,000)(20%) =	$ 10,000
	(Collections on 1984 sales)(1984 Gross profit percentage)	
	($200,000)(21%) =	42,000
	(Collections on 1985 sales)(1985 Gross profit percentage)	
	($350,000)(22%) =	77,000
	Total	$129,000

[5] Ibid.

POINT-OF-SALE ACCOUNTING			
	1983	**1984**	**1985**
Revenue recognized	$400,000	$550,000	$600,000
Cost of goods sold	320,000	434,500	468,000
Gross profit recognized	$ 80,000	$115,500	$132,000

The above comparisons indicate the significant differences in revenue recognition that can occur under the two methods. As discussed in Chapter 17, the installment sales method is permitted for tax purposes in some cases when this method would not be appropriate for financial reporting purposes, thus creating deferred federal income tax credits. For example, if the point-of-sale method were used for financial reporting purposes and the installment sales method were used for tax purposes for 1983, Red Star would record a deferred credit for an amount equal to its tax rate multiplied by the $58,000 difference between the two methods. See Chapter 17 for the concepts and for the methods of deferring federal income tax.

For financial accounting purposes, the installment sales method results in deferrals of gross profit that would be recognized under the point-of-sale method. The following schedule summarizes the computation of the deferred gross profits related to Red Star's outstanding installment sales receivables:

	YEAR-END DEFERRALS		
	12/31/83	**12/31/84**	**12/31/85**
1983 Sales	$400,000	$400,000	$400,000
Less: Cash collected to date on 1983 sales	110,000	320,000	370,000
Outstanding 1983 installment sales receivable	$290,000	$ 80,000	$ 30,000
1983 Gross profit percentage	20%	20%	20%
Gross profit deferred	$ 58,000	$ 16,000	$ 6,000
1984 Sales		$550,000	$550,000
Less: Cash collected to date on 1984 sales		220,000	420,000
Outstanding 1984 installment sales receivable		$330,000	$130,000
1984 Gross profit percentage		21%	21%
1984 Gross profit deferred		$ 69,300	$ 27,300
Gross profit deferred		$ 85,300	
1985 Sales			$600,000
Less: Cash collected to date on 1985 sales			350,000
Outstanding 1985 installment sales			$250,000
1985 Gross profit percentage			22%
1985 Gross profit deferred			$ 55,000
Gross profit deferred			$ 88,300

The accounting procedures generally used to accomplish the deferrals shown above include the initial recording of sales and cost of goods sold in the normal way. An adjusting entry is then used to close the sales and the cost of goods sold balances to a Deferred Gross Profit account. Another period-end adjusting entry is used to record the recognition of the gross profit related to cash collections. All of these entries can be summarized as follows for the Red Star Department Stores example:

DATE	ACCOUNTS	($000) 1983		1984		1985	
During year	Installments receivable	400		550		600	
	Installment sales		400		550		600
	Cost of installment sales	320		434.5		468	
	Inventory		320		434.5		468
	Cash	110		430		600	
	Installments receivable		110		430		600
12/31	Installment sales	400		550		600	
	Cost of installment sales		320		434.5		468
	Deferred gross profit		80		115.5		132
12/31	Deferred gross profit	22		88.2		129	
	Recognized gross profit		22		88.2		129

Balance sheet classification of the Deferred Gross Profit account is not intuitively clear. In practice, it is often shown as an offset to Installments Receivable. The above example would result in balance sheet disclosures as follows:

	($000)		
	12/31/83	12/31/84	12/31/85
Current assets			
Installments receivable	$290.0	$410.0	$410.0
Deferred gross profit	(58.0)	(85.3)	(88.3)
Net installments receivable	$232.0	$324.7	$321.7

Note that the net installments receivable amount equals the cost of installment sales for the outstanding receivables at each year-end.

Default and Repossession on Installment Sales

Because installment sales contracts are frequently used for "big-ticket" durables, they are written in a way that will facilitate repossession in the event of nonpayment. The repossessed merchandise can then be resold to different customers in completely separate transactions. In the event of **default and repossession,** the installment sales accounting method calls for (1) the recording of the repossessed merchandise at its current fair market value, (2) the write-off of all accounts related to the original installment sale, and (3) the recording of a gain or a loss on the repossession.

To illustrate the repossession technique, assume that on July 15, 1984, Red Star Department Stores repossesses an item that has the following history:

Date of sale	11/1/83
Original invoice price	$22,500
Cash collected through 7/15/84	12,000
Fair market value at 7/15/84	8,000

The following journal entry would record the repossession:

7/15/84	Deferred gross profit	2,100[a]	
	Inventory of repossessed merchandise	8,000[b]	
	Loss on repossession	400	
	Installment accounts receivable		10,500[c]
	(To record repossession of merchandise sold on an installment sales contract in 1983 when the gross profit percentage was 20%)		

[a] ($22,500 − $12,000) × 20%, = $2,100
[b] Fair market value.
[c] $22,500 − $12,000 = $10,500.

A subsequent sale of the repossessed merchandise would be recorded according to the terms of that sale with the cost of goods sold being $8,000.

FRANCHISE FEE REVENUE RECOGNITION

When one party (franchisor) grants business rights to operate a franchised business to another party (franchisee), questions arise concerning the accounting status of the initial consideration paid or promised upon the initiation of the contract. These questions are prompted by uncertainties relating to the collectibility of receivables from the franchisee and the cost of performance or ability to perform required services on the part of the franchisor. A great deal of professional judgment is required in making such determinations. Although promulgated standards on this topic provide broad guidelines,[6] the general criteria for revenue recognition govern the accountant's actions in specific cases.

Individual Franchise Sales

Consider the case where Dutch Chocolate House, Inc. (DCH), (franchisor) initiates a franchise agreement with Amanda O'Neal (franchisee) under which $50,000 is paid on July 1, 1983, and a 3-year, 14 percent, note with a maturity amount of $74,075 is signed for the remainder of the initial franchise fee. How much should DCH recognize as revenue in the current period? To answer this question, the specific conditions of the franchise contract must be analyzed in light of the general revenue-recognition criteria. Is the $74,075 collectible? Have the agreed-to franchisor services been performed? If we assume that the initial franchise fee is paid for the right to retail DCH chocolates and that no equipment, displays, or other assets are involved and no services are to be performed by DCH, then revenue is recognized immediately for the present value of required cash flows, after taking into consideration estimated uncollectibles:

7/1/83	Cash	50,000	
	Notes receivable	50,000	
	Franchise fee revenue		100,000
	(Assuming the note is deemed collectible, the following present-value computation is made: [P/F, 3, .14] [$74,075] = $50,000.)		

[6] *Statement of Financial Accounting Standards No. 45,* "Accounting for Franchise Fee Revenue" (Stamford, CT: FASB, 1981).

Deferral of revenue recognition is required when "substantial performance" of franchisor services has not been completed. Assume, for instance, that before operations can commence in Ms. O'Neal's establishment, a lease has to be negotiated at a particular shopping center mall, which is not scheduled to open until January 1, 1984. DCH must secure the lease in Ms. O'Neal's name by March 15, 1984, or return the cash payment and cancel the note. In addition, DCH is obliged to aid Ms. O'Neal in obtaining various state and local permits and licenses. Under such circumstances, GAAP would call for deferral of revenue recognition until evidence of service performance was available. The best evidence, of course, would be the commencement of operations of the franchise outlet, and this point in time is specifically mentioned in **FASB Statement No. 45.**[7]

If we assume that DCH, whose fiscal year ends on December 31, secures the lease and the permits on February 1, 1984, and operations commence at that time, the following journal entries would be appropriate:

7/1/83	Cash	50,000	
	Notes receivable	50,000	
	Deferred franchise fee revenue		100,000
During 1983	Prepaid cost of services	6,000	
	Cash		6,000
	(Assuming $6,000 was expended to perform required services)		
12/31/83	Interest receivable	3,500[a]	
	Interest revenue		3,500

[a] (.14)($50,000)(1/2).

2/1/84	Deferred franchise fee revenue	100,000	
	Initial franchise services expense	6,000	
	Franchise fee revenue		100,000
	Prepaid cost of services		6,000

Note that the costs related to the initial franchise services are deferred and matched with revenues during the second fiscal period. This is a straightforward application of the matching concept sanctioned by the **FASB Statement No. 45.** Continuing with this rationale, if revenue is recognized before all related costs are incurred, such costs should be accrued. It would seem that the same logic should be used for other recurring costs related to continuing franchise fees, but that is not the case. Although **FASB Statement No. 45** requires deferral of certain continuing franchise fee revenue in much the same manner as that described above, it explicitly states that related costs are to be expensed as incurred.[8]

In summary, then, GAAP require deferral of revenue recognition until both collectibility can be reasonably estimated and all material commitments (either expressed or implied) have been substantially performed.[9] In rare cases when collectibility cannot reasonably be estimated, deferral may be extended by means of installment sales or other gross profit deferral techniques.[10] In some cases, tangible assets

[7] Ibid., par. 5.

[8] Ibid., par. 14.

[9] Ibid.

[10] Ibid., par. 6.

EXHIBIT
23–2

EXAMPLES OF FRANCHISE FEE DISCLOSURES

MR. STEAK, INC.
Excerpt from Income Statement

	($000)	
	1980	**1979**
Revenues:		
Company-affiliated restaurant food sales	$28,355	$29,050
Sales and services to franchisees:		
Food products	20,375	24,279
Operating fees	4,177	4,254
Equipment and supplies	1,902	2,158
Other services	766	508
Franchise sales—net	62	205
Other revenue	681	845
	$56,318	$61,299

Excerpt from Notes

Recognition of initial franchise sales:

Revenue from sales of franchises is deferred when received and recorded as income at the time the franchisee commences operations.

SHONEY'S, INC., AND SUBSIDIARIES
Excerpt from Income Statement

	($000)	
	Years Ended	
	OCTOBER 26, 1980	**OCTOBER 23, 1979**
Revenues		
Net sales	$210,609	$183,504
Franchise fees	4,907	4,619
Other income	583	563
Total revenues	$216,099	$188,687

Excerpt from Notes

Franchise Fees

Initial franchise fees are recorded as income when the restaurant begins operation and the cash payment is received. Franchise fees based on sales of franchisees are accrued as earned.

DUNKIN DONUTS, INC.
Excerpt from Income Statement

	($000)	
	1980	**1979**
Gross Revenues:		
Sales by company-operated shops	$26,331	$29,623
Rental income (notes 1 and 8)	18,596	17,270
Continuing franchise fee income	13,653	12,424
Initial franchisee fee income (note 1)	1,778	1,374
Gain on sales of property, plant and equipment at existing locations (note 1)	1,443	1,169
Interest and other income	1,666	1,340
	$63,467	$63,200

EXHIBIT 23-2 (continued)

are sold to the franchisee as part of the initial agreement. In our deferral example, if DCH transfers title to displays, counters, and signs to Ms. O'Neal on July 1, 1983, and no return is allowed on such items, the gain on the sale of such items could be recognized upon transfer of title as follows:

7/1/83	Cash	$50,000	
	Notes receivable	50,000	
	Deferred franchise fee revenue		$87,000
	Gain on sale of equipment		3,000
	Equipment		10,000
	(Assuming the equipment had a book value of $10,000 and a fair value of $13,000)		

Other Franchise Considerations

The preceding discussion described the accounting for sales for individual franchise outlets. Sometimes a franchisor transmits the rights to a geographical area in which a franchisee can open several outlets. If the franchisor's obligations under the agreement are in terms of the entire geographical area rather than individual outlet openings, performance of service would have to be determined on a geographical area basis. If all the services required for the entire geographical area were substantially performed, then revenue could be recognized. If, however, the franchisor's obligations depend on the number of outlets actually opened, initial franchise fees would be recognized on a pro rata basis depending on the obligations related to each outlet.

Franchisors occasionally have the right to repossess franchises. In such cases, previously recognized revenue would have to be canceled against the period of repossession's franchise revenue if the franchise fee is refunded. If no refund is made upon repossession, the franchisor would make adjustments to any uncollectible receivables, eliminate deferred revenues, and recognize any revenue on any retained, but not previously recognized, consideration. Exhibit 23-2 shows several financial statement disclosures of franchise fee revenues.

REAL ESTATE SALES

The installment method is often used to defer the gross profit on certain real estate sales that have small down payments and payment periods extending beyond the seller's current accounting period. Again, justification for use of the installment sales method is contingent on lack of reasonable estimates of cash collections, which is common for this class of transactions. Deferral of revenue recognition is also justified by the fact that the seller may have committed himself or herself to performing services that will take considerable time to perform, such as drainage, grading, and access road construction.

Recognition of revenue at the date of the initial contract signing is recommended under AICPA guidelines only if the seller is in essence a secured creditor with no remaining unperformed substantial services, and if the buyer's commitment and ability to pay for the property are assured.[11] If these criteria are not met, the installment or other method of gross profit deferral would be applied.

SALES WITH RIGHT OF RETURN

In some industries, customers usually have the right to return products to sellers for credits or refunds. In such cases, the status of the original sale as a revenue-generating event may be questioned. For instance, a publisher may encourage bookstores to "overstock" by a certain percentage with the anticipation of returns for unsold books. In sales to final customers, sellers often allow full returns if the customer is dissatisfied with the product. Both of these examples are fundamentally different from warranties that oblige the seller to repair or replace damaged or defective products, events that do not negate the original sale.

In all cases of delivery of products or services, accountants must decide whether a sale has been accomplished. In cases where the **right of return** exists, accountants must ask two additional questions: (1) What evidence exists to confirm or disconfirm the finality of the sale? and (2) If there is a clear-cut possibility of return, can reasonable estimates be made of future returns? **FASB Statement No. 48** gives criteria relating to these questions.[12]

When the right of return exists, the following evidence confirms or disconfirms the finality of the sale:

1. **Selling price determination.** Is it determinable at the date of sale?
2. **The nature of the buyer's obligations.** Is the buyer obliged to pay a certain amount regardless of other events taking place? Examples of such events include resale to another party, theft of the product, and physical destruction of the product.
3. **The independence of the buyer.** Is the buyer a viable economic entity independent of the seller?
4. **The nature of the seller's obligation.** Is the seller free of responsibility to bring about a resale of the product?

If all four questions can be answered affirmatively, evidence exists supporting the finality of the sale, and **FASB Statement No. 48** sanctions the recognition of revenue at the time of sale if reasonable estimates can be made of future returns.[13]

The rationale is that even though the attributes of a sale with right of return may point to a final sale, the right of return still exists and estimates of probable

---

[11] See the AICPA's Industry Accounting Guide, *Accounting for Profit Recognition on Sales of Real Estate* (New York: AICPA, 1973).

[12] *Statement of Financial Accounting Standards No. 48,* "Revenue Recognition When Right of Return Exists" (Stamford, CT: FASB, 1981).

[13] Ibid.

returns must be possible in order that revenue not be overstated. As long as any of the above questions are answered negatively or as long as a reasonable estimate of returns cannot be made, both the sales revenue and the cost of sales are deferred until the right of return expires.

For example, assume that Ropex, Inc., a calendar-fiscal-year company, commences sales of its new personal computers in 1984 with the following results: On December 1, 1984, 200 units with a sales price of $4,500 each and total manufacturing cost of $3,000 each are delivered to distributors. The distributors have the right to return the product within 4 months of the delivery date. Payment and returns for the initial shipments were as follows:

	CASH RECEIPTS		RETURNS	
	UNITS	AMOUNT	UNITS	AMOUNT
Dec. 1984	50	$225,000	—	—
Jan. 1985	40	180,000	3	$13,500
Feb. 1985	35	157,500	10	45,000
Mar. 1985	45	202,500	5	22,500
	170	$765,000	18	$81,000

Ropex has used similar contracts with distributors in the past for such transactions and has experienced a 10 percent return rate on similar sales. If all four questions in the above list can be answered affirmatively and if Ropex has confidence in its estimate of returns, the following journal entries would be appropriate:

12/1/84	Accounts receivable	900,000	
	Sales		900,000
	(To record sale of 200 units @ $4,500)		
12/31/84	Cash	225,000	
	Accounts receivable		225,000
	(To record receipts of cash for 50 units @ $4,500)		
	Cost of goods sold	600,000	
	Inventory		600,000
	(To record cost of goods sold for 200 units @ $3,000)		
	Sales	90,000	
	Cost of goods sold		60,000
	Deferred gross profit on estimated returns		30,000
	(To record estimate of returns: [10%][200][$4,500] and [10%][200][$3,000])		
1/1/85 to 3/31/85	Cash	540,000	
	Accounts receivable		540,000
	(To record cash receipts)		
	Inventory	54,000	
	Deferred gross profit on estimated returns	27,000	
	Accounts receivable		81,000
	(To record returns)		

3/31/85	Cost of goods sold	6,000	
	Deferred gross profit on estimated re-		
	turns	3,000	
	Sales		9,000
	(To record expiration of return privilege		
	by eliminating the deferral balance)		

Note that revenue and cost of goods sold recognized in 1984 are based on the number of units expected not to be returned. The deferred gross profit balance is carried forward to 1985 and is eliminated when items are returned and/or when the right-of-return privilege expires.

If we assume that any one of the criteria for revenue recognition (page 894) is not met, then revenue would be recognized only upon receipt of cash or upon expiration of the return privilege. In the Ropex case, if we assume that the company has had no experience with such return policies and that the product is unique in the industry, sales and cost of sales would not be recognized until the sale is confirmed through cash collections or on March 31, 1985, upon expiration of the return right. Based on the cash receipts and returns facts on page 895, Ropex could make the following entries:

12/1/84	Accounts receivable	900,000	
	Sales		900,000
	(To record sale of 200 units @ $4,500)		
12/31/84	Cash	225,000	
	Accounts receivable		225,000
	(To record receipt of cash for 50 units		
	@ $4,500)		
	Cost of goods sold	600,000	
	Inventory		600,000
	(To record cost of goods sold for 200		
	units @ $3,000)		
	Sales	675,000[a]	
	Cost of goods sold		450,000[b]
	Deferred gross profit		225,000[c]
	(To defer revenue recognition on sales		
	for which right of return applies on		
	12/31/84)		

[a] 150 units @ $4,500 = $675,000.
[b] 150 units @ $3,000 = $450,000.
[c] 150 units @ $1,500 = $225,000.

1/1/85 to			
3/31/85	Cash	540,000[a]	
	Accounts receivable		540,000
	Cost of goods sold	360,000[b]	
	Deferred gross profit	180,000[c]	
	Sales		540,000
	(To recognize revenue and cost of		
	goods sold on cash collections)		

[a] 120 units @ $4,500 = $540,000.
[b] 120 units @ $3,000 = $360,000.
[c] 120 units @ $1,500 = $180,000.

1/1/85 to 3/31/85			
	Inventory	54,000[a]	
	Deferred gross profit	27,000[b]	
	Accounts receivable		81,000[c]
	(To record return of 18 units)		

[a] 18 units @ $3,000 = $54,000.
[b] 18 units @ $1,500 = $27,000.
[c] 18 units @ $4,500 = $81,000.

3/31/85			
	Cost of goods sold	36,000[a]	
	Deferred gross profit	18,000[b]	
	Sales		54,000[c]
	(To record expiration of return privilege on 12 units)		

[a] 12 units @ $3,000 = $36,000.
[b] 12 units @ $1,500 = $18,000.
[c] 12 units @ $4,500 = $54,000.

In both Ropex examples above, we ignored estimated uncollectibles and potential losses in value due to the return process. Because there is no reason to believe that customers with a return privilege will on average pose lower risks of bad debts than other customers, to the extent that revenue is recognized on sales for which receivables are outstanding, ordinary bad debt estimation procedures should be applied (see Chapter 8). By the same logic, if any costs or losses are expected on estimated returns, they should be accrued in conformance with the normal accounting for loss contingencies (see Chapter 16).

SUMMARY

Although this chapter is titled "Special Revenue-Recognition Problems," it should be obvious that the general concepts covered in Chapters 2 and 3 are applicable to the "special" events discussed here. What makes these events different is that they all share a common attribute: Revenue is recognized at a time other than the ordinary point of sale, where point of sale is usually the point of delivery of the product or service. It must be emphasized, however, that these are not all exceptions to the general concept but merely special subsets for which the criteria for revenue recognition at point of sale are not met. Percentage of completion methods do result in revenue recognition in advance of delivery, and this is justified by the need for timely information. All the other "special" cases discussed in this chapter relate to deferring revenue recognition because the criteria of estimating collectibles or determining all material costs have not been met.

QUESTIONS

Q23–1 When is revenue recognized?

Q23–2 What is the relationship between the definition of *asset* and revenue recognition?

Q23–3 Give an example of revenue recognition *before* the point of sale. Explain why revenue is recognized before the sale.

Q23-4 Give examples of revenue recognition *after* the point of sale. Explain why revenue is recognized after the sale in each case.

Q23-5 What is the justification for the percentage-of-completion method of accounting for revenues and expenses on long-term construction contracts?

Q23-6 When is the installment sales method permitted for financial accounting purposes?

Q23-7 When is the franchise fee revenue recognized by the franchisor if there are no remaining obligations of any kind to the franchisee?

Q23-8 What amortization period does the franchisor use for deferred franchise fee revenues?

Q23-9 When is the latest point at which profit may be recognized on long-term installment sales?

Q23-10 Explain how the concepts of revenue recognition, matching, and periodicity affect the choice of accounting method for long-term construction contracts.

Q23-11 Explain how the percentage-of-completion method of profit recognition for long-term contracts is an application of the method of accounting for changes in estimates.

Q23-12 How are anticipated losses for long-term construction contracts disclosed prior to the completion of a project?

Q23-13 What "elements" from the conceptual framework discussed in Chapter 2 argue against the use of the installment sales method?

Q23-14 *Gross profit on sales* is defined under the installment sales procedure. Can you think of another method of accounting for sales that would have the same effect on the income statement as the installment sales method but would have a different effect on the balance sheet?

Q23-15 What is meant by the notion of "substantial performance" that a franchisor uses to determine revenue recognition?

Q23-16 What is the correct timing of revenue recognition in the case of real estate sales, and does it differ from point-of-sale recognition?

CASES

C23-1 (CPA ADAPTED) Income determination for long-term construction contracts can present special problems because the construction work often extends over two or more accounting periods. The two methods commonly followed are the percentage-of-completion method and the completed contract method.

REQUIRED Evaluate the use of the percentage-of-completion method for income determination purposes for long-term construction contracts. Discuss only theoretical arguments.

C23-2 (CPA ADAPTED) In accounting for long-term contracts (those taking longer than 1 year to complete), the two methods commonly followed are the percentage-of-completion method and the completed contract method.

REQUIRED

1. Discuss how earnings on long-term contracts are recognized and computed under these two methods.
2. Under what circumstances is one method preferable to the other?
3. Why is earnings recognition as measured by interim billings not generally accepted for long-term contracts?
4. How are job costs and interim billings reflected on the balance sheet under the percentage-of-completion method and the completed contract method?

C23-3 Installment sales of equipment to be paid for over a long term are said to be similar to capital lease arrangements (or sales-type leases) from the lessor's point of view.

REQUIRED Is there a parallel between capital leases and long-term installment sales? Identify the differences and similarities between these two situations.

C23-4 The conventional method of installment sales accounting calls for partial recognition of the profit on the installment sale over the period of collection. An extreme version of revenue deferral calls for deferral of *all* the gross profit on installment sales until the payments have completely recovered the cost of the sale.

REQUIRED Describe how you would determine which deferral method should be used in a given situation, and describe a situation where you might defer all gross profit recognition until the end of the payment term.

C23-5 Certain retail land sales call for deferral of revenue recognition beyond the point of sale. These sales are governed by a special AICPA pronouncement that was necessary because of the problems encountered by real estate developers in collecting on sales of lots during the early 1970s. In some cases, the signed purchase contracts were considered to be null and void by the courts even though the buyers had signed purchase contracts and then failed to make payments in accordance with the contract schedule.

REQUIRED

1. Explain why you think that the revenues from certain land sales are deferred (not recognized) until some time after the point of sale where the buyer and seller sign a legal contract to buy and sell, respectively, a parcel of land.
2. Would you, as an auditor, ever permit the recognition of revenue from the sale of land at the point of sale (when the legal contract to purchase/sell is signed)? Explain.

C23-6 Franchise arrangements have become increasingly popular in the past 20 years. The franchisor demands a franchise fee from the franchisee. For example, a franchise for a certain pizza outlet calls for a fee to be paid by the owner of the outlet to the franchisor. This franchise fee is sometimes recognized as revenue immediately and at other times is deferred until future periods.

REQUIRED How is the determination of franchise fee revenue on the franchisor's books made?

EXERCISES

E23-1 Jason, Inc., a book publisher, allows its customers (mostly book stores) to return all unsold books for a 100 percent refund. At the end of its fiscal year, Jason has $100,000 of accounts receivable outstanding on which the right of return applies and for which normal sales revenue has been recorded. Jason has no means of estimating the number of returns. Jason's gross profit percentage is 60 percent.

REQUIRED How would Jason adjust its books at year-end to reflect uncertainty about the number of returns assuming that all normal year-end entries have been made?

E23-2 Consider the facts in the preceding exercise.

REQUIRED What adjustments would be necessary at year-end if Jason had a reasonable basis to estimate that 25 percent of the accounts receivable with return rights would in fact be returns? Assume that all conditions of the sales support revenue recognition in the current period.

E23-3 Samuel Web Corporation is contemplating using the installment sales method to record sales of electronic games to arcades in college dormitories. The company's controller feels that normal revenue recognition is not appropriate because of the complete lack of experience with sales of these items to this class of customers. Each machine sells for $2,400 and is paid for over 2 years at $100 per month plus 20 percent interest on the unpaid balance.

REQUIRED Prepare a schedule that compares the income statement and balance sheet effects of the installment sales and normal sales methods for one electronic game, assuming delivery is at the beginning of a fiscal year and the average cost per unit is $1,600.

E23-4 You are given the following data for the Delta Construction Company for contract 101, which has a fixed bid price of $900,000:

CONTRACT 101	1981	1982	1983	1984
Actual costs for year	40,000	95,000	140,000	205,000
Estimated remaining cost	740,000	665,000	550,000	320,000
Billed to customer	200,000	200,000	200,000	300,000
Received on account	150,000	200,000	200,000	150,000

REQUIRED Based on the above data, answer the following questions. (Show your computations.)

1. What is the gross profit to be recognized in 1984 under the completed contract method?
2. What is the total gross profit earned on this contract through 1983 under the percentage-of-completion method?
3. What is the gross profit to be recognized in 1984 under the percentage-of-completion method?

E23-5 Bagit Construction Company entered into a contract to build a bridge for the city of Medicine Hat for a flat fee of $800,000. The contract specified that engineers from both parties provide estimates of percentage of completion each period. Construction activities can be summarized as follows:

1983	Costs incurred during the year, $240,000; estimated costs to complete the project, $400,000
1984	Costs incurred during the year, $300,000; estimated costs to complete the project, $180,000
1985	Costs incurred during the year to complete the project, $160,000.

REQUIRED Indicate the gross profit to be recognized in each of the 3 years using the percentage-of-completion method.

E23-6 Washington Shipbuilders, Inc., is currently involved in one contract that is being accounted for under the percentage-of-completion method. As of December 31, 1984, the following cost history and estimates apply to this project:

	1983	1984
Bid price	$2,500,000	$2,500,000
Cost to date	850,000	900,000
Billing to date	800,000	1,000,000
Estimated total cost	1,000,000	1,000,000

All entries related to the contract have been recorded as of December 31, 1984, except for the revenue-recognition entry.

REQUIRED Show and explain what entry is still needed.

E23-7 Teche Construction Company has the following preclosing ledger account balances related to long-term construction contracts at year-end:

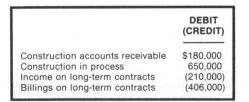

	DEBIT (CREDIT)
Construction accounts receivable	$180,000
Construction in process	650,000
Income on long-term contracts	(210,000)
Billings on long-term contracts	(406,000)

REQUIRED Show how these accounts would be reported on the income statement and the balance sheet for the current year-end.

E23–8 Des Moines Restaurant Suppliers outfits new restaurants and uses the installment sales method to account for sales to some of its customers. The following schedule applies to installment sales outstanding:

	1982	1983
Installment sales	$60,000	$80,000
Gross profit	15,000	20,000
1982 sales cash collections	30,000	20,000
1983 sales cash collections		45,000

REQUIRED Compute the approximate amount to be reported as deferred gross profit on the December 31, 1983, balance sheet.

E23–9 Giant TV Mart, Inc., has the following income statement items for 1983:

	1983
Sales (cash)	$150,000
Sales (installment basis)	320,000
Total sales	$470,000
Cost of sales	376,000
Less: Gross profit deferred on uncollected installment sales contracts	32,000
Gross profit recognized	$ 62,000

REQUIRED Compute the amount of cash collected on installment sales during 1983 assuming that 1983 was the first year of installment sales and that no repossessions took place.

E23–10 (CPA ADAPTED)

_____ 1. When progress billings are sent on a long-term contract, what type of account should be credited under the completed contract method and percentage-of-completion method?

COMPLETED CONTRACT METHOD	PERCENTAGE-OF-COMPLETION METHOD
a. Revenue	Revenue
b. Revenue	Contra asset
c. Contra asset	Revenue
d. Contra asset	Contra asset

_____ 2. Mercer Construction Company recognizes income under the percentage-of-completion method of reporting income from long-term construction contracts. During 1978 Mercer entered into a fixed-price contract to construct a bridge for $15,000,000. Contract costs incurred and estimated costs to complete the bridge were as follows:

	CUMULATIVE CONTRACT COSTS INCURRED	ESTIMATED COSTS TO COMPLETE
At 12/31/78	$ 1,000,000	$8,000,000
At 12/31/79	5,500,000	5,500,000
At 12/31/80	10,000,000	2,000,000

How much income should Mercer recognize on the above contract for the year ended December 31, 1980?

a. $500,000
b. $833,333
c. $1,350,000
d. $2,500,000

PROBLEMS

P23–1 The Karp Construction Company began operations in 1980. The following data summarize the cost and revenue information on all four projects contracted for to date at 12/31/82:

Cost Data ($000 omitted):

| | PROJECT | | | |
	101	102	103	104
Actual costs—1980	$ 7	$30	$18	$ 0
Actual costs—1981	25	12	12	20
Actual costs—1982	13	0	13	25
Estimated costs to complete	15	0	0	15
Estimated total costs	$60	$42	$43	$60

Revenue Data ($000 omitted):

| | PROJECT | | | |
	101	102	103	104
Total contract price	$80	$55	$45	$57
Billings to December 31, 1982	60	55	43	40
Collections to December 31, 1982	55	49	43	40

REQUIRED

1. Assume that Karp uses the percentage-of-completion method for reporting profit. Also assume that estimated total costs for project 101 as of the end of *1981* were $64,000. (Estimated total costs = Total actual costs plus estimated costs to complete.) Compute the profit to be reported for project 101 *only* for the year 1982. Be careful to read the dates and data correctly.

2. Identify the balance sheet accounts related to project 101 as of December 31, 1982, and illustrate what their balances would be, if any, as of that date.

3. Ignore requirements 1 and 2. Assume that Karp used the completed contract method of accounting for construction contracts. What would be the reported profit or loss for 1982 (consider all four projects)?

P23–2 Smith Brothers Builders, Inc., a newly formed corporation, has been asked to bid on an addition to a hospital. The president of the company has found a team to work up the estimates necessary to make a bid, including two engineers and the controller. The following estimates of costs and time schedules are made on November 1, 1982:

	1983	1984	TOTAL
Labor costs	$ 6,050,000	$ 7,500,000	$13,550,000
Material costs	12,000,000	9,000,000	21,000,000
Other	1,800,000	1,450,000	3,250,000
	$19,850,000	$17,950,000	$37,800,000

The president decides to bid $50,400,000, which would provide a 25 percent gross profit rate on the bid price. The president is very concerned about the effect of such a contract on the financial statements.

REQUIRED   As controller of Smith Brothers Builders, make up an analysis of the income statement impact of the above contract, assuming perfect estimates under (1) the completed contract method and (2) the percentage-of-completion method. (Assume a calendar-year accounting period.)

P23–3   Refer to the estimates shown in the preceding problem. Assume that Smith Brothers Builders, Inc., was granted the contract on January 1, 1983, and had the following experience:

	1983	1984	1985
Total costs incurred during year	$10,500,000	$17,400,000	$12,000,000
Billings during year	12,000,000	22,000,000	16,400,000
Cash received during year	8,300,000	24,000,000	18,100,000
Estimates of costs to complete at 12/31	27,300,000	11,500,000	0

REQUIRED

1. Assuming that the percentage-of-completion method is used, show all the necessary journal entries for the life of the contract.

2. Regardless of requirement 1, what entry would be necessary on December 31, 1984, if the estimate of the cost to complete was $30,000,000 at that time under both the percentage-of-completion and the completed contract methods?

P23–4   Chet Ludville's Burgers, Inc., sells franchised fast-food outlets in western Michigan. Thirty-five outlets have been opened since the chain was established on January 1, 1982. On January 1, 1983, the thirty-sixth outlet is established with 50 percent of the $100,000 franchise fee paid immediately, and the remaining $50,000 to be paid in four payments of $12,500 each December 31 of each year until 1986. The implied interest rate charged the franchisee is 10 percent, which is considered an appropriate rate because the owner of the thirty-sixth franchise has an excellent credit rating.

REQUIRED

1. Assume that Chet must refund all payments for the franchise if any of the services to be provided are not rendered through December 31, 1986. How should Chet account for the franchise-fee payments made in 1983 for the thirty-sixth outlet?

2. Assume that only the down payment is nonrefundable, and that the amount of the down payment and the timing of the remaining payments are representative of the portion of the total effort provided by the franchisor that has actually been performed to date. Record the first 2 years of the thirty-sixth franchise arrangement on Chet's books.

P23–5   Darren's Disco Discount Discs is a record-franchising company with over 300 stores in 22 states. Judy and Joe Halverson opened up the three hundredth franchise on January 1, 1983. Darren has charged an initial franchise fee of $35,000. In exchange for this fee, Darren has helped Judy and Joe to obtain a location and a building, to set up an accounting record-keeping system, and to design and construct a new storefront. The franchise arrangement calls for payments to Darren of an additional $1,000 per year by each outlet to support the cost of nationwide advertising.

Assume that Judy and Joe have agreed to pay Darren the $35,000 franchise fee with six equal payments of $8,042 beginning January 1, 1983, and on December 31 from 1983 to 1987. Judy and Joe can get outside financing at 15 percent interest.

REQUIRED

1. If it seems that the down payment for the franchise fee may have to be refunded to Judy and Joe and that Darren is required to provide substantial future services in the area of accounting systems design and implementation, how should the franchise fee be recorded by Darren in 1983?

2. If the down payment is not refundable and Darren is considered to have substantially performed all the major conditions of the franchise arrangements, how should the franchise fee be recorded by Darren in 1983 assuming the collectibility of the remaining franchise payments is very uncertain?

3. Repeat requirement 2 assuming the collectibility of the remaining franchise payments is very certain.

P23–6 (CPA ADAPTED) The Deytyme Construction Company began operations January 1, 1984. During the year, Deytyme entered into a contract with Redbeard Razor Corporation to construct a manufacturing facility. At that time, Deytyme estimated that it would take 5 years to complete the facility at a total cost of $4,800,000. The total contract price for construction of the facility is $6,000,000. During the year, Deytyme incurred $1,250,000 in construction costs related to the construction project. The estimated cost to complete the contract is $3,750,000. Redbeard was billed and paid 30 percent of the contract price.

REQUIRED Prepare schedules to compute the amount of gross profit to be recognized for the year ended December 31, 1984, and the amount to be shown as "cost of uncompleted contract in excess of related billings" or "billings on uncompleted contract in excess of related costs" at December 31, 1984, under each of the following methods:

1. Completed contract method
2. Percentage-of-completion method

P23–7 On April 1, 1984, Butler, Inc., entered into a fixed-fee contract to construct an electric generator for Dalton Corporation. At the contract date, Butler estimated that it would take 2 years to complete the project at a cost of $2,000,000. The fixed fee stipulated in the contract is $2,300,000. Butler appropriately accounts for this contract under the percentage-of-completion method. During 1984 Butler incurred costs of $700,000 related to the project, and the estimated cost at December 31, 1984, to complete the contract is $1,400,000. Dalton was billed $500,000 under the contract.

REQUIRED Prepare a schedule to compute the amount of gross profit to be recognized by Butler under the contract for the year ended December 31, 1984. Show supporting computations.

P23–8 (CPA ADAPTED) The Maple Corporation sells farm machinery on the installment plan. On July 1, 1984, Maple entered into an installment sale contract with Agriculture, Inc., for an 8-year period. Equal annual payments under the installment sale are $100,000 and are due on July 1. The first payment was made on July 1, 1984.

Additional information:

1. The amount that would be realized on an outright sale of similar farm machinery is $556,000.
2. The cost of the farm machinery sold to Agriculture is $417,000.
3. The finance charges relating to the installment period are $244,000 based on a stated interest rate of 12 percent, which is appropriate.
4. Circumstances are such that the collection of the installments due under the contract is reasonably assured.

REQUIRED What income or loss before income taxes should Maple record for the year ended December 31, 1984, as a result of the above transaction? Show supporting computations.

P23–9 In 1983 International Computers started to sell computers in several foreign countries. Some of these countries are rather unstable, and the controller is thinking of using the installment sales method to account for the sales that involve long-term paybacks.

The controller asks you to analyze the relative income statement effects of "normal" sales recognition and installment sales recognition given the schedule of sales over three years—1983, 1984, and 1985—shown at the top of page 905. Assume that all repossessions have a fair value equal to 75 percent of their original selling price.

REQUIRED Prepare the analysis requested by the controller.

P23–10 Water Haven, Inc., started building inexpensive portable cabins in a remote fishing area during 1983. Each cabin is constructed at a central location and transported by truck to camp sites. All sales contracts require

	1983	1984	1985
Sales	$10,000,000	$15,000,000	$20,000,000
Gross profit percentage	18%	20%	20%
Cash collections on sales	50%/1983 sales	50%/1984 sales 20%/1983 sales	50%/1985 sales 20%/1984 sales 20%/1983 sales
Defaults and repossessions	$1,000,000 of 1983 sales on which $500,000 has been collected	$1,500,000 of 1984 sales on which $750,000 has been collected $500,000 of 1983 sales on which $300,000 has been collected	$2,000,000 of 1985 sales on which $1,000,000 has been collected $500,000 of 1984 sales on which $400,000 has been collected $500,000 of 1983 sales on which $450,000 has been collected

installment payments over 3 years. The company sells two types of cabins—Economy and Deluxe—with the following cost and selling price characteristics:

	ECONOMY		DELUXE	
	1983	1984	1983	1984
Selling price	$6,500	$7,000	$9,000	$9,600
Cost to manufacture	4,550	4,900	5,850	6,240
Gross profit	$1,950	$2,100	$3,150	$3,360

During the 1983 and 1984 selling seasons the company had the following sales and cash collections:

	ECONOMY		DELUXE	
	1983	1984	1983	1984
Units sold	100	110	50	60
Cash collected:				
1983 Sales	$201,500	$255,000	$148,500	$130,000
1984 Sales		250,000		160,000

There were seven repossessions during 1984 as follows:

	NUMBER OF UNITS REPOSSESSED		PER UNIT AVERAGE RECEIVABLE AT DATE OF REPOSSESSION		PER UNIT AVERAGE FAIR VALUE AT DATE OF REPOSSESSION	
	ECONOMY	DELUXE	ECONOMY	DELUXE	ECONOMY	DELUXE
1983 Sales	2	3	$3,900	$5,580	$4,000	$6,500
1984 Sales	1	1	5,000	7,000	4,500	7,000

REQUIRED Show all journal entries for the above transactions assuming the installment sales method is used for accounting purposes.

P23–11 The Moriarity Construction Company accounts for its long-term construction contracts on a percentage-of-completion basis. You have been assigned to account for contract #87-6503, a bridge under construction in Kansas. The following information is available for the first 3 years of the $90,000,000 bridge:

	($000 OMITTED)		
	1983	**1984**	**1985**
Costs—current year	$ 5,000	$15,000	$15,000
Costs—prior year(s)	-0-	5,000	20,000
Total actual costs	$ 5,000	$20,000	$35,000
Estimated costs to complete	60,000	48,000	35,000
Estimated *total* costs	$65,000	$68,000	$70,000
Billings to date	7,000	25,000	40,000
Collections on billings to date	4,000	20,000	35,000
Estimated *total* profit	25,000	22,000	20,000

During 1986 the costs incurred on contract #87-6503 amounted to $25,000,000, and the estimated costs to complete were $15,000,000 at the end of 1986. A total of $28,000,000 was billed during 1986, and $25,000,000 was collected during the year.

REQUIRED

1. Compute the profit to be reported on contract #87-6503 for the year 1986.
2. Record all entries necessary to summarize the 1986 activity on contract #87-6503.
3. Indicate the balance sheet accounts that would appear at the end of 1986 pertaining to the contract, and their balances.

P23–12 (CPA ADAPTED) Curtiss Construction Company, Inc., entered into a firm fixed-price contract with Axelrod Associates on July 1, 1984, to construct a four-story office building. At that time Curtiss estimated that it would take between 2 and 3 years to complete the project. The total contract price for construction of the building is $4,000,000. Curtiss appropriately accounts for this contract under the completed contract method in its financial statements and for income tax reporting. The building was deemed substantially completed on December 31, 1986. Estimated percentage of completion, accumulated contract costs, and accumulated billings to Axelrod under the contract were as follows:

	AT DECEMBER 31, 1984	AT DECEMBER 31, 1985	AT DECEMBER 31, 1986
Percentage of completion	10%	60%	100%
Contract costs incurred	$ 350,000	$2,500,000	$4,250,000
Estimated costs to complete the contract	3,150,000	1,700,000	—
Billings to Axelrod	720,000	2,160,000	3,600,000

REQUIRED

1. Prepare schedules to compute the amount to be shown as "cost of uncompleted contract in excess of related billings" or "billings on uncompleted contract in excess of related costs" at December 31, 1984, 1985, and 1986. Ignore income taxes. Show supporting computations.
2. Prepare schedules to compute the profit or loss to be recognized as a result of this contract for the years ended December 31, 1984, 1985, and 1986. Ignore income taxes. Show supporting computations.

P23-13 (CPA ADAPTED) Tulip Corporation engages in long-term construction. Long-term contracts recorded under the percentage-of-completion method aggregate $6,000,000. Costs incurred on these contracts were $1,500,000 in 1984 and $3,000,000 in 1985. Estimated additional costs of $1,000,000 are required to complete these contracts. Revenues of $1,740,000 were recognized in 1984 and a total of $4,800,000 has been billed, of which $4,600,000 has been collected. No long-term contracts recorded under the percentage-of-completion method were completed in 1985. Note that the $1,740,000 is gross *revenue,* not gross *profit.*

The two long-term contracts recorded under the completed contract method were started in 1984. One is a $5,000,000 contract. Costs incurred were $1,400,000 in 1984 and $1,600,000 in 1985. A total of $3,100,000 has been billed and $2,800,000 collected. Although it is difficult to estimate the additional costs required to complete this contract, indications are that this contract will be profitable.

The second contract is for $4,000,000. Costs incurred were $1,200,000 in 1984 and $2,600,000 in 1985. A total of $3,300,000 has been billed and $2,900,000 collected. Although it is difficult to estimate the additional costs required to complete this contract, indications are that there will be a loss of approximately $550,000.

REQUIRED Prepare schedules to support the income statement effects of Tulip's long-term contracts for 1985.

P23-14 (CPA ADAPTED) The Birch Company sells computers. On January 1, 1985, Birch entered into an installment sale contract with the Grove Company for a 7-year period expiring December 31, 1991. Equal annual payments under the installment sale are $1,000,000 and are due on January 1. The first payment was made on January, 1, 1985.
Additional information:

1. The cash selling price of the computer, that is, the amount that would be realized on an outright sale, is $5,355,000.
2. The cost of sales relating to the computer is $4,284,000.
3. The finance charges relating to the installment period are $1,645,000 based on a stated interest rate of 10 percent, which is appropriate. For tax purposes, Birch appropriately uses the accrual basis for recording finance charges.
4. Circumstances are such that the collection of the installment sale is reasonably assured.
5. The installment sale qualifies for the installment method of reporting for tax purposes, but the normal sales method is used for financial accounting purposes.
6. Assume that the income tax rate is 40 percent.

REQUIRED

1. What income (loss) before income taxes should Birch appropriately record as a result of this transaction for the year ended December 31, 1985? Show supporting computations.
2. What provision for deferred income taxes, if any, should Birch appropriately record as a result of this transaction for the year ended December 31, 1985? Show supporting computations.

24

Accounting Changes and Errors

OVERVIEW   In this chapter we reconsider the accounting disclosure issues related to accounting changes, and the analysis and correction of accounting errors that were introduced in Chapter 3. In much of the text we have been concerned with accounting methods, their underlying concepts, and their implications for financial statement disclosure. Here we focus on financial statement disclosure for situations where changes in accounting occur. The primary characteristics of accounting information discussed in Chapter 2 that the generally accepted accounting principles are attempting to stress are **comparability** and **consistency.** This basic objective underlying generally accepted accounting procedures that affect the reporting of changes in accounting principles, estimates, entities, and errors is fundamental to understanding the efforts of accounting policy makers to enhance the usefulness of accounting reports.

ALTERNATIVE DISCLOSURES

Because of the dynamic environment within which business entities operate, it is not uncommon to observe an entity changing one or more of its methods of accounting over time. There are several different ways in which an entity might report the impact of changes in accounting methods. In general, one or more of three possible time periods may be affected by changes in accounting methods, resulting in the following possible treatments:

1. **Retroactive treatment:** The financial report data of prior accounting periods are altered because of the change.
2. **Current treatment:** The current year's financial report data are altered because of the change.
3. **Prospective treatment:** Only the future years' financial report data will be altered from what they would otherwise have been because of the change.

Historically, the correct treatment for accounting changes was not well defined, and changes were not uniformly handled across entities. This inconsistency created a need for disclosure rules to unify the methods of reporting accounting changes. Perhaps the major problem was the erosion of confidence on the part of external users of financial data because of the frequent application of accounting changes to prior years—that is, retroactive adjustments. Excessive use of retroactive adjustments tends to reduce the credibility of accounting information. To illustrate, assume that you noticed the following summarized data in Gamma Corporation's 1982 annual report:

GAMMA CORPORATION 1982 Annual Report Selected Data			
	1982	**1981**	**1980**
Net income	$ 14,565,000	$ 13,105,000	$ 11,876,000
Earnings per share	$2.87	$2.40	$2.10
Total assets	$150,000,000	$145,000,000	$143,000,000

At the end of the next year, 1983, you noticed the following summarized data in Gamma Corporation's annual report:

GAMMA CORPORATION 1983 Annual Report Selected Data			
	1983	**1982**	**1981**
Net income	$ 12,805,000	$ 11,276,000	$ 10,000,000
Earnings per share	$2.60	$2.35	$2.08
Total assets	$152,000,000	$149,000,000	$142,000,000

In both years you are left with the impression that Gamma has steadily been improving, but when you refer back to your 1982 report you realize that the accounting numbers for comparative years reported in 1983 have changed from those reported in 1982. A situation such as this would generally leave financial report readers with an uneasy feeling about the use of accounting information, perhaps wondering when and if the final income number for a given year will be known with certainty or reported.

Types of Accounting Changes

The lack of confidence in accounting data created by retroactive adjustments caused accounting policy makers to consider the disclosure implications of accounting changes and to address their lack of uniform treatment by business entities. The main pronouncement governing such changes and errors is **APB Opinion No. 20,** "Accounting Changes."[1] **Opinion No. 20** classifies errors and changes as follows:

1. Changes in accounting principles—current treatment
2. Changes in accounting principles—retroactive treatment
3. Changes in accounting estimates
4. Changes in accounting entities
5. Changes due to errors of prior years

Each of these five categories of accounting change and its related disclosure requirements will be dealt with in turn. Keep the Gamma Corporation example in mind and the problems created by retroactive adjustments, as it will help you understand the disclosure rules that have evolved since 1970.

Changes in Accounting Principles— Current Treatment

The accounting procedures for **most changes in accounting principles call for "current treatment"** disclosure. The impact of the principle change is to be reported in the financial statement in the year of the change. A **principle** is considered to be any accounting method that is systematically applied to the accounting data. It would include such things as the method of depreciation, amortization, inventory measurement, revenue recognition, accounting for investments, accounting for pensions, accounting for deferred taxes, doubtful account measurement, and any other accounting method having **one or more alternatives that have materially different effects on the measurement of income.**

Some accounting methods have alternatives that do *not* alter income measurement, and changes may be made in such accounting methods without considering the disclosure requirements discussed here. As examples of alternative **accounting methods that do not alter the measurement of income,** refer to the earlier discussion concerning the net and gross methods of accounting for purchase discounts (Chapter 9), the net and gross methods of recording long-term lease receivables (Chapter 15), the alternative methods of recording write-downs to market for inventory (Chapter 9), and the alternative ways to reconcile cash (Chapter 7). Prior to **APB Opinion No. 20,** most accounting method changes were accorded **retroactive treatment.** However, as a result of **APB Opinion No. 20,** all but a few accounting method changes now receive **current treatment.**

Common examples of changes in accounting principles that require current treatment disclosures are[2]

1. Change *to* LIFO inventory method
2. Change in method of accounting for leases

[1] *Accounting Principles Board Opinion No. 20,* "Accounting Changes" (New York: AICPA, July 1971).

[2] See *Accounting Trends and Techniques* (New York: AICPA, 1980–1982).

3. Change in method of accounting for interest costs related to construction
4. Change in method of accounting for oil and gas operations
5. Change in depreciation methods
6. Change in method of accounting for investment tax credit

We can evaluate the nature of accounting principle changes and determine what impact they have had on the entity's financial statements by carefully studying the statements and footnotes. If we ignore tax consequences, nearly all the accounting changes can be viewed as having *little or no direct consequence* on the firm's economic wealth position or economic performance. In other words, the funds flows of the entity (either cash or working capital) are generally unaffected by accounting changes.

Analysis of method changes Because of the noneconomic nature of most changes in accounting methods, a number of research studies have tried to determine whether external users react to reported income numbers that have been affected by accounting changes. If users were to react in such a way that the market price of the entity's stocks and bonds would be positively or negatively affected by changes in reported income numbers resulting from changes in accounting methods, it would be difficult to argue that these changes had little direct economic consequences. To date, most of these research studies have found that **stock prices are not affected by changes in accounting methods** that do not have a **direct** impact on the cash flows of the entity.[3] Accounting changes that do not have cash (economic) consequences are considered "artificial," even though they have an impact on income measurement.

The research results reported to date raise the question of why corporations would want to change accounting methods. Many possible reasons and theories for accounting changes have been suggested, but few seem to have the support of a majority. The belief that managers seek to enhance their own well-being by attempting to deceive owners and directors concerning the financial position of the entity may be somewhat naïve. Yet we cannot deny that accounting changes continue to take place with little apparent justification.

Some recent studies have found that stock prices do seem to react to certain accounting changes that do not have a known economic impact on the wealth position of the firm.[4] It has been suggested that investor reactions (as measured by changes in market prices) to accounting method changes that do not in and of themselves have any **direct** impact on the entity's cash flows are indications that the **indirect** effects of such changes may have economic significance to outside users. The economic impact of changes in accounting methods will undoubtedly continue to be an active area for accounting research, and the controversy over the direct and in-

---

[3] For several good sources of reviews of such literature, see George Foster, *Financial Statement Analysis* (Englewood Cliffs, NJ: Prentice-Hall, 1978); Baruch Lev, *Financial Statement Analysis: A New Approach* (Englewood Cliffs, NJ: Prentice-Hall, 1974); and Thomas Dyckman, David Downes, and Robert Magee, *Efficient Capital Markets and Accounting: A Critical Analysis* (Englewood Cliffs, NJ: Prentice-Hall, 1975).

[4] For example, see the following articles on oil and gas accounting methods: Dan Collins and Warrent Dent, "The Proposed Elimination of Full Cost Accounting in the Extractive Petroleum Industry," *Journal of Accounting and Economics,* Spring 1979, pp. 3–44; and Baruch Lev, "Impact of Accounting Regulation on the Stock Market: The Case of Oil and Gas Companies," *The Accounting Review,* July 1979, pp. 485–503.

direct consequences of accounting changes will probably remain unsettled for some time.

The LIFO effect   The most frequent change in accounting principles over the past few years has been the change *to* LIFO inventory measurement procedures. This change also happens to be the only one that, because of the tax laws, has an obvious **direct economic impact** on the entity. Before LIFO is approved for tax purposes, it must also be used as the basis for financial reporting (or "book" purposes). In this instance, the IRS has a direct impact on the accounting methods used for financial reporting. In periods of rising costs, taxable income will normally be lowest when using the LIFO cost-flow assumption, but so too will financial statement income measurement. As a result, a change to LIFO normally results in **a direct economic benefit through tax savings,** and **a noneconomic cost of lower income** in financial statements. If the *direct* economic effects were the only thing to be considered in selecting an inventory method, we would find it difficult to explain why many companies still use FIFO for financial statement purposes without the prediction of a forthcoming period of no cost increases or sustained deflation. The *indirect* effects and entity-specific factors that affect the choice of inventory method, as well as other accounting alternatives, have not been adequately explained by the research that has been conducted up to now. This area will probably receive increasing attention from accounting researchers in the future.

Example of current treatment—change in principle   To illustrate the **current treatment,** consider a change in the method of accounting for the investment tax credit. The Phelps Corporation changed from the deferral method to the flow-through method of accounting for the investment tax credit in 1983. Exhibit 24–1 summarizes the impact of the change in principle as of December 31, 1983.

In Exhibit 24–1, the tax credit that would have been taken in 1983 under the deferral method is $600,000 and would have resulted in an income tax expense of $6,600,000 in the 1983 income statement and an ending balance in the Deferred Investment Tax Credit account of $7,813,000 as of December 31, 1983. By changing to the flow-through method, the entire $1,000,000 investment tax credit available from 1983 purchases is recognized in 1983 to reduce income tax expense to $6,200,000 in the 1983 income statement. Because the flow-through method does not require a Deferred Investment Tax Credit account, the entire opening balance of $7,413,000, which represents the cumulative prior years' effect of the difference in the two methods, would be taken into income in 1983 as the cumulative "catch-up" effect of the accounting change, illustrating current treatment. The elimination of the Deferred Investment Tax Credit account would result in an increase in net income and would appear as a separate item in the lower portion of the income statement (similar to the disclosure accorded extraordinary items). This accounting change, like most others, has no direct impact on the economic flows of the entity. The entity is no better off in any real sense even though income is increased, as illustrated below.

The following journal entry would record the cumulative prior years' effect of the change in principle to the flow-through method:

12/31/83	Deferred investment tax credit	7,413,000	
	Cumulative effect of accounting		
	change		7,413,000
	(To record change to flow-through		
	method of accounting for invest-		
	ment tax credit)		

EXHIBIT 24-1

COMPARATIVE METHOD ANALYSIS—PHELPS CORPORATION

ALTERNATIVE TAX CREDIT METHODS	TAX CREDIT DATA: 1983			OTHER DATA			
	BALANCE IN DEFERRED INVESTMENT TAX CREDIT AS OF JANUARY 1, 1983	AMOUNT OF TAX CREDIT AMORTIZED	INCOME TAX EXPENSE PER INCOME STATEMENT	NET INCOME		EARNINGS PER SHARE	
				PER 1983 INCOME STATEMENT	PER 1982 INCOME STATEMENT	PER 1983 INCOME STATEMENT	PER 1982 INCOME STATEMENT
Deferral (old method)	$7,413,000	$ 600,000	$6,600,000	$ 9,685,000	$8,647,000 (as reported)	$7.21	$6.40 (as reported)
Flow-through (new method)	0	$1,000,000	$6,200,000	$10,085,000	$8,918,000 (revised)	$7.51	$6.60 (revised)
Difference	$7,413,000	$ 400,000	$ 400,000	$ 400,000	$ 271,000	$ .30	$ .20

The following entry would record the tax credit of $1,000,000 for the qualifying 1983 capital expenditures:

12/31/83	Income tax payable	1,000,000	
	Income tax expense		1,000,000
	(To record tax credit for 1983)		

Because the tax credit is a tax amount, the cumulative prior years' effect, net of taxes, is the same as the pretax amount of $7,413,000. The partial comparative statements for the years ending December 31, 1982 and 1983, would appear as follows:

PHELPS CORPORATION
Partial Balance Sheet
As of December 31

	1983	1982
Long-term liabilities		
Deferred investment tax credit	$ 0	$ 7,413,000

Partial Income Statement
For the Years Ended December 31

	1983	1982
Income before taxes	$16,285,000	$14,447,000
Income tax expense	6,200,000	5,800,000
Net income before cumulative effect of accounting change	$10,085,000	$ 8,647,000
Cumulative effect of accounting change (see Note 14)	7,413,000	0
Net income	$17,498,000	$ 8,647,000
Earnings per share before accounting change	$ 7.51	$ 6.40
Per share effect of accounting change	5.52	.00
Earnings per share	$ 13.03	$ 6.40

PRO FORMA AMOUNTS	1983	1982
Net income	$10,085,000	$ 8,918,000
Earnings per share	$ 7.51	$ 6.60

Note that the 1982 financial statement data reported for comparison purposes in the body of the statements would be *exactly the same* as the data reported in 1982 (see Exhibit 24–1), and would not be retroactively adjusted because of the change to flow-through in 1983. The total cumulative prior years' effect of $7,413,000 is treated *currently* in the 1983 income statement and balance sheet. This method of accounting for the impact of accounting changes reduces the confusion created by retroactive types of adjustments, and it clearly discloses the effect of such changes. An example of the disclosure of such a change in accounting principle is illustrated in Exhibit 24–2.

Pro forma disclosures   Although current treatment avoids the confusion created by the retroactive adjustment noted in the Gamma Corporation example on page 909, the comparability of the Phelps Corporation's financial results for 1982 and 1983 is impaired because the results for 1982 are based on the deferral method, whereas those for 1983 are based on the flow-through method. To improve the compara-

EXHIBIT 24-2

NL INDUSTRIES, INC.
Consolidated Statement of Income and Retained Earnings

(IN THOUSANDS, EXCEPT PER SHARE AMOUNTS)

YEARS ENDED DECEMBER 31	1980	PER SHARE OF COMMON STOCK	1979	PER SHARE OF COMMON STOCK	1978	PER SHARE OF COMMON STOCK
Revenues:						
Net sales	$2,117,552		$1,810,235		$1,538,412	
Equity in partially-owned companies (Note 4)	33,443		16,855		7,722	
Other income (loss), net (Note 9 and Page 25)	(7,324)		(574)		(3,974)	
	2,143,671		1,826,516		1,542,160	
Costs and expenses:						
Cost of goods sold	1,392,925		1,221,773		1,034,295	
Selling, general and administrative	439,710		364,424		312,145	
Interest (Note 11)	41,975		48,876		34,468	
Minority interest	4,565		2,869		1,745	
	1,879,175		1,637,942		1,382,653	
Income before items shown below	264,496		188,574		159,507	
Provision for income taxes (Page 27)	96,823		73,998		72,334	
Income from continuing operations	167,673	$4.94	114,576	$3.36	87,173	$2.55
Discontinued operations (Note 1):						
Income (loss) from discontinued operations, net of income taxes—$3,517,000 in 1979 and (3,662,000) in 1978	—		6,469		(897)	
(Loss) from disposal of discontinued operations, net of $28,227,000 income tax benefit	—		(35,359)			
Income before cumulative effect of accounting change	167,673		85,686		86,276	
Cumulative effect of accounting change (Note 3)	—		26,257		—	
Net income	167,673	4.94	111,943	3.28	86,276	2.52
Retained earnings at beginning of year	641,447		573,224		530,274	
Less dividends paid:						
Common: 1980, $1.30 per common share; 1979 and 1978, $1.20 per common share	42,993		39,407		39,013	
Preferred	4,313		4,313		4,313	
Retained earnings at end of year	$ 761,814		$ 641,447		$ 573,224	
Pro Forma Information (Note 3):						
Income from continuing operations (Pro-Forma)	$ 167,673	$4.94	$ 114,576	$3.36	$ 92,922	$2.72
Net income (Pro-Forma)	167,673	4.94	85,686	2.48	93,026	2.73

bility of current disclosures called for by most changes in accounting principles, **APB Opinion No. 20** requires that **pro forma** ("as if") data be reported on the face of the income statement below the regular income statement data.[5] The pro forma data should disclose the key income statement information **as it would have been reported** had the new method been used in the prior years reported for comparison purposes. These pro forma data are sometimes reported below the partial comparative income statements, as illustrated in the Phelps example. At a minimum, the pro forma disclosures should include net income before extraordinary items (when appropriate), net income, and earnings-per-share data for all the years reported in the comparative financial statements. The NL Industries statement in Exhibit 24–2 illustrates such pro forma disclosure.

If space does not permit reporting pro forma amounts on the face of the income statement, they should be prominently disclosed in the notes to the financial statements with the appropriate cross-reference to the financial statements. Disclosing the pro forma amounts in the footnotes is a common practice. If for some reason these pro forma amounts are not determinable because of the nature of the accounting change, the reason for not reporting the pro forma effects should be clearly stated in the notes to the financial statements.

The pro forma disclosures are designed to eliminate problems that might be encountered concerning the *comparability* of current financial reports prepared using one accounting method with prior reports using other methods. At the same time, **the formal financial statements of prior years should remain as originally reported.**

When current treatment is impossible or not required In the following two instances, a change in accounting principle that should receive current treatment may *not* result in the normal (current treatment) disclosure of the cumulative prior years' effect:

1. A change in principle where the cumulative prior years' effect is not determinable
2. A change in principle applicable to current and future periods only

Income statement disclosure of the cumulative prior years' effect of a change in accounting principle may not be possible because accounting records may be unable to provide sufficient data on what the prior years' differences between the two methods would have been. The primary example of such a case is the change to the LIFO inventory method, in which the measurement of the cumulative prior years' effect may be impossible because of insufficient data regarding historical inventory costs. Normally, a complete reconstruction of what an entity's inventory would have been had the LIFO method been used from the beginning of the business is either impossible to accomplish or economically impractical. In such a case, there simply is no cumulative prior-period effect measured or disclosed. Exhibit 24–3 illustrates the type of disclosure that would be made when a company changes to LIFO.

The second variation occurs when a new principle is adopted for future periods only. For example, if a new depreciation method is to be applied to equipment purchased in the current and future years, and the old depreciation method is to be used for the partly depreciated equipment, then no cumulative prior years' effect would be reported in the year of the change.

[5] *Accounting Principles Board Opinion No. 20,* "Accounting Changes," par. 21.

EXHIBIT
24–3

DISCLOSURE OF ACCOUNTING CHANGE WHERE CUMULATIVE EFFECT CANNOT BE DETERMINED—CHANGE TO LIFO

EASCO CORPORATION AND SUBSIDIARIES
Notes to Consolidated Financial Statements, 1980

Note 1–Accounting Policies and Business Segments

Inventories. Inventories are valued at the lower of cost or market with cost for substantially all product inventories determined using the last-in, first-out (LIFO) method in 1980. Cost was determined using the average cost method for 59% in 1979 and 64% in 1978 of the consolidated inventory balance (76% in 1979 and 83% in 1978 of Hand Tools segment inventories). See Note 2 for additional information.

Note 2—Change in Accounting Method and Inventories

In 1980, the company changed from the average cost method to the last-in, first out (LIFO) method for valuing inventories of its principal hand tools manufacturing subsidiary.

Management believes the LIFO method is more appropriate since LIFO has the effect of matching more closely current costs against current revenues in the statement of income and minimizing the impact of price level changes upon inventory. The effect of this change was to reduce 1980 net income by $613,000, or 19 cents per common share. There is no cumulative effect of the change on prior years since the December 31, 1979 inventory as previously reported is also the amount of the beginning inventory under the LIFO method.

For both of these cases where cumulative prior years' effects are not reported, the current financial statement data should disclose (in footnotes) the impact of the change on the current year's statements, and the pro forma effect (if measurable) on those prior years' data that are provided in the current financial statements for comparison purposes.

Changes in Accounting Principles— Retroactive Treatment

There are five types of exceptions to the general rule of reporting the cumulative prior years' effect currently and not restating prior years' results in accounting for changes in principles. These special cases, where **retroactive treatment is required,** are the following:

1. Change *from* LIFO *to* any other inventory method
2. Change to or from the full-cost method of accounting by entities in extractive industries
3. Change to or from the completed-contract method for long-term construction contracts
4. Change in any and all accounting methods for reports of entities that are "going public" (selling equity capital in the open market for the first time) or are seeking to merge with another entity. (These changes may be made retroactively one time only.)
5. Changes where promulgated GAAP require retroactive treatment as a result of a new accounting standard (for example, FASB Statement No. 43 on compensated absences)

The first three situations are straightforward specifications of accounting alternatives, whereas the fourth and fifth describe general situations where retroactive changes may be applied. In these five instances, retroactive adjustments to previously published results are called for, largely due to the potential magnitude of such changes and their significance to the overall comparability of the financial re

EXHIBIT 24–4

BAXENDALE CONSTRUCTION COMPANY
Historical Summary ($000)

		1983			1984			1985	
PRO-JECT NUM-BER	CON-TRACT PRICE (FIXED)	TOTAL ESTI-MATED PROFIT AT 12/31/83	PERCENT COM-PLETED TO DATE	REPORTED PROFIT— 1983	TOTAL ESTI-MATED PROFIT AT 12/31/84	PERCENT COM-PLETED TO DATE	REPORTED PROFIT— 1984	TOTAL ESTI-MATED PROFIT AT 12/31/85	PERCENT COM-PLETED TO DATE
101	$3,500	$ 735	100%	$ 735	—	—	—	—	—
102	500	50	50	25	$ 45	100%	$ 20	—	—
103	8,200	3,200	10	320	3,000	50	1,180	$2,700	80%
104	2,400	450	20	90	460	100	370	—	—
105	600	—	—	—	60	30	18	58	100
106	1,480	—	—	—	250	10	25	210	80
107	3,250	—	—	—	—			240	50
Total profit as reported				$ 1,170			$ 1,613		
Tax expense as reported[a]				$ 468			$ 645		
Retained earnings—end of period[a]				$10,450			$13,118		
Construction in process—end of period[a]				$ 1,550			$ 4,428		

[a] Assumed amounts for illustration purposes.

ports. Retroactive adjustment of prior data is accomplished by actually using pro forma-type data in the formal financial statements instead of in the footnotes. The major drawback of retroactive adjustment is that it produces the kind of year-to-year fluctuations in a given year's data experienced by the Gamma Corporation illustrated earlier in this chapter.

Example of retroactive treatment—change in principle To illustrate **retroactive disclosure** for changes in accounting principles, consider the historical data in Exhibit 24–4 for the Baxendale Construction Company. This company began operations in 1983 using the percentage-of-completion method of accounting for its long-term contracts for financial-reporting purposes only. In 1985 Baxendale decided to switch to the completed-contract method because of the uncertainty in predicting profit on long-term contracts. The following table compares the company's 2 years of operations under the two alternative methods:

BAXENDALE CONSTRUCTION COMPANY
Comparison of profits on long-term contracts under two methods

	1984	1983	TOTAL TO 12/31/84
Percentage-of-completion method	$1,613,000	$1,170,000	$ 2,783,000
Completed-contract method	− 505,000	− 735,000	−1,240,000
Difference	$1,108,000	$ 435,000	$ 1,543,000

To restate profits of prior years from the percentage-of-completion method to the completed-contract method assuming a 40 percent tax rate, the following entry would be recorded:

12/31/85	Retained earnings	925,800[a]	
	Deferred income tax	617,200[b]	
	Construction in progress		1,543,000
	(To eliminate profit recognized under the percentage-of-completion basis from retained earnings and inventory)		

[a] .60 × $1,543,000.
[b] .40 × $1,543,000.

This entry removes the profit that had been added to the inventory account Construction in Progress during 1983–1984 for the yet to be completed projects, and it also reverses the tax deferral that had been increasing because of the different methods used for book and tax purposes. The total balance in deferred taxes (assuming no other deferral items) would be zero after the above entry is recorded.[6] Also, retained earnings is reduced for the after-tax effect of the change.

The partial comparative statements that would be *reported in 1985* as a result of the change to the completed-contract method are illustrated in Exhibit 24–5. When compared with the data summarized in Exhibit 24–4, several differences should be noted in the 1984 comparative financial data *reported in 1984,* compared with the 1984 financial data *reported in 1985.* The comparative data reported in 1985 on the

EXHIBIT 24–5

CHANGE TO COMPLETED-CONTRACT METHOD		
BAXENDALE CONSTRUCTION COMPANY	1985	1984 (RESTATED)
Partial Income Statement Data		
Profit on construction contracts	$ 58,000	$ 505,000
Tax expense	(23,000)	(202,000)
Net income	$ 05,000	$ 303,000
Partial Retained Earnings Statement Data		
Beginning balance as previously reported	$12,192,000	$12,450,000
Less: Cumulative prior years' effect of accounting change (net of 40% tax effect)		(261,000)
Adjusted balance in beginning retained earnings	$12,192,000	$12,189,000
Plus net income	58,000	303,000
Less dividends	(50,000)	(000,000)
Ending balance in retained earnings	$12,200,000	$12,192,000
Partial Balance Sheet Data Assets		
Construction in progress	$ 6,721,000	$ 3,320,000

[6] For a review of the use of the Deferred Income Tax account for timing differences such as the one illustrated here, see Chapter 17.

completed-contract basis are entirely different from the data reported in 1984 on the percentage-of-completion basis.

The completed-contract application for the year 1983 is reflected in the adjustment of the December 31, 1983, retained earnings figure ($12,450,000) in the 1984 comparative retained earnings statement. Note that the opening retained earnings balance of $12,450,000 is the figure that had been previously reported as January 1, 1984, retained earnings *before* the effect of the change in method. The $261,000 adjustment to this opening balance accounts for the difference in the two methods from *before* Janaury 1, 1984 (=1983) net of taxes, or ($435,000) × (1 − .40) = $261,000. The 1984 net income added to the adjusted beginning retained earnings of $303,000 for 1984 reflects the new method for 1984. Finally, the new method alone is applied in the year of the change to arrive at the 1985 net income of $35,000.

Changing income of prior years   One of the difficult aspects of the retroactive adjustment illustrated in Exhibit 24–5 consists of understanding how the prior years' numbers are affected without any apparent journal entry support. Keep in mind that *no journal entry* made during 1985 is capable of affecting income statement account balances of previous years. All income statement (nominal) accounts of previous periods have been closed to, and are reflected in, the current retained earnings balance. As a result, the only journal entry necessary (or possible) to reflect the prior years' impact is to retained earnings (a debit of $925,800 in this case). However, entries to prior years' income statement accounts are not necessary to alter the reported comparative numbers of prior years. The retroactive adjustment process requires **restatement of prior years' data that are reported for comparative purposes,** and **revision of the opening retained earnings balance to reflect the impact of the change for prior years not being presented in the comparative statements.**

Changes in
Accounting
Estimates

The accounting treatment for changes in accounting estimates calls for **current and prospective treatment** according to **APB Opinion No. 20.** No retroactive changes are permitted or required as a result of a change in an accounting estimate. As emphasized in many instances throughout this text, accounting information is often based on uncertain facts or situations, and estimates play a major role in preparing financial report data. Most assets and liabilities are subject to estimates of one kind or another, and it is only reasonable to assume that we may eventually encounter new facts or situations which will suggest that previous estimates are no longer appropriate. These changes in estimates are *not* errors. Revised estimates should be applied prospectively so that the accounting reports will reflect the best estimates available at the time of the reports.

Revisions in estimates are generally made in an effort *to enhance the reliability of the accounting data,* but often this can be accomplished only by sacrificing consistency in the data. This trade-off in two of the major qualitative characteristics of accounting information suggests that revisions in estimates should not necessarily be automatic but should be weighed against the impact on the consistency of the financial data. That is *not* to say that it is better to be consistently wrong. By definition, there can be no absolute right or wrong when dealing with estimates, because they are forecasts of future events or activities.

The following are common examples of assets that are often subject to estimates (the nature of the estimates is listed in parentheses):

1. Accounts and notes receivable (estimated uncollectibles)
2. Inventory (estimated normal profit, and so forth, in determining LCM application; estimated percentage of completion on construction in process inventories, and so forth)
3. Plant and equipment (estimated life, salvage value, and so forth)
4. Resources (estimated total resources for depletion measurement)
5. Intangibles (estimated period of benefit)
6. Leases (estimated life and salvage value of leased assets)
7. Long-term investments (estimated holding period, estimated influence over unconsolidated subsidiaries, and so forth)

Examples of estimates that may affect the accounting for liabilities are

1. Estimated accrued vacation and sick pay payable
2. Estimated warranty obligations
3. Estimated federal, state, and local taxes
4. Estimated pension liability
5. Estimated deferred tax liability
6. Estimated future claims for litigation, coupon offers, and so forth

Of course, the estimation process plays a major role in the measurement and communication of accounting information. Understanding that accounting data are based in part on uncertain and imprecise measurement procedures is important if accounting data are to be used effectively in decision making.

Example of current and prospective treatment — change in estimate As an example of a change in accounting estimate, assume that Gulf-Texas Minerals has been depleting an oil discovery that had an initial cost of $4,800,000 based on the assumption (estimate) that the size of the discovery was 2,400,000 barrels of oil. The original depletion rate was, therefore, $2 per barrel for the extracted oil ($4,800,000/2,400,000). Assume also that in 1985, a revised estimate of the *total* reserve was 3,000,000 barrels based on a recent geological survey. On June 1, 1985, the date of the revision, the following data were available:

	BARRELS OF OIL	DOLLARS
Original estimate	2,400,000	$4,800,000
Balance remaining at 1/1/85	1,200,000	2,400,000
Extracted before 6/1/85	300,000	
Revised remaining reserve at 6/1/85	1,500,000	
Extracted between 6/1/85 and 12/31/85	350,000	

The accounting procedure for changes in estimates requires **application of the new estimate as of the beginning of the period in which the revised estimate is made.** Assuming Gulf-Texas is a calendar-year company, the revised estimate of 3,000,000 barrels would be applied from January 1, 1985, *to 1985 and future years* (currently and prospectively) by taking the net book value of the asset at January 1, 1985 ($2,400,000) and depleting it over the estimated 1,800,000 remaining barrels (3,000,000 less 1,200,000 already extracted) as of January 1, 1985. The revised rate would be

$$\frac{\$2,400,000}{1,800,000 \text{ barrels}} = \$1.333 \text{ per barrel}$$

The rate of $1.333 per barrel would be used for 1985 and future periods or until another change in estimate occurred in the future. The following entry would record the depletion for the extraction of 650,000 barrels of oil for 1985:

12/31/85	Depletion expense	866,667[a]	
	Accumulated depletion		866,667

[a] 650,000 × $1.3333333.

The partial comparative balance sheet data at December 31, 1985 would appear as follows:

Partial Comparative Balance Sheet		
	1985	**1984**
Assets		
Natural resources (oil)	$4,800,000	$4,800,000
Less accumulated depletion	3,267,000	2,400,000
Net resources	$1,533,000	$2,400,000

Changes in estimates will always receive current and prospective treatment and will never require a cumulative catch-up entry for prior years' effects or the restatement of prior years' amounts. When changes in estimates have a material impact on the comparability and consistency of the accounting reports, a footnote should explain the nature and impact of the change in estimate.

Changes in Accounting Entities

A merger or an acquisition will frequently have a major impact on the nature of an accounting entity. As a result, it would make very little sense to report comparative data without retroactively adjusting prior years' reports as if the merger or acquisition had taken place in some earlier period. Therefore, when the group of companies reported on in the consolidated financial statements changes due to mergers or acquisitions, **the change should be accounted for on a retroactive adjustment basis.** This process may be quite complex because of the retroactive accounting required for minority interests, incompatible fiscal year-ends, fair market-value estimates required by the purchase method for prior years, intercompany business transactions of prior years, and so on.

Because of the complexity involved in accounting for changes in an accounting entity, it is not possible to provide a complete example of such an accounting change. The underlying concepts, however, are similar to those applied in Chapter 14 to illustrate the change to the equity method of accounting for long-term investments.

Changes Due to Errors

Changes in accounting that result from the discovery of an error made in a prior period that has already been reported should receive retroactive adjustment. Such errors should not be allowed to remain in the statements of prior years that are being reported currently for comparison purposes. The accounting treatment to correct for errors made in prior periods is very similar to that illustrated for those changes in principle that receive retroactive treatment.

Example of retroactive treatment—error corrections To illustrate an error correction, assume that the Booth Bay Company acquired a piece of fish-netting machinery in January 1982 at a cost of $125,000. The equipment, which was expected to have a 10-year life and no salvage value, was to be depreciated on a straight-line basis. Due to the loss of the invoice, the purchase was incorrectly identified as "other expense" during 1982 for both book and tax purposes. The following results were reported at the end of 1982:

BOOTH BAY COMPANY

Selected Income Statement Data for the Years Ended December 31

	1982	1981
Depreciation expense	$ 1,000,000	$ 980,000
Income tax expense (40%)	3,800,000	3,400,000
Net income	5,700,000	5,100,000

Selected Balance Sheet Data as of December 31

	1982	1981
Equipment	$14,000,000	$13,200,000
Accumulated depreciation	10,120,000	(9,120,000)
Net equipment	$ 3,880,000	$ 4,080,000

Retained Earnings Statement as of December 31

	1982	1981
Retained earnings—Jan. 1	$46,600,000	$46,000,000
Net income	5,700,000	5,100,000
Dividends	(4,500,000)	(4,500,000)
Retained earnings—Dec. 31	$47,800,000	$46,600,000

Assume that the error was discovered during 1983. The following entries would be required sometime during 1983 to account for the accounting change due to the error:

1983	Equipment	125,000	
	Accumulated depreciation		12,500
	Retained earnings		112,500
	(To record netting equipment erroneously expensed during 1982)		
1983	Retained earnings	45,000[a]	
	Income taxes payable		45,000
	(To record taxes payable from understating 1982 net income for tax and book)		

[a] ($125,000 − $12,500) × .40 = $45,000

Also, the following entry would be required at year-end to record 1983 depreciation on the netting equipment:

```
12/31/83    Depreciation expense                        12,500
              Accumulated depreciation                             12,500
              (To record 1983 depreciation expense)
```

The following comparative statements would be reported at the end of 1983.

BOOTH BAY COMPANY
Selected Income Statement Data
For the Year Ended December 31

	1983	RESTATED 1982
Depreciation expense	$ 1,012,500	$ 1,012,500
Income tax expense (40%)	3,866,667	3,845,000
Net income	5,800,000	5,767,500

Selected Balance Sheet Data as of December 31

	1983	RESTATED 1982
Equipment	$14,125,000	$14,125,000
Accumulated depreciation	(11,145,000)	(10,132,500)
Net equipment	$ 2,980,000	$ 3,992,500

Retained Earnings Statement as of December 31

	1983	RESTATED 1982
Retained earnings—Jan. 1	$47,867,500	$46,600,000
Net income	5,800,000	5,767,500
Dividends	(5,000,000)	(4,500,000)
Retained earnings—Dec. 31	$48,667,500	$47,867,500

In Booth Bay's comparative statements for 1983, the error correction does not call for an adjustment to the retained earnings balance at January 1, 1982, because the error did not affect periods prior to 1982. Recall that the retroactive adjustment for the Baxendale Construction Company illustrated in Exhibit 24–5 did require an adjustment to the opening retained earnings balance *because the income of years prior to*

BOOTH BAY COMPANY
Retained Earnings Statement

	1983	RESTATED 1982
Retained earnings—Jan. 1	$47,860,000	$46,600,000
Correction due to error made in 1981 (net of taxes)		67,500
Corrected retained earnings—Jan. 1	$47,860,000	$46,667,500
Net income	5,800,000	5,692,500
Dividends	(5,000,000)	(4,500,000)
Retained earnings—Dec. 31	$48,660,000[a]	$47,860,000

[a] Note that the difference in retained earnings at 12/31/83 between the two assumptions of (1) error made in 1982 and (2) error made in 1981 is simply one year's depreciation expense after taxes: $12,500 × (1 − .4) = $48,667,500 − 48,660,000 = 7,500.

---

the date of the opening retained earnings were affected. In the Booth Bay case, if the same error had been made in 1981 instead of 1982 and was not discovered until 1983, the 1983 comparative retained earnings statement shown at the bottom of p. 924 would have been reported. The retroactive treatment required in accounting for errors is the same as the retroactive treatment for certain changes in accounting principles illustrated earlier.

SUMMARY OF TREATMENT OF ACCOUNTING CHANGES

As pointed out at the beginning of this chapter, all accounting changes are recorded by using one or more of the three types of change, which can be summarized as follows:

1. Retroactive treatment
   a. Errors
   b. Changes in principles—selected cases
   c. Changes in entity
2. Current treatment
   a. Changes in principles—general case
   b. Changes in estimates
3. Prospective treatment
   Changes in estimate affecting more than one year

Understanding how these accounting changes affect the financial reports is essential if report readers are to understand the nature of the financial statements and changes in financial reports from period to period. Although accounting changes do not occur so often as to affect most financial statements in most years, they tend to have a significant impact on the financial results when they do occur. However, the significance of their impact is normally in the magnitude of their effect on the reported numbers rather than their real economic impact on the position of the entity.

Proper financial statement disclosure of all material accounting changes should permit users of financial data *to determine the effect of the accounting change.* In the general case of a change in principle, the pro forma disclosures facilitate this determination. In all other cases, footnote disclosure of the change should permit the financial statement user to determine the impact of the change on current and comparative prior years' results. Whether the disclosure takes the form of pro forma data or a footnote is less important than whether the impact of the change is *clearly determinable, thus maintaining the comparability and consistency of the accounting data* as much as possible.

Preferability Statement

In 1975 the Securities and Exchange Commission issued **Accounting Series Release No. 177,** which requires the management of all companies making an accounting change in a filing with the SEC to include a statement explaining why the new accounting treatment is preferable.[7] Also, the auditor's report must indicate whether or not the auditor agrees with the preferability of the new method. One of the most common accounting changes in recent years has been the change to the LIFO inventory method. Most preferability statements have pointed out that LIFO is being elected because of its superior ability to match costs with revenues in periods of rising prices. However, the argument could also be made that FIFO results in a more

---

[7] *Accounting Series Release No. 177,* "Notice of Adoption of Amendments to Form 10–Q and Regulation S–X Regarding Interim Financial Reporting" (Washington, DC: SEC, 1975).

appropriate ending inventory value in periods of rising prices. It is difficult to argue consistently that one accounting alternative is superior or inferior to another, particularly for the auditor who must consider the preferences of many diverse client companies.

Interim Reporting Accounting changes for interim financial statements do not follow the exact same procedures discussed above. The disclosures for interim accounting changes, as covered by **FASB Statement No. 3,** are examined in detail in Chapter 27 of this text.

PRIOR PERIOD ADJUSTMENTS

The phrase **prior period adjustments** is used to identify those items of profit and loss not recognized in the income statement of the period but instead recognized as adjustments to the retained earnings balance of previous periods. In the context of the "all inclusive" (as opposed to "current operating") form of income statement disclosure (see Chapter 3), prior period adjustments are viewed as one of the primary exceptions. Other exceptions to the all-inclusive concept include the direct charges and credits to other owners' equity accounts allowed by GAAP governing long-term investments in marketable equity securities per **FASB Statement No. 12** (see Chapter 14) and foreign currency translations per **FASB Statement No. 52.** The following two items qualify for prior period adjustment treatment:[8]

1. Errors of prior years
2. Tax loss carryforward benefits that were in existence *before* the acquisition of an acquired subsidiary but realized *after* the acquisition

These two items receive retroactive treatment by adjusting retained earnings. Because errors were illustrated above as one of the accounting changes, we shall not illustrate such retroactive treatment again.

The definition of prior period adjustments has become narrower over time, and current GAAP are relatively restrictive as to what types of items may be considered prior period adjustments. The historical evolution of **APB Opinions No. 9** and **No. 20,** and **FASB Statements No. 5** and **No. 16,** have combined to narrow the use of retroactive adjustments of any kind to the following items:

1. Prior period adjustments
   a. Errors
   b. Subsidiary loss carryforwards
2. Changes in accounting principles—selected cases
3. Changes in accounting entity

This list of items may seem extensive until one considers the relatively low frequency of such situations. As a result of the series of pronouncements noted above, instances of retroactive adjustments are relatively few in comparison with earlier prepronouncement periods. Because of the reduction in retroactive adjustments, the problems associated with the Gamma Corporation example at the beginning of this chapter have been significantly reduced. Note that the accounting treatment for

---

[8] See *Statement of Financial Accounting Standards No. 16,* "Prior Period Adjustments" (Stamford, CT: FASB, June 1977), par. 11.

prior period adjustments is the same as that used for changes in principle that receive retroactive treatment even though these two types of "changes" are not the same.

ERROR ANALYSIS AND CORRECTION

Few errors made by modern corporate accounting systems go undetected by the internal and external audit process and are carried forward to some future period. However, it is not uncommon to find recording or measurement errors in the audit and review process. The analysis of errors and their correction is a rather difficult subject to deal with in an abstract setting. In the following section we present a three-step procedure for dealing with errors. This method is considered to be extremely useful in a real-world context.

Basic Approach to Analysis and Correction of Errors

Accounting errors can be one of the most confusing problems that accountants have to deal with. This is largely due to the lack of sufficient information and a proper framework for gathering and using the necessary information. All accounting errors, no matter how complex, can be analyzed and corrected by obtaining answers to the following three questions about a discovered error:

1. What was recorded in error?
2. What should have been recorded?
3. How do you now go from the entry in answer 1 to the entry in answer 2?

To illustrate how this framework can be applied, assume that on March 3, 1983, Star Ship Enterprises wrote off a $1,400 receivable from a customer—Speed Sprocket, Inc. Speed Sprocket was also a supplier of Star Ship, and on June 24, 1983, Star Ship purchased $2,100 in goods on account from Speed Sprocket. On July 15, Star Ship received a check from Speed Sprocket for $1,400. Because there was no receivable remaining due to the write-off, Star Ship erroneously credited "Accounts Payable—Speed Sprocket." Consider the following analysis:

1. What was recorded in error?

| 7/15/83 | Cash | 1,400 | |
| | Accounts payable | | 1,400 |

2. What should have been recorded?

7/15/83	Accounts receivable	1,400	
	Allowance for bad debts		1,400
7/15/83	Cash	1,400	
	Accounts receivable		1,400

3. How should we record situation 2 given that situation 1 has occurred?

12/31/83	Accounts payable	1,400	
	Accounts receivable		1,400
	(To correct entry of 7/15/83)		
12/31/83	Accounts receivable	1,400	
	Allowance for bad debts		1,400

Note that answering the third question simply involves (1) correcting the error observed in answering question 1 (that is, debit to accounts payable to *reverse* the erroneous part of the first entry) and (2) recording the correct parts of the entries in answer 2 *that have not already been recorded.* Because the debit to cash in answer 1 was correct, it was not a necessary part of the correcting entry in answer 3. It should be noted that *the Cash account is rarely part of a correcting entry unless the correction concerns the reconciliation of cash.* In nearly every case, increases and decreases to the Cash account reflect real economic activity in the form of arm's-length transactions not associated with errors.

Errors and Adjusting Entries

One of the most common accounting-recording errors occurs in the adjusting process that takes place at the end of an accounting period. Examples of such accounting errors would include situations where there is a *failure to accrue an asset or a liability* because of an omitted adjusting journal entry. The following are common adjusting entries that might not be accrued, resulting in an accounting error:

Accrued assets sometimes omitted

1. Interest receivable on interest-bearing accounts or notes
2. Interest receivable on interest-bearing investments
3. Interest on long-term leases accounted for as capital leases by the lessor
4. Earnings of an unconsolidated subsidiary being accounted for on an equity basis

Accrued liabilities sometimes omitted

1. Wages payable to employees
2. Interest payable on interest-bearing obligations, such as notes and accounts payable
3. Unearned revenue received in advance and recorded as earned revenue prior to the adjustment process at the end of a period
4. Income taxes and various other taxes (payroll, and so on) not properly accrued at year-end

To illustrate the general treatment for failure to accrue these assets or liabilities properly, assume that on December 31, 1984, Jiambalvo, Inc., failed to accrue $48,975 in wages payable that had been earned at that date. On January 3, 1985, Jiambalvo paid its weekly payroll of $78,968, which included the $48,975 that had not been accrued on December 31, 1984. This error was not discovered until the end of 1985. The following analysis and correction would occur at the end of 1985:

1. What was recorded in error?
   —No entry on December 31, 1984, when entry should have been made
   —Entry on January 3, 1985, incorrectly expensing all $78,968 in wages in 1985, as follows:

1/3/85	Wage expense	78,968	
	Cash		78,968

2. What should have been recorded?

12/31/84	Wage expense	48,975	
	Wage payable		48,975

1/3/85	Wage expense	29,993	
	Wage payable	48,975	
	Cash		78,968

3. How do we record situation 2 *given* that situation 1 has occurred?

12/31/85	Retained earnings	48,975	
	Wage expense		48,975
	(To correct wage expense incurred during 1984 but recorded in 1985 in error)		

The process of recording adjusting entries might also be the source of errors from the standpoint that **an adjustment to an existing asset or liability is omitted.** Examples of adjustments to existing assets and liabilities that are commonly recorded but might be omitted in a given instance include the following:

Asset adjustments sometimes omitted

1. Adjusting the allowance to reduce temporary investments to market (LCM)
2. Adjustments to allowance for bad debts
3. Adjustments to prepaid expenses
4. Adjustments to record depreciation
5. Adjustments to record amortization
6. Adjustments to record depletion
7. Adjustments to record sale of inventory

Liability adjustments sometimes omitted

1. Adjustments to warranty liability
2. Adjustments to deferred tax credits
3. Adjustments to unearned revenue received in advance when it is recorded as a liability at the time cash is received and then adjusted (downward) at the end of the period

To illustrate, assume that on July 1, 1983, R. Shockley, Inc., paid $6,000 for a 3-year insurance policy on its warehouse and contents, establishing the asset Prepaid Insurance for $6,000 on that date. No other entry is recorded in 1983. In 1984 Shockley discovers the error when preparing its December 31, 1984, adjustments. The following analysis and correction would occur at the end of 1984:

1. What was recorded in error?
   —No entry on December 31, 1983, when entry should have been made
2. What should have been recorded?

12/31/83	Insurance expense	1,000	
	Prepaid insurance		1,000
	(To record ½ year insurance expense)		

3. How do we record situation 2 *given* that situation 1 has occurred?

| 12/31/84 | Retained earnings | 1,000 | |
| | Prepaid insurance | | 1,000 |

We have seen that errors affecting income statements of **prior periods** cannot be corrected by using the income statement accounts of the current period. Instead, the Retained Earnings account must be used. Assume, for example, that $2,000 of depreciation expense on a properly recorded machine was not recorded in 1983 due to a clerical error. In 1984 the error was discovered, and the following analysis was performed (assuming no tax effect):

1. What was recorded in error?
   —No entry was made for depreciation expense for 1983.
2. What should have been recorded?

1983	Depreciation expense	2,000	
	Accumulated depreciation		2,000

3. How should we record situation 2 given that situation 1 has occurred?

1984	Retained earnings	2,000	
	Accumulated depreciation		2,000

The analysis suggested here should lead to a correcting entry in each case where an error was made in either the current period or a prior period. Note that the last three examples illustrated above have *all* been examples of correcting income statement errors from prior periods.

Prior Period
Errors Versus
Current Period
Errors

At what point does an error become a prior period error? Once the books have been closed for an accounting period and formal financial statements have been issued to owners and other external users, errors that are discovered must be treated as prior period adjustments. However, the process of closing and preparing year-end financial statements is rather time consuming, and it often takes 2 to 3 months to prepare the necessary reports and to complete an audit. As a result, errors discovered *after* year-end but *before* the books are closed may be treated as current period errors, and adjusting entries may be made and dated the last day of the just ended fiscal year. For instance, assume that on February 21, 1985, a company with a December 31 year-end learned of an error made prior to December 31, 1984. Assume also that the annual reports have not yet been issued. An entry to correct the error would be made on February 21, 1985, and dated December 31, 1984, thereby treating the error as a 1984 error.

Both management and the outside auditor have an obligation to notify external users about material errors of prior periods that are discovered shortly after the issuance of the annual reports. Such instances are rare in practice. In some cases, a material error is associated with gross mismanagement or fraud, and knowledge of the material error is disseminated through the press and news media.

Counter-
balancing
Errors

A most confusing type of error is the **counterbalancing error,** which is an error of one period that automatically corrects itself in the next period by way of a second error. These errors are difficult to analyze unless *both errors* are observed. Fortunately, the discovery of one error will normally lead the accountant to search for the error that has a counterbalancing effect. For example, assume that $1,000 interest income receivable from savings accounts was not accrued at the end of 1983. The receipt of a $2,000 interest check on March 31, 1984, would normally reveal the error because of the failure to accrue interest income and interest receivable at the end of 1983. However, if the error was not discovered until 1985, both the 1983 year-end accrual and the 1984 receipt of interest would normally be considered in evaluating the error. Let us consider these two alternative points of error identification, first assuming the error is discovered in 1984 after the books for 1983 have been closed:

1. What was recorded in error?
   —No adjustment for interest at 12/31/83
2. What should have been recorded?

12/31/83	Interest receivable	1,000	
	Interest income		1,000

3. How should we record situation 2 given that situation 1 has occurred?

12/31/84	Interest receivable	1,000	
	Retained earnings		1,000

Subsequent to this error correction, the interest payment received in 1984 would be recorded in the usual way:

3/31/84	Cash	2,000	
	Interest receivable		1,000
	Interest income		1,000

Next assume that a second error is made in 1984. This case is *a counterbalancing error involving two errors that offset one another* and can be analyzed as follows *as of 1985:*

1. What was recorded in error?

12/31/83	No adjusting entry was made.		
3/31/84	Cash	2,000	
	Interest income		2,000

2. What should have been recorded?

12/31/83	Interest receivable	1,000	
	Interest income		1,000
3/31/84	Cash	2,000	
	Interest receivable		1,000
	Interest income		1,000

3. How should we record situation 2 given that situation 1 has occurred?
   —No adjustment for these entries is required at this time. As of 1985, total income as reflected by current retained earnings is correct.

This counterbalancing error does *not* require any adjusting entries because the understatement of 1983 income by $1,000 has been offset by the overstatement of 1984 income by the same amount. Once the books for 1984 have been closed out, the error is counterbalanced.

No adjustments are required for such counterbalancing errors, however, if the errors are material, it is necessary to restate the incorrect data of prior years that are currently being reported for comparison purposes. For example, if the

1983 and 1984 income statements were being reported for comparison purposes in the 1985 financial report (with 1985 as the year the error was discovered), then 1983 interest income would be $1,000 higher than previously reported, and 1984 interest income would be $1,000 lower than previously reported in the comparative statements for the 1985 year-end. These report changes should be made for such counterbalancing errors even though no adjusting journal entries are required.

FUNDS FLOW EFFECTS

Most accounting changes related to changes in principles and changes in estimates have no impact on the entity's cash flows. Only in the case of LIFO, where there are direct tax implications, would changes in principles necessarily affect cash flows. Working capital flows, however, would probably be affected by changes in estimates and changes in principles. To the extent that these accounting changes affect the entity's working capital position, the net source or use of funds measurement in the statement of changes in financial position will be affected.

Because there will normally be a tax effect, cash flows and working capital flows will often be affected by errors. The errors themselves will generally have no direct impact on cash, but cash flows will be altered indirectly because of the discovery of an error. Because errors may affect any account, there is always the possibility that the net source or use of working capital will be altered because of the discovery of an error.

SUMMARY

Accounting changes and errors can have a significant impact on an entity's financial statements. External users seeking to evaluate an entity's position and performance should understand the impact of accounting changes and errors and how best to compensate for any inconsistency in the financial reports from one period to the next. They should also be able to determine the impact of such changes on the financial statements if meaningful comparisons are to be made within a firm over time or among firms at a point in time. To simply evaluate the "bottom line" accounting data such as earnings per share or net income or total assets without considering the items affecting these data is likely to lead to inappropriate comparative analyses and uninformed decision making.

A major aspect of the accounting changes and errors described in this chapter is their disclosure in the entity's financial reports. Based on our discussion of accounting changes and errors, it should be possible to decide whether any given financial report has been significantly affected by one or more of these items.

In reviewing the accounting changes and error corrections considered in this chapter, it should be noted that seldom do such items have *direct* economic significance. Even though the entity's financial statements may be significantly affected by the accounting for these changes or errors, the entity is usually the same before and after these items have been reported. The main exception to this occurs when the company changes to LIFO, which may have *direct* economic significance due to the impact on income tax payments. However, because of the general absence of direct economic significance, it may be even more important for external users to be able to determine the effects of accounting changes and error corrections on the financial statements of the entity.

Q24-1 What are *changes in accounting estimates* and how are they treated?

Q24-2 What are *changes in accounting principles* and how are they treated?

Q24-3 What are *changes due to errors* and how are they treated?

Q24-4 What is a *change in entity* and how is it treated?

Q24-5 What are *prior period adjustments* and how are they treated?

Q24-6 What are the three methods of treating accounting changes?

Q24-7 What are the disadvantages of retroactive adjustments?

Q24-8 What is the main advantage of retroactive adjustment?

Q24-9 What changes in accounting principles receive retroactive adjustment?

Q24-10 What is the correct disclosure of the prior years' impact for changes in accounting principles that do not receive retroactive adjustment?

Q24-11 What are *pro forma disclosures?* When are they used and why?

Q24-12 Give an example of a change in accounting principle where the cumulative effect is not disclosed because it is not determinable. How is this change in principle reported?

Q24-13 What is the correct treatment for a policy change from one depreciation method to another only for those assets acquired in the current and future years? (For example, the old method remains in use for the old depreciable assets.)

Q24-14 What three questions can accountants ask themselves as they seek to correct accounting errors?

Q24-15 What are *counterbalancing errors?* Give an example.

Q24-16 How are errors of previous years treated?

Q24-17 How are errors of the most recently completed year treated before the books are closed? After the books are closed?

C24-1 The Traster Corporation owns ten different stocks as part of its Temporary Investment in Marketable Securities account. One of the stocks is AT&T, of which Traster owns a total of 1,500 shares purchased at prices ranging from $25 to $180 per share. Traster has historically costed the sales of stocks held as temporary investments on a specific identification basis. On July 4, 1984, a fire in the corporation's vault destroyed the AT&T stock certificates. Subsequently AT&T replaced the burned stock certificates with new shares (certificates), and on November 3, 1984, Traster sold 150 shares of AT&T at $210 per share.

REQUIRED What cost should be assigned to the 150 shares sold on November 3, and how should the sale be disclosed in the financial statements? Does this situation involve an accounting change?

C24-2 As an analyst of securities in the steel industry, you noted in evaluating the published financial reports for a recent accounting period that nearly all the steel companies had changed from straight-line depreciation to accelerated depreciation. The steel companies have been complaining to Congress that they are paying taxes on income that does not really exist, and that the government is actually taxing the steel industry on its use of capital assets that are undervalued in its accounting reports.

REQUIRED Is this change in accounting method going to help solve the unfair tax problem cited by the steel industry? Explain.

C24-3 (CPA ADAPTED) The various types of accounting changes may significantly affect the presentation of both the financial position and results of operations for an accounting period and the trends shown in comparative financial statements and historical summaries.

REQUIRED

1. Describe a change in accounting principle and how it should be reported in the income statement of the period of the change.
2. Describe a change in accounting estimate and how it should be reported in the income statement of the period of the change.
3. Describe a change in reporting entity and how it should be reported. Give an appropriate example of a change in reporting entity.

C24–4 Some accounting researchers have argued that it is appropriate for a company to use LIFO inventory measurement in periods of rising prices, and that those entities that use FIFO are, in effect, paying taxes that they could have avoided. They state that this is like paying taxes to the government instead of dividends to shareholders. At the same time, we can observe many publicly traded entities that use non–LIFO inventory measurements for both book and tax purposes.

REQUIRED   Identify as many rational economic reasons as possible for explaining this apparent paradox between theory and practice.

C24–5 The change to the LIFO method of inventory measurement is probably the most discussed and debated accounting change of all.

REQUIRED   Why does this change receive more attention than most? List the potential advantages and disadvantages of changing to the LIFO inventory method.

C24–6 Assume that you are the top manager of a corporation that is 80 percent owned by another corporation. Assume also that your profit objective in reporting net income is to smooth income in such a way that it seems as if net income is increasing evenly at a rate of about 16 percent per year. You are in an economy where prices are strictly increasing over time at less than a 16 percent rate. To achieve your target net income figure in any given year, you sometimes elect to change your accounting methods.

REQUIRED

1. Assume that you need to *increase* net income this year in order to achieve your target of 16 percent growth in net income. What kind of accounting changes might help you to achieve the target?
2. Assume that you need to *decrease* net income this year in order to achieve your target. What kind of accounting changes might be made?
3. Which of the changes suggested in requirements 1 and 2 will have a real economic effect on your company?
4. What do you see as the potential limitations of using accounting changes to help you smooth net income over time?
5. What alternatives might help you to smooth net income more effectively than changes in accounting methods?

C24–7 K-Kar-Korp has $80,000,000 in long-term notes payable to a group of New York banks. The notes are not due until 1989 unless K-Kar-Korp's current ratio falls below 1.8 to 1, in which case the notes are due immediately. At the end of 1983, K-Kar-Korp's preliminary financial report indicated that its current ratio would be 1.4 to 1 unless something was done to correct the situation. This would mean that the entire $80,000,000 would have to be paid right away to the banks holding the notes.

REQUIRED

1. Assuming it is not yet December 31, 1983, what kind of actions can be taken so that the loans will not become due?
2. Assuming it is after December 31, 1983, what can be done to prevent their coming due?

C24–8 (CMA ADAPTED)   Barrow Co. is a publicly held regional manufacturer of western style clothes that uses a calendar year for financial reporting. During 1983 Barrow purchased a small chain of retail specialty clothing stores. The retail stores were privately owned and had been a good customer of Barrow's for a number of years.

Ron Hardy was hired as Controller of Barrow in May 1984. In preparation for the 1985 budget he personally completed a detailed comparison of the 1984 performance (current year) with the 1983 actual figures as reported. Through this analysis he has discovered the following items which affected the reported figures for 1983.

1. The accounts receivable at December 31, 1983 were understated by $63,000. A subsidiary ledger had a balance with a transposed number. The accounts receivable control account was reduced by this amount in the adjusting entries for 1983.

2. In May 1984, $60,000 was received in settlement for a $130,000 claim against a vendor for defective merchandise. The claim was filed in March 1983, but no receivable was recorded by Barrow because the vendor's financial condition was very weak.

3. Barrow paid $48,000 of additional income tax in 1983. This was the amount of additional tax due for 1980 as determined by an IRS audit of 1980 federal income tax return. Additional tax was treated as an extraordinary expense.

4. Barrow paid $75,000 in August 1984 to settle an employee discrimination suit. The suit was filed by a Barrow labor union charging bias in promotion practices in September 1983. No liability had been recorded in 1983 but the suit had been disclosed in the footnotes to the 1983 annual financial statements.

5. The retail chain Barrow acquired in 1983 recorded its bad debts on the direct-write-off basis even though the chain had significant credit sales and bad debt losses. The chain was included in the consolidated earnings of Barrow for 1983. Ron Hardy estimated that the chain would have had an allowance for doubtful accounts of $50,000 had an allowance system been used.

REQUIRED Discuss how Ron Hardy should handle each of the five situations to comply with *FASB Statement No. 16,* "Prior Period Adjustments." Include the pretax impact, if any, on 1983 and 1984 earnings to support your answer. Do not be concerned with the impact on earnings reported in interim financial statements.

EXERCISES

E24–1 For the past three accounting periods, the Haggerman Corporation has failed to record depreciation on the equipment in Plant 47.

REQUIRED Assuming this error is corrected in the current period, what will the effect of this error correction be on the following?

1. Taxes payable, current year
2. Beginning retained earnings
3. Net income, current year
4. Net cash flow from operations

E24–2

_____ 1. Prior period adjustments that affect the reported income numbers of prior years
a. Are reported as adjustments to current and future periods
b. Are treated on a prospective basis only
c. Are never reported in the operating income section of the income statement
d. Will always result in a change in the Deferred Income Tax Payable account
e. None of the above

_____ 2. On January 1, 1984, the Eaton Corporation decided to account for its interest in Nova Associates on the lower-of-cost-or-market basis. Eaton had previously accounted for Nova on the equity-method basis but changed due to shifts in ownership control.
a. This is a change in accounting method that is to be accounted for like a change in estimate, affecting only 1984 and future periods.
b. This change should receive retroactive treatment.
c. This change should be treated as a prior period adjustment.
d. No adjustment is required during 1984 to account for this accounting change.
e. None of the above

_____ 3. Assume that you acquired a building in 1981 and elected to use the sum-of-the-years'-digits depreciation method at that time. Ten years later (in 1990) you switch to the straight-line depreciation method. Your Accumulated Depreciation—Building account at the end of 1990 would show a balance equal to
   a. 10 years' depreciation on a straight-line basis, and your income statement would show a large "loss due to change in accounting principles"
   b. One year's depreciation on a straight-line basis plus 9 years on the sum-of-the-years'-digits basis, and your depreciation expense would be less than in prior years for the remaining life
   c. 10 years' depreciation on a straight-line basis, and the retained earnings statement would show a large correction to the beginning balance for "gain due to change in accounting principles"
   d. None of the above

_____ 4. The Z Company's bookkeeper forgot to record $1,500 of depreciation on the company's delivery truck. As a result of this omission, Z Company's
   a. Current assets were overstated   d. Total assets were unaffected
   b. Total equities were overstated   e. None of the above
   c. Working capital was overstated

_____ 5. _According to APB Opinion No. 20,_ which of the following is an example of a change in accounting estimate?
   a. A change from the percentage-of-sales method to the percentage-of-gross-accounts-receivable method of estimating bad debt expense
   b. A change from an accelerated depreciation method to the straight-line method for long-term depreciable assets
   c. The provision for "notes receivable discounted" in situations where notes are sold prior to maturity date and a contingent liability exists
   d. Selection of the percentage-of-completion method of accounting for long-term construction contracts
   e. None of the above

E24–3 The following events were discovered by Mavidson, Stickley, and Deil, CPAs, in the first audit of the Jaedicke Corporation for the year ending December 31, 1984. Fill in the grid by indicating whether the event overstated (O), understated (U), or had no effect (N) on the items indicated.

EVENT DISCOVERED BY AUDITORS	1984 NET INCOME	1984 NET ASSETS	1984 WORKING CAPITAL FROM OPERATIONS
1. Failed to record depreciation on an asset acquired in 1984.			
2. Failed to accrue wages payable for Ng, Foster, and Demski for 1984.			
3. Failed to record purchase of supplies received on 1/3/85 terms F.O.B. shipping point (shipped 12/31/84).			
4. Recorded interest on investments as interest receivable for all earned interest up to 12/31/84 but did not amortize discounts on long-term investments in bonds until the semiannual interest was received on 3/31/85.			
5. Did not amortize goodwill in long-term equity investments that had appreciated in value			

E24–4 On June 30, 1982, the World of Wheels roller-skating rink acquired capital assets with an expected useful life of 15 years. These assets were to be depreciated on a straight-line basis, with the estimated net scrap value equal to 5 percent of their original $83,700 purchase price. One-half year's depreciation was taken on December 31, 1982. During 1984 World of Wheels decides to change to the double-declining balance depreciation method for financial-reporting purposes, which it has been using for tax purposes for all of its capital assets. The tax rate has been 40 percent each year.

REQUIRED

1. Prepare the necessary entries to account for these assets for 1982, 1983, and 1984, including adjustments.
2. Illustrate how the partial comparative income statements would appear for 1982–1984 assuming that the following net income before taxes and depreciation expense applies to the three years: 1982, $100,000; 1983, $104,000; and 1984, $98,000.

E24–5 The Bar K Ranch has a December 31 year-end, but because of the seasonal nature of the business of raising and selling cattle, the ending inventory is estimated annually at year-end and is then adjusted annually during the spring roundup. The following data are available:

Beginning inventory, 1/1/83	15,760 head (adjusted)
Increase from breeding, 1983	4,800 head (estimated)
Sold in fall of 1983	10,000 head (actual count)
Ending inventory, 12/31/83	10,560 head (estimated)

The actual count during the 1984 spring roundup revealed a total of 10,950 head of cattle. The "cost of cattle sold" for 1983 was $3,750,000. Cattle are currently selling for $400 a head.

REQUIRED Record the journal entry in the spring of 1984 to adjust the beginning 1984 inventory for this change in estimate.

E24–6 Fill in the following grid to identify the type of accounting treatment appropriate for the situations described.

TYPE OF EVENT	THIS EVENT WILL RECEIVE THE (NEW) (OLD) FOLLOWING TYPE OF TREATMENT		
	PROSPECTIVE	CURRENT	RETROACTIVE
1. Change to the LIFO inventory method	✓		
2. Change to a 25-year depreciable life for machinery _estimate_	✓		
3. Change to the straight-line depreciation method for book purposes _principle / method_		✓	
4. Change to the successful efforts method of accounting for oil and gas reserves _full cost, successful_			✓
5. Change from LIFO to FIFO for inventories			✓
6. Change from the LCM method to the equity method for long-term investment			✓
7. Change to the completed-contract method of accounting for construction contracts			✓
8. Change in the percentage of sales estimated to require future warranty costs _change of estimate_	✓		
9. Change in depreciable assets caused by reclassification of prior years' expenses as assets due to their long-term benefits _error / estimate_	✓		
10. Change in the expected salvage value of assets due to change in their expected life	✓		

E24–7 During 1984 S. Todt, CPA, discovered the following errors in your financial records concerning inventory:

	INVENTORY	COST OF GOODS SOLD	NET INCOME
		AS REPORTED	
1983	Overstated by $19,870	$287,000	$37,800
1982	Understated by $23,740	312,000	18,350
1981	Understated by $16,500	234,000	20,170

Assume a 40 percent tax rate in solving this problem.

REQUIRED

1. Describe the effect of these inventory errors on the 1984
   a. Net income
   b. Working capital provided by operations
   c. Net assets
2. Record the error correction.
3. Illustrate the partial comparative income and retained earnings statements for 1982, 1983, and 1984 assuming that the 1984 cost of goods sold and net income measures were $337,000 and $41,000, respectively, *before* adjustment for the errors discovered by Todt. Retained earnings reported at December 31, 1981, was $400,000.

E24–8 In December 1984 S. Lambrose, Inc., decided to change to the sum-of-the-years'-digits method of depreciation for both of its hotels, which has been used for tax purposes since they were acquired. The hotels are being leased by Lambrose, Inc., on a long-term basis and are considered to be capital leases. However, the hotels will both be returned to their title holder, Metro Properties Corporation, in 19 years (2003) at a guaranteed residual value of $2,000,000. As of the end of 1984 the hotels have an expected remaining useful life of 28 years and have been leased for the past 31 years (including 1984) by Lambrose (since they were built for Metro Properties at an original cost of $12,000,000). Lambrose has been using straight-line depreciation for the past 31 years. Lambrose originally recorded the long-term lease at $12,000,000, less the present value of the guaranteed residual value of $2,000,000 assuming a 10 percent interest rate. The residual value is guaranteed by a third-party insurance company.

REQUIRED

1. Record the change in the depreciation method and the 1984 depreciation expense for S. Lambrose, Inc. Assume the tax rate has always been 40 percent.
2. Assume that Lambrose's operating income before taxes and depreciation was $1,946,000 for 1983 and $1,896,000 for 1984. Assume also that the tax rate is 40 percent for both years. Illustrate the partial comparative income statements for 1983 and 1984.
3. What is the impact of this change on Lambrose's debt-to-equity ratio?

E24–9 M. Walz's initial audit of the Sound Stage Studio at the end of the 1983 calendar year revealed the following errors and irregularities, which had been made by the bookkeeper during the first 3 years of operations:

1. Failed to accrue interest receivable at the end of 1982 ($650) and 1983 ($725) on Sound Stage's short-term investment in money market funds.
2. Failed to reduce the Unearned Studio Revenues liability account for advances that were actually earned in 1981 ($750); 1982 ($950); and 1983 ($450).
3. Failed to include unused recording tapes in the supplies inventory at the end of 1982. The tapes originally cost $1,850.

4. Expensed three new microphones acquired at the beginning of 1981, which had cost $4,880 and were expected to last 4 years. Sound Stage used the straight-line depreciation method for all depreciable assets.

5. Failed to accrue studio wages payable at the end of 1981 ($1,720) and again at the end of 1983 ($2,635).

REQUIRED

1. Prepare a schedule to correct these errors, starting with the following income numbers as previously reported, and arriving at the corrected amounts (ignore taxes):

	NET INCOME (UNAUDITED)
1981	$17,360
1982	18,920
1983	21,250

2. Record the necessary adjusting entries as of December 31, 1983, assuming the books for 1983 have not yet been completely closed out (that is, no annual report has been *issued* for 1983).

E24-10 (CMA ADAPTED)

_____ 1. If a firm, in preparing the data for its 1984 financial statements, discovers that a material error was made in 1983, it should
  a. Correct the effect of the error in the income statement for 1984 as an extraordinary item. No change should be made in the 1983 statements reported as part of the 1984 report.
  b. Correct the effect of the error in the income statement for 1984 as an extraordinary item. The 1983 statements, reported as part of the 1984 report, should be corrected to reflect the correct information.
  c. Reflect the effect of the error at its cumulative effect and report it on the balance sheet for 1984 as an element of owners' equity.
  d. Correct the effect of the error on the statement of retaining earning for 1984 as a prior period adjustment. No change should be made in the 1983 statements reported as part of the 1984 report.
  e. Correct the 1983 statements, reported as part of the 1984 report, to reflect the correct information.

_____ 2. The adjustment of the accumulated depreciation of an asset arising from a revision in the estimated useful life of an individual asset would
  a. Be recognized as an extraordinary item on the current income statement and require presentation of pro forma data on net income and earnings per share for all prior periods
  b. Require a retroactive adjustment so that all prior financial statements are corrected
  c. Require an adjustment directly to retained earnings
  d. Require no adjustment of the accumulated depreciation account but would be reflected in the current and future depreciation charges
  e. Be satisfied by any of the above treatments as long as there was proper disclosure

_____ 3. An asset purchased in 1983 was expensed rather than being capitalized. This material error was discovered in 1987 and would require
  a. Recognition of an extraordinary item on the 1987 income statement and presentation of pro forma data on net income and earnings per share for all prior periods
  b. A retroactive adjustment so that all prior financial statements are corrected
  c. An adjustment directly to retained earnings
  d. Recognition of the asset, net of accumulated depreciation since acquisition, on current and future financial statements but no adjustment of past financial statement
  e. Any of the above treatments as long as there was proper disclosure

_____ 4. On October 27, 1984, the Beta Company purchased inventory on account for $11,500. Due to an error, the transaction was not recorded. This $11,500 inventory was overlooked and was not counted as of the year ending October 31, 1984, and consequently was not included in the ending inventory figure. Beta uses the FIFO method of inventory valuation. These errors will cause the net income before taxes for the year ended October 31, 1984

a. To be overstated by $11,500
b. To be understated by $11,500
c. To be overstated by $23,000
d. To be understated by $23,000
e. To be unaffected

_____ 5. *Accounting Principles Board Opinion No. 20,* "Accounting Changes," lists certain changes in accounting principles that necessitate a restatement of prior period statements rather than use of the Cumulative Effect of Change in Accounting Principles account on the current income statement. A restatement of prior periods is required for a change from

a. Accelerated depreciation to straight-line depreciation
b. Bad debts estimated as a percentage of credit sales to a percentage of ending accounts receivable
c. FIFO inventory method to another inventory method
d. LIFO inventory method to another inventory method
e. The cash basis method to the accrual method for recording warranty costs

_____ 6. *Statement of Financial Accounting Standards No. 16,* "Prior Period Adjustments," greatly limited the number of prior period adjustments. Which one of the following items would be classified as a prior period adjustment?

a. Adjustments that result from realization of income tax benefits of preacquisition operating loss carryforwards of purchased subsidiaries
b. Gains or losses on disposal of a segment of a business
c. Gains or losses resulting from major devaluations and revaluations of foreign currencies
d. Gains or losses from sale or abandonment of property, plant, or equipment used in the business
e. Out-of-court settlement of litigation

PROBLEMS

P24–1 Because the accounting system has failed to account properly for inventory out on consignment, the ending inventory for the past 3 years has been recorded in error. This error, discovered by Karl Reichardt (CPA, CMA) at the end of year 4, is summarized as follows:

END OF YEAR	CORRECT MEASURE	RECORDED MEASURE
1	$135,700	$122,000
2	146,800	112,000
3	158,325	140,000
4	163,950	

REQUIRED

1. Prepare the necessary correcting entries at December 31, year 4 (ignore taxes).
2. Describe the impact of this failure on the measurement of net income and working capital from operations as reported in year 3.

P24–2 The following situations related to *Accounting Principles Board Opinion 20,* "Accounting Changes," occurred during 1985. Do the situations described below directly affect the reported amounts or accounts in segments of the financial statements identified in the columns? Fill in the grid using *Y* for *yes* and *N* for *no*.

SITUATION	NET INCOME BEFORE EXTRAORDINARY ITEMS (NIBEI)—1985	BELOW NIBEI IN THE 1985 INCOME STATEMENT	A CORRECTION TO THE RETAINED EARNINGS (1/1/85) BALANCE	IN THE 1984 COMPARATIVE INCOME STATEMENT REPORTED IN 1985
1. Changed from equity basis to the LCM basis of accounting for long-term investments in Zero Corporation common stock				
2. Due to favorable credit collection experience, adjusted the percentage of net credit sales that were thought to be uncollectible				
3. Discovered that research and development costs relating to a product introduced last year were capitalized as part of the patent cost				
4. Changed from the full-cost method to the successful-efforts method of accounting for oil exploration costs				
5. Changed the expected total construction costs on an incomplete building that is being accounted for on the percentage-of-completion basis but resulted in a projected net loss on the building				
6. Changed from FIFO inventory value to LIFO inventory value				

P24-3 (CPA ADAPTED) On January 1, 1985, the Wing Company purchased a machine for $240,000. At the date of acquisition, the machine had an estimated useful life of ten years and an estimated salvage value of $20,000. The machine is being depreciated on a straight-line basis. On January 1, 1988, Wing appropriately adopted the sum-of-the-years'-digits method of depreciation for this machine.

REQUIRED

1. Prepare a schedule computing the book value of this machine, net of accumulated depreciation, that would be included in Wing's balance sheet at December 31, 1988. Show supporting computations.
2. Prepare a schedule computing the cumulative effect on prior years of changing to a different depreciation method for the year ended December 31, 1988. Assume that the direct effects of this change are limited to the effect on depreciation and the related tax provision, and that the income tax rate for all the years was 50 percent. Show supporting computations.

P24-4 On January 1, 1990, Ohio Corporation acquired a machine that cost $50,000. The machine had a scrap value of $5,000 and an expected life of 5 years. Ohio decided to use the straight-line depreciation method for the machine. On December 15, 1991, Ohio decided to change from straight-line depreciation to sum-of-the-years'-digits depreciation. Ohio closes its books and prepares statements once a year, on December 31.

REQUIRED

1. Record the necessary journal entries or adjusting entries or both for the year 1991 on Ohio Corporation's books for the change described above. Give an *explanation* for all entries.
2. Indicate *how* and *where* the entries made in requirement 1 would affect the income statement and retained earnings statement. Be as specific as possible.
3. Assume that Ohio reports comparative balance sheets in 1991 (that is, 1990 and 1991 balance sheets). Indicate the balances to be reported in the Machinery account and the Accumulated Depreciation—Machinery account for *both* 1990 and 1991 at December 31, 1991.

P24-5 On December 1, 1980, Roman, Inc., a calendar-year company, acquired equipment that cost $185,350. The equipment had an expected life of 18 years and qualified for a 10 percent investment tax credit. Roman recorded a half year's depreciation in 1980 using the straight-line method. In December 1981 Roman revised the estimated useful life of the equipment to 16 years and changed the estimated scrap value from $5,350 (original estimate) to $7,950. On June 30, 1983, Roman decided to change to the sum-of-the-years'-digits depreciation method because this method would better match costs with benefits from the use of the equipment. On March 31, 1984, Roman traded in the old equipment along with $75,000 in cash for some rare paintings that had an appraisal value of $175,000.

REQUIRED Record all the journal entries necessary to account for the equipment from date of purchase to date of sale. Assume that Roman uses the flow-through method of accounting for the investment tax credit. Roman takes a half year's depreciation on all assets in the year of disposition.

P24-6 The Mountain State Bank has asked you to perform the initial audit of the Double D Ranch so that lending negotiations can be conducted between the ranch and the bank. The ranch has kept financial records for the past 3 years since being acquired by J. R. Youuwing. Although the records have been kept on an accrual basis, you discover the following omitted items during your audit of the 3-year period ending December 31, 1984:

1. Wages payable to ranch hands at December 31 year-ends have not been accrued. These accrued year-end amounts were as follows:

12/31/82	$14,675
12/31/83	29,320
12/31/84	61,145

2. Supplies inventories have always been expensed as incurred. The supplies on hand at December 31, 1984, amounted to $26,300.
3. Cattle inventories have never been reconciled at the Double D. There were 5,000 head on hand at January 1, 1982, at an original cost of $500,000, and it has been estimated that the number of cattle will increase at the rate of 20 percent each summer. Cattle are sold in the fall of each year, with the actual head of cattle sold over the past 3 years along with cost of goods sold and ending inventory as follows:

YEAR	NUMBER OF CATTLE SOLD	COST OF SALES	ENDING INVENTORY
1982	800	$ 90,150	$586,000
1983	1,000	112,180	587,820
1984	900	107,350	642,650

The actual physical count at December 31, 1984, revealed a total of 7,000 head of cattle on hand.

REQUIRED

1. Assume that the reported pretax income of Double D prior to your audit was as follows:

1982	$180,000
1983	25,000
1984	65,000

Prepare a schedule showing how the data in items 1–3 above would revise the pretax income previously reported for 1982–1984.

2. Prepare the necessary adjusting entries as of December 31, 1984.

P24–7 The December 31, 1983, balance sheet of J. Butt Enterprises included the following data:

		BALANCE
Assets		
Inventory (weighted average)	$109,745	
Less allowance to reduce to market	16,830	$ 92,915
Liabilities		
Deferred federal income taxes		$187,350

In 1984 Butt decided to switch to LIFO. The 1984 ending inventory under the weighted-average method and the LIFO method were measured as follows:

	1984
Weighted average	$125,340
LIFO	81,385

Inventory purchases during 1984 amounted to $6,847,215. The 1984 statutory tax rate is 46 percent. The effective tax expense per books before the change in inventory method is 22 percent on income from continuing operations before taxes, extraordinary items, and accounting changes of $400,000. Because of recent investments in capital assets, Butt qualified for $200,000 in investment tax credits during 1984, which are being accounted for under the deferral method. None of the December 31, 1983, balance in deferred income taxes is attributable to timing differences from inventory measurement.

REQUIRED

1. Record any entries necessary to account for the change to LIFO.
2. What is the cumulative prior years' impact of this accounting change? Explain.
3. Prepare the partial 1984 income statement after the change, beginning with pretax income from continuing operations.
4. What is the real economic benefit to J. Butt Enterprises in 1984 as a result of the switch to LIFO?

P24 8 During your initial audit of D. Haynes, Inc., you discovered the following items:

1. No allowance for uncollectibles had ever been set up by Haynes in accounting for its receivables. The write-offs taken over the past 4 years were as follows:

	WRITTEN OFF IN			
FROM	**1980**	**1981**	**1982**	**1983**
1980 sales	$ 4,830	$ 1,330	$ 120	0
1981 sales		5,340	1,895	$ 150
1982 sales			7,610	2,105
1983 sales				8,105
Net sales	$400,000	$520,000	$640,000	$745,000
Net credit sales	315,000	370,000	490,000	535,000

2. The wages payable at December 31 for the past 3 years were not accrued by the bookkeeper but should have been:

	1981	1982	1983
December 31	$4,820	$3,190	$6,730

3. Cash of $1,950 received on December 10, 1982, was recorded as service revenue, but the services were not actually performed until January 3, 1983.
4. The estimated taxes payable of $15,000 were recorded as income taxes payable on December 31, 1981, but were not paid until April 15, 1982, the date these taxes were actually due. Haynes's effective tax rate has always been 40 percent.
5. Equipment with an undepreciated net book value of $3,800 was taken out of service at the end of 1983, and based on the estimated salvage value of $1,200 as of the end of 1983, the following entry was recorded:

12/31/83	Other assets	1,200	
	Accumulated depreciation	70,400	
	Loss on equipment	2,600	
	Equipment		74,200

The book value of the equipment for tax purposes was zero. No other entries regarding the equipment were recorded in 1983.

REQUIRED Record any journal entries necessary to prepare Haynes's financial statements for December 31, 1983, in accordance with GAAP. Convert all percentages to numbers rounded to two decimal places.

P24–9 (CPA ADAPTED) The Topanga Manufacturing Company manufactures two products: Mult and Tran. At December 31, 1984, Topanga uses the first-in, first-out (FIFO) inventory method. Effective January 1, 1985, Topanga changed to the last-in, first-out (LIFO) inventory method. The cumulative effect of this change is not determinable, and, as a result, the ending inventory of 1984, for which the FIFO method was used, is also the beginning inventory for 1985 for the LIFO method. Any layers added during 1985 should be costed by reference to the first acquisitions of 1985, and any layers liquidated during 1985 should be considered a permanent liquidation.
The following information was available from Topanga's inventory records for the two most recent years:

	MULT		TRAN	
	UNITS	UNIT COST	UNITS	UNIT COST
1984 purchases				
January 7	5,000	$4.00	22,000	$2.00
April 16	12,000	4.50		
November 8	17,000	5.00	18,500	2.50
December 13	10,000	6.00		
1985 purchases				
February 11	3,000	7.00	23,000	3.00
May 20	8,000	7.50		
October 15	20,000	8.00		
December 23			15,500	3.50
Units on hand				
December 31, 1984	15,000		14,500	
December 31, 1985	16,000		13,000	

REQUIRED Compute the effect on income before income taxes for the year ended December 31, 1985, resulting from the change from the FIFO inventory method.

P24–10 The A. R. Roberts Corporation, a large closely held company, has never issued debt and has never had an audit in its entire 6-year history. Its president, Al Roberts, has decided to undertake a new project that will require a $1,500,000 bank loan. The bank insists that Roberts prepare audited financial statements for the past 3 years before the loan is granted. The following table summarizes the net income and retained earnings data that Roberts has previously prepared for financial-reporting purposes:

YEAR	NET INCOME	ENDING RETAINED EARNINGS	DIVIDENDS
1979	$119,000	$ 69,000	$ 50,000
1980	273,000	222,000	120,000
1981	175,000	277,000	120,000
1982	119,000	276,000	120,000
1983	233,000	389,000	120,000

Roberts has hired your firm, the Joseph L. Schultz CPA Firm, to conduct the audit. The preliminary net income for 1984 before your audit is $99,000. Dividends of $100,000 have been declared and paid in 1984. Mr. Roberts has noted that the bank is not certain that it will lend the $1,500,000 needed to finance the new project because of the apparently volatile nature of the A. R. Roberts Corporation's reported income.

During the course of your audit, you discover the following facts:

1. An asset acquired and placed into use in 1979 at the beginning of operations was erroneously left off of the property records until 1982. In 1982 this error was discovered, and the asset, which had originally cost $150,000, was placed on the books. The first year's depreciation of $10,000 was taken in 1982. The asset was originally expected to last 15 years. An additional $10,000 annual depreciation was taken in 1983 and 1984, and the net book value of the asset is $120,000 as of December 31, 1984.

2. In 1983 A. R. Roberts Corporation changed its estimated annual warranty obligation rate, which was based on gross sales of those products covered by warranty. The favorable experience encountered by Roberts indicated that warranty expense for 1981 and 1982, the first two years in which the warranty was offered, were overstated by an estimated $46,000 and $41,000, respectively. The rate was adjusted in 1983, and the 1981 and 1982 net income figures were increased to $175,000 and $119,000, respectively.

3. As a result of the audit, it was discovered that the 1983 ending inventory had included $49,000 of inventory that was assumed to be held on consignment by a dealer in North Platt when, in fact, the dealer had purchased the inventory outright from Roberts.

4. As a result of the audit, it was also learned that the 1983 amortization of goodwill and excess depreciation from Roberts's long-term equity investments in unconsolidated subsidiaries, which amounted to $16,000, was not adjusted for at the end of 1983.

5. The audit of Roberts's accounts and notes receivable revealed that the estimated rate of uncollectibles had been considerably overstated over the past 3 years. The allowance balance prior to the 1984 year-end adjustment to bad debt expense of $89,000 was $112,000. An analysis of the receivables indicated that receivables worth $77,500 should probably be written off as uncollectible, and that an allowance balance of about $54,500 would be sufficient as of December 31, 1984. The uncollectible rate as a percentage of the aged receivables was modified accordingly. Had these modified aging rates been used in the prior 3 years (1981–1983) the respective net income amounts would have been $236,500; $157,000; $280,000.

In your management letter to Roberts at the end of your audit, you suggested the following two accounting changes in an effort to better match the costs and benefits of Roberts's operating activities:

1. Roberts should change to the flow-through method of accounting for its investment tax credits. As of December 31, 1984, Roberts has $100,000 balance in the Deferred Investment Tax Credit account. No new tax credits occurred in 1984, but $20,000 of the January 1, 1984, balance in the Deferred Investment Tax Credit account was taken into income in 1984.

2. Roberts should change to the percentage-of-completion method of accounting for its construction contract operations, which make up a significant part of Roberts's overall activities. The change to the percentage-of-completion method would have the following pretax effect on the income numbers for 1979–1984:

1979	+ $71,000	1982	+ $187,000
1980	− 63,000	1983	+ 112,000
1981	+ 96,000	1984	− 17,000

Roberts, having considered the conceptual merits of your proposed accounting changes, has agreed to make the changes you suggested.

REQUIRED

1. Ignore taxes completely. Prepare a schedule for 1979–1984 to compute the corrected net income numbers based on the facts provided in the problem. Clearly label each adjustment.

2. Prepare the comparative income and retained earnings figures for the 3 years ending December 31, 1984, for A. R. Roberts Corporation as they would appear in the audited financial statements. Ignore taxes.

3. Discuss the audit's possible impact on the bank's lending decision.

4. Discuss the preferability argument presented by Schultz in the management letter to Roberts Corporation. Is the argument agreeable to you?

5. Identify those changes, if any, that were made to Roberts's income as a result of the audit and that have had an effect on Roberts's cash flows.

P24–11 Refer to the data in problem 24–10 regarding the Roberts Corporation. Assume that Roberts had been using the percentage-of-completion method for tax purposes since its inception in 1979, and that the switch to the percentage-of-completion method for book purposes occurred in 1984. Assume also that the effective tax rate for book purposes as reflected in the Income Tax Expense account has been 40 percent each year since 1979.

REQUIRED

1. Record the data identified in the problem that require adjusting or correcting entries as of December 31, 1984.

2. Prepare the comparative income statement data that would be reported for the 3 years ending December 31, 1984, after the audit.

P24–12 (CMA ADAPTED) The Bulloch Company is considering changing its inventory valuation method from the first-in, first-out method (FIFO) to the last-in, first-out method (LIFO) because of the potential tax savings. Before making the final decision, however, the management wishes to consider all the effects these changes would have on the company, including its annual reports.

The inventory account, currently valued on the FIFO basis, consists of 1,000,000 units at $7 per unit on January 1, 1982. There are 1,000,000 shares of common stock outstanding as of January 1, 1982. The cash balance on January 1, 1982, is $400,000.

The company has made the following forecasts for the period 1982–1984:

	1982	1983	1984
1. Unit sales (in millions of units)	1.1	1.0	1.3
2. Sales price per unit	$10	$10	$12
3. Unit purchases (in millions of units)	1.0	1.1	1.2
4. Purchase price per unit	$7	$8	$9
5. Annual depreciation (in thousands of dollars)	$300	$300	$300
6. Cash dividends per share	$0.15	$0.15	$0.15
7. Cash payments for additions to and replacement of plant and equipment (in thousands of dollars)	$350	$350	$350
8. Income tax rate	40%	40%	40%
9. Operating expense (exclusive of depreciation) as a percentage of sales	15%	15%	15%
10. Common shares outstanding (in millions)	1	1	1

REQUIRED

1. Prepare a schedule that illustrates and compares the following data for Bulloch Company under the FIFO inventory method and under the LIFO inventory method for 1982, 1983, and 1984, assuming the company would begin LIFO at the beginning of 1982:

   a. Year-end inventory balances   c. Earnings per share

   b. Annual net income after taxes   d. Cash balance

   Assume that all sales are collected in the year of sale and that all purchases, operating expenses, and taxes are paid during the year incurred.

2. Using the data in the question, your answer to requirement 1, and any additional issues you believe need to be considered, prepare a report that recommends whether or not Bulloch Company should change to the LIFO inventory method. Support your conclusions with appropriate arguments.

P24–13 (CPA ADAPTED)   The Paul Brown Corporation is in the process of negotiating a loan with a New York City bank for expansion purposes. The books and records have never been audited, and the bank has requested that an audit be performed. Brown has prepared the following comparative financial statements for the years ended December 31, 1983 and 1984.

THE PAUL BROWN CORPORATION
Balance Sheet
As of December 31, 1983 and 1984

	1984	1983
Assets		
Current assets		
Cash	$163,000	$ 82,000
Accounts receivable	392,000	296,000
Allowance for uncollectible accounts	(37,000)	(18,000)
Marketable securities, at cost	78,000	78,000
Merchandise inventory	207,000	202,000
Total current assets	803,000	640,000
Fixed assets		
Property, plant, and equipment	167,000	169,500
Accumulated depreciation	(121,600)	(106,400)
Total fixed assets	45,400	63,100
Total assets	$848,400	$703,100
Liabilities and Stockholders' Equity		
Liabilities		
Accounts payable	$121,400	$196,100
Stockholders' equity		
Common stock, par value $10 (authorized, 50,000 shares; issued and outstanding, 20,000 shares)	260,000	260,000
Retained earnings	467,000	247,000
Total stockholders' equity	727,000	507,000
Total liabilities and stockholders' equity	$848,400	$703,100

THE PAUL BROWN CORPORATION
Statement of Income
For the Years Ended December 31, 1983 and 1984

	1984	1983
Sales	$1,000,000	$900,000
Cost of sales	430,000	395,000
Gross profit	570,000	505,000
Operating expenses	210,000	205,000
Administrative expenses	140,000	105,000
	350,000	310,000
Net income	$ 220,000	$195,000

During the course of the audit, the following additional facts were determined:

1. An analysis of collections and losses on accounts receivable during the past 2 years indicates a drop in antici- pated losses due to bad debts. After consultation with management it was agreed that the loss experience rate on sales should be reduced from the recorded 2 percent to 1 percent, beginning with the year ended Decem- ber 31, 1984.

2. An analysis of marketable securities revealed that this investment portfolio consisted entirely of short-term investments in marketable equity securities that were acquired in 1983. The total market valuation for these investments as of the end of each year was as follows:

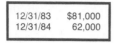

| 12/31/83 | $81,000 |
| 12/31/84 | 62,000 |

3. The merchandise inventory at December 31, 1983, was overstated by $4,000; and the merchandise inventory at December 31, 1984, was overstated by $6,100.

4. On January 2, 1983, equipment costing $12,000 (estimated useful life of 10 years and residual value of $1,000) was incorrectly charged to operating expenses. Brown records depreciation on the straight-line method. In 1984 fully depreciated equipment (with no residual value) that originally cost $17,500 was sold as scrap for $2,500. Brown credited the proceeds of $2,500 to property and equipment.

5. An analysis of 1983 operating expenses revealed that on January 15, 1983, Brown charged to expense a 3-year insurance premium of $2,700.

REQUIRED

1. Prepare the journal entries to correct the books at December 31, 1984. The books for 1984 have not been closed. *Ingore income taxes.*

2. Prepare a schedule showing the computation of corrected net income for the years ended December 31, 1983 and 1984, assuming that any adjustments are to be reported on comparative statements for the 2 years. The first items on your schedule should be the net income for each year. *Ignore income taxes. (Do not prepare finan- cial statements.)*

P24–14 (CPA ADAPTED)   The Quality Company's financial statements showed income before income taxes of $4,030,000 for the year ended December 31, 1985, and $3,330,000 for the year ended December 31, 1984. Addi- tional information follows.

1. Capital expenditures were $2,800,000 in 1985 and $4,000,000 in 1984. Included in the 1985 capital expen- ditures is equipment purchased for $1,000,000 on January 1, 1985, with no salvage value. In its financial statements, Quality used straight-line depreciation based on a 10-year estimated life. As a result of additional information now available, it is estimated that this equipment should have only an 8-year life.

2. Quality made an error in its financial statements which should be regarded as material. A payment of $180,000 was made in January 1985 and charged to expense in 1985 for insurance premiums applicable to policies commencing and expiring in 1984. No liability had been recorded for this item at December 31, 1984.

3. The allowance for doubtful accounts reflected in Quality's financial statements was $7,000 at December 31, 1985, and $97,000 at December 31, 1984. During 1985 $90,000 of uncollectible receivables was written off against the allowance for doubtful accounts. In 1984 the provision for doubtful accounts was based on a per- centage of net sales. The 1985 provision has *not* yet been recorded. Net sales were $58,500,000 for the year ended December 31, 1985, and $49,230,000 for the year ended December 31, 1984. Based on the latest available facts, and 1985 provision for doubtful accounts is estimated to be 0.2 percent of net sales.

4. A review of the estimated warranty liability at December 31, 1985, which is included in "other liabilities" in Quality's financial statements, has disclosed that this estimated liability should be increased $170,000.

5. Quality uses two large blast furnaces in its manufacturing process. Periodically these furnaces must be relined. Furnace A was relined in January 1979 at a cost of $230,000 and in January 1984 at a cost of $280,000. Furnace B was relined for the first time in January 1985 at a cost of $300,000. In Quality's finan- cial statements, these costs were expensed as incurred.

Because a relining will last for 5 years, a more appropriate matching of revenues and costs would have resulted if the cost of the relining had been capitalized and depreciated over the productive life of the relining. Quality has decided to make a change in accounting principle from expensing relining costs as incurred to capitalizing them and depreciating them over their productive life on a straight-line basis with a full year's depreciation in the year of relining. This change meets the requirements for a change in accounting principle under *APB Opinion No. 20*, "Accounting Changes."

REQUIRED

1. For the years ended December 31, 1984 and 1985, prepare a worksheet reconciling income before income taxes as given above with income before income taxes and cumulative effect of a change in accounting principle as adjusted for the above additional information. Show supporting computations. *Ignore income taxes and deferred tax considerations in your answer.* The worksheet should have the following format:

YEAR ENDED DECEMBER 31	1985	1984
Income before income taxes	$4,030,000	$3,330,000
Adjustments:		
Net adjustments		
Income before income taxes and cumulative effect of a change in accounting principle, after adjustments	$	$

2. For the year ended December 31, 1985, compute the cumulative effect before income taxes of the change in accounting principle from expensing to capitalizing relining costs. *Ignore income taxes and deferred tax considerations in your answer.*

P24–15 (CPA ADAPTED) The following data have been taken from the published financial statements of the Braken Corporation:

BRAKEN CORPORATION
Statement of Income and Retained Earnings
For the Year Ended August 31, 1984

Sales		$3,500,000
Less returns and allowances		35,000
Net sales		3,465,000
Less cost of goods sold		1,039,000
Gross margin		2,426,000
Less:		
Selling expenses	$1,000,000	
General and administrative expenses (Note 1)	1,079,000	2,079,000
Operating earnings		347,000
Add other revenue:		
Purchase discounts	10,000	
Gain on increased value of investments in real estate	100,000	
Gain on sale of treasury stock	200,000	
Correction of error in last year's statement	90,000	400,000
Ordinary earnings		747,000
Add extraordinary item—gain on sale of fixed asset		53,000
Earnings before income tax		800,000
Less income tax expense		380,000
Net earnings		420,000
Add beginning retained earnings		2,750,000
		3,170,000
Less:		
Dividends (12% stock dividend declared but not yet issued)		120,000
Contingent liability (Note 4)		300,000
Ending unappropriated retained earnings		$2,750,000

BRAKEN CORPORATION
Balance Sheet
As of August 31, 1984

ASSETS

Current assets		
Cash	$ 80,000	
Accounts receivable, net	110,000	
Inventory	130,000	
Total current assets		$ 320,000
Other assets		
Land and building, net	4,000,000	
Investments in real estate (current value)	1,508,000	
Investment in Gray, Inc., at cost (Note 2)	160,000	
Goodwill (Note 3)	250,000	
Discount on bonds payable	42,000	
Total other assets		5,960,000
Total assets		$6,280,000

LIABILITIES AND STOCKHOLDERS' EQUITY

Current liabilities		
Accounts payable	$ 140,000	
Income taxes payable	320,000	
Stock dividends payable	120,000	
Total current liabilities		$ 580,000
Other liabilities		
Due to Grant, Inc. (Note 4)	300,000	
Liability under employee pension plan	450,000	
Bonds payable (including portion due within one year)	1,000,000	
Deferred taxes	58,000	
Total other liabilities		1,808,000
Total liabilities		2,388,000
Stockholders' Equity		
Common stock	1,000,000	
Paid-in capital in excess of par	142,000	
Unappropriated retained earnings	2,750,000	
Total stockholders' equity		3,892,000
Total liabilities and stockholders' equity		$6,280,000

Footnotes to the Financial Statements

1. Depreciation expense is included in general and administrative expenses. During the fiscal year, the company changed from the straight-line method of depreciation to the sum-of-the-years'-digits method.
2. The company owns 40 percent of the outstanding stock of Gray, Inc. Because the ownership is less than 50 percent, consolidated financial statements with Gray cannot be presented.
3. In accordance with federal income tax laws, goodwill is not amortized. The goodwill was "acquired" in 1973.
4. The amount due to Grant, Inc., is contingent upon the outcome of a lawsuit that is currently pending. The amount of loss, if any, is not expected to exceed $300,000.

REQUIRED   Identify and explain the deficiencies in the presentation of Braken's financial statements. There are *no* arithmetical errors in the statements. Organize your answer as follows:

1. Deficiencies in the statement of earnings and retained earnings
2. Deficiencies in the statement of financial position
3. General comments

If an item appears on both statements, identify the deficiencies for each statement separately.

P24–16 (CPA ADAPTED) On January 1, 1984, Jeffries, Inc., paid $700,000 for 10,000 shares of Wolf Company's voting common stock which was a 10 percent interest in Wolf. At that date the net assets of Wolf totaled $6,000,000. The fair values of all of Wolf's identifiable assets and liabilities were equal to their book values. Jeffries does not have the ability to exercise significant influence over the operating and financial policies of Wolf. Jeffries received dividends of $.90 per share from Wolf on October 1, 1984. Wolf reported net income of $400,000 for the year ended December 31, 1984.

On July 1, 1985, Jeffries paid $2,300,000 for 30,000 additional shares of Wolf Company's voting common stock which represents a 30 percent investment in Wolf. The fair values of all of Wolf's identifiable assets net of liabilities were equal to their book values of $6,500,000. As a result of this transaction, Jeffries has the ability to exercise significant influence over the operating and financial policies of Wolf. Jeffries received dividends of $1.10 per share from Wolf on April 1, 1985, and $1.35 per share on October 1, 1985. Wolf reported net income of $500,000 for the year ended December 31, 1985, and $200,000 for the 6 months ended December 31, 1985. Jeffries amortizes goodwill over a 40-year period.

REQUIRED

1. Prepare a schedule showing the income or loss before income taxes for the year ended December 31, 1984, that Jeffries should report from its investment in Wolf in its income statement issued in March 1985.
2. During March 1986 Jeffries issues comparative financial statements for 1984 and 1985. Prepare schedules showing the income or loss before income taxes for the years ended December 31, 1984 and 1985, that Jeffries should report from its investment in Wolf. (Note that this problem assumes that Chapter 14 has been covered.)

25

The Statement of Changes in Financial Position

OVERVIEW   The statement of changes in financial position (SCFP) was introduced in Chapter 4, along with the basic definitions, formats, and relationships to other financial statements, and funds flow effects were discussed at the end of each chapter in Parts II and III. This chapter analyzes the elements of SCFPs, with special emphasis on how these elements relate to other financial statements and how they are developed from an analysis of each major element of the other statements.

The SCFP is a *required* financial statement, as are income statements, balance sheets, and retained earnings statements. In 1963 the AICPA issued **APB Opinion No. 3,** which *recommended* that the statement be called "statement of sources and applications of funds" and that it be presented as *supplemental* information in financial reports.[1] This opinion did not make inclusion in the annual reports mandatory, and it left optional the question of whether it should be covered in the independent accountant's report. The definition of funds to be used, and the format and organizational structure of the statement, were all left to the firm presenting the statement. The basic purpose

[1] *Accounting Principles Board Opinion No. 3,* "The Statement of Source and Application of Funds" (New York: AICPA, October 1963).

of **Opinion No. 3** was to encourage companies to present and use the "funds" statement. And it succeeded in that sense. A substantial increase in the number of companies presenting a statement of sources and applications of funds resulted.

APB Opinion No. 19 was issued in 1971 to establish more definitive standards for the preparation and presentation of the statement of changes in financial position.[2] The board required that such a statement be presented and that it be covered by the auditor's opinion. In addition, the board stated that the objectives of the SCFP were "(1) to summarize the financing and investing activities of the entity, including the extent to which the enterprise has generated funds from operations during the period, and (2) to complete the disclosure of changes in financial position during the period."[3] Within such stated broad objectives, any number of specific aspects of a firm's operations could be emphasized, such as liquidity. Which of these aspects should be emphasized? Should the emphasis change between years depending upon changing circumstances? In **Opinion No. 19** the board left questions regarding the exact form and structure of the SCFP unanswered.

APB Opinion No. 19 allows **funds** to be defined as either "cash" or "working capital." It is also possible to interpret **APB Opinion No. 19** as allowing other definitions of funds, such as "cash plus current marketable securities" or "quick assets." In practice, however, the choice is virtually always cash or working capital, and we shall concentrate on these definitions of funds.

Perhaps the SCFP's major contribution is its emphasis on funds flows within the business entity that are not based on accrual accounting, directing the analysis to those activities that involve funds flows. Increasing concern about liquidity has generated more interest in the SCFP. And to the extent that cash flows represent more of a pure (less contaminated by allocation methods or accounting procedures) economic flow than working capital, the use of, and interest in, the cash-flow data have become increasingly important to financial statement users.[4] Because of the greater interest in, and use of, the SCFP since it was required by **APB Opinion No. 19,** the FASB is reconsidering the disclosure of SCFP-type data in an attempt to refine and unify the nature of such disclosures, and changes in the content and SCFP's format will undoubtedly be forthcoming.[5]

RELATIONSHIPS OF FUNDS TO OTHER BALANCE SHEET CLASSIFICATIONS

The SCFP presents the changes in funds for an accounting period. Exhibit 25–1 shows the relationship of working capital (one definition of funds) to all the other major balance sheet classifications. Note how the changes in the current asset and current liability accounts, which represent the change in working capital, are related

---

[2] *Accounting Principles Board Opinion No. 19,* "Reporting Changes in Financial Position" (New York: AICPA, March 1971).

[3] Ibid., par. 4.

[4] Emphasis on the importance of cash flows can be found in the more recent theoretical pronouncements of the FASB and AICPA discussed in Chapter 2 of this text.

[5] *FASB Discussion Memorandum,* "Reporting Funds Flows, Liquidity, and Financial Flexibility" (Stamford, CT: FASB, 1980).

EXHIBIT 25–1

WORKING CAPITAL CHANGE AS A FUNCTION OF OTHER BALANCE SHEET CLASSIFICATIONS

Balance Sheet Example

BALANCE SHEET CLASSIFICATION	BALANCES END OF YEAR	BEGINNING OF YEAR	CHANGE (Δ) DURING YEAR
Current assets (CA)	$100	$ 80	+$20
Long-term assets (LTA)	405	390	+15
Current liabilities (CL)	70	60	+10
Noncurrent liabilities (NCL)	125	120	+5
Owner's equity (OE)	310	290	+20

Definitions of Working Capital and Change in Working Capital

$$\text{Working capital (WC)} = \text{CA} - \text{CL}$$
$$\text{Change in WC } (\Delta\text{WC}) = \Delta\text{CA} - \Delta\text{CL}$$

Relationship of Change in Working Capital to Changes in Other Balance Sheet Classifications

$$\text{CA} + \text{LTA} = \text{CL} + \text{NCL} + \text{OE}$$
$$\text{CA} - \text{CL} = \text{NCL} + \text{OE} - \text{LTA}$$
$$\Delta\text{CA} - \Delta\text{CL} = \Delta\text{NCL} + \Delta\text{OE} - \Delta\text{LTA}$$
$$\Delta\text{WC} = \Delta\text{NCL} + \Delta\text{OE} - \Delta\text{LTA}$$

Computation of the Change in Working Capital Using Amounts from the Example

$$\Delta\text{WC} = \Delta\text{NCL} + \Delta\text{OE} - \Delta\text{LTA}$$
$$\Delta\text{WC} = \$5 + \$20 - \$15$$
$$\Delta\text{WC} = \$10$$

EXHIBIT 25–2

CASH CHANGE AS A FUNCTION OF OTHER BALANCE SHEET CLASSIFICATIONS

Balance Sheet Example

BALANCE SHEET CLASSIFICATION	BALANCES END OF YEAR	BEGINNING OF YEAR	CHANGE (Δ) DURING YEAR
Cash (C)	$ 20	$ 25	−$ 5
Noncash current assets (NCA)	80	55	+25
Long-term assets (LTA)	405	390	+15
Current liabilities (CL)	70	60	+10
Noncurrent liabilities (NCL)	125	120	+5
Owners' equity (OE)	310	290	+20

Relationship of Change in Cash to Changes in Other Balance Sheet Classifications from the Example

$$\text{C} + \text{NCA} + \text{LTA} = \text{CL} + \text{NCL} + \text{OE}$$
$$\text{C} = \text{CL} + \text{NCL} + \text{OE} - \text{NCA} - \text{LTA}$$
$$\Delta\text{C} = \Delta\text{CL} + \Delta\text{NCL} + \Delta\text{OE} - \Delta\text{NCA} - \Delta\text{LTA}$$
$$\Delta\text{C} = +\$10 + \$5 + \$20 - \$25 - \$15$$
$$\Delta\text{C} = -\$5$$

to (explained by) changes in the other balance sheet accounts. In the example provided, the $10 increase in working capital is explained by a $5 increase in noncurrent liabilities (that is, the debt issuance effect), plus a $20 increase in owners' equity (that is, the net income effect), less a $15 decrease due to use of working capital to acquire long-term assets.

Exhibit 25–2 shows the relationship between the change in cash (another definition of funds) and changes in the other major balance sheet classifications. Note that the cash format is basically a finer partitioning of working capital. The example illustrates how the $5 decrease in cash resulted from a combination of events. In terms of net results, $35 of cash flowed in from operations and increased debt, but $40 of cash flowed out because of asset additions.

The analyses in Exhibits 25–1 and 25–2 demonstrate that a thorough description of changes in nonfund classifications completely explains the changes in funds. The term **nonfund** is defined depending on the definition of **funds** used in the given SCFP. If the cash basis is used, *nonfund* is defined as all noncash accounts. If the working capital basis is used, *nonfund* means all noncurrent accounts. We shall first consider balance sheet data, along with other financial statements and explanations. We shall then analyze each change in nonfund balance sheet items in order to derive the causes of fund flows.

THE STATEMENT OF CHANGES IN FINANCIAL POSITION: A COMPREHENSIVE CORPORATE CASE

The financial statement data for Staye-Cool Corporation in Exhibits 25–3, 25–4, and 25–5 will be used throughout the remainder of this chapter. Many of the items in the financial statements relate to accounting issues that have previously been discussed in this text, and a thorough understanding of the principles and procedures applicable to each is assumed in the following analysis.

The "building block" approach to SCFP construction will be demonstrated first. This approach analyzes all the changes in nonfund balance sheet items starting with nonfund assets and proceeding in the listed order to all the other nonfund balance sheet items. Subsequent to the illustration of the "building block" approach, another equally effective approach (worksheet analysis) will be demonstrated. Appendix G demonstrates a third approach—the T-account method.

We shall begin with a **working capital** definition of funds and at the end of the chapter show how the same techniques can be used when **cash** is chosen for the definition of funds. The working capital approach is not only the most widely used in practice, but it is also somewhat easier to consider the cash basis as an extension of the working capital basis rather than vice versa.

Computation of Working Capital Changes

The goal of the SCFP is to explain what caused the change in working capital during the period. An appropriate first step would be to determine the change in working capital. **APB Opinion No. 19** requires that a schedule showing the changes in working capital items be presented in the SCFP. Typically, this schedule is provided at the bottom of the SCFP. Any number of formats is possible; the following is one possibility:

```
                    STAYE-COOL CORPORATION
                  Schedule of Working Capital Changes
                  For the Year Ended December 31, 1985

                                              12/31/85      12/31/84

Current assets
  Cash                                      $    25,000   $    32,000
  Short-term investments                        280,000       179,000
  Trade accounts receivable (net)               650,000       724,000
  Notes receivable from officers                 76,000        33,000
  Inventory                                      294,000       298,000
  Prepaid insurance                               16,000        12,000
    Total current assets                     $1,341,000    $1,278,000
Current liabilities
  Accounts payable                          $   379,000   $   397,000
  Customer advances                              62,000        51,000
  Income taxes payable                           53,000        62,000
  Accrued salesmen salaries payable              27,000        21,000
  Notes payable—banks                           146,000       175,000
    Total current liabilities                   667,000       706,000
      Working capital: 12/31/85             $   674,000   $   572,000
                       12/31/84                 572,000
        Increase in working capital during 1985  $  102,000
```

Because the schedule above repeats what appears in the comparative balance sheet, the following format might be preferred:

```
                    STAYE-COOL CORPORATION
                  Schedule of Working Capital Changes
                  For the Year Ended December 31, 1985

                                          EFFECTS OF CHANGES IN
                                             CURRENT ITEMS ON
                                            WORKING CAPITAL

                                          INCREASE      DECREASE

Current assets
  Cash                                                  $    7,000
  Short-term investments                  $101,000
  Trade accounts receivable (net)                           74,000
  Notes receivable from officers            43,000
  Inventory                                                  4,000
  Prepaid insurance                          4,000
Current liabilities
  Accounts payable                          18,000
  Customer advances                                         11,000
  Income taxes payable                       9,000
  Accrued salesmen salaries payable                          6,000
  Notes payable—banks                       29,000
                                          $204,000      $102,000
    Deduct: Decreases                      102,000
      Increase in working capital during 1985  $102,000
```

The Basic SCFP Format Current GAAP call for an explicit reconciliation of "income from operations" and "working capital from operations." This is usually accomplished by means of a for-

EXHIBIT 25-3

STAYE-COOL CORPORATION
Comparative Balance Sheet

	DECEMBER 31, 1985		DECEMBER 31,1984	
Current assets				
Cash		$ 25,000		$ 32,000
Short-term investments		280,000		179,000
Trade accounts receivable (net)		650,000		724,000
Notes receivable from officers		76,000		33,000
Inventory		294,000		298,000
Prepaid insurance		16,000		12,000
Total current assets		$1,341,000		$1,278,000
Plant, property, and equipment				
Land		$1,200,000		$ 850,000
Buildings—cost	$2,800,000		$1,750,000	
Less: Accumulated depreciation	560,000	2,240,000	410,000	1,340,000
Machinery and equipment—cost	$1,750,000		$2,100,000	
Less: Accumulated depreciation	1,050,000	700,000	1,250,000	850,000
Total plant, property, and equipment		4,140,000		3,040,000
Intangibles				
Patents (net of amortization of $66,000 and $44,000 for 1985 and 1984, respectively)		$ 154,000		$ 176,000
Goodwill (net of amortization of $30,000 and $20,000 for 1985 and 1984, respectively)		370,000		380,000
Total intangibles		524,000		556,000
Total assets		$6,005,000		$4,874,000
Current liabilities				
Accounts payable		$ 379,000		$ 397,000
Customer advances		62,000		51,000
Income taxes payable		53,000		62,000
Accrued salesmen salaries payable		27,000		21,000
Notes payable—banks		146,000		175,000
Total current liabilities		$ 667,000		$ 706,000
Long-term liabilities				
Bonds payable—maturity amount	$2,500,000		$2,600,000	
Add: Unamortized bond premium	250,000		190,000	
Total long-term liabilities		2,750,000		2,790,000
Total liabilities		$3,417,000		$3,496,000
Stockholders' equity				
Common stock—$10 par value		$1,000,000		$ 500,000
Additional paid-in capital		500,000		225,000
Total paid-in capital		$1,500,000		$ 725,000
Retained earnings		1,088,000		653,000
Total stockholders' equity		2,588,000		1,378,000
Total liabilities and equities		$6,005,000		$4,874,000

mat similar to the one shown in Exhibit 25–6. The statement starts with "income before extraordinary items" (or some other reported income statement subtotal that approximates income from operations). *Next, an elimination is made of the impact of those items that are in this initial number but that* (1) *did not affect funds or* (2) *were nonoperating in nature and are eliminated in computing funds provided by operations.* We shall show how Staye-Cool's transactions are incorporated into a series of incomplete SCFPs in Exhibits 25–6 through 25–10, culminating in a complete SCFP in Exhibit 25–11. Exhibit 25–6 highlights the two initial entries into the incomplete SCFP: "Income before extraordinary items" and the bottom line, "Change in working capital."

EXHIBIT
25–4

STAYE-COOL CORPORATION
1985 Income Statement

Sales revenue		$6,850,000
Less: Cost of goods sold		3,975,000
Gross profit		$2,875,000
Operating expenses:		
Selling	$580,000	
General and administrative	624,000	
Depreciation	400,000	
Total operating expenses		1,604,000
Operating income before income taxes		$1,271,000
Other income:		
Gain on sale of buildings	$100,000	
Income from short-term investments	28,000	128,000
		$1,399,000
Other expenses:		
Loss on sale of machinery and equipment		30,000
Income before extraordinary item and income taxes		$1,369,000
Income tax expense		574,000
Income before extraordinary item		$ 795,000
Extraordinary item:		
Loss on expropriation of land (less income tax saving of $73,000).		110,000
Net income		$ 685,000

STAYE-COOL CORPORATION
1985 Retained Earnings Statement

Balance, 12/31/84	$ 653,000
Income for 1985	685,000
	$1,338,000
Dividends declared on common stock	250,000
Balance, 12/31/85	$1,088,000

EXHIBIT
25–5

STAYE-COOL CORPORATION
Additional Data for 1985

1. Land that had cost $800,000 was taken over by the state for highway construction. The state made a cash payment in compensation for the land. All additions to land were made by cash purchases.
2. A building that originally cost $500,000 was sold for $450,000 during the year. The book value at the date of sale was $350,000. All additions were paid for in cash.
3. The only activity in the Machinery and Equipment account was for dispositions for cash during the year. Total accumulated depreciation on items sold was $300,000.
4. Patents were acquired on December 1, 1983, and are being amortized over 10 years. Patent amortization expense is included as part of general and administrative expenses.
5. Goodwill amortization is $10,000 per year and is also included in general and administrative expenses.
6. Bonds with a total maturity value of $729,500 were converted into common stock. This was the only event affecting common stock during the year. The "book value" method was used in recording the conversion, which means that no gains or losses were recorded.
7. Bonds were issued during the year at a premium of $140,000.
8. Interest expense is included in general and administrative expenses.
9. Short-term investments costing $50,000 were sold for $50,000. All other activity in short-term investments involved purchases of securities.

EXHIBIT
25–6

STAYE-COOL CORPORATION Incomplete SCFP	
Sources of Funds	
Provided by operations	
Income before extraordinary items	$795,000
Deduct: Revenues and other credits not affecting working capital	XXX
Add: Expenses and other debits not affecting working capital	XXX
Working capital from operations	$ XXX
Plus *other sources* (a list of specific sources)	XXX
Total sources	$ XXX
Less *Uses of Funds* (a list of specific uses)	XXX
Change in working capital	$102,000

**Analysis
of Changes
in Nonfund
Classifications**

Changes in nonfund assets

LAND   The first nonfund item in Staye-Cool Corporation's balance sheet is land, which in total decreased by $350,000 during 1985. Partial evidence as to the nature of this decrease is found in the additional data, item 1, in Exhibit 25–5. Certain land with an original cost of $800,000 was taken over by the state for highway construction. The income statement shows an extraordinary loss of $110,000 net of $73,000 in taxes. Thus, we can reconstruct the journal entry to record the decrease in land as follows:

Cash	617,000	
Income taxes payable	73,000	
Extraordinary loss	110,000	
Land		800,000

In addition, since we started the year with $850,000 in the Land account and ended it with $1,200,000, it follows that additional land must have been acquired. The following journal entry shows how the purchase of $1,150,000 of land must have been recorded:[6]

Land	1,150,000	
Cash		1,150,000

What were the working capital effects of these two transactions? Working capital was increased by $690,000 (an increase in Cash of $617,000 and a decrease in Income Taxes Payable of $73,000) by the first transaction and reduced by $1,150,000 by the second. How would they be reported in the Staye-Cool SCFP? The "funds provided by operations" section is not affected because the only income statement item in these two journal entries is an extraordinary item that is not included in the $795,000 of "income before extraordinary items." Both the "other sources" and the "uses of funds" section of the SCFP would be affected as shown in Exhibit 25–7.

DEPRECIABLE ASSETS   The next nonfund assets on Staye-Cool's balance sheet are Buildings and Machinery and Equipment accounts, along with their accumulated depreciation accounts. We see in item 2 of the additional data (Exhibit 25–5) that a

[6] In an actual situation, we would be able to verify from the ledger and journal details that land was acquired for cash. In text books' problem settings, we shall observe that logical assumptions regarding unspecified data (such as the credit to cash) are made.

EXHIBIT
25–7

STAYE-COOL CORPORATION

Incomplete SCFP

Sources of Funds	
Provided by operations	
Income before extraordinary items	$ 795,000
Deduct: Credits not affecting working capital	XXX
Add: Debits not affecting working capital	XXX
Working capital from operations	$ XXX
Other Sources	
Compensation for expropriation of land	690,000
Total sources	$ XXX
Uses of Funds	
Acquisition of land	$1,150,000
Total uses	$ XXX
Change in working capital	$ 102,000

building that cost $500,000 was sold for $450,000 and that additions to buildings were paid for in cash. What effect did this activity and the depreciation charges have on funds? A reconstruction of the journal entries will answer these questions:

Cash	450,000[a]	
Accumulated depreciation—buildings	150,000[b]	
Buildings		500,000[a]
Gain on sale of buildings		100,000[c]

[a] Given in additional data.
[b] Forced given data available.
[c] From income statement.

Buildings	$1,550,000	
Cash		$1,550,000
(The ending balance in the Buildings account is $2,800,000 and the beginning balance was $1,750,000, which combined with the reduction of $500,000 shown in the previous entry forces an acquisition of $1,550,000.)		

It can now be seen that the Accumulated Depreciation—Buildings account has been affected by the disposition ($150,000) and the normal depreciation charge:

Depreciation expense	300,000	
Accumulation depreciation—buildings		300,000
(The beginning balance was $410,000 and the ending balance was $560,000, resulting in a $150,000 increase. Given the $150,000 decrease caused by the disposition, the normal depreciation charge must be $300,000.)		

The next account is Machinery and Equipment. Item 3 in the additional data indicates that no machinery or equipment was acquired during the year. All the change resulted from dispositions when total accumulated depreciation for the items sold was $300,000. With the loss of $30,000 on the sale of machinery and equipment reflected in the income statement, we can reconstruct the following summary entry for dispositions during the year:

Cash	20,000	
Loss on sale of machinery and equipment	30,000	
Accumulated depreciation—machinery and equipment	300,000	
Machinery and equipment		350,000

We can also determine what brought about the changes in accumulated depreciation—machinery and equipment:

Ending balance (12/31/85)		$1,050,000
Beginning balance (12/31/84)	$1,250,000	
Reduction due to sales of machinery and equipment	300,000	950,000
Increase due to recording 1985 depreciation expense		$ 100,000

As a result, the following entry must have been made to record 1985 depreciation expense for machinery and equipment:

Depreciation expense	100,000	
Accumulated depreciation— machinery and equipment		100,000

Exhibit 25–8 shows the effect of inserting the funds activity for depreciable assets into the incomplete SCFP. Note that both the loss on the sale of machinery and equipment ($30,000) and the depreciation expense ($300,000 for buildings and $100,000 for machinery and equipment) are deductions in "income before extraordinary items" (IBEI), which *do not* consume working capital, and thus they are added back to IBEI in computing working capital from operations.

However, the sale of the building did provide working capital (cash) of $450,000, but it is not included in "working capital from *operations*" because it is considered to be a *nonoperating* source of working capital. Note that the entire $450,000 cash from the sale of the building is reported in the "other sources" of funds section in Exhibit 25–8.

INTANGIBLES Patents decreased $22,000 and goodwill decreased $10,000 during the year. Based on the information provided in additional data items 4 and 5 (Exhibit 25–5), both assets decreased as a result of the following amortization entry:

General and administrative expense	32,000	
Patents		22,000
Goodwill		10,000

The analysis here is exactly the same as that for depreciation expense. The $32,000 must be added to "income before extraordinary items" (IBEI) because it decreased IBEI but did *not* consume working capital. Our incomplete SCFP, brought up to date, appears in Exhibit 25–9.

EXHIBIT
25–8

STAYE-COOL CORPORATION

Incomplete SCFP

Sources of Funds		
Provided by operations		
Income before extraordinary items		$ 795,000
Deduct: Gain on sale of building	$100,000	
Add: Loss on sale of machinery and equipment	30,000	
Depreciation expense	400,000	
Working capital from operations		$ XXX
Other Sources		
Compensation for expropriation of land		690,000
Sale of building		450,000
Sale of machinery and equipment		20,000
Total sources		$ XXX
Uses of Funds		
Acquisition of land		1,150,000
Acquisition of building		1,550,000
Total uses		$ XXX
Change in working capital		$ 102,000

Changes in nonfund liabilities and equities

BONDS PAYABLE AND COMMON STOCK   Bonds Payable decreased by a net amount of $100,000, and its related Unamortized Bond Premium account increased by a net amount of $60,000 during the year. The additional data items 6 and 7 (Exhibit 25–5) state directly (1) that bonds with a maturity value of $729,500 were converted into common stock, (2) that this was the only transaction during the year affecting common stock, and (3) that the book value method was used in recording the conversion—that is, no gain or loss on conversion is recorded. We can reconstruct the conversion entry as follows:

EXHIBIT
25–9

STAYE-COOL CORPORATION

Incomplete SCFP

Sources of Funds		
Provided by operations		
Income before extraordinary items		$ 795,000
Deduct: Gain on sale of building	$100,000	
Add: Loss on sale of machinery and equipment	30,000	
Depreciation expense	400,000	
Patent amortization	22,000	
Goodwill amortization	10,000	
Working capital from operations		$ XXX
Other Sources		
Compensation for expropriation of land		690,000
Sale of building		450,000
Sale of machinery and equipment		20,000
Total sources		$ XXX
Uses of Funds		
Acquisition of land		1,150,000
Acquisition of buildings		1,550,000
Total uses		$ XXX
Change in working capital		$ 102,000

Bonds payable	729,500	
Unamortized bond premium	45,500	
Common stock		500,000
Additional paid-in capital		275,000

Must the event be reflected in the SCFP? **APB Opinion No. 19** requires that the SCFP be prepared on the basis of "all financial resources," although within that broad concept of funds, working capital or cash changes can be emphasized. Any material change in noncurrent liabilities and owners' equity, except for stock dividends, stock splits, and retained earnings appropriations, must be reflected in the SCFP even though funds are not affected. These include such events and transactions as the direct exchange of one long-term liability for another long-term liability and the conversion of long-term debt into preferred or common stock. Whenever the noncurrent asset structure and noncurrent liability and owners' equity structure are changed simultaneously, they must be reflected in the SCFP, even when funds are not affected. For example, noncurrent assets could be acquired directly upon issuance of long-term debt, preferred stock, or common stock. Thus, the conversion must be reflected in the SCFP.

Up to now, the events reflected in our partial SCFP were reflected in that statement only once, as either funds provided or funds used. When an event that must be disclosed in the SCFP does not affect working capital (or cash in the case of a cash-basis SCFP), it is normally cited both as a source and as a use so that the net effect will be zero. This can be justified if you assume intermediate cash transactions. Under this assumption, the preceding event can be viewed as shown in the following *hypothetical* entries:

Cash	775,000	
Common stock		500,000
Additional paid-in capital		275,000
Bonds payable	729,500	
Unamortized bond premium	45,500	
Cash		775,000

The cash entries net out to zero, and *no cash actually changed hands,* but the assumption of the intermediate cash events allows you to see clearly that resources were "provided" by the issuance of common stock in exchange for bonds, and resources were "used" in the conversion of bonds to common stock.

We can now finish our analysis of bonds payable and unamortized premium as follows:

Bonds payable		
Ending balance		$2,500,000
Beginning balance	$2,600,000	
Reduction due to conversion	729,500	1,870,500
Increase due to new issuances		$ 629,500
Unamortized premium		
Ending balance		$ 250,000
Beginning balance	$ 190,000	
Reduction due to conversion	45,500	144,500
Increase during the year		$ 105,500
Increase due to new issuances		140,000
Decrease due to premium amortization		$ 34,500

Thus, we can reconstruct the entry at the time of the issuance of new bonds:

Cash	769,500	
Bonds payable		629,500
Unamortized bond premium		140,000

And we can summarize the entries for the amortization of premiums:

Interest expense	244,500	
Unamortized bond premium	34,500	
Cash or interest payable		279,000

Working capital increased by $769,500, so that should go into the SCFP as a resource provided. But what about the premium amortization of $34,500? We know that income is reduced by the effective interest charges of $244,500 (cash paid of $279,000 in this case less premium amortization). Therefore, because of the $34,500 premium amortization, the expense is less than the funds consumed by the transaction and must be deducted from IBEI in arriving at "working capital provided by operations." All of the bond and common stock entries have been inserted into the partial SCFP in Exhibit 25–10.

DIVIDENDS The only remaining item is the dividends declared of $250,000. The following entry reflects the declaration:

Retained earnings	250,000	
Dividends payable		250,000

Therefore, working capital was reduced, and this item would go into the SCFP as a resource used. Because there is no ending balance in dividends payable, we also know that all the dividends declared were paid, but this is irrelevant from a working

EXHIBIT
25–10

STAYE-COOL CORPORATION		
Incomplete SCFP		
Sources of Funds		
Provided by operations		
Income before extraordinary items		$ 795,000
Deduct: Gain on sale of building	$100,000	
Bond premium amortization	34,500	134,500
Add: Loss on sale of machinery and equipment	30,000	
Depreciation expense	400,000	
Patent amortization	22,000	
Goodwill amortization	10,000	462,000
Working capital from operations		$1,122,500
Other Sources		
Compensation for expropriation of land		690,000
Sale of building		450,000
Sale of machinery and equipment		20,000
Issuance of bonds		769,500
Issuance of common stock in exchange for bonds		775,000
Total sources		$3,827,000
Uses of Funds		
Acquisition of land		1,150,000
Acquisition of buildings		1,550,000
Conversion of bonds into common stock		775,000
Total uses		$ XXX
Change in working capital		$ 102,000

EXHIBIT
25–11

STAYE-COOL CORPORATION

Statement of Changes in Financial Position
For the Year Ended December 31, 1985

Sources of Funds
  Provided by operations
    Income before extraordinary items $ 795,000

Income before extraordinary items		$ 795,000
Deduct: Credits (additions) not affecting working capital:		
Gain on sale of building	$ 100,000	
Bond premium amortization	34,500	134,500
		$ 660,500
Add: Charges (deductions) not affecting working capital:		
Loss on sale of machinery and equipment	$ 30,000	
Depreciation expense	400,000	
Patent amortization	22,000	
Goodwill amortization	10,000	462,000
Working capital provided by operations, exclusive of extraordinary items		$1,122,500
Other Sources		
Compensation for expropriation of land		690,000
Sale of building		450,000
Sale of machinery and equipment		20,000
Issuance of bonds		769,500
Issuance of common stock in exchange for bonds		775,000
Total sources of working capital		$3,827,000
Uses of Funds		
To acquire land	$1,150,000	
To acquire buildings	1,550,000	
Declaration of dividends	250,000	
Conversion of bonds into common stock	775,000	
Total uses of working capital		3,725,000
Increase in working capital during 1985		$ 102,000

capital view. When dividends were paid, the following entry was made:

Dividends payable	250,000	
Cash		250,000

Because the decrease in the current liability of $250,000 is exactly offset by the decrease in the current asset cash of $250,000, this event is completely within the confines of working capital. There is no net impact on working capital, and it is not reported in the SCFP. Only dividends declared are reported when working capital is being emphasized. The same logic is used for many other transactions that involve offsetting increases and decreases in working capital, such as the payment of an account payable or the collection of an account receivable.

The insertion of dividends into our SCFP completes the analysis and will result in the formal SCFP shown in Exhibit 25–11.

Alternative Format for Funds from Operations

Statement format What is called the **statement format** could be used instead of the **reconciliation format** as shown in Exhibit 25–11 to derive "working capital provided by operations." The statement format shows more detail in terms of inflows and outflows of "funds" from operations than does the reconciliation format.[7] But which is better?

---

[7] For a discussion, see J. W. Giese and T. P. Klammer, "Achieving the Objectives of ABP Opinion No. 19," *Journal of Accountancy,* March 1974, pp. 54–61.

Those supporting the reconciliation approach use two main arguments to support their position: (1) there should be a direct tie-in of the SCFP to the income statement, and (2) it is the *net* figure that reflects the financial effects of operating activity.

Those supporting the statement format argue that using nonfund items to reconcile "income" on an accrual basis to "funds" provided by operations encourages many to believe that these items are sources or uses of funds, even though in fact they are not. Also, many feel that the statement format provides more complete and useful data regarding the flow of cash or working capital from operations because it reflects both the major inflows and outflows as opposed to only the *net* inflow or outflow. **APB Opinion No. 19** allows either format to be used.

The following data are needed to prepare and present the SCFP using the statement format:

1. *Sales.* The inflow of working capital from sales must equal $6,850,000. The sales were for cash, on account, or a reduction of customer advances, all of which are working capital (WC) items:

Cash, accounts receivable, etc. (WC)	6,850,000	
Sales		6,850,000

2. *Cost of goods sold.* Cost of goods sold may have originated from the following type of entry:

Cost of goods sold	3,975,000	
Inventory (WC)		3,975,000

3. *Selling expenses.* Our analyses revealed no nonfund debits (or credits). Therefore, everything affecting selling expenses also had an impact on (reduced) working capital:

Selling expenses	580,000	
Cash, accounts payable, or accrued sales staff salaries payable (WC)		580,000

4. *General and administrative expenses.* Everything contributing to this expense also affected working capital, except for amortization of bond premium, patents, and goodwill. Thus, in summary form, the following entry must have been made:

General and administrative expenses	624,000	
Unamortized bond premium	34,500	
Patents		22,000
Goodwill		10,000
Cash, accounts payable, prepaid insurance, or other working capital accounts (WC)		626,500

5. *Tax expense.* Tax expense must have been recorded as follows because there are no deferred tax accounts:

Tax expense	574,000	
Cash or income taxes payable (WC)		574,000

6. *Income from short-term investments.* Working capital from this item must have been recorded as follows:

| Cash or short-term receivable (WC) | 28,000 | |
| Income from short-term investments | | 28,000 |

7. *All other items.* Gains, losses, and depreciation in this example have no effect on working capital and are therefore excluded in preparing the SCFP.

Using items 1 through 7, we could prepare the "operations" portion of the SCFP following the statement format. The remainder of the SCFP is identical to that previously presented, once we arrive at "working capital provided by operations," and, therefore, it is not repeated here.

STAYE-COOL CORPORATION
Partial Statement of Changes in Financial Position
For the Year Ended December 31, 1985

Sources of Funds
  Provided by operations
    Working capital provided:

By sales		$6,850,000
By short-term investments		28,000
		$6,878,000
Working capital used in generating income:		
Cost of goods sold	$3,975,000	
Selling expense	580,000	
General and administrative expense	626,500	
Income taxes	574,000	5,755,500
Working capital provided by operations, exclusive of extraordinary items		$1,122,500

Some Additional Considerations

APB Opinion No. 19 indicates that certain changes falling completely within the common stockholders' equity section are not to be reflected in the SCFP. The changes involved are usually stock dividends and stock splits. Consider the entries made in these two cases. For a "large" stock dividend, either no entry or one similar to the following is made:

| Retained earnings | 1,000,000 | |
| Common stock—par value | | 1,000,000 |

When a "small" common stock dividend is declared, retained earnings must be capitalized at an amount equal to the fair market value of the stock at the date of declaration, resulting in the following type of entry:

Retained earnings	1,500,000	
Common stock—par value		1,000,000
Additional paid-in capital		500,000

In neither of these cases is the asset structure of the firm changed, and no significant realignment of owners' equity has taken place. The APB therefore concluded that these events should not be reflected in the SCFP. However, note that if a preferred stock dividend is declared in common stock of the firm, this represents a realignment of equities that must be reflected in the SCFP.

Use of a Worksheet

A more compact and structured technique for assembling the data needed to prepare a statement of changes in financial position involves the use of a **worksheet**.

We emphasize again that the concepts and basic analysis are the same. Using the data from the Staye-Cool Corporation example, we can construct the worksheet in Exhibit 25–12. In the first column we place the balance sheet data as of the beginning of the year. In the fourth column we place the balance sheet data as of the end of the year. The second and third columns are the *debit* and *credit* columns used in reconciling the beginning and ending balances and reflecting resources provided and used. In other words, our basic tasks remain the same: determining the causes of *net* changes in *all* nonfund balance sheet items and using those that affect working capital to help prepare the SCFP. In line with this, note that the first items in the worksheet indicate working capital at the beginning and end of the year. We need not list working capital items individually (see p. 956 for a detailed analysis.)

Explanation of worksheet   Each worksheet entry is numbered and explained in the following pages. Our schedule of working capital changes on p. 956 indicates that working capital increased by $102,000 during 1985. The increase in working capital is recorded on the worksheet as follows:

(1)	Working capital	102,000	
	Resources used—increase in working capital		102,000

To set up the first item in the SCFP using the reconciliation format, the following worksheet entry is necessary:

(2)	Resources provided—income before extraordinary items	795,000	
	Retained earnings		795,000

Beyond this point, instead of debiting or crediting a current asset or current liability as we analyze the changes, we simply debit or credit "resources provided" or "resources used." For example, recall that we constructed the original entry for the expropriation of the land as follows:

Cash	617,000	
Income taxes payable	73,000	
Extraordinary loss (net of income taxes of $73,000)	110,000	
Land		800,000

Our reconciliation entry on the worksheet becomes:

(3)	Resources provided—expropriation of land	690,000	
	Retained earnings	110,000	
	Land		800,000

Why do we debit retained earnings for $110,000? The loss of $110,000 was extraordinary. As such it was not deducted in arriving at the $795,000 figure for income before extraordinary items, and resources provided by operations therefore does not have to be adjusted for this figure. However, net income and, hence, retained earnings were reduced by this amount. Therefore, in order to reconcile retained earnings on January 1, 1985, with retained earnings on December 31, 1985, the $110,000 must be deducted. The $690,000 figure is the sum of cash received of $617,000 and the decrease in income tax payable of $73,000 (an increase in working

EXHIBIT 25–12

STAYE-COOL CORPORATION
Worksheet for Preparing a Statement of Changes in Financial Position
For the Year Ended December 31, 1985

	BALANCE 1/1/85	DEBIT (SOURCES)		CREDIT (USES)		BALANCE 12/31/85
Debits						
Working capital	572,000	(1)	102,000			674,000
Land	850,000	(4)	1,150,000	(3)	800,000	1,200,000
Buildings	1,750,000	(6)	1,550,000	(5)	500,000	2,800,000
Machinery and equipment	2,100,000			(7)	350,000	1,750,000
Patents	176,000			(9)	22,000	154,000
Goodwill	380,000			(9)	10,000	370,000
	5,828,000					6,948,000
Credits						
Accumulated depreciation—buildings	410,000	(5)	150,000	(8)	300,000	560,000
Accumulated depreciation—machinery and equipment	1,250,000	(7)	300,000	(8)	100,000	1,050,000
Bonds payable—maturity amount	2,600,000	(10)	729,500	(11)	629,500	2,500,000
Unamortized bond premium	190,000	(10)	45,500	(11)	140,000	250,000
		(12)	34,500			
Common stock—$10 par value	500,000			(10)	500,000	1,000,000
Additional paid-in capital	225,000			(10)	275,000	500,000
Retained earnings	653,000	(3)	110,000	(2)	795,000	1,088,000
		(13)	250,000			
	5,828,000		4,421,500		4,421,500	6,948,000
Resources Provided						
Income before extraordinary items		(2)	795,000			
Deduct: Nonfund credits:						
Gain on sale of buildings				(5)	100,000	
Bond premium amortization				(12)	34,500	
Add: Nonfund debits:						
Loss on sale of machinery and equipment		(7)	30,000			
Depreciation expense		(8)	400,000			
Patent amortization		(9)	22,000			
Goodwill amortization		(9)	10,000			
			1,257,000		134,500	
			134,500			
Working capital provided by operations before extraordinary items			1,122,500			
Expropriation of land		(3)	690,000			
Sale of buildings		(5)	450,000			
Sale of machinery and equipment		(7)	20,000			
Issuance of common stock for bonds		(10)	775,000			
Issuance of bonds for cash		(11)	709,500			
Resources Used						
To increase working capital				(1)	102,000	
To acquire land				(4)	1,150,000	
To acquire buildings				(6)	1,550,000	
Conversion of bonds to common stock				(10)	775,000	
To declare dividends on common stock				(13)	250,000	
Total resources provided			3,827,000			
Total resources used					3,827,000	

capital totaling $690,000). Thus, whenever our analysis indicates that a current asset or a current liability was debited by the firm at the time the transaction originally took place, we must debit some properly described item indicating the source under "resources provided" on the worksheet. Whenever an ordinary loss (nonfund debit) is involved, we must debit resources provided by operations in order to get

EXHIBIT 25-13

COMPARISON OF ORIGINAL ENTRIES TO WORKSHEET RECONCILING ENTRIES

ORIGINAL ENTRY			WORKSHEET RECONCILIATION ENTRIES			WORKSHEET ENTRY NUMBER
Cash	450,000		Resources provided—sale of buildings	450,000		5
Accumulated depreciation—buildings	150,000		Accumulated depreciation—buildings	150,000		
Buildings		500,000	Buildings		500,000	
Gain on sale of buildings		100,000	Resources provided—income before extraordinary items		100,000	
Buildings	1,550,000		Buildings	1,550,000		6
Cash		1,550,000	Resources used—to acquire buildings		1,550,000	
Cash	20,000		Resources provided—sale of machinery and equipment	20,000		7
Loss on sale of machinery and equipment	30,000		Resources provided—income before extraordinary items	30,000		
Accumulated depreciation—machinery and equipment	300,000		Accumulated depreciation—machinery and equipment	300,000		
Machinery and equipment		350,000	Machinery and equipment		350,000	
Depreciation expense	400,000		Resources provided—income before extraordinary items	400,000		8
Accumulated depreciation—buildings		300,000	Accumulated depreciation—buildings		300,000	
Accumulated depreciation—machinery and equipment		100,000	Accumulated depreciation—machinery and equipment		100,000	
General and administrative expenses	32,000		Resources provided—income before extraordinary items	22,000		9
Patents		22,000	Resources provided—income before extraordinary items	10,000		
Goodwill		10,000	Patents		22,000	
			Goodwill		10,000	

EXHIBIT 25-13
(continued)

ORIGINAL ENTRY			WORKSHEET RECONCILIATION ENTRIES			WORKSHEET ENTRY NUMBER
Bonds payable	729,500		Resources provided— issuance of com- mon stock in exchange for bonds			10
Unamortized bond premium	45,500					
Common stock		500,000		775,000		
Additional paid-in capital		275,000	Bonds payable	729,500		
			Unamortized bond premium	45,500		
			Resource used— bonds converted to common stock		775,000	
			Common stock		500,000	
			Additional paid-in capital		275,000	
Cash	769,500		Resources provided— issuance of bonds for cash			11
Bonds payable		629,500		769,500		
Unamortized bond premium		140,000	Bonds payable		629,500	
			Unamortized bond premium		140,000	
Interest expense	244,500		Unamortized bond premium	34,500		12
Unamortized bond premium	34,500		Resources provided —income before extraordinary items		34,500	
Cash or interest payable		279,000				
Retained earnings	250,000		Retained earnings	250,000		13
Dividends payable		250,000	Resources used— to declare dividends on common stock		250,000	

from IBEI to "working capital provided by operations." Whenever the analyses indicate that a current asset or a current liability was credited by the firm when the original event or transaction took place, we must credit some properly described item indicating the use under "resources used" on the worksheet. Whenever an ordinary gain (nonfund credit) is involved, we must credit (reduce) resources provided by operations in order to get from IBEI to "working capital provided by operations before extraordinary items."

When land was acquired, we reconstructed the original entry as follows:

| Land | 1,150,000 | |
| Cash | | 1,150,000 |

Therefore, our **worksheet entry** is:

| (4) | Land | 1,150,000 | |
| | Resources used—to acquire land | | 1,150,000 |

Since the analyses are complete in previous pages, and we now see how to prepare the reconciliation entries for the worksheet, Exhibit 25–13 shows how all the remaining original entries translate into worksheet entries.

The worksheet is now complete. Individual items reconcile horizontally. For example, the beginning land balance of $850,000 less the amount expropriated of $800,000 plus the land acquired of $1,150,000 equals the ending balance of $1,200,000. Using the data under "resources provided" and "resources used," we can construct the SCFP in Exhibit 25–11.

Exhibit 25–14 shows a working-capital-based SCFP from a published annual report.

EXHIBIT
25–14

PUBLISHED STATEMENT OF CHANGES IN FINANCIAL POSITION: WORKING CAPITAL BASIS

COLT INDUSTRIES INC. AND SUBSIDIARIES
Consolidated Statement of Changes in Financial Position

	($000)		
	1980	**1979**	**1978**
Source of Funds			
Net earnings	$ 97,751	$111,375	$ 87,020
Items not requiring use of working capital—			
Depreciation and amortization	57,851	47,876	44,192
Deferred income taxes	73	784	(4,141)
Working capital provided from operations	155,675	160,035	127,071
Long-term debt	36,631	8,251	24,847
	192,306	168,286	151,918
Application of Funds			
Capital expenditures	108,413	65,713	55,981
Decrease in long-term debt	16,967	30,797	41,359
Dividends paid	39,198	34,437	28,774
Purchase of treasury stock, net of stock options exercised	2,630	20,951	—
Other—net	3,674	1,181	(4,519)
	170,882	153,079	121,595
Working Capital			
Increase in working capital	21,424	15,207	30,323
At beginning of year	518,648	503,441	473,118
At end of year	$540,072	$518,648	$503,441

	INCREASE (DECREASE) IN WORKING CAPITAL		
	1980	**1979**	**1978**
Changes in Components of Working Capital			
Cash, including certificates of deposit	$ 7,187	$ 12,945	$ (15,344)
Marketable securities	26,658	(78,607)	76,483
Accounts and notes receivable	14,477	37,654	29,310
Inventories	12,321	42,694	33,022
Deferred income taxes	8,810	2,859	1,246
Other current assets	1,282	684	2,307
Notes payable to banks	(1,433)	9,512	(7,057)
Current maturities of long-term debt	2,948	3,819	(1,090)
Accounts payable	(38,515)	(5,892)	(43,162)
Accrued expenses	(12,311)	(10,461)	(45,392)
	$ 21,424	$ 15,207	$ 30,323

STATEMENT OF CHANGES IN FINANCIAL POSITION—
A CASH EMPHASIS

The analytical approach to cash-based SCFPs is essentially the same as that for working-capital-based SCFPs. First, we must determine the change that occurred in the cash balance during the year. That change becomes the amount of net sources or uses of cash that we are trying to explain by analyzing the change in all the other balance sheet accounts except cash. The major difference when emphasizing cash changes is determining the impact of all changes in current assets and current liabilities other than cash. This is not necessary for the working capital approach because the changes in these other current accounts are a part of the overall change in working capital.

To apply the cash basis, we must be able to distinguish between operating and nonoperating current assets and current liabilities. **Operating current assets and current liabilities** are those that affect the operating activity reported in the income statement (accounts receivable, inventories, wages payable, accrued expenses, and so on). It is necessary to use the changes in these items to determine "cash provided by operations." **APB Opinion No. 19** requires that changes in these items be shown in appropriate detail in the body of the statement. **Nonoperating current assets and current liabilities** are those that do not affect the operating activity reported in the income statement (receivables from employees, short-term notes payable to banks, dividends payable, and so on). Thus, these items are not used in determining "cash flow from operations." To the extent that cash is affected by nonoperating items, they are reported in sections of the SCFP as other than "cash flow from operations."

The data from the Staye-Cool example will be used to illustrate the cash-based SCFP, and therefore Exhibits 25–3, 25–4, and 25–5 should be reviewed before continuing. Cash decreased by $7,000 during 1985 ($32,000 − $25,000). Our objective in the SCFP, therefore, is to explain what brought about this decrease. The previous analyses for Staye-Cool all remain exactly the same and are reflected in the SCFP *except* in determining "funds flows from operations." Here the cash emphasis results in different amounts than does the working capital emphasis. The schedule at the top of p. 974 shows how to do this, starting with "income before extraordinary items."

Remember that we are starting here with "income before extraordinary items" (which is a "net" figure after deducting expenses and ordinary losses from net revenues) and reconciling it with "cash flow from operations." Why, then, do we add the beginning accounts receivable balance and deduct the ending balance? On an accrual basis, beginning accounts receivable resulted from sales of previous years (usually the immediately preceding one) that were reflected in income before extraordinary items of those previous years. However, we assume that those beginning receivables (net) would have been collected in cash in the current year. Therefore, to convert "income before extraordinary items" on an accrual basis to "cash flow from operations before extraordinary items," we must add beginning accounts receivable (net). By similar logic, the net ending accounts receivable balance (assumed to be from sales of the current year) will not be collected until future years, and therefore it must be deducted in computing "cash flow from operations."

Consider prepaid insurance. Cash flowed out before the current year as evidenced by the beginning balance, and so it should have been deducted in arriving at cash flow from operations of a prior year. Under generally accepted accounting prin-

SCHEDULE OF CASH FLOW FROM OPERATIONS

Income before extraordinary items		$ 795,000
Add: Beginning accounts receivable (net)	$724,000	
Beginning prepaid insurance	12,000	
Beginning inventories	298,000	
Ending accounts payable	379,000	
Ending customer advances	62,000	
Ending income taxes payable[a]	126,000	
Ending accrued salesmen salaries payable	27,000	1,628,000
		$2,423,000
Deduct: Ending accounts receivable (net)	$650,000	
Ending prepaid insurance	16,000	
Ending inventories	294,000	
Beginning accounts payable	397,000	
Beginning customer advances	51,000	
Beginning income taxes payable[a]	62,000	
Beginning accrued salesmen salaries payable	21,000	1,491,000
		$ 932,000
Add: Nonfund charges:		
Loss on sale of machinery and equipment	$ 30,000	
Depreciation expense	400,000	
Patent amortization	22,000	
Goodwill amortization	10,000	462,000
		$1,394,000
Deduct: Nonfund credits:		
Gain on sale of buildings	$100,000	
Bond premium amortization	34,500	134,500
Cash flow from operations		$1,259,500

[a] The income taxes payable was decreased by $73,000 due to expropriation of land, an extraordinary event. Thus, the ending balance from an operating perspective would have been $126,000 ($53,000 + $73,000).

ciples, however, the beginning balance would often be expensed in the current year on the accrual basis in arriving at income before extraordinary items. Hence, we must add beginning prepaid insurance to convert to cash flow from operations. We assume that the ending balance resulted from a cash outflow in the current year and must be deducted in arriving at cash flow from operations. Therefore, we deduct the ending balance of prepaid insurance.

All operating current assets are analyzed and handled in essentially the same manner. The rule with regard to operating current assets, *assuming you are starting with income before extraordinary items, is "add the beginning balances and deduct the ending balances."*

Consider one operating current liability as an illustration. The beginning accounts payable arose at some time prior to the current year. It is reasonable to assume that these liabilities were all paid during the current year. The operating events of the prior year giving rise to them would affect the cash flow of the current period, and therefore we must deduct beginning accounts payable from income before extraordinary items. The operating event giving rise to ending accounts payable would normally have been deducted as an expense during the current period on the accrual basis but does not result in a cash outflow until the following period. Therefore, we must add ending accounts payable.

All other *operating* current liabilities should be analyzed and handled in the same manner. The rule for operating current liabilities, when using the reconciliation format, is *"add the ending balances and deduct beginning balances."*

Some accountants prefer to work with changes in the account balances rather than use beginning and ending balances. Consequently, they would add decreases and deduct increases in operating current asset balances, and add increases and deduct decreases in operating current liability balances, when reconciling from "income before extraordinary items" to "cash flow from operations."

But what about the nonoperating current assets and current liabilities? In our illustration, these include short-term investments, notes receivable from officers, and notes payable—banks. As indicated, they are nonoperating and therefore are not used in determining cash flow from operations before extraordinary items. However, to the extent that cash was affected as the net changes in these accounts were brought about, the events must be reflected in the SCFP as indicated in the following analyses.

SHORT-TERM INVESTMENTS This account increased by a net of $101,000 during the year. The data in Exhibit 25-5 (item 9) indicate that short-term investments costing $50,000 were sold for $50,000 during 1985, resulting in the following entry at the time of sale:

Cash	50,000	
Short-term investments		50,000

Cash was increased, so this event would be reflected in the SCFP under "funds provided." If nothing else had happened during the period, the ending balance would have been $129,000 ($179,000 − $50,000). Because the ending balance is $280,000, Staye-Cool Corporation must have acquired short-term investments of $151,000 ($280,000 − $129,000). We don't know exactly how, but if we assume that cash was used, the following original entry must have been made:

Short-term investments	151,000	
Cash		151,000

This must be reflected in the SCFP under "funds used."

NOTES RECEIVABLE FROM OFFICERS This account increased by a net amount of $43,000 during the period. Because we have no data indicating what caused this net change, a reasonable assumption is that an additional $43,000 was lent to officers, the original entry being as follows:

Notes receivable from officers	43,000	
Cash		43,000

Because cash was reduced, this event would be reported in the SCFP as "funds used."

NOTES PAYABLE—BANKS This account decreased by a *net* amount of $29,000 during 1985. With no additional data, we may assume that banks were paid cash of $29,000 during the year, reflected as follows:

Notes payable—banks	29,000	
Cash		29,000

This event would be reported in the SCFP as "funds used."

Thus, our SCFP with a cash emphasis would appear as follows (see Exhibit 25–11 for items that are the same for the cash and working capital bases):

STAYE-COOL CORPORATION
Statement of Changes in Financial Position
For the Year Ended December 31, 1985

Sources of Funds

By operations:

Cash provided by operations, exclusive of extraordinary item (detail not repeated—see page 974)	$1,259,500
By extraordinary item—inflow of cash due to expropriation of land	617,000
Sale of buildings	450,000
Sale of machinery and equipment	20,000
Issuance of bonds for cash	769,500
Sale of short-term investments	50,000
Issuance of common stock in exchange for bonds	775,000
Total Sources of Cash	$3,941,000

Uses of Funds

To acquire land	$1,150,000	
To acquire buildings	1,550,000	
To acquire short-term investments	151,000	
To pay short-term notes to banks	29,000	
Additional loans to officers on short-term notes	43,000	
Payment of dividends	250,000	
Conversion of bonds to common stock	775,000	
Total Uses of Cash		3,948,000
Decrease in cash during 1985		$ 7,000

Comparing this statement with the SCFP in Exhibit 25–11, which emphasizes changes in working capital, reveals the following:

1. The analyses of all the changes in noncurrent assets and noncurrent liabilities remain the same under a cash emphasis as under a working capital emphasis and are identical in both statements of changes in financial position. This general principle prevails with two major exceptions: (a) **Reclassifications.** If a long-term debt is reclassified to current, or a long-term asset (such as marketable equity securities) is reclassified to current, working capital would be affected, but not cash. (b) **Extraordinary items.** Because extraordinary items can impact working capital items (such as income taxes payable) other than cash, working capital flow from such items can vary from cash flow (as reflected in our illustration).

2. The changes in *nonoperating* current assets and current liabilities must be reflected separately in appropriate sections of the SCFP under a cash emphasis, but not under a working capital emphasis.

3. The analyses of changes in retained earnings brought about by net income and dividends for the period may, and usually will, have different consequences under a cash versus a working capital emphasis.

4. The special items previously discussed that must be reflected in the SCFP even when working capital is not affected, such as conversions of debt to common stock, would be reflected in the same fashion when cash changes are emphasized.

Exhibit 25–15 shows a cash-based SCFP from a published annual report. Note that, although it emphasizes cash, it reports working capital effects also.

EXHIBIT
25–15

PUBLISHED STATEMENT OF CHANGES IN FINANCIAL POSITION: CASH BASIS

KNIGHT-RIDDER NEWSPAPER, INC.

Consolidated Statement of Changes in Financial Position

	($000)		
	YEAR ENDED DECEMBER 31		
	1980	**1979**	**1978**
Cash Provided by Operations			
Net income	$ 92,858	$ 88,360	$ 76,756
Charges to income not affecting working capital			
Depreciation	27,756	22,258	18,326
Provision for non-current deferred taxes	8,290	3,577	951
Amortization of goodwill, publication and broadcast rights	4,987	4,069	3,495
Deferred and other items, net	3,610	4,205	2,633
Total working capital provided by operations	137,501	122,469	102,161
Changes in certain working capital components			
Accounts receivable increase	(11,000)	(12,821)	(16,271)
Inventories (increase) decrease	(21,091)	2,396	2,865
Other current assets increase	(1,833)	(1,884)	(1,903)
Payables and accruals increase	17,635	12,225	9,365
Net cash provided by operations	120,332	122,385	97,217
Additional Sources of Cash			
Sale of Common Stock to employees	6,288	5,254	5,511
Collections on and sale of non-current assets	2,732	1,564	2,030
Total	9,020	6,818	7,541
Cash Used for Acquisitions			
Net tangible assets, excluding total debt	7,789	4,121	10,204
Goodwill, publication and broadcast rights	34,786	16,727	65,281
Less total debt	(35,975)		(26,170)
Less cash acquired	(3,614)	(1,557)	(4,306)
Total	2,986	19,291	45,009
Additional Uses of Cash			
Expenditures for property, plant and equipment (net of mortgage issued of $7,500 in 1979)	60,045	59,243	51,972
Payment of cash dividends	23,293	21,306	17,990
Purchase of treasury stock	18,963	17,179	61
Investment in newsprint mill			14,535
Reduction of total debt	4,288	7,139	1,308
Other items, net	5,388	7,246	2,836
Total	111,977	112,113	88,702
Net increase (decrease) in cash	14,389	(2,201)	(29,060)
Cash and short-term cash investments at beginning of year	43,684	45,885	74,838
Cash and short-term cash investments at end of year	$ 58,073	$ 43,684	$ 45,885
Working capital at end of year	$ 77,921	$ 63,789	$ 67,276

SUMMARY Financial statements that describe funds flow are an integral part of complete financial reporting. Current GAAP allow some flexibility in the definition of funds and the format of funds statements. GAAP do require that the basic funds-flow analysis (defined as cash or working capital) be augmented by disclosure of transactions that, although they do not affect funds, do represent significant financing and investing activities. Thus, the required statement is broader than funds flow, leading to the prescribed title "statement of changes in financial position," which encompasses all financial sources.

This chapter has emphasized analysis techniques involving the construction of

SCFPs. These analyses require considerable accounting knowledge. Each step requires the reconstruction of the effects of many transactions and an understanding of each affected account's relationship to other accounts.

The subject matter of this chapter, therefore, accomplishes two objectives: (1) It describes the concepts and techniques immediately relevant to the construction of SCFPs, and (2) it reviews and integrates the concepts and techniques discussed throughout the text.

APPENDIX G
The T-Account Approach to Preparation of the Statement of Changes in Financial Position

Many accountants who prepare statements of changes in financial position feel that the T-account approach not only is less time-consuming and cumbersome than the worksheet approach but also provides the structure missing in the "building block" approach we started with. We emphasize again that the concepts underlying all three approaches are the same. The T-account approach is simply another technique for accomplishing the same objectives. Just as the journal entries used in the worksheet are for analytical purposes only and *are not entered* into the firm's normal records, the T-accounts used here are also for analytical purposes only and do not become part of the firm's general ledger.

If we assume that working capital changes are to be emphasized in the SCFP, and use the data in our illustration for Staye-Cool Corporation, we can summarize the steps in a T-account approach as follows:

1. Set up a T-account for working capital. Calculate the increase or decrease during the period. If an increase, place the figure on the left; if a decrease, on the right. Section the T-account in order to reflect different sources and uses of working capital.

2. Set up T-accounts for all nonworking capital accounts, that is, noncurrent assets, noncurrent liabilities, and stockholders' equity.

3. Calculate the net change in all accounts. Place *net* increases of noncurrent assets on the left and *net* decreases on the right. For *net* changes in noncurrent liabilities and stockholders' equity accounts, place *net* increases on the right and *net* decreases on the left.

4. Analyze the *net* changes in all noncurrent assets, noncurrent liabilities, and stockholders' equity accounts. When working capital is increased, debit the working capital account and credit the other account or accounts. When working capital is decreased, credit the working capital account and debit the other account or accounts. When working capital is not affected but the event must be reflected in the SCFP, place a debit in the T-account set up in step 2 when resources are provided and credit the other accounts affected. Credit the account when resources

are used, debiting the other accounts affected. Because there must be equal debits and credits, the *net* impact will be zero.

5. In all the accounts except the working capital account, all the debits and credits to each account should equal the *net* change put in that account in step 3.

6. Use the information in the working capital account and the nonworking capital accounts to prepare a SCFP.

Because all the analyses for Staye-Cool Corporation have already been made, we shall not repeat them here. If desired, journal entries as reflected there can be prepared first and then posted to the T-accounts. This is not essential, however. As the analyses are being made, the conclusions reached can be reflected directly in the T-accounts. Note that entry 1 on page 968 ("working capital") should not be used in the T-account approach. It is made in the worksheet to balance the columns. In the T-account approach, it is taken care of when the net change of $102,000 is placed on the debit side of the working capital account. The remaining entries are keyed into the various T-accounts.

The T-accounts would appear as follows after posting the initial *net* changes and the effects of the events and transactions during the year in summarized form.

WORKING CAPITAL

NET CHANGE	102,000		
Sources of Funds		*Uses of Funds*	
Operating activity		Operating activity	
(2) Income before extraordinary items	795,000	(5) Gain on sale of buildings	100,000
(7) Loss on sale of machinery and equipment	30,000	(12) Bond premium amortization	34,500
(8) Depreciation expense	400,000		134,500
(9) Patent amortization	22,000		
(9) Goodwill amortization	10,000		
	1,257,000		
Nonoperating activity		*Nonoperating activity*	
(3) Expropriation of land	690,000	(4) To acquire land	1,150,000
(5) Sale of buildings	450,000	(6) To acquire buildings	1,550,000
(7) Sale of machinery and equipment	20,000	(13) Declaration of a cash dividend	250,000
(11) Issuance of bonds for cash	769,500		2,950,000
	1,929,500		
(10) Issuance of common stock for bonds	775,000	(10) Bonds converted into common stock	775,000
Total Sources	3,961,500	Total Uses	3,859,500

LAND

NET CHANGE	350,000		
(4) Acquisition of land	1,150,000	(3) Expropriation of land	800,000

BUILDINGS

NET CHANGE	1,050,000		
(6) Acquisition of buildings	1,550,000	(5) Sale of buildings	500,000

ACCUMULATED DEPRECIATION—BUILDINGS

			NET CHANGE	150,000
(5) Sale of buildings	150,000	(8) Depreciation for 1985		300,000

MACHINERY AND EQUIPMENT

			NET CHANGE	350,000
		(7) Sale of machinery and equipment		350,000

ACCUMULATED DEPRECIATION—MACHINERY AND EQUIPMENT

NET CHANGE	200,000			
(7) Sale of machinery and equipment	300,000	(8) Depreciation for 1985		100,000

PATENTS

			NET CHANGE	22,000
		(9) Patent amortization for 1985		22,000

GOODWILL

			NET CHANGE	10,000
		(9) Goodwill amortization for 1985		10,000

BONDS PAYABLE

NET CHANGE	100,000			
(10) Conversion into common stock	729,500	(11) Issuance of bonds for cash		629,500

UNAMORTIZED BOND PREMIUM

			NET CHANGE	60,000
(10) Conversion into common stock	45,500	(11) Issuance of bonds for cash		140,000
(12) Premium amortization for 1985	34,500			
	80,000			

COMMON STOCK

			NET CHANGE	500,000
		(10) Issued in exchange for bonds		500,000

ADDITIONAL PAID-IN CAPITAL

			NET CHANGE	275,000
		(10) Stock issued in exchange for bonds		275,000

RETAINED EARNINGS			
		NET CHANGE	435,000
(3) Loss on expropriation of land (net of tax savings of $73,000)	110,000	(2) Income for the year before extraordinary items	795,000
(13) Declaration of a cash dividend	250,000		
	360,000		

QUESTIONS

Q25–1 What are the basic objectives of the statement of changes in financial position as required by *APB Opinion No. 19?*

Q25–2 Which definition of funds must be followed in preparing a statement of changes in financial position under generally accepted accounting principles? Why?

Q25–3 In reflecting "funds" provided by continuing operations, what is the purpose of starting the disclosure with an income number?

Q25–4 In reflecting "working capital" provided by continuing operations, indicate four nonfund debits that will be added to, and four nonfund credits that will be deducted from, income from continuing operations. Why are these adjustments necessary?

Q25–5 What are the uses of the statement of changes in financial position? What types of questions will the SCFP help users answer with regard to the firm that cannot be answered by analysis of other statements?

Q25–6 In the SCFP, what are the advantages and disadvantages of emphasizing the change in cash as opposed to emphasizing the change in working capital for the year?

Q25–7 Name two types of events or transactions that must be reflected in the SCFP even if cash or working capital is not affected. Why must these be reflected?

Q25–8 What is the reconciliation format in a SCFP?

Q25–9 What are the advantages and disadvantages of using the reconciliation format for reflecting cash or working capital provided by continuing operations?

Q25–10 What is the statement format in a SCFP?

Q25–11 What are the advantages and disadvantages of using the statement format for reflecting cash or working capital provided by continuing operations?

CASES

C25–1 As controller of a large manufacturing company, you are often asked to explain accounting issues to nonaccounting professional personnel. Your current assignment is to explain the concept of funds flow as presented in statements of changes in financial position to members of a training session for middle-level production managers.

REQUIRED Draft an outline of the major points for such an address.

C25–2 After making the address described in C25–1, the first questions you are asked by the audience are, "Why do accountants add depreciation and amortization to get funds from operations?" and "How does depreciation generate funds?"

REQUIRED Answer these questions.

C25–3 Your company is applying for a short-term loan from a local bank. You supply the bank with audited financial statements for the last 5 years and a 1-year forecast of the statement of changes in financial position. The loan officer requests that the historic and forecasted SCFP be recast from the working capital basis to the cash basis.

When asked the reason for this request, the officer replies that cash-based SCFPs are always requested for loans of less than 1 year.

REQUIRED Present a rationale for such a policy.

C25-4 On January 1, 1984, you are involved in a meeting to forge strategy for the acquisition of a vast tract of timber costing $75,000,000 in the Northwest. The options are to sell common stock to the open market, with the proceeds of $75,000,000 being used to acquire the tract, or to sign a note with Washington Trisben, the current owner of the tract. This would require a $15,000,000 down payment plus two year-end payments of $30,000,000 plus interest on December 31, 1984, and December 31, 1985. It is expected that the down payment could be covered by selling current marketable securities that have a current book value of $10,000,000 and a fair value of $15,000,000. The first year-end payment could be covered by signing a mortgage loan with a long-term maturity.

REQUIRED Construct a schedule showing the probable effect of each alternative on the company's statement of changes in financial position for the 1984 calendar year, which will be prepared on a working capital basis. Ignore interest and dividends.

C25-5 Consider the following assertion: "A thorough analysis of comparative balance sheets, income statements, and retained earnings statements gives a complete history of an entity's performance and change in financial status." Compose a counterargument that stresses the need for a statement of changes in financial position.

REQUIRED Cite several common sources and uses of funds that could not be ascertained by an analysis of the other financial statements alone.

C25-6 The changes in funds flow for a period can be explained by analyzing the changes in all nonfund accounts.

REQUIRED Why is this true? What differences in the nonfund accounts must be analyzed between cash and working capital methods of computing funds flow?

C25-7 Consider the following working capital components for companies A and B on December 31, 1983:

	COMPANY A	COMPANY B
Current assets		
Cash	$ 781,000	$ 340,000
Accounts receivable	1,200,000	1,000,000
Inventory	3,500,000	6,400,000
Marketable equity securities	410,000	0
Prepaid expenses	320,000	0
Total current assets	$6,211,000	$7,740,000
Current liabilities		
Accounts payable (due by 1/31/84)	$ 800,000	$3,320,000
Taxes payable (due 3/15/84)	1,200,000	1,320,000
Notes payable (due 8/1/84)	501,000	—
Bonds payable (due 10/15/84)	1,110,000	—
Total current liabilities	$3,611,000	$4,640,000
Working capital	$2,600,000	$3,100,000

REQUIRED Discuss the relative liquidity positions of each company. What kinds of questions would you want answered in order to appraise the credit worthiness of each company for a $1,000,000 6-month loan and why?

C25-8 (CPA ADAPTED) The statement of changes of financial position is normally a required basic financial statement for each period for which an earnings statement is presented. The reporting entity has flexibility in the form, content, and terminology of this statement to meet the objectives of differing circumstances. For example, the concept of "funds" may be interpreted to mean, among other things, cash or working capital. However, the statement should be prepared based on the "all financial resources" concept.

REQUIRED

1. What is the "all financial resources" concept?
2. What two general types of financial transactions would be disclosed under the "all financial resources" concept but would not be disclosed without it?

C25–9 (CPA ADAPTED)   What effect, if any, would each of the following seven items have upon the preparation of a statement of changes in financial position prepared in accordance with generally accepted accounting principles using the cash concept of funds? Explain.

1. Accounts receivable—trade
2. Inventory
3. Depreciation
4. Deferred income tax credit from interperiod allocation
5. Issuance of long-term debt in payment for a building
6. Payoff of current portion of debt
7. Sale of a fixed asset resulting in a loss

EXERCISES

E25–1   Consider the following transactions in terms of their effects on funds:

1. A period-end accrual of wages
2. An increase in the Accounts Receivable account balance during the fiscal period
3. The sale of a marketable equity security that had been classified as a current asset for a cash amount equal to its book value
4. The write-off of a bad debt
5. The acquisition of a building by issuing common stock in payment

REQUIRED   How would each transaction affect funds defined as working capital? Defined as cash?

E25–2   A company sold a building and recorded the following journal entry:

8/1/83	Cash	100,000	
	Notes receivable (due 8/1/85)	250,000	
	Loss	50,000	
	Accumulated depreciation	45,000	
	Building		445,000

REQUIRED   If the company reports its statement of changes in financial position on the working capital basis, what effect will the above transaction have on funds-flow presentation?

E25–3   Mainline Trucking, Inc., lost all of its timber-moving equipment during the eruption of a volcano. The following journal entries were recorded regarding the event:

Extraordinary loss	4,650,000	
Accumulated depreciation	800,000	
Trucking equipment		5,450,000
Insurance claim receivable	2,500,000	
Extraordinary loss		2,500,000
Federal income taxes payable	860,000	
Extraordinary loss		860,000

REQUIRED Show how the above events would affect the company's statement of changes in financial position in the year of the loss if (1) the cash basis is used and (2) the working capital basis is used.

E25-4 DDX, Inc., has a preliminary SCFP that shows working capital from operations of + $14,250,000 and net change in working capital of $13,713,000. A year-end transaction was ignored in the preliminary statement, however. The company sold a factory building and recorded the following journal entry on December 31, the last day of the fiscal period (the sale was reflected in net income):

Loss	1,731,000	
Accumulated depreciation	22,500,000	
Cash	10,000,000	
Building		34,231,000

REQUIRED How will the above transaction affect working capital from operations and net change in working capital? (Ignore tax effects.)

E25-5 Consider the following summarized income statement:

Sales	$214,910,000
Cost of goods sold	176,400,000
Administrative expenses	23,910,000
Federal income taxes (40%)	5,840,000
Income before extraordinary item	8,760,000
Loss from fire damage (net of taxes of $1,800,000)	2,700,000
Net income	$ 6,060,000

The loss from fire damage resulted from the destruction of uninsured inventory by fire.

REQUIRED Describe how the extraordinary item would be reflected in the SCFP on the working capital basis.

E25-6 Collins, Inc., has net income before income taxes of $310,000 during 1983. The company's taxable income (on its tax return) for 1983 is $170,000. The following reconciliation is available:

Taxable income	$170,000
(Timing difference) depreciation differences	50,000
(Permanent difference) municipal bond interest	90,000
Net income before income tax	$310,000

The effective tax rate is 40 percent.

REQUIRED Show how the above tax considerations affect the "funds provided by operations" section of the SCFP if the working capital method is being used.

E25-7 Belville Airconditioners, Inc., had the following transactions relating to bonds during the fiscal year January 1, 1983–December 31, 1983:

1. On January 1, 1983, 15,000 bonds were sold at par of $1,000 each. Interest of $80 per bond outstanding is paid on June 30 and December 31 of each year.
2. On July 1, 1983, 500 bonds were purchased in the open market at $1,020 each and retired.

REQUIRED In 1983, what effect would the above bond transactions have on (1) cash from operations, (2) net cash flow, (3) working capital from operations, and (4) net working capital flow?

E25-8 On October 31, 1984, the end of its fiscal year, Robics Corporation has a note payable of $550,000 due on December 31, 1984. This note had previously appeared on balance sheets dated October 31, 1982, and October 31, 1983.

REQUIRED Is the current fiscal year's working capital affected by the note? Explain fully.

E25–9 Library Supplies Company had one marketable equity security classified as a current asset on its December 31, 1982, balance sheet. Transactions affecting the company's investments in 1983 are as follows:

		BALANCE IN INVESTMENT ACCOUNT
1/1/83	Beginning balance at cost which was less than market (X Company, 100,000 shares)	$450,000
6/1/83	Purchased 10,000 Y Company shares at $20 per share	200,000
7/15/83	Sold 50,000 X Company shares at $8 per share	(225,000)
12/31/83	Ending balance	$425,000
12/31/83	Market value per share: X Company, $6; Y Company, $11	

REQUIRED How will the above transactions affect the working capital flow presentation on Library Supplies Company's 1983 SCFP? Explain fully.

PROBLEMS

P25–1 Builtright, Inc., has the following postclosing trial balance on December 31, 1984:

Debits	
Treasury stock	108,000
Cash	329,076
Accounts receivable	785,000
Unamortized discount on bonds payable	122,050
Deferred federal income taxes (noncurrent)	450,000
Plant and equipment	1,880,000
Intangibles	1,650,000
Short-term prepayments	593,234
	5,917,360
Credits	
Allowance for uncollectibles	4,660
Accumulated depreciation	501,000
Current maturities of long-term debt	1,000,000
Notes payable (18-month note)	500,000
Accounts payable	234,000
Accrued taxes payable	35,700
Dividends payable	22,000
Bonds payable (due 12/31/90)	1,500,000
Capital stock	1,700,000
Retained earnings	420,000
	5,917,360

REQUIRED Compute Builtright's working capital at December 31, 1984.

P25–2 Jones and Merchant Coal Corporation has the following summarized income statement for 1984:

Sales	$137,870,000
Cost of goods sold	88,200,000
Depreciation expense	11,160,000
Depletion expense	4,050,000
Interest expense	5,580,000
Amortization of goodwill	750,000
Income tax expense	12,872,000
Net income	$15,258,000

Additional information:

1. Total depreciation for the year was $20,380,000. The amount not charged to depreciation expense was charged to cost of goods sold. there was no beginning or ending inventory.

2. Interest expense included the amortization of bond discount of $340,000.

3. Deferred income tax increased by a net credit of $1,200,000 resulting from differences in depreciation schedules used for book and tax purposes.

REQUIRED Construct a schedule showing the corporation's working capital from operations for 1984.

P25-3 Consider the following excerpt from W Corporation's first-quarter financial report: "Although sales and net income are down by 10 percent compared with last year, our working capital position has been materially enhanced by the adoption of accelerated depreciation for tax and accounting purposes as of the beginning of this fiscal year."

REQUIRED In what sense can this statement be said to be valid? Invalid?

P25-4 Consider Newsprint Corporation's comparative balance sheets and supplementary information:

	DECEMBER 31	
	1984	1983
Current assets		
Cash	$ 40,000	$ 30,000
Accounts receivable	300,000	380,000
Inventory	1,200,000	1,050,000
Marketable equity securities	61,000	100,000
Noncurrent assets		
Land	2,700,000	1,000,000
Buildings (net)	3,200,000	2,500,000
Equipment (net)	1,500,000	1,200,000
Total assets	$9,001,000	$6,260,000
Current liabilities		
Accounts payable	$ 600,000	$ 550,000
Taxes payable	150,000	200,000
Noncurrent liabilities		
Notes payable	1,200,000	1,000,000
Owners' equity		
Common stock—no par	4,500,000	4,000,000
Retained earnings	2,551,000	510,000
Total liabilities and owners' equity	$9,001,000	$6,260,000

Additional information:

1. Net income for 1984 was $3,551,000.

2. Dividend payments were $1,510,000.

3. Marketable equity securities were sold at a recorded loss of $20,000. No other entries affected that account.

4. Land was purchased for cash.

5. The only transactions to affect the Buildings account were the write-off of a building that had been fully depreciated and abandoned and the purchase of several new buildings for $800,000 cash plus a $200,000 note payable.

6. Equipment was acquired through the issuance of common stock.

7. Depreciation expense on building and equipment amounted to $500,000.

REQUIRED Construct a statement of changes in financial position using the working capital basis.

P25-5 Skelly Corporation uses the cash definition of funds in its SCFP. The following preliminary draft of the cash-flow analysis has been roughed out by your assistant:

Net income	$1,500,000
Add: Depreciation	400,000
Funds from operations	$1,900,000
Other sources	
Issuance of stock	$ 400,000
Issuance of bonds	1,100,000
Total sources	$3,400,000
Other uses	
Payment of dividends	300,000
Acquisition of building	405,000
Total uses	$ 705,000
Net funds flow	$2,695,000

You discover that three accounts were ignored in this preliminary analysis:

ACCOUNTS RECEIVABLE

1/1 Balance	$ 802,000	Collection	$4,500,000
Sales	5,500,000		
12/31 Balance	$1,802,000		

ACCOUNTS PAYABLE

Payments	$5,750,000	1/1 Balance	$ 419,000
		Purchases	6,050,000
		12/31 Balance	$ 719,000

INVENTORY

1/1 Balance	$1,500,000	Cost of Goods Sold	$3,000,000
Purchases	6,050,000		
12/31 Balance	$4,550,000		

REQUIRED Revise the funds-flow analysis in light of the effects of these three accounts.

P25–6 Ranger Shoe Company shows a working capital increase of $399,670 in its preliminary 1983 statement of changes in financial position. Several transactions, however, have not been reflected in that preliminary number:

1. A sale of idle land for cash. The land had a book value of $100,000 and was sold for $210,000.
2. A loss of $421,000 (tax effect of $200,000) from an out-of-court settlement in a patent infringement suit. The amount will be paid within 30 days of the end of the fiscal period.
3. The write-off of accounts receivable from a major customer who has filed for bankruptcy in the amount of $47,500. Ranger uses the allowance method for bad debts.
4. The reclassification from short-term to long-term of a note payable in the amount of $250,000, which the creditor has agreed to extend for 2 more years.

REQUIRED Recompute the change in working capital resulting from the above transactions. Give explanations for each.

P25–7 Memory Systems, Inc. had the following balances in its working capital accounts at the end of 1982 and 1983:

	12/31/83	12/31/82
Cash	$ 210,000	$ 189,000
Accounts receivable	1,400,000	1,200,000
Inventories	3,500,000	2,950,000
Notes receivable	45,000	0
Marketable securities	100,000	90,000
Accounts payable	237,000	211,000
Income taxes payable	140,500	100,600

Additional information about 1983 activities:

1. Net income for the year was $480,000.
2. Extraordinary loss was $290,000 after a tax effect of $116,000.
3. Premium amortization on bonds payable amounted to $30,000.
4. Depreciation expenses amounted to $159,500.
5. The journal entry to record tax expense included a credit to "deferred federal income taxes" of $39,500, which was classified as noncurrent.

REQUIRED

1. Compute the change in working capital for 1983.
2. Show the "working capital from operations" section of the SCFP for the above data.

P25–8 The comparative balance sheet and income statement for 1984 and 1985 for Sturdy Furniture Company are as follows:

STURDY FURNITURE COMPANY
Comparative Balance Sheet
As of December 31

ASSETS	1985	1984
Current assets		
Cash	$ 750,000	$ 500,000
Marketable securities	200,000	0
Accounts receivable (net)	2,100,000	1,450,000
Inventory	1,650,000	1,050,000
Prepaid expenses	250,000	125,000
Total current assets	$4,950,000	$3,125,000
Plant, property, and equipment	$2,825,000	$1,500,000
Less: Accumulated depreciation	275,000	125,000
	$2,550,000	$1,375,000
Total assets	$7,500,000	$4,500,000

LIABILITIES AND STOCKHOLDERS' EQUITY		
Current liabilities		
Accounts payable	$1,325,000	$1,100,000
Accrued expenses	350,000	325,000
Dividends payable	175,000	0
Total current liabilities	$1,850,000	$1,425,000
Bonds payable—long-term	1,250,000	0
Total liabilities	$3,100,000	$1,425,000
Stockholders' equity		
Common stock, no par	$3,000,000	$2,250,000
Retained earnings	1,400,000	825,000
Total stockholders' equity	$4,400,000	$3,075,000
Total equities	$7,500,000	$4,500,000

Comparative Income Statement
for Years Ended December 31

	1985	1984
Net revenues	$16,000,000	$10,000,000
Cost of goods sold	12,500,000	8,000,000
Gross profit	$ 3,500,000	$ 2,000,000
Expenses	2,500,000	1,300,000
Net income	$ 1,000,000	$ 700,000

No additional information is available.

REQUIRED

1. Prepare a statement of changes in financial position emphasizing working capital changes. Clearly state all assumptions.
2. Prepare a statement of changes in financial position emphasizing the change in cash. Clearly state all assumptions.

P25-9 The income statement for the Georgia Peach Company follows.

GEORGIA PEACH COMPANY
Income Statement
For the Year Ended December 31, 1985

Sales revenue		$5,600,000
Less: Bad debts, returns, and allowances		60,000
Net revenue		$5,540,000
Cost of goods sold		3,120,000
Gross profit		$2,420,000
Selling expenses (including depreciation of $35,000)	$242,000	
Administration expenses (including depreciation of $67,000)	325,000	
Income taxes (including deferred income tax of $72,000)	746,000	1,313,000
Operating income after taxes		$1,107,000
Gain on sale of building	$ 25,000	
Loss on sale of equipment	37,000	12,000
Income from continuing operations		$1,095,000
Extraordinary gain on condemnation of property (net of tax of $48,000)		165,000
Net income		$1,260,000

REQUIRED

1. Determine the working capital provided by operations using the reconciliation approach.
2. Determine the working capital provided by operations using the statement approach.
3. Assuming the proceeds received on the property condemned were $475,000, indicate how these data can be presented in the SCFP.

P25-10 (CPA ADAPTED) The management of Hatfield Corporation, concerned about a decrease in working capital, provided you with the comparative analysis of changes in account balances between December 31, 1983, and December 31, 1984, shown at the top of p. 990. During 1984 the following transactions occurred:

1. New machinery was purchased for $386,000. In addition, certain obsolete machinery that had a book value of $61,000 was sold for $48,000. No other entries were recorded in Machinery and Equipment or related accounts other than provisions for depreciation.
2. Hatfield paid $2,000 legal costs in a successful defense of a new patent. Amortization of patents amounting to $4,200 was recorded.
3. Preferred stock, par value $100, was purchased at 110 and was subsequently canceled. The premium paid was charged to retained earnings.
4. On December 10, 1984, the board of directors declared a cash dividend of $.20 per share payable to holders of common stock on January 10, 1985.

DEBIT BALANCES	1984	1983	INCREASE (DECREASE)
Cash	$ 145,000	$ 186,000	$ (41,000)
Accounts receivable	253,000	273,000	(20,000)
Inventories	483,000	538,000	(55,000)
Securities held for plant expansion purposes	150,000	—	150,000
Machinery and equipment	927,000	647,000	280,000
Leasehold improvements	87,000	87,000	—
Patents	27,800	30,000	(2,200)
Totals	$2,072,800	$1,761,000	$311,800
CREDIT BALANCES			
Allowance for uncollectible accounts receivable	$ 14,000	$ 17,000	$ (3,000)
Accumulated depreciation of machinery and equipment	416,000	372,000	44,000
Allowance for amortization of leasehold improvements	58,000	49,000	9,000
Accounts payable	232,800	105,000	127,800
Cash dividends payable	40,000	—	40,000
Current portion of 6% serial bonds payable	50,000	50,000	—
6% serial bonds payable	250,000	300,000	(50,000)
Preferred stock	90,000	100,000	(10,000)
Common stock	500,000	500,000	—
Retained earnings	422,000	268,000	154,000
Totals	$2,072,800	$1,761,000	$311,800

5. A comparative analysis of retained earnings as of December 31, 1984 and 1983 follows.

	1984	1983
Balance, January 1	$268,000	$131,000
Net income	195,000	172,000
	463,000	303,000
Dividends declared	(40,000)	(35,000)
Premium on preferred stock repurchased	(1,000)	—
	$422,000	$268,000

REQUIRED

1. Prepare Hatfield Corporation's statement of changes in financial position for the year ended December 31, 1984, based upon the information presented above. The statement should be prepared using a working capital format.

2. Prepare Hatfield Corporation's schedule of changes in working capital for the year ended December 31, 1984.

P25–11 (CMA ADAPTED)   The following financial statements pertain to the Sparton Corporation. Sparton is considering purchasing Archco, Inc. The statements presented did not include a statement of changes in financial position. Sparton's controller would like to have this statement, as well as other relevant financial information, before he makes a financial analysis of Archco, Inc.

The following additional information is available to explain the Archco, Inc., financial results for 1984:

1. The significant decline in cash and treasury bills occurred because funds from these two sources were used to retire the bonds at a favorable time.

2. Equipment with a cost of $35,000,000 and a book value of $18,000,000 was sold for $14,400,000.

3. A portion of the preferred stock was issued to provide cash to purchase outstanding bonds in the market. The remaining amount was issued to JIS Inc. for land and the related plant and equipment on the land.

ARCHCO, INC.
Statement of Financial Position
As of December 31
(000 omitted)

ASSETS	1984	1983
Cash	$ 16,800	$120,000
Accounts receivable	81,900	73,200
Inventories	119,700	97,500
U.S. treasury bills	33,450	79,500
Total current assets	$251,850	$370,200
Land	217,500	195,000
Plant and equipment (net of accumulated depreciation)	391,500	387,000
Patents (less accumulated amortization)	28,500	31,500
Total assets	$889,350	$983,700

LIABILITIES AND OWNERS' EQUITY		
Accounts payable	$136,500	$198,500
Taxes payable	3,000	2,500
Interest payable	6,000	4,500
Notes payable	30,000	21,750
Total current liabilities	$175,500	$227,250
Deferred income taxes	11,400	9,750
Long term bonds	150,000	300,000
Total liabilities	$336,900	$537,000
Preferred stock	111,000	45,000
Common stock	360,000	337,500
Retained earnings	81,450	64,200
Total liabilities and owners' equity	$889,350	$983,700

Income Statement
For the Year Ended December 31, 1984
(000 omitted)

Sales	$441,600	
Gain on retirement of bonds	9,900	$451,500
Expenses, taxes, and losses:		
Cost of goods sold	$252,000	
Wages and salaries	51,000	
Depreciation	18,000	
Amortization	3,000	
Other	28,200	
Interest	19,500	
Loss on sale of equipment	3,600	
Income taxes	16,950	392,250
Net income		$ 59,250

4. Cash dividends of $4,500,000 and $15,000,000 were paid to the preferred and common shareholders, respectively. The common shareholders received a stock dividend that had market value of $22,500,000.

5. The Income Tax Expense account and the Deferred Income Tax account that appear in the statements properly account for all of Archco's income tax situations.

REQUIRED

1. Prepare, in good form, a statement of changes in financial position for the year ended December 31, 1984. The statement should emphasize working capital.

2. Identify and explain the probable reasons why the Sparton controller would want Archco's statement of changes in financial position.

P25–12 (CMA ADAPTED)   Motel Enterprises operates and owns many motels throughout the United States. The company has expanded rapidly over the past few years, and company officers are concerned that they may have overexpanded.

The following financial statements and other financial data have been supplied by the controller of Motel Enterprises.

MOTEL ENTERPRISES
Income Statement
For Years Ended October 31
(unaudited)
(000 omitted)

	1984	1983
Revenue	$2,230	$1,920
Costs and expenses		
Direct room and related services	$ 400	$ 350
Direct food and beverage	740	640
General and administrative	302	250
Advertising	57	44
Repairs and maintenance	106	82
Interest expense	280	220
Depreciation	120	95
Lease payment	100	73
Total costs and expenses	$2,105	$1,754
Income before taxes	$ 125	$ 166
Provision for income tax	25	42
Net income	$ 100	$ 124

MOTEL ENTERPRISES
Statement of Financial Position
As of October 31
(unaudited)
(000 omitted)

ASSETS	1984	1983
Current assets		
Cash	$ 100	$ 125
Accounts receivable (net)	250	200
Inventory	60	50
Other	5	5
Total current assets	$ 415	$ 380
Long-term investments	$ 605	$ 710
Property and equipment		
Buildings and equipment (net)	$3,350	$2,540
Land	370	410
Construction in progress	150	450
Total property and equipment	$3,870	$3,400
Other assets	$ 110	$ 110
Total assets	$5,000	$4,600

LIABILITIES AND STOCKHOLDERS' EQUITY

	1984	1983
Current liabilities		
Accounts payable	$ 40	$ 30
Accrued liabilities	190	190
Notes payable to bank	30	10
Current portion of long-term notes	80	50
Total current liabilities	$ 340	$ 280
Long-term debt		
Long-term notes	$2,785	$2,325
Subordinated debentures (due May 1989)	800	800
Total long-term debt	$3,585	$3,125
Total liabilities	$3,925	$3,405
Stockholders' equity		
Common stock ($1 par)	$ 300	$ 300
Paid-in capital in excess of par	730	730
Net unrealized loss on long-term investments	(105)	—
Retained earnings	150	165
Total stockholders' equity	$1,075	$1,195
Total liabilities and stockholders' equity	$5,000	$4,600

Additional information:

1. *Accounts receivable.* The allowance for uncollectible accounts had a balance of $3,000 on October 31, 1983, and $4,000 on October 31, 1984.

2. *Long-term investments.* Motel Enterprises has investments in preferred stocks of public utilities, which are carried on the books at the lower-of-cost-or-market. The market values of the investments were as follows:

Oct. 31, 1983	$725,000
Oct. 31, 1984	$605,000
Dec. 1, 1984	$670,000

3. *Property and equipment.* Motel Enterprises acquires parcels of land for future sites and disposes of land if the site does not prove to be advantageous; this is a frequent and regular activity of the company. In addition, the company acquires existing motels, constructs motels on new sites, and builds additions to motels at existing sites.

During the 1983–1984 fiscal year, construction was completed on building additions at a total cost of $350,000.

New buildings were purchased during the year at a cost of $620,000; 40 percent of the purchase price was paid in cash and the balance will be due in 2 years. A total of $40,000 of the purchase price was allocated to Land.

Land no longer needed was sold on June 15, 1984, for $100,000; the land had a book value of $80,000.

Motel Enterprises has several operating leases that are not capitalized; this is the proper accounting treatment for the leases. The present value of the minimum lease commitments was $430,000 on October 31, 1983, and $520,000 on October 31, 1984.

4. *Long-term notes.* The long-term notes of Motel Enterprises consist mainly of term loans and mortgage loans. A major portion of the property and equipment and investments of Motel Enterprises are pledged as collateral for long-term notes.

Long-term notes become due as follows:

By October 31, 1985	$ 80,000
By October 31, 1986	150,000
By October 31, 1987	550,000
By October 31, 1988	350,000
By October 31, 1989	425,000
Over 5 years	1,310,000

5. *Dividends.* The company declared and paid to its stockholders $115,000 of cash dividends during the 1983–1984 fiscal year.

REQUIRED Prepare an estimated statement of changes in financial position for the year ended October 31, 1984. Use the working capital basis.

P25–13 (CMA ADAPTED) Odon Company has not yet prepared a formal statement of changes in financial position for the 1984 fiscal year. Comparative statements of financial position as of December 31, 1983 and 1984, and a statement of income and retained earnings for the year ended December 31, 1984, follow.

ODON COMPANY
Statement of Financial Position
December 31
(000 omitted)

ASSETS	1984	1983	LIABILITIES AND OWNERSHIP	1984	1983
Current assets			*Current liabilities*		
Cash	$ 60	$ 100	Accounts payable	$ 360	$ 300
U.S. treasury notes	0	50	Taxes payable	25	20
Accounts receivable	610	500	Notes payable	400	400
Inventory	720	600	Total current liabilities	$ 785	$ 720
Total current assets	$1,390	$1,250	Term notes payable—due 1989	200	200
Long-term assets			Total liabilities	$ 985	$ 920
Land	$ 80	$ 70	*Owners' equity*		
Buildings and equipment	710	600	Common stock outstanding	$ 830	$ 700
Accumulated depreciation	(180)	(120)	Retained earnings	290	310
Patents (less amortization)	105	130	Total owners' equity	$1,120	$1,010
Total long-term assets	$ 715	$ 680	Total liabilities and equity	$2,105	$1,930
Total assets	$2,105	$1,930			

```
                    ODON COMPANY
        Statement of Income and Retained Earnings
                Year Ended December 31, 1984
                      (000 omitted)

Sales                                        $2,408
Less expenses and interest
   Cost of goods sold            $1,100
   Salaries and benefits            850
   Heat, light, and power            75
   Depreciation                      60
   Property taxes                    18
   Patent amortization              25
   Miscellaneous expense           10
   Interest                          55      2,193
Net income before income taxes             $  215
   Income taxes                               105
Net income                                 $  110
Retained earnings—Jan. 1, 1984                310
                                           $  420
Stock dividend paid in shares                 130
Retained earnings—Dec. 31, 1984           $  290
```

REQUIRED   Prepare a statement of changes in financial position that reconciles the change in cash balance. Your statement should distinguish between sources of funds from sales operations, asset liquidations, and other sources. The uses section should identify debt retirement, asset acquisition, and income distribution.

P25–14 (CPA ADAPTED)   The income statement of Kenwood Corporation for the year ended December 31, 1984, follows.

```
                         KENWOOD CORPORATION
                           Income Statement
                    For the Year Ended December 31, 1984

Sales                                                          $1,000,000

Expenses:
   Cost of sales                                                  560,000
   Salary and wages                                               190,000
   Depreciation                                                    20,000
   Amortization                                                     3,000
   Loss on sale of equipment                                        4,000
   Interest                                                        16,000
   Miscellaneous                                                    8,000
Total expenses                                                    801,000
Income before income taxes and extraordinary item                199,000
Income taxes
   Current                                                         50,000
   Deferred                                                        40,000
Provision for income taxes                                         90,000
Income before extraordinary item                                 109,000
Extraordinary item—gain on repurchase of long-term bonds (net of $10,000 income tax)   12,000
Net income                                                     $  121,000

Earnings per share:
   Income before extraordinary item                                 $2.21
   Extraordinary item                                                 .24
   Net income                                                       $2.45
```

Comparative statements of financial position of Kenwood Corporation as of December 31, 1984, and December 31, 1983, follow.

KENWOOD CORPORATION
Statement of Financial Position

ASSETS	DECEMBER 31, 1984	DECEMBER 31, 1983	INCREASE (DECREASE)
Current assets			
Cash	$ 100,000	$ 90,000	$ 10,000
Accounts receivable (net of allowance for uncollectible accounts of $10,000 and $8,000, respectively)	210,000	140,000	70,000
Inventories	260,000	220,000	40,000
Total current assets	570,000	450,000	120,000
Land	325,000	200,000	125,000
Plant and equipment	580,000	633,000	(53,000)
Less: Accumulated depreciation	(90,000)	(100,000)	10,000
Patents	30,000	33,000	(3,000)
Total assets	$1,415,000	$1,216,000	$199,000

LIABILITIES AND SHAREHOLDERS' EQUITY			
Liabilities			
Current liabilities			
Accounts payable	$ 260,000	$ 200,000	$ 60,000
Accrued expenses	200,000	210,000	(10,000)
Total current liabilities	460,000	410,000	50,000
Deferred income taxes	140,000	100,000	40,000
Long-term bonds (due Dec. 15, 1990)	130,000	180,000	(50,000)
Total liabilities	730,000	690,000	40,000
Shareholders' equity			
Common stock, par value $5 (authorized, 100,000 shares; issued and outstanding, 50,000 and 42,000 shares, respectively)	250,000	210,000	40,000
Additional paid-in capital	233,000	170,000	63,000
Retained earnings	202,000	146,000	56,000
Total shareholders' equity	685,000	526,000	159,000
Total liabilities and shareholders' equity	$1,415,000	$1,216,000	$199,000

Additional information:

1. On February 2, 1984, Kenwood issued a 10 percent stock dividend to shareholders of record on January 15, 1984. The market price per share of the common stock on February 2, 1984, was $15.
2. On March 1, 1984, Kenwood issued 3,800 shares of common stock for land. The common stock and land had current market values of approximately $40,000 on March 1, 1984.
3. On April 15, 1984, Kenwood repurchased long-term bonds with a face value of $50,000. The gain of $22,000 was reported as an extraordinary item on the income statement.
4. On June 30, 1984, Kenwood sold equipment costing $53,000, with a book value of $23,000, for $19,000 cash.
5. On September 30, 1984, Kenwood declared and paid a $.04 per share cash dividend to shareholders of record August 1, 1984.
6. On October 10, 1984, Kenwood purchased land for $85,000 cash.
7. Deferred income taxes represent timing differences relating to the use of accelerated depreciation methods for income tax reporting and straight-line depreciation methods for financial statement reporting.

REQUIRED By means of a worksheet and using the working capital concept of funds, prepare a statement of changes in financial position of Kenwood Corporation for the year ended December 31, 1984. (Do not prepare a schedule of changes in working capital.)

P25-15 (CMA ADAPTED) The following schedule presents the *net* changes in the balance sheet accounts as of December 31, 1984, as compared with December 31, 1983, for the Lock Company. Lock's statement of changes in financial position has not yet been prepared for the year ended December 31, 1984. Additional information regarding Lock's operations during 1984 follows the schedule.

	NET CHANGE
DEBIT BALANCE ACCOUNTS	INCREASE (DECREASE)
Cash	$ (340,000)
Accounts receivable (net)	440,000
Inventories	580,000
Property, plant, and equipment	1,800,000
Total	$2,480,000
CREDIT BALANCE ACCOUNTS	
Accumulated depreciation	$ 950,000
Accounts payable	1,250,000
Notes payable—current	(150,000)
Serial bonds payable	(2,000,000)
Common stock, $10 par value	9,000,000
Capital contributed in excess of par value	1,300,000
Retained earnings	(7,870,000)
Total	$2,480,000

Additional information:

1. Lock Company incurred a net after-tax loss from regular operations of $500,000 for the year ended December 31, 1984. In addition, Lock had an extraordinary gain from the sale of condemned land in the amount of $1,400,000 net of tax of $600,000. The condemned land had a book value of $2,500,000.

2. Accounts receivable of $650,000 were written off during 1984 by charging allowance for doubtful accounts. The provision for bad debts for 1984 amounted to $1,250,000.

3. Machinery acquired in 1979 at a cost of $2,000,000 was sold for $550,000. The machinery had a net book value of $350,000 at the date of sale.

4. A new parcel of land was purchased during April 1984. The market value of the land was $6,300,000. Cash of $1,500,000 and 400,000 shares of Lock's common stock were given in exchange for the land.

5. The serial bonds mature at a rate of $2,000,000 each year. The bonds were sold at par value.

6. A 5 percent stock dividend was declared January 15, 1984, on 10,000,000 shares of Lock common stock. The stock dividend was issued on February 10, 1984, to all stockholders of record as of January 31, 1984. The market value of the stock at these three dates was

January 15, 1984	$11.00 per share
January 31, 1984	$10.45 per share
February 10, 1984	$10.60 per share

7. A cash dividend of $.30 per share of common stock was declared on December 31, 1984, to all stockholders of record as of January 15, 1985, to be payable on January 31, 1985.

REQUIRED

1. Prepare a schedule of changes in working capital for the Lock Company as of December 31, 1984.

2. Prepare a statement of changes in financial position for Lock Company for the year ended December 31, 1984. Prepare the statement using an "all financial resources" concept with the working capital format.

P25–16 (CPA ADAPTED) The following schedule showing *net* changes in balance sheet accounts at December 31, 1985, compared with December 31, 1984, was prepared from the records of the Sodium Company. The statement of changes in financial position for the year ended December 31, 1985, has not yet been prepared.

	NET CHANGE
ASSETS	**INCREASE (DECREASE)**
Cash	$ 50,000
Accounts receivable, net	76,000
Inventories	37,000
Prepaid expenses	1,000
Property, plant, and equipment, net	64,000
Total assets	$228,000
LIABILITIES	
Accounts payable	$ (55,500)
Notes payable—current	(15,000)
Accrued expenses	33,000
Bonds payable	(28,000)
Less: Unamortized bond discount	(1,200)
Total liabilities	(64,300)
STOCKHOLDERS' EQUITY	
Common stock, $10 par value	500,000
Capital contributed in excess of par value	200,000
Retained earnings	(437,700)
Appropriation of retained earnings for possible future inventory price decline	30,000
Total stockholders' equity	292,300
Total liabilities and stockholders' equity	$228,000

Additional information:

1. The net income for the year ended December 31, 1985, was $172,300. There were no extraordinary items.
2. During the year ended December 31, 1985, uncollectible accounts receivable of $26,400 were written off by a charge to allowance for doubtful accounts.
3. A comparison of property, plant, and equipment as of the end of each year follows:

	DECEMBER 31, 1985	DECEMBER 31, 1984	NET INCREASE (DECREASE)
Property, plant, and equipment	$570,500	$510,000	$60,500
Less: Accumulated depreciation	224,500	228,000	(3,500)
Property, plant, and equipment, net	$346,000	$282,000	$64,000

During 1985 machinery was purchased at a cost of $45,000. In addition, machinery that was acquired in 1968 at a cost of $48,000 was sold for $3,600. At the date of sale, the machinery had an undepreciated cost of $4,200. The remaining increase in property, plant, and equipment resulted from the acquisition of a tract of land for a new plant site.

4. The bonds payable mature at the rate of $28,000 every year.
5. In January 1985 the company issued an additional 10,000 shares of its common stock at $14 per share upon the exercise of outstanding stock options held by key employees. In May 1985 the company declared and issued a 5 percent stock dividend on its outstanding stock. During the year, a cash dividend was paid on the common stock. On December 31, 1985, there were 840,000 shares of common stock outstanding.
6. The appropriation of retained earnings for possible future inventory price decline was provided by a charge against retained earnings, in anticipation of an expected future drop in the market related to goods in inventory.

REQUIRED

1. Prepare a statement of changes in financial position for the year ended December 31, 1985, based upon the information presented above. The statement should be prepared using a *working capital format*.
2. Prepare a schedule of changes in working capital for the year 1985.

P25–17 (CPA ADAPTED) Comparative statements of financial position of Area Corporation as of December 31, 1984, and December 31, 1983, follow.

ASSETS	DECEMBER 31 1984	DECEMBER 31 1983	INCREASE (DECREASE)
Current assets			
Cash	$ 450,000	$ 287,000	$163,000
Notes receivable	45,000	50,000	(5,000)
Accounts receivable (net of allowance for uncollectible accounts of $17,100 and			
$24,700, respectively)	479,200	380,000	99,200
Inventories	460,000	298,000	162,000
Total current assets	1,434,200	1,015,000	419,200
Investment in common stock of Reading Company	—	39,000	(39,000)
Investment in common stock of Zip Corporation	246,300	—	246,300
Total	246,300	39,000	207,300
Machinery and equipment	455,000	381,000	74,000
Less: Accumulated depreciation	(193,000)	(144,000)	49,000
Total	262,000	237,000	25,000
Patents (less accumulated amortization)	26,000	19,000	7,000
Total assets	$1,968,500	$1,310,000	$658,500
LIABILITIES AND SHAREHOLDERS' EQUITY			
Liabilities			
Dividends payable	$ 181,000	$ —	$181,000
Accounts payable	156,000	40,800	115,200
Accrued expenses	92,000	84,000	8,000
Total liabilities	429,000	124,800	304,200
Shareholders' equity			
Preferred stock, par value $2 (authorized, 50,000 shares; issued and outstanding, 30,000 shares and 26,500 shares, respectively)	60,000	53,000	7,000
Capital contributed in excess of par—preferred stock	6,000	2,500	3,500
Common stock, par value $10 (authorized, 100,000 shares; issued and outstanding, 75,200 shares and 70,000 shares, respectively)	752,000	700,000	52,000
Capital contributed in excess of par—common stock	20,000	9,600	10,400
Earnings appropriated for contingencies	85,000	—	85,000
Retained earnings	616,500	420,100	196,400
Total shareholders' equity	1,539,500	1,185,200	354,300
Total liabilities and shareholders' equity	$1,968,500	$1,310,000	$658,500

Additional information:

1. For the year ended December 31, 1984, Area Corporation reported net income of $496,000.
2. Uncollectible accounts receivable of $4,000 were written off against the allowance for uncollectible accounts receivable.
3. Area's investment in the common stock of Reading Company was made in 1980 and represented a 3 percent interest in the outstanding common stock of Reading. During 1984, Area sold this investment for $26,000.
4. Amortization of patents charged to operations during 1984 was $3,000.
5. On January 1, 1984, Area acquired 90 percent of the outstanding common stock of Zip Corporation (45,000 shares, par value $10 per share) in a transaction appropriately accounted for as a purchase. To consummate this transaction, Area paid $72,000 cash and issued 3,500 shares of its preferred stock and 2,400 shares of its

common stock. The consideration paid was equal to the underlying book value of the assess acquired. The fair market value of area's stock on the date of the transaction was as follows:

Preferred	$ 3
Common	12

Zip Corporation is considered to be an unrelated business and not compatible with the operations of Area Corporation; and therefore, consolidation of the two companies is *not* required. For the year ended December 31, 1984, Zip Corporation reported net income of $150,000.

6. During 1984 the machinery and equipment that was acquired in 1977 at a cost of $22,000 was sold as scrap for $3,200. At the date of sale, this machinery had an undepreciated cost of $4,400. In addition, Area acquired new machinery and equipment at a cost of $81,000. The remaining increase in machinery and equipment resulted from major repairs made to machinery that were accounted for as capital expenditures.

7. On January 1, 1984, Area declared and issued a 4 percent stock dividend on its common stock. The market value of the shares on that date was $12 a share. The market value of the shares was not affected by the dividend distribution. On December 31, 1984, cash dividends were declared on both the common and the preferred stock as follows:

Common	$145,000
Preferred	36,000

8. In December 1984 a reserve for a contingent loss of $85,000 arising from a lawsuit was established by a charge against retained earnings.

REQUIRED   Prepare a statement of changes in financial position of Area Corporation for the year ended December 31, 1984, based upon the information presented above. The statement should be prepared using a *working capital format*. (Note: Do *not* prepare a schedule of working capital.)

26

Accounting for Changing Prices

OVERVIEW   Thus far we have dealt primarily with generally accepted accounting principles (GAAP) that are based on a historical-cost accounting information system. However, the conventional financial statements of publicly traded entities do not represent a pure historical-cost accounting model. As pointed out in Chapter 6 and in various sections of the chapters throughout Parts II and III of this text, the conventional model permits and sometimes requires departures from historical cost. The lower-of-cost-or-market measurement concept is perhaps the main example of a departure from the pure historical-cost model that is widely applied in preparing conventional financial statements. Other examples of departures from cost include the equity method of accounting for long-term investments and the recording of asset exchanges in certain cases.

The early exposure to historical-cost alternatives that was provided in Chapter 6 on a broad conceptual level should help you understand and evaluate the historical-cost departures encountered within GAAP. The material in Chapter 6 should also help you understand the supplementary "current-value" disclosure requirements considered in this chapter.

This chapter focuses on the specific supplementary financial statement disclosures required by the FASB. The disclosures provide unaudited footnote information to users of financial statements regarding the impact of changing prices on the conventional financial statement data. The material covered in this chapter should provide sufficient information for understanding the nature and source of the required disclosures for changing prices.

In the first part of the chapter we discuss the general concept of accounting for changing prices. In the second part we discuss the required minimum disclosures under GAAP for reporting the impact of price changes. In the third part of the chapter we illustrate comprehensive disclosures concerning price changes that are also permissible. And in the fourth part of the chapter we outline the uses and the limitations of the supplementary disclosures on price changes required by generally accepted accounting standards.

ACCOUNTING FOR CHANGING PRICES

Without the prompting from accounting policy makers, it is unlikely that widespread corporate disclosures concerning the impact of changing prices would have evolved. Although accounting academics had professed the merits of such **current-value** information for decades, it was not until the rapid price changes of the late 1960s and early 1970s occurred that accounting policy makers took action.[1] The Securities and Exchange Commission's disclosure requirement **(ASR 190),** which took effect in 1976, called for a restatement of inventories, plant assets, cost of goods sold, and depreciation expense on a replacement cost basis from the largest 1,000 SEC registrants. Then in 1979, on an experimental basis, the FASB called for specific current-value information as a footnote to the financial reports of public entities meeting a certain size requirement (see p. 1004).

The practice of measuring the alternatives to historical-cost accounting is still in the experimental stage, and the measurements are frequently misused or misunderstood. However, the *concept* of current-value measurements has gained favor with sophisticated users of financial statement data, who consider such measures more relevant than historical cost in certain decision-making situations.[2] Recall from Chapter 6 that the basic difference between the alternative accounting models was in the way each viewed the financial "well-offness" of the firm. The conventional accounting information system produces a balance sheet that reports the "well offness" of the entity **in terms of original transaction dollar amounts.** It was demonstrated that this measure of well-offness was not particularly useful for certain types of management decisions during periods of changing prices, and that alternative measures might be more relevant in some instances.

Chapter 6 also illustrated how using any of the accounting models without understanding their strengths and weaknesses could lead to serious decision-making

[1] Although the accounting literature in the United States has included articles on the impact of changing prices since the early 1900s, Henry Sweeney is generally credited with writing the first major text developing a price-level-adjusted accounting system—*Stabilized Accounting* (New York: Harper & Brothers, 1936). Many accounting classics have been published since that time and are being studied today by accounting historians.

[2] See the November 10, 1980, issue of *Forbes* (pp. 230–236) for an example of the type of coverage given the current-value information in the popular business press after only a single year's exposure to FASB Statement No. 33 data. See *Statement of Financial Accounting Standards No. 33,* "Financial Reporting and Changing Prices" (Stamford, CT: FASB, September 1979).

errors on the part of management and investors. The required disclosures based on these alternative models have evolved as a result of the accounting profession's recognizing that the conventional accounting model cannot, in periods of rapidly changing prices, accurately portray the well-offness of an entity in a way that is useful for decision making.

Given the dynamic nature of the economy that we live in and the tremendous variations in the decision-making perspectives for which accounting data are sought and employed, it is obvious that a single measurement system based on original transaction amounts cannot possibly satisfy all the demands placed on accounting information. Given the basic objective of accounting—**to provide relevant economic information for decision making**—it is necessary to consider alternatives to the historical-cost-based accounting information system. Understanding the strengths and weaknesses of the alternatives to historical-cost measures will enable financial statement users to benefit from the current set of supplementary disclosures. Future changes in non-historical-cost-based disclosure may be more understandable once a fundamental knowledge of the underlying purpose of these alternative accounting models is obtained.

Alternative Measures

There are many alternatives to historical cost, but all cost measurements can be broadly classified as **entry value** or **exit value.** An example of an exit-value cost would be the net realizable value of an asset as measured by its selling price less the expected normal costs needed to complete the sale (for example, a salesperson's commission). Recall that this value was used as the "ceiling" price in measuring inventory under the LCM valuation method. Although exit values are sometimes used within GAAP, their acceptance as an overall valuation method has been minimal, generally on the grounds that exit-value models anticipate profits (recognize revenue) at a point when there is still too much uncertainty concerning the eventual collection of the exit value.

Entry-value models have received nearly all the attention in discussions of alternative accounting measurement systems. Note that historical cost is an entry-value measurement, which uses *original entry price* as its basis. Two common alternatives have been proposed within the entry-value paradigm. The first is an original entry value adjusted for changes in the **general purchasing power of the monetary measurement unit.** This general inflation-adjusted measure is known by many different names, including the general-price-level-adjusted model (GPLA), the purchasing power units model, the constant-dollar model (CD), and the uniform measurement unit model. It may take various forms, depending on which of the general price indexes is selected as a basis for the measurements.

The second commonly discussed alternative is original entry cost adjusted for **specific entry-price changes.** This alternative is also known by many different names, including the specific-price-level-adjusted model (SPLA), the replacement-cost model, the current-cost model (CC), and the current-entry-value model. This model takes on a number of slightly different forms but it generally attempts to measure the *current replacement cost of the equivalent productive capacity* represented by the firm's net assets.

Measurement Method

The conversion of historical-cost dollar measurements to either constant-dollar (GPLA) or current-cost (SPLA) measurements is best illustrated, and most often accomplished in practice, by applying indexes to the historical amounts. Once an index

TABLE 26–1

	GROSS NATIONAL PRODUCT IMPLICIT PRICE DEFLATOR (GNP DEFLATOR)[a]	CONSUMER PRICE INDEX OF URBAN CONSUMERS (CPI–U)[b]	PRODUCER PRICE INDEX OF ALL COMMODITIES[b]	FOOD[b]	HOUSING[b]	TRANSPORTATION[b]
GENERAL AND SPECIFIC PRICE INDEXES						
YEAR						
1981	193.6	272.4	293.4	274.6	293.5	280.0
1980	177.4	246.8	268.8	254.6	263.3	249.7
1979	162.8	217.4	235.6	234.5	227.6	212.0
1978	150.0	195.4	209.3	211.4	202.8	185.5
1977	139.8	181.5	194.2	192.2	186.5	177.2
1976	132.1	170.5	183.0	180.8	177.2	165.5
1975	125.6	161.2	174.9	175.4	166.8	150.6
1974	114.9	147.4	160.1	161.7	150.6	137.7
1973	105.7	133.1	134.7	141.4	135.0	123.8
1972	100.0	125.3	119.1	123.5	129.2	119.9
1971	96.0	121.3	114.0	118.4	124.3	118.6
1970	91.4	116.3	110.4	114.9	118.9	112.7
1969	86.8	109.8	106.5	108.9	110.8	107.2
1968	82.5	104.2	102.5	103.6	104.2	103.2
1967	79.1	100.0	100.0	100.0	100.0	100.0
1966	76.8	97.2	99.8	99.1	97.2	97.2
1965	74.4	94.5	96.6	94.4	94.9	95.9
1964	72.8	92.9	94.7	92.4	93.8	94.3
1963	71.7	91.7	94.5	91.2	92.7	93.0
1962	70.6	90.6	94.8	89.9	91.7	92.5
1961	69.3	89.6	94.5	89.1	90.9	90.6
1960	68.7	88.7	94.9	88.0	90.2	89.6

[a] *Source:* Bureau of Commerce, 1972 = 100
[b] *Source:* Bureau of Labor Statistics, 1967 = 100

has been developed or identified, the conversion process is a straightforward exercise in multiplication. Some examples of general and specific indexes are shown in Table 26–1. The general form of this multiplication is simply

$$\text{Historical cost (in dollars)} \times \frac{\text{Current index (GPLA or SPLA)}}{\text{Historical index (GPLA or SPLA)}}$$

To illustrate, assume that 20 automobiles were acquired in 1979 when the general consumer price index was 217.4 percent and the specific transportation index was 212 percent.[3] The company originally paid $160,000 for these 20 automobiles, which were expected to have a useful life of 8 years. Assume that also at the end of 1983, the general price index was 260.0 percent and the specific transportation index was 300.0 percent. The 1983 year-end GPLA and SPLA gross book values for the automobiles would be computed as follows:

$$GPLA: \quad \$160,000 \times \frac{260.0}{217.4} = \underline{\$191,352}$$

$$SPLA: \quad \$160,000 \times \frac{300.0}{212.0} = \underline{\$226,415}$$

[3] The percentages used in these two indexes can be found in Table 26–1. In other words, transportation in 1979 cost 212 percent (or 2.12 times) the 1967 cost.

If we assume that the assets are 50 percent depreciated, the comparative data would appear as follows:

	HISTORICAL COST	CONSTANT DOLLAR (GPLA)	CURRENT COST (SPLA)
Automobiles	$160,000	$191,352	$227,920
Less accumulated depreciation	80,000	95,676	113,960
Net book value	$ 80,000	$ 95,676	$113,960

Index data for various goods and services are prepared by the U.S. government, and most current-cost and constant-dollar data have been developed using specific indexes such as those in Table 26–1. For current-cost information, however, it is possible to use other sources of data, such as current vendor price lists. Note that a specific price index could be constructed by following vendor prices for specific goods or services over a period of time, which is essentially how all specific indexes are developed.

MINIMUM DISCLOSURE UNDER FASB STATEMENT NO. 33

FASB Statement No. 33 calls for supplementary disclosures concerning **inventories and plant, property, and equipment on both a constant-dollar (GPLA) and a current-cost (replacement-cost) basis.** Although the FASB does not call for comprehensive financial statements on either a constant-dollar or a current-cost basis, the impact of these selected items on the overall financial statements should be apparent from the required disclosures.

As a result of **FASB Statement No. 33,** the SEC deleted its replacement-cost disclosure requirement originally established in **ASR No. 190.** The FASB statement applies to publicly held corporations with over $125,000,000 in inventories and gross plant, property, and equipment, or with total assets in excess of $1 billion. It was expected that such disclosures would eventually be applicable to all publicly traded entities.

Specific Disclosure Requirements

The minimum disclosures required by **FASB Statement No. 33** consist of the following:[4]

1. *Constant-dollar disclosures* (*current year*)
   An enterprise is required to disclose:
   a. Information on income from continuing operations for the current fiscal year on a historical-cost/constant-dollar basis
   b. The purchasing power gain or loss on net monetary items for the current fiscal year
   The purchasing power gain or loss on net monetary items shall *not* be included in income from continuing operations.

2. *Current-cost disclosures* (*current year*)
   An enterprise is required to disclose:
   a. Information on income from continuing operations for the current fiscal year on a current-cost basis

[4] *Statement of Financial Accounting Standards No. 33,* "Financial Reporting and Changing Prices," pars. 29, 30, 35, 51, and 52.

b. The current-cost amounts of inventory and property, plant, and equipment at the end of the current fiscal year

c. Increases or decreases for the current fiscal year in the current-cost amounts of inventory and property, plant, and equipment, net of inflation

The increases or decreases in current-cost amounts shall *not* be included in income from continuing operations.

3. *Five-year summary data*
    a. Net sales and other operating revenues
    b. Historical-cost/constant-dollar information
        (1) Income from continuing operations
        (2) Income per common share from continuing operations
        (3) Net assets at fiscal year-end
    c. Current-cost information (except for individual years in which the information was excluded from the current year disclosures)
        (1) Income from continuing operations
        (2) Income per common share from continuing operations
        (3) Net assets at fiscal year-end
        (4) Increases or decreases in the current cost amounts of inventory and property, plant, and equipment, net of inflation
    d. Other information
        (1) Purchasing power gain or loss on net monetary items
        (2) Cash dividends declared per common share
        (3) Market price per common share at fiscal year-end.

4. *Limitation*
    Whenever the recoverable amount of an asset is less than either the constant-dollar value or the current-cost value, the recoverable amount should be used to value the asset. "Recoverable amount" means the current value of the net cash flow expected to be realized from the use or sale of the asset.

5. *Methodology*
    a. The constant-dollar method should use the CPI–U index.
    b. The current-cost method may use internally or externally developed specific price indexes or evidence such as vendors' invoice prices or price lists to determine the current cost of an asset. The method selected should be based on availability, reliability, and cost and should be applied consistently.
    c. The constant-dollar amounts should be based on *average-for-the-year indexes*.
    d. The current costs should be based on average current costs of the period for the restatement of items required to compute operating income (cost of goods sold, depreciation, and depletion), and should be restated at end-of-period current costs net of general inflation for measuring the increases or decreases in inventory, plant, property, and equipment. This latter statement requires the use of year-end current costs restated in average-of-the-period constant dollars.

Some of the specific requirements discussed in **FASB Statement No. 33** do not pertain to most situations and have not been included in this outline.[5] However,

---

[5] Several FASB pronouncements dealing with special situations have also been issued subsequent to *FASB Statement No. 33*. These include FASB Statement No. 39, "Financial Reporting and Changing Prices: Specialized Assets—Mining and Oil and Gas," October 1980; *FASB Statement No. 40*, "Financial Reporting and Changing Prices: Specialized Assets—Timberlands and Growing Timber," November 1980; *FASB Statement No. 41*, "Financial Reporting and Changing Prices: Specialized Assets—Income Producing Real Estate," November 1980; and *FASB Statement No. 46*, "Financial Reporting and Changing Prices: Specialized Assets—Motion Pictures and Video Films" (March 1981). Also under consideration are "Financial Reporting and Changing Prices: Foreign Currency Translation" and "Financial Reporting and Changing Prices: Investment Companies," which should be released prior to publication of this text.

the requirements listed above will be sufficient to demonstrate the major impact of **FASB Statement No. 33** on financial reporting.

The disclosure requirements of **FASB Statement No. 33** call for parallel disclosure of *certain selected* current-cost and constant-dollar items. This piecemeal approach is *not* a comprehensive application of either the current-cost or the constant-dollar model. The following examples are based on the Sun Company, whose conventional financial statement data are provided in Exhibit 26–1. The examples will show how to construct the constant-dollar and current-cost data, *given* a set of conventional accounting data.

Converting conventional accounting data to constant-dollar data requires information about the general price index (CPI–U), and converting to current-cost data requires information about the specific price indexes appropriate for the specific entity. Table 26–2 summarizes all the assumed general and specific price indexes required for generating the **FASB Statement No. 33** type of disclosures for the Sun Company example.

The primary footnote disclosure required by **FASB Statement No. 33** for the

**EXHIBIT
26–1**

CONVENTIONAL FINANCIAL STATEMENTS		

SUN COMPANY
Balance Sheet as of December 31, 1985

Assets

Cash and accounts receivable		$ 350,000
Inventories (at LIFO cost)		420,000
Temporary investments		80,000
Plant and equipment (net of $500,000 accumulated depreciation)		600,000
Property		175,000
Patents and licenses (net)		45,000
Total assets		$1,670,000

Liabilities and equities

Accounts and accrued payables		$ 350,000
Long-term notes (due 2010)		500,000
Common stock (no par)		600,000
Retained earnings		220,000
Total liabilities and shareholders' equity		$1,670,000

SUN COMPANY
Income Statement for the Year Ended December 31, 1985

Sales revenue		$2,700,000
Cost of goods sold		
Beginning inventory	$ 350,000	
Net purchases	1,300,000	
Goods available for sale	$1,650,000	
Less ending inventory	420,000	
Cost of goods sold		$1,230,000
Gross margin		$1,470,000
Other expenses:		
Selling and administrative expense	$ 800,000	
Amortization expense	5,000	
Depreciation expense	41,375	
Income tax expense	311,812	$1,158,187
Net income		$ 311,813

TABLE 26–2

PRICE INDEX DATA

	GENERAL PRICE INDEX	SPECIFIC PRICE INDEX			
	ALL ITEMS	INVENTORY	PLANT[a]	EQUIPMENT[b]	PROPERTY
12/31/85	220%	320%	410%	210%	575%
Average 1985	215	300	400	200	550
12/31/84	205	290	390	190	525
Average 1984	205	275	375	180	500
12/31/83	205				
Average 1983	200	250		180	
12/31/82	195				
Average 1982	190				
12/31/81	180				
Average 1981	175				
12/31/80	165			150	
Average 1980	164				
12/31/79	162				
Average 1979	160				
12/31/78	155				
Average 1978	150	175			
12/31/77	145				
Average 1977	135				
12/31/76	125			120	
Average 1976	123				
12/31/75	120				
Average 1975	116				
12/31/74	110	100	100	100	100

[a] Plant was acquired on 1/1/75 for $500,000.
[b] Equipment was acquired on 1/1/75 ($150,000), as well as on 1/1/77 ($150,000), 12/31/80 ($150,000), and 6/30/83 ($150,000).

Sun Company is shown in Exhibit 26–2. This illustrated disclosure is divided into three parts—*A, B,* and *C*—for identification purposes in the explanations that follow. Note that *only* Exhibit 26–2 presents the required minimum disclosures, and that all the supporting exhibits (Exhibits 26–3 to 26–8) referred to here are provided to explain the type of analysis that would go into the preparation of these required disclosures.

The steps involved in restating the historical data to arrive at the disclosures illustrated in Exhibit 26–2 are as follows:

Step 1: Restate historical (nominal) dollars to average-of-the-period constant dollars for income statement items that require restatement (cost of goods sold, depreciation, and depletion).

Step 2: Compute the purchasing power gain or loss from holding monetary items during the period, measured in terms of average-of-the-period constant dollars.

Step 3: Restate historical (nominal) dollars to average-of-the-period current-cost (nominal) dollars for income statement items that require restatement (cost of goods sold, depreciation, and depletion).

Step 4: Restate historical (nominal) dollars to end-of-period current-cost (nominal) dollars for the items that require restatement (inventory, plant, property, and equipment), and measure the price increase of the current year in terms of current costs (nominal dollars).

Step 5: Restate the results from step 4 above—the current period's price increase in terms of current costs (nominal dollars)—in terms of current costs (constant dollars) using average-of-the-period constant dollars.

EXHIBIT
26–2

SUN COMPANY

Statement of Operating Income,
Impact of General and Specific Price Changes,
For the Year Ended December 31, 1985

	CONVENTIONAL ACCOUNTING	CONSTANT DOLLAR (GPLA)	CURRENT COST (SPLA)
Part A			
Sales revenue	$2,700,000	$2,700,000	$2,700,000
Cost of goods sold	$1,230,000	$1,230,000[a]	$1,230,000[c]
Selling and administrative expense	800,000	800,000	800,000
Advertising expense	5,000	5,000	5,000
Depreciation expense	41,375	67,073[b]	94,000[d]
Income tax expense	311,812	311,812	311,812
Total operating expense	$2,388,187	$2,413,885	$2,440,812
Income (loss) from operations	$ 311,813	$ 286,115	$ 259,188
Part B			
Purchasing power gain on net monetary items		$ 32,827	$ 32,827
Part C			
Increase in specific prices (current cost) of inventory and plant, property, and equipment held during the year			$ 276,830[e]
Effect of increase in general price level			254,701
Excess of increase in specific prices over increase in the general price level			$ 22,129

[a] See Exhibit 26–3 for details.
[b] See Exhibit 26–5 for details.
[c] See Exhibit 26–4 for details.
[d] See Exhibit 26–6 for details.
[e] See Exhibit 26–8 for details.

These are essentially the steps followed to prepare the data in Exhibit 26–2, as shown in the supporting schedules in Exhibits 26–3 to 26–8. We will illustrate that the order of these steps is not important except for the fact that step 5 cannot be accomplished until after step 4.

Part A—operating income   Part A of Exhibit 26–2 provides the comparative operating income statement data on a conventional basis; a constant-dollar, or GPLA (general-price-level-adjusted), basis; and a current-cost, or SPLA (specific-price-level-adjusted), basis. Note that in the comparative operating income data in part A, sales revenue does not differ among the three models. **FASB Statement No. 33** does *not* call for the adjustment of revenues under either constant-dollar or current-cost disclosures. For Sun Company the only items in the operating income data in part A that would differ (under the minimum disclosure requirements of **FASB Statement No. 33**) would be (1) cost of goods sold and (2) depreciation expense. In the Sun Company example, the only difference in the three models is the depreciation expense figures because Sun is using LIFO to measure cost of goods sold. When LIFO is used, the FASB does not **require** cost of goods to be restated for the SPLA measurement, provided that all beginning inventory layers remain in ending inventory.

Part B—purchasing power gain   Part B of Exhibit 26–2 simply reports the single net measurement of the purchasing power gain or loss experienced during the period. This computation, which was illustrated in Chapter 6, measures the impact of holding monetary items in periods of changing prices. Table 6–1 in Chapter 6 lists the monetary assets and liabilities that would ordinarily be used in computing the monetary gains or losses. Recall that monetary assets and liabilities are those items that represent a fixed claim to a specified number of dollars. As a result, the measurement of monetary items will not change in either a constant-dollar or a current-cost measurement system. The measurement of the purchasing power gain or loss is a hypothetical measure of the net cost or benefit to the entity resulting from its net monetary assets or liabilities during a period of *general* price change.

Note that the amount of the purchasing power gain is the same in both the GPLA and the SPLA column in Exhibit 26–2 and will always be the same because the gain or loss is based on *general* price changes. In this case, the reported purchasing power gain resulted from holding net monetary liabilities during a period when the general price level *increased*. The actual balance sheet measurements of monetary assets and liabilities (cash, accounts receivable, accounts payable, notes payable, and other fixed claims to dollars) are *the same* for the GPLA model, the SPLA model, *and* the conventional model. Holding monetary items during inflation will have an impact on the entity regardless of the model being used for preparing the financial statements. For example, holding cash during a period when the general inflation measure (such as the CPI–U) increases by 20 percent means that you can purchase 20 percent less with the cash at the end of the period than at the beginning, and thus a purchasing power loss has been incurred.

Although not enough data are provided to actually compute the net purchasing power effect on the statements, with a few additional assumptions the shortcut method allowed per **FASB Statement No. 33** can be accomplished, thereby illustrating step 2 in the restatement process.[6] Assume the following net monetary position for the end of 1984 in addition to the 1985 data provided:

	DECEMBER 1985	DECEMBER 1984
Monetary assets	$ 350,000	$ 280,000
Monetary liabilities	(850,000)	(720,000)
Net monetary liabilities	$(500,000)	$(440,000)

	NOMINAL DOLLARS	CONVERSION FACTOR	AVERAGE 1985 DOLLARS
Net monetary balance at 1/1/85	$440,000	215/205	$461,463
Increase in net monetary liabilities	00,000	215/215	00,000
			$521,463
Net monetary balance at 12/31/85	$500,000	215/220	−488,636
Purchasing power gain on net monetary liabilities			$ 32,827

This shortcut method is different than the method illustrated in Chapter 6, but it provides a good approximation of the purchasing power gain or loss providing cash inflows and outflows were reasonably even throughout the period.

The single net number for purchasing power gain or loss lets the financial statement reader know the effects of general inflation on the net monetary position of the entity. A purchasing power gain could be explained by one of two possible

[6] *Statement of Financial Accounting Standards No. 33*, "Financial Reporting and Changing Prices," par. 232.

situations: (1) a company was in a net monetary liability position on average during a period of general inflation, or (2) a company was in a net monetary asset position on average during a period of general deflation. During a period of inflation (decreasing purchasing power in the monetary unit of measure), holding monetary assets will result in losses while holding monetary liabilities will result in gains. Conversely, during a period of deflation, monetary assets generate purchasing power gains while liabilities generate purchasing power losses. In the case of Sun Company, the first explanation—a liability position during a period of inflation—explains the purchasing power gain of $32,827.

Part C—price increases   Part C of Exhibit 26–2 summarizes the effects of the current-cost price increases stated in terms of both nominal current costs ($276,830) and current costs stated in terms of average 1985 purchasing power units ($22,129), with the difference between the two ($254,701) representing the *general* inflation portion of the total nominal current-cost price increase. For the Sun Company, the statement indicates that Sun's inventory, plant, property, and equipment experienced specific price increases during the year totaling $276,830. The effect of the general inflation experienced during 1985 is said to account for $254,701 of this increase. After adjusting for the effect of general inflation, the 1985 current-cost price increase stated in average 1985 constant dollars is measured to be $22,129.

It might be pointed out that some of these measurements are related to material covered earlier in Chapter 6 and discussed in other sources using somewhat different terminology. The $276,830 amount is essentially the *total holding gain* (observed in Chapter 6 in the replacement-cost model) for 1985 stated in current costs.[7] This amount represents the sum of the 1985 holding gains resulting from the 1985 changes in the current costs of inventory, plant, property, and equipment. The $22,129 amount is an effort to measure the total holding gain of the current-cost model restated in terms of average-of-the-period constant dollars. This restatement represents an attempt to integrate the current-cost and the constant-dollar models in a way not previously illustrated in this text. It is an effort to report the net difference between the specific price changes ($276,830) and the general price changes ($254,701). In this case, it appears as though specific prices have increased more rapidly than general prices. Keep in mind, however, that the current-cost price changes are from January 1, 1985, to December 31, 1985, while the constant-dollar factors reflect the change in general prices from the 1984 average to the 1985 average. In addition, the methodology is clearly not an accurate measure of the difference in holding gains for the period between the GPLA and the SPLA models. This will become clearer in the analyses of the supporting schedules.

Detailed Analysis of Supplementary Disclosure
In the following sections we examine the details of each item in the supplementary disclosure requirement illustrated in Exhibit 26–2. The details of each item will help you to understand the basis for the required disclosures. In analyzing Exhibits 26–3 through 26–8, keep in mind that these items are provided *for illustration purposes only*. They are *not* required disclosures.

---

[7] Note that the FASB in *Statement No. 33* specifically avoided use of the term "holding gains" in discussing the effects of price changes. Still, the effects of price changes on assets are commonly referred to as holding gains.

Cost of goods sold   Why doesn't cost of goods sold change in the Sun Company example? The answer is that Sun Company used the LIFO cost-flow assumption for pricing inventory in its conventional accounting statements. Since there was a real increase in inventory units during 1985, cost of goods sold was priced out using the prices from purchases made during 1985. Cost of goods sold is made up of 1985 purchases only, and, therefore, their historical cost is equal to their GPLA value (see Exhibit 26–3 for details). Exhibit 26–3 represents an application of step 1 in preparing **FASB Statement No. 33** disclosures.

According to **FASB Statement No. 33,** companies using LIFO for conventional accounting purposes need not report different cost of goods sold for either of the alternative models **unless a layer of beginning inventory is used (sold) during the period.** In the Sun Company example, if the ending inventory would have been less than $350,000 on a historical-cost basis for 1985, some of the beginning 1985 inventory would have been consumed. This would have caused the cost of goods sold measurement for the three models to differ. To illustrate, assume that Sun Company's ending inventory was $240,000 (historical cost) at the end of 1985 rather than $420,000. The following cost of goods sold on a constant-dollar basis (step 1 above) would have resulted:

	HISTORICAL COST (NOMINAL DOLLARS)	CONSTANT DOLLARS (AVERAGE 1985 DOLLARS)
Beginning inventory	$ 350,000	$ 524,795
Purchases	1,300,000	1,300,000
Goods available for sale	$1,650,000	$1,824,795
Ending inventory	240,000	406,545
Cost of goods sold	$1,410,000	$1,418,250

The ending constant-dollar measurement is the sum of the 1975 and 1978 inventory layers, which had originally cost $120,000 each, restated in terms of average 1985 dollars ($234,545 + $172,000 = $406,545).

EXHIBIT 26–3

ITEM	DATE OF PURCHASE	GPLA AT PURCHASE	COST OF PURCHASE ×	GPLA INDEX FOR AVERAGE 1985 PRICES −	GPLA VALUATION FOR 1985
SUN COMPANY Constant-Dollar Model—Supporting Data for Cost of Goods Sold and Ending Inventory For the Year Ended December 31, 1985						
Beginning inventory	1/1/75	110	$ 120,000	215/110	$ 234,545
	6/30/78	150	120,000	215/150	172,000
	6/30/83	200	110,000	215/200	118,250
			$ 350,000		$ 524,795
Purchases		215	1,300,000	215/215	1,300,000
			$1,650,000		$1,824,795
Ending inventory	1/1/75	110		215/110	
	6/30/78	150	350,000	215/150	524,795
	6/30/83	200		215/200	
	6/30/85	215	70,000	215/215	70,000
			$ 420,000		$ 594,795
Cost of goods sold			$1,230,000		$1,230,000

Inventory   Changes in inventory prices are measured only within the current-cost model. Although measuring price changes is possible for both the GPLA and SPLA models, many feel that measuring changing prices on a GPLA basis is not appropriate. As a result, Exhibit 26–3 does not measure any price change (or holding gain) in the ending balance sheet value of inventory but simply measures GPLA cost of goods sold. However, Exhibit 26–4 provides both the current-cost measurement of cost of goods sold ($1,230,000 from step 3) and the current-cost price change (holding gain) in terms of both nominal dollars and constant dollars. We see that the price changes (holding gains) measured in Exhibit 26–4 result from application of steps 4 and 5 in the restatement process. In this case since there are no realized holding gains in a LIFO inventory measure, the total holding gain may be measured by **comparing the ending asset values given the price changes ($818,896 and**

EXHIBIT 26–4

				CURRENT COSTS (NOMINAL DOLLARS)		**CURRENT COSTS (CONSTANT DOLLARS)**
ITEM	**HISTORICAL COST**	×	**SPLA INDEX**	=	× **GPLA INDEX** =	

SUN COMPANY
Current Cost Model—Supporting Data for Cost of Goods Sold and Inventory Price Increase in Terms of Current Costs and Constant Dollars for the Year Ended December 31, 1985

ITEM	HISTORICAL COST	× SPLA INDEX =	CURRENT COSTS (NOMINAL DOLLARS)	× GPLA INDEX =	CURRENT COSTS (CONSTANT DOLLARS)
Beginning inventory (1/1/85)	$ 120,000	290/100	$ 348,000		
	120,000	290/175	198,857		
	110,000	290/250	127,600		
	$ 350,000		$ 674,457	215/205	$ 707,357
Purchases	$ 1,300,000	300/300	$ 1,300,000	215/215	$ 1,300,000
Cost of goods sold	$(1,230,000)	300/300	$(1,230,000)ª	215/215	$(1,230,000)
Ending inventory (12/31/85)	$ 120,000	320/100	$ 384,000		
	120,000	320/175	219,429		
	110,000	320/250	140,800		
	70,000	320/300	74,667		
	$ (420,000)		$ (818,896)ᵇ	215/220	$ (800,285)
Increase in current costs— nominal dollars			$ 74,439ᶜ		
Increase in current costs— constant dollars					$ 22,928ᶜ

ª This may also be computed by taking the average unit cost of inventory during the year and multiplying by the number of units sold.

ᵇ This may also be computed by taking the year-end cost per unit and multiplying by the number of units in ending inventory.

ᶜ The amounts are computed by taking the difference between ending inventory measures based on current costs ($818,896 and $800,285) and ending inventory without the current cost changes, computed as follows:

	CURRENT COSTS	
	NOMINAL DOLLARS	CONSTANT DOLLARS
Beginning inventory	$ 674,457	$ 707,357
+ Purchases	1,300,000	1,300,000
Goods available for sale	1,974,457	2,007,357
− Cost of goods sold	1,230,000	1,230,000
Ending inventory (no price changes)	$ 744,457	$ 777,357
Ending inventory after price changes	$ 818,896	$ 800,285
Ending inventory ignoring price changes	744,457	777,357
Increase in current costs	$ 74,439	$ 22,928

$800,285) **with the ending asset values that would have resulted without the price changes** ($744,457 and $777,357 respectively). This is, by definition, an unrealized holding gain that results from the impact of changing prices on asset measurement. If there had been no general or specific price changes during the year, no holding gains would have resulted on either a nominal-dollar or a constant-dollar basis.

Depreciation expense The depreciation expense figures reported in Exhibit 26–2 are supported by the computations in Exhibits 26–5 and 26–6, representing additional applications of steps 1 and 3, respectively. The constant dollar depreciation is larger than historical cost depreciation because the general price level has increased since the depreciable assets were acquired. The current-cost (SPLA) depreciation is

EXHIBIT
26–5

SUN COMPANY

Constant-Dollar Model—Supporting Data for
Depreciation Expense for the Year Ended
December 31, 1985

Beginning Balance

ITEM	DATE OF ACQUISITION	GPLA INDEX AT ACQUISITION	HISTORICAL COST NET BOOK VALUE 1/1/85	GPL INDEX FOR AVERAGE 1984 PRICES	GPLA NET BOOK VALUE AT 1/1/85
Plant	1/1/75	110	$382,308	205/110	$ 712,483
Equipment	1/1/75	110	114,692	205/110	213,744
Equipment	1/1/77	125	34,375	205/125	56,375
Equipment	12/31/80	165	42,000	205/165	52,182
Equipment	6/30/83	200	68,000	205/200	69,700
			$641,375		$1,104,484

Plus Acquisitions — None · 215/215 · None

Less Depreciation

ITEM	DATE OF ACQUISITION	GPLA INDEX AT ACQUISITION	HISTORICAL COST DEPRECIATION	GPL INDEX FOR AVERAGE 1985 PRICES	GPLA DEPRECIATION
Plant	1/1/75	110	$ 13,077	215/110	$ 25,560
Equipment	1/1/75	110	3,923	215/110	7,667
Equipment	1/1/77	125	9,375	215/125	16,125
Equipment	12/31/80	165	7,000	215/165	9,121
Equipment	6/30/83	200	8,000	215/200	8,600
			$ 41,375		$ 67,073

Less Disposals (Sales) — None · 215/215 · None

Ending Balance

ITEM	DATE OF ACQUISITION	GPLA INDEX AT ACQUISITION	HISTORICAL COST NET BOOK VALUE 12/31/85	GPLA INDEX FOR AVERAGE 1985 PRICES	GPLA NET BOOK VALUE AT 12/31/85
Plant	1/1/75	110	$369,231	215/110	$ 721,679
Equipment	1/1/75	110	110,769	215/110	216,503
Equipment	1/1/77	125	25,000	215/125	43,000
Equipment	12/31/80	165	35,000	215/165	45,606
Equipment	6/30/83	200	60,000	215/200	64,500
			$600,000		$1,091,288

EXHIBIT
26–6

SUN COMPANY

Current Cost Model—Supporting Data for Depreciation Expense and Plant and Equipment Price Increase in Terms of Current Costs and Constant Dollars
For the Year Ended December 31, 1985

ITEM	HISTORICAL COST	× SPLA INDEX =	CURRENT COSTS (NOMINAL DOLLARS)	× GPLA INDEX =	CURRENT COSTS (CONSTANT DOLLARS)
Beginning balance					
Plant	$ 382,308	390/100	$ 1,491,001		
Equipment	114,692	190/100	217,915		
Equipment	34,375	190/120	54,427		
Equipment	42,000	190/150	53,200		
Equipment	68,000	190/180	71,778		
	$ 641,375		$ 1,888,321	215/205	$ 1,980,434
Plus acquisitions	None		None	215/215	None
Less depreciation	$ (41,375)[a]		$ (94,000)[a]	215/215	$ (94,000)
Less disposals (sales)	None		None	215/215	None
Ending balance					
Plant	$ 369,231	410/100	$ 1,513,847		
Equipment	110,769	210/100	232,615		
Equipment	25,000	210/120	43,750		
Equipment	35,000	210/150	49,000		
Equipment	60,000	210/180	70,000		
	$ 600,000		$ 1,909,212	215/220	$ 1,865,821
Increase in current costs— nominal dollars			$ 114,891[b]		
Decrease in current costs— constant dollars					$ (20,613)[b]

[a] These amounts are computed as follows:

HISTORICAL-COST DEPRECIATION	SPLA INDEX FOR AVERAGE 1985 PRICES	SPLA DEPRECIATION
$13,077	400/100	$52,308
3,923	200/100	7,846
9,375	200/120	15,625
7,000	200/150	9,333
8,000	200/180	8,888
$41,375		$94,000

[b] These amounts are computed by taking the difference in the ending balances with and without the current cost changes, computed as follows:

	CURRENT COST	
	NOMINAL DOLLARS	CONSTANT DOLLARS
Beginning balance	$1,888,321	$1,980,434
Less depreciation	94,000	94,000
Ending Balance (no price changes)	$1,794,321	$1,886,434
Ending balance after price changes	$1,909,212	$1,865,821
Ending balance ignoring price changes	1,794,321	1,886,434
Increase (decrease) in current costs	$ 114,891	$ (20,613)

more than the constant-dollar (GPLA) depreciation because the specific price levels for the depreciable assets have experienced greater price increases than the general price level. Specific prices will not necessarily increase (or decrease) more rapidly than the increase (or decrease) in general prices in every situation. For some assets the general price index may be increasing more rapidly than their specific price index.

The general framework for Exhibits 26–5 and 26–6 provide for acquisitions and disposals as well as for depreciation. Acquisitions would normally be added at average-of-the-period prices for both GPLA and SPLA computations and as a result would have an equal effect on historical and current-value measurements. Disposals would be accounted for like depreciation, with the historical book values of the sold assets being restated to GPLA or SPLA values. Disposals would *not* be included in depreciation expense.

Note that in Table 26–2 the specific price index of the equipment increased from 100 percent in 1975 to 180 percent in 1984, an increase of 80 percent, whereas the general price level index increased from 110 to 205 percent, an 86.4 percent increase during the same period. As a result, the January 1, 1985, GPLA value of the equipment purchased in 1975 ($213,744) was greater than the January 1, 1985, SPLA value ($206,446). Note also that this order changes during 1985 when the specific index overtakes the general index in the Sun Company example.

Plant and equipment The computation of the specific price increases in the plant and equipment account parallel those of inventory. There is no price increase measured in Exhibit 26–5 for the GPLA model. In Exhibit 26–6, however, steps 3, 4, and 5 of the restatement process are illustrated. First, depreciation expense (reported in part A of Exhibit 26–2) on a current cost (nominal dollars) basis is computed by taking the historical-cost amounts and converting them to current costs ($94,000). Then the price increase for 1985 included in the price-adjusted ending balances of plant and equipment are computed by comparing them with the ending balances that would have been reported if there had been no price changes during 1985. These no-price-change balances are found by the following formula:

	BEGINNING BALANCE	+	ACQUISITIONS	–	DEPRECIATION EXPENSE	–	DISPOSALS	=	BALANCE (NO PRICE CHANGE)
Historical cost	$ 641,375	+	0	–	$41,375	–	0	=	$ 600,000
Current costs—nominal dollars	$1,888,321	+	0	–	$94,000	–	0	=	$1,794,321
Current costs—constant dollars	$1,980,434	+	0	–	$94,000	–	0	=	$1,886,434

The difference between these balances and the price-adjusted balances represents the effect of the price increase during the period, or the realized and unrealized holding gains. In this case, the price increase (the total holding gain) on a current-cost/nominal-dollar basis was $114,891, while the price *decrease* on a current-cost/constant-dollar basis was $20,613.[8] These price increases, along with those

[8] See *Statement of Financial Accounting Standards No. 33*, par. 236. We find it very difficult to interpret the current-cost/constant-dollar measurements in the context of the statement. The $20,613 decrease seems to imply that general price changes were larger than specific price changes during the period since the general inflation effect ($114,891 + $20,613 = $135,504) is greater than the specific price change ($114,891). This may be observed by placing the $114,891 and the $(20,613) values into part C of Exhibit 26–2. Note from the index data in Table 26–2, however, that specific price increases for 1985 for both plant (over 5 percent) and equipment (over 10 percent) were greater than the change in the general price index—(215 – 205)/205 = 4.9 percent.

EXHIBIT 26–7

SUN COMPANY
Increase in Current Costs on Property
For the Year Ended December 31, 1985

ITEM	HISTORICAL COST	×	SPLA INDEX	=	CURRENT COSTS (NOMINAL DOLLARS)	×	GPLA INDEX	=	CURRENT COSTS (AVERAGE 1985 DOLLARS)
Beginning balance	$175,000		525/100		$ 918,750		215/205		$963,567
Plus purchases	—		—		—		215/215		—
Less depletion or amortization	—		—		—		215/215		—
Less disposals	—		—		—		215/215		—
Ending balance	$175,000		575/100		$1,006,250		215/220		$983,381
Increase in current costs—nominal dollars					$ 87,500				
Increase in current costs—constant dollars									$ 19,814

from inventory (Exhibit 26–4) and property (Exhibit 26–7) are summarized in Exhibit 26–8 to reconcile with part C of Exhibit 26–2.

Land   Exhibit 26–7 reconstructs the computations for measuring the price change in the Property account during 1985. There is no impact on operating income in part A of Exhibit 26–2. The price increases on a current cost/nominal dollar basis ($87,500) and on a current-cost/constant-dollar basis ($19,814) resulting from the Property account are summarized along with the other holding gains in Exhibit 26–8. The net result of this summary is the basis for the required disclosures illustrated in part C of Exhibit 26–2, with the difference between the specific-price-level effects and the general-price-level effects on the balance sheet assets reported in part C of Exhibit 26–2 ($22,129).

Other minimum disclosure data   In addition to the information illustrated in Exhibit 26–2, **FASB Statement No. 33** calls for 5-year summary data as outlined in item 3 on page 1005. These data are GPLA, SPLA, and historical in nature and are designed to provide trends in the current-value data in comparison with their historical-cost counterparts. An example of such disclosures for the General Motors Corporation (GM) is given in Schedule A of Exhibit 26–9.

EXHIBIT 26–8

SUN COMPANY
Summary of Current Cost Increases for 1985

Current Costs—Nominal Dollars	
From Inventory (Exhibit 26–4)	$ 74,439
From Plant and Equipment (Exhibit 26–6)	114,891
From Property (Exhibit 26–7)	87,500
Increase in specific prices for 1985—nominal dollars	$276,830
Current Costs—Constant Dollars	
From Inventory (Exhibit 26–4)	$ 22,928
From Plant and Equipment (Exhibit 26–6)	(20,613)
From Property (Exhibit 26–7)	19,814
Increase in specific prices for 1985—constant dollars	$ 22,129

Summary The kind of summary used in the primary current-cost and constant-dollar disclosures in Exhibit 26–2 is similar to that used in practice. Exhibits 26–3 to 26–8 are not normally reported and are not required but have been provided for the Sun Company example to illustrate the conversion of historical-cost data to GPLA and SPLA data. Schedule B of Exhibit 26–9 provides an actual example of **FASB Statement No. 33** disclosure for the General Motors Corporation. Note that for GM, both of the alternative models applied to inventory and plant assets alone

EXHIBIT 26–9

Schedule A

GENERAL MOTORS CORPORATION
Comparison of Selected Data Adjusted for Effects of Changing Prices
(Dollars in Millions Except Per Share Amounts)
Historical Cost Data Adjusted for General Inflation (Constant Dollar)
and Changes in Specific Prices (Current Cost)[a]

	1980	1979	1978	1977	1976
Net sales—as reported	$57,728.5	$66,311.2	$63,221.1	$54,961.3	$47,181.0
—in constant 1967 dollars	23,390.8	30,501.9	32,354.7	30,281.7	27,672.1
Net income (loss)—as reported	$ (762.5)	$ 2,892.7	$ 3,508.0	$ 3,337.5	$ 2,902.8
—in constant 1967 dollars	(1,023.8)[b]	817.0	1,384.5	1,580.9	1,485.4
—in current cost 1967 dollars	(829.5)[b]	829.5			
Earnings (loss) per share of common stock—as reported	$ (2.65)	$ 10.04	$ 12.24	$ 11.62	$ 10.08
—in constant 1967 dollars	(3.52)[b]	2.83	4.83	5.50	5.15
—in current cost 1967 dollars	(2.86)[b]	2.87			
Dividends per share of common stock—as reported	$ 2.95	$ 5.30	$ 6.00	$ 6.80	$ 5.55
—in constant 1967 dollars	1.20	2.44	3.07	3.75	3.26
Net income (loss) as a percent of sales—as reported	(1.3%)	4.4%	5.5%	6.1%	6.2%
—in constant 1967 dollars	(4.4)	2.7	4.3	5.2	5.4
—in current cost 1967 dollars	(3.5)	2.7			
Net income (loss) as a percent of stockholders' equity— as reported	(4.3%)	15.1%	20.0%	21.2%	20.2%
—in constant 1967 dollars	(9.4)	6.7	11.2	13.1	14.8
—in current cost 1967 dollars	(7.3)	6.4			
Net assets at year end—as reported	$17,814.6	$19,179.3	$17,569.9	$15,766.9	$14,385.2
—in constant 1967 dollars	10,887.6	12,163.4	12,351.3	12,041.4	10,007.7
—in current cost 1967 dollars	11,377.2	12,982.7			
Unrealized gain from decline in purchasing power of dollars of net amounts owed	$ 182.3	$ 83.8			
Increase in specific prices of inventory and property over increase in the general price level—net decrease	$ (689.2)	$ (221.8)			
Market price per common share at year-end—unadjusted	$ 45.00	$ 50.00	$ 53.75	$ 62.88	$ 78.50
—in constant 1967 dollars	18.23	23.00	27.51	34.64	46.04
Average Consumer Price Index	246.8	217.4	195.4	181.5	170.5

[a] Adjusted data have been determined by applying the Consumer Price Index—Urban to the data with 1967 (CPI–100) as the base year as specified by SFAS No. 33. Depreciation has been calculated on a straight-line basis for this calculation.

[b] These amounts will differ from those shown for constant dollar and current cost in Schedule B because a different base year has been used (1967 in Schedule A and 1980 in Schedule B) in order to illustrate the impact of changing prices in alternative forms.

EXHIBIT 26-9 (cont.)

Schedule B

Schedule of Income (Loss) Adjusted for Changing Prices
For the Year Ended December 31, 1980
(Dollars in Millions Except Per Share Amounts)

	AS REPORTED IN THE FINANCIAL STATEMENTS (HISTORICAL COST)	SELECTED DATA ADJUSTED FOR GENERAL INFLATION (1980 CONSTANT DOLLAR)	ADJUSTED FOR CHANGES IN SPECIFIC PRICES (1980 CURRENT COST)
Net sales	$57,728.5	$57,728.5	$57,728.5
Cost of sales	52,099.8	53,278.6	52,483.2
Depreciation and amortization expense	4,177.7	4,763.0	5,078.9
Other operating and nonoperating items—net	2,598.8	2,598.8	2,598.8
United States and other income taxes (credit)	(385.3)	(385.3)	(385.3)
Total costs and expenses	58,491.0	60,255.1	59,775.6
Net income (loss)	$ (762.5)	$ (2,526.6)[a]	$ (2,047.1)[a]
Earnings (loss) per share of common stock	$ (2.65)	$ (8.69)[a]	$ (7.05)[a]
Unrealized gain from decline in purchasing power of dollars of net amounts owed		$ 449.8	$ 449.8
Increase in specific prices of inventory and property over increase in general price level—net decrease			$ (1,700.9)[b]

[a] These amounts will differ from those shown for constant dollar and current cost in Schedule A because a different base year has been used (1967 in Schedule A and 1980 in Schedule B) in order to illustrate the impact of changing prices in alternative forms.

[b] At December 31, 1980 current cost of inventory was $9,015.7 million and current cost of real estate, plants and equipment (including special tools), net of accumulated depreciation and amortization, was $23,467.3 million. The current cost of property owned and the related depreciation and amortization expense were calculated by applying selected producer price indices to historical book values of machinery and equipment, the Marshall Valuation Service index to buildings and the use of assessed values for land.

Impact of Inflation on Financial Data

In recent years, the accounting profession has given a great deal of consideration to the question of reporting the impact of inflation on financial data. Many complex theories have been proposed and studied but none has received general acceptance. Nevertheless, all interested parties agree that inflation has an impact on financial data. Thus, in September 1979 the Financial Accounting Standards Board (FASB) issued Statement No. 33, *Financial Reporting and Changing Prices.* Statement No. 33 establishes standards for reporting certain effects of price changes on financial data. No one method is required by the Statement; instead, alternative methods are required in order to display various effects. The Statement is intended to help readers of financial data assess results in the following specific areas:
   a. The erosion of general purchasing power,
   b. Enterprise performance,
   c. The erosion of operating capability, and
   d. Future cash flows.
The accompanying Schedules display the basic historical cost financial data adjusted for general inflation (constant dollar) and also for changes in specific prices (current cost) for use in such assessments.
In reviewing these Schedules, the following comments may be of assistance in understanding the reasons for the different ''income'' amounts and the uses of the data.

Financial statements—historical cost base
The objective of financial statements, and the primary purpose of accounting, is to furnish, to the fullest extent practicable, objective, quantifiable summaries of the results of financial transactions to those who need or wish to judge management's ability to manage. The data are prepared by management and independently verified by the independent public accountants.

EXHIBIT 26-9 (cont.)

The present accounting system in general use in the United States and the financial statements prepared by major companies from that system were never intended to be measures of relative economic value, but instead are basically a history of transactions which have occurred and by which current and potential investors and creditors can evaluate their expectations. There are many subjective, analytical, and economic factors which must be taken into consideration when evaluating a company. Those factors cannot be quantified objectively. Just as the financial statements cannot present in reasonable, objective, quantifiable form all of the data necessary to evaluate a business, they also should not be expected to furnish all the data needed to evaluate the impact of inflation on a company.

Data adjusted for general inflation—constant dollar base

Financial reporting is, of necessity, stated in dollars. It is generally recognized that the purchasing power of a dollar has deteriorated in recent years, and the costs of raw materials and other items as well as wage rates have increased and can be expected to increase further in the future. It is not as generally recognized, however, that profit dollars also are subject to the same degree of reduction in purchasing power. Far too much attention is given to the absolute level of profits rather than the relationship of profits to other factors in the business and to the general price level. For example, as shown in the accompanying Schedule A, adjusting the annual amount of sales and net income (loss) to a constant 1967 dollar base, using the U.S. Bureau of Labor Statistics' Consumer Price Index for Urban Consumers, demonstrates that constant dollar profits have not increased in recent years in line with the changes in sales volume. This is reflected in the general decline in the net income as a percent of sales over that period as well as the decrease in the dividend paid in terms of constant dollars of purchasing power.

Data adjusted for changes in specific prices—current cost

Another manner in which to analyze the impact of inflation on financial data (and thus the business) is by adjusting the historical cost data to the current costs for the major balance sheet items which have been accumulated through the accounting system over a period of years and which thus reflect different prices for the same commodities and services.

The purpose of this type of restatement is to furnish estimates of the impact of price increases for replacement of inventories and property on the potential future net income of the business and thus assess the probability of future cash flows. Although these data may be useful for this purpose, they do not reflect specific plans for the replacement of property. A more meaningful estimate of the impact of such costs or future earnings is the estimated level of future capital expenditures which is set forth in the Financial Review: Management's Discussion and Analysis (page 12).

Summary

In the accompanying Schedules, the effects of the application of the preceding methods on the past five years' and the current year's operations are summarized. Under both the constant dollar and the current cost methods, the net income (loss) of the business is lower (higher) than that determined under the historical cost method. What does this mean? It means that business, as well as individuals, is affected by inflation and that the purchasing power of business dollars also has declined. In addition, the costs of maintaining the productive capacity, as reflected in the current cost data (and estimate of future capital expenditures), have increased, and thus management must seek ways to cope with the impact of inflation through accounting methods such as the Last-In, First-Out (LIFO) method of inventory valuation, which matches current costs with current revenues, and through accelerated methods of depreciation.

Another significant adjustment is the restatement of stockholders' equity—the investment base. The adjustment for general inflation (constant dollar) puts all the expenditures for these items on a consistent purchasing power basis—the average 1967 dollar. This adjustment decreases the historical stockholders' equity, as represented by net assets in Schedule A, of about $17.8 billion to a constant dollar basis of $10.9 billion. In other words, the $17.8 billion represented in the financial statements has only $10.9 billion of purchasing power expressed in 1967 dollars. The net assets adjusted for specific prices (current cost restated in 1967 dollars), as shown in Schedule A, amounted to $11.4 billion. This is $0.5 billion higher than that shown on a constant dollar basis due to the fact that the CPI–U index is accelerating more rapidly than the indices of specific prices applicable to General Motors.

Finally, it must be emphasized that there is a critical need for national monetary and fiscal policies designed to control inflation and to provide adequate capital for future business growth which, in turn, will mean increased productivity and employment.

resulted in losses well over $1 billion greater than the loss reported on a historical-cost basis, as reported in Schedule B.

The general impression from the comparative data provided in Schedule B is that, although GM's operations reported a loss for the historical-cost model, the magnitude of the reported operating loss would have been considerably greater if either the GPLA or SPLA model had been used. Based on the GPLA adjustments to cost of goods sold and depreciation expense alone, GM's shareholders are told that the operating loss would have been over $2.5 billion, more than three times that reported on a historical basis, causing each common shareholder's share of the loss to increase by over $6.00 per share.

The magnitude of the impact of GM's operating results adjusted for price changes is certainly substantial. While interpretations of such piecemeal disclosures must be made with caution, it seems clear that from a current-value perspective, GM's operating results were much worse than reported under the historical-cost model. The summary data in Schedule A also reveal that net income from 1976 to 1979 as reported on a historical basis was overstated when compared to net income measured on a constant-dollar basis. Note that if the constant-dollar earnings per share data were considered to be a more appropriate measure of the change in wealth than historical-cost EPS, GM would be considered to have paid dividends in excess of earnings from 1976 to 1980 since the actual cash dividends ($2.95 in 1980, $5.30 in 1979, and so on) exceeded the constant-dollar ESP data—($3.52) in 1980, $2.83 in 1979, and so on—each year! The concept of liquidating dividends by GM seems consistent with the changes in the market price of GM stock over the 1976 to 1980 period, which declined by about 43 percent from the 1976 price of $78.50 per share to the 1980 price of $45.00 per share.

COMPREHENSIVE DISCLOSURE UNDER FASB STATEMENT NO. 33

The Sun Company example in the previous section illustrated the minimum disclosures required by **FASB Statement No. 33**. These disclosures are what virtually all companies affected by this pronouncement have provided. However, *comprehensive current-cost and/or constant-dollar data* are also permitted by the FASB pronouncements. Because some companies may report comprehensive current-cost or constant-dollar financial statement data, we shall now illustrate comprehensive constant-dollar data for the Sun Company.

Comprehensive
Constant-
Dollar Data

The balance sheet and income statement data for the Sun Company that were illustrated under the minimum disclosure requirements may be somewhat misleading in that only selective data were reported at their constant-dollar or current-cost amounts. We might argue that if either constant-dollar or current-cost data are useful for inventory, plant, property, and equipment, why aren't they useful for other assets and liabilities as well? The answer is that the above-mentioned assets were singled out for special treatment because of their significance relative to other assets. Still, for some entities, other assets may be of equal or greater importance, and therefore comprehensive statements may be necessary to provide users with a better estimate of the impact of changing prices on the entity's financial position.

To compare the minimum disclosures with comprehensive disclosures, consider the Sun Companay data once again. The conventional balance sheet and income statement for 1985 shown in Exhibit 26–1 are completely converted to constant-dollar statements stated **in terms of 1985 year-end dollars** in the exhibits that follow.

It should be noted that one of the differences between the minimum and the comprehensive disclosures is the general or specific index that may be used. For minimum levels of disclosure, **average-of-the-period price indexes** must be used for the constant-dollar model. However, if comprehensive disclosure is elected, **end-of-period price indexes may be used.** The illustrations for the Sun Company's comprehensive constant-dollar statements are based on the year-end price index data, and the other price index data are taken from Table 26–2.

In Exhibit 26–10 the conventional balance sheet for 1985 is converted to constant dollars (GPLA) based on 1985 year-end dollars. All nonmonetary items are

EXHIBIT
26–10

		SUN COMPANY		
		Balance Sheet		
		As of December 31, 1985		
	HISTORICAL COST BALANCE	**GPLA FACTOR**	**GPLA BALANCE**
Assets			
Cash and accounts receivable	$ 350,000	Monetary asset	$ 350,000
Inventories	420,000	[a]	608,628
Temporary investments	80,000	[b]	94,865
Plant and equipment (net of $300,000 accumulated depreciation)	600,000	[c]	1,116,667
Property	175,000	220/110	350,000
Patents and licenses (net)	45,000	220/180	55,000
Total assets	$1,670,000		$2,575,160
Liabilities			
Accounts and accrued payables	$ 350,000	Monetary liability	$ 350,000
Long-term note (due 2010)	500,000	Monetary liability	500,000
Common stock (no par)	600,000	220/110	1,200,000
Retained earnings	220,000		525,160
Total liabilities and shareholders' equity	$1,670,000		$2,575,160

[a] See Exhibit 26–12 for details.
[b] See Exhibit 26–14 for details.
[c] See Exhibit 26–13 for details.

converted, with monetary items remaining the same in both conventional and GPLA balance sheets. Because the composition of three of the assets—inventories, plant and equipment, and temporary investments—is complex (made up of a number of items at different costs), the details of their conversion to 1985 year-end values are provided in supplementary schedules in Exhibits 26–12, 26–13, and 26–14. Also, the conventional and GPLA income statements illustrated in Exhibit 26–11 refer to the supporting details of Exhibits 26–12, 26–13, and 26–14.

Inventories/cost of goods sold Note that the GPLA cost of goods sold in Exhibit 26–11 ($1,258,605) is different from the GPLA cost of goods sold in Exhibit 26–2 ($1,230,000). This difference is attributable to the use of year-end GPLA values in the comprehensive illustration. Because year-end prices are used, even the purchases of $1,300,000 stated in terms of average 1985 prices must be converted to year-end constant dollars. The ending inventory at year-end constant dollars ($608,628) is $13,833 greater than it was in the earlier example (Exhibit 26–3) based on average 1985 constant dollars. Since everything in the comprehensive disclosure for inventory and cost of goods sold (Exhibit 26–12) is being converted to index 220 dollars instead of index 215 dollars, we would expect Exhibits 26–3 and 26–12 to be completely different. Note, however, that all of the amounts in Exhibit

EXHIBIT
26–11

SUN COMPANY

Income Statement

For the Year Ended December 31, 1985

		HISTORICAL COST BALANCE	GPLA FACTOR	GPLA BALANCE
Sales revenue		$2,700,000	220/215	$2,762,791
Cost of goods sold				
Beginning inventory	$ 350,000			
Plus net purchases	1,300,000			
Goods available for sale	$1,650,000			
Less ending inventory	420,000	1,230,000	a	1,258,605
Gross margin		$1,470,000		$1,504,186
Other expenses				
Selling and administrative expense		800,000	220/215	818,605
Amortization expense		5,000	220/180	6,111
Depreciation expense		41,375	b	68,633
Income tax expense		311,812	220/220	311,812
Income from operations		$ 311,813		$ 299,025
Net monetary gain (loss)		0		33,590
Net income		$ 311,813		$ 332,615

ᵃ See Exhibit 26–12 for details.

ᵇ See Exhibit 26–13 for details.

26–3 when multiplied by 220/215 will result in their Exhibit 26–12 counterparts. For example, ending inventory in Exhibit 26–3 would be reconciled with ending inventory in Exhibit 26–12 as follows:

INDEX 215 DOLLARS				INDEX 220 DOLLARS
$594,795	×	220/215	=	$608,628

Of course this relationship is true for other assets as well.

EXHIBIT
26–12

SUN COMPANY

Constant-Dollar Model—Supporting Data for
Inventory and Cost of Goods Sold—Comprehensive Disclosure

ITEM	DATE OF PURCHASE	GPLA AT PURCHASE	HISTORICAL COST OF PURCHASE	GPLA FACTOR	GPLA VALUATION
Beginning inventory	1/1/75	110	$ 120,000	220/110	$ 240,000
	6/30/78	150	120,000	220/150	176,000
	6/30/83	200	110,000	220/200	121,000
			$ 350,000		$ 537,000
Purchases	1/1/85–12/31/85	215	$1,300,000	220/215	$1,330,233
Cost of goods available			$1,650,000		$1,867,233
Ending inventory (LIFO)	1/1/75	110	$ 120,000	220/110	$ 240,000
	6/30/78	150	120,000	220/150	176,000
	6/30/83	200	110,000	220/200	121,000
	6/30/85	215	70,000	220/215	71,628
			$ 420,000		$ 608,628
Cost of goods sold			$1,230,000		$1,258,605

Plant and equipment The comprehensive restatement of plant and equipment in terms of 1985 end-of-period constant dollars follows a process similar to that illustrated in Exhibit 26–5. Note that the GPLA depreciation expense in Exhibit 26–13 is simply the depreciation expense from Exhibit 26–5 multiplied by 220/215 ($67,073 × 220/215 = $68,633). The same is true for all the other comparative data between the two exhibits.

Temporary investments The conversion of the historical-cost values of temporary investments to end-of-period GPLA values requires information about the general price index at the date of acquisition just as the price index of inventory layers was necessary for converting inventory. The assumed layers provided in Exhibit 26–14 indicate three different purchases of temporary investments have been made. The GPLA value of $94,865 is $14,865 greater than the price paid for the temporary investments. We should point out that the GPLA value of $94,865 may not even be

EXHIBIT
26–13

SUN COMPANY
Constant-Dollar Model—Supporting Data for Depreciation Expense and Ending Plant and Equipment— Comprehensive Disclosure

Beginning Balance

ITEM	DATE OF ACQUISITION	GPLA INDEX AT ACQUISITION	HISTORICAL COST NET BOOK VALUE 1/1/85	GPLA INDEX FOR ENDING 1985 PRICES	GPLA NET BOOK VALUE AT 1/1/85
Plant	1/1/75	110	$382,308	205/110	$ 712,483
Equipment	1/1/75	110	114,692	205/110	213,744
Equipment	1/1/77	125	34,375	205/125	56,375
Equipment	12/31/80	165	42,000	205/165	52,182
Equipment	6/30/83	200	68,000	205/200	69,700
			$641,375		$1,104,484

Less Depreciation

ITEM	DATE OF ACQUISITION	GPLA INDEX AT ACQUISITION	HISTORICAL COST DEPRECIATION	GPLA INDEX FOR ENDING 1985 PRICES	GPLA DEPRECIA- TION
Plant	1/1/75	110	$ 13,077	220/110	$ 26,154
Equipment	1/1/75	110	3,923	220/110	7,846
Equipment	1/1/77	125	9,375	220/125	16,500
Equipment	12/31/80	165	7,000	220/165	9,333
Equipment	6/30/83	200	8,000	220/200	8,800
			$ 41,375		$ 68,633

Ending Balance

ITEM	DATE OF ACQUISITION	GPLA INDEX AT ACQUISITION	HISTORICAL COST NET BOOK VALUE 12/31/85	GPLA INDEX FOR ENDING 1985 PRICES	GPLA NET BOOK VALUE AT 12/31/85
Plant	1/1/75	110	$369,231	220/110	$ 738,462
Equipment	1/1/75	110	110,769	220/110	221,538
Equipment	1/1/77	125	25,000	220/125	44,000
Equipment	12/31/80	165	35,000	220/165	46,667
Equipment	6/30/83	200	60,000	220/200	66,000
			$600,000		$1,116,667

EXHIBIT
26–14

SUN COMPANY				
Constant-Dollar Model—Supporting Data for				
Temporary Investments—Comprehensive Disclosure				
Ending Balance—December 31, 1985				
DATE OF ACQUISITION	GPLA AT DATE OF ACQUISITION	HISTORICAL COST AT DATE OF ACQUISITION	GPLA FACTOR	GPLA VALUATION
6/30/79	160	$20,000	220/160	$27,500
12/31/81	180	30,000	220/180	36,667
6/30/85	215	30,000	220/215	30,698
		$80,000		$94,865

close to the actual fair market value of the temporary investments. The $94,865 is the original cost of $80,000 restated in terms of 1985 year-end (index 220) dollars.

Income statement and balance sheet Without the comparative balance sheet data on either a constant-dollar or a conventional basis for December 31, 1984, there is no way to completely relate the GPLA income statement and balance sheet to one another or to the conventional statements. However, several additional points might be noted regarding the comprehensive example. First, GPLA revenues are *not* the same as conventional revenues. This is the result of using a 1985 year-end index rather than the 1985 average index. The extension of revenues as well as selling and administrative expense by 220/215 suggests that these revenues and expenditures took place evenly throughout 1985. Alternatively, tax payments were made in year-end (index 220) dollars, whereas amortization related to intangibles acquired with 1981 year-end (index 180) dollars.

Note that the 1985 GPLA income from operations and net monetary gain are different from those reported for the earlier GPLA example. These differences are the result of stating everything in terms of *year-end* (index 220) dollars instead of average-of-the-period (index 215) dollars, plus the fact that all nonmonetary items are adjusted in the comprehensive case, but only inventory, plant, property, and equipment are adjusted in the minimum disclosure case.

Although most companies affected by **FASB Statement No. 33** have provided the minimum disclosure as an unaudited footnote to their annual reports, some entities have provided *comprehensive* disclosures of current-cost and constant-dollar financial statements. An example of such comprehensive disclosure in Alcan Aluminum Limited's 1980 annual report is provided in Exhibit 26–15.

USING CURRENT-VALUE DISCLOSURES

In order to use current-value disclosures effectively for economic decision making, it is necessary to understand the underlying nature of these alternatives to the historical-cost model.[9] Two major aspects of current-value data must be understood before using these data for decision making:

[9] Certainly a great deal of time could be consumed in reading all the literature that discusses the strengths, weaknesses, and assumptions of the models that offer alternatives to historical cost. The basic notion that is considered to be pivotal, however, is the underlying definition of wealth or well-offness being measured by any given alternative model. If the wealth measure makes sense for a given decision-making situation, then the model applying that wealth measure is likely to provide useful information for decision making.

1. What exactly is being measured in the alternative models?
2. Is one model more relevant than the others for decision making?

What Is Being Measured? The historical-cost (conventional accounting) data, the constant-dollar data, and the current-cost data are all measuring the wealth position (balance sheet) and change in wealth (income and funds statements) of the accounting entity. Each of the three

EXHIBIT 26-15

COMPREHENSIVE CONSTANT-DOLLAR AND CURRENT-COST DISCLOSURES EXAMPLE

ALCAN ALUMINUM LIMITED

Inflation Accounting

The need for inflation accounting is becoming more obvious, but confusion as to method persists. However, most people in North America seem to agree that the historical cost basis should be retained for the basic financial statements and that the effects of inflation should be presented as supplementary data.

    The Financial Accounting Standards Board (FASB) in the United States in their FAS 33 has now called for a five-year period of experimentation, with the two methods—Current Purchasing Power (CPP) and Current Cost (CC)—being reported in parallel. Accordingly, Alcan presents several statements which compare the financial results for 1979 and 1980 under these different methods of accounting, as well as certain data required by FAS 33 for the past five years.

    Historical cost (HC) is the actual cost which was incurred to acquire an asset or service, and is that reported in the basic financial statements.

    CPP starts with HC and, using the U.S. Consumer Price Index (CPI), restates HC amounts into dollars having equal purchasing power. Thus, for example, a dollar spent in 1976 would be equal to $1.48 in terms of 1980 current purchasing power. It is important to note that these results do not reflect the current cost of particular assets, goods or services in the 1980 market; rather they reflect a general rate of inflation. Also, CPP does not change the generally accepted accounting principles used in recording transactions at historical costs; only the unit of measurement is changed.

    CC focuses upon the changing prices of specific assets, goods and services and measures the current value in terms of what those items would have cost when they were used or sold.

CC Methodology

Alcan's larger subsidiaries have reviewed their assets in detail and have developed the current cost by using reliable market prices or by applying appropriate specific price indexes to the historical costs of specific assets or groups of assets. For smaller subsidiaries where the amounts are not significant and for the equity-accounted companies, the CPI was applied to historical costs as in the CPP method. Straight-line depreciation was calculated using the same method and asset life as in the basic HC financial statements. CC cost of sales was determined by adjusting historical costs by the estimated inflation which occurred during the period between the time of production and the time of sale. The amounts so derived were then computed in terms of year-end 1980 dollars for the accompanying statements.

    For property, plant and equipment, this method measures the current cost of replacement of assets using existing technology in current dollars.

    Although FAS 33 only calls for a restatement of certain HC items on the CC basis, we have developed a comprehensive set of statements in which inventories and property, plant and equipment were determined by application of the CC method described above and all other accounts, except shareholders' equity and minority interests, were derived by application of the CPP concept.

Conclusions

Both the CPP and CC methods undoubtedly give more realistic results than HC by eliminating the effects of inflation, but the audience is less familiar with these. The CPP method is precise but the results are only approximate for given assets. The CC method permits application of judgment in determining many amounts and is therefore open to some degree of scepticism by the reader. Alcan's use of specific price indexes has for the most part removed the judgment factor.

    Both methods confirm that Alcan's HC earnings are dramatically reduced when the effects of inflation are taken into account as evidenced by the resulting rates of return.

    It is interesting to note that over the years, since Alcan's property, plant and equipment were acquired, the effects of inflation in the construction industry have been much greater than the general rate of inflation as indicated by the CPI. However, during the last two years the reverse situation has prevailed.

    There are criticisms of the general index used in CPP, as a measurement of the general rate of inflation, and there are also many pitfalls in the CC method, particularly the subjective judgment aspect, which are troublesome. We welcome the FASB's policy of introducing a five-year period of experimentation with both methods and we believe this will allow time for development of the concepts and for resolution of at least some of the problems of implementation which are bound to arise. Hopefully this will enable everybody to agree on a method of inflation accounting which is conceptually sound and precise, and is intelligible to the users of the statements.

EXHIBIT 26–15 (cont.)

Inflation Accounting

Consolidated Balance Sheet—31 December
In Millions of U.S. Dollars

	HISTORICAL AS REPORTED		CPP IN TERMS OF YEAR-END 1980 DOLLARS		CC IN TERMS OF YEAR-END 1980 DOLLARS	
	1980	1979	1980	1979	1980	1979
Current assets excluding inventories	1,131	1,055	1,131	1,186	1,131	1,186
Inventories	1,436	1,134	1,561	1,383	1,538	1,361
Deferred receivables and charges	136	133	136	149	136	149
Investments in companies owned 50% or less	326	253	568	492	568	492
Property, plant and equipment—net	2,441	1,915	3,339	2,961	4,068	3,796
	5,470	4,490	6,735	6,171	7,441	6,984
Current liabilities	1,194	914	1,194	1,027	1,194	1,027
Long-term debt	910	759	910	854	910	854
Deferred income taxes and credits	629	510	629	573	629	573
Minority interests	274	275	406	428	431	474
Shareholders' equity	2,463	2,032	3,596	3,289	4,277	4,056
	5,470	4,490	6,735	6,171	7,441	6,984
Rate of return on average capital employed (%)	16	16	9	8	7	7
Rate of return on average shareholders' equity (%)	24	23	12	10	9	7

Consolidated Net Income Information
In Millions of U.S. Dollars

	AS REPORTED IN THE FINANCIAL STATEMENTS (HC)		AS ADJUSTED FOR GENERAL INFLATION (CPP)		AS ADJUSTED FOR CHANGES IN SPECIFIC PRICES (CC)	
	IN HISTORICAL DOLLARS		IN YEAR-END 1980 DOLLARS		IN YEAR-END 1980 DOLLARS	
	1980	1979	1980	1979	1980	1979
Sales and operating revenues	5,215	4,390	5,461	5,218	5,461	5,218
Cost of sales and operating expenses	3,682	3,240	3,993	3,998	3,976	3,952
Depreciation expense	162	149	311	313	370	383
Selling, research and administrative expenses	352	308	369	366	369	366
Interest	107	114	112	135	112	135
Income taxes	393	211	412	251	412	251
Other	(23)	(38)	(24)	(45)	(24)	(45)
Indexing adjustments	—	—	10	53	32	54
	4,673	3,984	5,183	5,071	5,247	5,096
Income from continuing operations	542	406	278	147	214	122
Extraordinary item	—	21	—	(7)	—	(7)
Holding gain on monetary items	—	—	145	171	145	171
Net income for the year	542	427	423	311	359	286
Inventories and property, plant and equipment						
Increase in general price level (CCP)					616	720
Increase in specific prices (CC)					522	316
Excess of increase in general price level over increase in specific prices					94	404

financial statement measurements is different simply because each measurement defines wealth differently from the others.

Historical cost Historical cost measures the entity's financial position and changes in financial position in terms of original transaction values. The balance sheets reported under a historical-cost model are based on the original transaction amounts for assets, liabilities, and equities year after year, and historical-cost income flows and funds are measured in terms of original transaction values. As a result, the entity's reported net assets or wealth position and flow of wealth in the financial statements include dollar unit measures from a number of different time periods as the result of basic computations' being performed on dollar measures from different time periods.

Constant dollar The constant-dollar model defines wealth and changes in wealth in terms of uniform purchasing power units. The uniform purchasing power unit may take various forms, but for current GAAP reporting requirements it must be defined in terms of CPI–U purchasing power units. The constant-dollar model accounts for assets, liabilities, and equities in terms of uniform dollar units of purchasing power. Also, the income flows and funds flows are measured in terms of uniform dollars. The uniform dollar measure (or purchasing power unit) required for use in constant-dollar information is the *current* purchasing power unit. In other words, all dollars are converted (restated) in terms of current period dollars (current period purchasing power units).

The constant-dollar financial statements permit users to assess the impact of the changes in the unit of measure (the dollar) on the entity's financial well-being and to evaluate the entity's performance in light of changes in the unit of measure. For example, operating profits attributable to changes in the measurement unit ("holding gains") could be part of the historical-dollar operating income measure. Constant-dollar financial statements are based on mathematical manipulations of like measurements that are defined in terms of purchasing power units of a particular period.

Current cost The current-cost model defines wealth in terms of the replacement cost of the entity's existing productive capacity. This model seeks to measure wealth by holding constant the ability to produce at a desired level of activity. Whereas the capital maintenance concept underlying historical cost is based on original transaction amounts, and the constant-dollar model is oriented toward capital maintenance in terms of purchasing power, the current-cost model seeks to maintain capital in terms of productive capacity. In theory, under the current-cost model, income would not be recognized unless the entity's productive capacity (net assets stated at their current replacement values net of depreciation, and so on) at the end of the period (prior to the distribution of dividends) were greater than its productive capacity at the beginning of the period.

The current-cost model measures assets, liabilities, and equities in terms of their current replacement values, or the cost that would be incurred to replace their equivalent productive capacity (utility) to the entity. The income flows and funds flows are similarly defined in the context of current replacement values. Current-cost operating income would *not* include a profit component attributable to changes in the specific prices of assets consumed in the income-generating process. As a result, operating income from the current-cost model is a measure of the profitability of operations without the effects of holding gains from price changes in the assets used in the income-generating process (inventory, machinery, labor, and so on). As in the constant-dollar model, the current-cost model performs mathematical manipulations on like measures, which in this case are defined in terms of current replacement dollar units of measure.

Current cost/constant dollars Under the minimum disclosures per **FASB Statement No. 33** we illustrated a measure of price change called current costs/constant dollars (see Exhibits 26–4 and 26–6), which adjusts the sum of the current-cost holding gains for the effects of general inflation in a way that is somewhat unique. While many have advocated combining the GPLA model with other current-value models, the current-cost/constant-dollar method illustrated earlier was provided because it is required under GAAP. We do not refer to minimum **FASB Statement No. 33** disclosures as resulting from any model per se because of the fact that they are fragmented disclosures that are incomplete.

Capital
Maintenance
and Change
in Wealth

The difference between the three measurement alternatives (historical cost, constant dollar, and current cost) might best be viewed from the balance sheet perspective. The balance sheet can be viewed as a statement of the entity's wealth position at a point in time, with changes in the balance sheet reflecting changes in wealth. Consider the example in Exhibit 26–16. The Wrobleski Corporation balance sheets for the three alternative models at the end of period 1 are all different because of the different measurement unit employed in each model. By comparing the data at the end of period 1, we can conclude that general price levels of prior periods have changed more rapidly than specific price levels because the constant-dollar asset measurement is greater than the current-cost (nominal dollars) measurement.

Assume that during period 2, Wrobleski has *no operating activity.* Note that although the historical-cost model would record *no change* in wealth position between period 1 and period 2, the constant-dollar and current-cost models record increases in wealth during period 2.[10] Based on the assumed circumstances, there were increases in both the general price level (10 percent) and the specific price levels (various) during period 2; hence the change in the Wrobleski Corporation's wealth position.

Assume that during period 3 there are *no* general or specific price changes and that the single event that occurs is the sale of all inventory for $100. All three models once again result in different positions. The change in wealth under histori-

---

[10] Specifically, the GPLA change in wealth was $2.5, measured as follows:

	IN TERMS OF END-OF-PERIOD 2 DOLLARS
Ending retained earnings	$195.0
− Beginning retained earnings	
($175 × 1.10%)	192.5
Increase in retained earnings	$ 2.5

The SPLA change in wealth is measured in several different ways but would equal $25 including both realized and unrealized holding gains, but *not* including the purchasing power gain from being in a net monetary liability position during a period of inflation.

cal cost is $+\$25$, whereas constant-dollar wealth change is $-\$10$ and current-cost wealth change is $+\$5$. These three concepts of wealth will, by definition, result in different measures of financial position, and changes in financial position, from one period to another.

Is One Model More Relevant Than the Others for Decision Making? Understanding the differences between the various accounting models will help us to decide whether one particular model is most relevant in a specific situation. In a general sense, given no information about the objective of a specific decision maker who is seeking to use accounting information, the question cannot be answered. Put another way, each one of the alternatives may be the most relevant given certain specific decision-making goals and objectives on the part of the user. It is impossible to provide specific examples concerning which type of accounting information is the most relevant to certain user decisions, even for relatively common decisions such as

EXHIBIT 26–16

ALTERNATIVE WEALTH MEASURES

THE WROBLESKI CORPORATION

END OF PERIOD 1		END OF PERIOD 2		END OF PERIOD 3	
HISTORICAL-COST BALANCE SHEET		**HISTORICAL-COST BALANCE SHEET**		**HISTORICAL-COST BALANCE SHEET**	
ASSETS	LIABILITIES AND EQUITIES	ASSETS	LIABILITIES AND EQUITIES	ASSETS	LIABILITIES AND EQUITIES
Cash $ 25	Accounts	Cash $ 25	Accounts	Cash $125	Accounts
Inventory 75	payable $ 50	Inventory 75	payable $ 50	Inventory 0	payable $ 50
Plant 100	Stock 50	Plant 100	Stock 50	Plant 100	Stock 50
	Retained earnings 100		Retained earnings 100		Retained earnings 125
$200	$200	$200	$200	$225	$225

CONSTANT-DOLLAR BALANCE SHEET		**CONSTANT-DOLLAR BALANCE SHEET**		**CONSTANT-DOLLAR BALANCE SHEET**	
ASSETS	LIABILITIES AND EQUITIES	ASSETS	LIABILITIES AND EQUITIES	ASSETS	LIABILITIES AND EQUITIES
Cash $ 25	Accounts	Cash $ 25	Accounts	Cash $125	Accounts
Inventory 100	payable $ 50	Inventory 110	payable $ 50	Inventory 0	payable $ 50
Plant 200	Stock 100	Plant 220	Stock 110	Plant 220	Stock 110
	Retained earnings 175		Retained earnings 195		Retained earnings 185
$325	$325	$355	$355	$345	$345

CURRENT-COST BALANCE SHEET		**CURRENT-COST BALANCE SHEET**		**CURRENT-COST BALANCE SHEET**	
ASSETS	LIABILITIES AND EQUITIES	ASSETS	LIABILITIES AND EQUITIES	ASSETS	LIABILITIES AND EQUITIES
Cash $ 25	Accounts	Cash $ 25	Accounts	Cash $125	Accounts
Inventory 85	payable $ 50	Inventory 95	payable $ 50	Inventory 0	payable $ 50
Plant 165	Stock 50	Plant 180	Stock 50	Plant 180	Stock 50
	Retained earnings 175		Retained earnings 200		Retained earnings 205
$275	$275	$300	$300	$305	$305

TABLE 26-3

CORPORATE MANAGEMENT'S VIEWS REGARDING USEFULNESS OF FASB STATEMENT NO. 33

ON THE HISTORICAL-COST/CONSTANT-DOLLAR BASIS

		(NUMBER OF RESPONSES INDICATING)			
RESTATED AMOUNT	AVERAGE SCORE OF RESPONSES[a]	VERY USEFUL	SOMEWHAT USEFUL	NOT USEFUL	NO RESPONSE
1. Dividends per share	1.9	57	97	39	5
2. Five-year trend data	2.0	52	100	45	1
3. Effective tax rate	2.1	59	65	69	5
4. Market price per share	2.1	44	85	67	2
5. Purchasing power gain or loss	2.1	32	106	59	1
6. Income from continuing operations	2.2	25	100	72	1
7. Dividend payout ratio	2.3	29	77	81	11
8. Return on investment	2.3	18	85	82	13
9. Net assets	2.4	9	96	90	3

ON THE CURRENT-COST BASIS

		(NUMBER OF RESPONSES INDICATING)			
RESTATED AMOUNT	AVERAGE SCORE OF RESPONSES[a]	VERY USEFUL	SOMEWHAT USEFUL	NOT USEFUL	NO RESPONSE
1. Effective tax rate	1.9	72	65	50	11
2. Five-year trend data	1.9	50	98	36	14
3. Income from continuing operations	2.0	40	104	47	7
4. Dividends per share	2.1	34	69	46	49
5. Dividend payout ratio	2.1	34	84	58	22
6. Purchasing power gain or loss	2.2	27	81	56	34
7. Net assets	2.2	18	118	53	9
8. Return on investment	2.2	24	92	61	21
9. Market price per share	2.3	21	63	68	46
10. Net holding gain or loss[b]	2.3	12	102	74	10

[a] The average score is based on the weighted average of responses; "very useful" = 1, "somewhat useful" = 2, "not useful" = 3.
[b] Not applicable under the historical cost/constant dollar method.
Source: Arthur Young & Company, *Financial Reporting and Changing Prices: A Survey of Preparers' Views and Practices* (New York: Arthur Young & Company, 1981), p. 9.

credit granting or investing, because of the differences between individuals. People make choices and economic decisions based on their own individual preferences, which are sometimes referred to as their individual **utility functions.** Because there is no reason to believe that these sets of preferences are or should be the same for everyone, relevance becomes a matter of individual choice. The fact that no single type of accounting data can be judged superior for all users in all decision-making situations is precisely the reason why alternatives to historical-cost (conventional) accounting data have gained wide support.

Although it is not possible to make definitive statements regarding the preferability of one accounting model over another, it is interesting nevertheless to learn that certain information is becoming the "most acceptable" alternative information. A great deal of research has attempted to discover what aspect of the supplementary disclosures certain interest groups prefer and why. In a survey taken by a major CPA firm after 2 years' experience with **FASB Statement No. 33,** over 200 corporations (all of which prepare the current-value disclosures) indicated a 2-to-1 preference for current-cost data over constant-dollar data.[11] In this survey, the corporations were asked what they considered to be the most useful of the current-cost and constant-dollar restated data reported as a result of **FASB Statement No. 33**.[12] As Table 26–3 indicates, different items were considered useful for the two different sets of restated data. Note in particular the increased significance of income from continuing operations on a current-cost basis versus the constant-dollar equivalent. The tax rate and dividend data were also considered useful from management's perspective. Although these views do not necessarily represent those of all corporate managers, and may have little similarity with the views of external users of financial statement data, they are probably indicative of the trend that will develop in future current-value disclosures since management is the group responsible for preparing the financial statements.

Despite our being unable to make absolute statements about the preferability of one type of accounting data to another, we can make broad generalizations. Users who are interested in data that will enable them to evaluate their financial position (wealth) in terms of general purchasing power units will probably prefer constant-dollar accounting data. Also, individuals interested in evaluating their wealth and change in wealth in terms of current values (either current-dollar units or current replacement values or perhaps current market values) will not find historical-cost data useful in periods of changing prices. In certain situations, however, such as those involving debt contracts that are written with various covenants based on historical-cost data, historical costs may be the most relevant. Decisions related to the debt agreement would probably ignore the accounting data based on alternative models.

[11] Arthur Young & Company, *Financial Reporting and Changing Prices: A Survey of Preparers' Views and Practices* (New York: Arthur Young & Company, 1981), p. 7.

[12] Ibid., p. 9.

SUMMARY

In this chapter we focused on the generally accepted accounting principles for measuring the impact of changing prices on the entity. The first part of the chapter covered the fundamental measurement methodology (price index manipulation) and illustrated the basic minimum disclosures required by **FASB Statement No. 33.** Using the average of the current year's general (GPLA) and specific (SPLA) prices, the balance sheet and operating income effect of price changes on inventory, plant, property, and equipment were measured for the Sun Company. These selected current-value measurements were reported in a comparative format in accordance with the required disclosures.

The second part of the chapter repeated the exercise on a general-price-level (constant-dollar) basis for the Sun Company's entire balance sheet and income statement in order to illustrate the optional comprehensive disclosures permitted under GAAP.

The last part of the chapter showed how the alternative accounting data are compared and contrasted from a wealth measurement point of view. The difference in their definitions of wealth is at the heart of the difference in these alternative models. We noted that without detailed knowledge of the preferences of individual decision makers, there is no satisfactory way to determine whether one model is superior or inferior to any other. It was suggested, however, that in periods where general or specific price changes are material, the relevance of historical-cost data as a basis for business decisions is reduced. It is because of the price changes experienced in recent periods that the alternatives to historical cost have gained the support and attention of both the users and the preparers of financial statements. The development of alternatives to historical cost will undoubtedly be tied to the rate of general and specific price changes that will be experienced in the future.

QUESTIONS

Q26-1 What was the first major disclosure requirement for current-value information by publicly traded entities?

Q26-2 Who must now report current-value data in conformance with *FASB No. 33*?

Q26-3 What major economic factor generated an awareness of the merits of current-value data in the 1970s?

Q26-4 What minimum current-value disclosures does *FASB Statement No. 33* require?

Q26-5 What is the accepted measure used to convert historical-cost data to constant-dollar data?

Q26-6 How are SPLA indexes developed for converting historical-cost data to current-cost data?

Q26-7 When is it possible to report "cost of goods sold" expense in *FASB Statement No. 33* disclosures that are the same for historical-cost, current-cost, and constant-dollar measures?

Q26-8 Is the measurement of purchasing power gains (or losses) relevant for constant-dollar disclosures alone? Explain.

Q26-9 Explain the nature of the unrealized holding gains in inventory as measured within the constant-dollar model.

Q26-10 Explain the nature of the unrealized holding gains in inventory as measured within the current-cost (nominal dollar) model.

Q26-11 Explain how the effects of price changes on ending asset balances are measured under minimum *FASB Statement No. 33* disclosures.

Q26-12 Explain the relationship between *FASB Statement No. 33* disclosures for price changes in ending asset values and the concepts of realized and unrealized holding gains.

Q26-13 How do holding gains (or losses) differ from operating income (or loss)?

Q26-14 Why does *FASB Statement No. 33* require restatement of only inventory and plant, property, and equipment?

Q26-15 When may comprehensive current-cost and/or constant-dollar restatements be reported?

Q26-16 According to *FASB Statement No. 33,* what is the reference point in time (for example, month-end dollars, year-end dollars) of the GPLA and SPLA price indexes required for minimum disclosures?

Q26-17 According to *FASB Statement No. 33,* when can end-of-period GPLA and/or SPLA price indexes be employed?

CASES

C26-1 (CMA ADAPTED) In September 1979 the *Statement of Financial Accounting Standards No. 33,* "Financial Reporting and Changing Prices," was issued. No changes are required in the basic financial statements, but information required by *FASB Statement No. 33* is to be presented in supplementary statements, schedules, or notes in the financial reports.

REQUIRED

1. A number of terms are defined and used in *FASB Statement No. 33:*
   a. Differentiate between the terms *constant dollar* and *current cost.*
   b. Explain what is meant by *current-cost—constant-dollar accounting* and how it differs from *historical-cost—nominal-dollar accounting.*
2. Identify the accounts for which an enterprise must measure the effects of changing prices in order to present the supplementary information required by *FASB Statement No. 33.*
3. *FASB Statement No. 33* is based upon the *Statement of Financial Concepts No. 1,* "Objectives of Financial Reporting by Business Enterprises," which concludes that financial reporting should provide information to help investors, creditors, and other financial statement users assess the amounts, timing, and uncertainty of prospective net cash inflows to the enterprise.
   a. Explain how *FASB Statement No. 33* can help attain this objective.
   b. Identify and discuss two ways in which the information required by *FASB Statement No. 33* may be useful for internal management decisions.

C26–2 (CMA ADAPTED) Financial reporting for both external and internal purposes is affected by generally accepted accounting principles. One of these principles or assumptions has been that dollar amounts on financial statements be based on historical unadjusted prices. This assumption implies that inflation does not affect the amounts presented on the financial statements. Therefore, financial reports prepared under this assumption are at variance with economic reality. This has troubled financial managers, the accounting profession, and the government, all of whom have been seeking a solution.

REQUIRED

1. When historical unadjusted prices are used in financial reporting, explain what effect inflation has on a firm's
   a. Statement of financial position
   b. Statement of income
2. Based upon your answers to requirements 1a and 1b, explain what erroneous conclusions could be made about a firm's financial performance by analyzing financial statements that have been prepared without considering the effects of inflation.
3. Discuss the steps a firm could take to reflect the effect of inflation in its internal reports.

C26–3 (CPA ADAPTED) Advocates of current-value accounting propose several methods for determining the valuation of assets to approximate current values. Two of the methods proposed are *replacement cost* and *present value of future cash flows.*

REQUIRED Describe each of the two methods cited above, and discuss the pros and cons of the various procedures used to arrive at the valuation for each method.

C26–4 (CPA ADAPTED) Proponents of price level restatement of financial statements assert that a basic weakness of financial statements not adjusted for price-level changes is that they are made up of mixed dollars.

REQUIRED

1. What is meant by the term *mixed dollars,* and why is this a weakness of unadjusted financial statements?
2. Explain how financial statements restated for price-level changes eliminate this weakness. Use property, plant, and equipment as your example in this discussion.

C26–5 (CPA ADAPTED) Price-level adjusted financial statements are prepared in an effort to eliminate the effects of inflation or deflation. An integral part of determining restated amounts and applicable gain or loss from restatement is the segregation of all assets and liabilities into monetary and nonmonetary classifications. One reason for this classification is that price-level gains and losses for monetary items are currently matched against earnings.

REQUIRED What factors determine whether an asset or liability is classified as monetary or nonmonetary? Include in your answer the justification for recognizing gains and losses from monetary items and not for nonmonetary items.

E26–1   Indicate whether each of the following items is a *monetary* or a *nonmonetary* asset:

Cash	Bond Sinking Fund	Leased assets
Accounts receivable	Franchise fee	Leases receivable
Allowance for uncollectible accounts	Plant, property, and equipment	Organization costs
Notes receivable	Accumulated depreciation	Office supplies inventory
Short-term investments at LCM	Accumulated amortization	Unamortized bond issue costs
Equity investment in unconsolidated subsidiary	Patents	Deferred income taxes
Prepaid insurance	Copyrights	Prepaid pension costs

E26–2   Indicate whether each of the following items is a *monetary* or a *nonmonetary* liability or equity:

Accounts payable	Mortgage payable (18%)	Unemployment insurance payable
Wages payable	Unearned service revenue	Minority interest
Federal income taxes payable	Warranty liability	Preferred stock
Bond discount	Contingent liability—legal claims pending	Common stock
Bond premium	Unfunded pension liability	Capital in excess of par value
Bonds payable	State and Federal withholding taxes payable	

E26–3   B. Lewis, Inc., held the following assets and liabilities throughout the last accounting period (with *no* change in their respective balances) as the general price level increased from 150 to 165.

	BALANCE
Cash	$ 60,000
Accounts receivable	80,000
Inventory	130,000
Notes payable (10%)	75,000
Accounts payable	68,000
Wages payable	29,000
Taxes payable	42,000

REQUIRED   Compute the net monetary gain or loss for the period.

E26–4 (CPA ADAPTED)   The following schedule lists the average Consumer Price Index (all urban consumers) of the indicated year:

1982	100
1983	125
1984	150

Carl Corporation's equipment account at December 31, 1984, is as follows:

YEAR ACQUIRED	ORIGINAL COST	EXPECTED USEFUL LIFE
1982	$ 36,000	5 years
1983	65,000	10 years
1984	40,000	8 years
	$141,000	

Depreciation is calculated, using the sum-of-the-years'-digits method. A full year's depreciation is charged in the year of acquisition. There were no disposals in 1984.

REQUIRED

1. What amount of depreciation expense would be included in the income statement adjusted for general inflation (historical-cost–constant-dollar accounting) for 1984?
2. What is the amount of the 1984 historical-cost depreciation expense?

E26–5 (CPA ADAPTED) Details of Monmouth Corporation's assets at December 31, 1983, are as follows:

YEAR ACQUIRED	PERCENT DEPRECIATED	HISTORICAL COST	ESTIMATED CURRENT COST
1981	30	$50,000	$70,000
1982	20	15,000	19,000
1983	10	20,000	22,000

Monmouth calculates depreciation at 10 percent per annum, using the straight-line method. A full year's depreciation is charged in the year of acquisition. There were no disposals of fixed assets. Monmouth prepared supplementary information for inclusion in its 1983 annual report as required by the Financial Accounting Standards Board.

REQUIRED

1. What is the net amount to be reported at December 31, 1983, on a historical-cost basis?
2. In Monmouth's supplementary information restated into current cost, what is the net current cost (after accumulated depreciation) of the fixed assets as of December 31, 1983?

E26–6 (CPA ADAPTED) Valuation to reflect general-price-level adjustments, as opposed to replacement cost, would yield differing amounts on a firm's financial statements.

Several transactions concerning one asset of a calendar-year company are summarized as follows:

1984	Purchased land for $40,000 cash on December 31. Replacement cost at year-end was $40,000.
1985	Held this land all year. Replacement cost at year-end was $52,000.
1986	Sold this land for $68,000 on October 31.

The general-price-level index was as follows:

12/31/84	100
12/31/85	110
10/31/86	120

REQUIRED On your answer sheet, duplicate the following schedules and complete the information required based upon the transactions described above.

VALUATION OF LAND ON BALANCE SHEET	GENERAL PRICE LEVEL	REPLACEMENT COST
12/31/84	$	$
12/31/85		

GAINS IN INCOME STATEMENT	GENERAL PRICE LEVEL	REPLACEMENT COST
1984	$	$
1985		
1986		
Total		

E26-7 Carol and Jim are schoolteachers who are also in the business of building houses during their summer vacations. In 1978 they purchased a 10-acre plot of land for $180,000 with the intention of dividing the land into 20 half-acre parcels for construction purposes. In 1982 they built their first house on one of the half-acre parcels of land. The house cost $71,300 to build, which included all materials, labor, and subcontractor costs but did not include any costs for their own labor. According to appraisals made at the beginning of 1982, the lot was worth $15,000 prior to construction of the house. The estimated replacement cost of the house and lot was $95,800 at the date of completion. In the fall of 1982 the house was put up for sale for $135,000 (including the lot). Carol and Jim did not sell the house until the spring of 1984, but the market price and the replacement cost had changed several times prior to the sale, as follows:

	MARKET PRICE	BUILDERS' REPLACEMENT COST INCLUDING COST OF LOT
1/1/83	$140,000	$114,950
5/1/83	148,000	119,500
8/30/83	145,000	120,350
12/31/83	145,000	124,000
1/31/84	152,000	126,400
4/30/84	156,000	125,350

On May 5, 1984, the house was sold for $153,000. The replacement cost on the date of the sale was estimated at $125,000 (including the lot).

REQUIRED

1. Prepare historical-cost and comprehensive current-cost (nominal dollars) income statements for the period 1982–1984 on an annual basis (calendar year).

2. Some have argued that since the current-cost basis recognizes income before the point of sale, in cases such as the one above it is very unrealistic because Jim and Carol do not receive anything of value until the time of sale. How might Jim and Carol realize their current-cost profits prior to 1984?

E26-8 (CMA ADAPTED) *Statement of Financial Accounting Standards No. 33,* "Financial Reporting and Changing Prices," is applicable only to larger businesses, and there are two size tests that determine which businesses must comply with this statement.

_____ 1. The first dollar-size test is that the dollar amount of inventories and of property, plant, and equipment (before deducting accumulated depreciation, depletion, and amortization) be greater than
   a. $75,000,000
   b. $100,000,000
   c. $125,000,000
   d. $150,000,000
   e. $200,000,000

_____ 2. The second dollar-size test is that the dollar amount of total assets (after deducting accumulated depreciation) be greater than
   a. $1 billion
   b. $1.5 billion
   c. $2 billion
   d. $500,000,000
   e. $750,000,000

_____ 3. *FASB Statement No. 33* adopted a price index for the computations to convert historical-cost information to a constant-dollar basis. The price index to be used is the

a. Capital equipment price index
b. Consumer price index—urban
c. Gross national product (GNP) deflator

d. Retail price index
e. Wholesale price index

_____ 4. Which of the following is *not* a monetary item?
a. Accounts receivable
b. Wages payable
c. Long-term notes payable

d. Common stock outstanding
e. None of the above

_____ 5. Which of the following is not reported on a constant-dollar basis under minimum FASB disclosures?
a. Inventory
b. Land
c. Temporary investments

d. Equipment
e. Capital leases

E26–9 Gwen and Art Galleries purchased equipment on January 1, 1980, when the general price index was 185 percent. The equipment had a 20-year life, no scrap value, and cost $280,000 at that time. By December 31, 1983, the general price index had risen to 245 percent, and by December 31, 1984, the general price index was 280 percent. Gwen and Art uses straight-line depreciation.

REQUIRED

1. Compute the amount of gross and net equipment to be reported in Gwen and Art's balance sheet at December 31, 1983, and also at the end of 1984 on a GPLA (end-of-year-dollars) basis.
2. Illustrate how the 1983 and 1984 comparative GPLA balance sheet data for the gross and net value of the equipment would appear in a comprehensive GPLA balance sheet at the end of 1984 where *all* amounts are reported in terms of index 280 dollars.

E26–10 IXL Glass Company is owned by Kate and Gene. On December 31, 1978, they purchased a glass-cutting machine for $160,000. The machine was considered to be somewhat experimental but was expected to last at least 10 years with no scrap value. The equipment was new to the industry, and it proved to be so efficient at cutting glass that nearly every glass installer in the country had it by 1982. The price of the cutting machine had increased to $320,000 by the end of 1982. At the end of 1983 Kate and Gene expanded their operations and purchased a second cutting machine for $352,000. IXL Glass uses the sum-of-the-years'-digits depreciation method for all of its depreciable assets.

REQUIRED

1. Compute the amount of gross and net equipment to be reported in the balance sheet at the end of 1982, and also at the end of 1983 on a year-end current-cost basis.
2. Compute the 1983 holding gain for IXL Glass on the original glass-cutting machine. How much of this holding gain was realized in 1983, and how much is yet to be realized (unrealized)?
3. Compute the 1983 depreciation expense and the 1983 price increases on a current-cost basis per *FASB Statement No. 33* minimum disclosure requirements assuming the following GPLA values:

DATE	GPLA INDEX
12/31/82	100
12/31/83	110
Average-1983	105

PROBLEMS

P26–1 The Sonoco Corporation had the following activities in its Plywood Inventory Control account during the most recent accounting period:

DATE	ACTIVITY	AMOUNT UNITS (SQUARE FEET)	UNIT COST	GENERAL PRICE INDEX
Jan. 1.	Beginning balance	40,000	$1.00	180
Mar. 15	Purchase	80,000	1.03	189
Mar. 31	Sales, 1st quarter	90,000	—	—
June 15	Purchase	100,000	1.07	202
June 30	Sales, 2nd quarter	110,000	—	—
Sept. 15	Purchase	75,000	1.10	214
Sept. 30	Sales, 3rd quarter	60,000	—	—
Dec. 15	Purchase	40,000	1.15	223
Dec. 31	Sales, 4th quarter	35,000	—	—
Dec. 31	Ending balance	40,000	—	—

The year-end general price index was 225, and the year-end cost per square foot was $1.16. Sonoco uses a FIFO cost-flow assumption for financial reporting.

REQUIRED

1. Compute cost of goods sold on both a historical-cost FIFO basis *and* a general price-level adjusted basis using average-of-the-period general price levels. Do not round the price level index.
2. Compute the general-price-level-adjusted holding gain (loss) for the period using average-of-the-period general price levels. Assume that the average price level of the prior year was 180.

P26–2 Refer to the data in problem 26–1.

REQUIRED Repeat requirements 1 and 2 in problem 26–1 using the end-of-period general price levels.

P26–3 Refer to the data in problem 26–1.

REQUIRED

1. Compute the cost of goods sold on both a historical-cost FIFO basis and a current-cost (SPLA) basis using average-of-the-period specific levels. (*Hint:* You should develop a specific-price-level index from the data provided.)
2. Compute the holding gain for the period on a current-cost basis.

P26–4 Refer to the data in problem 26–1.

REQUIRED Repeat requirements 1 and 2 of problem 26–3 using end-of-period specific price levels.

P26–5 The Carol Mowrey Art Supplies Company carries an inventory of canvas, which comes in rolls of 1,000 feet at widths of 2½', 3', 4' and 6'. The ending inventory at December 31, 1983, consisted of the following:

SIZE	NUMBER OF ROLLS	HISTORICAL (FIFO) COST PER ROLL	REPLACEMENT COST PER ROLL
2½'	25	$1,000	$1,000
3'	32	1,250	1,250
4'	6	1,500	1,500
6'	7	1,800	1,800

The ending inventory of canvas rolls at the end of 1984 consisted of the following items:

SIZE	NUMBER OF ROLLS	HISTORICAL (FIFO) COST PER ROLL	REPLACEMENT COST PER ROLL
2½'	30	$1,200	$1,200
3'	20	1,450	1,450
4'	15	1,700	1,700
6'	10	2,000	2,000

The sales for 1984 indicated that 100 of the 2½' rolls, 150 of the 3' rolls, 62 of the 4' rolls, and 34 of the 6' rolls were sold evenly during the year. Purchases of $485,700 took place evenly throughout the year. The price increases noted in the data provided occurred evenly throughout 1984. Carol Mowrey uses the FIFO cost-flow assumption for inventory measurement.

REQUIRED

1. Compute cost of goods sold and ending inventory on a historical-cost basis.
2. Compute cost of goods sold and the ending inventory using *average-of-the-period* current costs.
3. Compute the cost of goods sold and the ending inventory using *end-of-period* current costs.
4. Compute cost of goods sold and the current-cost price increases as they would be computed per *FASB Statement No. 33* minimum disclosure requirements. To do so, assume the following GPLA data:

DATE	GPLA INDEX
12/31/83	1.00
12/31/84	1.12
Average-1984	1.06

P26–6 (CPA ADAPTED) The financial statements of a business entity could be prepared by using historical cost or current value as a basis. In addition, the basis could be stated in terms of unadjusted dollars or dollars restated for changes in purchasing power. The various permutations of these two separate and distinct areas are shown in the following matrix:

	UNADJUSTED DOLLARS	DOLLARS RESTATED FOR CHANGES IN PURCHASING POWER
Historical cost	1	2
Current value	3	4

Block 1 of the matrix represents the traditional method of accounting for transactions in accounting today, wherein the absolute (unadjusted) amount of dollars given up or received is recorded for the asset or liability obtained (relationship between resources). Amounts recorded in the method described in block 1 reflect the original cost of the asset or liability and do not take account of any change in value of the unit of measure (standard of comparison). This method assumes the validity of the accounting concepts of a going concern and stable monetary unit. Any gain or loss (including holding and purchasing power gains or losses) resulting from the sale or satisfaction of amounts recorded under this method is deferred in its entirety until sale or satisfaction.

REQUIRED For each of the remaining matrix blocks (2, 3, and 4), answer the following questions. *Limit your discussion to nonmonetary assets only.*

1. How will this method of recording assets affect the relationship between resources and the standard of comparison?
2. What is the theoretical justification for using each method?
3. How will each method of asset valuation affect the recognition of gain or loss during the life of the asset and ultimately from the sale or abandonment of the asset? Your answer should include a discussion of the timing

and magnitude of the gain or loss and conceptual reasons for any difference from the gain or loss computed using the traditional method.

P26-7 The following income statement data are taken from the Buckmaster Corporation for the year ending December 31, 1984.

	HISTORICAL COST	
Sales		$15,863,000
Cost of sales:		
Beginning inventory	$1,485,000	
Purchases	6,328,000	
Goods available	7,813,000	
Ending inventory	2,030,000	
Cost of goods sold		5,783,000
Gross margin		$10,080,000
Other expenses:		
Depreciation expense	$4,395,000	
Salaries and wages	3,820,000	
Income tax expense	839,250	9,054,250
Net income		$1,025,750

The CPI–U index at January 1, 1984, was 215 percent and increased by 20 percent to 258 percent by December 31, 1984. The increase occurred evenly throughout the year, as did Buckmaster's activities. The buildings and equipment being depreciated by Buckmaster were acquired when the CPI–U price index was 120 percent. The beginning inventory costed on a LIFO basis, with layers added to inventory at average cost of the period, represents a weighted-average price index of 130 percent. The net monetary items resulted in a net monetary gain of $2,125,000 for 1984. Taxes were paid at the end of the year. Do not round price index data in this problem.

REQUIRED

1. Prepare a constant-dollar income statement for Buckmaster for 1984. Because you are preparing a complete statement, use end-of-period constant-dollar units.
2. Illustrate how the constant-dollar income statement data required for minimum *FASB Statement No. 33* disclosures would appear in Buckmaster's 1984 annual report. Use average-of-the-period constant-dollar units.
3. Which data are more relevant, those in requirement 1 or requirement 2? Explain.

P26-8 Hipple, Inc., reported the following historical-cost data:

Balance Sheet				
December 31, 1983				
Assets			*Liabilities and Equities*	
Cash	$ 21,000		Accounts payable	$ 13,500
Inventory (LIFO)	42,000		Wages payable	6,800
Plant and equipment	285,000		Common stock	180,000
Accumulated depreciation	(99,750)		Retained earnings	157,950
Land	110,000			
	$358,250			$358,250

The following index information was available:

	CPI–U		SPECIFIC PRICE INDEXES		
	ORIGINAL	12/31/83	ORIGINAL	12/31/83	12/31/84
Inventory	185%	275%	200%	296%	355%
Plant and equipment	135	275	160	285	328
Land	125	275	150	260	235
Common stock	120	275	145	210	245

During 1984 Hipple had the following activities as reported on a historical-cost basis:

	AMOUNT	COMMENTS
Sales	$758,000	All cash
Purchases	347,000	All but $18,000 were paid for by 12/31/84
Wages and salaries expense	295,000	All but $7,200 were paid for by 12/31/84
Income tax expense	38,600	All paid in cash at 12/31/84
Depreciation expense	14,250	Amount equals 5% of original plant and equipment
Dividends	60,000	All paid in cash at 12/31/84

The CPI–U increased evenly throughout 1984 to a year-end level of 330 percent. Hipple paid all the December 31, 1983, payables early in 1984. The ending inventory, priced out on a LIFO basis and with layers added to inventory at average cost of the period, was $45,000 at December 31, 1984. Do not round index data.

REQUIRED

1. Prepare a historical-cost income statement and balance sheet for Hipple for 1984.
2. Prepare a constant-dollar income statement and balance sheet for Hipple for 1984 based on *year-end* prices. Also prepare the 1983 balance sheet on a constant-dollar basis as it appeared at the end of 1983.

P26–9   Refer to the data in problem 26–8 for Hipple, Inc.

REQUIRED

1. Prepare current-cost balance sheets for Hipple for 1984 and for 1983 based on their respective *year-end* current costs.
2. Prepare a 1984 current-cost income statement for Hipple *without* including realized or unrealized holding gains (just operating income for 1984). Assume that Hipple's wages and salaries are changing at the same rate as the CPI–U. Use year-end current costs.
3. (Optional) Complete the current-cost income statement by computing the realized and unrealized holding gains. Also reconcile net income with the change in retained earnings.

P26–10   Refer to the data in problem 26–8 for Hipple, Inc. In addition, assume that the following price index data are available:

	CPI–U		SPECIFIC PRICE INDEXES	
	AVERAGE 1983	AVERAGE 1984	AVERAGE 1983	AVERAGE 1984
Inventory	263%	302.5%	285.5%	325.5%
Plant and equipment	263	302.5	280.0	306.5
Land	263	302.5	260.0	260.0
Common stock	263	302.5	205.5	227.5

REQUIRED

1. Using the data from problem 26–8 plus the data provided above, prepare the necessary disclosure to conform with the minimum requirement of *FASB Statement No. 33* on a constant-dollar basis.
2. Repeat requirement 1 for the current-cost basis.

P26–11   The following conventional accounting balance sheet for the Stockton Corporation was taken from the annual report for the year ended December 31, 1983. The company has been in business for 2 full years.

```
                    STOCKTON CORPORATION
                         Balance Sheet
                    As of December 31, 1983

        ASSETS                    LIABILITIES AND OWNERS' EQUITY

Cash                 $  1,000    Accounts payable              $10,000
Inventory (FIFO)       50,000    Wages payable                   2,000
Prepaid rent            2,400
Equipment              60,000
Accumulated depreciation (20,000)  Owners' equity               81,400
                     $93,400                                   $93,400
```

The following additional information pertains to Stockton's balance sheet as of December 31, 1983:

```
Inventory:    Consists of 1,000 units, replacement cost at December 31, 1983, was $55 per unit, items sold for $75 per unit in
              1983.
Prepaid rent: Represents rent for first 6 months of 1984.
Equipment:    Straight-line depreciation has been used, the scrap value is zero, replacement cost at December 31, 1983, was
              $75,000, another firm offered Stockton $50,000 for the equipment "as is" on December 31, 1983.
```

During 1984, the third year of operations, the following events took place:

1. On January 2, 1984, another 3,000 units of inventory were purchased on account for $55 per unit. A total of $160,000 was paid on accounts payable *evenly* throughout 1984.
2. Sales of 3,000 units at $75 per unit took place *evenly* throughout 1981. All sales were for cash.
3. During 1984 the average cost to replace goods similar to those carried by Stockton was $62, with the year-end replacement cost up to $70. Stockton decided to increase the selling price to $82 per unit in 1985 to offset the cost increase.
4. Cash payments for wages of $15,000 were made evenly throughout 1984. At year-end, wages payable totaled $1,600.
5. On July 1, 1984, Stockton paid $6,000 for 1 year's rental of the facilities currently occupied.
6. At the end of 1984, another firm offered to buy Stockton's equipment for $50,000. Stockton discovered that the cost to replace the same equipment new at December 31, 1984, was $90,000. Stockton decided to keep the old equipment.
7. The following general-price-level readings were available during 1984:

```
        1/1/84      137.5%
        12/31/84    165.0
Average for 1984    150.0
```

REQUIRED

1. Prepare the conventional balance sheet and income statement for 1984 based on the data provided.
2. Assume that the balance sheet position at December 31, 1983, given in the problem is stated in terms of index 137.5 dollars. In other words, the balance sheet is already in a GPLA form as of December 31, 1983. Prepare the GPLA balance sheet and income statement for 1984 using year-end dollars on a GPLA basis.

P26–12 Refer to the Stockton Corporation data in problem 26–11.

REQUIRED

1. Reconstruct the beginning balance sheet position on a replacement-cost basis as of December 31, 1983.

2. Based on the activities that took place during 1984, prepare the balance sheet and income statement for 1984 on a replacement-cost basis. Use average-for-the-year replacement costs.

P26–13 Refer to the Stockton Corporation data in problem 26–11.

REQUIRED

1. Reconstruct Stockton's balance sheet at December 31, 1983, on a market-value basis.
2. Based on the activities that took place during 1984, prepare the balance sheet for 1984 on a market-value basis. Use end-of-period market values. What was income for 1984 on a market value basis?

P26–14 Refer to the Stockton Corporation data in problem 26–11. Assume the following additional information concerning the historical-cost balance sheet data given for December 31, 1983:

	ORIGINAL COST	GPLA AT DATE OF ACQUISITION
Inventory:		
500 units	$22,000	125%
500 units	28,000	130
Prepaid rent	2,400	125
Equipment	60,000	105

REQUIRED

1. Reconstruct the Stockton Corporation's GPLA balance sheet as of December 31, 1983, in terms of index 137.5 dollar units.
2. Prepare a GPLA income statement and balance sheet for 1984 based on the events that occurred during 1984 as described in problem 26–11. Use end-of-period GPLA dollar units to prepare your statements.

27

Full Disclosure, an Introduction to SEC Reporting, and Financial Statement Analysis

OVERVIEW

The premise that underlies and motivates financial accounting is that accounting data will ultimately be used in analyses. Because the specific goals of all possible analyses are so diverse, the accounting profession has adopted a **full-disclosure** philosophy. Accountants supplement the primary financial statement data with auxiliary schedules, exhibits, and notes. As we have stressed throughout the text, specific items in the financial statements often require clarifying supplementary footnote information. In this chapter we consider the overall package of accounting information typically found in annual reports to shareholders, and we introduce techniques used in the analysis of such information. Emphasis is placed on the sequence of information items, the cross-referencing of various items of financial statement data with their related notes, the nature of the specific note that describes accounting policies, and other supplementary financial and nonfinancial data. In addition to the general disclosure patterns found in published annual reports, two very important disclosure requirements are considered. (1) **segmental reporting** and (2) **interim reporting.** The chapter also surveys form 10–K, the major annual report required by the SEC. Emphasis is placed on the relationship between SEC requirements and general financial-reporting requirements. In conclusion, some basic techniques of financial statement analysis are presented.

ANNUAL REPORTS TO SHAREHOLDERS

An annual report to shareholders can be viewed as a package of interrelated information, with each section having unique characteristics and formats. Some sections are highly standardized, showing little variation across reporting entities; however, flexibility in format is usually permitted by GAAP. Although few reports, if any, will have exactly the same sequence of information items, the general patterns that exist make it possible to analyze a typical annual report framework.

The common sequencing patterns are illustrated below, followed by a discussion of each annual report section in turn. Particular attention is given to the relationships between the financial statements and the explanatory notes.

The Sequencing of Report Data

Exhibit 27–1 identifies six major sections of information normally found in the annual reports to shareholders: (1) management's discussion, (2) financial statements (audited), (3) other financial data, (4) management's representation, (5) auditor's attestation, and (6) miscellaneous. Because GAAP do not specify the order of these data, it is not uncommon to find alternative sequencing patterns. For instance, the inflation-adjusted data (shown in Exhibit 27–1 as part of item 3) may be part of Management's Discussion (item 1).

Management's discussion Management has wide latitude as to its style of communicating with stockholders and other interested parties. Formal accounting standards do not specify the formats of these summaries and discussions. As we shall see later, annual reports by firms registered with the SEC must include certain general areas of discussion, but few specifics are required. Auditing standards require that auditors review the content of the management's discussion to ensure that references to financial results do not contradict the substance of the audited financial statements.

Financial statements and notes The four primary financial statements typically precede the notes, with either the income statement or the balance sheet leading off. Although the general nature of the primary financial statements is the same for all firms, the exact content of each statement may vary widely among firms. Except in regulated industries where considerable uniformity is required, the formats of the financial statement disclosures may differ significantly even for firms within the same industry. Also, the level of aggregation encountered in the published reports is generally quite high. For example, whereas a typical chart of accounts (an entity's list of ledger accounts) might include over 100 income statement accounts, it is not uncommon to find ten or fewer revenue and expense items reported in the income statement.

The major accounting policies of the reporting entity are normally found in the first footnote. This is followed by the specific notes, which are often cross-referenced to the related items on the financial statements. Sometimes no explicit cross-referencing by note number is used, as is the case with the accounting policies note, which usually is not specifically cross-referenced. For example, even though the explanation of the accounting policies concerning inventory may be critical to an understanding of "cost of goods sold" in the income statement and "inventory" in the balance sheet, such cross-referencing is usually omitted.

Exhibit 27–2 gives one sequence of the notes that might be found in an annual report.

EXHIBIT
27–1

TYPICAL SEQUENCING OF ANNUAL REPORT DATA

MAJOR SECTION	COMMON TITLE	TYPICAL CONTENTS
Management's discussion	Financial highlights	Columnar summaries of key financial indicators for several comparative periods. These data usually include sales, net income, earnings per share, and funds from operations. There may also be ratios, quarterly data, dividend data, and stock price figures.
	Letter to stockholders	The chairman of the board of directors and the president (or chief executive officer) normally use this medium to discuss and explain the performance of the past period as well as the plans for the future.
	Operating summaries and financial review	Extended discussion concerning the performance of major operating units and the factors affecting them. Financial information from the financial statements for each unit may be included in this section.
Financial statements	Consolidated income statement Consolidated balance sheet Consolidated statement of stockholders' equity Consolidated statement of changes in financial position	The formal financial statements with comparative data from prior years.
	Notes	The first note is usually a summary of significant accounting policies and is followed by other notes that augment the presentations in the formal financial statements.
Other financial data	Data adjusted for inflation	These data include the *FASB Statement No. 33* required constant-dollar and current-cost disclosures. Entities will often expand and augment the required information.
	Quarterly data	Selected key financial data for each quarter, usually including sales, operating income, net income, dividends, earnings per share, and stock prices.
Auditor's attestation	Report of independent accountants	The report in which the auditors state the scope of their work and their opinion as to fairness of presentation.
Management's representation	Report of management	This short note states that management has prepared the financial statements and other data and that it is responsible for their content.
Miscellaneous	Key personnel	List of the names of key officers and members of the board of directors.
	Locations	A list of addresses of headquarters, manufacturing plants, major facilities, transfer agents, legal counsel, and auditors.

EXHIBIT
27-2

EXAMPLES OF COMMON TITLES OF NOTES TO FINANCIAL STATEMENTS

Note 1	Summary of Significant Accounting Policies
	Principles of Consolidation
	Net Income per Share
	Acquisitions and Dispositions
	Inventory Valuation
	Property, Plant, and Equipment
	Income Tax Policy
	Pension Plans
Note 2	Extraordinary Gains (Losses)
Note 3	Details of Working Capital Changes
Note 4	Long-Term Debt
Note 5	Taxes
Note 6	Pensions
Note 7	Leases
Note 8	Stock Options
Note 9	Litigation
Note 10	Contingencies
Note 11	Commitments
Note 12	Lines of Business

ACCOUNTING POLICIES NOTE   The number of alternative accounting techniques available to reporting entities has been reduced considerably over the past few decades, but there is still a certain latitude in many areas. For instance, a wide variety of depreciation and inventory valuation techniques are currently permissible. Entities with the same economic attributes may use different accounting techniques, resulting in significant differences in their financial reports. Single entities may use a variety of techniques as long as they are consistent from period to period. For example, it is not uncommon for one entity to use LIFO, FIFO, and averaging techniques in different aspects of its operations. In addition, industry practices may often call for special accounting applications that would not be considered acceptable in other industries.

Each reporting entity, therefore, can be characterized by the specific accounting techniques chosen from among those that are generally acceptable. The sum of these choices is referred to as an entity's **accounting policies,** and **APB Opinion No. 22** has mandated that those accounting policies be disclosed.[1] Although the APB suggested flexibility in the disclosing of accounting policies and, therefore, merely gave examples of the kinds of policies to be disclosed, a core of policy disclosure items seems to have evolved. Consolidation policy, depreciation and amortization policies, income tax policies, and inventory policies are almost always present, with others shown depending on the nature of the business.

OTHER SPECIFIC NOTES   Throughout the text we have seen situations that called for augmented disclosure in the form of notes to the financial statements. In some cases, pronouncements may require additional numerical data as well as descriptive narratives. These disclosure rules typically rely on professional judgment in determining the nature and extent of such augmentation. Increased disclosure must be judged by weighing the benefits expected in the form of better information for decision makers against the cost of providing the information. Although it is true that GAAP sometime call for additional disclosure, the accountant must always judge whether the item in question is of material consequence. The formal rules are

[1] *Accounting Principles Board Opinion No. 22,* "Disclosure of Accounting Policies" (New York: AICPA, April 1972).

viewed as the framework for accounting information. It is the professional accountant's responsibility to communicate as complete a financial picture as is practicable within that framework.

Other major annual report sections   Data adjusted for inflation is discussed in detail in Chapters 6 and 26. Quarterly data and the auditor's report are discussed later in this chapter.

The last three items in Exhibit 27–1 (report of management, key personnel, and locations) take on a variety of forms. The report of management clearly states that management and not the independent auditor has full responsibility for the content of the financial statements. Often these reports mention the purpose and nature of the system of internal controls. Another topic often discussed is the audit committee of the board of directors (which usually does not include officers of the company), which oversees the company's relationship with its independent auditor.

Most of the information in published financial statements is provided on an entity-wide basis in 1-year intervals. The next two sections of this chapter show how two reporting practices lead to disaggregated information—by product and geography for segmental reporting and by time periods for interim reports.

SEGMENTAL (LINE OF BUSINESS) REPORTING

Businesses range from those that operate in a single industry with one major class of customers to those that are conglomerates. Financial statements, however, reflect the consolidated picture for the economic entity taken as a whole. The **economic entity** concept calls for the disclosure of primary financial information as if all legal entities were merged into one. Consolidation procedures are designed to accomplish this. **Segmental reporting** does not disaggregate the entity into its *legal segments* but rather into its *significant products and markets*.

Information about the performance and status of the individual segments of a diversified business may be necessary in many decision contexts. To the extent that segments are affected by different economic conditions, a more precise interpretation of the consolidated results will be possible if financial information is given for each segment. Segmental information could *conceivably* range from simple descriptions of the major industries in which a business operates to full-blown financial statements for each industry. In addition, the geographical regions involved could be described either generally or in great detail. This section describes the segmental disclosure that is currently required for certain corporations.

In response to the growing complexity and diversity in business entities, **FASB Statement No. 14** instituted the requirement that information on industry segments, foreign operations, and major customers be disclosed,[2] and **FASB Statement No. 21** limited the application of such requirements to publicly traded companies.[3] Application of **FASB Statement No. 14** will result in the type of disclosures illustrated for a hypothetical case in Exhibit 27–3, consisting of two major sections: (1) industry segment data and (2) geographical data. Both the rules and the disclosure formats that apply to the content of each section are similar. The main thrust of

[2] *Statement of Financial Accounting Standards No. 14,* "Financial Reporting for Segments of a Business Enterprise" (Stamford, CT: FASB, December 1976).

[3] *Statement of Financial Accounting Standards No. 21,* "Suspension of the Reporting of Earnings per Share and Segment Information by Nonpublic Enterprises" (Stamford, CT: FASB, April 1978).

EXHIBIT 27-3

RELIANCE PRODUCTS, INC.
Information on Industry Segments

($000)

| | INDUSTRIES | | | | |
	BUILDING SUPPLIES	TIMBER	OTHER	ELIMINATIONS	CONSOLIDATED
Sales to Outsiders	$905	$256	$35	$ —	$1,196
Intersegment Sales	25	—	—	(25)	—
Total Sales	$930	$256	$35	$(25)	$1,196
Operating Profit	$ 70	$ 12	$ 5	$ (2)	$ 85
Unallocated (Expense) Income, Net					6
Interest (Expense) Income, Net					9
Income from Continuing Operations Before Taxes					$ 100
Identifiable Assets	$790	$194	$20	$(10)	$ 994
Unallocated Assets					120
Total Assets					$1,114
Depreciation and Amortization	$ 60	$ 50	$10		$ 120
Capital Expenditures	$210	$ 85	$15		$ 310

Information on Operations in Different Geographical Areas

	UNITED STATES	EUROPE	SOUTH AMERICA	ELIMINATIONS	CONSOLIDATED
Sales to Outsiders	$750	$326	$120	$ —	$1,196
Intergeographic Area Transfers	50			(50)	—
Total Revenue	$800	$326	$120	$(50)	$1,196
Operating Profit	$ 54	$ 20	$ 15	$ (4)	$ 85
Unallocated (Expenses) Income, Net					6
Interest (Expense) Income, Net					9
Income from Continuing Operations Before Taxes					$ 100
Identifiable Assets	$775	$130	$100	$(11)	$ 994
Unallocated Assets					120
Total Assets					$1,114

the pronouncement is to establish criteria for "reportable" industry segments and "reportable" geographical areas and to prescribe the minimum information to be reported for each category.

What is an industry segment? The standard states that although no one criterion can govern in all cases, the similarities in the products, the production processes, and the markets should be considered in deciding on industry segmentation. Once the business has been segmented, the segments must be judged significant, termed *reportable,* in order to require mandatory disclosure.

Foreign operations can be significant in comparison with all operations. Foreign operations can also be capable of segmentation by geographical areas, which are defined as countries or groups of countries. Again, no strict rules are given for the determination of geographical areas, but such characteristics as proximity, economic affinity, and business environments are mentioned in FASB Statement No. 14 as being important considerations. Once geographical segments have been determined, tests are performed to identify reportable segments under the FASB standards.

Tests for Reportable Industry Segments

If *one or more* of the following tests are met, certain information on the industry segment must be disclosed:

TEST	CRITERIA FOR DISCLOSURE
Revenues test	Revenues of the segment must be greater than or equal to 10 percent of the combined revenues of all segments.
Operating profit or loss test	The operating profit or loss of the segment must be greater than or equal to 10 percent of the higher of the combined profits of all the segments reporting profits or the combined losses of those reporting losses.
Identifiable assets test	The identifiable assets of the segment must be greater than or equal to 10 percent of the sum of the identifiable assets of all segments.

For purposes of the tests described above, revenues include both sales to unaffiliated entities and sales and transfers to affiliated entities. Once reportable segments have been identified, it is necessary to make these segments aggregate to a substantial portion of overall operations. To accomplish this, **FASB Statement No. 14** requires that the aggregate sales to unaffiliated customers of all reportable segments be equal to at least 75 percent of such sales by all segments, even though this may necessitate reporting additional segments. For instance, consider a company that has the following segmental results for sales:

	SEGMENT 1	SEGMENT 2	OTHER	TOTAL
Sales	43%	20%	37%	100%

The "other" category actually includes five smaller divisions no one of which meets the 10% criterion:

Segment 3	9%
Segment 4	8%
Segment 5	7%
Segment 6	7%
Segment 7	6%

In order to report at least 75 percent of sales, the following segments would have to be shown:

	SEGMENT 1	SEGMENT 2	SEGMENT 3	SEGMENT 4	OTHER	TOTAL
Sales	43%	20%	9%	8%	20%	100%

A maximum of ten industry segments is allowed; therefore, the possible number of segments for those entities that meet the criterion of at least one test can range from a minimum of two to a maximum of ten.

If one segment dominates—that is, if one industry segment has more than 90 percent of the revenue, operating profit, and identifiable assets of all segments and no other segment meets *any* of the 10 percent criteria—then no segment disclosure is required, except for a discussion of the nature of the dominant industry. Such entities would be unaffected by the industry disclosures required by **FASB Statement No. 14.**

In the Reliance Products, Inc., example (Exhibit 27–3), the company's operations met one or more of the above tests. Building supplies and timber are industry segments based on product characteristics. Note that *both* unaffiliated parties' sales and intersegment sales are shown and that the "eliminations" reconcile the segments sales with the consolidated sales balance appearing in the consolidated financial statements. The 75 percent test is met, which ensures that segmentation encompasses a significant portion of total operations; and no one segment exceeds the 90 percent dominant industry criterion.

Required Disclosure

FASB Statement No. 14 gives a detailed list of specific items to be disclosed. We merely highlight the following major items:

1. *Revenue:* Sales to unaffiliated customers and sales or transfers to other industry segments
2. *Profitability:* Operating profit or loss for each reportable segment
3. *Identifiable assets:* The aggregate carrying amount of identifiable assets

Each of these items requires many specific definitions and detailed analysis if **FASB Statement No. 14** is to be fully implemented. Our examples are greatly simplified to emphasize the major objectives of the standard.

Tests for Reportable Geographical Areas

The identification of reportable foreign operations and the more specific geographical areas is a sequential process. First, it must be determined whether foreign operations taken as a whole are significant. If **either of two criteria is met,** foreign operations are considered significant and certain information must be disclosed:

TEST	CRITERIA FOR DISCLOSURE
Sales to unaffiliated parties test	Foreign operations' sales to unaffiliated parties must be greater than or equal to 10 percent of consolidated revenue.
Identifiable assets test	The identifiable assets of foreign operations must be greater than or equal to 10 percent of consolidated total assets.

If either one of the above criteria is met, foreign operations must be shown separately from domestic operations. A duplicate pair of tests is made for the detection of significant geographical areas within the overall foreign operations category. The Reliance Products, Inc., example (Exhibit 27–3) shows three distinct geographical areas. Note that Europe and South America are listed rather than the specific countries. The rules give a considerable degree of latitude in making such determinations. If there were another geographical area, Asia for instance, which did not meet the 10 percent tests, it would show up as an "other" foreign geographical area without specific identification.

The required disclosure items for foreign operations relate to: (1) revenue, with sales to unaffiliated customers and sales or transfers between areas shown separately; (2) operating profit or net income; and (3) identifiable assets. Again, this standard is detailed and complex, and we merely highlight it here.

Other
Disclosure
Tests
Two additional disclosure items may be necessary. One is concerned with major customers. If sales to a single customer are equal to or greater than 10 percent of consolidated revenues, then disclosure must be made of the revenues earned from each such customer. The names of the major customers need not be disclosed.

A test is also made for the disclosure of export sales. If export sales from an enterprise's home country to unaffiliated customers in foreign countries are equal to or greater than 10 percent of consolidated revenues, disclosure of export sales is required.

INTERIM REPORTING

Timeliness is certainly a necessary attribute for accounting information if it is to be relevant for decision making. Timely information, however, can be quite costly and can often be achieved only at the expense of accuracy and completeness. **Interim financial reports** have evolved in response to a need for more timely information than that provided in annual reports. Most major corporations publish interim (quarterly) financial statements that contain summarized and unaudited data. In addition, entities that file with the SEC may be required to file quarterly statements. Accounting rules were developed to provide some uniformity in these interim disclosures. Although not requiring entities to report interim statements in order to be in conformance with GAAP, current policy does prescribe the accounting principles to be used for interim reports if a publicly traded entity chooses to publish such reports. In essence, within the realm of practicality the current rule **(APB Opinion No. 28)** views each interim period as a complete accounting period (with some exceptions) and requires that the same accounting principles be applied to the interim period as are applied to the annual period.[4]

Interim
Revenue
Recognition
The recognition of revenue for an interim period follows the same logic as that for an annual period. Generally, revenue is recognized as it is being earned or according to the other revenue-recognition techniques used by the entity; for example, if the percentage-of-completion method is being used for annual reporting, then it would be used for the interim period as well.

The revenue-recognition procedures required by **APB Opinion No. 28** force **interim revenue recognition** to reflect the seasonal fluctuations in sales activity.[5] This rule avoids the use of accruals and deferrals to smooth revenue recognition in such a way that each quarter is depicted as having earned equal revenues. For example, assume that the Great Midwest Amusement Park, Inc., has the following flow of earned revenue from admissions (in millions of dollars):

	JAN.	FEB.	MAR.	APR.	MAY	JUNE	JULY	AUG.	SEPT.	OCT.	NOV.	DEC.
Earned admissions revenue:	$0	$0	$1	$4	$10	$30	$30	$20	$4	$1	$0	$0
Quarterly (seasonal) revenue earned		$1			$44			$54			$1	

[4] *Accounting Principles Board Opinion No. 28,* "Interim Financial Reporting" (New York: AICPA, May 1973).

[5] Ibid.

This seasonal revenue pattern is consistent with the firm's actual economic activity as opposed to the following smoothed pattern for the total yearly revenue:

Quarterly (smoothed) revenue recognized	$25	$25	$25	$25

Interim Cost Recognition

Given that revenues are to reflect the actual earned amounts for each interim period, what is the logical pattern for expense recognition? According to **APB Opinion No. 28,** all cost directly associated with revenue is recognized in the interim period in which the revenue is recognized.[6] In other words, costs are *matched* with revenue in the period of the recognition of revenue. Although some costs (such as material and labor) are readily matched with units of sales, other costs are allocated to time periods of expenditure because of the difficulty in determining how they are related to revenue generation. Consider some additional data for the Great Midwest Amusement Park, Inc., example. Exhibit 27–4 lists the quarterly cash flows and expense recognition for several different types of expenditures. Note that the *quarterly allocation* procedures for maintenance and insurance (expenditures 3 and 4) fol-

EXHIBIT 27–4

ANALYSIS OF CASH FLOWS AND EXPENSES IN QUARTERLY FINANCIAL STATEMENTS

GREAT MIDWEST AMUSEMENT PARK, INC.

TYPE OF EXPENDITURE	CASH OUTFLOW IN EACH QUARTER (IN MILLIONS OF DOLLARS)				EXPENSE RECOGNIZED IN EACH QUARTER[a] (IN MILLIONS OF DOLLARS)			
	QUARTER				**QUARTER**			
	1	**2**	**3**	**4**	**1**	**2**	**3**	**4**
1. Security services	.3	.4	.5	.3	.3	.4	.5	.3
2. Operators' wages	.4	16.6	21.6	.4	.4	16.6	21.6	.4
3. Preparation of rides	1.2	.5	.4	2.4	.045	1.980	2.430	.045
4. Fire insurance	2.0	—	—	—	.5	.5	.5	.5

[a] Explanation of money amounts:

1. Expense recognition for security services follows the timing of the payment because the benefits of security services are assumed to be spread throughout the year regardless of revenues.
2. Operators' wages depend on the amount of time the attractions are open for business; therefore, expense recognition follows cash flow.
3. Preparation expenditures come primarily during the off season, but the benefits accrue during the open season. These costs are allocated on the basis of relative revenues for each quarter. For instance, if we have perfect estimates of revenues of $100,000,000 as discussed on page 1052 and perfect estimates of the preparation expenditures of $4,500,000, the proportions assigned to each quarter would be as follows (in millions):

$$\text{Quarter 1} \quad \frac{\$1}{\$100}\ (\$4.5) = \$\ .045$$

$$2 \quad \frac{\$44}{\$100}\ (\$4.5) = 1.980$$

$$3 \quad \frac{\$54}{\$100}\ (\$4.5) = 2.430$$

$$4 \quad \frac{\$1}{\$100}\ (\$4.5) = \underline{\ \ .045}$$

$$\text{Total} \qquad \underline{\$4.500}$$

4. Fire insurance premium expenditures benefit all periods; and, therefore, they are recorded as prepaid and are allocated on a straight-line basis.

[6] Ibid.

EXHIBIT
27-5

GREAT MIDWEST AMUSEMENT PARK, INC.

Representative Journal Entries

EXPENDITURE NUMBER		DEBIT	CREDIT
1	Security service expense	X	
	Cash		X
	(Recorded at each payment)		
2	Wages expense	X	
	Cash		X
	(Recorded on each payday)		
3	(a) Deferred preparation costs	X	
	Cash		X
	(Recorded at each payment)		
	(b) Preparation expense	X	
	Deferred maintenance		X
	(Recorded at end of each interim period)		
4	(a) Prepaid insurance	X	
	Cash		X
	(Recorded at each payment)		
	(b) Insurance expense	X	
	Prepaid insurance		X
	(Recorded at end of each interim period)		

low the same logic as that for allocations between annual accounting periods. The allocation of such expenditures is required to achieve the matching of revenues and costs called for in both quarterly and annual statements. The sample journal entries to record the interim expenditures in Exhibit 27–4 appear in Exhibit 27–5.

Although arbitrary assignments of costs to interim periods are not allowed, the costs incurred during a period are sometimes recognized as expenses immediately because their benefits are consumed within one interim period. Gains and losses in interim periods follow the same rules as those for a complete annual period. If, given their characteristics, they would be recognized in a current annual report, then they would also be recognized in the interim reporting period in which they were incurred.

There are many other specific provisions in currently promulgated GAAP on interim reporting. In most instances, however, these provisions treat each interim period as if it were an annual period. For example, extraordinary items, segment disposals, and unusual and nonrecurring items are not deferred but are recognized in the interim period in which they occur.

Interim Accounting Changes

Changes in estimates   The rules for changes in *estimates* in interim reports, as stated in **APB Opinion No. 28** can be summarized as follows:

> The interim period in which an accounting estimate change is made must be treated as if the new estimate had been in effect throughout that interim period. In addition, if the period of change is not the first interim period of the year, the adjustments to the current year's preceding interim periods are recorded in the period of the change.[7]

For example, assume that the estimated salvage value of a computer purchased on January 1, 1983, was originally $20,000 and that this value is changed to zero during

[7] Ibid, pars. 23–29.

the second quarter of 1984. The following standard analysis would be necessary to compute the new depreciation charges (assuming straight-line depreciation):

Original cost (1/1/83)	$100,000
Estimated useful life	4 years
Original depreciation charge per quarter	$ 5,000[a]
Revised depreciation charge per quarter	$ 6,667[b]

[a] $100,000 − 20,000 = $80,000; $80,000 ÷ 16 = $5,000.
[b] Book value at 1/1/84 = 80,000 ÷ 12 = $6,667 per quarter.

During the first quarter of 1984, $5,000 was recorded as depreciation expense. During the second quarter, $6,667 is charged to expense for the second quarter, and $1,667 is charged to expense to adjust the first quarter as follows:

Depreciation expense	8,334	
Accumulated depreciation		8,334

Cumulative-effect type of principles changes   Accounting *principles* changes, if occurring in the first interim period, are handled much the same as for annual reports. Where applicable, the cumulative effect on prior periods is taken into income during the first interim period. If a cumulative-effect type of accounting change (see Chapter 24) takes place in any quarter other than the first, the cumulative effect is not reflected in income in the interim period of change.[8] Previous quarterly results are adjusted to reflect the new method, with the cumulative effect on prior years being reflected in the restated net income of the first quarter.

For example, if equipment is purchased on January 1, 1983, for $24,000 and is depreciated over 4 years with zero estimated salvage using straight-line depreciation, the following depreciation charge per quarter for 1983 would have been reported:

1ST	2ND	3RD	4TH	TOTAL 1983
$1,500	$1,500	$1,500	$1,500	$6,000

If during the *first quarter* of 1984 the sum-of-the-years'-digits method is initiated, the following depreciation schedule would become applicable:

ANNUAL DEPRECIATION		1984 QUARTERLY DEPRECIATION	
SUM-OF-THE-YEARS'-DIGITS METHOD		SUM-OF-THE-YEARS'-DIGITS METHOD	
PERIOD	AMOUNT	PERIOD	AMOUNT
1983	$ 9,600	Q1	$1,800
1984	7,200	Q2	1,800
1985	4,800	Q3	1,800
1986	2,400	Q4	1,800
Total	$24,000	Total	$7,200

[8] *Statement of Financial Accounting Standards No. 3,* "Reporting Accounting Changes in Interim Financial Statements" (Stamford, CT: FASB, December 1974).

The cumulative effect of the change is $3,600 ($9,600 − $6,000), the difference in 1983 depreciation under the two methods. Note that the new 1984 depreciation amount ($7,200) is allocated equally to the four 1984 quarterly periods ($1,800 per quarter). The following journal entries would record the cumulative prior year's adjustment and the ordinary quarterly depreciation:

3/31/84	Cumulative effect of accounting change	3,600	
	Accumulated depreciation		3,600
3/31/84	Depreciation expense	1,800	
	Accumulated depreciation		1,800

The $3,600 cumulative change is reflected in first-quarter income.

If, however, the change was made effective in the *second quarter of 1984,* the cumulative effect would be handled retroactively as if it had taken place in the first quarter:

6/30/84	Retained earnings (as of 4/1/84)	3,900	
	Accumulated depreciation		3,900
	(To adjust 4/1/84 retained earnings by the cumulative effect, as of 4/1/84, of an accounting change)		
6/30/84	Depreciation expense	1,800	
	Accumulated depreciation		1,800
	(Second quarter depreciation charge)		

The first quarter income statement would be restated in any subsequent comparisons to reflect the $300 increase in depreciation expense and the $3,600 cumulative effect as of 1/1/84.

In summary, then, cumulative-effect types of accounting changes occurring in interim periods other than the first are generally treated as retroactive adjustments to beginning-of-the-quarter retained earnings. Only when an accounting change whose effect is normally reported in current income as a "cumulative effect" takes place during the first quarter of a fiscal year is the "cumulative effect of accounting change" reported separately in that quarterly income statement.

Previous quarterly data from the current or prior fiscal years that are reported for comparison purposes should provide sufficient information to enable the impact of the change in estimate or change in principal to be determinable. This is accomplished by restating prior data and providing a footnote disclosure.

Interim Income Tax Considerations

Another important consideration in interim reporting is the measurement of income tax expense. GAAP, as promulgated in **FASB Interpretation No. 18,** require that estimates be made at each balance sheet date of the **effective annual income tax rate.**[9] This estimated annual rate should be used to record tax expense each interim period. Assume that an entity has the following quarterly pretax operating income and estimated annual tax rates at the end of each quarter:

	AS OF THE END OF QUARTER			
	1	2	3	4
Pretax operating income	$100,000	$200,000	$400,000	$200,000
Estimated effective annual tax rate	30%	32%	36%	34%

[9] *Interpretation of Financial Accounting Standards No. 18,* "Accounting for Income Taxes in Interim Periods" (Stamford, CT: FASB, March 1977).

Note that the effective tax rate estimates change during the year based on varying estimates of investment and foreign tax credits, depletion allowances, capital gains, and many other considerations. Accounting for the tax expense at the end of each quarter would be as follows:

3/31/84	Tax expense	30,000	
	Tax payable		30,000
	[(30%)($100,000)]		
6/30/84	Tax expense	66,000	
	Tax payable		66,000
	[(32%)($300,000) − $30,000 = $66,000]		
9/30/84	Tax expense	156,000	
	Tax payable		156,000
	[(36%)($700,000) − $96,000 = $156,000]		
12/31/84	Tax expense	54,000	
	Tax payable		54,000
	[(34%)($900,000) − $252,000 = $54,000]		

The accounting treatment for changes in the estimated annual tax rate is the same as that accorded other changes in estimates. The changes affect only current and future periods, with the current-period expense compensating for differences between prior and current estimates.

Required Disclosure

Promulgated GAAP dealing with interim reporting are extensive, and the above considerations are merely highlights. Exhibit 27–6 lists the disclosure items required when publicly traded companies publish interim financial reports. The information is required for the current quarter, the current year to date, or the last 12 months to date, and comparable data for the preceding year.

AN INTRODUCTION TO SEC ANNUAL REPORTS

As discussed in Chapter 1, the Securities and Exchange Commission has very broad powers to prescribe the financial information distributed to the public by entities under its jurisdiction. It has the ultimate authority to set accounting principles and the formats of financial statements used both in SEC filings and in published financial reports. Although the SEC has influenced the FASB and its predecessors by ini-

EXHIBIT 27–6

DISCLOSURE ITEMS REQUIRED IN INTERIM REPORTS

1. Income statement items:
   a. Sales or gross revenues
   b. Income tax expense
   c. Extraordinary items
   d. Cumulative effect of a change in accounting principle
   e. Net income
   f. Earnings per share (primary and fully diluted)
2. Discussion of the following if applicable:
   a. Seasonal revenue, costs, or expenses
   b. Significant changes in estimates or provisions for income taxes
   c. Disposal of segments, extraordinary, unusual, or infrequently recurring items
   d. Contingent items
   e. Changes in accounting principles or estimates
   f. Significant changes in financial position

tiating new requirements on its own, operating control over accounting standards has remained in the private sector.

Currently there is a great deal of similarity between the financial statement requirements for general purposes and the financial statement requirements for SEC filings. Since the SEC's adoption of an integrated disclosure system philosophy in 1980, the similarities between the two systems have increased. Among other things, the integration philosophy instituted a certain amount of substitutability of general financial statements from published annual reports for financial statements required in SEC filings. In other words, instead of having different financial statements in reports to shareholders and those required in SEC filings (known as **Form 10–K**), the current SEC rules encourage a published annual report to be included "by reference" to meet the 10–K requirements. The rules encourage conformance of the primary financial disclosure items found in published annual reports with those required in SEC filings. In making this change, publicly traded companies were required to modify their published annual reports to (1) expand management discussion and analysis, (2) provide a new summary of financial data, and (3) include three comparative years for income statements, statements of changes in financial position, and their related notes. The requirement of two comparative years for balance sheets has not changed.

All in all, the changes made by the SEC have reaffirmed that GAAP generated in the private sector govern public reporting. The impact of these recent changes has been to make statements that are in compliance with GAAP acceptable for other types of financial-reporting requirements as well.

Form 10–K

As is true of all SEC filings, the format of the annual report is not as completely specified as that of income tax forms, for instance. In other words, there are no blank forms to fill in. Instead, the instructions for Form 10–K (and other SEC forms) list the information categories required from the registrant. In its completed form, the annual report is a lengthy document consisting of four major parts (see Exhibit 27–7).

Prior to the changes made in 1980, the instructions for Form 10–K called for far more detail than that found in published annual reports. More importantly, there were often differences in the information items. The SEC now divides the financial information into two broad classes:

1. Information to be disclosed in all annual reports submitted to the SEC or made available to stockholders (included in this class are all the data described in part II of Exhibit 27–7)
2. Information that is important to a limited and sophisticated group of users (included in this class are all the data described in parts I, III, and IV of Exhibit 27–7)

Any or all of the information described in parts I and II may be incorporated into Form 10–K by referring to the annual reports to shareholders, and part II information *must* appear in the shareholders' annual report.

Other SEC Filings

The kinds of forms that businesses under the jurisdiction of the SEC have to file depend on the nature of the securities they issue. The filings can be categorized into (1) those pursuant to the 1933 Securities Act, which deals with the registration of new security offerings; and (2) those pursuant to the 1934 Securities Exchange Act,

EXHIBIT
27–7

CONTENTS OF FORM 10-K

MAJOR SECTION	DATA ITEM NUMBER	DESCRIPTION OF INFORMATION REQUIRED
Cover Page		
Part I	1	*Business:* Includes (a) business history and development, (b) industry segments, (c) description of business, and (d) foreign operations. (*Note:* Much of this information is required for stockholders' reports and is to be incorporated by reference.)
	2	*Properties:* Descriptions of plants and facilities, leasing arrangements, and statement about the general state of properties.
	3	*Legal proceedings:* Description of material litigation and governmental actions.
	4	*Security ownership of certain beneficial owners and management*
Part II	5	*Market for the registrant's common stock and related security matters*
	6	*Selected financial data and comparison of selected financial data adjusted for the effects of changing prices:* A 5-year summary of net sales or operating revenues, income or loss from continuing operations, total assets, long-term debt, and cash dividends.
	7	*Management's discussion and analysis of financial conditions and results of operations:* A discussion of financial statements covering liquidity, capital resources, and results of operations. Trends and significant events and uncertainties are to be stressed. Also, effects of inflation are to be discussed.
	8	*Financial statements and supplementary data:* Includes (a) opinion of independent certified public accountants, (b) consolidated balance sheet (2 years), (c) consolidated income statement (3 years), (d) consolidated statement of changes in financial position (3 years), (e) consolidated statement of shareholders' equity (3 years), and (f) notes to financial statements.
Part III	9	*Directors and executive officers of registrant*
	10	*Management remuneration and transactions*
Part IV	11	*Exhibits, financial statement schedules, and reports on significant events:* Includes elaborations of many financial statement disclosures. Schedules could contain (1) details of property, plant, and equipment, (2) accumulated depreciation, depletion, and amortization, and (3) short-term debt, etc. Exhibits include, among others, details concerning the computations of net income per common share and certain subsidiary information, and a summary of other significant events that have a material impact on the registrant, if any.
Signature Page		Signatures are required from the principal executive officer(s), principal financial officer, controller or principal accounting officer, and at least a majority of the board of directors.

which deals with periodic disclosure required of publicly held companies. The latter group includes the form 10–K discussed above.

The SEC has an elaborate system of guidelines and rules that govern the makeup and content of the filings under the securities acts. **Regulation S–X** is a lengthy document that contains the specific rules relating to financial information to be reported in all types of filings. Most of the part II (Exhibit 27–7) information on Form 10–K is governed by Regulation S–X, for instance. **Regulation S–K,** on the other hand, is primarily concerned with the disclosure of nonfinancial information in SEC filings.

Registration statements consist of two major parts: (1) prospectuses, which are provided to potential security holders, contain financial statements and such information as the nature of the securities being issued and the planned use of the proceeds; and (2) information not required in prospectuses, such as expenses of issuance, expenses of distribution, and indemnifications of officers and directors.

Periodic reports for established security issuers include forms 10–K, 10–Q, 8–K, and several other specialized forms. **Form 10–Q** is the financial report required by the SEC within 45 days of the end of fiscal quarters one, two, and three. The **APB Opinion No. 28** rules for interim financial reporting discussed earlier in this chapter are used as the basis for the 10–Q's summarized financial statement disclosures.[10] Certain management discussions and footnotes are also required. **Form 8–K** must be filed within 15 days of a material event, such as changes in the controlling shareholder group, bankruptcy, and auditor changes.

AN INTRODUCTION TO FINANCIAL STATEMENT ANALYSIS

Annual reports are available to many different types of decision makers who may use all or parts of the information provided and who, in many instances, rely on other individuals for preliminary analysis. It is unrealistic to suppose that most decision makers read a report from cover to cover. In most cases, users will have some prior knowledge of an entity's history and current performance. Individual investors may also rely on professional analysts' summaries of performance that are based on thorough reviews of annual reports and other relevant economic data. Banks often employ specialists to analyze clients' financial statements. Bond raters analyze an entity's history, current state, and prospects and assign it a rating that they feel indicates the riskiness of the proposed bonds. In this section we introduce certain basic analytical procedures that can be used as inputs in a wide variety of decision-making situations. It is important to realize that none of the following types of analysis is foolproof and that a great deal of research is needed to determine the value of such analyses.

The Company and Its Environment

Individual companies cannot be viewed in isolation. They are affected by the dynamic settings in which they operate—the world economy, the home-country economy, the industry or industries, the locale, and the governmental regulatory environment in each setting. Nevertheless, an individual company can be portrayed in various time frames, depending on the nature of the decision process. For example, current debt-paying ability may be important for short-term credit decisions, long run career opportunities may influence a prospective employee's decision to accept an employment offer, the past year's performance may be suitable for income tax assessment, and so on.

The Company and Its Industry

There are many factors that a company cannot control directly but that are often crucial to its economic well-being. For instance, an industry can be characterized by its regulatory environment, its industrial organization, its supply factors, its demand factors, its basic operating cycle, and so forth. For example, on each of these dimensions, the fast-food industry is probably different from the electric utilities industry. This has to be well understood before a company's potential can be evaluated. A

---

[10] *Accounting Principles Board Opinion No. 28,* "Interim Financial Reporting."

company can respond to industry factors by diversification. Segmental disclosures, as discussed in this chapter, may aid analysts in evaluating such responses.

The Company and Its Peers

Despite the more or less imposed factors, the company has a history of past actions and a current package of resources, skills, and organizational structure that may give clues to its future performance. All analysis techniques must be viewed in a relative sense. That is, we analyze *relative* market-share track record, *relative* growth in sales, *relative* research and development capabilities, *relative* diversification of customers and products, *relative* labor relations, *relative* input costs, *relative* age of plant and equipment. A major class of attributes that may be impossible to measure directly is management skills. Often the former kinds of measurable factors are taken as indicators of the latter. In any event, it is the determination of the relationship of the specific entity to other relevant entities that is the starting point of most analyses.

The Company's Accounting Characteristics

Once the company's environment and peer relationships are understood with some degree of confidence, it is necessary, before more specific accounting-based measurements are evaluated, to understand how accounting numbers are generated in the specific entity. The auditor's opinion is often relied on for an indication of GAAP compliance. The different possible opinions mean very different things and will be examined in a later section. But even if GAAP compliance is accepted, many other accounting decisions can affect the accounting statements. Analysis of the inventory techniques employed, the amortization and depreciation policies, the revenue-recognition policies, and many others can be used to evaluate management's degree of conservatism. Such analysis can also be useful, of course, in evaluating the more specific measures discussed below.

Ways of Viewing a Given Entity

An entity can be analyzed by means of many sorts of comparisons. We shall concentrate on certain common methods of structuring the financial statement data without delving into the murky area of how final decisions are made.

Comparing entity A with other similar entities gives an interentity **relational view** of entity A. This can be particularly helpful in deciding between several prospective merger candidates, for instance. By comparing entity A's current performance or state with that of previous periods, decision makers can obtain an intraentity **sequential view** of entity A. Such a view may be useful in helping decision makers to project entity A's performance or state into the future, or to evaluate management's forecasts if they are made available. Management often provides forecasted financial statements to bankers and bond raters for use in lending and bond-rating decisions. Time series (sequential) analyses of past performance and comparisons of past forecast accuracy are used to judge the value of the current management projections.

Another general approach to financial statement analysis can be termed the **normative view** in that certain generally held beliefs about the normal relationships in financial statements are used as reference points. This approach can be misleading if the bases for the norms are not carefully selected and understood. For instance, what is "normal" for the proportion of current assets to current liabilities in one industry may not be "normal" in another industry. However, certain conditions may cause an entity that is "normal" in most respects to be viewed as "unusual" by the decision maker.

STATEMENT ANALYSIS BY ABSTRACTING
AWAY FROM ABSOLUTE DOLLARS

Certain transformations of the accounting data are used to aid analysis. These include the conversion of dollar amounts into percentages and ratios as a means of abstracting away from absolute size or as a means of pinpointing emerging problems that can be obscured by dollar amounts. We shall use the Hewlett-Packard (HP) financial statement data shown in Exhibit 27–8 to demonstrate certain basic analytical structures. (To emphasize the analytical aspects of the following material, actual years are relabeled: 19X1 = 1976 and 19X2 = 1977.) Keep in mind that analysis itself is not demonstrated in what follows. Only certain structural aspects of this subtle and complex process can be introduced in this short space.[11]

The HP income statement data could be converted into the following percentages if patterns in expenses over time were considered important:

	PERCENTAGE OF NET SALES		
	19X2	19X1	INCREASE (DECREASE)
Net sales	100%	100%	—
Other income (net)	1.0	1.1	(.1)
Total revenues	101.0	101.1	(.1)
Cost and expenses			
Cost of goods sold	45.8	48.2	(2.4)
Research and development	9.2	9.7	(.5)
Marketing	15.3	15.9	(.6)
Administrative and general	13.6	12.5	1.1
Interest	.3	.4	(.1)
Taxes on income	8.0	6.3	1.7
Net earnings	8.9	8.2	.7

Recasting to a "common size" can be done on balance sheets as well as income statements by assigning 100 percent to total assets and to total liabilities and owners' equity and showing all other balance sheet categories as percentages of these items.

Ratio Analysis   A **ratio** is the percentage computed by dividing one amount by another amount. In the context of financial statement analysis, the amounts are often in terms of dollars or some other relevant magnitude, such as number of shares outstanding or some time measurement. *Ratios are particularly useful in abstracting away from absolute amounts in that the resulting percentages facilitate comparisons of the performance or current status of entities of different sizes or of a given entity over different periods.*

Remember that the financial statement data themselves result from "analysis" of basic transactions. Computation of ratios can be viewed as second-order analyses of data that have already been analyzed and modified by the various accounting procedures used to construct financial statements. Users of ratios, therefore, must be aware of the limitations of both accounting analysis and ratio analysis. Ratios are *not* perfect indicators of an entity's performance or status. Their usefulness is constrained by the limitations of the financial statement data upon which they are based and the logic used in their computations.

[11] See George Foster, *Financial Statement Analysis* (Englewood Cliffs, NJ: Prentice-Hall, 1978), for a thorough discussion of financial statement analysis.

EXHIBIT
27–8

FINANCIAL STATEMENTS FOR HEWLETT-PACKARD COMPANY AND SUBSIDIARIES

HEWLETT-PACKARD COMPANY AND SUBSIDIARIES
Consolidated Statement of Earnings
For the Years Ended October 31, 19X2 and 19X1

	19X2	19X1
	(MILLIONS)	
Net sales	$1,360.0	$1,111.6
Other income, net	13.9	12.0
	1,373.9	1,123.6
Costs and expenses		
Cost of goods sold	622.2	535.6
Research and development	125.4	107.6
Marketing	207.5	176.6
Administrative and general	185.4	139.1
Interest	4.2	4.1
	1,144.7	963.0
Earnings before taxes on income	229.2	160.6
Taxes on income	107.7	69.8
Net earnings	$ 121.5	$ 90.8
Net earnings per share	$ 4.27	$ 3.24

HEWLETT-PACKARD COMPANY AND SUBSIDIARIES
Consolidated Statement of Financial Position
October 31, 19X2 and 19X1

	19X2	19X1
ASSETS	(MILLIONS)	
Current assets		
Cash, including time deposits (19X2—$113.4; 19X1—$77.7)	$ 130.9	$ 95.1
Marketable securities, at cost which approximates market	41.9	11.7
Notes and accounts receivable, less allowance for doubtful accounts (19X2—$1.0; 19X1—$0.8)	272.4	234.3
Inventories		
Finished goods	88.6	70.7
Work in process	104.6	80.8
Raw materials	85.6	86.4
Deferred taxes on income, deposits and prepaid expenses	27.9	25.6
Total Current Assets	751.9	604.6
Property, plant, and equipment, at cost		
Land	36.9	32.0
Buildings and improvements	279.8	210.3
Machinery and equipment	163.8	141.7
Other	56.1	43.1
Leaseholds and leasehold improvements	11.9	11.6
Construction in progress	33.3	46.3
	581.8	485.0
Accumulated depreciation and amortization	203.4	170.0
	378.4	315.0
Other assets		
Investment in unconsolidated Japanese affiliate	8.4	6.2
Patents and other intangible assets	2.4	2.7
Other	17.0	12.7
	27.8	21.6
	$1,158.1	$941.2

EXHIBIT
27–8
(cont.)

LIABILITIES AND SHAREOWNERS' EQUITY		19X2	19X1
		(MILLIONS)	
Current liabilities			
Notes payable		$ 46.9	$ 58.4
Accounts payable		45.9	31.9
Accrued expenses		137.5	105.6
Accrued taxes on income		61.6	34.7
Total Current Liabilities		291.9	230.6
Long-term debt, less current portion included in notes payable above (19X2—$2.9; 19X1—$0.7)		12.1	7.6
Deferred taxes on income		29.7	26.2
Total liabilities		333.7	264.4
Shareowners' equity			
Common stock, par value $1 a share:			

	19X2	19X1	19X2	19X1
	(THOUSANDS OF SHARES)			
Authorized	40,000	40,000		
Reserved for:				
Stock option plans	625	683		
Stock purchase plans	950	374		
Service award plan	103	14		
Issued and outstanding	28,479	27,996	28.5	28.0
Capital in excess of par value			208.3	171.4
Retained earnings			587.6	477.4
Total Shareowners' Equity			824.4	676.8
			$1,158.1	$941.2

HEWLETT-PACKARD COMPANY AND SUBSIDIARIES

Consolidated Statement of Changes in Financial Position
For the Years Ended October 31, 19X2 and 19X1

	19X2	19X1
	(MILLIONS)	
Working capital provided:		
Net earnings	$121.5	$ 90.8
Add charges (deduct credits) not affecting working capital:		
Depreciation and amortization	47.6	39.5
Deferred taxes on income	3.5	3.7
Stock purchase and award plans	9.3	8.3
Other	(1.9)	—
Working capital provided from operations	180.0	142.3
Proceeds from sale of common stock	27.8	24.2
Proceeds of additional long-term debt	7.8	3.4
Other, net	.5	(3.5)
Total working capital provided	216.1	166.4
Working capital used:		
Investment in property, plant and equipment	115.5	103.4
Dividends to shareowners	11.3	8.4
Reduction in long-term debt	3.3	0.7
Total working capital used	130.1	112.5
Increase in working capital	86.0	53.9
Working capital at beginning of year	$374.0	320.1
Working capital at end of year	$460.0	$374.0
Increase in working capital consisted of:		
Increase (decrease) in current assets:		
Cash and marketable securities	$ 66.0	$ 29.2
Notes and accounts receivable	38.1	29.5
Inventories	40.9	32.7
Deferred taxes on income, deposits and prepaid expenses	2.3	10.0
	147.3	101.4

EXHIBIT
27–8
(cont.)

Decrease (increase) in current liabilities:		
Notes payable	11.5	(25.2)
Accounts payable and accrued expenses	(45.9)	(24.6)
Accrued taxes on income	(26.9)	2.3
	(61.3)	(47.5)
Increase in working capital	$ 86.0	$ 53.9

HEWLETT-PACKARD COMPANY AND SUBSIDIARIES

Consolidated Statements of Capital in Excess of Par Value and Retained Earnings
For the Years Ended October 31, 19X2 and 19X1

	19X2	19X1
	(MILLIONS)	
Capital in excess of par value:		
Amount at beginning of year	$171.4	$138.4
Excess of market value of proceeds received, less expenses, over par value of common stock issued under:		

	19X2	19X1		
	(THOUSANDS OF SHARES)			
Stock option plans	48	58		
Stock purchase plans	424	289		
Service award plan	11	11		
			36.6	32.1
Income tax benefit from employees' compensation relating to stock options			0.3	0.9
Amount at end of year			$208.3	$171.4
Retained earnings:				
Amount at beginning of year			$477.4	$395.0
Net earnings			121.5	90.8
Dividends paid			(11.3)	(8.4)
Amount at end of year			$587.6	$477.4

Despite these limitations, many ratios are useful in statement analysis. By using ratios, decision makers can obtain information concerning such things as the liquidity, activity (turnover) or asset utilization, profitability, and financial leverage of a firm. We shall discuss specific ratios within each of those broad categories. Again we shall use portions of the consolidated financial statements of Hewlett-Packard (HP) Company and Subsidiaries (Exhibit 27–8).

Liquidity ratios **Liquidity ratios** attempt to measure the debt-paying ability of a firm—its prospects of being able to meet its maturing obligations. Business failures result primarily from an inability to meet obligations as they mature. Liquidity ratios are usually considered by credit lenders before making funds available to a firm, particularly on a short-term basis. Four ratios can be used to determine liquidity: the **current ratio;** the **quick,** or **acid-test ratio;** the **defensive interval ratio;** and the **SCFP ratio.**

CURRENT RATIO   The current ratio is calculated by dividing current assets by current liabilities: **current assets ÷ current liabilities.** Using the HP data, the current ratios would be:

19X2

$$\frac{\$751.9}{\$291.9} = 2.58 \text{ to } 1$$

19X1

$$\frac{\$604.6}{\$230.6} = 2.62 \text{ to } 1$$

Thus, the company had $2.58 of current assets for every $1 of current liabilities owed at the end of 19X2, as compared with $2.62 at the end of 19X1. Whether this is adequate for enabling the firm to pay its liabilities as they come due depends on a number of other considerations that relate to the accounting definitions of current assets and current liabilities and certain accounting measurement problems. For instance, although all the balance sheet classifications used in the computation of the current ratio are termed *current,* they do not all have the same life cycle. A current receivable could be a week or a year away from conversion to cash or even longer because the definition of *current assets* includes the phrase ". . . a year or operating cycle whichever is longer." Other potentially troublesome working capital items are marketable equity securities and inventories. Recall that marketable equity securities are carried on a lower-of-cost-or-market basis, which results in a conservative bias. Inventories can be carried at LIFO, which usually has little relationship to current value. This is particularly troublesome in that two similar entities could have the same units in actual physical inventory and could legitimately have vastly different accounting numbers on their primary financial statements.

QUICK, OR ACID-TEST RATIO   This ratio is calculated by dividing **quick assets** —cash, marketable securities, and accounts receivable (net) by current liabilities: **quick assets ÷ current liabilities.** Using the HP data, the quick ratios would be:

19X2

$$\frac{\$130.9 + \$41.9 + \$272.4}{\$291.9} = 1.53 \text{ to } 1$$

19X1

$$\frac{\$95.1 + \$11.7 + \$234.3}{\$230.6} = 1.48 \text{ to } 1$$

The quick ratio can be viewed as a test of the firm's ability to pay its immediate obligations. Inventories and other items included in the current ratio are excluded because they are often two or three steps removed from cash.

DEFENSIVE-INTERVAL RATIO   The **defensive-interval ratio** is calculated by dividing cash, marketable securities, and net accounts receivable (quick assets) by projected daily "operational" expenditures: **quick assets ÷ daily operational expenditures.** The daily operational expenditures figure is calculated by dividing the sum of cost of goods sold expense, research and development, selling expenses, general and administrative expenses, interest, and taxes, minus noncash expenses (such as depreciation and amortization) by 365 days:

19X2

$$\frac{\$130.9 + \$41.9 + \$272.4}{\dfrac{\$1,144.7 + \$107.7 - \$47.6}{365}} = 135 \text{ days}$$

19X1

$$\frac{\$95.1 + \$11.7 + \$234.3}{\dfrac{\$963.0 + \$69.8 - \$39.5}{365}} = 125 \text{ days}$$

This ratio indicates the time span (interval) over which operational needs could be covered by the quick assets. Such factors as the nature of the firm, credit terms on sales and purchases, and timing of cash inflows and outflows should also be considered before a decision is made concerning the adequacy of the coverage.

SCFP LIQUIDITY RATIOS   A ratio using data from the statement of changes in financial position can also be useful in judging a firm's liquidity position: **working capital from operations ÷ current liabilities.** Using the HP data, this ratio would be:

19X2

$$\frac{\$180.0}{\$291.9} = 61.66\%$$

19X1

$$\frac{\$142.3}{\$230.6} = 61.71\%$$

This ratio may be a useful indicator of a firm's ability to generate working capital from operations relative to current obligations.

Activity ratios   **Activity ratios** attempt to show how the firm is using its assets in carrying out its objectives. Assets that turn over too slowly may be an indication that there is too much of an investment in those assets. Major examples of ratios in this category are **accounts receivable turnover, inventory turnover,** and **total asset turnover.**

ACCOUNTS RECEIVABLE TURNOVER   This ratio is calculated by dividing net credit sales on account by average net receivables (beginning-of-the-period receivables plus end-of-the period receivables divided by 2): **net credit sales ÷ average net receivables.** Using the HP data (we assume that all the sales were on account), receivable turnover would be (beginning net accounts receivable balance for 19X1 is $204.8 million):

19X2

$$\frac{\$1,360.0}{\dfrac{\$272.4 + \$234.3}{2}} = 5.37 \text{ times per year}$$

19X1

$$\frac{\$1,111.6}{\dfrac{\$234.3 + \$204.8}{2}} = 5.06 \text{ times per year}$$

Dividing 365 by each of these results shows that receivables are being collected on the average of every 68 days in 19X2 and every 72 days in 19X1. To use these ratios, other factors normally need to be considered. If a firm's credit terms were $^2/_{10}$, n/30 and it had a receivable turnover less than 12, for example, this would indicate that a percentage of the receivables would be past due. In such a case, perhaps credit is being extended too liberally or the firm's collection procedures are lax.

INVENTORY TURNOVER   This ratio is calculated by dividing cost of goods sold expense by average inventory (beginning-of-the-period inventory plus end-of-the-period inventory divided by 2): **cost of goods sold ÷ average inventory.** Using the HP data, the inventory turnover ratios would be (beginning inventory for 19X1 is $205.2 million):

19X2

$$\frac{\$622.2}{\dfrac{\$278.8 + \$237.9}{2}} = 2.41 \text{ times per year}$$

19X1

$$\frac{\$535.6}{\dfrac{\$237.9 + \$205.2}{2}} = 2.42 \text{ times per year}$$

These ratios suggest an inventory turnover rate of once every 151 days for both 19X2 and 19X1 (dividing 365 by the turnover ratios). All else being equal, the more rapidly inventory turns over, the better.

TOTAL ASSET TURNOVER   This ratio is calculated by dividing net sales by average total assets (beginning-of-the-period total assets plus end-of-the-period total assets divided by 2): **net sales ÷ average total assets.** Using the HP data, the asset turnover would be (total assets at the beginning of 19X1 were $767.7 million):

19X2

$$\frac{\$1,360.0}{\dfrac{\$1,158.1 + \$941.2}{2}} = 1.30 \text{ times per year}$$

19X1

$$\frac{\$1,111.6}{\dfrac{\$941.2 + \$767.7}{2}} = 1.30 \text{ times per year}$$

This ratio attempts to indicate how efficiently management utilizes the resources of a firm. Ideally, current values should be used for assets in computing this ratio. The use of book values may create the impression that firms using old assets (relatively low book values) are more efficient than firms using new assets when this may not actually be the case. Significant differences between book values and current values, therefore, may create problems when using ratios involving long-term assets or liabilities.

Leverage ratios **Leverage ratios** attempt to help the user understand the investment of the owners relative to the firm's creditors and can indicate the firm's ability to cover interest on debt.

DEBT TO EQUITY   This ratio is calculated by dividing total debt by total stockholder's equity: **total debt ÷ total stockholders' equity.** Using the HP data, the ratios would be:

$$\text{19X2}$$

$$\frac{\$333.7}{\$824.4} = 40\%$$

$$\text{19X1}$$

$$\frac{\$264.4}{\$676.8} = 39\%$$

It is not uncommon to see ratios of over 100 percent (that is, debt greater than owners' equity). The leverage of U.S. manufacturing firms has tended to increase since World War II, and modern financial theory suggests that a low debt ratio may not be as good (or a high debt ratio as bad) as was once believed. However, higher debt ratios are associated with higher market risk and higher expected market returns.

TIMES-INTEREST-EARNED RATIO   This ratio is calculated by dividing net income before taxes and interest charges by interest charges: **net income + tax expense + interest charges ÷ interest charges).** Using the HP data, the ratios would be:

$$\text{19X2}$$

$$\frac{\$121.5 + \$107.7 + \$4.2}{\$4.2} = 55.6 \text{ times}$$

$$\text{19X1}$$

$$\frac{\$90.8 + \$69.8 + \$4.1}{\$4.1} = 40.2 \text{ times}$$

This ratio is based on an "income" figure, and all the uncertainties implicit in that measurement must be weighed. Note that income tax is added back because the interest charge is tax deductible; as interest is incurred, taxable income is reduced.

Profitability ratios **Profitability ratios** attempt to measure the firm's overall operating efficiency and effectiveness in attaining its primary objective of profit maximization. Major examples of ratios in this category are **profit margin on sales, rate of return on assets employed, rate of return on stockholders' equity,** and **earnings per share.**

PROFIT MARGIN ON SALES   This ratio is calculated by dividing net income from continuing operations by net sales: **net income from continuing operations ÷ net sales.** Using the HP data, this ratio would be:

19X2

$$\frac{\$121.5}{\$1,360.0} = 8.9\%$$

19X1

$$\frac{\$90.8}{\$1,111.6} = 8.2\%$$

Using income from continuing operations rather than net income is preferred because the ratio then reflects the rate of return on sales from the normal, recurring, operating activities of the firm. (In our HP data, income from continuing operations and net income are equal because there are no special items on the HP income statement.) This is particularly true of comparisons across entities.

RATE OF RETURN ON ASSETS EMPLOYED The "profit margin on sales" ratio, taken by itself, does not give a complete picture of how profitable the firm was for a given period of time. Many feel that because return on investment relates profits to the assets that generated them, it is a better indicator of profitability. The rate of return on assets employed equals the profit margin on sales ratio (above) times the asset turnover ratio. Using the HP data, this would be:

19X2: 1.30 × 8.9% = 11.6%
19X1: 1.30 × 8.2% = 10.7%

Note that this is equivalent to net income over average total assets:

$$19X2: \frac{\$121.5}{\$1,049.7} = 11.6\%$$

$$19X1: \frac{\$90.8}{\$854.5} = 10.6\% \text{ (rounding difference)}$$

To determine whether these rates of return are at least commensurate with the risks assumed in the venture, comparisons would be made with industry averages and target rates of return. This ratio emphasizes the importance of rapid asset turnover. Large grocery stores, for example, often have very low margins on sales. However, the items they sell turn over so rapidly that the successful firms earn an attractive rate of return on assets employed. Other firms, such as jewelry stores selling high-priced items, must have a much higher margin on sales in order to stay in business because products turn over so slowly.

RETURN ON STOCKHOLDERS' EQUITY This ratio is calculated by dividing income from continuing operations (net of preferred stock dividends, if any) by average stockholders' equity (stockholders' equity at the beginning of 19X1 was $561.0 million): **income from continuing operations ÷ average equity.** Using the HP data, this ratio would be:

19X2

$$\frac{\$121.5}{\frac{\$824.4 + \$676.8}{2}} = 16.2\%$$

$$\frac{\$90.8}{\dfrac{\$676.8 + \$561.0}{2}} = 14.7\%$$

EARNINGS PER SHARE (EPS)   The calculation of this ratio can be very complex and is covered in detail in Chapter 22. It often represents the use of complex data combined into a single calculation. Decision makers should realize that EPS can be misleading when used for comparison purposes, because of differences in accounting methods employed.

Market-based ratios   Market-based ratios are ratios that attempt to deal more directly with the returns to owners. As discussed in earlier chapters in this book (such as Chapter 6), one of the commonly identified objectives of accounting information is to help external users predict the future cash flows of the entity. The future cash flows to both owners and creditors are necessarily related to the cash flows of the entity's operations in the long run. Hence, accounting is often considered to be useful in helping external users predict the long-run cash-generating ability of the entity. Market-based ratios, however, deal more directly with the cash flows of immediate significance to the stockholders. Two popular ratios that fall into this category are the **price-earnings (P/E) ratio,** and the ratio of systemic risk called **market beta.**

PRICE EARNINGS RATIO   The **P/E ratio** is the ratio of the market price per share of common stock over the earnings per share. In the HP example, assume the market price per share of common is $38 at the end of 19X2 and $40 at the end of 19X1, the P/E ratios would be:

$$19X2: \frac{\$38.00}{4.27} = 8.9$$

$$19X1: \frac{\$40.00}{3.24} = 12.3$$

P/E ratios will often range between 4 or 5 at the low end and 18 or 19 at the high end, with lower P/E stocks generally considered to be less speculative than high P/E stocks. P/E ratios are very popular and are often quoted along with the stock prices in the financial press.

MARKET BETA   **Systematic market risk,** called **market beta,** is a direct measure of the relationship between the implicit cash return to the common shareholder for a period of time for a specific stock and the implicit cash returns on all common stocks. **The implicit cash return on the stock is the sum of dividends plus price change** (increase or decrease) for a period of time. The formula for computing market beta is:

$$\beta_i = \frac{\mathrm{Cov}(R_i, R_m)}{\sigma_{R_m}^2}$$

where:

β_i = market beta for firm i

R_i = the return (cash dividends plus price change for the period) on firm i's stock.

R_m = the return on the market (a weighted average return of all stocks in the market)

$\text{Cov}(R_i, R_m)$ = the covariance between R_i and R_m

$\sigma^2_{R_m}$ = the variance of the market returns (a measure of the dispersion of returns on all stocks)

Beta is essentially a description of how the implicit cash returns from one stock compared with the implicit cash returns of all stocks for the most recent period (where the period may be monthly, quarterly, annually, and so on). Betas generally range from about .7 to about 1.7. This relationship is sometimes displayed graphically as shown in Figure 27–1. The line labeled β_B is at a 45° angle from the R_m axis and, therefore, the slope of the line which describes the change in R_i (ΔR_i) relative to the change in R_m (ΔR_m) is 1.0. In other words, the change in the returns from firm i will be equal to the change in the returns from all stocks in the market. Stocks with a beta equal to about 1.0 are said to be at the same expected risk and return level as the weighted average risk and return of all stocks in the market.

The line labeled β_A has a slope greater than 1.0, which means that it has higher expected returns than the market when the return on the market is positive, and lower expected returns than the market when the market returns are negative (such as when the average price of stocks experiences a decline). Stocks with betas greater than 1.0 are considered to be above average in risk.

The line labeled β_C has a slope of less than 1.0, which means that the return on the security changes less than the return on the market. If the market return is, on average, increasing at 10 percent, stocks with betas of less than 1.0 will normally increase (return) less than 10 percent. Conversely, if the market return declines by 10 percent, these low-beta stocks should experience less than a 10 percent decrease in returns.

FIGURE
27–1
Market beta

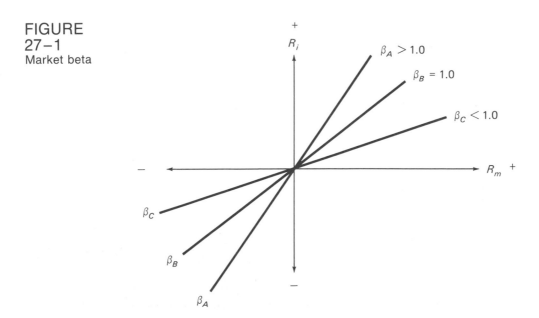

Systematic market risk or beta is somewhat more complicated than this brief introduction might suggest. For more thorough treatment, you can consult a text on investments. The basic concept introduced here is provided because of the increasing popularity of this ratio. Major investment services consider a stock's beta to be a key financial ratio. The ratio may change somewhat from period to period, but it will normally not change a great deal.

The Auditor's Report as a Form of Analysis

The financial statements presented in annual reports are those of the management of the firm. Management is, in essence, reporting on its accomplishments to the financial statement users. The independent auditor conducts certain tests of the firm's records in order to be able to state whether or not the financial statements fairly present the information in accordance with generally accepted accounting principles. In so doing, the auditor adds credence to those statements and the user receives independent evidence as to the reliability of management's representations.

In Exhibit 27–9 we illustrate the so-called **short-form audit report** for the Hewlett-Packard Company. In all such reports, the auditor must follow certain standards. In the first paragraph, often called the **scope paragraph,** the auditor must indicate the character of the auditor's examination and the degree of responsibility being taken. In the Hewlett-Packard report, the auditor indicates that the financial statements were examined and that the examination was in accordance with generally accepted auditing standards and therefore included such tests of the accounting records as were deemed necessary in the circumstances.

The last paragraph is called the **opinion paragraph.** If the auditor has been able to conduct an adequate examination and finds that the financial statements are in conformance with GAAP and are consistently prepared, this paragraph will state that the financial statements present fairly the firm's financial position, operating results, and changes in financial position in conformity with generally accepted accounting principles consistently applied. By so stating, this implies that the informative disclosures accompanying the financial statements, such as footnotes, are also adequate. Thus, the Hewlett-Packard Company received an **unqualified** (or what is often called a **"clean") opinion.**

EXHIBIT 27–9

AUDITOR'S REPORT

HEWLETT-PACKARD COMPANY AND SUBSIDIARIES
Report of Independent Certified Public Accountants

The Board of Directors and Shareowners
Hewlett-Packard Company:

We have examined the consolidated statement of financial position of Hewlett-Packard Company and subsidiaries as of October 31, 19X2 and 19X1 and the related consolidated statements of earnings, capital in excess of par value, retained earnings and changes in financial position for the years then ended. Our examinations were made in accordance with generally accepted auditing standards and, accordingly, included such tests of the accounting records and such other auditing procedures as we considered necessary in the circumstances.

In our opinion, such financial statements present fairly the consolidated financial position of Hewlett-Packard Company and subsidiaries at October 31, 19X2 and 19X1 and the consolidated results of their operations and the changes in their financial position for the years then ended, in conformity with generally accepted accounting principles applied on a consistent basis.

San Francisco, California
December 18, 19X2

When there are special circumstances or problems that the auditor wishes to discuss, paragraphs are inserted between the scope paragraph and the opinion paragraph for that purpose. The possible variety of these special circumstances or problems is almost limitless. Sometimes these problems, though significant, are not so severe as to invalidate the statements as a whole, and the auditor will render what is called a **qualified opinion.** Attention will be called to the problems creating the necessity for qualification, and the opinion paragraph will then indicate that the statements are fairly presented subject to the situation bringing about the qualification. A variety of problems can cause the auditor to qualify the opinion, such as having the scope of the audit examination limited by existing conditions, determining that certain generally accepted accounting principles were not followed, or deciding that the disclosures are inadequate.

Of course, the problems involved could be so severe that the auditor will express an **adverse opinion.** In such cases, the auditor feels that the statements are not fairly presented, and this will be stated in the auditor's report after discussing the specific problems of the company.

Disclaimers of opinion are given in cases where uncertainties are such that the auditor cannot determine whether the statements are fairly presented. For example, what if there is considerable doubt as to whether the firm will be able to continue as a going concern? Or, what if the scope of the auditor's examination has been so severely limited that there is insufficient evidence on which to express an opinion? In both of these cases, the auditor may give a disclaimer. Such information may be useful to users in deciding to what extent they can rely on the financial presentations.

As an example of a disclaimer of opinion, consider the report in Exhibit 27–10 relating to Chrysler's 1980 financial statements. Although the conditions had been developing for a number of years, by 1979 Chrysler was in a precarious financial position. Suppliers were not being paid on time and were threatening to refuse to extend additional credit. Chrysler was having difficulty getting loans refinanced and found that borrowing additional funds was nearly impossible. Many felt that the only thing that could save Chrysler would be loan guarantees by the federal government. Chrysler officials were discussing that possibility with government officials, but by the end of 1979 no final decisions had been made. During 1980, however, the government guarantees came through. Nevertheless, a great deal of uncertainty still existed on February 27, 1981, when the report shown in Exhibit 27–10 was published.

After describing the various financial difficulties Chrysler was having, indicating some question as to whether or not Chrysler could continue as a going concern, the auditor indicated that an opinion could not be expressed as to the fairness of presentation of the statements because of uncertainty as to whether Chrysler Corporation was a going concern, an underlying assumption upon which the statements had been prepared.

The auditor's report is complex, and we have merely introduced it here to show that financial statement users can and do draw on the analyses made by independent auditors. The auditors use their skills, professional standards, and techniques to test the financial statements, and their formal opinions become the starting point for further analysis. Such a division of analysis effort, between the auditor and the individual financial statement user, seems to be cost effective. The auditor provides publicly available signals to all decision makers, and the individual decision

EXHIBIT
27–10

DISCLAIMER OF OPINION—CHRYSLER CORPORATION

Accountants' Report

Shareholders and Board of Directors
Chrysler Corporation, Detroit, Michigan

We have examined the accompanying consolidated balance sheet of Chrysler Corporation and consolidated subsidiaries at December 31, 1980 and 1979, and the related consolidated statements of operations, additional paid-in capital, net earnings retained, and changes in financial position for each of the three years in the period ended December 31, 1980. Our examinations were made in accordance with generally accepted auditing standards and accordingly included such tests of the accounting records and such other auditing procedures as we considered necessary in the circumstances.

The Corporation has incurred substantial losses in 1979 and 1980, and as more fully described in Note 2, the continuation of the Corporation is dependent upon a return to sustained profitable operations and the availability, if needed, of additional financing or concessions. The Corporation's ability to achieve sustained profitability will be affected by many factors which are beyond its control, such as the automobile market conditions, actions of competitors, availability of consumer financing, interest rates, other economic conditions and government regulation. Although the Corporation has been able to fund its losses through liquidation of assets, federally guaranteed loans and concessions from its lenders, employees and suppliers (which activities are characteristic of a company being restructured), deterioration in the Corporation's financial condition during 1980 has diminished its ability to absorb losses without further restructuring. As the Corporation further develops and executes strategies for a return to sustained profitable operations, and a special committee of the Board of Directors reviews alternative methods for obtaining infusions of new capital, future actions may result in adjustments of assets and liabilities and changes in the relative interests of Corporation's equity owners, in amounts that could be significant in relation to the accompanying financial statements. The foregoing matters raise a question as to whether or not the use of generally accepted accounting principles applicable to a going concern is appropriate in the circumstances.

In addition, the Corporation is continuing its negotiations for an industrial cooperation agreement with Peugeot S.A. (see Note 5), and accordingly continues to value its 14% ownership in Peugeot as a long-term investment. However, the carrying value of the Peugeot stock may require adjustment if the nature of this investment changes.

In our opinion, the accompanying financial statements have been prepared in conformity with generally accepted accounting principles applicable to a going concern applied on a consistent basis, except for the capitalization of interest in 1980 with which we concur (see Note 11). The financial statements do not purport to give effect to adjustments, if any, that may be appropriate should the Corporation be unable to operate as a going concern and therefore be required to realize its assets and liquidate its liabilities, contingent obligations and commitments in other than the normal course of business and at amounts different from those in the accompanying financial statements.

In view of the uncertainties and the ongoing restructuring described in the preceding paragraphs, we are unable to express an opinion as to whether or not the accompanying financial statements are presented fairly because we are unable to determine whether or not the use of generally accepted accounting principles applicable to a going concern is appropriate in the circumstances.

TOUCHE ROSS & CO.
Certified Public Accountants

February 27, 1981 Detroit, Michigan

---

makers then can concentrate on the types of analysis needed in their specific decision contexts.

Financial statement analysis, therefore, is affected by a broad range of activities, starting with the initial recording and classification of transactions through the work of the independent auditor to the specific analyses of individual decision makers. Decisions made at all stages of the financial reporting process affect the ultimate use of accounting information.

SUMMARY

Financial-reporting processes usually culminate in interim and annual reports that are made available to various external user groups. The package of materials, of which the formal financial statements constitute one part, is composed of several sections. Each of these sections tells part of the overall story about the current state and past performance of the entity. In this chapter we have reviewed the commonly encountered annual report sections, including those not directly governed by GAAP. We also discussed the purpose and nature of the accounting policies note and the other notes.

Segmental reporting seeks to disaggregate reporting entities into significant segments along industry and geographical lines. Motivated by the belief that multisegment businesses cannot be fully evaluated without disclosure of segmental characteristics, GAAP prescribe the disclosure items necessary for those segments that meet a variety of tests.

Interim reporting is motivated by the timeliness objective. Although GAAP do not adopt a completely consistent view of the nature of interim reporting, the overall thrust of current practice is to have each interim report reflect the quarter's economic activity with a minimum smoothing of revenues and expenses. The result is an interim reporting system that tracks seasonal variations.

The SEC is a major force in financial reporting, and Form 10–K is the primary document used for formal filings of annual financial statements. Although an integration initiative has considerably simplified the required financial disclosures by making them conform, more or less, to GAAP, there are still many unique aspects in SEC reporting. Registration statements are required when certain new securities issues are proposed. The system of financial disclosure for both registrations with, and regular reporting to, the SEC were introduced.

Properly determined and utilized, ratios and other forms of financial statement analysis can help financial statement users understand the stories told by those statements. But ratios have the same limitations as the data on which they are based. This does not negate their usefulness, but it does indicate they should be used with care.

Ratios are interrelated and interdependent; therefore, too much emphasis should not be placed on one or two ratios taken alone. Weaknesses in one ratio can be counterbalanced by strengths in other ratios, and they must be considered in a total setting if the operational story of the firm is to be understood. However, an unlimited number of ratios could be calculated because almost any item in one statement could be related to almost any other item in that statement or others. Such an approach would not be useful because many such ratios would be meaningless, if not misleading. Therefore, care must be exercised in the selection of ratios. They should reflect something substantive regarding the liquidity, activity, leverage, and operating activities and conditions of the firm.

We have emphasized that judgment is critical in accounting. As a consequence, approximations are necessary in deriving many of the data presented in financial statements. Because ratios are based on these data, they too are approximations, necessary and useful, but approximations nonetheless. They should be considered in this light.

Despite all these caveats, the analyses we have presented are useful in assessing the performance and status of a firm. Analyses and ratios other than those discussed might be calculated and used, and they often are. The ones discussed can act as a springboard for calculating and understanding others.

Ratio analysis is not the only consideration in understanding financial statements. Footnotes contain much useful information that not only amplifies and clarifies the data in the body of the statements but presents data that can have an impact on the future of the firm, such as commitments and contingencies. And the auditor's report should not be overlooked. If the report contains no qualifications or disclaimers, the user knows at least that a competent professional did not find anything of substance challenging the fairness of the financial statement presentations. This adds credence to the statements and helps the user determine their reliability. However, when something of significance challenges the fairness of the presentations—which indicates that the statements were not presented in conformance with generally accepted accounting principles–the auditor will describe and discuss the exception.

QUESTIONS

Q27-1 Financial statement analaysis is performed on existing financial statements. In what sense are the financial statements themselves the results of analyses?

Q27-2 What are the basic differences between the accounting policies' note and the other notes found in financial statements?

Q27-3 If you were assigned to evaluate a company's annual report and were given very little time to do it, what one item would you read first and why?

Q27-4 In general terms, contrast the perspectives of the "management discussion" and the "auditor's report." Is there ever any direct tie between the two?

Q27-5 Write a one-paragraph rule that tells when a financial statement note is needed. Are you satisfied with this rule? Explain.

Q27-6 Given the fact that financial analysts know a lot about major companies' diversification, what justifies the reporting requirements for lines of business?

Q27-7 Consider the specific percentage tests required by *FASB Statement No. 14* for segmental reporting. What are the advantages and disadvantages of general guidelines versus specific tests in accounting standards?

Q27-8 Develop arguments for and against the requirement that quarterly income statements reflect seasonal activity and should not be normalized.

Q27-9 Why, do you think, do GAAP not include a list of "generally accepted financial ratios"?

Q27-10 What role does the auditor's opinion play in analyzing a company's financial statements?

CASES

C27-1 (CMA ADAPTED) Firms prepare annual financial statements for internal management use and for distribution to outside parties. In addition, many firms prepare some type of summary reports or statements quarterly, monthly, and/or weekly for both internal use and external distribution. The frequency of reporting may affect the cost to prepare the reports or statements and their objectivity.

REQUIRED

1. Basic accounting theory assumes that the accounting period appropriate for internal and external reporting for most firms is 1 year. Explain why the year is used as the basic accounting reporting period.
2. Explain in general terms why summary reports or statements are prepared for reporting periods that are shorter than one year. In your explanation, give an example of why (a) internal management and (b) an outside party may want reports or statements that cover a shorter time period than one year.
3. Adjustments to the accounting records are made whenever summary reports or statements are prepared annually, quarterly, or monthly.

a. Explain why these adjustments are needed.

b. Cite specific examples of some adjustments that would have to be made to the accounting records.

4. How is the objectivity of financial information presented in summary reports or statements affected when more frequent reports are prepared? Explain your answer.

C27–2 (CPA ADAPTED)   To understand current generally accepted accounting principles with respect to accounting for, and reporting upon, segments of a business enterprise, as required by *FASB Statement No. 14,* it is necessary to be familiar with certain unique terminology.

REQUIRED

1. With respect to segments of a business enterprise, define
   a. Industry segment
   b. Revenue
   c. Operating profit and loss
   d. Identifiable assets

2. A central issue in reporting upon industry segments of a business enterprise is the determination of which segments are reportable.
   a. What tests determine whether an industry segment is reportable?
   b. What test determines whether enough industry segments have been separately reported upon, and what guideline indicates the maximum number of industry segments to be shown?

C27–3 (CPA ADAPTED)   Interim financial reporting has become an important topic in accounting. There has been considerable discussion as to the proper method of reflecting results of operations at interim dates. Accordingly, the Accounting Principles Board issued an opinion clarifying some aspects of interim financial reporting.

REQUIRED

1. Discuss generally how revenue should be recognized at interim dates, and specifically how revenue should be recognized for industries subject to large seasonal fluctuations in revenue and for long-term contracts, using the percentage-of-completion method at annual reporting dates.

2. Discuss generally how product and period costs should be recognized at interim dates.

3. Discuss how the provision for income taxes is computed and reflected in interim financial statements.

C27–4 (CPA ADAPTED)   Many accountants and financial analysts contend that companies should report financial data for segments of the enterprise.

REQUIRED

1. What does financial reporting for segments of a business enterprise involve?
2. Identify the reasons for requiring financial data to be reported by segments.
3. Identify the possible disadvantages of requiring financial data to be reported by segments.
4. Identify the accounting difficulties inherent in segment reporting.

C27–5 (CMA ADAPTED)   The following excerpt is from paragraphs 9 and 10 of *Accounting Principles Board Opinion No. 28,* "Interim Financial Reporting": "Interim financial information is essential to provide investors and others with timely information as to the progress of the enterprise. The usefulness of such information rests on the relationship that it has to the annual results of operations. Accordingly, the Board has concluded that each interim period should be viewed primarily as an integral part of an annual period."

In general, the results for each interim period should be based on the accounting principles and practices used by an enterprise in the preparation of its latest annual financial statements unless a change in an accounting practice or policy has been adopted in the current year. However, the board has concluded that certain accounting principles and practices followed for annual reporting purposes may require modification at interim reporting dates so that the reported results for the interim period may better relate to the results of operations for the annual period.

REQUIRED   Listed below are six independent cases that describe how accounting facts might be reported on an individual company's interim financial reports. For any four of the six cases, state whether the method proposed for interim reporting would be acceptable under GAAP applicable to interim financial data. Support each answer with a brief explanation.

1. Coe Company is reasonably certain that it will have an employee strike in the third quarter. As a result, it ships heavily during the second quarter but plans to defer the recognition of the sales in excess of the normal sales volume. The deferred sales will be recognized as sales in the third quarter when the strike is in progress. Coe Company management thinks this is more nearly representative of normal second- and third-quarter operations.

2. Day Company takes a physical inventory at year-end for annual financial statement purposes. Inventory and cost of sales reported in the interim quarterly statements are based on estimated gross profit rates because a physical inventory would result in a cessation of operations. Day Company does have reliable perpetual inventory records.

3. Ball Company is planning to report one-fourth of its pension expense each quarter.

4. Fragle Company wrote inventory down to reflect lower-of-cost-or-market in the first quarter of 1985. At year-end the market exceeds the original acquisition cost of this inventory. Consequently, management plans to write the inventory back up to its original cost as a year-end adjustment.

5. Good Company realized a large gain on the sale of investments at the beginning of the second quarter. The company wants to report one-third of the gain in each of the remaining quarters.

6. Jay Company has estimated its annual audit fee. It plans to prorate this expense equally over all four quarters.

C27–6 (CMA ADAPTED) Identify and explain what financial characteristic of a firm would be measured by an analysis in which the following four ratios were calculated: current; quick (or acid-test); accounts receivable turnover; inventory turnover.

Do these ratios provide adequate information to measure this characteristic or are additional data required? If so, give two examples of the additional data.

C27–7 (CPA ADAPTED) Following are the financial statements issued by Allen Corportion for its fiscal year ended October 31, 1983.

ALLEN CORPORATION
Statement of Financial Position
October 31, 1983

ASSETS

Cash	$ 15,000
Accounts receivable, net	150,000
Inventory	120,000
Total current assets	285,000
Trademark (Note 3)	250,000
Land	125,000
Total assets	$660,000

LIABILITIES

Accounts payable	$ 80,000
Accrued expenses	20,000
Total current liabilities	100,000
Deferred income tax payable (Note 4)	80,000
Total liabilities	180,000

STOCKHOLDERS' EQUITY

Common stock, par $1 (Note 5)	$100,000	
Additional paid-in capital	180,000	
Retained earnings	200,000	480,000
Total liabilities and stockholders' equity		$660,000

```
                 ALLEN CORPORATION
                  Earnings Statement
          For the Fiscal Year Ended October 31, 1983

Sales                                          $1,000,000
Cost of goods sold                                750,000
   Gross margin                                   250,000
Expenses:
   Bad debt expense              $ 7,000
   Insurance                      13,000
   Lease expenses (Note 1)        40,000
   Repairs and maintenance        30,000
   Pensions (Note 2)              12,000
   Salaries                       60,000         162,000
   Earnings before provision for income tax       88,000
   Provision for income tax                        28,740
      Net earnings                                $59,260

Earnings per common share outstanding              $0.5926
```

```
                 ALLEN CORPORATION

             Statement of Retained Earnings
          For the Fiscal Year Ended October 31, 1983

Retained earnings, Nov. 1, 1982          $150,000
Extraordinary gain, net of income tax      25,000
Net earnings for the fiscal year ended Oct.
31, 1983                                   59,260
                                          234,260
Dividends ($.3426 per share)               34,260
Retained earnings, Oct. 31, 1983         $200,000
```

Note 1—Long-Term Lease

Under the terms of a 5-year noncancelable lease for buildings and equipment, the company is obligated to make annual rental payments of $40,000 in each of the next four fiscal years. At the conclusion of the lease period, the company has the option of purchasing the leased assets for $20,000 (a bargain puchase option) or entering into another 5-year lease of the same property at an annual rental of $5,000.

Note 2—Pension Plan

Substantially all employees are covered by the company's pension plan. Pension expense is equal to the total of pension benefits paid to retired employees during the year.

Note 3—Trademark

The company's trademark was purchased from Apex Corporation on January 1, 1981, for $250,000.

Note 4—Deferred Income Tax Payable

The entire balance in the deferred income tax payable account arose from tax-exempt municipal bonds that were held during the previous fiscal year giving rise to a difference between taxable income and reported net earnings for the fiscal year ended Octobe 31, 1982. The deferred liability amount was calculated on the basis of expected tax rates in future years.

Note 5—Warrants

On January 1, 1982, one common stock warrant was issued to stockholders of record for each common share owned. An additional share of common stock is to be issued upon exercise of ten stock warrants and receipt of an amount equal to par value. For the 6 months ended October 31, 1983, the average market value for the company's common stock was $5 per share and no warrants had yet been exercised.

Note 6—Contingent Liability

On October 31, 1983, the company was contingently liable for product warranties in an amount estimated to aggregate $75,000.

REQUIRED Review the preceding financial statements and related footnotes. Identify any inclusions or exclusions from them that would be in violation of generally accepted accounting principles, and indicate corrective action to be taken. Do *not* comment as to format or style. Respond in the following order:

1. Statement of financial position
2. Footnotes
3. Earnings statement
4. Statement of retained earnings
5. General

C27-8 (CMA ADAPTED) The Johnson Company is a closely held corporation with six stockholders. The company has been managed by one of its stockholders since it was formed in 1962. The remaining five stockholders have previously been inactive in company affairs and have been content with an annual financial report. They have now asked the management to present interim financial statements for their review.

REQUIRED Identify and discuss three major accounting issues that must be resolved in order to present interim statements.

C27-9 (CMA ADAPTED) The following three financial ratios were among many presented in the financial analysis of a retail organization:

1. Inventory turnover
2. Acid-test (quick ratio)
3. Times interest earned

REQUIRED

1. How is each of these ratios calculated?
2. What does each ratio tell you about the operation of the business?

C27-10 (CMA ADAPTED) Multipro, Inc., manufactures a wide variety of pharmaceuticals, medical instruments, and other related medical supplies. Eighteen months ago the company developed and began to market a new product line of antihistamine drugs under various trade names. Sales and profitability of this product line during the current fiscal year greatly exceeded management's expectations. The new product line will account for 10 percent of the company's total sales and 12 percent of the company's operating income for the fiscal year ending June 30, 1984. Management believes sales and profits will be significant for several years.

Multipro is concerned about its market position relative to its competitors should disclosure be made about the volume and profitability of its new product line in its annual financial statements. Management is not sure how *FASB Statement No. 14*, "Financial Reporting for Segments of a Business Enterprise," applies in this case.

REQUIRED

1. What is the purpose for requiring that segment information be disclosed in financial statements?
2. Identify and explain the factors that should be considered when attempting to decide how products should be grouped to determine a single business segment.
3. What options, if any, does Multipro have regarding the disclosure of its new antihistamine product line? Explain your answer.

C27–11 (CPA ADAPTED) Three independent, unrelated statements follow regarding financial accounting. Each statement contains some unsound reasoning.

STATEMENT 1 One function of financial accounting is to measure a company's net earnings for a given period of time. An earnings statement will measure a company's true net earnings if it is prepared in accordance with generally accepted accounting principles. Other financial statements are basically unrelated to the earnings statement. Net earnings would be measured as the difference between revenues and expenses. Revenues are an inflow of cash to the enterprise and should be realized when recognized. This may be accomplished by using the sales basis or the production basis. Expenses should be matched with revenues to measure net earnings. Usually, variable expenses are assigned to the product, and fixed expenses are assigned to the period.

STATEMENT 2 One function of financial accounting is to present a company's financial position accurately at a given point in time. This is done with a statement of financial position (balance sheet), which is prepared using historical-cost valuations for all assets and liabilities except inventories. Inventories are stated at first-in, first-out (FIFO); last-in, first-out (LIFO); or average valuations. The statement of financial position must be prepared on a consistent basis with prior years' statements.

In addition to reflecting assets, liabilities, and stockholders' equity, a statement of financial position should, in a separate section, reflect a company's reserves. The section should include three different types of reserves: depreciation reserves, product warranty reserves, and retained earnings reserves. All three of these types of reserves are established by a credit to the reserve account.

STATEMENT 3 Financial statement analysis involves using ratios to test the past performance of a given company. Past performance is compared with a predetermined standard, and the company is evaluated accordingly. One such ratio is the current ratio, which is computed as current assets divided by current liabilities, or as monetary assets divided by monetary liabilities. A current ratio of 2-to-1 is considered good for companies; but the higher the ratio, the better the company's financial position is assumed to be. The current ratio is dynamic because it helps to measure funds flows.

REQUIRED Identify the areas that are not in accordance with GAAP or are untrue with respect to the financial statement analysis discussed in each of the statements, and explain why the reasoning is incorrect. Complete your identification and explanation of each statement before proceeding to the next statement.

C27–12 (CMA ADAPTED) Primier Paint Company, a publicly held corporation, is preparing its interim financial report for the first quarter of the current year. Primier's external auditor is scheduled to review the interim financial information for the quarter before the report is issued to the stockholders. The external audit firm performing the review has conducted the annual audit for the last 5 years.

James Sullivan, Primier's president, wants the interim report to be released as soon as possible and would like to minimize the external auditor's fee. He has asked the controller, Edward Kare, to take the necessary steps to expedite the external auditor's review. Kare has been Primier's controller for 8 years.

REQUIRED

1. Explain the objective of the review of Primier Paint Company's interim financial information by its external auditor before the interim report is released to stockholders.
2. Identify the information Edward Kare might be expected to furnish during the review of Primier Paint Company's interim financial information by its external auditor.

EXERCISES

E27–1 Diamond Products, Inc., has three distinct operating units:

UNIT	REVENUES	NET INCOME	ASSETS
Foods	$51,000,000	4,495,000	$ 60,000,000
Chemicals (industrial)	19,500,000	(275,000)	40,000,000
Pharmaceuticals	6,000,000	(20,000)	5,000,000
Total	$76,500,000	$4,200,000	$105,000,000

REQUIRED Perform all the tests required to determine segments under *FASB Statement No. 14.* Which of the above operating units would be reported as a segment in Diamond's published financial statements?

E27–2 A United States-based company has the following geographical breakdown of operations:

GEOGRAPHICAL AREA	SALES	ASSETS
United States	$181,200,000	$260,000,000
Europe		
France	14,300,000	12,000,000
West Germany	20,100,000	2,500,000
Other	11,400,000	1,700,000
Canada	6,200,000	31,300,000
Total	$233,200,000	307,500,000

REQUIRED Discuss the possible disclosures required under GAAP for this situation.

E27–3 Golden Meadows Raceway, Inc., has a season that runs from April 1 to the end of September, and a calendar fiscal year. Discuss how each of the following expenditures should appear on the company's quarterly income statements?

	ACTUAL QUARTERLY EXPENDITURES			
	1ST	2ND	3RD	4TH
1. Grounds crew	5,000[a]	45,000	50,000	15,000[a]
2. Insurance on facilities	$100,000	$100,000	$100,000	$100,000
3. Cost of concessions sold	0	350,000	400,000	0
4. Attendants' wages	40,000[b]	200,000	210,000	40,000[b]

[a] Cost during March and October to get track prepared for the season.
[b] Year-round employees who perform regular maintenance duties throughout the year.

E27–4 Consider the facts in exercise 27–3. Assume that a fire destroyed part of the grandstand on June 12, 1983. This was recorded as follows:

Extraordinary loss	1,427,400	
Accumulated depreciation	321,000	
Federal income taxes payable	951,600	
Grandstand		2,700,000

REQUIRED How would this loss affect the quarterly and year-end income statements for 1983 and why?

E27–5 During the third fiscal quarter of 1983, Runkel Corporation changed its method of depreciation of buildings from a straight-line to an accelerated depreciation method for both book and tax purposes. The following schedule summarizes the differences in methods:

ACCUMULATED DEPRECIATION THROUGH THE BEGINNING OF	ACCUMULATED DEPRECIATION	
	STRAIGHT LINE	ACCELERATED
Current fiscal year	$3,000,000	$4,880,000
2nd quarter	3,250,000	5,136,000
3rd quarter	3,500,000	5,392,000
4th quarter	3,750,000	5,648,000

REQUIRED How would the change in depreciation method affect the third-quarter financial statements? How would it affect the financial statements for the year?

E27–6 Harvey Engines, Inc., started operations in 1983 and has the following quarterly net income before taxes. Also shown is the company's best estimate of the "full-year net income before taxes" made at the end of each quarter.

QUARTER	ACTUAL NET INCOME (LOSS) BEFORE TAXES (NIBT)	ESTIMATE OF FULL-YEAR NIBT MADE AT END OF EACH QUARTER
1st	$31,000	$150,000
2nd	42,000	160,000
3rd	48,000	170,000
4th	(57,000)	64,000ª
1983 NIBT	$64,000	

ª Actual.

Assume that there are no differences between book and tax returns and that the following schedule applies for tax liability:

TAXABLE INCOME ($)	TAX RATE (%)
0–25,000	15
25,001–50,000	18
50,001–75,000	30
75,001–100,000	40
Over $100,000	46

REQUIRED What quarterly tax expense amounts would have been shown on the quarterly statements? Explain.

E27–7 Portland Electrical Company has the following financial data in its current financial statements:

	BEGINNING BALANCE	ENDING BALANCE
Sales (all credit)	0	$261,000
Cost of goods sold	0	187,000
Inventories (merchandise)	$49,000	61,000
Accounts receivable	23,000	27,000
Cash	16,000	10,500
Working capital	10,000	6,000

REQUIRED Using the appropriate ratios from the chapter as a basis, answer the following questions:

1. How long does it take on average from sales to cash collection from customers? Explain.
2. How long does it take on average from inventory acquisition to sale of inventory? Explain.

E27–8 A corporation has the following summarized financial information for 1983 and 1984:

	12/31/84	1984	12/31/83	1983
Current assets	15,000,000		16,000,000	
Noncurrent assets	22,000,000		27,000,000	
Current liabilities	4,000,000		7,000,000	
Noncurrent liabilities	11,000,000		14,000,000	
Net income		7,000,000		8,000,000

REQUIRED Compute the debt-to-equity ratio at December 31, 1983 and 1984, and comment on its use as an indicator of the corporation's financial strength.

P27-1 Federal Chemicals Corporation operates in several industries and in several countries. A portion of its industry segment information disclosure in its 1983 annual report follows:

	LINES OF BUSINESS ($000,000)						
	CHEMICAL						
	SPECIALTY	AGRI-CULTURAL	NATURAL RESOURCES	RESTAU-RANT	RE-TAIL	OTHER	TOTAL
Sales	$1,818	$ 549	$ 341	$ 85	$360	$ 980	$4,133
Operating profit	190	71	61	20	25	103	470
Identifiable assets	3,280	1,300	1,918	563	469	1,900	9,430

REQUIRED

1. Perform the 10 percent tests called for by *FASB Statement No. 14* for determining reportable segments.
2. Give potential reasons why the segments that do not meet these tests were disclosed above.

P27-2 Brookline Publishers, Inc., specializes in greeting cards. Sales billed and cash expenditures flows for 1983 were as follows (income tax expense is expected to be 40 percent of net income before taxes and there are no beginning or ending inventories):

	1ST QUARTER	2ND QUARTER	3RD QUARTER	4TH QUARTER
Sales	$ 880,000	$ 640,000	$2,780,000	$1,350,000
Production costs	1,300,000	1,100,000	600,000	250,000
Advertising costs	55,000	60,500	601,000	330,500
Administrative costs	250,000	255,000	258,000	270,000

REQUIRED With the information given combined with your own assumptions about the relationships of revenues and expenses, construct a schedule that shows summarized quarterly income statements for 1983. List your assumptions.

P27-3 At the end of the second quarter of 1984, Leather Goods, Inc., a wholesaler of all types of leather products, has the following preliminary results:

	1ST QUARTER	2ND QUARTER	FORECASTED TOTALS FOR 1984
Sales	$850,000	$925,000	$20,500,000
Cost of goods sold	422,000	510,000	10,100,000
Administrative expense	120,000	140,000	1,500,000
Federal income taxes			3,560,000
Net income			$ 5,340,000

A comparison of the to-date amount and the projections show that the company has most of its sales in the third and fourth quarters. At the end of the second quarter, the company made an accounting method change that will have the following effect on reported results:

	PRIOR YEARS	1ST QUARTER	2ND QUARTER	FORECASTED TOTAL FOR 1984
Administrative expense increase	$20,000	$3,000	$3,000	$12,000

The projected tax rate is not affected by the change in accounting method, and the change is effective for both accounting and tax purposes. Assume that the tax rate for 1984 was the same as for prior years.

REQUIRED   Using the data given, show the comparative first- and second-quarter interim income statements. Give complete explanations, and show all assumptions and computations.

P27-4   The following data relate to Betts, Inc.

BETTS, INC.

Balance Sheet

As of December 31, 1984

ASSETS		LIABILITIES AND STOCKHOLDERS' EQUITY	
Cash	$ 122,000	Accounts payable	$ 147,000
Receivables (net of allowance of $29,000)	276,000	Accrued liabilities	14,000
Inventory	384,000	Notes payable (Due 6/30/86)	88,000
Prepaid insurance	8,500	Capital stock	776,000
Land	58,000	Retained earnings	317,500
Equipment (net)	494,000		
	$1,342,500		$1,342,500

BETTS, INC.

Income Statement

For the Year Ended December 31, 1984

Sales revenue (all on credit)		$3,150,000
Cost of goods sold:		
inventory, 1/1/84	$ 297,000	
Purchases (net)	2,350,000	
Cost of goods available for sale	$2,647,000	
Less: Inventory, 12/31/84	384,000	
Cost of goods sold		2,263,000
Gross profit		$ 887,000
Operating expenses		535,000
Net income		$ 352,000

REQUIRED

1. Compute the following ratios for Betts, Inc. Assume that beginning and ending balances are the same unless the information indicates otherwise.
    a. Current ratio
    b. Quick ratio
    c. Inventory turnover
    d. Receivables turnover
    e. Profit margin on sales
    f. Rate of return on assets
    g. Rate of return on stockholders' equity
2. Indicate for each of the following independent transactions whether the quick ratio of Betts, Inc., would be increased, be decreased, or remain the same.

a. Write-off of uncollectible accounts of $7,000
b. Issuance of common stock for cash of $20,000
c. Pay $28,000 of the notes payable
d. Collect $55,000 of the accounts receivable
e. Purchase land on a long-term mortgage payable
f. Acquire inventory on account

P27–5 Xanadu, Inc., has the following operating results and asset items related to its various segments of operations and geographical areas:

	SALES	OPERATING PROFIT	ASSETS
Manufacture of records and tapes	162,000,000	34,000,000	254,000,000
Distribution of movies	38,000,000	(30,000,000)	30,000,000
Agents for concerts	50,000,000	6,000,000	2,000,000
Home office (not distributed)	—	—	14,000,000
Total	250,000,000	10,000,000	300,000,000
United States	170,000,000		230,000,000
Canada	50,000,000		31,000,000
Great Britain	30,000,000		25,000,000
Home office (not distributed)	—		14,000,000
Total	250,000,000		300,000,000

REQUIRED Discuss the required line of business and geographical disclosures for Xanadu, and give a detailed explanation of the reasons for your decisions, including the necessary computations.

P27–6 (CMA ADAPTED) The Locke Company is a publicly held manufacturing company whose fiscal year ends March 31. On December 1, 1983, after several months of discussion and analysis, the management of Locke decided for financial-reporting purposes to change from accelerated depreciation to straight-line depreciation and to increase the warranty expense accrual. These revisions are to be effective immediately, but they will not affect tax-accounting procedures.

The following table presents the accelerated depreciation for the past two quarters and the estimated amount for the third quarter of the current fiscal year as reported for financial statement purposes. The table also presents the recalculated figures for the same periods under the straight-line method. The accumulated depreciation as of April 1, 1983, amounted to $980,000 under the accelerated depreciation method but would only have been $700,000 if straight-line depreciation had been used.

FISCAL QUARTER	ACCELERATED DEPRECIATION (ACTUAL AMOUNT USED FOR FINANCIAL-REPORTING PURPOSES)	STRAIGHT-LINE DEPRECIATION (RECALCULATED AMOUNTS)
Fiscal year ending 3/31/84		
First (4/1/83–6/30/83)	$62,000	$50,000
Second (7/1/83–9/30/83)	58,000	50,000
Third (10/1/83–12/31/83, estimated)	55,000	50,000

Locke Company has a 1-year warranty on its products. Management has been accruing warranty expense at the rate of 1.00 percent of net sales. The balance of the accrued warranty account as of April 1, 1983, was $47,000. The data presented in the following table show the actual warranty accruals and expenditures for the past six quarters and the estimates for the current third quarter. Actual warranty expenditures have exceeded the accrual for the past three quarters and are expected to exceed the accrual for future quarters if a 1.00 percent accrual rate continues to be used. Consequently, management has decided to increase the accrual rate to 1.25 percent of net sales effective with the third quarter of the current year.

FISCAL QUARTER	ACCRUED WARRANTY EXPENSES @ 1%	ACTUAL WARRANTY EXPENDITURES
Fiscal year ending 3/31/83		
First (4/1/82–6/30/82)	$40,000	$32,000
Second (7/1/82–9/30/82)	42,000	35,000
Third (10/1/82–12/31/82)	45,000	42,000
Fourth (1/1/83–3/31/83)	35,000	44,000
Fiscal year ending 3/31/84		
First (4/1/83–6/30/83)	43,000	47,000
Second (7/1/83–9/30/83)	46,000	55,000
Third (10/1/83–12/31/83, estimated)	50,000	58,000

The estimated financial results and related earnings per share for the third quarter and for the 9 months ending December 31 for the current fiscal year are shown in the following table. The third quarter and 9-month data presented for the current fiscal year were compiled before the two accounting revisions were implemented. The company has issued only common stock and has no dilutive securities. One million shares of common stock have been outstanding for the past 2 years. Locke Company is subject to a 40 percent income tax rate.

	FISCAL YEAR ENDING 3/31/84	
	THIRD QUARTER	NINE MONTHS
	(10/1/83– 12/31/83)	(4/1/83– 12/31/83)
Income before extraordinary items	$600,000	$1,500,000
Extraordinary loss, net of related income tax effect	400,000	1,000,000
Net income	$200,000	$ 500,000
Earnings per share		
Earnings before extraordinary loss	$.60	$1.50
Extraordinary loss	.40	1.00
Net earnings	$.20	$ .50

REQUIRED

1. Discuss the disclosure requirements for current- and prior-year data that Locke Company would need to make in its interim financial statements as a consequence of the change in depreciation method and increase in warranty expense accrual.

2. Locke Company will prepare and distribute to its stockholders interim financial statements at the end of the third quarter of the current fiscal year. These statements will present third-quarter and year-to-date data following generally accepted accounting procedures. Present the financial results and related earnings-per-share data as they would appear in the interim financial statements issued at the end of the third quarter reflecting the change in depreciation method and increase in warranty expense accrual. Explain your presentation and show the supporting calculations.

P27–7 (CPA ADAPTED)   The Printing Company is listed on the New York Stock Exchange. The market value of its common stock was quoted at $10 per share on December 31, 1984 and 1985. Printing's balance sheet on December 31, 1984 and 1985, and its statement of income and retained earnings for the years then ended, are shown on p. 1089.

REQUIRED   Based on the information given, compute (for the year 1985 only) the following:

1. Current (working capital) ratio
2. Quick (acid-test) ratio
3. Number of days' sales in average receivables, assuming a business year consisting of 300 days and all sales on account
4. Inventory turnover
5. Book value per share of common stock

PRINTING COMPANY
Balance Sheet

	DECEMBER 31,	
ASSETS	**1985**	**1984**
Current assets		
Cash	$ 3,500,000	$ 3,600,000
Marketable securities, at cost which approximates market	13,000,000	11,000,000
Accounts receivable, net of allowance for doubtful accounts	105,000,000	95,000,000
Inventories, lower-of-cost-or-market	126,000,000	154,000,000
Prepaid expenses	2,500,000	2,400,000
Total current assets	250,000,000	266,000,000
Property, plant, and equipment, net of accumulated depreciation	311,000,000	308,000,000
Investments, at equity	2,000,000	3,000,000
Long-term receivables	14,000,000	16,000,000
Goodwill and patents, net of accumulated amortization	6,000,000	6,500,000
Other assets	7,000,000	8,500,000
Total assets	$590,000,000	$608,000,000

LIABILITIES AND STOCKHOLDERS' EQUITY

	1985	1984
Current liabilities		
Notes payable	$ 5,000,000	$15,000,000
Accounts payable	38,000,000	48,000,000
Accrued expenses	24,500,000	27,000,000
Income taxes payable	1,000,000	1,000,000
Payments due within one year on long-term debt	6,500,000	7,000,000
Total current liabilities	75,000,000	98,000,000
Long-term debt	169,000,000	180,000,000
Deferred income taxes	74,000,000	67,000,000
Other liabilities	9,000,000	8,000,000
Stockholders' equity		
Common stock, par value $1 per share (authorized, 20,000,000 shares; issued and outstanding, 10,000,000 shares)	10,000,000	10,000,000
5% cumulative preferred stock, par value $100 per share; $100 liquidating value (authorized, 50,000 shares; issued and outstanding 40,000 shares)	4,000,000	4,000,000
Additional paid-in capital	107,000,000	107,000,000
Retained earnings	142,000,000	134,000,000
Total stockholders' equity	263,000,000	255,000,000
Total liabilities and stockholders' equity	$590,000,000	$608,000,000

PRINTING COMPANY
Statement of income and Retained Earnings

	YEAR ENDED DECEMBER 31,	
	1985	**1984**
Net sales	$600,000,000	$500,000,000
Costs and expenses:		
Cost of goods sold	490,000,000	400,000,000
Selling, general, and administrative expenses	66,000,000	60,000,000
Other, net	7,000,000	6,000,000
Total costs and expenses	563,000,000	466,000,000
Income before income taxes	37,000,000	34,000,000
Income taxes	16,800,000	15,800,000
Net income	20,200,000	18,200,000
Retained earnings at beginning of period	134,000,000	126,000,000
Dividends on common stock	12,000,000	10,000,000
Dividends on preferred stock	200,000	200,000
Retained earnings at end of period	$142,000,000	$134,000,000

6. Earnings per share on common stock
7. Price-earnings ratio on common stock

Show supporting computations.

P27–8 (CMA ADAPTED)

_____ 1. A company's current ratio is 2.2-to-1 and its quick (acid-test) ratio is 1.0-to-1 at the beginning of the year. At the end of the year, the company has a current ratio of 2.5-to-1 and a quick ratio of .8-to-1. Which of the following could help explain the divergence in the ratios from the beginning to the end of the year?
   a. An increase in inventory levels during the current year
   b. An increase in credit sales in relationship to cash sales
   c. An increase in the use of trade payables during the current year
   d. An increase in the collection rate of accounts receivable
   e. The sale of marketable securities at a price below cost

_____ 2. Which of the following will cause a decrease in a company's accounts receivable turnover ratio?
   a. Tighten credit standards
   b. Enforce credit terms more aggressively
   c. Ease enforcement of credit terms
   d. Factor all accounts receivable
   e. Require customers to use bank credit cards, and eliminate the company's own card

_____ 3. If just prior to a period of rising prices, a company changed its inventory measurement method from FIFO to LIFO, the effect in the next period would be to
   a. Increase both the current ratio and the inventory turnover
   b. Decrease both the current ratio and the inventory turnover
   c. Increase the current ratio and decrease the inventory turnover
   d. Decrease the current ratio and increase the inventory turnover
   e. Leave the current ratio and the inventory turnover unchanged

   The following data apply to items 4 and 5: Mr. Sparks, the owner of School Supplies, Inc., is interested in keeping control over accounts receivable. He understands that accounts receivable turnover will give a good indication of how well receivables are being managed. School Supplies, Inc., does 70 percent of its business during June, July, and August. The terms of sale are 2/10, n/60.
   Net sales for the year ended December 31, 1983, and receivables balances are as follows:

Net sales	$1,500,000
Receivables, less allowance for doubtful accounts of $8,000 at Jan. 1, 1983	72,000
Receivables, less allowance for doubtful accounts of $10,000 at Dec. 31, 1983	60,000

_____ 4. The average accounts receivable turnover calculated from the data above is
   a. 20.0 times   d. 18.75 times
   b. 25.0 times   e. 20.8 times
   c. 22.7 times

_____ 5. The average accounts receivable turnover computed for School Supplies, Inc., in item 4 is
   a. Representative of the entire year
   b. Overstated
   c. Understated
   d. Comparable with turnover that would be experienced in June, July, and August
   e. Absolutely correct

P27–9 (CMA ADAPTED) The following 1984 financial statements for Johanson Company apply to items 1–5.

JOHANSON COMPANY
Statement of Financial Position
December 31

	($000)	
ASSETS	**1983**	**1984**
Current assets		
Cash and temporary investments	$ 380	$ 400
Accounts receivable (net)	1,500	1,700
Inventories	2,120	2,200
Total current assets	$4,000	$4,300
Long-term assets		
Land	$ 500	$ 500
Building and equipment (net)	4,000	4,700
Total long-term assets	$4,500	$5,200
Total assets	$8,500	$9,500
LIABILITIES AND EQUITIES		
Current liabilities		
Accounts payable	$ 700	$1,400
Current portion of long-term debt	500	1,000
Total current liabilities	$1,200	$2,400
Long-term debt	4,000	3,000
Total liabilities	$5,200	$5,400
Stockholders' equity		
Common stock	$3,000	$3,000
Retained earnings	300	1,100
Total stockholders' equity	$3,300	$4,100
Total liabilities and equities	$8,500	$9,500

JOHANSON COMPANY
Statement of Income and Retained Earnings
For the Year Ended December 31, 1984

	($000)	
Net sales		$28,800
Less: Cost of goods sold	$15,120	
Selling expenses	7,180	
Administrative expenses	4,100	
Interest	400	
Income taxes	800	27,600
Net income		$ 1,200
Retained earnings, Jan. 1		300
Subtotal		$ 1,500
Cash dividends declared and paid		400
Retained earnings, Dec. 31		$ 1,100

1. The acid-test ratio for 1984 for Johanson Company is
   a. 1.1 to 1
   b. .9 to 1
   c. 1.8 to 1
   d. .2 to 1
   e. .17 to 1

2. The average number of days sales outstanding in 1984 for Johanson Company is
   a. 18 days
   b. 360 days
   c. 20 days
   d. 4.4 days
   e. 80 days

_____ 3. The times interest earned ratio in 1984 for Johanson Company is
    a. 3.0 times   d. 2.0 times
    b. 1.0 times   e. 6.0 times
    c. 72.0 times

_____ 4. The asset turnover in 1984 for Johanson Company is
    a. 3.2 times   d. 1.1 times
    b. 1.7 times   e. .13 times
    c. .4 times

_____ 5. The inventory turnover in 1984 for Johanson Company is
    a. 13.6 times   d. 7.0 times
    b. 12.5 times   e. 51.4 times
    c. .9 times

P27–10 (CMA ADAPTED) The following data apply to items 1–6: Depoole Company manufactures industrial products and uses a calendar year for financial-reporting purposes. Items 1–6 present several of Depoole's transactions during 1984. Assume that total quick assets exceeded total current liabilities both before and after each transaction described. Assume also that Depoole has positive profits in 1984 and a credit balance throughout 1984 in its Retained Earnings account.

_____ 1. Payment of a trade account payable of $64,500 would
    a. Increase the current ratio, but the quick ratio would not be affected
    b. Increase the quick ratio, but the current ratio would not be affected
    c. Increase both the current and the quick ratios
    d. Decrease both the current and the quick ratios
    e. Have no effect on the current and quick ratios

_____ 2. The purchase of raw materials for $85,000 on open account would
    a. Increase the current ratio
    b. Decrease the current ratio
    c. Increase net working capital
    d. Decrease net working capital
    e. Increase both the current ratio and the net working capital

_____ 3. The collection of a current accounts receivable of $29,000 would
    a. Increase the current ratio   d. Decrease the quick ratio
    b. Decrease the current ratio   e. Not affect the current or quick ratios
    c. Increase the quick ratio

_____ 4. Obsolete inventory of $125,000 was written off during 1984. This would
    a. Decrease the quick ratio   d. Decrease the current ratio
    b. Increase the quick ratio   e. Decrease both the current and the quick
    c. Increase net working capital   ratios

_____ 5. The issuance of serial bonds in exchange for an office building with the first installment of the bonds due in late 1984 would
    a. Decrease net working capital   d. Affect all of the above as indicated
    b. Decrease the current ratio   e. Affect none of the above as indicated
    c. Decrease the quick ratio

_____ 6. The early liquidation of a long-term note with cash would
    a. Affect the current ratio to a greater degree than the quick ratio
    b. Affect the quick ratio to a greater degree than the current ratio
    c. Affect the current and quick ratios to the same degree
    d. Affect the current ratio, but not the quick ratio
    e. Affect the quick ratio, but not the current ratio

P27–11 (CMA ADAPTED)

_____ 1. Adequacy of disclosure in the financial statements and the footnotes is the primary responsibility of
    a. The management of the company presenting the statements

b. The public accounting firm auditing the statements

c. The internal auditors of the company presenting the statements

d. The attorneys of the company presenting the statements

e. The financial analysts using the statements for investment purposes

2. Footnotes to financial statements are beneficial in meeting the disclosure requirements of financial reporting. The footnotes should not be used to
   a. Describe significant accounting policies
   b. Describe depreciation methods employed by the company
   c. Describe principles and methods peculiar to the industry in which the company operates when these principles and methods are predominantly followed in that industry
   d. Disclose the basis of consolidation for consolidated statements
   e. Correct an improper presentation in the financial statements

3. Full-disclosure reporting often requires the use of footnotes. All but one of the following items are usually covered by footnotes to the financial statements. Which item would have to be reflected in the body of the balance sheet?
   a. Data regarding the amortization of intangible assets, including the method and period of amortization
   b. Pension accruals data, the difference between the cost provisions and the amounts paid to the pension fund
   c. Employee stock option plans data, including the number of shares under option, option prices, and the number of shares under options that are currently exercisable
   d. Data concerning capital leases, including a description of leasing arrangements and future minimum lease payments as of the date of the balance sheet
   e. Data concerning events, contracts, or transactions that have occurred since the balance sheet date and may have a bearing on future values or earnings of the company

P27–12 (CMA ADAPTED) Warford Corporation was formed 5 years ago through a public subscription of common stock. Lucinda Street, who owns 15 percent of the common stock, was one of the organizers of Warford and is its current president. The company has been successful but is now experiencing a shortage of funds. On June 10 Street approached the Bell National Bank, asking for a 24-month extension on two $30,000 notes, which are due on June 30, 1983, and September 30, 1983. Another note of $7,000 is due on December 31, 1983, but she expects no difficulty in paying this note on its due date. Street explained that Warford's cash-flow problems are due primarily to the company's desire to finance a $300,000 plant expansion over the next two fiscal years through internally generated funds.

The commercial loan officer of Bell National Bank requested financial reports for the last 2 fiscal years. These reports are shown below:

WARFORD CORPORATION

Income Statement

For the Fiscal Years Ended March 31

	1983	1982
Sales	$3,000,000	$2,700,000
Cost of goods sold[a]	1,902,500	1,720,000
Gross margin	1,097,500	$ 980,000
Operating expenses	845,000	780,000
Net income before taxes	$ 252,500	$ 200,000
Income taxes (40%)	101,000	80,000
Income after taxes	$ 151,500	$ 120,000

[a] Depreciation charges on the plant and equipment of $100,000 and $102,500 for the fiscal years ended March 31, 1982 and 1983, respectively, are included in cost of goods sold.

REQUIRED

1. Calculate the following items for Warford Corporation:
   a. Current ratio for fiscal years 1982 and 1983
   b. Acid-test (quick) ratio for fiscal years 1982 and 1983
   c. Inventory turnover for fiscal year 1983
   d. Return on assets for fiscal years 1982 and 1983

2. Identify and explain what other financial reports and/or financial analyses might be helpful to the commercial loan officer of Bell National Bank in evaluating Street's request for a time extension on Warford's notes.

3. Assume that the percentage changes experienced in fiscal year 1983 as compared with fiscal year 1982 for sales, cost of goods sold, gross margin, and net income after taxes will be repeated in each of the next 2 years. Is Warford's desire to finance the plant expansion from internally generated funds realistic? Explain your answer.

4. Should Bell National Bank grant the extension on Warford's notes considering Street's statement about financing the plant expansion through internally generated funds? Explain your answer.

APPENDIX H
Compound-Interest

TABLE H-1

THE FUTURE VALUE OF A PRESENT AMOUNT OF 1 (F/P)

n	1%	2%	3%	4%	5%	6%	7%	8%	9%	10%	11%	12%	13%	14%
1	1.0100	1.0200	1.0300	1.0400	1.0500	1.0600	1.0700	1.0800	1.0900	1.1000	1.1100	1.1200	1.1300	1.1400
2	1.0201	1.0404	1.0609	1.0816	1.1025	1.1236	1.1449	1.1664	1.1881	1.2100	1.2321	1.2544	1.2769	1.2996
3	1.0303	1.0612	1.0927	1.1249	1.1576	1.1910	1.2250	1.2597	1.2950	1.3310	1.3676	1.4049	1.4429	1.4815
4	1.0406	1.0824	1.1255	1.1699	1.2155	1.2625	1.3108	1.3605	1.4116	1.4641	1.5181	1.5735	1.6305	1.6890
5	1.0510	1.1041	1.1593	1.2167	1.2763	1.3382	1.4026	1.4693	1.5386	1.6105	1.6851	1.7623	1.8424	1.9254
6	1.0615	1.1262	1.1941	1.2653	1.3401	1.4185	1.5007	1.5869	1.6771	1.7716	1.8704	1.9738	2.0820	2.1950
7	1.0721	1.1487	1.2299	1.3159	1.4071	1.5036	1.6058	1.7138	1.8280	1.9487	2.0762	2.2107	2.3526	2.5023
8	1.0829	1.1717	1.2668	1.3686	1.4775	1.5938	1.7182	1.8509	1.9926	2.1436	2.3045	2.4760	2.6584	2.8526
9	1.0937	1.1951	1.3048	1.4233	1.5513	1.6895	1.8385	1.9990	2.1719	2.3579	2.5580	2.7731	3.0040	3.2520
10	1.1046	1.2190	1.3439	1.4802	1.6289	1.7908	1.9671	2.1589	2.3674	2.5937	2.8394	3.1059	3.3946	3.7072
11	1.1157	1.2434	1.3842	1.5395	1.7103	1.8983	2.1049	2.3316	2.5804	2.8531	3.1518	3.4786	3.8359	4.2262
12	1.1268	1.2682	1.4258	1.6010	1.7959	2.0122	2.2522	2.5182	2.8127	3.1384	3.4984	3.8960	4.3345	4.8179
13	1.1381	1.2936	1.4685	1.6651	1.8856	2.1329	2.4098	2.7196	3.0658	3.4523	3.8833	4.3635	4.8980	5.4924
14	1.1495	1.3195	1.5126	1.7317	1.9799	2.2609	2.5785	2.9372	3.3417	3.7975	4.3104	4.8871	5.5348	6.2614
15	1.1610	1.3459	1.5580	1.8009	2.0789	2.3966	2.7590	3.1722	3.6425	4.1772	4.7846	5.4736	6.2543	7.1379
16	1.1726	1.3728	1.6047	1.8730	2.1829	2.5403	2.9522	3.4259	3.9703	4.5950	5.3109	6.1304	7.0673	8.1373
17	1.1843	1.4002	1.6528	1.9479	2.2920	2.6928	3.1588	3.7000	4.3276	5.0545	5.8951	6.8661	7.9861	9.2765
18	1.1961	1.4282	1.7024	2.0258	2.4066	2.8543	3.3799	3.9960	4.7171	5.5599	6.5435	7.6900	9.0243	10.5752
19	1.2081	1.4568	1.7535	2.1068	2.5269	3.0256	3.6165	4.3157	5.1417	6.1159	7.2633	8.6128	10.1974	12.0557
20	1.2202	1.4859	1.8061	2.1911	2.6533	3.2071	3.8697	4.6609	5.6044	6.7275	8.0623	9.6463	11.5231	13.7435
21	1.2324	1.5157	1.8603	2.2788	2.7860	3.3996	4.1406	5.0338	6.1088	7.4002	8.9491	10.8039	13.0211	15.6676
22	1.2447	1.5460	1.9161	2.3699	2.9253	3.6035	4.4304	5.4365	6.6586	8.1403	9.9336	12.1003	14.7139	17.8611
23	1.2572	1.5769	1.9736	2.4647	3.0715	3.8197	4.7405	5.8714	7.2579	8.9543	11.0262	13.5524	16.6267	20.3616
24	1.2697	1.6084	2.0328	2.5633	3.2251	4.0489	5.0724	6.3412	7.9111	9.8497	12.2391	15.1787	18.7881	23.2122
25	1.2824	1.6406	2.0938	2.6658	3.3864	4.2919	5.4274	6.8485	8.6231	10.8347	13.5854	17.0001	21.2306	26.4620
26	1.2953	1.6734	2.1566	2.7725	3.5557	4.5494	5.8073	7.3963	9.3991	11.9181	15.0798	19.0401	23.9906	30.1666
27	1.3082	1.7069	2.2213	2.8834	3.7335	4.8223	6.2139	7.9880	10.2451	13.1100	16.7386	21.3249	27.1094	34.3900
28	1.3213	1.7410	2.2879	2.9987	3.9201	5.1117	6.6488	8.6271	11.1671	14.4210	18.5798	23.8839	30.6336	39.2046
29	1.3345	1.7758	2.3566	3.1186	4.1161	5.4184	7.1142	9.3172	12.1722	15.8631	20.6236	26.7500	34.6159	44.6932
30	1.3478	1.8114	2.4273	3.2434	4.3219	5.7435	7.6122	10.0626	13.2677	17.4494	22.8922	29.9600	39.1160	50.9503
31	1.3613	1.8476	2.5001	3.3731	4.5380	6.0881	8.1451	10.8676	14.4617	19.1943	25.4104	33.5552	44.2011	58.0833
32	1.3749	1.8845	2.5751	3.5081	4.7649	6.4534	8.7152	11.7370	15.7633	21.1137	28.2055	37.5818	49.9473	66.2150
33	1.3887	1.9222	2.6523	3.6484	5.0032	6.8406	9.3253	12.6760	17.1820	23.2251	31.3081	42.0917	56.4404	75.4851
34	1.4026	1.9607	2.7319	3.7943	5.2533	7.2510	9.9781	13.6901	18.7284	25.5476	34.7520	47.1427	63.7777	86.0530
35	1.4166	1.9999	2.8139	3.9461	5.5160	7.6861	10.6765	14.7853	20.4139	28.1023	38.5747	52.7998	72.0688	98.1004
36	1.4308	2.0399	2.8983	4.1039	5.7918	8.1472	11.4239	15.9681	22.2512	30.9126	42.8179	59.1358	81.4377	111.8350
37	1.4451	2.0807	2.9852	4.2681	6.0814	8.6361	12.2236	17.2456	24.2538	34.0038	47.5279	66.2321	92.0246	127.4910
38	1.4595	2.1223	3.0748	4.4388	6.3855	9.1542	13.0792	18.6252	26.4366	37.4042	52.7560	74.1799	103.9880	145.3400
39	1.4741	2.1647	3.1670	4.6164	6.7047	9.7035	13.9948	20.1152	28.8159	41.1446	58.5591	83.0815	117.5060	165.6880
40	1.4889	2.2080	3.2620	4.8010	7.0400	10.2857	14.9744	21.7244	31.4094	45.2591	65.0006	93.0513	132.7820	188.8840
41	1.5038	2.2522	3.3599	4.9931	7.3920	10.9028	16.0226	23.4624	34.2362	49.7850	72.1507	104.2170	150.0440	215.3280
42	1.5188	2.2972	3.4607	5.1928	7.7616	11.5570	17.1442	25.3394	37.3175	54.7635	80.0872	116.7240	169.5490	245.4740
43	1.5340	2.3432	3.5645	5.4005	8.1497	12.2504	18.3443	27.3665	40.6760	60.2398	88.8968	130.7300	191.5910	279.8400
44	1.5493	2.3901	3.6715	5.6165	8.5571	12.9854	19.6284	29.5558	44.3369	66.2638	98.6754	146.4180	216.4980	319.0180
45	1.5648	2.4379	3.7816	5.8412	8.9850	13.7646	21.0024	31.9203	48.3272	72.8902	109.5300	163.9880	244.6420	363.6800
46	1.5805	2.4866	3.8950	6.0748	9.4342	14.5904	22.4725	34.4739	52.6766	80.1792	121.5780	183.6670	276.4460	414.5950
47	1.5963	2.5363	4.0119	6.3178	9.9060	15.4658	24.0456	37.2318	57.4175	88.1971	134.9520	205.7070	312.3840	472.6390
48	1.6122	2.5871	4.1323	6.5705	10.4013	16.3938	25.7288	40.2104	62.5851	97.0168	149.7960	230.3920	352.9940	538.8080
49	1.6283	2.6388	4.2562	6.8333	10.9213	17.3774	27.5298	43.4272	68.2177	106.7190	166.2740	258.0390	398.8830	614.2410
50	1.6446	2.6916	4.3839	7.1067	11.4674	18.4201	29.4569	46.9014	74.3573	117.3900	184.5640	289.0030	450.7380	700.2350

TABLE H−1 (Cont.)

n	15%	16%	17%	18%	19%	20%	21%	22%	23%	24%	25%
1	1.1500	1.1600	1.1700	1.1800	1.1900	1.2000	1.2100	1.2200	1.2300	1.2400	1.2500
2	1.3225	1.3456	1.3689	1.3924	1.4161	1.4400	1.4641	1.4884	1.5129	1.5376	1.5625
3	1.5209	1.5609	1.6016	1.6430	1.6852	1.7280	1.7716	1.8158	1.8609	1.9066	1.9531
4	1.7490	1.8106	1.8739	1.9388	2.0053	2.0736	2.1436	2.2153	2.2889	2.3642	2.4414
5	2.0114	2.1003	2.1924	2.2878	2.3864	2.4883	2.5937	2.7027	2.8153	2.9316	3.0518
6	2.3131	2.4364	2.5652	2.6996	2.8398	2.9860	3.1384	3.2973	3.4628	3.6352	3.8147
7	2.6600	2.8262	3.0012	3.1855	3.3793	3.5832	3.7975	4.0227	4.2593	4.5077	4.7684
8	3.0590	3.2784	3.5115	3.7589	4.0214	4.2998	4.5950	4.9077	5.2389	5.5895	5.9605
9	3.5179	3.8030	4.1084	4.4355	4.7854	5.1598	5.5599	5.9874	6.4439	6.9310	7.4506
10	4.0456	4.4114	4.8068	5.2338	5.6947	6.1917	6.7275	7.3046	7.9259	8.5944	9.3132
11	4.6524	5.1173	5.6240	6.1759	6.7767	7.4301	8.1403	8.9117	9.7489	10.6571	11.6415
12	5.3503	5.9360	6.5801	7.2876	8.0642	8.9161	9.8497	10.8722	11.9912	13.2140	14.5519
13	6.1528	6.8858	7.6987	8.5994	9.5964	10.6993	11.9182	13.2641	14.7491	16.3863	18.1899
14	7.0757	7.9875	9.0075	10.1473	11.4198	12.8392	14.4210	16.1822	18.1414	20.3191	22.7374
15	8.1371	9.2655	10.5387	11.9738	13.5895	15.4070	17.4494	19.7423	22.3140	25.1956	28.4217
16	9.3576	10.7480	12.3303	14.1290	16.1715	18.4884	21.1138	24.0856	27.4462	31.2426	35.5271
17	10.7613	12.4677	14.4265	16.6723	19.2441	22.1861	25.5477	29.3844	33.7588	38.7408	44.4089
18	12.3755	14.4625	16.8790	19.6733	22.9005	26.6233	30.9127	35.8490	41.5233	48.0386	55.5112
19	14.2318	16.7765	19.7484	23.2145	27.2516	31.9480	37.4044	43.7358	51.0737	59.5679	69.3890
20	16.3666	19.4608	23.1056	27.3931	32.4294	38.3376	45.2593	53.3576	62.8206	73.8642	86.7362
21	18.8216	22.5745	27.0336	32.3238	38.5910	46.0052	54.7637	65.0963	77.2694	91.5916	108.4200
22	21.6448	26.1864	31.6293	38.1421	45.9233	55.2062	66.2641	79.4175	95.0413	113.5740	135.5250
23	24.8915	30.3762	37.0062	45.0077	54.6487	66.2474	80.1796	96.8893	116.9010	140.8310	169.4070
24	28.6252	35.2364	43.2973	53.1091	65.0320	79.4969	97.0173	118.2050	143.7880	174.6310	211.7580
25	32.9190	40.8743	50.6579	62.6688	77.3881	95.3963	117.3910	144.2100	176.8590	216.5420	264.6980
26	37.8569	47.4142	59.2697	73.9491	92.0918	114.4760	142.0430	175.9360	217.5370	268.5120	330.8720
27	43.5354	55.0004	69.3455	87.2600	109.5890	137.3710	171.8720	214.6420	267.5700	332.9550	413.5900
28	50.0657	63.8005	81.1343	102.9670	130.4110	164.8450	207.9650	261.8640	329.1120	412.8640	516.9880
29	57.5756	74.0086	94.9271	121.5010	155.1890	197.8140	251.6380	319.4740	404.8070	511.9520	646.2350
30	66.2119	85.8500	111.0650	143.3710	184.6750	237.3760	304.4820	389.7580	497.9130	634.8200	807.7940
31	76.1437	99.5860	129.9460	169.1780	219.7640	284.8520	368.4230	475.5040	612.4330	787.1770	1009.7400
32	87.5653	115.5200	152.0360	199.6300	261.5190	341.8220	445.7920	580.1150	753.2930	976.0990	1262.1800
33	100.7000	134.0030	177.8830	235.5630	311.2073	410.1870	539.4080	707.7410	926.5500	1210.3600	1577.7200
34	115.8050	155.4430	208.1230	277.9650	370.3370	492.2240	652.6840	863.4400	1139.6600	1500.8500	1972.1500
35	133.1760	180.3140	243.5040	327.9980	440.7010	590.6690	789.7470	1053.4000	1401.7800	1861.0500	2465.1900
36	153.1520	209.1640	284.8990	387.0380	524.4340	708.8000	955.5940	1285.1500	1724.1900	2307.7100	3081.4900
37	176.1250	242.6010	333.3320	456.7050	624.0760	850.5630	1156.2700	1567.8800	2120.7500	2861.5600	3851.8600
38	202.5440	281.4520	389.9990	538.9120	742.6510	1020.6800	1399.0900	1912.8200	2608.5200	3548.3300	4814.8300
39	232.9260	326.4840	456.2980	635.9160	883.7540	1224.8100	1692.8900	2333.6400	3208.4800	4399.9300	6018.5300
40	267.8650	378.7220	533.8690	750.3810	1051.6700	1469.7700	2048.4000	2847.0300	3946.4300	5455.9100	7523.1700
41	308.0440	439.3170	624.6270	885.4490	1251.4800	1763.7300	2478.5700	3473.3800	4854.1100	6765.3700	9403.9600
42	354.2510	509.6080	730.8130	1044.8300	1489.2700	2116.4700	2999.0000	4237.5300	5970.5600	8389.0200	11754.9000
43	407.3880	591.1450	855.0520	1232.9000	1772.2300	2539.7700	3628.8700	5169.7800	7343.7800	10402.4000	14693.7000
44	468.4970	685.7280	1000.4100	1454.8200	2108.9500	3047.7200	4390.9300	6307.1300	9032.8600	12898.9000	18367.1000
45	538.7710	795.4450	1170.4800	1760.6900	2509.6500	3657.2700	5313.0300	7694.7000	11110.4000	15994.7000	22958.9000
46	619.5870	922.7160	1369.4600	2025.6900	2986.4800	4388.7200	6428.7600	9387.5400	13665.8000	19833.4000	28698.6000
47	712.5250	1070.3500	1602.2700	2390.3200	3553.9200	5266.4600	7778.8000	11452.8000	16808.9000	24593.4000	35873.2000
48	819.4040	1241.6100	1874.6600	2820.5800	4229.1600	6319.7600	9412.3500	13972.4000	20675.0000	30495.9000	44841.0000
49	942.3150	1440.2600	2193.3500	3328.2800	5032.7000	7583.7100	11388.0000	17046.3000	25430.2000	37814.9000	56051.9000
50	1083.6600	1670.7100	2566.2200	3927.3700	5988.0100	9100.4500	13780.6000	20796.5000	31279.2000	46890.6000	70064.9000

TABLE H-2

THE PRESENT VALUE OF A FUTURE AMOUNT OF 1 (P/F)

n	1%	2%	3%	4%	5%	6%	7%	8%	9%	10%	11%	12%	13%	14%	15%
1	.9901	.9804	.9709	.9615	.9524	.9434	.9346	.9259	.9174	.9091	.9009	.8929	.8850	.8772	.8696
2	.9803	.9612	.9426	.9246	.9070	.8900	.8734	.8573	.8417	.8264	.8116	.7972	.7831	.7695	.7561
3	.9706	.9423	.9151	.8890	.8638	.8396	.8163	.7938	.7722	.7513	.7312	.7118	.6931	.6750	.6575
4	.9610	.9239	.8885	.8548	.8227	.7921	.7629	.7350	.7084	.6830	.6587	.6355	.6133	.5921	.5718
5	.9515	.9057	.8626	.8219	.7835	.7473	.7130	.6806	.6499	.6209	.5934	.5674	.5428	.5194	.4972
6	.9420	.8880	.8375	.7903	.7462	.7050	.6663	.6302	.5963	.5645	.5346	.5066	.4803	.4556	.4323
7	.9327	.8706	.8131	.7599	.7107	.6651	.6228	.5835	.5470	.5132	.4817	.4524	.4251	.3996	.3759
8	.9235	.8535	.7894	.7307	.6768	.6274	.5820	.5403	.5019	.4665	.4339	.4039	.3762	.3506	.3269
9	.9143	.8368	.7664	.7026	.6446	.5919	.5439	.5002	.4604	.4241	.3909	.3606	.3329	.3075	.2843
10	.9053	.8204	.7441	.6756	.6139	.5584	.5084	.4632	.4224	.3855	.3522	.3220	.2946	.2697	.2472
11	.8963	.8043	.7224	.6496	.5847	.5268	.4751	.4289	.3875	.3505	.3173	.2875	.2607	.2366	.2149
12	.8874	.7885	.7014	.6246	.5568	.4970	.4440	.3971	.3555	.3186	.2858	.2567	.2307	.2076	.1869
13	.8787	.7730	.6810	.6006	.5303	.4688	.4150	.3677	.3262	.2897	.2575	.2292	.2042	.1821	.1625
14	.8700	.7579	.6611	.5775	.5051	.4423	.3878	.3405	.2993	.2633	.2320	.2046	.1807	.1597	.1413
15	.8614	.7430	.6419	.5553	.4810	.4173	.3625	.3152	.2745	.2394	.2090	.1827	.1599	.1401	.1229
16	.8528	.7284	.6232	.5339	.4581	.3936	.3387	.2919	.2519	.2176	.1883	.1631	.1415	.1229	.1069
17	.8444	.7142	.6050	.5134	.4363	.3714	.3166	.2703	.2311	.1978	.1696	.1456	.1252	.1078	.0929
18	.8360	.7002	.5874	.4936	.4155	.3503	.2959	.2502	.2120	.1799	.1528	.1300	.1108	.0946	.0808
19	.8277	.6864	.5703	.4746	.3957	.3305	.2765	.2317	.1945	.1635	.1377	.1161	.0981	.0829	.0703
20	.8195	.6730	.5537	.4564	.3769	.3118	.2584	.2145	.1784	.1486	.1240	.1037	.0868	.0728	.0611
21	.8114	.6598	.5375	.4388	.3589	.2942	.2415	.1987	.1637	.1351	.1117	.0926	.0768	.0638	.0531
22	.8034	.6468	.5219	.4220	.3418	.2775	.2257	.1839	.1502	.1229	.1007	.0826	.0680	.0560	.0462
23	.7954	.6342	.5067	.4057	.3256	.2618	.2109	.1703	.1378	.1117	.0907	.0738	.0601	.0491	.0402
24	.7876	.6217	.4919	.3901	.3101	.2470	.1971	.1577	.1264	.1015	.0817	.0659	.0532	.0431	.0349
25	.7798	.6095	.4776	.3751	.2953	.2330	.1842	.1460	.1160	.0923	.0736	.0588	.0471	.0378	.0304
26	.7721	.5976	.4637	.3607	.2812	.2198	.1722	.1352	.1064	.0839	.0663	.0525	.0417	.0332	.0264
27	.7644	.5859	.4502	.3468	.2678	.2074	.1609	.1252	.0976	.0763	.0597	.0469	.0369	.0291	.0230
28	.7568	.5744	.4371	.3335	.2551	.1956	.1504	.1159	.0896	.0693	.0538	.0419	.0326	.0255	.0200
29	.7493	.5631	.4244	.3206	.2429	.1846	.1406	.1073	.0821	.0630	.0485	.0374	.0289	.0224	.0174
30	.7419	.5521	.4120	.3083	.2314	.1741	.1314	.0994	.0754	.0573	.0437	.0334	.0256	.0196	.0151
31	.7346	.5412	.4000	.2965	.2204	.1643	.1228	.0920	.0692	.0521	.0394	.0298	.0226	.0172	.0131
32	.7273	.5306	.3883	.2851	.2099	.1550	.1147	.0852	.0634	.0474	.0354	.0266	.0200	.0151	.0114
33	.7201	.5202	.3770	.2741	.1999	.1462	.1072	.0789	.0582	.0431	.0319	.0238	.0177	.0133	.0099
34	.7130	.5100	.3660	.2635	.1903	.1379	.1002	.0731	.0534	.0391	.0288	.0212	.0157	.0116	.0086
35	.7059	.5000	.3554	.2534	.1813	.1301	.0937	.0676	.0490	.0356	.0259	.0189	.0139	.0102	.0075
36	.6989	.4902	.3450	.2437	.1727	.1227	.0875	.0626	.0449	.0324	.0234	.0169	.0123	.0089	.0065
37	.6920	.4806	.3350	.2343	.1644	.1158	.0818	.0580	.0412	.0294	.0210	.0151	.0109	.0078	.0057
38	.6852	.4712	.3252	.2253	.1566	.1092	.0765	.0537	.0378	.0267	.0190	.0135	.0096	.0069	.0049
39	.6784	.4620	.3158	.2166	.1492	.1031	.0715	.0497	.0347	.0243	.0171	.0120	.0085	.0060	.0043
40	.6717	.4529	.3066	.2083	.1420	.0972	.0668	.0460	.0318	.0221	.0154	.0107	.0075	.0053	.0037
41	.6650	.4440	.2976	.2003	.1353	.0917	.0624	.0426	.0292	.0201	.0139	.0096	.0067	.0046	.0033
42	.6584	.4353	.2890	.1926	.1288	.0865	.0583	.0395	.0268	.0183	.0125	.0086	.0059	.0041	.0028
43	.6519	.4268	.2805	.1852	.1227	.0816	.0545	.0365	.0246	.0166	.0113	.0077	.0052	.0036	.0025
44	.6454	.4184	.2724	.1781	.1169	.0770	.0509	.0338	.0226	.0151	.0101	.0068	.0046	.0031	.0021
45	.6391	.4102	.2644	.1712	.1113	.0727	.0476	.0313	.0207	.0137	.0091	.0061	.0041	.0027	.0019
46	.6327	.4021	.2567	.1646	.1060	.0685	.0445	.0290	.0190	.0125	.0082	.0054	.0036	.0024	.0016
47	.6265	.3943	.2493	.1583	.1010	.0647	.0416	.0269	.0174	.0113	.0074	.0049	.0032	.0021	.0014
48	.6203	.3865	.2420	.1522	.0961	.0610	.0389	.0249	.0160	.0103	.0067	.0043	.0028	.0019	.0012
49	.6141	.3790	.2350	.1463	.0916	.0575	.0363	.0230	.0147	.0094	.0060	.0039	.0025	.0016	.0011
50	.6080	.3715	.2281	.1407	.0872	.0543	.0340	.0213	.0135	.0085	.0054	.0035	.0022	.0014	.0009

TABLE H–2 (Cont.)

n	16%	17%	18%	19%	20%	21%	22%	23%	24%	25%	30%	35%	40%	45%	50%
1	.8621	.8547	.8475	.8403	.8333	.8264	.8197	.8130	.8065	.8000	.7692	.7407	.7143	.6897	.6667
2	.7432	.7305	.7182	.7062	.6944	.6830	.6719	.6610	.6504	.6400	.5917	.5487	.5102	.4756	.4444
3	.6407	.6244	.6086	.5934	.5787	.5645	.5507	.5374	.5245	.5120	.4552	.4064	.3644	.3280	.2963
4	.5523	.5337	.5158	.4987	.4822	.4665	.4514	.4369	.4230	.4096	.3501	.3011	.2603	.2262	.1975
5	.4761	.4561	.4371	.4190	.4019	.3855	.3700	.3552	.3411	.3277	.2693	.2230	.1859	.1560	.1317
6	.4104	.3898	.3704	.3521	.3349	.3186	.3033	.2888	.2751	.2621	.2072	.1652	.1328	.1076	.0878
7	.3538	.3332	.3139	.2959	.2791	.2633	.2486	.2348	.2218	.2097	.1594	.1224	.0949	.0742	.0585
8	.3050	.2848	.2660	.2487	.2326	.2176	.2038	.1909	.1789	.1678	.1226	.0906	.0678	.0512	.0390
9	.2630	.2434	.2255	.2090	.1938	.1799	.1670	.1552	.1443	.1342	.0943	.0671	.0484	.0353	.0260
10	.2267	.2080	.1911	.1756	.1615	.1486	.1369	.1262	.1163	.1074	.0725	.0497	.0346	.0243	.0173
11	.1954	.1778	.1619	.1476	.1346	.1229	.1122	.1026	.0938	.0859	.0558	.0368	.0247	.0168	.0116
12	.1685	.1520	.1372	.1240	.1122	.1015	.0920	.0834	.0757	.0687	.0429	.0273	.0176	.0116	.0077
13	.1452	.1299	.1163	.1042	.0935	.0839	.0754	.0678	.0610	.0550	.0330	.0202	.0126	.0080	.0051
14	.1252	.1110	.0986	.0876	.0779	.0693	.0618	.0551	.0492	.0440	.0254	.0150	.0090	.0055	.0034
15	.1079	.0949	.0835	.0736	.0649	.0573	.0507	.0448	.0397	.0352	.0195	.0111	.0064	.0038	.0023
16	.0930	.0811	.0708	.0618	.0541	.0474	.0415	.0364	.0320	.0281	.0150	.0082	.0046	.0026	.0015
17	.0802	.0693	.0600	.0520	.0451	.0391	.0340	.0296	.0258	.0225	.0116	.0061	.0033	.0018	.0010
18	.0691	.0592	.0508	.0437	.0376	.0324	.0279	.0241	.0208	.0180	.0089	.0045	.0023	.0012	.0007
19	.0596	.0506	.0431	.0367	.0313	.0267	.0229	.0196	.0168	.0144	.0068	.0033	.0017	.0009	.0004
20	.0514	.0433	.0365	.0308	.0261	.0221	.0187	.0159	.0135	.0115	.0053	.0025	.0012	.0006	.0003
21	.0443	.0370	.0309	.0259	.0217	.0183	.0154	.0129	.0109	.0092	.0040	.0018	.0008	.0004	.0002
22	.0382	.0316	.0262	.0218	.0181	.0151	.0126	.0105	.0088	.0074	.0031	.0014	.0006	.0003	.0001
23	.0329	.0270	.0222	.0183	.0151	.0125	.0103	.0085	.0071	.0059	.0024	.0010	.0004	.0002	.0001
24	.0284	.0231	.0188	.0154	.0126	.0103	.0085	.0070	.0057	.0047	.0018	.0007	.0003	.0001	.0001
25	.0245	.0197	.0160	.0129	.0105	.0085	.0069	.0056	.0046	.0038	.0014	.0005	.0002	.0001	.0000
26	.0211	.0169	.0135	.0109	.0087	.0070	.0057	.0046	.0037	.0030	.0011	.0004	.0002	.0001	.0000
27	.0182	.0144	.0115	.0091	.0073	.0058	.0047	.0037	.0030	.0024	.0008	.0003	.0001	.0000	.0000
28	.0157	.0123	.0097	.0077	.0061	.0048	.0038	.0030	.0024	.0019	.0006	.0002	.0001	.0000	.0000
29	.0135	.0105	.0082	.0064	.0051	.0040	.0031	.0025	.0019	.0015	.0005	.0002	.0001	.0000	.0000
30	.0116	.0090	.0070	.0054	.0042	.0033	.0026	.0020	.0016	.0012	.0004	.0001	.0000	.0000	.0000
31	.0100	.0077	.0059	.0045	.0035	.0027	.0021	.0016	.0013	.0010	.0003	.0001	.0000	.0000	.0000
32	.0087	.0066	.0050	.0038	.0029	.0022	.0017	.0013	.0010	.0008	.0002	.0001	.0000	.0000	.0000
33	.0075	.0056	.0043	.0032	.0024	.0018	.0014	.0011	.0008	.0006	.0002	.0001	.0000	.0000	.0000
34	.0064	.0048	.0036	.0027	.0020	.0015	.0012	.0009	.0007	.0005	.0001	.0000	.0000	.0000	.0000
35	.0055	.0041	.0030	.0023	.0017	.0013	.0010	.0007	.0005	.0004	.0001	.0000	.0000	.0000	.0000
36	.0048	.0035	.0026	.0019	.0014	.0011	.0008	.0006	.0004	.0003	.0001	.0000	.0000	.0000	.0000
37	.0041	.0030	.0022	.0016	.0012	.0009	.0006	.0005	.0003	.0003	.0001	.0000	.0000	.0000	.0000
38	.0036	.0026	.0019	.0014	.0010	.0007	.0005	.0004	.0003	.0002	.0001	.0000	.0000	.0000	.0000
39	.0031	.0022	.0016	.0011	.0008	.0006	.0004	.0003	.0002	.0002	.0000	.0000	.0000	.0000	.0000
40	.0026	.0019	.0013	.0010	.0007	.0005	.0003	.0002	.0002	.0001	.0000	.0000	.0000	.0000	.0000
41	.0023	.0016	.0011	.0008	.0006	.0004	.0003	.0002	.0002	.0001	.0000	.0000	.0000	.0000	.0000
42	.0020	.0014	.0010	.0007	.0005	.0003	.0002	.0002	.0001	.0001	.0000	.0000	.0000	.0000	.0000
43	.0017	.0012	.0008	.0006	.0004	.0003	.0002	.0001	.0001	.0001	.0000	.0000	.0000	.0000	.0000
44	.0015	.0010	.0007	.0005	.0003	.0002	.0002	.0001	.0001	.0001	.0000	.0000	.0000	.0000	.0000
45	.0013	.0008	.0006	.0004	.0003	.0002	.0001	.0001	.0001	.0000	.0000	.0000	.0000	.0000	.0000
46	.0011	.0007	.0005	.0003	.0002	.0002	.0001	.0001	.0001	.0000	.0000	.0000	.0000	.0000	.0000
47	.0009	.0006	.0004	.0003	.0002	.0001	.0001	.0001	.0000	.0000	.0000	.0000	.0000	.0000	.0000
48	.0008	.0005	.0003	.0002	.0002	.0001	.0001	.0001	.0000	.0000	.0000	.0000	.0000	.0000	.0000
49	.0007	.0005	.0003	.0002	.0001	.0001	.0001	.0000	.0000	.0000	.0000	.0000	.0000	.0000	.0000
50	.0006	.0004	.0002	.0002	.0001	.0001	.0001	.0000	.0000	.0000	.0000	.0000	.0000	.0000	.0000

TABLE H-3

THE PRESENT VALUE OF AN ORDINARY ANNUITY OF 1 (P/A)

n	1%	2%	3%	4%	5%	6%	7%	8%	9%	10%	11%	12%	13%	14%	15%
1	.9901	.9804	.9709	.9615	.9524	.9434	.9346	.9259	.9174	.9091	.9009	.8929	.8850	.8772	.8696
2	1.9704	1.9416	1.9135	1.8861	1.8594	1.8334	1.8080	1.7833	1.7591	1.7355	1.7125	1.6901	1.6681	1.6467	1.6257
3	2.9410	2.8839	2.8286	2.7751	2.7232	2.6730	2.6243	2.5771	2.5313	2.4869	2.4437	2.4018	2.3612	2.3216	2.2832
4	3.9020	3.8077	3.7171	3.6299	3.5459	3.4651	3.3872	3.3121	3.2397	3.1699	3.1024	3.0374	2.9745	2.9137	2.8550
5	4.8534	4.7135	4.5797	4.4518	4.3295	4.2124	4.1002	3.9927	3.8897	3.7908	3.6959	3.6048	3.5172	3.4331	3.3522
6	5.7955	5.6014	5.4172	5.2421	5.0757	4.9173	4.7666	4.6229	4.4859	4.3553	4.2305	4.1114	3.9976	3.8887	3.7845
7	6.7282	6.4720	6.2303	6.0021	5.7864	5.5824	5.3893	5.2064	5.0330	4.8684	4.7122	4.5638	4.4226	4.2883	4.1604
8	7.6517	7.3255	7.0197	6.7328	6.4632	6.2098	5.9713	5.7466	5.5348	5.3349	5.1461	4.9676	4.7988	4.6389	4.4873
9	8.5660	8.1622	7.7861	7.4353	7.1078	6.8017	6.5152	6.2469	5.9953	5.7590	5.5371	5.3282	5.1317	4.9464	4.7716
10	9.4713	8.9826	8.5302	8.1109	7.7217	7.3601	7.0236	6.7101	6.4177	6.1446	5.8892	5.6502	5.4262	5.2161	5.0188
11	10.3676	9.7868	9.2526	8.7605	8.3064	7.8869	7.4987	7.1390	6.8052	6.4951	6.2065	5.9377	5.6869	5.4527	5.2337
12	11.2551	10.5753	9.9540	9.3851	8.8633	8.3839	7.9427	7.5361	7.1607	6.8137	6.4924	6.1944	5.9177	5.6603	5.4206
13	12.1338	11.3484	10.6349	9.9857	9.3936	8.8527	8.3577	7.9038	7.4869	7.1034	6.7499	6.4235	6.1218	5.8424	5.5832
14	13.0037	12.1062	11.2961	10.5631	9.8986	9.2950	8.7455	8.2442	7.7862	7.3667	6.9819	6.6282	6.3025	6.0021	5.7245
15	13.8651	12.8492	11.9379	11.1184	10.3797	9.7123	9.1079	8.5595	8.0607	7.6061	7.1909	6.8109	6.4624	6.1422	5.8474
16	14.7179	13.5777	12.5611	11.6523	10.8378	10.1059	9.4467	8.8514	8.3126	7.8237	7.3792	6.9740	6.6039	6.2651	5.9542
17	15.5623	14.2919	13.1661	12.1657	11.2741	10.4773	9.7632	9.1216	8.5436	8.0216	7.5488	7.1196	6.7291	6.3729	6.0472
18	16.3983	14.9920	13.7535	12.6593	11.6896	10.8276	10.0591	9.3719	8.7556	8.2014	7.7016	7.2497	6.8399	6.4674	6.1280
19	17.2260	15.6785	14.3238	13.1339	12.0853	11.1581	10.3356	9.6036	8.9501	8.3649	7.8393	7.3658	6.9380	6.5504	6.1982
20	18.0456	16.3514	14.8775	13.5903	12.4622	11.4699	10.5940	9.8181	9.1285	8.5136	7.9633	7.4694	7.0248	6.6231	6.2593
21	18.8570	17.0112	15.4150	14.0292	12.8212	11.7641	10.8355	10.0168	9.2922	8.6487	8.0751	7.5620	7.1016	6.6870	6.3125
22	19.6604	17.6580	15.9369	14.4511	13.1630	12.0416	11.0612	10.2007	9.4424	8.7715	8.1757	7.6446	7.1695	6.7430	6.3587
23	20.4558	18.2922	16.4436	14.8569	13.4886	12.3034	11.2722	10.3711	9.5802	8.8832	8.2664	7.7184	7.2297	6.7921	6.3988
24	21.2434	18.9139	16.9355	15.2470	13.7987	12.5504	11.4693	10.5288	9.7066	8.9847	8.3481	7.7843	7.2829	6.8352	6.4338
25	22.0232	19.5234	17.4132	15.6221	14.0940	12.7834	11.6536	10.6748	9.8226	9.0770	8.4217	7.8431	7.3300	6.8729	6.4641
26	22.7952	20.1210	17.8768	15.9828	14.3752	13.0032	11.8258	10.8100	9.9290	9.1610	8.4880	7.8956	7.3717	6.9061	6.4906
27	23.5596	20.7069	18.3270	16.3296	14.6430	13.2106	11.9867	10.9352	10.0266	9.2372	8.5478	7.9425	7.4086	6.9352	6.5135
28	24.3165	21.2813	18.7641	16.6631	14.8981	13.4062	12.1371	11.0511	10.1161	9.3066	8.6016	7.9844	7.4412	6.9607	6.5335
29	25.0658	21.8444	19.1885	16.9837	15.1411	13.5908	12.2777	11.1584	10.1983	9.3696	8.6501	8.0218	7.4701	6.9831	6.5509
30	25.8077	22.3964	19.6005	17.2920	15.3725	13.7649	12.4091	11.2578	10.2737	9.4269	8.6938	8.0552	7.4957	7.0027	6.5660
31	26.5423	22.9377	20.0005	17.5885	15.5928	13.9291	12.5318	11.3498	10.3428	9.4790	8.7331	8.0850	7.5183	7.0199	6.5791
32	27.2696	23.4683	20.3888	17.8736	15.8027	14.0841	12.6466	11.4350	10.4062	9.5264	8.7686	8.1116	7.5383	7.0350	6.5905
33	27.9897	23.9885	20.7658	18.1477	16.0026	14.2303	12.7538	11.5139	10.4644	9.5694	8.8005	8.1353	7.5560	7.0483	6.6005
34	28.7027	24.4986	21.1319	18.4112	16.1929	14.3682	12.8540	11.5870	10.5178	9.6086	8.8293	8.1565	7.5717	7.0599	6.6091
35	29.4086	24.9986	21.4872	18.6646	16.3742	14.4983	12.9477	11.6546	10.5668	9.6442	8.8552	8.1755	7.5856	7.0701	6.6166
36	30.1075	25.4888	21.8323	18.9083	16.5469	14.6211	13.0352	11.7172	10.6118	9.6765	8.8786	8.1924	7.5979	7.0790	6.6231
37	30.7995	25.9694	22.1673	19.1426	16.7113	14.7368	13.1170	11.7752	10.6530	9.7059	8.8996	8.2075	7.6087	7.0868	6.6288
38	31.4847	26.4406	22.4925	19.3679	16.8679	14.8461	13.1935	11.8289	10.6908	9.7327	8.9186	8.2210	7.6183	7.0937	6.6338
39	32.1631	26.9026	22.8082	19.5845	17.0171	14.9491	13.2650	11.8786	10.7255	9.7570	8.9356	8.2330	7.6269	7.0998	6.6380
40	32.8347	27.3555	23.1148	19.7928	17.1591	15.0464	13.3317	11.9246	10.7574	9.7791	8.9510	8.2438	7.6344	7.1051	6.6418
41	33.4997	27.7995	23.4124	19.9931	17.2944	15.1381	13.3941	11.9672	10.7866	9.7991	8.9649	8.2534	7.6410	7.1097	6.6450
42	34.1581	28.2348	23.7014	20.1857	17.4232	15.2246	13.4525	12.0067	10.8134	9.8174	8.9774	8.2619	7.6469	7.1138	6.6478
43	34.8100	28.6615	23.9819	20.3708	17.5459	15.3062	13.5070	12.0432	10.8380	9.8340	8.9886	8.2696	7.6522	7.1173	6.6503
44	35.4555	29.0799	24.2543	20.5489	17.6628	15.3833	13.5579	12.0771	10.8605	9.8491	8.9988	8.2764	7.6568	7.1205	6.6524
45	36.0945	29.4901	24.5187	20.7201	17.7741	15.4559	13.6055	12.1084	10.8812	9.8628	9.0079	8.2825	7.6609	7.1232	6.6543
46	36.7273	29.8923	24.7755	20.8847	17.8801	15.5244	13.6500	12.1374	10.9002	9.8753	9.0161	8.2880	7.6645	7.1256	6.6559
47	37.3537	30.2866	25.0247	21.0430	17.9810	15.5891	13.6916	12.1643	10.9176	9.8866	9.0235	8.2928	7.6677	7.1277	6.6573
48	37.9740	30.6731	25.2667	21.1952	18.0772	15.6501	13.7305	12.1891	10.9336	9.8969	9.0302	8.2972	7.6705	7.1296	6.6585
49	38.5881	31.0521	25.5017	21.3415	18.1687	15.7077	13.7668	12.2122	10.9482	9.9063	9.0362	8.3010	7.6730	7.1312	6.6596
50	39.1961	31.4236	25.7298	21.4822	18.2559	15.7619	13.8008	12.2335	10.9617	9.9148	9.0416	8.3045	7.6753	7.1327	6.6605

TABLE H–3 (Cont.)

PV ann (handwritten)

								i							
n	16%	17%	18%	19%	20%	21%	22%	23%	24%	25%	30%	35%	40%	45%	50%
1	.8621	.8547	.8475	.8403	.8333	.8264	.8197	.8130	.8065	.8000	.7692	.7407	.7143	.6897	.6667
2	1.6052	1.5852	1.5656	1.5465	1.5278	1.5095	1.4915	1.4740	1.4568	1.4400	1.3609	1.2894	1.2245	1.1653	1.1111
3	2.2459	2.2096	2.1743	2.1399	2.1065	2.0739	2.0422	2.0114	1.9813	1.9520	1.8161	1.6959	1.5889	1.4933	1.4074
4	2.7982	2.7432	2.6901	2.6386	2.5887	2.5404	2.4936	2.4483	2.4043	2.3616	2.1662	1.9969	1.8492	1.7195	1.6049
5	3.2743	3.1993	3.1272	3.0576	2.9906	2.9260	2.8636	2.8035	2.7454	2.6893	2.4356	2.2200	2.0352	1.8755	1.7366
6	3.6847	3.5892	3.4976	3.4098	3.3255	3.2446	3.1669	3.0923	3.0205	2.9514	2.6428	2.3852	2.1680	1.9831	1.8244
7	4.0386	3.9224	3.8115	3.7057	3.6046	3.5079	3.4155	3.3270	3.2423	3.1611	2.8021	2.5075	2.2628	2.0573	1.8830
8	4.3436	4.2072	4.0776	3.9544	3.8372	3.7256	3.6193	3.5179	3.4212	3.3289	2.9247	2.5982	2.3306	2.1085	1.9220
9	4.6065	4.4506	4.3030	4.1633	4.0310	3.9054	3.7863	3.6731	3.5655	3.4631	3.0190	2.6653	2.3790	2.1438	1.9480
10	4.8332	4.6586	4.4941	4.3389	4.1925	4.0541	3.9232	3.7993	3.6819	3.5705	3.0916	2.7150	2.4136	2.1681	1.9653
11	5.0286	4.8364	4.6560	4.4865	4.3271	4.1769	4.0354	3.9019	3.7757	3.6564	3.1474	2.7519	2.4383	2.1849	1.9769
12	5.1971	4.9884	4.7932	4.6105	4.4392	4.2785	4.1274	3.9852	3.8514	3.7251	3.1903	2.7792	2.4559	2.1965	1.9846
13	5.3423	5.1183	4.9095	4.7147	4.5327	4.3624	4.2028	4.0530	3.9124	3.7801	3.2233	2.7994	2.4685	2.2045	1.9897
14	5.4675	5.2293	5.0081	4.8023	4.6106	4.4317	4.2646	4.1082	3.9616	3.8241	3.2487	2.8143	2.4775	2.2100	1.9932
15	5.5755	5.3242	5.0916	4.8759	4.6755	4.4890	4.3152	4.1530	4.0013	3.8593	3.2682	2.8254	2.4839	2.2138	1.9954
16	5.6685	5.4053	5.1624	4.9377	4.7296	4.5364	4.3567	4.1894	4.0333	3.8874	3.2833	2.8337	2.4885	2.2164	1.9970
17	5.7487	5.4746	5.2223	4.9897	4.7746	4.5755	4.3908	4.2190	4.0591	3.9099	3.2948	2.8397	2.4918	2.2182	1.9980
18	5.8179	5.5338	5.2732	5.0333	4.8122	4.6079	4.4187	4.2431	4.0799	3.9279	3.3037	2.8443	2.4941	2.2195	1.9986
19	5.8775	5.5845	5.3163	5.0701	4.8435	4.6346	4.4415	4.2627	4.0967	3.9424	3.3106	2.8476	2.4958	2.2203	1.9991
20	5.9289	5.6278	5.3528	5.1009	4.8696	4.6567	4.4603	4.2786	4.1103	3.9539	3.3158	2.8501	2.4970	2.2209	1.9994
21	5.9732	5.6648	5.3837	5.1268	4.8913	4.6749	4.4756	4.2915	4.1212	3.9631	3.3199	2.8519	2.4979	2.2213	1.9996
22	6.0113	5.6964	5.4099	5.1486	4.9094	4.6900	4.4882	4.3021	4.1300	3.9705	3.3230	2.8533	2.4985	2.2216	1.9997
23	6.0443	5.7234	5.4321	5.1669	4.9245	4.7025	4.4985	4.3106	4.1371	3.9764	3.3254	2.8543	2.4989	2.2218	1.9998
24	6.0726	5.7465	5.4510	5.1823	4.9371	4.7128	4.5070	4.3176	4.1428	3.9811	3.3272	2.8550	2.4992	2.2219	1.9999
25	6.0971	5.7662	5.4669	5.1952	4.9476	4.7213	4.5139	4.3232	4.1474	3.9849	3.3286	2.8556	2.4994	2.2220	1.9999
26	6.1182	5.7831	5.4805	5.2060	4.9563	4.7284	4.5196	4.3278	4.1511	3.9879	3.3297	2.8560	2.4996	2.2221	1.9999
27	6.1364	5.7975	5.4919	5.2152	4.9636	4.7342	4.5243	4.3316	4.1541	3.9903	3.3306	2.8563	2.4997	2.2221	2.0000
28	6.1521	5.8099	5.5016	5.2228	4.9697	4.7390	4.5281	4.3346	4.1566	3.9923	3.3312	2.8565	2.4998	2.2221	2.0000
29	6.1656	5.8204	5.5099	5.2293	4.9747	4.7430	4.5312	4.3371	4.1585	3.9938	3.3317	2.8567	2.4998	2.2222	2.0000
30	6.1772	5.8294	5.5168	5.2347	4.9789	4.7463	4.5338	4.3391	4.1601	3.9950	3.3321	2.8568	2.4999	2.2222	2.0000
31	6.1873	5.8371	5.5227	5.2392	4.9825	4.7490	4.5359	4.3407	4.1614	3.9960	3.3324	2.8569	2.4999	2.2222	2.0000
32	6.1959	5.8437	5.5277	5.2431	4.9854	4.7512	4.5376	4.3420	4.1624	3.9968	3.3326	2.8569	2.4999	2.2222	2.0000
33	6.2034	5.8493	5.5320	5.2463	4.9878	4.7531	4.5390	4.3431	4.1632	3.9975	3.3328	2.8570	2.5000	2.2222	2.0000
34	6.2098	5.8541	5.5356	5.2490	4.9898	4.7546	4.5402	4.3440	4.1639	3.9980	3.3329	2.8570	2.5000	2.2222	2.0000
35	6.2154	5.8582	5.5386	5.2512	4.9915	4.7559	4.5411	4.3447	4.1644	3.9984	3.3330	2.8571	2.5000	2.2222	2.0000
36	6.2201	5.8617	5.5412	5.2531	4.9930	4.7569	4.5419	4.3453	4.1649	3.9987	3.3331	2.8571	2.5000	2.2222	2.0000
37	6.2243	5.8647	5.5434	5.2547	4.9941	4.7578	4.5425	4.3458	4.1652	3.9990	3.3332	2.8571	2.5000	2.2222	2.0000
38	6.2278	5.8673	5.5453	5.2561	4.9951	4.7585	4.5431	4.3461	4.1655	3.9992	3.3332	2.8571	2.5000	2.2222	2.0000
39	6.2309	5.8695	5.5468	5.2572	4.9959	4.7591	4.5435	4.3464	4.1657	3.9993	3.3332	2.8571	2.5000	2.2222	2.0000
40	6.2335	5.8713	5.5482	5.2582	4.9966	4.7596	4.5438	4.3467	4.1659	3.9995	3.3333	2.8571	2.5000	2.2222	2.0000
41	6.2358	5.8729	5.5493	5.2590	4.9972	4.7600	4.5441	4.3469	4.1660	3.9996	3.3333	2.8571	2.5000	2.2222	2.0000
42	6.2377	5.8743	5.5500	5.2596	4.9977	4.7603	4.5444	4.3471	4.1662	3.9997	3.3333	2.8571	2.5000	2.2222	2.0000
43	6.2394	5.8755	5.5511	5.2602	4.9980	4.7606	4.5446	4.3472	4.1663	3.9997	3.3333	2.8571	2.5000	2.2222	2.0000
44	6.2409	5.8765	5.5518	5.2607	4.9984	4.7608	4.5447	4.3473	4.1663	3.9998	3.3333	2.8571	2.5000	2.2222	2.0000
45	6.2422	5.8773	5.5523	5.2611	4.9986	4.7610	4.5448	4.3474	4.1664	3.9998	3.3333	2.8571	2.5000	2.2222	2.0000
46	6.2432	5.8781	5.5528	5.2614	4.9989	4.7611	4.5450	4.3475	4.1665	3.9999	3.3334	2.8571	2.5000	2.2222	2.0000
47	6.2442	5.8787	5.5533	5.2617	4.9991	4.7613	4.5450	4.3475	4.1665	3.9999	3.3334	2.8571	2.5000	2.2222	2.0000
48	6.2450	5.8792	5.5536	5.2619	4.9992	4.7614	4.5451	4.3476	4.1665	3.9999	3.3334	2.8571	2.5000	2.2222	2.0000
49	6.2457	5.8797	5.5539	5.2621	4.9994	4.7615	4.5452	4.3476	4.1666	3.9999	3.3334	2.8571	2.5000	2.2222	2.0000
50	6.2463	5.8801	5.5542	5.2623	4.9995	4.7615	4.5452	4.3477	4.1666	3.9999	3.3334	2.8571	2.5000	2.2222	2.0000

TABLE H-4

THE FUTURE VALUE OF AN ORDINARY ANNUITY OF 1 (F/A)

n	1%	2%	3%	4%	5%	6%	7%	8%	9%	10%	11%	12%	13%	14%
1	1.0000	1.0000	1.0000	1.0000	1.0000	1.0000	1.0000	1.0000	1.0000	1.0000	1.0000	1.0000	1.0000	1.0000
2	2.0100	2.0200	2.0300	2.0400	2.0500	2.0600	2.0700	2.0800	2.0900	2.1000	2.1100	2.1200	2.1300	2.1400
3	2.0301	3.0604	3.0909	3.1216	3.1525	3.1836	3.2149	3.2464	3.2781	3.3100	3.3421	3.3744	3.4069	3.4396
4	4.0604	4.1216	4.1836	4.2465	4.3101	4.3746	4.4399	4.5061	4.5731	4.6410	4.7097	4.7793	4.8498	4.9211
5	5.1010	5.2040	5.3091	5.4163	5.5256	5.6371	5.7507	5.8666	5.9847	6.1051	6.2278	6.3528	6.4803	6.6101
6	6.1520	6.3081	6.4684	6.6330	6.8019	6.9753	7.1533	7.3359	7.5233	7.7156	7.9129	8.1152	8.3227	8.5355
7	7.2135	7.4343	7.6625	7.8983	8.1420	8.3938	8.6540	8.9228	9.2004	9.4872	9.7833	10.0890	10.4047	10.7305
8	8.2857	8.5830	8.8923	9.2142	9.5491	9.8975	10.2598	10.6366	11.0285	11.4359	11.8594	12.2997	12.7573	13.2328
9	9.3685	9.7546	10.1591	10.5828	11.0266	11.4913	11.9780	12.4876	13.0210	13.5795	14.1640	14.7757	15.4157	16.0853
10	10.4622	10.9497	11.4639	12.0061	12.5779	13.1808	13.8164	14.4866	15.1929	15.9374	16.7220	17.5487	18.4197	19.3373
11	11.5668	12.1687	12.8078	13.4864	14.2068	14.9716	15.7836	16.6455	17.5603	18.5312	19.5614	20.6546	21.8143	23.0445
12	12.6825	13.4121	14.1920	15.0258	15.9171	16.8699	17.8885	18.9771	20.1407	21.3843	22.7132	24.1331	25.6502	27.2707
13	13.8093	14.6803	15.6178	16.6268	17.7130	18.8821	20.1406	21.4953	22.9534	24.5227	26.2116	28.0291	29.9847	32.0887
14	14.9474	15.9739	17.0863	18.2919	19.5986	21.0151	22.5505	24.2149	26.0192	27.9750	30.0949	32.3926	34.8827	37.5811
15	16.0969	17.2934	18.5989	20.0236	21.5786	23.2760	25.1290	27.1521	29.3609	31.7725	34.4054	37.2797	40.4175	43.8424
16	17.2579	18.6393	20.1569	21.8245	23.6575	25.6725	27.8881	30.3243	33.0034	35.9497	39.1899	42.7533	46.6717	50.9804
17	18.4304	20.0121	21.7616	23.6975	25.8404	28.2129	30.8402	33.7502	36.9737	40.5447	44.5008	48.8837	53.7391	59.1176
18	19.6147	21.4123	23.4144	25.6454	28.1324	30.9057	33.9990	37.4502	41.3013	45.5992	50.3959	55.7497	61.7251	68.3941
19	20.8109	22.8406	25.1169	27.6712	30.5390	33.7600	37.3790	41.4463	46.0185	51.1591	56.9395	63.4397	70.7494	78.9692
20	22.0190	24.2974	26.8704	29.7781	33.0660	36.7856	40.9955	45.7620	51.1601	57.2750	64.2028	72.0524	80.9468	91.0249
21	23.2392	25.7833	28.6765	31.9692	35.7193	39.9927	44.8652	50.4229	56.7645	64.0025	72.2651	81.6987	92.4699	104.7684
22	24.4716	27.2990	30.5368	34.2480	38.5052	43.3923	49.0057	55.4568	62.8733	71.4027	81.2143	92.5026	105.4910	120.4360
23	25.7163	28.8450	32.4529	36.6179	41.4305	46.9958	53.4361	60.8933	69.5319	79.5430	91.1479	104.6029	120.2048	138.2970
24	26.9735	30.4219	34.4265	39.0826	44.5020	50.8156	58.1767	66.7648	76.7898	88.4973	102.1742	118.1552	136.8315	158.6586
25	28.2432	32.0303	36.4593	41.6459	47.7271	54.8645	63.2490	73.1059	84.7009	98.3471	114.4133	133.3339	155.6196	181.8708
26	29.5256	33.6709	38.5530	44.3117	51.1135	59.1564	68.6765	79.9544	93.3240	109.1818	127.9988	150.3339	176.8501	208.3327
27	30.8209	35.3443	40.7096	47.0842	54.6691	63.7058	74.4838	87.3508	102.7231	121.0999	143.0786	169.3740	200.8406	238.4993
28	32.1291	37.0512	42.9309	49.9676	58.4026	68.5281	80.6977	95.3388	112.9682	134.2099	159.8173	190.6989	227.9499	272.8892
29	33.4504	38.7922	45.2189	52.9663	62.3227	73.6398	87.3465	103.9659	124.1354	148.6309	178.3972	214.5828	258.5834	312.0937
30	34.7849	40.5681	47.5754	56.0849	66.4388	79.0582	94.4608	113.2832	136.3075	164.4940	199.0209	241.3327	293.1992	356.7868
31	36.1327	42.3794	50.0027	59.3283	70.7608	84.8017	102.0730	123.3459	149.5752	181.9434	221.9132	271.2926	332.3151	407.7370
32	37.4941	44.2270	52.5028	62.7015	75.2988	90.8898	110.2182	134.2135	164.0370	201.1378	247.3236	304.8477	376.5161	465.8202
33	38.8690	46.1116	55.0778	66.2095	80.0638	97.3432	118.9334	145.9506	179.8003	222.2515	275.5292	342.4294	426.4632	532.0350
34	40.2577	48.0338	57.7302	69.8579	85.0670	104.1838	128.2588	158.6267	196.9823	245.4767	306.8374	384.5210	482.9034	607.5199
35	41.6603	49.9945	60.4621	73.6522	90.3203	111.4348	138.2369	172.3168	215.7108	271.0244	341.5896	431.6635	546.6808	693.5727
36	43.0769	51.9944	63.2759	77.5983	95.8363	119.1209	148.9135	187.1021	236.1247	299.1268	380.1644	484.4631	618.7493	791.6729
37	44.5076	54.0343	66.1742	81.7022	101.6281	127.2681	160.3374	203.0703	258.3759	330.0395	422.9825	543.5987	700.1868	903.5071
38	45.9527	56.1149	69.1594	85.9703	107.7095	135.9042	172.5610	220.3159	282.6298	364.0434	470.5106	609.8305	792.2110	1030.9981
39	47.4123	58.2372	72.2342	90.4092	114.0950	145.0585	185.6403	238.9412	309.0665	401.4478	523.2667	684.0102	896.1985	1176.3378
40	48.8864	60.4020	75.4013	95.0255	120.7998	154.7620	199.6351	259.0565	337.8824	442.5926	581.8261	767.0914	1013.7043	1342.0251
41	50.3752	62.6100	78.6633	99.8265	127.8398	165.0477	214.6096	280.7810	369.2919	487.8518	646.8269	860.1424	1146.4858	1530.9086
42	51.8790	64.8622	82.0232	104.8196	135.2318	175.9505	230.6322	304.2435	403.5281	537.6370	718.9779	964.3595	1296.5290	1746.2359
43	53.3978	67.1595	85.4839	110.0124	142.9933	187.5076	247.7765	329.5830	440.8457	592.4007	799.0655	1081.0826	1466.0777	1991.7089
44	54.9318	69.5027	89.0484	115.4129	151.1430	199.7580	266.1209	356.9496	481.5218	652.6408	887.9627	1211.8125	1657.6679	2271.5481
45	56.4811	71.8927	92.7199	121.0294	159.7002	212.7435	285.7493	386.5056	525.8587	718.9048	986.6386	1358.2300	1874.1647	2590.5648
46	58.0459	74.3306	96.5015	126.8706	168.6852	226.5081	306.7518	418.4261	574.1860	791.7953	1096.1688	1522.2176	2118.8061	2954.2439
47	59.6263	76.8172	100.3965	132.9454	178.1194	241.0986	329.2244	452.9002	626.8628	871.9748	1217.7474	1705.8838	2395.2509	3368.8381
48	61.2226	79.3535	104.4084	139.2632	188.0254	256.5645	353.2701	490.1322	684.2804	960.1723	1352.6996	1911.5898	2707.6335	3841.4754
49	62.8348	81.9406	108.5406	145.8337	198.4267	272.9584	378.9990	530.3427	746.8656	1057.1896	1502.4966	2141.9806	3060.6259	4380.2820
50	64.4632	84.5794	112.7969	152.6671	209.3480	290.3359	406.5289	573.7702	815.0835	1163.9085	1668.7712	2400.0182	3459.5072	4994.5215

FUANN

						i					
n	15%	16%	17%	18%	19%	20%	21%	22%	23%	24%	25%
1	1.0000	1.0000	1.0000	1.0000	1.0000	1.0000	1.0000	1.0000	1.0000	1.0000	1.0000
2	2.1500	2.1600	2.1700	2.1800	2.1900	2.2000	2.2100	2.2200	2.2300	2.2400	2.2500
3	3.4725	3.5056	3.5389	3.5724	3.6061	3.6400	3.6741	3.7084	3.7429	3.7776	3.8125
4	4.9934	5.0665	5.1405	5.2154	5.2913	5.3680	5.4457	5.5242	5.6038	5.6842	5.7656
5	6.7424	6.8771	7.0144	7.1542	7.2966	7.4416	7.5892	7.7396	7.8926	8.0484	8.2070
6	8.7537	8.9775	9.2068	9.4420	9.6830	9.9299	10.1830	10.4423	10.7079	10.9801	11.2588
7	11.0668	11.4139	11.7720	12.1415	12.5227	12.9159	13.3214	13.7396	14.1708	14.6153	15.0735
8	13.7268	14.2401	14.7733	15.3270	15.9020	16.4991	17.1109	17.7623	18.4300	19.1229	19.8419
9	16.7858	17.5185	18.2847	19.0059	19.9234	20.7989	21.7139	22.6700	23.6690	24.7125	25.8023
10	20.3037	21.3215	22.3931	23.5213	24.7089	25.9587	27.2738	28.6574	30.1128	31.6434	33.2529
11	24.3493	25.7329	27.1999	28.7551	30.4035	32.1504	34.0013	35.9620	38.0388	40.2379	42.5661
12	29.0017	30.8502	32.8239	34.9311	37.1802	39.5805	42.1416	44.8737	47.7877	50.8950	54.2077
13	34.3519	36.7862	39.4040	42.2187	45.2445	48.4966	51.9913	55.7455	59.7788	64.1097	68.7596
14	40.5047	43.6720	47.1027	50.8180	54.8409	59.1959	63.9095	69.0100	74.5280	80.4961	86.9495
15	47.5804	51.6595	56.1101	60.9653	66.2607	72.0351	78.3305	85.1922	92.6694	100.8151	109.6868
16	55.7175	60.9250	66.6488	72.9390	79.8502	87.4421	95.7799	104.9345	114.9834	126.0108	138.1085
17	65.0751	71.6730	78.9792	87.0680	96.0218	105.9306	116.8937	129.0201	142.4295	157.2534	173.6357
18	75.8364	84.1407	93.4056	103.7403	115.2659	128.1167	142.4413	158.4045	176.1883	195.9942	218.0446
19	88.2118	98.6032	110.2846	123.4135	138.1664	154.7400	173.3540	194.2535	217.7116	244.0328	273.5558
20	102.4436	115.3797	130.0329	146.6280	165.4180	186.6880	210.7584	237.9893	268.7853	303.6006	342.9447
21	118.8101	134.8405	153.1385	174.0210	197.8474	225.0256	256.0176	291.3469	331.6059	377.4648	429.6809
22	137.6316	157.4150	180.1721	206.3448	236.4385	271.0307	310.7813	356.4432	408.8753	469.0563	538.1011
23	159.2764	183.6014	211.8013	244.4868	282.3618	326.2369	377.0454	435.8607	503.9166	582.6298	673.6264
24	184.1678	213.9776	248.8076	289.4945	337.0105	392.4842	457.2249	532.7501	620.8174	723.4610	843.0329
25	212.7930	249.2140	292.1049	342.6035	402.0425	471.9811	554.2422	650.9551	764.6055	898.0916	1054.7912
26	245.7120	290.0883	342.7627	405.2721	479.4306	567.3773	671.6330	795.1653	941.4647	1114.6336	1319.4890
27	283.5688	337.5024	402.0323	479.2211	571.5224	681.8528	813.6760	971.1016	1159.0016	1383.1457	1650.3612
28	327.1041	392.5028	471.3778	566.4809	681.1116	819.2233	985.5479	1185.7440	1426.5720	1716.1007	2063.9515
29	377.1697	456.3032	552.5121	669.4474	811.5228	984.0680	1193.5130	1447.6077	1755.6835	2128.9648	2580.9394
30	434.7451	530.3117	647.4391	790.9480	966.7122	1181.8815	1445.1507	1767.0814	2160.4907	2640.9164	3227.1743
31	500.9569	616.1616	758.5038	934.3186	1151.3875	1419.2579	1749.6323	2156.8393	2658.4036	3275.7363	4034.9678
32	577.1005	715.7475	888.4494	1103.4960	1371.1511	1704.1094	2118.0551	2632.3439	3270.8364	4062.9131	5044.7098
33	664.6655	831.2671	1040.4858	1303.1252	1632.6698	2045.9313	2563.8467	3212.4500	4024.1288	5039.0122	6306.8873
34	765.3654	965.2698	1218.3684	1538.6878	1943.8771	2456.1176	3103.2545	3920.2007	4950.6784	6249.3751	7884.6091
35	881.1702	1120.7130	1426.4910	1816.6516	2314.2137	2948.3411	3755.9380	4783.6448	6090.3344	7750.2252	9856.7614
36	1014.3457	1301.0270	1669.9945	2144.6489	2754.9143	3539.0093	4545.6849	5837.0467	7492.1113	9611.2702	12321.9517
37	1167.4975	1510.1914	1954.8936	2531.6857	3279.3480	4247.8112	5501.2788	7122.1970	9216.2970	11918.9862	15403.4396
38	1343.6222	1752.8220	2288.2255	2988.3801	3903.4241	5098.3734	6657.5474	8690.0803	11337.0453	14780.5428	19255.2996
39	1546.1655	2034.2735	2678.2238	3527.2991	4646.0747	6119.0481	8056.6323	10602.8979	13945.5657	18328.8733	24070.1243
40	1779.0903	2360.7573	3134.5218	4163.2130	5529.8289	7343.8577	9749.5250	12936.5355	17154.0459	22728.8027	30088.6553
41	2046.9539	2739.4784	3668.3905	4913.5913	6581.4964	8813.6293	11797.9253	15783.5734	21100.4763	28184.7153	37611.8193
42	2354.9969	3178.7950	4293.0169	5799.0378	7832.9807	10577.3551	14276.4897	19256.9595	25954.5859	34950.0469	47015.7739
43	2709.2465	3688.4022	5023.8298	6843.8646	9322.2471	12693.8260	17275.5525	23494.4905	31925.1406	43339.0586	58770.7178
44	3116.6335	4279.5465	5878.8809	8076.7602	11094.4740	15233.5913	20904.4187	28664.2786	39268.9229	53741.4326	73464.3965
45	3585.1285	4965.2739	6879.2906	9531.5770	13203.4240	18281.3096	25295.3464	34971.4199	48301.7754	66640.3760	91831.4961
46	4123.8978	5760.7178	8049.7700	11248.2609	15713.0746	21938.5713	30608.3694	42666.1323	59412.1836	82635.0664	114790.3701
47	4743.4824	6683.4326	9419.2310	13273.9479	18699.5586	26327.2856	37037.1270	52053.6812	73077.9863	102468.4824	143488.9629
48	5456.0048	7753.7818	11021.5002	15664.2584	22253.4749	31593.7427	44815.9233	63506.4912	89886.9220	127061.9180	179362.2031
49	6275.4055	8995.3870	12896.1553	18484.8250	26482.0350	37913.4912	54228.2676	77478.9189	110561.9150	157557.7700	224203.7539
50	7217.7164	10435.6488	15089.5010	21813.0935	31515.3357	45497.1895	65617.2041	94625.2812	135992.1562	195372.6465	280255.6914

INDEX

American Institute of Accounting (AIA), 10
American Institute of Certified Public Accountants
     (AICPA), 10
  as accounting policy maker, 16, 18
  Accounting Principles Board (APB) of (see Accounting
     Principles Board)
  Accounting Standards Division of, 16
  organization of (fig.), 17
  Private Companies Section of, 18
  Public Oversight Board of, 18
  Securities and Exchange Commission Practice Section of,
     18
  Statements of Position of, 16
Amortization (amortization schedules), 161
  of bond discount, effective interest method of, 491–495,
     684
  of bond discount or premium, straight-line method of, 494
  of bond issue costs, 688
  for bond issuers and bondholders, 680–681
  of bonds, fiscal period consideration and, 689
  of a capital lease, 555
  defined, 414
  of past and prior service pension benefits, 728–737
  of serial bonds, 697–698
Analysis-of-sales method of estimating uncollectibles, 274–
     277
Annual reports, 1044–1094
  compensated absences disclosure in, 600
  convertibility feature of outstanding bonds in, 694
  current liabilities disclosure in, 592
  notes payable disclosure in, 597
  Securities and Exchange Commission (SEC), 1057–1060
     Form 8-K, 1060
     Form 10-K, 1058
     Form 10-Q, 1060
     Regulation S-K, 1059
     Regulation S-X, 1059
  segmental (line of business) reporting in, 1048–1052
  sequencing of report data in, 1045–1048
  serial bonds in, 698
  treasury stock disclosure in, 779, 781
  troubled debt restructuring in, 706–707
  warrants issued with debt in, 696
  (see also Financial statements)
Annuities due, 154, 162–163
Annuity (-ies):
  accounting for, 160–162
  capital recovery factors and, 164
  ordinary:
     future value of, 158
     present value, 154–158
  present value of, 154–158
     annual compounding, 154–157
     semiannual compounding, 157–158
  semiannual payments and, 157–158
  sinking fund factors and, 163–164
Annuity method of depreciation, 421–422
Annuity obligation amount of bonds, 678
Annuity payment date of bonds, 678
Antidilutive securities, 849, 850
Arbitrage, 832

ASR (see Accounting Series Releases)
Assets (asset accounting):
  in accrual accounting, 46–48
  after acquisition, 225–226
  at acquisition, 225
  in balance sheets, 120–124
     current assets, 120–122
     noncurrent assets, 122–124
     similarities among assets, 120
  cash (see Cash)
  cash-equivalent price of, 224
  changes in economic potential of, 225–226
  common attributes of, 223–225
     entity's ability to utilize economic potential, 223–224
     future economic potential, 223
     objective measurement in monetary terms, 224–225
  current, 120–122
  defined, 32, 450
  depletable, in balance sheets, 123
  disposals and retirements of, 226
  equities as sources of, 588
  expenses distinguished from, 226–227
  intangible (see Intangibles)
  long-term (see Intangibles; Long-term investments; Plant,
     property, and equipment)
  means of payment and valuation of, 537–538
  near-cash, 229
  noncurrent, 122–124
  wasting versus nonconsumable, 386–387
Assigning of accounts receivable, 280–281
Auditing Standards Executive Committee (AudSEC), 16
Auditors, independent, as accounting information user
     group, 7–9
Auditor's report, 1073–1075
Average-cost method of inventory assignment, 314

B

Bad Debt Expense account, 269–276
Balances:
  compensating, 229
  minimum, 229
Balance sheet, 39, 119–129
  assets in, 120–124
     current assets, 120–122
     noncurrent assets, 122–124
     similarities among assets, 120
  defined, 45
  equity sections of, 762–764
  format of, 128, 129
  general-price-level-adjusted, 192–193
  incomes statements, retained earning statements, and, 93–
     94
  LCM disclosures in, 324–326
  liabilities and equities in, 124–127
     current liabilities, 126
     determining when a liability exists, 124–126
     noncurrent liabilities, 126–127
     similarities between liabilities and equities, 124
  mortgage or other collateral terms related to liabilities in,
     678, 679

Key Accounting Pronouncements continued

No.	Title	Date Issued
28.	Accounting for Sales with Leasebacks	May 1979
29.	Determining Contingent Rentals	June 1979
30.	Disclosure of Information about Major Customers	Aug. 1979
31.	Accounting for Tax Benefits Related to U.K. Tax Legislation Concerning Stock Relief	Sept. 1979
32.	Specialized Accounting and Reporting Principles and Practices in AICPA Statements of Position and Guides on Accounting and Auditing Matters	Sept. 1979
33.	Financial Reporting and Changing Prices	Sept. 1979
34.	Capitalization of Interest Cost	Oct. 1979
35.	Accounting and Reporting by Defined Benefit Pension Plans	Mar. 1980
36.	Disclosure of Pension Information	May 1980
37.	Balance Sheet Classification of Deferred Taxes	July 1980
38.	Accounting for Preacquisition Contingencies of Purchased Enterprises	Sept. 1980
39.	Financial Reporting and Changing Prices: Specialized Assets—Mining and Oil and Gas	Oct. 1980
40.	Financial Reporting and Changing Prices: Specialized Assets—Timberlands and Growing Timber	Nov. 1980
41.	Financial Reporting and Changing Prices: Specialized Assets—Income-Producing Real Estate	Nov. 1980
42.	Determining Materiality for Capitalization of Interest	Nov. 1980
43.	Accounting for Compensated Absences	Nov. 1980
44.	Accounting for Intangible Assets of Motor Carriers	Dec. 1980
45.	Accounting for Franchise Fee Revenue	Mar. 1981
46.	Financial Reporting and Changing Prices: Motion Picture Films	Mar. 1981
47.	Disclosure of Long-Term Obligations	Mar. 1981
48.	Revenue Recognition When Right of Return Exists	June 1981
49.	Accounting for Product Financing Arrangements	June 1981
50.	Financial Reporting in the Record and Music Industry	Nov. 1981
51.	Financial Reporting by Cable Television Companies	Nov. 1981
52.	Foreign Currency Translation	Dec. 1981
53.	Financial Reporting by Producers and Distributors of Motion Picture Films	Dec. 1981
54.	Financial Reporting and Changing Prices: Investment Companies	Jan. 1982
55.	Determining Whether a Convertible Security Is a Common Stock Equivalent	Feb. 1982
56.	Designation of AICPA Guide and Statement of Position (SOP) 81–1 on Contractor Accounting and SOP 81–2 Concerning Hospital-Related Organizations as Preferable for Purposes of Applying APB Opinion No. 20	Mar. 1982
57.	Related Party Disclosures	Mar. 1982
58.	Capitalization of Interest Cost in Financial Statements That Include Investments Accounted for by the Equity Method	Apr. 1982
59.	Deferral of the Effective Date of Certain Accounting Requirements for Pension Plans of State and Local Government Units	Apr. 1982
60.	Accounting and Reporting by Insurance Enterprises	June 1982
61.	Accounting for Title Plant	June 1982
62.	Capitalization of Interest Cost for Tax-Exempt Borrowings, Certain Gifts, and Grants	June 1982
63.	Financial Reporting by Broadcasters	June 1982

Statements of Financial Accounting Concepts (SFACs)

No.	Title	Date Issued
1.	Objectives of Financial Reporting by Business Enterprises	Nov. 1978
2.	Qualitative Characteristics of Accounting Information	May 1980
3.	Elements of Financial Statements of Business Enterprises	Dec. 1980
4.	Objectives of Financial Reporting by Nonbusiness Enterprises	Dec. 1980